Research Navigator— Reliable, Relevant, and Resourceful!

This page contains your personal access code for Research Navigator™

Use your unique personal access code to register for **Research Navigator**™ today!
All you will need to register is a valid e-mail address and your access code below.*

To register for **Research Navigator**™ :

1. Go to **http://www.researchnavigator.com**

2. Click **Register**, under New Users on the left side of your screen.

3. Enter your access code exactly as it appears below:

YOUR PERSONAL ACCESS CODE

PSPHCS-JEHAD-MOTEL-COPED-TAPIR-MOLES

4. Follow the instructions on the screen to complete your registration—click the **Help** button at anytime if you are unsure how to respond.

5. Once you have successfully completed registration, write down the **Login Name** and **Password** you just created in a safe place.

Once you register, you have access to all of the resources in **Research Navigator**™ for six months!

After you register, you can log in anytime:
Simply go to **http://www.researchnavigator.com**, and type your personal **Login Name** and **Password** (that you created during registration) into the spaces under Returning Users.

*This access code can only be used to complete one registration.

Media and Research Update

INVITATION TO
PSYCHOLOGY

Media and Research Update

INVITATION TO
PSYCHOLOGY

SECOND EDITION

CAROLE WADE
Dominican University of California

CAROL TAVRIS

PEARSON

Prentice
Hall

Upper Saddle River, New Jersey 07458

Editor-in-Chief: Leah Jewell
Executive Editor: Jennifer Gilliland
Editorial Assistant: Blythe Ferguson
Editor-in-Chief of Development: Rochelle Diogenes
Development Editor: Leslie Carr
AVP/Director of Production and Manufacturing: Barbara Kittle
Project Manager: Maureen Richardson
Managing Editor: Joanne Riker
Manufacturing Manager: Nick Sklitsis
Prepress and Manufacturing Buyer: Tricia Kenny
Creative Design Director: Leslie Osher
Interior Design: Anne DeMarinis / Laura Gardner
Cover Design: Anne DeMarinis / Laura Gardner
Cover Art: Piero Guzzi
Photo Researcher: Diana Gongora
Image Specialist: Beth Boyd
Manager, Rights & Permissions: Zina Arabia
Director, Image Resource Center: Melinda Reo
Production/Formatting/Art Manager: Guy Ruggiero
Formatting, Media Update: Rosemary Ross
Anatomical Art: Medical and Scientific Illustration
Electronic Art Corrections: Maria Piper
Director of Marketing: Beth Mejia
Marketing Manager: Jeff Hester
Marketing Assistant: Jeanette Laforet

Photo Credits appear on pp. 525–527, which constitute a continuation of the copyright page.

This book was set in 9.75/12 Meridien Roman by TSI Graphics and was printed and bound by R.R. Donnelley. The cover was printed by Phoenix Color Corp.

ISBN 0-13-177879-X

Pearson Education Ltd.
Pearson Education Australia PTY, Limited
Pearson Education Singapore, Pte. Ltd.
Pearson Education North Asia Ltd.
Pearson Education, Canada, Ltd.
Pearson Educación de Mexico, S.A. de C.V.
Pearson Education–Japan
Pearson Education Malaysia, Pte. Ltd.
Pearson Education, Upper Saddle River, NJ

MEDIA UPDATE CONTENTS

WHAT IS PSYCHOLOGY?

More PSYCHOLOGY IN THE NEWS

Do Vaccines Cause Autism?

Correlational findings reported in the media and on the Internet are sometimes based on rumor or anecdote and turn out to be small, nonexistent, or questionable. Here's an example involving autism, the neurological disorder described in Chapter 1 on page 14.

Children with autism typically do not connect well with others. Sometimes they don't speak or make eye contact. They may endlessly repeat some actions, such as tapping their fingers, and some become self-destructive.

For several years, the media have featured stories about children who first showed such symptoms at age two after being vaccinated for measles, mumps, and rubella. Many parents have concluded that vaccines caused the disorder in their children. Some have filed lawsuits against vaccine manufacturers, charging that Thimerosal, a mercury-based preservative used since the 1930s (but phased out of vaccines for young children a few years ago) is to blame. They point to the timing of the first symptoms and to skyrocketing rates of autism in the United States and Canada, which suggest some sort of environmental trigger for the condition.

The critical-thinking guidelines in Chapter 1, and information on correlations, can help us evaluate these arguments. First, and most important, *correlations do not establish causation* (page 23). The fact that the symptoms of autism are often recognized at the same age that vaccines are given does not necessarily mean that the vaccines are *causing* autism; it could be just coincidence. Second, other explanations for the increase in cases are possible (see the "Consider Other Interpretations" guideline on page 16). Some other environmental factor could be operating, or the apparent increase could be due to better reporting.

The second possibility is, in fact, a highly plausible one. Better educational services are now available for autistic children, which not only encourages better reporting, but may also encourage a diagnosis of autism where once the diagnosis might have been mental retardation. (Government statistics show that the number of children getting services for mental retardation has fallen at the same time that the number getting services for autism has swelled.) In addition, in recent years the definition of autism has been broadened to include a greater range of symptoms, some of them milder than in "classic" autism, and that too could boost the number of reported cases.

Of course, it is also possible that rates of autism have truly increased, and that environmental factors are activating the condition in genetically susceptible children. Are vaccines one of those factors?

Critical thinkers decide by examining the evidence (page 13). In 1998, a British study of 12 patients did link autism with the measles-mumps-rubella vaccine, but the evidence was anecdotal and there was no control group, an essential feature of any good study (pages 25–26). Since then, several other studies have found no link, including an exhaustive Danish study that examined the health records of 537,303 children—every child born in Denmark between 1991 and 1998 (Madsen et al., 2002). The National Institutes of Health is funding further research, but at present there seems to be little reason to think that vaccines contribute to autism (Nelson & Bauman, 2003).

This issue is not merely academic. Many parents, reading about the vaccine debate, have panicked and have refused to let their children be immunized, putting them at risk for serious childhood diseases. Ironically, girls who have not been immunized are later vulnerable to developing German measles (rubella) during pregnancy—and thus face an increased risk of having an autistic child.

References

Madsen, Kreesten M.; Hviid, Anders; Vestergaard, Mogens; et al. (2002). A population-based study of measles, mumps, and rubella vaccination and autism. *New England Journal of Medicine, 347*(19), 1477–1482.

Nelson, Karen B., & Bauman, Margaret L. (2003). Thimerosal and autism? *Pediatrics, 111*(3), 674–679.

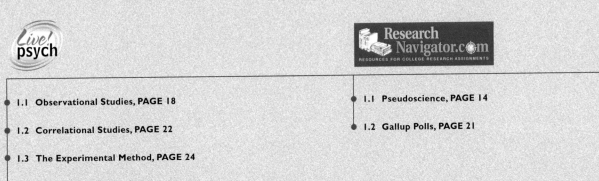

THEORIES OF PERSONALITY

More PSYCHOLOGY IN THE NEWS

Who is the "Real" John Walker Lindh?

On October 4, 2002, John Walker Lindh, the "American Taliban," was sentenced to 20 years in prison without possibility of parole in exchange for pleading guilty to two counts of "supplying services to the Taliban." Lindh, now 21, attended militant training camps in Afghanistan and later joined the Taliban's fight against the Northern Alliance, America's ally.

His lawyers and family claimed that Lindh was a lonely young man on a spiritual quest who got in over his head when he went to the Middle East. In his mid-teens he became a Muslim, calling himself Suleyman al-Lindh. He traveled to Yemen, where he became convinced that a proper Muslim should train for a military jihad (holy war) to create a pure Islamic state. Eventually he made his way to Pakistan and then Afghanistan, where he fell in with the Taliban, who knew him as Abdul Hamid. During the U.S. war in Afghanistan following the attacks of September 11, 2001, the Americans captured him. In prison, he remains a faithful Muslim, praying toward Mecca five times a day.

Like the story that opens this chapter—of Kathleen Ann Soliah, who became Sara Jane Olson—the case of John Walker Lindh's transformation into Abdul Hamid raises many questions about the nature of personality. Did Lindh's personality change, or just the circumstances of his life?

A psychodynamic theorist would look for unconscious motives in Lindh's rejection of his family and embrace of a radically different culture. Was his anger at the American way of life a displacement of his anger toward his parents (who had divorced) or toward other authority figures, as Olson's might have been? Was his attraction to a rigidly all-male environment an unconscious reflection of homosexual feelings? (*Time* magazine reported that a Pakistani mentor had claimed to have had a sexual relationship with the young man, a claim he later denied making.)

Psychologists taking a biological view of personality would point out that young people in their late teens—the period of Lindh's restless travels to the Middle East—are as a group the most neurotic (emotionally negative), the least agreeable and conscientious, and the most open to new experience (page 46). However, other traits characterizing this young man, such as the likely one of introversion, probably remained stable over the years.

Psychologists who take a learning perspective would say that when people are in a situation in which aggressive behavior is rewarded—with attention, excitement, comradeship, and feelings of power—they may become political revolutionaries, as Olson did, or religious "warriors," as Lindh did. For Lindh, who by all accounts felt lonely and alienated from his peers in America, finding a group of welcoming, like-minded peers in the Middle East must have been exhilarating. A social-cognitive learning theorist would add that just as the situation rewarded certain traits and attitudes in Lindh, his own traits and attitudes would have attracted him to that situation to begin with (page 49).

Cultural psychologists might observe that although Lindh tried hard to shed his identity as an American, his behavior in fact reflects a deeply ingrained American cultural value: individualism. Lindh (and his parents) took for granted his right to seek spiritual fulfillment in any way he chose, even when such a quest took him away from his family and meant placing his own goals and wishes above those of his parents.

Finally, humanist psychologists might ask us to see the world through Lindh's eyes instead of through our own. They would remind us to be cautious about forming impressions based solely on what we hear others say about him. And they might point out that whatever the contributing factors to his personality, ultimately his choices and his actions were governed by his free will.

References

Mayer, Jane (2003, March 10). Lost in the Jihad. *The New Yorker*, 50–59.

Roche, Timothy, et al., The Making of John Walker Lindh (2002, *Time*, 45–54.

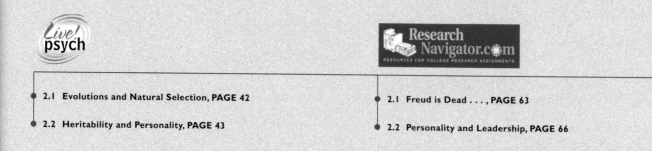

DEVELOPMENT OVER THE LIFE SPAN

More PSYCHOLOGY IN THE NEWS

Send in the Clones

In January, 2003, an astonishing story exploded into the news: A biotech company called Clonaid claimed it had produced the world's first human clone, a miracle baby named Eve. Clonaid's president is a member of the Order of Angels of the Raelians, a group of people who believe that all human beings are descended from clones planted here 25,000 years ago by 4-foot-tall green space aliens. (How do the Raelians know the "aliens' " height and color, we wonder?) The story made headlines for a few days, and then it quickly disappeared after the Raelians refused to submit the mother and baby to genetic tests.

Scientists were extremely upset about this sensational story, because it became a lightning rod for the public's fears and misconceptions about cloning. Many people mistakenly believe that because a clone shares all of its sole parent's DNA, it will therefore become an exact replica of that individual—that it will walk, talk, think, and feel just as its parent does. That false belief is the very reason some people would like to clone themselves—to achieve immortality—and others fear the notion of having an identical (younger) version of themselves wandering around.

But as this chapter shows, human development throughout life is a complex braid of genetics, experience, and circumstances. Genetics are certainly a powerful contributor in human maturation and personality, but prenatal development can be affected by harmful substances (page 75); thinking and moral reasoning are affected by culture, experience, and situations (pages 86 and 88); gender schemas are shaped by learning and experience (pages 91–92); parents and peers affect a child's values and beliefs (pages 93–95); life's transitions, expected and unexpected, affect the timing and course of development (pages 101–103); and experiences can alter the path from childhood to adulthood (page 106).

For all these reasons, even identical twins are often not "identical" in every respect. They might differ in sexual orientation, mental health, opinions, and values, and in many other ways. If you had a clone made of yourself, it would not become you—because you are also the result of the countless experiences you have had, your interpretations of those experiences, the chance events that caused you to make one decision over another, your friendships. . . .

The Clonaid claim was also distressing to good scientists because it violated the accepted rules of scientific practice. All scientific research must go through careful scrutiny, publication in professional journals, and review by fellow scholars; Clonaid's president avoided all of this, instead going directly to the media with her announcement. She was basically asking the public to take her word about Clonaid's claims. But scientists know that animal cloning produces high rates of spontaneous abortion and severe birth defects that lead to heart disease, kidney failure, and other causes of premature death; the same would be true of any efforts to clone humans. Indeed, the risks for humans would be higher than in animals because human brain development is so much more complex (Schatten, Prather, & Wilmut, 2003).

Scientists are also concerned that Clonaid's ethically questionable and high-risk efforts to clone a human being are being confused with the quite different but potentially life-saving research on stem cells. "No one wants to see 100 copies of Madonna or Michael Jordan," said Robert Lanza, medical director of another biotech firm that has pioneered in cloning human embryos for stem-cell research (Gibbs, 2003). "But it would be tragic if this outrage spills over into legitimate medical research that could cure millions of patients."

References

Gibbs, Nancy (2003, January 13). Abducting the cloning debate. *Time*, 46–49.

Schatten, G.; Prather, R.; & Wilmut, I. (2003, January 17). Cloning claim is science fiction, not science. [Letters] *Science*, 299, 344.

Live! psych

Research Navigator.com
RESOURCES FOR COLLEGE RESEARCH ASSIGNMENTS

NEURONS, HORMONES, AND THE BRAIN

More PSYCHOLOGY IN THE NEWS

Christopher Reeve's Surprising Progress

In December, 2002, seven years after actor Christopher Reeve fractured his neck in a horseback-riding accident, a surprising report on his progress appeared in the news. In a study conducted at Washington University, Reeve had followed a video image of a tennis ball and indicated the direction it was going by moving either his tongue or his left index finger. MRI scans taken during the study showed that the actor has retained an usual degree of brain activity in response to motor and sensory signals from the paralyzed parts of his body.

Scientists have long assumed that the rule governing the brain is "use it or lose it." When the spinal cord is severed, as was Reeve's, signals are prevented from traveling between the brain and the body. The brain then usually reorganizes itself, and areas that would normally respond to these signals become incapable of doing so. Reeve's brain seems to show such organization in certain areas. But during the tennis ball task, Reeve's MRI patterns differed little from those of a healthy 23-year-old who served as a control.

The actor, known for playing Superman and other roles, has been following a rigorous exercise program and undergoing electrical muscle stimulation ever since his accident. Most of the neural pathways in the spine that carry signals between the brain and the body were severed, paralyzing him from the shoulders down, yet he has recovered some limited sensation and movement. He can move his right wrist and the fingers of his left hand. In a swimming pool, he can take a step and push off against the wall. He can breathe for two hours without his respirator. And he now has some sensation on about two-thirds of his body; he can feel his wife's hand resting on his.

How can the concepts discussed in Chapter 4 help us understand Reeve's unexpected progress? First, we should keep in mind that it is too soon to know whether these results from a single case study will generalize to other patients. However, Reeve's improvement does demonstrate the often surprising *plasticity* of the brain (page 120). Not all the neural connections in his spinal cord were severed; perhaps some of those left intact were able to get enough signals through to keep the brain responding normally.

As Chapter 4 discusses, plasticity depends in part on a person's experiences. Perhaps Reeve's physical therapy has kept neurons alive that might otherwise have died or become dysfunctional, or has prodded some neurons in the spinal cord to regenerate. (Some studies with spine-injured rats suggest this might be possible.) Perhaps it has even caused some neurogenesis, the production of new cells (page 119).

The research Reeve took part in demonstrates the usefulness of MRI and other brain-scanning techniques for studying the brain and even for evaluating the prospects of recovery in the case of spinal-cord or brain damage. But as we point out in the chapter (page 126), brain scans alone cannot answer all our questions; in this case, scans do not tell us *why* or *how* the recovery occurred. The possibilities mentioned above are still just speculations.

Neuroscientists have probably learned more about the brain in the past few decades than in all of human history, but many puzzles remain, including the puzzle of Christopher Reeve's progress. In a way, this is good news. As Reeve said in commenting on his results, "It means that there are no absolutes, and patients should be encouraged to push as far as they can."

Reference
Corbetta, M.; Burton, H.; Sinclair, R. J.; et al. (2002). Functional reorganization and stability of somatosensory-motor cortical topography in a tetraplegic subject with late recovery. *Proceedings of the National Academy of Science, 99*(26), 17066–17071.

SENSATION AND PERCEPTION

More PSYCHOLOGY IN THE NEWS

Bad Vibrations

In 2001, Americans were mesmerized by the tragic story of Chandra Levy. Levy, age 24, had worked in Washington, D.C. as an intern for a California congressman, with whom she'd had an affair. In April she disappeared, and many people wondered whether the congressman was involved in some way. There were few clues in the case, but plenty of tips.

Hundreds of those tips came from psychics saying they knew where Chandra was: She was hiding in a mansion; being held hostage in a cave; drowned in the Potomac River; stuffed in a California storage locker; or located in countless other places across the country.

Psychics claim to be capable of "remote viewing," the ability to see things that are not present. Remote viewing is a form of extrasensory perception (ESP), the purported ability to perceive things beyond the reach of the normal organs of perception (page 181). Can psychics and others who say they have ESP really see what no one else can? Can they perceive someone who is hundreds or thousands of miles away, or pick up psychic "vibrations" from them? In Chapter 5 we discuss the lack of evidence for such claims. The Chandra Levy case shows why it is important to think critically about them.

One characteristic of many psychic "visions" is vagueness. For example, one well-known psychic, Sylvia Browne, in an interview with Paula Zahn on the Fox News Channel, said that Levy's body was located near "some trees in a marshy area." And a state representative from Georgia, Dorothy Pelote, said she had communicated with Levy's ghost and could see Levy's body lying in a ditch—again, in a wooded area. These are pretty safe conjectures. After all, when a person has been missing for a considerable length of time, the odds of her turning up alive are small; Levy

disappeared near a wooded area; and bodies are usually buried where there are trees and water. Hardly anyone buries their victim on the main floor of Bloomingdale's.

When a psychic claim is vague, the psychic can later "retrofit" it after the victim is found, adjusting the prediction to fit the facts. (Finding the victim amid potted plants on the patio counts as "trees and water.") Other psychic practices are using information already available and making a lot of different guesses in the hope that one will be right. If one guess happens to hit the target, people remember that one and forget the others. But psychics usually disagree with one another. In the Levy case, Washington, D.C., police chief Charles H. Ramsey remarked to the *Washington Post*, "How can all these psychic radars be all over the country? Who's right"? (It turns out no one was. In May, 2002, a man walking his dog discovered Levy's remains in a Washington park; the case remains unsolved.)

In thinking about psychic claims and extrasensory perception, we also need to base conclusions on more than anecdotes. You may have heard seemingly impressive stories about a particular psychic's success. But what about all the cases psychics do not solve? Why couldn't psychics find 15-year-old Elizabeth Smart during the nine months after she was kidnapped from her family home, while she was living with her captors only a few miles away? Why haven't they been able to find Osama bin Laden?

Not all psychics are con artists; some sincerely believe they have special powers. But that does not mean they are harmless. Most police departments consider psychic "help" to be useless, but they must investigate all tips. Thus psychics can waste valuable police resources. And when psychics offer their services to the desperate parents of missing children, they can raise false hopes, leaving families devastated when their information proves to be worthless.

Research Navigator.com
RESOURCES FOR COLLEGE RESEARCH ASSIGNMENTS

THINKING AND INTELLIGENCE

More PSYCHOLOGY IN THE NEWS

Fear of Flying

At a press conference in March, 2003, the Air Transport Association (ATA), a group representing the nation's major airlines, predicted that a war with Iraq would have a devastating impact on the airline industry. The ATA based its forecast on the sharp drop in advance bookings a month earlier, when the United States went on "orange alert," and on the fact that air travel plummeted after the September 11, 2001, terrorist attacks.

Are public fears of flying during or after national emergencies warranted? Did the thousands of people who chose to drive instead of flying after 9/11 make a rational decision?

The information in Chapter 6, and recent research on risk, can help us answer these questions. First, we know that the *availability heuristic* (page 196) causes people to overestimate the danger of flying, because disasters such as those that befell the four airliners hijacked on September 11 are so vivid and come so easily to mind. We also know that people have a bias to avoid or minimize loss, risk, and negative outcomes (page 197). So when they think of flying in terms of risk instead of its advantages, they are apt to avoid it.

In reality, flying within the United States remains far safer than driving, even when we take into account the deaths of the 232 airline passengers on September 11. Michael Sivak and Michael J. Flannagan (2003) calculated the risks of flying by considering fatalities during the period from 1992 through 2001 on 10 major commercial airlines. The average nonstop flight during that period was about 1,150 kilometers, and the risk of dying from driving that distance was about 65 times that from flying. The risk of dying on any given nonstop domestic flight was less than one in 10 million. (Distance does not make much difference, since the main risks occur at takeoff and landing.)

On the basis of these and other statistics, Sivak and Flannagan concluded that "for any distance that is long enough for flying to be an option, driving even on the safest roads is more risky than flying with the major airlines." It really is true: The most dangerous part of any airplane trip is the drive to and from the airport.

If you are thinking critically, you might ask what all this has to do with the *future*, when further terrorist attacks might make flying riskier than it has been in the past. Sivak and Flannagan thought of that, too. They calculated that for flying to have been as risky as driving was between 1992 and 2001, airline disasters on the scale of those of September 11 would have had to occur 120 times—about once a month for *10 years*.

The same kind of analysis applies to other kinds of risk. In 2002, when two snipers randomly shot at people in the Washington, D.C., suburbs, people began to vary their route to work, zigzag their way to their parked cars, and take other evasive actions, although the risk of being shot at remained exceedingly low. And when an unknown person sent anthrax through the post office in 2001, many people were afraid to open their mail, although again, the actual risk for any given individual was tiny. A total of five people died during the anthrax attacks; in contrast, in the year 2000, some 3,600 U.S. residents died from fires, most of them in the home (Ropeik & Gray, 2002).

Now, doesn't that make you feel better?

References

Ropeik, David, & Gray, George (2002). *Risk: A practical guide for deciding what's really safe and what's really dangerous in the world around you.* Boston: Houghton Mifflin.

Sivak, Michael, & Flannagan, Michael J. (2003). Flying and driving after the September 11 attacks. *American Scientist, 91,* 6–8.

MEMORY

More PSYCHOLOGY IN THE NEWS

They All Knew What They Saw

If you read the news item for Chapter 6 on the previous page, you know that the risk of dying on a commercial jet is minuscule, and that flying is far, far safer than driving. *Now don't forget that* as you read this item, because it's about an airplane crash.

On November 12, 2001, American Airlines Flight 587 crashed near Kennedy International Airport shortly after takeoff. In the months following the disaster, the National Transportation Safety Board (NTSB) took statements from 349 eyewitnesses. More than half reported seeing a fire in the plane while it was still in the air. Many said the fire was in the fuselage, but others said it was in the left engine, or the right engine, or the left wing, or the right wing. Nearly three-fifths of the witnesses said something fell off the plane, and 13 percent of those said it was a wing. These reports spurred speculation that the crash had been caused by a terrorist bomb or missile.

When the NTSB investigated, however, it came to a different conclusion. According to evidence in the wreckage and on the flight recorders, no in-flight fire actually occurred. Something did fall off the plane, but it was the vertical portion of the tail, not an engine or a wing. These findings incensed some of the eyewitnesses. One, who said he saw two separate explosions, told the *New York Post* (January 7, 2002), "There were no falling parts until the second explosion of flames—I'll go to my grave with that."

In Chapter 8, we note that memory is reconstructive, an active process that involves imagination and inference along with direct recollection (page 229). Our sensory memory of an event is fleeting (page 240). Our short-term memory

is just that: short. Because we do not have a mental tape recording of an event residing in long-term memory, but only a partial encoding of the event, we often must piece together what must have happened. This is true even for "flashbulb" memories of events that are shocking or tragic, such as accidents and disasters.

To recall a complex past event, we may draw on our beliefs, expectations, and knowledge about such events—our *cognitive schemas*, which are based on past experiences (page 228). Flight 587 took only 93 seconds to crash, but the witnesses had had a lifetime of witnessing plane crashes in movies and on TV. And in those fictional depictions, airplane crashes usually involve a lot of smoke and fire while the plane is still in the air. The witnesses therefore had cognitive schemas for "airplane crash" that primed them to "see" a fire.

The manner in which investigators question witnesses can also lead to mistakes of memory (page 232). In another airline disaster, the crash of TWA Flight 800 in 1996, many people thought they saw a missile streak upward into the sky when it was actually the body of the plane itself, after the forward portion had fallen off following a fuel tank explosion. FBI investigators asked witnesses where the missile came from—a leading question, because it presupposed the presence of a missile.

Of course, safety officials have to gather eyewitness accounts, in case they provide an important lead. But after the investigation into Flight 587, a spokesman for the NTSB told reporters, "I don't think I'm making any news by saying that eyewitness testimony at a plane crash and probably at many traumatic events is unreliable" (quoted in Wald, 2002).

Reference

Wald, Matthew L. (2002, June 23). For air crash detectives, seeing isn't believing. *The New York Times*, WK5.

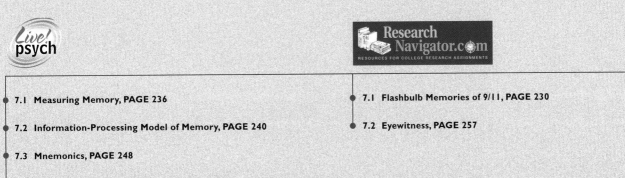

CHAPTER EIGHT

LEARNING

More PSYCHOLOGY IN THE NEWS

Tough Love or Child Abuse?

In late December, 2002, a jury in Orange County, California, acquitted a couple of felony conspiracy to abuse their teenage son and deadlocked on a misdemeanor charge of child abuse. The case drew widespread attention, in part because it revealed how conflicted Americans are about the use of punishment by parents.

The alleged abuse started when the boy was 12. Grady Machnick, a sheriff's sergeant, and Deborah Machnick, a former school principal, often forced their son to sleep outside on a dog mat when he failed to do his homework. On one occasion, Ms. Machnick sent him to school with dog feces in his backpack as punishment for not picking up after the family dog. The teenager also said that to punish him for leaving the house unlocked, she once humiliated him by taking nude photographs of him.

Many of the jurors, themselves parents, said they disapproved of the Machnicks' methods but shared their frustration in trying to discipline a difficult child. (The boy had been earning poor grades, refused to do chores, had shoplifted from a local supermarket, and stole money from his parents.) Many jurors also said that although they would never use these kinds of harsh discipline on their own children, they did not consider such punishments to be a crime. In February, 2003, a judge ruled that the prosecutor could retry the couple on the misdemeanor charge.

How would you have voted in this case? As we discuss in Chapter 8, punishment can sometimes be effective; for example, it deters some young criminals from repeating their offenses (page 281). And some psychologists argue that the occasional, moderate use of punishment in the home—even spanking—has no long-term detrimental outcomes for most middle-class children, so long as it occurs in an otherwise loving context and as a quick action of last resort when a child is misbehaving (Baumrind, Larzelere, & Cowan, 2002).

As a routine method of parental discipline, however, punishment often makes matters worse (page 282). For example, teenagers who have been routinely punished may become even more rebellious. Or they may run away, which is what the Machnick boy did at age 14, when he arrived at his best friend's house at 1:00 a.m. with his hair soaking wet. His father, he said, had awakened him by dousing him with water because he had arrived home late from school. Authorities ultimately placed the boy in custody with the friend's family.

Although the defense lawyers in the Machnick case denied that the methods used by their clients had any adverse impact on their son, routine or severe punishment often does have long-term negative consequences. When parents insult or ridicule a child, the results are especially devastating. This makes the alleged episodes involving the photographs and dog feces particularly disturbing.

In a public statement, Grady Machnick said, "One of my biggest regrets is I was unable to find a form of behavior modification that would work." Too bad he didn't take Introductory Psychology! He would have learned what behavior modification really is and how to properly apply it. In Chapter 8 we discuss alternatives to punishment, including the reinforcement of desirable behavior and the combination of reinforcement with extinction of undesirable behavior (page 283). And in Chapter 3, we discuss the effectiveness of *induction*—appealing to the child's own resources, abilities, sense of responsibility, and feelings for others. We suspect that the family now caring for the Machnick boy is using those methods. They report that he is behaving well.

Reference

Baumrind, Diana; Larzelere, Robert E.; & Cowan, Philip A. (2002). Ordinary physical punishment: Is it harmful? Commentary on Gerhoff (2002). *Psychological Bulletin, 128,* 580–589.

BEHAVIOR IN SOCIAL AND CULTURAL CONTEXT

More PSYCHOLOGY IN THE NEWS

Conformity and Dissent in Anxious Times

On March 3, 2003, Stephen Downs, age 60, and his son Roger, age 31, were shopping at a mall in Guilderland, New York. They each bought an antiwar T-shirt. Steve's said "Peace on Earth" on the front and "Give Peace a Chance" on the back; Roger's said "No War With Iraq" and "Let Inspections Work." Almost immediately, two security guards asked the men to remove their shirts or leave the mall. Roger complied, but Stephen, a lawyer with the state Commission on Judicial Conduct and a former Peace Corps volunteer, refused. He was handcuffed, arrested, hauled into court, and charged with trespass.

This was not the first time that the mall authorities had demanded that peace protesters leave. Just before Christmas, they had ejected two dozen antiwar protesters wearing pro-peace shirts and carrying signs.

Two days after Downs was arrested, 100 antiwar demonstrators marched through the mall in protest. "We just want to know what the policy is and why it's being randomly enforced," said Erin O'Brien, an organizer of the noontime rally. "It's only the people in the recent months who have anti-war or peace T-shirts that are being asked to leave the mall."

The next day, officials at the mall dropped charges against Stephen Downs.

This small news story illustrates many of the principles of social psychology discussed in Chapter 9. Consider a few of them:

- *Obedience to authority:* Roger obeyed the guards' demand to remove his shirt, although he felt their order was "ridiculous" and morally wrong. He wanted to be polite (see page 301) and not make trouble.
- *Disobedience to authority:* Stephen felt that the guards' demands were not only immoral, but illegal; the American Constitution guarantees his freedom of speech in public places. His conscience and knowledge of his legal rights led him to make a different decision from that of his son.
- *Conformity:* When a nation gears up for war, public conformity to the government's position tends to increase. Whenever the majority feels threatened by dissenters, it puts enormous pressure on them to conform to the majority view (page 310).
- *Dissent:* Because of the power of authority, social roles, norms, and group pressure to conform (see page 312), it is often difficult for individuals to stand up for a point of view that is unpopular or not shared by the majority. Stephen Downs' independence probably stemmed from his own history in the Peace Corps and his legal work. "I'm not trying to convert anybody," he told the Albany *Times-Union*. "This was a statement of where I was in my life."
- *The importance of allies.* Dissent, protest, and social influence increase when an individual has allies (page 313). When 100 people showed up to support Stephen Downs' constitutional right to wear a T-shirt with his political opinion on it, the mall authorities backed down.
- *Social identities, ethnocentrism, and conflict.* When two groups are competing, in conflict, or at war, "us-them" thinking and social identities are strengthened (page 316). As war with Iraq loomed, therefore, the social identity of "American" was heightened. Many Americans started thinking that because "we" are good and right, anyone who disagrees with "us" is aiding the enemy, "them."

In times of threat and conflict, the voices of dissenters are all the more crucial to the democratic process. Unfortunately, as principles of social psychology help us understand, the majority is even more likely than usual to try to silence them.

Live! psych

Research Navigator.com
RESOURCES FOR COLLEGE RESEARCH ASSIGNMENTS

PSYCHOLOGICAL DISORDERS

More PSYCHOLOGY IN THE NEWS

The Invention of "Female Sexual Dysfunction"

Almost everywhere you look nowadays, you can read about a brand-new disorder that millions of American women allegedly suffer from: "female sexual dysfunction" (FSD), which is supposed to be the female version of male erectile dysfunction. The discovery of FSD is said to be a medical breakthrough. Unlike the old diagnosis of "frigidity," it has nothing to do with a woman's psychological inhibitions or problems in her relationship; it is due entirely to problems with blood flow to the female genitals. Accordingly, if Viagra is the right treatment for men, it's right for women, too.

Two high-profile sisters, Jennifer Berman (a urologist) and Laura Berman (a psychotherapist), have written a popular book about FSD; they have their own sex clinic to treat it; and they have a popular show on the Discovery Channel. As a gushing article in *O*, the Oprah magazine reported, "more than 40 percent of women suffer from some sort of sexual dysfunction"; fortunately for them, "two smart sisters are riding in on white horses to give women equal access to joy."

As this chapter shows, the public needs to be especially cautious and think critically when reading about "new" psychological disorders, because of all the subjective problems in defining disorders and diagnosing them (pages 332–336). In particular, the chapter describes the dangers of overdiagnosis once a new label has been invented; the power of labels to persuade people that there is only one explanation of their problems; the confusion between normal problems and serious "disorders" or "dysfunctions"; and the illusion of objectivity conveyed by an official label. The chapter also cautions against oversimplified biological explanations of complex disorders, such as alcohol abuse (pages 354–355).

All of these concerns apply to FSD. Consider just a few problems with this diagnosis:

- There is no evidence that women who complain of sexual problems or low libido actually have problems with genital blood flow.
- No one has agreed on what "normal" sexual functioning is in women, let alone on definitions of "sexual dysfunction." Most sexual problems and psychological problems, as the chapter discusses, are not comparable to medical conditions or diseases like gout.
- There is no evidence that Viagra or hormones help most women who have low sexual desire or responsiveness.

Of course some women have sexual problems. But "blood flow" isn't necessarily the reason they do. A group of sex therapists and sex researchers have proposed a new way of understanding and treating sexual problems (Kaschak & Tiefer, 2001). Their approach includes problems due to medical and hormonal factors, but also problems due to cultural factors (such as lack of sex education, or the belief that "good" women do not enjoy sex); psychological factors (such as fear, inhibition, or a history of abuse); and relational factors (such as anger and conflict in the relationship).

As the discussion of "multiple personality disorder" suggests (pages 350–352), sometimes a "disorder" becomes a hugely successful fad because it fits certain trends in the popular culture, addresses people's needs or anxieties, and is promoted through the media. In the case of FSD, several factors make the medicalization of female sexual problems popular. One is that sex research is now largely funded by the pharmaceutical industry, which is continually looking for new miracle sex drugs (see also Chapter 11, page 373). Another is that many people are much more comfortable seeing sex as a matter of genital mechanics than of the heart or brain or relationship. It's so much easier to take a pill than to talk.

Reference

Kaschak, Ellyn, & Tiefer, Leonore (eds.) (2001). *A new view of women's sexual problems.* New York: Haworth Press.

Live psych

APPROACHES TO TREATMENT AND THERAPY

More PSYCHOLOGY IN THE NEWS

Should a Mentally Ill Defendant be Forcibly Medicated?

Suppose a person who commits a crime has a severe mental illness and is therefore unable to participate in his or her trial. Suppose medication might allow the individual to become competent enough to stand trial. As this chapter discusses, antipsychotic medication can often reduce the symptoms of mental illness, but it doesn't always work, and it often has side effects that are unpleasant or unsettling (pages 372–373). What if the individual, because of these drawbacks, chooses not to be medicated? Does the state have the right to forcibly medicate the person?

In March, 2003, the Supreme Court heard both sides of the issue in the case of a dentist, Charles Sell, who was indicted in 1997 for fraud and conspiring to murder a witness and an FBI agent. Because Sell believed that the FBI was plotting against him, he was diagnosed as having "delusional disorder, persecutory type" and was ordered to take antipsychotic medication so the government could try him. He appealed, claiming that forcible administration of medication would violate his constitutional rights.

Both sides agreed that every citizen has an interest in avoiding unwanted medication that alters the mind. Both sides agreed that the government therefore has an "extra burden" to justify the need for forced treatment. But the government prosecutor argued that this burden had been met, and that the government has a "compelling interest" in bringing criminal defendants to trial in order to maintain "social order and peace" (Greenhouse, 2003). Medication, he said, can restore mentally ill defendants "to a point of rationality" where they can decide whether to go to trial or remain "warehoused" in a mental health institution, which is what happened to Charles Sell after his arrest.

Sell's lawyer countered that his client was not dangerous to himself or others; that his years of pretrial confinement were already longer than any jail sentence that might have been imposed; and that he has a fundamental human right to refuse medication. He agreed that Sell was legally incompetent to stand trial, but maintained that he was "medically competent" to understand what was happening to him and to decide whether to take medication.

As of this writing, the Supreme Court is debating this case, but even more challenging cases await them. In a close 6-to-5 decision, an appeals court ruled in February, 2003, that a death-row inmate who is mentally ill can be forcibly medicated in order to make him "competent" enough to be executed. It's curious reasoning: The law in many states prohibits the execution of a mentally ill person—but if medication can alleviate the symptoms, the person is considered "cured" and can be put to death.

The issue of forced medication has divided psychologists (who treat disorders with psychotherapy) and psychiatrists (who can prescribe medication; see Chapter 1). In the Sell case, the American Psychological Association sided with the defendant, noting that the same drug that makes a person seem more competent at trial "can prejudice the defendant in the eyes of the jury" because many drugs increase restlessness or the appearance of boredom. But the American Psychiatric Association sided with the government, arguing that medications are usually the most appropriate treatment for psychotic disorders, so the court "should not ignore the real costs of leaving a defendant untreated."

As one exasperated Supreme Court justice said to Sell's defense attorney: "We can't try him because his mind is not working properly but you say he's entitled to refuse the drugs that would make his mind work properly. It's just a crazy situation."

Reference

Greenhouse, Linda (2003, March 4). Forcing mentally ill on trial to take drugs is pondered. *The New York Times*, A18.

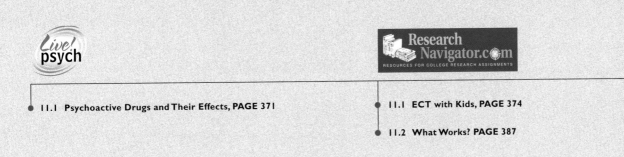

CHAPTER TWELVE

EMOTION, STRESS, AND HEALTH

More PSYCHOLOGY IN THE NEWS

A Crime of Passion

On Valentine's Day, 2003, Clara Harris, a 45-year-old Texas dentist, was sentenced to 20 years in prison for the first-degree murder of her husband. Enraged at discovering that he was having an affair, she had run over him repeatedly with her Mercedes-Benz in the parking lot of the hotel where they had been married 11 years before—as her stepdaughter watched in horror. Although Harris had become aware earlier of her husband's affair and had hired a private detective to spy on him, the jury found that Harris had killed him with "sudden passion" rather than cold deliberation, so she will be eligible for parole in only 10 years. Otherwise her conviction could have put her in prison for up to 99 years.

This story illustrates the centuries-old conflict that humans have about our emotions: Do we control them, or do they control us? The law acknowledges the difference between illegal actions committed in "the heat of anger" or "sudden passion" and those committed with "cool" premeditation—in Clara Harris's case, a potential difference of some 89 years in prison!

This chapter begins with discussion of the two-way relationship between emotion and cognition (page 398) and explores the connections between emotion and stress. It describes what is known about the physiology of arousal during emotional states and responses to stressful events (pages 401–403, and 411). When we are feeling extreme emotions or when major stressors require the body to cope with threat, fear, or danger, the body whirls into action to give us the energy to respond. Just about everyone has had the unpleasant experience of a racing heart, sweaty palms, and other emotional symptoms upon seeing a current or former lover with a new partner. When Harris found her husband in the hotel lobby with his mistress, we can all imagine how physically upset she would have felt.

But biology does not give us the whole picture. It is equally important to understand the role of perceptions, beliefs, explanations, and expectations, both in generating emotions (pages 404–405) and in responding to stress (pages 413–415). It may seem obvious that Harris blamed her husband entirely for having an affair and betraying her—and rage was the resulting emotion. Indeed, he had humiliated her by comparing her physical attributes with those of his mistress. But had she interpreted his behavior as evidence of childish immaturity and selfishness, she might have reacted to his affair with other emotions, such as regret and contempt.

The chapter also discusses the importance of believing that one has control over events, and the helplessness and panic that can ensue when people lose that perception of control. Westerners, particularly, tend to have a philosophy of fighting back against unwelcome events rather than of accepting inevitable disappointments and losses (page 415). When Harris, a former beauty queen, discovered her husband's affair, she tried to recover control of her marriage and win her husband back by dyeing her hair and making plans to have cosmetic surgery. When these efforts failed, she did not know what else to do.

Finally, this chapter discusses ways of coping that are healthier than shooting the person causing anger and stress! These include rethinking the problem, learning from it, comparing oneself to others less fortunate, cultivating a sense of humor, and finding a good, strong support group of others in your boat (pages 422–423). Clara Harris might not have been able to control her pounding heart and emotional distress when she saw her husband with another woman. But if she had had better ways of managing her distress, she could have controlled her behavior. She could have walked away.

Live! psych

Research Navigator.com
RESOURCES FOR COLLEGE RESEARCH ASSIGNMENTS

THE MAJOR MOTIVES OF LIFE

More PSYCHOLOGY IN THE NEWS

Dying to be Thin

Many Americans will go to any lengths to lose weight—especially if the "magic cure" is an herb or pill that offers the promise of rapid weight loss without having to exercise, eat less, or diet.

In October, 2002, Jennifer Rosenthal, age 28, of Long Beach, California, was persuaded by a friend to take usnic acid, a chemical found in certain lichen plants. Although usnic acid is not approved as a dietary aid, the label on the bottle (sold over the Internet, $39.95 for 90 capsules) said the chemical would make the body burn calories "at an accelerated rate." "It was like you're doing aerobic exercise while you're just sitting there," Jennifer said.

So Jennifer Rosenthal, who was not overweight but wanted to "stay in shape," took the pills for 17 days. A month later she suffered complete liver failure and went into a coma. If she had not received a liver transplant as quickly as she did, she would have died. It now turns out that usnic acid has been implicated in liver disease or death in a significant number of cases. One weight-loss product (Lipokinetix) containing a form of usnic acid was taken off the market, but its manufacturer continues to sell other pills on its Web site that allegedly build muscle and burn fat.

Rosenthal's story came right on the heels of the death of Steve Bechler, a 23-year-old pitcher for the Baltimore Orioles who collapsed and died during a spring-training workout. His death was linked to ephedra, another substance widely promoted for weight loss. The Food and Drug Administration has received more than 100 reports of deaths among ephedra users, and of many other problems, such as strokes, seizures, heart disorders, and psychotic breakdowns (Grady, 2003).

The dietary supplements industry has sales of more than $17 billion a year, much of it through the Internet, and it is almost entirely unregulated. As long as manufacturers do not promise that these products will treat or cure disease, the FDA cannot do much about them; it must prove the product has an unreasonable risk of harm before it can be banned. In March, 2003, the FDA attempted to impose minimum guidelines assuring that dietary supplements at least contain what they are supposed to contain (products vary enormously in the amount of active ingredient they contain), but the ruling has no provisions for enforcement.

Because of the lack of regulation, consumers need to be skeptical about claims and promises made by weight-loss products. Unfortunately, Jennifer Rosenthal never thought to ask whether usnic acid had been tested on humans or studied for its effectiveness (or ineffectiveness), risks, and side effects. She did not ask whether it had been approved by the FDA. "I didn't think about that kind of stuff," she told a reporter from the *New York Times* (Grady, 2003). "Not very smart."

Indeed, not very smart—and her story is an object lesson in why consumers should call upon their own good critical-thinking skills to assess claims of "miracle pills" and to demand evidence of a product's safety and effectiveness. As we saw in this chapter, the mechanisms that govern weight gain and loss, appetite, eating, and hunger are enormously complex and interrelated, involving genetics, hormones, exercise, social pressures, and culture. No wonder so many people yearn for a simple solution—one that does not require them to change their eating or exercise habits.

Jennifer Rosenthal can be grateful to pills at last. She takes 47 of them a day, to prevent her body from rejecting her new liver.

Reference

Grady, Denise (2003, March 4). Seeking to fight fat, she lost her liver. *The New York Times*, Science Section, 1, 6.

CONTENTS AT A GLANCE

CONTENTS

Psychology textbooks have always had a little problem with length. William James's two-volume classic, *Principles of Psychology* (1890), took him twelve long years to write and weighed in at a hefty 1,393 pages. (And today's students think *they* have it hard!) Just two years after it was published, James followed it with *Psychology, Briefer Course,* which was much shorter, under 500 pages. But James was not happy with his briefer book; in a letter to his publishers, he complained that he had left out "all bibliography and experimental details, all metaphysical subtleties and digressions, all quotations, all humor and pathos, all *interest* in short. . . ." (quoted in Weiten & Wight, 1992).

The great James was probably too hard on himself; he was entirely incapable of writing anything dull or disjointed. Nevertheless, we kept his words in mind as we were working on our own "briefer" introduction to psychology. From the outset, we were guided by a philosophy that we hoped would help us avoid some of the pitfalls of the genre:

1. A brief book should be brief—not only in terms of pages, but in the number of chapters.

2. The book's organization should be appealing and meaningful.

3. Students at all levels need critical-thinking tools for evaluating psychological issues intelligently.

4. Brief or long, a textbook needs to use examples, analogies, lively writing, and a strong narrative sense to pull students into the material and make it meaningful to their lives.

5. Students remember more if they learn actively.

6. Research on culture, gender, and ethnicity is as integral to psychology as is research on the brain, genetics, and hormones.

In the rest of this preface, we describe how we have tried to translate our philosophy about writing this book into reality, and what is new in this second edition.

1. Brevity

Even with a brief textbook consisting of 14 or 15 chapters, instructors often feel hard-pressed to cover the material in a semester or quarter. We decided, therefore, that 13 chapters would be ideal: enough to cover all the major topics, but few enough to give instructors some breathing room. A 13-chapter book allows you to spend some extra time on topics that students sometimes find difficult, such as the brain; to develop your favorite topics in greater depth; to take time at the beginning of the semester to get to know your students; or to use time at the end of the term to summarize and review.

2. A Meaningful Organization

We wanted the organization of this book to do two things: engage students quickly and provide a logical "scaffolding" for the diverse topics in psychology. The first chapter, which introduces students to the field and to the fundamentals of critical and scientific thinking, is followed by six sections consisting of two chapters each. The title of each section invites the reader to consider how the discipline of psychology can illuminate aspects of his or her own life and provides the reader with a personal frame of reference for assimilating the information:

■ PART ONE: YOUR SELF examines major theories of personality (Chapter 2) and development (Chapter 3). These are extremely high-interest topics for students, and will draw them into the course right away. Moreover, starting off with these chapters allows us to avoid redundancy in coverage of the major schools of psychology—biological, learning, cognitive, sociocultural, and psychodynamic. Instead of introducing these perspectives in the first chapter and then having to explain them again in a much later personality chapter, we cover them once, in this section.

■ PART TWO: YOUR BODY explores the many ways in which the brain, neurons, and hormones affect psychological functioning (Chapter 4), and the neurological and psychological underpinnings of sensation and perception (Chapter 5).

■ PART THREE: YOUR MIND discusses the impressive ways in which human beings think and reason—and why they so often fail to think and reason well (Chapter 6)—and explores the puzzles and paradoxes of memory (Chapter 7).

■ PART FOUR: YOUR ENVIRONMENT covers basic principles of learning (Chapter 8) and the impact of social and cultural contexts on behavior (Chapter 9). Combining learning and social psychology in the same part is a break from convention, but we think it makes wonderful sense, for these two fields share an emphasis on "extrapsychic" factors in behavior.

■ PART FIVE: YOUR MENTAL HEALTH reviews the major mental and emotional disorders (Chapter 10) and evaluates the therapies designed to treat them (Chapter 11).

■ PART SIX: YOUR LIFE shows how mind, body, and environment influence emotions, stress, and health (Chapter 12) and the fundamental motives that drive people: eating and appetite, love and sex, and work and achievement (Chapter 13).

Naturally, a brief book will not include every topic that might be found in a longer book, but we have tried to retain all of those that are truly essential in an introductory course. In most cases, you will find these topics in the chapters where you expect them to be, but there are a few exceptions. For example, eating disorders are not discussed in the chapter on psychological disorders; instead, we discuss them in the context of psychological, genetic, and cultural factors in eating, overweight, and dieting (Chapter 13). Likewise, because we wanted to limit the book to 13 chapters, we chose not to include a separate chapter on consciousness, but we have not ignored this material; sleep and dreams are discussed in the brain chapter (Chapter 4), hypnosis in the memory chapter (Chapter 6), and drugs in a section on addiction in the disorders chapter (Chapter 10). If at first you do not see a topic that interests you, we urge you to look for it in the table of contents or the index.

3. Critical and Creative Thinking

Since we introduced critical thinking in the first edition of our longer book, in the 1980s, we have been gratified to see its place in the study of psychology grow. Without critical-thinking skills, learning ends at the classroom door.

In this book, too, our goal is to get students to reflect on what they learn, resist leaping to conclusions on the basis of personal experience alone (so tempting in psychological matters), apply rigorous standards of evidence, and listen to competing views. As in our longer book, we introduce eight basic guidelines to critical and creative thinking right away, in the first chapter, and then teach and model these guidelines throughout the book.

We use a critical-thinking icon—a lightbulb—together with a "tab" like the one in the sample on this page—to draw the reader's attention to some (but not all) of the critical-thinking discussions in the text. The lightbulb and tab are meant to say to students, "Listen up! As you read about this topic, you will need to be especially careful about assumptions, evidence, and conclusions." The critical-thinking lightbulb also appears in Quick Quizzes (see the discussion of active learning on page xiv) to alert students to quiz items that give them practice in critical thinking.

True critical thinking, we have always maintained, cannot be reduced to a set of rhetorical questions or to a formula for analyzing studies. It is a *process of evaluating claims and ideas, and thus it must be woven into a book's narrative.* We try to model critical thinking for students in our evaluations not only of popular but unsupported cultural ideas, such as ESP and subliminal perception, but also of popular but unsupported academic ideas, such as Carol Gilligan's notion that the sexes differ in moral reasoning or Maslow's

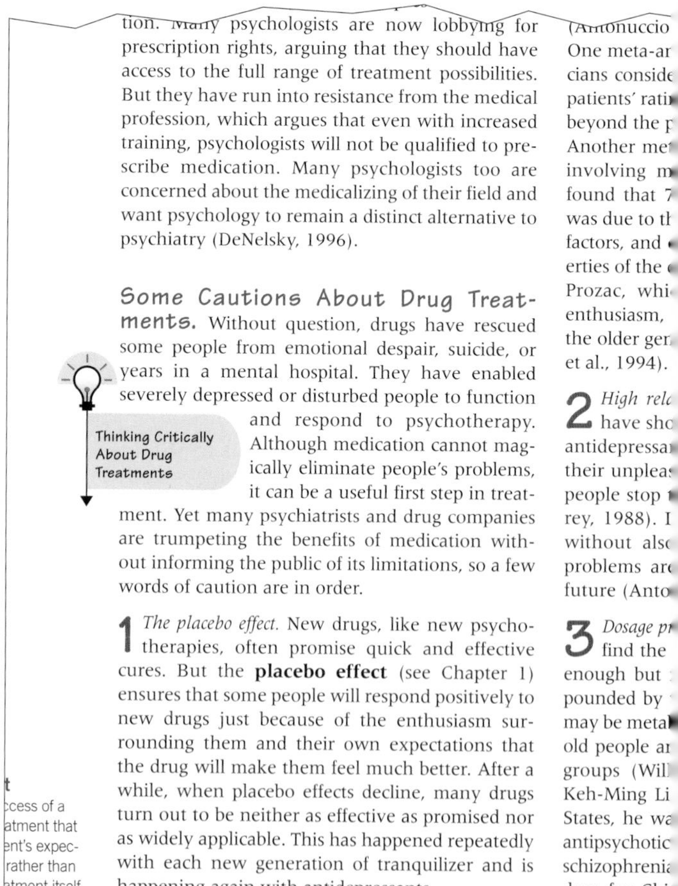

---

tion. Many psychologists are now lobbying for prescription rights, arguing that they should have access to the full range of treatment possibilities. But they have run into resistance from the medical profession, which argues that even with increased training, psychologists will not be qualified to prescribe medication. Many psychologists too are concerned about the medicalizing of their field and want psychology to remain a distinct alternative to psychiatry (DeNelsky, 1996).

Some Cautions About Drug Treatments.
Without question, drugs have rescued some people from emotional despair, suicide, or years in a mental hospital. They have enabled severely depressed or disturbed people to function and respond to psychotherapy. Although medication cannot magically eliminate people's problems, it can be a useful first step in treatment. Yet many psychiatrists and drug companies are trumpeting the benefits of medication without informing the public of its limitations, so a few words of caution are in order.

1 *The placebo effect.* New drugs, like new psychotherapies, often promise quick and effective cures. But the **placebo effect** (see Chapter 1) ensures that some people will respond positively to new drugs just because of the enthusiasm surrounding them and their own expectations that the drug will make them feel much better. After a while, when placebo effects decline, many drugs turn out to be neither as effective as promised nor as widely applicable. This has happened repeatedly with each new generation of tranquilizer and is happening again with antidepressants.

[text partially cut off on right margin]

(Antonuccio
One meta-an
cians conside
patients' rati
beyond the p
Another met
involving m
found that 7
was due to th
factors, and
erties of the
Prozac, whi
enthusiasm,
the older gen
et al., 1994).

2 High rela
have sho
antidepressa
their unpleas
people stop
rey, 1988). I
without also
problems are
future (Anto

3 Dosage pr
find the
enough but
pounded by
may be metal
old people ar
groups (Wil
Keh-Ming Li
States, he wa
antipsychotic
schizophrenia
dose for Chi

[text partially cut off on left margin near bottom]
t
ccess of a
atment that
ent's expec-
rather than
atment itself.

---

326 | PART 4 *Your Environment*

TAKING PSYCHOLOGY WITH YOU

Travels Across the Cultural Divide

A French salesman worked for a company that was bought by Americans. When the new American manager ordered him to step up his sales within the next three months, the employee quit in a huff, taking his customers with him. Why? In France, it takes years to develop customers; in family-owned businesses, relationships with customers may span generations. The American wanted instant results, as Americans often do, but the French salesman knew this was impossible and quit. The American view was, "He wasn't up to the job; he's lazy and disloyal, so he stole my customers." The French view was, "There is no point in explaining anything to a person who is so stupid as to think you can acquire loyal customers in three months" (Hall & Hall, 1987).

Both men were committing the fundamental attribution error: assuming that the other person's behavior was due to personality rather than the situation—in this case, a situation governed by cultural rules. Many corporations now realize that such rules are not trivial and that success in a global economy depends on understanding them. You, too, can benefit from the psychological research on culture, whether you plan to do

Or suppose that you are shopping in the Middle East or Latin America, where bargaining on a price is the usual practice. If you are not used to bargaining, the experience is likely to be exasperating—you will not know whether you got taken or got a great buy. On the other hand, if you are from a bargaining culture, you will feel just as exasperated if a seller offers you a flat price. "Where's the fun in this?" you'll say. "The whole human transaction of shopping is gone!" Whichever kind of culture you come from, you may need a "translator" to help you navigate the unfamiliar system. For example, in Los Angeles, a physician we know could not persuade his Iranian patients that office fees are fixed, not negotiable. They kept offering him half, then 60 percent . . . and each time he said "no" they thought he was just taking a hard negotiating position. It took a bicultural relative of the patients to explain the odd American custom of fixed prices for service.

● *When in Rome, do as the Romans do—as much as possible.* Most of the things you really need to know about a culture are not to be found in the guidebooks or travelogues. To learn the unspoken rules of a culture,

accept the reality of different customs, but most of us will still feel uncomfortable trying to change our own ways.

● *Avoid stereotyping.* Try not to let your awareness of general cultural differences cause you to overlook individual variations within cultures. During a dreary Boston winter, social psychologist Roger Brown (1986) went to the Bahamas for a vacation. To his surprise, he found the people he met unfriendly, rude, and sullen. He decided that the reason was that Bahamians had to deal with spoiled, demanding foreigners, and he tried out this hypothesis on a cab driver. The cab driver looked at Brown in amazement, smiled cheerfully, and told him that Bahamians don't mind tourists; just *unsmiling* tourists.

And then Brown realized what had been going on. "Not tourists generally, but this tourist, myself, was the cause," he wrote. "Confronted with my unrelaxed wintry Boston face, they had assumed I had no interest in them and had responded non-committally, inexpressively. I had created the Bahamian national character. Everywhere I took my face it sprang into being. So I began smiling a lot,

---

concept of a motivational hierarchy. Similarly, we try to model the importance of critical thinking and empirical evidence in our coverage of psychological issues that have evoked emotional debate, such as children's eyewitness testimony, multiple personality disorder, "recovered" memories, parental versus peer influence on children, the role of biology in addiction, definitions of racism and sexism, and many others. An emphasis on critical thinking is also integral to the book's new on-line media program (see below); students are not just given links to relevant web sites—they are encouraged to think critically about the material they find there.

4. Liveliness and Relevance

Virginia Woolf once said that fiction is not dropped like a pebble upon the ground, but, like a spider's web, is attached to life at all four corners. The same principle applies to good textbook writing. Authors of texts at all levels have a unique opportunity to combine scholarly rigor and authority with warmth and compassion in

conveying what psychologists know (and still seek to know) about the predicaments and puzzles of life.

The predicaments and puzzles that people care most about, of course, are those that arise in their own lives. **Taking Psychology with You,** a feature that concludes each chapter, draws on research reported in the chapter to tackle practical topics such as living with chronic pain (Chapter 5), becoming more creative (Chapter 6), improving study habits (Chapter 8), getting along with people of other cultures (Chapter 9), and evaluating self-help programs and books (Chapter 11).

However, we also want students to see that psychology can deepen our understanding of events and problems that go beyond the personal. Each chapter therefore begins with a real story from the news—about a 63-year-old woman giving birth, an eyewitness whose mistaken testimony sent a man to prison for 11 years, the apparent rise of "Internet addiction," a child who died during a session of "rebirthing" therapy in Colorado—and asks students how they might think critically about the issues the story raises.

PSYCHOLOGY IN THE NEWS

Age Record Broken as 63-Year-Old Woman Gives Birth

LOS ANGELES, APRIL 10, 1997. A fertility specialist at the University of Southern California has announced that a 63-year-old patient, Arceli Keh, gave birth last year to a healthy baby girl. The child was conceived through in vitro ("test tube") fertilization, with sperm from the woman's 60-year-old husband and an egg donated by a younger woman. Previously, the oldest woman on record to give birth was a 53-year-old Italian woman who had a child in 1994 through the use of similar procedures.

Although the USC infertility program has a policy of rejecting patients over age 55, the California woman lied about her age and did not confess the truth until she was 13 weeks pregnant. The woman's own 86-year-old mother, unaware of her daughter's pregnancy until the delivery, is reportedly

The oldest woman ever to give birth, Arceli Keh, age 63, cuddles her daughter Cynthia.

This **Psychology in the News** feature is not merely a "motivator" to be quickly forgotten; each story is revisited at the end of the chapter, where concepts and findings from the chapter are used to analyze and evaluate the questions raised earlier. We think this device helps promote critical thinking and also helps students appreciate that psychology is indeed "attached to life at all four corners."

5. Active Learning

One of the soundest findings about learning is that you can't just sit there like a flounder while it happens. You have to be actively involved, whether practicing a new skill or encoding new material. In this textbook, we have included several pedagogical features designed to encourage students to become actively involved in what they are reading.

What's Ahead introduces each major section within a chapter. This feature consists of a brief set of questions that are not merely rhetorical but are intended to be provocative or intriguing enough to arouse students' curiosity and draw them into the material: Why do some people get depressed even though they "have it all"? Why are people who are chronically angry and mistrustful their own worst enemy? What's the difference between ordinary techniques of persuasion and the coercive techniques used by cults?

Looking Back, at the end of each chapter, lists all of the *What's Ahead* questions along with page numbers to show where the material for each question was covered. This way, students can check their retention and can easily review if they find that they can't answer a question. This feature also has another purpose: Students will gain a sense of how much they are learning about matters of personal and social importance, and will be able to appreciate how much more psychology offers beyond "common sense." Some instructors may want to turn some of these questions into essay or short-answer test items or written assignments.

Quick Quizzes have been retained and adapted from our longer text because of their track record in promoting active learning. These periodic self-tests encourage students to check their progress while they are reading and to go back and

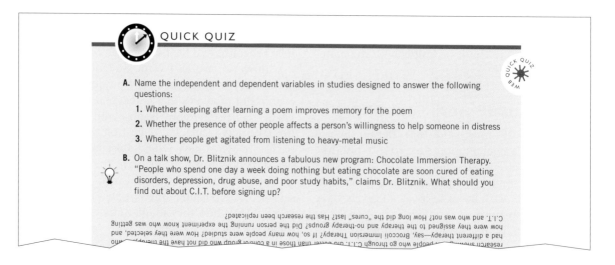

QUICK QUIZ

A. Name the independent and dependent variables in studies designed to answer the following questions:

1. Whether sleeping after learning a poem improves memory for the poem

2. Whether the presence of other people affects a person's willingness to help someone in distress

3. Whether people get agitated from listening to heavy-metal music

B. On a talk show, Dr. Blitznik announces a fabulous new program: Chocolate Immersion Therapy. "People who spend one day a week doing nothing but eating chocolate are soon cured of eating disorders, depression, drug abuse, and poor study habits," claims Dr. Blitznik. What should you find out about C.I.T. before signing up?

research shows... people who go through C.I.T. did better than those in a control group who did not have the therapy... who had a different therapy—say, Broccoli Immersion Therapy? If so, how many people were studied? How were they selected, and how were they assigned to the therapy and no-therapy groups? Did the person running the experiment know who was getting C.I.T. and who was not? How long did the "cures" last? Has the research been replicated?

review if necessary. The quizzes do more than test for memorization of definitions; they tell students whether they comprehend the issues. Mindful of the common tendency to skip quizzes or to peek at the answers, we have used various formats and have included entertaining examples in order to motivate students to test themselves.

As mentioned earlier, many of the quizzes also include critical-thinking questions, identified by the lightbulb symbol. They invite the student to reflect on the implications of findings and to consider how psychological principles might illuminate real-life issues. For example: What kinds of questions should a critical thinker ask about a new drug for depression? If a woman's job performance is declining, what else besides low achievement might be the reason? How should a critical consumer evaluate some expert's claim that health is entirely a matter of "mind over matter"? Although we offer some possible responses to such questions, most of them do not have a single correct answer, and students may be able to come up with some valid, well-reasoned answers that differ from our own.

Get Involved exercises provide an entertaining approach to active learning. Some consist of quick demonstrations (e.g., swing a flashlight in a dark closet to see how images remain briefly in sensory memory); some are simple mini-studies (e.g., violate a social norm and see what happens); and some help students relate course material to their own lives (e.g., list the extrinsic and intrinsic reinforcers that might be involved in a diverse array of activities, from studying to prayer). Instructors may want to assign some of these exercises to the entire class and then discuss the results and what they mean.

Other pedagogical features include **graphic illustrations** of complex concepts; **summary tables;** a **running glossary** that defines boldfaced technical terms on the pages where they occur for handy reference and study; a **cumulative glossary** at the back of the book; a list of **key terms** at the end of each chapter with page numbers so that students can find the sections where the terms are covered; **chapter outlines;** and **chapter summaries** in paragraph form to help students review major concepts.

6. Coverage of Human Diversity

When the first edition of our longer textbook came out, some considered our goal of mainstreaming issues of gender, ethnicity, and culture into introductory psychology quite radical—either a sop to political correctness or a fluffy and superficial fad in psychology. Today, the issue is no longer whether to include these topics, but how best to do it.

From the beginning, our own answer has been to raise relevant studies and issues about

---

work for you?)

Facial expressions are important clues to a person's emotions, but they are only part of the emotional picture. Even Ekman, who has been studying them for years, concludes, "There is obviously emotion without facial expression and facial expression without emotion." Later we will see that culture and circumstance play an

The two cerebral hemispheres also play different roles in the experience of positive and negative emotions (Davidson, 1992). Regions of the left hemisphere appear to be specialized for positive emotions such as happiness, whereas regions of the right hemisphere are specialized for negative emotions such as fear and sadness. People with damage to the left hemisphere sometimes experience

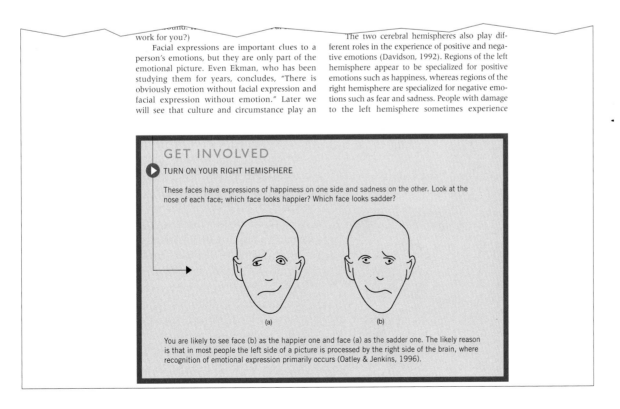

GET INVOLVED

TURN ON YOUR RIGHT HEMISPHERE

These faces have expressions of happiness on one side and sadness on the other. Look at the nose of each face; which face looks happier? Which face looks sadder?

(a)   (b)

You are likely to see face (b) as the happier one and face (a) as the sadder one. The likely reason is that in most people the left side of a picture is processed by the right side of the brain, where recognition of emotional expression primarily occurs (Oatley & Jenkins, 1996).

gender and culture in the main body of the text, and we continue to do so. Are there sex differences in the brain? This controversial and fascinating issue belongs in the brain chapter (Chapter 4). Do people from all cultures experience and express emotion the same way, and do women and men differ in "emotionality"? These topics belong in the emotion chapter (Chapter 12). In addition, Chapter 9, "Behavior in Social and Cultural Context," highlights the sociocultural perspective in psychology and includes an extended discussion of ethnic identity, ethnocentrism, prejudice, and cross-cultural relations.

We include important findings on gender differences—and similarities—in our discussions of many psychological topics, including (among others) adolescent development, the brain, social norms and roles, depression, eating disorders and body-image problems (in both sexes), emotion, socialization, hormones, love, menopause and menstruation, moral reasoning, object-relations theories of personality development, pain, weight and dieting, and work motivation. And of course we consider not only differences and similarities

in sexuality—in biology, attitudes, motives, orientation, scripts, and "drive"—but also the evolutionary, psychological, and cultural theories that have been proposed to explain those differences and similarities.

Similarly, we discuss findings on culture and ethnicity to show how a cultural level of analysis helps us better understand group differences in addiction rates, emotional disorders such as anxiety and panic, the diagnosis of mental disorder, behavioral rules and norms for such "personality" traits as cleanliness and risk-taking, conversational distance, notions of time, sexual attitudes and behavior, the effectiveness of medication and psychotherapy for various disorders, the display of emotion, IQ scores, attitudes about the ideal body and how those attitudes affect physical and psychological health, and cognitive processes such as moral reasoning and the fundamental attribution error. We discuss cultural influences on universal human processes such as infant development, attachment and bonding, the "Big Five" personality traits, language, perception, memory, taste preferences, cognitive development, self-identity, and performance in school. And we discuss cultural universals such as ethnocentrism, prejudice, ethnic identity, stereotyping, and group conflict, as well as findings from social psychology and cross-cultural psychology about ways that groups in conflict might resolve their differences or at least learn to live with them.

A book's coverage of gender and culture, however, cannot be adequately assessed solely in terms of the number of times group differences and characteristics are mentioned. There are hundreds of gender and cultural differences that, though reliable, are trivial and do not warrant space in an introductory textbook. We would rather devote space to in-depth discussions of issues where differences between the sexes or between ethnic groups really matter. For example, it is not enough to say, in passing, that women are more likely than men to seek treatment for depression, or that Japanese schoolchildren have higher math scores than American children, without explaining why these differences might exist. Mainstreaming gender and culture also means discussing the larger controversies that these sensitive topics invariably produce. Do men and women differ in the nature of the "sex drive," and how should we assess evolutionary and cultural explanations of gender differences in sexuality and love? (See Chapter 13.) What, exactly, do we mean when we say someone is "racist" or "sexist"—is this a matter of unconscious attitudes, conscious beliefs, or actual behavior? (See Chapter 9.)

cled were laborers and farmers, so being physically strong and muscular was a sign of being working class. In the past decade, pressures have increased for middle-class men to be "fit," highly toned, and strong (Bordo, 2000).

Why did these changes occur? One explanation is that white men and women associate overweight, in either sex, with softness, laziness, and weakness (Crandall & Martinez, 1996). In particular, the curvy, big-breasted female body is associated in people's minds with femininity, nur-

mothers—such as after [War] II, when women were encouraged to give up their wartime jobs and have many children (Bennett & Gurin, 1982; Stearns, 1997). However, people also associate femininity with incompetence. Thus, whenever women have entered traditionally male spheres of education and work, as they did in the 1920s and between the 1970s and the present, bright, ambitious women have tried to look boyishly thin and muscular in order to avoid appearing "soft," feminine, and dumb (Silverstein & Perlick, 1995; Silverstein, Peterson, & Perdue,

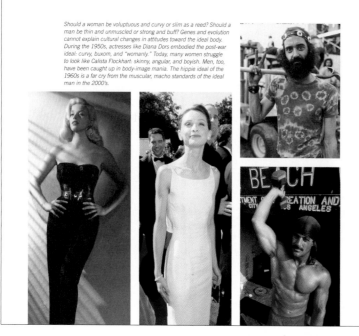

Should a woman be voluptuous and curvy or slim as a reed? Should a man be thin and unmuscled or strong and buff? Genes and evolution cannot explain cultural changes in attitudes toward the ideal body. During the 1950s, actresses like Diana Dors embodied the post-war ideal: curvy, buxom, and "womanly." Today, many women struggle to look like Calista Flockhart: skinny, angular, and boyish. Men, too, have been caught up in body-image mania. The hippie ideal of the 1960s is a far cry from the muscular, macho standards of the ideal man in the 2000's.

What's New in this Edition?

In this second edition of *Invitation to Psychology,* we have retained the first edition's basic approach, organization, and pedagogy. Many of its features have been tested by time and student reaction; students and instructors like them.

Any new edition, however, offers its authors and publisher an opportunity to expand and improve a book's features. For the second edition of *Invitation to Psychology,* Prentice Hall has created a smashing new on-line **media program,** accessed through the book's website: **www.prenhall.com/wade.** Marginal icons throughout the text direct students to web links related to the material, video clips, simulations and animations of figures and tables, readings, activities, and an on-line study guide—all intended to promote active learning and stimulate intellectual curiosity.

A new edition also permits authors to streamline language, cast a fresh eye on the internal organization of chapters, and replace dated examples or stories with more current ones. This we have done. And of course, we have carefully updated material throughout the book with cutting-edge research and critical discussions of current issues, as users of our books have come to expect. Here are just a few examples from each chapter.

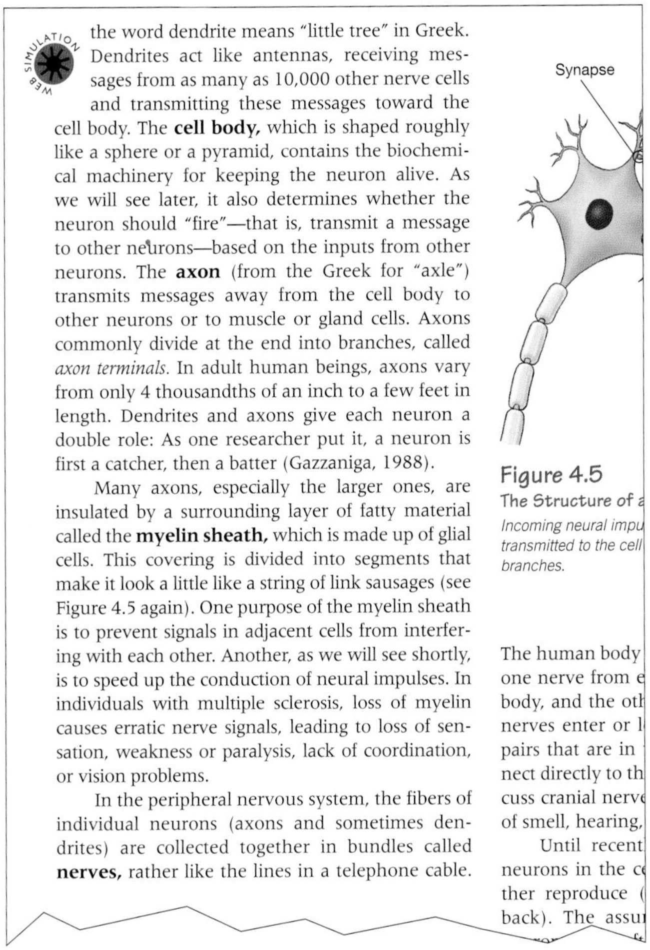

■ CHAPTER 1 (WHAT IS PSYCHOLOGY?): We clarified two of our critical-thinking guidelines and added a discussion of why control groups are crucial in nonexperimental as well as experimental studies.

■ CHAPTER 2 (THEORIES OF PERSONALITY): We reorganized the section on temperaments; modified and sharpened the section on evaluating genetic theories of personality; and added findings on regional variations in cultural expectations regarding personality traits.

■ CHAPTER 3 (DEVELOPMENT OVER THE LIFE SPAN): We made significant changes in the organization of this chapter. We also added important new material, including, for example, a discussion of parental versus peer influence on children's development and recent research questioning Ainsworth's explanation for differing attachment styles in children.

■ CHAPTER 4 (NEURONS, HORMONES, AND THE BRAIN): We updated and expanded our discussion of the exciting research on precursor cells and neurogenesis; added a description of functional MRI; and added research showing the effects of experience on the brains of musicians, cab drivers, and bilingual persons.

■ CHAPTER 5 (SENSATION AND PERCEPTION): We added several recent studies and significantly reorganized the discussion of pain, which now includes material on Ronald Melzack's neuromatrix theory.

■ CHAPTER 6 (THINKING AND INTELLIGENCE): We revised the section on culture and testing, deleting some material but adding a discussion of stereotype threat; added recent criticisms of the "intelligences" approach; and added recent findings on numerical abilities in nonhuman primates.

■ CHAPTER 7 (MEMORY): We revised and updated the section on children's eyewitness memory, devoting considerable space to this topic because of its social and legal relevance, and because research on this topic shows the important role that psychological research can play in real life; and we replaced the short section on motivated forgetting with a longer discussion on psychogenic amnesia and the controversy over repression.

the word dendrite means "little tree" in Greek. Dendrites act like antennas, receiving messages from as many as 10,000 other nerve cells and transmitting these messages toward the cell body. The **cell body,** which is shaped roughly like a sphere or a pyramid, contains the biochemical machinery for keeping the neuron alive. As we will see later, it also determines whether the neuron should "fire"—that is, transmit a message to other neurons—based on the inputs from other neurons. The **axon** (from the Greek for "axle") transmits messages away from the cell body to other neurons or to muscle or gland cells. Axons commonly divide at the end into branches, called *axon terminals.* In adult human beings, axons vary from only 4 thousandths of an inch to a few feet in length. Dendrites and axons give each neuron a double role: As one researcher put it, a neuron is first a catcher, then a batter (Gazzaniga, 1988).

Many axons, especially the larger ones, are insulated by a surrounding layer of fatty material called the **myelin sheath,** which is made up of glial cells. This covering is divided into segments that make it look a little like a string of link sausages (see Figure 4.5 again). One purpose of the myelin sheath is to prevent signals in adjacent cells from interfering with each other. Another, as we will see shortly, is to speed up the conduction of neural impulses. In individuals with multiple sclerosis, loss of myelin causes erratic neural signals, leading to loss of sensation, weakness or paralysis, lack of coordination, or vision problems.

In the peripheral nervous system, the fibers of individual neurons (axons and sometimes dendrites) are collected together in bundles called **nerves,** rather like the lines in a telephone cable.

Synapse

Figure 4.5
The Structure of a
Incoming neural impu
transmitted to the cell
branches.

The human body
one nerve from e
body, and the oth
nerves enter or l
pairs that are in
nect directly to th
cuss cranial nerve
of smell, hearing,

Until recent
neurons in the c
ther reproduce (
back). The assu

■ CHAPTER 8 (LEARNING): We deleted the discussion of classical conditioning's role in drug tolerance and withdrawal, which involves compensatory responses and thus is difficult for introductory students to grasp. Instead, we now discuss the role of classical conditioning in reactions to medical treatments—both misery and relief. We also revised our discussion of punishment to include research on the effectiveness of consistent punishment in reducing recidivism in young criminals.

■ CHAPTER 9 (BEHAVIOR IN SOCIAL AND CULTURAL CONTEXT): This chapter contains major organizational changes, along with new research on deindividuation, the difference between hostile and "benevolent" sexism, and implicit measures of prejudice.

■ CHAPTER 10 (PSYCHOLOGICAL DISORDERS): We strengthened our critical discussion of the Rorschach because of new research questioning much of its reliability and validity; added research on antisocial personality disorder (including a study of APD-like behavior in chimpanzees); and added research supporting the view that addiction can be the result as well as the cause of drug abuse.

■ CHAPTER 11 (APPROACHES TO TREATMENT AND THERAPY): We updated and expanded our discussion of the "scientist-practitioner gap"; added a critical discussion of the growing alliance between researchers and pharmaceutical companies that fund their work; and updated the list of problems for which cognitive and behavioral therapies are the treatments of choice.

■ CHAPTER 12 (EMOTIONS, STRESS, AND HEALTH): We reorganized and updated the section on stressors that affect the body; added research on how locus of control affects health; and added work on the benefits of overcoming adversity.

■ CHAPTER 13 (THE MAJOR MOTIVES OF LIFE): We revised and updated much of the material in this chapter, in our discussions of male and female sexuality, biological theories of sexual orientation, and the genetics, psychology, and culture of weight and body shape. In the latter section, we added new research that questions set-point theory, which cannot account for the worldwide obesity epidemic. We discuss the role of cultural norms in determining the "ideal body," and the risks to health when that ideal is either too thin or obese. And we have added new studies suggesting that North American men are succumbing to body image problems, too.

A more complete list of additions, deletions, and changes is available from your Prentice Hall representative.

Invitation to Psychology, Second Edition, also contains a brand-new art program. We have replaced graphic illustrations with those found in our longer book, which are pedagogically clearer. We are especially delighted with the new anatomical art, which was prepared by exceptional artists who are also physicians; they really know what they are doing! We think you will find their anatomical drawings to be colorful, accurate, and, above all, student-friendly.

The Supplements Package
For the Instructor

Instructor's Resource Manual

Prepared by Virginia Diehl of Western Illinois University, this manual contains a wealth of material to help you plan and manage your course, including: "teacher-to-teacher" discussions, chapter learning objectives and outlines, detailed lecture suggestions and ideas, demonstrations and activities, review and critical-thinking exercises, handout masters, transparency suggestions, and video and media resources for each chapter.

Test Item File

Prepared by Cathleen McGreal of Kalamazoo College, this test bank contains over 3,000 multiple-choice, true/false, short-answer, and essay questions that test factual, applied, and conceptual knowledge.

Prentice Hall Test Manager

One of the most popular test-generating software programs on the market, Test Manager is available in Windows and Macintosh formats and contains a Gradebook, Online Network Testing, and many tools to help you edit and create tests. The program comes with full technical support and telephone "Request a Test" service.

Prentice Hall's Introductory Psychology Transparencies, Series V

Designed in large-type format for lecture settings, these full-color overhead transparencies add visual appeal to your lectures by augmenting the visuals in the text with a variety of new illustrations.

Powerpoint Slides and Online Graphics Archive

Available in the Faculty Module of the Premium Companion Website, each chapter's art has been digitized and is availabe for download into any presentation software. Powerpoint lectures for each chapter are also available for download.

Prentice Hall Video Libraries

Prentice Hall has assembled a superior collection of video materials, which range from short lecture launchers to full-length detailed features for use in the Introductory Psychology course. The videos below are available to qualified adopters.

ABC News Videos for Introductory Psychology, Series III consists of segments from ABC Nightly News with Peter Jennings, Nightline, 20/20, Prime Time Live, and The Health Show.

The Alliance Series: The Annenberg/CPB Collection is the most extensive collection of professionally produced videos available with any introductory psychology textbook. Selections include videos in the following Annenberg series: The Brain, The Brain Teaching Modules, Discovering Psychology, The Mind, and The Mind Teaching Modules.

Films for the Humanities and Sciences A wealth of videos from the extensive library of Film for the Humanities and Sciences, on a variety of topics in psychology, are available to qualified adopters. Contact your local Prentice Hall representative for a list of videos.

Media Support for *Invitation to Psychology*, Second Edition

Both professors and students will find many useful resources in the media program accompanying this text.

www.prenhall.com/wade
Premium Companion Website

Every new book comes with FREE access to this extensive online study resource, prepared by Lynne Blesz-Vestal, Ph.D. Designed to reinforce each chapter's main concepts, this site includes extensive online support and information—simulations, activities, weblinks, videos, readings, and quizzes. These features are keyed to specific material and are identified by icons throughout the text.

The online Study Guide portion of the site allows students to review each chapter's material,

take practice tests, research topics for course projects, and more. Professors should visit the Faculty Module of the site to download electronic versions of the Instructor's Resource Manual, Powerpoint Slides for each chapter, and an Online Graphics Archive.

Video Classics in Psychology

Using the power of video to clarify key concepts presented in each chapter of **Invitation to Psychology**, Second Edition, this CD-ROM includes many of the best-known classic experiments and interviews with renowned contributors to the field of psychology. It includes clips of Milgram's obedience study, the visual cliff, Little Albert, Pavlov's dog, Harlow's monkeys, and Bandura's bo-bo doll study, to name a few, and conversations with Skinner, Lorenz, Piaget, Erikson, Jung, and Hilgard. The CD-ROM is packaged FREE with each new text, and it works in conjunction with the Premium Companion Website.

ContentSelect Research Database

Prentice Hall and EBSCO, the world leader in online journal subscription management, have developed a customized research database for students of psychology. This database provides free and unlimited access to the text of over 75 peer-reviewed psychology publications. You can access this research database by going to the **Invitation to Psychology**, Second Edition Premium Companion Website and clicking on the ContentSelect button.

Mind Matters CD-ROM

Free when packaged with a new text, **Mind Matters** features interactive learning modules on history, methods, biological psychology, learning, memory, sensation, and perception. Each module combines text, video, graphics, simulations, games, and assessment to reinforce key psychological concepts.

Online Course Management

For professors interested in using the Internet and online course management in their courses, Prentice Hall offers fully customizable online courses in WebCT, BlackBoard, and Pearson's Course Compass powered by BlackBoard to accompany this textbook. Contact your local Prentice Hall representative or visit www.prenhall.com/demo for more information.

For the Student

Study Guide

Written by Sherri Jackson of Jacksonville University and Richard Griggs of University of Florida, this student workbook helps students master the core concepts in each chapter. Every study-guide chapter contains chapter overviews, guided-review exercises, key terms, quizzes, sample answers for the "What's Ahead" questions from the text, and multiple-choice practice tests.

Psychology on the Internet: Evaluating Online Resources

This hands-on Internet tutorial features Web sites related to psychology and general information about using the Internet for research. This supplement is available FREE when packaged with the text and helps students capitalize on all the resources that the World Wide Web has to offer.

Supplementary Textbooks Available for Packaging

The following workbooks and supplementary textbooks are available in specially discounted packages with the textbook or as stand-alone supplements:

Psychobabble and Biobunk, Second Edition by Carol Tavris. This expanded and updated collection of opinion essays, written for *The Los Angeles Times, The New York Times, Scientific American,* and other publications, encourages debate in the classroom by applying psychological research and the principles of scientific and critical thinking to issues in the news.

Forty Studies that Changed Psychology, Fourth Edition by Roger Hock of Mendocino College presents forty seminal research studies that have shaped modern psychological study. This paperback supplement provides an overview of each ground-breaking study, its findings, the impact these findings have had on current thinking in the discipline, and the most notable extensions and follow-up studies.

How to Think Like a Psychologist: Critical Thinking in Psychology, Second Edition by Donald McBurney of the University of Pittsburgh. This brief paperback uses a question-and-answer format to explore some of the most common questions students ask about psychology.

The Psychology Major: Career and Strategies for Success by Eric Landrum, Idaho State University, Stephen Davis, Emporia State University, and Terri Landrum, Idaho State University. This brief paperback provides valuable information on career options available to psychology majors, tips for improving academic performance, and a guide to the APA style of research reporting.

Experiencing Psychology by Gary Brannigan, SUNY, Plattesburg. This hands-on activity book contains 39 active-learning experiences corresponding to major topics in psychology to provide students experience in "doing" psychology.

Acknowledgments

Like any other cooperative effort, writing a book requires a support team. We are indebted to the following reviewers for their many insightful and substantive suggestions during the development of the first and second editions. (We apologize if any affiliations have changed.)

Paul Ackerman, Wichita State University

Lloyd Anderson, Bismarck State College

Eva Glahn Atkinson, Brescia University

Ronald Baenninger, Temple University

Judith Barker, Cuyahoga Community College

Linda M. Bastone, SUNY-Purchase College

Jim Beers, John Jay College of Criminal Justice

John Bouseman, Hillsborough Community College

Michael A. Britt, Marist College

Robert Bruel, Kean College

Dan Brunsworth, Kishwaukee College

Sharon K. Calhoun, Indiana University – Kokomo

Sally Carr, Lakeland Community College

Loren Cheney, Community College of Rhode Island

Norman Culbertson, Yakima Valley College

Mark Cummins, Dason College

William Curtis, Camden County College

Gregory Cutler, Bay de Noc Community College

Betty Davenport, Campbell University

Nat DeAnda, Los Medanos College

Virginia Diehl, Western Illinois University

Lynn Dodson, Seattle Central Community College

Evelyn Doody, Community College of Southern Nevada

Laurel End, Mt. Mary College

and her associates at TSI Graphics did the layouts with their customary efficiency and skill. And we are especially grateful to Piero Guzzi for creating the beautiful, original painting for the cover illustration; molto grazie, Piero.

As always, our greatest thanks go to Howard Williams and Ronan O'Casey, who for so many years and editions have bolstered us with their love, humor, good cheer, and good coffee, even when we are suffering from Impossible Deadline

Dysphoria Disorder (IDDD, under consideration for the next DSM).

We hope that you will enjoy reading and using *Invitation to Psychology,* and that your students will find it a true invitation to the field we love. We welcome your reactions, experiences using it, and suggestions for improvements or for teaching from it.

—*Carole Wade*
—*Carol Tavris*

If you are reading this introduction, you are starting your introductory psychology course on the right foot. It always helps to get a general picture of what you are about to read before charging forward.

Our goal in this book is to guide you to think critically and imaginatively about psychological issues, and to help you apply what you learn to your own life and the world around you. We ourselves have never gotten over our initial excitement about psychology, and we have done everything we can think of to make the field as absorbing for you as it is for us. However, what you bring to this book is as important as what we have written—we can pitch ideas at you, but you have to step up to the plate to connect with them. This text will remain only a collection of pages with ink on them unless you choose to read actively. The more involved you are in your own learning, the more successful the book and your course will be, and the more enjoyable, too.

Getting Involved

To encourage you to read and study actively, we have included some special features:

■ Every chapter opens with **Psychology in the News,** an actual story from the media related to issues that will be discussed in the chapter. *Do not skip these stories!* We return to them at the end of the chapter, to show you how findings from psychology might help you understand each story in particular and others like it that you will encounter. How do you feel about a 63-year-old woman who gives birth to a baby? Why would star athletes who could easily attract consenting sexual partners nonetheless commit date rape? What motivates a man to recover from cancer and go on to win the Tour de France bicycle race? As you read the chapter, try to link its findings and ideas to the opening story and come up with your own insights. If you do this, you will find that studying psychology will not only help you with your own problems and goals, but will also increase your understanding of the world around you.

■ Each chapter contains several **Get Involved** exercises, entertaining little experiments or explorations you can do that demonstrate what you are reading about. In Chapter 2, for instance, you get to see where you fall on an inventory of basic personality traits, and in Chapter 11, we will show you how your own thoughts affect your moods. Some Get Involved exercises take only a minute; others are "mini-studies" that you can do by observing or interviewing others.

■ Before each major section, a feature called **What's Ahead** lists some preview questions to stir your curiosity and indicate what that section will cover. For example: Why does paying children for good grades sometimes backfire? Do people remember better when they're hypnotized? What do psychologists think is the "sexist sex organ"? Do men and women differ in the ability to love? When you finish the chapter, you will encounter these questions again, under the heading **Looking Back.** Use this list as a self-test; if you can't answer a question, go to the page indicated after the question and review the material.

■ In Chapter 1, we will introduce you to the basic guidelines of **critical and creative thinking**—the principles we hope will help you distinguish unsupported claims or "psychobabble" from good, scientific reasoning. The identifying icon for critical thinking is a lightbulb. Throughout the book, some (but not all) of our critical-thinking discussions are signaled in the text by a small tab that includes the lightbulb and the topic being critically examined, like the one shown here. We will be telling you about many lively and passionate debates in psychology—about sex and gender differences, therapy, memory, "multiple personality disorder," and many other topics—and we hope our coverage of these debates will increase your involvement with the ongoing discoveries of psychology.

Thinking Critically About "Multiple Personalities"

■ Every chapter contains several **Quick Quizzes** that test your understanding, retention, and ability to apply what you have read to examples. Do not let the word "quiz" give you a sinking feeling. These quizzes are for your practical use and, we hope, for your enjoyment. When you have trouble with a question, do not go on; pause right then and there, review what you have read, and then try again.

■ Some of the Quick Quizzes contain a *critical-thinking item,* denoted by the lightbulb symbol. The answers we give for these items are only suggestions; feel free to come up with different ones.

Quick Quizzes containing critical-thinking items are not really so quick, because they ask you to reflect on what you have read and to apply the guidelines to critical thinking described in Chapter 1. But if you take the time to respond thoughtfully to them, we think you will become more engaged with the material, learn more, and become a more sophisticated user of psychology.

■ At the end of each chapter, a feature called **Taking Psychology with You** draws on research to suggest ways you can apply what you have learned to everyday problems and concerns (such as how to boost your motivation, improve your memory, and become more creative) as well as more serious ones, such as how to live with chronic pain or help a friend who seems suicidal.

■ Throughout each chapter you will find **media icons** directing you to on-line activities, quizzes, simulations, videos, web sites, and readings that will reinforce your learning and help you do well in your course. First read the chapter; then, to get to these features, simply go to **www.prenhall.com/wade,** using the access code provided when you purchased your new book.

How to Study

In our years of teaching, we have found that certain study strategies can vastly improve learning, and so we offer the following suggestions. (Reading Chapter 7, on memory, and Chapter 8, on learning, will also be helpful.)

■ Before starting the book, read *Contents at a Glance* (p. v) to get an overall view of the book's organization. Before starting a chapter, read the chapter title and major headings to get an idea of what is in store. Browse through the chapter, looking at the pictures and reading the rest of the headings.

■ Do not read the text as you might read a novel, taking in large chunks at a sitting. To get the most from your studying, we recommend that you read only a part of each chapter at a time.

■ Instead of simply reading silently, nodding along saying "hmmmmm" to yourself, try to restate what you have read in your own words at the end of each major section. Some people find it helpful to write down main points. Others prefer to recite main points aloud to someone else—or even into a tape recorder. Do not count on getting by with just one reading of a chapter. Most people need to go through the material at least twice, and then review the main points several times before an exam.

■ When you have finished a chapter, read the **Summary.** Some students tell us they find it useful to write down their own summaries first, then compare them with the book's. Use the list of **Key Terms** at the end of each chapter as a checklist. Try to define and discuss each term in the list to see how well you understand and remember it. If you need to review a term, a page number is given to tell you where it is first mentioned in the chapter. Finally, review the **Looking Back** questions to be sure you can answer them.

■ Important new terms in this textbook are printed in **boldface** and are defined in the margin of the page on which they appear or on the facing page. The **marginal glossary** permits you to find these terms and concepts easily, and will help you when you study for exams. A complete glossary also appears at the end of the book.

■ The **Study Guide** for this book, available at your bookstore, is an excellent learning resource. It contains review materials, exercises, and practice tests to help you understand and apply the concepts in the book.

■ If you are assigned a term project or a report, you may need to track down some references or do further reading. Throughout the book, discussions of studies and theories include *citations* that look like this: (Aardvark & Zebra, 2001). A citation tells you who the authors of a book or paper are and when their work was published. The full reference can then be looked up in the alphabetical **Bibliography** at the end of the book. At the back of the book you will also find a *Name Index* and a *Subject Index.* The name index lists the name of every author cited and the pages where each person's work is discussed. If you remember the name of a psychologist but not where he or she was mentioned, look up the name in the name index. The subject index lists all the major topics mentioned in the book. If you want to review material on, say, depression, you can look up "depression" in the subject index and find each place it is mentioned.

We have done our utmost to convey our own enthusiasm about psychology, but, in the end, it is your efforts as much as ours that will determine whether you find psychology to be exciting or boring, and whether the field will make a difference in your own life. This book is our way of inviting you into the world of psychology. Our warmest welcome!

—*Carole Wade*
—*Carol Tavris*

Carole Wade earned her Ph.D. in cognitive psychology at Stanford University. She began her academic career at the University of New Mexico, where she taught courses in psycholinguistics and developed the first course at the university on the psychology of gender. She was professor of psychology for ten years at San Diego Mesa College, then taught at the College of Marin, and is now affiliated with Dominican University of California. She is author, with Carol Tavris, of *Psychology, Psychology in Perspective,* and *The Longest War: Sex Differences in Perspective.* Dr. Wade has a long-standing interest in making psychology accessible to students and the general public through lectures, workshops, and general interest articles. For many years she has focused her efforts on the teaching and promotion of critical-thinking skills, diversity issues, and the enhancement of undergraduate education in psychology. She chaired the APA Board of Educational Affairs Task Force on Diversity Issues at the Precollege and Undergraduate Levels of Education in Psychology, is a past chair of the APA's Public Information Committee, has been a G. Stanley Hall Lecturer, and currently serves on the steering committee for the National Institute on the Teaching of Psychology. Dr. Wade is a Fellow of the American Psychological Association and a charter member of the American Psychological Society. When she isn't busy with her professional activities, she can be found riding the trails of northern California on her Arabian horse, Condé.

Carol Tavris earned her Ph.D. in the social psychology program at the University of Michigan, and as a writer and lecturer she has sought to educate the public about the importance of critical and scientific thinking in psychology. She is author of *The Mismeasure of Woman; Anger: The Misunderstood Emotion;* and, with Carole Wade, *Psychology; Psychology in Perspective;* and *The Longest War: Sex Differences in Perspective.* She has written on psychological topics for a wide variety of magazines and professional publications; many of her opinion essays and book reviews for *The Los Angeles Times, The New York Times Book Review, Scientific American,* and other publications have recently been collected in *Psychobabble and Biobunk: Using Psychology to Think Critically About Issues in the News.* Dr. Tavris lectures widely on, among other topics, critical thinking, pseudoscience in psychology and psychiatry, anger, and the science and politics of research on gender. She has taught in the psychology department at UCLA and at the Human Relations Center of the New School for Social Research in New York. She is a Fellow of the American Psychological Association and a charter Fellow of the American Psychological Society; a member of the board of the Council for Scientific Clinical Psychology and Psychiatry; and a member of the editorial board of the APS's *Psychological Science in the Public Interest.* When she is not writing or lecturing, she can be found walking the trails of the Hollywood Hills with her border collie, Sophie.

PSYCHOLOGY IN THE NEWS

Authorities Remove Obese Child from Parents

ALBUQUERQUE, NM, AUGUST 28, 2000. A controversy has erupted over the removal of 3-year-old Anamarie Martinez-Regino from her parents. State authorities blame the parents for the fact that the toddler eats enormous amounts of food and weighs an unhealthy 117 pounds. Anamarie's parents say that they have tried in every way to help the child, but that from early infancy her weight has ballooned. "I just don't understand how they could think I'm doing this to her," says her mother.

Alabama Honors Rosa Parks

MONTGOMERY, AL, AUGUST 28, 2000. Forty-five years after Rosa Parks was convicted of violating segregation laws by refusing to give up her bus seat to a white man, her home state has finally honored her by inducting her into the Alabama Academy of Honor. Parks's calm courage during her arrest triggered a successful 381-day black boycott of city buses and launched the modern civil-rights movement. She eventually moved to Detroit and has devoted her life to promoting racial harmony and helping young African-Americans.

▲ Simon Rodia in front of his life's work, the famed Watts Towers.

Watts Towers Reopened to Public

LOS ANGELES, CA, OCTOBER 1, 2000. The world-famous Watts Towers, damaged in the 1994 Northridge earthquake, reopened Saturday to gasps of admiration. The wire-mesh towers were built single-handedly by Italian laborer Simon Rodia in his backyard over a period of 33 years, beginning in the 1920s. Rodia covered them with colored glass, pottery pieces, seashells, and many other "treasures." One visitor called the towers "a testament to an iron will," and another said he took away the message, "Never give up on your vision."

Vermont Allows Gay Civil Unions

WOODSTOCK, VT, JULY 20, 2000. Gays and lesbians from many states are flocking to Vermont to take advantage of a recent law permitting civil unions for same-sex couples. The law confers insurance benefits, hospital visitation rights, and other benefits of marriage. Legal battles are looming, as gay couples who "tied the knot" in Vermont prepare to ask their home states to recognize their unions.

▼ San Francisco Mayor Willie Brown conducts a domestic partnership ceremony for gay and lesbian couples. Vermont has legalized such unions, but the issue continues to divide the public.

WHAT IS PSYCHOLOGY?

I f you were reading the newspaper in the year 2000, you might have come across the five stories shown here. Newspapers and magazines are full of tales of heroism and courage, murder and mayhem, personal accomplishment and emotional controversies. But why, you may be wondering, are we starting this book with these stories? What on earth do they have to do with psychology?

The answer is: Everything.

People usually associate psychology with mental and emotional disorders, personal problems, and psychotherapy. But psychologists take as their subject the entire spectrum of beautiful and brutish things that human beings do—the kinds of things you read or hear about every day. Psychologists reading these particular stories would want to know whether Anamarie Martinez-Regino's obesity could be the result of a genetic problem rather than parental neglect. They would want to find out why some people, although perfectly pleasant to friends and relatives, burn with hatred for people of different ethnicities, religions, or nationalities; and why some people put their own lives in jeopardy to stand up for a cause or help others. They would wonder why people become straight, gay, or bisexual—and why so many people fear or detest homosexuality. And they would be curious to know what motivates some individuals to confidently pursue their dreams—for example, by building fanciful towers in their backyard—whereas others give up before they even start.

If you want to know what psychology is about, then, a newspaper is a pretty good place to start! Indeed, in this book we will be discussing all the issues raised by these stories. But psychology is not just about martyrs and murderers, heroes and haters, or behavior that is newsworthy. Psychologists are also interested in how ordinary human beings—and other animals, too—learn, remember, solve problems, perceive, feel, and get along (or fail to get along) with others. They are therefore as likely to study commonplace experiences—rearing children, gossiping, remembering a shopping list, daydreaming, making love, and making a living—as exceptional ones.

If you have ever wondered what makes people tick, or if you want to gain some insight into your own behavior, then you have enrolled in the right course. We invite you now to step into the world of psychology, the discipline that dares to explore the most complex topic on earth: *you.*

What's Ahead

- **What's the difference between psychology and plain old common sense?**

- **How old is the science of psychology?**

- **Was Sigmund Freud the official founder of scientific psychology?**

- **What are the five major perspectives in psychology?**

1.1 The Science of Psychology

Psychology can be defined as *the discipline concerned with behavior and mental processes and how they are affected by an organism's physical state, mental state, and external environment.* This definition, however, is a little like defining a car as a vehicle for transporting people from one place to another, without explaining how a car differs from a train or a bus, how a Ford differs from a Ferrari, or how a catalytic converter works. To get a clear picture of what psychology is, you are going to need to know more about its methods, its findings, and its ways of interpreting information.

psychology
The discipline concerned with behavior and mental processes and how they are affected by an organism's physical state, mental state, and external environment; often represented by Ψ, the Greek letter psi (usually pronounced "sy").

empirical
Relying on or derived from observation, experimentation, or measurement.

Psychology, Pseudoscience, and Common Sense

Let's begin by considering what psychology is *not.* First, the psychology that you are about to study bears little relation to the popular psychology ("pop psych") found in many self-help books and on many TV and radio talk shows. In recent years, the public's appetite for psychological information has created a huge market for what R. D. Rosen (1977) called "psychobabble": pseudoscience and quackery covered by a veneer of psychological language. Serious psychology is more complex, more informative, and, we think, far more helpful than psychobabble because it is based on rigorous research and **empirical** evidence, evidence gathered by careful observation, experimentation, and measurement. Today, more than ever, when so many simplistic pop-psych ideas have filtered into public consciousness, the media, education, and even the law, people need to distinguish between psychobabble and serious psychology.

Second, serious psychology differs radically from such nonscientific competitors as graphology, fortune telling, numerology, and the most popular, astrology. Like psychologists, promoters of these competing systems try to explain people's problems and predict their behavior. If you are having romantic problems, for example, an astrologer may advise you to choose an Aries instead of an Aquarius as your next love, and a "past-lives channeler" may say it's because you were jilted in a former life. But whenever the claims of psychics, astrologers, and the like are put to the test, those claims turn out to be so vague that they're meaningless—or they are just plain wrong (Dean, 1987; Rowe, 1993; Shermer, 1997).

I see you as being less gullible in the future.

Third, psychology is not just a fancy name for common sense. True, psychological research does sometimes confirm what people commonly believe. When that happens, it may be tempting to conclude that scientific studies are a waste of time. Often, however, the obviousness of a psychological finding is only an illusion. Armed with the wisdom of hindsight, people may maintain that they "knew it all along" when in fact they did not.

Moreover, psychological research often produces findings that contradict common sense. For example, according to popular belief, early experiences determine how a person turns out, for better or for worse; people speak of their "formative years" and the supposedly lifelong effects of childhood traumas. Yet, as we will see in later chapters, many abilities and attributes can change throughout life in response to new situations, and even children traumatized by abuse, neglect, or war can become happy, secure adults if their circumstances improve (Garmezy, 1991; Werner, 1989).

You will be learning about many other findings that violate current "common sense" or popular opinion. Are unhappy memories "repressed" and then accurately recalled years later, as if they had been recorded on videotape? Are most abused children destined to become abusive parents themselves? Do policies of abstinence from alcohol reduce rates of alcoholism? All of these common beliefs and many others are contradicted by empirical evidence.

However, although psychologists often challenge prevailing beliefs, psychological findings do not have to be surprising to be important. Psychologists also seek to extend and deepen our understanding of generally accepted facts. After all, everyone knows that an apple will fall to the ground if it drops from a tree, but it took Isaac Newton to discover the laws of gravity and to explain why the apple falls and why it travels at a particular speed. Psychologists, like scientists in other fields, strive not only to discover new phe-nomena, but also to deepen our understanding of an already familiar world.

The Birth of Modern Psychology

Most of the great thinkers of history, from Aristotle to Zoroaster, raised questions that today would be called psychological. They wanted to know how people take in information through their senses, use information to solve problems, and become motivated to act in brave or villainous ways. They wondered about the elusive nature of emotion, and whether it controls us or is something we can control. Like today's psychologists, they wanted to *describe, predict, understand,* and *modify* behavior in order to add to human knowledge and increase human happiness. But unlike modern psychologists, scholars of the past did not rely heavily on empirical evidence. Often, their observations were based simply on anecdotes or descriptions of individual cases.

This does not mean that the forerunners of modern psychology were always wrong. On the contrary, they often had insights and made observations that were verified by later work. Hippocrates (c. 460 B.C.–c. 377 B.C.), the Greek physician known as the founder of modern medicine, observed patients with head injuries and inferred that the brain must be the ultimate source of "our pleasures, joys, laughter, and jests as well as our sorrows, pains, griefs, and tears." And so it is. In the first century A.D., the Stoic philosophers observed that people do not become angry or sad or anxious because of actual events but because of their explanations of those events. And so they do.

But without empirical methods, the forerunners of psychology also committed some terrible blunders. A good example comes from the early 1800s, when the theory of *phrenology* (Greek for "study of the mind") became wildly popular.

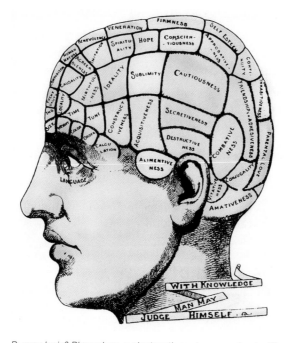

Bumpy logic? Phrenology, a nineteenth-century pseudoscientific fad, linked bumps on the skull with character traits. On this phrenological "map," notice the tiny space allocated to self-esteem and the large one devoted to cautiousness!

Inspired by the writings and lectures of Austrian physician Joseph Gall (1758–1828), phrenologists argued that different brain areas accounted for specific character and personality traits, such as "stinginess" and "religiosity," and that such traits could be "read" from bumps on the skull. Thieves, for example, supposedly had large bumps above the ears. When phrenologists examined people who had "stealing bumps" but who were *not* thieves, they explained away this counterevidence by saying that other brain bumps represented positive traits that were holding the person's thieving impulses in check. In the United States, parents, teachers, and employers flocked to phrenologists for advice (Benjamin, 1998). But phrenology was a classic pseudoscience—sheer nonsense.

At about the time that phrenologists were reaching the peak of their popularity, several pioneering men and women in Europe and America were starting to study psychological issues using scientific methods. In 1879, the first psychological laboratory was officially established, in Leipzig, Germany, by Wilhelm Wundt (VIL-helm Voont). Wundt, who was trained in medicine and philosophy, promoted a method called *trained introspection*, in which volunteers were taught to carefully observe, analyze, and describe their own sensations, mental images, and emotional reactions. Wundt's introspectors might take as long as 20 minutes to

report their inner experiences during a 1.5-second experiment. The goal was to break behavior down into its most basic elements, much as a chemist might analyze water into hydrogen plus oxygen. Most psychologists eventually rejected trained introspection as too subjective, but Wundt still is usually credited for formally initiating the movement to make psychology a science.

Another early approach to scientific psychology, called **functionalism,** emphasized the function, or purpose, of behavior, instead of its analysis and description. One of functionalism's leaders was William James (1842–1910), an American philosopher, physician, and psychologist. Attempting to grasp the nature of the mind through introspection, wrote James (1890/1950), is "like seizing a spinning top to catch its motion, or trying to turn up the gas quickly enough to see how the darkness looks." Inspired in part by the evolutionary theories of British naturalist Charles Darwin (1809–1882), James and other functionalists instead asked how various actions help a person or animal adapt to the environment. This emphasis on the causes and consequences of behavior was to set the course of psychological science.

Psychology also has roots in Vienna, Austria, where it first developed as a method of psychotherapy. While researchers were at work in their laboratories, struggling to establish psychology as a science, Sigmund Freud, an obscure neurologist, was in his office listening to his patients' reports of depression, nervousness, and obsessive habits. Freud became convinced that their symptoms had mental, not bodily, causes. His patients' distress was due, he concluded, to conflicts, memories, and emotional traumas that had originated in early childhood and were too threatening to be remembered consciously. Freud's ideas eventually evolved into a broad theory of personality, and both his theory and his methods of treating people with emotional problems became known as **psychoanalysis.**

From these early beginnings in philosophy, natural science, and medicine, psychology eventually grew into a complex discipline encompassing many different specialties, perspectives, and methods. Today the field is like a large, sprawling family. The members of this family share common great-grandparents, but some of the cousins have formed alliances, some are quarreling, and a few are barely speaking to one another.

Psychology's Present

Five major theoretical perspectives now predominate in psychology. These approaches reflect differ-

functionalism
An early psychological approach that emphasized the function or purpose of behavior and consciousness.

psychoanalysis
A theory of personality and a method of psychotherapy, originally formulated by Sigmund Freud, which emphasizes unconscious motives and conflicts.

What makes us who we are? Psychologists approach questions about human behavior from five major perspectives: biological, learning, cognitive, sociocultural, and psychodynamic.

this perspective, *behaviorists* focus on the environmental conditions—the rewards and punishers—that maintain or discourage specific behaviors. Behaviorists do not invoke the mind to explain behavior; they prefer to stick to what they can observe and measure directly: acts and events taking place in the environment. *Social-cognitive learning theorists,* on the other hand, combine elements of classic behaviorism with research on thoughts, values, and intentions. They believe that people learn not only by adapting their behavior to the environment, but also by imitating others and by thinking about the events happening around them.

3 The **cognitive perspective** emphasizes what goes on in people's heads—how people reason, remember, understand language, solve problems, explain experiences, acquire moral standards, and form beliefs. (The word *cognitive* comes from the Latin for "to know.") One of the most important contributions of this perspective has been to show how our explanations and perceptions affect what we do and feel. All of us are constantly seeking to make sense of the world and of our own physical and mental states. Our ideas may not always be realistic or sensible, but they continually influence our actions and choices.

4 The **sociocultural perspective** goes beyond the study of the individual, focusing on how social and cultural forces shape every aspect of human behavior, from how (and whether!) we kiss to what and where we eat. Most of us underestimate the impact of other people, the social context, and cultural rules on nearly everything we do: how we perceive the world, express joy or grief, manage our households, and treat our friends and enemies. We are like fish that are unaware they live in water, so obvious is water in their lives. Sociocultural psychologists study the water—the social and cultural environments that people "swim" in every day.

5 The **psychodynamic perspective** deals with unconscious dynamics within the individual, such as inner forces, conflicts, or instinctual energy. This approach is associated most closely with Freudian psychoanalysis, but many other psychodynamic theories also exist. Psychodynamic psychologists try to dig below the surface of a person's behavior to get to the roots of personality; they think of themselves as archeologists of the mind. As we will see in Chapter 2, psychodynamic psychology is the thumb on the hand of

ent questions that psychologists ask about human behavior, different assumptions about how the mind works, and, most important, different ways of explaining why people do what they do.

1 The **biological perspective** focuses on how bodily events affect behavior, feelings, and thoughts. Electrical impulses shoot along the intricate pathways of the nervous system. Hormones course through the bloodstream, signaling internal organs to slow down or speed up. Chemical substances flow across the tiny gaps that separate one microscopic brain cell from another. Biological psychologists want to know how these physical events interact with events in the external environment to produce behavior, perceptions, memories, emotions, and mental disorders. They also investigate the contribution of genes and other biological factors to the development of abilities and personality traits.

2 The **learning perspective** is concerned with how the environment and experience affect a person's (or a nonhuman animal's) actions. Within

biological perspective
A psychological approach that emphasizes bodily events and changes associated with actions, feelings, and thoughts.

learning perspective
A psychological approach that emphasizes how the environment and experience affect a person's or animal's actions; it includes *behaviorism* and *social-cognitive learning theories.*

cognitive perspective
A psychological approach that emphasizes mental processes in perception, memory, language, problem solving, and other areas of behavior.

sociocultural perspective
A psychological approach that emphasizes social and cultural influences on behavior.

psychodynamic perspective
A psychological approach that emphasizes unconscious dynamics within the individual, such as inner forces, conflicts, or the movement of instinctual energy.

psychology—connected to the other fingers, but also set apart from them because it differs radically from the others in its language, methods, and standards of acceptable evidence.

We will be encountering the major findings and methods of these five approaches in the rest of this book. The differences among these schools of thought are very real; a psychoanalyst's explanation of your personality will not be the same as a cognitive psychologist's, and neither account will be the same as a biological or learning psychologist's.

However, not all psychologists feel they must swear allegiance to one approach or another.

Many, if not most, are *eclectic*, using what they believe to be the best features of diverse schools of thought. Moreover, whatever their theoretical convictions, most psychological scientists agree on certain basic guidelines about what is and what is not acceptable in their discipline. Nearly all reject supernatural explanations of events— evil spirits, psychic forces, miracles, and so forth. Most believe in the importance of gathering empirical evidence and not relying on hunches or personal belief. This insistence on rigorous standards of proof is what sets psychology apart from other, nonscientific explanations of human experience.

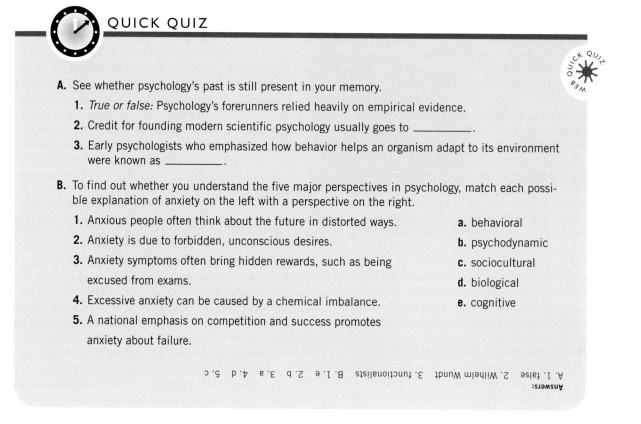

QUICK QUIZ

A. See whether psychology's past is still present in your memory.

1. *True or false:* Psychology's forerunners relied heavily on empirical evidence.

2. Credit for founding modern scientific psychology usually goes to _____.

3. Early psychologists who emphasized how behavior helps an organism adapt to its environment were known as _____.

B. To find out whether you understand the five major perspectives in psychology, match each possible explanation of anxiety on the left with a perspective on the right.

1. Anxious people often think about the future in distorted ways.

2. Anxiety is due to forbidden, unconscious desires.

3. Anxiety symptoms often bring hidden rewards, such as being excused from exams.

4. Excessive anxiety can be caused by a chemical imbalance.

5. A national emphasis on competition and success promotes anxiety about failure.

a. behavioral

b. psychodynamic

c. sociocultural

d. biological

e. cognitive

Answers:

A. 1. false   2. Wilhelm Wundt   3. functionalists   B. 1. e   2. b   3. a   4. d   5. c

What's Ahead •————————▶

- If someone tells you that he or she is a psychologist, why can't you assume the person is a therapist?

- If you decided to call yourself a "psychotherapist," would you be breaking the law?

- What's the difference between a clinical psychologist and a psychiatrist?

1.2 What Psychologists Do

Now you know the main viewpoints that guide psychologists in their work. But what do psychologists actually do with their time between breakfast and dinner?

The professional activities of psychologists generally fall into three broad categories: (1) teach-

Table 1.1 What Is a Psychologist?

Many psychologists are psychotherapists, but others do research, teach, work in business, or consult.

Academic/Research Psychologists	Clinical Psychologists	Psychologists in Industry, Law, or Other Settings
Specialize in areas of pure or applied research, such as:	*May work in any of these settings:*	*Do research or serve as consultants to institutions on, for example:*
Human development	Private practice	Sports
Psychometrics (testing)	Mental-health clinics or services	Consumer issues
Health	Hospitals	Advertising
Education	Research laboratories	Organizational problems
Industrial/organizational psychology	Colleges and universities	Environmental issues
Physiological psychology		Public policy
Sensation and perception		Survey research and opinion polls

ing and doing research in colleges and universities; (2) providing health or mental health services, often referred to as *psychological practice;* and (3) conducting research or applying its findings in nonacademic settings such as business, sports, government, law, and the military (see Table 1.1). Some psychologists move flexibly across these areas. A researcher might also provide counseling services in a mental-health setting, such as a clinic or a hospital; a university professor might teach, do research, and serve as a consultant in legal cases.

Psychological Research

Most psychologists who do research have doctoral degrees (Ph.D.s or Ed.D.s, doctorates in education). Some, seeking knowledge for its own sake, work in **basic psychology;** others, concerned with the practical uses of knowledge, work in **applied psychology.** A psychologist doing basic research might ask, "How do children, adolescents, and adults differ in their approach to moral issues such as honesty?" An applied psychologist might ask, "How can knowledge about moral development be used to prevent teenage violence?"

Research psychologists' findings fill most of this book, so you can get a good idea of what psychologists study and teach by scanning the Table of Contents on pages vii–x. Psychologists doing basic and applied research have made important contributions in areas as diverse as health, education, child development, testing, conflict resolution, marketing, industrial design, worker productivity, and urban planning.

Psychological Practice

Psychological practitioners, whose goal is to understand and improve physical and mental health, work in mental hospitals, general hospitals, clinics, schools, counseling centers, and private practice. Since the late 1970s, the proportion of psychologists who are practitioners has steadily increased; today, practitioners account for well over two-thirds of new psychology doctorates and members of the American Psychological Association (APA), psychology's largest professional organization (APA Research Office, 1998).

Some practitioners are *counseling psychologists,* who generally help people deal with problems of everyday life, such as test anxiety, family conflicts, or low job motivation. Others are *school psychologists,* who work with parents, teachers, and students to enhance students' performance and resolve emotional difficulties. The majority, however, are *clinical psychologists,* who diagnose, treat, and study mental or emotional problems. Clinical psychologists are trained to do psychotherapy with severely disturbed people, as well as with those who are simply troubled or unhappy and want to learn to handle their problems better.

In almost all states, a license to practice clinical psychology requires a doctorate. Most clinical psychologists have a Ph.D., some have an Ed.D.,

basic psychology
The study of psychological issues in order to seek knowledge for its own sake rather than for its practical application.

applied psychology
The study of psychological issues that have direct practical significance; also, the application of psychological findings.

and a smaller but growing number have a Psy.D. (doctorate in psychology, pronounced "sy-dee"). Clinical psychologists typically do four or five years of graduate work in psychology, plus at least a year's internship under the direction of a practicing psychologist. Clinical programs leading to a Ph.D. or Ed.D. are usually designed to prepare a person both as a scientist and as a practitioner; they require completion of a dissertation, a major scholarly project (usually involving research) that contributes to knowledge in the field. Programs leading to a Psy.D. focus on professional practice and do not usually require a dissertation, although they typically require the student to complete a study, theoretical paper, literature review, or other scholarly project.

People often confuse *clinical psychologist* with three other terms: *psychotherapist, psychoanalyst,* and *psychiatrist,* but these terms mean different things. A *psychotherapist* is simply someone who does any kind of psychotherapy. The term is not legally regulated; in fact, in most states, anyone can say that he or she is a "therapist" of one sort or another without having any training at all. A *psychoanalyst* is a person who practices one particular form of therapy, psychoanalysis. To call yourself a psychoanalyst, you must have an advanced degree, get specialized training at a psychoanalytic institute, and undergo extensive psychoanalysis yourself. A *psychiatrist* is a medical doctor (M.D.) who has done a three-year residency in psychiatry to learn to diagnose and treat mental disorders under the supervision of more experienced physicians. Like some clinical psychologists, some psychiatrists do research on mental problems, such as depression or schizophrenia, instead of working with patients.

Psychiatrists and clinical psychologists do similar work, but psychiatrists, because of their medical training, tend to focus more on possible biological causes of mental disorders and often treat these problems with medication. They can write prescriptions, and clinical psychologists cannot (or at least not yet; in many states, psychologists are pressing for prescription-writing privileges). Psychiatrists, however, are often untrained in current psychological theories and methods (Luhrmann, 2000).

Clinical social workers, counselors with various specialties, and marriage, family, and child counselors also do mental-health work. These professionals ordinarily treat general problems rather than serious mental disturbance, although

their work may bring them into contact with people with serious problems—violent delinquents, sex offenders, and individuals involved in domestic violence or child abuse. Licensing requirements vary from state to state but usually include

Psychological researchers and practitioners work in many settings, from classrooms to courtrooms. On the top, sports psychologist Sean McCain helps an Olympic athlete mentally rehearse what he would do during an actual athletic event. In the middle, a clinical psychologist helps a couple in therapy. On the bottom, Louis Herman studies a dolphin's ability to understand an artificial language comprised of hand signals; in response to the gestural sequence "person" and "over," the dolphin will leap over the person in the pool.

Table 1.2 Types of Psychotherapists

Psychotherapist	A person who does psychotherapy: may have anything from no degree to an advanced professional degree; the term is unregulated
Clinical psychologist	Has a Ph.D., an Ed.D., or a Psy.D.
Psychoanalyst	Has specific training in psychoanalysis after an advanced degree (usually, but not always, an M.D. or a Ph.D.)
Psychiatrist	A medical doctor (M.D.) with a specialty in psychiatry
Licensed clinical social worker (LCSW); counselors with various specialties; marriage, family, and child counselor (MFCC)	Licensing requirements vary; generally has at least an M.A. in psychology or social work

a master's degree in psychology or social work and one or two years of supervised experience. (For a summary of the types of psychotherapists and the training they receive, see Table 1.2.)

Many research psychologists, and some practitioners, are worried about an increase in the number of psychotherapists who are unschooled in research methods and the empirical findings of psychology, and who use unvalidated therapy techniques (Beutler, 2000; Dawes, 1994; Poole et al., 1995). In 1987, such concerns contributed to the formation of the American Psychological Society (APS), an organization devoted to the needs and interests of psychology as a science. Many practitioners, on the other hand, argue that psychotherapy is an art, and that research findings are largely irrelevant to the work they do with clients. In Chapter 11, we will return to the important issue of the widening gap in training and attitudes between scientists and many therapists.

Partly because of these tensions, and partly because the media and the public persist in equating "psychologist" with "psychotherapist," some psychological scientists think it is time to use other labels to describe what they do and to yield the word *psychologist* to its popular meaning. Research psychologists, they say, should call themselves "cognitive scientists," "behavioral scientists," "neuroscientists," and so forth, depending on their area of study. This change in language is already under way. At present, however, the word *psychologist* still embraces all the cousins in psychology's sprawling family.

Psychology in the Community

Since World War II, psychology has expanded rapidly in terms of scholars, publications, and specialties. The American Psychological Association now has 52 divisions. Some represent major fields such as developmental psychology or physiological psychology. Others represent specific research or professional interests, such as the psychology of women, the psychology of men, ethnic minority issues, sports, the arts, environmental concerns, gay and lesbian issues, peace, psychology and the law, and health.

As psychology has grown, psychologists have found ways to contribute to their communities in about as many fields as you can think of. They consult with companies to improve worker satisfaction and productivity. They establish programs to improve race relations and reduce ethnic tensions. They advise commissions on how pollution and noise affect mental health. They do rehabilitation training for people who are physically or mentally disabled. They educate judges and juries about eyewitness testimony. They assist the police in emergencies involving hostages or disturbed persons. They conduct public-opinion surveys. They run suicide-prevention hot lines. They advise zoos on the care and training of animals. They help coaches improve the athletic performances of their teams. And on and on.

Is it any wonder that people are a little fuzzy about what a psychologist is?

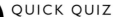

QUICK QUIZ

Can you match the specialties on the left with their defining credentials and approaches on the right?

1. psychotherapist
2. psychiatrist
3. clinical psychologist
4. research psychologist
5. psychoanalyst

a. Trained in a therapeutic approach started by Freud

b. Has a Ph.D., Psy.D, or Ed.D. and does research on, or psychotherapy for, mental-health problems

c. May have any credential, or none

d. Has an advanced degree (usually a Ph.D.) and does applied or basic research

e. Has an M.D.; tends to take a medical approach to emotional problems

Answers:
1.c 2.e 3.b 4.d 5.a

What's Ahead

- What guidelines can help you evaluate psychological claims?

- Why is a psychological theory unscientific if it explains anything that could conceivably happen?

- What's wrong with drawing conclusions about behavior from a collection of anecdotes?

1.3 Critical and Scientific Thinking in Psychology

One of the greatest benefits of studying psychology is that you learn not only how the brain works in general but also how to use yours in particular—by thinking critically. **Critical thinking** is the ability and willingness to assess claims and make objective judgments on the basis of well-supported reasons and evidence, rather than emotion and anecdote. Critical thinkers are able to look for flaws in arguments and to resist claims that have no supporting evidence. Critical thinking, however, is not merely negative thinking. It includes the ability to be creative and constructive—to come up with alternative explanations for events, think of implications of research findings, and apply new knowledge to social and personal problems.

critical thinking
The ability and willingness to assess claims and make objective judgments on the basis of well-supported reasons and evidence, rather than emotion or anecdote.

Most people know that you have to exercise the body to keep it in shape, but they may not realize that clear thinking also requires effort and practice. All around us we can see examples of flabby thinking. Sometimes people justify their mental laziness by proudly telling you they are open-minded. "It's good to be open-minded," philosopher Jacob Needleman once replied, "but not so open that your brains fall out."

Critical thinking is not only indispensable in ordinary life; it is also fundamental to all science, including psychological science. By exercising critical thinking, you will be able to distinguish serious psychology from the psychobabble that clutters the airwaves and bookstores. Critical thinking requires logical skills, but other skills and dispositions are also important (Halpern, 1995; Levy, 1997; Paul, 1984; Ruggiero, 1997). Here are eight essential critical-thinking guidelines that we will be emphasizing throughout this book.

Ask Questions; Be Willing to Wonder.
What is the one kind of question that most exasperates parents of young children? "Why is the sky blue, Mommy?" "Why doesn't the plane fall?" "Why don't pigs have wings?" Unfortunately, as children grow up, they tend to stop asking "why" questions like these. (Why do you think this is?)

"The trigger mechanism for creative thinking is the disposition to be curious, to wonder, to inquire," observed Vincent Ruggiero (1988). "Asking 'What's wrong here?' and/or 'Why is this the way it is, and how did it come to be that way?'

It is not enough to say that something "could be" true. Critical thinkers decide which explanation is most likely to be true, based on the best available evidence.

leads to the identification of problems and challenges." We hope that you will not approach psychology as received wisdom but will ask many questions about the theories and findings we present in this book. Be on the lookout, too, for questions about human behavior that have not been answered. If you do that, you will not only be learning psychology; you will also be learning to think the way psychologists do.

Define Your Terms. Once you have raised a general question, the next step is to frame it in clear and concrete terms. Vague or poorly defined terms in a question can lead to misleading or incomplete answers. For example, have you ever wondered whether animals can use language? The answer depends on how you define "language." If you mean "a system of communication," then birds do it, bees do it, and even trees do it. But if you mean "a system of communication that combines sounds or gestures into an infinite number of structured utterances that convey meaning" (which is how linguists define it), then as far as anyone can tell, only people use language, though some animals are able to acquire some aspects of language in special settings (see Chapter 6).

For scientists, defining terms means being precise about just what it is that they're studying. Researchers often start out with a **hypothesis,** a statement that attempts to describe or explain a given behavior, and initially, this hypothesis may be stated quite generally, as in, say, "Misery loves company." But before any research can be done, the hypothesis must be made more precise. For example, "Misery loves company" might be rephrased as

"People who are anxious about a threatening situation tend to seek out others facing the same threat."

A hypothesis, in turn, leads to explicit predictions about what will happen in a particular situation. In a prediction, terms such as *anxiety* or *threatening situation* are given **operational definitions,** which specify how the phenomena in question are to be observed and measured. "Anxiety" might be defined operationally as a score on an anxiety questionnaire; "threatening situation" might be defined as the threat of an electric shock. The prediction might be, "If you raise people's anxiety scores by telling them they are going to receive electric shocks, and then you give them the choice of waiting alone or with others in the same situation, they will be more likely to choose to wait with others than they would be if they were not anxious." The prediction can then be tested.

Examine the Evidence. Have you ever heard someone in the heat of argument exclaim, "I just know it's true, no matter what you say" or "That's my opinion; nothing's going to change it"? Have you ever made such statements yourself? Accepting a conclusion without evidence, or expecting others to do so, is a sure sign of lazy thinking. A critical thinker asks, "What evidence supports or refutes this argument and its opposition? How reliable is the evidence?" If checking the reliability of the evidence directly is not possible, the person considers whether it came from a reliable source.

In scientific research, an idea may initially generate excitement because it is plausible, imaginative,

hypothesis
A statement that attempts to predict or to account for a set of phenomena; scientific hypotheses specify relationships among events or variables and are empirically tested.

operational definition
A precise definition of a term in a hypothesis, which specifies the operations for observing and measuring the process or phenomenon being defined.

When demonstrating "levitation" and other "magical abilities," illusionists such as André Kole exploit people's tendency to trust the evidence of their own eyes even when such evidence is misleading. Critical thinkers ask questions about the nature and reliability of the evidence for a phenomenon.

principle of falsifiability
The principle that a scientific theory must make predictions that are specific enough to expose the theory to the possibility of disconfirmation; that is, the theory must predict not only what will happen, but also what will not happen.

or appealing, but as we have seen, eventually it must be backed by empirical evidence if it is to be taken seriously. A collection of anecdotes or an appeal to authority will not do.

Here's an example involving childhood autism, a serious mental disorder. Autistic children often will not look you in the eye; they live in a silent world of their own, cut off from normal social interaction. They may rock back and forth for hours, and sometimes they do self-destructive things, such as poking pencils in their ears. At one time, many clinicians thought that autism was caused by rejecting, cold "refrigerator mothers." Their belief was influenced by the writings of the eminent psychoanalyst Bruno Bettelheim. Bettelheim drew his conclusions from just a few case studies of autistic children whose mothers had psychological problems—and he exaggerated the number of cases he had examined (Pollak, 1997). Yet Bettelheim's authority was so great that many people accepted his claims despite his meager data. When proper studies were finally done, using objective testing procedures and a larger, representative group of autistic children and their parents, scientists learned that

parents of autistic children are as psychologically healthy as any other parents. Today we know that autism stems from a neurological problem rather than from any psychological problems of the mothers. But because so many people accepted Bettelheim's claims, thousands of women blamed themselves for their children's disorder and suffered needless guilt and remorse.

Analyze Assumptions and Biases.

Assumptions are beliefs that are taken for granted, and *biases* are assumptions that keep us from considering the evidence fairly or that cause us to ignore the evidence entirely. Critical thinkers try to identify and evaluate the unspoken assumptions on which claims and arguments may rest—in the books they read, the political speeches they hear, and the ads that bombard them every day. And in science, a questioning attitude toward assumptions is what drives progress. Some of the greatest scientific advances have been made by those who dared to doubt what everyone else assumed to be true: that the sun revolves around the earth, that illness can be cured by applying leeches to the skin, that madness is a sign of demonic possession.

Critical thinkers are willing to analyze and test not only other people's assumptions, but also their own (which is a lot harder). Researchers put their own assumptions to the test by stating a hypothesis in such a way that it can be *refuted,* or disproved by counterevidence. This principle, known as the **principle of falsifiability,** does not mean that the hypothesis *will* be disproved, only that it *could* be if contrary evidence were to be discovered. Another way of saying this is that a scientist must risk disconfirmation by predicting not only what will happen, but also what will *not* happen. In the "misery loves company" study, the hypothesis would be refuted if most anxious people went off alone to sulk and worry, or if anxiety had no effect on their behavior (see Figure 1.1). A willingness to make "risky" predictions forces the scientist to take such negative evidence seriously and to abandon mistaken assumptions. Any researcher who refuses to go out on a limb and risk disconfirmation is not a true scientist; and any theory that purports to explain everything that could conceivably happen is unscientific.

If you keep your eyes open, you will find that violations of the principle of falsifiability abound in everyday life. For example, some police officers and therapists believe that murderous satanic cults are widespread, even though research psychologists, the FBI, and police investigators have been unable

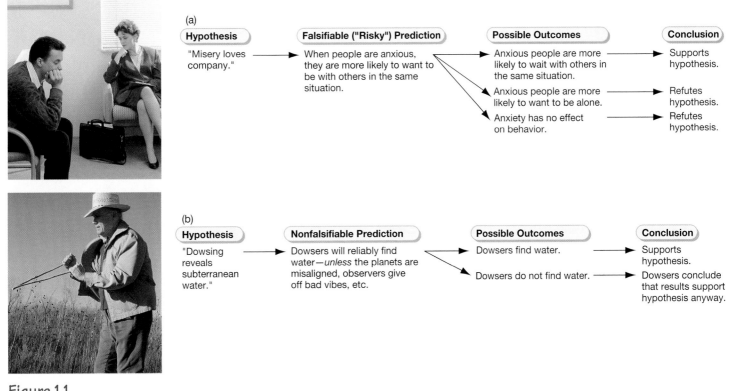

Figure 1.1
The Principle of Falsifiability

The scientific method requires researchers to expose their ideas to the possibility of counterevidence, as in row (a). In contrast, pseudoscientists and people claiming psychic powers, such as dowsers (who say they can find underground water with a "dowsing rod" that bends when water is present), typically interpret all possible outcomes as support for their assertions, as in row (b). Their claims are therefore untestable.

to substantiate this claim (Burgess et al., 1998; Spitz, 1997). Believers say they are not surprised by the lack of evidence because satanic cults cover up their activities by eating bodies or burying them. The FBI's failure to find the evidence is "proof," they say, that the FBI is part of a conspiracy to support the satanists. To believers, then, the lack of evidence of satanic cults is actually a sign of the cults' success. But think about that claim. If a lack of evidence can count as evidence, then what could possibly count as counterevidence? What could ever get believers to change their minds, to admit they were wrong?

Avoid Emotional Reasoning. Emotion has a place in critical thinking and in science, too. Passionate commitment to a view motivates people to think boldly, to defend unpopular ideas, and to seek evidence for creative new theories. But emotional conviction alone cannot settle arguments. As Nobel Prize–winning scientist Peter Medawar (1979) once wrote, "The intensity of the conviction that a hypothesis is true has no bearing on whether it is true or not."

You probably already hold strong beliefs about child rearing, drugs, the causes of crime, racism, the origins of intelligence, gender differences, homosexuality, and many other issues of concern to psychologists. As you read this book, you may find yourself quarreling with findings that you dislike. Disagreement is fine; it means that you are reading actively. All we ask is that you think about why you are disagreeing: Is it because the evidence is unpersuasive or because the results make you feel anxious or annoyed?

Don't Oversimplify. A critical thinker looks beyond the obvious, resists easy generalizations, and rejects either–or thinking. For example, is it better to feel you have control over what happens to you, or to accept with tranquility whatever life serves up? Either answer oversimplifies. As we will see in Chapter 12, control has many important benefits, but sometimes it's best to "go with the flow."

One common form of oversimplification is *argument by anecdote*—generalizing from a personal experience or a few examples to everyone: One crime committed by a paroled ex-convict means that parole should be abolished; one friend who hates his or her school means that everybody who goes there hates it. Anecdotes are often the source of stereotyping, as well: One dishonest welfare mother means they are all dishonest; one encounter with an unconventional Californian means they are all flaky. Critical and scientific thinkers want more evidence than one or two stories before drawing such sweeping conclusions.

Consider Other Interpretations.

A critical thinker creatively formulates hypotheses that offer reasonable explanations of the topic at hand. In science, the goal is to arrive at a **theory,** an organized system of assumptions and principles that purports to explain certain phenomena and how they are related. A scientific theory is not just someone's personal opinion, as people imply when they say "It's only a theory." Theories that come to be accepted by the scientific community make as few assumptions as possible and account for many empirical findings (Stanovich, 1996).

Before settling on an explanation of some behavior, however, critical thinkers are careful not to shut out alternative possibilities. They generate as many interpretations of the evidence as they can before settling on the most likely one. For example, suppose a news magazine reports that people who are chronically depressed are more likely than nondepressed people to develop cancer. Before concluding that depression causes cancer, you would need to consider some other possibilities. Perhaps depressed people are more likely to smoke and to drink too much, and it is those unhealthful habits that increase their cancer risk. Or perhaps, in studies of depression and cancer, early, undetected cancers were responsible for the patients' feelings of depression.

Tolerate Uncertainty.

Ultimately, learning to think critically teaches us one of the hardest lessons of life: how to live with uncertainty. Sometimes there is little or no evidence available to examine. Sometimes the evidence permits only tentative conclusions. Sometimes the evidence seems strong enough to permit strong conclusions . . . until, exasperatingly, new evidence throws our beliefs into disarray. Critical thinkers are willing to accept this state of uncertainty. They are not afraid to say, "I don't know" or "I'm not sure."

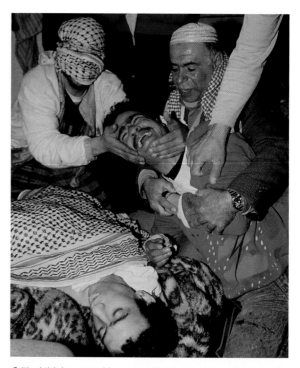

Critical thinkers consider competing explanations. For example, many North Americans believe that men are "naturally" less emotionally expressive than women, but this difference may be due less to gender than to culture, as we will see in Chapter 12. This Palestinian man, grieving over his dead son, does not fit Western stereotypes of male emotionality.

In science, tolerating uncertainty means that researchers must avoid drawing firm conclusions until other researchers have repeated, or *replicated,* their studies and verified their findings. Secrecy is a big "no-no" in science; you must be willing to tell others where you got your ideas and how you tested them so that others can challenge the findings if they think the findings are wrong. Replication is an essential part of the scientific process because sometimes what seems to be a fabulous phenomenon turns out to be only a fluke.

The need to accept a certain amount of uncertainty does not mean that we must abandon all assumptions, beliefs, and convictions. That would be impossible, in any case: We all need values and principles to guide our actions. As Vincent Ruggiero (1988) wrote, "It is not the embracing of an idea that causes problems—it is the refusal to relax that embrace when good sense dictates doing so."

As you read this book, you will have many opportunities to think critically about psychological theories and about the personal and social issues that affect us all. From time to time, a blue tab with a lightbulb symbol (like the one shown here)

Thinking Critically About . . .

theory
An organized system of assumptions and principles that purports to explain a specified set of phenomena and their interrelationships.

will highlight a discussion where one or more of our critical-thinking guidelines is especially relevant. Also, in Quick Quizzes, the lightbulb will indicate questions that give you practice in applying the guidelines. Keep in mind, however, that critical thinking is important throughout the book, not only where the lightbulb appears.

Critical thinking is a tool to guide us on a lifelong quest for understanding—a tool that we must keep sharpening. And it is as much an attitude as it is a set of skills. True critical thinking, in the words of philosopher Richard W. Paul (1984), is "fair-mindedness brought into the heart of everyday life."

 QUICK QUIZ

Can you identify how the guidelines to critical thinking were violated in each of the following cases?

1. For years, writer Norman Cousins told how he had cured himself of a rare, life-threatening disease through a combination of humor and vitamins. In a best-selling book about his experience, he recommended the same approach to others.

2. Benjamin Rush, an eighteenth-century physician, believed that yellow fever should be treated by bloodletting. Many of his patients died, but Rush did not lose faith in his approach; he attributed each recovery to his treatment and each death to the severity of the disease (Stanovich, 1996).

Answers:
1. Cousins oversimplified, arguing by anecdote instead of examining evidence from controlled studies that included people who were *not* helped by humor and vitamins; and he may have been reasoning emotionally because of his own dramatic recovery. 2. Rush failed to analyze and test his assumptions; he violated the principle of falsifiability, interpreting a patient's survival as support for his hypothesis and explaining away each death by saying that the person had been too ill for the treatment to work. Thus, there was no possible counterevidence that could refute the theory (which, by the way, was dead wrong—the "treatment" was actually as dangerous as the disease).

What's Ahead

- When are psychological case studies informative, and when are they useless?

- Why do psychologists often observe people in laboratories instead of in everyday situations?

- Why should you be skeptical about psychological tests in magazines and newspapers?

- What's the difference between a psychological survey and a poll of listeners conducted by a radio talk-show host?

1.4 Descriptive Studies: Establishing the Facts

Psychologists gather evidence to support their hypotheses by using different methods, depending on the kinds of questions they want to answer. These methods are not mutually exclusive, however. Just as a police detective may use a magnifying glass *and* a fingerprint duster *and* interviews of suspects to figure out "who done it," psychological sleuths often draw on different techniques at different stages of an investigation. As you read about these methods, you may want to list their advantages and disadvantages, to help you remember them better, then check your list against the one in Table 1.3 on page 29.

We will begin with **descriptive methods**, which allow researchers to describe and predict behavior but not necessarily to choose one explanation over competing ones.

Case Studies

A **case study** (or *case history*) is a detailed description of a particular individual. It may be based on careful observation or on formal psychological testing. It may include information about a person's childhood, dreams, fantasies, experiences, relationships, and hopes—anything that will provide insight into the person's behavior. Case studies are most commonly used by clinicians, but

descriptive methods
Methods that yield descriptions of behavior but not necessarily causal explanations.

case study
A detailed description of a particular individual being studied or treated.

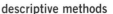

This picture, drawn by Genie, a young girl who endured years of isolation and mistreatment, shows one of her favorite pastimes: listening to researcher Susan Curtiss play the piano. Genie's drawings were used along with other case material to study her mental and social development.

1.1

sometimes academic researchers use them as well, especially when they are just beginning to study a topic or when practical or ethical considerations prevent them from gathering information in other ways.

For example, suppose you want to know whether the first few years of life are critical for acquiring language. Can children who have missed out on hearing speech (or, in the case of deaf children, seeing signs) "catch up" later? Obviously, psychologists cannot answer this question by isolating children and seeing what happens! So instead they have studied unusual cases of language deprivation.

One such case involved a 13-year-old girl who had been cruelly locked up in a small room since infancy. Her mother, a battered wife, barely cared for her, and no one in the family spoke a word to her. If she made the slightest sound, her severely disturbed father beat her with a large piece of wood. When she was finally rescued, "Genie," as researchers called her, did not know how to chew or to stand erect, and her only sounds were high-pitched whimpers. Eventually, she began to use words and understand short sentences, but even after many years, her grammar and pronunciation remained abnormal. She never learned to use pronouns correctly, ask questions, produce proper negative sentences, or use the little word endings that communicate tense, conjunction, and posses-

observational study
A study in which the researcher carefully and systematically observes and records behavior without interfering with the behavior; it may involve either naturalistic or laboratory observation.

sion (Curtiss, 1977, 1982; Rymer, 1993). This sad case, along with similar ones, suggests that a critical period exists for language development, with the likelihood of mastering a first language declining steadily after early childhood and falling off drastically at puberty (Pinker, 1994).

Case studies illustrate psychological principles in a way that abstract generalizations and cold statistics never can, and they produce a more detailed picture of an individual than other methods do. In biological research, cases of patients with brain damage have yielded important clues to how the brain is organized (see Chapter 4). But in most instances, case studies have serious drawbacks. Information is often missing or is hard to interpret. And the person who is the focus of the study may be *unrepresentative* of the group that the researcher is interested in. For example, it is possible that Genie was born with mental deficits that made her unlike most other children. That is why case studies are usually only sources, rather than tests, of hypotheses. You should be extremely cautious about pop-psych books and TV programs that present only testimonials and vivid case histories as evidence.

Observational Studies

In **observational studies,** the researcher observes, measures, and records behavior while taking care to avoid intruding on the people (or animals) being observed. The primary purpose of *naturalistic observation* is to find out how people or other animals act in their normal social environments. Psychologists use naturalistic observation wherever people happen to be—at home, on playgrounds or streets,

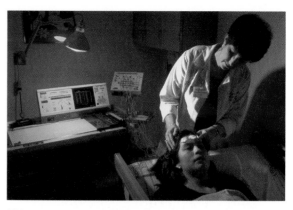

This woman is slumbering for science. By sleeping in the laboratory instead of in the natural environment of their own homes, volunteers can provide researchers with valuable information about brain and muscle activity during sleep.

GET INVOLVED

A STUDY OF "PERSONAL SPACE"

Try a little naturalistic observation of your own. Go to a public place where people seat themselves, such as a movie theater or a cafeteria with large tables. If you choose a setting where many people enter at once, you might recruit some friends to help you; you can divide the area into sections and assign each observer one section to observe. As individuals and groups sit down, note how many seats they leave between themselves and the next person. On the average, how far do people tend to sit from strangers? Once you have your results, see how many possible explanations you can come up with.

in schoolrooms, or in offices. Often, however, researchers prefer making their observations in a laboratory setting. In *laboratory observation,* they have more control. They can use sophisticated equipment, determine how many people will be observed at once, maintain a clear line of vision, and so forth.

Suppose that you wanted to know how infants of different ages respond when left with a stranger. The most efficient approach might be to have parents and their infants come to your laboratory, observe them playing together for a while through a one-way window, then have a stranger enter the room and, a few minutes later, have the parent leave. You could record signs of distress, interactions with the stranger, and other behavior, checking your observations against those of others to ensure accuracy. If you did this, you would find that very young infants carry on cheerfully with whatever they are doing when the parent leaves. However, by the age of about 8 months, children will often burst into tears or show other signs of what child psychologists call "separation anxiety" (see Chapter 3).

One shortcoming of laboratory observation is that the presence of researchers and special equipment may cause subjects to behave differently than they would in their usual surroundings. Further, observational studies, like other descriptive studies, are more useful for describing behavior than for explaining it. If we observe infants protesting whenever a parent leaves the room, we cannot be sure *why* they are protesting. Is it because they have become attached to their parents and want them nearby, or have they learned from experience that crying brings an adult with a cookie and a cuddle? Observational studies alone cannot answer such questions.

Tests

Psychological tests, sometimes called *assessment instruments,* are procedures for measuring and evaluating personality traits, emotional states, aptitudes, interests, abilities, and values. Typically, such tests require people to answer a series of written or oral questions. The answers may then be totaled to yield a single numerical score, or a set of scores. *Objective tests,* also called "inventories," measure beliefs, feelings, or behaviors of which an individual is aware; *projective tests* are designed to tap unconscious feelings or motives (see Chapter 10).

At one time or another, you have no doubt taken a psychological test, such as an intelligence test, achievement test, or vocational-aptitude test. Hundreds of psychological tests are used in industry, education, the military, and the helping professions. Some are given to individuals, others to large groups. These measures help clarify differences among individuals, as well as differences in the reactions of the same individual on different occasions or at different stages of life. They may be used to promote self-understanding, to evaluate treatments and programs, or, in scientific research, to draw generalizations about human behavior. Well-constructed psychological tests are a great improvement over simple self-evaluation because many people have a distorted view of their own abilities and traits.

One test of a good test is whether it is **standardized**—that is, whether uniform procedures exist for giving and scoring the test. It would hardly be fair to give some people detailed instructions and plenty of time and others only vague instructions and limited time. Those who administer the test must know exactly how to explain the

psychological tests
Procedures used to measure and evaluate personality traits, emotional states, aptitudes, interests, abilities, and values.

standardize
In test construction, to develop uniform procedures for giving and scoring a test.

Many people attach a lot of importance to their test scores!

tasks involved, how much time to allow, and what materials to use. Scoring is usually done by referring to **norms,** or established standards of performance. The usual procedure for developing norms is to give the test to a large group of people who resemble those for whom the test is intended. Norms determine which scores can be considered high, low, or average.

Test construction presents many challenges. For one thing, the test must be **reliable**—that is, it must produce the same results from one time and place to the next. A vocational-interest test is not reliable if it tells Tom that he would make a wonderful engineer but a poor journalist, but then it gives different results when Tom retakes the test a week later. Nor is it reliable if alternate forms of the test, intended to be comparable, yield different results.

To be useful, a test must also be **valid;** that is, it must measure what it is designed to measure. A creativity test is not valid if what it actually measures is verbal sophistication. The validity of a test is often measured by its ability to predict other, independent measures, or criteria, of the trait in question. The criterion for a scholastic aptitude test might be college grades; the criterion for a test of shyness might be behavior in social situations. Among psychologists, controversy exists about the validity of even some widely used tests. For example, an evaluation of the Graduate Record Exam (GRE) found it to be somewhat useful for predicting first-year grades in graduate psychology programs, but *not* second-year grades, professors' ratings of students, or the quality of students' dissertations (Sternberg & Williams, 1997).

Criticisms and reevaluations of psychological tests keep psychological assessment scientifically rigorous and can lead to better, more sophisticated testing. In contrast, the pseudoscientific tests frequently found in magazines and newspapers usually have not been evaluated for either validity or reliability. These questionnaires often have inviting headlines such as "Are You Self-destructive?" or "The Seven Types of Lover," but they are merely lists of questions that someone thought sounded good.

Surveys

Psychological tests usually generate information about people indirectly. In contrast, **surveys** are questionnaires and interviews that gather information by asking people directly about their experiences, attitudes, or opinions. Most of us are familiar with surveys in the form of national opinion polls, such as the Gallup and Roper polls. Surveys have been done on many topics, from Internet use to sexual preferences. They produce bushels of data—but they are not easy to do well.

The biggest hurdle is getting a **representative sample,** a group of subjects that accurately represents the larger population that the researcher wishes to describe. Suppose you wanted to know about drug use among college sophomores. Questioning every college sophomore in the country would not be practical; instead, you would need to recruit a sample. You could use special selection procedures to ensure that this sample contained the same proportion of women, men, blacks, whites, poor people, rich people, Catholics, Jews, and so on as in the general population of college sophomores. Even then, a sample drawn just from your own school or town might not yield results applicable to the entire country.

A sample's size is less critical than its representativeness; a small but representative sample may yield extremely accurate results, whereas a survey or poll that fails to use proper sampling methods may yield questionable results, no matter how large the sample. For example, a radio talk-show host who asks listeners to call in to vote on a controversial question is hardly conducting a scientific poll, even if thousands of people respond. Why? As a group, people who listen to talk radio are likely to hold different opinions on certain topics than those who prefer, say, a classical music station. Moreover, such polls suffer from a **volunteer bias:**

Thinking Critically About Opinion Polls and Surveys

norms
In test construction, established standards of performance.

reliability
In test construction, the consistency of scores derived from a test, from one time and place to another.

validity
The ability of a test to measure what it was designed to measure.

surveys
Questionnaires and interviews that ask people directly about their experiences, attitudes, or opinions.

representative sample
A group of subjects, selected from a population for study, which matches the population on important characteristics such as age and sex.

Every time I think I'm part of a normal relationship...

Someone publishes a new survey.

Those who feel strongly enough to volunteer their opinions may differ from those who stay silent. When you read about a survey (or any other kind of study), always ask who participated. A biased, nonrepresentative sample does not necessarily mean that a survey is worthless or uninteresting, but it does mean that the results may not hold true for other groups.

Another problem with surveys is that people sometimes lie, especially when the survey is about a touchy topic ("What? Me do that disgusting/dishonest/fattening thing? Never!"). The likelihood of lying is reduced when respondents are guaranteed anonymity. Also, there are ways to check for lying—for example, by asking a question several times with different wording. But not all surveys use these techniques, and even when people are trying to be truthful, they may misinterpret the survey questions or misremember the past.

When you hear about the results of a survey or opinion poll, you also need to check to see how the questions were phrased. It is easy to word questions in ways that elicit a particular answer. For example, political pollsters often design questions to produce the results they want. A Republican might ask people whether they support "increasing the amount spent on Medicare at a slower rate," whereas a Democrat might ask whether people favor "cuts in the projected growth of Medicare." The two phrases mean exactly the same thing, but respondents are likely to react more negatively when the word "cuts" is used (Kolbert, 1995).

As you can see, although surveys can be extremely informative, they must be conducted and interpreted carefully.

1.2

volunteer bias
A shortcoming of findings derived from a sample of volunteers instead of a representative sample, the volunteers may differ from those who did not volunteer.

QUICK QUIZ

A. Which descriptive method would be most appropriate for studying each of the following topics? (All of them, by the way, have been investigated by psychologists.)

1. Ways in which the games of boys differ from those of girls

2. Changes in attitudes toward nuclear disarmament after a TV movie about nuclear holocaust

3. The math skills of children in the United States versus Japan

4. Physiological changes that occur when people watch violent movies

5. The development of a male infant who was reared as a female after his penis was accidentally burned off during a routine surgery

a. case study

b. naturalistic observation

c. laboratory observation

d. survey

e. test

B. Professor Flummox gives her new test of aptitude for studying psychology to her psychology students at the start of the year. At the end of the year, she finds that those who did well on the test averaged only a C in the course. The test lacks _____ .

Answers:
A. 1.b 2.d 3.e 4.c 5.a B. validity

- If grades and TV watching are "negatively" correlated, what is the relationship between them?

- If TV watching and aggressiveness in children are positively correlated, does that mean that TV watching causes aggressiveness?

1.5 Correlational Studies: Looking for Relationships

In descriptive research, psychologists often want to know whether two or more phenomena are related and, if so, how strongly. For example, are students' grade-point averages related to the number of hours they spend watching television? To find out, a psychologist would do a **correlational study.**

The word **correlation** is often used as a synonym for relationship. Technically, however, a correlation is a numerical measure of the *strength* of the relationship between two things. The "things" may be events, scores, or anything else that can be recorded and tallied. In psychological studies, such things are called **variables** because they can vary in quantifiable ways. Height, weight, age, income, IQ scores, number of items recalled on a memory test, number of smiles in a given time period—anything that can be measured, rated, or scored can serve as a variable.

A **positive correlation** means that high values of one variable are associated with high values of the other, and that low values of one variable are associated with low values of the other:

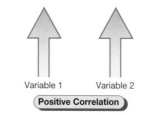

Height and weight are positively correlated, for example; so are IQ scores and school grades. Rarely is a correlation perfect, however. Some tall people weigh less than some short ones; some people with average IQs are superstars in the classroom, and some with high IQs get poor grades. Figure 1.2a shows a positive correlation between men's educational level and their annual income.

A **negative correlation** means that high values of one variable are associated with *low* values of the other:

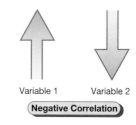

Figure 1.2b shows a negative correlation between average income and the incidence of dental disease for groups of 100 families; in general, as you can see, the higher the income, the fewer the dental problems. In the automobile business, the older the car, the lower the price, except for antiques and models favored by collectors. As for human beings, in general, the older adults are, the fewer miles they can run, the fewer crimes they are likely to commit, and the fewer hairs they have on their heads. And remember that correlation between hours spent watching TV and grade-point averages? It's a negative one: Lots of hours in front of the television are associated with lower grades (Potter, 1987; Ridley-Johnson, Cooper, & Chance, 1983). See whether you can think of other variables that are negatively correlated. Remember, though, a negative correlation means that a certain kind of relationship exists. If there is no relationship between two variables, we say that they are *uncorrelated*. Adult shoe size and IQ scores are uncorrelated.

The statistic used to express a correlation is called the **coefficient of correlation.** This number conveys both the size of the correlation and its direction. A perfect positive correlation has a coefficient of +1.00, and a perfect negative correlation has a coefficient of −1.00. Suppose you weighed ten people and listed them in order, from lightest to heaviest, then measured their heights and listed them in order, from shortest to tallest. If the names on the two lists were in exactly the same order, the correlation between weight and height would be +1.00. If the correlation between two variables is +.80, it means that the two are strongly related. If the correlation is −.80, the relationship is just as strong, but it is negative. When there is no association between two variables, the coefficient is zero or close to zero.

Correlational studies are common in psychology and are often reported in the news. But beware; correlations can be misleading. The important thing to remember is that *a correlation does not show causation.* It is easy to assume that if A predicts

correlational study
A descriptive study that looks for a consistent relationship between two phenomena.

correlation
A measure of how strongly two variables are related to one another.

variables
Characteristics of behavior or experience that can be measured or described by a numeric scale; variables are manipulated and assessed in scientific studies.

positive correlation
An association between increases in one variable and increases in another—or between decreases in one and in the other.

negative correlation
An association between increases in one variable and decreases in another.

coefficient of correlation
A measure of correlation that ranges in value from −1.00 to +1.00.

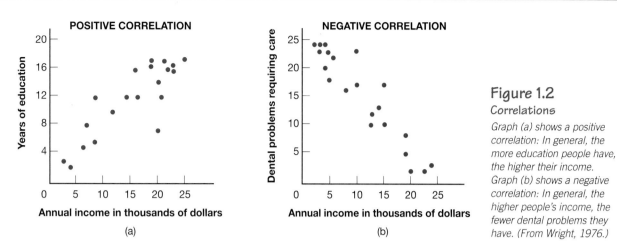

Figure 1.2
Correlations

Graph (a) shows a positive correlation: In general, the more education people have, the higher their income. Graph (b) shows a negative correlation: In general, the higher people's income, the fewer dental problems they have. (From Wright, 1976.)

B, A must be causing B—that is, making B happen—but that is not necessarily so. The number of storks nesting in some European villages is reportedly correlated (positively) with the number of human births in those villages. Therefore, knowing when the storks nest allows you to predict when more births than usual will occur. But that doesn't mean that storks bring babies or that babies attract storks! Human births seem to be somewhat more frequent at certain times of the year (you might want to speculate on the reasons), and the peaks just happen to coincide with the storks' nesting periods.

> **Thinking Critically About Correlation and Causation**

The coincidental nature of the correlation between nesting storks and human births is obvious, but in other cases, unwarranted conclusions about causation are more tempting. For example, if TV watching is correlated with children's aggressiveness, it is possible that violent programs are causing aggressiveness. But it is also possible that aggressive kids are drawn to television violence, or that some third factor accounts for both aggressiveness and attraction to violent programs (see Chapter 8). Similarly, the negative correlation between TV watching and grades might exist because heavy TV watchers have less time to study, but it is also possible that they have some personality trait that attracts them to TV and makes them dislike studying, or that they use TV as an escape when their grades are low, or that TV is especially appealing to people who are not academically inclined . . . you get the idea.

The moral of the story: When two variables are associated, one variable may or may not be causing the other.

QUICK QUIZ

A. Are you clear about correlations? Find out by identifying each of the following as a positive or negative correlation:

1. The higher a male monkey's level of the hormone testosterone, the more aggressive he is likely to be.

2. The older people are, the less frequently they tend to have sexual intercourse.

3. The hotter the weather, the more crimes against persons (such as muggings) tend to occur.

B. Now see whether you can generate two or three alternative explanations for each of the preceding findings.

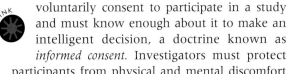

What's Ahead

- Why do psychologists rely so heavily on experiments?
- What, exactly, do control groups control for?
- In a double-blind experiment, who is "blind," and what aren't they supposed to "see"?

1.3

1.6 The Experiment: Hunting for Causes

Researchers often propose explanations of behavior on the basis of descriptive studies, but when they want to actually track down the causes of behavior, they rely heavily on the experimental method. An **experiment** allows the researcher to *control* or manipulate the situation being studied. Instead of being a passive recorder of what is going on, the researcher actively does something that he or she believes will affect people's behavior and then observes what happens. These procedures allow the experimenter to draw conclusions about cause and effect—about what causes what.

All psychological studies must conform to certain ethical guidelines, but such guidelines are especially important in experimental research because of this element of manipulation. In most colleges and universities, an ethics committee must approve all proposed studies. In addition, the American Psychological Association (APA) has a code of ethics, stating that human subjects must voluntarily consent to participate in a study and must know enough about it to make an intelligent decision, a doctrine known as *informed consent.* Investigators must protect participants from physical and mental discomfort or harm, and if any risk exists, they must warn the subjects in advance and give them an opportunity to withdraw at any time.

The APA's code also covers the humane treatment of research animals, which are used in only a small minority of psychological studies but are crucial to progress in some fields, especially biological psychology and behavioral research. Because of heated debates over animal rights and welfare, the APA's guidelines for using animals have been made more comprehensive in recent years. In addition, federal regulations governing the housing and care of animals have been strengthened and are constantly being reviewed. Every experiment involving vertebrates must now be reviewed by a committee that includes representatives from the research institution and the community.

Experimental Variables

Suppose you are a psychologist and you come across reports that cigarette smoking improves reaction time on simple tasks. You have a hunch that nicotine may have the opposite effect, however, when the task is as complex and demanding as driving a car. Therefore you decide to do an experiment to test your hypothesis. In a laboratory, you ask smokers to "drive" using a computerized driving simulator equipped with a stick shift and a gas pedal. The object, you tell them, is to maximize distance by driving as fast as possible on a winding road while avoiding rear-end collisions. At your request, some of the subjects smoke a cigarette immediately before climbing into the driver's seat. Others do not. You are interested in comparing how many collisions the two groups have. The basic design of this experiment is illustrated in Figure 1.3, which you may want to refer back to as you read the next few pages.

The aspect of an experimental situation manipulated or varied by the researcher is known as the **independent variable.** The reaction of the subjects—the behavior that the researcher tries to predict—is the **dependent variable.** Every experiment has at least one independent and one dependent variable. In our example, the independent variable is nicotine use: one cigarette versus none. The dependent variable is the number of collisions.

Ideally, everything in the experimental situation *except* the independent variable is held constant—that is, kept the same for all participants. You would not have some people use a stick shift and others an automatic, unless shift type were an independent variable. Similarly, you would not have some people go through the experiment alone and others perform in front of an audience. Holding everything but the independent variable constant ensures that whatever happens is due to the researcher's manipulation and nothing else. It allows you to rule out other interpretations.

Understandably, students often have trouble keeping independent and dependent variables straight. You might think of it this way: The dependent variable—the outcome of the study—*depends* on the independent variable. When psychologists set up an experiment, they think, "If I do X, the subjects in my study will do Y." The "X"

experiment
A controlled test of a hypothesis in which the researcher manipulates one variable to discover its effect on another.

independent variable
A variable that an experimenter manipulates.

dependent variable
A variable that an experimenter predicts will be affected by manipulations of the independent variable.

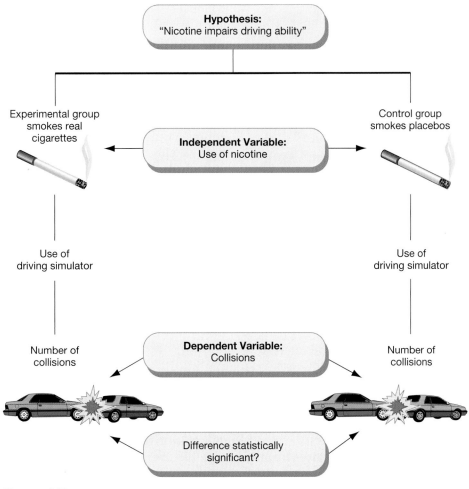

Figure 1.3
Do Smoking and Driving Mix?
The text describes this experimental design to test the hypothesis that nicotine in cigarettes impairs driving skills.

represents the independent variable; the "Y" represents the dependent variable:

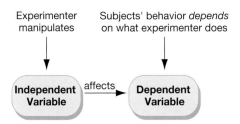

Most variables may be either independent or dependent, depending on what the experimenter wishes to find out. If you want to know whether eating chocolate makes people nervous, then the amount of chocolate eaten is the independent variable. If you want to know whether feeling nervous makes people eat chocolate, then the amount of chocolate eaten is the dependent variable.

Experimental and Control Conditions

Experiments usually require both an experimental condition and a comparison, or **control condition.** In the control condition, subjects are treated exactly like those in the experimental condition, except that they are not exposed to the same treatment, or manipulation of the independent variable. Without a control condition, you can't be sure that the behavior you are interested in would not have occurred anyway, even without your manipulation. In some studies, the same subjects can be used in both the control and the experimental conditions;

control condition
In an experiment, a comparison condition in which subjects are not exposed to the same treatment as in the experimental condition.

Control groups are crucial in experiments and other kinds of studies. For example, if a child is fascinated with the genitals of an anatomically realistic doll, does that mean the child has been sexually abused? Many people thought so, until studies using control groups showed that the doll play of nonabused children is no different from that of abused children (Koocher et al., 1995; Poole & Lamb, 1998). This child, who was not abused, is poking a pencil into the doll's vagina.

random assignment
A procedure for assigning people to experimental and control groups in which each individual has the same probability as any other of being assigned to a given group.

placebo
An inactive substance or fake treatment used as a control in an experiment or given by a medical practitioner to a patient.

single-blind study
An experiment in which subjects do not know whether they are in an experimental or a control group.

they are said to serve as their own controls. In other studies, subjects are assigned to either an *experimental group* or a *control group.*

In the nicotine experiment, the people who smoke before driving make up the experimental group, and those who do not smoke make up the control group. We want these two groups to be roughly the same in terms of average driving skill. It would not do to start out with a bunch of reckless roadrunners in the experimental group and a bunch of tired tortoises in the control group. We probably also want the two groups to be similar in average intelligence, education, smoking history, and other characteristics, so that none of these variables will affect our results. One way to accomplish this is to use **random assignment** of people to one group or another. If we have enough participants in our study, individual characteristics that could possibly affect the results are likely to be roughly balanced in the two groups, so we can ignore them.

We now have two groups. We also have a problem. In order to smoke, the experimental subjects must light up and inhale. These acts might set off certain expectations—of feeling relaxed, getting nervous, feeling confident, or

whatever. These expectations, in turn, might affect driving performance. It would be better to have the control group do everything the experimental group does except use nicotine.

Therefore, let's change our experimental design a bit. Instead of having the control subjects refrain from smoking, we will give them a **placebo,** a fake treatment. Placebos, which are critical when testing new drugs, often take the form of pills or injections containing no active ingredients. In our study, we will use phony cigarettes that taste and smell like the real thing but contain no active ingredients. Our control subjects will not know their cigarettes are fake and will have no way of distinguishing them from real ones. Now if they have substantially fewer collisions than the experimental group, we will feel safe in concluding that nicotine increases the probability of an auto accident.

Control groups, by the way, are also important in nonexperimental studies. Consider one highly publicized, long-running descriptive study of 80 children whose parents divorced when the children were young (Wallerstein, Lewis, & Blakeslee, 2000). In lengthy interviews over the years, the children, who are now in their thirties, have revealed many psychological problems and difficulties in relationships. The clinical researchers who did the study interpret these results as a strong indictment of divorce. But these children all grew up in one extremely affluent county in California, so the sample was nonrepresentative. Even more important, the study did not include a critical control group: children growing up with unhappy parents in an intact family. Without such a control group, the results cannot tell us much. For the record, better designed, large-scale research finds that children of divorce, although indeed at risk for certain psychological problems, usually surmount those problems and go on to live well-adjusted lives. Their adjustment depends on many factors, such as the amount of conflict between the parents before and after the divorce (Amato, 1994; Amato & Keith, 1991).

Experimenter Effects

Because expectations can influence the results of a study, subjects should not know whether they are in an experimental or a control group. When this is so (as it usually is), the experiment is said to be a **single-blind study.** But subjects are not the only ones who bring expectations to the laboratory; so do researchers. And researchers' expectations

GET INVOLVED

▶ THE POWER OF A SMILE

Prove to yourself how easily nonverbal cues from an experimenter can affect the behavior of a study's participants. As you walk around campus, quickly glance at individuals approaching you and either smile or maintain a neutral expression, then observe the other person's expression. Try to keep the duration of your glance the same whether you smile or not. You might record the results as you collect them instead of relying on your memory. Chances are that people you smile at will smile back, whereas those you approach with a neutral expression will return that expression. What does this tell you about the importance of doing double-blind studies?

and hopes for a particular result may cause them to inadvertently influence the participants' responses through facial expressions, posture, tone of voice, or some other cue.

Many years ago, Robert Rosenthal (1966) demonstrated how powerful such **experimenter effects** can be. He had students teach rats to run a maze. Half the students were told that their rats had been bred to be "maze bright," and half were told that their rats had been bred to be "maze dull." In reality, there were no genetic differences between the two groups of rats, yet the supposedly brainy rats actually did learn the maze more quickly, apparently because of the way the students treated them. If an experimenter's expectations can affect a rodent's behavior, reasoned Rosenthal, surely they can affect a human being's. He went on to demonstrate this point in many other studies (Rosenthal, 1994). Even an experimenter's friendly smile can affect people's responses in a study.

One solution to the problem of experimenter effects is to do a **double-blind study.** In such a study, the person running the experiment, the one having actual contact with the subjects, also does not know which subjects are in which groups until the data have been gathered. Double-blind procedures are standard in drug research. Different doses of a drug are coded in some way, and the person administering the drug is kept in the dark about the code's meaning until after the experiment. To run our nicotine study in a double-blind fashion, we would keep the person dispensing the cigarettes from knowing which ones were real and which were placebos. In psychological research, double-blind studies are often more difficult to design than those that are single-blind. The goal,

however, is always to control everything possible in an experiment.

Advantages and Limitations of Experiments

Because experiments allow conclusions about cause and effect, and because they permit researchers to distinguish real effects from placebo effects, they have long been the method of choice in psychology.

However, like all methods, the experiment has its limitations. Just as in other kinds of studies, the participants are not always representative of the larger population. Most volunteers in academic experiments are college students, who differ in many ways from people who are not in school. Moreover, in an experiment, the researcher determines which questions are asked and which behaviors are recorded, and the participants try to do as they are told. In their desire to cooperate, advance scientific knowledge, or present themselves in a positive light, they may act in ways that they ordinarily would not (Kihlstrom, 1995).

Thus, research psychologists confront a dilemma: The more control they exercise over the situation, the more unlike real life it may be. For this reason, many psychologists have called for more **field research,** the careful study of behavior in natural contexts such as schools and the workplace, using both descriptive and experimental methods.

Now that we have come to the end of our discussion of research methods, how did you do on your list of their advantages and disadvantages? You can find out by comparing your list with the one in Table 1.3 on page 29.

experimenter effects
Unintended changes in subjects' behavior due to cues inadvertently given by the experimenter.

double-blind study
An experiment in which neither the subjects nor the individuals running the study know which subjects are in the control group and which are in the experimental group until after the results are tallied.

field research
Descriptive or experimental research conducted in a natural setting outside the laboratory.

QUICK QUIZ

A. Name the independent and dependent variables in studies designed to answer the following questions:

1. Whether sleeping after learning a poem improves memory for the poem

2. Whether the presence of other people affects a person's willingness to help someone in distress

3. Whether people get agitated from listening to heavy-metal music

B. On a talk show, Dr. Blitznik announces a fabulous new program: Chocolate Immersion Therapy. "People who spend one day a week doing nothing but eating chocolate are soon cured of eating disorders, depression, drug abuse, and poor study habits," claims Dr. Blitznik. What should you find out about C.I.T. before signing up?

Answers:

A. 1. Opportunity to sleep after learning is the independent variable; memory for the poem is the dependent variable. 2. The presence of other people is the independent variable; willingness to help others is the dependent variable. 3. Exposure to heavy-metal music is the independent variable; agitation is the dependent variable. B. Some questions to ask: Is there research showing that people who go through C.I.T. did better than those in a control group who did not have the therapy, or who had a different therapy—say, Broccoli Immersion Therapy? If so, how many people were studied? How were they selected, and how were they assigned to the therapy and no-therapy groups? Did the person running the experiment know who was getting C.I.T. and who was not? How long did the "cures" last? Has the research been replicated?

What's Ahead

- How can psychologists tell whether a finding is impressive or trivial?

- Why are some findings statistically significant but unimportant in practical terms?

1.4

1.7 Evaluating the Findings

If you are a psychologist who has just done an observational study, a survey, or an experiment, your work has only just begun. Once you have some results in hand, you must do three things with them: (1) describe them, (2) assess how reliable and meaningful they are, and (3) figure out how to explain them.

Why Psychologists Use Statistics

Let's say that 30 people in the nicotine experiment smoked real cigarettes, and 30 smoked placebos. We have recorded the number of collisions for each person on the driving simulator. Now we have 60 numbers. What can we do with them?

descriptive statistics
Statistics that organize and summarize research data.

arithmetic mean
An average that is calculated by adding up a set of quantities and dividing the sum by the total number of quantities in the set.

The first step is to summarize the data. The world does not want to hear how many collisions each person had. It wants to know what happened in the nicotine group as a whole, compared with what happened in the control group. To provide this information, we need numbers that sum up our data. Such numbers, known as **descriptive statistics,** are often depicted in graphs and charts.

A good way to summarize the data is to compute group averages. The most commonly used type of average is the **arithmetic mean.** (For two other types, see the Appendix.) The mean is calculated by adding up all the individual scores and dividing the result by the number of scores. We can compute a mean for the nicotine group by adding up the 30 collision scores and dividing the sum by 30. Then we can do the same for the control group. Now our 60 numbers have been boiled down to 2. For the sake of our example, let's assume that the nicotine group had an average of 10 collisions, whereas the control group's average was only 7.

We must be careful, however, about how we interpret these averages. It is possible that no one in our nicotine group actually had 10 collisions. Perhaps half the people in the group were motoring maniacs and had 15 collisions, whereas the others were more cautious and had only 5. Perhaps almost all the subjects had 9, 10, or 11 collisions. Perhaps the number of accidents

Table 1.3 Research Methods in Psychology: Their Advantages and Disadvantages

Method	Advantages	Disadvantages
Case study	Good source of hypotheses. Provides in-depth information on individuals. Unusual cases can shed light on situations or problems that are unethical or impractical to study in other ways.	Vital information may be missing, making the case hard to interpret. The person's memories may be selective or inaccurate. The individual may not be representative or typical.
Naturalistic observation	Allows description of behavior as it occurs in the natural environment. Often useful in first stages of a research program.	Allows researcher little or no control of the situation. Observations may be biased. Does not allow firm conclusions about cause and effect.
Laboratory observation	Allows more control than naturalistic observation. Allows use of sophisticated equipment.	Allows researcher only limited control of the situation. Observations may be biased. Does not allow firm conclusions about cause and effect. Behavior may differ from behavior in the natural environment.
Test	Yields information on personality traits, emotional states, aptitudes, abilities.	Difficult to construct tests that are reliable and valid.
Survey	Provides a large amount of information on large numbers of people.	If sample is nonrepresentative or biased, it may be impossible to generalize from the results. Responses may be inaccurate or untrue.
Correlational study	Shows whether two or more variables are related. Allows general predictions.	Does not permit identification of cause and effect.
Experiment	Allows researcher to control the situation. Permits researcher to identify cause and effect, and to distinguish placebo effects from treatment effects.	Situation is artificial, and results may not generalize well to the real world. Sometimes difficult to avoid experimenter effects.

ranged from 0 to 15. The mean does not tell us about such variability in the subjects' responses. For that, we need other descriptive statistics. For example, the **standard deviation** tells us how clustered or spread out the individual scores are around the mean; the more spread out they are, the less "typical" the mean is. (For details, see the Appendix.) Unfortunately, when research is reported in newspapers or on the nightly news, you usually hear only about the mean.

At this point in our nicotine study, we have one group with an average of 10 collisions and another with an average of 7. Should we break out the champagne? Try to get on TV? Call our moth-

ers? Better hold off. Perhaps if one group had an average of 15 collisions and the other an average of 1, we could get excited. But rarely does a psychological study hit you between the eyes with a sensationally clear result. In most cases, there is some possibility that the difference between the two groups was due simply to chance. Perhaps the people in the nicotine group just happened to be a little more accident-prone, and their behavior had nothing to do with the nicotine.

To find out how impressive the data are, psychologists use **inferential statistics.** These statistics do not merely describe or summarize the data; they permit a researcher to draw *inferences*

standard deviation
A commonly used measure of variability that indicates the average difference between scores in a distribution and their mean.

inferential statistics
Statistical procedures that allow researchers to draw inferences about how statistically meaningful a study's results are.

Averages can be misleading if you don't know the extent to which events deviated from the statistical mean and how they were distributed.

(conclusions based on evidence) about how meaningful the findings are. Like descriptive statistics, inferential statistics involve the application of mathematical formulas to the data (again, see the Appendix for details). The most commonly used inferential statistics are **significance tests,** which tell researchers how likely a result was to have occurred by chance. In our nicotine study, a significance test will tell us how likely it is that the difference between the nicotine group and the placebo group occurred by chance. It is not possible to rule out chance entirely, but if the likelihood that a result occurred by chance is extremely low, we say that the result is *statistically significant.* This means that the probability that the difference is "real" is overwhelming—not certain, mind you, but overwhelming.

By convention, psychologists consider a result to be significant if it would be expected to occur by chance 5 or fewer times in 100 repetitions of the study. Another way of saying this is

that the result is significant at the .05—"point oh five"—level. If the difference could be expected to occur by chance in 6 out of 100 studies, we would have to say that the results failed to support the hypothesis—that the difference we obtained might well have occurred merely by chance—although we might still want to do further research to be sure. You can see that psychologists refuse to be impressed by just any old result.

By the way, a nicotine study similar to our hypothetical example has actually been done, using somewhat more complicated procedures (Spilich, June, & Renner, 1992). Smokers who lit up before driving got a little farther on the simulated road, but they also had significantly more rear-end collisions on average (10.7) than did temporarily abstaining smokers (5.2) or nonsmokers (3.1). After hearing about this research, the head of Federal Express banned smoking on the job among all of the company's drivers (George Spilich, personal communication).

significance tests
Statistical tests that assess how likely it is that a study's results occurred merely by chance.

QUICK QUIZ

Check your understanding of the descriptive–inferential distinction by mentally placing a check in the appropriate column for each phrase:

	Descriptive statistics	Inferential statistics
1. Summarize the data	_____	_____
2. Give likelihood of data occurring by chance	_____	_____
3. Include the mean	_____	_____
4. Give a measure of statistical significance	_____	_____
5. Tell you whether to call your mother about your results	_____	_____

Answers:
1. descriptive 2. inferential 3. descriptive 4. inferential 5. inferential

From the Laboratory to the Real World

The last step in any study is to figure out what the findings mean. Trying to understand behavior from uninterpreted findings is like trying to become fluent in Swedish by reading a Swedish–English dictionary. Just as you need the grammar of Swedish to tell you how the words fit together, the psychologist needs hypotheses and theories to explain how the facts that emerge from research fit together.

Choosing the Best Explanation.

Sometimes it is hard to choose between competing explanations. Does nicotine disrupt driving by impairing coordination, by increasing a driver's vulnerability to distraction, by interfering with the processing of information, by distorting the perception of danger—or by some combination of these factors? In interpreting any study, we must not go too far beyond the facts. Several explanations may fit those facts equally well, which means that more research will be needed to determine the best explanation.

Sometimes the best interpretation of a finding does not emerge until a hypothesis has been tested in different ways. If the findings of studies using different methods converge, there is greater reason to be confident about them. On the other hand, if they conflict, researchers will know they must modify their hypotheses or do more research.

Here's an example. When psychologists compare the mental-test scores of young people and old people, they usually find that younger people consistently outscore older ones. This type of research, in which groups are compared at a given time, is called **cross-sectional:**

Cross-sectional Study
Different groups compared at one time:

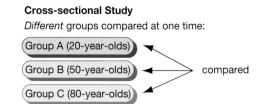

But **longitudinal studies** can also be used to investigate mental abilities across the life span. In a longitudinal study, the same people are followed over a period of time and are reassessed at regular intervals:

Longitudinal Study
Same group compared at different times:

In contrast to cross-sectional studies, longitudinal studies find that as people age, they sometimes continue to perform as well as they ever did on certain mental tests. A *general* decline in ability may not occur until people reach their 70s or 80s (Salthouse, 1998; Schaie, 1993). Why do results from the two types of studies conflict? Probably because cross-sectional studies measure generational differences; younger generations tend to outperform older ones because they are better educated or are more familiar with the tests used. Without longitudinal studies, we might falsely conclude that all kinds of mental ability inevitably decline sharply with age.

Judging the Result's Importance.

Sometimes psychologists agree on the reliability and meaning of a finding, but not on its ultimate relevance for theory or practice. Statistical significance alone does not provide the answer. A result may be statistically significant at the "point oh five level" yet be small and of little consequence in everyday life because the independent variable does not explain most of the variation in people's behavior. On the other hand, a result may not quite reach statistical significance yet be worth following up on (Falk & Greenbaum, 1995; Hunter, 1997). Because of these problems, many psychologists now prefer other statistical procedures that reveal how powerful the independent variable really is—how much of the variation in the data the variable accounts for.

> **Thinking Critically About "Significant" Research Findings**

One popular statistical technique, called **meta-analysis,** combines and analyzes data from many studies, instead of assessing each study's results separately. Meta-analysis tells the researcher how much of the variation in scores across *all* the studies examined can be explained by a particular variable. For example, a meta-analysis of nearly 50 years of research found that gender accounts for a good deal of the variance in performance on certain spatial–visual tasks, with males doing better than females on the average (Voyer, Voyer, & Bryden, 1995). In contrast, other meta-analyses have shown that gender accounts for only 1 to 5 percent of the variance on tests of verbal ability, math ability, and aggressiveness (Feingold, 1988; Hyde, 2000;

cross-sectional study
A study in which subjects of different ages are compared at a given time.

longitudinal study
A study in which subjects are followed and periodically reassessed over a period of time.

meta-analysis
A procedure for combining and analyzing data from many studies; it determines how much of the variance in scores across all studies can be explained by a particular variable.

Psychologists use scientific methods to study many puzzles of human behavior. Why do people lose their inhibitions when they dress up in funny outfits? Why do some people strive to become champion athletes in spite of physical disabilities? Why do some people become anorexic, in some cases starving themselves to death? And why do many people "forget themselves" in a mob, and do destructive things they would never dream of doing on their own?

Hyde, Fennema, & Lamon, 1990; Hyde & Linn, 1988). Although gender differences on these tests are reliable, they are small, and scores for males and females greatly overlap.

Techniques such as meta-analysis are useful because rarely does one study prove anything, in psychology or any other field. That is why you should be suspicious of headlines that announce a sudden, major scientific breakthrough. Scientific progress usually occurs gradually, not in one fell swoop.

PSYCHOLOGY IN THE NEWS, REVISITED

Now that you have finished the first chapter of this book, you are ready to explore more deeply what psychologists have learned about human behavior. We hope you will resist the temptation to skip descriptions of how these findings were obtained and will keep in mind that what we know about human behavior cannot be separated from how we know it.

At the start of each of the remaining chapters, we will present a real story from the news, one that raises some intriguing psychological questions. Then, at the end of the chapter, we will revisit the story to show how the material you have learned can help answer those questions. If you are ready to share the excitement of studying human behavior; if you love mysteries and want to know not only who did it but also why they did it; if you are willing to reconsider what you think you think . . . then you are ready to read on.

TAKING PSYCHOLOGY WITH YOU

What Psychology Can Do for You—and What It Can't

If you intend to become a psychologist or a mental-health professional, you have an obvious reason for taking a course in psychology. But psychology can contribute to your life in many ways, whether you plan to work in the field or not. Here are a few things psychology can do for you:

● *Make you a more informed person.* One purpose of education is to acquaint people with their cultural heritage and with humankind's achievements in literature, the humanities, and science. Because psychology plays a large role in contemporary society, being a well-informed person requires knowing something about psychological methods and findings.

● *Satisfy your curiosity about human nature.* When the Greek philosopher Socrates admonished his students to "know thyself," he was only telling them to do what they wanted to do anyway. The topic that fascinates human beings most is human beings. Psychology—along with the other social sciences, literature, history, and philosophy—can contribute to a better understanding of yourself and others.

● *Help you increase control over your life.* Psychology cannot solve all your problems, but it does offer techniques that may help you handle your emotions, improve your memory, and eliminate unwanted habits. It can also foster an attitude of objectivity that is useful for analyzing your behavior and your relationships with others.

● *Help you on the job.* A bachelor's degree in psychology is useful for getting a job in a helping profession, for example, as a welfare caseworker or a rehabilitation counselor. Anyone who works as a nurse, doctor, member of the clergy, police officer, or teacher can also put psychology to work on the job. So can waiters, flight attendants, bank tellers, salespeople, receptionists, and others whose jobs involve customer service. Finally, psychology can be useful to those whose jobs require them to predict people's behavior—for example, labor negotiators, politicians, advertising copywriters, managers, product designers, buyers, market researchers, magicians. . . .

● *Give you insights into political and social issues.* Crime, drug abuse, discrimination, and war are not only social issues but also psychological ones. Psychological knowledge alone cannot solve the complex political, social, and ethical problems that plague every society, but it can help you make informed judgments about them. For example, if you know that involuntary crowding often leads to stress, hostility, and difficulty concentrating, this knowledge may affect your views on which programs to support for schools and prisons.

● *Help you become a more critical thinker.* If you master and truly understand the material in this course, you will become less likely to confuse correlation and causation, to be swayed by stereotypes, or to accept glib generalizations that are unsupported by evidence. You will be suspicious when a "scientific survey" in the mail comes with a solicitation for funds from a political organization. You will resist drawing conclusions about "most people" on the basis of casual observations of yourself or your friends. And you will make better decisions about the claims and arguments you hear every day ("Buy this!" "Believe that!").

We are optimistic about psychology's role in the world, but we want to caution you that sometimes people expect things from psychology that it can't deliver. For example, psychology can't tell you the meaning of life. A philosophy about the purpose of life requires not only knowledge but also reflection and a willingness to learn from life's experiences. Nor does psychological understanding relieve people of responsibility for their actions. Knowing that your short temper is a result, in part, of your unhappy childhood does not give you a green light to yell at your family. Similarly, understanding the origins of child beating may help us to reduce child abuse and to treat offenders, but we can still hold child beaters accountable for their behavior.

Most important, psychology will not provide you with simple answers to complex questions. You have already learned that psychologists, like other scientists, often disagree among themselves. This disagreement is a normal result of their differing perspectives and methods, and it reflects the fact that most human phenomena do not lend themselves to one-note explanations. Therefore, rather than becoming attached to any one approach ("Medication will one day cure all mental illnesses"; "With the right environment, any child can become a Mozart"), the critical thinker will try to integrate the best contributions of each. In the final chapter of this book, we suggest how findings from several perspectives might help us understand some of the most fundamental activities and motives of life.

Despite the complexity of behavior and the lack of simple answers to human problems, psychologists have made enormous progress in unraveling the secrets of the human brain, mind, and heart. At the end of each chapter, starting with the next one, the "Taking Psychology with You" feature will suggest ways to apply psychological findings to your own life—at school, on the job, or in your relationships.

SUMMARY

The Science of Psychology

● *Psychology* is the discipline concerned with behavior and mental processes and how they are affected by an organism's external and internal environment. Psychology's methods and reliance on *empirical evidence* distinguish it from pseudoscience and "psychobabble."

● Psychological findings sometimes confirm, but often contradict, common sense. In any case, a result does not have to be surprising to be scientifically important.

● Psychology's forerunners made some valid observations and had some useful insights, but without rigorous empirical methods, they also made serious errors in the description and explanation of behavior, as in the case of phrenology.

● The official founder of scientific psychology was Wilhelm Wundt, who established the first psychological laboratory in 1879, in Leipzig, Germany. Wundt emphasized the analysis of experience into basic elements, through *trained introspection*. A competing approach, *functionalism*, was inspired in part by the evolutionary theories of Charles Darwin; it emphasized the purpose of behavior. One of its leading proponents was William James. Psychology as a method of psychotherapy was born in Vienna, with the work of Sigmund Freud and the establishment of *psychoanalysis*.

● Five points of view predominate today in psychology. The *biological perspective* emphasizes bodily events associated with actions, thoughts, and feelings. The *learning perspective* emphasizes how the environment and a person's history affect behavior; *behaviorists* reject mentalistic explanations and *social–cognitive learning theorists* combine elements of behaviorism with the study of thoughts, values, and intentions. The *cognitive perspective* emphasizes mental processes in perception, problem solving, belief formation, and other human activities. The *sociocultural perspective* explores how the social context and cultural rules affect an individual's beliefs and behavior. And the *psychodynamic perspective*, which originated with Freud's theory of *psychoanalysis*, emphasizes unconscious motives, conflicts, and desires; it differs greatly from the other approaches in its methods and standards of accept-

able evidence. Each approach has made important contributions to psychology, but many, if not most, psychologists are eclectic, drawing on more than one school of thought.

What Psychologists Do

● Psychologists do research and teach in colleges and universities, provide mental-health services (*psychological practice*), and conduct research and apply findings in a wide variety of nonacademic settings. *Applied psychology* is concerned with the practical uses of psychological knowledge. *Basic psychology* is concerned with knowledge for its own sake.

● *Psychotherapist* is an unregulated word for anyone who does therapy, including persons who have no credentials or training at all. Licensed therapists differ according to their training and approach. *Clinical psychologists* have a Ph.D., an Ed.D., or a Psy.D.; *psychiatrists* have an M.D.; *psychoanalysts* are trained in psychoanalytic institutes; and clinical social workers, counselors with various specialties, and marriage, family, and child counselors may have a variety of postgraduate degrees. Many psychologists are concerned about an increase in poorly trained psychotherapists who lack credentials or a firm understanding of research methods and findings.

Critical and Scientific Thinking in Psychology

● One benefit of studying psychology is the development of *critical-thinking* skills and attitudes. The critical thinker asks questions, defines terms clearly, examines the evidence, analyzes assumptions and biases, avoids emotional reasoning, avoids oversimplification, considers alternative interpretations, and tolerates uncertainty. These activities not only are useful in ordinary life but also are the basis of the scientific method. For example, scientists are required to state *hypotheses* and predictions precisely and formu-late operational definitions ("define your terms"); to gather empirical evidence; to comply with the *principle of falsifiability* ("analyze assumptions"); to be cautious in settling on a *theory* ("consider other interpretations"); and to resist drawing firm conclusions until results are *replicated* ("tolerate uncertainty").

Descriptive Studies: Establishing the Facts

- *Descriptive methods* allow psychologists to describe and predict behavior but not necessarily to choose one explanation over others. Such methods include case studies, observational studies, psychological tests, and surveys, as well as correlational methods.

- *Case studies* are detailed descriptions of individuals. They are often used by clinicians, and they can be valuable in exploring new research topics and addressing questions that would otherwise be difficult to study. But because the person under study may not be representative of people in general, case studies are typically sources rather than tests of hypotheses.

- In *observational studies*, the researcher systematically observes and records behavior without interfering in any way with the behavior. *Naturalistic observation* is used to find out how subjects behave in their natural environments. *Laboratory observation* allows more control and the use of special equipment; behavior in the laboratory, however, may differ in certain ways from behavior in natural contexts.

- *Psychological tests* are used to measure and evaluate personality traits, emotional states, aptitudes, interests, abilities, and values. A good test is one that has been *standardized*, is scored using established *norms*, and is both *reliable* and *valid*. Critics have questioned the reliability and validity of even some widely used tests.

- *Surveys* are questionnaires or interviews that ask people directly about their experiences, attitudes, and opinions. Researchers must take precautions to obtain a *sample* that is *representative* of the larger population that the researcher wishes to describe and that yields results that are not skewed by a *volunteer bias*. Findings can also be affected by the fact that respondents sometimes lie, misremember, or misinterpret the questions.

Correlational Studies: Looking for Relationships

- In descriptive research, studies that look for relationships between phenomena are known as *correlational*. A *correlation* is a measure of the strength of a positive or negative relationship between two variables, and is expressed by the *coefficient of correlation*. A correlation does *not* demonstrate a causal relationship between the variables.

The Experiment: Hunting for Causes

- *Experiments* allow researchers to control the situation being studied, manipulate an *independent variable*, and assess the effects of the manipulation on a *dependent variable*. Experimental studies usually require a comparison or *control condition*, and often involve *random assignment* of subjects to experimental and control groups. In some studies, control subjects receive a *placebo*. *Single-blind* and *double-blind* procedures can be used to prevent the expectations of the subjects or the experimenter from affecting the results. Because experiments allow conclusions about cause and effect, they have long been the method of choice in psychology. However, like laboratory observations, experiments create a special situation that may call forth behavior not typical in other environments. Many psychologists, therefore, have called for more *field research*.

Evaluating the Findings

- Psychologists use *descriptive statistics*, such as the *arithmetic mean* and *standard deviation*, to summarize data. They use *inferential statistics* to find out how impressive the data are. *Significance tests* tell the researcher how likely it is that the results of a study occurred merely by chance. The results are said to be *statistically significant* if this likelihood is very low.

- Choosing among competing interpretations of a finding can be difficult, and care must be taken to avoid going beyond the facts. Sometimes the best interpretation does not emerge until a hypothesis has been tested in more than one way—for example, by using both *cross-sectional* and *longitudinal* methods.

- Statistical significance does not always imply real-world importance because the amount of variation in the data accounted for by a particular variable may be small. Conversely, a result that does not quite reach significance may be potentially useful. Therefore, many psychologists are now turning to other statistical measures. The technique of *meta-analysis*, for example, reveals how much of the variation in scores across many different studies can be explained by a particular variable.

KEY TERMS

Use this list to check your understanding of terms and people in this chapter. If you have trouble with a term, you can find it on the page listed.

psychology 4
empirical 4
Wilhelm Wundt 6
trained introspection 6
functionalism 6
William James 6
Sigmund Freud 6
psychoanalysis 6
biological perspective 7
learning perspective 7
behaviorists 7
social–cognitive learning theorists 7
cognitive perspective 7
sociocultural perspective 7
psychodynamic perspective 7
psychological practice 9
basic psychology 9
applied psychology 9
counseling psychologist 9
school psychologist 9
clinical psychologist 9
psychotherapist 10

psychiatrist 10
critical thinking 12
hypothesis 13
operational definition 13
principle of falsifiability 14
theory 16
replicate 16
descriptive methods 17
case study 17
observational studies 18
naturalistic observation 18
laboratory observation 19
psychological tests 19
standardization 20
norms 20
reliability 20
validity 20
surveys 20
representative sample 20
volunteer bias 21
correlational study 22
correlation 22
variable 22

positive correlation 22
negative correlation 22
coefficient of correlation 22
experiment 24
independent variable 24
dependent variable 24
control condition 25
experimental/control groups 26
random assignment 26
placebo 26
single-blind study 26
experimenter effects 27
double-blind study 27
field research 27
descriptive statistics 28
arithmetic mean 28
standard deviation 29
inferential statistics 29
significance tests 30
cross-sectional study 31
longitudinal study 31
meta-analysis 31

LOOKING BACK

Now that you have read this chapter, see whether you can answer the "What's Ahead" questions that preceded each major section. By using these questions to "look back," you can find out how much you have learned—and what you may need to review.

- What's the difference between psychology and plain old common sense? (p. 5)

- How old is the science of psychology? (p. 6)

- Was Sigmund Freud the official founder of scientific psychology? (p. 6)

- What are the five major perspectives in psychology? (pp. 7–8)

- If someone tells you that he or she is a psychologist, why can't you assume the person is a therapist? (pp. 8–9)

- If you decided to call yourself a "psychotherapist," would you be breaking the law? (p. 10)

- What's the difference between a clinical psychologist and a psychiatrist? (p. 10)

- What guidelines can help you evaluate psychological claims? (pp. 12–16)

- Why is a psychological theory unscientific if it explains anything that could conceivably happen? (p. 14)

- What's wrong with drawing conclusions about behavior from a collection of anecdotes? (p. 16)

- When are psychological case studies informative, and when are they useless? (p. 18)

- Why do psychologists often observe people in laboratories instead of in everyday situations? (p. 19)

- Why should you be skeptical about psychological tests in magazines and newspapers? (p. 20)

- What's the difference between a psychological survey and a poll of listeners conducted by a radio talk-show host? (p. 21)

- If grades and TV watching are "negatively" correlated, what is the relationship between them? (p. 22)

- If TV watching and aggressiveness in children are positively correlated, does that mean that TV watching causes aggressiveness? (p. 23)

- Why do psychologists rely so heavily on experiments? (p. 24)

- What, exactly, do control groups control for? (p. 25)

- In a double-blind experiment, who is "blind," and what aren't they supposed to "see"? (p. 27)

- How can psychologists tell whether a finding is impressive or trivial? (pp. 29–30)

- Why are some findings statistically significant but unimportant in practical terms? (p. 31)

Bomb-Plot Suspect Talks of Life on the Lam

ST. PAUL, MN, JUNE 16, 1999. Sara Jane Olson, a Midwestern mother and homemaker who hid "in plain sight" from the law for over two decades, was finally arrested today. The FBI acted on tips from viewers of the television program "America's Most Wanted," which featured Olson in a segment last month.

In the 1970s, Olson, who was then known as Kathleen Ann Soliah, allegedly enlisted as a foot soldier in the radical Symbionese Liberation Army, a group that kidnapped newspaper heiress Patty Hearst, robbed banks, and battled police. In 1976, she was about to be indicted in Los Angeles for plotting to kill police officers by blowing up squad cars with pipe bombs. But instead of standing trial, Soliah went underground

Kathleen Soliah, who for decades was wanted by the FBI, is shown in a 1974 photo (left) at a rally in Berkeley's Ho Chi Minh Park. Over the years Soliah, a former revolutionary, transformed herself into Sara Jane Olson (right, in a photo taken after her arrest).

and started a new, entirely different life: She married a Minnesota physician, had three children, and became a respectable suburbanite known for her community involvement and her work as a local stage actress.

Friends and neighbors have had trouble reconciling the woman they have known for years as a solid citizen with the militant revolutionary pictured in old photos and "wanted" posters. Even Olson seems to have trouble connecting with her former self. When police cars, lights flashing, surrounded her automobile in her upscale St. Paul neighborhood, she says, her first thought was that it was "odd."

THEORIES OF PERSONALITY

How was Kathleen Soliah able to transform herself into Sara Jane Olson? Was her earlier personality a fluke, the result of a temporary aberration, or was the self she presented to the world for nearly a quarter of a century a lie, just one of the roles she played over the years as an actress? How was Olson able to suppress her past so well that her husband, children, and closest friends never suspected she was living with a dark secret? Is her true personality militant and angry or serene and dignified? Who is the *real* Sara Jane?

In psychology, **personality** refers to a distinctive pattern of behavior, thoughts, motives, and emotions that characterizes an individual over time. This pattern reflects specific **traits,** habitual ways of behaving, thinking, and feeling: shy, brave, reliable, friendly, hostile, confident, and so on. The schools of psychology described in Chapter 1 differ in the traits they consider most important, and in their views of the origins and stability of those traits. Biological psychologists seek evidence for genetically influenced qualities that remain entrenched throughout life. In the learning tradition, many behavioral psychologists argue that people are influenced more by their learning histories and immediate circumstances than by any permanent, individual traits. Social–cognitive learning theorists, who draw on both the learning and the cognitive perspectives, emphasize the perceptions, values, and beliefs that contribute to an individual's distinctive personality. Cultural psychologists trace the cultural origins of traits and typical ways of behaving. Psychodynamic psychologists search for personality in the dark, unconscious recesses of the mind. And humanists, who belong to a modern philosophical branch of psychology, regard personality as the private self, the "true self" behind the masks that people wear in daily life.

In this chapter, we will describe these major approaches to personality, and when we are done, we will return to the puzzle of Sara Jane Olson. As you read, ask yourself: Is personality really stable, or are some qualities and traits utterly changeable? Are we, by nature, aggressive, loving, cooperative, or hostile, or are these qualities learned? To what extent are we conscious of the motives and conflicts that shape our personalities? And which has more influence on our behavior: our personality or the situation we are in?

What's Ahead

- How can psychologists tell which personality traits are basic?

- Which five dimensions of personality seem to describe people the world over?

2.1 The Elements of Personality

Psychological tests provide information about particular aspects of personality, such as needs, values, interests, and typical ways of responding to situations. Using these tests, psychologists have identified a broad array of personality traits, from sensation seeking (the enjoyment of risk) to "erotophobia" (the fear of sex).

One of the most influential trait theorists was Gordon Allport (1897–1967). Allport (1937, 1961) recognized that not all traits have equal weight and significance in people's lives. Most of us have five to ten *central traits* that reflect a characteristic way of behaving, dealing with others, and reacting to new situations. For instance, some people see the world as a hostile, dangerous place, whereas others see it as a place for fun and frolic. *Secondary traits*, in contrast, are more changeable aspects of personality, such as musical preferences, habits, casual opinions, and the like.

Another influential personality theorist, Raymond B. Cattell, essentially confirmed Allport's idea that traits vary in their "centrality" to the individual. Cattell advanced the study of personality by applying a statistical method called **factor analysis.** This procedure identifies clusters of correlated items that seem to be measuring some common, underlying factor. For example, the traits of assertiveness, willingness to tell jokes in large groups, and pleasure in meeting new people might share the common factor of extroversion. Using questionnaires, life descriptions, and observations, Cattell (1965, 1973) measured dozens of personality traits in thousands of people, including humor, intelligence, creativity, leadership, and emotional disorder. He concluded that 16 factors are necessary to describe the complexities of personality, although later in his career he noted that only a few of them had been repeatedly confirmed.

Today, the evidence for a small cluster of fundamental personality traits is overwhelming. Although researchers are still debating exactly how many traits belong to this inner group, most agree on the centrality of five "robust factors," known informally as the *Big Five* (Digman, 1996; Jang et al., 1998; McCrae & Costa, 1996; Wiggins, 1996). These

personality
A distinctive and relatively stable pattern of behavior, thoughts, motives, and emotions that characterizes an individual.

trait
A characteristic of an individual, describing a habitual way of behaving, thinking, and feeling.

factor analysis
A statistical method for analyzing the intercorrelations among different measures or test scores; clusters of measures or scores that are highly correlated are assumed to measure the same underlying trait or ability (factor).

The four basic personality types

Former basketball player Dennis Rodman, whose costumes and antics amused some people and appalled others, is a perfect example of extroversion, one of the "Big Five" personality factors.

factors are remarkably stable over a person's lifetime and have been identified all over the world, in places as diverse as China, the Netherlands, Japan, Spain, the Philippines, Hawaii, Germany, Portugal, Israel, Korea, Russia, and Australia (Benet-Martinez & John, 1998; Digman & Shmelyov, 1996; Katigbak, Church, & Akamine, 1996; McCrae & Costa, 1997; Yang & Bond, 1990):

1 *Extroversion versus introversion* describes the extent to which people are outgoing or shy. It includes such traits as being talkative or silent, sociable or reclusive, adventurous or cautious, eager to be in the limelight or inclined to stay in the shadows.

2 *Neuroticism,* or negative emotionality, includes such traits as anxiety, an inability to control impulses, and a tendency to feel negative emotions such as anger, guilt, and resentment. Neurotic individuals are worriers, complainers, and defeatists, even when they have no major problems. They are always ready to see the sour side of life and none of its sweetness.

3 *Agreeableness* describes the extent to which people are good-natured or irritable, gentle or headstrong, cooperative or abrasive, secure or suspicious and jealous. It reflects the tendency to have friendly relationships or hostile ones.

4 *Conscientiousness* describes the degree to which people are responsible or undependable, persevering or quick to give up, steadfast or fickle, tidy or careless.

5 *Openness to experience* describes the extent to which people are original, imaginative, questioning, artistic, and capable of creative thinking, or conforming, unimaginative, and predictable.

The Big Five do not represent all of the traits that make up personality, but they do seem to capture its essential dimensions. The logical next question is, "Where do those traits come from?"

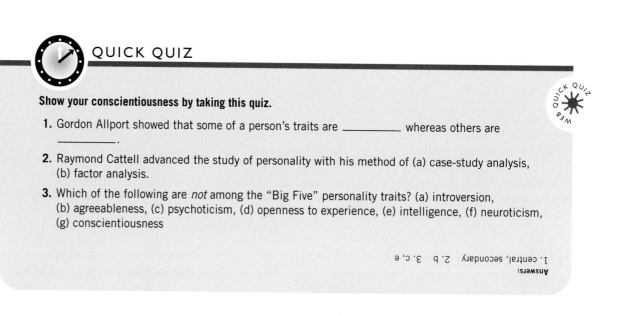

QUICK QUIZ

Show your conscientiousness by taking this quiz.

1. Gordon Allport showed that some of a person's traits are _____ whereas others are _____ .

2. Raymond Cattell advanced the study of personality with his method of (a) case-study analysis, (b) factor analysis.

3. Which of the following are *not* among the "Big Five" personality traits? (a) introversion, (b) agreeableness, (c) psychoticism, (d) openness to experience, (e) intelligence, (f) neuroticism, (g) conscientiousness

Answers:

1. central, secondary   2. b   3. c, e

2.1

What's Ahead

- Is it possible to be born irritable or easygoing?

- Why are twins important in studying the heritability of traits?

- To what extent are personality differences among people influenced by their genetic differences?

- Are people who have highly heritable personality traits stuck with them forever?

2.2 The Biological Contribution

A mother we know was describing her two children: "My daughter has always been emotionally intense and a little testy," she said, "but my son is the opposite, placid and good-natured. They came out of the womb that way." Was this mother right? Is it possible to be born touchy or easygoing? What aspects of personality might have an inherited component?

Psychologists who take a biological perspective try to answer these questions in two ways: by studying temperaments in infants and young children and by doing heritability studies with twins and adopted children. They hope that genes underlying temperaments and traits will one day be identified (Plomin et al., 1998).

Heredity and Temperament

Even in the first weeks after birth, infants differ in activity level, mood, responsiveness, soothability, and attention span (Belsky, Hsieh, & Crnic, 1996; Kagan, 1994). Some are irritable and cranky; others are calm and sweet-natured. Some will cuddle up in an adult's arms and snuggle; others squirm and fidget, as if they dislike being held. Some smile easily; others fuss and cry. These differences appear early, even when you control for possible prenatal influences such as the mother's nutrition, drug use, or problems with the pregnancy. Most psychologists, therefore, believe that babies are born with genetically determined **temperaments,** physiological dispositions to respond to the environment in relatively stable, typical ways.

temperaments
Physiological dispositions to respond to the environment in certain ways; they are present in infancy and are assumed to be innate.

Extreme shyness and fear of new situations tend to be biologically based, stable aspects of temperament—both in human beings and in monkeys. On the right, a timid infant rhesus monkey cowers behind a friend in the presence of an outgoing stranger.

Such temperaments may later form the basis of specific personality traits.

How can heredity affect a baby's temperament? **Genes,** the basic units of heredity, are made up of elements of *DNA* (deoxyribonucleic acid). These elements form chemical codes for the synthesis of proteins; proteins, in turn, affect virtually every aspect of the body, from its structure to the chemicals that keep it running. Genes can affect a child's temperament through their effects on the child's brain and nervous system.

Jerome Kagan (1994, 1998a, 1998b) has been studying two temperamental styles, which he calls "reactive" and "nonreactive." About 20 percent of all children are at one extreme or the other, and the rest (about 80 percent) fall somewhere in between. Highly reactive infants, even at 4 months of age, are excitable, nervous, and fearful; they overreact to any little thing, even a colorful picture placed in front of them. At 5 years, many are still timid and uncomfortable in new situations, and at 7 years, many need to sleep with the light on and are afraid of sleeping in an unfamiliar house—even if they have never been traumatized. In contrast, nonreactive infants, says Kagan (1998a), are "California, laid-back babies." They rarely cry, they are outgoing and curious about new toys and events, and they continue to be easygoing and extroverted throughout childhood.

Children with these two temperaments differ physiologically. During mildly stressful tasks, reactive children are more likely than nonreactive children to show signs of activity in the sympathetic nervous system, the part of the nervous system that is generally responsible for physiological arousal (see Chapter 4). Their heart rate increases, the pupils of their eyes dilate, they show height-

ened brain activity, and they produce high levels of two stress hormones, norepinephrine and cortisol. Stephen Suomi (1987, 1991) has found exactly the same physiological symptoms in shy, anxious infant rhesus monkeys. Starting early in life, these "uptight" monkeys respond with anxiety to novelty and challenge, just as overreactive children do. They, too, have high heart rates and elevated levels of stress hormones. When uptight rhesus monkeys grow up, they usually continue to be anxious when challenged, and they act traumatized even though nothing bad has ever happened to them (Higley et al., 1991).

Heredity and Traits

Another way to study the biological basis of personality is to estimate the **heritability** of specific traits within groups of people. This method is favored by **behavioral geneticists,** scientists concerned with the genetic bases of ability and personality. Within any group, individuals will vary in shyness, cheerfulness, impulsiveness, or any other quality. "Heritability" gives us a statistical estimate of the *proportion of the total variation in a trait that is attributable to genetic variation within a group.* Because the heritability of a trait is expressed as a proportion, the maximum value it can have is 1.0.

We know that heritability is a tough concept to understand at first, so here's an example. Suppose that your entire psychology class takes a test of shyness, and you compute an average shyness score for the group. Some individuals will have scores close to the average, whereas others will have scores that are much higher or lower than the average. Heritability gives you an estimate of the

2.2

genes
The functional units of heredity; they are composed of DNA and specify the structure of proteins.

heritability
A statistical estimate of the proportion of the total variance in some trait that is attributable to genetic differences among individuals within a group.

behavioral genetics
An interdisciplinary field of study concerned with the genetic bases of behavior and personality.

extent to which this variation in shyness is due to genetic differences among the students who took the test. Note, however, that this estimate applies only to the group as a whole. It does not tell you anything about the impact of genetics on any *particular* individual's shyness or extroversion. You might be shy primarily because of your genes, but your friend Henrietta might be shy because she comes from a culture that values modesty and social reserve in females.

One obvious example of a highly heritable trait is height: Within a group of equally well-nourished individuals, most of the variation among them will be accounted for by their genetic differences. In contrast, table manners have low heritability because most variation among individuals is accounted for by differences in upbringing. Even highly heritable traits, however, can be modified by the environment. For example, although height is highly heritable, malnourished children may not grow up to be as tall as they would have, given sufficient food. Conversely, if children eat an extremely nutritious diet, they may grow up to be taller than anyone thought they could.

Computing Heritability.

Scientists have no way to estimate the heritability of a trait or behavior directly, so they must *infer* it by studying people whose degree of genetic similarity is known. You might think that the simplest approach would be to compare blood relatives within families; everyone knows of families that are famous for some talent or personality trait. But the fact that a trait "runs" in a family doesn't tell us much, because close relatives usually share environments as well as genes. If Carlo's parents and siblings all love lasagna, that doesn't mean a taste for lasagna is heritable! The same applies if everyone in Carlo's family is shy, neurotic, or moody.

A better approach is to study adopted children (e.g., Loehlin, Horn, & Willerman, 1996; Plomin & DeFries, 1985). Such children share half of their genes with each birth parent, but they grow up in a different environment, apart from their birth parents. On the other hand, they share an environment with their adoptive parents and siblings, but not their genes. Researchers can compare correlations between the children's traits and those of their biological and adoptive relatives and can then use the results to estimate heritability.

Another approach is to compare **identical (monozygotic) twins** with **fraternal (dizygotic) twins.** *Identical twins* develop when a fertilized egg (zygote) divides into two parts that then become separate embryos. Because the twins come from the same fertilized egg, they share all their genes, barring genetic mutations. (Identical twins may differ slightly at birth, however, because of differences in the blood supply to the two fetuses, or other chance factors.) In contrast, *fraternal twins* develop when a woman's ovaries release two eggs instead of one, and each egg is fertilized by a different sperm. Fraternal twins are wombmates, but they are no more alike genetically than any other two siblings (they share, on average, only half their genes), and they may be of different sexes. Behavioral geneticists can estimate the heritability of a trait by comparing groups of same-sex fraternal twins with groups of identical twins. The assumption is that if identical twins are more alike than fraternal twins, then the increased similarity must be genetic.

Perhaps, however, environments shared by identical twins differ from those shared by fraternal twins. People may treat identical twins, well, identically, or they may go to the other extreme by emphasizing the twins' differences. To avoid these problems, investigators have studied identical twins who were separated early in life and were reared apart. (Until recently, adop-

Identical twins Gerald Levey (left) and Mark Newman, separated shortly after birth, have been studied at the Minnesota Center for Twin and Adoption Research. When Gerald and Mark were reunited at age 31, they discovered that they shared some astounding similarities. Both men were volunteer firefighters, wore mustaches, and were bachelors. Both liked to hunt, watch old John Wayne movies, and eat Chinese food after a night on the town. They also drank the same brand of beer, held the can with the little finger curled under it, and crushed the can when it was empty. The challenge for researchers is to determine which of these traits and behaviors are influenced strongly by heredity, which result mainly from environmental factors such as upbringing, and which are due merely to chance.

identical (monozygotic) twins
Twins that develop when a fertilized egg divides into two parts that develop into separate embryos.

fraternal (dizygotic) twins
Twins that develop from two separate eggs fertilized by different sperm; they are no more alike genetically than any other pair of siblings.

tion policies often permitted such separations to occur.) In theory, separated identical twins share all their genes but not their environments. Any similarities between them should therefore be primarily genetic and should permit a direct estimate of heritability.

How Heritable Are Personality Traits?

Behavioral geneticists are finding that many traits are, in fact, highly heritable. Whether the trait in question is one of the Big Five, selflessness, aggressiveness, or overall happiness and well-being, heritability is typically around .50 (Bouchard, 1997a; Jang et al., 1998; Loehlin, 1992; Lykken & Tellegen, 1996; Waller et al., 1990). This means that within a group of people, about 50 percent of the variation in such traits is attributable to genetic differences. These findings have been replicated in many countries.

Some researchers have even reported high heritability for such specific behaviors as getting divorced (McGue & Lykken, 1992) and watching a lot of television in childhood (Plomin et al., 1990)! These results are puzzling: How can divorce and TV watching be heritable? Our prehistoric ancestors didn't get married, let alone divorced, and they certainly didn't watch TV. What could be the personality traits or temperaments underlying these behaviors?

Here's an even more startling finding: In numerous behavioral–genetic studies, the only environmental contribution to personality differences comes from having unique experiences not shared with other family members, such as being in Mrs. Miller's class in the fourth grade or winning the lead in the school play (Bouchard, 1997a; Hur, McGue, & Iacono, 1998; Loehlin, 1992). Shared environment—the family you grew up with and the experiences you shared with your siblings and parents—seems to have no significant effect on your personality. (We are speaking only of personality traits; of course, your family experiences do affect your feelings toward your parents and siblings.)

Understandably, behavioral geneticists are excited about these findings, which have huge implications for the age-old debate over the relative contributions of "nature" (genetic dispositions) and "nurture" (upbringing and environment) in the development of personality. They believe this evidence undermines the conventional wisdom that child-rearing practices and experiences in the home are central to personality development

Separated at birth, the Mallifert twins meet accidentally.

(as we will discuss further in Chapter 3). "It will doubtless seem incredible to many readers that variables such as social class, educational opportunities, religious training, and parental love and discipline have no substantial influence on adult personality," wrote Robert McCrae and Paul Costa (1988), "but imagine for a moment that it is correct. What will it mean for research in developmental psychology? How will clinical psychology and theories of therapy be changed?"

Good questions! What *do* these findings mean for education, for raising children, or for the treatment of personality problems? Does the environment count for nothing?

Evaluating Genetic Theories

Findings on the heritability of personality are impressive—so impressive that many people forget that if heredity accounts for about half of the reason people differ in their traits, then the environment (and errors in measurement) must account for the other half. As Robert Plomin (1989) observed, "The wave of acceptance of genetic influence on behavior is growing into a tidal wave that threatens to engulf the second message of this research: These same data provide the best available evidence for the importance of environmental influences."

Let's consider some other reasons not to jump to the conclusion that "genes are everything":

Thinking Critically About Genes and Personality

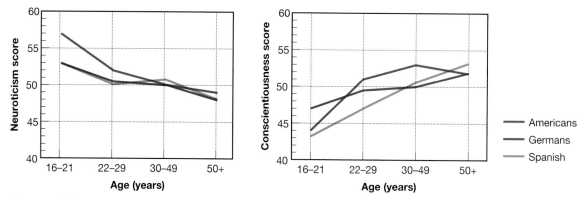

Figure 2.1

Consistency and Change in Personality

Studies of thousands of people in many different cultures find that although the Big Five traits remain fairly stable, changes do occur over the life span. As you can see here, neuroticism (negative emotionality) is highest among young adults and then declines; and conscientiousness is lowest among young adults, and then steadily increases. These changes probably reflect common experiences that occur as young people leave home and grow up (Costa et al., 1999).

1 *Not all traits are equally heritable or unaffected by shared environment.* Religious orthodoxy, intellectual interests, feelings of inadequacy, adherence to traditional notions of masculinity and femininity, and many other traits are strongly affected by the environment a child shares with his or her family and larger culture (Beer, Arnold, & Loehlin, 1998).

2 *Some studies may underestimate the impact of the environment.* Heritability gives us the *relative* impact of genetics and the environment on behavior. To estimate heritability, therefore, you need sensitive measures for gauging both the genetic similarity or dissimilarity of individuals *and* the similarities or differences in their environments. Measures of environmental influences on behavior are still fairly crude, often relying on vague, grab-bag categories such as "social class" or "religious affiliation," and possibly failing to detect some important environmental influences. If the influence of the environment is underestimated, the influence of heredity will necessarily be overestimated.

3 *Even traits that are highly heritable are not rigidly fixed.* Experience can strengthen or diminish a person's traits. For some traits, experiences at certain periods in life become particularly influential and therefore heritability decreases. For example, studies of thousands of people in ten countries found that young people, ages 16 to 21, are the most neurotic (emotionally negative) and the least agreeable and conscientious (see Figure 2.1). By age 30, however, perhaps as a result of the new responsibilities of adulthood, they become more agreeable and conscientious and less negative and bitter (Costa et al., 1999).

Even individuals at the extremes of some temperament often change as they grow older, depending on how parents and others react to them. Kagan, who has been following reactive and nonreactive children for many years, puts it this way: What proportion of extremely reactive babies become vivacious, fearless, and extroverted? Zero. But what proportion remain extremely shy, subdued, and fearful as older children? Only about 15 percent. And what proportion become average, neither extremely shy nor extremely outgoing? All the rest. "The environment acts on fearful children to move them toward health, toward the center," Kagan (1998a) explains.

The lesson to take away from behavioral–genetic research, then, is that a genetic predisposition does not imply genetic *inevitability* (Sapolsky, 1998). A shy man may never become Robin Williams and a timid woman probably won't become Whoopi Goldberg, but both can learn to become more comfortable and sociable in new situations. Our personalities develop in a context in which biology and experience are inextricably intertwined.

QUICK QUIZ

We hope you will be agreeable about taking this quiz.

1. What two broad areas of research support the hypothesis that personality differences are due in part to genetic differences?

2. In behavioral–genetic studies, the heritability of personality traits, including the Big Five, is typically about (a) .50, (b) .90, (c) .10 to .20, (d) zero.

3. Diane hears that timidity is an inherited temperament. She tells her roommate that her own fear of meeting people and going to parties must be due mostly to genes, and that there is nothing she can do about it. What's wrong with her reasoning?

4. A newspaper headline announces, "Couch Potatoes Born, Not Made: Kids' TV Habits May Be Hereditary." Why is this headline misleading? What other explanations of the finding are possible? What aspects of TV watching *could* have a hereditary component?

Answers:

1. research on temperaments and on heritability   2. a   3. Diane could be shy for any number of reasons, but even if her extreme shyness is inherited, it could be modified by experience.   4. The headline implies that there is a "TV-watching gene," but the writer is failing to consider other explanations. For example, perhaps some temperaments dispose people to be sedentary or passive, and this disposition can lead to a tendency to watch a lot of television.

What's Ahead

- Why don't behaviorists have a theory of personality?

- How would a social–cognitive learning theorist explain habitual hostility or aggressiveness?

- What's the difference between people who think they control their own destiny and those who think that destiny controls them?

2.3 The Learning Contribution

On a hot summer day, James Peters shot and killed his next-door neighbor, Ralph Galluccio. Peters had reached the end of his patience in a ten-year dispute with Galluccio over their common property line. Shocked friends said that the intensity of this feud was not predictable from the men's personalities. Galluccio, his employer reported, was "a likable person with a good, even disposition." Peters, said his employer, was a "very mild-mannered, cooperative" man, an "all-around good guy."

A biological psychologist might say that this violent episode demonstrates the aggressive capac-ity of human nature in general and of violence-prone personalities in particular. A learning theorist, however, would emphasize each man's past learning and present environment. In Chapter 8, we will discuss in detail the principles that govern learning and the major findings of this approach. Here we will be concerned only with what psychologists from the learning perspective have had to say about personality.

The Behavioral School

In 1913, a psychologist named John B. Watson (1878–1958) published a paper that rocked the still-young science of psychology. In "Psychology as the Behaviorist Views It," Watson argued that if psychology were ever to be as objective as physics, chemistry, and biology, psychologists would have to avoid terms such as *mental state* and *mind,* and stick to what they could observe and measure directly—acts and events taking place in the environment. In short, they should give up mentalism for **behaviorism.**

In his own research, Watson focused on reflexive behavior, such as trembling and sweating when you are scared. Later, B. F. Skinner (1904–1990) extended the behavioral view, but with important modifications. Calling his approach

behaviorism
An approach to psychology that emphasizes the study of observable behavior and the role of the environment as a determinant of behavior.

Learning theorists emphasize the powerful influence of the situation on a person's "personality." Which is the "real" Boris Yeltsin? The former Russian president was serious and restrained during a speech to military leaders, but merry and extroverted during the political campaign of 1996, when he got up on stage to dance with a rock band.

radical behaviorism, Skinner emphasized **operant conditioning** as the fundamental form of learning. In operant conditioning, which involves voluntary rather than reflexive behavior, the consequences of any act powerfully affect the probability that the act will occur again. In brief, acts followed by pleasant consequences (**reinforcers**) are more likely to be repeated, whereas acts followed by unpleasant consequences (punishment or withdrawal of reinforcers) are likely to decrease. For Skinner, the explanation of behavior was to be found primarily by looking outside the individual, rather than within.

But if explanations lie outside the individual, then it does not really make much sense to talk about "personality." Indeed, in the behavioral view, people do not have "traits"; they simply show certain behavior patterns. Labels such as "aggressive," "ambitious," or "conscientious" are simply shorthand descriptions of responses that tend to occur in particular situations. We may say that one job applicant, for example, is "calm and confident," whereas another is "anxious and shy," but all this means is that the two applicants tend to respond differently when being interviewed for a job. Skinner would say that if we looked into the behavioral histories of the two applicants, we would discover different patterns of reinforcement and punishment. For the first person, calm, confident behavior probably paid off in the past. For the second person, attempts at self-expression in school or at home may have been met with ridicule or sarcasm.

Behaviorists do not deny that people have feelings, thoughts, or values. However, they believe that these mental states are as subject to the laws of learning as, say, riding a bike. In this view, mental states, values, and personality traits do not explain behavior; they are behaviors to be explained. Thus, Skinner would say that it is meaningless to say that "Juanita works hard because she is ambitious" or that "Gary procrastinates because he's lazy." Instead, Skinner would say, hard work probably earns rewards for Juanita, which is why she continues to work hard, and procrastination may get Gary sympathy when he fails, which is why he continues to avoid finishing his work. Thus, to a behaviorist, the rewards and punishers in the particular situation are critical.

The Social–Cognitive Learning School

Behaviorism was the predominant American school of psychological research until the early 1960s. In that decade, a "cognitive revolution" swept psychology, and researchers began to focus on the ways in which thoughts and beliefs affect behavior. But even earlier, some psychologists within the learning tradition had begun to doubt that behavioral principles were sufficient to explain behavior and personality. Eventually, these doubts led to an outgrowth of behaviorism known as *social-learning theory,* which today is usually called **social–cognitive learning theory.**

Habits, Beliefs, and Behavior. As we will see in more detail in Chapter 8, social–cognitive learning theorists depart from classic behaviorism

operant conditioning
The process by which a response becomes more likely to occur or less so, depending on its consequences.

reinforcer
A stimulus or event that strengthens or increases the probability of the response it follows.

social–cognitive learning theory
A theory that emphasizes how behavior is learned and maintained through the interaction between individuals and their environments, an interaction strongly influenced by such cognitive processes as observations, expectations, perceptions, and motivating beliefs.

by emphasizing three things: (1) observational learning and the role of models, such as parents, teachers, and celebrities; (2) cognitive processes, such as perceptions and interpretations of events; and (3) motivating values, emotions, and beliefs, such as enduring expectations of success or failure or confidence in your ability to achieve goals.

Whereas behaviorists see "personality" as a set of habits and beliefs that have been rewarded over a person's lifetime, social–cognitive learning theorists maintain that these habits and beliefs eventually acquire a life of their own, coming to exert their own effects on behavior. For example, you may grow up to be emotionally restrained because your parents rarely expressed their emotions and rewarded you for controlling your feelings; but once you have this trait, it will influence how you respond to others, whom you associate with, and many other aspects of your behavior (Bandura, 1994; Mischel & Shoda, 1995).

Social–cognitive learning theorists also emphasize how mental processes—such as thoughts, values, and goals—affect what individuals will do at any given moment and, more generally, the kinds of personalities they develop. A behaviorist would say that a man who is quick to behave aggressively has learned to do so because his actions get him what he wants. But a social–cognitive learning theorist would add that aggressive people have characteristic perceptions and beliefs that fuel their behavior. Nonviolent people are able to take another person's perspective. If someone does something they dislike, they are apt to say, "He's had a rotten day" instead of "He's a rotten person." In contrast, aggressive people assume that others are insulting them, even in the absence of evidence. If someone does something they dislike, they attribute the action to the person's meanness and malice. They see provocation everywhere.

Perceptions of Control.

One of the most important aspects of personality studied by social–cognitive learning theorists is the extent to which people believe they control what happens to them. Much of the original work on this topic was done by Julian Rotter, who started out as a behaviorist. Rotter was working as both a psychotherapist and a researcher, trying to treat his patients' persistent, self-defeating actions according to behavioral principles. But these methods were not working. Rotter saw that his clients had formed entrenched attitudes as a result of their lifetimes of experience, and that these attitudes were affecting their decisions and actions (Hunt, 1993; Rotter, 1982, 1990).

Rotter concluded that people learn over time that certain of their acts will be rewarded and others punished, and thus they develop general expectations about whether their efforts will be successful. A child who studies hard and gets good grades, attention from teachers, admiration from friends, and praise from parents will come to expect that hard work in other situations will also pay off. A child who studies hard and gets poor grades, is ignored by teachers and parents, and is rejected by friends for being a grind will come to expect that hard work isn't worth it.

Once acquired, these expectations often create a *self-fulfilling prophecy:* The person's expectations lead to behavior that makes the prediction come true (R. Jones, 1977). You expect to succeed, so you work hard—and succeed. Or you expect to fail, so you don't do much work, and as a result you do poorly. Self-fulfilling prophecies also occur in love affairs: People who expect to be rejected ("No one could love a schlub like me") often behave in ways that cause their partners to eventually reject them (Downey et al., 1998).

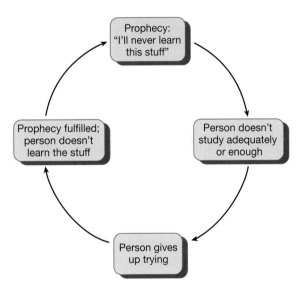

Rotter and his colleagues demonstrated the power of expectancies in many experiments. At the same time, both in his private practice and in his research, Rotter was observing people whose expectations of success never went up even when they were actually successful. "Oh, that was just a fluke," they would say, or "I was lucky; it will never happen again."

Rotter therefore decided that people's feelings or beliefs about the forces that govern their behavior are as important as anything that actually happens to them. He chose the term **locus of control**

locus of control
A general expectation about whether the results of your actions are under your own control (internal locus) or beyond your control (external locus).

GET INVOLVED

▶ WHO'S IN CONTROL?

Think back to the last time you did well on a test or on some task. Which of the following phrases best describes how you explained your success to yourself?

- I'm really competent (or smart, skillful, etc.).
- I worked hard, and it paid off.
- I was lucky.
- The test (or task) was pretty easy.
- I did well, but only because someone else helped me.

▼ Now think about a time you did *not* do well on a test or task. Which phrase best describes how you accounted for your disappointing performance?

- I'm just not good at this.
- I didn't work (or try) hard enough.
- I was unlucky.
- I did poorly, but the test (or task) wasn't fair.
- I did poorly, but only because I got bad instruction or too little help.

What do your answers tell you about your locus of control? Do you tend to be internal for success, or external? What about for failure? Do your beliefs about the results of your actions motivate you to further effort, or discourage you?

---

to refer to people's beliefs about whether the results of their actions are under their own control. People who have an *internal locus of control* ("internals") tend to believe that they are responsible for what happens to them, that they control their own destiny. People who have an *external locus of control* ("externals") tend to believe that their lives are controlled by luck, fate, or other people.

To measure these traits, Rotter (1966) developed an Internal/External (I/E) Scale consisting of pairs of statements. You have to choose the statement in each pair with which you most strongly agree, as in these two items:

1. a. Many of the unhappy things in people's lives are partly due to bad luck.
   b. People's misfortunes result from mistakes they make.
2. a. Becoming a success is a matter of hard work; luck has little or nothing to do with it.
   b. Getting a good job depends mainly on being in the right place at the right time.

Research on locus of control took off like a shot, and over the years more than 2,000 studies based on the I/E scale (including a version for children) have been published, involving people of all ages and from many different ethnic groups. An internal locus of control emerges at an early age and is associated with many aspects of life, including health, academic achievement, and political activism (Nowicki & Strickland, 1973; Strickland, 1989). (In Chapter 12, we will discuss in greater detail how a sense of control affects a person's health.)

Your locus of control can change, however, depending on your experiences and your perceptions of them. During the 1960s, when the American civil-rights movement was gathering steam, civil-rights activists and black student leaders were more likely to score at the internal end of the scale than were their counterparts who were uninvolved in civil-rights efforts (Gore & Rotter, 1963). By the mid-1970s, however—after the assassinations of Martin Luther King, Jr., Malcolm X, and John and Robert Kennedy, and after many Americans had become disillusioned with the Vietnam War—scores on the I/E Scale changed. Civil-rights leaders and college students became less internal—that is, less confident that they, as individuals, could improve social conditions (Strickland, 1989).

Today, many Americans seem to have an external locus of control, reflected in the growing

These members of the Communications Workers Union have an internal locus of control, motivating them to protest their city's budget cuts. What social forces and events might promote an internal locus of control, and which ones might reduce it?

numbers who do not vote and who believe their fates are determined by the stars or by destiny. Where would you place your own locus of control? How do you think it influences your actions, or apathy, as a student and citizen? How does it affect your beliefs about the possibility of changing yourself or improving the world?

Evaluating Learning Theories

Why did James Peters kill Ralph Galluccio? Behaviorists would investigate why these two men failed to learn the skills to negotiate their differences, and how each had learned over time that aggressive actions would make other people knuckle under. Social–cognitive learning theorists would investigate not only the environmental conditions of the quarrel, but also each man's perceptions of it, and why Peters and Galluccio thought there was no way out other than violence. Both learning approaches would have no trouble explaining how these two men, who were so hostile toward each other, could be described by their friends and employers as mild-mannered and likeable. A behaviorist would say that different situations evoke and reinforce different "traits." A social–cognitive learning theorist would say that a person can be hostile and obnoxious in one situation and pleasant and friendly in another, depending on how the person interprets the two situations.

Some psychologists criticize the behavioral branch of the learning perspective for implying that individuals are as soft as jellyfish, and that with the right environment, anyone can become anything. They also complain that behaviorism treats people as passive recipients of environmental events. These common charges are not really fair. Skinner, for instance, often stated that people's genetic constitutions and temperaments place limits on what they can learn, and he argued that people can choose to change their environments and thus their own behavior.

Thinking Critically About the Environment and Personality

A more valid criticism is that learning approaches to personality sometimes attribute behavior to the "environment" without defining exactly what the environment consists of or how it affects people. Or they explore one influence on learning at a time: a parental model, a teacher's reactions, the pattern of reinforcers in a given situation, media messages, and so forth. In real life, though, people are surrounded by hundreds of interacting influences. This fact poses a problem for learning theories: When nearly anything can have an influence on you, it can be frustratingly difficult to show that any one thing actually is having an influence. It's like trying to grab a fistful of fog; you know it's there, but somehow it keeps getting away from you.

For example, how strongly do role models in the media influence the personality traits the sexes value and cultivate in themselves? For many people, the answer is obvious—"very strongly." Yet as social–cognitive learning theorists would be the first to agree, not everyone reacts to the same images in the same way. Some men admire action heroes like those played by Arnold Schwarzenegger or Wesley Snipes but others regard them as silly cartoon figures. Some women see gaunt models and think they should look that way, too, but others are repelled by these images and want to buy the models a decent meal. Thus, it is difficult to specify *which* media images are having an effect, and on whom; and it is difficult to disentangle the effects of the media from all the other events and factors that influence people's ideas about men and women.

Nevertheless, the learning approach to personality makes an essential point: Personality is shaped in part by your environment, your experiences, and your beliefs and expectations. To understand personality, we need to know not only about people's genetics, but also about their minds, their pasts, and, as we will see next, their culture.

Calvin and Hobbes

by Bill Watterson

As social–cognitive theorists would admit, not everyone responds to media images and role models in the same way.

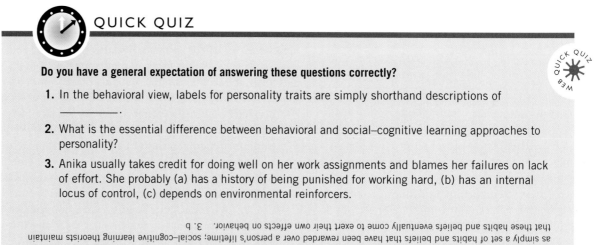

QUICK QUIZ

Do you have a general expectation of answering these questions correctly?

1. In the behavioral view, labels for personality traits are simply shorthand descriptions of _____.

2. What is the essential difference between behavioral and social–cognitive learning approaches to personality?

3. Anika usually takes credit for doing well on her work assignments and blames her failures on lack of effort. She probably (a) has a history of being punished for working hard, (b) has an internal locus of control, (c) depends on environmental reinforcers.

Answers:

1. behavioral patterns—that is, behavioral responses that tend to occur in specific situations   2. Behaviorists regard "personality" as simply a set of habits and beliefs that have been rewarded over a person's lifetime; social–cognitive learning theorists maintain that these habits and beliefs eventually come to exert their own effects on behavior.   3. b

---

What's Ahead

- Why are risk-taking, aggressiveness, and punctuality more than just individual personality traits?

- How does belonging to an individualist or a collectivist culture influence your personality— and even whether you think you have a stable "self"?

- Why might an Arab and a Swede agree on everything the other is saying, and still feel uncomfortable with each other?

2.4 The Cultural Contribution

Are you the kind of person who takes risks—say, by smoking cigarettes, driving 100 mph on the highway without a seat belt, or having unprotected sex with a stranger?

Most Western psychologists regard risk-taking as a personality trait that is embedded in an individual, because of either a genetic predisposition or lessons learned from experience. But culture has a profound effect on people's behavior, attitudes, and

Collectivist Chinese workers in Beijing do their morning T'ai Chi exercises in identical, harmonious fashion. Individualistic Americans exercise by running, walking, bicycling, and skating, all in different directions and wearing different clothes.

the traits they value or reject. Cultural values, for example, affect people's feelings about risk: People in the Netherlands or Britain are more likely than Germans and Austrians to take risks and less likely to favor rules and regulations intended to promote public safety, such as the requirement to carry citizen identification cards (Cvetkovich & Earle, 1994). The reason, according to cultural psychologists, is that Germans and Austrians place a high value on avoiding uncertainty and thus welcome laws that reduce danger to individuals and communities.

A **culture** is a program of shared rules that govern the behavior of members of a community or society, and a set of values and beliefs shared by most members of that community and passed from one generation to another (Lonner, 1995). In this section, we will consider some of the contributions of the cultural approach to understanding personality.

Culture and Personality

People learn their culture's rules as effortlessly as they learn its language. These rules are major contributors to the package of traits we call personality. It can be hard to see this because the power of culture often feels less real than our private sense of self. But here's a demonstration. Who are you? Take as much time as you like to complete this sentence: "I am _____."

Your response to the "Who am I?" test will be greatly influenced by your cultural background, particularly whether your culture emphasizes individualism or community (Hofstede & Bond, 1988; Markus & Kitayama, 1991; Triandis, 1996). In **individualist cultures,** the independence of the individual takes precedence over the needs of the group, and the self is often defined as a col-

lection of personality traits ("I am outgoing, agreeable, and ambitious") or in occupational terms ("I am a psychologist"). In **collectivist cultures,** group harmony takes precedence over the wishes of the individual, and the self is defined in the context of relationships and the community ("I am the son of a farmer, descended from three generations of storytellers on my mother's side . . .").

As Table 2.1 on the next page shows, individualist and collectivist ways of defining the self influence which personality traits we value, how we express emotions, and how much we value having relationships or maintaining freedom (Campbell et al., 1996; Kashima et al., 1995). Individualist and collectivist outlooks even affect whether we believe that personality is stable across situations. In a revealing study comparing Japanese and Americans, the Americans reported that their sense of self changes only 5 to 10 percent in different situations, whereas the Japanese said that 90 to 99 percent of their sense of self changes (de Rivera, 1989). For the group-oriented Japanese, it is important to enact *tachiba,* to perform your social roles correctly so that there will be harmony with others. Americans, in contrast, tend to value "being true to your self" and having a "core identity." Thus, even basic ideas about what personality means and whether it is consistent across situations are deeply affected by culture.

Because people fail to understand the power of culture on behavior, they often attribute another person's mysterious or annoying actions to individual personality when they are really due to cultural norms. Consider, for example, *conversational distance:* how close people usually stand to one another when they are speaking (Hall, 1959, 1976). Arabs like to stand close enough to feel your breath,

culture
A program of shared rules that govern the behavior of members of a community or society, and a set of values, beliefs, and attitudes shared by most members of that community.

individualist cultures
Cultures in which the self is regarded as autonomous, and individual goals and wishes are prized above duty and relations with others.

collectivist cultures
Cultures in which the self is regarded as embedded in relationships, and harmony with one's group is prized above individual goals and wishes.

Table 2.1 — Some Average Differences Between Individualist and Collectivist Cultures

Members of Individualist Cultures	Members of Collectivist Cultures
Define the self as autonomous, independent of groups	Define the self as an interdependent part of groups
Give priority to individual, personal goals	Give priority to the needs and goals of the group
Value independence, leadership, achievement, self-fulfillment	Value group harmony, duty, obligation, security
Give more weight to an individual's attitudes and preferences than to group norms as explanations of behavior	Give more weight to group norms than to individual attitudes as explanations of behavior
Attend to the benefits and costs of relationships; if costs exceed advantages, a person is likely to drop a relationship	Attend to the needs of group members; if a relationship is beneficial to the group but costly to the individual, the individual is likely to stay in the relationship

Source: Triandis, 1996.

Arabs tend to stand much closer to one another than Westerners do. This "personality difference" is due to different cultural norms for conversational distance.

monochronic cultures
Cultures in which time is organized sequentially; schedules and deadlines are valued over people.

polychronic cultures
Cultures in which time is organized horizontally; people tend to do several things at once and value relationships over schedules.

touch your arm, and see the pupils of your eyes—a distance that makes most white Americans, Canadians, and northern Europeans uneasy, unless they are talking intimately with a lover. The English and the Swedes stand farthest apart when they converse; southern Europeans stand closer; and Latin Americans and Arabs stand the closest (Keating, 1994; Sommer, 1969). One of our students from the Middle East told us he always thought his Anglo classmates were cold and aloof, even prejudiced against him, because they kept moving away from him in conversation. They, in turn, thought he had a "pushy" personality. They were all simply trying to reestablish the conversational distance that made them comfortable.

Cultural psychologists have studied the impact of cultural norms on many personality traits. Take cleanliness. How often do you take baths or showers? Do you regard baths as healthy and invigorating, or as a disgusting wallow in dirty water? How often, and where, do you wash your hands—or feet? A person who might seem obsessively clean in one culture might seem an appalling slob in another (Fernea & Fernea, 1994).

Or consider tardiness. Individuals differ in whether they try to be places "on time" or are always late, but cultural norms affect how individuals regard time in the first place. In **monochronic cultures,** such as those of northern Europe, Canada, and the United States, time is organized into linear segments in which people do one thing "at a time" (Hall, 1983; Hall & Hall, 1990). The day is divided into appointments, schedules, and routines, and because time is a precious commodity, people don't like to "waste" time or "spend" too much time on any one activity. In such cultures, therefore, it is considered the height of rudeness (or high status) to keep someone waiting. But in southern Europe, South America, and Africa, you are more likely to find **polychronic cultures,** where time is organized along parallel lines. People do many things at once, and the needs of friends and family supersede those of the appointment book. People in Latin America and the Middle East think nothing of waiting all day, or even a week, to see someone. The idea of having to be somewhere "on time," as if time were more important than a person, is unthinkable.

In culturally diverse North America, the two time systems keep bumping into each other. Business, government, and other institutions are organized monochronically, but many Native

Americans, Latinos, and other people tend to operate on polychronic principles. The result is repeated misunderstandings. An Anglo judge in Miami got into hot water when he observed that "Cubans always show up two hours late for weddings"—late in his culture's terms, that is. The judge was accurate in his observation; the problem was his implication that something was wrong with Cubans for being "late." And "late" compared to what, by the way? The Cubans were perfectly on time for Cubans.

Evaluating Cultural Theories

A woman we know, originally from England, married a Lebanese man. They were happy together but had the usual number of marital misunderstandings and squabbles. After a few years, they visited his home town in Lebanon, where she had never been. "I was stunned," she told us. "All the things I thought he did because of his *personality* turned out to be because he's *Lebanese!* Everyone there was just like him!"

Thinking Critically About Culture and Personality

Our friend's reaction illustrates both the contributions and the limitations of cultural theories of personality. She was right in recognizing that some of her husband's behavior was attributable to his culture—for example, his Lebanese notions of time were very different from her English notions. But she was wrong to infer that the Lebanese are all "like him": Individuals are affected by their culture, but they vary within it.

Cultural psychologists face the key problem of how to describe cultural influences on personality without stereotyping (Church & Lonner, 1998). As one student of ours put it, "How come when we students speak of 'the' Japanese or 'the' blacks or 'the' whites or 'the' Latinos, it's called stereotyping, and when you do it, it's called 'cross-cultural psychology'?" This question shows excellent critical thinking! The study of culture does not rest on the assumption that all members of a culture behave the same way. As we have already seen in this chapter, individuals vary according to their temperaments, beliefs, and learning histories, and this variation occurs within every culture. Moreover, regional variations occur in every society. In America, the most collectivist region is the Deep South, with its history of strong regional identity, whereas the West, with its history of rugged frontier individualism, is the least (Vandello & Cohen, 1999). The Chinese and the Japanese both value group harmony, but the Chinese are more likely to promote individual achievement, whereas the Japanese are more likely to strive for group consensus (Dien, 1999).

Yet the fact that individuals vary within a culture does not negate the existence of cultural rules that, on average, make Swedes different from Bedouins or Cambodians different from Italians. Cultural theories of personality remind us, therefore, that what we value, how we behave, and the qualities we like or dislike in ourselves start with the culture or ethnic group in which we are raised.

QUICK QUIZ

Are you from a culture that values taking quizzes?

1. Cultures whose members regard the "self" as a collection of stable personality traits are (individualist/collectivist).

2. Cultures whose members do many things at once and value relationships over schedules and appointments are (monochronic/ polychronic).

3. Which of the terms in Items 1 and 2 apply to the majority culture in the United States and Canada?

Answers:
1. individualist 2. polychronic 3. individualist, monochronic

- In Freud's theory of personality, why are the id and the superego always at war?

- When people say you're being "defensive," what defenses might they be thinking of?

- How do psychologists regard Freud today—as a genius or a fraud?

- What would Carl Jung have to say about Darth Vader?

- What are the "objects" in the object-relations approach to personality?

2.5 The Psychodynamic Contribution

Of all the theories of personality, the psychodynamic approach is the one most embedded in popular culture. A man apologizes for "displacing" his frustrations at work onto his family. A woman suspects that she is "repressing" a childhood trauma. An alcoholic reveals that he is no longer "in denial" about his drinking. A teacher informs a divorcing couple that their 8-year-old child is "regressing" to immature behavior. All of this language—about displacing, repressing, denying, and regressing—can be traced to the first psychodynamic theory of personality, Sigmund Freud's theory of **psychoanalysis.**

Freud's theory is called **psychodynamic** because it emphasizes the movement of psychological energy within the person, in the form of attachments, conflicts, and motivations. Today many psychodynamic theories exist, differing from Freudian theory and from one another, but they all share five general elements:

1. An emphasis on unconscious **intrapsychic** dynamics, the movement of mental (psychic) forces within the mind.

2. A belief in the primacy of the first 5 years— that is, an assumption that adult personality and ongoing problems are formed primarily by experiences in early childhood.

3. A belief that psychological development occurs in fixed stages, during which predictable mental events occur and unconscious issues or crises must be resolved.

4. A focus on fantasies and symbolic meanings of events as the unconscious mind perceives

them, rather than on actual experiences, as the main influences on personality and behavior.

5. A reliance on subjective rather than objective methods of getting at the truth of a person's life—for example, through analysis of dreams, myths, folklore, symbols, and, most of all, the revelations uncovered in psychotherapy.

In this section, we will introduce you to Freud's ideas, and to two of the many psychodynamic theories that have added new rooms and levels to the original Freudian edifice. Then we will try to show you why attitudes toward Freud today range from reverence to contempt, and why he evokes such controversy.

Freud and Psychoanalysis

To enter the world of Sigmund Freud (1856–1939) is to enter a realm of unconscious motives, passions, guilty secrets, unspeakable yearnings, and conflicts between desire and duty. These unseen forces, Freud believed, have far more power over us than our conscious intentions do. The unconscious reveals itself, said Freud, in dreams, in *free association*—talking about anything that pops into your head, without worrying about what anyone will think of you—and in jokes, apparent accidents, and slips of the tongue. The British member of Parliament who referred to the "honourable member from Hell" when he meant to say "Hull," said Freud (1920/1960), was revealing his actual, unconscious appraisal of his colleague.

The Structure of Personality. In Freud's theory, personality consists of three major systems: the id, the ego, and the superego (see Table 2.2). Any action we take or problem we have results from the interaction and degree of balance among these systems (Freud, 1905b, 1920/1960, 1923/1962).

The **id,** which is present at birth, is the reservoir of unconscious psychological energies and the motives to avoid pain and obtain pleasure. The id contains two competing groups of instincts: the life, or sexual, instinct (fueled by psychic energy called the **libido**) and the death, or aggressive, instinct. As energy builds up in the id, tension results. The id may discharge this tension in the form of reflexive actions, physical symptoms, or uncensored mental images and unbidden thoughts.

The **ego,** the second system to emerge, is a referee between the needs of instinct and the demands of society. It bows to the realities of life,

---

psychoanalysis
A theory of personality and a method of psychotherapy originally developed by Sigmund Freud; it emphasizes unconscious motives and conflicts.

psychodynamic theories
Theories that explain behavior and personality in terms of unconscious energy dynamics within the individual.

intrapsychic
Within the mind (psyche) or self.

id
In psychoanalysis, the part of personality containing inherited psychological energy, particularly sexual and aggressive instincts.

libido [li-BEE-dough]
In psychoanalysis, the psychic energy that fuels the sexual or life instincts of the id.

ego
In psychoanalysis, the part of personality that represents reason, good sense, and rational self-control.

Table 2.2   Summary of Freud's Model of the Mind

	Id	**Ego**	**Superego**
What it does	Expresses sexual and aggressive instincts	Mediates between desires of the id and demands of the superego; uses defense mechanisms to ward off unconscious anxiety	Represents conscience and the rules of society; follows internalized moral standards
How conscious it is	Entirely unconscious	Partly conscious, partly unconscious	Partly conscious, mostly unconscious
When it develops	Present at birth	Emerges after birth, with early formative experiences	Last system to develop; becomes internalized after the phallic (Oedipal) stage
Example	"I'm so mad I could kill you" (felt unconsciously)	Might make a conscious choice ("Let's talk about this") or resort to an unconscious defense mechanism, such as denial ("What, me angry? Never.")	"Thou shalt not kill."

putting a rein on the id's desire for sex and aggression until a suitable, socially appropriate outlet for them can be found. The ego, said Freud, is both conscious and unconscious, and it represents "reason and good sense."

The **superego,** the last system of personality to develop, represents morality, the rules of parents and society, and the power of authority; it includes the conscience, the inner voice that says you did something wrong. The superego, which is partly conscious but largely unconscious, judges the activities of the id, handing out good feelings of pride and satisfaction when you do something well and handing out miserable feelings of guilt or shame when you break the rules.

An old joke summarizes the role of the id, ego, and superego this way: The id says, "I want it, and I want it now"; the superego says, "You can't have it; it's bad for you"; and the ego, the rational mediator, says, "Well, maybe you can have some of it—later." According to Freud, the healthy personality must keep all three systems in balance. Someone who is too controlled by the id is governed by impulse and selfish desires. Someone who is too controlled by the superego is rigid, moralistic, and bossy. Someone who has a weak ego is unable to balance personal needs and wishes with social duties and realistic limitations.

If a person feels anxious or threatened when the wishes of the id conflict with social rules, the ego has weapons at its command to relieve the tension. These unconscious weapons, called **defense mechanisms,** deny or distort reality, but they also protect us from conflict and anxiety. They become unhealthy only when they cause self-defeating behavior and emotional problems. Freud described 17 defense mechanisms; later, other psychoanalysts revised his list. Here are some of the primary defenses identified by Freud's daughter Anna (1967), who became a psychoanalyst herself, and by most contemporary psychodynamic psychologists (Vaillant, 1992):

1 *Repression* occurs when a threatening idea, memory, or emotion is blocked from consciousness. A woman who had a frightening childhood experience that she cannot remember, for example, is said to be repressing her memory of it.

2 *Projection* occurs when a person's own unacceptable or threatening feelings are repressed and then attributed to someone else. A person who is embarrassed about having sexual feelings toward members of a different ethnic group, for example, may project this discomfort onto them, saying, "Those people are dirty-minded and oversexed."

3 *Displacement* occurs when people direct their emotions (especially anger) toward things, animals, or other people that are not the real object of their feelings. A boy who is forbidden to express

superego
In psychoanalysis, the part of personality that represents conscience, morality, and social standards.

defense mechanisms
Methods used by the ego to prevent unconscious anxiety or threatening thoughts from entering consciousness.

"I'm sorry, I'm not speaking to anyone tonight. My defense mechanisms seem to be out of order."

anger toward his father, for example, may "take it out" on his toys or his younger sister. When displacement serves a higher cultural or socially useful purpose, as in the creation of art or inventions, it is called *sublimation.* Freud argued that society has a duty to help people sublimate their unacceptable impulses, for the sake of civilization. Sexual passion may be sublimated into the creation of art or literature; aggressive impulses may be sublimated into competitive sports.

4 *Reaction formation* occurs when a feeling that produces unconscious anxiety is transformed into its opposite in consciousness. A woman who is afraid to admit to herself that she fears her husband may instead cling to the belief that she loves him deeply. A person who is aroused by erotic images may angrily assert that pornography is disgusting. How does such a transformed emotion differ from a true emotion? In reaction formation, the professed feeling is excessive, and the person is extravagant and vehement about demonstrating it. ("Of course I love him! I *never* have any bad thoughts about him! He's perfect!")

5 *Regression* occurs when a person reverts to a previous phase of psychological development. An 8-year-old boy who is anxious about his parents' quarreling may regress to earlier habits of thumb sucking or clinging. Adults may regress to immature behavior when they are under pressure—for example, by having a temper tantrum when they don't get their way.

6 *Denial* occurs when people refuse to admit that something is unpleasant, such as mistreatment by a partner; that they have a prob-

lem, such as drinking too much; or that they are feeling a forbidden emotion, such as anger. Denial protects a person's self-image and preserves the illusion of invulnerability ("It can't happen to me").

The Development of Personality. Freud maintained that personality develops in a series of *psychosexual stages,* in which sexual energy takes different forms as the child matures. Each new stage produces a certain amount of frustration, conflict, and worry. If these become too great, normal development may be interrupted, and the child may remain *fixated,* or stuck, at the current stage.

For example, said Freud, people may remain fixated at the *oral stage,* in the first year of life (when babies experience the world through their mouths), because they were either overindulged as infants when nursing or weaned too abruptly. They will seek oral gratification in smoking, overeating, nail biting, or chewing on pencils. They may be clinging and dependent, or they may deny their dependence by acting brash and tough. Those who remain fixated at the *anal stage,* at about age 2 to 3 (when toilet training and control of bodily wastes are the key issues), may become "anal retentive," holding everything in, obsessive about neatness and cleanliness. Or they may become just the opposite, "anal expulsive"— messy and disorganized.

For Freud, however, the most crucial stage for the formation of personality was the *phallic stage,* which lasts roughly from age 3 to age 5 or 6. At this stage, said Freud, the child unconsciously

A Freudian would say that this woman's smoking and nail-biting are signs of an oral fixation.

wishes to possess the parent of the other sex and to get rid of the parent of the same sex. Children often announce proudly that "I'm going to marry Daddy (or Mommy) when I grow up," and they reject the same-sex "rival." Freud (1924a, 1924b) labeled this phenomenon the **Oedipus complex,** after the Greek legend of King Oedipus, who unwittingly killed his father and married his mother.

Boys and girls, Freud believed, experience the Oedipal complex differently. Boys at this stage are discovering the pleasure and pride of having a penis. When they see a naked girl for the first time, they are horrified. Their unconscious exclaims (in effect), "Her penis has been cut off! Who could have done such a thing to her? Why, it must have been her powerful father. And if he could do it to her, my father could do it to me!" This realization, said Freud, causes the boy to repress his desire for his mother and identify with his father. He accepts his father's authority and the father's standards of conscience and morality; the superego has emerged.

Freud admitted that he did not quite know what to make of girls, who, lacking the penis, could not go through the same steps. He speculated that a girl, upon discovering male anatomy, would panic that she had only a puny clitoris instead of a stately penis. She would conclude, said Freud, that she already had lost her penis. As a result, he said, girls do not have the powerful motivating fear that boys do to give up their Oedipal feelings and develop a strong superego; they have only a lingering sense of "penis envy."

By about age 5 or 6, when the Oedipus complex is resolved, said Freud, the child's fundamental personality patterns are formed. Unconscious conflicts with parents, unresolved fixations and guilts, and attitudes toward the same and the other sex will continue to replay themselves throughout life. The child settles into a supposedly nonsexual *latency stage,* in preparation for the *genital stage,* which begins at puberty. (Modern research, however, shows that most "latency"-age children are curious about sex, masturbate, and experiment with sexual play [Friedrich, 1998; Reynolds, 1998]).

In Freud's view, then, your adult personality is shaped by how you progressed through the early psychosexual stages, which defense mechanisms you have learned to use to reduce anxiety, and whether your ego is strong enough to balance the conflict between the id (what you'd like to do) and the superego (your conscience).

As you might imagine, Freud's ideas were not exactly received with yawns. Sexual feelings in 5-year-olds! Repressed longings in respectable adults! Unconscious meanings in dreams! Penis envy! This was strong stuff in the early years of the twentieth century, and before long, psychoanalysis had captured the public imagination in Europe and America. But it also produced a sharp rift with the emerging schools of empirical psychology (Hornstein, 1992).

This rift continues to divide psychologists and other scholars today. Some revere Freud as a hero who battled public censure and ridicule in his unwavering pursuit of scientific truth (Gay, 1988). Others acknowledge that some of Freud's ideas have proved faulty, but they believe that the overall framework of his theory is timeless and brilliant (Westen, 1998). Still others think psychoanalytic theory is nonsense, with little empirical support (Cioffi, 1998). Citing evidence from long unpublished papers, these critics argue that Freud was not the brilliant theoretician, impartial scientist, or even successful clinician that he claimed to be. On the contrary, Freud often pressured his patients into accepting his explanations of their symptoms; and he ignored all evidence disconfirming his ideas (Crews, 1998; Powell & Boer, 1995; Sulloway, 1992; Webster, 1995).

Consider the story of Freud's 18-year-old patient "Dora" (Freud, 1905a). Dora had been spurning sexual advances made by her father's friend, "Herr K," since she was 14 (Lakoff & Coyne, 1993). Dora's father wanted her to accept Herr K's overtures, perhaps because he himself

Oedipus complex
In psychoanalysis, a conflict in which a child desires the parent of the other sex and views the same-sex parent as a rival; this is the key issue in the phallic stage of development.

was having an affair with Herr K's wife; so he sent Dora off to Freud, who attempted to cure her of her "hysterical" refusal to have sex with Herr K. Freud tried to convince Dora that it was not the ugly situation involving her father and his friend that was distressing her, but her own repressed desires for sex. He actually advised Herr K to "press his suit with a passion" and to ignore Dora's repeated rejections. Dora angrily left treatment after three months, and Freud was never able to accept her "obstinate" rejection of his analysis of her symptoms.

On the positive side, Freud welcomed women into the profession of psychoanalysis, wrote eloquently about the devastating results for women of society's suppression of their sexuality, and argued, ahead of his time, that homosexuality was neither a sin nor a perversion but a "variation of the sexual function" that was "nothing to be ashamed of" (Freud, 1961). Freud was thus a mixture of intellectual vision and blindness, sensitivity and arrogance. His provocative ideas left a powerful legacy to psychology—one that others began to tinker with immediately.

QUICK QUIZ

Have Freudian concepts registered in the unconscious part of your mind? If so, which Freudian concepts do these events suggest?

1. A 4-year-old girl wants to snuggle on Daddy's lap but refuses to kiss her mother.

2. A celibate priest writes poetry about sexual passion.

3. A man who is angry at his boss shouts at his kids for making noise.

4. A woman whose father was cruel to her when she was little insists over and over that she loves him dearly.

5. A racist justifies segregation by saying that black men are only interested in sex with white women.

6. A 9-year-old boy who moves to a new city starts having tantrums.

Answers:
1. Oedipus complex   2. sublimation   3. displacement   4. reaction formation   5. projection   6. regression

Two Other Psychodynamic Approaches

Some of Freud's followers stayed in the psychoanalytic tradition and modified Freud's theories from within. Karen Horney [HORN-eye], for example, argued that it is insulting philosophy and bad science to claim that half the human race is dissatisfied with its anatomy. When women feel inferior to men, she said, we should look for explanations in the disadvantages that women live with and their second-class status. In fact, said Horney, if anyone has an envy problem, it is men. Men have "womb envy": They envy women's ability to bear and nurse children.

Others broke away from Freud, or were actively rejected by him, and went off to start their own schools. Today, there are many psychodynamic approaches, but two are especially popular: the work of Carl Jung and that of the object-relations theorists.

Jungian Theory. Carl Jung (1875–1961) was originally one of Freud's closest friends, but by 1914 he had left Freud's inner circle. His greatest difference with Freud concerned the nature of the unconscious. In addition to the individual's own unconscious, said Jung (1967), there is a **collective unconscious** shared by all human beings, containing universal memories, symbols, and images that are the legacy of human history. In his studies of myths, art, and folklore in cultures all over the world, Jung identified a number of these common themes, which he called **archetypes.**

An archetype can be a picture, such as the "magic circle," called a *mandala* in Eastern religions, which Jung thought symbolizes the unity of life and "the totality of the self." Or it can be a

collective unconscious
In Jungian theory, the universal memories and experiences of humankind, represented in the symbols, stories, and images (archetypes) that occur across all cultures.

archetypes (AR-ki-tipes)
Universal, symbolic images that appear in myths, art, stories, and dreams; to Jungians, they reflect the collective unconscious.

figure found in fairy tales, legends, and popular stories, such as the Hero, the nurturing Earth Mother, the Powerful Father, or the Wicked Witch. It can even be an aspect of the self. For example, the *shadow* archetype reflects the prehistoric fear of wild animals and represents the bestial, evil side of human nature.

Two of the most important archetypes, in Jung's view, are those of maleness and femaleness. Jung (like Freud) recognized that "masculine" and "feminine" qualities exist in both sexes. The *anima* represents the feminine archetype in men; the *animus* represents the masculine archetype in women. Problems can arise, however, if a person tries to repress his or her internal, opposite archetype—that is, if a man denies his softer "feminine" side or if a woman denies her "masculine" aspects. People also create problems in relationships when they expect the partner to behave like the ideal archetypal man or woman, instead of a real human being who has both sides (Young-Eisendrath, 1993).

Many of Jung's ideas were more suited to mysticism and philosophy than to empirical psychology, which may be why so many Jungian ideas are popular with New Age movements today. But some basic archetypes, such as the Hero and the Earth Mother, do appear in the stories and images of virtually every society, taking different forms (Campbell, 1949/1968; Neher, 1996). Jung would recognize dragons, Darth Vader, and Dracula as expressions of the shadow archetype.

Although Jung shared with Freud a fascination with the darker aspects of the personality, he (along with other dissenters from Freudian orthodoxy) had confidence in the positive, forward-moving strengths of the ego. He believed that people are motivated not only by past conflicts, but also by their future goals and their desire to fulfill themselves. Jung was also among the first to identify extroversion/introversion as a basic dimension of personality.

Modern Jungians are interested in how universal images and stories affect the way people see their own lives. When Dan McAdams (1988) asked 50 people to tell their life stories in a two-hour session, he found that people tended to report a common archetype, a mythic character, at the heart of their life narratives. For example, many individuals told stories that could be symbolized by the myth of the Greek god Dionysus, the pleasure seeker who escapes responsibility. Archetypes, says McAdams, repre-

In The Wizard of Oz, *the Wicked Witch of the West is a beloved example of the archetype of evil.*

sent "the main characters in the life stories we construct as our identities."

The Object-Relations School.

In the late 1950s, John Bowlby (1958), a British psychoanalyst, contested the Freudian view that an infant's attachment to its mother is due to her ability to gratify the baby's oral needs. Bowlby observed that infants who were deprived of normal contact with parents and other adults suffered catastrophically, and he argued for the primacy of attachment needs—social stimulation, warmth, and contact. Bowlby's work influenced other psychoanalysts to acknowledge the fundamentally social nature of human development. Although the need for social contact in infancy now seems obvious, this change in emphasis was a significant departure from the classic Freudian view, for Freud essentially regarded the baby as if it were an independent little organism ruled by its own instinctive desires.

Today, an emphasis on relationships is associated with the **object-relations school,** which was developed in Great Britain by Melanie Klein, W. Ronald Fairbairn, and D. W. Winnicott (Horner, 1991; Hughes, 1989). In contrast to Freud's emphasis on the Oedipal period, object-relations theorists hold that the first two years of life are the most critical for development of the inner core of personality. Freud emphasized

object-relations school
A psychodynamic approach that emphasizes the importance of the infant's first two years of life and the baby's formative relationships, especially with the mother.

the child's fear of the powerful father; object-relations analysts emphasize the child's need for the powerful mother, who is usually the baby's caregiver in the first critical years. Freud's theory was based on the dynamics of inner drives; object-relations theory holds that the basic human drive is not impulse gratification but the need to be in relationships.

The reason for the clunky word "object" in object-relations theory (instead of the warmer word "human" or even "parent") is that the infant's attachment is not only to a real person (usually the mother) but also to the infant's evolving perception of her. The child creates a *representation* of the mother—someone who is kind or fierce, protective or rejecting—that is not literally the same as the woman herself. The child's representations of important adults, whether realistic or distorted, unconsciously affect personality throughout life, influencing how the person relates to others: with trust or suspicion, acceptance or criticism (Westen, 1998).

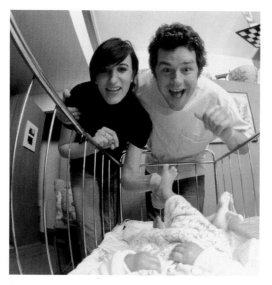

According to object-relations theory, a baby constructs unconscious representations of his or her parents, which will influence the child's relations with others throughout life.

In Freudian theory, other people are relevant to an infant only insofar as they gratify the infant's drives or block them. But to object-relations theorists, other people are important as sources of attachment. The central problem in life is to find a healthy balance between the need for others and the need for independence. This balance requires constant adjustment to separations and losses: small ones that occur during quarrels, moderate ones such as leaving home for the first time, and major ones such as divorce or death. The way we react to these separations, according to object-relations theorists, is largely determined by our experiences in the first year or two of life.

The object-relations school also departs from Freudian theory regarding the nature of male and female development (Sagan, 1988; Winnicott, 1957/1990). In the object-relations view, children of both sexes identify first with the mother. Girls, who are the same sex as the mother, do not need to separate from her; the mother treats a daughter as an extension of herself. But boys, if they are to develop a masculine identity, must break away from the mother; the mother encourages a son to be independent and separate. Thus, men develop more rigid boundaries between themselves and other people than women do.

The result, in the object-relations view, is that men tend to be less secure than women because their identity is based on *not* being like women. Later in life, the typical psychological problem for women is how to increase their autonomy and assert their own needs in close relationships. In contrast, the typical problem for men is how to permit close attachments (Gilligan, 1982). Some object-relations theorists believe that this gender difference is inevitable because women are biologically suited to be the primary nurturers. Others argue that if men played a greater role in nurturing infants and small children, the sex difference in the need for separation from the mother would fade, and so would men's need to be "opposite" from women (Chodorow, 1978, 1992).

Evaluating Psychodynamic Theories

Although modern psychodynamic theorists differ in many ways, they share a general belief that the way to understand personality is by exploring its unconscious dynamics (Westen, 1998). Many psychologists in other fields, however, regard psychodynamic ideas as literary metaphors that can never be tested, rather than as scientific hypotheses (Cioffi, 1998; Crews, 1998). Critics argue that psychodynamic theories are guilty of three scientific failings:

Thinking Critically About Psychodynamic Ideas

1 *Violating the principle of falsifiability.* As we saw in Chapter 1, a theory that is impossible to disconfirm in principle is not scientific. Many psychodynamic ideas about unconscious motivations are, in fact, impossible to confirm or disconfirm. If your experience seems to support these ideas, it is taken as evidence of their correctness, but if you doubt them or offer disconfirming evidence, you must be "defensive," lack observational skills, or (a favorite accusation) be "in denial." This way of responding to criticism is neither scientific nor fair!

2 *Drawing universal principles from the experiences of a few atypical patients.* Freud and most of his followers generalized from a few individuals, often patients in therapy, to all human beings. Of course, the problem of overgeneralizing from small samples occurs in other areas of psychology, too, and sometimes valid insights about human behavior can be obtained from case studies. The problem occurs when the observer fails to confirm these observations by studying larger, more representative samples and incorrectly infers that what applies to some individuals must apply to all. For example, to confirm Freud's ideas about penis envy, you would need to observe or talk to many young children. Freud himself did not do this; however, when research psychologists interview preschool-age children, they typically find that many children of *both* sexes envy one another. In one charming study of 65 preschool-age boys and girls, 45 percent of the girls had fantasized about having a penis or being male in other ways—and 44 percent of the boys had fantasized about being pregnant (Linday, 1994).

3 *Basing theories of personality development on the retrospective accounts and fallible memories of patients.* Most psychodynamic theorists have not observed random samples of children at different ages, as modern child psychologists do, to construct their theories of development. Instead, they have worked backward, creating theories based on themes in adults' recollections. The analysis of memories can be an illuminating way to achieve insights about our lives; in fact, it is the only way we can think about our own lives! But as we will see in Chapter 7, memory does not work like a tape recorder; it is often inaccurate, influenced as much by what is going on in our lives now as what happened in the past. If you are currently not getting along with your mother, you may remember all the times in your childhood when she was hard on you and forget the counterexamples of her kindness.

Retrospective analysis has another problem: It creates an *illusion of causality* between events. People often assume, without justification, that if A came before B, then A must have caused B. For example, if your mother spent three months in the hospital when you were 5 years old and today you feel shy and insecure in college, an object-relations analyst might draw a connection between the two facts. But a lot of other things could be causing your shyness and insecurity, as we have seen: your

Some psychodynamic ideas can be tested empirically. For example, Freud thought that playing or observing aggressive sports would "displace" aggressive energy into socially accepted activities, and hence reduce it. But behavioral research finds that aggressive sports actually stimulate increased violence among players and among spectators, like these soccer fans.

temperament, your learning history, the norms of your culture, or the fact that your college is large and impersonal.

In response to the concerns of critics, some psychodynamic psychologists and researchers in other areas are using empirical methods to reformulate or refine psychodynamic theories and concepts. For example, some have developed objective tests of specific defense mechanisms to find out how these strategies protect self-esteem and reduce anxiety (Cramer, 2000; Plutchik et al., 1988). Cognitive psychologists are investigating nonconscious processes in thought and memory (Epstein, 1994; Kihlstrom, Barnhardt, & Tataryn, 1992). Social psychologists are studying how people unconsciously relive past relationships in their present ones (Andersen & Berk, 1998). And some social and learning psychologists are identifying the situations and conditions under which people "displace" aggressive feelings onto innocent bystanders (Marcus-Newhall et al., 2000).

Psychodynamic ideas will continue to be controversial, but these ideas have encouraged researchers to tackle large, fascinating, and difficult questions, such as why some symbols are universal; why men and women often regard each other with envy and animosity instead of love; why individuals are sometimes unaware of their own motives; and why people unconsciously repeat patterns of behavior that seem irrational to others.

2.1

QUICK QUIZ

Do you have a psychodynamic conflict about quizzes?

1. An 8-year-old boy is behaving aggressively, hitting classmates, and refusing to obey his teacher. Match each explanation of his behavior with the appropriate theorist: Freud, Jung, or object-relations theorists.

   a. The boy has repressed his internal *anima* archetype.

   b. The boy is expressing the aggressive energy of the id and has not developed enough ego control.

   c. The boy has had unusual difficulty separating emotionally from his mother and is compensating by behaving aggressively.

2. In the 1950s and 1960s, many psychoanalysts, observing unhappy gay men who had sought therapy, concluded that homosexuality was a mental illness. What violation of the scientific method were they committing?

Answers:

1. a. Jung   b. Freud   c. object-relations theorists   2. The analysts were drawing inappropriate conclusions from atypical patients in therapy, failing to test these conclusions with heterosexuals or gay men who were not in therapy. When such research was done, using appropriate control groups, it turned out that gay men were not more mentally disturbed or depressed than heterosexuals (Hooker, 1957).

What's Ahead

- How does the humanist vision of human nature differ from the visions of behaviorism and psychoanalysis?

- In the humanist view, what's wrong with saying to a child, "I love you because you've been good"?

2.6 The Humanist Contribution

A final way to look at personality starts with the person's own view of the world—his or her subjective interpretation of what is happening right now. Psychologists who take a *humanist* approach to personality believe that personality is influenced less by our genes, past learning, or unconscious conflicts than by our uniquely human capacity to shape our own futures. It is defined, they say, by the human abilities that separate us from other animals: freedom of choice and free will.

The Inner Experience

Humanist psychology was launched as a movement within psychology in the early 1960s.

humanist psychology
A psychological approach that emphasizes personal growth and the achievement of human potential rather than the scientific understanding and assessment of behavior.

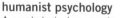

Humanists rejected the psychoanalytic emphasis on hostility, instincts, and repressed conflicts. They also rejected behaviorism, with its emphasis on reinforcers, punishers, and specific behaviors. The movement's chief leaders—Abraham Maslow (1908–1970), Carl Rogers (1902–1987), and Rollo May (1909–1994)—argued that it was time for a "third force" in psychology, one that would draw a fuller picture of human potential.

The trouble with psychology, said Maslow (1971), was that it had focused too much on negative traits and had forgotten such positive aspects of human nature as joy, laughter, love, happiness, and *peak experiences,* rare moments of rapture caused by the attainment of excellence or the experience of beauty. The traits that Maslow thought most important to personality were not the Big Five, but rather the qualities of the *self-actualized person*—the person who strives for a life that is meaningful, challenging, and satisfying. Personality development could be viewed, he thought, as a gradual progression toward a state of self-actualization. As Maslow (1971) wrote, "When you select out for careful study very fine and healthy people, strong people, creative people, saintly people, sagacious people . . . then you get a very different view of mankind. You are asking how tall can people grow, what can a human being become?"

Abraham Maslow regarded self-actualization as a lifelong process, one you are never too old to begin. Hulda Crooks, shown here at age 91 climbing Mt. Fuji, took up mountain climbing at 54. "When I come down from the mountain," she said, "I feel like I can battle in the valley again." She died at the age of 101.

Carl Rogers, like Freud, derived many of his ideas from observing his clients in therapy. As a clinician, Rogers (1951, 1961) was interested not only in why some people cannot function well, but also in what he called the fully functioning individual. How you behave depends on your subjective reality, Rogers said, not on the external reality around you. Fully functioning people experience *congruence,* or harmony, between the image they project to others and their true feelings and wishes. They are trusting, warm, and open, not defensive or intolerant. Their beliefs about themselves are realistic.

To become fully functioning people, Rogers maintained, we all need **unconditional positive regard,** love and support for the people we are, without strings (conditions) attached. This doesn't mean that Winifred should be allowed to kick her brother when she is angry with him or that Wilbur may throw his dinner out the window because he doesn't like pot roast. In these cases, a parent can correct the child's behavior without withdrawing love from the child. The child can learn that the behavior, not the child, is what is

bad. "House rules are 'no violence,' Winifred," is a very different message from "You are a horrible person, Winifred."

Unfortunately, Rogers observed, many children are raised with *conditional* positive regard: "I'll love you if you behave well, and I won't love you if you behave badly." Adults often treat each other this way, too. People treated with conditional regard begin to suppress or deny feelings or actions that they believe are unacceptable to those they love. The result is incongruence, a sense of being "out of touch with your feelings," of not being true to your "real self." The suppression of feelings and parts of oneself produces low self-regard, defensiveness, and unhappiness. The result is an individual who scores high on neuroticism—who is bitter, unhappy, and negative.

Not all humanists have been optimistic about human nature. For example, Rollo May (1994) emphasized some of the inherently difficult and tragic aspects of the human condition, including loneliness, anxiety, and alienation. In books such as *Love and Will* and *The Meaning of Anxiety,* May brought to American psychology elements of the European philosophy of *existentialism.* This doctrine holds that free will confers on us responsibility for our actions. The price is often anxiety and despair, which is why many people try to escape from freedom into narrow certainties and blame others for their misfortunes. Our personalities reflect the ways we cope with the inevitable struggles of life: to find meaning in existence, to use our freedom wisely, and to face suffering and death bravely. May popularized the humanist idea that we can draw on inner resources to make the best of ourselves, but he added that we can never escape the harsh realities of life and death.

Evaluating Humanist Theories

As with psychodynamic theories, the major criticism of humanist psychology is that many of its assumptions are untestable. Freud looked at humanity and saw destructive drives, selfishness, and lust. Maslow and Rogers looked at humanity and saw cooperation, selflessness, and love. May looked at humanity and saw fear of freedom, loneliness, and the struggle for

Thinking Critically About Testing Humanist Ideas

unconditional positive regard
To Carl Rogers, love or support given to another person, with no conditions attached.

William Fabricius, Arizona State University

Vivian Ferry, Community College of Rhode Island

Andrew Geoghegan, Longview Community College

Richard Girard, New Hampshire Community Technical College

Randy Gold, Cuesta College

Peter Graham, Pensacola Junior College

David Grilly, Cleveland State University

Bea Gattuso Grosh, Millersville University

Roger Harnish, Rochester Institute of Technology

James E. Hart, Edison Community College

Jack Harnett, Virginia Commonwealth University

Peter C. Hill, Grove City College

Gene Indenbaum, SUNY-Farmingdale

Sherri Jackson, Jacksonville University

Craig Johnson, Towson State University

Jim Jokerst, Aims Community College

David Klein, Stark State College of Technology

Katherine Kocel, Jackson State University

Anne Kollath, Allan Hancock College

Patsy Lawson, Volunteer State Community College

Gary Levy, University of Wyoming

John F. Lindsay, Jr., Georgia College and State University

Peter Maneno, Normandale Community College

Lyla Maynard, Des Moines Area Community College

Cynthia McCormick, Armstrong Atlantic State University

Rafael Mendez, Bronx Community College

Judi Misale, Truman State University

Benjamin Newberry, Kent State University

Diana P. Nagel, Northwest Arkansas Community College

Orlando Olivares, Bridgewater State College

David Perkins, College of St. Elizabeth

Wade Pickren, Southeastern Oklahoma State University

Paula M. Popovich, Ohio University

Jack Powell, University of Hartford

Shirley Pritchett, Northeast Texas Community College

Steven Richman, Nassau Community College

Mark Rittman, Cuyahoga Metro Community College

Lee Schrock, Kankakee Community College

Charles Slem, Cal Poly-San Luis Obispo

Angela Simon, El Camino College

Christina S. Sinisi, Charleston Southern University

Holly Straub, University of South Dakota

Ed Valsi, Oakland Community College

Matthew Westra, Longview community College

Fred Whitford, Montana State University

Edmond Zuromski, Community College of Rhode Island

We are also grateful to our superb editorial and production teams at Prentice Hall. "Cooperation in pursuit of mutual goals" is known to build strong alliances, and we have certainly forged an alliance with this remarkable group. Our deepest thanks to the indefatigable Jennifer Gilliland, Senior Acquisitions Editor, who supervised the revision from start to finish with enthusiasm, skill, and plenty of great ideas; to Nicole Girrbach, her extraordinarily talented and efficient assistant; Senior Production Editor Maureen Richardson, who is simply a genius at putting all the elements of a book together calmly and capably, all the while soothing her authors' frazzled nerves; and our loyal and witty copyeditor, Shari Dorantes Hatch, who has been minding our prose for many editions and still laughs at our jokes. Our thanks also to Media Editor Karen Branson, who worked hard to coordinate the complex media program and the icons found throughout the book, and to Lynn Blesz-Vestal for selecting the web links in the program, preparing the online study guide, and writing questions that enable students to use the web links intelligently and think critically about the material. Our special appreciation to Vice President and Editorial Director of Social Sciences and Psychology, Laura Pearson; to Editor-in-Chief of Development Susanna Lesan; to Development Editor Leslie Carr; and to Senior Marketing Manager Sharon Cosgrove—all of whom helped enormously in the initial launch of this revision.

We are delighted with the book's design, inside and out. Our heartfelt gratitude to Anne DeMarinis for giving this edition its warm new look while keeping its visual connection to the earlier edition, and to Maria Piper, who made necessary corrections to the line art. We are indebted to Dr. William Ober and Claire Garrison at Medical and Scientific Illustration for their beautiful and highly accurate anatomical art. Connie Blacker

meaning. These differences, say the critics, may tell us more about the observers than about the observed.

Many humanist concepts, although intuitively appealing, are hard to define operationally (see Chapter 1). How can we know whether a person is self-fulfilled or self-actualized? How can we tell whether a woman's decision to quit her job and become a professional rodeo rider represents an "escape from freedom" or a freely made choice? And what exactly is unconditional positive regard? If it is defined as unquestioned support of a child's efforts at mastering a new skill, or as assurance that the child is loved in spite of his or her mistakes, then it is clearly a good idea. But in the popular culture, it has often been interpreted as an unwillingness ever to say "no" to a child, or to offer constructive criticism and set limits, which children need.

Despite such concerns, humanist psychologists have added balance to the study of personality. Influenced in part by the humanists, psychologists in other perspectives are studying many positive human traits, such as courage, helpfulness to others, the motivation to excel, and self-confidence. Stress researchers have discovered the healing powers of humor and hope. Developmental psychologists are studying ways to foster children's empathy and creativity. And the humanist argument that we have the power to choose our own destinies, even when fate delivers us into tragedy, has fostered an appreciation of human resilience in the face of adversity.

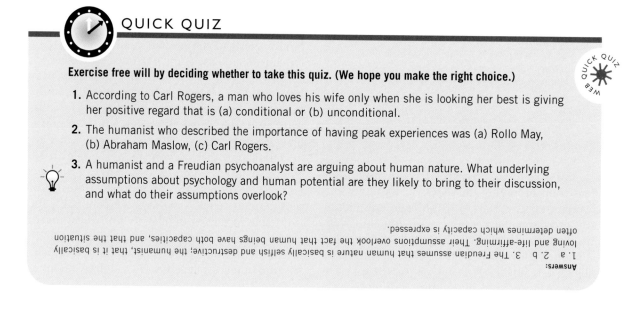

QUICK QUIZ

Exercise free will by deciding whether to take this quiz. (We hope you make the right choice.)

1. According to Carl Rogers, a man who loves his wife only when she is looking her best is giving her positive regard that is (a) conditional or (b) unconditional.

2. The humanist who described the importance of having peak experiences was (a) Rollo May, (b) Abraham Maslow, (c) Carl Rogers.

3. A humanist and a Freudian psychoanalyst are arguing about human nature. What underlying assumptions about psychology and human potential are they likely to bring to their discussion, and what do their assumptions overlook?

Answers:

1. a 2. b 3. The Freudian assumes that human nature is basically selfish and destructive; the humanist, that it is basically loving and life-affirming. Their assumptions overlook the fact that human beings have both capacities, and that the situation often determines which capacity is expressed.

Together, the five approaches to personality discussed in this chapter portray a complex constellation of qualities that make up a human being: biological dispositions, habits born of experience, beliefs and expectations, traits influenced by cultural forces, unconscious motives and defenses, and modes of behavior developed in the struggle to become our best selves. (For a summary of these approaches, see Table 2.3.)

One way to integrate these different theories may lie in recognizing that personality has two broad dimensions. Each of us has a public personality that we present to the world, consisting of our characteristic habits and temperaments and our basic traits. This is the personality that biological, learning, and cultural theories address. But we also have a private personality that reflects our interior sense of self, consisting of our subjective experience of emotions, memories, dreams, wishes, and worries (Singer, 1984). This is the personality that psychodynamic and humanistic theories address. Each of us weaves these two dimensions of personality together in the narratives we tell to explain our lives, our inconsistencies, our failures and successes—to explain, in short, why we are the way we are.

Table 2.3   Theories of Personality Contrasted

	Basic Method of Inquiry	Explanation of Personality Traits	Possibility of Personal Change
Biological theories	Empirical study of temperaments, heritability of traits.	Temperaments are inborn, and many traits are highly influenced by genes.	Limited by biology, but partly modifiable by experience.
Learning theories Behaviorism	Empirical study of behavior in specific situations.	"Trait" labels are a shorthand for behavior patterns resulting from reinforcement and punishment.	Good, if the environment changes.
Social–cognitive learning theories	Empirical study of behavior, cognitions, internalized beliefs and values.	Cognitions and situational demands interact to produce traits.	Good, because people can alter their situations and beliefs.
Cultural theories	Empirical study of behavior, cognitions, and values within and across cultures.	Cultural values and rules determine which traits are encouraged or discouraged.	Depends on whether a culture values personal change or stability.
Psychodynamic theories	Subjective analysis of unconscious dynamics and early childhood memories.	Unconscious dynamics stemming from childhood produce adult defenses, inner conflicts, and motives.	Limited by unconscious processes and the difficulty of overcoming early experiences.
Humanist theories	Subjective analysis of a person's perceptions of reality.	A person's subjective reality and choices shape personality, decisions, and behavior.	Good, if the person exercises free will and takes responsibility for change.

PSYCHOLOGY IN THE NEWS, REVISITED

How are the dimensions of personality woven together in the case of Kathleen Soliah, a.k.a. Sara Jane Olson, whose apparent change of personality was described in the news item at the start of this chapter?

Psychologists taking a biological view of personality would say that despite Olson's apparent transformation, many of her personality traits probably remained stable over the years, merely taking a different form as she grew older. For example, she may always have been an extrovert, as suggested by her early activism and later acting career.

Yet Olson's story also shows that despite the general stability of many traits and temperaments, personality does sometimes change—and some-

times it changes big-time! What accounts for this? Psychologists who take a learning perspective would say that the stability or flexibility of a person's behavior depends largely on the situation. When people are in a situation in which militant or aggressive behavior is rewarded—with attention, excitement, comradeship, and a sense of power over what they view as a corrupt system—they may become revolutionaries. If the situation changes drastically, with their behavior now threatened with severe punishments (prison, the loss of friends), they may change accordingly; in Olson's case, an entirely different way of living, more conventional, was rewarded. A social–cognitive learning theorist would add that a person's beliefs and perceptions are also critical in any "personality transplant." One young revolutionary might respond to the threat of imprisonment with fear and a determination to escape. But someone else might interpret the situation differently and respond with resignation ("They got me; I'll get through this the best I can") or with angry determination ("I'll remain committed to this cause until I die, no matter what the price").

Cultural psychologists would observe that Soliah/Olson's change of personality did not occur in a cultural void. The late 1960s and early 1970s were turbulent times, when many young people expressed their outrage over social injustices and the quagmire of the Vietnam War by joining movements that promised sweeping social change—an end to the war, to discrimination, to poverty. Some despaired of changing "the system" with peaceful methods and resorted to violent action as a means to that end. But by the mid-1970s and early 1980s, many activists had become disillusioned with the slow progress of change (and, as we saw, became more "external"), and there was no longer a war to serve as a focus for protest. The 1980s began an era of conservative politics and the pursuit of affluence, and countless former revolutionaries entered traditional roles and occupations. One famous anti-establishment radical, Jerry Rubin, became a stockbroker!

A psychodynamic theorist would be dissatisfied with all of these explanations and would instead look for unconscious motives in Soliah/Olson's early involvement with the Symbionese Liberation Army. Was her anger at the system a displacement of anger toward her parents or other authority figures? Did her personality soften when she came to terms with this anger or was able to "sublimate" it into more constructive activities?

Finally, humanist psychologists might speculate that the private woman, the one who lives inside Olson's skin, could be quite different from the one presented in interviews. Accordingly, we should be wary of forming impressions based solely on her public persona—either the persona of her rebellious youth or that of her conventional middle age.

Ultimately, we can only guess at who the "real" woman is: Sara, Kathleen, both, . . . or neither. All of us, however, can use the insights of the theorists in this chapter to better understand ourselves and the people in our lives. Genetic influences, learned habits, cultural norms, unconscious fears and conflicts, and visions of possibility, filtered through our interior sense of self and our life story, give each of us the stamp of our personality—one that is as distinctive as a fingerprint.

TAKING PSYCHOLOGY WITH YOU

How to Avoid the Barnum Effect

How well does the following paragraph describe you?

Some of your aspirations tend to be pretty unrealistic. At times you are extroverted, affable, sociable, while at other times you are introverted, wary, and reserved. You have found it unwise to be too frank in revealing yourself to others. You pride yourself on being an independent thinker and do not accept others' opinions without satisfactory proof. You prefer a certain amount of change and variety, and you become dissatisfied when hemmed in by restrictions and limitations. At times you have serious doubts as to whether you have made the right decision or done the right thing.

When people believe that this description was written just for them—the result of a personalized horoscope or handwriting analysis—they all say the same thing:

"It's me! It describes me *exactly!*" Magician James Randi often gives audiences of college students a similar "personalized profile" and asks them to rate it for its accuracy. Students invariably rate their profiles as highly accurate—until Randi asks them to exchange profiles with a neighbor, and they realize that all the descriptions are identical.

The reason everyone thinks this description is accurate is that it is vague enough to apply to almost everyone and it is flattering (don't we all consider ourselves to be "independent thinkers"?). And if people pay money for a profile, take the time to write away for it, or provide detailed information about themselves, they are even more likely to believe that the profile is eerily accurate. This is why many psychologists worry about the "Barnum effect" (Snyder & Shenkel, 1975). P. T. Barnum was the great circus showman who said,

"There's a sucker born every minute." He knew that the formula for success was to "have a little something for everybody"— and that is just what unscientific personality profiles, horoscopes, and handwriting analysis (graphology) have in common. They have "a little something for everybody" and hence are nonfalsifiable.

Pseudosciences such as graphology have failed to predict personality accurately whenever they have been tested empirically (Beyerstein, 1996; Klimoski, 1992). Pesky, disconfirming facts are simply explained away after the fact. For example, when one graphologist learned that Mohandas Gandhi did not display the large writing she said was typical of great leaders, she explained that his writing showed he was modest and preferred to lead from a position of inferiority. Yet unless they see a demonstration like the one Randi does, most people continue to fall for bogus personality profiles, seeing what they want to see and ignoring the rest.

If you do not want to be taken in by the Barnum effect, research offers this advice:

• *Beware of all-purpose descriptions that could apply to anyone.* We know a couple who were terribly impressed when an astrologer told them that "each of you needs privacy and time to be independent," along with "but don't become too independent, or you will lose your bond." Such observations,

which play it safe by playing it both ways, apply to just about all couples.

• *Beware of your own selective perceptions.* Most of us are so impressed when a horoscope, psychic, or graphologist gets something right that we overlook all the descriptions that are plain wrong.

• *Resist flattery.* This is a hard one. It is easy to reject a profile that describes you as selfish, stupid, or unoriginal. Watch out

for the ones that tell you how wonderful and smart you are, what a great leader you will be, or how modest you are about your superior abilities.

If you keep your critical faculties with you, you won't end up paying hard cash for soft answers, pawning the piano because Geminis should invest in gold this month, or taking a job you despise because it fits your "personality type." In other words, you will prove Barnum wrong.

SUMMARY
The Elements of Personality

• *Personality* refers to an individual's distinctive and relatively stable pattern of behavior, motives, thoughts, and emotions; it reflects different *traits*, characteristics that describe a person across situations.

• Gordon Allport argued that people have a few *central traits* that are key to their personalities, and a greater number of *secondary traits* that are less fundamental. Raymond Cattell used *factor analysis* to identify clusters of traits that he considered the basic components of personality. Today, there is strong evidence for the *Big Five* dimensions of personality: extroversion versus introversion, neuroticism (negative emotionality), agreeableness, conscientiousness, and openness to experience.

The Biological Contribution

• Individual differences in *temperaments*—ways of reacting to the environment—emerge early in life and can influence subsequent personality development. Temperamental differences in extremely reactive and nonreactive children (and monkeys) may be due to variations in the responsiveness of the sympathetic nervous system to change and novelty.

• *Behavioral–genetic* data from studies of *identical and fraternal twins* and adopted children suggest that the *heritability* of many adult personality traits is around .50, with most of the remaining variation accounted for by people's unique experiences rather than those they share with family members. But *genes* tell only part of the story. Not all traits are equally heritable or unaffected by shared environ-

ment; some studies may underestimate the impact of the environment; and some temperaments and traits that are highly heritable can be modified by experience.

The Learning Contribution

• Learning theories of personality emphasize the role of experience. *Behaviorists,* inspired by the work of B. F. Skinner, argue that personality is only a convenient fiction because behavior depends on environmental (external) *reinforcers* and punishers (i.e., *operant conditioning*). *Social-cognitive learning theorists* agree that personality consists of acquired patterns, but they argue that learned expectations, habits, perceptions, and beliefs—a person's personality—come to influence and regulate behavior. For example, behavior is influenced by the extent to which people believe they have control over their lives (have an *internal* or *external locus of control*). A person's expectations about success or failure can lead to a *self-fulfilling prophecy.*

• One problem with learning theories of personality is that behavior is sometimes attributed to a vague category called "the environment" without specifying which aspects of it are having effects. Another problem is that so many situational factors influence people's behavior that it can be difficult to single out the impact of any one of them.

The Cultural Contribution

• Many qualities that Western psychologists treat as individual personality traits, such as risk-taking or a preference for a certain *conversational distance,* are heavily influenced by culture. People from *individualist cultures* define themselves in different terms than those from *collectivist cultures,* and they perceive their "selves" as more stable across situations. People from *monochronic cultures* are more concerned with punctuality and doing things "one at a time" than are people from *polychronic cultures,* who value relationships above time schedules.

- Cultural theories of personality face the problem of describing broad cultural characteristics and their influence on personality without promoting stereotypes.

The Psychodynamic Contribution

- Sigmund Freud was the founder of *psychoanalysis,* which was the first *psychodynamic theory.* Modern psychodynamic theories share an emphasis on (a) *intrapsychic dynamics,* (b) the formative role of childhood experiences and conflicts, (c) the idea that psychological development occurs in stages, (d) the importance of a person's unconscious perceptions of events rather than what actually happened, and (e) subjective methods of understanding a person's life and personality.

- To Freud, the personality consists of the *id* (the source of *libido* or sexual energy and the aggressive instinct), the *ego* (the source of reason), and the *superego* (the source of conscience). *Defense mechanisms* protect the ego from unconscious anxiety. They include, among others, *repression, projection, displacement* (one form of which is *sublimation*), *reaction formation, regression,* and *denial.*

- Freud believed that personality develops in a series of *psychosexual stages:* oral, anal, phallic (Oedipal), latency, and genital. During the phallic stage, Freud believed, the *Oedipus complex* occurs in which the child desires the parent of the other sex and feels rivalry with the same-sex parent. When the Oedipus complex is resolved, the child identifies with the same-sex parent, but females retain a lingering sense of inferiority and "penis envy"—a notion contested by another psychoanalyst, Karen Horney.

- Carl Jung believed that people share a *collective unconscious* that contains universal memories and images, or *archetypes.* Personality, in this view, includes such archetypes as the *shadow* (evil) and the *anima* and the *animus.*

- The *object-relations school* emphasizes the importance of the first two years of life, rather than the Oedipal phase; the infant's relationships to important figures, especially the mother, rather than sexual needs and drives; and the problem in male development of breaking away from the mother.

- Psychodynamic approaches have been criticized for violating the principle of falsifiability; for overgeneralizing from atypical patients to everyone; and for basing theories on the unreliable memories and retrospective accounts of patients, which can lead to an *illusion of causality* between events. But some psychodynamic ideas, especially about nonconscious processes and defenses, are being studied empirically and have made important contributions to psychology.

The Humanist Contribution

- *Humanist psychologists* focus on a person's subjective sense of self and free will to change. They emphasize human potential and the strengths of human nature, as in Abraham Maslow's concepts of *peak experiences* and *self-actualization.* Carl Rogers stressed the importance of *unconditional positive regard* in creating a "fully functioning" person. Rollo May helped bring *existentialism* into American psychology, emphasizing the inherent dilemmas of human existence, such as the search for meaning in life. Critics observe that these ideas are subjective and difficult to study, but they have added depth to the study of personality.

- Biological, learning, and cultural theories of personality tend to emphasize the public personality that we present to the world; psychodynamic and humanist theories emphasize the private, interior sense of self. Together these approaches portray a complex vision of human personality.

KEY TERMS

personality 39	Raymond Cattell 40	genes 43
trait 39	factor analysis 40	heritability 43
Gordon Allport 40	"Big Five" personality traits 40	behavioral genetics 43
central and secondary traits 40	temperament 42	identical and fraternal twins 44

LOOKING BACK ◀

- How can psychologists tell which personality traits are basic? (p. 40)

- Which five dimensions of personality seem to describe people the world over? (pp. 41–42)

- Is it possible to be born irritable or easygoing? (pp. 42–43)

- Why are twins important in studying the heritability of traits? (p. 44)

- To what extent are personality differences among people influenced by their genetic differences? (p. 45)

- Are people who have highly heritable personality traits stuck with them forever? (p. 46)

- Why don't behaviorists have a theory of personality? (p. 48)

- How would a social-cognitive learning theorist explain habitual hostility or aggressiveness? (p. 49)

- What's the difference between people who think they control their own destiny and those who think that destiny controls them? (pp. 49–50)

- Why are risk-taking, aggressiveness, and punctuality more than just individual personality traits? (pp. 52–53)

- How does belonging to an individualist or a collectivist culture influence your personality—and even whether you think you have a stable "self"? (pp. 53–54)

- Why might an Arab and a Swede agree on everything the other is saying, and still feel uncomfortable with each other? (pp. 53–54)

- In Freud's theory of personality, why are the id and the superego always at war? (p. 57)

- When people tell you that you're being "defensive," what defenses might they be thinking of? (pp. 57–58)

- How do psychologists regard Freud today—as a genius or a fraud? (p. 59)

- What would Carl Jung have to say about Darth Vader? (p. 61)

- What are the "objects" in the object-relations approach to personality? (p. 62)

- How does the humanist vision of human nature differ from the visions of behaviorism and psychoanalysis? (p. 64)

- In the humanist view, what's wrong with saying to a child, "I love you because you've been good"? (p. 65)

Age Record Broken as 63-Year-Old Woman Gives Birth

LOS ANGELES, APRIL 10, 1997. A fertility specialist at the University of Southern California has announced that a 63-year-old patient, Arceli Keh, gave birth last year to a healthy baby girl. The child was conceived through in vitro ("test tube") fertilization, with sperm from the woman's 60-year-old husband and an egg donated by a younger woman. Previously, the oldest woman on record to give birth was a 53-year-old Italian woman who had a child in 1994 through the use of similar procedures.

Although the USC infertility program has a policy of rejecting patients over age 55, the California woman lied about her age and did not confess the truth until she was 13 weeks pregnant. The woman's own 86-year-old mother, unaware of her daughter's pregnancy until the delivery, is reportedly

The oldest woman ever to give birth, Arceli Keh, age 63, cuddles her daughter Cynthia.

delighted at becoming a grandparent, and the rest of the close-knit Filipino family has also been supportive. But some fertility experts and ethicists have misgivings. Dr. Mark Sauer, who pioneered the use of donor eggs in older women, said, "I lose my comfort level after 55 because I have to believe that there are quality-of-life issues involved in raising a child at [the parent's] age. When [the baby] is 5, her mother will be 68. And I have to believe that a 78-year-old dealing with a teenager may have some problems."

DEVELOPMENT OVER THE LIFE SPAN

How do *you* react to the idea of a 63-year-old woman having a baby? Would it make any difference if the mother were "only" 55 years old, or 50, or 45? What if she were older than 63? Do you feel the same about older fathers as you do about older mothers? Is there a "right" time to become a parent? For that matter, is there a "right" time to do anything in life—go to school, get married, retire, . . . die?

Until the late nineteenth century, people of different ages often inhabited the same social world. Children and teenagers worked alongside adults on farms and in factories; several generations often shared one household. Neither children nor old people were set apart from the rest of society on the grounds that they were too young or too old to participate (Chudacoff, 1990).

Then, during the first half of the twentieth century, social and economic changes in industrialized countries led to the notion that life unfolds in a progression of distinct stages. Childhood came to be seen as a special time, when "formative" experiences determine the kind of adult a person will become. Adolescence, the years between the physical changes of puberty and the social markers of adulthood, became longer and longer, and its defining characteristics were said to be turmoil and turbulence. Adulthood was conceptualized as a series of predictable stages, from marriage and parenthood to retirement. Elderly people were increasingly

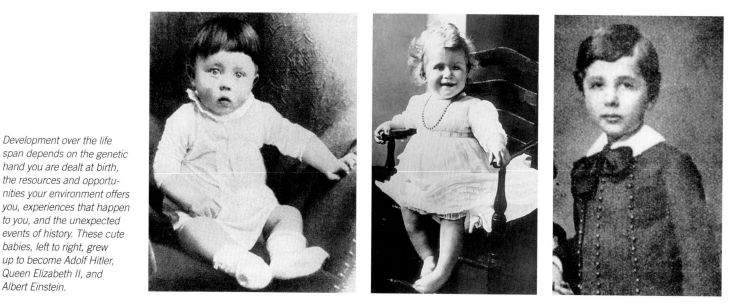

Development over the life span depends on the genetic hand you are dealt at birth, the resources and opportunities your environment offers you, experiences that happen to you, and the unexpected events of history. These cute babies, left to right, grew up to become Adolf Hitler, Queen Elizabeth II, and Albert Einstein.

separated from the rest of society on the grounds that they could not keep up with the fast-moving world.

Today, we are undergoing another revolution in the way we think about the universal human journey from birth to death. Because of improvements in health care, a changing economy, a high divorce rate, and advances in reproductive technology, events over the life span are no longer as predictable as they were just a few decades ago. Most college students are still in their late teens or 20s, but many are older. A person might marry or start a career at 25, and do so again at 55.

Psychologists are probably no better equipped than anyone else to address the many ethical issues raised by these changes—such as whether a woman should forgo pregnancy if she can't realistically expect to be around until her child grows up. But *developmental psychologists,* who study universal aspects of life–span development as well as cultural and individual variations, can help us think critically about the question of "natural" life stages.

Developmental psychologists focus on physiological and cognitive changes across the life span, and on **socialization,** the processes by which children learn the attitudes and behaviors expected of them by society. In this chapter, we will explore some of their major findings, starting at the very beginning of human development, with the period from conception to birth, and continuing through adulthood into old age. As you read, ask yourself what it means, in psychological terms, to be young,

socialization
The processes by which children learn the behaviors, attitudes, and expectations required of them by their society or culture.

middle-aged, or old—and why so many people feel uneasy about the prospect of postmenopausal motherhood.

What's Ahead

- How can a pregnant woman reduce the risk of damage to the embryo or fetus?

- Given a choice, what do newborns prefer to look at?

- How does culture affect a baby's physical maturation?

- Why is cuddling so important for infants (not to mention adults)?

- If you have a 1-year-old, why shouldn't you worry if your baby cries when left with a new babysitter?

3.1 From Conception to the First Year

A baby's development, before and after birth, is a marvel of *maturation,* the unfolding of genetically influenced behavior and physical characteristics. In only 9 months of a mother's pregnancy, a cell grows from a dot this big (.) to a squalling bundle of energy that looks just like Aunt Sarah. In another 15 months, that bundle of energy grows into a babbling toddler who is curious about everything. No other time in human development brings so many changes, so fast.

Prenatal Development

Prenatal development is divided into three stages: the germinal, the embryonic, and the fetal. The *germinal stage* begins at conception, when the male sperm unites with the female ovum (egg). A day or so after conception, the fertilized egg, or *zygote*, begins to divide into two parts and, in 10 to 14 days, it attaches itself to the wall of the uterus. The outer portion of the zygote will form part of the placenta and umbilical cord, and the inner portion becomes the embryo. The placenta, connected to the embryo by the umbilical cord, serves as the growing embryo's link for food from the mother; it allows nutrients to enter and wastes to exit, and it screens out some, but not all, harmful substances.

Once implantation of the zygote is completed, about two weeks after conception, the *embryonic stage* begins, lasting until the eighth week after conception. The embryo develops webbed fingers and toes, a tail, eyes, ears, a nose, a mouth, a heart and circulatory system, and a spinal cord—although at 8 weeks, the embryo is only 1½ inches long. During the fourth to eighth week, the hormone testosterone is secreted by rudimentary testes in embryos that are genetically male; without this hormone, the embryo will develop to be anatomically female.

After eight weeks, the *fetal stage* begins. The organism, now called a *fetus*, further develops the organs and systems that existed in rudimentary form in the embryonic stage. By 28 weeks, the nervous and respiratory systems are developed enough to allow most fetuses to live if born prematurely. (Technological advances allow many to survive if born even earlier, but the risks are much higher.) The greatest gains in brain and nervous-system development occur during the last 12 weeks of a full-term pregnancy.

Although the womb is a fairly sturdy protector of the growing embryo or fetus, some harmful influences can cross the placental barrier. These influences, which are particularly damaging during the embryonic stage, include the following:

1 *German measles* (rubella), especially early in the pregnancy, can affect the fetus's eyes, ears, and heart. The most common consequence is deafness. Rubella is preventable if the mother has been vac-

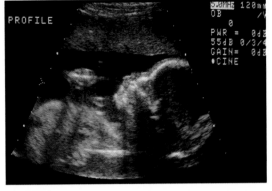

The first picture that many parents have of their offspring is a fetal sonogram, like this one taken during the twenty-third week of pregnancy.

cinated, which can be done up to three months before pregnancy.

2 *X-rays or other radiation, or toxic chemicals* such as lead, can cause fetal abnormalities and deformities. Exposure to lead is also associated with attention problems and lower IQ scores, as we will see in Chapter 6.

3 *Sexually transmitted diseases* can cause mental retardation, blindness, and other physical disorders. Genital herpes can affect the fetus if the mother has an outbreak at the time of delivery, which exposes the newborn to the virus as the baby passes through the birth canal. (This risk can be avoided by having a cesarean section.) HIV, the virus that causes AIDS, can also be transmitted to the fetus, especially if the mother has developed AIDS and has not been treated. However, not all babies of HIV-infected mothers become infected; estimates range from 13 to 30 percent (Bee, 1997).

4 *Cigarette smoking* during pregnancy increases the likelihood of miscarriage, premature birth, abnormal fetal heartbeat, and an underweight baby. The negative effects may last long after birth, showing up in increased rates of infant sickness, sudden infant death syndrome (SIDS), and, in later childhood, hyperactivity and learning difficulties. Cigarette smoking is actually more dangerous to the fetus than cocaine use (Slotkin, 1998).

5 *Having more than two alcoholic drinks every day* significantly increases the risk of a baby's having *fetal alcohol syndrome (FAS)*. FAS infants are often smaller than normal, have smaller brains, have facial deformities, are uncoordinated, and are mentally retarded. Even when babies do not have FAS, frequent

3.1

exposure to alcohol during pregnancy can impair their later mental abilities, attention span, and academic achievement (Streissguth et al., 1999). The most dangerous stage for these effects is the first trimester (first 12 weeks). But the consequences of lighter drinking—a drink or two every so often—are less clear. Some longitudinal studies find no effects, whereas others find small intellectual deficits (Forrest et al., 1991; Hunt et al., 1995).

6 *Drugs other than alcohol* can be harmful to the fetus, whether they are illicit ones such as morphine, cocaine, and heroin, or commonly used legal substances such as antibiotics, antihistamines, tranquilizers, acne medication, and diet pills. Fathers' drug use can also cause fetal defects; cocaine, for example, does so by binding to sperm (Yazigi, Odem, & Polakoski, 1991). Longitudinal studies of children exposed to cocaine in the womb have dispelled the myth of the "crack baby" who is severely damaged for life (Newman & Buka, 1991). Nonetheless, cocaine can cause small, subtle impairments in children's cognitive and language abilities (Lester, LaGasse, & Seifer, 1998).

The lesson is clear. A pregnant woman does well to abstain from smoking completely, to avoid alcohol or drink very little of it, and to take no other drugs of any kind unless they are medically necessary and have been adequately tested for safety—and then to accept the fact that her child will never be properly grateful for all that sacrifice!

The Infant's World

Newborn babies could never survive on their own, but they are far from being passive and inert. As a result of evolution, many abilities, tendencies, and characteristics are universal in human beings and are present at birth or develop very early, given certain experiences.

Newborns begin life with several *motor reflexes,* automatic behaviors that are necessary for survival (see Table 3.1). They will grasp tightly a finger pressed on their palms. They will turn their heads toward a touch on the cheek or corner of the mouth and search for something to suck on, a handy "rooting reflex" that allows them to find the breast or bottle. Many of these reflexes eventually disappear, but others—such as the knee-jerk, eye-blink, and sneeze reflexes—remain.

Babies are also equipped with a set of inborn perceptual abilities. They can see, hear, touch, smell, and taste (bananas and sugar water are in; rotten eggs are out). A newborn's visual focus range is only about 8 inches, the average distance between the baby and the face of the person holding the baby, but visual ability develops rapidly. Newborns can distinguish contrasts, shadows, and edges. They can discriminate their mother or other primary caregiver on the basis of smell, sight, or sound almost immediately. Within a couple of months, they show evidence of depth perception (see Chapter 5).

Table 3.1   Reflexes of the Newborn Baby

Reflex	Description
Rooting	An infant touched on the cheek or corner of the mouth will turn toward the touch and search for something to suck on.
Sucking	An infant will suck on anything suckable, such as a nipple or finger.
Swallowing	An infant can swallow, though this reflex is not yet well coordinated with breathing.
Moro or "startle"	In response to a loud noise or a physical shock, an infant will throw its arms outward and arch its back.
Babinski	In response to a touch on the bottom of the foot, the infant's toes will splay outward and then curl in. (In adults, the toes just curl in.)
Grasp	In response to a touch on the palm of the hand, an infant will grasp.
Stepping	If held so that the feet just touch the ground, an infant will show "walking" movements, alternating the feet in steps.

Babies are born with a special delight in looking at faces and imitating expressions.

Infants do not use their perceptual abilities in a random manner. When given a choice, they show a surprising interest in looking at and listening to unfamiliar things—which, of course, includes most of the world. A baby will even stop nursing if someone new enters his or her range of vision. Infants are also primed to gaze at human faces. Babies who are only *9 minutes old* will turn their heads to watch a drawing of a face if it moves in front of them, but they will not turn if the "face" consists of scrambled features or is only the outline of a face (Goren, Sarty, & Wu, 1975; Johnson et al.,

1991). A preference for faces over other stimuli in the environment probably has survival value because it helps babies recognize where their next meal is likely to come from.

Despite such commonalities, however, many aspects of infants' maturation depend on cultural customs that govern how their parents hold, touch, feed, and talk to them (Super & Harkness, 1994). For example, infants in many African cultures surpass American infants in their rate of learning to sit and to walk. Parents in these cultures routinely bounce babies on their feet, exercise the newborn's walking reflex, prop young infants in sitting positions, and discourage crawling. In contrast, infants of the Ache people, who live in the rain forest of South America, are physically restricted in their first year, as it is too dangerous for them to venture far from their mothers. Ache children begin walking at about 23 months, nearly a year later than children in North America (Feldman, 1997). Eventually, though, healthy children everywhere are able to crawl, sit, and walk.

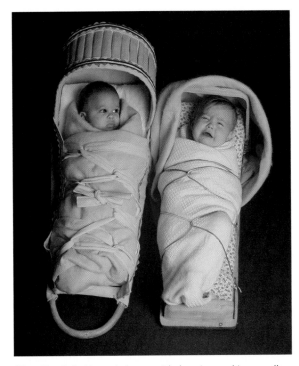

Most Navajo babies calmly accept being strapped to a cradle board (left), whereas white babies often protest vigorously (right). Yet despite cultural differences in such practices, babies everywhere eventually sit, crawl, and walk.

Attachment

Emotional attachment is a universal capacity of all primates and is important all through life. By becoming attached to a caregiver, children gain a secure base from which they can explore the environment, and a haven of safety to return to when they are afraid (Bowlby, 1969).

Attachment begins with physical touching and cuddling between infant and parent. Margaret and Harry Harlow first demonstrated the importance of touching, or **contact comfort,** by raising infant rhesus monkeys with two kinds of artificial mothers (Harlow, 1958; Harlow & Harlow, 1966). The first was a forbidding construction of wires and warming lights, with a milk bottle connected to it. The second was

contact comfort
In primates, the innate pleasure derived from close physical contact; it is the basis of an infant's first attachment.

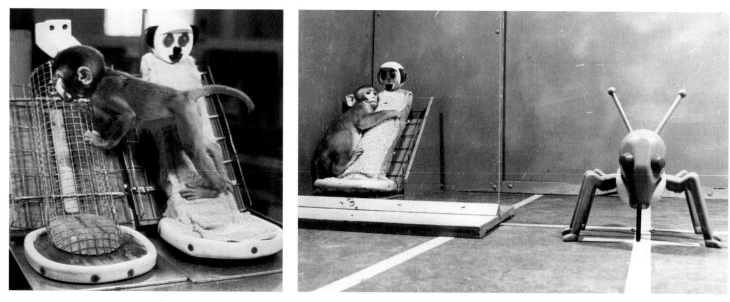

Figure 3.1
The Comfort of Contact

Infants need cuddling as much as they need food. In Margaret and Harry Harlow's studies, infant rhesus monkeys were reared with a cuddly terry-cloth "mother" and with a bare wire "mother" that provided milk (left). The infants would cling to the terry mother when they weren't being fed, and when they were frightened (as by a toy spider, right), it was the terry mother they ran to.

separation anxiety
The distress that most children develop, at about 7 to 9 months of age, when their primary caregivers temporarily leave them with strangers or in a new situation; it varies according to cultural practices.

constructed of wire and covered in foam rubber and cuddly terry cloth (see Figure 3.1). At the time, psychologists thought that babies become attached to their mothers because mothers provide food and warmth. But the Harlows' baby monkeys ran to the terry-cloth "mother" when they were frightened or startled, and cuddling up to it calmed them down. Human children, too, often seek contact comfort when they are in an unfamiliar situation, are scared by a nightmare, or fall and hurt themselves.

Once babies are emotionally attached to the mother or other caregiver, separation can be a wrenching experience. Between 7 and 9 months of age, most children become wary or fearful of strangers. They wail if they are put in an unfamiliar setting or are left with an unfamiliar person. And they show **separation anxiety** if the primary caregiver temporarily leaves them. This reaction usually continues until the middle of the second year, but many children show signs of distress at parental separation until they are about 3 years old. Western children do, in any case: Child-rearing practices influence how strongly the anxiety is felt and how long it lasts. In cultures where babies are raised with lots of adults and other children, "separation anxiety" is not as intense or as long-lasting as it can be in cultures where babies form attach-

ments primarily with parents and only a few other adults (Kagan, Kearsley, & Zelazo, 1978; Rothbaum et al., 2000).

To determine the nature of the attachment between mothers and babies, Mary Ainsworth (1973, 1979) devised an experimental method called the *Strange Situation.* A mother brings her baby into an unfamiliar room containing lots of toys. After a while a stranger comes in and attempts to play with the child. The mother leaves the baby with the stranger. She then returns and plays with her child, and the stranger leaves. Finally, the mother leaves the baby alone for three minutes and then returns. In each case, observers carefully note how the baby behaves with the mother, with the stranger, and when the baby is alone.

Ainsworth divided children into three categories on the basis of their reactions to the Strange Situation. Some babies are *securely attached:* They cry or protest if the parent leaves the room; they welcome her back and then play happily again; and they are clearly more attached to the mother than to the stranger. Other babies are *insecurely attached,* and this insecurity can take two forms. The child may be *avoidant,* not caring whether the mother leaves the room, making little effort to seek contact with her on her return, and treating the stranger about the same as the mother. Or the child may be *anxious or ambivalent,* resisting contact with the mother at reunion but protesting loudly if she leaves. Anxious or ambivalent babies may cry to be picked up and then demand to be put down, or they may behave as if they are angry with the mother and may resist her efforts to comfort them. Insecure attachment is of great concern to psychologists because it can lead to emotional and behavioral problems in childhood and possibly throughout life (Mickelson, Kessler, & Shaver, 1997; Shaw, Keenan, & Vondra, 1994).

Ainsworth believed that insecure attachment results primarily from the way mothers treat their babies during the first year. Mothers who are sensitive and responsive to their babies' needs, she said, create securely attached infants; mothers who are uncomfortable with or insensitive to their babies create insecurely attached infants. To many, the implication was that babies needed exactly the "right kind" of mothering from the very first in order to become securely attached, and that putting a baby or child in daycare would retard this important development—notions that caused insecurity among many mothers!

However, the belief that it is entirely the mother who creates a securely or insecurely attached child has turned out to be incorrect. It is true that neglect, abuse, and extreme deprivation adversely affect a child's attachment (Bowlby, 1973). But today we know that differences in *normal* child-rearing practices do not affect a child's attachment style (De Wolff & van IJzendoorn, 1997). About two-thirds of all children become securely attached under a wide range of parental practices. German babies are frequently left on their own for a few hours at a stretch by mothers who believe that even babies should become self-reliant (Kagan, 1998b). Among the Efe of Africa, babies spend about half their time away from their mothers, in the care of older children and other adults, and they do not develop the intense one-on-one attachment that Western children do (Tronick, Morelli, & Ivey, 1992). Yet German and Efe children are not insecure, and they develop normally. Japanese babies seem "insecure-ambivalent" to Western observers, because the babies appear to be "excessively" clingy, dependent, unwilling to explore new environments, and passive. Yet all of these behaviors characterize what the Japanese regard as normal feelings and expressions of connection to others, which they value more than "independence" (Rothbaum et al., 2000). In some cultures and

Thinking Critically About Attachment Theory

families, children who are exposed to many adults may seem to be "avoidant" in the Strange Situation because they don't panic when their mothers leave. But all that shows, many psychologists believe, is that they have learned to be comfortable with strangers (Harris, 1998)!

Likewise, time spent in daycare has no effect on the security of a child's attachment. One major longitudinal study of more than 1,000 children compared infants who were in child care 30 hours or more a week, from age 3 months to age 15 months, with children who spent less than 10 hours a week in child care. The two groups did not differ on any measure of attachment (NICHD Early Child Care Research Network, 1997; see also McKim et al., 1999).

What factors, then, do promote the development of insecure attachment? One is the child's own genetically influenced temperament. Babies who are fearful and prone to crying from birth are more likely to show insecure behavior in the Strange Situation. Another is stressful circumstances in the child's family. Infants and young children are likely to shift from secure to insecure attachment if their families are undergoing a period of chronic stress, as during a divorce or a family member's chronic illness (Belsky et al., 1996; Lewis, 1997).

Along with outright rejection by parents, these factors can produce insecure attachment. But infants can and do thrive in many kinds of environments, and "good care" covers a lot of territory and many different customs. As long as caregivers are affectionate and responsive, most babies get along fine.

Longitudinal and cross-cultural studies repeatedly find that good daycare does not affect the security of children's attachment. On the contrary, it often produces many social and cognitive benefits (NICHD Early Child Care Research Network, 1997).

QUICK QUIZ

Are you feeling secure, anxious, or avoidant about quizzes?

1. Name as many potentially harmful influences on fetal development as you can.

2. Melanie is playing happily on a jungle gym at her child-care center when she falls off and scrapes her knee. She runs to her caregiver for a consoling cuddle. Melanie is seeking _____.

3. A baby left in the Strange Situation does not protest when his mother leaves the room, and he seems to ignore her when she returns. What style of attachment is this behavior said to reflect?

4. In Item 3, what else besides the child's style of attachment could be causing the child's reaction?

Answers:
1. German measles early in pregnancy; exposure to radiation or toxic chemicals; sexually transmitted diseases; the mother's use of cigarettes, alcohol, or other drugs 2. contact comfort 3. insecure (avoidant) 4. the child's own temperament; frequent exposure to and therefore comfort with other adults; the child's familiarity with being left alone temporarily

What's Ahead

- Why do so many parents speak "baby talk"?

- Is language an innate ability or an acquired one?

- What important accomplishment are infants revealing when they learn to play "peekaboo"?

- Why will most 5-year-olds choose a tall, narrow glass of lemonade over a short, fat glass containing the same amount?

- When reasoning about moral issues, are women more compassionate and caring than men?

3.2 Cognitive Development

Our friend Joel reports how thrilled he was when his 13-month-old daughter Alison looked at him one day and said, for the first time, "Daddy!" His delight was deflated somewhat, though, when the doorbell rang and she ran to the door, calling, "Daddy!" And his delight was completely shattered when the phone rang and Alison ran to it, shouting, "Daddy!" Later Joel learned that there was a 2-year-old child in Alison's daycare group whose father would ring the doorbell when he picked her up. Alison had acquired her friend's enthusiasm for doorbells but did not quite get the hang of "Daddy." She will soon enough, though. She will also be able to reason and see the world from Daddy's viewpoint. And soon, too, she will be able to understand what her daddy means when he praises her for being a "good girl"—or scolds her for being a naughty one.

Language

Try to read this sentence aloud:

Kamaunawezakusomamanenohayawewenimtuwamaanasana.

Can you tell where one word begins and another ends? Unless you know Swahili, the syllables of this sentence will sound like gibberish.[1]

Well, to a baby learning its native tongue, *every* sentence must, at first, be gibberish. How, then, does an infant pick out discrete syllables and words from the jumble of sounds in its environment, much less figure out what those words mean? And how is it that in only a few short years, children not only understand thousands of words, but can also produce and understand an endless number of new word combinations?

From Cooing to Communicating. The process of acquiring language begins in the first months, with crying and cooing. Even at this early stage, babies are highly responsive to the pitch, intensity, and sound of language, and to the

[1]In Swahili, *kama unaweza kusoma maneno haya, wewe ni mtu wa maana sana* means, "If you can read these words, you are a remarkable person."

emotions in people's voices. As Anne Fernald (1990) put it, for babies, "the melody is the message." Adults seem to know this; when they speak to babies, their pitch is higher and more varied than usual, and their intonation is more exaggerated. Adult use of "baby talk"—researchers call it *"parentese"*—has been documented all over the world, in countries as different as Sweden and Japan. Parentese helps babies learn the "melody" and rhythm of their native language (Fernald & Mazzie, 1991; Kuhl et al., 1997).

By 4 to 6 months of age, babies can often recognize their own names and other words that are regularly spoken with emotion, such as "mommy" and "daddy." They also know many of the key consonant and vowel sounds (phonemes) of their native language and can distinguish such sounds from those of other languages (Kuhl et al., 1992). Over time, exposure to the baby's native language reduces the child's ability to perceive speech sounds in other languages. Thus, Japanese infants can hear the difference between the English sounds "la" and "ra," but older Japanese children and Japanese adults cannot. Because this contrast does not exist in their language, they become insensitive to it.

Between 6 months and 1 year, infants become increasingly familiar with the sound structure of their native language. They are able to distinguish words from the flow of speech. They will listen longer to words that violate their expectations of what words should sound like and even to sentences that violate their expectations of how sentences should be structured (Jusczyk, 1997; Marcus et al., 1999). They start to babble, making many "ba-ba" and "goo-goo" sounds, endlessly repeating sounds and syllables. Then, at about a year of age, though the timing varies considerably, children start to name things. They already have some mental concepts for familiar people and objects, and their first words represent these concepts ("mama," "doggie," "fly").

Starting at about 11 months, babies develop a repertoire of symbolic gestures, another important tool of communication. They gesture to refer to objects (e.g., sniffing to indicate "flower"), to request things (e.g., smacking the lips for "food"), to describe objects (e.g., raising the arms for "big"), and to reply to questions (e.g., opening the palms or shrugging the shoulders for "I don't know"). They clap in response to pictures of things they like, from Teletubbies to baseball games. Children whose parents encourage them to use gestures acquire larger vocabularies, have better comprehension, are better listeners, and are less frustrated

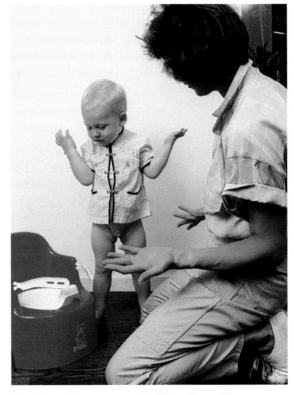

Symbolic gestures emerge early! This mother and her son are clearly having a "conversation."

in their efforts to communicate than babies who are not encouraged to use gestures (Goodwyn & Acredolo, 1998).

Between the ages of 18 months and 2 years, toddlers begin to produce words in two- or three-word combinations ("Mama here," "go 'way bug," "my toy"). The child's first combinations of words have a common quality: They are **telegraphic.** When people had to pay for every word in a telegram, they quickly learned to drop unnecessary articles (*a, an,* or *the*) and auxiliary verbs (such as *is* or *are*), but they still conveyed the message. Similarly, the two-word "telegrams" of toddlers omit articles, auxiliary verbs, other parts of speech, and word endings, but they are still remarkably accurate in conveying meanings. Children use two-word "telegrams" to locate things ("here toy"), make demands ("more milk"), negate actions ("no want," "all-gone milk"), describe events ("Bambi go," "hit ball"), describe objects ("pretty dress"), show possession ("Mama dress"), and ask questions ("Where Daddy?"). Pretty good for a little kid, don't you think?

At about this age, children reveal another impressive talent: the rapid acquisition of new words. They absorb new words as they hear them,

telegraphic speech
A child's first word combinations, which omit (as a telegram did) unnecessary words.

forming a quick impression of a word's likely meaning by using their knowledge of grammatical contexts and the rules for formulating words. The process of absorbing and understanding thousands of new words continues throughout childhood.

How on earth do children do all this?

The Innate Capacity for Language. At one time, most psychologists assumed that children learned to speak—or in the case of deaf children, to use the gestures of American Sign Language (ASL) or other gestural languages—by imitating adults and paying attention when adults corrected their mistakes. Then along came linguist Noam Chomsky (1957, 1980), who argued that language was far too complex to be learned bit by bit, as one might learn a list of world capitals. Language, he noted, is not just any old communication system. It is a system that enables us to combine elements that are themselves meaningless into utterances that convey meaning—and to reject utterances that are not acceptable in our native tongue. It permits us to express and comprehend an infinite number of novel utterances, created on the spot—and this is essential, because except for a few fixed phrases ("How are you?" "Get a life"), most of the utterances we produce or hear over a lifetime are new.

The task facing children, said Chomsky, is far more complicated than merely figuring out which sounds form words. They must also take the *surface structure* of a sentence—the way the sentence is actually spoken or signed—and apply grammatical rules (*syntax*) in order to infer an underlying *deep structure* that contains meaning. For example, although "Mary kissed John" and "John was kissed by Mary" have different surface structures, any 5-year-old knows that the two sentences have essentially the same deep structure, in which Mary is the actor and John gets the kiss. The human brain, said Chomsky, must therefore contain a **language acquisition device,** an innate mental module that allows young children to develop language if they are exposed to an adequate sampling of conversation. Just as a bird is designed to fly, human beings are designed to use language.

Over the years, linguists and psycholinguists (researchers who study the psychology of language) have gathered many types of evidence to support this position (Crain, 1991; Pinker, 1994):

1 *Children in different cultures go through similar stages of linguistic development.* For example, they will often use double negatives ("He don't want no milk"; "Nobody don't like me"), even when their language does not allow such constructions (Klima & Bellugi, 1966; McNeill, 1966). Such commonalities suggest that children's brains are disposed to notice the features common to all languages (nouns and verbs, certain phrase structures, and so forth), even in languages as seemingly different as Mohawk and English, or Okinawan and Bulgarian (Baker, 1999; Cinque, 1999; Pesetsky, 1999).

2 *Children combine words in ways that adults never would.* They reduce a parent's sentences ("Let's go to the store!") to their own two-word version ("Go store!") and make many charming errors that an adult would not ("The alligator goed kerplunk," "Daddy taked me," "Hey, Horton heared a Who") (Ervin-Tripp, 1964; Marcus et al., 1992). Such errors, which linguists call *overregularizations,* are not random; they show that the child has grasped a grammatical rule (add the *t* or *d* sound to make a verb past tense, as in *walked* and *hugged*) and is merely overgeneralizing it (*taked, goed*). Of course, children cannot state such rules explicitly (neither can most adults), but their errors show that they have an implicit knowledge of the rules and can apply them.

3 *Adults do not consistently correct their children's syntax.* Explanations of language acquisition that emphasize learning assume that children are rewarded for saying the right words and punished for making errors. But parents do not stop to correct every error in their children's speech, so long as they can understand what the child is trying to say (Brown, Cazden, & Bellugi, 1969). Indeed, par-

language acquisition device

According to many psycholinguists, an innate mental module that allows young children to develop language if they are exposed to an adequate sampling of conversation.

Human beings appear to have an inborn facility for acquiring language, even when they cannot hear speech. In North America, where many hearing-impaired people use American Sign Language, deaf children learn to sign in ASL as easily as hearing children learn to speak.

ents often *reward* children for incorrect statements! The 2-year-old who says "Want milk!" is likely to get it; most parents would not wait for a more grammatical (or polite) request.

Chomsky's ideas so revolutionized thinking about language development that some linguists refer to the initial publication of his ideas as The Event (Rymer, 1993). Although Chomsky himself avoided the evolutionary implications of his argument, others maintain that the capacity for language evolved in human beings because it permitted our ancestors to convey precise information about time, space, objects, and events, and to negotiate alliances that were necessary for survival (Pinker, 1994).

It thus seems likely that genes contribute to our ability to acquire language. As we saw in Chapter 2, however, nature and nurture usually interact in the development of any behavior, and this includes language. Although most children have an inborn capacity to acquire language from mere exposure to it, parents help things along. They may not go around correcting their children's speech all day, but neither do they ignore their children's errors. For example, they are more likely to repeat verbatim a child's well-formed sentence than a sentence with errors ("That's a horse, mommy!" "Yes, that's a horse"). And when the child makes a mistake or produces a clumsy sentence, parents almost invariably respond by recasting it or expanding its elements ("Monkey climbing!" "Yes, the monkey is climbing the tree") (Bohannon & Stanowicz, 1988). Children then imitate these correct adult sentences. They also imitate their parents' accents, inflections, and tone of voice, and they will repeat some words that the parent tries to teach ("This is a ball, Erwin." "Baw").

Language therefore depends on both biological readiness and social experience. Abused children who are not exposed to language during their early years (such as Genie, whom we mentioned in Chapter 1), rarely speak normally. Such sad evidence suggests a *critical period* in language development during the first few years of life or possibly the first decade (Curtiss, 1977; Lenneberg, 1967). During these years, children need exposure to language and opportunities to practice their emerging linguistic skills in conversation with others.

Thinking

As anyone who has ever observed a young child knows, children do not think the way adults do. At age 2, they may call all large animals by one

name (say, *horsie*) and all small animals by another (say, *bug*). At 4, they may protest that a sibling has "more" fruit juice when it is only the shapes of the glasses that differ, not the amount of juice.

In the 1920s, Swiss psychologist Jean Piaget [Zhan Pee-ah-ZHAY] (1896–1980) proposed a theory of cognitive development to explain these childish mistakes. Piaget was to child development what Freud was to psychoanalysis and Skinner to behaviorism: a figure of towering influence (Flavell, 1996). His keen observations of children and his brilliant ideas caused a revolution in thinking about how thinking develops.

Piaget's great insight was that children's errors are as interesting as their correct responses. Children will say things that seem cute or wildly illogical to adults, but the strategies children use to think and solve problems, said Piaget, are not stupid or meaningless; they reflect a predictable interaction between the child's maturational stage and the child's experience in the world.

Piaget's Theory of Cognitive Stages.
According to Piaget (1929/1960, 1952a, 1952b, 1984), as children develop, they must make constant mental adaptations to new observations and experiences. This adaptation takes two forms: assimilation and accommodation.

Assimilation is what you do when you fit new information into your present system of knowledge and beliefs or into your mental *schemas* (networks of associations, beliefs, and expectations about categories of things and people). Suppose that little Harry learns a schema for "dog" by playing with the family spaniel. If he then sees the neighbor's collie and says "doggie!" he has assimilated the new information about the neighbor's pet into his schema for dogs. **Accommodation** is what you do when, as a result of undeniable new information, you must change or modify your existing schemas. If Harry sees the neighbor's Siamese cat and still says "doggie!" his parents are likely to laugh and correct him. Harry will have to modify his schema for *dogs* to exclude cats, and he will have to create a schema for *cats*. In this way, he accommodates the new information that a Siamese cat is not a dog.

Using these concepts, Piaget proposed that all children go through four stages of cognitive development:

1 *The sensorimotor stage (birth to age 2).* In this stage, the infant learns through concrete actions: looking, touching, hearing, putting things in the

assimilation
In Piaget's theory, the process of absorbing new information into existing cognitive structures.

accommodation
In Piaget's theory, the process of modifying existing cognitive structures in response to experience and new information.

Figure 3.2
Piaget's Principle of Conservation

In a typical test for conservation of number (left), the child must say whether one of the sets of blocks has "more." His answer shows whether he understands that the two sets contain the same number, even though the larger blocks in one set take up more space. In a test for conservation of quantity (right), the child is shown two short, fat glasses with equal amounts of liquid. Then the contents of one glass are poured into a tall, narrow beaker, and the child is asked whether one container now has more. Her answer shows whether she understands that pouring liquid from a short, fat glass into a tall, narrow glass leaves the amount of liquid unchanged.

3.2

object permanence
The understanding, which develops late in the first year, that an object continues to exist even when you cannot see it or touch it.

operations
In Piaget's theory, mental actions that are cognitively reversible.

egocentric thinking
Seeing the world from only your own point of view; the inability to take another person's perspective.

conservation
The understanding that the physical properties of objects—such as the number of items in a cluster or the amount of liquid in a glass—can remain the same even when their form or appearance changes.

mouth, sucking, grasping. "Thinking" consists of coordinating sensory information with bodily movements. Gradually, these movements become more purposeful, as the child explores the environment and learns that specific movements will produce specific results. Swatting a cloth away will reveal a hidden toy; letting go of a fuzzy toy duck will cause it to drop out of reach; banging on the table with a spoon will produce dinner (or Mom, taking the spoon away).

A major accomplishment at this stage, said Piaget, is **object permanence,** the understanding that something continues to exist even if you cannot see it or touch it. In the first few months, he observed, infants seem to follow the motto "out of sight, out of mind." They will look intently at a toy, but if you hide it behind a piece of paper they will not look behind the paper or make an effort to get the toy. By about 6 months of age, however, infants begin to grasp the idea that a toy exists and the family cat exists, whether or not they can see the toy or the cat. If a baby of this age drops a toy from her playpen, she will look for it; she also will look under a cloth for a toy that is partially hidden. By 1 year of age, most babies have developed an awareness of the permanence of (some) objects; even if a toy is covered by a cloth, it must

be under there. This is when they love to play peekaboo.

Object permanence, said Piaget, represents the beginning of the child's capacity to use mental imagery and other symbolic systems. The child is able for the first time to hold a concept in mind, to learn that the word *fly* represents an annoying, buzzing creature, and that *Daddy* represents a friendly, playful one.

2 *The preoperational stage (ages 2 to 7).* In this stage, the use of symbols and language accelerates. A 2-year-old is able to pretend, for instance, that a large box is a house, table, or train. But Piaget described this stage largely in terms of what (he thought) the child cannot do. Although children can think, said Piaget, they cannot reason, and they lack the mental abilities necessary for understanding abstract principles or cause and effect. Piaget called these missing abilities **operations,** by which he meant reversible actions that the child performs in the mind. An operation is a sort of "train of thought" that can be run backward or forward. Multiplying 2 times 6 to get 12 is an operation; so is the reverse operation, dividing 12 by 6 to get 2.

Piaget also believed (mistakenly, as we will see) that preoperational children cannot take another person's point of view because their thinking is **egocentric.** They see the world only from their own frames of reference, said Piaget, and they cannot imagine that others see things differently.

Further, said Piaget, preoperational children cannot grasp the concept of **conservation**—the notion that physical properties do not change when their forms or appearances change. Children at this age are unable to understand that an amount of liquid, a number of pennies, or a length of rope remains the same even if you pour the liquid from one glass to another, stack the pennies, or coil the rope (see Figure 3.2). If you pour liquid from a short, fat glass into a tall, narrow glass, preoperational children will say there is more liquid in the second glass. They attend to the appearance of the liquid (its height in the glass) to judge its quantity, so they are misled.

3 *The concrete operations stage (ages 7 to 12).* In this stage, Piaget said, children's thinking is still grounded in *concrete* experiences and concepts, rather than in abstractions or logical deductions. However, the nature and quality of their thought processes change significantly. They come to understand the principles of conservation, reversibility, and cause and effect. They learn to categorize things (e.g., oaks as trees) and to order things serially from smallest to largest, lightest to darkest, and shortest to tallest. And they understand the nature of identity; for example, they know that a girl does not turn into a boy by wearing a boy's hat, and that a brother will always be a brother, even if he grows up.

4 *The formal operations stage (age 12 to adulthood).* In this last stage, teenagers become capable of abstract reasoning. They understand that ideas can be compared and classified, just as objects can. They are able to reason about situations they have not experienced firsthand, and they can think about future possibilities. They are able to search systematically for answers to problems. They are able to draw logical conclusions from premises common to their culture and experience.

Table 3.2 summarizes Piaget's stages of cognitive development.

Evaluating Piaget. Piaget transformed the field of developmental psychology, providing an entirely new vision of the nature of children. However, findings from modern research have challenged some key aspects of his theory:

1 *The changes from one stage to another are neither as clear-cut nor as sweeping as Piaget implied.* Cognitive abilities develop in overlapping waves rather than discrete steps (Siegler, 1996). At any given age, a child may use several different strategies in trying to solve a problem, some more complex or accurate than others. Moreover, children's reasoning ability often depends on the circumstances—who is asking them questions, the specific words used, the materials used, and what they are reasoning *about*—not just on the stage they are in.

2 *Children can understand far more than Piaget gave them credit for.* Taking advantage of the fact that infants look longer at novel or surprising stimuli than at familiar ones, psychologists have used delightfully imaginative methods to show that

---

Table 3.2 Summary of Piaget's Stages of Cognitive Development

Stage	Major Accomplishments
Sensorimotor (0–2)	Object permanence Beginning of representational thought
Preoperational (2–7)	Accelerated use of symbols and language
Concrete operations (6 or 7–11)	Understanding of conservation Understanding of identity Understanding of serial ordering
Formal operations (12–adulthood)	Abstract reasoning Ability to compare and classify ideas

Possible event

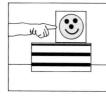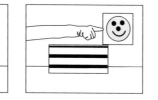

Impossible event

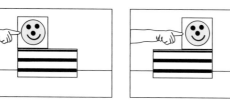

Figure 3.3

Testing Infants' Knowledge

In this clever procedure, a baby watches as a box is pushed from left to right along a striped platform. The box is pushed until it reaches the end of the platform (a possible event) or until only a bit of it rests on the platform (an impossible event). Babies look longer at the impossible event, suggesting that it surprises them; somehow they know that an object needs physical support and can't just float on air (Baillargeon, 1994).

babies know more than Piaget could have dreamed. For example, clever studies show that infants as young as 4 months seem to understand some basic principles of physics (see Figure 3.3)! Babies that young will look longer at a ball if it seems to roll through a solid barrier, or leap between two platforms, or hang in midair, than they do when an action obeys the laws of physics. Infants as young

Experience and culture influence cognitive development. Children who work with clay, wood, and other materials, such as this young potter in India, tend to understand the concept of conservation sooner than children who have not had this kind of experience.

as 2½ to 3½ months are aware that objects exist even when masked by other objects, a form of object permanence that Piaget never imagined possible in babies so young (Baillargeon, 1994). Further, by the age of only *1 week,* babies will spend more time looking at a novel set of three items after getting used to a set of two items, or vice versa, which means that they can recognize the difference in number (Geary, 1995). Such findings suggest that babies may be biologically programmed to understand some things about how the world works.

Children also advance more rapidly in their symbolic abilities than Piaget thought. Between the ages of 2½ and 3, toddlers become able to think of a miniature model of a room in two ways at once: as a room in its own right and as a symbol of the larger room it represents (DeLoache, 1995). This ability is a big step toward adult symbolic thought, in which anything can stand for anything else: a flag for a country, a logo for a company.

3 *Preschoolers are not as egocentric as Piaget thought.* Most 3- and 4-year-olds *can* take another person's perspective. When 4-year-olds play with 2-year-olds, for example, they simplify their speech so the younger children will understand (Shatz & Gelman, 1973). And even very young children are capable of touching acts of empathy, understanding when another child or adult is sad and offering comfort. In one study, a toddler of only 13 months offered her beloved doll to a grieving adult (Hoffman, 1990).

By about age 4 to 5, children begin to figure out that another person might see things differently than they do. One 5-year-old we know showed her teacher a picture she had drawn of a cat and an unidentifiable blob. "The cat is lovely," said the teacher, "but what is this thing here?" "That has nothing to do with you," said the child. "That's what the *cat* is looking at."

4 *Cognitive development depends on the child's education and culture.* Traditional nomadic hunting peoples, such as the Inuit of Canada and the Aborigines of Australia, do not quantify things and do not need to (Dasen, 1994). The Aborigines have number words only up to five; after that, all quantities are described as "many." In such cultures, the ability to understand the conservation of quantity or number develops late, if at all. But nomadic hunters excel in spatial abilities, because spatial orientation is crucial for finding water holes and finding successful hunting routes. In contrast, children who live in settled agricultural communities, such as the Baoulé of the Ivory

Coast, develop rapidly in the ability to quantify and much more slowly in spatial reasoning. In all cultures, however, education affects cognitive abilities: Many unschooled children of the Wolof, a rural group in Senegal, do not acquire an understanding of conservation, as do their peers who attend school, but brief training can speed its development (Greenfield, 1976).

5 *Just as Piaget underestimated the cognitive skills of young children, he overestimated those of many adults.* As we discuss in Chapter 6, not all adolescents and adults develop the ability for formal reasoning and reflective judgment. Some never develop the capacity for formal operations, and others continue to think concretely unless a specific problem requires abstract thought.

These findings have altered our understanding of cognitive development. Nevertheless, most psychologists accept Piaget's major point: New reasoning abilities depend on the emergence of previous ones; you cannot learn algebra before you can count, or philosophy before you understand logic. Perhaps the most enduring legacy of Piaget's work is his emphasis on the fact that children are not passive vessels into which education and experience are poured. Children actively interpret their worlds, using their developing schemas and abilities to assimilate new information and figure things out.

Moral Reasoning

Piaget (1932) pioneered in the study of another important aspect of cognitive development: moral reasoning, which changes according to a child's cognitive maturity. A young child, he observed, will say that a child who breaks a vase by accident is as naughty as one who breaks it intentionally. Older children, because of their maturing cognitive abilities, are able to evaluate moral behavior in terms of a person's intentions and motives.

In the 1960s, Lawrence Kohlberg (1964), inspired by Piaget's work, outlined a stage theory of moral reasoning that became highly influential. Your moral stage, said Kohlberg, can be determined by the answers you give to hypothetical dilemmas. For example, suppose a man's wife is dying and needs a special drug. The man cannot afford the drug and the druggist refuses to lower his price. Should the man steal the drug? What if he no longer loves his wife? If the man is caught, should the judge be lenient? To Kohlberg, as to Piaget, the reasoning behind the answers was more important than the decisions themselves.

Kohlberg (1964, 1976, 1984) proposed that children progress through three levels of moral development, each consisting of two stages:

1. *Preconventional morality.* Very young children obey rules because they fear being punished if they disobey and later because they think it is in their best interest to obey. Their moral reasoning is hedonistic, self-centered, and lacking in empathy; what is "right" is what feels good.

2. *Conventional morality.* At about ages 10 or 11, according to Kohlberg, children shift to the conventional morality of adult society, which is at first based on conformity and loyalty to others and later based on an understanding of law and justice.

3. *Postconventional ("principled") morality.* Some adults, said Kohlberg, realize that certain laws—such as those that legitimize the mistreatment of minorities—are themselves immoral. They recognize that people hold different values and standards, and that laws are important but can be changed. A very few postconventional individuals develop a moral standard based on universal human rights. When faced with a conflict between law and conscience, they follow conscience, even at great personal risk.

According to Kohlberg, Mohandas Gandhi (called the "Mahatma," or wise one) reached the highest level of morality because of his commitment to nonviolence and peaceful change. But people's moral behavior is not the same in every situation or relationship. Gandhi, for example, was aloof from his family and followers, whom he often treated in a harsh and callous manner.

Kohlberg's theory of moral reasoning generated much discussion, and research has confirmed the general shift from preconventional to conventional morality in many cultures. However, the theory has three significant limitations:

1 *Kohlberg's theory tends to overlook educational and cultural influences on moral reasoning.* College-educated people tend to give "higher-level" explanations of moral decisions than people who have not attended college, but all that shows, say Kohlberg's critics, is that college-educated people are more verbally sophisticated and have learned to think in legalistic terms (Eckensberger, 1994). Indeed, the cruelest lawyer could get a higher moral-reasoning score than the kindest 8-year-old (Schulman & Mekler, 1994)! Moreover, cultural factors play a major role in children's moral reasoning (Shweder, Mahapatra, & Miller, 1990; Wygant, 1997). In China, for example, moral decisions and values based on social harmony and devotion to parents are considered the highest form of moral reasoning, in contrast to the analytic, individualistic thinking emphasized by Kohlberg (Dien, 1982).

2 *People's moral reasoning is often inconsistent across situations.* The reasoning behind people's moral choices depends on the situation and on the nature of the dilemma (Wygant, 1997). For example, you might show conventional morality by overlooking a racial slur at a dinner party because you do not want to upset anyone, but reveal postconventional reasoning by protesting a governmental policy you regard as immoral. In one study using Kohlberg's

"It all depends on how you define 'chop.'"

A child or adult may be verbally sophisticated in rationalizing bad behavior, and still do the wrong thing!

dilemmas, most of the participants gave responses spanning three to six substages; only one young man had scores that reflected a single stage (Wark & Krebs, 1996).

3 *Moral reasoning is often unrelated to moral behavior.* Moral-reasoning ability increases during the school years, but so do cheating, lying, cruelty, and the cognitive ability to rationalize these actions (Kagan, 1993). College students usually draw on lofty principles of justice and fair play to justify moral decisions, yet about one-third of American and Canadian college men say they would force a woman into sexual acts if they could get away with it—the lowest form of moral reasoning (Malamuth & Dean, 1990). As Thomas Lickona (1983) wryly summarized, "We can reach high levels of moral reasoning, and still behave like scoundrels."

Another popular approach to moral reasoning was proposed in the early 1980s by Carol Gilligan (1982). Gilligan argued that men tend to base their moral choices on abstract principles of law and justice, asking questions such as "Whose rights should take precedence here?", whereas women tend to base their moral decisions on principles of compassion and caring, asking questions such as "Who will be hurt least?" This was an appealing theory—especially to many women! But most studies have not supported Gilligan's view of a significant gender difference in moral reasoning (Cohn, 1991; Friedman, Robinson, & Friedman, 1987; Jaffee & Hyde, 2000; Thoma, 1986; Walker, 1995). Moreover, as with Kohlberg's theory, the kind of reasoning that people use depends on what they are reasoning about. Both sexes tend to use justice-based reasoning when they are thinking about abstract ethical dilemmas, and care-based reasoning when they are thinking about intimate dilemmas in their own lives (Clopton & Sorell, 1993; Walker, de Vries, & Trevethan, 1987).

As children develop, their ability to understand right from wrong depends not just on their reasoning skills, but also on the emergence of conscience and "moral emotions" such as shame, guilt, and empathy (Hoffman, 1990). The capacity for moral feeling, like that for language, seems to be inborn. As Jerome Kagan (1984) wrote, "Without this fundamental human capacity, which nineteenth-century observers called a *moral sense*, the child could not be socialized." The moral sense, however, can be nurtured or extinguished by experiences in a child's life, as we will see.

QUICK QUIZ

Do you feel a moral obligation to answer these questions on cognitive development?

1. "More cake!" and "Mommy come" are examples of _____ speech.

2. What did Chomsky mean by a "language acquisition device"?

3. Understanding that two rows of six pennies are equal in number, even if one row is spread out and the other is stacked up, is an example of _____.

4. Understanding that a toy exists even after Mom puts it in her purse is an example of _____, which develops during the _____ stage.

5. List five findings that challenge aspects of Piaget's theory.

6. Margo says she pays her taxes because she believes in obeying the law. Manny says he pays because he is afraid of getting caught. According to Kohlberg, what level of moral reasoning has each of them achieved?

Answers:
1. telegraphic speech 2. an innate mental module that permits young children to develop language if they are exposed to it 3. conservation 4. object permanence, sensorimotor 5. The changes from one stage to another are not as clear as Piaget implied; children know more and know it earlier than Piaget thought; they are less egocentric than Piaget thought; their cognitive development is affected by their culture; and not all adolescents and adults achieve the ability for formal operations. 6. Margo is at a conventional level, Manny at a preconventional level.

What's Ahead

- How would a biologically oriented psychologist explain why most little boys and girls are "sexist" in their choice of toys?

- What happens to children's notions about gender once they are able to distinguish males from females?

- How do teachers unintentionally reinforce assertiveness in boys?

- If a little girl "knows" that girls can't be doctors, does this mean she will never go to med school?

3.3 Gender Development

No parent ever excitedly calls a relative to exclaim, "It's a baby! It's a 7½-pound, black-haired baby!" The baby's sex is the first thing everyone notices and announces. Most babies, unless they have rare abnormalities, are born unambiguously male or female—an anatomical and physiological distinction. But how do children learn the rules of masculinity and femininity—the things that boys do that are supposedly different from what girls do? Why, as one psychologist we know put it, do most preschool children act like the Gender Police, rigidly insisting, say, that boys can't be nurses and girls can't be doctors?

Many psychologists use the terms *sex* and *gender* to capture the distinction between anatomy and behavior (Deaux, 1985; Lott, 1997). *Sex* refers to the physiological or anatomical attributes of males and females; thus, we might speak of a "sex difference" in the frequency of baldness or color blindness. *Gender* is used to refer to the cultural and psychological attributes that children learn are appropriate for the sexes; thus, we might speak of a "gender difference" in sexual attitudes, dishwashing, and fondness for romance novels.

Toddlers can label themselves as boys or girls, but it is not until the age of 4 or 5 that most children develop a secure **gender identity,** a fundamental sense of maleness or femaleness that exists regardless of what they wear or how they behave. Only then do they understand that what boys and girls do does not necessarily indicate what sex they are: A girl remains a girl even if she can climb a tree, and a boy remains a boy even if he has long hair. In contrast, **gender typing** reflects society's

gender identity
The fundamental sense of being male or female; it is independent of whether the person conforms to the social and cultural rules of gender.

gender typing
The process by which children learn the abilities, interests, personality traits, and behaviors associated with being masculine or feminine in their culture.

ideas about which abilities, interests, traits, and behaviors are appropriately "masculine" or "feminine." A person can have a strong gender identity and not be gender typed: A man may be confident in his maleness and not feel threatened by doing "unmasculine" things such as needlepointing a pillow; a woman may be confident in her femaleness and not feel threatened by doing "unfeminine" things such as serving in combat.

Influences on Gender Development

Developmental psychologists study the influence of biology, cognition, and learning in the emergence of gender identity, gender differences in behavior, and gender typing.

Biological Factors. Starting in the preschool years, boys and girls congregate primarily with other children of their sex (Maccoby, 1998). They will play together if required to, but given their druthers, they immediately choose to play with friends of their own sex. This preference occurs all over the world, almost regardless of how adults treat children—whether they encourage boys and girls to play together or separate them

gender schema
A cognitive schema (mental network) of knowledge, beliefs, metaphors, and expectations about what it means to be male or female.

Look familiar? In a scene typical of many nursery schools and homes, the boy builds a gun out of anything he can, and the girl dresses up in any pretty thing she can find. Psychologists (and parents) debate whether such gender typing is biologically based or a result of subtle reinforcements and the emergence of gender schemas.

(Lytton & Romney, 1991; Maccoby, 1998). Similarly, although many parents lament that they try to give their children the same toys, often it makes no difference; their sons want trucks and their daughters want dolls.

Biological researchers believe that these play and toy preferences must have a biological basis, perhaps in prenatal hormones, genes, or brain organization. They point out that girls who were exposed to prenatal androgens (masculinizing hormones) in the womb are later more likely than nonexposed girls to prefer "boys' toys," such as cars, fire engines, and Lincoln logs (Berenbaum & Snyder, 1995). And in all primate species, young males are more likely than females to go in for physical roughhousing (Maccoby, 1998).

Cognitive Factors. Cognitive psychologists explain the mystery of children's gender segregation and toy preferences not in terms of biology but in terms of the child's own unfolding cognitive abilities. As children mature, they develop a **gender schema,** a mental network of beliefs, metaphors, and expectations about what it means to be male or female (Bem, 1993; Fagot, 1985; Spence, 1985). And as soon as children have a gender schema, they change their behavior to conform to it.

Before you can have a gender schema, of course, you have to be able to recognize that there are two sexes. This ability starts to emerge even before children can speak. By the age of 9 months, most babies can discriminate male from female faces (Fagot & Leinbach, 1993), and they can match female faces with female voices (Poulin-Dubois et al., 1994). But it takes a couple of years before they can label themselves and others consistently as a "boy" or "girl."

Once children can do that, they begin to prefer same-sex playmates and sex-traditional toys, without being explicitly taught to do so. They become more gender typed in their toy play, games, aggressiveness, and verbal skills than children who still cannot consistently label males and females. Most notably, girls stop behaving aggressively (Fagot, 1993). It is as if they go along, behaving like boys, until they know they are girls. At that moment, but not until that moment, they seem to decide, "Girls don't do this; I'm a girl; I'd better not either."

One interesting aspect of gender development is that virtually all over the world, boys' gender schemas are more rigid than girls' are. That is, boys express stronger preferences for "masculine" toys and activities than girls do for "feminine" ones, and boys are harsher on themselves and on other boys when they fail to behave in sex-typed ways (Bussey & Bandura, 1992; Maccoby, 1998). One reason may be that most societies value masculine occupations and traits more than feminine ones, and they give males higher status. So when boys behave like (or play with) girls, they lose status, and when girls behave like boys, they gain status (Serbin, Powlishta, & Gulko, 1993).

With increasing experience and cognitive sophistication, older children construct their own standards of what boys and girls may or may not do. Eventually, they become aware of the exceptions to their gender schemas; they understand that women can be engineers and men can be cooks. From middle childhood on, many people become more flexible about gender roles and rules, especially if they have friends of the other sex and if their families, jobs, or cultures encourage such flexibility (Katz & Ksansnak, 1994). Other people, however,

retain rigid gender schemas throughout their lives, feeling uncomfortable or angry at the prospect of a male nurse or a female drill sergeant. How flexible are your own gender schemas?

Learning Factors. A third influence on gender development is the environment, which is full of subtle and not-so-subtle messages about what girls and boys are supposed to do. Behavioral and social–cognitive learning theorists study how the process of *gender socialization* instills these messages in children (Yoder, 1999).

For example, many adults say they treat boys and girls equally or that "my little girl was just naturally feminine but my boy was born feisty," but learning theorists dispute such claims. Gender socialization begins at the moment of birth, when the newborn is enveloped in a blanket of the "right" color and dressed in clothes that the culture considers "male" or "female." Adults will actually respond to the same baby differently depending on how the child is dressed (Stern & Karraker, 1989).

Adults will also respond to boys and girls differently even when the children are behaving in *exactly the same way*. In one observational study, 12- to 16-month-old boys and girls were similar in assertiveness (e.g., in their efforts to get an adult's attention) and in attempts to communicate. But teachers responded far more often to assertive boys than to shy ones, and to verbal girls than to nonverbal ones. In other words, the teachers reinforced gender-typed behavior in the children. When the researchers observed the same children a year later, a gender difference was now apparent, with boys behaving more assertively and girls talking more to teachers (Fagot et al., 1985).

Parents, teachers, and other adults convey their beliefs and expectations about gender even when they are entirely unaware that they are doing so. For example, when parents believe that boys are naturally better at math or sports and that girls are naturally better at English, they unwittingly communicate those beliefs by how they respond to a child's success or failure. They may tell a son who did well in math, "You're a natural math whiz, Johnny!" But if a daughter gets good grades, they may say "Wow, you really worked hard in math, Janey, and it shows!" The implication is that girls have to try hard but boys have a natural gift. Messages like these are not lost on the children. Parents' beliefs about the "natural" abilities of the two sexes in math, English, and sports are related to their children's interest in these areas and feelings of competence in pursuing them—even among boys and girls who have equal abilities (Eccles, 1993; Frome & Eccles, 1998).

Gender over the Life Span

In today's fast-moving world, gender development has become a lifelong process, in which people's gender schemas, attitudes, and behavior shift as they have new experiences and as society itself changes. In some areas, gender rules are still being negotiated. For example, for many people, the rules governing a date are in flux: Which partner pays? Who asks whom out? Who makes sexual overtures? In other situations, such as working on an assembly line, gender is usually irrelevant.

Gender differences in personality traits and motivations are greatest in childhood and adolescence, but in North America they decline significantly in adulthood (Cohn, 1991). By middle age, many people report a "gender crossover," as they explore aspects of their personalities and interests they had previously suppressed: Women often become more achievement oriented, men more nurturant and family oriented (Franz, 1997; James & Lewkowicz, 1997; Stewart & Ostrove, 1998).

In sum, 3-year-old children may behave like sexist piglets while they are trying to figure out what it means to be male or female; their behavior may be driven by genes and hormones, cognitive schemas, parental and social lessons, or a combination of all of these factors. But their behavior as 3-year-olds often has little to do with how they will behave at 23 or 43. Children can grow up in an extremely gender-typed family, and yet, as adults, find themselves in careers or relationships they would never have imagined for themselves (Maccoby, 1998). If 3-year-olds are the Gender Police, many adults end up breaking the law.

These images once had the power to startle or offend people; today, they are commonplace. Economic changes have required the participation of women in every kind of work, and the participation of men in family life.

QUICK QUIZ

Males and females are equally capable of taking this quiz.

1. Two-year-old Jeremy thinks that if he changed from wearing pants to wearing dresses, he could become a girl. He still lacks a stable _____.

2. A biological psychologist would say that a 3-year-old boy's love of going "vroom, vroom" with his truck collection is probably a result of _____; a learning theorist would say that it results from _____ by parents and teachers.

3. Which statement about gender schemas is *false?* (a) They are present in early form by 1 year of age; (b) they are permanent conceptualizations of what it means to be masculine or feminine; (c) they probably reflect the status of men and women in society.

4. Herb hopes his 4-year-old daughter will be a doctor, but she refuses to play with the toy stethoscope he bought her and insists that only boys can be doctors. What conclusions about gender differences can Herb draw?

Answers:

1. gender identity   2. biological factors such as hormones or brain processes; gender socialization   3. b   4. Not many; His daughter's rigid gender-typed behavior is typical of children acquiring gender schemas, but it does not predict much of anything about the career she will choose as an adult.

What's Ahead

- What's wrong with "because I say so" as a way of getting children to behave?

- What two key factors limit parents' influence on their children's personalities and behavior?

3.4 How Much do Parents Matter?

Can parents determine how their children will turn out, as if their children were a batch of cookies? Are parents the strongest influence on their children's personalities, behavior, and emotional problems? Until recently, most psychologists (and parents) would not have dreamed of even asking these questions. The answers, they would have said, are self-evident: Of course parents are the most important influence on their children's development. The question is not *whether* they influence children, but *how.*

In the past few years, however, some psychologists have begun to chip away at this widely held belief. Parents are important, they say, but other factors play an equally important role—maybe a

more important role—in children's personality and behavior. We turn now to this lively debate.

The Power of Parents

Much of the research on children's social and emotional development has focused on how parents discipline their kids. One common method is **power assertion,** which includes threats, shouting, scolding, physical punishment, depriving the child of privileges, and generally taking advantage of being bigger, stronger, and more powerful ("Do it because I say so"). Power assertion, however, is associated with a *lack* of moral feeling and behavior in children, poor self-control, and a failure to internalize moral values, as well as low self-esteem, low grades, and poor social skills. When parents are verbally abusive—insulting and ridiculing the child—the results are particularly devastating for children (Moore & Pepler, 1998).

Longitudinal studies show how power assertion by parents can lead to aggressiveness and poor impulse control in children. Parents of aggressive children do a lot of shouting, scolding, and spanking, but they fail to connect the punishment with the child's behavior. They do not state clear rules, require compliance, consistently punish violations,

power assertion
A method of child rearing in which the parent uses punishment and authority to correct the child's misbehavior.

or praise good behavior. Instead, they nag and shout, occasionally and unpredictably tossing in a slap or a loss of privileges. This combination of power assertion with intermittent discipline causes the children's aggressiveness to increase and eventually get out of hand. The child becomes withdrawn, manipulative, and difficult to control, which causes the parents to try to assert their power even more forcefully, which makes the child angrier . . . and a vicious cycle is generated (Patterson, Reid, & Dishion, 1992; Snyder & Patterson, 1995).

A far more successful method of disciplining children is **induction,** in which the parent appeals to the child's own resources, helpful nature, affection for others, and sense of responsibility. A parent using induction might explain to a misbehaving child that the child's actions could harm, inconvenience, or disappoint another person ("You made Doug cry; it's not nice to bite"; "You must never poke anyone's eyes because that could hurt them seriously"). Or the parent might appeal to the child's own helpful inclinations ("I know you're a person who likes to be good to others"), which is far more effective than citing external reasons to be good ("You'd better be nice or you won't get dessert") (Eisenberg, 1995). Children whose parents use induction tend to feel guilty if they hurt others. They internalize standards of right and wrong, confess rather than lie if they misbehave,

induction
A method of child rearing in which the parent appeals to the child's own resources, abilities, sense of responsibility, and feelings for others in correcting the child's misbehavior.

accept responsibility for their misbehavior, and are considerate of others (Hoffman, 1994; Radke-Yarrow, Zahn-Waxler, & Chapman, 1983).

The use of induction is not the same as permissiveness—letting children do anything they want—which tends to produce children who are impulsive, unmotivated, and irresponsible. Parents who use induction tend to be *authoritative* rather than arbitrarily authoritarian or permissive; that is, they give emotional support to the child and are willing to listen to the child's concerns and wishes, but they also set reasonable expectations and teach their children how to meet them (Baumrind, 1989, 1991). Children of authoritative parents tend to be thoughtful and helpful, and also to have high self-esteem and do well in school.

Limits on Parental Influence

Parenting styles, however, are not the only influence on a child's psychological development. For one thing, most parents are inconsistent in their parenting practices, depending on their own stresses, moods, and other factors (Holden & Miller, 1999). They may be permissive on Tuesday when they are feeling cheerful, and authoritarian on Friday when they are stressed out from

Thinking Critically About Parental Influence

Power Assertion
The parent uses threats, physical force, or other kinds of power to get the child to obey.

Example:
"Do it because I say so"; "Stop that right now."

Result:
The child obeys, but only when the parent is present; the child often feels resentful.

Induction
The parent appeals to the child's good nature, empathy, love for the parent, and sense of responsibility to others, and offers explanations of rules.

Example:
"You're too grown up to behave like that"; "Fighting hurts your little brother."

Result:
The child tends to internalize reasons for good behavior.

a tiring week. Further, even when parents are consistent in the way they treat their children, there may be little relation between what they do and how the children turn out (Harris, 1998). Some children of troubled and abusive parents are resilient and do not suffer lasting emotional damage; some children of the kindest and most nurturing parents succumb to drugs, mental illness, or gangs. Why?

Temperaments. One explanation has to do with the child's own inborn temperament (see Chapter 2). Just as the parent influences the child, the child influences the parent. For example, many parents become authoritarian because they are dealing with a difficult child who has been impulsive or disruptive from an early age (Henry et al., 1996). Parents are more permissive with easygoing children and more punitive with defiant ones. And children respond in different ways to a parent's discipline. When a mother "authoritatively" insists that her two sons do their homework, one son may do so conscientiously while another complains that she is crushing his "freedom."

Peers. The other powerful influence on how children behave is their peers. Children, like adults, have two socializing environments: their homes and their world outside the home (Harris, 1998). Their behavior, like that of adults, depends on the

situation they are in. Thus, children who are competitive with their siblings may be cooperative with friends. They can be honest at home and deceitful at school, or vice versa. At home, children learn how their parents want them to behave and what they can get away with; as soon as they leave home, they conform to the dress, habits, language, and rules of their peers. Children who were law-abiding in the fifth grade may start breaking the law in high school, if that is what it takes—or what they think it takes—to win the respect of their peers.

Parents lament the conformity of their children to their peer groups and worry about their kids falling into the wrong clique, but, according to Judith Harris (1998), children's attachment to their peer groups makes perfect sense. Identification with the peer group, not identification with the parent, Harris argues, is the key to survival of the next generation. That is why children have their own traditions, words, rules, and games, and why their culture often operates in opposition to adult rules.

It has been difficult to tease apart the effects of parents and peers, Harris observes, because children's environments usually duplicate parental values, language, and customs. (Many parents see to it that they do!) To see which factors are strongest, therefore, we must look at situations in which these environments clash. For example, when parents value academic achievement and their child's peers do not, who wins? Typically, the answer is peers.

In a study of 15,000 students at nine different American high schools, researchers sought reasons for the average difference in school performance of Asian-Americans, African-Americans, Latinos, and whites (Steinberg, Dornbusch, & Brown, 1992). Asian-American students, who had the highest grades on the average, reported having the highest level of peer support for academic achievement. They studied together in groups, cheered one another on, and praised one another's success. But many African-American students regarded academic success as a sign of selling out to the white establishment. High-achieving black students often said they had few black friends for this reason; they felt they had to choose between doing well in school and being popular with their peers. This dilemma affects students of *any* ethnicity or gender whose peer group thinks that academic success is only for nerds and sellouts (Arroyo & Zigler, 1995).

The first day of day care can be a rude awakening for an only child raised at home.

COMMITTED reprinted by permission of United Feature Syndicate, Inc.

Of course, some children have the resources, because of their temperaments or close family bonds, to resist peer pressure. But exceptions should not detract from the rule: that children, like adults, look to their peers for their standards about how to dress, think, speak, and behave.

Well, then, do parents matter? Clearly the answer depends on how we define our terms: matter for what? As discussed in Chapter 2, research has repeatedly shown that when it comes to personality traits, the influence of genetics is very strong, and the influence of child-rearing practices and family life is weak to non-existent (Cohen, 1999). Child-rearing techniques seem to have little impact on children's basic temperaments and traits, such as timidity or extroversion. But child-rearing techniques can make a big difference in children's behavior and social development if parents keep the children's temperaments in mind.

Parents may not be able to control their children's behavior in peer groups, but they can help their children resist the appeal of delinquent or violent ones. Consider the factors that predict which boys at high risk of delinquency and crime will be less vulnerable: consistent parental discipline and close supervision, parental affection and close parent–child attachment, and high parental standards and expectations (McCord, 1992; Patterson et al., 1998; C. Smith et al., 1997).

Most of all, what parents do affects the quality of their relationship with their children—whether their children feel loved, secure, and valued, or humiliated, frightened, and worthless. Surely this is the most important way that parents "matter"! But once children leave home, starting in preschool, parental influence on children's behavior outside the home begins to wane. Peers and culture take over. The conflict a child might feel between parents and peers typically reaches its peak during adolescence, to which we now turn.

Research Navigator.com
RESOURCES FOR COLLEGE RESEARCH ASSIGNMENTS

3.2

QUICK QUIZ

Would your peers encourage you to take this quiz?

1. Which method of parental discipline tends to create children who have internalized values of helpfulness and empathy? (a) induction, (b) punishment, (c) power assertion

2. Most developmental psychologists believe that what parents do affects children profoundly. Most behavioral geneticists believe that most personality traits have a genetic component and emerge almost regardless of what parents do (see Chapter 2). How might these two positions be reconciled?

Answers:

1. a 2. We can avoid either-or thinking by asking which qualities may be due largely to genetic influences (such as timidity and extroversion) and which are strongly affected by parental lessons (such as aggressiveness and empathy). Also, we can recognize that how a child turns out depends on the interaction between a child's temperament and the parents' behavior.

What's Ahead

- What are the advantages and disadvantages of experiencing puberty earlier than most of your classmates do?

- During adolescence, are extreme turmoil and unhappiness the exception or the rule?

- When teenagers and their parents quarrel, what is it typically about?

3.5 Adolescence

Adolescence refers to the period of development between **puberty,** the age at which a person becomes capable of sexual reproduction, and adulthood. In some cultures, the time span between puberty and adulthood is only a few months; a sexually mature boy or girl is expected to marry and assume adult tasks. In modern Western societies, however, teenagers are not considered emotionally mature enough to assume the rights, responsibilities, and roles of adulthood.

The Physiology of Adolescence

Until puberty, boys and girls produce roughly the same levels of "male hormones" (androgens) and "female hormones" (estrogens). At puberty, the brain's pituitary gland begins to stimulate hormone production in the adrenal and reproductive glands (see Chapter 4). From puberty on, boys have a higher level of androgens than girls do, and girls have a higher level of estrogens than boys do.

In boys, the reproductive glands are the testes (testicles), which produce sperm; in girls, the reproductive glands are the ovaries, which release ova (eggs). During puberty, these sex organs mature and the individual becomes capable of reproduction. In girls, the development of breasts and **menarche,** the onset of menstruation, are signs of sexual maturity. In boys, the signs are the onset of nocturnal emissions and the growth of the testes, scrotum, and penis. Hormones are also responsible for the emergence of *secondary sex characteristics,* such as a deepened voice and facial and chest hair in boys and pubic hair in both sexes.

The onset of puberty depends on both genetic and environmental factors. Menarche, for example, depends on a female's having a critical level of body fat, which is necessary to sustain a pregnancy; body fat triggers the hormonal changes associated with puberty (Chehab et al., 1997). An increase in body fat among children in developed countries may help explain why the average age of puberty has been declining in Europe and North America. A study of more than 17,000 girls found that black girls begin developing breasts and pubic hair at an average age of just under 9 years, meaning that nearly half show these signs by age 8; the average for white girls is slightly over a year later (Herman-Giddens et al., 1997). But this finding is highly controversial, and the average age of menarche itself has not appreciably declined in the last half century, occurring at about 12 years and 8 months in white girls and a few months earlier in black girls. Other explanations have been proposed for the earlier appearance of breasts and pubic hair, such as environmental toxins and hormones in food, but there is as yet no evidence to support these theories.

The physical changes of puberty are part of the last "growth spurt" on the child's road to adulthood.

To their embarrassment, children typically reach puberty at different times. These girls are all the same age, but they differ considerably in physical maturity.

For girls, the adolescent growth spurt begins, on average, at age 10, peaks at 12 or 13, and stops at about age 16, by which time most girls are sexually mature. For boys, the average adolescent growth spurt starts at about age 12 and ends at about age 18. This difference in rates of development is often a source of misery to adolescents, because most girls mature sooner than most boys.

The figures we have given you are only averages; individuals vary enormously in the onset and length of puberty. If you entered puberty before most of your classmates, or if you matured much later than they did, you know that your experience of adolescence was different from that of the average teenager (whoever that is). Early-maturing boys generally have a more positive view of their bodies, and their relatively greater size and strength gives them a boost in sports and the prestige that being a good athlete brings young men. But they are also more likely to smoke, drink alcohol, use other drugs, and break the law than later-maturing boys, and to have less self-control and emotional stability (Duncan et al., 1985).

Likewise, some early-maturing girls have the prestige of being socially popular. But, partly because others in their peer group regard them as being sexually precocious, they are also more likely to fight with their parents, drop out of school, have

puberty
The age at which a person becomes capable of sexual reproduction.

menarche (men-ARR-kee)
The onset of menstruation.

a negative body image, and have emotional problems (Caspi & Moffitt, 1991; Stattin & Magnusson, 1990). Early menarche itself does not cause these problems; rather, it tends to accentuate existing behavioral problems and family conflicts. Girls who go through puberty relatively late, in contrast, have a more difficult time at first, but by the end of adolescence many are happier with their appearance and more popular than their early-maturing classmates (Feldman, 1997).

The Psychology of Adolescence

In April, 1999, an eruption of violence at Columbine High School in Littleton, Colorado, put adolescent suffering on full public display. Two teenagers, enraged at the popularity of school jocks and resentful about their own inadequacies, killed 12 classmates and a teacher in a coldly premeditated plan and then committed suicide. In the national self-scrutiny that followed these murders, hundreds of people—adolescents and adults—wrote to newspapers and called in to talk shows to describe the misery of being an unpopular teenager. They spoke of what it was like to be excluded, bullied by the popular kids, and considered nerds or losers. How typical are these experiences? Are most teenagers angry and unhappy?

Turmoil and Adjustment.
Feelings of insecurity, anger, and rejection are, in fact, common in adolescence, but they are not typical of all teenagers all the time. In studies of representative samples, only a minority are seriously troubled, angry, or

Thinking Critically About "Adolescent Turmoil"

unhappy. Most teenagers have supportive families, a sense of purpose and self-confidence, good friends, and the skill to cope with their problems. Extreme turmoil and unhappiness are the exception, not the rule (Steinberg, 1990).

Nevertheless, three kinds of problems are more common during adolescence than during childhood or adulthood: conflict with parents, mood swings and depression, and higher rates of reckless, rule-breaking, and risky behavior (Arnett, 1999). The years of adolescence can be difficult and challenging because teenagers are developing their own standards and values, often by trying on the styles, actions, and attitudes of their peers, in contrast to those of their parents. This is one reason for the appeal of breaking adult rules. They do not do this just to annoy their parents. The peer group represents the values and style of the generation that they identify with, the generation that they will share experiences with as adults (Harris, 1998). That is why the peer group becomes especially important during adolescence.

Adolescent culture often consists of many different peer groups, organized by interests (jocks, nerds, musicians, artists, etc.), ethnicity, or status and popularity. Children and teenagers who are temperamentally fearful and shy, have few or no friends, or are physically unattractive or weak are more likely than other kids to be bullied, victimized, and rejected by their peers (Hodges & Perry, 1999). Peer acceptance is so important to children and adolescents that these experiences are often far more traumatic and memorable than is punitive treatment by parents. In one Canadian study, college students were asked, "What made you most unhappy when you were a child?" Only 9 percent mentioned their parents; 37 percent described humiliation or rejection by peers (Ambert, 1997).

Adolescents who are lonely, depressed, worried, or angry tend to express these concerns in ways characteristic of their sex. Boys are more likely than girls to *externalize* their emotional problems in acts of aggression and other antisocial behavior; the killers at Columbine High School were an extreme example of this kind of "acting out." Girls, in contrast, are more likely than boys to *internalize* their problems, for example, by becoming withdrawn or developing eating disorders (Zahn-Waxler, 1996).

Separation and Connection.
During the transition from childhood to adulthood, conflicts with adults typically focus on the adolescent's increased desire for autonomy. The Michigan Study of Adolescent Life Transitions followed 1,500 adolescents as they moved from the sixth to the seventh grade. Some teenagers became less motivated to study and began to misbehave—not because of hormonal changes but because, in essence, they were still being treated like children. For example, their parents, perhaps worried about their maturing children's sexuality and possible drug use, were using increasingly punitive measures of controlling them. Thus, the researchers concluded, just when adolescents' cognitive abilities are maturing to enable them to do more complex academic tasks and make responsible personal decisions, some teachers and parents are stifling these needs (Eccles et al., 1993).

Adolescence can be a time of turmoil and rebellion (left), but most teens feel good about themselves and their communities, as do the young people on the right, who have volunteered to remove graffiti.

When teenagers have conflicts with their parents over autonomy, they are usually trying to *individuate,* to develop their own opinions, values, and style of dress and look; they do not want to sever the connection entirely. In one typical study, adolescents described quarrels over issues like these: "why my mother manipulates the conversation to get me to hate her"; "how much of a bastard my father is to my sister"; "how ugly my mom's taste is"; "how pig-headed my mom and dad are" (Csikszentmihalyi & Larson, 1984). But these fights—over what is important, who should set the rules, differences of opinion and taste, and the like—rarely reflected a true rift between parent and adolescent.

For young men and women in Western societies, then, quarrels with parents tend to signify a change from one-sided parental authority to a more reciprocal, adult relationship (Laursen & Collins, 1994). But in the many collectivist and traditionalist cultures around the world, such as India, adolescents would not dream of rebelling against their parents, to whom they feel they owe allegiance and loyalty, nor would the goal of autonomy be more important than family harmony (Arnett, 1999; Segall et al., 1999).

QUICK QUIZ

If you are not in the midst of adolescent turmoil, try these questions.

1. The onset of menstruation is called _____ .
2. *True or false:* Puberty is the same thing as adolescence.
3. Extreme turmoil and rebellion in adolescence are (a) nearly universal, (b) the exception rather than the rule, (c) rare.
4. In Western societies, conflicts between teenagers and their parents are typically over issues of _____ .

Answers:

1. menarche   2. false (can you say why?)   3. b   4. autonomy or individuation

What's Ahead

- What's wrong with thinking that life occurs in a series of predictable stages?

- What feelings are common when people fail to marry, start working, or have children at the "right" time?

- Does menopause make most women depressed or irrational?

- Do men go through a male version of menopause?

- What mental abilities decline in old age, and which ones do not?

3.6 Adulthood

According to ancient Greek legend, the Sphinx was a monster—half lion, half woman—who terrorized passersby on the road to Thebes. The Sphinx would ask each traveler a question and then murder those who failed to answer correctly. (The Sphinx was a pretty tough grader.) The question was this: What animal walks on four feet in the morning, two feet at noon, and three feet in the evening? Only one traveler, Oedipus, knew the solution to the riddle. The animal, he said, is Man, who crawls on all fours as a baby, walks upright as an adult, and limps in old age with the aid of a staff.

The Sphinx was the first life-span theorist. Since then, many philosophers, writers, and scientists have speculated on the course of adult life. Are the changes of adulthood predictable, like those of childhood? What are the major psychological issues of adult life? Is mental and physical deterioration in old age inevitable?

Stages and Ages

As we saw in Chapter 2, Freud believed that personality is formed by age 5 or 6, when the Oedipus complex is resolved. A fuller theory of develop- ment, stretching from birth to death, was proposed by psychoanalyst Erik H. Erikson (1902–1994). Just as children progress through stages, he said, so do adults. Erikson (1950/1963, 1982) wrote that all individuals go through eight stages in their lives, resolving an inevitable "crisis" at each one:

1. *Trust versus mistrust* is the crisis that occurs during the baby's first year, when the baby depends on others to provide food, comfort, cuddling, and warmth. If these needs are not met, the child may never develop the essential trust necessary to get along in the world, especially in relationships.

2. *Autonomy (independence) versus shame and doubt* is the crisis that occurs when the child is a toddler. The young child is learning to be independent and must do so without feeling too ashamed or doubtful of his or her actions.

3. *Initiative versus guilt* is the crisis that occurs as the preschooler develops. The child is acquiring new physical and mental skills and enjoying newfound talents but must also learn to control impulses. The danger lies in developing too strong a sense of guilt over his or her wishes and fantasies.

4. *Competence versus inferiority* is the crisis for school-age children, who are learning to make things, use tools, and acquire the skills for adult life. Children who fail these lessons of mastery and competence risk feeling inadequate and inferior.

5. *Identity versus role confusion* is the crisis of adolescence, when teenagers must decide what they are going to be and what they hope to make of their lives. The term *identity crisis* describes what Erikson considered to be the primary conflict of this stage. Those who resolve this crisis will come out of this stage with a strong identity, ready to plan for the future. Those who do not will sink into confusion, unable to make decisions.

6. *Intimacy versus isolation* is the crisis of young adulthood. Once you have decided who you are, said Erikson, you must share yourself with another and learn to make commitments. No matter how successful you are in work, you are not complete until you are capable of intimacy.

7. *Generativity versus stagnation* is the crisis of the middle years. Will you sink into complacency and selfishness, or will you experience generativity, the pleasure of creativity and renewal? Parenthood is the most common means for the successful resolution of this stage, but people can be productive, creative, and nurturant in other ways, in their work or their relationships with the younger generation.

8. *Ego integrity versus despair* is the crisis of old age. As they age, people strive to reach the ultimate goal—wisdom, spiritual tranquility, an acceptance of their lives. Just as the healthy child will not fear life, said Erikson, the healthy adult will not fear death.

According to Erik Erikson, children must resolve the crisis of competence and older adults must resolve the crisis of generativity. This child and her grandmother are certainly meeting their respective developmental tasks, but are the needs for competence and generativity confined to a particular stage of life?

Erikson recognized that cultural and economic factors affect psychological development. Some societies, for example, make the passage between stages relatively easy. If you know you are going to be a farmer like your parents and you have no alternative, then moving from adolescence into young adulthood is not a terribly painful step (unless you hate farming). If you have many choices, however, as adolescents in urban societies often do, the transition can become prolonged. Some people put off making choices and never resolve their "identity crisis." Similarly, cultures that place a high premium on independence and individualism will make it difficult for many of their members to resolve Erikson's sixth crisis, that of intimacy versus isolation.

Erikson showed that development is never finished; it is an ongoing process, and the issues of one period of life may be reawakened during another. His work was important because he placed adult development in the context of family and society, and he specified many of the essential concerns of adulthood: trust, competence, identity, generativity, and the ability to enjoy life and accept death.

However, Erikson's stages are far from universal, and the psychological concerns he identified do not necessarily occur at only one stage of life. Although in Western societies adolescence *is* often a time of confusion about identity and aspirations, an identity crisis is not limited to the teen years. A man who has worked in one job all his life, and then is laid off and must find an entirely new career, may have an identity crisis, too. Likewise,

competence is not mastered once and for all in childhood. People learn new skills and lose old ones throughout their lives, and their sense of competence rises and falls accordingly. Moreover, people who are highly generative (in terms of being committed to helping the next generation) tend to be so throughout their lives, doing volunteer work or choosing occupations that allow them to help others (Mansfield & McAdams, 1996).

Stage theories, therefore, are no longer considered an adequate approach to capturing life development. As one psychologist summarized, "There is not one process of aging, but many; there is not one life course followed, but multiple courses. . . . The variety is as rich as the historic conditions people have faced and the current circumstances they experience" (Pearlin, 1982).

The Transitions of Life

Today, theories of adult development emphasize the *transitions* and milestones that mark adult life (Baltes, 1983; Schlossberg, 1984). Having a child has strong effects on you and will affect your life in predictable ways, whether you become a parent for the first time at 16 or 46. Entering the workforce affects your self-confidence and ambition regardless of whether you start work at 18 or 48. Some experiences are hallmarks of major life transitions, notably getting a job, getting married or becoming committed to a partner, having children, retiring, and becoming a grandparent. But the transitions themselves are less important, psychologically speaking, than whether they are expected or unexpected—and whether or not you are sharing them with others of your generation.

Starting Out: The Social Clock. In all societies, people evaluate their transitions according to a *social clock* that determines whether they are "on time" for their age or "off time" (Helson & McCabe, 1993; Neugarten, 1979). Cultures have different social clocks that define the "right" time to marry, start work, and have children. In some societies young men and women are supposed to marry and start having children right after puberty, and work responsibilities come later. In others, a man may not marry until he has shown that he can support a family, which might not be until his 30s. Society's reactions to people who are "off time" vary as well, from amused tolerance ("Oh, when will he grow up?") to pity, scorn, and outright rejection.

Doing the right thing at the right time, compared to your friends and age-mates, is reassuring.

When nearly everyone in your group goes through the same experience or enters a new role at the same time—going to school, driving a car, voting, marrying, having a baby, retiring—adjusting to these *anticipated transitions* is relatively easy. Conversely, if hardly anyone you know is doing these things, you will not feel out of step if you don't do them either.

As we have noted, though, traditional social clocks in Western societies are changing. Many people face *unanticipated transitions,* the events that happen without warning, such as being fired from a job because of downsizing. And many people have to deal with *"nonevent transitions,"* the changes they expect to happen that do not: for example, not getting married at the age they expected to, not getting promoted, not being able to afford to retire, or realizing that they cannot have children (Schlossberg & Robinson, 1996).

One of the reasons that young adulthood is often the most stressful time in people's lives is that young adults are often making many rapid transitions at once: leaving home for college or a job, starting a career, finding a serious relationship. These transitions will be more difficult for those who feel they are not keeping up with their peers: "I'm a junior and haven't declared a major," "I'm almost 30 and not even in a serious relationship" (Helson & McCabe, 1993). Being freed of a cultural social clock can be liberating, but people who cannot do things "on time," for reasons out of their control, may feel depressed and anxious.

The Middle Years. Most people think that the most important issues of the middle years are, for women, the misery of menopause and the "empty nest" (when grown children leave home), and, for men, a corresponding "midlife crisis." But they are wrong.

Actually, according to a large-scale research project that has followed 8,000 Americans for 10 years, for most women and men the midlife years—between 35 and 65—are the prime of life (MacArthur Foundation, 1999). It is true that these years are often a time of reflection and reassessment, as people look back on what they have accomplished, take stock of what they regret not having done, and think about what they want to do with their remaining years (Stewart & Vandewater, 1999). But far from being a time of turmoil, midlife is typically a time of psychological well-being, good health, productivity, and community involvement. American women in their 50s today are more likely than those in any other age group to describe their lives as being "first-rate" and to report having a high quality of life (Mitchell & Helson, 1990). Midlife crises are the exception, and when they occur it is not for reasons related to aging but to specific events, such as the loss of a job or spouse. Another stereotype bites the dust!

But doesn't menopause make most midlife women depressed, irritable, and irrational? **Menopause,** which usually occurs between ages 45 and 55, is the cessation of menstruation after the ovaries stop producing estrogen and progesterone. Menopause does produce physical symptoms in many women, notably "hot flashes," as the vascular system adjusts to the decrease in estrogen. But only about 10 percent of all women have unusually severe physical symptoms.

Thinking Critically About Menopause

The negative view of menopause as a syndrome that causes depression and other negative emotional reactions is based on women who have had an early menopause following a hysterectomy (removal of the uterus) or who have had a lifetime history of depression. But these women are not typical. According to many surveys of thousands

menopause
The cessation of menstruation and of the production of ova; it is usually a gradual process lasting up to several years.

Doonesbury

BY GARRY TRUDEAU

of healthy, randomly chosen women in the general population, most view menopause positively (with relief that they no longer have to worry about pregnancy or menstrual periods) or with no particular feelings at all. The vast majority have only a few, temporarily bothersome symptoms and do not become depressed; only 3 percent even report regret at having reached menopause (MacArthur Foundation, 1999; Matthews et al., 1990; McKinlay, McKinlay, & Brambilla, 1987).

What about men? Although testosterone diminishes throughout life, it never drops as sharply in men as estrogen does in women, and men do not lose their fertility, although their sperm count may slowly diminish. In short, there is no "male menopause," and hormones do not cause a midlife crisis in men any more than in women. For both sexes, the physical changes of midlife do not predict how people will feel about aging or how they will respond to it (Ryff & Keyes, 1995).

Old Age

Not long ago you would have been considered old in your 60s. Today, the fastest-growing segment of the population in North America consists of people over the age of 85. There were 4 million Americans age 85 or older in 2000, and there may be as many as 31 million by 2050 (Schneider, 1999). Of these, more than 600,000 will be over the age of 100. How will these people function?

First, the bad news. Alas, it is true that various aspects of intelligence, memory, and other forms of mental functioning decline significantly with age: Older adults score lower on tests of reasoning, spatial ability, and complex problem solving than do younger adults (Verhaeghen & Salthouse, 1997). As people age, it takes them longer to retrieve names, dates, and other information; in fact, the speed of cognitive processing in general slows down (Bashore, Ridderinkhof, & van der Molen, 1997). The decline in short-term memory and

speed of processing actually begins much earlier, in the twenties, and gradually drops off over the life span (Parks, 2000).

But not all cognitive abilities worsen with age (see Figure 3.4). *Gerontologists*—researchers who study aging and the old—distinguish two kinds of cognitive ability. **Fluid intelligence** is the capacity for deductive reasoning and the ability to use new information to solve problems. It reflects an inherited predisposition, and it parallels other biological capacities in its growth and, in later years, decline (Baltes & Graf, 1996; Bosworth & Schaie, 1999). **Crystallized intelligence** consists of the knowledge and skills that are built up over a lifetime—the kind of intelligence that gives us the ability to solve math problems, define words, or take political positions. It depends heavily on education and experience, and it tends to remain stable or even improve over the life span. This is why physicians, lawyers, teachers, farmers, musicians, insurance agents, politicians, psychologists, and people in many other occupations can continue working well into old age (Baltes & Graf, 1996).

Fortunately, gerontologists have made great strides in separating conditions once thought to be an inevitable part of old age from those that are preventable or treatable. For example, apparent senility in the elderly is often caused by prescription medications, harmful combinations of medications, and even by over-the-counter drugs (such as sleeping pills and antihistamines), all of which can be hazardous to old people. Weakness and frailty are often caused by sedentary lifestyles; exercise and moderate levels of weight training can restore muscle strength and flexibility (Rowe & Kahn, 1998). Other problems once thought to be inevitable in old age, such as depression and passivity, often result from the loss of meaningful activity, intellectual stimulation, and control over events (Langer, 1989; Schaie, 1994).

Thinking Critically About "Inevitable" Declines in Old Age

fluid intelligence
The capacity for deductive reasoning and the ability to use new information to solve problems; it is relatively independent of education and tends to decline in old age.

crystallized intelligence
Cognitive skills and specific knowledge of information acquired over a lifetime; it depends heavily on education and tends to remain stable over the lifetime.

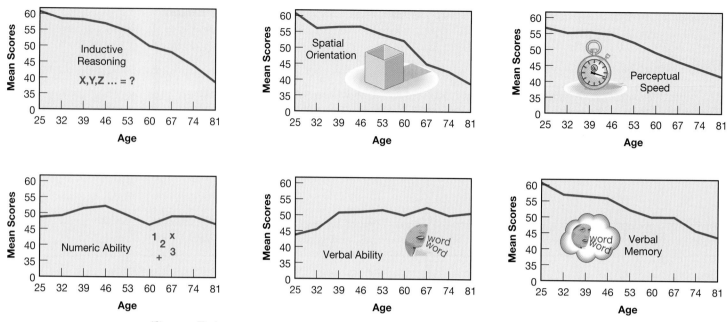

Figure 3.4
Changes in Intellectual Functioning over the Life Span

As these graphs show, some intellectual abilities tend to dwindle with age, but numerical and verbal abilities remain relatively steady over the years.

A longitudinal Canadian study of 250 middle-aged and older adults found that those who remained involved in intellectually challenging activities did not show declines in cognitive ability (Hultsch et al., 1999). The researchers could not rule out the possibility that people with high cognitive functioning continue to pursue intellectual challenges because they are able to. But other research shows that mental stimulation does increase mental functioning. Older adults can sometimes do as well on memory tests as people in their 20s, when given guidance and cues for encoding and retrieving memories—for example, when they are taught to use effective encoding strategies rather than merely making lists (Loewen, Shaw, & Craik, 1990). Short-term training programs for people between 60 and 80 years old produce gains in mental test scores that are as large as the losses typical for that age group (Baltes, Sowarka, & Kliegl, 1989; Willis, 1987).

Although some losses are inevitable with age, physical exercise and mental stimulation promote the growth of synapses in the human brain, even well into old age (Kleim et al., 1998). Also, as people age, their brains seem to compensate for cognitive losses by recruiting areas that previously had not been involved in a given task. In PET-scan studies comparing younger adults (ages 18 to 30) and older adults (ages 65 to 75) on memory tests, the younger people showed lateralization in performing the tasks: left hemispheric activation for verbal memory, and right hemispheric activation for spatial memory. But in the older people, both halves of their frontal lobes were activated for both types of memory (Reuter-Lorenz, Stanczak, & Miller, 1999; Reuter-Lorenz et al., 2000).

Stereotypes about old people are breaking down as more and more people are living long, healthy, active lives.

Perhaps the best news is that as many people get older, they get happier, they become calmer, and their well-being improves; they learn to control negative feelings and emphasize the positive (Mroczek & Kolarz, 1998). And older couples, compared with younger couples, are less likely to express anger, belligerence, and whining when they quarrel (Carstensen & Charles, 1998). Perhaps age really does bring wisdom!

Some researchers who study aging are therefore optimistic. In their view, people who have challenging occupations and interests, and who adapt flexibly to change, are likely to maintain their cognitive abilities (Diamond, 1993; Kolb & Whishaw, 1998). "Use it or lose it," they say. Other researchers, however, are less optimistic. "When you've lost it, you can't use it," they reply. They are worried about the growing numbers of people living into their 90s and 100s, when rates of cognitive impairment and dementia rise dramatically (Baltes & Graf, 1996; Thomassen, van Schaick, & Blansjaar, 1998). The challenge for society is to make sure that the many people who will be living into their 90s can keep using their brains instead of losing them.

QUICK QUIZ

People of any age can answer this quiz.

1. The key psychological issue during adolescence, said Erikson, is a(n) _____ crisis.

2. Ernie wants to go to law school but is failing his prelaw classes. Ernie is about to undergo a(n) _____ transition.

3. Most women react to menopause by (a) feeling depressed, (b) regretting the loss of femininity, (c) going a little crazy, (d) feeling relieved or neutral.

4. Which of these statements about the decline of mental abilities in old age is *false?* (a) It can often be lessened by training programs; (b) it inevitably happens to all old people; (c) it is sometimes a result of malnutrition or disease, rather than aging; (d) it is slowed when people live in stimulating environments.

5. Almost overnight, your 80-year-old grandmother has become confused and delusional. Before concluding that old age has made her senile, what other explanation should you rule out?

Answers:
1. identity 2. nonevent 3. d 4. b 5. You should rule out the possibility that she is taking too many medications or other drugs that can be hazardous in older people.

What's Ahead

• Do traumatic childhood experiences affect a person forever?

• Do most abused children become abusive parents?

3.7 Are Adults Prisoners of Childhood?

Most people take for granted that the path from childhood to adolescence to adulthood is a fairly straight one. We think of the lasting attitudes, habits, and values our parents taught us. We continue to have deep emotional attachments to our families, even when we are fighting with them. And many people carry with them the scars of emotional wounds they suffered as children.

Moreover, when children have been beaten or neglected, have been constantly subjected to verbal and physical abuse by their parents, or live in violent communities, they are more likely than other children to have emotional problems, become delinquent and violent themselves, commit crimes, have low IQs, drop out of school, or attempt suicide (Malinosky-Rummell & Hansen, 1993; Maxfield & Widom, 1996; Moore & Pepler, 1998). Yet studies that follow people from childhood to adulthood

The actress Audrey Hepburn nearly starved to death in her native Belgium during the Nazi occupation in World War II. But she, like many children who live through war and other traumas, triumphed over her early adversity. Until the end of her life, Hepburn worked tirelessly on behalf of children suffering from the effects of illiteracy, famine, and war.

challenge the widespread assumption that childhood traumas always have specific and inescapable effects:

- *Recovery from war.* After World War II, many European children, made homeless by the war, were adopted by American families. About 20 percent of the children had problems at first, but over the years they all made good progress in school; none had psychiatric problems; and all established happy, affectionate relationships with their new parents (Rathbun, DiVirgilio, & Waldfogel, 1958).

- *Recovery from abusive or alcoholic parents.* Compared to children of healthy parents, more children of abusive or alcoholic parents become abusive or alcoholic themselves, but the majority do not (Cohen, 1999; Kaufman & Zigler, 1987; West & Prinz, 1987).

- *Recovery from sexual abuse.* Children who have been sexually abused have more emotional and behavioral symptoms than nonabused children, especially if the abuse is severe, repeated, and part of other chronically stressful experiences in a child's life. Yet the

research shows, much to people's surprise, that by adulthood, most victims are as well adjusted as people in the general population. Meta-analyses of studies of nearly 37,000 college students and of more than 12,000 adults have found no overall link between childhood sexual abuse and later emotional disorders or unusual psychological problems (Rind & Tromovitch, 1997; Rind, Tromovitch, & Bauserman, 1998).

Many clinicians have found these results difficult to accept because, by virtue of the work they do, they see the people who are having trouble coping with the effects of difficult or traumatic childhoods. They do not see the people in the general population who have overcome their pasts or vow not to repeat their parents' mistakes. Moreover, many clinicians accept the assumption of psychodynamic approaches that childhood traumas often have specific and long-lasting effects on adult personality and problems. But if we question this assumption, avoid emotional reasoning, and consider the evidence fairly, then we get a different picture.

Because of the heartening discoveries about children's recovery from trauma, many psychologists today are studying the origins of *resilience* in the children of violent, neglectful, abusive, or alcoholic parents (Cowen et al., 1990; Garmezy, 1991). Many of these children have easygoing temperaments or personality traits that affect how they respond to adversity; they roll with fairly severe punches. Other resilient children are rescued by love and attention from their siblings, peers, or caring adults other than their parents. And some have experiences outside the family—in schools, places of worship, or other organizations—that give them a sense of competence, moral support, solace, religious faith, and self-esteem (Masten & Coatsworth, 1998).

This encouraging news does not mean that recovery from severe hardship is easy. The abuse and neglect of children are widespread problems, and society cannot afford to be indifferent to children's suffering. Unlike Canada and most European nations, the United States places a low priority on child-care services and education; one in five American children lives in poverty, more than in any other industrialized nation.

But as children develop, they are subject to other influences, too. Perhaps the most powerful reason for the resilience of so many children, and for the changes that adults make throughout their lives, is that we are all constantly interpreting our experiences. We can unthinkingly decide to repeat our parents' mistakes or make conscious efforts to learn from them. We can decide that we want to remain prisoners of childhood or to strike out in new directions at 20, 50, . . . or 80. Because we have minds and can think about our setbacks and victories, our problems and our accomplishments, the link between childhood and adulthood is more like a dotted curve than a straight line.

PSYCHOLOGY IN THE NEWS, REVISITED

Has our review of events across the life span helped you to clarify your thoughts about the woman who gave birth at age 63? The concept of the social clock can help us understand why so many people feel queasy about a woman getting pregnant so late in life: She is obviously "off time"! Of course, plenty of older people, required by unforeseen circumstances to rear their grandchildren, have risen to the challenge. But, as we have seen, age brings cognitive, not to mention physical, changes, so it seems legitimate to worry about whether elderly parents—of either sex—will have the mental resources and energy to guide their children through the many hurdles of childhood and adolescence.

On the other hand, we have also learned that the whole concept of "natural stages" is far more valid for children than for adults. Children do go through predictable stages in their cognitive, linguistic, and social development. But the terrain of adulthood can vary tremendously, depending on a person's genes, culture, generation, and individual experiences. As we saw, the issues explored by Erikson, including identity crises and generativity, can arise at any age. Reaching a certain age has few if any inevitable consequences; increasingly, age is what we make of it.

In the years to come, many people will be charting their travels through life in ways that challenge conventional notions of what the guiding road map should look like. In the absence of clear signposts, will they get disoriented and lose their way, or will the result be a more creative and satisfying adventure?

TAKING PSYCHOLOGY WITH YOU

Bringing Up Baby

How should you treat your children? Should you be strict or lenient, powerful or permissive? Should you require your child to stop having tantrums, to clean up his or her room, to be polite? Should you say, "Oh, nothing I do will matter, anyway"? Even granted the limitations of parental influence, certain child-rearing practices are effective in teaching children to be confident, considerate, and helpful at home:

● *Set high expectations that are appropriate to the child's age, and teach the child how to meet them* (Damon, 1995). Some parents make few demands on their children, either unintentionally or because they believe a parent should not impose standards. Others make many demands, such as requiring children to be polite, help with chores, control their anger, be thoughtful of others, and do well in school. The children of parents who make few demands tend to be aggressive, impulsive, and immature. The children of parents who have high expectations tend to be helpful and above average in competence and self-confidence. But the demands must be appropriate for the child's age. You can't expect 2-year-olds to dress themselves, and before you can expect children to get up on time, they have to know how to work an alarm clock.

● *Explain, explain, explain.* Induction—telling a child why you have applied a rule—teaches a child to be responsible. Punitive methods ("Do it or I'll spank you") may result in compliance, but the child will tend to disobey as soon as you are out of sight. Explanations also teach children how to reason and understand; they reward curiosity and open-mindedness. This does not mean you have to argue with a 4-year-old about the merits of table manners. But, while setting standards for your children, you can also allow them to express disagreements and feelings.

● *Encourage empathy.* Call the child's attention to the effect of his or her actions on others, appeal to the child's sense of fair play and desire to be good, and teach the child to take another person's point of view. Vague orders, such as "Don't fight," are less effective than showing the child how fighting disrupts and hurts others. For boys especially, aggression and empathy are strongly and negatively related: the higher the one, the lower the other (Eisenberg et al., 1996).

● *Notice, approve of, and reward good behavior.* Many parents punish behavior they dislike, a form of attention that may actually be rewarding to the child. It is much more effective to praise the behavior you do want, which teaches the child what is right.

Even the best parenting cannot create the "ideal child"—that is, one who is an exact replica of you. You cannot control everything that happens to your child, or your child's basic temperament. "The idea that we can make our children turn out any way we want is an illusion. Give it up," advises Judith Harris (1998). But, she adds, you do have the power to make their lives miserable or secure, and to affect the quality of the relationship you will have with them throughout your life: one filled with conflict and resentment, or one that is close and loving.

SUMMARY

From Conception to the First Year

• Prenatal development consists of the *germinal, embryonic,* and *fetal* stages. Harmful influences that can adversely affect the fetus's development include German measles, toxic chemicals, some sexually transmitted diseases, cigarettes, alcohol (which in excess can cause *fetal alcohol syndrome*), illegal drugs, and even over-the-counter medications.

• Babies are born with certain physical abilities, including motor reflexes necessary for survival and a number of perceptual abilities. Newborns are also naturally attracted to novelty and to human faces. Cultural practices affect the timing of physical milestones such as walking, but eventually all healthy children crawl, sit, and walk.

• Babies' survival depends on physical and emotional attachment to their caregivers. Their innate need for *contact comfort* gives rise to emotional attachment to their caregivers, and by the age of 7 to 9 months, they begin to feel *separation anxiety.* Studies of the *Strange Situation* have identified three styles of infant attachment: *secure, avoidant,* and *anxious–ambivalent.* Insecurely attached children may develop long-term emotional and behavioral problems.

• Styles of attachment are relatively unaffected by the normal range of child-rearing practices, including whether babies spend time in daycare. Insecure attachment may be caused by the child's own fearful, insecure temperament, by stressful family situations, by upsetting events in later childhood, and by parents who are extremely neglectful or rejecting of their babies.

Cognitive Development

• Infants are responsive to the pitch, intensity, and sound of language, which may be why adults in many cultures speak to babies in *parentese*—using higher-pitched words and exaggerated intonation. At 4 to 6 months of age, babies begin to recognize the sounds of their own language; they go through a babbling phase from age 6 months to 1 year. At about 1 year, they start saying single words and using symbolic gestures. At age 2, children speak in two- or three-word *telegraphic* sentences that convey a variety of messages.

• Language allows us to express and comprehend an infinite number of novel utterances. Noam Chomsky argued that the ability to take the *surface structure* of any utterance and apply rules of *syntax* to infer its underlying *deep structure* must depend on an innate faculty for language, a *language acquisition device.* Many findings support this view: Children from different cultures go through similar stages of language development; children's language is full of *overregularizations,* reflecting grammatical rules; and adults do not consistently correct their children's syntax.

• Nonetheless, parental practices, such as repeating correct sentences verbatim and recasting incorrect ones, aid in language acquisition. Biological readiness and experience probably interact in the development of language. Case studies of children deprived of exposure to language suggest that a *critical period* exists for acquiring a first language.

• Jean Piaget argued that cognitive development depends on an interaction between maturation and a child's experiences in the world. Children's thinking changes and adapts through *assimilation* and *accommodation.* Piaget proposed four stages of cognitive development: *sensorimotor* (birth to age 2), during which the child learns *object permanence; preoperational* (ages 2 to 7), during which language and symbolic thought develop; *concrete operations* (ages 6 or 7 to 11), during which the child comes to understand *conservation,* identity, and serial ordering; and *formal operations* (age 12 to adulthood), during which abstract reasoning develops.

• Researchers have found that the changes from one stage to another are not as clear-cut as Piaget implied; that young children have more cognitive abilities, at earlier ages, than Piaget thought; and that young children are not always egocentric in their thinking. Cultural practices affect the pace and content of cognitive development, and not all adults develop the ability for formal operations.

● Lawrence Kohlberg's theory of moral development proposed three levels of moral reasoning, each with two stages: *preconventional morality* (based on rules, punishment, and self-interest), *conventional morality* (based on relationships and rules of justice and law), and *postconventional* ("principled") *morality* (based on higher principles of human rights). Carol Gilligan argued that women tend to base moral decisions on principles of compassion, whereas men tend to base theirs on abstract principles of justice. Most research, however, finds no gender differences in moral reasoning.

● Stage theories of moral reasoning have three limitations: They tend to overlook the influence of culture and education; moral reasoning is often inconsistent across situations; and moral reasoning and moral behavior are often unrelated.

Gender Development

● Gender development includes the emerging awareness of *gender identity,* the cognitive understanding that a person is biologically male or female, regardless of what he or she does or wears, and *gender typing,* the process by which boys and girls learn what it means to be masculine or feminine.

● Biological psychologists account for gender differences in behavior in terms of genetics, hormones, and brain organization, observing that universally, young children tend to prefer same-sex toys and playing with other children of their sex. Cognitive psychologists study how children develop *gender schemas* of "male" and "female" categories and qualities, which in turn shape their gender-typed behavior. Gender schemas tend to be inflexible at first but often becomes more flexible as the child cognitively matures and assimilates new information. Learning theorists study the direct and subtle reinforcers and social messages that foster gender typing.

● Gender development changes over the life span, depending on people's experiences with work and family life, and on the gender composition of the situations they are in.

How Much Do Parents Matter?

● Parental discipline methods have different consequences for a child's behavior. *Power assertion* is associated with children who have a sense of external control, are aggressive and destructive, and show a lack of empathy and moral behavior. *Induction* is associated with children who develop empathy and internalized moral standards and who can resist temptation. In general, *authoritative* parents, who use induction and set limits, have better results with their children than do *authoritarian* or *permissive* parents.

● Two major factors limit the influence that parents have on their children: the child's own genetically influenced temperament, which affects the child's behavior, and also how the child perceives the parent's actions and intentions, and the child's peer groups. But parents strongly affect the quality of their relationships with their children.

Adolescence

● *Adolescence* begins with the physical changes of *puberty.* In girls, puberty is signaled by *menarche* and the development of breasts; in boys, it begins with the onset of nocturnal emissions and the development of the testes and scrotum. Boys and girls who enter puberty early tend to have a more difficult adjustment than do those who enter puberty later than average, possibly because early puberty intensifies already existing problems from childhood.

● Most adolescents do not go through extreme emotional turmoil, anger, or rebellion. However, conflict with parents, mood swings and depression, and reckless behavior are more common in adolescence than in childhood or adulthood. The peer group becomes especially important for teenagers, and rejection by peers can lead to psychological problems. Boys tend to *externalize* their emotional problems in acts of aggression and other antisocial behavior; girls tend to *internalize* their problems by becoming withdrawn or developing eating disorders. One challenge of adolescence in Western cultures is *individuation*, breaking away from parents to develop autonomy and a more reciprocal relationship with them.

Adulthood

● Erik Erikson proposed that life consists of eight stages, each with a unique psychological crisis that must be resolved, such as an *identity crisis* in adolescence. Erikson made an important contribution by recognizing the essential concerns of adulthood and by showing that development is a lifelong process. However, unlike stages of child development, adult stages are not universal and psychological issues or crises are not confined to particular chronological periods.

• The *transitions* approach to development emphasizes the changes in people's lives regardless of when they occur. Adults often evaluate their development according to a *social clock* that determines whether they are "on time" or "off time" for a particular event. Transitions may be *anticipated, unanticipated,* and *"nonevent"* (expected changes that do not occur).

• The middle years are generally not a time of turmoil or crisis, but the prime of most people's lives. In women, *menopause* begins in the late 40s or early 50s. Many women have temporary physical symptoms but most do not regret the end of fertility or become depressed and irritable. In middle-aged men, hormone production slows down, but fertility continues.

• *Gerontologists* have revised our ideas about old age, now that people are living longer and healthier lives. Many supposedly inevitable results of aging—such as osteoporosis, senility, and depression—are often the result of disease, inappropriate medication, poor nutrition, and lack of stimulation and control of one's environment. But certain cognitive processes do diminish with age. The speed of cognitive processing slows down, and *fluid intelligence* parallels other biological capacities in its eventual decline. *Crystallized intelligence,* in contrast, depends heavily on culture, education, and experience, and it tends to remain stable or even improve over the life span.

Are Adults Prisoners of Childhood?

• Children who experience violence or neglect are at risk of many serious problems later in life. But the majority of children are resilient, able to overcome early traumas and even parental abuse. Psychologists now study the origins of children's resilience, as well as the consequences of childhoods of poverty and trauma.

KEY TERMS

socialization 74
maturation 74
germinal, embryonic, fetal stages 75
fetal alcohol syndrome (FAS) 75
motor reflexes 76
contact comfort 77
separation anxiety 78
Strange Situation 78
kinds of attachment: secure, avoidant, and anxious–ambivalent 78
"parentese" 81
telegraphic speech 81
syntax 82
surface structure and deep structure 82
language acquisition device 82
overregularizations 82

critical period (for language acquisition) 83
Jean Piaget 83
assimilation 83
accommodation 83
sensorimotor stage 83
object permanence 84
preoperational stage 84
operations 84
egocentric thinking 84
conservation 84
concrete operations stage 84
formal operations stage 85
preconventional, conventional, and postconventional moral reasoning (Kohlberg) 87
care–based versus justice-based moral reasoning (Gilligan) 88
gender identity 89

gender typing 89
gender schema 90
power assertion 93
induction 94
authoritative parenting 94
adolescence 96
puberty 96
menarche 97
secondary sex characteristics 97
Erik Erikson 100
identity crisis 100
social clock 101
transitions: anticipated, unanticipated, and nonevent 102
menopause 102
gerontology 103
fluid intelligence 103
crystallized intelligence 103

LOOKING BACK

- How can a pregnant woman reduce the risk of damage to the embryo or fetus? (pp. 75–76)

- Given a choice, what do newborns prefer to look at? (p. 77)

- How does culture affect how a baby's physical maturation? (p. 77)

- Why is cuddling so important for infants (not to mention adults)? (p. 78)

- If you have a 1-year-old, why shouldn't you worry if your baby cries when left with a new babysitter? (p. 78)

- Why do so many parents speak "baby talk"? (p. 81)

- Is language an innate ability or an acquired one? (pp. 82–83)

- What important accomplishment are infants revealing when they learn to play "peekaboo"? (p. 84)

- Why will most 5-year-olds choose a tall, narrow glass of lemonade over a short, fat glass containing the same amount? (p. 84)

- When reasoning about moral issues, are women more compassionate and caring than men? (p. 88)

- How would a biologically oriented psychologist explain why most little boys and girls are "sexist" in their choice of toys? (p. 90)

- What happens to children's notions about gender once they are able to distinguish males from females? (p. 90)

- How do teachers unintentionally reinforce assertiveness in boys? (p. 92)

- If a little girl "knows" that girls can't be doctors, does this mean she will never go to med school? (p. 92)

- What's wrong with "because I say so" as a way of getting children to behave? (p. 93)

- What two key factors limit parents' influence on their children's personalities and behavior? (p. 95)

- What are the advantages and disadvantages of experiencing puberty earlier than most of your classmates do? (pp. 97–98)

- During adolescence, are extreme turmoil and unhappiness the exception or the rule? (p. 98)

- When teenagers and their parents quarrel, what is it typically about? (p. 99)

- What's wrong with thinking that life occurs in a series of predictable stages? (p. 101)

- What feelings are common when people fail to marry, start working, or have children at the "right" time? (p. 102)

- Does menopause make most women depressed or irrational? (pp. 102–103)

- Do men go through a male version of menopause? (p. 103)

- What mental abilities decline in old age, and which ones do not? (pp. 103–104)

- Do traumatic childhood experiences affect a person forever? (pp. 105–106)

- Do most abused children become abusive parents? (p. 106)

Fox Tapes Final "Spin City"

NEW YORK, MARCH 17, 2000. Perennially youthful actor Michael J. Fox, 38, taped an emotional final episode of "Spin City" tonight before a teary-eyed studio audience. Two years ago, Fox revealed to a surprised public that he had been diagnosed in 1991 with Parkinson's disease, a debilitating condition that causes tremors, rigidity, and sometimes, in its advanced stages, intellectual impairment.

Fox left the popular sitcom, which he helped to create, to help in the fight against Parkinson's and to spend more time with his family. He was also motivated by the fact that his symptoms were milder during vacations, when he was not under the stress of working 14-hour days.

Medication has helped the popular actor deal with his physical symptoms, and the support of family, friends, and fans, he says,

After four seasons, Michael J. Fox waves good-bye after a tearful taping of his final episode of "Spin City." Fox left the show to spend more time with his family and to raise money for Parkinson's research.

has helped him cope with the mental challenge of living with his disease while in the public eye. Much of his energy will now go into the Michael J. Fox Foundation for Parkinson's Research, although he intends to continue acting and producing. Someday, he says, he may write a book on "how to lose your brain without losing your mind."

NEURONS, HORMONES, AND THE BRAIN

Although Michael J. Fox is younger than most Parkinson's patients, he is not alone: The disabling disorder affects millions of people worldwide. Along with other conditions affecting the brain and nervous system, such as Alzheimer's disease and stroke, Parkinson's reminds us that the 3-pound organ inside our skulls is the bedrock of behavior and mental activity. Change it and you inevitably change the person, either physically or mentally. Neuropsychologists, along with neuroscientists from other disciplines, study the brain and the rest of the nervous system in hopes of gaining a better understanding of consciousness, perception, memory, emotion, stress, mental disorders, and even self-identity.

At this very moment, your own brain, assisted by other parts of your nervous system, is busily taking in these words. Whether you are excited, curious, or bored, your brain is registering some sort of emotional reaction. As you continue reading, your brain will (we hope) store away much of the information in this chapter. Later on, your brain may enable you to smell a flower, climb the stairs, greet a friend, solve a personal problem, or chuckle at a joke. But the brain's most startling accomplishment is its knowledge that it is doing all these things. This self-awareness makes brain research different from the study of anything else in the universe. Scientists must use the cells, biochemistry, and circuitry of their own brains to understand the cells, biochemistry, and circuitry of brains in general.

"THEN IT'S AGREED—YOU CAN'T HAVE A MIND WITHOUT A BRAIN, BUT YOU CAN HAVE A BRAIN WITHOUT A MIND."

Because the brain is the site of consciousness, people disagree about what language to use in discussing it. If we say that your brain stores events or registers emotions, we imply a separate "you" that is "using" that brain. But if we leave "you" out of the picture and just say the brain does these things, we risk implying that brain mechanisms alone explain behavior (which is untrue), and we lose sight of the person. No one has ever resolved this dilemma to everyone's satisfaction.

William Shakespeare called the brain "the soul's frail dwelling house." Actually, this miraculous organ is more like the main room in a house filled with many alcoves and passageways—the "house" being the nervous system as a whole. Before we can understand the windows, walls, and furniture of this house, we need to become acquainted with the overall floor plan. It's a pretty technical plan, which means that you will be learning many new terms, but you will need to know these terms in order to understand how biological psychologists go about explaining psychological topics. As you read, keep Michael J. Fox in mind. Which parts of his brain have been affected by his disease? What can be done about such disorders? Most important, can you "lose your brain without losing your mind"?

central nervous system (CNS)
The portion of the nervous system consisting of the brain and spinal cord.

spinal cord
A collection of neurons and supportive tissue running from the base of the brain down the center of the back, protected by a column of bones (the spinal column).

What's Ahead

- Why do you automatically pull your hand away from something hot, "without thinking"?
- Is it possible to consciously control your heartbeat or blood pressure?
- In an emergency, which part of your nervous system whirls into action?

4.1 The Nervous System: A Basic Blueprint

The function of a nervous system is to gather and process information, produce responses to stimuli, and coordinate the workings of different cells. Even the lowly jellyfish and the humble worm have the beginnings of such a system. In very simple organisms that do little more than move, eat, and eliminate wastes, the "system" may be no more than one or two nerve cells. In human beings, who do such complex things as dance, cook, and take psychology courses, the nervous system contains billions of cells. Scientists divide this intricate network into two main parts: the central nervous system and the peripheral (outlying) nervous system (see Figure 4.1).

The Central Nervous System

The **central nervous system (CNS)** receives, processes, interprets, and stores incoming sensory information—information about tastes, sounds, smells, color, pressure on the skin, the state of internal organs, and so forth. It also sends out messages destined for muscles, glands, and internal organs. The CNS is usually conceptualized as having two components: the brain, which we will consider in detail later, and the **spinal cord.** The spinal cord is actually an extension of the brain. It runs from the base of the brain down the center of the back, protected by a column of bones (the spinal column), and it acts as a bridge between the brain and the parts of the body below the neck.

The spinal cord produces some behaviors on its own, without any help from the brain. These *spinal reflexes* are automatic, requiring no con-

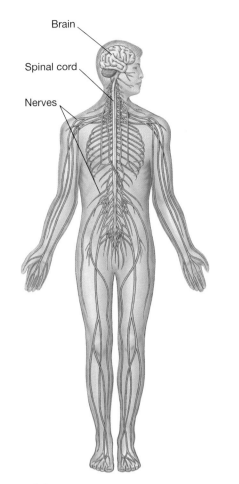

Figure 4.1
The Central and Peripheral Nervous Systems

The central nervous system includes the brain and the spinal cord. The peripheral nervous system consists of 43 pairs of nerves that transmit information to and from the central nervous system. Twelve pairs of cranial nerves in the head enter the brain directly; 31 pairs of spinal nerves enter the spinal cord at the spaces between the vertebrae of the spine.

scious effort. For example, if you accidentally touch a hot iron, you will immediately pull your hand away, even before your brain has had a chance to register what has happened. Nerve impulses bring a message to the spinal cord (hot!), and the spinal cord immediately sends out a command via other nerve impulses, telling muscles in your arm to contract and pull your hand away from the iron. (Reflexes above the neck, such as sneezing and blinking, involve the lower part of the brain, rather than the spinal cord.)

The neural circuits underlying many spinal reflexes are linked to other neural pathways that run up and down the spinal cord, to and from the brain. Because of these connections, reflexes can sometimes be influenced by thoughts and emotions. An example is erection in men, a spinal reflex that can be inhibited by anxiety or distracting thoughts, and initiated by erotic thoughts. Some reflexes can be brought under conscious control. If you concentrate, you may be able to keep your knee from jerking when it is tapped, as it normally would. Similarly, most men can learn to voluntarily delay ejaculation, another spinal reflex.

The Peripheral Nervous System

The **peripheral nervous system (PNS)** handles the central nervous system's input and output. It contains all portions of the nervous system outside the brain and spinal cord, right down to nerves in the tips of the fingers and toes. If your brain could not collect information about the world by means of a peripheral nervous system, it would be like a radio without a receiver. In the peripheral nervous system, *sensory nerves* carry messages from special receptors in the skin, muscles, and other internal and external sense organs to the spinal cord, which sends them along to the brain. These nerves put us in touch with both the outside world and the activities of our own bodies. *Motor nerves* carry orders from the central nervous system to muscles, glands, and internal organs. They enable us to move, and they cause glands to contract and to secrete substances, including chemical messengers called *hormones.*

Scientists further divide the peripheral nervous system into two parts: the somatic (bodily) nervous system and the autonomic (self-governing) nervous system. The **somatic nervous system,** sometimes called the *skeletal nervous system,* consists of nerves that are connected to sensory receptors and to the skeletal muscles that permit voluntary action. When you sense the world around you, or when you turn off a light or write your name, your somatic system is active. The **autonomic nervous system** regulates the functioning of blood vessels, glands, and internal (visceral) organs such as the bladder, stomach, and heart. When you see someone you have a crush on, and your heart pounds, your hands get sweaty, and your cheeks feel hot, you can blame your autonomic nervous system.

The autonomic nervous system works more or less automatically, without a person's conscious control. However, some people can learn to heighten or suppress their autonomic responses

peripheral nervous system (PNS)
All portions of the nervous system outside the brain and spinal cord; it includes sensory and motor nerves.

somatic nervous system
The subdivision of the peripheral nervous system that connects to sensory receptors and to skeletal muscles; sometimes called the *skeletal nervous system.*

autonomic nervous system
The subdivision of the peripheral nervous system that regulates the internal organs and glands.

intentionally. In India, some yogis can slow their heartbeats and metabolisms so dramatically that they can survive in a sealed booth long after most of us would have died of suffocation. During the 1960s and 1970s, Neal Miller and his colleagues showed that many other people can also learn to control their visceral responses by using a technique called *biofeedback* (Miller, 1978).

In biofeedback, monitoring devices track the bodily process in question and produce a signal, such as a light or a tone, whenever a person makes the desired response. The person may either use a prearranged method to produce the desired response or simply try to increase the signal's frequency in any way that he or she chooses. Using biofeedback, some people have learned to control such autonomic responses as blood pressure, blood flow, heart rate, and skin temperature. Some clinicians are therefore using biofeedback training to treat high blood pressure, asthma, and migraine headaches, although there is controversy about success rates and about what, exactly, is being controlled—the actual autonomic

responses, or responses that can be voluntarily produced, such as breathing, which then in turn affect the autonomic system.

The autonomic nervous system is itself divided into two parts: the **sympathetic nervous system** and the **parasympathetic nervous system.** These two parts work together, but in opposing ways, to adjust the body to changing circumstances (see Figure 4.2). The sympathetic system acts like the accelerator of a car, mobilizing the body for action and an output of energy. It makes you blush, sweat, and breathe more deeply, and it pushes up your heart rate and blood pressure. As we will see in Chapter 12, when you are in a situation that requires you to fight, flee, or cope, the sympathetic nervous system whirls into action. The parasympathetic system is more like a brake: It does not stop the body, but it does tend to slow things down or keep them running smoothly. It enables the body to conserve and store energy. If you have to jump out of the way of a speeding motorcyclist, sympathetic nerves increase your heart rate. Afterward, parasympathetic nerves slow it down again and keep its rhythm regular.

sympathetic nervous system
The subdivision of the autonomic nervous system that mobilizes bodily resources and increases the output of energy during emotion and stress.

parasympathetic nervous system
The subdivision of the autonomic nervous system that operates during relaxed states and that conserves energy.

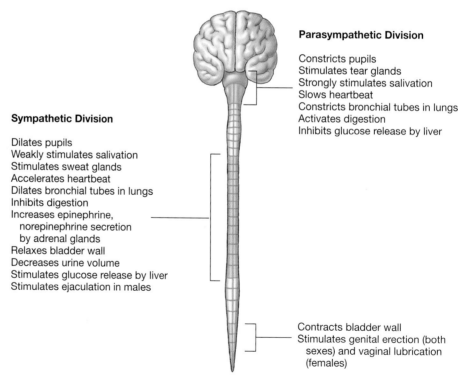

Sympathetic Division

Dilates pupils
Weakly stimulates salivation
Stimulates sweat glands
Accelerates heartbeat
Dilates bronchial tubes in lungs
Inhibits digestion
Increases epinephrine,
   norepinephrine secretion
   by adrenal glands
Relaxes bladder wall
Decreases urine volume
Stimulates glucose release by liver
Stimulates ejaculation in males

Parasympathetic Division

Constricts pupils
Stimulates tear glands
Strongly stimulates salivation
Slows heartbeat
Constricts bronchial tubes in lungs
Activates digestion
Inhibits glucose release by liver

Contracts bladder wall
Stimulates genital erection (both
   sexes) and vaginal lubrication
   (females)

Figure 4.2

The Autonomic Nervous System

In general, the sympathetic division of the autonomic nervous system prepares the body to expend energy, and the parasympathetic division restores and conserves energy. Sympathetic nerve fibers exit from areas of the spinal cord shown in red in this illustration; parasympathetic fibers exit from the base of the brain and from spinal cord areas shown in green.

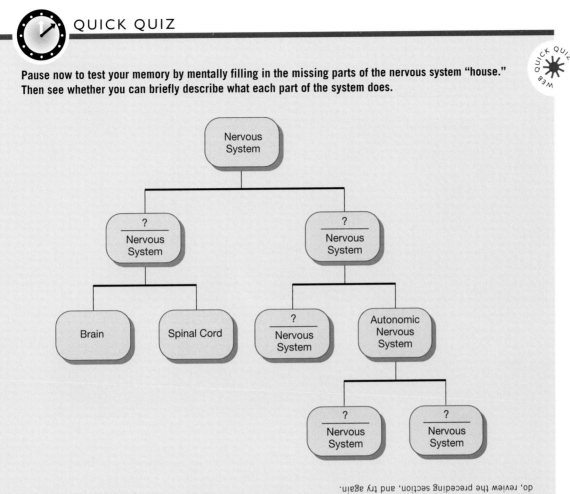

QUICK QUIZ

Pause now to test your memory by mentally filling in the missing parts of the nervous system "house." Then see whether you can briefly describe what each part of the system does.

Answers:
Check your answers against Figure 4.3 on the next page. If you had difficulty, or if you could label the parts but forgot what they do, review the preceding section, and try again.

What's Ahead

- Which cells are the nervous system's "communication specialists," and how do they "talk" to each other?

- How do learning and experience alter the brain's circuits?

- Why do neural impulses travel more slowly in babies than in adults?

- What happens when levels of brain chemicals called neurotransmitters are too low or too high?

- Which substances in the brain mimic the effects of morphine by dulling pain and promoting pleasure?

- Which hormones can improve your memory?

4.2 Communication in the Nervous System

The blueprint we have just described provides only a general idea of the nervous system's structure. Now let's turn to the details.

The nervous system is made up in part of **neurons,** or *nerve cells.* These neurons are held in place by **glial cells** (from the Greek for "glue"). Glial cells, which greatly outnumber neurons, also provide the neurons with nutrients, insulate the neurons, and remove cellular debris when the neurons die. Many neuroscientists suspect that glial cells carry electrical or chemical signals between parts of the nervous system, signals that affect neighboring neurons. It is the neurons,

neuron
A cell that conducts electrochemical signals; the basic unit of the nervous system; also called a *nerve cell.*

glial cells
Nervous-system cells that aid the neurons by providing them with nutrients, insulating them, and removing cellular debris when they die.

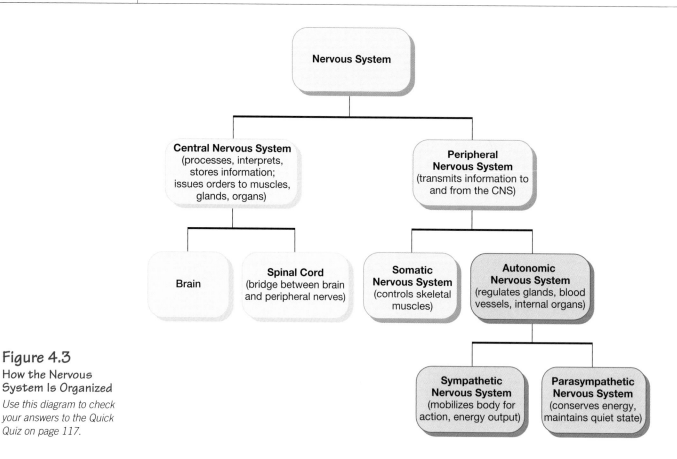

Figure 4.3
How the Nervous
System Is Organized

*Use this diagram to check
your answers to the Quick
Quiz on page 117.*

4.1

dendrites
The branches of a neuron
that receive information from
other neurons and transmit it
toward the cell body.

however, that are the communication specialists, transmitting signals to, from, or within the central nervous system.

Although neurons are often called the building blocks of the nervous system, in structure they are more like snowflakes than blocks, exquisitely delicate and differing from one another greatly in size and shape (see Figure 4.4). In the giraffe, a neuron that runs from the spinal cord down the animal's hind leg may be 9 feet long! In the human brain, neurons are microscopic. No one is sure how many neurons the human brain contains, but a typical estimate is 100 billion, about the same number as there are stars in our galaxy—and some estimates go much higher.

The Structure of the Neuron

As you can see in Figure 4.5, a neuron has three main parts: *dendrites,* a *cell body,* and an *axon.* The **dendrites** look like the branches of a tree; indeed,

Figure 4.4
Different Kinds of Neurons

*Neurons vary in size and shape, depending on their location and
function. More than 200 types of neurons have been identified
in mammals.*

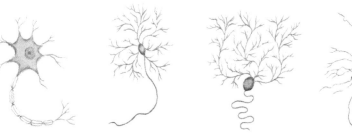

Spinal cord   Thalamus   Cerebellum   Cortex
(motor neuron)

the word dendrite means "little tree" in Greek. Dendrites act like antennas, receiving messages from as many as 10,000 other nerve cells and transmitting these messages toward the cell body. The **cell body,** which is shaped roughly like a sphere or a pyramid, contains the biochemical machinery for keeping the neuron alive. As we will see later, it also determines whether the neuron should "fire"—that is, transmit a message to other neurons—based on the inputs from other neurons. The **axon** (from the Greek for "axle") transmits messages away from the cell body to other neurons or to muscle or gland cells. Axons commonly divide at the end into branches, called *axon terminals.* In adult human beings, axons vary from only 4 thousandths of an inch to a few feet in length. Dendrites and axons give each neuron a double role: As one researcher put it, a neuron is first a catcher, then a batter (Gazzaniga, 1988).

Many axons, especially the larger ones, are insulated by a surrounding layer of fatty material called the **myelin sheath,** which is made up of glial cells. This covering is divided into segments that make it look a little like a string of link sausages (see Figure 4.5 again). One purpose of the myelin sheath is to prevent signals in adjacent cells from interfering with each other. Another, as we will see shortly, is to speed up the conduction of neural impulses. In individuals with multiple sclerosis, loss of myelin causes erratic nerve signals, leading to loss of sensation, weakness or paralysis, lack of coordination, or vision problems.

In the peripheral nervous system, the fibers of individual neurons (axons and sometimes dendrites) are collected together in bundles called **nerves,** rather like the lines in a telephone cable.

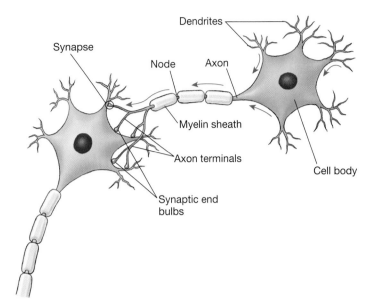

Figure 4.5
The Structure of a Neuron
Incoming neural impulses are received by the dendrites of a neuron and are transmitted to the cell body. Outgoing signals pass along the axon to terminal branches.

The human body has 43 pairs of peripheral nerves; one nerve from each pair is on the left side of the body, and the other is on the right. Most of these nerves enter or leave the spinal cord, but the 12 pairs that are in the head, the *cranial nerves,* connect directly to the brain. In Chapter 5, we will discuss cranial nerves that are involved in the senses of smell, hearing, and vision.

Until recently, neuroscientists thought that neurons in the central nervous system could neither reproduce (multiply) nor regenerate (grow back). The assumption was that no new CNS neurons arose after infancy, and that if cells in the brain or spinal cord were injured or damaged, nothing could be done. But then the conventional wisdom got overthrown. Animal studies showed that severed axons in the spinal cord *can* regrow if you treat them with certain nervous-system chemicals (Schnell & Schwab, 1990). And Canadian neuroscientists working with mice discovered that immature cells, called *precursor cells,* will give birth to new neurons (a process called *neurogenesis*) when immersed in a growth-promoting protein in the laboratory. The new neurons will then continue to divide and multiply (Reynolds & Weiss, 1992). One of the researchers, Samuel Weiss, said that this result "challenged everything I had read;

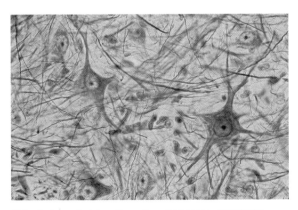

This photograph, taken through a microscope, reveals the delicate fibers of human motor neurons.

cell body
The part of the neuron that keeps it alive and determines whether it will fire.

axon
A neuron's extending fiber, which conducts impulses away from the cell body and transmits them to other neurons or to muscle or gland cells.

myelin sheath
A fatty insulation that may surround the axon of a neuron.

nerve
A bundle of nerve fibers (axons and sometimes dendrites) in the peripheral nervous system.

everything I had learned when I was a student" (quoted in Barinaga, 1992).

We now know that the human brain also contains precursor cells (sometimes called *progenitor* or *stem cells*), and that these cells, too, give rise to new neurons when treated in the laboratory. Even more astonishing, in rodents and monkeys, precursor cells in an area associated with learning and memory continue to divide and mature throughout adulthood (Gage et al., 1998; Gould et al., 1998). Researchers who studied the brains of five elderly people who had died of cancer found evidence of the very same process (Eriksson et al., 1998). Animal studies suggest that we have some control over that process, because physical and mental exercise promote the production and survival of these new cells (Gould et al., 1999; Kempermann, Brandon, & Gage, 1998; van Praag, Kempermann, & Gage, 1999). On the other hand, stress can inhibit the production of new cells (Gould et al., 1998), and nicotine can kill them (Berger, Gage, & Vijayaraghavan, 1998).

Each year brings ever more findings that only a short time ago would have seemed like science fiction. Animal research has raised hopes that regenerated axons will someday enable people with spinal-cord injuries to use their limbs again, and that transplanted precursor cells from embryos or adults will help people recover from brain damage. Some experimental surgeries have already been performed, and although the results are still uncertain, such daring experiments will continue. Eventually, treatments inspired by basic research on neurons may be among the most stunning contributions of biological research.

synapse
The site where a nerve impulse is transmitted from one nerve cell to another; it includes the axon terminal, the synaptic cleft, and receptor sites in the membrane of the receiving cell.

How Neurons Communicate

Neurons do not directly touch each other, end to end. Instead, they are separated by a minuscule space called the *synaptic cleft,* where the axon terminal of one neuron nearly touches a dendrite or the cell body of another. The entire site—the axon terminal, the cleft, and the covering membrane of the receiving dendrite or cell body—is called a **synapse.** Because a neuron's axon may have hundreds or even thousands of terminals, a single neuron may have synaptic connections with a great many others. As a result, the number of communication links in the nervous system runs into the trillions or perhaps even the quadrillions.

When we are born, most of these synapses have not yet formed (see Figure 4.6). Throughout life, axons and dendrites continue to grow, and tiny projections on dendrites, called *spines,* increase in size and in number, producing more complex connections among the brain's nerve cells. Just as new learning and stimulating environments promote the production of new neurons, they also produce the greatest increases in synaptic complexity (Diamond, 1993; Greenough & Anderson, 1991; Greenough & Black, 1992; Rosenzweig, 1984). Throughout life, too, some unused synaptic connections are lost as cells or their branches die and are not replaced. Thus, the brain's circuits are continually changing in response to information, challenges, and changes in the environment.

This remarkable *plasticity* (flexibility) may help explain why people with brain damage sometimes experience amazing recoveries—why individuals who cannot recall simple words after a stroke may be speaking normally within a matter of months, and why patients who cannot move an arm after a head injury may regain full use of it after physical therapy. Their brains have rewired themselves to adapt to the damage! Recent research with 13 stroke patients who each had a paralyzed arm suggests that the brain can actually be coaxed to perform such rewiring (Liepert et al., 2000). The patients' good arms were immobilized so that they had to try to use their paralyzed limbs. After only a

Contrary to what scientists once thought, the brain produces new neurons throughout life. In an area associated with learning and memory, new cells develop from immature "precursor" cells, and physical and mental stimulation promotes their production and survival. These mice, who have toys to play with, tunnels to explore, wheels to run on, and other mice to share their cage with, will grow more cells than mice living in standard cages.

few weeks of intensive therapy, the patients regained nearly full use of their limbs. What's more, an area on the injured side of the brain responsible for arm movements had nearly doubled! Further studies of this promising therapy are currently under way.

Neurons speak to one another, or in some cases to muscles or glands, in an electrical and chemical language. When a nerve cell is stimulated, a change in electrical potential occurs between the inside and the outside of the cell. The physics of this process involves the sudden, momentary inflow of positively charged sodium ions across the cell's membrane, followed by the outflow of positively charged potassium ions. The result is a brief change in electrical voltage—an *action potential*—which produces an electrical current or impulse.

If an axon is unmyelinated, the action potential at each point in the axon gives rise to a new action potential at the next point; thus, the action potential travels down the axon somewhat as fire travels along the fuse of a firecracker. But in myelinated axons, the process is a little different. Conduction of a neural impulse beneath the sheath is impossible, in part because sodium and potassium ions cannot cross the cell's membrane except at the breaks (nodes) between the myelin's "sausages." Instead, the action potential "hops" from one node to the next. (More specifically, positively charged ions flow down the axon at a very fast rate, causing regeneration of the action potential at each node.) This arrangement allows the impulse to travel faster than it could if the action potential had to be regenerated at every point along the axon. Nerve impulses travel more slowly in babies than in older children and adults because when babies are born, the myelin sheaths on their axons are not yet fully developed.

When a neural impulse reaches the axon terminal's buttonlike tip, it must get its message across the synaptic cleft to another cell. At this point, *synaptic vesicles,* tiny sacs in the tip of the axon terminal, open and release a few thousand molecules of a chemical substance called a **neurotransmitter.** Like sailors carrying a message from one island to another, these molecules then diffuse across the synaptic cleft (see Figure 4.7).

When they reach the other side, the neurotransmitter molecules bind briefly with *receptor sites,* special molecules in the membrane of the receiving neuron, fitting these sites much as a key fits a lock. Changes occur in the receiving neuron's membrane, and the ultimate effect is either

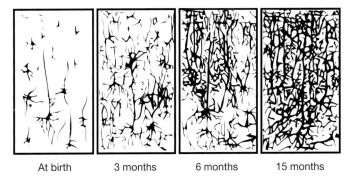

Figure 4.6
Getting Connected

Neurons in a newborn's brain are widely spaced, but they immediately begin to form connections. These drawings show the marked increase in the size and number of neurons from birth to age 15 months.

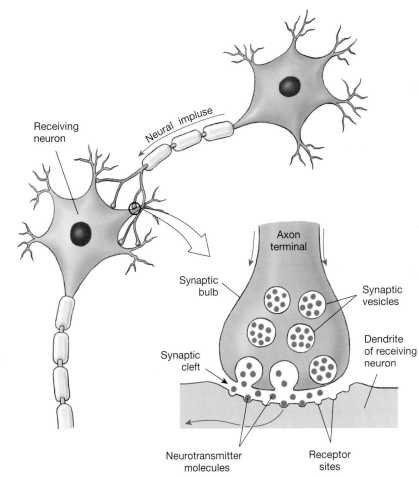

Figure 4.7
Neurotransmitter Crossing a Synapse

Neurotransmitter molecules are released into the synaptic cleft between two neurons from vesicles (chambers) in the transmitting neuron's axon terminal. The molecules then bind to receptor sites on the receiving neuron. As a result, the electrical state of the receiving neuron changes, and the neuron becomes either more or less likely to fire an impulse, depending on the type of transmitter substance.

excitatory (a voltage shift in a positive direction) or *inhibitory* (a voltage shift in a negative direction), depending on which receptor sites have been activated. If the effect is excitatory, the probability that the receiving neuron will fire increases; if it is inhibitory, the probability decreases. Inhibition in the nervous system is extremely important. Without it, we could not sleep or coordinate our movements. Excitation of the nervous system would be overwhelming, producing convulsions.

What any given neuron does at any given moment depends on the net effect of all the messages being received from other neurons. Only when the cell's voltage reaches a certain threshold will it fire. Thousands of messages, both excitatory and inhibitory, may be coming into the cell. Essentially, the neuron must average them. But how it does this, and how it "decides" whether to fire, is still not well understood. The message that reaches a final destination depends on the rate at which individual neurons are firing, how many are firing, what types of neurons are firing, and where the neurons are located. It does *not* depend on how strongly the neurons are firing, however, because a neuron always either fires or it doesn't. Like the turning on of a light switch, the firing of a neuron is an *all-or-none* event.

Chemical Messengers in the Nervous System

The nervous system "house" would remain forever dark and lifeless without chemical couriers such as the neurotransmitters. Let's look more closely now at these substances, and at two other types of chemical messengers: endorphins and hormones.

Neurotransmitters: Versatile Couriers.
As we have seen, neurotransmitters make it possible for one neuron to excite or inhibit another. Neurotransmitters exist not only in the brain, but also in the spinal cord, the peripheral nerves, and certain glands. Through their effects on specific nerve circuits, these substances can affect mood, memory, and well-being. The nature of the effect depends on the level of the neurotransmitter and its location. Hundreds of substances are known or suspected to be neurotransmitters, and the number keeps growing. Here are a few of the better-understood neurotransmitters and some of their known or suspected effects:

- *Serotonin* affects neurons involved in sleep, appetite, sensory perception, temperature regulation, pain suppression, and mood.

- *Dopamine* affects neurons involved in voluntary movement, learning, memory, and emotion.

- *Acetylcholine* affects neurons involved in muscle action, cognitive functioning, memory, and emotion.

- *Norepinephrine* affects neurons involved in increased heart rate and the slowing of intestinal activity during stress, and neurons involved in learning, memory, dreaming, waking from sleep, and emotion.

- *GABA (gamma-aminobutyric acid)* functions as the major inhibitory neurotransmitter in the brain.

Harmful effects can occur when neurotransmitter levels are too high or too low. Low levels of serotonin and norepinephrine have been associated with severe depression. Abnormal GABA levels have been implicated in sleep and eating

The brains of Alzheimer's patients produce an abnormally low level of the neurotransmitter acetylcholine, which may help account for some of the memory losses associated with this tragic disease.

neurotransmitter
A chemical substance that is released by a transmitting neuron at the synapse and that alters the activity of a receiving neuron.

disorders and in convulsive disorders, including epilepsy (Bekenstein & Lothman, 1993). People with Alzheimer's disease—a devastating condition that leads to memory loss, personality changes, and eventual disintegration of all physical and mental abilities—lose brain cells responsible for producing acetylcholine, and this deficit may help account for their memory problems. Later, we will see that a loss of dopamine is responsible for the symptoms of Parkinson's disease.

We want to warn you, however, that pinning down the relationship between neurotransmitter abnormalities and behavioral abnormalities is extremely difficult. Each neurotransmitter plays multiple roles, and the functions of different substances often overlap. Further, it is always possible that something about a disorder leads to abnormal neurotransmitter levels, instead of the other way around. Although drugs that boost or decrease levels of particular neurotransmitters are sometimes effective in treating disorders, that does not necessarily mean that abnormal neurotransmitter levels are causing the disorders. After all, aspirin can relieve a headache, but headaches are not caused by a lack of aspirin!

Many of us regularly do things that affect our own neurotransmitters, usually without knowing it. Most recreational drugs produce their effects by blocking or enhancing the actions of neurotransmitters. So do some herbal remedies. For example, St. John's Wort, which many people take for depression, prevents the cells that release serotonin from reabsorbing excess molecules that have remained in the synaptic gap; as a result, serotonin levels rise. Many people do not realize that such remedies, because they affect the nervous system's biochemistry, can interact with other medications and can be harmful in high doses. Even ordinary foods can influence the availability of neurotransmitters in the brain, as we discuss in "Taking Psychology with You."

Endorphins: The Brain's Natural Opiates.
Another intriguing group of chemical messengers is known collectively as *endogenous opioid peptides,* or more popularly as **endorphins.** Endorphins have effects similar to those of natural opiates; that is, they reduce pain and promote pleasure. They are also thought to play a role in appetite, sexual activity, blood pressure, mood, learning, and memory. Some endorphins function as neurotransmitters, but most act primarily as *neuromodulators,* which alter the effects of neuro-

transmitters—for example, by limiting or prolonging those effects.

Endorphins were identified in the early 1970s. Candace Pert and Solomon Snyder (1973) were doing research on morphine, a pain-relieving and mood-elevating opiate derived from heroin, which is made from poppies. They found that morphine works by binding to receptor sites in the brain. This seemed odd. As Snyder later recalled, "We doubted that animals had evolved opiate receptors just to deal with certain properties of the poppy plant" (quoted in Radetsky, 1991). Pert and Snyder reasoned that if opiate receptors exist, then the body must produce its own internally generated, or *endogenous,* morphinelike substances, which they named "endorphins." Soon they and other researchers confirmed this hypothesis.

Endorphin levels seem to shoot up when an animal or a person is afraid or under stress. This is no accident; by making pain bearable in such situations, endorphins give a species an evolutionary advantage. When an organism is threatened, it needs to do something fast. Pain, however, can interfere with action: A mouse that pauses to lick a wounded paw may become a cat's dinner; a soldier who is overcome by an injury may never get off the battlefield. But, of course, the body's built-in system of counteracting pain is only partly successful, especially when painful stimulation is prolonged.

A link may also exist between endorphins and the pleasures of social contact. When young puppies, guinea pigs, and chicks are injected with low doses of either morphine or endorphins, the animals show much less distress than usual when separated from their mothers. (In all other respects, they behave normally.) The morphine or endorphins seem to provide a biochemical replacement for the mother, or, more precisely, for the endorphin surge presumed to occur during contact with her. Conversely, when young guinea pigs and chicks received a chemical that *blocks* the effects of opiates, their crying increases (Panksepp et al., 1980). These findings suggest that endorphin-stimulated euphoria may be a child's initial motive for seeking affection and cuddling—that, in effect, a child attached to a parent is a child addicted to love.

Hormones: Long-Distance Messengers.
Hormones, which make up the third class of chemical messengers, are substances that are produced primarily in **endocrine glands.** They are released directly into the bloodstream,

4.1

endorphins (en-DOR-fins)
Chemical substances in the nervous system that are similar in structure and action to opiates; they are involved in pain reduction, pleasure, and memory, and are known technically as *endogenous opioid peptides.*

hormones
Chemical substances, secreted by organs called *glands,* that affect the functioning of other organs.

endocrine glands
Internal organs that produce hormones and release them into the bloodstream.

which carries them to organs and cells that may be far from their point of origin. Hormones have dozens of jobs, from promoting bodily growth to aiding digestion to regulating metabolism.

Neurotransmitters and hormones are not always chemically distinct; the two classifications are like clubs that admit some of the same members. A particular chemical, such as norepinephrine, may belong to more than one classification, depending on where it is located and what function it is performing. Nature has been efficient, giving some substances more than one task to perform.

The following hormones, among others, are of particular interest to psychologists:

1 Melatonin, which is secreted by the *pineal gland,* deep within the brain, promotes sleep. It also helps to regulate (and in turn is regulated by) a "biological clock" in the brain—a cluster of cells that coordinates an array of bodily rhythms, including the 24-hour wake–sleep cycle (Haimov & Lavie, 1996). The pineal gland responds to light and dark via complex connections that originate in the back of the eye. When you go to sleep in a darkened room, your melatonin level rises; when you wake up in the morning to a lightened room, it falls. Melatonin treatments have been used to synchronize the disturbed sleep–wake cycles of blind people who lack light perception and whose melatonin production does not cycle normally (Sack & Lewy, 1997). However, efforts to treat the insomnia of sighted people by giving them melatonin have been sparse, and the results have been mixed (*UC Berkeley Wellness Letter,* May 2000). Melatonin supplements sold over the counter should be used with caution, if at all, because there are no federal standards for quality or dosage, and the long-term safety of such treatments is not yet known.

2 Adrenal hormones, which are produced by the *adrenal glands* (organs that are perched right above the kidneys), are involved in emotion and stress (see Chapter 12). These hormones also rise in response to nonemotional conditions, such as heat, cold, pain, injury, burns, and physical exercise, and in response to some drugs, such as caffeine and nicotine. The outer part of each adrenal gland produces *cortisol,* which increases blood-sugar levels and boosts energy. The inner part produces *epinephrine* (popularly known as adrenaline) and *norepinephrine.* When adrenal hormones are released in your body, they activate the sympathetic nervous system, which in turn increases your arousal level and prepares you for action.

Adrenal hormones also enhance memory. If you give people a drug that prevents their adrenal glands from producing these hormones, they will remember less about emotional stories they heard than control subjects will (Cahill et al., 1994). Conversely, if you give epinephrine to animals right after learning, their memories will improve (McGaugh, 1990). In real life, the hormones that flood the body during a traumatic or upsetting experience may make the event *too* memorable and may even account for the persistent "flashbacks" that some survivors of trauma suffer. Work is now under way to find out whether drugs that block these hormones immediately after such an event will help prevent the later development of these troubling symptoms (McGaugh, 1999). For ordinary learning, however—the kind of learning you do in school—high hormone levels may interfere with memory, and a moderate level is optimal. You should therefore aim for an arousal level somewhere between "hyper" and "laid back."

3 Sex hormones, which are secreted by tissue in the gonads (testes in men, ovaries in women), and also by the adrenal glands, include three main types, all occurring in both sexes but in differing amounts and proportions in males and females after the onset of puberty. *Androgens* (the most important of which is *testosterone*) are masculinizing hormones produced mainly in the testes but also in the ovaries and the adrenal glands. Androgens set in motion the physical changes males experience at puberty—for example, a deepened voice and facial and chest hair—and cause pubic and underarm hair to develop in females. Testosterone also influences sexual arousal in both sexes. *Estrogens* are feminizing hormones that bring on physical changes in females at puberty, such as breast development and the onset of menstruation, and that influence the course of the menstrual cycle. *Progesterone* contributes to the growth and maintenance of the uterine lining in preparation for a fertilized egg, among other functions. Estrogens and progesterone are produced mainly in the ovaries but are also produced in the testes and the adrenal glands. Researchers are now studying the possible involvement of sex hormones in behavior not directly related to sex and reproduction. For example, many researchers believe that estrogen may contribute to improved learning and memory by promoting the formation of synapses in certain areas of the brain (Sherwin, 1998a; Wickelgren, 1997).

melatonin
A hormone, secreted by the pineal gland, that is involved in the regulation of daily biological rhythms.

adrenal hormones
Hormones that are produced by the adrenal glands and that are involved in emotion and stress.

sex hormones
Hormones that regulate the development and functioning of reproductive organs and that stimulate the development of male and female sexual characteristics; they include androgens, estrogens, and progesterone.

QUICK QUIZ

You can activate your neurotransmitters by taking this quiz.

A. Which word in parentheses best fits each of the following definitions?

1. Basic building blocks of the nervous system (*nerves/neurons*)

2. Cell parts that receive nerve impulses (*axons/dendrites*)

3. Site of communication between neurons (*synapse/myelin sheath*)

4. Opiate-like substance in the brain (*dopamine/endorphin*)

5. Chemicals that make it possible for neurons to communicate (*neurotransmitters/hormones*)

6. Hormone closely associated with emotional excitement (*epinephrine/estrogen*)

B. *True or false:* To remember the material in this chapter well, you should be as relaxed as possible while studying.

C. Imagine that you are depressed, and you hear about a treatment that affects the levels of several neurotransmitters thought to be involved in the disorder. Based on what you have learned, what questions would you want to ask before deciding whether to try the treatment?

Answers:

A. 1. neurons 2. dendrites 3. synapse 4. endorphin 5. neurotransmitters 6. epinephrine B. false (Can you say why?) C. You might want to ask, among other things, about side effects (each neurotransmitter has several functions, all of which might be affected by the treatment); about evidence that the treatment works; and about whether there is any reason to believe that your own neurotransmitter levels are abnormal or whether there may be other reasons for your depression.

What's Ahead

- Why are patterns of electrical activity in the brain called "brain waves"?

- What scanning techniques allow psychologists to view changes in brain activity while people listen to music or solve math problems?

4.3 Mapping the Brain

We come now to the main room of the nervous system "house": the brain. A disembodied brain stored in a formaldehyde-filled container is unexciting—a putty-colored, wrinkled glob of tissue that looks a little like an oversized walnut. It takes an act of imagination to envision this modest-looking organ writing *Hamlet*, discovering radium, or inventing the paper clip.

In a living person, of course, the brain is encased in a thick protective vault of bone. How, then, can scientists study it? One approach is to study patients who have had a part of the brain damaged or removed because of disease or injury. Another, called the *lesion method,* involves damag-ing or removing sections of brain in animals, then observing the effects.

The brain can also be probed with devices called *electrodes.* Some electrodes are coin-shaped and are simply pasted or taped onto the scalp. They detect the electrical activity of millions of neurons in particular regions of the brain and are widely used in research and medical diag-nosis. The electrodes are connected by wires to a machine that translates the electrical energy from the brain into wavy lines on a moving piece of paper or visual patterns on a screen. That is why electrical patterns in the brain are known as "brain waves." Different wave patterns are associated with sleep, relaxation, and mental concentration.

A brain-wave recording is called an **electro-encephalogram (EEG).** A standard EEG is useful but not very precise because it reflects the activities of many cells at once. "Listening" to the brain with an EEG machine is like standing outside a sports stadium: You know when something is happen-ing, but you can't be sure what it is or who is doing it. Fortunately, computer technology can be combined with EEG technology to get a clearer picture of brain activity patterns associated with specific events and mental processes; the computer

electroencephalogram (EEG)
A recording of neural activity detected by electrodes.

Electroencephalograms (EEGs) use electrodes to produce an overall picture of electrical activity in different areas of the brain.

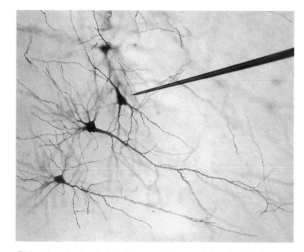

This microelectrode is being used to record the electrical impulses generated by a single cell in the brain of a monkey.

suppresses all the background "noise," leaving only the "melody"—the pattern of electrical responses to the event being studied.

For even more precise information, researchers use *needle electrodes,* very thin wires or hollow glass tubes that can be inserted into the brain, either directly in an exposed brain or through tiny holes in the skull. Only the skull and the membranes covering the brain need to be anesthetized; the brain itself, which processes all sensation and feeling, paradoxically feels nothing when touched. Therefore, a human patient or an animal can be awake and not feel pain during the procedure. Needle electrodes can be used both to record electrical activity from the brain and to stimulate the brain with weak electrical currents. Stimulating a given area often results in a specific sensation or movement. *Microelectrodes* are so fine that they can be inserted into single cells.

Since the mid-1970s, even more amazing doors to the brain have opened. The **PET scan (positron-emission tomography)** goes beyond anatomy to record biochemical changes in the brain as they are happening. One type of PET scan takes advantage of the fact that nerve cells convert glucose, the body's main fuel, into energy. A researcher can inject a patient with a glucoselike substance that contains a harmless radioactive element. This substance accumulates in brain areas that are particularly active and are consuming glucose rapidly. The substance emits radiation, which is a telltale sign of activity, like cookie crumbs on a child's face. The radiation is detected by a scanning device, and the result is a computer-processed picture of biochemical activity on a display screen, with different colors indicating different activity levels. Other kinds of PET scans measure blood flow or oxygen consumption, which also reflect brain activity.

PET scans, which were originally designed to diagnose abnormalities, have produced evidence that certain brain areas in people with emotional disorders are either unusually quiet or unusually active. But PET technology can also show which parts of the brain are active during ordinary activities and emotions. It lets researchers see which areas are busiest when a person hears a song, recalls a sad memory, works on a math problem, or shifts attention from one task to another. The

PET scan (positron-emission tomography)
A method for analyzing biochemical activity in the brain, using injections of a glucose-like substance containing a radioactive element.

MRI (magnetic resonance imaging)
A method for studying body and brain tissue, using magnetic fields and special radio receivers.

PET scans in Figure 4.8 show what an average healthy brain looks like when a person is doing different tasks.

Another technique, **MRI (magnetic resonance imaging),** allows the exploration of "inner space" without injecting chemicals. Powerful magnetic fields and radio frequencies are used to produce vibrations in the nuclei of atoms making up body organs, and the vibrations are then picked up as signals by special receivers. A computer analyzes the signals, taking into account their strength and duration, and converts them into a high-contrast picture of the organ (see Figure 4.9). An ultrafast version of MRI, called *functional MRI,* can capture brain changes many times a second as a person performs a task, such as reading a sentence or solving a puzzle.

Still other scanning methods are becoming available with each passing year. Some even produce a moving picture that shows ongoing changes in the brain. A word of caution, though: Brain scans alone do not tell us precisely what is happening inside a person's head, either mentally or physiologically. Enthusiasm for new technology has produced a mountain of findings, but also some unwarranted conclusions about "brain centers" or "critical circuits" for this or that behavior. One scientist (cited in Wheeler, 1998) drew this analogy: A researcher scans the brains of gum-chewing volunteers, finds out which parts of their brains are active, and concludes that he or she has found the brain's "gum-chewing center"!

Descriptive studies using brain scans, then, are just a first step in understanding brain processes. Nonetheless, they are an exciting first step. We will

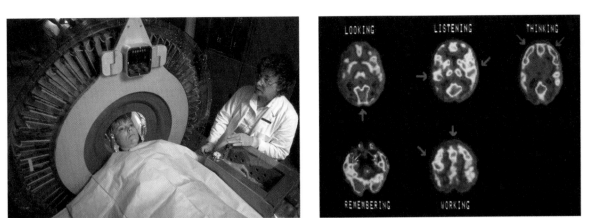

Figure 4.8
PET Scans of Metabolic Activity in the Brain

On the left, a woman lies with her head in a PET scanner, which will detect biochemical activity in specific brain areas. In the scans on the right, red indicates areas of highest activity and violet indicates areas of lowest activity. Clockwise starting from the upper left, the arrows point to regions that are most active when the person looks at a complicated visual scene, listens to a sound, performs a mental task, moves the right hand, or recalls stories heard previously.

be reporting many findings from PET-scan and MRI research throughout this book. The brain can no longer hide from researchers behind the fortress of the skull. It is now possible to get a clear visual image of our most enigmatic organ without so much as lifting a scalpel.

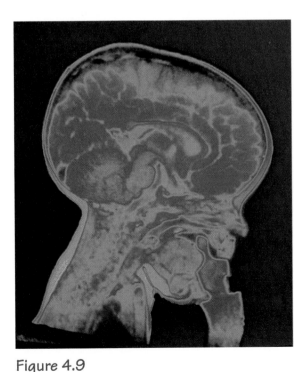

Figure 4.9
MRI of a Child's Brain

This MRI shows a child's brain—and the bottle he was drinking from while the image was obtained.

What's Ahead

- Which brain part acts as a "traffic officer" for incoming sensations?

- Which brain part is the "gateway to memory"— and what cognitive catastrophe occurs when it is damaged?

- Why is it a good thing that the outer covering of the human brain is so wrinkled?

- How did a bizarre nineteenth-century accident illuminate the role of the frontal lobes?

4.4 A Tour Through the Brain

All modern brain theories assume that different brain parts perform different (though overlapping) tasks. This concept, known as **localization of function,** goes back at least to Joseph Gall (1758–1828), the Austrian anatomist who thought that personality traits were reflected in the development of specific areas of the brain (see Chapter 1). Gall's theory of *phrenology* was completely wrongheaded (so to speak), but his general notion of specialization in the brain had merit.

To learn about what the various brain structures do, let's take an imaginary stroll through the brain. Pretend, now, that you have shrunk to a

4.3

localization of function
Specialization of particular brain areas for particular functions.

microscopic size and that you are wending your way through the "soul's frail dwelling house," starting at the lower part, just above the spine. Figure 4.10 shows the major structures we will encounter along the tour; you may want to refer to it as we proceed.

The Brain Stem

We begin at the base of the skull with the **brain stem,** which began to evolve some 500 million years ago in segmented worms. The brain stem looks like a stalk rising out of the spinal cord. Pathways to and from upper areas of the brain pass through its two main structures: the **medulla** and the **pons.** The pons is involved in (among other things) sleeping, waking, and dreaming. The medulla is responsible for bodily functions that do not have to be consciously willed, such as breathing and heart rate. Hanging has long been used as a method of execution because when it breaks the neck, nervous pathways from the medulla are severed, stopping respiration.

brain stem
The part of the brain at the top of the spinal cord, consisting of the medulla and the pons.

medulla
A structure in the brain stem responsible for certain automatic functions, such as breathing and heart rate.

pons
A structure in the brain stem involved in, among other things, sleeping, waking, and dreaming.

reticular activating system (RAS)
A dense network of neurons found in the core of the brain stem; it arouses the cortex and screens incoming information.

Extending upward from the core of the brain stem is the **reticular activating system (RAS).** This dense network of neurons, which extends above the brain stem into the center of the brain and has connections with higher areas, screens incoming information and arouses the higher centers when something happens that demands their attention. Without the RAS, we could not be alert or perhaps even conscious.

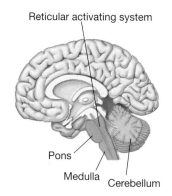

The Cerebellum

Standing atop the brain stem and looking toward the back part of the brain, we see a structure about the size of a small fist. It is the **cerebellum,** or "lesser brain," which contributes to a sense of balance and coordinates the muscles so that movement is smooth and precise. If your cerebellum were damaged, you would probably become exceedingly clumsy and uncoordinated. You might have trouble using a pencil, threading a needle, or even walking. In addition, this structure is involved in remembering certain simple skills and acquired reflexes (Daum & Schugens, 1996; Krupa, Thompson, & Thompson, 1993). Some researchers think that the cerebellum also plays a role in analyzing sensory information, solving problems, and understanding words (Fiez, 1996; Gao et al., 1996; Müller, Courchesne, & Allen, 1998).

The Thalamus

Deep in the brain's interior, we can see the **thalamus,** the busy traffic officer of the brain. As sensory messages come into the brain, the thalamus directs them to higher centers. For example, the sight of a sunset sends signals that the thalamus directs to a vision area, and the sound of an oboe sends signals that the thalamus sends on to an auditory area. The only sense that completely bypasses the thalamus is the sense of smell, which

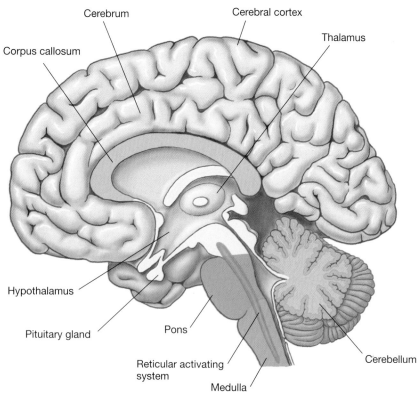

Figure 4.10
The Human Brain
This cross section depicts the brain as if it were split in half. The view is of the inside surface of the right half, and shows the structures described in the text.

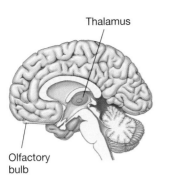

Thalamus

Olfactory
bulb

has its own private switching station, the *olfactory bulb.* The olfactory bulb lies near areas involved in emotion. Perhaps that is why particular odors—the smell of fresh laundry, gardenias, a steak sizzling on the grill—often rekindle memories of important personal experiences.

The Hypothalamus and the Pituitary Gland

Beneath the thalamus sits a structure called the **hypothalamus** (*hypo* means "under"). It is involved in drives associated with the survival of both the individual and the species—hunger, thirst, emotion, sex, and reproduction. It regulates body temperature by triggering sweating or shivering, and it controls the complex operations of the autonomic nervous system. It also contains the biological clock that controls the body's daily rhythms.

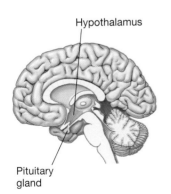

Hypothalamus

Pituitary
gland

Hanging down from the hypothalamus, connected to it by a short stalk, is a cherry-sized endocrine gland called the **pituitary gland.** The pituitary is often called the body's "master gland" because the hormones it secretes affect many other endocrine glands. The master, however, is really only a supervisor. The true boss is the hypothalamus, which sends chemicals to the pituitary, telling it when to "talk" to the other endocrine glands. The

pituitary, in turn, sends hormonal messages out to these glands.

The Limbic System

The hypothalamus has many connections to a set of loosely interconnected structures called the **limbic system,** shown in Figure 4.11 on the next page. (*Limbic* comes from the Latin for "border": These structures form a sort of border between the higher and lower parts of the brain.) Some anatomists include the hypothalamus and parts of the thalamus in the limbic system. Although the usefulness of speaking of the limbic system as an integrated set of structures is now in dispute, it is clear that structures in this region are heavily involved in emotions, such as rage and fear, that we share with other animals (MacLean, 1993).

Many years ago, James Olds and Peter Milner reported finding "pleasure centers" in the limbic system (Olds, 1975; Olds & Milner, 1954). Olds and Milner trained rats to press a lever in order to get a buzz of electricity delivered through tiny electrodes to the limbic system. Some rats would press the bar thousands of times an hour, for 15 or 20 hours at a time, until they collapsed from exhaustion. When they revived, they went right back to the bar. When forced to make a choice, the hedonistic rodents opted for electrical stimulation over such temptations as water, food, and even an attractive rat of the other sex that was making provocative gestures. Today, researchers believe that brain stimulation activates neural pathways rather than discrete "centers," and that changes in neurotransmitter or neuromodulator levels are involved.

The Amygdala.
One limbic structure that especially concerns psychologists is the **amygdala,** which appears to be responsible for evaluating sensory information, quickly determining its emotional importance, and contributing to the initial decision to approach or withdraw from a person or situation (see Chapter 12). For example, it instantly assesses danger or threat. The amygdala also plays an important role in mediating anxiety and depression; PET scans find that depressed and anxious patients show increased neural activity in this structure (Schulkin, 1994).

The Hippocampus.
Another important limbic area is the **hippocampus,** which has a shape that must have reminded someone of a sea horse, for that is what its name means. This structure

cerebellum
A brain structure that regulates movement and balance, and that is involved in the learning of certain kinds of simple responses.

thalamus
A brain structure that relays sensory messages to the cerebral cortex.

hypothalamus
A brain structure involved in emotions and drives vital to survival, such as fear, hunger, thirst, and reproduction; it regulates the autonomic nervous system.

pituitary gland
A small endocrine gland at the base of the brain, which releases many hormones and regulates other endocrine glands.

limbic system
A group of brain areas involved in emotional reactions and motivated behavior.

amygdala
A brain structure involved in the arousal and regulation of emotion and the initial emotional response to sensory information.

hippocampus
A brain structure involved in the storage of new information in memory.

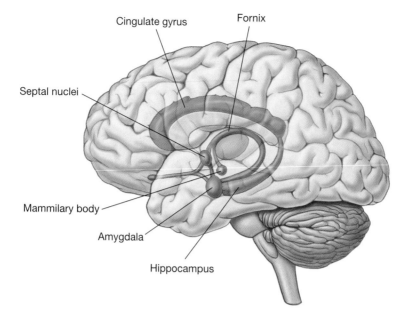

Figure 4.11
The Limbic System
Structures of the limbic system play an important role in memory and emotion. The text describes two of these structures, the amygdala and the hippocampus.

compares sensory information with what the brain has learned to expect about the world. When expectations are met, it tells the reticular activating system to "cool it." There's no need for neural alarm bells to go off every time a car goes by, a bird chirps, or you feel your saliva trickling down the back of your throat!

The hippocampus has also been called the "gateway to memory." It enables us to form spatial memories so that we can accurately navigate through our environment (Maguire et al., 2000). And, along with adjacent brain areas, it enables us to form new memories about facts and events—the kind of information you need to identify a flower, tell a story, or recall a vacation trip. This information is then stored in the cerebral cortex, which we will be discussing shortly. For example, when you recall meeting someone yesterday, various aspects of the memory—information about the person's greeting, tone of voice, appearance, and location—are probably stored in different locations in the cortex (Damasio et al., 1996; Squire, 1987). But without the hippocampus, the information would never get to these destinations (Mishkin et al., 1997; Squire & Zola-Morgan, 1991).

We know about the "gateway" function of the hippocampus in part from research on brain-damaged patients with severe memory problems. The case of one man, known to researchers as H. M., is probably the most intensely studied in the annals of medicine (Corkin, 1984; Corkin et al., 1997; Milner, 1970; Ogden & Corkin, 1991).

In 1953, when H. M. was 27, surgeons removed most of his hippocampus, along with part of his amygdala. The operation was a last-ditch effort to relieve H. M.'s severe and life-threatening epilepsy. People who have *epilepsy*, a neurological disorder that has many causes and takes many forms, often have seizures. Usually, the seizures are brief, mild, and controllable by drugs, but in H. M.'s case, they were unrelenting and uncontrollable.

The operation did achieve its goal: Afterward, the young man's seizures were milder and could be managed with medication. His memory, however, had been affected profoundly. Although H. M. continued to recall most events that had occurred before the operation, he could no longer remember new experiences for much longer than 15 minutes; they vanished like water down the drain. With sufficient practice, H. M. could acquire new manual or problem-solving skills, such as playing tennis or solving a puzzle, but he could not remember the training sessions in which he learned these skills. He would read the same magazine over and over without realizing it. He could not recall the day of the week, the year, or even his last meal. Most scientists attribute these deficits to an inability to form new memories for long-term storage.

Today, many years later, H. M. will occasionally recall an unusually emotional event, such as the assassination of someone named Kennedy. He sometimes remembers that both his parents are dead, and he knows he has memory problems. But, according to Suzanne Corkin, who has studied

H. M. extensively, these "islands of remembering" are the exceptions in a vast sea of forgetfulness. This good-natured man still does not know the scientists who have studied him for decades. He thinks he is much younger than he is, and he can no longer recognize a photograph of his own face; he is stuck in a time warp from the past.

Scientists are starting to understand just what happens in the hippocampus and in nearby structures during the formation of a long-term memory. For example, some synaptic pathways become more easily excitable and therefore more receptive to further impulses (McNaughton & Morris, 1987). But these changes and others take time, which may explain why memories remain vulnerable to disruption for a while after they are stored. Just as concrete takes time to set, memories require a period of *consolidation,* or stabilization, before they solidify.

The Cerebrum

At this point in our tour, the largest part of the brain still looms above us. It is the cauliflower-like **cerebrum,** where the higher forms of thinking take place. The complexity of the human brain's circuitry far exceeds that of any computer in existence, and much of its most complicated wiring is packed into this structure. Compared with many other creatures, we humans may be ungainly, feeble, and thin-skinned, but our well-developed cerebrum enables us to overcome these limitations and creatively control our environment (and, some would say, to mess it up).

The cerebrum is divided into two separate halves, or **cerebral hemispheres,** connected by a large band of fibers called the **corpus callosum.** In general, the right hemisphere is in charge of the left side of the body and the left hemisphere is in charge of the right side of the body. As we will see shortly, the two hemispheres also have somewhat different tasks and talents, a phenomenon known as **lateralization.**

The Cerebral Cortex. Working our way right up through the top of the brain, we find that the cerebrum is covered by several thin layers of densely packed cells known collectively as the **cerebral cortex.** Cell bodies in the cortex, as in many other parts of the brain, produce a grayish tissue; hence the term *gray matter.* In other parts of the brain (and in the rest of the nervous system), long, myelin-covered axons prevail, providing the brain's *white matter.* Although the cortex is only about 3 millimeters thick, it contains almost three-fourths of all the cells in the human brain. The cortex has many deep crevasses and wrinkles, which enable it to contain its billions of neurons without requiring us to have the heads of giants—heads that would be too big to permit us to be born. In other mammals, which have fewer neurons, the cortex is less crumpled; in rats, it is quite smooth.

Lobes of the Cortex. On each cerebral hemisphere, deep fissures divide the cortex into four distinct regions, or lobes (see Figure 4.12):

- The **occipital lobes** (from the Latin for "in back of the head") are at the lower back part of the brain. Among other things, they contain the *visual cortex,* where visual signals are processed. Damage to the visual cortex can cause impaired visual recognition or even blindness.

- The **parietal lobes** (from the Latin for "pertaining to walls") are at the top of the brain. They contain the *somatosensory cortex,* which receives information about pressure, pain, touch, and temperature from all over the body. The areas of the somatosensory cortex that receive signals from the hands and the face are disproportionately large because these body parts are particularly sensitive.

cerebrum (suh-REE-brum)
The largest brain structure, consisting of the upper part of the brain; it is in charge of most sensory, motor, and cognitive processes. (From the Latin for "brain.")

cerebral hemispheres
The two halves of the cerebrum.

corpus callosum
The bundle of nerve fibers connecting the two cerebral hemispheres.

lateralization
Specialization of the two cerebral hemispheres for particular operations.

cerebral cortex
A collection of several thin layers of cells covering the cerebrum; it is largely responsible for higher mental functions; cortex is Latin for "bark" or "rind."

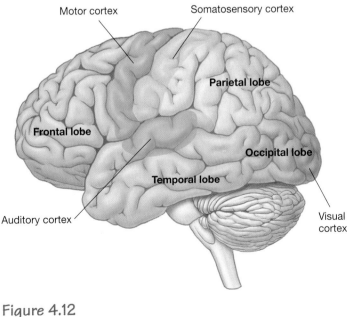

Figure 4.12
Lobes of the Cerebral Cortex
Deep fissures divide the cortex of each cerebral hemisphere into four regions.

4.2

occipital [ahk-SIP-uh-tuhl] lobes
Lobes at the lower back part of the brain's cerebral cortex; they contain areas that receive visual information.

parietal [puh-RYE-uh-tuhl] lobes
Lobes at the top of the brain's cerebral cortex; they contain areas that receive information on pressure, pain, touch, and temperature.

temporal lobes
Lobes at the sides of the brain's cerebral cortex; they contain areas involved in hearing, memory, perception, emotion, and (in the left lobe, typically) language comprehension.

frontal lobes
Lobes at the front of the brain's cerebral cortex; they contain areas involved in short-term memory, higher-order thinking, initiative, social judgment, and (in the left lobe, typically) speech production.

■ The **temporal lobes** (from the Latin for "pertaining to the temples") are at the sides of the brain, just above the ears, behind the temples. They are involved in memory, perception, and emotion, and they contain the *auditory cortex,* which processes sounds. An area of the left temporal lobe known as *Wernicke's area* is involved in language comprehension.

■ The **frontal lobes,** as their name indicates, are located toward the front of the brain, just under the skull in the area of the forehead. They contain the *motor cortex,* which issues orders to the 600 muscles of the body that produce voluntary movement. In the left frontal lobe, a region known as *Broca's area* handles speech production. During short-term memory tasks, areas in the frontal lobes are especially active (Goldman-Rakic, 1996). The frontal lobes are also involved in the ability to make plans, think creatively, and take initiative.

When a surgeon probes these four pairs of lobes with an electrode, different things tend to happen (although there is some overlap). If a surgeon applied electrical current to your somato-sensory cortex in the parietal lobes, for example, you would probably feel a tingling in your skin or a sense of being gently touched. If your visual cortex in the occipital lobes were electrically stimulated, you might report a flash of light or swirls of color. And, eerily, many areas of your cortex, when stimulated, would do nothing at all.

The "silent" areas are sometimes called the *association cortex,* because they are involved in higher mental processes. Psychologists are especially interested in the forwardmost part of the frontal lobes, the *prefrontal cortex.* This area barely exists in mice and rats and takes up only 3.5 percent of the cerebral cortex in cats, about 7 percent in dogs, and 17 percent in chimpanzees. In human beings, it accounts for fully 29 percent of the cortex.

Scientists have long known that the frontal lobes, and the prefrontal cortex in particular, must have something to do with personality. The first clue appeared in 1848, when a bizarre accident drove an inch-thick, 3½-foot-long iron rod clear through the head of a young railroad worker named Phineas Gage. As you can see in Figure 4.13, the rod (which is still on display at Harvard University, along with Gage's skull) entered beneath his left eye and exited

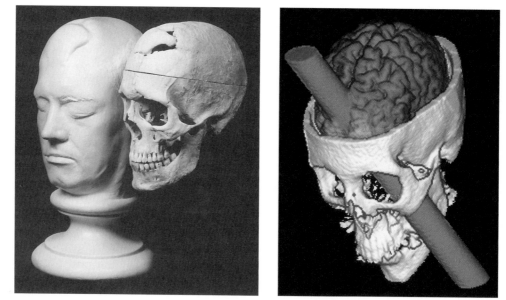

Figure 4.13
A Famous Skull

On the left is Phineas Gage's skull and a cast of his head. You can see where an iron rod penetrated his skull, altering his behavior and personality dramatically. The exact location of the brain damage remained controversial for almost a century and a half, until Hanna and Antonio Damasio and their colleagues (1994) used measurements of Gage's skull and MRIs of normal brains to plot possible trajectories of the rod. The reconstruction on the right shows that the damage occurred in an area of the prefrontal cortex associated with emotional processing and rational decision making.

through the top of his head, destroying much of his prefrontal cortex (H. Damasio et al., 1994). Miraculously, Gage survived this trauma and retained the ability to speak, think, and remember. But his friends complained that he was "no longer Gage." In a sort of Jekyll-and-Hyde transformation, he had changed from a mild-mannered, friendly, efficient worker into a foul-mouthed, ill-tempered, undependable lout who could not hold a steady job or stick to a plan. His employers had to let him go, and he was reduced to exhibiting himself as a circus attraction.

This sad case and others suggest that parts of the frontal lobes are involved in social judgment, rational decision making, and the ability to set goals and to make and carry through plans (Klein & Kihlstrom, 1998). As neurologist Antonio Damasio (1994) wrote, "Gage's unintentional message was that observing social convention, behaving ethi-cally, and, in general, making decisions advanta-geous to one's survival and progress, require both knowledge of rules and strategies and the integrity of specific brain systems." Interestingly, the mental deficits that characterize damage to these areas are accompanied by a flattening out of emotion and feeling, which suggests that normal emotions are necessary for everyday reasoning and the ability to learn from mistakes.

The frontal lobes also govern the ability to do a series of tasks in the proper sequence and to stop doing them at the proper time. The pioneering Soviet psychologist Alexander Luria (1980) studied many cases in which damage to the frontal lobes disrupted these abilities. One man observed by Luria kept trying to light a match after it was already lit. Another planed a piece of wood in the hospital carpentry shop until it was gone, and then went on to plane the workbench!

QUICK QUIZ

It's time again to see how your own brain is working. Match each description on the left with a term on the right.

1. Filters out irrelevant information

2. Known as the "gateway to memory"

3. Controls the autonomic nervous system; involved in drives associated with survival

4. Consists of two hemispheres

5. Wrinkled outer covering of the brain

6. Site of the motor cortex; associated with planning and taking initiative

a. reticular activating system

b. cerebrum

c. hippocampus

d. cerebral cortex

e. frontal lobes

f. hypothalamus

Answers:
1.a 2.c 3.f 4.b 5.d 6.e

What's Ahead

- If the two cerebral hemispheres were out of touch, would they feel different emotions and think different thoughts?

- Why do researchers often refer to the left hemisphere as "dominant"?

- Should you sign up for a program that promises to perk up the right side of your brain?

4.5 The Two Hemispheres of the Brain

We have seen that the cerebrum is divided into two hemispheres that control opposite sides of the body. Although similar in structure, these hemi-spheres have somewhat separate talents, or areas of specialization.

Split Brains: A House Divided

In a normal brain, the two hemispheres communicate with one another across the corpus callosum, the bundle of fibers that connects them. Whatever happens in one side of the brain is instantly flashed to the other side. What would happen, though, if the two sides were cut off from one another?

In 1953, Ronald E. Myers and Roger W. Sperry took the first step toward answering this question by severing the corpus callosum in cats. Normally,

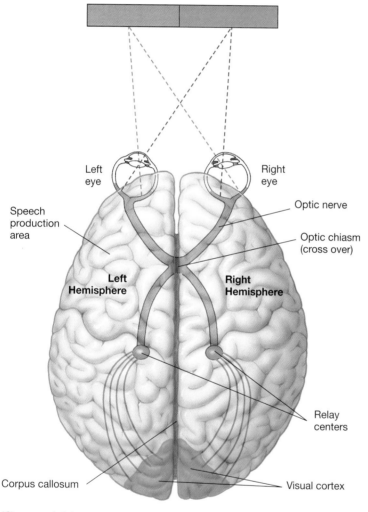

Speech production area

Left eye

Right eye

Optic nerve

Optic chiasm (cross over)

Left Hemisphere

Right Hemisphere

Relay centers

Corpus callosum

Visual cortex

Figure 4.14
Visual Pathways

Each brain hemisphere receives information from the eyes about the opposite side of the visual field. Thus, if you stare directly at the corner of a room, everything to the left of the juncture is represented in your right cerebral hemisphere and vice versa. This is so because half of the axons in each optic nerve cross over (at the optic chiasm) to the opposite side of the brain. Normally, each hemisphere immediately shares its information with the other one, but in split-brain patients, severing the corpus callosum prevents such communication.

each eye (in cats and in humans) transmits messages to both sides of the brain (see Figure 4.14). After this procedure, a cat's left eye sent information only to the left hemisphere and its right eye sent information only to the right hemisphere.

At first, the cats did not seem to be affected much by this drastic operation. But Myers and Sperry showed that something profound had happened. They trained the cats to perform tasks with one eye blindfolded. For example, a cat might have to push a panel with a square on it to get food but ignore a panel with a circle. Then the researchers switched the blindfold to the cat's other eye and tested the animal again. Now the cats behaved as if they had never learned the trick. Apparently, one side of the brain did not know what the other side was doing. It was as if the animals had two minds in one body. Later studies confirmed this result with other species, including monkeys (Sperry, 1964).

In all the animal studies, ordinary behavior, such as eating and walking, remained normal. Encouraged by this finding, in the early 1960s, a team of surgeons decided to try cutting the corpus callosum in patients with debilitating, uncontrollable epilepsy. In severe forms of this disease, disorganized electrical activity spreads from an injured area to other parts of the brain. The surgeons reasoned that cutting the connection between the two halves of the brain might stop the spread of electrical activity from one side to the other.

The results of this *split-brain surgery* generally proved successful. Seizures were reduced and sometimes disappeared completely. As an added bonus, these patients gave scientists a chance to find out what each half of the brain can do when it is quite literally cut off from the other. It was already known that the two hemispheres are not mirror images of each other. In most people, language is largely handled by the left hemisphere; thus, a person who suffers brain damage because of a stroke—a blockage in or rupture of a blood vessel in the brain—is much more likely to have language problems if the damage is in the left side than if it is in the right. How would splitting the brain affect language and other abilities?

In their daily lives, split-brain patients did not seem much affected by the fact that the two sides of their brains were incommunicado. Their personalities and intelligence remained intact; they could walk, talk, and in general lead normal lives. Apparently, connections in the undivided brain stem kept body movements normal. But in a series of ingenious studies, Sperry and his colleagues (and later other researchers) showed that perception and memory had been affected, just as they had been in earlier animal research. In 1981, Sperry won a Nobel Prize for his work.

To understand this research, refer again to Figure 4.14. If you look straight ahead, everything in the left side of the scene before you—the "visual field"—goes to the right half of your brain, and everything in the right side of the scene goes to the left half of your brain. This is true for both eyes.

The experimental procedure was to present information to only one or the other side of the subjects' brains. In one early study (Levy, Trevarthen, & Sperry, 1972), the researchers took photographs of different faces, cut them in two, and pasted different halves together. The reconstructed photographs were then presented on slides. The person was told to stare at a dot on the middle of the screen, so that half the image fell to the left of this point and half to the right. Each image was flashed so quickly that the person had no time to move his or her eyes. When the subjects were asked to say what they had seen, they named the person in the right part of the image (which would be the little boy in Figure 4.15). But when they were asked to point with their left hands to the face they had seen, they chose the person in the left side of the image (the mustached man in the figure). Further, they claimed they had noticed nothing unusual about the original photographs! Each side of the

brain saw a different half-image and automatically filled in the missing part. Neither side knew what the other side had seen.

Why did the patients name one side of the picture but point to the other? Speech centers are in the left hemisphere. When the person responded with speech, it was the left side of the brain doing the talking. When the person pointed with the left hand, which is controlled by the right side of the brain, the right hemisphere was giving its version of what the person had seen.

In another study, the researchers presented slides of ordinary objects and then suddenly flashed a slide of a nude woman. Both sides of the brain were amused, but because only the left side has speech, the two sides responded differently. When the picture was flashed to one woman's left hemisphere, she laughed and identified it as a nude. When it was flashed to her right hemisphere, she said nothing but began to chuckle. Asked what she was laughing at, she said, "I don't know . . . nothing . . . oh—that funny machine." The right hemisphere could not describe what it had seen, but it reacted emotionally, just the same (Gazzaniga, 1967).

A Question of Dominance

Dozens of people have undergone the split-brain operation since the mid-1960s, and research on left–right differences has also been done with people whose brains are intact (Springer & Deutch,

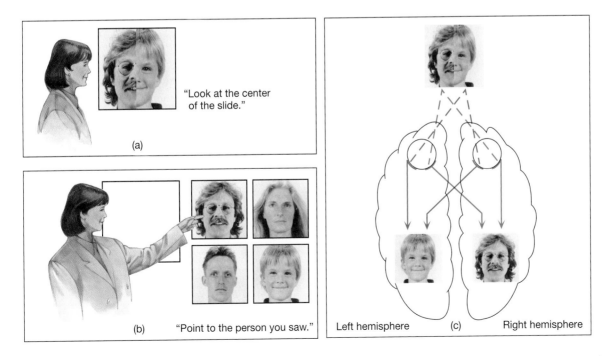

(a) "Look at the center of the slide."

(b) "Point to the person you saw."

Left hemisphere   (c)   Right hemisphere

Figure 4.15
Divided Brain, Divided View

When split-brain patients were shown composite photographs (a) and were then asked to pick out the face they had seen from a series of intact photographs (b), they said they had seen the face on the right side of the composite—yet they pointed with their left hands to the face that had been on the left. Because the two cerebral hemispheres could not communicate, the verbal left hemisphere was aware of only the right half of the picture, and the relatively mute right hemisphere was aware of only the left half (c).

1998). Electrodes and PET scans have been used to gauge activity in the left and right hemispheres while people perform different tasks. The results confirm that nearly all right-handed people and a majority of left-handers process language mainly in the left hemisphere. The left side is also more active during some logical, symbolic, and sequential tasks, such as solving math problems and understanding technical material. Because of its cognitive talents, many researchers refer to the left hemisphere as *dominant.* They believe that the left hemisphere usually exerts control over the right hemisphere. One well-known split-brain researcher, Michael Gazzaniga (1983), has argued that without help from the left side, the right side's mental skills would probably be "vastly inferior to the cognitive skills of a chimpanzee." He and others also believe that a mental "module" in the left hemisphere is constantly trying to explain actions and emotions generated by brain parts whose workings are nonverbal and outside of awareness.

You can see in split-brain patients how the left hemisphere concocts such explanations. In one classic example, a picture of a chicken claw was flashed to a patient's left hemisphere, a picture of a snow scene to his right. The task was to point to a related image for each picture from an array, with a chicken the correct choice for the claw and a shovel for the snow scene. The patient chose the shovel with his left hand and the chicken with his right. When asked to explain why, he responded (with his left hemisphere) that the chicken claw went with the chicken, and the shovel was for cleaning out the chicken shed. The left hemisphere had seen the left hand's response but did not know about the snow scene, so it interpreted the response by using the information it did have (Gazzaniga, 1988). In people with intact brains, says Gazzaniga, the left side's interpretations account for the sense of a unified, coherent identity.

Other researchers, including Sperry (1982), have rushed to the right hemisphere's defense. The right side, they point out, is no dummy. It is superior in problems requiring spatial–visual ability, the ability you use to read a map or follow a dress pattern, and it excels in facial recognition and the ability to read facial expressions. It is active during the creation and appreciation of art and music. It recognizes nonverbal sounds, such as a dog's barking. The right hemisphere also has some language ability. Typically, it can read a word briefly flashed to it and can understand an experimenter's instructions. In a few split-brain patients, the right hemisphere's language ability has been quite well developed.

Some researchers have credited the right hemisphere with having a cognitive style that is intuitive and holistic (in which things are seen as wholes), in contrast to the left hemisphere's more rational and analytic mode. However, many researchers are concerned about popular misinterpretations of this conclusion. Books and programs that promise to make you more "right-brained," they observe, ignore the fact that the right hemisphere is not always a hero: It contains regions that process negative emotions like fear and sadness and it is associated with the tendency to withdraw from others (Davidson, 1995; Harmon-Jones & Allen, 1998). Further, the differences between the two sides are relative, not absolute—a matter of degree. In most real-life activities, the two hemispheres cooperate naturally, with each making a valuable contribution. As Sperry (1982) himself once noted, "The left–right dichotomy . . . is an idea with which it is very easy to run wild."

Thinking Critically About "Right Brain/Left Brain" Theories

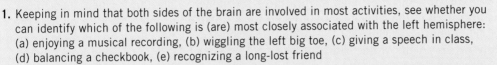

QUICK QUIZ

Use as many parts of your brain as necessary to answer these questions.

1. Keeping in mind that both sides of the brain are involved in most activities, see whether you can identify which of the following is (are) most closely associated with the left hemisphere: (a) enjoying a musical recording, (b) wiggling the left big toe, (c) giving a speech in class, (d) balancing a checkbook, (e) recognizing a long-lost friend

2. Over the past decades, thousands of people have taken courses and bought tapes that promise to develop the "creativity" and "intuition" of their right hemispheres. What characteristics of human thought might explain the eagerness of some people to glorify "right-brainedness" and disparage "left-brainedness" (or vice versa)?

Answers:

1. c, d 2. One possible answer: Human beings like to make sense of the world, and one easy way to do that is to divide humanity into opposing categories. This kind of either-or thinking can lead to the conclusion that fixing up one brain hemisphere (e.g., making "left-brained" types more "right-brained") will make individuals happier and the world a better place. If only it were that simple!

What's Ahead

- How do biological theories of dreaming differ from the familiar Freudian view?

- Do men talk about sports and women about feelings because their brains are different?

4.6 Two Stubborn Issues in Brain Research

If you have mastered the definitions and descriptions in this chapter, you are prepared to read popular accounts of advances in neuropsychology. But many questions remain about how the brain works, and we will end this chapter with two of them.

Why Do We Dream?

One of the oldest mysteries about the brain is why it seems to "shut down" for sleep yet remains active by providing us with strange and colorful nightly dreams.

One obvious function of sleep is to provide a time-out period, so that the body can eliminate waste products from muscles, repair cells, strengthen the immune system, and recover physical abilities lost during the day. Our nightly slumbers also

appear to help the brain function efficiently. After the loss of even a single night's sleep, mental flexibility, attention, and creativity all suffer. In chronic sleep deprivation, high levels of the stress hormone cortisol may damage or impair brain cells that are necessary for learning and memory (Leproult et al., 1997). Not surprisingly, when people are sleepy, traffic and work accidents become far more likely (Coren, 1996; Maas, 1998). And after several days of sleep deprivation, people become extremely irritable and begin to have hallucinations and delusions (Dement, 1978).

Sleep, then, is obviously necessary for alert mental functioning. But why do we spend a good part of each night flying through the air, battling monsters, or having

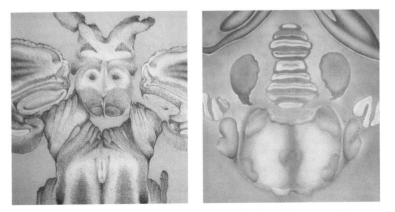

These drawings from a dream journal show how fanciful dream imagery can be.

weird conversations in the fantasy world of our dreams? Biological research is beginning to reveal the answers.

The Realms of Sleep.

Until the early 1950s, little was known about dreaming. Then a breakthrough occurred in the laboratory of physiologist Nathaniel Kleitman, who at the time was the only person in the world who had spent an entire career studying sleep. Kleitman had given one of his graduate students, Eugene Aserinsky, the tedious task of finding out whether the slow, rolling eye movements that characterize the onset of sleep continue throughout the night. To both men's surprise, eye movements did indeed occur, but they were rapid, not slow (Aserinsky & Kleitman, 1955). Using the electroencephalograph to measure the brain's electrical activity, these researchers, along with another of Kleitman's students, William Dement, were able to correlate the rapid eye movements with changes in sleepers' brain-wave patterns (Dement, 1992). Adult volunteers were soon spending their nights sleeping in laboratories while scientists observed them and measured changes in their brain activity, muscle tension, breathing, and other physiological responses.

As a result of this research, today we know that during sleep, periods of **rapid eye movement (REM)** alternate with periods of fewer eye movements, or *non-REM (NREM)*, in a cycle that recurs about every 90 minutes or so. The REM periods last from a few minutes to as long as an hour, averaging about 20 minutes. Whenever they begin, the pattern of electrical activity from the sleeper's brain changes to resemble that of alert wakefulness. Non-REM periods are themselves divided into four shorter stages, each associated with a particular brain-wave pattern.

In the first stage, you feel yourself drifting on the edge of consciousness. In the second, you are sleeping soundly enough to be undisturbed by minor noises. In the third, your brain waves, breathing, and pulse have slowed down considerably, and you are hard to arouse. And in the fourth, you are in deep sleep and are difficult to awaken, though oddly, this is when sleeptalking and sleepwalking are most likely to occur. (The causes of sleepwalking, which occurs more often in children than adults, are still under investigation.)

Then you move back up the ladder, from Stage 4 to 3 to 2 to 1. At that point, about 70 to 90 minutes after the onset of sleep, something peculiar happens. Stage 1 does not turn into drowsy wakefulness, as one might expect. Instead, your brain begins to emit long bursts of very rapid, somewhat irregular waves. Your heart rate increases, your blood pressure rises, and your breathing becomes faster and more irregular. Small twitches in your face and fingers may occur. In men, the penis becomes somewhat erect, as vascular tissue relaxes and blood fills the genital area more quickly than it exits. In women, the clitoris enlarges and vaginal lubrication increases. At the same time, most of your skeletal muscles go limp, preventing your aroused brain from producing physical movement. You have entered the realm of REM.

Because the brain is extremely active while the body is entirely inactive, REM sleep has also been called "paradoxical sleep." It is during these periods that you are most likely to dream. Even people who claim they never dream at all will report dreams if awakened in a sleep laboratory during REM sleep. But dreaming is also reported during non-REM sleep, though the dreams tend to be shorter and to be less vivid and fantastical (Foulkes, 1962).

REM and non-REM sleep continue to alternate throughout the night, with the REM periods tending to get longer and closer together as the hours pass. An early REM period may last only a few minutes, whereas a later one may go on for 20 or 30 minutes and sometimes as long as an hour. This pattern explains why you are likely to be dreaming when the alarm clock goes off in the morning.

The Dreaming Brain.

In the past, most theories of dreaming have been psychological. Sigmund Freud, for example, proposed that we dream in order to gratify unconscious wishes and longings, often sexual or violent in nature (Freud, 1900/1953). If the dream arouses anxiety, said Freud, the rational part of the mind disguises its message; otherwise the dream would intrude into consciousness and waken the dreamer. To Freud,

Live! psych
4.5

rapid eye movement (REM) sleep
Sleep periods characterized by fast eye movement, loss of muscle tone, and dreaming.

Because cats sleep so much—up to 80 percent of the time—it is easy to catch them in the various stages of slumber. A cat in non-REM sleep (left) remains upright, but during the REM phase (right), its muscles go limp and it flops onto its side.

every dream had a hidden meaning, no matter how absurd the images might seem.

Others have emphasized the ongoing conscious preoccupations of waking life, such as concerns about relationships, work, sex, or health (Domhoff, 1996; Punamaeki & Joustie, 1998; Webb & Cartwright, 1978). For example, college students often dream that they are unprepared for an exam, or that they have shown up for the wrong exam, or that they can't find the room where the exam is being given (Halliday, 1993; Van de Castle, 1994). And, you may be gratified to know, instructors often dream that they have forgotten their lecture notes at home, or that their notes contain only blank pages and they have nothing to say!

Biological researchers, however, believe that dreams originate not in the psyche but in the physiological workings of the brain. For example, Francis Crick and Graeme Mitchison (1995) argue that during REM sleep a sort of "reverse learning" occurs. Unused synaptic connections in the brain, they say, become weaker, making memory more efficient and accurate and protecting us from becoming obsessed by unwanted thoughts and images. In this view, dreams are merely mental garbage, and there's no point in trying to remember or analyze them. Other researchers emphasize the *strengthening* of synaptic connections associated with recently stored memories; they find that disruptions of REM sleep impair memory for a task and normal REM sleep enhances it (Karni et al., 1994). This research does not really explain why we dream, however.

Probably the most influential biological theory is the **activation-synthesis theory,** proposed by Allan Hobson (1988, 1990). To Hobson, dreams have a most unromantic source: neurons that are firing spontaneously in the lower part of the brain, in the pons. These neurons control eye movement, gaze, balance, and posture, and they send messages to areas of the cerebral cortex responsible for visual processing and voluntary action during wakefulness.

According to the activation-synthesis theory, signals originating in the pons have no psychological meaning in themselves. But the cortex tries to make sense of them by synthesizing, or combining, them with existing knowledge and memories to produce some sort of coherent interpretation—just as it would if the signals had come from sense organs during wakefulness. When neurons fire in the part of the brain that handles balance, for instance, the cortex may generate a dream

ACTIVATION-SYNTHESIS THEORY OF DREAMS

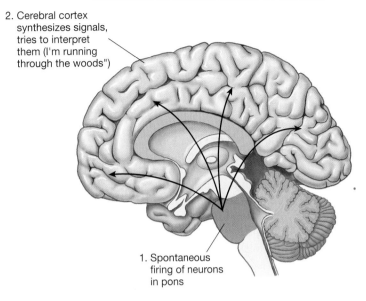

2. Cerebral cortex synthesizes signals, tries to interpret them (I'm running through the woods")

1. Spontaneous firing of neurons in pons

about falling. When signals occur that would ordinarily produce running, the cortex may manufacture a dream about being chased. Because the signals from the pons occur randomly, the cortex's interpretation—the dream—is likely to be incoherent and confusing. And because cortical neurons that control the initial storage of new memories are turned off during sleep, we typically forget our dreams upon waking unless we write them down or immediately recount them to someone else.

Wishes, in this view, do not cause dreams; brain-stem mechanisms do. But that does not mean that dreams are meaningless. Hobson (1988) has argued that the brain "is so inexorably bent upon the quest for meaning that it attributes and even creates meaning when there is little or none to be found in the data it is asked to process." By studying these attributed meanings, you can learn about your unique perceptions, conflicts, and concerns—not by trying to dig below the surface of the dream, as Freud would, but by examining the surface itself. Or you can relax and just enjoy the nightly entertainment that dreams provide.

This theory, like all other theories of dreaming, has come in for criticism (Squier & Domhoff, 1998). Not all dreams are as disjointed or bizarre as the theory predicts, and not all dreams occur during REM sleep. Perhaps it will turn out that different kinds of dreams have different purposes and origins. We all know from experience that some of our dreams seem to be related to daily problems,

activation-synthesis theory
The theory that dreaming results from the cortical synthesis and interpretation of neural signals triggered by activity in the lower part of the brain.

some are vague and incoherent, and some are anxiety dreams that occur when we are tense and worried. Biological approaches, however, present a challenge to traditional psychological theories and show us that much remains to be learned about the functions of dreaming and even of sleep itself.

Are There "His" and "Hers" Brains?

A second stubborn issue concerns the existence of sex differences in the brain. Historically, findings on male–female brain differences have often flip-flopped in a most suspicious manner, a result of the biases of the observers rather than the biology of the brain (Shields, 1975). For example, in the 1960s, scientists speculated that women were more "right-brained" and men were more "left-brained," which supposedly explained why men were "rational" and women "intuitive." Then, when the virtues of the right hemisphere were discovered, such as creativity and artistic ability, some researchers decided that men were more right-brained. But it is now clear that the abilities popularly associated with the two sexes do not fall neatly into the two hemispheres of the brain. The left side is more verbal (presumably a "female" trait), but it is also more mathematical (presumably a "male" trait). The right side is more intuitive ("female"), but it is also more spatially talented ("male").

To intelligently evaluate the issue of sex differences in the brain, we need to ask two questions: Do male and female brains differ physically? And if so, what, if anything, does this difference have to do with behavior?

Let's consider the first question. Several anatomical and biochemical sex differences have been found in animal brains, especially in areas related to reproduction, such as the hypothalamus (McEwen, 1983). Human sex differences, however, have been more elusive. Of course, we would expect to find male–female brain differences that are related to the regulation of sex hormones and other aspects of reproduction. But many researchers want to know whether there are differences that affect how men and women think or behave—and here, the picture is murkier.

For example, in 1982, two anthropologists autopsied 14 human brains and reported an average sex difference in the size and shape of the *splenium,* a small section at the end of the corpus cal-losum, the bundle of fibers dividing the cerebral hemispheres (de Lacoste-Utamsing & Holloway, 1982). The researchers concluded that women's brains are less lateralized for certain tasks than men's are—that men rely more heavily on one or the other side of the brain, whereas women tend to use both sides. This conclusion quickly made its way into newspapers, magazines, and even text-books as a verified sex difference.

Today, however, the picture has changed. In a review of the available studies, neuroscientist William Byne (1993) found that only the 1982 study reported the splenium to be larger in women. Two very early studies (in 1906 and 1909) found that it was larger in men, and 21 later studies found no sex difference at all. More-over, a Canadian analysis of 49 studies found only trivial differences between the two sexes, differences that paled in comparison with the huge individual variations *within* each sex (Bishop & Wahlsten, 1997). Most people are unaware of these findings because studies that find no differences rarely make headlines.

Researchers are now looking for other sex differences in the brain, such as in the density of neurons in specific areas. One team, examining nine brains from autopsied bodies, found that the women had an average of 11 percent more cells in areas of the cortex associated with the processing of auditory information; all of the women had more of these cells than did any of the men (Witelson, Glazer, & Kigar, 1994).

Some researchers are using high-tech methods to search for average sex differences in the brain areas that are active when people work on a particular task. In one study (Shaywitz et al., 1995), 19 men and 19 women were asked to say whether pairs of nonsense words rhymed, a task that required them to process and compare sounds. MRI scans showed that in both sexes an area at the front of the left hemisphere was activated. But in 11 of the women and none of the men, the corresponding area in the right hemisphere was also active (see Figure 4.16). These findings and similar ones are further evidence for a sex difference in lateralization, at least for this one type of language function. Such a difference could help explain why left-hemisphere damage is less likely to cause language problems in women than in men after a stroke (Inglis & Lawson, 1981; McGlone, 1978).

Over the next few years, research may reveal additional anatomical and information-processing differences in the brains of males and females. But even if such differences exist, we must then ask our

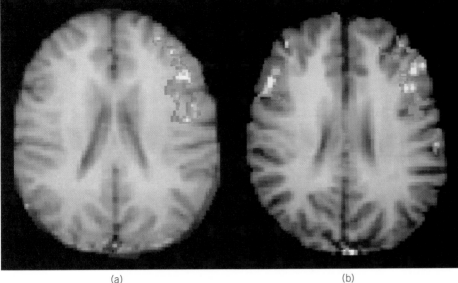

(a)   (b)

Figure 4.16
Gender and the Brain

These MRIs show that the brains of men and women tend to function differently during a task involving the comparison of sounds. (Because of the orientation of the images, the left hemisphere is seen on the right and vice versa.) During the first step in the task, the sounding out of words, the left-hemisphere area associated with speech production was active in all of the men's brains (a) and in 8 of the 19 women's brains. However, the other 11 women showed activity in both hemispheres (b). In spite of these brain differences, the two sexes performed equally well on the task. The researchers concluded that nature has provided the brain with different routes to the same ability (Shaywitz et al., 1995).

second question: *What do the differences mean for the behavior of men and women in real life—if anything?*

Some popular writers have been quick to assume that brain differences explain, among other things, women's allegedly superior intuition, women's love of talking about feelings and men's love of talking about sports, women's greater verbal ability, men's edge in math ability, and why men won't ask for directions when they're lost. But there are at least three problems with these conclusions:

Thinking Critically About Sex Differences in the Brain

1 *These supposed gender differences are stereotypes;* in each case, the overlap between the sexes is greater than the difference between them. As we saw in Chapter 1, even differences that are statistically significant are often quite small in practical terms (Hyde, 2000).

2 *A biological difference does not necessarily have behavioral implications.* Amid all the excitement about the MRI differences in the rhyme-judgment study, for example, hardly anyone seemed to notice that both sexes did equally well on the test!

So what are the MRI patterns actually explaining? Speculations are as plentiful as ants at a picnic, but at present they remain just that—speculations. To know whether sex differences in the brain translate into significant behavioral differences, we would need to know much more about how brain organization and chemistry affect human abilities and traits (Blum, 1997; Hoptman & Davidson, 1994).

3 *Sex differences in the brain could be the result rather than the cause of behavioral differences.* Remember that experiences in life are constantly sculpting the circuitry of the brain, affecting the way brains are organized and how they function—and males and females often have different experiences.

Thus, the answer to our second question, whether physical differences are linked to behavior, is "No one really knows." It is important to keep an open mind about new findings on sex differences in the brain, but because the practical significance of these findings (if any) is not clear, it is also important to be cautious and aware of how such results might be exaggerated and misused.

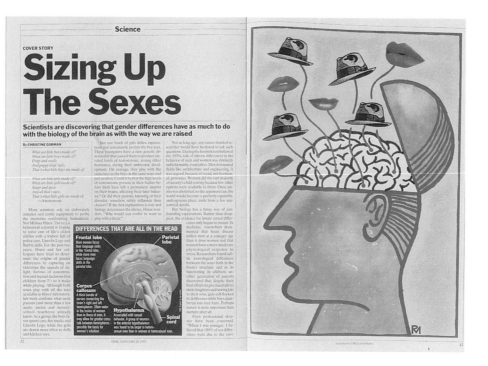

The press has been quick to run stories on differences in male and female brains. Many articles, such as this one from Time, conclude from interesting but tentative findings that gender differences in behavior must be biologically based. Is this conclusion justified? Why do you think the media give so much less attention to studies reporting similarities between the sexes?

QUICK QUIZ

Men and women alike have brains that can answer these questions.

1. Why is REM sleep called "paradoxical sleep"?

2. In the activation-synthesis theory of dreaming, what gets synthesized and what brain part does the synthesizing?

3. Name three reasons we should not assume that sex differences in the brain explain reported gender differences in behavior or cognition.

Answers:

1. The body is inactive but the brain is active and producing dreams. 2. The cortex synthesizes random signals from the pons with existing knowledge and memories to produce a coherent interpretation of the signals. 3. Most of the reported gender differences are stereotypes and small; in practical terms, a biological difference does not necessarily have important behavioral implications; and brain differences could be the result rather than the cause of behavioral differences.

The study of the brain illuminates the capacities we all share as human beings—thought, language, memory, emotion. But we want to close this chapter by underscoring a point we made in the previous section, in our discussion of sex differences: that each brain is unique, because each person's life experiences are unique. If you are a string musician, the area in your brain associated with music production is likely to be larger than that of nonmusicians (Jancke, Schlaug, & Steinmetz, 1997). If you are a cab driver, the area in your hippocampus responsible for visual representations of the environment is likely to be larger than average (Maguire et al., 2000). If you are bilingual and learned both of your languages in early childhood, you will probably use a single, uniform Broca's area to generate complex sentences in the two languages; but if you learned your second language during adolescence, your Broca's area will be divided into two distinct regions, one for each language (Kim et al., 1997).

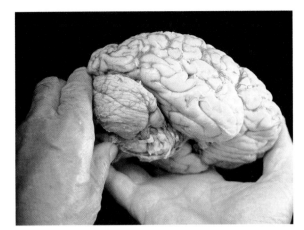

Experience sculpts the brain, so each brain is unique.

Roger Sperry (1982) once put it well: "The individuality inherent in our brain networks makes that of fingerprints or facial features gross and simple by comparison."

PSYCHOLOGY IN THE NEWS—REVISITED

Now that you know more about the workings of the brain, let's return to the problem of Parkinson's disease, the disorder suffered by Michael J. Fox.

The first symptom that Fox noticed, in 1991, was a persistent twitch in the little finger of his left hand. Eventually, the twitch spread to the entire hand, and as time went on, he developed tremors in his entire left side. Many Parkinson's patients experience not only tremors, but also stiffness, weakness, and rigidity. They may develop a shuffling walk, a rigid stoop, halting speech, and an unblinking expression. Individuals with advanced cases may seem to "freeze" for minutes or even hours, and about a third of them eventually show signs of dementia.

Parkinson's symptoms are due to the degeneration of brain cells that produce and use the neurotransmitter dopamine, which, as we saw, is involved in voluntary movement. The cause of this degeneration, like so much else about the brain, is still unknown. Injections of dopamine do not help, because dopamine molecules cannot cross the *blood–brain barrier,* a system of densely packed capillary and glial cells whose function is to prevent potentially harmful substances from entering the brain. Symptoms can be lessened by the administration of levodopa (L-dopa), which is a precursor (building block) of dopamine, but patients must take larger and larger doses to achieve the desired result. After a while, adverse effects, including depression, confusion, and even episodes of psychosis, may be worse than the disease itself.

Brain surgery has also been tried. In 1996, Fox underwent a surgical procedure that destroyed a part of the thalamus involved in movement control, and the worst of his tremors were relieved. During the 1990s, surgeons pioneered another dramatic approach. They grafted dopamine-producing brain tissue from aborted fetuses into the brains of Parkinson's patients and of patients with similar symptoms caused by use of a synthetic "designer" drug (Freed et al., 1993; Lindvall et al., 1994; Uchida & Toya, 1996; Widner et al., 1993). This method seemed promising but recently, controlled research—comparing patients receiving cell grafts with those getting only sham surgery—showed no overall benefits, and about 15 percent of the patients who got the grafts became much worse (Kolata, 2001). Nonetheless, some researchers are still hopeful that brain research will ultimately yield effective treatments.

Those are the physiological and medical facts. Fox's story, however, illustrates that to understand human beings we need to understand more than their brain chemistry. For one thing, the way the brain functions depends in part on a person's experiences: Overwork, you may recall, aggravated the actor's symptoms, and vacations reduced them. Nor can brain chemistry explain the grace and humor that Fox has brought to his battle—why he was able to joke that before his operation, his tremors were sometimes so uncontrollable that he "could mix a margarita in five seconds" (quoted in Perry, 2000). To understand how people step up to the curve balls that life throws their way, we need to consider not just their neurons but also their relationships, their cultural traditions, their life histories, and the way they explain and interpret the events that befall them.

The study of our most miraculous organ, the brain, helps us understand the abilities we all rely on and the memories and emotions that make us human. But analyzing a human being in terms of physiology alone is like analyzing the Taj Mahal solely in terms of the materials that were used to build it. Even if we could monitor every cell and circuit of the brain, we would still need to understand the circumstances, thoughts, and cultural rules that affect whether we are gripped by hatred, consumed by grief, lifted by love, or transported by joy.

TAKING PSYCHOLOGY WITH YOU

Food for Thought—Diet and Neurotransmitters

"Vitamin improves sex!" "Mineral boosts brainpower!" "Chocolate chases the blues!" Claims such as these have long given nutritional theories of behavior a bad reputation. In the late 1960s, when Nobel laureate Linus Pauling proposed that some mental disorders be treated with massive doses of vitamins, few researchers listened. Mainstream medical authorities classified Pauling's vitamin therapy with such infamous cure-alls as snake oil and leeches.

Today, most mental-health professionals remain skeptical of nutritional cures for mental illness. But the underlying premise of nutritional treatments—that diet affects the brain and therefore behavior—is no longer considered a fringe idea. Claims that sugar or common food additives lead to undesirable behavior in otherwise normal people have not been supported, but in some types of disorders, diet may make a difference. In one double-blind study, researchers asked depressed patients to abstain from refined sugar and caffeine. Over a three-month period, these patients showed significantly more improvement in their symptoms than did another group of patients who refrained from eating red meat and using artificial sweeteners (Christensen & Burrows, 1990).

Some of the most exciting work on diet and behavior has looked at the role played by nutrients in the synthesis of neurotransmitters, the brain's chemical messengers. *Tryptophan,* an amino acid found in protein-rich foods (dairy products, meat, fish, and poultry), is a precursor (building block) of serotonin. *Tyrosine,* another amino acid found in proteins, is a precursor of norepinephrine, epinephrine, and dopamine. *Choline,* a component of the lecithin found in egg yolks, soy products, and liver, is a precursor of acetylcholine.

In the case of tryptophan, the path between the dinner plate and the brain is indirect. Tryptophan leads to the production of serotonin, which reduces alertness, promotes relaxation, and hastens sleep. Because tryptophan is found in protein, you might think that a high-protein meal would make you drowsy and that carbohydrates (sweets, bread, pasta, potatoes) would make you relatively alert. Actually, the opposite is true. High-protein foods contain several amino acids, not just tryptophan, and they all compete for a ride on carrier molecules headed for brain cells. Because tryptophan occurs in foods in small quantities, it doesn't stand much of a chance if all you eat is protein. It is in the position of a tiny child trying to push aside a crowd of adults for a seat on the subway.

Carbohydrates, however, stimulate the production of the hormone insulin, and insulin causes all the other amino acids to be drawn out of the bloodstream while having little effect on tryptophan. So carbohydrates increase the odds that tryptophan will make it to the brain (Wurtman, 1982). Paradoxically, then, a high-carbohydrate, no-protein meal is likely to make you relatively calm or lethargic, and a high-protein one is likely to promote alertness, all else being equal (Spring, Chiodo, & Bowen, 1987; Wurtman & Lieberman, 1982–1983).

How else might nutrition affect mental and physical performance? In a report commissioned by the U.S. Army, the National Academy of Sciences reviewed existing animal and human studies on this question (Marriott, 1994). These studies suggest that (1) tyrosine can reduce symptoms that occur in extreme cold and at high altitudes, such as fuzzy thinking, headache, and nausea; (2) carbohydrates can prolong endurance under stressful conditions, increase fine-motor coordination, improve mood, and help people sleep; (3) choline can enhance memory and strengthen muscles and the immune system; and (4) caffeine improves alertness and mental performance (although in high doses it can cause anxiety and insomnia).

Keep in mind, though, that many other factors influence mood and behavior, that the effects of nutrients are subtle, and that some of these effects depend on a person's age, the circumstances, and even the time of day. Further, nutrients interact with each other in complex ways. If you don't eat protein, you won't get enough tryptophan, but if you go without carbohydrates, the tryptophan found in protein will be useless. Many people try to rev themselves up with nutritional supplements, but in the United States, herbal remedies and other dietary supplements are currently exempt from regulation by the Food and Drug Administration. Brands vary enormously in quality and in the amount of each active ingredient they contain (Angell & Kassirer, 1998).

In sum, if you're looking for brain food, you are most likely to find it in a well-balanced diet.

SUMMARY

- The brain is the bedrock of consciousness, perception, memory, emotion, and self-awareness.

The Nervous System: A Basic Blueprint

- The function of the nervous system is to gather and process information, produce responses to stimuli, and coordinate the workings of different cells. Scientists divide it into the *central nervous system (CNS)* and the *peripheral nervous system (PNS)*. The CNS, which includes the brain and *spinal cord,* receives, processes, interprets, and stores information and sends messages destined for muscles, glands, and organs. The PNS transmits information to and from the CNS by way of *sensory* and *motor nerves.*

- The peripheral nervous system consists of the *somatic nervous system,* which permits sensation and voluntary actions, and the *autonomic nervous system,* which regulates blood vessels, glands, and internal (visceral) organs. The autonomic system usually functions without conscious control, although some people can learn to heighten or suppress autonomic responses, using *biofeedback* techniques.

• The autonomic nervous system is divided into the *sympathetic nervous system,* which mobilizes the body for action, and the *parasympathetic nervous system,* which conserves energy.

Communication in the Nervous System

• *Neurons* are the basic units of the nervous system and are held in place by *glial cells.* Each neuron consists of *dendrites,* a *cell body,* and an *axon.* In the peripheral nervous system, axons (and sometimes dendrites) are collected together in bundles called *nerves.* Many axons are insulated by a *myelin sheath* that speeds up the conduction of neural impulses and prevents signals in adjacent cells from interfering with one another. Recent research has challenged the old assumption that neurons in the human central nervous system cannot be induced to regenerate or multiply. Scientists have also learned that *precursor cells* in brain areas associated with learning and memory continue to divide and mature throughout adulthood. A stimulating environment enhances this process of *neurogenesis.*

• Communication between two neurons occurs at the *synapse.* Many synapses have not yet formed at birth. During development, axons and dendrites continue to grow as a result of both physical maturation and experience with the world, and throughout life, new learning results in new synaptic connections in the brain. Thus, the brain's circuits are not fixed and immutable but are continually changing in response to information, challenges, and changes in the environment.

• When a wave of electrical voltage (*action potential*) reaches the end of a transmitting axon, *neurotransmitter* molecules are released into the *synaptic cleft.* When these molecules bind to *receptor sites* on the receiving neuron, that neuron becomes either more or less likely to fire. The message that reaches a final destination depends on how frequently particular neurons are firing, how many are firing, what types are firing, and where they are located.

• Through their effects on neural circuits, neurotransmitters play a critical role in mood, memory,

and psychological well-being. Abnormal levels of neurotransmitters have been implicated in several disorders, including depression, Alzheimer's disease, and Parkinson's disease.

• *Endorphins,* which act primarily as *neuromodulators* that affect the action of neurotransmitters, reduce pain and promote pleasure. Endorphin levels seem to shoot up when an animal or person is afraid or is under stress. Endorphins may also be linked to the pleasures of social contact.

• *Hormones,* produced mainly by the *endocrine glands,* affect and are affected by the nervous system. Psychologists are especially interested in *melatonin,* which promotes sleep and regulates a "biological clock" that coordinates bodily rhythms; *adrenal hormones* such as *epinephrine* and *norepinephrine,* which are involved in emotions, memory, and stress; and the *sex hormones,* which are involved in the physical changes of puberty, the menstrual cycle (*estrogens* and *progesterone*), sexual arousal (*testosterone*), and some nonreproductive functions—including, many researchers believe, mental functioning.

Mapping the Brain

• Researchers study the brain by observing patients with brain damage, by using the *lesion method* with animals, and by using such techniques as *electroencephalograms (EEGs), positron-emission tomography (PET scans),* and *magnetic resonance imaging (MRI).*

A Tour Through the Brain

• All modern brain theories assume *localization of function.* In the lower part of the brain, in the *brain stem,* the *medulla* controls automatic functions such as heartbeat and breathing, the *pons* is involved in sleeping, waking, and dreaming, and the *reticular activating system (RAS)* screens incoming information and is responsible for alertness. The *cerebellum* contributes to balance and coordination, and may also play a role in some higher mental operations.

• The *thalamus* directs sensory messages to appropriate higher centers. The *hypothalamus* is involved in emotion and in drives associated with survival. It also controls the operations of the autonomic nervous system and sends out chemicals that tell the *pituitary gland* when to "talk" to other endocrine glands.

• The *limbic system* is involved in emotions that we share with other animals, and it contains pathways involved in pleasure. Within this system, the *amygdala* is responsible for evaluating sensory information and quickly determining its emotional importance, and for the initial decision to approach or withdraw from a person or situation. The *hippocampus* has been called the "gateway to memory" because it plays a critical role in the formation of long-term memories for facts and events.

• Much of the brain's circuitry is packed into the *cerebrum,* which is divided into two *cerebral hemispheres* and is covered by thin layers of cells known collectively as the *cerebral cortex.* The *occipital, parietal, temporal,* and *frontal lobes* of the cortex have specialized (but partially overlapping) functions. The *association cortex* appears to be responsible for higher mental processes. The frontal lobes, particularly areas in the *prefrontal cortex,* are involved in social judgment, the making and carrying out of plans, and decision making.

The Two Hemispheres of the Brain

• Studies of *split-brain* patients, who have had the *corpus callosum* cut, show that the two cerebral hemispheres have somewhat different talents, a phenomenon known as *lateralization.* In most people, language is processed mainly in the left hemisphere, which generally is specialized for logical, symbolic, and sequential tasks. The right hemisphere is associated with spatial–visual tasks, facial recognition, the creation and appreciation of art and music, and the processing of negative emotions. In most mental activities, however, the two hemispheres cooperate as partners, with each making a valuable contribution.

Two Stubborn Issues in Brain Research

• Sleep appears to be necessary not only for bodily restoration but also for normal brain function. During sleep, periods of *rapid eye movement,* or *REM,* alternate with *non-REM* sleep. Dreams are reported most often during the REM periods. Freud argued that dreams arise because of unconscious wishes and longings, whereas many contemporary sleep researchers believe that dreams express the conscious conflicts of waking life. Biological theories, however, emphasize the physiological origins of dreams. For example, the *activation-synthesis theory* holds that dreams occur when the cortex tries to make sense of spontaneous neural firing initiated in the pons.

• Sex differences have been observed in anatomical and biochemical studies of animal brains. Sex differences in human brains, however, have been more elusive, and there is controversy about their existence and their meaning. Biological differences do not necessarily explain behavioral ones, and sex differences in experience could affect brain organization rather than the other way around.

• In evaluating research on the brain and behavior, it is important to remember that findings about the brain are most illuminating when they are integrated with psychological and cultural ones.

KEY TERMS

central nervous system (CNS) 114

spinal cord 114

spinal reflex 114

peripheral nervous system (PNS) 115

sensory nerves 115

motor nerves 115

somatic nervous system 115

autonomic nervous system 115

biofeedback 116

sympathetic nervous system 116

parasympathetic nervous system 116

neuron 117

glial cell 117

dendrite 118

cell body 119

axon 119

axon terminal 119

myelin sheath 119

nerve 119

precursor cells 119

neurogenesis 119

synaptic cleft 120

synapse 120

plasticity 120

action potential 121

synaptic vesicle 121

neurotransmitter 121

receptor sites 121

endorphins 123

neuromodulator 123

hormones 123

endocrine gland 123

melatonin 124

adrenal hormones 124

cortisol 124

epinephrine and norepinephrine 124

sex hormones (androgens, estrogens, progesterone) 124

LOOKING BACK

- Why do you automatically pull your hand away from something hot, "without thinking"? (pp. 114–115)

- Is it possible to consciously control your heartbeat or blood pressure? (pp. 115–116)

- In an emergency, which part of your nervous system whirls into action? (p. 116)

- Which cells are the nervous system's "communication specialists," and how do they "talk" to each other? (pp. 117–118)

- How do learning and experience alter the brain's circuits? (p. 120)

- Why do neural impulses travel more slowly in babies than in adults? (p. 121)

- What happens when levels of brain chemicals called neurotransmitters are too low or too high? (pp. 122–123)

- Which substances in the brain mimic the effects of morphine by dulling pain and promoting pleasure? (p. 123)

- Which hormones can improve your memory? (p. 124)

- Why are patterns of electrical activity in the brain called "brain waves"? (p. 125)

- What scanning techniques allow psychologists to view changes in the brain while people listen to music or solve math problems? (p. 126)

- Which brain part acts as a "traffic officer" for incoming sensations? (p. 128)

- Which brain part is the "gateway to memory"—and what cognitive catastrophe occurs when it is damaged? (p. 130)

- Why is it a good thing that the outer covering of the human brain is so wrinkled? (p. 131)

- How did a bizarre nineteenth-century accident illuminate the role of the frontal lobes? (pp. 132–133)

- If the two cerebral hemispheres were out of touch, would they feel different emotions and think different thoughts? (pp. 134–135)

- Why do researchers often refer to the left hemisphere as "dominant"? (p. 136)

- Should you sign up for a program that promises to perk up the right side of your brain? (p. 136)

- How do biological theories of dreaming differ from the familiar Freudian view? (p. 139)

- Do men talk about sports and women about feelings because their brains are different? (pp. 140–141)

UFO Sighting over St. Louis

St. Louis, MO, January 28, 2000. A motorist has reported that two weeks ago she spotted three unidentified flying objects hovering over the highway during rush-hour traffic. Stacy McKenna, 28, a college student and waitress, said the objects were shaped like triangles with white lights at each point. "At first they were just two bouncing, glowing lights," she said. "Then another one dropped out of the sky. It was so huge, I screamed because I thought I was going to hit it." McKenna said she didn't believe in UFOs before, but now she is "intrigued."

Many people who viewed these odd objects in the skies above Santos, Brazil, were convinced they were seeing UFOs.

Dozens of other area residents have reported seeing alien spacecraft this month. They are not alone: UFO sightings have occurred all over the world, especially in North America. California leads in the number of reported sightings, with Washington state in second place. A private pilot helped coin the term "flying saucer" many decades ago after seeing nine shiny disks skipping through the air, and thousands of reports of saucers and other mysterious objects have come in ever since then.

One of the earliest UFO accounts occurred in the late 1940s, when a rancher noticed some strange pieces of metal strewn about his property near Roswell, New Mexico. When the Air Force quickly blocked off and cleared the site, stories circulated that a spacecraft had crashed and that alien corpses had been recovered. Today, thousands of believers in UFOs still flock to the International UFO Museum and Research Center's headquarters in Roswell.

SENSATION AND PERCEPTION

We have all heard stories about UFOs and "flying saucers." Some of us laugh and some take them seriously. Why are they so common? Are UFO sightings reported only by people who are silly or gullible, or do smart, savvy people also see alien aircraft? If such sightings are illusions, then why do they include specific details? And why is one report often followed by several others in the same location: because there really are a lot of UFOs in the area or because of the power of suggestion?

In this chapter, we will try to answer these questions by exploring how we sense information from the environment and how we use this information to construct a model of the world—a model that is not always accurate.

Sensation is the detection of physical energy emitted or reflected by physical objects. The cells that do the detecting are located in the *sense organs*—the eyes, ears, tongue, nose, skin, and internal body tissues. Sensory processes produce an immediate awareness of sound, color, form, and other building blocks of consciousness. They tell us what is happening, both inside our bodies and in the world beyond our own skins. Without sensation, we would lose touch—literally—with reality. But to make sense of the world impinging on our senses, we also need **perception,** a set of processes that organize sensory impulses into meaningful patterns. Our sense of vision produces a two-dimensional image on the back of the eye, but we *perceive* the world in three dimensions.

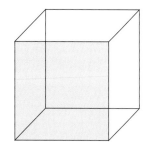

If you stare at this cube, the surface on the outside and front will suddenly be on the inside and back or vice versa, because your brain can interpret the sensory image in two different ways.

Our sense of hearing brings us the sound of a C, an E, and a G played simultaneously on the piano, but we *perceive* a C-major chord.

Sensation and perception are the foundation of learning, thinking, and acting, and findings on these topics can often be put to practical use—for example, in the design of hearing aids and industrial robots. Findings in this area have also been used to improve the training of flight controllers, astronauts, and others who must make crucial decisions based on what they sense and perceive.

An understanding of sensation and perception can also help us think more critically about our own experiences. As you read this chapter, ask yourself why people sometimes perceive things that are not there, and, conversely, why they sometimes miss things that are there—looking without seeing, listening without hearing.

What's Ahead

- What kind of code in the nervous system helps explain why a pinprick and a kiss feel different?

- Why does your dog hear a "silent" doggie whistle when you can't?

- What kind of bias can influence whether you think you hear the phone ringing when you're in the shower?

- What happens when people are deprived of all external sensory stimulation?

5.1 Our Sensational Senses

At some point, you probably learned that there are five senses, corresponding to five sense organs: vision (eyes), hearing (ears), taste (tongue), touch (skin), and smell (nose). Actually, there are more than five senses, though scientists disagree about the exact number. The skin, which is the organ of touch or pressure, also senses heat, cold, and pain, not to mention itching and tickling. The ear, which is the organ of hearing, also contains receptors that account for a sense of balance. The skeletal muscles contain receptors responsible for a sense of bodily movement.

All of our senses evolved to help us survive. Even pain, which causes so much human misery, is an indispensable part of our evolutionary heritage, for it alerts us to illness and injury. Sensory experiences also contribute immeasurably to our quality of life, even when they are not directly helping us stay alive. They entertain us, amuse us, soothe us, inspire us. If we really pay attention to our senses, said poet William Wordsworth, we can "see into the life of things" and hear "the still, sad music of humanity."

The Riddle of Separate Sensations

Sensation begins with the **sense receptors,** cells located in the sense organs. When these receptors detect an appropriate stimulus—light, mechanical pressure, or chemical molecules—they convert the energy of the stimulus into electrical impulses that travel along nerves to the brain. Sense receptors are like military scouts who scan the terrain for signs of activity. These scouts cannot make many decisions on their own. They must transmit what they learn to field officers—sensory neurons in the peripheral nervous system. The field officers in turn must report to generals at a command center—the cells of the brain. The generals are responsible for analyzing the reports, combining information brought in by different scouts, and deciding what it all means.

The "field officers" in the sensory system all use exactly the same form of communication: a neural impulse. It is as if they must all send their messages on a bongo drum and can only go "boom." How, then, are we able to experience so many different kinds of sensations? The answer is that the nervous system *encodes* the messages. One kind of code, which is *anatomical,* was first described in 1826 by the German physiologist Johannes Müller, in his **doctrine of specific nerve energies.** According to this doctrine, different sensory modalities (such as vision and hearing) exist because signals

---

sensation
The detection of physical energy emitted or reflected by physical objects; it occurs when energy in the external environment or the body stimulates receptors in the sense organs.

perception
The process by which the brain organizes and interprets sensory information.

sense receptors
Specialized cells that convert physical energy in the environment or the body to electrical energy that can be transmitted as nerve impulses to the brain.

doctrine of specific nerve energies
The doctrine that different sensory modalities, such as vision and hearing, exist because signals received by the sense organs stimulate different nerve pathways leading to different areas of the brain.

received by the sense organs stimulate different nerve pathways leading to different areas of the brain. Signals from the eye cause impulses to travel along the optic nerve to the visual cortex. Signals from the ear cause impulses to travel along the auditory nerve to the auditory cortex. Light and sound waves produce different sensations because of these anatomical differences.

The doctrine of specific nerve energies implies that what we know about the world ultimately reduces to what we know about the state of our own nervous system. Therefore, if sound waves could stimulate nerves that end in the visual part of the brain, we would "see" sound. In fact, a similar sort of crossover does occur when you close your right eye, press lightly on the right side of the lid, and "see" a flash of light seemingly coming from the left. The pressure produces an impulse that travels up the optic nerve to the visual area in the right side of the brain, where it is interpreted as coming from the left side of the visual field.

Anatomical encoding, however, does not completely solve the riddle of separate sensations. For one thing, linking the different skin senses to distinct nerve pathways has proven difficult. The doctrine of specific nerve energies also fails to explain variations of experience *within* a particular sense—the sight of pink versus red, the sound of a piccolo versus the sound of a tuba, or the feel of a pinprick versus the feel of a kiss. An additional kind of code is therefore necessary. This second kind of code has been called *functional* (Schneider & Tarshis, 1986).

Functional codes rely on the fact that sensory receptors and neurons fire, or are inhibited from firing, only in the presence of specific sorts of stimuli. At any particular time, then, some cells in the nervous system are firing, and some are not. Information about *which* cells are firing, *how many* cells are firing, the *rate* at which cells are firing, and the *patterning* of each cell's firing constitutes a functional code. You might think of such a code as the neurological equivalent of the Morse code. Functional encoding may occur all along a sensory route, starting in the sense organs and ending in the brain.

Measuring the Senses

Just how sensitive are our senses? The answer comes from the field of *psychophysics,* which is concerned with how the physical properties of stimuli are related to our psychological experience of them. Drawing on principles from both physics and psychology, psychophysicists have studied how the strength or intensity of a stimulus affects the strength of sensation in an observer.

Absolute Thresholds. One way to find out how sensitive the senses are is to show people a series of signals that vary in intensity and ask them to say which signals they can detect. The smallest amount of energy that a person can detect reliably is known as the **absolute threshold.** The word *absolute* is a bit misleading because people detect borderline signals on some occasions and miss them on others. "Reliable" detection is said to occur when a person can detect a signal 50 percent of the time.

If you were having your absolute threshold for brightness measured, you might be asked to sit in a dark room and look at a wall or screen. You would then be shown flashes of light, varying in brightness, one flash at a time. Your task would be to say whether you noticed a flash. Some flashes you would never see. Some you would always see. And sometimes you would miss seeing a flash, even though you had noticed one of equal brightness on other trials. Such errors seem to occur in part because of random firing of cells in the nervous system, which produces fluctuating background noise, something like the background noise in a stereo system.

By studying absolute thresholds, psychologists have found that our senses are very sharp indeed. If you have normal sensory abilities, you can see a candle flame on a clear, dark night from 30 miles away. You can hear a ticking watch in a perfectly quiet room from 20 feet away. You can taste a teaspoon of sugar diluted in two gallons of water, smell a drop of perfume diffused through a three-room apartment, and feel the wing of a bee falling on your cheek from a height of 1 centimeter (Galanter, 1962).

Yet despite these impressive sensory skills, our senses are tuned in to only a narrow band of physical energies. For example, we are visually sensitive to only a tiny fraction of all electromagnetic energy; we do not see radio waves or microwaves (see Figure 5.1 on the next page). Other species can pick up signals that we cannot. Dogs can detect high-frequency sound waves that are beyond our range, as you know if you have ever called your pooch with a "silent" doggie whistle. Bats and porpoises can hear sounds two octaves beyond our range, and bees can see ultraviolent light, which merely gives human beings a sunburn.

absolute threshold
The smallest quantity of physical energy that can be reliably detected by an observer.

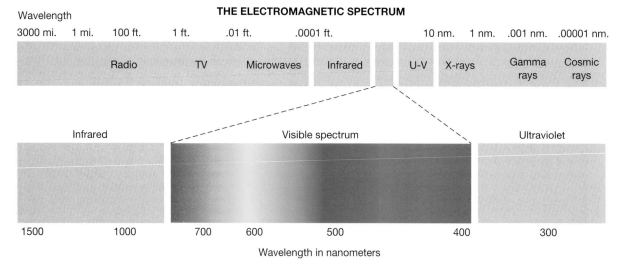

THE ELECTROMAGNETIC SPECTRUM

Wavelength

3000 mi.   1 mi.   100 ft.   1 ft.   .01 ft.   .0001 ft.   10 nm.   1 nm.   .001 nm.   .00001 nm.

Radio   TV   Microwaves   Infrared   U-V   X-rays   Gamma rays   Cosmic rays

Infrared   Visible spectrum   Ultraviolet

1500   1000   700   600   500   400   300

Wavelength in nanometers

Figure 5.1
Visible Spectrum of
Electromagnetic Energy
*Our visual system detects
only a small fraction of the
electromagnetic energy
around us.*

Difference Thresholds. Psychologists also study sensory sensitivity by having people compare two stimuli and judge whether they are the same or different. For example, a person might be asked to compare the weight of two blocks, the brightness of two lights, or the saltiness of two liquids. The smallest difference in stimulation that a person can detect reliably (again, half of the time) is called the **difference threshold,** or *just noticeable difference (jnd)*. When you compare two stimuli, A and B, the difference threshold will depend on the intensity or size of A. The larger or more intense A is, the greater the change must be before you can detect a difference. If you are comparing the weights of two pebbles, you might be able to detect a difference of only a fraction of an ounce, but you would not be able to detect such a subtle difference if you were comparing two massive boulders.

In everyday life, we may sometimes think we can detect a difference between stimuli when we cannot. Years ago, as a class project, undergraduate students at Williams College offered tasters three glasses of cola, two of one leading brand and one of the other (or vice versa), and asked them which drink they liked most and least. Each taster was given three trials. Most of the tasters were inconsistent in their preferences, indicating that they had trouble telling the two brands apart (Solomon, 1979). Apparently, the difference between the two tastes exceeded the students' difference thresholds.

Signal-Detection Theory. Despite their usefulness, the procedures we have described have a serious limitation. Measurements for any given individual may be affected by the person's general tendency, when uncertain, to respond, "Yes, I noticed a signal (or a difference)" or "No, I didn't

difference threshold
The smallest difference in stimulation that can be reliably detected by an observer when two stimuli are compared; also called just noticeable difference (jnd).

Different species sense the world differently. The flower on the left was photographed in normal light. The one on the right, photographed under ultraviolet light, is what a butterfly might see, because butterflies have ultraviolet receptors. The hundreds of tiny bright spots are nectar sources.

notice anything." Some people are habitual yea-sayers, willing to gamble that the signal was really there. Others are habitual naysayers, cautious and conservative. In addition, alertness, motives, and expectations can influence how a person responds on any given occasion. If you are in the shower and you are expecting an important call, you may think you heard the telephone ring when it didn't. In laboratory studies, when observers want to impress the experimenter, they may lean toward a positive response.

Fortunately, these problems of *response bias* are not insurmountable. According to **signal-detection theory,** an observer's response in a detection task can be divided into a *sensory process,* which depends on the intensity of the stimulus, and a *decision process,* which is influenced by the observer's response bias. Methods are available for separating these two components. For example, the researcher can include some trials in which no stimulus is present and others in which a weak stimulus is present. Under these conditions, four kinds of responses are possible: The person (1) detects a signal that was present (a "hit"), (2) says the signal was there when it was not (a "false alarm"), (3) fails to detect the signal when it was present (a "miss"), or (4) correctly says the signal was absent when it was absent (a "correct rejection"):

RESPONSES IN SIGNAL DETECTION

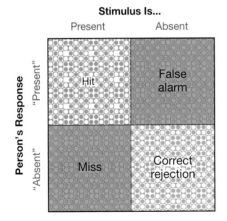

Yea-sayers will have more hits than naysayers, but they will also have more false alarms because they are too quick to say "Yup, it was there." Naysayers will have more correct rejections than yea-sayers, but they will also have more misses, because they are too quick to say "Nope, nothing was there." This information can be fed into a mathematical formula that yields separate estimates of a person's response bias and sensory capacity. The individual's true sensitivity to a signal of any particular intensity can then be predicted.

The old method of measuring thresholds assumed that a person's ability to detect a stimulus depended solely on the stimulus. Signal-detection theory assumes that there is no single "threshold," because at any given moment, a person's sensitivity to a stimulus depends on a decision that he or she actively makes. Signal-detection methods have many real-world applications, from screening applicants for jobs requiring keen hearing to training air-traffic controllers, whose decisions about the presence or absence of a blip on a radar screen may mean the difference between life and death.

Sensory Adaptation

Variety, they say, is the spice of life. It is also the essence of sensation, for our senses are designed to respond to change and contrast in the environment. When a stimulus is unchanging or repetitious, sensation often fades or disappears. Receptors or nerve cells higher up in the sensory system get "tired" and fire less frequently. The resulting decline in sensory responsiveness is called **sensory adaptation.** Such adaptation is usually useful because it spares us from having to respond to unimportant information; for example, most of the time you have no need to feel your watch sitting on your wrist. Sometimes, however, adaptation can be hazardous, as when you no longer smell a gas leak that you noticed when you first entered the kitchen.

We never completely adapt to extremely intense stimuli—a terrible toothache, the odor of ammonia, the heat of the desert sun. And we rarely adapt completely to visual stimuli, whether they are weak or intense. Eye movements, voluntary and involuntary, cause the location of an object's image on the back of the eye to keep changing, so that visual receptors don't have a chance to "fatigue." But in the laboratory, researchers can stabilize the image of a simple pattern, such as a line, at a particular point on the back of a person's eye. They use an ingenious device consisting of a tiny projector mounted on a contact lens. Although the eyeball moves, the image of the object stays focused on the same receptors. In minutes, the image begins to disappear.

What would happen if our senses adapted to *most* incoming stimuli? Would we sense nothing, or would the brain substitute its own images

signal-detection theory
A psychophysical theory that divides the detection of a sensory signal into a sensory process and a decision process.

sensory adaptation
The reduction or disappearance of sensory responsiveness that occurs when stimulation is unchanging or repetitious.

GET INVOLVED

NOW YOU SEE IT, NOW YOU DON'T

Sensation depends on change and contrast in the environment. Hold your hand over one eye and stare at the dot in the middle of the circle on the right. You should have no trouble maintaining an image of the circle. However, if you do the same with the circle on the left, the image will fade. The gradual change from light to dark does not provide enough contrast to keep your visual receptors firing at a steady rate. The circle reappears only if you close and reopen your eye or shift your gaze to the X.

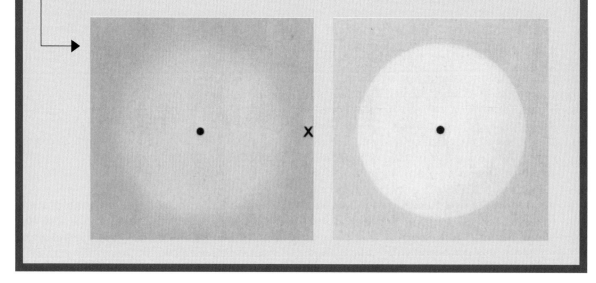

for the sensory experiences no longer available by way of the sense organs? In early studies of **sensory deprivation,** researchers studied this question by isolating male volunteers from all patterned sight and sound. Vision was restricted by a translucent visor; hearing by a U-shaped pillow and background noise from an air conditioner and fan; and touch by cotton gloves and cardboard cuffs. The volunteers took brief breaks to eat and use the bathroom, but otherwise they lay in bed, doing nothing. The results were dramatic. Within a few hours, many of the men felt edgy. Some were so disoriented that they quit the study the first day. Those who stayed longer became confused, restless, and grouchy. Many reported bizarre visions, such as a squadron of marching squirrels or a procession of marching eyeglasses. Few were willing to remain in the study for more than two or three days (Heron, 1957).

But the notion that sensory deprivation is unpleasant or even dangerous turned out to be an oversimplification (Suedfeld, 1975). In many of the studies, the experimental procedures them-selves probably aroused anxiety: Participants were told about "panic buttons" and were asked to sign "release from legal liability" forms.

Later research, using better methods, showed that hallucinations are less dramatic and less disorienting than was thought at first. In fact, many people enjoy time-limited periods of deprivation, and some perceptual and intellectual abilities actually improve. The response to sensory deprivation depends on your expectations and interpretations of what is happening. Reduced sensation can be scary if you are locked in a room for an indefinite period, but relaxing if you have retreated to that room voluntarily for a little time out—at, say, a luxury spa or a monastery.

Thinking Critically About Sensory Deprivation

Still, it is clear that the human brain requires a minimum amount of sensory stimulation in order to function normally. This need may help explain why people who live alone often keep the radio or television set running continuously and why prolonged solitary confinement is used as a form of punishment or even torture.

sensory deprivation
The absence of normal levels of sensory stimulation.

The effects of sensory deprivation depend on the circumstances. Being isolated against your will can be terrifying, but many people have found an hour alone in a "flotation tank" to be pleasantly relaxing.

Sensory Overload

If too little stimulation can be bad for you, so can too much, because it can lead to fatigue and men-

tal confusion. If you have ever felt exhausted, nervous, and headachy after a day crammed with hectic activities and deadlines, you know first-hand about sensory overload.

When people find themselves in a state of overload, they often cope by blocking out unimportant sights and sounds and focusing only on those they find interesting or useful. Psychologists have dubbed this the "cocktail party phenomenon" because at a cocktail party, a person typically focuses on just one conversation, ignoring other voices, the clink of ice cubes, music, and bursts of laughter across the room. The competing sounds all enter the nervous system, enabling the person to pick up anything important—even the person's own name, spoken by someone several yards away. Unimportant sounds, though, are not fully processed by the brain.

The capacity for **selective attention** protects us in daily life from being overwhelmed by all the sensory signals impinging on our receptors. The brain is not forced to respond to everything the sense receptors send its way. The "generals" in the brain can choose which "field officers" get past the command center's gates. Those that do not seem to have anything important to say are turned back.

selective attention
The focusing of attention on selected aspects of the environment and the blocking out of others.

QUICK QUIZ

If you are not overloaded, try answering these questions.

1. Even on the clearest night, some stars cannot be seen by the naked eye because they are below the viewer's _____ threshold.

2. If you jump into a cold lake, but moments later the water no longer seems so cold, sensory _____ has occurred.

3. If you are immobilized in a hospital bed, with no roommate and no TV or radio, and you feel edgy and disoriented, you may be suffering the effects of _____.

4. During a break from your job as a waiter, you decide to read. For 20 minutes, you are so engrossed that you fail to notice the clattering of dishes or orders being called out to the cook. This is an example of _____.

5. In real-life detection tasks, is it better to be a naysayer or a yea-sayer?

Answers:
1. absolute   2. adaptation   3. sensory deprivation   4. selective attention   5. Neither; it depends on the consequences of a "miss," or a "false alarm," and the probability of an event occurring. You might want to be a yea-sayer if you are "miss," or a "false alarm," and the probability of an event occurring. You might want to be a naysayer if you are you think you hear the phone ringing, and you are expecting a call about a job interview. You might want to be a naysayer if you are just out the door, you think you hear the phone and you are on your way to a job interview and don't want to be late.

What's Ahead

- How does the eye differ from a camera?

- Why can we describe a color as bluish green but not as reddish green?

- If you were blind in one eye, why might you misjudge the distance of a painting on the wall but not of buildings a block away?

- As a friend approaches, her image on your retina grows larger; why do you continue to see her as the same size?

- Why are perceptual illusions so valuable to psychologists?

5.2 Vision

Vision is the most frequently studied of all the senses, and with good reason. More information about the external world comes to us through our eyes than through any other sense organ. (Perhaps that is why people say "I see what you mean" instead of "I hear what you mean.") Because we are most active in the daytime, we are "wired" to take advantage of the sun's illumination. Animals that are active at night tend to rely more heavily on hearing.

What We See

The stimulus for vision is light; even cats, raccoons, and other creatures famous for their ability to get around in the dark need *some* light to see. Visible light comes from the sun and other stars and from lightbulbs, and is also reflected off objects. Light travels in the form of waves, and the characteristics of these waves affect three aspects of our visual world: hue, brightness, and saturation.

1 Hue, the dimension of visual experience specified by color names, is related to the *wavelength* of light—that is, to the distance between the crests of a light wave. Shorter waves tend to be seen as violet and blue, and longer ones as orange and red. (We say "tend to" because other factors also affect color perception, as we will see later.) The sun produces white light, a mixture of all the visible wavelengths. Sometimes, drops of moisture in the air act like a prism: They separate the sun's white light into the colors of the visible spectrum, and we are treated to a rainbow.

2 Brightness is the dimension of visual experience related to the amount, or *intensity,* of the light an object emits or reflects. Intensity corresponds to the amplitude (maximum height) of the wave. Generally speaking, the more light an object reflects, the brighter it appears. However, brightness is also affected by wavelength: Yellows appear brighter than reds and blues when physical intensities are actually equal. (For this reason, many fire departments have switched from red engines to yellow ones.)

3 Saturation (colorfulness) is the dimension of visual experience related to the *complexity of light*—that is, to how wide or narrow the range of wavelengths is. When light contains only a single wavelength, it is said to be "pure," and the resulting color is said to be completely saturated. At the other extreme is white light, which lacks any color and is completely unsaturated. In nature, pure light is extremely rare. Usually, we sense a mixture of wavelengths, and we see colors that are duller and paler than completely saturated ones.

Hue, brightness, and saturation are all *psychological* dimensions of visual experience, whereas wavelength, intensity, and complexity are all *physical* properties of the visual stimulus, light.

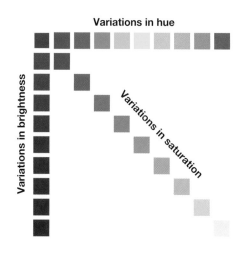

Variations in hue

Variations in brightness

Variations in saturation

An Eye on the World

Light enters the visual system through the eye, a wonderfully complex and delicate structure. As you read this section, examine Figure 5.2. Notice that the front part of the eye is covered by the transparent *cornea*. The cornea protects the eye and bends incoming light rays toward a *lens* located behind it. A camera lens focuses incoming light by moving closer to or farther from the shutter

hue
The dimension of visual experience specified by color names and related to the wavelength of light.

brightness
Lightness or luminance; the dimension of visual experience related to the amount of light emitted from or reflected by an object.

saturation
Vividness or purity of color; the dimension of visual experience related to the complexity of light waves.

opening. However, the lens of the eye works by subtly changing its shape, becoming more or less curved to focus light from objects that are close by or far away. The amount of light that gets into the eye is controlled by muscles in the *iris,* the part of the eye that gives it color. The iris surrounds the round opening, or *pupil,* of the eye. When you enter a dim room, the pupil widens, or dilates, to let more light in. When you emerge into bright sunlight, the pupil contracts to allow in less light. You can see these changes by watching your eyes in a mirror as you change the lighting.

The visual receptors are located in the back of the eye, or **retina.** In a developing embryo, the retina forms from tissue that projects out from the brain, not from tissue destined to form other parts of the eye; thus, the retina is actually an extension of the brain. As Figure 5.3 shows, when the lens of the eye focuses light on the retina, the result is an upside-down image (which can actually be seen with an instrument used by eye specialists). Light from the top of the visual field stimulates light-sensitive receptor cells in the bottom part of the retina, and vice versa. The brain interprets this upside-down pattern of stimulation as something that is right side up.

About 120 to 125 million receptors in the retina are long and narrow and are called **rods.** Another 7 or 8 million receptors are cone-shaped and are called, appropriately enough, **cones.** The center of the retina, or *fovea,* where vision is sharpest, contains only cones, clustered densely together. From the center to the periphery, the ratio of rods to cones increases, and the outer edges contain virtually no cones.

Rods are more sensitive to light than cones are. They enable us to see in dim light and at night. (Cats see well in dim light in part because they have a high proportion of rods.) Because

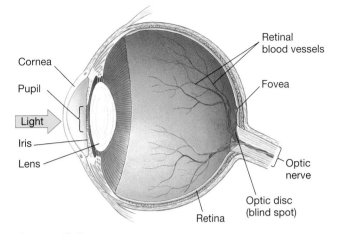

Figure 5.2
Major Structures of the Eye
Light passes through the pupil and lens and is focused on the retina at the back of the eye. The point of sharpest vision is at the fovea.

rods occupy the outer edges of the retina, they also handle peripheral (side) vision. That is why you can sometimes see a star from the corner of your eye even though it is invisible to you when you gaze straight at it. But rods cannot distinguish different wavelengths of light and therefore are not sensitive to color. That is why it is often hard to distinguish colors clearly in dim light. The cones, on the other hand, are differentially sensitive to specific wavelengths of light and allow us to see colors. However, the cones need much more light than rods do to respond. Therefore they don't help us much when we are trying to find a seat in a darkened movie theater. (These differences are summarized in Table 5.1.)

We have all noticed that it takes some time for our eyes to adjust fully to dim illumination. This process of **dark adaptation** involves chemical

5.1

retina
Neural tissue lining the back of the eyeball's interior, which contains the receptors for vision.

rods
Visual receptors that respond to dim light.

cones
Visual receptors involved in color vision.

dark adaptation
A process by which visual receptors become maximally sensitive to dim light.

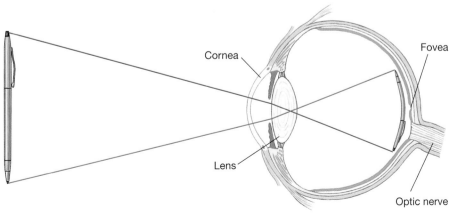

Figure 5.3
The Retinal Image
When we look at an object, the light pattern on the retina is upside down. René Descartes (1596–1650) was probably the first person to demonstrate this fact. He cut a piece from the back of an ox's eye and replaced the piece with paper. When he held the eye up to the light, he saw an upside-down image of the room on the paper!

Table 5.1   Differences Between Rods and Cones

	Rods	Cones
How many?	120–125 million	7–8 million
Where most concentrated?	Periphery of retina	Center (fovea) of retina
How sensitive?	High sensitivity	Low sensitivity
Sensitive to color?	No	Yes

changes in the rods and cones. The cones adapt quickly, within 10 minutes or so, but they never become very sensitive to the dim illumination. The rods adapt more slowly, taking 20 minutes or longer, but are ultimately much more sensitive. After the first phase of adaptation, you can see better but not well; after the second phase, your vision is as good as it ever will get.

Rods and cones are connected by synapses to *bipolar neurons,* which in turn communicate with

neurons called **ganglion cells** (see Figure 5.4). The axons of the ganglion cells converge to form the *optic nerve,* which carries information out through the back of the eye and on to the brain. Where the optic nerve leaves the eye, at the *optic disc,* there are no rods or cones. The absence of receptors produces a blind spot in the field of vision. Normally, we are unaware of the blind spot because (1) the image projected on the spot is hitting a different, "nonblind" spot in the other

ganglion cells
Neurons in the retina of the eye, which gather information from receptor cells (by way of intermediate bipolar cells); their axons make up the optic nerve.

Figure 5.4
The Structures of the Retina

For clarity, all cells in this drawing are greatly exaggerated in size. In order to reach the receptors for vision (the rods and cones), light must pass through the ganglion cells and bipolar neurons as well as the blood vessels that nourish them (not shown). Normally, we do not see the shadow cast by this network of cells and blood vessels because the shadow always falls on the same place on the retina, and such stabilized images are not sensed. But when an eye doctor shines a moving light into your eye, the treelike shadow of the blood vessels falls on different regions of the retina and you may see it—a rather eerie experience.

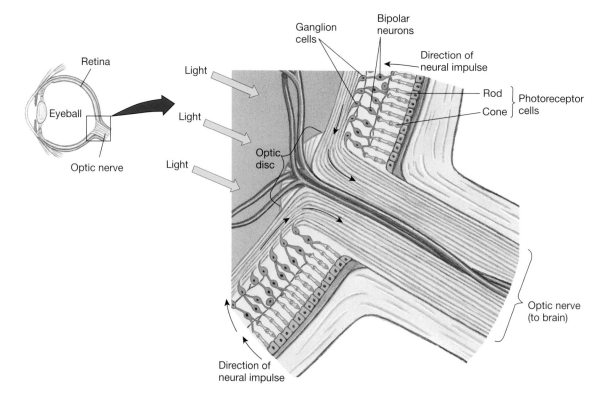

eye; (2) our eyes move so fast that we can pick up the complete image; and (3) the brain fills in the gap. You can find your blind spot by following the instructions in the Get Involved exercise on this page.

Why the Visual System Is Not a Camera

Although the eye is often compared with a camera, the visual system, unlike a camera, is not a passive recorder of the external world. Instead of simply registering spots of light and dark, as in a photograph, neurons in the visual system build up a picture of the world by detecting its meaningful features.

Ganglion cells and neurons in the thalamus of the brain respond to simple features in the environment, such as spots of light and dark. In mammals, special **feature-detector** cells in the visual cortex respond to more complex features. This fact was first demonstrated by David Hubel and Torsten Wiesel (1962, 1968), who painstakingly recorded impulses from individual cells in the brains of cats and monkeys. (In 1981, they received a Nobel Prize for their work.) Hubel and Wiesel found that different neurons were sensitive to different patterns projected on a screen in front of the animal's eyes. Most cells responded maximally to moving or stationary lines that were oriented in a particular direction and located in a particular part of the visual field. One type of cell might fire most rapidly in response to a horizontal line in the lower right part of the visual field, another to a diagonal line at an angle in the upper left part of the visual field. In the real world, such features make up the boundaries and edges of objects.

Since this pioneering work was done, scientists have found that other cells in the visual system have more complex kinds of specialties. For example, in primates, the visual cortex contains cells that respond maximally to bull's-eyes, spirals, or concentric circles (Gallant, Braun, & Van Essen, 1993). Even more intriguing, some cells in the temporal lobe respond maximally to *faces* (Ó Scalaidhe, Wilson, & Goldman-Rakic, 1997; Young & Yamane, 1992). That may help explain why a person with brain damage may continue to recognize faces even after losing the ability to recognize other objects. In one case (Moscovitch, Winocur, & Behrmann, 1997), a man could recognize a face made up entirely of vegetables (see the photograph on the next page), but he could not recognize the vegetables!

The brain's job is to take fragmentary information about lines, angles, shapes, motion, brightness, texture, and patterns, and come up with a unified view of what and where things are. How on earth does it do this? We saw in Chapter 4 that as neurons converge at a synapse, their overall pattern of firing determines whether the neuron

feature detectors
Cells in the visual cortex that are sensitive to specific features of the environment.

Cases of brain damage support the idea that particular systems of brain cells are highly specialized. One man's injury left him unable to identify ordinary objects, which he said often looked like "blobs." Yet he had no trouble with faces, even when they were upside down or incomplete. When shown this painting, he could easily see the face, but he could not see the vegetables comprising it (Moscovitch, Winocur, & Behrmann, 1997).

trichromatic theory
A theory of color perception, which proposes three mechanisms in the visual system, each sensitive to a certain range of wavelengths; their interaction is assumed to produce all the different experiences of hue.

opponent-process theory
A theory of color perception, which assumes that the visual system treats pairs of colors as opposing or antagonistic.

on the other side of the synapse is excited or inhibited. The firing (or inhibition) of that neuron, then, actually conveys information to the *next* neuron along the sensory route about what was happening in many other cells. Eventually, a single cell in the cortex of the brain may receive information that was originally contained in the firing of thousands of different visual receptors. The perception of a visual stimulus may ultimately depend on the activation of many cells in far-flung parts of the brain, and on the overall pattern and rhythm of their activity (Bower, 1998).

How We See Colors

Why do we see the world in living color instead of shades of gray? For 300 years, scientists have been trying to figure out the answer.

The Trichromatic Theory.

The **trichromatic theory** (also known as the *Young–Helmholtz theory*) applies to the first level of processing, which occurs in the retina of the eye. The retina contains three basic types of cones. One type responds maximally to blue (or more precisely, to a range of wavelengths near the short end of the spectrum, which give rise to the experience of blue), another to green, and a third to red. The hundreds of colors we see result from the combined activity of these three types of cones. Subtypes of the basic cone types exist, however, and people with different subtypes for red actually see the color red somewhat differently (Neitz & Neitz, 1995).

Total color blindness is usually due to a genetic variation that causes cones of the retina to be absent or malfunctional. The visual world then consists of black, white, and shades of gray. Many species of animals are totally color-blind, but the condition is extremely rare in human beings. Most "color-blind" people are actually *color deficient*. Usually, the person is unable to distinguish red and green; the world is painted in shades of blue, yellow, brown, and gray. In rarer instances, a person may be blind to blue and yellow and may see only reds, greens, and grays. Color deficiency is found in about 8 percent of white men, 5 percent of Asian men, and 3 percent of black men and Native American men (Sekuler & Blake, 1994). Because of the way the condition is inherited, it is rare in women.

The Opponent-Process Theory.

The **opponent-process theory** applies to the second stage of color processing, which occurs in ganglion cells in the retina and in neurons in the thalamus and visual cortex of the brain. These cells, known as *opponent-process cells,* either respond to short wavelengths but are inhibited from firing by long wavelengths, or vice versa (DeValois & DeValois, 1975). Some opponent-process cells respond in opposite fashion to red and green; that is, they fire in response to one and turn off in response to the other. Others respond in opposite fashion to blue and yellow. (A third system responds in opposite fashion to white and black and thus yields information about brightness.) The net result is a color code that is passed along to the higher visual centers. Because this code treats red and green, and also blue and yellow, as antagonistic, we can describe a color as bluish green or yellowish green but not as reddish green or yellowish blue.

Opponent-process cells that are *inhibited* by a particular color seem to produce a burst of firing when the color is removed, just as they would if the opposing color were present. Similarly, cells that *fire* in response to a color stop firing when the color is removed, just as they would if the opposing

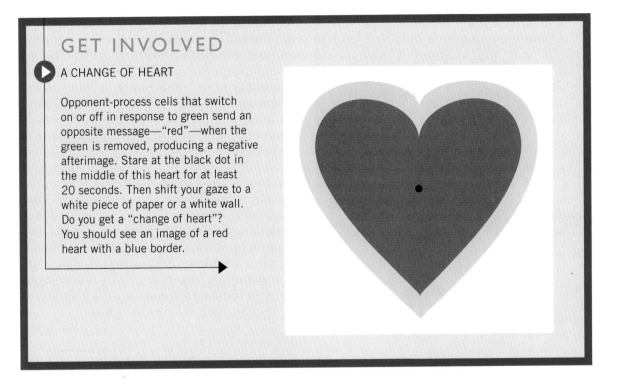

A CHANGE OF HEART

Opponent-process cells that switch on or off in response to green send an opposite message—"red"—when the green is removed, producing a negative afterimage. Stare at the black dot in the middle of this heart for at least 20 seconds. Then shift your gaze to a white piece of paper or a white wall. Do you get a "change of heart"? You should see an image of a red heart with a blue border.

color were present. These facts explain why we are susceptible to *negative afterimages* when we stare at a particular hue—why we see, for instance, red after staring at green (see the Get Involved exercise on this page). A sort of neural rebound effect occurs: The cells that switch on or off to signal the presence of "green" send the opposite signal ("red") when the green is removed—and vice versa.

Color in Context. The perceived color of an object also depends on the wavelengths reflected by everything around it, a fact well known to artists and interior designers (see Figure 5.5). Thus, you never see a good, strong red unless other objects in the surroundings reflect the green and blue part of the spectrum. Edwin Land (1959), inventor of the Polaroid camera, worked out precise rules that predict exactly how an object will appear, given the wavelengths reflected by all the objects in a scene, and the brain may use similar rules, although the details still need to be worked out.

Constructing the Visual World

We do not see a retinal image; that image is merely grist for the mill of the mind, which actively interprets the image and constructs the world from the often fragmentary data of the senses. In the brain, sensory signals that give rise to vision, hearing,

taste, smell, and touch are combined from moment to moment to produce a unified model of the world. This is the process of perception.

Form Perception. To make sense of the world, we have to know where one thing ends and another begins. In vision, we must separate the

Figure 5.5
Color in Context

The way you perceive a color depends on the colors around it. In this work by Joseph Albers, the adjacent Xs in each pair are actually the same color, but against different backgrounds they look different.

Figure 5.6
Figure and Ground

Do you see the goblins or angels? The woodcut Heaven and Hell *by M. C. Escher shows both, depending on whether you see the black or white sections as figure or ground.*

5.2

is nowhere in the film, which consists of separate static frames projected at 24 frames per second.

The Gestalt psychologists noted that we always organize the visual field into *figure* and *ground*. The figure stands out from the rest of the environment (see Figure 5.6). Some things stand out as figure by virtue of their intensity or size; it is hard to ignore the blinding flash of a camera or a tidal wave approaching your piece of beach. Unique objects also stand out, such as a banana in a bowl of oranges. Moving objects in an otherwise still environment, such as a shooting star, will usually be seen as figure. Indeed, it is hard to ignore a sudden change of any kind in the environment because our brains are geared to respond to change and contrast. However, selective attention, the ability to concentrate on some stimuli and to filter out others, gives us some control over what we perceive as figure and ground.

Here are some other **Gestalt principles** that describe how the visual system groups sensory building blocks into perceptual units:

1 *Proximity.* Things that are near each other tend to be grouped together. Thus, you perceive the dots on the left as two groups of dots, not as eight separate, unrelated ones. Similarly, you perceive the pattern on the right as vertical columns of dots, not as horizontal rows:

2 *Closure.* The brain tends to fill in gaps in order to perceive complete forms. This is fortunate because we often need to decipher less-than-perfect images. The following figures are easily perceived as a triangle, a face, and the letter *e,* even though none of the figures is complete:

3 *Similarity.* Things that are alike in some way (for example, in color, shape, or size) tend to be perceived as belonging together. In the figure below, you see the circles on the left as forming an *x,* and on the right, you see horizontal bars rather

teacher from the lectern; in hearing, we must separate the piano solo from the orchestral accompaniment; and in taste, we must separate the marshmallow from the hot chocolate. This process of dividing up the world occurs so rapidly and effortlessly that we take it completely for granted—until we must make out objects in a heavy fog or words in the rapid-fire conversation of someone speaking a foreign language.

The *Gestalt psychologists,* who belonged to a movement that began in Germany and was influential in the 1920s and 1930s, were among the first to study how people organize the world visually into meaningful units and patterns. In German, *gestalt* means "pattern" or "configuration." The Gestalt psychologists' motto was "The whole is more than the sum of its parts." They observed that when we perceive something, properties emerge from the whole configuration that are not found in any particular component. When you watch a movie, for example, the motion you "see"

Gestalt principles
Principles that describe the brain's organization of sensory building blocks into meaningful units and patterns.

than vertical columns because the horizontally aligned stars share the same color:

4 *Continuity.* Lines and patterns tend to be perceived as continuing in time or space. You perceive the figure on the left as a single line partially covered by an oval rather than as two separate lines touching an oval. In the figure on the right, you see two lines, one curved and one straight, instead of two curved and two straight lines, touching at one focal point:

Consumer products are sometimes designed with little thought for visual principles such as those formulated by the Gestalt psychologists—which is why it can be a major challenge to find the pause button on your VCR's remote control (Norman, 1988). Good design requires, among other things, that crucial distinctions be visually obvious. For instance, knobs and switches with different functions should differ in color, texture, or shape, and they should stand out as "figure."

 Depth and Distance Perception. Ordinarily we need to know not only what something is, but also where it is. Touch gives us this information directly, but vision does not, so we must *infer* an object's location by estimating its distance or depth.

To perform this remarkable feat, we rely in part on **binocular cues**—cues that require the use of two eyes. One such cue is **convergence,** the turning of the eyes inward, which occurs when they focus on a nearby object. The closer the object, the greater the convergence, as you know if you have ever tried to "cross" your eyes by looking at your own nose. As the angle of convergence changes, the corresponding muscular changes provide information to the brain about distance.

The two eyes also receive slightly different retinal images of the same object. You can prove this by holding a finger about 12 inches in front of

your face and looking at it with only one eye at a time. Its position will appear to shift when you change eyes. Now hold up two fingers, one closer to your nose than the other. Notice that the amount of space between the two fingers appears to change when you switch eyes. The slight difference in lateral (sideways) separation between two objects as seen by the left eye and the right eye is called **retinal disparity.** Because retinal disparity increases as the distance between two objects increases, the brain can use it to infer depth and calculate distance.

Binocular cues help us estimate distances up to about 50 feet. For objects farther away, we use only **monocular cues,** cues that do not depend on using both eyes. One such cue is *interposition:* When an object is interposed between the viewer and a second object, partly blocking the view of the second object, the first object is perceived as being closer. Another monocular cue is *linear perspective:* When two lines known to be parallel appear to be coming together or converging, they imply the existence of depth. For example, if you are standing between railroad tracks, they appear to converge in the distance. These and other monocular cues are illustrated on pages 164–165.

Visual Constancies: When Seeing Is Believing. Your perceptual world would be a confusing place without another important perceptual skill. Lighting conditions, viewing angles, and the distances of stationary objects are all continually changing as we move about, yet we rarely confuse these changes with changes in the objects themselves. This ability to perceive objects as stable or unchanging even though the sensory patterns they produce are constantly shifting is called **perceptual constancy.** The best-studied constancies are visual, and they include the following:

1 *Shape constancy.* We continue to perceive objects as having a constant shape even though the shape of the retinal image produced by an object changes when our point of view changes. If you hold a Frisbee directly in front of your face, its image on the retina will be round. When you set the Frisbee on a table, its image becomes elliptical, yet you continue to identify the Frisbee as round.

2 *Location constancy.* We perceive stationary objects as remaining in the same place, even though the retinal image moves about as we move our eyes, heads, and bodies. As you drive

5.3

binocular cues
Visual cues to depth or distance requiring two eyes.

convergence
The turning inward of the eyes, which occurs when they focus on a nearby object.

retinal disparity
The slight difference in lateral separation between two objects as seen by the left eye and the right eye.

monocular cues
Visual cues to depth or distance that can be used by one eye alone.

perceptual constancy
The accurate perception of objects as stable or unchanged despite changes in the sensory patterns they produce.

along the highway, telephone poles and trees fly by—on your retina. But you know that these objects do not move on their own, and you also know that your body is moving, so you perceive the poles and trees as staying put.

3 *Size constancy.* We continue to see an object as having a constant size even when its retinal image becomes smaller or larger. A friend approaching on the street does not seem to be growing; a car pulling away from the curb does not seem to be shrinking. Size constancy depends in part on familiarity with objects. You *know* that people and cars don't change size from moment to moment. It also depends on the apparent distance of an object. When you move your hand toward your face, your brain registers the fact that the hand is getting closer, and you correctly perceive its unchanging size. There is, then, an intimate relationship between perceived size and perceived distance.

4 *Brightness constancy.* We continue to see objects as having a relatively constant brightness, even though the amount of light they reflect changes as the overall level of illumination changes. Thus, we

BIZARRO   By DAN PIRARO

I HAVE NO SENSE OF DEPTH PERCEPTION. COULD YOU TELL ME— IS THAT SOMEONE STANDING WAY UP THERE ON THE CORNER, OR IS THERE A LITTLE MAN IN YOUR HAIR?

When size constancy fails.

MONOCULAR CUES TO DEPTH

Most cues to depth do not depend on having two eyes. Some monocular (one-eyed) cues are shown here.

LIGHT AND SHADOW

Both of these attributes give objects the appearance of three dimensions.

INTERPOSITION

An object that partly blocks or obscures another one must be in front of the other one and is therefore seen as closer.

MOTION PARALLAX

When an observer is moving, objects appear to move at different speeds and in different directions. The closer an object, the faster it seems to move; and close objects appear to move backward, whereas distant ones seem to move forward.

perceive that snow remains white even on a cloudy day. We are not fooled because the brain registers the total illumination in the scene, and we automatically take this information into account in our perception of the snow's brightness.

5 *Color constancy.* We see an object as maintaining its hue despite the fact that the wavelengths of light reaching our eyes from the object may change somewhat as the illumination changes. For example, outdoor light is "bluer" than indoor light, and objects outdoors therefore reflect more "blue" light than those indoors. Conversely, indoor light from a lamp is rich in long wavelengths and is therefore "yellower." Yet objects usually look the same color in both places. The explanation involves sensory adaptation, which we discussed earlier. Outdoors, we quickly adapt to short-wavelength (bluish) light, and indoors, we adapt to long-wavelength light. As a result, our visual responses are similar in the two situations. Also, as we saw earlier, the brain takes into account all the wavelengths in the visual field when computing the color of a particular object. If a lemon is bathed in bluish light, so, usually, is everything else around it. The increase in blue light reflected by the lemon is "canceled" in the visual cortex by the increase in blue light reflected by the lemon's surroundings, so the lemon continues to look yellow.

Visual Illusions: When Seeing Is Misleading. Perceptual constancies allow us to make sense of the world. Occasionally, however, we can be fooled, and the result is a **perceptual illusion.** For psychologists, illusions are valuable because they are *systematic* errors that provide us with hints about the perceptual strategies of the mind.

Although illusions can occur in any sensory modality, visual illusions have been the best studied. Visual illusions sometimes occur when the strategies that normally lead to accurate perception are overextended to situations where they don't apply. Compare the lengths of the two vertical lines in Figure 5.7. If you are like most people, you perceive the line on the right as slightly longer than the one on the left—yet they are exactly the same length. This is the Müller–Lyer illusion, named after the German sociologist who first described it in 1889.

perceptual illusion
An erroneous or misleading perception of reality.

RELATIVE SIZE

The smaller an object's image on the retina, the farther away the object appears.

TEXTURE GRADIENTS

Distant parts of a uniform surface appear denser; that is, its elements seem spaced more closely together.

RELATIVE CLARITY

Because of particles in the air—from dust, fog, or smog—distant objects tend to look hazier, duller, or less detailed.

LINEAR PERSPECTIVE

Parallel lines will appear to be converging in the distance; the greater the apparent convergence, the greater the perceived distance. This cue is often exaggerated by artists to convey an impression of depth.

Figure 5.7
The Müller-Lyer Illusion

The two lines in (a) are exactly the same length. (If you don't believe it, measure them!) We are probably fooled into perceiving them as different because the brain interprets the one with the outward-facing branches as farther away, as if it were the far corner of a room, and the one with the inward-facing branches as closer, as if it were the near edge of a building (b).

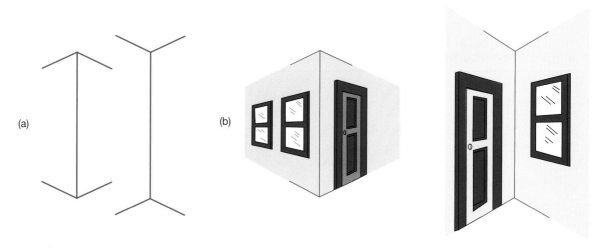

Live! psych

5.4

One explanation for the Müller–Lyer illusion is that the branches on the lines serve as perspective cues that normally suggest depth (Gregory, 1963). The line on the left is like the near edge of a building; the one on the right is like the far corner of a room (see part b of the figure). Although the two lines produce the same-size retinal image, the one with the outward-facing branches suggests greater distance. We are fooled into perceiving it as longer because we automatically apply a rule about the relationship between size and distance that is normally useful: When two objects produce the same-size retinal image and one is farther away, the farther one is larger. The problem, in this case, is that there is no actual difference in the distance of the two lines, so the rule is inappropriate.

Just as there are size, shape, location, brightness, and color constancies, so there are size, shape, location, brightness, and color illusions. Some illusions are simply a matter of physics.

Thus, a chopstick in a half-filled glass of water looks bent because water and air refract light differently. Other illusions occur due to misleading messages from the sense organs, as in sensory adaptation. Still others, like the Müller–Lyer illusion, seem to occur because the brain misinterprets sensory information. Figure 5.8 shows some other startling illusions.

In everyday life, most illusions are harmless, or even useful or entertaining. Occasionally, however, an illusion interferes with the performance of some skill. In baseball, two types of pitches that drive batters batty are the rising fastball, in which the ball seems to jump a few inches when it reaches home plate, and the breaking curveball, in which the ball seems to loop toward the batter and then fall at the last moment; both of these pitches are physical impossibilities. According to one explanation, they are illusions that occur when batters wrongly estimate a ball's speed and

Figure 5.8
Fooling the Eye

Although perception is usually accurate, our eyes can play tricks on us. In (a), the cats as drawn are all the same size; in (b), the diagonal lines are all parallel. To see the illusion depicted in (c), hold your index fingers 5 to 10 inches in front of your eyes as shown, then focus straight ahead. Do you see a floating "fingertip frankfurter"? Can you make it shrink or expand?

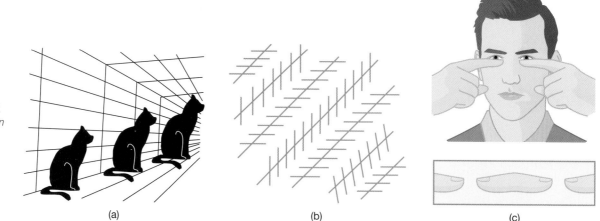

(a)   (b)   (c)

momentarily shift their gaze to where they think it will cross home plate (Bahill & Karnavas, 1993). Illusions may also lead to industrial and automobile accidents. For example, because large objects often appear to move more slowly than small ones, drivers sometimes underestimate the speed of onrushing trains at railroad crossings and think they can "beat" the train, with tragic results.

QUICK QUIZ

Can you accurately perceive these questions?

1. How can two Gestalt principles help explain why you can make out the Big Dipper on a starry night?

2. *True or false:* Binocular cues help us locate objects that are very far away.

3. Hold one hand about 12 inches from your face and the other one about 6 inches away. (a) Which hand will cast the smaller retinal image? (b) Why don't you perceive that hand as smaller?

Answers:

1. *Proximity* of certain stars encourages you to see them as clustered together to form a pattern; *closure* allows you to "fill in the gaps" and see the contours of a "dipper." 2. false 3. a. The hand that is 12 inches away will cast a smaller retinal image. b. Your brain takes the differences in distance into account in estimating size; also, you know how large your hands are.

What's Ahead

- Why does a note played on a flute sound different from the same note on an oboe?

- If you habitually listen to loud music through headphones, what kind of hearing impairment are you risking?

- To locate the source of a sound, why does it sometimes help to turn or tilt your head?

5.3 Hearing

Like vision, the sense of hearing, or *audition*, provides a vital link with the world around us. Because social relationships rely so heavily on hearing, when people lose their hearing they sometimes come to feel socially isolated. That is why many hearing-impaired people feel strongly about teaching deaf children American Sign Language (ASL) or other gestural languages, which allow them to communicate with and forge close relationships with other signers.

What We Hear

The stimulus for sound is a wave of pressure created when an object vibrates (or when compressed air is released, as in a pipe organ). The vibration (or release of air) causes molecules in a transmitting substance to move together and apart. This movement produces variations in pressure that radiate in all directions. The transmitting substance is usually air, but sound waves can also travel through water and solids, as you know if you have ever put your ear to the wall to hear voices in the next room.

As with vision, psychological aspects of our auditory experience are related in a predictable way to physical characteristics of the stimulus—in this case, a sound wave:

1 **Loudness** is the dimension of auditory experience related to the *intensity* of a wave's pressure. Intensity corresponds to the amplitude, or maximum height, of the wave. The more energy contained in the wave, the higher it is at its peak. Perceived loudness is also affected by how high or low a sound is. If low and high sounds produce waves with equal amplitudes, the low sound may seem quieter.

Sound intensity is measured in units called *decibels* (dB). A decibel is one-tenth of a *bel*, a unit named for Alexander Graham Bell, the inventor of the telephone. The average absolute threshold of hearing in human beings is zero decibels. Decibels are not equally distant, as inches on a ruler are. A 60-decibel sound (such as that of a sewing machine) is not 50 percent louder than a 40-decibel sound (such as that of a whisper); it is 100 times louder. Table 5.2 shows the intensity in decibels of some common sounds.

loudness
The dimension of auditory experience related to the intensity of a pressure wave.

Table 5.2   Sound Intensity Levels in the Environment

The following decibel levels apply at typical working distances. Each ten-point increase represents a tenfold increase in sound intensity over the previous level. Even some everyday noises can be hazardous to hearing if exposure goes on for too long a time.

Typical Level (Decibels)	Examples	Dangerous Time Exposure
0	Lowest sound audible to human ear	
30	Quiet library, soft whisper	
40	Quiet office, living room, bedroom away from traffic	
50	Light traffic at a distance, refrigerator, gentle breeze	
60	Air conditioner at 20 feet, conversation, sewing machine	
70	Busy traffic, noisy restaurant (constant exposure)	Critical level begins
80	Subway, heavy city traffic, alarm clock at 2 feet, factory noise	More than 8 hours
90	Truck traffic, noisy home appliances, shop tools, lawn mower	Less than 8 hours
100	Chain saw, boiler shop, pneumatic drill	Less than 2 hours
120	Rock concert in front of speakers, sandblasting, thunderclap	Immediate danger
140	Gunshot blast, jet plane at 50 feet	Any length of exposure time is dangerous
180	Rocket launching pad	Hearing loss inevitable

Source: Reprinted with permission from the American Academy of Otolaryngology—Head and Neck Surgery, Washington, D.C.

2 **Pitch** is the dimension of auditory experience related to the frequency of the sound wave and, to some extent, its intensity. *Frequency* refers to how rapidly the air (or other medium) vibrates—that is, the number of times per second the wave cycles through a peak and a low point. One cycle per second is known as 1 *hertz* (Hz). The healthy ear of a young person normally detects frequencies in the range of 16 Hz (the lowest note on a pipe organ) to 20,000 Hz (the scraping of a grasshopper's legs).

3 **Timbre** is the distinguishing quality of a sound. It is the dimension of auditory experience related to the *complexity* of the sound wave—to the relative breadth of the range of frequencies that make up the wave. A pure tone consists of only one frequency, but in nature, pure tones are extremely rare. Usually what we hear is a complex wave consisting of several subwaves with different frequencies. A particular combination of frequencies results in a particular timbre. Timbre is what

makes a note played on a flute, which produces relatively pure tones, sound entirely different from the same note played on an oboe, which produces very complex sounds.

When many frequencies are present but are not in harmony, we hear noise. When all the frequencies of the sound spectrum occur, they produce a hissing sound called *white noise*. White noise is named by analogy to white light. Just as white light includes all wavelengths of the visible light spectrum, so white noise includes all frequencies of the audible sound spectrum.

An Ear on the World

As Figure 5.9 shows, the ear has an outer, a middle, and an inner section. The soft, funnel-shaped outer ear is well designed to collect sound waves, but hearing would still be quite good without it. The essential parts of the ear are hidden from view, inside the head.

pitch
The height or depth of a tone; the dimension of auditory experience related to the frequency of a pressure wave.

timbre
The distinguishing quality of a sound; the dimension of auditory experience related to the complexity of the pressure wave.

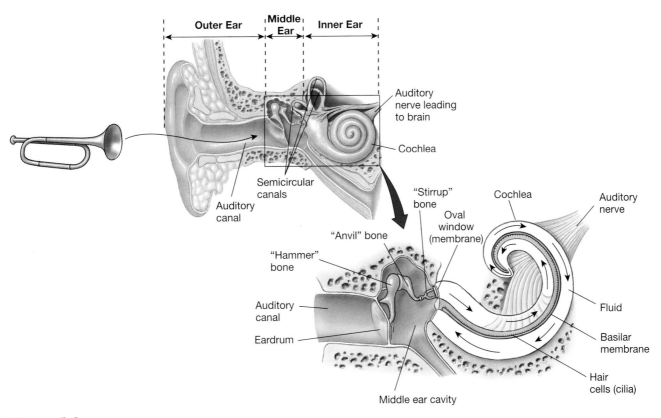

Figure 5.9
Major Structures of the Ear

Sound waves collected by the outer ear are channeled down the auditory canal, causing the eardrum to vibrate. These vibrations are then passed along to the tiny bones of the middle ear. Movement of these bones intensifies the force of the vibrations and funnels them to a small membrane separating the middle and inner ear. The receptor cells for hearing (hair cells), located in a small organ within the snail-shaped cochlea, initiate nerve impulses that travel along the auditory nerve to the brain.

A sound wave passes into the outer ear and through an inch-long canal to strike an oval-shaped membrane called the *eardrum.* The eardrum is so sensitive that it can respond to the movement of a single molecule! A sound wave causes it to vibrate with the same frequency and amplitude as the wave itself. This vibration is passed along to three tiny bones in the middle ear, the smallest bones in the human body. These bones, known informally as the "hammer," the "anvil," and the "stirrup," move one after the other, which has the effect of intensifying the force of the vibration. The innermost bone, the stirrup, pushes on a membrane that opens into the inner ear.

The actual organ of hearing is a chamber inside the **cochlea,** a snail-shaped structure within the inner ear. This organ plays the same role in hearing that the retina plays in vision. It contains the all-important receptor cells, which in this case look like bristles and are called hair cells, or *cilia.* Exposure to extremely loud noise for a brief period, or more moderate levels of noise for a sustained period, can damage these fragile cells. They flop over, like broken blades of grass, and if the damage reaches a critical point, hearing loss occurs. In our society, with its millions of office machines, automobiles, power saws, leaf blowers, jackhammers, and stereos (often played at full blast and listened to through headphones), such impairment is common. Many college students already have impaired hearing because of damage to the cilia.

The hair cells of the cochlea are embedded in the rubbery *basilar membrane,* which stretches across the interior of the cochlea. When pressure reaches the cochlea, it causes wavelike motions in fluid within the cochlea's interior. These motions push on the basilar membrane, causing it to move in a wavelike motion, too. Just above the hair cells is yet another membrane. As the hair cells rise and fall, their tips brush against it, and they bend. This causes the hair cells to initiate a signal that is passed

5.5

cochlea (KOCK-lee-uh)
A snail-shaped, fluid-filled organ in the inner ear, containing the receptors for hearing.

along to the *auditory nerve,* which then carries the message to the brain. The particular pattern of hair-cell movement is affected by the manner in which the basilar membrane moves. This pattern determines which neurons fire and how rapidly they fire, and the resulting code in turn determines the sort of sound we hear. For example, we discriminate high-pitched sounds largely on the basis of where activity occurs along the basilar membrane; activity at different sites leads to different neural codes. We discriminate low-pitched sounds largely on the basis of the frequency of the basilar membrane's vibration; again, different frequencies lead to different neural codes.

Could anyone ever imagine such a complex and odd arrangement of bristles, fluids, and snail shells if it did not already exist?

Constructing the Auditory World

 Just as we do not see a retinal image, so we do not hear a chorus of brushlike tufts bending and swaying in the dark recesses of the cochlea. Just as we do not see a jumbled collection of lines and colors, so we do not hear a chaotic collection of disconnected pitches and timbres. Instead, we use our perceptual powers to organize patterns of sound and to construct a meaningful auditory world.

For example, in class, your psychology instructor hopes you will perceive his or her voice as *figure* and the hum of a passing airplane, cheers from the athletic field, or distant sounds of a construction crew as *ground.* Whether these hopes are realized will depend, of course, on where you choose to direct your attention. Other Gestalt principles also seem to apply to hearing. The *proximity* of notes in a melody tells you which notes go together to form phrases; *continuity* helps you follow a melody on one violin when another violin is playing a different melody; *similarity* in timbre and pitch helps you pick out the soprano voices in a chorus and hear them as a unit; *closure* helps you understand a radio announcer's words even when static makes some of the individual sounds unintelligible.

Besides needing to organize sounds, we also need to know where they are coming from. We can estimate the *distance* of a sound's source by using loudness as a cue. For example, we know that a train sounds louder when it is 20 yards away than when it is a mile off. To locate the *direction* a sound is coming from, we depend in part on the fact that we have two ears. A sound arriving from the right reaches the right ear a fraction of a second sooner than it reaches the left ear, and vice versa. The sound may also provide a bit more energy to the right ear (depending on its frequency) because it has to get around the head to reach the left ear. Localizing sounds that are coming from directly in back of you or from directly above your head is hard because such sounds reach both ears at the same time. When you turn or cock your head, you are actively trying to overcome this problem. Many animals do not have to do this; they can move their ears independently of their heads.

QUICK QUIZ

How well can you detect the answers to these questions on hearing?

1. Which psychological dimensions of hearing correspond to the intensity, frequency, and complexity of the sound wave?

2. Tom Petty has a nasal voice, and Bob Dylan has a gravelly voice. Which psychological dimension of hearing describes the difference?

3. An extremely loud or sustained noise can permanently damage the _____ of the ear.

4. During a lecture, a classmate draws your attention to a buzzing fluorescent light that you had not previously noticed. What will happen to your perception of figure and ground?

Answers:
1. loudness, pitch, timbre 2. timbre 3. hair cells (cilia) 4. The buzzing sound will become figure and the lecturer's voice will become ground, at least momentarily.

What's Ahead

- Why do saccharin and caffeine taste bitter to some people but not to others?
- Why do you have trouble tasting your food when you have a cold?
- Why do people often continue to "feel" limbs that have been amputated?

5.4 Other Senses

Psychologists have been particularly interested in vision and audition because of the importance of these senses to human survival. However, research on the other senses is growing dramatically, as awareness of how they contribute to our lives increases and new ways are found to study them.

Taste: Savory Sensations

Taste, or *gustation,* occurs because chemicals stimulate thousands of receptors in the mouth. These receptors are located primarily on the tongue, but some are also found in the throat, inside the cheeks, and on the roof of the mouth. If you look at your tongue in a mirror, you will notice many tiny bumps; they are called **papillae** (from the Latin for "pimple"), and they come in several forms. In all but one form, **taste buds** line the sides of each papilla (see Figure 5.10). The buds, which up close look a little like a segmented orange, are commonly referred to, mistakenly, as the receptors for taste. The actual receptor cells are *inside* the buds, 15 to

50 to a bud. These cells send tiny fibers out through an opening in the bud; the receptor sites are on these fibers. The receptor cells are replaced by new cells about every 10 days. However, after age 40 or so, the total number of taste buds (and therefore receptors) declines, which is probably why older people can often enjoy strong tastes that children may detest.

Most researchers believe that there are four basic tastes: *salty, sour, bitter,* and *sweet,* each produced by a different type of chemical. (Some think there are other basic tastes as well, including the taste of monosodium glutamate.) Until the 1990s, nearly all textbooks included a "tongue map," showing areas supposedly most sensitive to the four basic tastes. But then physiological psychologist Linda Bartoshuk (1993) found that the map was based on a misleading graph published in 1942—and it was simply wrong. The four basic tastes can be perceived at any spot on the tongue that has receptors, and differences among the areas are small. Interestingly, the center of the tongue contains no taste buds, and so it cannot produce *any* sort of taste sensation. But, as in the case of the eye's blind spot, you will not usually notice the lack of sensation because the brain fills in the gap.

When you bite into an egg or a piece of bread or an orange, its unique flavor is composed of some combination of the four basic taste types. The physiological details are still not well understood, and there is even uncertainty about whether distinct tastes are associated with different types of nerve fibers. Researchers have reported finding two possible taste receptors in rats, one for sweet tastes and

papillae (pa-PILL-ee)
Knoblike elevations on the tongue, containing the taste buds. (Singular: papilla.)

taste buds
Nests of taste-receptor cells.

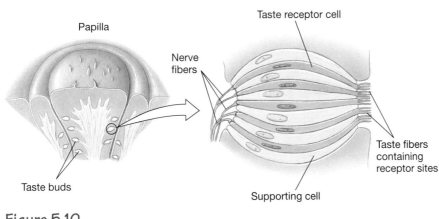

Figure 5.10
Taste Receptors
The illustration on the left shows taste buds lining the sides of a papilla on the tongue's surface. The illustration on the right shows an enlarged view of a single taste bud.

the other for bitter (Hoon et al., 1999). But this finding may or may not apply to human beings.

Some taste preferences, such as a liking for sweets, are universal, a part of our evolutionary heritage (Bartoshuk & Beauchamp, 1994). Others are a matter of culture. For example, many North Americans who enjoy raw oysters, raw smoked salmon, and raw herring are nevertheless put off by other forms of raw seafood that are popular in Japan, such as sea urchin and octopus. Individual tastes also vary; within a given culture, some people will greedily gobble up a dish that makes others turn green. These differences are due in part to learning (see Chapter 8). But they are also related to genetic differences in the density of taste buds; human tongues can have as few as 500 or as many as 10,000 taste buds (Miller & Reedy, 1990).

Because of genetic differences in sensitivity to particular tastes, people live in different "taste worlds" (Bartoshuk, 1993, 1998). For example, in the United States, about 25 percent of people are "supertasters" who find saccharin, caffeine, broccoli, and many other substances unpleasantly bitter. "Tasters," in contrast, detect less bitterness in these substances, and "nontasters" detect none

at all. Supertasters also perceive sweet tastes as sweeter and salty tastes as saltier than other people do, and they feel more "burn" from substances such as ginger, pepper, and hot chiles (Bartoshuk et al., 1998; Lucchina et al., 1998). The reason for these differences are found on the tongue: Supertasters have more taste buds, and certain papillae are smaller, are more densely packed, and look different than those in nontasters (Reedy et al., 1993).

The attractiveness of a food can be affected by its temperature and texture. As Goldilocks found out, a bowl of cold porridge is not nearly as delicious as one that is properly heated. And any peanut butter fan will tell you that chunky and smooth peanut butters just don't taste the same. Even more important for taste is a food's odor. Subtle flavors such as chocolate and vanilla would have little taste if we could not smell them (see Figure 5.11). The dependence of taste on smell explains why you have trouble tasting your food when you have a stuffy nose. Most people who chronically have trouble tasting things have a problem with smell, not taste per se.

Smell: The Sense of Scents

The great author and educator Helen Keller, who was blind and deaf from infancy, once called smell "the fallen angel of the senses." Yet our sense of smell, or *olfaction*, although seemingly crude when compared to a bloodhound's, is actually quite good—and is far more useful than most people realize.

The receptors for smell are specialized neurons embedded in a tiny patch of mucous membrane in the upper part of the nasal passage, just beneath the eyes (see Figure 5.12). Millions of receptors in each nasal cavity respond to chemical molecules in the air. When you inhale, you pull these molecules into the nasal cavity, but they can also enter from the mouth, wafting up the throat like smoke up a chimney. These molecules trigger responses in the receptors, and these responses combine to yield the yeasty smell of freshly baked bread or the spicy fragrance of a eucalyptus tree. Signals from the receptors are carried to the brain's olfactory bulb by the *olfactory nerve*, which is made up of the receptors' axons. From the olfactory bulb, they travel to a higher region of the brain.

Figuring out the neural code for smell has been a real challenge. Of the 10,000 or so smells we detect (rotten, burned, musky, fruity, spicy, flowery, resinous, putrid, . . .), none seems to be more

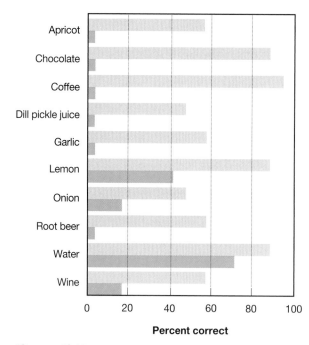

Figure 5.11

Taste Test

The tan bars show the percentages of people who could identify a substance dropped on the tongue when they were able to smell it. The blue bars show the percentages who could identify a substance when they were prevented from smelling it. (From Mozell et al., 1969.)

basic than any other. Moreover, a thousand kinds of receptors exist, each kind responding to a part of an odor molecule's structure (Axel, 1995; Buck & Axel, 1991). This complicated system is quite different from the one involved in vision, which uses only three basic receptor types, or in taste, which uses only four (or possibly five). But researchers are making progress; they have discovered that distinct odors activate unique combinations of receptor types, and they have succeeded in identifying some of those combinations (Malnic et al., 1999). Soon we may know the neural codes for all of the world's smells.

Although smell is less vital for human survival than for the survival of other animals, it is still important. We sniff out danger by smelling smoke, food spoilage, or poison gases. Thus, a deficit in the sense of smell is nothing to turn up your nose at. Such a loss can come about because of infection or disease, and smokers are nearly twice as likely as nonsmokers to have trouble detecting common odors. A person who has smoked two packs a day for 10 years must abstain from cigarettes for 10 more years before the sense of smell returns to normal (Frye, Schwartz, & Doty, 1990).

5.1

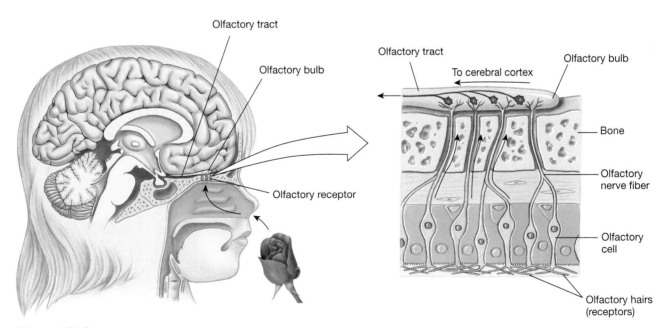

Figure 5.12
Receptors for Smell

Airborne chemical molecules (vapors) enter the nose and circulate through the nasal cavity, where the smell receptors are located. The receptors' axons make up the olfactory nerve, which carries signals to the brain. When you sniff, you draw more vapors into the nose and speed their circulation. Vapors can also reach the nasal cavity through the mouth by way of a passageway from the throat.

Smell has not only evolutionary but also cultural significance. These pilgrims in Japan are purifying themselves with holy incense for good luck and health. Incense has always been an important commodity; in the New Testament, the gifts of the Magi included frankincense and myrrh.

Human odor preferences, like taste preferences, vary. In some societies, people use rancid fat as a hair pomade, but anyone in North America who did so would quickly have a social problem. Within a particular culture, context and experience are all-important. The very same chemicals that contribute to unpleasant body odors and bad breath also contribute to the pleasant bouquet and flavor of cheese.

Senses of the Skin

The skin's usefulness is more than just skin deep. Besides protecting our innards, our 2 square yards of skin help us identify objects and establish intimacy with others. By providing a boundary between ourselves and everything else, the skin also gives us a sense of ourselves as distinct from the environment.

The basic skin senses include *touch* (or pressure), *warmth, cold,* and *pain.* Within these four types are variations such as itch, tickle, and painful burning. Although certain spots on the skin are especially sensitive to the four basic skin sensations, scientists have had difficulty finding distinct receptors for these sensations, except in the case of pressure. A few years ago, however, Swedish researchers found a new, thin kind of nerve fiber

gate-control theory
The theory that the experience of pain depends in part on whether pain impulses get past a neurological "gate" in the spinal cord and thus reach the brain.

that seems to be responsible for at least some types of itching (Schmelz et al., 1997).

Perhaps specialized fibers will also be discovered for other skin sensations. In the meantime, many aspects of touch continue to baffle science—for example, why gently touching adjacent pressure spots in rapid succession produces tickle; and why the simultaneous stimulation of warm and cold spots produces not a lukewarm sensation but the sensation of heat. Decoding the messages of the skin senses will eventually tell us how we are able to distinguish sandpaper from velvet and glue from grease.

The Mystery of Pain

Pain, which is not only a skin sense but also an internal sense, has come under special scrutiny. Pain differs from other senses in an important way: When the stimulus producing it is removed, the sensation may continue on—sometimes for years. Chronic pain disrupts lives, puts stress on the body, and causes depression and despair. (For ways of coping with pain, see "Taking Psychology with You.")

The Gate-Control Theory of Pain. For many years, the leading explanation of pain has been the **gate-control theory,** which was first proposed by Canadian psychologist Ronald Melzack and British physiologist Patrick Wall (1965). According to this theory, pain impulses must get past a "gate" in the spinal cord. The gate is not an actual structure, but rather a pattern of neural activity that either blocks pain messages coming from the skin, muscles, and internal organs or lets those signals through. Normally, the

THE GATE-CONTROL THEORY OF PAIN

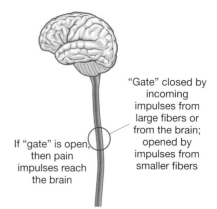

"Gate" closed by incoming impulses from large fibers or from the brain; opened by impulses from smaller fibers

If "gate" is open, then pain impulses reach the brain

gate is kept shut, either by impulses coming into the spinal cord from large fibers that respond to pressure and other kinds of stimulation or by signals coming down from the brain itself. But when body tissue is injured, the large fibers are damaged and smaller fibers open the gate, allowing pain messages to reach the brain unchecked.

Because the gate-control theory emphasizes the role of the brain in controlling the gate, it correctly predicts that thoughts and feelings can influence our reactions to pain. When we dwell on our pain, focusing on it and talking about it constantly instead of acting in spite of it, we often intensify our experience of it (Sullivan, Tripp, & Santor, 1998). Conversely, when we are distracted from our pain, we may not feel it as we usually would—as gymnast Kerri Strug demonstrated in 1996, when she won an Olympic gold medal despite having a sprained ankle. The gate-control theory also correctly predicts that mild pressure, or other kinds of stimulation, can interfere with severe or protracted pain by closing the spinal gate. When we vigorously rub a banged elbow, or apply ice packs, heating, or stimulating ointments to injuries, we are applying this principle.

The Neuromatrix Theory of Pain.

Although the gate-control theory has been extremely useful, it does not completely explain pain. Pain is now known to be far more complicated than scientists throughout when the theory was first proposed, involving complicated chemical changes at the site of injury and in the spinal cord and brain. Moreover, the gate-control theory does not fully explain the many instances of severe, chronic pain that occur without any sign of injury or disease whatsoever. In the strange phenomenon of *phantom pain*, for instance, a person continues to feel pain that seemingly comes from an amputated limb, or from an organ that has been surgically removed. An amputee may feel the same aching, burning, or sharp pain from gangrenous ulcers, calf cramps, throbbing toes, surgical wounds, or even ingrown toenails that he or she endured before the surgery. Even when the spinal cord has been completely severed, amputees often continue to report phantom pain from areas below the break. There are no nerve impulses for the spinal-cord gate to block or let through—so why is there pain?

These puzzles have led Ronald Melzack (1992, 1993) to propose a revised explanation of pain, the **neuromatrix theory.** According to this explana-

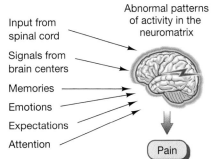

THE NEUROMATRIX THEORY OF PAIN

Input from spinal cord

Signals from brain centers

Memories

Emotions

Expectations

Attention

Abnormal patterns of activity in the neuromatrix

Pain

tion, the brain is capable of generating pain (and other sensations as well) entirely on its own, without any external stimulation. An extensive network of neurons in the brain—a neuromatrix—gives us a sense of our own bodies and body parts. When this network produces abnormal patterns of activity, the result is pain. Such abnormal patterns can occur not only because of input from peripheral nerves, but also as a result of memories, emotions, expectations, or signals from various brain centers. Or, in the case of phantom pain, the abnormal patterns may arise because of a lack of sensory stimulation, or because of the person's efforts to move a nonexistent limb. Evidence that brain areas associated with a missing limb continue to function in its absence is consistent with this view (Davis et al., 1998).

Pain is one of the most fascinating psychological mysteries of our time. It can rise and fall in epidemics, like the flu—as national outbreaks of back pain or whiplash or repetitive motion injuries reveal (Gawande, 1998). The people who suffer during such epidemics are not faking it, and their pain is not "just in their heads." But it may be in their brains.

The Environment Within

We usually think of our senses as pipelines to the "outside" world, but two senses keep us informed about the movements of our own bodies. **Kinesthesis** tells us where our body parts are located and lets us know when they move. This information is provided by pain and pressure receptors located in the muscles, joints, and tendons (tissues that connect muscles to bones). Without kinesthesis, you could not touch your finger to your nose with your eyes shut. In fact, you would have trouble with any voluntary movement. Think of how hard walking is when your leg has "fallen

neuromatrix theory
The theory that a matrix of neurons in the brain is capable of generating pain (and other sensations) in the absence of signals from sensory nerves.

kinesthesis (KIN-es-THEE-sis)
The sense of body position and movement of body parts; also called *kinesthesia*.

Dancers, divers, and gymnasts turn their kinesthetic talents into artistry.

equilibrium
The sense of balance.

semicircular canals
Sense organs in the inner ear, which contribute to equilibrium by responding to rotation of the head.

whether we are standing upright or on our heads and tells us when we are falling or rotating. Equilibrium relies primarily on three **semicircular canals** in the inner ear (see Figure 5.9 on page 169). These thin tubes are filled with fluid that moves and presses on hairlike receptors whenever the head rotates. The receptors initiate messages that travel through a part of the auditory nerve that is not involved in hearing.

Normally, kinesthesis and equilibrium work together to give us a sense of our own physical reality, something we take utterly for granted but should not. Oliver Sacks (1985) told the heartbreaking story of a young British woman named Christina, who suffered irreversible damage to her kinesthetic nerve fibers because of a mysterious inflammation. At first, Christina was as floppy as a rag doll; she could not sit up, walk, or stand. Then, slowly, she learned to do these things, relying on visual cues and sheer willpower. But her movements remained unnatural; she had to grasp a fork with painful force or she would drop it. More important, despite her remaining sensitivity to light touch on the skin, she could no longer experience herself as physically embodied: "It's like something's been scooped right out of me, right at the centre. . . . "

With equilibrium, we come, as it were, to the end of our senses. Every second, millions of sensory signals reach the brain, which combines and integrates them to produce a model of reality from moment to moment. How does it know how to do this? Are our perceptual abilities inborn, or must we learn them? We turn next to this issue.

asleep" or how clumsy chewing is when a dentist has numbed your jaw with novocaine.

Equilibrium, or the sense of balance, gives us information about our bodies as a whole. Along with vision and touch, it lets us know

QUICK QUIZ

Can you make some sense out of the following sensory problems?

1. April always has trouble tasting foods, especially those with subtle flavors. What is the most likely explanation of her difficulty?

2. May has chronic shoulder pain. How might the gate-control theory and the neuromatrix theory explain it?

3. June, a rock musician, does not hear as well as she used to. What is a likely explanation?

Answers:

1. An impaired sense of smell, possibly due to disease, illness, or cigarette smoking. 2. Nerve fibers that normally close the pain "gate" may have been damaged (the gate-control theory), or a matrix of cells in the brain may be producing abnormal activity (the neuromatrix theory). 3. Hearing impairment has many causes, but in June's case, we might suspect that prolonged exposure to loud music has damaged the hair cells of her cochlea.

What's Ahead

● Do babies see the world the way adults do?

● What could cause people to "see" the face of a religious figure on a wall or even a cinnamon bun?

5.5 Perceptual Powers: Origins and Influences

What happens when babies first open their eyes? Do they see the same sights, hear the same sounds, smell the same smells, taste the same tastes as an adult does? Are their strategies for organizing the world wired into their brains from the beginning? Or is an infant's world, as William James once suggested, only a "blooming, buzzing confusion," waiting to be organized by experience and learning? The truth lies somewhere between these two extremes.

Inborn Abilities and Perceptual Lessons

One way to study the origins of perceptual abilities is to see what happens when the usual perceptual experiences of early life fail to take place. To do so, researchers study animals whose sensory and perceptual systems are similar to our own, such as cats. What they find is that without certain experiences during critical periods of development, perception develops abnormally.

For example, when newborn animals are reared in total darkness for weeks or months, or are fitted with translucent goggles that permit only diffuse light to get through, or are allowed to see only one visual pattern and no others, visual development is impaired. In one famous study, kittens were exposed to either vertical or horizontal black and white stripes. Special collars kept them from seeing anything else, even their own bodies. After several months, the kittens exposed only to vertical stripes seemed blind to all horizontal contours; they bumped into horizontal obstacles, and they ran to play with a bar that an experimenter held vertically but not to a bar held horizontally. In contrast, those exposed only to horizontal stripes bumped into vertical obstacles and ran to play with horizontal bars but not vertical ones (Blakemore & Cooper, 1970).

Kittens are actually born with the ability to detect horizontal and vertical lines, and other orientations as well; at birth, their brains are equipped with the same kinds of feature-detector cells that adult cats have. But when kittens are kept from seeing horizontal or vertical lines during a critical period in their development, as in the study we described, the cells sensitive to those orientations deteriorate or change, and perception suffers (Crair, Gillespie, & Stryker, 1998; Hirsch & Spinelli, 1970). Similar critical periods may exist in human beings.

Many other visual skills are also present at birth, at least in rudimentary form, or they develop quite early, given normal experiences. For example, human infants can discriminate sizes and colors very early, possibly at birth. They can distinguish contrasts, shadows, and complex patterns after only a few weeks. Even some depth perception may be present from the beginning.

Testing an infant's perception of depth requires considerable ingenuity. One clever procedure that was used for decades was to place infants on a device called a *visual cliff* (Gibson & Walk, 1960). The "cliff" is a pane of glass covering a shallow surface and a deep one (see Figure 5.13 on the next page). Both surfaces are covered by a checkerboard pattern. The infant is placed on a board in the middle, and the child's mother tries to lure the baby across either the shallow or the deep side. Babies as young as 6 months of age will crawl across the shallow side but will refuse to crawl out over the "cliff." Their hesitation shows that they have depth perception.

Of course, by 6 months of age, a baby has had quite a bit of experience with the world. But infants younger than 6 months, even though they are unable to crawl, can also be tested on the visual cliff. At only 2 months of age, babies show a drop in heart rate when placed on the deep side of the cliff, but no change when they are placed on the shallow side. A slowed heart rate is usually a sign of increased attention. Thus, although these infants may not be frightened the way an older infant would be, it seems they can perceive the difference between the "shallow" and the "deep" sides of the cliff (Banks & Salapatek, 1984).

We have been talking only about vision, but other sensory abilities are also inborn or develop very early, as we saw in Chapter 3. Infants can distinguish salty from sweet and can discriminate among odors. They can distinguish a person's voice from other kinds of sounds. And they will startle to a loud noise and turn their heads toward

Floor as seen through glass

Figure 5.13
A Cliff-hanger
Infants as young as 6 months usually hesitate to crawl past the apparent edge of a visual cliff, which suggests that they are able to perceive depth.

its source, showing that they perceive sound as being localized in space. Because neurological connections in their brains and sensory systems are not completely formed, their senses are less acute than an adult's. However, an infant's world is far from the blooming, buzzing confusion that William James took it to be.

Psychological and Cultural Influences on Perception

The fact that some perceptual processes appear to be innate does not mean that all people perceive the world in the same way. A camera doesn't care what it "sees." A tape recorder doesn't ponder what it "hears." A robot arm on a factory assembly line holds no opinion about what it "touches." But because we human beings care about what we see, hear, taste, smell, and feel, psychological factors can influence what we perceive and how we perceive it. Here are a few of them:

1 *Needs.* When we need something, have an interest in it, or want it, we are especially likely to perceive it. For example, hungry individuals are faster than others at seeing words related to hunger when the words are flashed briefly on a screen (Wispé & Drambarean, 1953).

2 *Emotions.* Emotions can also influence our interpretation of sensory information. A small

perceptual set
A habitual way of perceiving, based on expectations.

child afraid of the dark may see a ghost instead of a robe hanging on the door, or a monster instead of a beloved doll. Pain, in particular, is affected by emotion. Soldiers who are seriously wounded often deny being in much pain, even though they are alert and are not in shock. Their relief at being alive may offset the anxiety and fear that contribute so much to pain (although other explanations are also possible). Conversely, negative emotions such as anger, fear, sadness, or depression can prolong and intensify a person's pain (Fernandez & Turk, 1992; Fields, 1991).

3 *Expectations.* Previous experiences often affect how we perceive the world (Lachman, 1996). The tendency to perceive what you expect is called a **perceptual set.** Perceptual sets can come in handy; they help us fill in words in sentences, for example, when we haven't really heard every one. But perceptaul sets can also cause misperceptions. In Center Harbor, Maine, local legend has it that veteran newscaster Walter Cronkite was sailing into port one day when he heard a small crowd on shore shouting "Hello, Walter . . . Hello, Walter." Pleased, he waved and took a bow. Only when he ran aground did he realize what they had really been shouting: "Shallow water . . . shallow water."

By the way, the previous paragraph has a misspelled word. Did you notice it? If not, probably it was because you expected all the words in this book to be spelled correctly.

4 *Beliefs.* What we hold to be true about the world can affect our interpretation of ambiguous sensory signals. A few years ago, people got excited when they saw an image of Mother Teresa, the Albanian nun famous for her work with the poor and the dying, in a cinnamon bun. Images that remind people of a crucified Jesus have been reported on walls, dishes, and food items, causing great excitement among those who believe that divine messages can be found on everyday objects—until other explanations emerge. In California, an image of Jesus on a garage door drew large crowds; it turned out to be caused by two streetlights that merged the shadows of a bush and a "For Sale" sign in the yard.

Our needs, emotions, expectations, and beliefs are all affected, in turn, by the culture we live in. Different cultures also provide people with different experiences, and these experiences can affect their perceptions. In a classic study done in the 1960s, researchers found that members of some African tribes were much less likely to be fooled by the Müller–Lyer illusion and other geometric illusions than were Westerners. In the West, the researchers observed, people live in a "carpentered" world, full of rectangular structures built with the aid of straightedges and carpenter's squares. Westerners are also used to interpreting two-dimensional photographs and perspective drawings as representations of a three-dimensional world. Therefore, they interpret the kinds of angles used in the Müller–Lyer illusion as right angles extended in space—just the sort of habit that would increase susceptibility to the illusion. The rural Africans in the study, living in a less carpentered environment and in round huts, seemed

People often see what they want to see. A man in Nashville bought a cinnamon bun at a coffee shop and thought he saw a likeness of Mother Teresa in it. The bun was duly shellacked and enshrined at the coffee shop, and hundreds traveled to see it.

more likely to take the lines in the figures literally, as two-dimensional, which could explain why they were less susceptible to the illusion (Segall, Campbell, & Herskovits, 1966).

This research was followed by a flurry of replications in the 1970s, showing that it was indeed culture that produced the differences between groups (Segall, 1994; Segall et al., 1999). Since then, little work has been done on the fascinating intersection of culture and visual illusions. However, culture affects perception in many other ways: by shaping our stereotypes, directing our attention, and telling us what is important to notice and what is not.

 **QUICK QUIZ**

Direct your perceptual attention now to this quiz.

1. Animal studies suggest that newborns and infants (a) have few perceptual abilities, (b) need visual experiences during a critical period for vision to develop normally, (c) see as well as adults.

2. On the visual cliff, 6-month-old babies (a) go right across because they cannot detect depth, (b) cross even though they are afraid, (c) will not cross because they can detect depth, (d) cry or get bored.

3. "Have a nice . . . " says Dewey, but then he gets distracted and doesn't finish the thought. Yet Clarence is sure he heard Dewey wish him a nice *day.* Why?

Answers:

1. b 2. c 3. Because of Clarence's perceptual set, due to his expectations

- Can "subliminal perception" tapes help you lose weight or reduce your stress?
- Why are most psychologists skeptical about ESP?

5.6 Puzzles of Perception

We come, finally, to two intriguing questions about perception that have captured the public's imagination for years. First, can we perceive what is happening in the world without being conscious of doing so? Second, can we pick up signals from the world or from other people without using our usual sensory channels at all?

Subliminal Perception

As we saw earlier in our discussion of the "cocktail party phenomenon," even when people are oblivious to speech sounds, they are processing and recognizing those sounds at some level. But these sounds are *above* people's absolute thresholds. Is it also possible to perceive and respond to messages that are *below* the absolute threshold—too quiet to be consciously heard, or too brief or dim to be consciously seen? Perhaps you have come across ads for products that will allow you to take advantage of such "subliminal perception."

Perceiving Without Awareness. First, a simple visual stimulus *can* affect your behavior even when you are unaware that you saw it. In one study, people subliminally exposed to a face tended to prefer that face over one they did not

"see" in this way (Bornstein, Leone, & Galley, 1987). In other studies, researchers have flashed words subliminally in a person's visual field while the person focuses on the middle of a screen. When the words are related to some personality trait, such as honesty, people are more likely later on to judge someone they read about as having that trait. They have been "primed" to evaluate the person that way (Bargh, 1999).

Findings such as these have convinced many psychologists that people often know more than they know they know. In fact, nonconscious processing appears to occur not only in perception, but also in memory, thinking, and decision making, as we will see in Chapters 6 and 7. However, the real-world implications of subliminal perception are not as dramatic as you might think. Even in the laboratory, where researchers have considerable control, the phenomenon is hard to demonstrate. The strongest evidence comes from studies using simple stimuli (faces or single words, such as *bread*), rather than complex stimuli such as sentences ("Eat whole-wheat bread, not white bread"). And even with single words, the influence of the subliminal stimulus usually disappears within seconds (Greenwald, Draine, & Abrams, 1996).

Perception Versus Persuasion. While subliminal *perception* may occur under certain conditions, subliminal *persuasion*, the subject of many popular books and magazine articles, is quite another matter. Empirical research has uncovered no basis whatsoever for believing that advertisers can seduce us into buying soft drinks or voting for political candidates by slipping subliminal slogans and images into television and magazine ads. Nor can anyone corrupt young minds with subliminal images or messages slipped into animated movies or rock songs.

Thinking Critically About Subliminal Perception

Zits

Reprinted with permission of King Features Syndicate.

What about those subliminal tapes that promise to help you lose weight, stop smoking, relieve stress, read faster, boost your motivation, lower your cholesterol, stop biting your nails, overcome jet lag, or stop taking drugs—all without any effort on your part? In study after study, placebo tapes—tapes that do not contain the messages that participants think they do—are just as "effective" as subliminal tapes (Eich & Hyman, 1992; Merikle & Skanes, 1992; Moore, 1992, 1995). In one typical study, people listened to tapes labeled "memory" or "self-esteem," but some heard tapes that were incorrectly labeled. About half of the participants showed improvement in the area specified by the label, *whether it was correct or not;* the improvement was due to expectations alone (Greenwald et al., 1991).

In sum, if advertisers want you to buy something, they would do better to spend their money on *above*-threshold messages. And if you want to improve yourself or your life, we encourage you to do so—but you'll probably have to do it the old-fashioned way: by working at it.

QUICK QUIZ

There are no subliminal messages in this quiz—trust us.

Suppose you hear about a study that appeared to find evidence of "sleep learning"—the ability to perceive and retain material played on an audiotape while a person sleeps. What would you want to know about this research before deciding to tape this chapter and play it by your bedside all night instead of studying it in the usual way?

Answer:

You might ask about the kinds of material used; did it consist of just single words or complex messages? You might ask whether the results were large enough to have practical consequences, and most important, how it was determined that the subjects were really asleep while the tape was playing. When brain-wave measurements are used to verify that subjects are actually sleeping, no "sleep learning" takes place. So if you want to learn the material in this chapter, you'll have to stay awake!

Extrasensory Perception: Reality or Illusion?

Eyes, ears, mouth, nose, skin—we rely on these organs for our experience of the external world. Some people, however, claim they can send and receive messages about the world without relying on the usual sensory channels, by using *extrasensory perception (ESP)*. Reported ESP experiences involve things like *telepathy,* the direct communication of messages from one mind to another without the usual sensory signals, and *precognition,* the perception of an event that has not yet happened.

Most ESP claims challenge everything we currently know to be true about the way the world and the universe operate. In the era of *The X Files,* a lot of people are ready to accept these claims. Should they?

Evidence—or Just Coincidence? Much of the "evidence" for extrasensory perception comes from anecdotal accounts. But people are not always reliable reporters of their own experiences. They often embellish and exaggerate, or recall only part of what happened. They also tend to forget incidents that don't fit their beliefs, such as "premonitions" of events that fail to occur. Many ESP experiences could merely be unusual coincidences that are memorable because they are dramatic. What passes for telepathy or precognition could also be based on what a person knows or deduces through ordinary means. If Joanne's father has had two heart attacks, her premonition that her father will die shortly (followed, in fact, by her father's death) may not be so impressive.

Thinking Critically About ESP

The scientific way to establish a phenomenon is to produce it under controlled conditions. Extrasensory perception has been studied extensively by researchers in the field of **parapsychology.** In a typical study, a person might be asked to guess which of five symbols will appear on a card presented at random. A "sender" who has already seen the card tries to transmit a mental image of the symbol to the person. Although most people do no better than chance at guessing the symbols, in some studies, a few people have consistently done somewhat better than chance. But ESP studies

5.2

parapsychology
The study of purported psychic phenomena such as ESP and mental telepathy.

have often been poorly designed, with inadequate precautions against fraud and improper statistical analysis. When skeptical researchers try to repeat the studies, they get negative results. After an exhaustive review, the National Research Council concluded that there was "no scientific justification . . . for the existence of parapsychological phenomena" (Druckman & Swets, 1988).

The history of research on psychic phenomena has been one of initial enthusiasm followed by disappointment when results cannot be replicated, and the thousands of studies done since the 1940s have failed to make a convincing case for ESP. In

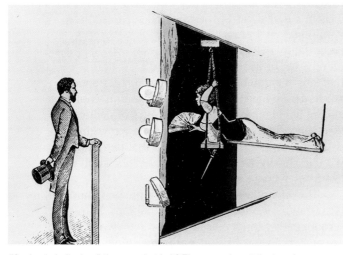

"Seeing is believing," they say, but is it? The engraving at the top shows a "living half-woman" seemingly swinging in mid-air. The sketch at the bottom shows how the trick is done. The woman reclines on an artificial bust, her body supported by another swing and hidden by black curtains. Due to a trick of lighting, the viewer sees only the swing, the face, the necklace, and the sword beneath the swing. The moral: Be skeptical about paranormal claims, even if you "saw it with your own eyes."

the 1990s, social psychologist Daryl Bem made waves in the psychological community when he reported a series of ESP studies carried out with the late Charles Honorton, a British parapsychologist. Bem and Honorton (1994) studied telepathy. A sender sat in a soundproof room and concentrated on a picture or video clip selected at random by a computer. A receiver sat in another soundproof room. At the end of the transmission period, the receiver was shown four pictures or video clips and was asked to pick out the one that most closely matched his or her mental imagery during the transmission period. If the receiver selected the stimulus that was "sent," that trial counted as a "hit." Bem and Honorton reported an overall hit rate of about 33 percent, whereas chance would predict only 25 percent.

But these findings quickly came under criticism. Although the methods used by Bem and Honorton were better than those used by previous researchers, possible flaws existed in the way the pictures and video clips were randomized and selected (Hyman, 1994). A meta-analysis of 30 studies using methods as rigorous as Bem and Honorton's found no evidence whatsoever for telepathy (Milton & Wiseman, 1999).

Lessons from a Magician. Despite the lack of evidence for ESP, about half of all Americans say they believe in it. Perhaps you yourself have had an experience that seemed to involve ESP or have seen a convincing demonstration by someone else. Surely you can trust the evidence of your own eyes—or can you? We will answer with a true story, one that contains an important lesson not only about ESP but about ordinary perception as well.

During the 1970s, Andrew Weil (who is now known for his efforts to promote alternative medicine) set out to investigate the claims of a self-proclaimed psychic named Uri Geller (Weil, 1974a, 1974b). Geller seemed able to bend keys without touching them, start broken watches, and guess the nature of simple drawings hidden in sealed envelopes. Although he had performed previously as a stage magician, he denied using trickery. His powers, he said, came from energy from another universe.

Weil, who believed in telepathy, felt that ESP might be explained by principles of modern physics and was receptive to Geller's claims. When he met Geller at a private gathering, he was not disappointed. Geller correctly identified a cross and a Star of David sealed inside separate envelopes. He made a stopped watch start running and a ring sag into an oval shape, apparently without touching them. He made keys change shape in front of Weil's very eyes. Weil came away a convert. What he had seen with his own eyes seemed impossible to deny . . . until he met The Amazing Randi.

James Randi is a famous magician who is dedicated to educating the public about psychic deception. To Weil's astonishment, Randi was able to duplicate what Geller had done. He, too, could bend keys and guess the contents of sealed envelopes. But Randi's feats were tricks, and he was willing to show Weil exactly how they were done. Weil suddenly experienced "a sense of how strongly the mind can impose its own interpretations on perceptions; how it can see what it expects to see, but not see the unexpected."

Weil was dis-illusioned—literally. He was forced to admit that the evidence of one's own eyes is not always reliable. Even when he knew what to look for in a trick, he could not catch The Amazing Randi doing it. Weil learned that our sense impressions of reality are not the same as reality. Our eyes, our ears, and especially our brains can play tricks on us.

PSYCHOLOGY IN THE NEWS, REVISITED

The great Greek philosopher Plato once said that "knowledge is nothing but perception." But simple perception is *not* always the best path to knowledge. As we have seen throughout this chapter, we do not passively register the world "out there"; we mentally construct it. If we are critical thinkers, therefore, we will be aware of how our beliefs and assumptions shape our perceptions.

This means that we should maintain a healthy skepticism when people report seeing spaceships and aliens, as in the story that started this chapter. Some individuals, as we have noted, are habitual yea-sayers who, because of their expectations, are quick to think they saw something that wasn't there. All of us, even those of us who are not usually gullible, have needs and beliefs that can fool us into seeing things that we *want* to see. And all of us occasionally read meanings into sensory experiences that are not inher-

ent in the experience itself. Who has not seen nonexistent water on a hot highway, or felt a nonexistent insect on the skin after merely thinking about bugs?

Many forces conspire to encourage epidemics of UFO sightings. Some come from the popular media, which generate a lot of money by promoting movies, TV shows, and talk-show accounts about extraterrestrials—and which usually portray skeptics as nerds or narrow-minded debunkers. Other forces are inherent in human psychology, including the fallibility of memory and the power of suggestion after an initial report of a sighting. And some reasons for UFO sightings can be traced to normal distortions of perception: When you are looking up at the sky, where there are few points of reference, it is difficult to judge how far away or how big an object is.

Whenever impartial investigators have looked into UFO reports, they have found that what people really saw were weather balloons, rocket launchings, swamp gas, military aircraft, or (in the majority of cases) ordinary celestial bodies, such as planets and meteors. The strange objects in the photo accompanying our news story, which looked so much like flying saucers, were really lenticular (lens-shaped) clouds. And the "alien bodies" reported in Roswell were really test dummies made of rubber, which the Air Force was dropping from high-altitude balloons before subjecting human beings to jumps from the same height. But even capable, intelligent people can be fooled. One astronomer who investigates UFO reports says, "I've been with Air Force pilots who thought they were seeing a UFO. But it was actually the moon. I've seen people look at Venus and say they could see portholes on a spaceship" (quoted in Ratcliffe, 2000).

None of this means that the only real world is the mundane one we see in everyday life. Because our sense organs evolved for particular purposes, our sensory windows on the world are partly shuttered. But we can use reason, ingenuity, and science to pry open those shutters. Ordinary perception tells us that the sun circles the earth, but the great astronomer Copernicus was able to figure out nearly five centuries ago that the opposite is true. Ordinary perception will never let us see ultraviolet and infrared rays directly, but we know they are there, and we can measure them. If science can enable us to overturn the everyday evidence of our senses, who knows what surprises about reality science still has in store for us?

TAKING PSYCHOLOGY WITH YOU

Living with Pain

Temporary pain is an unpleasant but necessary part of life, a warning of disease or injury. Chronic pain is another matter, a serious problem in itself. Back injuries, arthritis, migraine headaches, serious illnesses such as cancer—all can cause unrelieved misery to pain sufferers and their families. Chronic pain can also impair the immune system, putting patients at risk of further complications from their illnesses (Page et al., 1993).

At one time, the only way to combat pain was with drugs or surgery, which were not always effective. Today, we know that pain is affected by attitudes, actions, emotions, and circumstances, and that treatment must take these influences into account. Social roles, too, can influence a person's response to pain. For example, although women tend to report greater pain than men do, a real-world study of people who were in pain for more than six months found that men suffered more psychological distress than women did, possibly because the male role made it hard for them to admit their pain (Snow et al., 1986).

Many pain-treatment programs encourage patients to manage their pain themselves instead of relying entirely on health-care professionals. Usually, these programs combine several strategies:

• *Painkilling medication.* Doctors often worry that patients will become addicted to painkillers or will develop a tolerance to the drugs. The physicians will therefore give a minimal dose, then wait until the effects wear off and the patient is once again in agony before giving more. This approach is ineffective and is based on outdated notions about addiction. In reality, people who take painkillers to control their pain rarely become addicted (see Chapter 10).

The method now recommended by experts (although doctors and hospitals do not always follow the advice) is to give pain sufferers a continuous dose of painkiller in whatever amount is necessary to keep them pain-free, and to allow them to do this for themselves when they leave the hospital. This strategy leads to reduced dosages rather than larger ones and does not lead to drug dependence (Hill et al., 1990; Portenoy, 1994).

• *Involvement by family and friends.* When a person is in pain, friends and relatives understandably tend to sympathize and to excuse the sufferer from regular responsibilities. The sufferer takes to bed, avoids physical activity, and focuses on the pain. As we will see in Chapter 8, attention from others is a powerful reinforcer of whatever behavior produces the attention. Also, focusing on pain tends to increase it, and inactivity can lead to shortened muscles, muscle spasms, and fatigue. So sympathy and attention can sometimes backfire and may actually prolong the agony (Flor, Kerns, & Turk, 1987).

For this reason, many pain experts now encourage family members to resist rewarding or reinforcing the pain and to reward activity, exercise, and wellness instead. This approach, however, must be used carefully, preferably under the direction of a medical or mental-health professional, because a patient's complaints about pain are an important diagnostic tool for the physician.

• *Self-management.* When patients learn to identify how, when, and where their pain occurs, this knowledge helps them determine whether the pain is being maintained by external events. Just having a sense of control over pain can have a powerful pain-

reducing effect. In one study, students who monitored their pain while one hand was submerged in freezing water showed more rapid recovery from the pain than did students who had tried to suppress their awareness of pain sensations or distract themselves, apparently because the monitoring students had a sense of control (Cioffi & Holloway, 1993).

• *Relaxation, hypnosis, biofeedback, and acupuncture.* A blue-ribbon panel of experts concluded that relaxation techniques, hypnosis, and biofeedback often help reduce chronic pain from a variety of conditions (NIH Technology Assessment Panel, 1996). The evidence for acupuncture is weaker, however. Some studies find that acupuncture helps in reducing some kinds of pain, possibly by stimulating the release of endorphins (Holden, 1997). However, the best-designed studies are the least likely to find such an effect, so many medical experts remain skeptical.

• *Cognitive–behavioral therapy.* Cognitive–behavioral strategies teach people how to recognize the connections among thoughts, feelings, and pain; substitute adaptive thoughts for negative ones; and use coping strategies such as distraction, relabeling of sensations, and imagery to alleviate suffering (see Chapter 11). These techniques increase feelings of control and reduce feelings of inadequacy.

For further information, you can contact pain clinics or services in teaching hospitals and medical schools. There are many reputable clinics around the country, some specializing in specific disorders, such as migraines or back injuries. But take care: There are also many untested therapies and quack practitioners who only prey on people's pain.

SUMMARY

• *Sensation* is the detection and direct experience of physical energy as a result of environmental or internal events. *Perception* is the process by which sensory impulses are organized and interpreted.

Our Sensational Senses

• Sensation begins with the *sense receptors,* which convert the energy of a stimulus into electrical impulses that travel along nerves to the brain.

Separate sensations can be accounted for by *anatomical codes* (as set forth by the *doctrine of specific nerve energies*) and *functional codes* in the nervous system.

• Psychologists specializing in *psychophysics* have studied sensory sensitivity by measuring *absolute* and *difference thresholds*. *Signal-detection theory*, however, holds that responses in a detection task consist of both a sensory process and a decision process and will vary with the person's motivation, alertness, and expectations.

• Our senses are designed to respond to change and contrast in the environment. When stimulation is unchanging, *sensory adaptation* occurs. Too little stimulation can cause *sensory deprivation*. Too much stimulation can cause *sensory overload*, which is why we exercise *selective attention*.

Vision

• Vision is affected by the wavelength, intensity, and complexity of light, which produce the psychological dimensions of visual experience—*hue, brightness*, and *saturation*. The visual receptors—*rods* and *cones*—are located in the *retina* of the eye, and send signals (via other cells) to the *ganglion cells* and ultimately to the *optic nerve*, which carries visual information to the brain. Rods are responsible for vision in dim light; cones are responsible for color vision. *Dark adaptation* occurs in two stages.

• Specific aspects of the visual world, such as lines at various orientations, are detected by *feature-detector cells* in the visual areas of the brain. Some cells respond maximally to complex patterns, and even faces. The eye is not a camera; the brain takes in fragmentary information about lines, angles, shapes, motion, brightness, texture, and other features of what we see, and comes up with a unified view of the world.

• The *trichromatic* and *opponent-process* theories of color vision apply to different stages of processing. In the first stage, three types of cones in the retina respond selectively to different wavelengths of light. In the second, *opponent-process cells* in the retina and the thalamus respond in opposite fashion to short and long wavelengths of light.

• Perception involves the active construction of a model of the world from moment to moment. The *Gestalt principles* (e.g., *figure and ground, proximity, closure, similarity*, and *continuity*) describe visual strategies used by the brain to perceive forms.

• We localize objects in visual space by using both *binocular* and *monocular* cues to depth. Binocular cues include *convergence* and *retinal disparity*. Monocular cues include, among others, interposition and linear perspective. *Perceptual constancies* allow us to perceive objects as stable despite changes in the sensory patterns they produce. *Perceptual illusions* occur when sensory cues are misleading or when we misinterpret cues.

Hearing

• Hearing (*audition*) is affected by the intensity, frequency, and complexity of pressure waves in the air or other transmitting substance, corresponding to the experience of *loudness, pitch,* and *timbre* of the sound. The receptors for hearing are hair cells (*cilia*) embedded in the *basilar membrane,* in the interior of the *cochlea*. These receptors pass signals along to the auditory nerve. The sounds we hear are determined by patterns of hair-cell movement, which produce different neural codes. When we localize sounds, we use as cues subtle differences in how pressure waves reach each of our ears.

Other Senses

• Taste (*gustation*) is a chemical sense. Elevations on the tongue, called *papillae*, contain many *taste buds*. There are four basic tastes—salty, sour, bitter, and sweet—and possibly others, including the taste of monosodium glutamate. Responses to a particular taste depend on culture, genetic differences among individuals (for example, some people are "supertasters"), the texture and temperature of the food, and above all, the food's smell.

• Smell (*olfaction*) is also a chemical sense. Research on the neural code for smell has been complicated; no basic odors have been identified, as a thousand different receptor types exist. But researchers have discovered that distinct odors activate unique combinations of receptor types, and they have started to identify those combinations. Cultural and individual differences also affect people's responses to particular odors.

• The skin senses include touch (pressure), warmth, cold, and pain, and variations such as itch and tickle. Except in the case of pressure, it has been difficult to identify specialized receptors for these senses, although researchers have reported a receptor for one kind of itching.

• Pain is both a skin sense and an internal sense. According to the *gate-control theory,* the experience of pain depends on whether neural impulses get past a "gate" in the spinal cord and reach the brain. According to the *neuromatrix theory,* a matrix of neurons in the brain can generate pain even in the absence of signals from sensory neurons, which may explain the puzzling phenomenon of *phantom pain.*

• *Kinesthesis* tells us where our body parts are located, and *equilibrium* tells us the orientation of the body as a whole. Together, these two senses provide us with a feeling of physical embodiment.

Perceptual Powers: Origins and Influences

• Studies of animals and human infants suggest that many fundamental perceptual skills are inborn or acquired shortly after birth. By using the *visual cliff,* for example, psychologists have learned that babies have depth perception by the age of 6 months and possibly even earlier. However, without certain experiences early in life, cells in the nervous system deteriorate or change,

or fail to form appropriate neural pathways, and perception is impaired.

• Psychological influences on perception include needs, beliefs, emotions, and expectations (which produce *perceptual sets*). These influences are affected by culture, which gives people practice with certain kinds of experiences. Because psychological factors affect the way we construct the perceptual world, the evidence of our senses is not always reliable.

Puzzles of Perception

• In the laboratory, simple visual subliminal messages can influence behavior, at least briefly. However, there is no evidence that complex behaviors can be altered by "subliminal–perception" tapes or other subliminal techniques.

• *Extrasensory perception (ESP)* refers to paranormal abilities such as telepathy and precognition. Believers in ESP tend to overlook disconfirming evidence. Years of research in the field of *parapsychology* have failed to produce convincing evidence for ESP. Many so-called psychics take advantage of people's desire to believe in ESP, but what they do is no different from the tricks of any good magician. The story of ESP illustrates a central fact about human perception: It does not merely capture objective reality but also reflects our needs, biases, and beliefs.

KEY TERMS

sensation 149
perception 149
sense receptors 150
anatomical codes 150
doctrine of specific nerve energies 150
functional codes 151
absolute threshold 151
(just noticeable) difference threshold (jnd) 152
signal-detection theory 153
sensory adaptation 153
sensory deprivation 154
selective attention 155
hue 156

brightness 156
saturation 156
retina 157
rods and cones 157
dark adaptation 158
ganglion cells 158
optic nerve 158
feature-detector cells 159
trichromatic theory 160
opponent-process theory 160
negative afterimage 161
figure and ground 162
Gestalt principles 162
binocular cues 163
convergence 163

retinal disparity 163
monocular cues 163
perceptual constancy 163
perceptual illusion 165
audition 167
loudness 167
pitch 168
frequency (sound wave) 168
timbre 168
cochlea 169
basilar membrane 169
auditory nerve 170
gustation 171
papillae 171
taste buds 171

LOOKING BACK ◄

- What kind of code in the nervous system helps explain why a pinprick and a kiss feel different? (p. 151)

- Why does your dog hear a "silent" doggie whistle when you can't? (p. 151)

- What kind of bias can influence whether you think you hear the phone ringing when you're in the shower? (p. 153)

- What happens when people are deprived of all external sensory stimulation? (pp. 153–154)

- How does the eye differ from a camera? (p. 159)

- Why can we describe a color as bluish green but not as reddish green? (p. 160)

- If you were blind in one eye, why might you misjudge the distance of a painting on the wall but not of buildings a block away? (p. 163)

- As a friend approaches, her image on your retina grows larger; why do you continue to see her as the same size? (p. 164)

- Why are perceptual illusions so valuable to psychologists? (p. 165)

- Why does a note played on a flute sound different from the same note on an oboe? (p. 168)

- If you habitually listen to loud music through headphones, what kind of hearing impairment are you risking? (p. 169)

- To locate the source of a sound, why does it sometimes help to turn or tilt your head? (p. 170)

- Why do saccharin and caffeine taste bitter to some people but not to others? (p. 172)

- Why do you have trouble tasting your food when you have a cold? (p. 172)

- Why do people often continue to "feel" limbs that have been amputated? (p. 175)

- Do babies see the world the way adults do? (p. 178)

- What could cause people to "see" the face of a religious figure on a wall or even a cinnamon bun? (p. 179)

- Can "subliminal perception" tapes help you lose weight or reduce your stress? (pp. 180–181)

- Why are most psychologists skeptical about ESP? (pp. 181–183)

Robot Produces "Offspring"

CAMBRIDGE, MA, AUGUST 29, 2000. Scientists at Brandeis University have announced the creation of a robot that designs and builds other robots. Their achievement has touched off a debate among scientists and philosophers about the uniqueness of human intelligence.

The robot, named "Golem" after a mythical humanoid in medieval Jewish folklore, is made up of plastic cylinders, ball joints, and small motors. It uses a plastic model-making machine to plan and produce different kinds of self-propelled "offspring" that can skitter across the floor like a crab or an insect. The robot also mimics evolution by identifying which of its progeny are the "fittest" in terms of distance covered in a given period of time.

In recent years, machines designed by researchers in the field of artificial intelligence have learned to perform many other human tasks—recognizing speech, reacting to different tones of voice, solving a variety of challenging problems. In 1997, in a six-game chess match, an IBM computer named Deep Blue defeated Russian chess master Garry Kasparov, regarded by

Computer scientists Jordan Pollack (left) and Hod Lipson (right), of Brandeis University, proudly show off two of Golem's offspring.

many as the most talented chess player in history. Before the match, Kasparov had said he was "defending human superiority in a purely intellectual field . . . that defines human beings." After the machine's victory, the Internet began to be bombarded with messages like "It's over for mankind" and "This is the moment in which human beings begin to take to the sidelines."

Although the Brandeis robot does not actually replicate—its offspring cannot produce new robots themselves—many researchers believe this accomplishment is an important step in creating more humanlike machines. At a recent conference at the Massachusetts Institute of Technology, one scientist even predicted that by the year 2040, robots will be as smart as people.

THINKING AND INTELLIGENCE

Are lifelike robots really just around the corner? Can a machine think—and therefore be said to have a mind? Is it really "over for mankind"? To answer these questions intelligently, we first need to have a clear understanding of what thinking and intelligence are.

Each day, in the course of ordinary living, we all make plans, draw inferences, analyze relationships, and organize and reorganize our mental world. Descartes' famous declaration, "I think, therefore I am," could just as well have been reversed: "I am, therefore I think." Our powers of thought and intelligence inspired our forebears to give our species the immodest name *Homo sapiens*, Latin for wise or rational man. Certainly the human mind, which has managed to come up with poker, penicillin, and pantyhose, is a miraculous thing.

But the human mind has also managed to come up with traffic jams, junk mail, and war. To better understand why the same species that figured out how to get to the moon is also capable of breathtaking bumbling here on earth, we will examine in this chapter how people reason, solve problems, and grow in intelligence, as well as some sources of their mental shortcomings. As you read, ask yourself: Could a machine ever do this?

What's Ahead

- When you think of a bird, why are you more likely to recall a robin than a penguin?

- How are visual images like images on a computer screen?

- What is happening mentally when you mistakenly take your geography notes to your psychology class?

6.1 Thought: Using What We Know

Think for a moment about what *thinking* does for you. It frees you from the confines of the immediate present: You can think about a trip taken three years ago, a party planned for next Saturday, or the War of 1812. It carries you beyond the boundaries of reality: You can imagine unicorns and utopias, Martians and magic. Because you think, you do not need to grope your way blindly through your problems but, with some effort and knowledge, can solve them intelligently and creatively.

To explain such abilities, many cognitive psychologists liken the human mind to an information processor, somewhat analogous to a computer but far more complex. Information-processing approaches capture the fact that the brain does not passively record information but actively alters and organizes it. When we take action, we physi-cally manipulate the environment; when we think, we *mentally* manipulate internal representations of objects, activities, and situations.

The Elements of Cognition

One type of mental representation, or unit of thought, is the **concept,** a mental category that groups objects, relations, activities, abstractions, or qualities having common properties. The instances of a concept are seen as roughly similar. For example, *golden retriever, cocker spaniel,* and *border collie* are instances of the concept *dog,* and *anger, joy,* and *sadness* are instances of the concept *emotion.* Concepts simplify and summarize information about the world so that it is manageable, and so that we can make decisions quickly and efficiently. You may never have seen a *basenji* or eaten *escargots,* but if you know that the first is an instance of *dog* and the second an instance of *food,* you will know, roughly, how to respond (unless you do not like to eat snails, which is what escargots are).

The qualities associated with a concept do not necessarily apply to every instance: Some apples are not red; some dogs do not bark; some birds do not fly or perch on trees. But all the instances of a concept do share a "family resemblance." When we need to decide whether something belongs to a concept, we are likely to compare it to a **prototype,** a representative example of the concept (Rosch, 1973). For instance, which dog is doggier—a golden retriever or a chihuahua? Which fruit is more fruitlike—an apple or a pineapple? Which

concept
A mental category that groups objects, relations, activities, abstractions, or qualities having common properties.

prototype
An especially representative example of a concept.

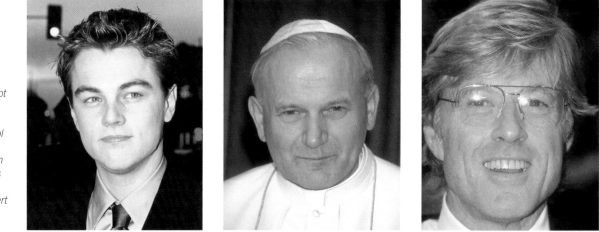

Some instances of a concept are more representative, or prototypical, than others. For example, Hollywood idol Leonardo deCaprio clearly qualifies as a "bachelor," an unmarried man (at least, as of 2001). But is the Pope a bachelor? What about Robert Redford, who is divorced and has not remarried?

activity is more representative of sports—football or weight lifting? Most people within a culture can easily tell you which instances of a concept are most representative, or *prototypical.*

Concepts are the building blocks of thought, but they would be of limited use if we merely stacked them up mentally. We must also represent their relationships to one another. One way we accomplish this may be by storing and using **propositions,** units of meaning that are made up of concepts and that express a unitary idea. A proposition can express nearly any sort of knowledge (e.g., *Hortense raises border collies*) or belief (e.g., *Border collies are smart*). Propositions, in turn, are linked together in complicated networks of knowledge, associations, beliefs, and expectations. These networks, which psychologists call **cognitive schemas,** serve as mental models of aspects of the world. For example, gender schemas represent a person's beliefs and expectations about what it means to be male or female (see Chapter 3). People also have schemas about cultures, occupations, animals, geographical locations, and many other features of the social and natural environment.

Mental images—especially visual images, pictures in the mind's eye—are also important in thinking and in the construction of cognitive schemas. Although no one can directly "see" another person's visual images, psychologists are able to study them indirectly. One method is to measure how long it takes people to rotate an image in their imaginations, scan from one point to another in an image, or read off some detail from an image. The results suggest that visual images are much like images on a computer screen: We can manipulate them, they occur in a mental "space" of a fixed size, and small ones contain less detail than larger ones (Kosslyn, 1980; Shepard & Metzler, 1971).

Most people also report auditory images (for instance, a song, slogan, or poem you can hear in your "mind's ear"), and many report images in other sensory modalities as well—touch, taste, smell, or pain. Some even report kinesthetic images, feelings in the muscles and joints. Athletes often imagine themselves performing a skill, such as diving or sprinting, and this visual and kinesthetic rehearsal seems to improve actual performance (Druckman & Swets, 1988). Brain scans show that such mental practice activates most of the brain circuits involved in the activity itself (Stephan et al., 1995).

Here, then, is a visual summary of the elements of cognition:

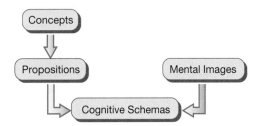

How Conscious Is Thought?

When we think about thinking, we usually have in mind those mental activities, such as solving problems, drawing up plans, or making decisions, that are carried out in a deliberate way with a conscious goal in mind. However, not all mental processing is conscious.

Subconscious processes lie outside of awareness but can be brought into consciousness with little effort when necessary. These processes allow us to handle more information and to perform more complex tasks than if we depended entirely on conscious thought, and they enable us to perform more than one task simultaneously (Kahneman & Treisman, 1984). Consider all the automatic routines performed "without thinking," though they might once have required careful, conscious attention: knitting, typing, driving a car, decoding the letters in a word in order to read it. Because of the capacity for automatic processing, people can even learn to perform simultaneously such complex

Some well-learned skills do not require much conscious thought, so this mother is able to do several things at the same time—to "multi-task."

proposition
A unit of meaning that is made up of concepts and expresses a single idea.

cognitive schema
An integrated mental network of knowledge, beliefs, and expectations concerning a particular topic or aspect of the world.

mental image
A mental representation that mirrors or resembles the thing it represents; it can occur in many and perhaps all sensory modalities.

subconscious processes
Mental processes occurring outside of conscious awareness but accessible to consciousness when necessary.

tasks as reading and taking dictation (Hirst, Neisser, & Spelke, 1978).

Nonconscious processes, in contrast, remain outside of awareness. For example, you have no doubt had the odd experience of having a solution to a problem "pop into mind" after you have given up trying to find one. With sudden insight, you see how to solve an equation, assemble a cabinet, or finish a puzzle, without quite knowing how you managed to find the solution. Similarly, people will often say they rely on "intuition"—hunches and gut feelings—rather than conscious reasoning to make decisions.

Insight and intuition probably involve two stages of mental processing (Bowers et al., 1990). In the first stage, clues in the problem automatically activate certain memories or knowledge, and you begin to see a pattern or structure in the problem, although you cannot yet say what it is. This nonconscious process guides you toward a hunch or a hypothesis. Then, in the second stage, your thinking becomes conscious, and you become aware of a possible solution. This stage may feel like a sudden revelation ("Aha, I've got it!"), but considerable nonconscious mental work has already occurred. Sometimes, however, people solve problems without experiencing the second stage. For example, some people learn to make good choices when playing a card game without ever consciously discovering the best strategy for winning (Bechara et al., 1997).

Usually, of course, much of our thinking is conscious—but we may not be thinking very *hard.* We may act, speak, and make decisions out of habit, without stopping to analyze what we are doing or why we are doing it. This sort of mental inertia, which Ellen Langer (1989) has called *mindlessness,* keeps people from recognizing when a change in context requires a change in behavior.

In one study by Langer and her associates, a researcher approached people as they were about to use a photocopier and made one of three requests: "Excuse me, may I use the Xerox machine?" "Excuse me, may I use the Xerox machine, because I have to make copies," or "Excuse me, may I use the Xerox machine, because I'm in a rush." Normally, people will let someone go before them only if the person has a legitimate reason for doing so, as in the third request. In this study, however, people also complied when the reason sounded like

"This CD player costs less than players selling for twice as much."

This salesman knows all about mindlessness.

an authentic explanation but was actually meaningless ("because I have to make copies"). They heard the form of the request, but they did not hear its content, and they mindlessly stepped aside (Langer, Blank, & Chanowitz, 1978).

The mindless processing of information has benefits: If we stopped to think twice about everything we did during the day, we would get nothing done ("Okay, now I'm reaching for my toothbrush; now I'm putting toothpaste on it; now I'm brushing my upper-right molars"). But mindlessness can also lead to errors and mishaps, ranging from the trivial (putting the butter in the dishwasher or locking yourself out of your apartment) to the serious (driving carelessly while on "automatic pilot").

Jerome Kagan (1989) has argued that fully conscious awareness is needed only when we must make a deliberate choice, when events happen that can't be handled automatically, and when unexpected moods and feelings arise. "Consciousness," he says, "can be likened to the staff of a fire department. Most of the time, it is quietly playing pinochle in the back room; it performs [only] when the alarm sounds." That may be so, but most of us would probably benefit if our mental firefighters paid a little more attention to their jobs. Cognitive psychologists have, therefore, devoted a great deal of study to mindful, conscious thought, decision-making, and the capacity to reason.

nonconscious processes
Mental processes occurring outside of and not available to conscious awareness.

QUICK QUIZ

Stay conscious while taking this quiz.

1. Stuffing your mouth with cotton candy, licking a lollipop, and chewing on a piece of beef jerky are all instances of the _____ *eating.*

2. Which example of the concept *chair* is prototypical: *high chair, rocking chair, dining-room chair?*

3. In addition to concepts and images, _____, which express a unitary idea, have been suggested as a basic form of mental representation.

4. Peter's mental representation of *Thanksgiving* includes associations (e.g., with turkeys), attitudes ("It's a time to be with relatives"), and expectations ("I'm going to gain weight from all that food"). They are all part of his _____ for the holiday.

5. Zelda discovers that she has dialed her boyfriend's number instead of her mother's, as she intended. Her error can be attributed to _____.

Answers:
1. concept 2. a plain, straight-backed dining-room chair will be prototypical for most people 3. propositions 4. cognitive schema 5. mindlessness

What's Ahead

- Mentally speaking, why is making a cake, well, a piece of cake?
- Why can't logic solve all of our problems?
- What kind of reasoning do juries need to be good at?
- When people say that all opinions and claims are equally valid, what error are they making?

6.2 Reasoning Rationally

Reasoning is purposeful mental activity that involves operating on information in order to reach conclusions. Unlike impulsive or nonconscious responding, reasoning requires us to draw specific inferences from observations, facts, or assumptions.

Formal Reasoning: Algorithms and Logic

In *formal reasoning problems*—the kind you might find, say, on an intelligence test or a college entrance exam—the information needed for drawing a conclusion or reaching a solution is specified clearly, and there is a single right (or best) answer.

In some formal problems and well-defined tasks, all you have to do is apply an **algorithm,** a set of procedures guaranteed to produce a solution even if you do not really know how it works. To solve a problem in long division, for example, you apply a series of operations that you learned in elementary school. To make a cake, you apply an algorithm called a *recipe.*

For other formal problems, the rules of formal logic are crucial tools to have in your mental toolbox. These tools include (among others) the processes of deductive and inductive reasoning. In *deductive reasoning*, a conclusion *necessarily* follows from a set of observations or propositions (*premises*):

6.1

DEDUCTIVE REASONING

For example, if the premises "All human beings are mortal" and "I am a human being" are true, then the conclusion "I am mortal" must also be true. In contrast, in *inductive reasoning,* a conclusion

reasoning
The drawing of conclusions or inferences from observations, facts, or assumptions.

algorithm
A problem-solving strategy guaranteed to produce a solution even if the user does not know how it works.

probably follows from certain propositions or premises, but it could conceivably be false:

INDUCTIVE REASONING

For example, if your premises are "I had a delicious meal at Joe's Restaurant on Monday," "I had a delicious meal there again on Tuesday," and "I had another delicious meal there on Wednesday," you might reasonably reach the conclusion that "Joe's Restaurant consistently serves good food." Deductive and inductive reasoning may seem pretty straightforward, but many of us have trouble thinking logically in our lives.

Informal Reasoning: Heuristics and Dialectical Thinking

Unfortunately, algorithms and logical reasoning cannot solve all of life's problems. In *informal reasoning problems,* there may be no clearly correct solution (Galotti, 1989). Many approaches, viewpoints, or possible solutions may compete, and you may have to decide which one is most reasonable. Moreover, information may be incomplete, or people may disagree on what the premises should be. Your position on the controversial issue of abortion, for example, will depend on your premises about when meaningful human life begins, what rights an embryo has, and what rights a woman has to control her own body. People on opposing sides of this issue even disagree on how the premises should be phrased because they have different emotional reactions to terms such as "rights," "meaningful life," and "control over one's body."

The differences between formal and informal reasoning problems are summarized in Table 6.1. These two types of problems typically call for different approaches. Whereas formal problems can often be solved with an algorithm, informal problems often call for a **heuristic**—a rule of thumb that suggests a course of action without guaranteeing an optimal solution. Anyone who has ever played chess or a card game such as Bridge or Hearts is familiar with heuristics (e.g., "Get rid of high cards first"). In these games, working out all the possible sequences of moves would take too long and be too difficult. Heuristics are also useful to an investor trying to predict the stock market, a renter trying to decide whether to lease an apartment, a doctor try-

heuristic
A rule of thumb that suggests a course of action or guides problem solving but does not guarantee an optimal solution.

Table 6.1 Two Kinds of Reasoning

In formal reasoning, we apply rules of logic to solve well-specified problems. In informal, everyday reasoning, we must solve problems that are less clearly defined. Here are some differences between the two modes of thought:

Formal	Informal
All premises are supplied.	Some premises are implicit and some are not supplied at all.
There is typically one correct answer.	There are typically several possible answers that vary in quality.
Established methods often exist for solving the problem.	Established procedures of inference that apply to the problem rarely exist.
You usually know when the problem is solved.	It is often unclear whether the current solution is good enough.
The problem is often of limited real-world interest.	The problem typically has personal relevance.
Problems are solved for their own sake.	Problems are often solved as a means of achieving other goals.

Source: Adapted from Galotti, 1989.

ing to determine the best treatment for a patient, and a factory owner trying to boost production: All are faced with incomplete information on which to base a decision and may therefore resort to rules of thumb that have proven effective in the past.

In thinking about real-life problems, a person must also be able to use **dialectical reasoning,** the process of comparing and evaluating opposing points of view. Philosopher Richard Paul (1984) has described dialectical reasoning as movement "up and back between contradictory lines of reasoning, using each to critically cross-examine the other":

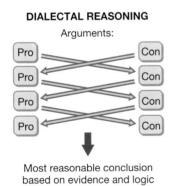

DIALECTAL REASONING

Arguments:

Most reasonable conclusion based on evidence and logic

Dialectical reasoning is what juries are supposed to do to arrive at a verdict: consider arguments for and against the defendant's guilt, point and counterpoint. It is also what voters are supposed to do when thinking about whether the government should raise taxes or lower them, or about the best way to improve public education.

Reflective Judgment

Many adults clearly have trouble thinking dialectically—they take one position, and that's that. To find out precisely how people reason and justify their conclusions, Karen Kitchener and Patricia King interviewed adolescents and adults of all ages and occupations, asking them where they stood on issues such as nuclear power, the safety of food additives, and the objectivity of the news media. Kitchener and King did not care how much people knew about these issues, or even how they felt about them; they just wanted to know how their respondents had reached their conclusions. More specifically, they wanted to know whether people use *reflective judgment* in thinking about everyday problems (King & Kitchener, 1994; Kitchener & King, 1990). Reflective judgment is basically what we have called critical thinking: the ability to evaluate and integrate evidence, relate that evidence to a theory or opinion, and reach a conclusion that can be defended as reasonable or plausible, while standing ready to reassess those conclusions in the face of new information.

The researchers began by providing their interviewees with statements that described opposing viewpoints on various topics. Then the interviewer asked, What do you think about these statements? How did you come to hold that point of view? On what do your base your position? Can you ever know for sure that your position is correct? Why do you suppose disagreement exists about this issue?

Based on the responses, King and Kitchener were able to identify seven cognitive stages on the road to reflective thought, some occurring in childhood and others unfolding throughout adolescence and adulthood. At each stage, people make different kinds of assumptions about how things are known and use different ways of justifying or defending their beliefs. Each stage builds on the skills of the prior one and lays a foundation for successive ones.

dialectical reasoning
A process in which opposing facts or ideas are weighed and compared, with a view to determining the best solution or to resolving differences.

We will not be concerned here with the details of these stages, but only with their broad outlines. In general, people in the two early, *prereflective stages* assume that a correct answer always exists and that it can be obtained directly through the senses ("I know what I've seen") or from authorities ("They said so on the news"; "That's what I was brought up to believe"):

Pre-reflective judgment

"I was brought up to believe…"
"I just know what I know."

If authorities don't yet have the truth, prereflective thinkers tend to reach conclusions on the basis of what "feels right" at the moment. They do not distinguish between knowledge and belief, or between belief and evidence, and they don't see any reason for justifying a belief (King & Kitchener, 1994):

INTERVIEWER: Can you ever know for sure that your position [on evolution] is correct?

RESPONDENT: Well, some people believe that we evolved from apes and that's the way they want to believe. But I would never believe that way and nobody could talk me out of the way I believe because I believe the way that it's told in the Bible.

During the three *quasi-reflective stages*, people recognize that some things cannot be known with absolute certainty, but they are not sure how to deal with these situations. They realize that judgments should be supported by reasons, but they pay attention only to evidence that fits what they already believe. They know that there are alternative viewpoints, but they seem to think that because knowledge is uncertain, any judgment about the evidence is purely subjective. Quasi-reflective thinkers will defend a position by saying that "We all have a right to our own opinion," as if all opinions are created equal:

Quasi-reflective judgment

"Knowledge is purely subjective."
"We all have a right to our opinion."

Here is the response of a college student who uses quasi-reflective reasoning:

INTERVIEWER: Can you say you will ever know for sure that chemicals [in foods] are safe?

STUDENT: No, I don't think so.

INTERVIEWER: Can you tell me why you'll never know for sure?

STUDENT: Because they test them in little animals, and they haven't really tested them in humans, as far as I know. And I don't think anything is for sure.

INTERVIEWER: When people differ about matters such as this, is it the case that one opinion is right and one is wrong?

STUDENT: No. I think it just depends on how you feel personally because people make their decisions based upon how they feel and what research they've seen. So what one person thinks is right, another person might think is wrong. . . . If I feel that chemicals cause cancer and you feel that food is unsafe without it, your opinion might be right to you and my opinion is right to me.

In the last two stages, a person becomes capable of *reflective judgment*. He or she understands that although some things can never be known with certainty, some judgments are more valid than others because of their coherence, their fit with the evidence, their usefulness, and so on. People at these stages are willing to consider evidence from a variety of sources and to reason dialectically. At the very highest stage, they are able to defend their conclusions as representing the most complete, plausible, or compelling understanding of an issue, based on currently available evidence:

Reflective judgment

"Based on the evidence, I believe…"
"Here are the reasons for my conclusions…"

This interview with a graduate student illustrates reflective thinking:

INTERVIEWER: Can you ever say you know for sure that your point of view on chemical additives is correct?

STUDENT: No, I don't think so [but] I think that we can usually be reasonably certain, given the information we have now, and considering our methodologies.

INTERVIEWER: Is there anything else that contributes to not being able to be sure?

STUDENT: Yes. . . . It might be that the research wasn't conducted rigorously enough. In other words, we might have flaws in our data or sample, things like that.

INTERVIEWER: How then would you identify the "better opinion"?

STUDENT: One that takes as many factors as possible into consideration. I mean one that uses the higher percentage of the data that we have, and perhaps that uses the methodology that has been most reliable.

INTERVIEWER: And how do you come to a conclusion about what the evidence suggests?

STUDENT: I think you have to take a look at the different opinions and studies that are offered by different groups. Maybe some studies offered by the chemical industry, some studies by the government, some private studies. . . . You wouldn't trust, for instance, a study funded by the tobacco industry that proved that cigarette smoking is not harmful . . . you have to try to interpret people's motives and that makes it a more complex soup to try to strain out.

Most people do not show evidence of reflective judgment until their middle or late twenties, if at all. And most undergraduates, regardless of age, tend to score at only Stage 3 during their first year of college. But here's the good news: When students get support for thinking reflectively and have opportunities to practice it, their reasoning tends to become more complex, sophisticated, and well-grounded (Kitchener et al., 1993). Moreover, higher education gradually moves people closer to reflective judgment. By their senior year, students typically score at Stage 4; most graduate students score at Stage 4 or 5; and many advanced doctoral students perform consistently at Stage 6 (King &

"I'm going to ask the jury to hold its applause until all the evidence has been introduced."

Jury members are supposed to make reflective judgments, but they don't always do so.

Kitchener, 1994). Longitudinal studies show that these differences do not occur only because lower-level thinkers are more likely to drop out of school along the way.

The gradual development of thinking skills among undergraduates, said Barry Kroll (1992), represents an abandonment of "ignorant certainty" in favor of "intelligent confusion." It may not seem so, but this is a big step forward! You can see why, in this book, we emphasize thinking about and evaluating psychological findings, and not just memorizing them.

QUICK QUIZ

Put on your thinking cap to answer these questions.

1. Most of the holiday gifts Mervin bought this year cost more than they did last year, so he concludes that inflation is increasing. Is he using inductive, deductive, or dialectical reasoning?

2. Yvonne is arguing with Henrietta about whether real estate is a better investment than stocks. "You can't convince me," says Yvonne. "I just know I'm right." Yvonne needs training in _____ reasoning.

3. Seymour thinks the media have a liberal political bias, and Selena thinks they are too conservative. "Well," says Seymour, "I have my truth and you have yours. It's purely subjective." Which of King and Kitchener's levels of thinking is Seymour at?

 4. What kind of evidence might resolve the issue that Seymour and Selena are arguing about?

Answers:
1. inductive 2. dialectical 3. quasi-reflective 4. Researchers might have raters watch a random sample of TV news shows and measure the amount of time devoted to conservative and liberal politicians or viewpoints. Or raters could read a random sample of newspaper editorials from all over the country and evaluate the editorials as liberal or conservative in outlook. You may be able to think of other strategies, as well. However, subjective TV program or newspapers ratings of *entire* TV programs or newspapers might not be informative because people often perceive only what they want or expect to perceive.

- Why do people worry about dying in an airplane crash but ignore dangers that are far more likely?

- How might your physician's choice of words about alternative treatments for your illness affect which one you choose?

- When "Monday morning quarterbacks" say they knew all along who would win Sunday's big game, what bias might they be showing?

- Why will a terrible hazing make you more loyal to the group that hazed you?

6.3 Barriers to Reasoning Rationally

Although most people have the capacity to think logically, reason dialectically, and make judgments reflectively, it is abundantly clear that they don't always do so. One obstacle is the need to be right; if your self-esteem depends on winning every argument, you will find it hard to listen with an open mind to competing views. Another obstacle is plain old mental laziness. Many social critics think such laziness is on the rise because television is replacing reading. Television programs often provide sound bites instead of fully developed arguments, encouraging viewers to form quick, impulsive opinions instead of carefully considered

availability heuristic
The tendency to judge the probability of a type of event by how easy it is to think of examples or instances.

Many of us overestimate the chances of dying in a plane crash and underestimate the chances of dying in a car crash. As the text explains, one reason is the availability heuristic: Although airline disasters are rare, we remember them better than the automobile accidents that take place every day.

ones. As writer Mitchell Stephens (1991) said, "All television demands is our gaze."

Human thought processes are also tripped up by many predictable biases and errors. Psychologists have studied dozens of these cognitive pitfalls; here we describe just a few of them.

Exaggerating the Improbable

A common cognitive bias is the inclination to exaggerate the probability of very rare events—a bias that helps explain why so many people enter lotteries and why they buy airline disaster insurance.

People are especially likely to exaggerate the likelihood of a rare event if its consequences are catastrophic. One reason is the **availability heuristic,** the tendency to judge the probability of an event by how easy it is to think of examples or instances (Tversky & Kahneman, 1973). Catastrophes stand out in our minds and are therefore more "available" mentally than are other kinds of negative events. In one study, people overestimated the frequency of deaths from tornadoes and underestimated the frequency of deaths from asthma, which occur 20 times as often but do not make headlines. These same people estimated deaths from accidents and disease to be equally frequent, even though 16 times as many people die each year from disease as from accidents (Lichtenstein et al., 1978).

People will sometimes work themselves into a froth about highly unlikely events, such as dying in an airplane crash, yet they will irrationally ignore dangers to human life that are harder to visualize, such as a growth in skin-cancer rates due to depletion of the ozone layer in the earth's atmosphere. Similarly, parents are often more frightened about real but unlikely threats to their children, such as being kidnapped by a stranger or dying from a routine immunization shot (both horrible but extremely rare), than they are about problems more common in children, such as depression, delinquency, and poor grades, or dangers that are far more likely, such as auto accidents or accidental drownings.

Avoiding Loss

In general, people try to avoid or minimize risks and losses when they make decisions. So when a choice is framed in terms of the risk of losing something, they will respond more cautiously than when the *same* choice is framed in terms of gain. They will, for example, choose a ticket that has a 10 percent chance of winning a raffle, rather than one that has a 90 percent chance of losing! Or they will rate a condom as effective when they are told it has a 95 percent success rate in protecting against the AIDS virus, but not when they are told it has a 5 percent failure rate—which is exactly the same thing (Linville, Fischer, & Fischhoff, 1992).

Here's another example. Suppose you had to choose between two health programs to combat a disease expected to kill 600 people. Which would you prefer: a program that would definitely save 200 people, or one with a one-third probability of saving all 600 people and a two-thirds probability of saving none? (Problem 1 in Figure 6.1 illustrates this choice.) When asked this question, most people, including physicians, say they prefer the first program. In other words, they reject the riskier though potentially more rewarding solution in favor of a sure gain. However, people *will* take a risk if they see it as a way to *avoid loss.* Suppose now that you have to choose between a program in which 400 people will definitely die and a program in which there is a one-third probability of nobody dying and a two-thirds probability that all 600 will die. If you think about it, you will see that the alternatives are exactly the same as in the first problem; they are merely worded differently (see Problem 2 in Figure 6.1). Yet this time, most people choose the second solution. They reject risk when they think of the outcome in terms of lives saved but accept risk when they think of the outcome in terms of lives lost (Tversky & Kahneman, 1981).

Few of us will have to face a decision involving hundreds of lives, but we may have to choose between different medical treatments for ourselves or a relative. Our decision may be affected by whether the doctor frames the choice in terms of chances of surviving or chances of dying.

The Confirmation Bias

When people want to make the most accurate judgment possible, they usually try to consider all of the relevant information. But when they are thinking about issues they already feel strongly about, they tend to give in to the **confirmation bias,** paying attention only to evidence that confirms what they want to believe, and finding fault with evidence or arguments that point in a different direction (Edwards & Smith, 1996; Kunda, 1990; Nickerson, 1998). You rarely hear someone say, "Oh, thank you for explaining to me why my lifelong philosophy of child raising (or politics, or

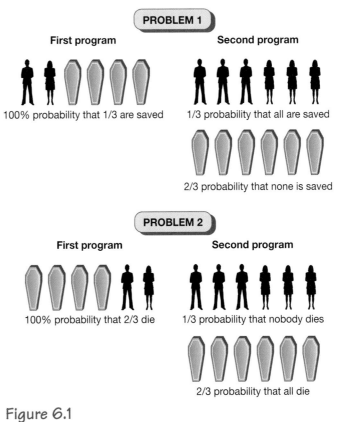

Figure 6.1
A Matter of Wording

The decisions we make depend on how the alternatives are framed. When asked to choose between the two programs in Problem 1, which are described in terms of lives saved, most people choose the first program. When asked to choose between the programs in Problem 2, which are described in terms of lives lost, most people choose the second program. Yet the alternatives in the two problems are actually identical.

investing) is wrong. I'm so grateful for the facts!" The person usually says, "Oh, buzz off, and take your cockamamie ideas with you."

We see the confirmation bias all around us. Politicians, for example, are likely to accept economic news that confirms their philosophies and dismiss counterevidence as biased or unimportant. Police officers who are convinced of a suspect's guilt are likely to take anything the suspect says or does as evidence that confirms it. The confirmation bias also affects jury members. In one study, people listened to an audiotaped reenactment of an actual murder trial and then said how they would have voted and why. Instead of considering and weighing possible verdicts in light of the evidence, many people quickly constructed a story about what had happened and then considered only the evidence that supported their version of events. These same people were the most confident in their decisions and were most likely

6.2

confirmation bias
The tendency to look for or pay attention only to information that confirms one's own belief.

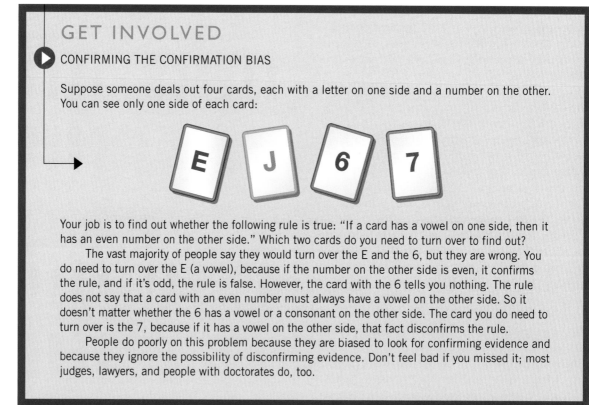

GET INVOLVED

CONFIRMING THE CONFIRMATION BIAS

Suppose someone deals out four cards, each with a letter on one side and a number on the other. You can see only one side of each card:

Your job is to find out whether the following rule is true: "If a card has a vowel on one side, then it has an even number on the other side." Which two cards do you need to turn over to find out?

The vast majority of people say they would turn over the E and the 6, but they are wrong. You do need to turn over the E (a vowel), because if the number on the other side is even, it confirms the rule, and if it's odd, the rule is false. However, the card with the 6 tells you nothing. The rule does not say that a card with an even number must always have a vowel on the other side. So it doesn't matter whether the 6 has a vowel or a consonant on the other side. The card you do need to turn over is the 7, because if it has a vowel on the other side, that fact disconfirms the rule.

People do poorly on this problem because they are biased to look for confirming evidence and because they ignore the possibility of disconfirming evidence. Don't feel bad if you missed it; most judges, lawyers, and people with doctorates do, too.

to vote for an extreme verdict (Kuhn, Weinstock, & Flaton, 1994).

The confirmation bias can also affect how you react to what you are learning. When students read about scientific findings that dispute one of their own cherished beliefs or that challenge the wisdom of their own actions, they tend to acknowledge but minimize the strengths of the research. In contrast, when a study supports their view, they will acknowledge any flaws (such as a small sample or a reliance on self-reports) but will give these flaws less weight than they otherwise would (Sherman & Kunda, 1989). Psychologists do the same thing! In thinking critically, it seems, people apply a double standard: They think most critically about results they don't like.

Biases Due to Mental Sets

Another barrier to rational thinking is the development of a **mental set,** a tendency to try to solve new problems by using the same heuristics, strategies, and rules that worked in the past on similar problems. Mental sets make human learning and problem solving efficient; because of them, we do not have to keep reinventing the wheel. But mental sets are not helpful when a problem calls for fresh insights and methods. They cause us to cling rigidly to the same old assumptions, hypotheses, and strategies, blinding us to better or more rapid solutions. (For an illustration of this point, try the "Get Involved" exercise on the next page.)

One common mental set is the tendency to find patterns in events. This tendency is adaptive because it helps us understand and exert some control over what happens in our lives. But it also leads us to see meaningful patterns even when they don't exist. For example, many people with arthritis think that their symptoms follow a pattern dictated by the weather. They suffer more, they say, when the barometric pressure changes or when it's damp or humid out. Yet when researchers followed 18 arthritis patients for 15 months, *no* association whatsoever emerged between weather conditions and the patients' self-reported pain levels, their ability to function in daily life, or a doctor's evaluation of their joint tenderness (Redelmeier & Tversky, 1996). Did the patients say, "Oh, thank you for pointing out that my belief was unfounded! How incredibly interesting"? No, they adamantly refused to believe the results.

mental set
A tendency to solve problems using procedures that worked before on similar problems.

GET INVOLVED

CONNECT THE DOTS

Copy the following figure, and see whether you can connect the dots by using no more than four straight lines, without lifting your pencil or pen. A line must pass through each point. Can you do it?

Most people have difficulty with this problem because they have a mental set to interpret the arrangement of dots as a square. Once having done so, they then assume that they can't extend a line beyond the "boundaries" of the square. Now that you know this, you might try again if you haven't yet solved the puzzle. Some possible solutions are given on page 225.

The Hindsight Bias

Would you have predicted, beforehand, that the quirky movie *American Beauty* would win the Oscar for best film of 2000 instead of a more traditional Hollywood blockbuster? When people learn the outcome of an event or the answer to a question, they are often sure that they "knew it all along." Armed with the wisdom of hindsight, they see the outcome that actually occurred as inevitable, and they overestimate their ability to have predicted what happened. Compared with judgments made *before* an event takes place, their judgments about their ability to have predicted the event in advance are inflated (Fischhoff, 1975; Hawkins & Hastie, 1990).

This **hindsight bias** shows up in political assessments ("I always knew my candidate would win"), medical judgments ("I could have told you that mole was cancerous"), and military opinions ("The generals should have known that Pearl Harbor would be attacked"). And when investors buy a stock and its price goes up, they are apt to think, in hindsight, that they were more confident about their purchase at the time they made it than they really were (Louie, 1999).

Like mental sets, the hindsight bias can be adaptive. When we try to make sense of the past, we focus on explaining just one outcome, the one that occurred, because explaining outcomes that did not take place can be a waste of time. As Scott

Hawkins and Reid Hastie (1990) wrote, "hindsight biases represent the dark side of successful learning and judgment" because when we are sure we knew something "all along," we are also less willing to find out what we need to know in order to make accurate predictions in the future. In medical conferences, for example, when doctors are told what the postmortem findings were for a patient who died, they tend to think the case was easier to diagnose than it actually was ("I would have known it was a brain tumor"), and so they learn less from the case than they should (Dawson et al., 1988).

Perhaps you feel that we're not telling you anything new because you have always known about the hindsight bias. If so, you may just have a hindsight bias about the hindsight bias!

The Need for Cognitive Consistency

The confirmation bias enables us to avoid evidence that contradicts our beliefs. But what happens when disconfirming evidence finally smacks us in the face, and we cannot ignore or discount it any longer? For example, as the twentieth century rolled to an end, predictions of doomsday—the end of the world—escalated. Similar predictions have been made throughout history. When these predictions fail, how come we never hear believers say, "Boy, what a jerk I was"?

hindsight bias
The tendency to overestimate one's ability to have predicted an event once the outcome is known; the "I knew it all along" phenomenon.

cognitive dissonance
A state of tension that occurs when a person simultaneously holds two cognitions that are psychologically inconsistent, or when a person's belief is incongruent with his or her behavior.

According to the theory of **cognitive dissonance,** people will resolve such conflicts in predictable, though not always obvious, ways (Festinger, 1957). *Dissonance*, the opposite of consistency (*consonance*), is a state of tension that occurs when you simultaneously hold either two cognitions (beliefs, thoughts, attitudes) that are psychologically inconsistent or a belief that is incongruent with your behavior. This tension is uncomfortable, so you will be motivated to reduce it. You may do this by rejecting or modifying one of those inconsistent beliefs, changing your behavior, denying the evidence, or rationalizing (Harmon-Jones et al., 1996):

COGNITIVE DISSONANCE

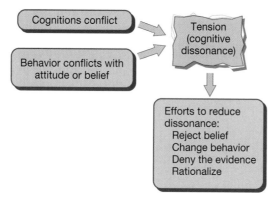

Many years ago, in a famous and clever field study, Leon Festinger and two associates explored people's reactions to failed prophecies by infiltrating a group of people who thought the world would end on December 21 (Festinger, Riecken, & Schachter, 1956). The group's leader, whom the researchers called Marian Keech, promised that the faithful would be picked up by a flying saucer and whisked to safety at midnight on December 20. Many of her followers quit their jobs and spent all their savings, waiting for the end. What would they do or say, Festinger and his colleagues wondered, to reduce the dissonance between "The world is still muddling along on the 21st" and "I predicted the end of the world and sold all my worldly possessions"?

The researchers predicted that believers who had made no public commitment to the prophecy, who awaited the end

of the world by themselves at home, would simply lose their faith. But those who had acted on their conviction by selling their property and waiting with Keech for the spaceship would be in a state of dissonance. They would, said the researchers, have to *increase* their religious belief to avoid the intolerable realization that they had behaved foolishly and others knew it. That is just what happened. At 4:45 A.M., long past the appointed hour of the saucer's arrival, the leader had a new vision. The world had been spared, she said, because of the impressive faith of her little band.

Cognitive–dissonance theory predicts that in more ordinary situations, too, people will resist or rationalize information that conflicts with their existing ideas. For example, if you are a cigarette smoker, your behavior is dissonant with your awareness that smoking causes illness. You might try to reduce the dissonance by trying to quit; by rejecting the evidence that smoking is bad; by persuading yourself that you will quit later on ("after these exams"); by emphasizing the benefits of smoking ("A cigarette helps me relax"); or by deciding that you don't want a long life, anyhow ("It will be shorter, but sweeter"). Likewise, cigarette manufacturers are good at reducing the dissonance between "this job makes a lot of money for the company and for me" and "cigarette smoking kills 400,000 people a year." When the president of one tobacco company was told that smoking during pregnancy increases the chances of having a low-birthweight baby, he replied, "Some women would prefer having smaller babies" (quoted in Kluger, 1996).

There are three conditions under which you are particularly likely to try to reduce dissonance (Aronson, Wilson, & Akert, 1999):

1 *When you need to justify a choice or decision that you freely made.* All car dealers know about "buyer's remorse": The second that people buy a car, they worry that they made the wrong decision, spent too much, or got a lemon. This is called *postdecision dissonance*, and cognitive–dissonance theory predicts that you will try to resolve it. You will probably decide that the car (or toaster, or house, or spouse) that you chose is really, truly the best in the world. However, if someone else made your decision for you, you will not feel much dissonance if it proves misguided. There is no dissonance between "The Army drafted me; I had no choice about being here" and "I hate basic training."

6.1

2 *When your actions violate your self-concept, particularly your sense of consistency.* If you have a concept of yourself as consistent in your convictions, you will probably experience dissonance if you are in a situation in which you suppress your feelings for the sake of group harmony. North Americans are especially likely to feel dissonance because they regard the "self" as being consistent across situations. In other cultures, where people think of themselves as being different in different situations, and where group harmony is highly valued, dissonance is less likely to occur.

3 *When you put a lot of effort into a decision, only to find the results less than you had hoped for.* The harder you work to reach a goal, or the more you suffer for it, the more you will try to convince yourself that you value the goal, even if the goal is not so great after all (Aronson & Mills, 1959). This explains why hazing, whether in social clubs or the military, turns new recruits into loyal members. You might think that people would hate a group that made them suffer. But the cognition "I went through a lot of awful stuff to join this group" is dissonant with the cognition "only to find I hate the group." Therefore, people must decide either that the hazing was not so bad or that they really like the group. This mental reevaluation is called the **justification of effort,** and it is one of the most popular methods of reducing dissonance.

Cognitive–dissonance theory has its limitations. Some people, like some cultures, do not have a strong need for consistency, and so they are less subject than others to experience cognitive dissonance (Cialdini, Trost, & Newsom, 1995). And some people are secure enough to own up to their mistakes instead of rationalizing them. Still, the need for cognitive consistency under certain conditions can lead to irrational, self-defeating decisions and actions.

Overcoming Our Cognitive Biases

The fact that our decisions and judgments, and the feelings of regret or pleasure that follow, are not always rational has enormous implications for the legal system, business, medicine, government—in fact, in all areas. But before you despair about the human ability to think clearly and rationally, we should tell you that the situation is not hopeless. For one thing, people are not equally irrational in

The more you must endure to reach a goal, the more highly you will value it. This "justification of effort" may be one reason that fraternities often subject pledges to disgusting, frightening, or even dangerous hazing. These initiates, blindfolded and forced to wear vomit-drenched T-shirts, were also covered with molasses and were urinated on by their new fraternity brothers. They probably became devoted members.

all situations. When they are doing things they have some expertise in, or making decisions that have serious consequences, cognitive biases often diminish. Accountants who audit companies' books, for example, are less subject to the confirmation bias than are undergraduates in psychology experiments, perhaps because auditors can be sued if they misjudge a firm's profitability or economic health (Smith & Kida, 1991).

Further, once we understand a bias, we may be able to reduce or eliminate it. For example, we have seen that doctors are vulnerable to the hindsight bias if they already know what caused a patient's death. But Hal Arkes and his colleagues (1988) were able to reduce a similar bias in neuropsychologists. The psychologists were given a case study and were asked to state one reason why each of three possible diagnoses—alcohol withdrawal, Alzheimer's disease, and brain damage—might have been applicable. This procedure forced the psychologists to consider all the evidence, not just evidence that supported the correct diagnosis. The hindsight bias evaporated when the psychologists realized that the correct diagnosis had not been so obvious at the time the patient was being treated.

Some people, of course, seem to think more clearly than others all the time; we call them "intelligent." But just what is intelligence, and how can we measure and improve it? We take up that question next.

justification of effort
The tendency of individuals to increase their liking for something that they have worked hard or suffered to attain; a common form of dissonance reduction.

QUICK QUIZ

In hindsight, will you say this quiz was easy?

1. Stu meets a young woman at the student cafeteria. They hit it off, start to see each other regularly, and eventually get married. Says Stu, "I knew that day, when I headed for the cafeteria, that something special was about to happen." What cognitive bias is affecting Stu's thinking, charmingly romantic though it is?

2. In a classic study of cognitive dissonance, students did some boring, repetitive tasks and then had to tell another student, who was waiting to participate in the study, that the work was interesting and fun (Festinger & Carlsmith, 1959). Half the students were offered $20 for telling this lie and the others only $1. Which students who lied decided later on that the tasks had been fun after all?

Answers:
1. the hindsight bias   2. The students who got only $1. They were in a state of dissonance because "the task was as dull as dishwater" is dissonant with "I said I enjoyed it"—and for a mere dollar, at that." Those who got $20 could rationalize that the large sum (which was *really* large in the 1950s) justified the lie.

What's Ahead

- How did the original purpose of intelligence testing change when IQ tests came to America?

- Is it possible to design intelligence tests that are not influenced by culture?

- Why do some psychologists defend traditional intelligence testing and others oppose it?

- What kind of intelligence allows you to master the unspoken rules for academic success?

- What is "EQ," and why is it as important as IQ?

6.4 Intelligence

Educator Sylvia Ashton-Warner once called intelligence "the tool to find the truth—a tool that must be kept sharpened." Yet psychologists disagree on just what this tool is. Some equate it with the ability to reason abstractly, others with the ability to learn and profit from experience in daily life. Some emphasize the ability to think rationally, others the ability to act purposefully. These qualities are all probably part of what most people mean by **intelligence,** but theorists weigh them differently.

One of the longest-running debates in psychology is whether a global quality called "intelligence" even exists. A typical intelligence test asks you to do several things: provide a specific bit of information, notice similarities between objects, solve arithmetic problems, define words, fill in the missing parts of incomplete pictures, arrange pictures in a logical order, arrange blocks to resemble a design, assemble puzzles, use a coding scheme, or judge what behavior would be appropriate in a particular situation. Researchers use a statistical method called *factor analysis* to try to identify which basic abilities underlie performance on the various items. As we saw in Chapter 2, this procedure identifies clusters of correlated items that seem to be measuring some common ability, or factor. Most scientists believe that a general ability, or **g factor,** underlies the specific abilities and talents measured by intelligence tests (Herrnstein & Murray, 1994; Spearman, 1927; Wechsler, 1955). But others dispute the existence of a g factor on the grounds that a person can excel in some tasks yet do poorly in others (Gould, 1994; Guilford, 1988). Disagreements over how to define intelligence have led some writers to argue that intelligence is "whatever intelligence tests measure."

Measuring Intelligence: The Psychometric Approach

The traditional approach to intelligence, the **psychometric** approach, focuses on how well people perform on standardized aptitude tests. The tests you take in your courses are called *achievement tests* because they are designed to measure skills and

---

intelligence
An inferred characteristic of an individual, usually defined as the ability to profit from experience, acquire knowledge, think abstractly, act purposefully, or adapt to changes in the environment.

g factor
A general intellectual ability assumed by many theorists to underlie specific mental abilities and talents.

psychometrics
The measurement of mental abilities, traits, and processes.

knowledge that you have already learned. *Aptitude tests,* in contrast, are designed to measure the ability to acquire skills or knowledge in the future. For example, vocational aptitude tests can help you decide whether you will do better as a mechanic or a musician, and IQ tests do a pretty good job of predicting school performance. But all mental tests are in some sense achievement tests because they assume past learning or experience with particular objects, words, or situations. The difference between achievement tests and aptitude tests is one of degree and intended use.

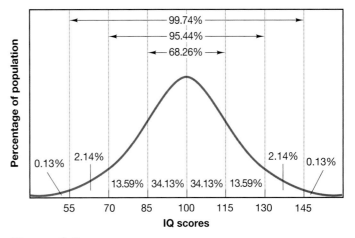

Figure 6.2

Expected Distribution of IQ Scores

In a large population, IQ scores tend to be distributed on a normal (bell-shaped) curve. On most tests, about 68 percent of all people will score between 85 and 115; about 95 percent will score between 70 and 130; and about 99.7 percent will score between 55 and 145. In any actual sample, however, the distribution will depart somewhat from the theoretical ideal.

The Invention of the IQ Test. The first widely used intelligence test was devised in 1904, when the French Ministry of Education asked psychologist Alfred Binet (1857–1911) to find a way to identify children who were slow learners so they could be given remedial work. The ministry was reluctant to let teachers identify such children, because the teachers might have prejudices about poor children or might assume that shy or disruptive children were mentally impaired. They wanted a more objective approach.

Wrestling with the problem, Binet had a great insight: In the classroom, the responses of "dull" children resembled those of ordinary children of younger ages. Bright children, on the other hand, responded like children of older ages. The thing to measure, then, was a child's **mental age (MA),** or level of intellectual development relative to other children's. Then instruction could be tailored to the child's capabilities.

The test devised by Binet and his colleague, Theophile Simon, measured memory, vocabulary, and perceptual discrimination. Items ranged from those that most young children could do easily to those that only older children could handle, as determined by the testing of large numbers of children. A scoring system developed later by others used a formula in which the child's mental age was divided by the child's chronological age to yield an **intelligence quotient,** or **IQ** (a quotient is the result of division). Thus a child of 8 who scored like an average 10-year-old would have a mental age of 10 and an IQ of 125 (10 divided by 8, times 100). All average children, regardless of age, would have an IQ of 100 because mental age and chronological age would be the same.

This method of figuring IQ had serious flaws, however. At one age, scores might cluster tightly around the average, whereas at another age they might be more dispersed. As a result, the score

necessary to be in the top 10 or 20 or 30 percent of your age group varied, depending on your age. Also, the IQ formula did not make much sense for adults: A 50-year-old who scores like a 30-year-old does not have low intelligence! Today, therefore, intelligence tests are scored differently. The average is usually set arbitrarily at 100, and tests are constructed so that about two-thirds of all people score between 85 and 115. Individual scores are computed from tables based on established norms. These scores are still informally referred to as "IQs," and they still reflect how a person compares with other people, either children of a particular age or adults in general. At all ages, the distribution of scores approximates a normal (bell-shaped) curve, with scores near the average (mean) most common and very high or very low scores rare (see Figure 6.2).

In the United States, Stanford psychologist Lewis Terman revised Binet's test and established norms for American children. His version, the Stanford–Binet Intelligence Scale, was first published in 1916 and has been updated several times since. (For some sample items, see Table 6.2.) Two decades later, David Wechsler designed another test expressly for adults, which became the Wechsler Adult Intelligence Scale (WAIS). It was followed by the Wechsler Intelligence Scale for Children (WISC). Although the Wechsler tests produce a general IQ score, they also provide specific scores for different kinds of ability. Verbal

mental age (MA)
A measure of mental development expressed in terms of the average mental ability at a given age.

intelligence quotient (IQ)
A measure of intelligence originally computed by dividing a person's mental age by his or her chronological age and multiplying the result by 100; now derived from norms provided for standardized intelligence tests.

Table 6.2 Sample Items from the Stanford-Binet Intelligence Test, Form L–M

The older the test taker is, the more the test requires in the way of verbal comprehension and fluency.

Age	Task
4	Fills in the missing word when asked, "Brother is a boy; sister is a _____." Answers correctly when asked, "Why do we have houses?"
9	Answers correctly when examiner says, "In an old graveyard in Spain they have discovered a small skull which they believe to be that of Christopher Columbus when he was about 10 years old." What is foolish about that? Examiner presents folded paper; child draws how it will look unfolded.
12	Completes "The streams are dry . . . there has been little rain." Tells what is foolish about statements such as "Bill Jones's feet are so big that he has to put his trousers on over his head."
Adult	Can describe the difference between *misery* and *poverty, character* and *reputation, laziness* and *idleness*. Explains how to measure 3 pints of water with a 5-pint and a 2-pint can.

Source: From Lewis M. Terman and Maud A. Merrill, *Stanford-Binet Intelligence Scale* (1972 norms ed.). Boston: Houghton Mifflin, 1973. (Currently published by the Riverside Publishing Company.) Items are copyright 1916 by Lewis M. Terman, 1937 by Lewis M. Terman and Maud A. Merrill, © 1960, 1973 by the Riverside Publishing Company. Reproduced or adapted by permission of the publisher.

items test a person's vocabulary, arithmetic abilities, immediate memory span, ability to recognize similarities (e.g., "How are books and movies alike?"), and general knowledge and comprehension (e.g., "Who was Thomas Jefferson?" "Why do people who want a divorce have to go to court?"). "Performance" items test a range of nonverbal skills (see Figure 6.3).

Binet had emphasized that his test merely *sampled* intelligence and did not measure everything covered by that term. A test score, he said, could be useful, along with other information, for predicting school performance, but it should not be confused with intelligence itself. The tests were designed to be given to each child individually, so the test-giver could see whether a child was ill or nervous, had poor vision, or was not trying. The purpose was to identify children with learning problems, not to rank all children.

But when intelligence testing was brought from France to the United States, its original purpose got lost at sea. In America, IQ tests became widely used not to bring slow learners up to the average, but to categorize people in school and in the armed services according to their presumed "natural ability." The testers overlooked the fact

that in America, with its many ethnic groups, people did not all share the same background and experience (Gould, 1981/1996).

Can IQ Tests Be "Culture Free"?

Intelligence tests developed between World War I and the 1960s for use in schools favored city children over rural ones, middle-class children over poor ones, and white children over nonwhite children. One item, for example, asked whether the Emperor Concerto was written by Beethoven, Mozart, Bach, Brahms, or Mahler. (The answer is Beethoven.) Critics complained that the tests did not measure the kinds of knowledge and skills that are intelligent in a minority neighborhood or in the hills of Appalachia. They feared that because teachers thought IQ scores revealed the limits of a child's potential, low-scoring children might not get the educational attention or encouragement they needed.

Thinking Critically About Culture and Intelligence Testing

Test makers responded by trying to construct tests that were *culture free.* Such tests were usually nonverbal; in some, instructions were even pantomimed. They also tried to design tests that were *culture fair:* Instead of trying to eliminate the influ-

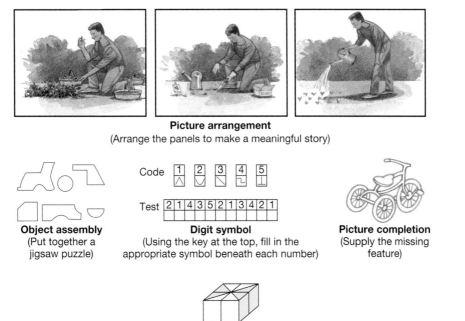

Picture arrangement
(Arrange the panels to make a meaningful story)

Object assembly
(Put together a
jigsaw puzzle)

Code

Test

Digit symbol
(Using the key at the top, fill in the
appropriate symbol beneath each number)

Picture completion
(Supply the missing
feature)

Block design
(Copy the design shown, using another set of blocks)

Figure 6.3

Performance Tasks on the Wechsler Tests

*Nonverbal items such as these are particularly useful for measuring the abilities of those who
have poor hearing, are not fluent in the tester's language, have limited education, or resist doing
classroom-type problems. A large gap between a person's verbal score and performance score
on a Wechsler test sometimes indicates a specific learning problem. (Object assembly, digit
symbol, and picture completion adapted from Cronbach, 1990.)*

ence of culture, they attempted to include items
that incorporated knowledge and skills common
to many different cultures. But both approaches
were less successful than originally hoped.

One reason for the disappointing results was
that cultures differ in the problem-solving strategies they emphasize (Serpell, 1994). In the West,
white, middle-class children typically learn to
classify things by category—to say that an apple
and a peach are similar because they are both
fruits, and that a saw and a rake are similar
because they are both tools. But children who are
not trained in middle-class ways of sorting things
may classify objects according to their sensory
qualities or functions. For example, they may say
that an apple and a peach are similar because they
both taste good. We think that's a charming and
innovative answer, but it is one that testers interpret as less intelligent (Miller-Jones, 1989).

It is also difficult to eliminate the influence of
culture because cultural values and experiences
affect a person's attitude toward tests, comfort in
the settings required for testing, motivation, rapport with the test-giver, competitiveness, and experience in solving problems independently rather
than with others (Anastasi & Urbina, 1997; López,
1995). For example, cultural stereotypes that portray women or members of particular ethnic, age,
or socioeconomic groups as unintelligent can actually depress the test performance of people in these
groups. You might think that a woman would say,
"So sexists think women are dumb at math? I'll
show *them*" or that an African-American would
say, "So racists believe that blacks aren't as smart as
whites? Just give me that exam." But often that is
not what happens.

On the contrary, such individuals commonly feel a burden of doubt about their
abilities that Claude Steele (1992, 1997)
has labeled **stereotype threat.** The threat
occurs when people believe that if they do not do
well, they will confirm the stereotypes about their
group. Their anxiety may then worsen their performance. Or they may cope by "disidentifying"
with the test, saying to themselves, in effect, "The
outcome of this test has no bearing on how I feel

stereotype threat
A burden of doubt a person
feels about his or her performance, due to negative
stereotypes about his or her
group's abilities.

An intelligence test is useful only if it is used intelligently. Testing by the U.S. army during World War I often occurred under noisy, crowded, and confusing conditions, and many items were culturally loaded. Nevertheless, many people concluded from the results that a high proportion of army recruits were "morons."

about myself" (Major et al., 1998). As a result, they may not be motivated to do well. Stereotype threat has been shown to affect the test performance of many African-Americans, low-income people, women, and elderly people—all of whom perform better on tests when they are not feeling self-conscious about themselves as members of negatively stereotyped groups (Brown & Josephs, 1999; Croizen & Claire, 1998; Levy, 1996; Steele & Aronson, 1995).

Beyond the IQ Test. In theory, it should be possible to reduce the impact of cultural bias and stereotype threat by throwing out test items on which white urban children get higher scores than others. A similar strategy was actually used years ago to eliminate sex differences in IQ. On early tests, girls scored higher than boys at every age (Samelson, 1979). No one was willing to conclude that males were intellectually inferior, so in the 1937 revision of the Stanford–Binet test, Lewis Terman simply deleted the items on which boys had done poorly. Poof! No sex differences.

But few people seem willing to do for cultural differences what Terman did for sex differences, and the reason reveals a dilemma at the heart of intelligence testing. Intelligence tests put some groups of children at a disadvantage, yet they also measure skills and knowledge useful in the classroom. How can educators recognize and accept cultural differences and, at the same time, require students to demonstrate mastery of the skills, knowledge, and attitudes that will help them succeed in school and in the larger society? How can test makers eliminate bias from tests, while preserving the purpose for which the tests were designed?

Many social scientists believe that it is important for society to keep using IQ tests. The tests predict school performance fairly well, and they identify not only the mentally retarded, but also gifted students who have not previously considered higher education. To supporters of IQ testing, concealing the effects of cultural disadvantage by rejecting conventional tests is "equivalent to breaking a thermometer because it registers a body temperature of 101" (Anastasi, 1988). When the tests reveal group differences, the pro-test camp maintains, the solution is to give individualized help to children who need it so they can do better—Binet's original goal. Indeed, many schools are already doing this.

Critics, however, point out that standardized tests tell us nothing about *how* a person goes about answering questions and solving problems. Nor do they explain why people with low scores on IQ tests often behave intelligently in real life—making smart consumer decisions, winning at the racetrack, and making wise personal choices (Ceci, 1996). Some researchers, therefore, have rejected the psychometric approach to the study and measurement of intelligence in favor of a cognitive approach.

Dissecting Intelligence: The Cognitive Approach

Cognitive psychologists, thinking critically, have questioned prevailing assumptions about the very meaning of intelligence and the best way to measure it. In contrast to the psychometric approach, which is concerned with how many answers a person gets right on a test, the cognitive approach emphasizes the *strategies* people use when thinking about problems and arriving at a solution.

Thinking Critically About What It Means to Be Smart

The Triarchic Theory. One well-known cognitive theory, Robert Sternberg's **triarchic theory of intelligence** (1988, 1995), distinguishes three aspects of intelligence:

GET INVOLVED
▶ ARE YOU A SAVVY STUDENT?

How good is your tacit knowledge about how to be a student? List as many strategies for success as you can think of. Consider what the successful student does when listening to lectures, participating in class discussions, communicating with professors, preparing for exams, writing term papers, and dealing with an unexpectedly low grade. Many of these strategies are never explicitly taught. You may want to do this exercise with a friend and compare lists. Are there some strategies that one of you thought of and the other did not?

1 *Componential intelligence* refers to the information-processing strategies that go on inside your head when you are thinking intelligently about a problem. These mental "components" include recognizing the problem, selecting a strategy for solving it, mastering and carrying out the strategy, and evaluating the result.

Some of these operations require **metacognition,** the knowledge or awareness of your own cognitive processes and the ability to monitor and control those processes. Metacognition is associated with strong academic achievement (Landine & Steward, 1998). Students who are weak in metacognition fail to notice when a passage in a textbook is especially difficult or they haven't understood it. As a result, they spend too little time on difficult material and too much time on material they already know (Nelson & Leonesio, 1988). In contrast, students who are strong in metacognition check their comprehension by restating what they have read, backtracking when necessary, and questioning what they are reading (Bereiter & Bird, 1985). (If they are reading this textbook, they also take the Quick Quizzes!)

2 *Experiential intelligence* refers to how well you transfer skills to new situations. People with experiential intelligence cope well with novelty and learn quickly to make new tasks automatic; those who are lacking in this area perform well only under a narrow set of circumstances. For example, a student may do well in school, where assignments have specific due dates and feedback is immediate, but be less successful after graduation if her job requires her to set her own deadlines and her employer doesn't tell her how she is doing.

3 *Contextual intelligence* refers to the practical application of intelligence, which requires you to take into account the different contexts in which you find yourself. If you are strong in contextual intelligence, you know when to adapt to the environment (you are in a dangerous neighborhood, so you become more vigilant). You know when to change environments (you had planned to be a teacher but discover that you dislike working with kids, so you switch to accounting). And you know when to fix the situation (your marriage is rocky, so you and your spouse go for counseling).

Without contextual intelligence, you will not acquire **tacit knowledge**—practical strategies for achieving your goals that are not formally taught but must instead be inferred from observing others (Sternberg et al., 1995). In studies of college professors, business managers, and salespeople, tacit knowledge is a strong predictor of effectiveness on the job (Sternberg, Wagner, & Okagaki, 1993). In college students, tacit knowledge about how to be a good student actually predicts academic success in college as well as entrance exams do (Sternberg & Wagner, 1989).

Domains of Intelligence.
Other psychologists, too, are expanding our understanding of what it means to be intelligent. They point out that someone who is intelligent in one area, or domain, is not necessarily intelligent in all others. A Nobel prize winner in physics may be a nitwit when it comes to making up a budget; a biologist who is cautious and careful in his own field may uncritically accept unscientific claims about human psychology (Ceci, 1996; Shermer, 1997).

Howard Gardner (1983, 1993, 1995) has proposed that the domains of intelligence be expanded to include musical aptitude, kinesthetic intelligence (the bodily grace and physical self-awareness of athletes and dancers), and the capacity for insight into oneself, others, or the natural world. These talents,

triarchic theory of intelligence
A cognitive theory of intelligence that emphasizes information-processing strategies, the ability to transfer skills to new situations, and the practical application of intelligence.

metacognition
The knowledge or awareness of one's own cognitive processes.

tacit knowledge
Strategies for success that are not explicitly taught but that instead must be inferred.

Some theorists who argue for an expanded definition of intelligence would say that a singer has musical intelligence, a surveyor has spatial intelligence, and a compassionate friend has emotional intelligence.

emotional intelligence
The ability to identify your own and other people's emotions accurately, express your emotions clearly, and regulate emotions in yourself and others.

Gardner argues, are relatively independent and may even have separate neural structures. People with brain damage often lose intelligence in one domain without losing their competence in the others. And some autistic and retarded individuals with *savant syndrome* (*savant* means "learned" in French) have exceptional talents in one area, such as music, art, or rapid mathematical computation, despite poor functioning in all others.

Two of Gardner's domains, understanding yourself and understanding others, overlap with what some psychologists call **emotional intelligence:** the ability to identify your own and other people's emotions accurately, express your emotions clearly, and regulate emotions in yourself and others (Goleman, 1995; Mayer & Salovey, 1997). People with high emotional intelligence—popularly known as "EQ"—use their emotions to motivate

People with emotional intelligence are skilled at reading nonverbal emotional cues. Which of these boys do you think feels the most confident and relaxed, which one is shyest, and which feels most anxious? What cues are you using to answer?

themselves, to spur creative thinking, and to deal empathically with others. People who are low in emotional intelligence are often unable to identify their own emotions; they may insist that they're not depressed when a relationship ends, for example, but meanwhile they start drinking too much, become irritable, and stop going out with friends. They express emotions inappropriately, such as by acting violently or impulsively when they are angry or worried. And they misread nonverbal signals from others; for example, they will give a long-winded account of all their problems even when the listener is obviously bored.

Studies of brain-damaged adults suggest a biological basis for emotional intelligence. Neuroscientist Antonio Damasio (1994) has studied patients with prefrontal-lobe damage that makes them incapable of experiencing strong feelings. Although they score in the normal range on conventional mental tests, these patients persistently make "dumb," irrational decisions in their lives because they cannot assign values to different options or read emotional cues from others.

Thinking Critically About Intelligence(s). Not everyone is enthusiastic about the proliferation of new "intelligences." Some argue that emotional intelligence is not a special cognitive ability but a collection of personality traits, such as empathy and extroversion, and that nothing is gained by giving "EQ" its own trendy new label (Davies, Stankov, & Roberts, 1998). Others maintain that abilities such as Gardner's musical and kinesthetic intelligences are better thought of as talents, or else the very concept of intelligence loses all meaning. What is to prevent someone from adding "handicraft intelligence" or "financial intelligence" or "farming intelligence"?

Broadening the notion of intelligence, however, has been useful for several reasons. It has forced us to think more critically about what we mean by intelligence. It has inspired a promising (though still unproven) new type of mental testing, in which the test-giver provides ongoing feedback to the test-taker during the test, so that the person can learn from the experience and improve his or her performance (Grigorenko & Sternberg, 1998). And it has led to a focus on teaching children practical strategies for improving their abilities in reading, writing, homework, and test-taking: for example, how to manage their time so they don't procrastinate, how to study differently for multiple-choice versus essay exams, and how to make a persuasive case for their ideas (Sternberg et al., 1995).

Most important, new approaches to intelligence encourage us to overcome the mental set of assuming that the only kind of intelligence necessary for a successful life is the kind captured by IQ tests.

6.2

 QUICK QUIZ

Are you feeling smart about intelligence?

1. In a sense, all mental tests are (aptitude/achievement) tests.

2. Hilda, age 66, is worried about taking an IQ test because she knows that older people are often assumed to have diminished mental abilities. Hilda is being affected by _____.

3. What goals do cognitive theories of intelligence have that psychometric theories do not?

4. Logan understands the material in his statistics class, but on tests, he spends the entire period on the most difficult problems and never even gets to the problems he can solve easily. According to the triarchic theory of intelligence, which aspect of intelligence does he need to improve?

5. Tracy does not have an unusually high IQ, but at work, she was quickly promoted because she knows how to set priorities, communicate with management, and make others feel valued. Tracy has _____ knowledge about how to succeed on the job.

6. What is wrong with defining intelligence as "whatever intelligence tests measure"?

Answers:

1. achievement 2. stereotype threat 3. to understand people's strategies for solving problems and to use this information to improve mental performance 4. componential intelligence (which includes metacognition) 5. tacit 6. This definition implies that a low score must be entirely the scorer's fault rather than the test's. But the test-taker may be intelligent in domains that the test fails to measure, and the test may be measuring traits other than intelligence. (By the way, the definition is also circular: How do we know someone is intelligent? Because he or she scored high on an intelligence test. Why did the person score high? Because the person is intelligent!)

What's Ahead

- If intelligence is highly heritable, does that mean group differences in IQ are genetic?

- What sorts of environmental "nutrients" nurture mental ability?

- Some gifted people are professionally successful, and others are not; what makes the difference?

- Why do Asian children perform much better in school than American students do, despite having worse school facilities?

6.5 The Origins of Intelligence

"Intelligence," as we have seen, can mean many things. But however we define or measure it, clearly some people think and behave more intelligently than others. What accounts for these differences?

Genes and Intelligence

Behavioral geneticists approach this question by doing heritability studies, focusing mainly on the kind of intelligence measured by IQ tests. In Chapter 2, we saw that **heritability** is the proportion of the total variance in a trait within a group that is attributable to genetic variation within the group. This proportion, which can have a maximum value of 1.0, is usually estimated by doing twin and adoption studies. (You might review pages 43 to 45 if you need to refresh your memory for these procedures.)

Genes and Individual Differences.

Behavioral–genetic studies show that the kind of intelligence that produces high IQ scores is highly heritable. For children and adolescents, heritability estimates average around .50; that is, about half of the variance in IQ scores, give or take a few percentage points, is explainable by genetic differences (Chipuer, Rovine, & Plomin, 1990; Devlin, Daniels, & Roeder, 1997; Plomin, 1989). For adults, the estimates are higher—in the .60 to .80 range (Bouchard, 1995; McClearn et al., 1997; McGue et al., 1993).

In studies of twins, the scores of identical twins are always much more highly correlated than those of fraternal twins, a difference that reflects the influence of genes. In fact, the scores of identical twins reared *apart* are more highly correlated than those of fraternal twins reared *together,* as you can see in Figure 6.4. In adoption studies, the scores of adopted children are more highly correlated with those of their birth parents than with those of

heritability
A statistical estimate of the proportion of the total variance in some trait that is attributable to genetic differences among individuals within a group.

biologically unrelated adoptive parents: The higher the birth parents' scores, the higher the child's score is likely to be. As adopted children grow into adolescence, the correlation between their IQ scores and those of their biologically unrelated family members diminishes, and in adulthood the correlation is *zero* (Bouchard, 1997b; Scarr, 1993; Scarr & Weinberg, 1994).

Overall, the research on the heritability of IQ-test performance is pretty impressive. Researchers are now looking for genes that might influence performance on IQ tests, and they have identified one possible candidate (Chorney et al., 1998). But behavioral–genetic findings do not mean that genes *determine* IQ. In Chapter 2, we saw that if heredity accounts for only part of why people differ on some trait, then the environment must account for the rest. We also saw that a highly heritable trait can nonetheless be highly modifiable by the environment.

The Question of Group Differences.
If genes influence individual differences in intelligence, do they also help account for differences between groups, as many people assume? This issue has tremendous political and social importance, so we are going to look at it closely.

Most of the focus has been on black–white differences, because African-American children score, on average, some 10 to 15 points lower on IQ tests than do white children. (We are talking about *averages;* the distributions of scores for black children and white children overlap considerably.) A few psychologists have proposed a genetic explanation of this difference (Jensen, 1969, 1981; Rushton, 1988). In their much-discussed book *The Bell Curve: Intelligence and Class Structure in American Life* (1994), the late psychologist Richard Herrnstein and political scientist Charles Murray cited heritability studies to imply that the gap in IQ scores between the average white child and the average black child can never be closed.

As you can imagine, this topic provokes much more controversy than does research on, say, the sex lives of sea lions. Racists have used theories of genetic differences between groups to justify their own hatreds, and politicians have used them to argue for cuts in programs that would benefit blacks and other minorities. Herrnstein and Murray themselves concluded that there was little point in spending money on programs that were trying to raise the IQs of low-scoring children.

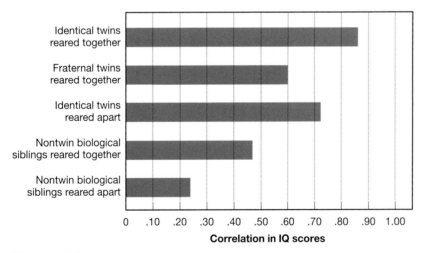

Figure 6.4
Correlations in Siblings' IQ Scores
The IQ scores of identical twins are highly correlated, even when they are reared apart. The data in this graph are based on average correlations across many studies (Bouchard & McGue, 1981).

Genetic explanations, however, have a fatal flaw: They use heritability estimates based mainly on white samples to estimate the role of heredity in *group* differences, a procedure that is not valid. This problem sounds pretty technical, but it is not really too difficult to understand, so stay with us.

Consider, first, not people but tomatoes. (Figure 6.5 will help you visualize the following "thought experiment.") Suppose you have a bag of tomato seeds that vary genetically; all things being equal, some will produce tomatoes that are puny and tasteless, and some will produce tomatoes that are plump and delicious. Now you take a bunch of these seeds in your left hand and another bunch from the same bag in your right hand. Though one seed differs genetically from another, there is no *average* difference between the seeds in your left hand and those in your right. You plant the left hand's seeds in pot A, with some soil that you have doctored with nitrogen and other nutrients, and you plant the right hand's seeds in pot B, with soil from which you have extracted nutrients. You sing to pot A and put it in the sun; you ignore pot B and leave it in a dark corner.

When the tomato plants grow, they will vary *within* each pot in terms of height, the number of tomatoes produced, and the size of the tomatoes, purely because of genetic differences. But there will also be an average difference between the plants in pot A and those in pot B: The plants in pot A will be healthier and bear more tomatoes. This difference *between* pots is due entirely to the different soils—even though the heritability of the *within*-pot differences is 100 percent (Lewontin, 1970).

The principle is the same for people as it is for tomatoes. Although intellectual differences *within* groups are at least partly genetic, that does not mean that differences *between* groups are genetic. Blacks and whites do not grow up, on average, in the same "pots" (environments). Because of a long legacy of racial discrimination and de facto segregation, black children (as well as Latino and other minority children) often receive far fewer nutrients—literally, in terms of food, and figuratively, in terms of education, encouragement by society, and intellectual opportunities. And as we have seen, negative stereotypes about ethnic groups may cause members of these groups to doubt their own abilities, become anxious and self-conscious, and perform more poorly than they otherwise would on tests.

Figure 6.5
The Tomato Plant Experiment

In the hypothetical experiment described in the text, even if the differences among plants within each pot were due entirely to genetics, the average difference between pots could be environmental. The same general principle applies to individual and group differences among human beings.

Doing good research on the origins of black–white differences in IQ is nearly impossible in the United States, where racism affects the lives of even affluent, successful African-Americans (Cose, 1994; Parker, 1997; Staples, 1994). However, the handful of studies that have overcome past methodological problems fail to reveal any genetic differences between blacks and whites in whatever it is that IQ tests measure. One study found, for example, that children fathered by black and white American soldiers in Germany after World War II and reared in similar German communities by similar families did not differ significantly in IQ (Eyferth, 1961). Another showed that degree of African ancestry (which can be roughly estimated from skin color, blood analysis, and genealogy) was not related to measured intelligence, as a genetic theory of black–white differences would predict (Scarr et al., 1977). And white and black infants do equally well on a test that measures their preference for novel stimuli, a predictor of later IQ scores (Fagan, 1992).

An intelligent reading of the research on intelligence, therefore, does not direct us to conclude that differences among cultural, ethnic, or national groups are permanent, genetically determined, or signs of any group's superiority. On the contrary, the research suggests that we should make sure that all children grow up in the best possible soil, with room for the smartest and the slowest to find a place in the sun.

The Environment and Intelligence

By now you may be wondering what kinds of experiences hinder intellectual development and what kinds of environmental "nutrients" promote it. Here are some of the influences associated with reduced mental ability:

- *Poor prenatal care.* If a pregnant woman is malnourished, contracts infections, takes certain drugs, smokes, drinks excessively, or is exposed to environmental pollutants, the fetus is at risk of having learning disabilities and a lower IQ.

- *Malnutrition.* The average IQ gap between severely malnourished and well-nourished children can be as high as 20 points (Stoch & Smythe, 1963; Winick, Meyer, & Harris, 1975).

- *Exposure to toxins.* Lead, for example, can damage the nervous system, producing attention problems, lower IQ scores, and poor school achievement (Needleman et al., 1996). Nearly 9 percent of all children in the United States ages 1 to 5 are exposed to dangerous levels of lead from lead paint and old lead pipes, and for black children ages 1 and 2, the percentage rises to 21.6 (Brody et al., 1994).

- *Stressful family circumstances.* Factors that predict reduced intellectual competence include a father who does not live with the family, a mother with a history of mental illness, limited parental work skills, and a history of stressful events during the child's early life (Sameroff et al., 1987). On average, each risk factor reduces a child's IQ score by 4 points. Children with no risk factors score more than *30 points higher* than those with seven risk factors.

In contrast, a healthy and stimulating environment can raise mental performance, sometimes dramatically (Guralnick, 1997; Ramey & Ramey, 1998). In one longitudinal study called the Abecedarian Project, inner-city children who got lots of mental enrichment at home and in child care or school, starting in infancy, had much better school performance throughout childhood than did children in a control group (Campbell & Ramey, 1995). In general, children's mental abilities improve when parents talk to their children about many topics and describe things accurately and fully; encourage them to think things through; read to them; and expect them to do well.

Perhaps the best evidence for the importance of environmental influences on intelligence is the fact that IQ scores in developed countries have been climbing for at least three generations (Flynn, 1987, 1999) (see Figure 6.6). Genes in these countries cannot possibly have changed enough to account for this rise in scores. The causes are still being debated, but most cognitive psychologists believe they include improvements in education, an increasing emphasis on the skills required by technology, and better nutrition (Neisser, 1998).

We see, then, that although heredity may provide the range of a child's intellectual potential—a Homer Simpson can never become an Einstein—many other factors affect where in that range the child will fall.

Figure 6.6
Climbing IQ Scores

Raw scores on IQ tests have been rising in developed countries for many decades, at a rate much too steep to be accounted for by genetic changes. Because test norms are periodically readjusted to set the average score at 100, most people are unaware that real IQ has been increasing. On this graph, average scores are calibrated according to 1989 norms. As you can see, performance was much lower in 1918 than in 1989. (Adapted from Horgan, 1995.)

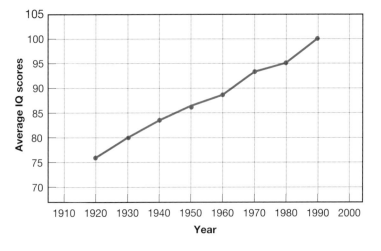

The children of migrant workers (left) often spend long hours in backbreaking field work and may miss out on the educational opportunities and intellectual advantages available to middle-class children (right).

Attitudes, Motivation, and Intellectual Success

Even with a high IQ, emotional intelligence, genetic advantages, talent, and practical know-how, you still might get nowhere at all. Talent, unlike cream, does not inevitably rise to the top; success also depends on drive and determination.

Consider a finding from one of the longest-running psychological studies ever conducted. Since 1921, researchers at Stanford University have been following more than 1,500 people with childhood IQ scores in the top 1 percent of the distribution. As boys and girls, these subjects were nicknamed "Termites," after Lewis Terman, who originally directed the research. The Termites started out bright, physically healthy, sociable, and well adjusted. As they entered adulthood, most became successful in the traditional ways of the times: men in careers and women as homemakers (Sears & Barbee, 1977; Terman & Oden, 1959). However, some gifted men failed to live up to their early promise, dropping out of school or drifting into low-level work. When the researchers compared the 100 most successful men with the 100 least successful, they found that motivation made the difference. The successful men were ambitious, were socially active, had many interests, and were encouraged by their parents. The least successful men drifted casually through life. There was *no* average difference in IQ between the two groups.

Motivation to work hard at intellectual tasks depends in turn on your attitudes about intelligence and achievement. For many years, Harold Stevenson and his colleagues have been studying such attitudes in Asia and the United States. Since 1980 they have been comparing large samples of grade-school children, parents, and teachers in Minneapolis, Chicago, Sendai (Japan), Taipei (Taiwan), and Beijing (Stevenson & Stigler, 1992). In 1990, Stevenson, along with Chuansheng Chen and Shin-ying Lee (1993), revisited the original schools to collect new data on fifth-graders, and they also retested many of the children who had been in the 1980 study and who were now in the eleventh grade. Their results have much to teach us about the cultivation of intellect.

In 1980, the Asian children far outperformed the American children on a broad battery of mathematical tests. (A similar gap existed between the Chinese and American children on reading tests.) On computations and word problems, there was virtually no overlap between schools, with the lowest-scoring Beijing schools doing better than the highest-scoring Chicago schools. By 1990, the gap between the Asian and American children had grown even greater. Only 4 percent of the Chinese children and 10 percent of the Japanese children had scores as low as those of the *average* American child. These differences could not be accounted for by educational resources: The Chinese schools had worse facilities and larger classes than the American ones, and on average,

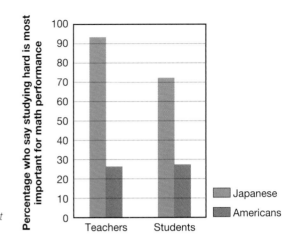

Figure 6.7

What's the Secret of Math Success?

Japanese school teachers and students are much more likely than their American counterparts to believe that the secret to doing well in math is working hard. Americans tend to think that you either have mathematical intelligence or you don't.

the Chinese parents were poorer and less educated than the American parents. Nor did it have anything to do with intellectual ability in general; the American children were just as knowledgeable and capable as the Asian children on tests of general information.

But this research found that Asians and Americans are worlds apart in their attitudes, expectations, and efforts:

- *Beliefs about intelligence.* American parents, teachers, and children are far more likely than Asians to believe that mathematical ability is innate (see Figure 6.7). They think that if you "have it," you don't have to work hard, and if you don't have it, there's no point in trying.

- *Standards.* American parents have far lower standards for their children's performance; they are satisfied with scores barely above

average on a 100-point test. In contrast, Chinese and Japanese parents are happy only with very high scores.

- *Values.* American students do not value education as much as Asian students do, and they are more complacent about mediocre work. When asked what they would wish for if a wizard could give them anything they wanted, more than 60 percent of the Chinese fifth-graders named something related to their education. Can you guess what the American children wanted? A majority said money or possessions.

When it comes to intellect, then, it's not just what you've got that counts but what you do with it. Complacency, fatalism, or low standards can prevent people from recognizing what they don't know and reduce their efforts to learn.

QUICK QUIZ

Are you feeling complacent about your quiz performance?

1. On average, behavioral–genetic studies estimate the heritability of intelligence to be (a) about .90, (b) low at all ages, (c) about .50 for children and adolescents.

2. *True or false:* If a trait such as intelligence is highly heritable within a group, then differences between groups must also be due mainly to heredity.

3. The available evidence (does/does not) show that ethnic differences in average IQ scores are due to genetic differences.

4. Name four environmental factors associated with reduced mental ability.

Answers:
1. c   2. false (can you say why, using the tomato-plant analogy?)   3. does not   4. poor prenatal care, malnutrition, exposure to toxins, stressful family circumstances

What's Ahead

- Why do some researchers think that animals can think?
- People love to talk to their pets—but can their pets learn to talk back?

6.6 Animal Minds

A green heron swipes some bread from a picnicker's table and scatters the crumbs on a nearby stream. When a minnow rises to the bait, the heron strikes, swallowing its prey before you can say "hook, line, and sinker." A sea otter, floating calmly on its back, bangs a mussel shell against a stone that is resting on its stomach. When the shell cracks apart, the otter devours the tasty morsel inside, tucks the stone under its flipper, and dives for another shell, which it will open in the same way.

Incidents such as these suggest that we are not the only animals with cognitive abilities—that "dumb beasts" are far smarter than we may think. Many best-selling books have described the amazingly humanlike emotions and "thoughts" of animals. But how humanlike are they?

Animal Intelligence

In the 1920s, Wolfgang Köhler (1925) put chimpanzees in situations in which some tempting bananas were just out of reach, then watched to see what the apes would do. Most did nothing, but a few turned out to be quite clever. If the bananas were outside the cage, the animal might pull them in with a stick. If they were hanging overhead, and there were boxes in the cage, the chimpanzee might pile up the boxes and climb on top of them to reach the fruit. Often the solution came after the animal had been sitting quietly for a while. It appeared as though the chimp had been thinking about the problem and was struck by a sudden insight.

Behaviorists, as you might imagine, felt that this seemingly impressive behavior could be accounted for perfectly well by the standard principles of operant learning (see Chapter 8). Because of their influence, for years any scientist who claimed that animals could think was likely to get laughed at, or worse. Today, however, the study of animal intelligence is enjoying a resurgence, especially in the interdisciplinary field of **cognitive ethology**. (*Ethology* is the study of animal behavior, especially in natural environments.) Cognitive ethologists argue that some animals can anticipate future events, make plans and choices, and coordinate their activities with those of their comrades—that they are, indeed, capable of thought.

When we think about animal cognition, though, we must be careful, because even complex behavior can be genetically prewired and automatic. The assassin bug of South America catches termites by gluing nest material on its back as camouflage, but it is hard to imagine how the bug's tiny dab of brain tissue could enable it to

cognitive ethology
The study of cognitive processes in nonhuman animals.

In an early study of animal intelligence, Sultan, a talented chimpanzee studied by Wolfgang Köhler, was able to figure out how to reach a cluster of bananas by stacking some boxes and climbing on top of them.

plan this strategy consciously. Even many cognitive ethologists are cautious about how much cognition they are willing to read into an animal's behavior. An animal could be aware of its environment and know some things, they say, without knowing that it knows and without being able to think about its own thoughts as human beings do—in short, without having metacognition (Budiansky, 1998; Hauser, 2000).

Yet explanations of animal behavior that leave out any sort of consciousness at all and that attribute animals' actions entirely to instinct do not seem to account for some of the amazing things that animals can do. Like the otter who uses a stone to crack mussel shells, many animals are capable of using objects in the natural environment as rudimentary tools. For example, mother chimpanzees occasionally show their young how to use stone tools to open hard nuts (Boesch, 1991).

How smart is this otter?

In the laboratory, too, nonhuman primates have accomplished some surprising things. In one study, chimpanzees compared two pairs of food wells containing chocolate chips. One pair might contain, say, five chips and three chips, the other four chips and three chips. Allowed to choose which pair they wanted, the chimps almost always chose the one with the higher total, showing some sort of summing ability (Rumbaugh, Savage-Rumbaugh, & Pate, 1988). Other chimps have learned to use numerals to label quantities of items and simple sums (Boysen & Berntson, 1989; Washburn & Rumbaugh, 1991). Two rhesus monkeys, Rosencrantz and Macduff, learned to order groups of up to four symbols according to the number of symbols in each group (e.g., one square, two trees, three ovals, four flowers). Later, when presented with pairs of symbol groups containing up to nine symbols, they were able to point to the group with more symbols, without any further training (Brannon & Terrace, 1998). This is not exactly algebra, but it does suggest that monkeys have a rudimentary sense of number.

Animals and Language

A primary ingredient of human cognition is *language,* the ability to combine elements that are themselves meaningless into an infinite number of utterances that convey meaning. As we saw in Chapter 3, language allows us to express and comprehend an infinite number of novel utterances, created on the spot. We seem to be the only species that evolved to do this naturally. Other primates use a variety of grunts and screeches to warn each other of danger, to attract attention, and to express emotions, but the sounds are not combined to produce original sentences (at least, as far as we can tell). Bongo may make a certain sound when he finds food, but he cannot say, "The bananas in the next grove are a lot riper than the ones we ate last week and sure beat our usual diet of termites."

Perhaps, however, some animals could acquire language if they got a little help from their human friends. Dozens of researchers have tried to provide chimpanzees with just such help. Because the vocal tract of an ape does not permit speech, most researchers have tried innovative approaches that rely on gestures or visual symbols. In one project, chimpanzees learned to use as words various geometric plastic shapes arranged on a magnetic board (Premack & Premack, 1983). In another, they learned to punch symbols on a computer-monitored keyboard (Rumbaugh, 1977). In yet another, they mastered hundreds of signs from American Sign Language (ASL) (Fouts & Rigby, 1977; Gardner & Gardner, 1969).

All of these animals learned to follow instructions, answer questions, and make requests. More important, they combined individual signs or symbols into longer utterances that they had never seen before. Before long, accounts of the apes' abilities were causing quite a stir. The animals were apparently using their newfound skills to apologize for being disobedient, scold their trainers, and even talk to themselves. Koko, a lowland gorilla, reportedly used signs to refer to past and future events, to mourn for her dead pet kitten, and to convey her yearning for a baby. She even lied on occasion, when she did something naughty (Patterson & Linden, 1981).

The animals in these studies were lovable, the findings appealing—so it was easy for emotional reasoning to prevail over critical thinking. But soon skeptics and some of the researchers themselves began to point out serious problems (Seidenberg & Petitto, 1979; Terrace, 1985). In their desire to talk to the animals and their affection for their primate friends, researchers had not always been objective. They had overinterpreted the animal's utterances, reading all sorts of meanings and intentions into a single sign or symbol, and unwittingly giving nonverbal cues that might enable the apes to respond correctly. Further, the animals appeared to be stringing signs and symbols together in no particular order,

Thinking Critically About Apes and Language

instead of using grammatical rules to produce novel utterances; "Me eat banana" seemed to be no different for them than "Banana eat me."

 These problems still plague some projects. In 1998, America Online sponsored a live chat with Koko. Her trainer, Francine Patterson, used sign language to relay questions from the audience to the gorilla. Critics felt Patterson read much too much into Koko's "replies":

QUESTION: Koko are you going to have a baby in the future?

KOKO: Pink

PATTERSON: Koko was commenting on the color of my shirt. We had an earlier discussion about colors today.

Q: Do you like to chat with people?

KOKO: Fine nipple.

PATTERSON: Nipple rhymes with people, she doesn't sign people per se, she was trying to do a "sounds like . . . "

Today, however, most researchers have taken the criticisms to heart and have greatly improved their procedures. They have shown that with careful training, chimps can indeed learn to use symbols to refer to objects. Some animals have even used signs spontaneously to converse with each other, suggesting that they are not merely imitating or trying to get a reward (Van Cantfort & Rimpau, 1982).

Bonobos (sometimes misleadingly called "pygmy chimps") are especially adept at language. One bonobo named Kanzi has learned to understand English words, short sentences, and keyboard symbols, *without formal training* (Savage-Rumbaugh & Lewin, 1994; Savage-Rumbaugh, Shanker, & Taylor, 1998). Kanzi responds correctly to commands such as "Put the key in the refrigerator" and "Go get the ball that is outdoors" even when he has never heard the words combined in that particular way before. He picked up language as children do—by observing others using it, and through normal social interaction. He has also learned, with training, to manipulate keyboard symbols to request favorite foods or activities (games, TV, visits to friends) or to announce his intentions.

You do not even have to be a primate to acquire some aspects of language. In Hawaii, Louis Herman and his colleagues have taught dolphins to respond to requests made in two artificial languages: one consisting of computer-generated whistles and another of hand and arm gestures

Kanzi, a bonobo with the most advanced linguistic skills yet acquired by a nonhuman primate, answers questions and makes requests by punching symbols on a specially designed computer keyboard. He also understands short English sentences. Kanzi is shown here with researcher Sue Savage-Rumbaugh.

(Herman, Kuczaj, & Holder, 1993; Herman & Morrel-Samuels, 1996). To interpret a request correctly, the dolphins must take into account both the meaning of the individual symbols in a string of whistles or gestures and the order of the symbols (syntax). For example, they must understand the difference between "To left Frisbee, right surfboard take" and "To right surfboard, left Frisbee take."

In another fascinating project, Irene Pepperberg (2000) has spent more than two decades teaching Alex, her African gray parrot, to count, classify, and compare objects by vocalizing English words. When Alex is shown up to six items and is asked how many there are, he responds with spoken (squawked?) English phrases, such as "two cork(s)" or "four key(s)." He can even respond correctly to questions about items specified on two dimensions, as in "How many blue key(s)?" Alex also makes requests ("Want pasta") and answers simple questions about objects ("What color [is this]?" "Which is bigger?"). When he is presented with a blue cork and a blue key and is asked "What's the same?," he will correctly respond "Color." He actually scores slightly better with new objects than with familiar ones, suggesting that he is not merely memorizing a set of stock phrases.

Alex is one clever bird—but how clever? His abilities raise intriguing questions about the intelligence of animals and their capacity for specific aspects of language.

Thinking About the Thinking of Animals

These results on animal cognition are impressive, but scientists are still divided over just what the animals in these studies are doing. Do they have true language? Are they "thinking," in human terms?

On one side are those who worry about *anthropomorphism,* the tendency to falsely attribute human qualities to nonhuman beings. They tell the story of Clever Hans, a "wonder horse" at the turn of the century, who was said to possess mathematical and other abilities (Spitz, 1997). Clever Hans would answer math problems by stamping his hoof the appropriate number of times and other problems by tapping in an established code. But a little careful experimentation by a psychologist, Oskar Pfungst (1911/1965), revealed that when Hans was prevented from seeing his questioners, or when they did not know the answers themselves, his "powers" left him. It seems that questioners were staring at the animal's feet and leaning forward expectantly after stating the problem, then lifting their eyes and relaxing as soon as he completed the right number of taps. Clever Hans was indeed clever, but not at math or other human skills. He was merely responding to nonverbal signals that people were inadvertently providing. (Perhaps he had a high EQ.)

On the other side are those who warn against *anthropocentrism,* the tendency to think, mistakenly, that human beings have nothing in common with other animals (de Waal, 1997; Fouts, 1997). The need to see our own species as unique, they say, may keep us from recognizing that other species, too, have cognitive abilities, even if not as intricate as our own. Those who take this position point out that most modern researchers have gone to great lengths to avoid the Clever Hans problem.

The outcome of this debate is bound to have an effect on how we view ourselves and our place among other species. As Donald Griffin (1992) wrote, "Cognitive ethology presents us with one of the supreme scientific challenges of our times, and it calls for our best efforts of critical and imaginative investigation." Perhaps, as cognitive ethologist Marc Hauser (2000) suggests, we can find a way to study and respect animal minds and emotions without assuming sentimentally that they are just like ours.

"It's always 'Sit,' 'Stay,' 'Heel'—never 'Think,' 'Innovate,' 'Be yourself.'"

QUICK QUIZ

Regrettably, your pet beagle can't help you answer these questions.

1. Which of the following abilities have primates demonstrated, either in the natural environment or the laboratory? (a) the use of objects as simple tools; (b) the summing of quantities; (c) the use of symbols to make requests; (d) an understanding of short English sentences

2. Barnaby thinks that his pet snake Curly is harboring angry thoughts about him because Curly has been standoffish and won't curl around his neck anymore. What error is Barnaby making?

Answers:
1. all of them   2. anthropomorphism

PSYCHOLOGY IN THE NEWS, REVISITED

We human beings have always thought of ourselves as the smartest species around, and for good reason. We have an astounding ability to adapt to change, solve problems in novel ways, invent endless new gizmos, and use language to create everything from puns to poetry. Yet as this chapter has shown, we are not always as wise in our thinking as we might think, and we may not even be the only animal capable of thought. As if that weren't bad enough, now some people are saying, as in our opening story, that machines are gaining on us in the mental-abilities department. Will computers and robots eventually be able to make crucial decisions for us on how to improve public education, manage a baseball team, or schedule the fall TV lineup?

That's hardly likely. Consider the chess-playing accomplishments of Deep Blue—or more accurately, the accomplishments of the human programmers who wrote the machine's software. Although Deep Blue's feats are impressive—it analyzed 200 million moves per second—real intelligence is more than the capacity to perform computations with lightning speed. As we have seen, it involves the ability to deal with informal reasoning problems, reason dialectically and reflectively, devise mental shortcuts, read emotions, and acquire tacit knowledge.

Intelligence also involves mental efficiency: Human beings are intelligent not because they can consider 200 million chess positions a second, but because they don't have to! During the contest between Garry Kasparov and Deep Blue, the computer, in a sense, cheated (Klopfenstein, 1997). The Russian was prevented by the traditional rules of play from consulting any books or experts; the machine had access to a complete historical library of chess strategy, stored in its electronic memory banks. But its raw calculating power disguised its inefficiency; it could not "prune" moves that were likely to be ineffective or draw analogies with moves that had been duds in similar circumstances. The only way it could win was to reject the same moves millions of times (McCarthy, 1997).

Golem, the robot that designs other robots, is even less of a challenge to human uniqueness.

At the robotics conference mentioned in our story, most of the participants disagreed with the researcher who predicted that robots will soon be as smart as we are. One of Golem's inventors, when asked whether self-reproducing robots could figure out how to become a doomsday machine and threaten the world, as in the movie *The Terminator,* said that such a prospect is "as far off as a fax machine is from a Star Trek transporter" (quoted in Chang, 2000). Others pointed out that robots lack the most important requirement for ruling the universe—a mind of their own.

Robots and computers, of course, are not the least bit troubled by their lack of cleverness, inasmuch as they lack a mind to be troubled. As computer scientist David Gelernter (1997) wrote after Deep Blue's victory, "How can an object that wants nothing, fears nothing, enjoys nothing, needs nothing, and cares about nothing have a mind?" Because machines are mindless, they also lack a trait that distinguishes human beings not only from computers but also from other species: *We try to understand our own misunderstandings.* We want to know what we don't know; we are motivated to overcome our mental shortcomings. Our uniquely human capacity for self-examination is probably the best reason to remain optimistic about our cognitive abilities.

TAKING PSYCHOLOGY WITH YOU

Becoming More Creative

Take a few moments to answer these items from the Remote Associates Test. Your task is to come up with a fourth word that is associated with each item in a set of three words (Mednick, 1962). For example, an appropriate answer for the set *news–clip–wall* is *paper.* Got the idea? Now try these (the answers are given on page 225):

1. piggy–green–lash

2. surprise–political–favor

3. mark–shelf–telephone

4. stick–maker–tennis

5. cream–cottage–cloth

Associating elements in new ways by finding a common connection among them is an important component of creativity. People who are uncreative rely on *convergent thinking,* following a particular set of steps that they think will converge on one correct solution. Once they have solved a problem, they tend to develop a mental set and approach future problems in the same way.

Creative people, in contrast, exercise *divergent thinking;* instead of stubbornly sticking to one tried-and-true path, they explore some side alleys and generate several possible solutions. They come up with new hypotheses, imagine other interpretations, and look for connections that may not be immediately obvious. As a result, they are able to use familiar concepts in unexpected ways. Creative thinking can be found in the auto mechanic who invents a new tool, the mother who designs and makes her children's clothes, or the office manager who devises a clever way to streamline work flow (Richards, 1991).

A high IQ does not guarantee creativity. Personality characteristics seem more important, especially these three (Helson, Roberts, & Agronick, 1995; MacKinnon, 1968; McCrae, 1987; Schank, 1988):

1. *Nonconformity.* Creative individuals are not overly concerned about what others think of them. They are willing to risk ridicule by proposing ideas that may initially appear foolish or off the mark. Geneticist Barbara McClintock's research was ignored or belittled by many for nearly 30 years. But she was sure she could show how genes move around and produce sudden changes in heredity. In 1983, when McClintock won the Nobel Prize, the judges called her work the second greatest genetic discovery of our time, after the discovery of the structure of DNA.

2. *Curiosity.* Creative people are open to new experiences; they notice when reality contradicts expectations, and they are curious about the reason. For example, Wilhelm Roentgen, a German physicist, was studying cathode rays when he noticed a strange glow on one of his screens. Other people had seen the glow, but they ignored it because it didn't

jibe with their understanding of cathode rays. Roentgen studied the glow, found it to be a new kind of radiation, and thus discovered X-rays (Briggs, 1984).

3. *Persistence.* After that imaginary lightbulb goes on over your head, you still have to work hard to make the illumination last. Or, as Thomas Edison, who invented the real lightbulb, reportedly put it, "Genius is one-tenth inspiration and nine-tenths perspiration." No invention or work of art springs forth full-blown from a person's head. There are many false starts and painful revisions along the way.

In addition to traits that foster creativity, there are *circumstances* that do so. One is the encouragement of *intrinsic* rather than *extrinsic* motivation. Intrinsic motives include a sense of accomplishment, intellectual fulfillment, the satisfaction of curiosity, and the sheer love of the activity. Extrinsic motives include a desire for money, fame, and attention, or the wish to avoid punishment. In one study, artworks created for extrinsic reasons (they were commissioned by art collectors) were judged to be less creative than works done by the same artists for the intrinsic pleasure of creation—and this was true even when the person commissioning the work allowed the artist complete freedom (Amabile, Phillips, & Collins, 1993). As Robert Frost once said, "One should never write a poem to pay a gas bill." But this does not mean that writers and artists should work for free! When people are trained to think divergently, and when extrinsic rewards are tied to creative effort and not just to doing the job, then rewards can promote further creativity (Eisenberger, Armeli, & Pretz, 1998).

Creativity also flourishes when people have control over how to perform a task or solve a problem; are evaluated unobtrusively, instead of being constantly observed and judged; and work independently (Amabile, 1983). Organizations encourage creativity when they let people take risks, give them plenty of time to think about problems, and welcome innovation.

In sum, if you hope to become more creative, there are two things you can do. One is to cultivate the personal qualities that lead to creativity. The other is to seek out the kinds of situations that permit you to express them.

SUMMARY

Thought: Using What We Know

- *Thinking* is the mental manipulation of information. Our mental representations simplify and summarize information from the environment.

- A *concept* is a mental category that groups objects, relations, activities, abstractions, or qualities that share certain properties. *Prototypical* instances of a concept are more representative than others. *Propositions* are made up of concepts and express a unitary idea. They may be linked together to form *cognitive schemas,* which serve as mental models of aspects of the world. *Mental images* also play a role in thinking.

- Not all mental processing is conscious. *Subconscious processes* lie outside of awareness but can be brought into consciousness when necessary. *Nonconscious processes* remain outside of awareness but nonetheless affect behavior and may be involved in what we call "intuition" and "insight." Conscious processing may be carried out in a *mindless* fashion if we overlook changes in context that call for a change in behavior.

Reasoning Rationally

- *Reasoning* is purposeful mental activity that involves drawing inferences and conclusions from observations, facts, or assumptions (premises).

- *Formal reasoning problems* can often be solved by applying an *algorithm,* a set of procedures that are guaranteed to produce a solution, or by using logical processes, such as *deductive* and *inductive reasoning.*

- *Informal reasoning problems* may have no clearly correct solution. Disagreement may exist about basic premises, information may be incomplete, and many viewpoints may compete. Such problems may call for the application of *heuristics,* rules of thumb that suggest a course of action without guaranteeing an optimal solution. They may also require *dialectical thinking* about opposing points of view.

- Studies of *reflective judgment* show that many people have trouble thinking dialectically. People in the *prereflective* stages do not distinguish between knowledge and belief, or between belief and evidence. Those in the *quasi-reflective* stages think that because knowledge is sometimes uncertain, any judgment about the evidence is purely subjective. Those whose thinking has reached the *reflective stages* understand that although some things cannot be known with certainty, some judgments are more valid than others because of their coherence, usefulness, fit with the evidence, and so on. Higher education moves people gradually closer to reflective judgment.

Barriers to Reasoning Rationally

- The need to be right is an obstacle to rational thinking, as is mental laziness, which many commentators think is encouraged by increased television watching.

- The ability to reason clearly and rationally is also affected by many cognitive biases. People tend to exaggerate the likelihood of improbable events, in part because of the *availability heuristic;* to be swayed in their choices by the desire to *avoid loss;* to attend mostly to evidence that confirms what they want to believe (the *confirmation bias*); to be mentally rigid, forming *mental sets* and seeing patterns where none exists; and to overestimate their ability to have made accurate predictions (the *hindsight bias*).

• The theory of *cognitive dissonance* holds that people are also motivated to reduce the tension that exists when two cognitions conflict—by rejecting or changing a belief, changing their behavior, or rationalizing. People are especially likely to do so when they need to justify a decision (i.e., reduce *postdecision dissonance*); when their actions violate their self-concept; or when they have put hard work into an activity (the *justification of effort*).

• Once we understand a bias, we may be able to reduce or eliminate it.

Intelligence

• Although we all wish to think intelligently, *intelligence* is hard to define. Some theorists believe that a general ability (a *g factor*) underlies the many specific abilities tapped by intelligence tests, whereas others do not.

• The traditional approach to intelligence, the *psychometric approach*, focuses on how well people perform on standardized *aptitude tests*. The *intelligence quotient*, or *IQ*, represents how a person has done on an intelligence test, compared to other people. Alfred Binet designed the first widely used intelligence test for the purpose of identifying children who could benefit from remedial work. But in the United States, people assumed that intelligence tests revealed "natural ability," and they used the tests to categorize people in school and in the armed services.

• IQ tests have been criticized for being biased in favor of white, middle-class people. However, efforts to construct *culture-free* and *culture-fair* tests have been disappointing. Culture affects nearly everything to do with taking a test, from attitudes to problem-solving strategies. Negative stereotypes about a person's ethnicity, gender, or age may cause the person to suffer *stereotype threat*, a burden of doubt about his or her own abilities, which can lead to anxiety or "disidentification" with the test.

• Many social scientists consider IQ tests useful for predicting school performance and diagnosing learning difficulties, but critics would like to dispense with the tests because they are so often misused or misinterpreted.

• In contrast to the psychometric approach, *cognitive approaches* to intelligence emphasize the strate-

gies people use to solve problems, not just whether they get the right answers. Sternberg's *triarchic theory of intelligence* proposes three aspects of intelligence: *componential* (including *metacognition*), *experiential*, and *contextual*. The theory also emphasizes the importance of *tacit knowledge*, which is important in an individual's personal and occupational success.

• Intelligence in one domain does not necessarily imply intelligence in another. Howard Gardner proposes that there are actually several "intelligences" besides those usually considered, including musical and kinesthetic intelligence, and the capacity to understand the natural world, yourself, or others. The latter two overlap with what many psychologists call *emotional intelligence*, which is associated with personal, academic, and occupational success.

The Origins of Intelligence

• Behavioral–genetic studies estimate the heritability of intelligence (as measured by IQ tests) to be high: about .50 for children and adolescents and .60 to .80 for adults. But these results do not mean that genes determine intelligence, or that *group* differences in intelligence are genetic. It is not valid to draw conclusions about ethnic differences in intelligence from estimates based on differences *within* a group. The available evidence fails to support genetic explanations of these differences.

• Environmental factors such as poor prenatal care, malnutrition, exposure to toxins, and stressful family circumstances are associated with lower performance on mental tests; and a healthy and stimulating environment can improve performance.

• Intellectual achievement also depends on motivation and attitudes. Cross-cultural work shows that beliefs about the origins of mental abilities, parental standards, and attitudes toward education can help account for differences in academic performance.

Animal Minds

• Some researchers, especially those in the field of *cognitive ethology*, argue that nonhuman animals have greater cognitive abilities than is usually thought. Some animals can use objects as rudimentary tools. Chimpanzees have learned to use numerals to label quantities of items and symbols to refer to objects. In several projects using visual symbol systems or American Sign Language (ASL), primates have acquired linguistic skills. Some animals (even some nonprimates) seem able to use simple grammatical ordering rules to convey or comprehend meaning. However, scientists are still divided as to how to interpret these findings, and they are trying to avoid both *authropomorphism* and *authropocentrism*.

KEY TERMS

LOOKING BACK

- When you think of a bird, why are you more likely to recall a robin than a penguin? (pp. 190–191)

- How are visual images like images on a television screen? (p. 191)

- What is happening mentally when you mistakenly take your geography notes to your psychology class? (p. 192)

- Mentally speaking, why is making a cake, well, a piece of cake? (p. 193)

- Why can't logic solve all of our problems? (p. 194)

- What kind of reasoning do juries need to be good at? (p. 195)

- When people say that all opinions and claims are equally valid, what error are they making? (p. 196)

- Why do people worry about dying in an airplane crash but ignore dangers that are far more likely? (p. 198)

- How might your physician's choice of words about alternative treatments for your illness affect which one you choose? (p. 199)

- When "Monday morning quarterbacks" say they knew all along who would win Sunday's big game, what bias might they be showing? (p. 201)

- Why will a terrible hazing make you more loyal to the group that hazed you? (p. 203)

- How did the original purpose of intelligence testing change when IQ tests came to America? (p. 206)

- Is it possible to design intelligence tests that are not influenced by culture? (pp. 206–208)

- Why do some psychologists defend traditional intelligence testing and others oppose it? (p. 208)

- What kind of intelligence allows you to master the unspoken rules for academic success? (p. 209)

mostly to evidence that confirms what they want to believe (the *confirmation bias*); to be mentally rigid, forming *mental sets* and seeing patterns where none exists; and to overestimate their ability to have made accurate predictions (the *hindsight bias*).

- The theory of *cognitive dissonance* holds that people are also motivated to reduce the tension that exists when two cognitions conflict—by rejecting or changing a belief, changing their behavior, or rationalizing. People are especially likely to do so when they need to justify a decision (i.e., reduce *postdecision dissonance*); when their actions violate their self-concept; or when they have put hard work into an activity (the *justification of effort*).

- Once we understand a bias, we may be able to reduce or eliminate it.

Intelligence

- Although we all wish to think intelligently, *intelligence* is hard to define. Some theorists believe that a general ability (a *g factor*) underlies the many specific abilities tapped by intelligence tests, whereas others do not.

- The traditional approach to intelligence, the *psychometric approach,* focuses on how well people perform on standardized *aptitude tests*. The *intelligence quotient,* or *IQ,* represents how a person has done on an intelligence test, compared to other people. Alfred Binet designed the first widely used intelligence test for the purpose of identifying children who could benefit from remedial work. But in the United States, people assumed that intelligence tests revealed "natural ability," and they used the tests to categorize people in school and in the armed services.

- IQ tests have been criticized for being biased in favor of white, middle-class people. However, efforts to construct *culture-free* and *culture-fair* tests have been disappointing. Culture affects nearly everything to do with taking a test, from attitudes to problem-solving strategies. Negative stereotypes about a person's ethnicity, gender, or age may cause the person to suffer *stereotype threat*, a burden of doubt about his or her own abilities, which can lead to anxiety or "disidentification" with the test.

- Many social scientists consider IQ tests useful for predicting school performance and diagnosing learning difficulties, but critics would like to dispense with the tests because they are so often misused or misinterpreted.

- In contrast to the psychometric approach, *cognitive approaches* to intelligence emphasize the strategies people use to solve problems, not just whether they get the right answers. Sternberg's *triarchic theory of intelligence* proposes three aspects of intelligence: *componential* (including *metacognition*), *experiential,* and *contextual.* The theory also emphasizes the importance of *tacit knowledge,* which is important in an individual's personal and occupational success.

- Intelligence in one domain does not necessarily imply intelligence in another. Howard Gardner proposes that there are actually several "intelligences" besides those usually considered, including musical and kinesthetic intelligence, and the capacity to understand the natural world, yourself, or others. The latter two overlap with what many psychologists call *emotional intelligence,* which is associated with personal, academic, and occupational success.

The Origins of Intelligence

- Behavioral–genetic studies estimate the heritability of intelligence (as measured by IQ tests) to be high: about .50 for children and adolescents and .60 to .80 for adults. But these results do not mean that genes determine intelligence, or that *group* differences in intelligence are genetic. It is not valid to draw conclusions about ethnic differences in intelligence from estimates based on differences *within* a group. The available evidence fails to support genetic explanations of these differences.

- Environmental factors such as poor prenatal care, malnutrition, exposure to toxins, and stressful family circumstances are associated with lower performance on mental tests; and a healthy and stimulating environment can improve performance.

- Intellectual achievement also depends on motivation and attitudes. Cross-cultural work shows that beliefs about the origins of mental abilities, parental standards, and attitudes toward education can help account for differences in academic performance.

Animal Minds

- Some researchers, especially those in the field of *cognitive ethology,* argue that nonhuman animals have greater cognitive abilities than is usually thought. Some animals can use objects as rudimentary tools. Chimpanzees have learned to use numerals to label quantities of items and symbols to refer to objects. In several projects using visual symbol systems or American Sign Language (ASL), primates have acquired linguistic skills. Some animals (even some nonprimates) seem able to use simple grammatical ordering rules to convey or comprehend meaning. However, scientists are still divided as to how to interpret these findings, and they are trying to avoid both *authropomorphism* and *authropocentrism*.

KEY TERMS

thinking   190
concept   190
prototype   190
proposition   191
cognitive schema   191
mental image   191
subconscious processes   191
nonconscious processes   192
mindlessness   192
reasoning   193
formal reasoning problems   193
algorithm   193
deductive reasoning   193
inductive reasoning   193
informal reasoning problems   194
heuristic   194
dialectical reasoning   195
reflective judgment   195
 prereflective stages   196
 quasi-reflective stages   196
 reflective stages   196

availability heuristic   198
avoidance of loss   198
confirmation bias   199
mental set   200
hindsight bias   201
cognitive dissonance   202
postdecision dissonance   202
justification of effort   203
intelligence   204
factor analysis   204
g factor   204
psychometric approach to intelligence   204
achievement versus aptitude tests   204
mental age (MA)   205
intelligence quotient (IQ)   205
Stanford–Binet Intelligence Scale   205
Wechsler Adult Intelligence Scale (WAIS)   205

Wechsler Intelligence Scale for Children (WISC)   205
culture-free and culture-fair tests   206
stereotype threat   207
cognitive approaches to intelligence   208
triarchic theory of intelligence   208
 componential intelligence   209
 experiential intelligence   209
 contextual intelligence   209
metacognition   209
tacit knowledge   209
emotional intelligence   210
heritability   212
cognitive ethology   217
anthropomorphism   220
anthropocentrism   220
convergent versus divergent thinking   221

LOOKING BACK

- When you think of a bird, why are you more likely to recall a robin than a penguin? (pp. 190–191)
- How are visual images like images on a television screen? (p. 191)
- What is happening mentally when you mistakenly take your geography notes to your psychology class? (p. 192)
- Mentally speaking, why is making a cake, well, a piece of cake? (p. 193)
- Why can't logic solve all of our problems? (p. 194)
- What kind of reasoning do juries need to be good at? (p. 195)
- When people say that all opinions and claims are equally valid, what error are they making? (p. 196)
- Why do people worry about dying in an airplane crash but ignore dangers that are far more likely? (p. 198)

- How might your physician's choice of words about alternative treatments for your illness affect which one you choose? (p. 199)
- When "Monday morning quarterbacks" say they knew all along who would win Sunday's big game, what bias might they be showing? (p. 201)
- Why will a terrible hazing make you more loyal to the group that hazed you? (p. 203)
- How did the original purpose of intelligence testing change when IQ tests came to America? (p. 206)
- Is it possible to design intelligence tests that are not influenced by culture? (pp. 206–208)
- Why do some psychologists defend traditional intelligence testing and others oppose it? (p. 208)
- What kind of intelligence allows you to master the unspoken rules for academic success? (p. 209)

- What is "EQ," and why is it as important as IQ? (p. 210)

- If intelligence is highly heritable, does that mean that group differences in IQ are genetic? (p. 213)

- What sorts of environmental "nutrients" nurture mental ability? (p. 214)

- Some gifted people are professionally successful, and others are not; what makes the difference? (p. 215)

- Why do Asian children perform much better in school than American students do, despite having worse school facilities? (p. 216)

- Why do some researchers think that animals can think? (pp. 217–218)

- Everyone loves to talk to their pets—but can their pets learn to talk back? (pp. 218–219)

Answers to the Remote Associates Test on page 221:
back, party, book, match, cheese

Some solutions to the nine-dot problem in the Get Involved exercise on page 201 (from Adams, 1986):

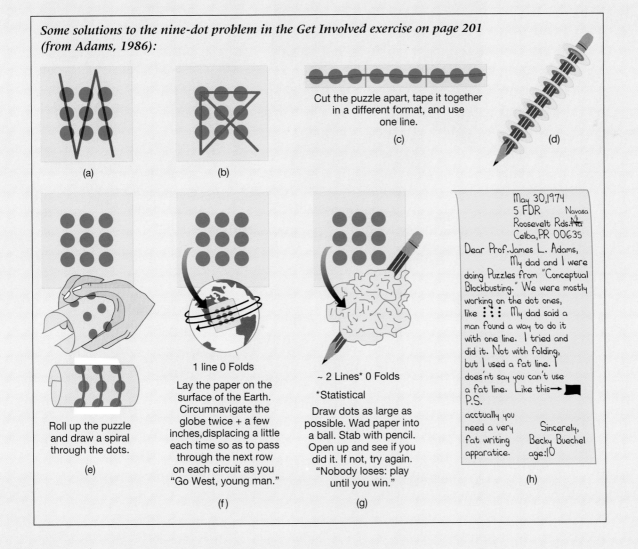

(a)

(b)

Cut the puzzle apart, tape it together in a different format, and use one line.

(c)

(d)

Roll up the puzzle and draw a spiral through the dots.

(e)

1 line 0 Folds

Lay the paper on the surface of the Earth. Circumnavigate the globe twice + a few inches, displacing a little each time so as to pass through the next row on each circuit as you "Go West, young man."

(f)

~ 2 Lines* 0 Folds

*Statistical

Draw dots as large as possible. Wad paper into a ball. Stab with pencil. Open up and see if you did it. If not, try again. "Nobody loses: play until you win."

(g)

May 30, 1974
5 FDR   Navasa
Roosevelt Rds.Na
Ceiba, PR 00635
Dear Prof. James L. Adams,
   My dad and I were doing Puzzles from "Conceptual Blockbusting." We were mostly working on the dot ones, like ⁚⁚⁚ My dad said a man found a way to do it with one line. I tried and did it. Not with folding, but I used a fat line. I does'nt say you can't use a fat line. Like this→ ◢
P.S.
acctually you need a very fat writing apparatice.
                 Sincerely,
                 Becky Buechel
                 age: 10

(h)

Appeal Fails, Man Sentenced to Two Life Terms for Rape

GREENSBORO, NC, 1987. An appeals court has sentenced Ronald Junior Cotton to two life sentences for the rape of Jennifer Thompson in 1984, upholding a 1985 conviction by a lower court. Thompson, a 22-year-old straight-A college student at the time of the attack, testified that during her ordeal, as a knife was being held to her throat, she made a conscious effort to memorize every detail of the rapist's face and to look for scars, tattoos, and other characteristics that would help her identify him later on.

An appeals court has upheld the conviction of Ronald Junior Cotton (left), identified by Jennifer Thompson as having raped her. Although a fellow inmate, Bobby Poole (right), has boasted of committing the crime, Thompson stands by her testimony.

On the same day that the rape occurred, Thompson helped police put together a composite sketch of her attacker. A few days after the attack, she identified Cotton in a series of police photos, and later she unhesitatingly picked him out from a lineup. She says she is completely confident in her identification of Cotton and knows he was the man who assaulted her. Cotton was convicted on the strength of Thompson's eyewitness testimony.

During a pretrial hearing for the appeal, Thompson learned that another inmate in the prison where Cotton was being held, Bobby Poole, has bragged that he was the one who committed the rape. But Thompson remains certain that she has identified the right man. When Poole was brought into court during the appeals hearing, Thompson was asked if she had ever seen him. "I have never seen him in my life," she answered. "I have no idea who he is."

CHAPTER SEVEN

MEMORY

At one time, most prosecutors and juries would have dismissed Jennifer Thompson's testimony outright. For many decades, it was hard for rape victims to get justice in the legal system because public opinion tended to blame them for having "provoked" the attack or for failing to fight back strongly enough. Then, as people became more aware of the horrific nature of rape and the unfairness of blaming victims, acceptance of women's testimony increased. Today, many defendants, like Ronald Junior Cotton, are being sent to prison or even sentenced to death primarily on the strength of the victim's testimony.

But is a witness's or a victim's account always reliable? In the absence of corroborating evidence, should a victim's certainty that she is accurate in her identification be sufficient for establishing guilt? Much is at stake in our efforts to answer these questions: getting justice for rape victims, and also not falsely convicting men who are innocent.

The Cotton case did not end in 1987. At the conclusion of this chapter, we will tell you what ultimately happened. Meanwhile, as you read, ask yourself, When should we trust our memories, and when should we be cautious about doing so? We all forget a great deal, of course: We watch the evening news and half an hour later can't recall the main story; we enjoy a meal and quickly forget what we ate; we study our heads off for an exam, only to find that some of the information isn't there when we need it most. Do we also "remember" things that never happened? Are memory malfunctions the exception to the rule, or could they be the norm? If memory is not always reliable, how can any of us hope to know the story of our own lives? And what are the implications for the legal system, which relies so much on the memories of witnesses and crime victims?

What's Ahead

- What's wrong with thinking of memory as a mental movie camera?

- Why do "flashbulb" memories of surprising or shocking events sometimes have less wattage than we think?

- If you have a strong emotional reaction to a remembered event, does that mean your memory is accurate?

7.1 Reconstructing the Past

Memory refers to the capacity to retain and retrieve information, and also to the structures that account for this capacity. Human beings are capable of astonishing feats of memory. Most of us can easily remember who fought whom in World War II, the tune of our national anthem, how to use an automated teller machine, the most embarrassing experience we ever had, zillions of details about our favorite sports or films, and hundreds of thousands of other bits of information, without hesitation.

Memory confers competence; without it we would be as helpless as newborns, unable to carry out even the most trivial of our daily tasks. Memory also confers a sense of personal identity; each of us is the sum of our recollections, which is why we feel so threatened when others challenge our memories. Individuals and cultures alike rely on a remembered history for a sense of coherence and meaning; memory gives us our past and guides our future.

The Manufacture of Memory

In ancient times, philosophers compared memory to a soft wax tablet that would preserve anything that chanced to make an imprint on it. Then, with the advent of the printing press, they began to think of memory as a gigantic library, storing specific events and facts for later retrieval. Today, in the audiovisual age, many people compare memory to a tape recorder or a movie camera, automatically recording every moment of their lives.

Films and novels reflect and influence popular assumptions about memory. In Alfred Hitchcock's 1945 film "Spellbound," an amnesia patient is suspected of murder, and the clues to the identity of the real killer appear in a dream he has. The surrealistic dream sequences, designed by artist Salvador Dali, conveyed the psychoanalytic idea that painful memories are never forgotten but are merely locked away in the unconscious with all the details intact, waiting to be recovered—a notion that modern research has questioned.

Popular and appealing though this belief about memory is, however, it is utterly wrong. Not everything that happens to us or impinges on our senses is tucked away for later use; memory is selective. If it were not, our minds would be cluttered with mental junk—the temperature at noon Thursday, the price of turnips two years ago, a phone number needed only once. Moreover, recovering a memory is not at all like replaying a videotape of an event; it is more like watching a few unconnected frames and then figuring out what the rest of the scene must have been like.

One of the first scientists to make this point was the British psychologist Sir Frederic Bartlett (1932). Bartlett asked people to read lengthy, unfamiliar stories from other cultures and then tell the stories back to him. As the volunteers tried to recall the stories, they made interesting errors: They often eliminated or changed details that did not make sense to them, and they added other details to make the story coherent, sometimes even adding a moral. Memory, Bartlett concluded, must therefore be largely a *reconstructive* process. We may reproduce some kinds of simple information by rote, said Bartlett, but when we remember complex information, we typically alter it in ways that help us make sense of the material, based on what we already know or think we know. Since Bartlett's time, hundreds of studies have found this to be true for everything from stories to conversations to personal experiences (Schacter, 1996).

In reconstructing their memories, people often draw on many sources. Suppose, for example, that someone asks you to describe one of your early birthday parties. You may have some direct recollection of the event, but you may also incorporate information from family stories, photographs, or home videos, and even from accounts of other people's birthdays and reenactments of birthdays on television. You take all these bits and pieces and build one integrated account. Later, you may not be able to separate your original experience from what you added after the fact—a phenomenon called **source amnesia,** or *source misattribution.*

A dramatic instance of reconstruction once occurred in the sad case of H. M., whom we described briefly in Chapter 4. Ever since 1953, when much of H. M.'s hippocampus and the adjacent cortex were surgically removed, he has been unable to form lasting memories for new events, facts, songs, stories, or faces, and so he does not remember much of anything that has happened since his operation (Hilts, 1995; Ogden & Corkin,

If these children remember their vacation later in life, their reconstruction may include information picked up from family photographs, videos, and stories. Because of source amnesia, they will probably be unable to distinguish their actual memories from information they got elsewhere.

1991). To cope with his devastating condition, H. M. will sometimes resort to reconstructions. On one occasion, after eating a chocolate Valentine's Day heart, H. M. stuck the shiny red wrapping in his shirt pocket. Two hours later, while searching for his handkerchief, he pulled out the paper and looked at it in puzzlement. When a researcher asked why he had the paper in his pocket, he replied, "Well, it could have been wrapped around a big chocolate heart. It must be Valentine's Day!" The researcher could hardly contain her excitement about H. M.'s possible recall of a recent episode. But a short time later, when she asked him to take out the paper again and say why he had it in his pocket, he replied, "Well, it might have been wrapped around a big chocolate rabbit. It must be Easter!"

Sadly, H. M. *had* to reconstruct the past; his damaged brain could not recall it in any other way. But those of us with normal memory abilities also reconstruct, far more often than we realize.

The Fading Flashbulb

Of course, some unusual, shocking, or tragic events, such as earthquakes or accidents, do seem to hold a special place in memory, especially when we were personally involved. Such events seem frozen in time, with all the details intact. Years ago, Roger Brown and James Kulik (1977) labeled these vivid recollections of emotional events "flashbulb memories" because that term captures the surprise, illumination, and seemingly photographic detail that characterize them. They

source amnesia
The inability to distinguish what you originally experienced from what you heard or were told about an event later.

THE FAR SIDE   By GARY LARSON

More facts of nature: All forest animals, to this very day, remember exactly where they were and what they were doing when they heard that Bambi's mother had been shot.

Research Navigator.com
RESOURCES FOR COLLEGE RESEARCH ASSIGNMENTS

7.1

confabulation
Confusion of an event that happened to someone else with one that happened to you, or a belief that you remember something when it never actually happened.

speculated that the capacity for flashbulb memories may have evolved because such memories had survival value. Remembering the details of a surprising or dangerous experience could have helped our ancestors avoid similar situations.

Despite their intensity, however, even flashbulb memories are not always complete or accurate records of the past (Wright, 1993). For example, people who saw the 1986 explosion of the space shuttle *Challenger* often swear that they know exactly where they were and what they were doing when the tragedy occurred. But research done after the explosion showed that memories like these grow dimmer with time. In one study, college students, on the morning after the *Challenger* tragedy, reported how they had heard the news. Three years later, when they again recalled how they learned of the incident, not one student was entirely correct and a third of them were *completely wrong*, although they felt confident that they were remembering accurately (Neisser & Harsch, 1992). More recently, psychologists interviewed 222 college students after the verdict was announced in the O. J. Simpson case in 1995. Fifteen months

later, half of the students' recollections were highly accurate, and only 11 percent contained major errors or distortions. But after 32 months, only 29 percent of the recollections remained accurate, and more than 40 percent contained distortions (Schmolck, Buffalo, & Squire, 2000).

Even with flashbulb memories, then, facts tend to get mixed with a little fiction. The conclusion is inescapable: Remembering is an *active* process, one that involves not only dredging up stored information but also putting two and two together to reconstruct the past. And sometimes we put two and two together and get five.

The Conditions of Confabulation

In Chapter 6, we saw that rational thinking is often hampered by the confirmation bias and the need to reduce dissonance. Memory, too, is biased: For example, after making a decision, we will remember information that supported the wisdom of our choice and conveniently "forget" information that might have led us to make an alternative choice (Mather, Shafir, & Johnson, 2000). These predictable memory distortions reduce feelings of regret, but they also make it harder for people to learn from their mistakes.

Of course, people don't forget that they made a decision to go to College X instead of College Y, or to marry Mindy rather than Cindy. But often, because memory is reconstructive, it is subject to **confabulation**—confusing an event that happened to someone else with one that happened to you, or coming to believe that you remember something that never happened. Such confabulations are especially likely to occur under four circumstances (Garry, Manning, & Loftus, 1996; Hyman & Pentland, 1996; Johnson, 1995):

1 *You have thought about the imagined event many times.* Suppose that at family gatherings you keep hearing about the time that Uncle Sam scared everyone at a New Year's party by pounding a hammer into the wall with such force that the wall collapsed. The story is so colorful that you can practically see Uncle Sam in your mind's eye. The more you think about this event, the more likely you are to believe that you were actually there, even if you were sound asleep in another house.

2 *The image of the event contains a lot of details.* Ordinarily, we can distinguish an imagined event from a real one by the amount of detail we recall; real events tend to produce more details. However, the longer you think about an imagined event, the more details you are likely to add—what Sam was wearing, the fact that he'd had too much to drink, the crumbling plaster, people standing around in party hats—and these details may in turn persuade you that the event really happened and that you have a direct memory of it.

3 *The event is easy to imagine.* If forming an image of an event takes little effort (as does visualizing a man pounding a wall with a hammer), then we tend to think that our memory is real. In contrast, when we must make an effort to form an image—for example, of being in a place we have never seen or doing something that is utterly foreign to us—our cognitive efforts apparently serve as a cue that the event did not really take place, or that we were not there when it did.

4 *You focus on your emotional reactions to the event rather than on what actually happened.* Emotional reactions to an imagined event can resemble those that would have occurred in response to a real event, and so they can mislead us. This means that your feelings about an event, no matter how strongly you hold them, are no guarantee that the event really happened. Consider again our Sam story, which happens to be true. A woman we know believed for years that she had been present in the room as an 11-year-old child when her uncle destroyed the wall. Because the story was so vivid and upsetting to her, she felt angry at him for what she thought was his mean and violent behavior, and she assumed that she must have been angry at the time as well. Then, as an adult, she learned that she was not at the party at all but had merely heard about it repeatedly over the years; and that Sam had not pounded the wall in anger, but as a joke—to inform the assembled guests that he and his wife were about to remodel their home. Nevertheless, our friend's family has had a hard time convincing her that her "memory" of this event is entirely wrong, and they are not sure she believes them yet.

As the Sam story illustrates, and as laboratory research verifies, false memories can be as stable over time as true ones (Brainerd, Reyna, & Brandse, 1995; Poole, 1995; Roediger & McDermott, 1995). Yet many people still believe that memories are permanently stored in the brain with perfect accuracy, and that there are accurate ways of getting them "out"—such as through hypnosis. We will see what is wrong with that assumption next.

NEVER FORGETS   SOMETIMES FORGETS   ALWAYS FORGETS

 QUICK QUIZ

See whether you can reconstruct what you have read in order to answer these questions.

1. Memory is like (a) a wax tablet, (b) a giant file cabinet, (c) a video recorder, (d) none of these.

2. *True or false:* Like other memories, flashbulb memories are vulnerable to distortion.

3. Which of the following confabulated "memories" might people be most inclined to accept as having really happened to them? (a) being lost in a shopping center at the age of 5, (b) taking a class in astrophysics, (c) visiting a monastery in Tibet as a child, (d) being bullied by another kid in the fourth grade

Answers:
1. d   2. true   3. a and d because they are common events that are easy to imagine and that contain a lot of vivid details. It would be harder to induce someone to believe that he or she had studied astrophysics or visited Tibet, because these are rare events that take an effort to imagine.

What's Ahead

- Can the question someone asks you about a past event affect what you remember about it?
- Can children's testimony about sexual abuse be trusted?
- Do people remember better when they're hypnotized?

7.2 Memory and the Power of Suggestion

The reconstructive nature of memory helps the mind work efficiently. Instead of cramming our brains with infinite details, we can store the essentials of an experience, then use our knowledge of the world to figure out the specifics when we need them. But precisely because memory is reconstructive, it is also vulnerable to suggestion—to ideas implanted in our minds after the event, which then become associated with it. This normal process raises some thorny problems in legal cases that involve eyewitness testimony or people's memories of what happened, when, and to whom.

The Eyewitness on Trial

Without the accounts of eyewitnesses, many guilty people would go free. But because memory is reconstructive, eyewitness testimony is not always reliable, even when the witness is certain about the accuracy of his or her report (Bothwell, Deffenbacher, & Brigham, 1987; Sporer et al., 1995). As a result, some convictions based solely or mostly on such testimony turn out to be tragic mistakes. Errors by eyewitnesses are especially likely to occur when the suspect's ethnicity differs from that of the witness. Perhaps prejudices or unfamiliarity prevent people from attending to the distinctive features of members of other groups, or perhaps ethnic stereotypes affect people's reconstructions of what happened (Brigham & Malpass, 1985; Chance & Goldstein, 1995; Sherman & Bessenoff, 1999).

Eyewitness accounts are also heavily influenced by the way in which questions are put to the witness and by suggestive comments made during an interrogation or interview. In a classic study of leading questions, Elizabeth Loftus and John Palmer (1974) showed people short films depicting car collisions. Afterward, the researchers asked some of the viewers, "About how fast were the cars going when they hit each other?" Other viewers were asked the same question, but with the verb changed to *smashed, collided, bumped,* or *contacted.* Estimates of how fast the cars were going varied, depending on which word was used. *Smashed* produced the highest average speed estimates (40.8 mph), followed by *collided* (39.3 mph), *bumped* (38.1 mph), *hit* (34.0 mph), and *contacted* (31.8 mph).

In a similar study, the researchers asked some participants, "Did you see *a* broken headlight?" but asked of others "Did you see *the* broken headlight?" (Loftus & Zanni, 1975). The question with *the* presupposes a broken headlight and merely asks whether the witness saw it, whereas the question with *a* makes no such presupposition. People who received questions with *the* were far more likely to report having seen something that had not really appeared in the film than were those who received questions with *a.* If a tiny word like *the* can lead people to "remember" what they never saw, you can imagine how the leading questions of police detectives and lawyers might influence a witness's recall.

Misleading information from other sources, too, can profoundly alter what we remember. In one study, students were shown the face of a young man who had straight hair, then heard a description of the face supposedly written by another witness—a description that wrongly said the man had light, curly hair (see Figure 7.1). When the students reconstructed the face using a kit of facial features, a third of their reconstructions contained the misleading detail, whereas only 5 percent contained it when curly hair was not mentioned (Loftus & Greene, 1980).

Leading questions, suggestive comments, and misleading information affect people's memories for their own experiences, as well as for events they have merely witnessed. In many studies, researchers have induced people to "recall" complicated events from early in life that never actually happened at all, such as getting lost in a shopping mall, being hospitalized for a high fever, being harassed by a bully, or spilling punch all over the mother of the bride at a wedding (Hyman & Pentland, 1996; Loftus & Pickrell, 1995; Mazzoni et al., 1999).

Children's Testimony

The power of suggestion can affect anyone, but many people are especially concerned about its impact on children being questioned about pos-

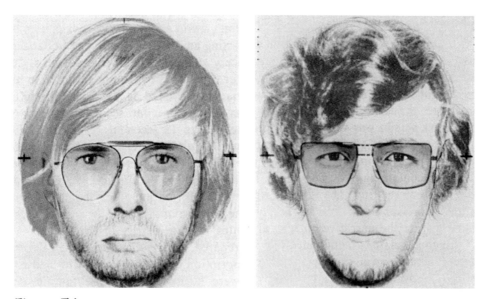

Figure 7.1
The Influence of Misleading Information

In a study described in the text, students saw a young man's face and then had to reconstruct it from memory. On the left is one student's reconstruction in the absence of misleading information about the man's hair; on the right is another person's reconstruction of the same face after exposure to the misleading information (Loftus & Greene, 1980).

sible sexual abuse. For many decades most adults believed that children's memories could not be trusted, because young children confuse fantasy with reality and tend to say whatever adults expect. Then, as the issue of child abuse came to public attention in the 1970s and 1980s, some people began to argue that no child would ever lie about or misremember such a traumatic experience.

Resolving this debate became critical as accusations of child abuse in daycare centers across the United States skyrocketed. The first was a case against the McMartin preschool in Los Angeles, in the mid-1980s, and it was soon followed by dozens of others. After being interviewed by therapists and police investigators, children in these schools were claiming that their teachers had molested them in the most terrible ways: by hanging them in trees, putting handcuffs on them, raping them, even forcing them to eat feces. Although in no case had parents actually seen the daycare teachers treating the children badly, although none of the children had complained to their parents, and although none of the parents had noticed any symptoms or problems in their children, most of the accused teachers were sentenced to many years in prison

Thinking Critically About Children's Testimony

(Nathan & Snedeker, 1995). Were these people guilty of unspeakably horrible acts, or had the children been somehow persuaded to make up fanciful stories?

After reviewing the research on this issue, Stephen Ceci and Maggie Bruck (1995) concluded that both extreme positions—"children always lie" and "children never lie"—are wrong. Ceci and Bruck found that most young children *do* recollect accurately most of what they have observed or experienced. On the other hand, some children *will* say that something happened when it did not. Like adults, they can be influenced to report an event in a certain way, depending on the frequency of the suggestions and the insistence of the person making them.

Therefore, instead of asking "Are children suggestible?" or "Are children's memories accurate?," Ceci and Bruck (1995) proposed asking a more useful question: "Under what conditions are children apt to be suggestible?" One such condition is being very young. Preschoolers' memories are more vulnerable to suggestive questions than are those of school-age children and adults. Preschoolers are also more likely to have source amnesia, failing to remember whether they actually saw or experienced something themselves or heard about it from an adult. And the boundary between reality and fantasy may blur for very young children, especially in emotionally charged situations, making it more likely that their accounts will include confabulations of imagined events (Poole & Lamb, 1998).

In addition, children's memories, just like adults' memories, can be influenced by pressure to conform to the interviewer's expectations and by the desire to please the interviewer. One team of researchers, having analyzed the transcripts of interrogations of children in the McMartin case, applied the same techniques in an experiment with preschool children (Garven et al., 1998). A young man visited children at their preschool, read them a story, and handed out treats. The man did nothing aggressive, inappropriate, or surprising. A week later the experimenter questioned the children about the man's visit. She asked children in one group leading questions ("Did he shove the teacher? Did he throw a crayon at a kid who was talking?"). She asked a second group the same questions, but also used influence techniques used by interrogators in the McMartin case and other cases of daycare workers accused of child abuse: for example, telling the children what "other kids"

had supposedly said, expressing disappointment if answers were negative, and praising children for making allegations.

In the first group, children said "yes, it happened" to about 15 percent of the false allegations about the man's visit. This finding alone refutes the notion that children never lie, misremember, or make things up. In the second group, the 3-year-olds, on average, said "yes" to *over 80 percent* of the false allegations suggested to them, and the 4- to 6-year-olds said yes to about half of the allegations (see Figure 7.2). Note that the interviews in this study lasted only 5 to 10 minutes, whereas in actual investigations, interviewers often question children repeatedly over many weeks.

Some people argue that children cannot be induced to report real-life traumatic experiences that never actually happened to them, but they can be. In one study, schoolchildren were asked for their recollections of an actual incident in which a sniper had terrorized their schoolyard. Many of the children who were not at the school during the shooting, including some who were on vacation at the time, reported memories of hearing shots, seeing someone lying on the ground, and other details

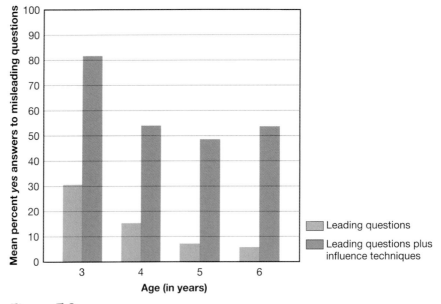

Figure 7.2
Social Pressure and Children's False Allegations

When researchers asked preschoolers whether a visitor had committed aggressive acts—acts that had not actually occurred—only a small minority of the 4- to 6-year-olds said yes (though fully 30 percent of the 3-year-olds said yes). But when the researchers used social-influence techniques taken from real-life child-abuse investigations, most *children said yes (Garven et al., 1998).*

they could not possibly have experienced directly. Apparently, they had been influenced by the accounts of the children who had been there (Pynoos & Nader, 1989).

In sum, children, like adults, can be accurate in what they report; and, also like adults, they can distort, forget, fantasize, and be misled. As research shows, their memory processes are only human.

Memory Under Hypnosis

Some people think that the limitations on memory that we have discussed can be overcome by using hypnosis. Let's see what research has to say about this.

Hypnosis is a procedure in which a practitioner suggests changes in the sensations, perceptions, thoughts, feelings, or behavior of the subject (Kirsch & Lynn, 1995). The subject, in turn, tries to alter his or her cognitive processes in accordance with the hypnotist's suggestions (Nash & Nadon, 1997). People usually report that this effort feels involuntary, but actually it is a voluntary one. Hypnosis has been used successfully to alleviate chronic pain; reduce stress and anxiety; anesthetize people undergoing dental work, surgery, or childbirth; and reduce nausea in cancer patients having chemotherapy (Kirsch, Montgomery, & Sapirstein, 1995; Nash & Nadon, 1997).

Hypnosis, however, does *not* increase the overall accuracy of memory. On the contrary: Under hypnosis, the natural tendency to confuse fact and speculation is increased by a desire to please the hypnotist and by the hypnotist's encouragement of fantasy and the reporting of detailed images ("Imagine that you are back in your grandmother's house when you were 7 . . . describe the room and what she is wearing . . ."). Although hypnosis does sometimes elicit new information about an event, it also increases *errors,* probably because hypnotized people are more willing than nonhypnotized people to guess or because they mistake vividly imagined possibilities for actual memories (Dinges et al., 1992; Kihlstrom, 1994; Nash & Nadon, 1997). In other words, hypnotized people confabulate.

Hypnosis also does not produce "age regression," a literal reexperiencing of long-ago events. When people are "regressed" to an early age, their brain waves, mental performance, moral

Thinking Critically About Hypnosis and Memory

reasoning, and emotions remain adultlike, and their memories are often wrong (Nash, 1987). They may use baby talk or say they *feel* 3 years old, but they are unconsciously playing a role, and they will do the same when they are hypnotically regressed to "past lives." Unfortunately, some psychotherapists who use hypnosis in their practice do not know this. In a survey of nearly 900 members of the American Association of Marriage and Family Therapists, more than half mistakenly believed that "hypnosis can be used to recover memories from as far back as birth" (Yapko, 1994). Between one-fourth and one-third of all therapists are using hypnosis and other suggestive techniques to try to uncover their clients' supposedly repressed memories, without knowing much about the limitations of these methods (Poole et al., 1995).

In a fascinating series of studies that demonstrated how false memories can be constructed under hypnotic suggestion, Nicholas Spanos and his colleagues (1991) directed hypnotized Canadian university students to regress past their own births to previous lives. About a third of the students reported being able to do so. But when they were asked, while supposedly reliving a past life, to name the leader of their country, say whether the country was at peace or at war, or describe the money used in their community, the students could not do it. One young man, who thought he was Julius Caesar, said the year was 50 A.D. and he was emperor of Rome. But Caesar died in 44 B.C. and was never crowned emperor, and dating years as A.D. or B.C. did not begin until several centuries later!

In these studies, many of the participants tried to fulfill the requirements of the role by weaving events, places, and persons from their present lives into their accounts, and by picking up cues from the experimenter. The researchers concluded that the act of "remembering" another "self" involves the construction of a fantasy that accords with the rememberer's own beliefs and also the beliefs of others—in this case, the authoritative hypnotist.

Because errors and pseudomemories are so common in hypnotically induced recall, the American Psychological Association has long opposed the use of "hypnotically refreshed" testimony in courts of law. But memory researchers do find hypnosis extremely useful—for studying how human suggestibility and the power of imagination affect the way we perceive the present and reconstruct the past.

hypnosis
A procedure in which the practitioner suggests changes in the sensations, perceptions, thoughts, feelings, or behavior of the subject, who cooperates by altering his or her normal cognitive functioning accordingly.

QUICK QUIZ

Being hypnotized is unlikely to help you with this quiz.

1. Research suggests that the best way to encourage truthful testimony by children is to (a) reassure them that their friends have had the same experience, (b) reward them for telling you that something happened, (c) scold them if you believe they are lying, (d) try to avoid leading questions.

2. Which statement about hypnosis is correct? (a) It reduces errors in memory; (b) it enables people to relive memories from infancy; (c) it permits people to relive a former life; (d) it demonstrates that memories are permanently and accurately stored in the brain; (e) all are correct; (f) none are correct.

3. Under hypnosis, Jim describes the chocolate cake at his fourth birthday and Joan remembers her former life as a twelfth-century French queen. But lemon cake was served at Jim's birthday and Joan can't speak twelfth-century French. What explanation best accounts for their vivid but incorrect memories?

4. In psychotherapy, hundreds of people have claimed to recall long-buried memories of having taken part in satanic rituals involving animal and human torture and sacrifice. Yet law-enforcement investigators and psychologists have been unable to confirm any of these reports (Goodman et al., 1995). Based on what you have learned so far, how might you explain such "memories"?

Answers:
1. d 2. f 3. They are playing the role of the hypnotized subject, using their imaginations to respond to the hypnotist's suggestions and trying to come up with a fanciful, plausible story. 4. Therapists who uncritically assume that satanic cults are widespread may ask leading questions and otherwise influence their patients. Patients, who are susceptible to their therapists' interpretations, may then confabulate and "remember" experiences that did not happen, borrowing details from fictionalized accounts or from other troubling experiences in their lives (Ofshe & Watters, 1994). The result may be source amnesia and the patient's mistaken conviction that the memory is real.

7.1

explicit memory
Conscious, intentional recollection of an event or of an item of information.

recall
The ability to retrieve and reproduce from memory previously encountered material.

recognition
The ability to identify previously encountered material.

What's Ahead

- In general, which is easier—a multiple-choice item or a short-answer essay item—and why?

- Can you know something without knowing that you know it?

- Why is the computer often used as a metaphor for the mind?

7.3 In Pursuit of Memory

Now that we have seen how memory *doesn't* work—namely, like a tape recorder, an infallible filing system, or a journal written in indelible ink—we turn to studies of how it *does* work. The ability to remember is not an absolute talent; it depends on the type of performance being called for. If you have a preference for multiple-choice, essay, or true-false exams, you already know this.

Measuring Memory

Conscious recollection of an event or an item of information is called **explicit memory.** It is usually measured using one of two methods. The first method tests for **recall,** the ability to retrieve and reproduce information encountered earlier. Essay and fill-in-the-blank exams and memory games such as Trivial Pursuit or Jeopardy require recall. The second method tests for **recognition,** the ability to identify information you have previously observed, read, or heard about. The information is given to you, and all you have to do is say whether it is old or new, or perhaps correct or incorrect, or pick it out of a set of alternatives. The task, in other words, is to compare the information you are given with the information stored in your memory. True-false and multiple-choice tests call for recognition.

Recognition tests can be tricky, especially when false items closely resemble correct ones. Under most circumstances, however, recognition is easier than recall. Recognition for visual images

GET INVOLVED

▶ RECALLING RUDOLPH'S FRIENDS

You can try this test of recall if you are familiar with the poem *'Twas the Night Before Christmas* or the song *Rudolph the Red-Nosed Reindeer*. Rudolph had eight reindeer friends; name as many of them as you can. After you have done your best, turn to the Get Involved exercise on page 238 for a recognition test on the same information.

is particularly impressive. If you show people 2,500 slides of faces and places, and later you ask them to identify which ones they saw out of a larger set, they will be able to accurately identify more than 90 percent of the original slides (Haber, 1970).

The superiority of recognition over recall was once demonstrated in a study of people's memories of their high school classmates (Bahrick, Bahrick, & Wittlinger, 1975). The participants, ages 17 to 74, first wrote down the names of as many classmates as they could remember. Recall was poor; even when prompted with yearbook pictures, the youngest people failed to name almost a third of their classmates, and the oldest failed to name most of them. Recognition, however, was far better. When asked to look at a series of cards, each of which contained a set of five photographs, and to say which picture in each set showed a former classmate, recent graduates were right 90 percent of the time—and so were people who had graduated 35 years earlier. The ability to recognize names was nearly as impressive.

Sometimes, information encountered in the past affects our thoughts and actions even though we do not consciously or intentionally remember it—a phenomenon known as **implicit memory** (Graf & Schacter, 1985; Schacter, Chiu, & Ochsner, 1993). To get at this subtle sort of knowledge, researchers must rely on indirect methods, instead of the direct ones used to measure explicit memory. One common method, **priming,** asks you to read or listen to some information and then tests you later to see whether the information affects your performance on another type of task.

For example, suppose that you had to read a list of words, some of which began with the letters *def* (such as *define, defend,* or *deform*). Later you might be asked to complete word stems (such as *def-*) with the first word that comes to mind. Even if you could not recognize or recall the original words very well, you would be more likely to complete the word fragments with words from the list than you would be if you had not seen the list. In this procedure, the original words "prime" certain responses on the word-completion task (that is, make them more available), showing that people can retain more knowledge about the past than they realize. They know more than they know that they know (Richardson-Klavehn & Bjork, 1988; Roediger, 1990).

Another method of measuring implicit memory, the **relearning method,** or *savings method,* straddles the boundary between implicit and explicit memory tests. Devised by Hermann Ebbinghaus (1885/1913) over a century ago, the relearning method requires you to relearn information or a task that you had learned earlier. If you master it more quickly the second time around, you must be remembering something from the first experience. One eminent memory researcher told us that he considers the relearning method to be a test of explicit memory. But another maintained that it can function as a test of implicit memory if the learner is unaware that the material being relearned was ever learned earlier.

implicit memory
Unconscious retention in memory, as evidenced by the effect of a previous experience or previously encountered information on current thoughts or actions.

priming
A method for measuring implicit memory in which a person reads or listens to information and is later tested to see whether the information affects performance on another type of task.

relearning method
A method for measuring retention that compares the time required to relearn material with the time used in the initial learning of the material.

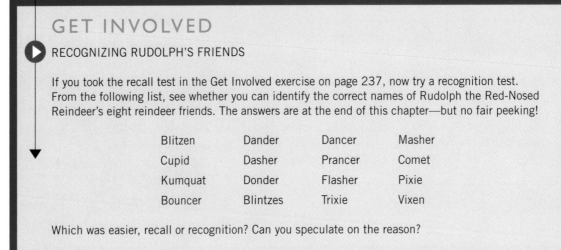

GET INVOLVED

RECOGNIZING RUDOLPH'S FRIENDS

If you took the recall test in the Get Involved exercise on page 237, now try a recognition test. From the following list, see whether you can identify the correct names of Rudolph the Red-Nosed Reindeer's eight reindeer friends. The answers are at the end of this chapter—but no fair peeking!

Blitzen	Dander	Dancer	Masher
Cupid	Dasher	Prancer	Comet
Kumquat	Donder	Flasher	Pixie
Bouncer	Blintzes	Trixie	Vixen

Which was easier, recall or recognition? Can you speculate on the reason?

Models of Memory

Although people usually refer to memory as a single faculty, as in "I must be losing my memory" or "He has a memory like an elephant's," the term *memory* actually covers a complex collection of abilities and processes. If tape recorders or video cameras are not accurate metaphors for capturing these diverse components of memory, then what metaphor would be better?

As we saw in Chapter 6, many cognitive psychologists liken the mind to an information processor, along the lines of a computer, though more complex. They have constructed *information-processing models* of cognitive processes, liberally borrowing computer-programming terms such as *input, output, accessing,* and *information retrieval.* When you type something on your computer's keyboard, the machine encodes the information into an electronic language, stores it on a disk, and retrieves it when you need to use it. Similarly, in information-processing models of memory, we *encode* information (convert it to a form that the brain can process and use), *store* the information (retain it over time), and *retrieve* the information (recover it for use). In storage, the information may be represented as concepts, propositions, images, or *cognitive schemas,* mental networks of knowledge, beliefs, and expectations concerning particular topics or aspects of the world. (If you can't retrieve these terms, see Chapter 6.)

In most information-processing models, storage takes place in three interacting memory systems. *Sensory memory* retains incoming sensory informa-

tion for a second or two, until it can be processed further. *Short-term memory (STM)* holds a limited amount of information for a brief period of time, perhaps up to 30 seconds or so, unless a conscious effort is made to keep it there longer. *Long-term memory (LTM)* accounts for longer storage— from a few minutes to decades (Atkinson & Shiffrin, 1968, 1971). Information can pass from sensory memory to short-term memory, and in either direction between short-term and long-term memory, as illustrated in Figure 7.3.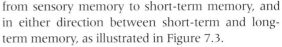

This model, which is often informally called the "three-box model," has dominated research on memory since the late 1960s. However, some psychologists argue that just one system exists, with different mental processes called on for different tasks. Critics of the three-box model also note that the human brain does not operate like your average computer. Most computers process instructions and data sequentially, and so the three-box model has emphasized sequential operations; but the human brain performs many operations simultaneously, in parallel. It recognizes patterns all at once rather than as a sequence of information bits, and it perceives new information, produces speech, and searches memory all at the same time. It can do this because millions of neurons are active at once, and each neuron communicates with thousands of others, which in turn communicate with millions more.

Because of these differences between human beings and machines, some cognitive scientists prefer a **parallel distributed processing (PDP),** or *connectionist,* model. Instead of representing infor-

parallel distributed processing (PDP)
A model of memory in which knowledge is represented as connections among thousands of interacting processing units, distributed in a vast network and all operating in parallel.

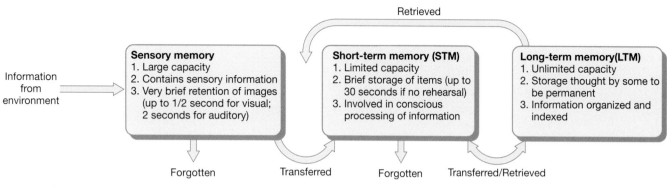

Figure 7.3
Three Memory Systems

In the "three-box model" of memory, information that does not transfer out of sensory memory or short-term memory is assumed to be forgotten forever. Once in long-term memory, information can be retrieved for use in analyzing incoming sensory information or performing mental operations in short-term memory.

mation as flowing from one system to another, a PDP model represents the contents of memory as connections among a huge number of interacting processing units, distributed in a vast network and all operating in parallel—just like the neurons of the brain (McClelland, 1994; Rumelhart, McClelland, & the PDP Research Group, 1986). As information enters the system, the ability of these units to excite or inhibit each other is constantly adjusted to reflect new knowledge.

Memory researchers are still arguing about which model of memory is most useful. In this chapter, we emphasize the three-box model, but keep in mind that the computer metaphor that inspired the model could one day be as outdated as the metaphor of memory as a camera.

 QUICK QUIZ

How well have you encoded what you just learned?

1. Alberta solved a crossword puzzle a few days ago. She no longer recalls the words in the puzzle, but while playing a game of Scrabble with her brother, she unconsciously tends to form words that were in the puzzle, showing that she has _____ memories of some of the words.

2. The three basic memory processes are _____, storage, and _____.

3. Do the preceding two questions ask for recall, recognition, or relearning? (And what about *this* question?)

4. If you know the story of Snow White and the Seven Dwarfs, identify which of the following are *not* among the Seven Dwarfs who loved Snow White: Dopey, Dumbo, Sneezy, Sleepy, Surly, Bashful, Horny, Doc, Wheezy, Grumpy, Happy, Mork. How do you know?

5. One objection to traditional information-processing theories of memory is that unlike most computers, the brain performs many independent operations _____.

Answers:

1. implicit 2. encoding, retrieval 3. The first two questions both measure recall; the third question measures recognition. 4. Dumbo, Surly, Horny, Wheezy, Mork. Presumably you know because you have no recognition memory for these names. 5. simultaneously, or in parallel

What's Ahead

- Why is short-term memory like a leaky bucket?

- When a word is on the tip of your tongue, what errors are you likely to make in recalling it?

- What's the difference between "knowing how" and "knowing that"?

Live! psych

7.2

7.4 The Three-Box Model of Memory

The information-processing model of three separate memory systems—sensory, short-term, and long-term—remains a leading approach because it offers a convenient way to organize the major findings on memory, does a good job of accounting for these findings, and is consistent with the biological facts about memory described in Chapter 4. Let us now peer into each of the "boxes."

Sensory Memory: Fleeting Impressions

In the three-box model, all incoming sensory information must make a brief stop in **sensory memory,** the entryway of memory. Sensory memory includes a number of separate memory subsystems, as many as there are senses. Visual images remain in a visual subsystem for a maximum of half a second. Auditory images remain in an auditory subsystem for a slightly longer time, by most estimates up to two seconds or so.

Sensory memory acts as a holding bin, retaining information in a highly accurate form until we can select items for attention from the stream of stimuli bombarding our senses. It gives us a brief time to decide whether information is extraneous or important; not everything detected by our senses warrants our attention. **Pattern recognition,** the identification of a stimulus on the basis of information already contained in long-term memory, occurs during the transfer of information from sensory memory to short-term memory.

Information that does not quickly go on to short-term memory vanishes forever, like a message written in disappearing ink. That is why people who see an array of 12 letters for just a fraction of a second can report only 4 or 5 of them; by the time they answer, their sensory memories are already fading (Sperling, 1960). The fleeting nature of sensory memory is actually beneficial; it prevents multiple sensory images—"double exposures"—that might interfere with the accurate perception and encoding of information.

Short-term Memory: Memory's Scratch Pad

Like sensory memory, **short-term memory (STM)** retains information only temporarily—for up to about 30 seconds by most estimates, although some researchers think that the maximum interval may extend to a few minutes. In short-term memory, the material is no longer an exact sensory image but is an encoding of one, such as a word or a phrase. This material either transfers into long-term memory or decays and is lost forever.

Individuals with brain injury, such as H. M., demonstrate the importance of transferring new information from short-term memory into long-term memory. H. M., you will recall, can store information on a short-term basis; he can hold a conversation and he appears to be fine when you first meet him. He also retains implicit memories. However, for the most part, H. M. cannot retain explicit information about new facts and events for longer than a few minutes. His terrible memory deficits involve a problem in transferring explicit memories from short-term storage into long-term storage. With a great deal of repetition and drill, H. M. can learn some new visual information, retain it in long-term memory, and recall it normally (McKee & Squire, 1992). But usually information does not get into long-term memory in the first place.

Besides retaining new information for brief periods while we are learning it, short-term memory holds information that has been retrieved from long-term memory for temporary use, providing the mental equivalent of a scratch pad. Thus short-term memory functions in part as a *working memory.* When you do an arithmetic problem, your working memory contains the numbers and the instructions for doing the necessary operations, plus the intermediate results from each step. The ability to bring information from long-term memory into working memory is not disrupted in patients like H. M. They can do arithmetic, converse, relate events that predate their injury, and do anything else that requires retrieval of information from long-term into short-term memory. Their problem is with the flow of information in

---

sensory memory
A memory system that momentarily preserves extremely accurate images of sensory information.

pattern recognition
The identification of a stimulus on the basis of information already contained in long-term memory.

short-term memory (STM)
In the three-box model of memory, a limited-capacity memory system involved in the retention of information for brief periods; it is also used to hold information retrieved from long-term memory for temporary use.

the other direction, from short-term memory to long-term.

People such as H. M. fall at the extreme end on a continuum of forgetfulness, but even those of us with normal memories know from personal experience how frustratingly brief short-term retention can be. We look up a telephone number, are distracted for a moment, and find that the number has vanished from our minds. We meet someone at a meeting and two minutes later find ourselves groping unsuccessfully for the person's name. Is it any wonder that short-term memory has been called a "leaky bucket"?

According to most memory models, if the bucket did not leak it would quickly overflow, because at any given moment, short-term memory can hold only so many items. Years ago, George Miller (1956) estimated its capacity to be "the magical number 7 plus or minus 2." Five-digit zip codes and 7-digit telephone numbers fall conveniently in this range; 16-digit credit card numbers do not. Some researchers have questioned whether Miller's magical number is so magical after all; estimates of STM's capacity have ranged from 2 items to 20. Everyone agrees, however, that the number of items that short-term memory can handle at any one time is small.

If this is so, then how do we remember the beginning of a spoken sentence until the speaker reaches the end? After all, most sentences are longer than just a few words. According to most models of memory, we overcome this problem by grouping small bits of information into larger units,

or **chunks.** The real capacity of STM, it turns out, is not a few bits of information but a few chunks. A chunk may be a word, a phrase, a sentence, or even a visual image, and it depends on previous experience. For most Americans, the acronym *FBI* is one chunk, not three, and the date *1492* is one chunk, not four. In contrast, the number *9214* is four chunks and *IBF* is three—unless your address is 9214 or your initials are IBF. To take a more visual example: If you are unfamiliar with football and look at a field full of players, you probably won't be

chunk
A meaningful unit of information; it may be composed of smaller units.

If you do not play chess, you probably will not be able to recall the positions of these chess pieces after looking away. But experienced chess players can remember the position of every piece after glancing only briefly at the board. They are able to "chunk" the pieces into a few standard configurations, instead of trying to memorize where each piece is located.

able to remember their positions when you look away. But if you are a fan of the game, you may see a single chunk of information—say, a wishbone formation—and be able to retain it.

Even chunking cannot keep short-term memory from eventually filling up. Fortunately, much of the information we take in during the day is needed for only a few moments. If you are multiplying two numbers, you need to remember them only until you have the answer. If you are talking to someone, you need to keep the person's words in mind only until you have understood them. But some incoming information is needed for longer periods and must be transferred to long-term memory. Items that are particularly meaningful, have an emotional impact, or relate to something already in long-term memory may enter long-term storage easily, with only a brief stay in STM. The destiny of other items depends on how soon new information displaces them in short-term memory. Material in short-term memory is easily displaced unless we do something to keep it there, as we will discuss shortly.

Long-term Memory: Final Destination

The third box in the three-box model of memory is **long-term memory (LTM).** The capacity of long-term memory seems to have no practical limits. The vast amount of information stored there enables us to learn, get around in the environment, and build a sense of identity and a personal history.

Organization in Long-term Memory.

Because long-term memory contains so much information, it must be organized in some way, so that we can find the particular items we're looking for. One way to organize words (or the concepts they represent) is by the *semantic categories* to which they belong. *Chair,* for example, belongs to the category *furniture.* In a classic study, people had to memorize 60 words that came from four semantic categories: animals, vegetables, names, and professions. The words were presented in random order, but when people were allowed to recall the items in any order they wished, they tended to recall them in clusters corresponding to the four categories (Bousfield, 1953). This finding has been replicated many times.

Evidence on the storage of information by semantic category also comes from cases of people with brain damage. In one such case, a patient called M. D. appeared to have made a complete

recovery after suffering several strokes, with one odd exception: He had trouble remembering the names of fruits and vegetables. M. D. could easily name a picture of an abacus or a sphinx but he drew a blank when he saw a picture of an apple or a carrot. He could sort pictures of animals, vehicles, and other objects into their appropriate categories but did poorly with pictures of fruits and vegetables. On the other hand, when M. D. was *given* the names of fruits and vegetables, he immediately pointed to the corresponding pictures (Hart, Berndt, & Caramazza, 1985). Apparently, M. D. still had information about fruits and vegetables, but his brain lesion prevented him from using their names to get to the information when he needed it, unless the names were provided by someone else. This evidence suggests that information about a particular concept (such as *apple*) is linked in some way to information about the concept's semantic category (such as *fruit*).

Indeed, many models of long-term memory represent its contents as a vast network of interrelated concepts and propositions (Anderson, 1990; Collins & Loftus, 1975). In these models, a small part of a conceptual network for *animals* might look something like the one in Figure 7.4. The way people use these networks, however, depends on experience and education. For example, studies of rural children in Liberia and Guatemala have shown that the more schooling children have, the more likely they are to use semantic categories in recalling lists

Culture affects the encoding, storage, and retrieval of information in long-term memory. Navajo healers, who use stylized, symbolic sand paintings in their rituals, must be able to commit to memory dozens of intricate visual designs because no exact copies are made and the painting is destroyed after each ceremony.

long-term memory (LTM)
In the three-box model of memory, the memory system involved in the long-term storage of information.

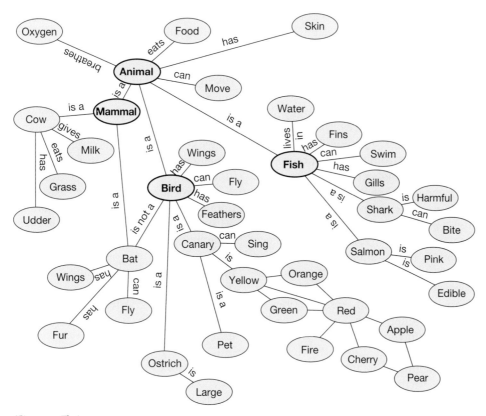

Figure 7.4
Part of a Conceptual Grid in Long-term Memory

Many models of memory represent the contents of long-term semantic memory as an immense network or grid of concepts and the relationships among them. This illustration shows part of a hypothetical grid for animals.

of objects (Cole & Cole, 1993). This makes sense, because in school, children must memorize a lot of information in a short time, and semantic grouping can help. Unschooled children, having less need to memorize lists, do not cluster items and do not remember them as well (Cole & Cole, 1993). But this does not mean that unschooled children have poor memories. When the task is meaningful to them—say, recalling objects that were in a story or a village scene—they remember extremely well (Mistry & Rogoff, 1994).

We organize information in long-term memory not only by semantic groupings but also in terms of the way words sound or look. Have you ever tried to recall some word that was on the "tip of your tongue"? Nearly everyone experiences such *tip-of-the-tongue (TOT) states,* especially when trying to recall the names of acquaintances or famous persons, the names of objects and places, or the titles of movies or books (Burke et al., 1991). TOT states are reported even by users of sign language, who call them tip-of-the-finger states!

One way to study this frustrating experience is to have people record tip-of-the-tongue episodes in daily diaries. Another is to give people the definitions of uncommon words and ask them to supply the words. When a word is on the tip of the tongue, people tend to come up with words that are similar in meaning to the right one before they finally recall it. For example, for "patronage bestowed on a relative, in business or politics" a person might say "favoritism" rather than the correct response, "nepotism." But verbal information in long-term memory also seems to be indexed by sound and form, and it is retrievable on that basis. Incorrect guesses often have the correct number of syllables, the correct stress pattern, the correct first letter, or the correct prefix or suffix (R. Brown & McNeill, 1966). For example, for the target word *sampan* (an Asian boat), a person might say "Siam" or "sarong."

Information in long-term memory may also be organized by its familiarity, relevance, or association with other information. The method used in any given instance probably depends on the nature of the memory; you would no doubt store information about the major cities of Europe differently from information about your first date. To understand the organization of long-term memory, then, we must know what kinds of information can be stored there.

The Contents of Long-term Memory.

Most theories of memory distinguish skills or habits ("knowing how") from abstract or representational knowledge ("knowing that"). **Procedural memories** are memories of knowing how to do something—for example, knowing how to comb your hair, use a pencil, solve a jigsaw puzzle, knit a sweater, or swim. Many researchers consider procedural memories to be implicit, because once skills and habits are well learned, they do not require much conscious processing. **Declarative memories,** on the other hand, are memories of knowing that something is true, as in knowing that Ottawa is the capital of Canada; they are usually assumed to be explicit.

Declarative memories, in turn, come in two varieties: semantic memories and episodic memories (Tulving, 1985). **Semantic memories** are internal representations of the world, independent of any particular context. They include facts, rules, and concepts—items of general knowledge. On the basis of your semantic memory of the concept *cat*, you can describe a cat as a small, furry mammal that typically spends its time eating, sleeping, prowling, and staring into space, even though a cat may not be present when you give this description, and you probably won't know how or when you first learned it. **Episodic memories** are internal representations of personally experienced events. When you remember how your cat once surprised you in the middle of the night by pouncing on your face as you slept, you are retrieving an episodic memory. Figure 7.5 summarizes these kinds of memories.

As we saw in Chapter 4, with sufficient practice, patients such as H. M., who cannot form new declarative memories because of damage to the hippocampus, can acquire new procedural memories; they can learn to solve a puzzle, read mirror-reversed words, or play tennis—even though they do not remember the training sessions in which they learned these skills. Apparently the parts of the brain involved in acquiring procedural memories have remained intact.

From Short-term to Long-term Memory: A Riddle.

The three-box model of memory is often invoked to explain an interesting phenomenon called the **serial-position effect.** If you are shown a list of items and are then asked immediately to recall them, your retention of any particular item will depend on its position in the list (Glanzer & Cunitz, 1966). Recall will be best for

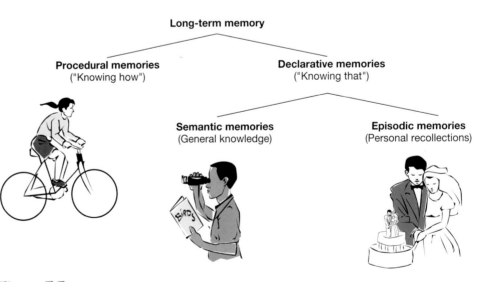

Figure 7.5
Types of Long-term Memories
This diagram summarizes the distinctions among long-term memories. Can you come up with other examples of each memory type?

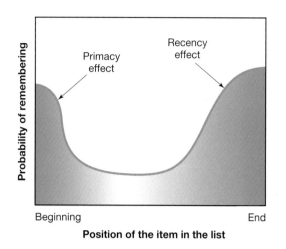

Figure 7.6

The Serial-Position Effect

When people try to recall a list of items immediately after learning it, they tend to remember the first and last items best and middle ones worst.

items at the beginning of the list (the *primacy effect*) and at the end of the list (the *recency effect*). When retention of all the items is plotted, the result is a U-shaped curve, as shown in Figure 7.6. A serial-position effect occurs when you are introduced to

a lot of people at a party and find you can recall the names of the first few people you met and the last, but almost no one in between.

According to the three-box model, the first few items on a list are remembered well because short-term memory was relatively "empty" when they entered, so these items did not have to compete with others to make it into long-term memory. They were thoroughly processed, so they remain memorable. The last few items are remembered for a different reason: At the time of recall, they are still sitting in short-term memory. The items in the middle of a list, however, are not so well retained because by the time they get into short-term memory, it is already crowded. As a result, many of these items drop out of short-term memory before they can be stored in long-term memory.

This explanation makes sense except for one thing: Under some conditions, the last items on a list are well remembered even when the test is delayed past the time when short-term memory has presumably been "emptied" and filled with other information (Greene, 1986). In other words, the recency effect occurs even when, according to the three-box model, it should not. At present, then, the serial position curve remains something of a puzzle.

QUICK QUIZ

Find out whether the findings just discussed have transferred from your short-term memory to your long-term memory.

1. _____ memory holds images for a fraction of a second.

2. For most people, the abbreviation *U.S.A.* consists of _____ informational chunk(s).

3. Suppose you must memorize a long list of words that includes the following: *desk, pig, gold, dog, chair, silver, table, rooster, bed, copper,* and *horse.* If you can recall the words in any order you wish, how are you likely to group them in recall? Why?

4. When you roller-blade, are you relying on procedural, semantic, or episodic memory? How about when you recall the months of the year? Or when you remember falling while roller-blading on an icy January day?

5. If a child is trying to memorize the alphabet, which sequence should present the greatest difficulty: *abcdefg, klmnopq,* or *tuvwxyz?* Why?

Answers:
1. sensory 2. one 3. *Desk, chair, table,* and *bed* would probably form one cluster; *pig, dog, rooster,* and *horse* a second; and *gold, silver,* and *copper* a third. Concepts tend to be organized in long-term memory in terms of semantic categories, such as furniture, animals, and metals. 4. procedural; semantic; episodic 5. *klmnopq,* because of the serial-position effect

What's Ahead

- What's wrong with trying to memorize in a rote fashion when you're studying—and what's a better strategy?

- Memory tricks are fun, but are they always useful?

7.5 How We Remember

Once we understand how memory works, we can use that understanding to encode and store information so that it "sticks" and will be there when we need it. What are the best strategies to use?

Effective Encoding

Our memories, as we have seen, are not exact replicas of experience. Sensory information is summarized and encoded—for example, as words or images—almost as soon as it is detected. When you hear a lecture, for example, you may hang on every word (we hope you do), but you do not memorize those words verbatim. You extract the main points and encode them.

To remember information well, you have to encode it accurately in the first place. With some kinds of information, accurate encoding takes place automatically, without effort. Think about where you usually sit in your psychology class. When were you last there? You can probably provide this

Encoding classroom material for later recall usually takes a deliberate effort. Which of these students do you think will remember best?

information easily, even though you never made a deliberate effort to encode it. In general, people automatically encode their location in space and time and the frequency with which they do certain things (Hasher & Zacks, 1984). But other kinds of information require *effortful encoding.* To retain such information, you might have to select the main points, label concepts, associate the information with personal experiences or with material you already know, or rehearse it until it is familiar.

Unfortunately, people sometimes count on automatic encoding when effortful encoding is needed. For example, some students wrongly assume that they can encode the material in a textbook as effortlessly as they encode where they sit in the classroom. Or they assume that the ability to remember and perform well on tests is innate and that effort will not make any difference. As a result, they wind up in trouble at test time. Experienced students know that most of the information in a college course requires effortful encoding and sometimes hard work.

Rehearsal

An important technique for keeping information in short-term memory and increasing the chances of long-term retention is *rehearsal,* the review or practice of material while you are learning it. When people are prevented from rehearsing, the contents of their short-term memories quickly fade.

In an early study of this phenomenon, people had to memorize meaningless groups of letters. Immediately afterward, they had to start counting backward by threes from an arbitrary number; this counting prevented them from rehearsing the letter groups. Within only 18 seconds, the subjects forgot most of the items. But when they did not have to count backward, their performance was much better, probably because they were rehearsing the items to themselves (Peterson & Peterson, 1959). You are taking advantage of rehearsal when you look up a telephone number and then repeat it over and over in order to keep it in short-term memory until you no longer need it.

A poignant demonstration of the power of rehearsal once occurred during a session with H. M. (Ogden & Corkin, 1991). The experimenter gave H. M. five digits to repeat and remember, but then she was unexpectedly called away. When she returned after more than an hour, H. M. was able to repeat the five digits correctly. He had been rehearsing them the entire time.

Short-term memory holds many kinds of information, including visual information and abstract meanings. But most people—or at least most hearing people—seem to favor speech for encoding and rehearsing the contents of short-term memory. The speech may be spoken aloud or to oneself. When people make errors on short-term memory tests that use letters or words, they often confuse items that sound the same or similar, such as *d* and *t,* or *bear* and *bare.* These errors suggest that they have been rehearsing verbally.

Some strategies for rehearsing are more effective than others. **Maintenance rehearsal** involves merely the rote repetition of the material. This kind of rehearsal is fine for keeping information in STM, but it will not always lead to long-term retention. A better strategy if you want to remember for the long haul is **elaborative rehearsal,** also called *elaboration of encoding* (Cermak & Craik, 1979; Craik & Tulving, 1975). Elaboration involves associating new items of information with material that has already been stored or with other new facts. It can also involve analyzing the physical, sensory, or semantic features of an item.

Suppose, for example, that you are studying the hypothalamus in Chapter 4. Simply memorizing the definition of the hypothalamus in a rote manner is unlikely to help much. Instead, when going over the concept, you could encode the information in the lower part of Figure 7.7. The more you elaborate the concept of the hypothalamus, the better you will remember it.

A related strategy for prolonging retention is **deep processing,** or the processing of meaning. If you process only the physical or sensory features of a stimulus, such as how the word *hypothalamus* is spelled and how it sounds, your processing will be shallow even if it is elaborated. If you recognize patterns and assign labels to objects or events ("The *hypo*thalamus is *below* the thalamus"), your processing will be somewhat deeper. If you fully analyze the meaning of what you are trying to remember (for example, by encoding the functions and importance of the hypothalamus), your processing will be deeper yet.

Shallow processing is sometimes useful; when you memorize a poem, for instance, you will want to pay attention to (and elaborately encode) the sounds of the words and the patterns of rhythm in the poem, and not just the poem's meaning. Usually, however, deep processing is more effective. Unfortunately, students often try to memorize information that has little or no meaning for them, which explains why the information doesn't stick.

maintenance rehearsal
Rote repetition of material in order to maintain its availability in memory.

elaborative rehearsal
Association of new information with already stored knowledge and analysis of the new information to make it memorable.

deep processing
In the encoding of information, the processing of meaning rather than simply the physical or sensory features of a stimulus.

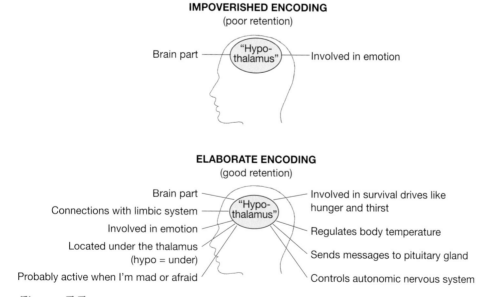

Figure 7.7
Elaboration of Encoding

In elaborated encoding, you encode the features of an item and its associations with other items in memory. When you studied the hypothalamus in Chapter 4, was your encoding elaborated or impoverished?

Live! psych

7.3

Mnemonics

In addition to using elaborative rehearsal and deep processing, people who want to give their powers of memory a boost sometimes use **mnemonics** [neh-MON-iks], formal strategies and tricks for encoding, storing, and retaining information. (Mnemosyne, pronounced neh-MOZ-eh-nee, was the ancient Greek goddess of memory. Can you remember her?) Some mnemonics take the form of easily memorized rhymes (e.g., "Thirty days hath September / April, June, and November . . . "). Others use formulas (e.g., "**E**very **g**ood **b**oy **d**oes **f**ine" for remembering which notes are on the lines of the treble clef in musical notation). Still others use visual images or word associations.

The best mnemonics force you to encode material actively and thoroughly. They may also reduce the amount of information by chunking it, which is why, in ads, many companies now use words for their phone numbers instead of unmemorable numbers (for example, "Dial GET RICH"). Many mnemonics make the material meaningful and thus easier to store and retrieve, say by having you weave unrelated facts and words into a coherent story (Bower & Clark, 1969). If you needed to remember the parts of the digestive system for a physiology course, you could construct a narrative about what happens to a piece of food from the moment it enters a person's mouth, then repeat the narrative aloud to yourself or to a study partner.

Some stage performers with amazing recall rely on more complicated mnemonics. We are

"YOU SIMPLY ASSOCIATE EACH NUMBER WITH A WORD, SUCH AS 'TABLE' AND 3,476,029."

not going to spend time on them here, because for ordinary memory tasks, such tricks are often no more effective than rote rehearsal, and sometimes they are actually worse (Wang, Thomas, & Ouellette, 1992). Most memory researchers do not use such mnemonics themselves. After all, why bother to memorize a grocery list using a fancy mnemonic when you can write down what you need to buy? The fastest route to a good memory is to follow the principles suggested by the findings in this section and by research reviewed in the "Taking Psychology with You" feature at the end of this chapter.

mnemonics (neh-MON-iks)
Strategies and tricks for improving memory, such as the use of a verse or a formula.

VERY QUICK QUIZ

Perhaps Mnemosyne will help you answer this question.

Camille is furious with her history professor. "I read the chapter three times, but I still failed the exam," she fumes. "The test must have been unfair." What's wrong with Camille's reasoning, and what are some other possible explanations for her poor performance, based on principles of critical thinking and what you have learned so far about memory?

Answer:
Camille is reasoning emotionally and is not examining the assumptions underlying her explanations. Perhaps she relied on automatic rather than effortful encoding, used maintenance instead of elaborative rehearsal, and used shallow instead of deep processing when she studied. She may also have tried to encode everything, instead of being selective.

What's Ahead

- How might new information "erase" old memories?

- What theory explains why you keep dialing an old area code instead of the one that has replaced it?

- Why is it easier to recall experiences from elementary school if you see pictures of your classmates?

- Why are many researchers skeptical about claims of "repressed" and "recovered" memories?

7.6 Why We Forget

Have you ever, in the heat of some deliriously happy moment, said to yourself, "I'll never forget this, never, *never*, NEVER"? Do you find that you can more clearly remember saying those words than the deliriously happy moment itself? Sometimes you encode an event, you rehearse it, you analyze its meaning, you tuck it away in long-term storage—and still, to your dismay, you forget it. Is it any wonder that most of us have wished, at one time or another, for a "photographic memory"?

Actually, having a perfect memory is not the blessing that you might suppose. The Russian psychologist Alexander Luria (1968) once told of a journalist, S., who could reproduce giant grids of numbers both forward and backward, even after the passage of many years. S. also remembered the exact circumstances under which he had originally learned the material. To accomplish his astonishing feats, he used mnemonics, especially the formation of visual images. But you should not envy him, for he had a serious problem: He could not forget even when he wanted to. Along with the diamonds of experience, he kept dredging up the pebbles. Images he had formed in order to remember kept creeping into consciousness, distracting him and interfering with his ability to concentrate. At times he even had trouble holding a conversation because the other person's words would set off a jumble of associations. In fact, Luria called him "rather dull-witted." Eventually, S. took to supporting himself by traveling from place to place, demonstrating his mnemonic abilities for audiences.

Thinking Critically About Having a Perfect Memory

Like remembering, then, a certain degree of forgetting contributes to our survival and our sanity. Think back; would you really want to recall every silly blunder, every angry argument, every embarrassing episode, every painful moment in your life? Could it be that self-confidence and optimism depend on locking some follies and grievances in a back drawer of memory? Nonetheless, most of us forget more than we would like to, and we would like to know why.

Over a century ago, in an effort to measure pure memory loss independent of personal experience, Hermann Ebbinghaus (1885/1913) memorized long lists of nonsense syllables, such as *bok, waf,* or *ged,* and then tested his retention over a period of several weeks. Most of his forgetting occurred soon after the initial learning and then leveled off (see Figure 7.8a on the next page). Ebbinghaus's method of studying memory was adopted by generations of psychologists, even though it did not tell them much about the kinds of memories that people care about most.

A century later, Marigold Linton decided to find out how people forget real events rather than nonsense syllables. Like Ebbinghaus, she used herself as a subject, but she charted the curve of forgetting over years rather than days. Every day for 12 years she recorded on a 4- × 6-inch card two or more things that had happened to her that day. Eventually, she accumulated a catalogue of thousands of discrete events, both trivial ("I have dinner at the Canton Kitchen: delicious lobster dish") and significant ("I land at Orly Airport in Paris"). Once a month, she took a random sampling of all the cards accumulated to that point, noted whether she could remember the events on them, and tried to date the events. Linton (1978) later told how she had expected the kind of rapid forgetting reported by Ebbinghaus. Instead, as you can see in Figure 7.8b, she found that long-term forgetting was slower and proceeded at a much more constant pace, as details gradually dropped out of her memories.

Of course, some memories, especially those that mark important transitions, are more memorable than others. You are not likely to forget your high school graduation or your first kiss. But why did Marigold Linton, like the rest of us, forget so many details of everyday events? Psychologists have proposed five mechanisms to account for forgetting: decay, replacement of old memories by new ones, interference, cue-dependent forgetting, and psychogenic amnesia.

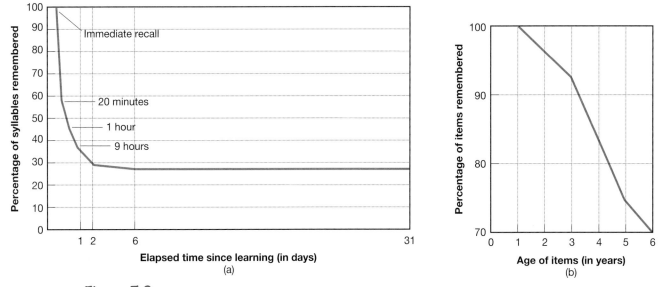

Figure 7.8
Two Kinds of Forgetting Curves
When Hermann Ebbinghaus tested his own memory for nonsense syllables, forgetting was rapid at first and then tapered off (a). In contrast, when Marigold Linton tested her own memory for personal events over a period of several years, her retention was excellent at first, but then it fell off at a gradual but steady rate (b).

Decay

One commonsense view, the **decay theory,** holds that memory traces fade with time if they are not "accessed" now and then. We have already seen that decay occurs in sensory memory and that it occurs in short-term memory as well, unless we keep rehearsing the material. However, the mere passage of time does not account so well for forgetting in long-term memory. People commonly forget things that happened only yesterday while remembering events from many years ago. Indeed, some memories, both procedural and declarative, can last a lifetime. If you learned to swim as a child, you will still know how to swim at age 30, even if you have not been in a pool or lake for 22 years. We are also happy to report that some school lessons have great staying power. In one study, people did well on a Spanish test some 50 years after taking Spanish in high school, even though most had hardly used Spanish at all in the intervening years (Bahrick, 1984). Decay alone, although it may play some role, cannot entirely explain lapses in long-term memory.

decay theory
The theory that information in memory eventually disappears if it is not accessed; it applies more to short-term than to long-term memory.

Motor skills, which are stored as procedural memories, can last a lifetime.

When people who saw a car with a yield sign (left) were later asked if they had seen "the stop sign" (a misleading question), many said they had. Similarly, when those shown a stop sign were asked if they had seen "the yield sign," many said yes. These false memories persisted even after the researchers revealed their use of misleading questions, suggesting that the misleading information had erased the subjects' original mental representations of the signs (Loftus, 1980).

Replacement

Another theory holds that new information entering memory can wipe out old information, just as rerecording on an audiotape or videotape will obliterate the original material. In one study supporting this view, researchers showed people slides of a traffic accident and used leading questions to get them to think that they had seen a stop sign when they had really seen a yield sign, or vice versa. People in a control group who were not misled in this way were able to identify the sign they had actually seen. Later, all the participants were told the purpose of the study and were asked to guess whether they had been misled. Almost all of those who had been misled continued to insist that they had *really, truly* seen the sign whose existence had been planted in their minds (Loftus, Miller, & Burns, 1978). The researchers interpreted these findings to mean that the subjects had not just been trying to please them, and that people's original perceptions had in fact been "erased" by the misleading information.

Interference

A third theory holds that forgetting occurs because similar items of information interfere with one another in either storage or retrieval; the information may get into memory, but it becomes confused with other information. Such interference, which occurs in both short- and long-term memory, is especially common when you have to recall isolated facts—names, addresses, personal identification numbers, area codes, and the like.

Suppose you are at a party and you meet someone named Julie. A little later you meet someone named Judy. You go on to talk to other people, and after an hour, you again bump into Julie, but by mistake you call her Judy. The second name has interfered with the first. This type of interference, in which new information interferes with the ability to remember old information, is called **retroactive interference:**

7.4

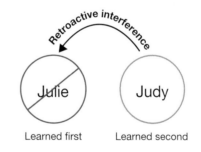

Retroactive interference is illustrated by the story of an absent-minded professor of ichthyology (the study of fish) who complained that whenever he learned the name of a new student, he forgot the name of a fish.

Because new information is constantly entering memory, we are all vulnerable to the effects of retroactive interference—or at least most of us are. H. M. is an exception; his memories of childhood and adolescence are unusually detailed, clear, and unchanging. H. M. can remember actors who were famous when he was a child, the films they were in, and who their costars were. He also knows the names of friends from the second grade.

retroactive interference Forgetting that occurs when recently learned material interferes with the ability to remember similar material stored previously.

Presumably, these early declarative memories were not subject to interference from memories acquired since the operation because H. M. has not acquired any new memories.

Interference also works in the opposite direction. Old information (such as the Spanish you learned in high school) may interfere with the ability to remember new information (such as the French you are trying to learn now). This type of interference is called **proactive interference:**

proactive interference
Forgetting that occurs when previously stored material interferes with the ability to remember similar, more recently learned material.

cue-dependent forgetting
The inability to retrieve information stored in memory because of insufficient cues for recall.

state-dependent memory
The tendency to remember something when the rememberer is in the same physical or mental state as during the original learning or experience.

```
          Proactive interference
       ┌──────────────────────────┐
       │                          ↓
    ( Julie )                  ( Judy )⊘

   Learned first           Learned second
```

Over a period of weeks, months, and years, proactive interference may cause more forgetting than retroactive interference does, because we have stored up so much information that can potentially interfere with anything new.

Cue-dependent Forgetting

Often, when we need to remember, we rely on *retrieval cues,* items of information that can help us find the specific information we're looking for. For example, if you are trying to remember the last name of an actor, it might help to know the person's first name or the name of a recent movie the actor starred in.

When we lack retrieval cues, we may feel as if we are lost among the stacks in the mind's library. In long-term memory, this type of memory failure, called **cue-dependent forgetting,** may be the most common type of all. Willem Wagenaar (1986), who, like Marigold Linton, recorded critical details about events in his life, found that within a year, he had forgotten 20 percent of those details, and after five years, he had forgotten 60 percent. However, when he gathered cues from witnesses about ten events that he thought he had forgotten, he was able to recall something about all ten, which suggests that some of his forgetting was cue dependent.

Cues that were present when you learned a new fact or had an experience are apt to be especially useful later as retrieval aids. That may explain why remembering is often easier when you are in the same physical environment as you were when an event occurred: Cues in the present context match those from the past. Some people have suggested that the overlap between present and past cues may also lead to a *false* sense of having been in exactly the same situation before; this is the eerie phenomenon of *déjà vu* (which means "already seen" in French). Ordinarily, however, contextual cues help us remember the past more accurately.

Your mental or physical state may also act as a retrieval cue, evoking a **state-dependent memory.** For example, if you are intoxicated when something happens, you may remember it better when you once again have had a few drinks than when you are sober. (This is not an endorsement of drunkenness! Your memory will be best if you are sober during both encoding and recall.) Likewise, if your emotional arousal is especially high or low at the time of an event, you may remember that event best when you are once again in the same emotional state. When victims of violent crimes have trouble recalling details of the experience, it may be in part because they are far less emotionally aroused than they were at the time of the crime (Clark, Milberg, & Erber, 1987).

You may also be better able to retrieve a memory when your current mood matches the *kind of material* you are trying to remember. You are likely to remember happy events better when

Charlie Chaplin's film City Lights *provides a classic illustration of state-dependent memory. After Charlie saves the life of a drunken millionaire, the two spend the rest of the evening in boisterous merrymaking. But the next day, after sobering up, the millionaire fails to recognize Charlie and gives him the cold shoulder. Then, once again, the millionaire gets drunk—and once again he greets Charlie as a pal.*

you are feeling happy than when you are sad (Mayer, McCormick & Strong, 1995). Similarly, you are likely to remember unhappy events better and remember more of them when you are feeling unhappy, which in turn creates a vicious cycle. The more unhappy memories you recall, the more depressed you feel, and the more depressed you feel, the more unhappy memories you recall . . . so you stay stuck in your depression and make it even worse (Lyubomirsky, Caldwell, & Nolen-Hoeksema, 1998). You can break out of this trap by deliberately focusing on memories of happy events instead of unpleasant ones.

Psychogenic Amnesia

A final theory of forgetting focuses on **psychogenic amnesia,** the loss of memory for painful events. *Amnesia,* the inability to remember important personal information, can result from organic conditions such as brain disease or head injury. In psychogenic amnesia, however, the causes are psychological: embarrassment, guilt, a desire to protect self-esteem, or, more typically, extreme emotional shock. For example, a woman who has been raped or a man who has been in a horrible car accident may have amnesia for the experience, although generally the memory returns within a fairly short period of time.

The mechanisms that might account for psychogenic amnesia are still murky. Perhaps people with this kind of memory loss are intentionally keeping themselves from retrieving their painful memories, say, by distracting themselves when a memory is awakened. Perhaps, understandably, they are not rehearsing these memories, so the memories become more likely to fade. Perhaps they are avoiding the retrieval cues that would evoke the memories. Psychogenic amnesia may occur for any or all of these reasons, or for others that remain to be discovered.

Thinking Critically About "Repression"

One especially controversial explanation of psychogenic amnesia, originally proposed by Sigmund Freud, is *repression*—the selective, involuntary pushing of threatening or upsetting information into the unconscious mind. The validity of this explanation has come under renewed scrutiny because of debates over recovered memories of sexual abuse. Beginning in the 1990s, many women and some men came to believe, during psychotherapy, that they were recalling long-buried memories of sexual victimization. A

wave of criminal charges took place against their "remembered" perpetrators, usually fathers or other relatives. In one typical case, a woman named Laura B. sued her father, claiming that he had molested her from the ages of 5 to 23 and had even raped her just days before her wedding. Laura B. said she had repressed these memories and had no recollection of them until they emerged during therapy.

Some people believe that such memories are accurate; they accept the psychodynamic view that painful memories can be repressed and remain inaccessible for years (Freyd, 1996; Pope, 1996). But others argue that although real abuse occurs, many false memories of victimization have been encouraged by naïve therapists who are unaware of the power of suggestion and the dangers of confabulation (Lindsay & Read, 1994; Loftus & Ketcham, 1994). These critics point out that repeated experiences of trauma like those claimed by Laura B. are more likely to be remembered than forgotten, even when the victims wish they could forget (Schacter, 1996). Only rarely have "recovered" memories been corroborated by objective evidence, so it is difficult and often impossible to determine their accuracy. Most research psychologists are skeptical of the whole concept of repression, which they consider vague and ill-defined (Holmes, 1990; Schacter, 1996).

Because of these concerns, courts, too, have recently become skeptical of accusations based solely on "repressed" and "recovered" memories. In an important ruling in the case of Laura B., the judge wrote that her recovered memories would not be admissible evidence because "the phenomenon of memory repression, and the process of therapy used in these cases to recover the memories, have not gained general acceptance in the field of psychology; and are not scientifically reliable" (*State of New Hampshire* v. *Joel Hungerford,* May 23, 1995).

The widespread misuse of the concept of repression has meant that psychotherapists and the public alike need to think critically about defining terms and gathering evidence. Of course, all psychologists realize that people can and do have psychogenic amnesia for troubling, embarrassing, and painful experiences, and that with the right cues, these memories may return. One clinician reported a case of a client who became upset when he saw several men reading X-rated magazines at a newsstand. Eventually he remembered that when he was 11, he had been sexually molested by his cousin

psychogenic amnesia
The partial or complete loss of memory (due to nonorganic causes) for threatening information or traumatic experiences.

and several other older boys—who had been reading the same kind of magazine (Nash, 1994). Obviously, therefore, not all recovered memories are false. But did this man unconsciously "repress" his bad memory or simply try to forget it?

How, then, should we respond to an individual's claim to have recovered once-repressed memories of abuse? As we will see in the next section, we should be skeptical if the person says that, thanks to therapy, he or she now has memories from the first year or two of life. In addition, we should be skeptical if, over time, the person's memories become more and more implausible—for instance, the person says that sexual abuse

continued day and night for 15 years without ever being remembered and without anyone else in the household noticing anything amiss. And we should hear alarm bells go off if a therapist used suggestive techniques, such as hypnosis and leading questions, to "help" a patient recall the alleged abuse (Loftus, 1996). In contrast, a person's recollections are more likely to be trustworthy if there is corroborating evidence from medical records or from the recollections of other family members, if the person reacted emotionally at the time, and if the person spontaneously recalled the event without pressure from others or the use of suggestive techniques in therapy.

QUICK QUIZ

If you have not repressed what you just learned, try these questions.

1. After reading *Even Cowgirls Get the Blues* many years ago, Wilma became a fan of novelist Tom Robbins. Later, she developed a crush on actor Tim Robbins, but every time she tries to recall his name she calls him "Tom." Why?

2. When a man at his twentieth high-school reunion sees his old friends, he recalls incidents he thought were long forgotten. Why?

Answers:
1. proactive interference 2. The sight of his friends provides retrieval cues for the incidents.

What's Ahead

- Why are the first few years of life a mental blank?

- Why have human beings been called the "story telling animal"?

7.7 Autobiographical Memories

For most of us, our autobiographical memories are by far the most fascinating. We use them as entertainment ("Did I ever tell you about the time . . . ?"); we manipulate them—some people even publish them—in order to create an image of ourselves; we analyze them to learn more about who we are.

Childhood Amnesia: The Missing Years

A curious aspect of autobiographical memory is that most adults cannot recall any events from earlier than their third or fourth year. A few people apparently can recall momentous experiences that occurred when they were as young as 2 years old, such as the birth of a sibling, but not earlier (Newcombe et al., 2000; Usher & Neisser, 1993). As adults, we cannot remember being fed in infancy by our parents, taking our first steps, or uttering our first halting sentences. We are victims of **childhood amnesia** (sometimes called *infantile amnesia*).

There is something disturbing about childhood amnesia—so disturbing that some people adamantly deny it, claiming to remember events from the second or even the first year of life. But

childhood (infantile) amnesia
The inability to remember events and experiences that occurred during the first two or three years of life.

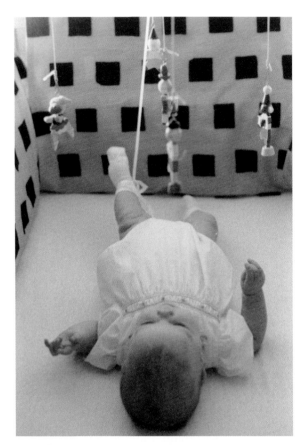

This infant, who is learning to kick in order to make a mobile move, may remember the trick a week later. However, when she is older, she will not remember the experience itself. Like the rest of us, she will fall victim to childhood amnesia.

like other false memories, these are merely reconstructions based on photographs, family stories, and imagination. The "remembered" event may not even have taken place. Swiss psychologist Jean Piaget (1952b) once reported a memory of nearly being kidnapped at the age of 2. Piaget remembered sitting in his pram, watching his nurse as she bravely defended him from the kidnapper. He remembered the scratches she received on her face. He remembered a police officer with a short cloak and white baton who finally chased the kidnapper away. But when Piaget was 15, his nurse wrote to his parents confessing that she had made up the entire story. Piaget noted, "I therefore must have heard, as a child, the account of this story . . . and projected it into the past in the form of a visual memory, which was a memory of a memory, but false."

Of course, we all retain procedural memories from the toddler stage, when we first learned to use a fork, drink from a cup, and pull a wagon. We also retain semantic memories acquired early in life: the rules of counting, the names of people and things, knowledge about objects in the world, words and meanings. Further, toddlers who are only 1 to 2 years old can often remember past experiences, and some 4-year-olds can remember experiences that occurred before age 2½ (Bauer & Dow, 1994; McDonough & Mandler, 1994). What young children do not do well is encode and retain their early episodic memories—memories of particular events—and carry them into later childhood or adulthood.

Sigmund Freud thought that childhood amnesia was another case of repression, but most memory researchers today think that repression has nothing to do with it. Biological psychologists believe that childhood amnesia occurs because brain areas involved in the formation or storage of events, and other areas involved in working memory and decision making (such as the prefrontal cortex), are not well developed until a few years after birth (McKee & Squire, 1993; Newcombe et al., 2000). Cognitive psychologists have proposed other explanations, which include the following:

Thinking Critically About "Memories" from Infancy

1 *Lack of a sense of self.* In one view, we cannot have an autobiographical memory of our*selves* until we have a self to remember. Indeed, autobiographical memories do not begin until the emergence of a self-concept, an event that occurs at somewhat different ages for different children, but not before the age of 2 (Howe, Courage, & Peterson, 1994).

2 *Impoverished encoding.* Preschoolers probably encode experiences far less elaborately than adults. Young children have not yet mastered the social conventions for reporting events; they do not know what is important and interesting to others. Instead, they tend to rely on adults' questions to provide retrieval cues ("Where did we go for breakfast?" "Who did you go trick-or-treating with?"), and this dependency on adults may prevent them from building up a stable core of remembered material that will be available when they are older (Fivush & Hamond, 1991).

3 *A focus on the routine.* Preschoolers tend to focus on the routine, familiar aspects of an experience, such as eating lunch or playing with toys, rather than the distinctive aspects that will provide retrieval cues and make an event memorable in the long run (Fivush & Hamond, 1991).

4 *Different ways of thinking about the world.* The cognitive schemas used by preschoolers are very different from those used by older children and adults. Only after acquiring language and starting school do children learn to think like adults do. Their new, adultlike schemas do not contain the information and cues necessary for recalling earlier experiences, so memories of those experiences are lost (Howe & Courage, 1993).

Whatever the explanation for childhood amnesia, our first memories, even when they are not accurate, may provide some useful insights into our personalities, current concerns, ambitions, and attitudes toward life (Kihlstrom & Harackiewicz, 1982). The psychologist Lloyd Morgan once wrote that an autobiography "is a story of oneself in the past, read in the light of one's present self." That is just what our private memories are.

Memory and Narrative: The Stories of Our Lives

The communications researcher George Gerbner once observed that our species is unique because we tell stories . . . and live by the stories we tell. This view of human beings as the "storytelling animal" has had a huge impact in cognitive psychology. The *narratives* we compose to simplify and make sense of our lives have a profound influence on our plans, memories, love affairs, hatreds, ambitions, and dreams.

Thus we say, "I am this way because, as a small child, this happened to me, and then my parents. . . ." We say, "Let me tell you the story of how we fell in love." We say, "When you hear what happened, you'll understand why I felt

entitled to take such cold-hearted revenge." These stories are not necessarily fictions, as in the child's meaning of "tell me a story." Rather, they are attempts to provide a unifying theme that organizes and gives meaning to the events of our lives. But because these narratives rely heavily on memory, and because memories are reconstructed and are constantly shifting in response to present needs, beliefs, and experiences, our stories are also, to some degree, works of interpretation and imagination. Adult memories thus reveal as much about the present as they do about the past (Ross, 1989).

Once we have formulated a story's central theme ("My parents opposed my plans," "My lover was domineering"), that theme may then serve as a cognitive schema that guides what we remember and what we forget (Mather, Shafir, & Johnson, 2000). The story's theme may also influence our judgments of events and people in the present. If you have a fight with your lover, for example, the central theme in your story about the fight might be negative ("He was a jerk") or neutral ("It was a mutual misunderstanding"). This theme may bias you to blame or forgive your partner long after you have forgotten what the conflict was all about or who said what (McGregor & Holmes, 1999). You can see that the "spin" you give a story is critical—so be careful about the stories you tell!

As we have seen throughout this chapter, many details about events, even those landmarks we are sure we remember clearly, are probably distorted, forgotten, or added after the fact. By now, you should not be surprised that memory can be as fickle as it can be accurate. As cognitive psychologists have shown repeatedly, we are not merely actors in our personal life dramas; we also write the scripts.

PSYCHOLOGY IN THE NEWS, REVISITED

At the start of this chapter, we promised to tell you what happened in the case of Ronald Junior Cotton, convicted of the 1984 rape of Jennifer Thompson on the strength of her eyewitness testimony.

In 1995, Thompson agreed to provide a blood sample so that DNA tests could be run on evidence that had been collected during the investigation. The tests revealed that Cotton was innocent. In fact it was Bobby Poole, the man who had bragged about the crime during Cotton's trial, who had raped her. Confronted with the evidence, Poole confessed, and Ronald Cotton, who had spent 11 years in prison, was released. In a *New York Times* editorial (June 18, 2000), Jennifer Thompson wrote, "The man I was so sure I had never seen in my life was the man who was inches from my throat, who raped me, who hurt me, who took my spirit away, who robbed me of my soul. And the man I had identified so emphatically on so many occasions was absolutely innocent."

How would you feel if your eyewitness testimony resulted in the conviction of an innocent person? Would you be able to admit your mistake, or would you, as some have, cling more resolutely than ever to the accuracy of your memory? Thompson decided to meet Cotton and apologize to him personally. Amazingly, they were both able to put this tragedy behind them, overcome the racial barrier that divided them (he is black, she is white), and become friends. Nevertheless, she wrote, she still lives "with the constant anguish that my profound mistake cost him so dearly. I cannot begin to imagine what would have happened had my mistaken identification occurred in a capital case." Thompson learned from personal experience what you have learned from this chapter: that eyewitnesses can and do make mistakes, that racial differences can increase these mistakes, that even memories for shocking or traumatic experiences are vulnerable to distortion and influence by others, and that our confidence in our memories is not a reliable guide to their accuracy.

The Cotton case is far from unique. A 1996 Justice Department report estimated that as many as 200,000 people, 10 percent of America's prison

Since Ronald Cotton was exonerated of the rape of Jennifer Thompson, the two have become friends. Thompson says she lives with constant anguish because of her mistaken identification.

population, may be innocent of the crimes for which they were convicted. When psychological scientists examined 40 cases where wrongful conviction had been established beyond doubt, they found that 90 percent of these cases had involved a false identification by one or more eyewitnesses (Wells et al., 1998).

Inspired by the Innocence Project at the Cordozo School of Law in New York City, grassroots organizations of lawyers and students have been successfully challenging questionable convictions and have been obtaining the release of innocent people. In 2000, the Republican governor of Illinois, George Ryan, imposed a moratorium on capital punishment in his state after 13 men were freed from death row after DNA evidence unequivocally exonerated them. One of the men, who had been on death row for 16 years, was just hours from execution when a group of Northwestern University journalism students produced evidence that another man had committed the crime.

Obviously, not all eyewitness testimony is erroneous, and such testimony certainly needs to be heard and taken into account. But the potential for errors in identification makes it extremely important to gather evidence carefully, ensure adequate legal representation for defendants, conduct police interviews using proper procedures, and obtain a DNA analysis whenever possible.

7.2

The most important lesson to be learned from the research in this chapter, the lesson Jennifer Thompson learned to her despair and to her credit, is that human memory has both tremendous abilities and tremendous weaknesses. Because in a sense we are our memories, this is a difficult truth to accept. If we can do so, we will be able to respect the great power of memory and at the same time retain humility about our capacity for error, confabulation, and self-deception.

TAKING PSYCHOLOGY WITH YOU

How to . . . Uh . . . Remember

Someday in the near future, drugs may be available to help people remember better. For the time being, however, those of us who hope to improve our memories must rely on mental strategies. Some simple mnemonics can be useful, but complicated ones are often more bother than they're worth. A better approach is to follow some general guidelines based on the principles in this chapter:

● *Pay attention!* It seems obvious, but often we fail to remember because we never encoded the information in the first place. For example, which of these is the real Lincoln penny?

Most Americans have trouble recognizing the real penny because they have never attended to the details of a penny's design (Nickerson & Adams, 1979). We are not advising you to do so, unless you happen to be a coin collector or a counterfeiting expert. Just keep in mind that when you do have something to remember, such as the material in this book,

you will do better if you encode it well. (The real penny, by the way, is the left one in the bottom row.)

● *Encode information in more than one way.* The more elaborate the encoding of information, the more memorable it will be. Use your imagination! For instance, in addition to remembering a telephone number by the sound of the individual digits, you might note the spatial pattern they make as you punch them in on the telephone.

● *Add meaning.* The more meaningful the material, the more likely it is to link up with information already in long-term memory. Meaningfulness also reduces the number of chunks of information you have to learn. Common ways of adding meaning include making up a story about the material (fitting the material into a cognitive schema) and forming visual images. (Some people find that the odder the image, the better.) If your license plate happens to be 236MPL, you might think of 236 maples. If you are trying to remember the concept of procedural memory from this chapter, you might make the concept meaningful by thinking of an example from your own life, such as your ability to ride a mountain bike, and then imagine a "P" superimposed on an image of yourself on your bike.

● *Take your time.* Leisurely learning, spread out over several sessions, usually produces better results than harried cramming (although *reviewing* material just before a test can be helpful). In terms of hours spent, "distributed" (spaced) learning sessions are more efficient than "massed" ones; in other words, three separate one-hour study sessions may result in more retention than one session of three hours.

● *Take time out.* If possible, minimize interference by using study breaks for rest or recreation. Sleep is the ultimate way to reduce interference. In a classic study, students who slept for eight hours after learning lists of nonsense syllables retained them better than students who went about their usual business (Jenkins & Dallenbach, 1924). Sleep is not always possible, of course, but periodic mental relaxation usually is.

● *Overlearn.* You can't remember something you never learned well in the first place. Overlearning—studying information even after you think you know it—is one of the best ways to ensure that you'll remember it.

● *Monitor your learning.* Test yourself frequently, rehearse thoroughly, and review periodically to see how you are doing. Don't just evaluate your learning immediately after reading the material, though; because the information is still in short-term memory, you are likely to feel a false sense of confidence about your ability to recall it later. If you delay making a judgment for at least a few minutes, your evaluation will probably be more accurate (Nelson & Dunlosky, 1991).

Whatever strategies you use, you will find that active learning produces more comprehension and better retention than does passive reading or listening. The mind does not gobble up information automatically; you must make the material digestible. Even then, you should not expect to remember everything you read or hear. Nor should you want to. Piling up facts without distinguishing the important from the trivial is just confusing. Popular books and tapes that promise a "perfect," "photographic" memory, or "instant recall" of everything you learn, fly in the face of what psychologists know about how the mind operates. Our advice: Forget them.

SUMMARY

Reconstructing the Past

- Unlike a tape recorder or video camera, human *memory* is highly selective and is *reconstructive:* People add, delete, and change elements in ways that help them make sense of information and events. They often have *source amnesia,* the inability to distinguish information stored during an event from information added later. Even *flashbulb memories,* emotionally powerful memories that seem particularly vivid, are often embellished or distorted and tend to become less accurate over time.

- Because memory is reconstructive, it is subject to *confabulation,* the confusion of imagined events with actual ones. Confabulation is more likely when people have thought about the imagined event many times, the image of the event contains many details, the event is easy to imagine, and the focus of attention is on emotional reactions to the event.

Memory and the Power of Suggestion

- The reconstructive nature of memory makes memory vulnerable to suggestion. Eyewitness testimony is especially vulnerable to error when the suspect's ethnicity differs from that of the witness, when *leading questions* are put to witnesses, or when the witnesses are given misleading information.

- Findings on memory help clarify the issues in the debate about whether children are capable of making up accounts of sexual abuse. Children, like adults, often remember the essential aspects of an event accurately. However, like adults, they can also be suggestible, especially when they are very young, are in emotionally charged situations that blur the line between fantasy and reality, are asked leading questions, or wish to please the interviewer or conform to what they believe other children have said.

- *Hypnosis,* although it has been used successfully for medical and psychological purposes, does not increase the overall accuracy of memory or permit people to "regress" to their childhoods. Because hypnosis encourages people to confuse facts and vividly imagined possibilities, "hypnotically refreshed" recall is often full of errors and pseudomemories.

In Pursuit of Memory

- The ability to remember depends in part on the type of performance called for. In tests of *explicit memory* (conscious recollection), *recognition* is usually better than *recall.* In tests of *implicit memory,* which is measured by indirect methods such as *priming,* past experiences may affect current thoughts or actions even when these experiences are not consciously and intentionally remembered. The *relearning method* seems to straddle the boundary between explicit and implicit tests of memory.

- In *information-processing models,* memory involves the *encoding, storage,* and *retrieval* of information. In the *three-box model,* there are three interacting systems: sensory memory, short-term memory, and long-term memory. Some cognitive scientists prefer a *parallel distributed processing (PDP)* or *connectionist model,* which represents knowledge as connections among numerous interacting processing units, distributed in a vast network and all operating in parallel. But the three-box model continues to offer a convenient way to organize the major findings on memory.

The Three-Box Model of Memory

- In the three-box model, incoming sensory information makes a brief stop in *sensory memory,* which momentarily retains it in the form of sensory images. *Pattern recognition* occurs during the transfer of information from sensory memory to short-term memory. Sensory memory gives us a little time to decide whether information is important enough to warrant further attention.

- *Short-term memory (STM)* retains new information for up to 30 seconds by most estimates (unless rehearsal takes place) and also serves as a *working memory* for the processing of information retrieved from long-term memory for temporary use. The capacity of STM is extremely limited but can be extended if information is organized into larger units by *chunking.* Items that are meaningful, have an emotional impact, or link up to something already in long-term memory may enter long-term storage easily, with only a brief stay in STM.

- *Long-term memory (LTM)* contains an enormous amount of information that must be organized to make it manageable. For example, words (or the concepts they represent) seem to be organized by *semantic categories*. Many models of LTM represent its contents as a network of interrelated concepts. The way people use these networks depends on experience and education. Research on *tip-of-the-tongue (TOT) states* shows that words are also indexed in LTM in terms of sound and form.

• *Procedural memories* ("knowing how") are memories for how to perform specific actions; *declarative memories* ("knowing that") are memories for abstract or representational knowledge. Declarative memories include *semantic memories* (general knowledge) and *episodic memories* (memories for personally experienced events.)

• The three-box model is often invoked to explain the *serial-position effect* in memory, but although it can explain the *primacy effect*, it cannot explain why a *recency effect* sometimes occurs even when the model predicts it should not.

How We Remember

• In order to remember material well, we must encode it accurately in the first place. Some kinds of information, such as material in a college course, require *effortful*, as opposed to *automatic*, *encoding*. Rehearsal of information keeps it in short-term memory and increases the chances of long-term retention. *Elaborative rehearsal* is more likely to result in transfer to long-term memory than is *maintenance rehearsal*, and *deep processing* is usually a more effective retention strategy than *shallow processing*.

• *Mnemonics* can also enhance retention by promoting elaborative encoding and making material meaningful, but for ordinary memory tasks, complex memory tricks are often ineffective or even counterproductive.

Why We Forget

• Forgetting can occur for several reasons. Information in sensory and short-term memory appears to *decay* if it does not receive further processing. New information may replace old information in long-term memory. *Proactive* and *retroactive interference* may take place. *Cue-dependent forgetting* may occur when retrieval cues are inadequate. The most effective *retrieval cues* are those that were present at the time of the initial experience. A person's mood or physical state may also act as a retrieval cue, evoking a *state-dependent memory*.

• Some lapses in memory may be due to *psychogenic amnesia*, the forgetting of disturbing or shocking events, but psychologists are divided about why this occurs. The psychodynamic explanation, *repression*, has met with skepticism among psychological scientists, who consider it vague and unverified. In cases involving claims of recovered memories of repressed events, courts have also become skeptical.

Autobiographical Memories

• Most people cannot recall any events from earlier than the third or fourth year. The reason for such *childhood amnesia* may be partly biological. Cognitive explanations include the lack of a sense of self until the age of 2 or 3, young children's impoverished encoding of their experiences, their focus on routine rather than distinctive aspects of an experience, and their immature cognitive schemas.

• A person's *narrative* "life story" organizes the events of his or her life and gives them meaning. Narratives change as people build up a store of episodic memories, and life stories are, to some degree, works of interpretation and imagination. The central themes of our stories can guide recall and influence our judgments of people and events.

KEY TERMS

LOOKING BACK ◀

- What's wrong with thinking of memory as a mental movie camera? (p. 229)

- Why do "flashbulb" memories of surprising or shocking events sometimes have less wattage than we think? (p. 230)

- If you have a strong emotional reaction to a remembered event, does that mean your memory is accurate? (p. 231)

- Can the question someone asks you about a past event affect what you remember about it? (p. 232)

- Can children's testimony about sexual abuse be trusted? (pp. 232–235)

- Do people remember better when they're hypnotized? (p. 235)

- In general, which is easier—a multiple-choice item or a short-answer essay item—and why? (p. 236)

- Can you know something without knowing that you know it? (p. 237)

- Why is the computer often used as a metaphor for the mind? (p. 238)

- Why is short-term memory like a leaky bucket? (p. 241)

- When a word is on the tip of your tongue, what errors are you likely to make in recalling it? (p. 243)

- What's the difference between "knowing how" and "knowing that"? (p. 244)

- What's wrong with trying to memorize in a rote fashion when you're studying—and what's a better strategy? (p. 247)

- Memory tricks are fun, but are they always useful? (p. 248)

- How might new information "erase" old memories? (p. 251)

- What theory explains why you keep dialing an old area code instead of the one that has replaced it? (p. 252)

- Why is it easier to recall experiences from elementary school if you see pictures of your classmates? (p. 252)

- Why are many researchers skeptical about claims of "repressed" and "recovered" memories? (p. 253)

- Why are the first few years of life a mental blank? (pp. 255–256)

- Why have human beings been called the "story telling animal"? (p. 256)

Answers to the Get Involved exercises on pages 237 and 238:
Rudolph's eight friends were Dasher, Dancer, Prancer, Vixen, Comet, Cupid, Donder, and Blitzen.

Tiny Chain Gets Girl Suspended

ATLANTA, GA, OCTOBER 1, 2000. An 11-year-old girl, Ashley Smith, has been suspended from a local middle school for carrying a Tweety Bird wallet with a small chain dangling from it. School authorities say that the chain qualifies as a weapon and thus falls under their "zero-tolerance" policy.

Such policies are gaining popularity across the nation after a series of tragic killings at schools in Colorado, Oregon, Arkansas, Mississippi, and Kentucky. The policies call for the immediate suspension or expulsion of any student who carries an object that can be used as a weapon, who is in possession of any kind of drug, or who writes an essay containing violent images.

Defenders of zero tolerance argue that increased school violence and a rise in disciplinary problems have made severe penalties for even minor infractions necessary. In one government survey, 18 percent of students said they had brought some kind of weapon to school recently, and fistfights and razor slashings are being reported in many places.

Critics, however, argue that zero-tolerance policies have gone too far. In Ohio, a

Because of her school's zero-tolerance policy, Ashley Smith got suspended for carrying this "Tweety Bird" chain on her wallet.

13-year-old honor student got in trouble for bringing Midol to class. In Pennsylvania, a 6-year-old was suspended for 10 days for possession of a nail clipper. In Virginia, an eighth-grade boy was suspended for four months after he took a knife away from a classmate who was contemplating suicide; the boy had put the knife in his locker, intending to give it to his mother.

LEARNING

A re zero-tolerance policies in schools, such as the ones mentioned in this story, justified? At the core of the zero-tolerance debate is a more general issue: What are the best ways to get people to behave well and to discourage them from behaving badly? Are punishment and "crackdowns" effective? If so, what forms should punishment take? And are there any alternatives?

These questions are central ones for researchers who study **learning,** which to psychologists means any relatively permanent change in behavior that occurs because of experience (except for changes due to fatigue, injury, or disease). Experience is the greatest teacher, providing the essential link between the past and the future and enabling an organism to adapt to changing circumstances in order to survive and thrive.

Research on learning has been heavily influenced by **behaviorism,** the school of psychology that accounts for behavior in terms of observable acts and events, without reference to mental entities, such as "mind" or "will." Behaviorists focus on a basic kind of learning called **conditioning,** which involves associations between environmental stimuli and responses. They have shown that two types of conditioning—*classical conditioning* and *operant conditioning*—can explain much of human behavior. But other approaches, known as *social–cognitive learning theories,* hold that omitting mental processes from explanations of human learning is like omitting passion from descriptions of sex: You may explain the form, but you miss the substance. To social–cognitive theorists and cognitive theorists, learning is not so much a change in behavior as a change in *knowledge* that has the potential for affecting behavior.

As you read about the principles of conditioning and learning in this chapter, ask yourself what they can teach us about the exercise of zero-tolerance policies. Are such policies likely to reduce disruptiveness and discipline problems in our schools? How can we most effectively modify other people's behavior—and our own?

What's Ahead

- Why would a dog salivate when it sees a light-bulb or hears a buzzer, even though it can't eat these things?

- How can classical conditioning help explain prejudice?

- If you have learned to fear collies, why might you also be scared of sheepdogs?

8.1 Classical Conditioning

At the turn of the century, the great Russian physiologist Ivan Pavlov (1849–1936) was studying salivation in dogs, as part of a research program on digestion. His work would shortly win him the Nobel Prize in physiology and medicine. One of Pavlov's procedures was to make a surgical opening in a dog's cheek and insert a tube that conducted saliva away from the animal's salivary gland so that the saliva could be measured. To stimulate the reflexive flow of saliva, Pavlov placed meat powder or other food in the dog's mouth. This procedure was later refined by others (see Figure 8.1).

Pavlov was a truly dedicated scientific observer. Many years later, as he lay dying, he even dictated his sensations for posterity! And he imbued his students with the same passion for detail. During his salivation studies, one of these students noticed something that most people would have overlooked or dismissed as trivial. After a dog had been brought to the laboratory a number of times, it would start to salivate *before*

the food was placed in its mouth. The sight or smell of the food, the dish in which the food was kept, even the sight of the person who delivered the food each day or the sound of the person's footsteps were enough to start the dog's mouth watering. This new salivary response clearly was not inborn, so it had to have been acquired through experience.

At first, Pavlov treated the dog's drooling as merely an annoying secretion. But he quickly realized that his student had stumbled onto an important phenomenon, one that Pavlov came to believe was the basis of all learning in human beings and other animals. He called that phenomenon a "conditional" reflex—conditional because it depended on environmental conditions. Later, an error in the translation of his writings transformed "conditional" into "conditioned," the word most commonly used today.

Pavlov soon dropped what he had been doing and turned to the study of conditioned reflexes, to which he devoted the last three decades of his life. Why were his dogs salivating to things other than food?

New Reflexes from Old

At first, Pavlov speculated about what his dogs might be thinking and feeling to make them drool before getting their food. Was the doggy equivalent of "Oh boy, this means chow time" going through their minds? Eventually, however, he decided that such speculation was pointless (Todes, 1997). Instead, he focused on the environment in which the conditioned reflex arose. The original salivary reflex, according to Pavlov, consisted of an **unconditioned stimulus (US),** food, and an **unconditioned response (UR),** salivation. By an *unconditioned stimulus,* Pavlov meant an event or thing that elicits a response automatically or reflexively. By an *unconditioned response,* he meant the response that is automatically produced:

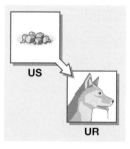

learning
A relatively permanent change in behavior (or behavioral potential) due to experience.

behaviorism
An approach to psychology that emphasizes the study of observable behavior and the role of the environment as a determinant of behavior.

conditioning
A basic kind of learning that involves associations between environmental stimuli and the organism's responses.

unconditioned stimulus (US)
The classical-conditioning term for a stimulus that elicits a reflexive response in the absence of learning.

unconditioned response (UR)
The classical-conditioning term for a reflexive response elicited by a stimulus in the absence of learning.

Figure 8.1
A Modification of Pavlov's Method

In the apparatus on the right, which was based on Ivan Pavlov's techniques, saliva from a dog's cheek flowed down a tube and was measured by the movement of a needle on a revolving drum. In the photo on the left, Pavlov is in the center, flanked by his students and a canine subject.

8.1

Learning occurs, said Pavlov, when a neutral stimulus is regularly paired with an unconditioned stimulus:

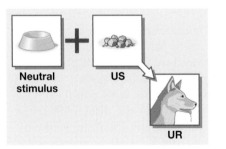

The neutral stimulus then becomes a **conditioned stimulus (CS),** which elicits a learned or **conditioned response (CR)** that is usually similar to the original, unlearned one. In Pavlov's laboratory, the sight of the food dish, which had not previously elicited salivation, became a CS for salivation:

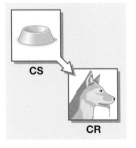

The procedure by which a neutral stimulus becomes a conditioned stimulus eventually became known as **classical conditioning,** also called *Pavlovian* or *respondent conditioning.* In his research, Pavlov and his students went on to show that all sorts of things can become conditioned stimuli for salivation if they are paired with food: the ticking of a metronome, the musical tone of a tuning fork, the vibrating sound of a buzzer, a triangle drawn on a large card, even a pinprick or an electric shock. And since Pavlov's day, many automatic, involuntary responses besides salivation have been classically conditioned—for example, heartbeat, stomach secretions, blood pressure, reflexive movements, blinking, and muscle contractions. The optimal interval between the presentation of the neutral stimulus and the presentation of the US depends on the kind of response involved; in the laboratory, the interval is often less than a second.

Principles of Classical Conditioning

Classical conditioning occurs in all species, from worms to *Homo sapiens*. Let's look more closely at some important features of this process: extinction, higher-order conditioning, and stimulus generalization and discrimination.

conditioned stimulus (CS)
The classical-conditioning term for an initially neutral stimulus that comes to elicit a conditioned response after being associated with an unconditioned stimulus.

conditioned response (CR)
The classical-conditioning term for a response that is elicited by a conditioned stimulus; it occurs after the conditioned stimulus is associated with an unconditioned stimulus.

classical conditioning
The process by which a previously neutral stimulus acquires the capacity to elicit a response through association with a stimulus that already elicits a similar or related response.

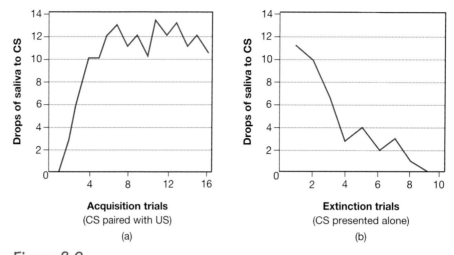

Figure 8.2
Acquisition and Extinction of a Salivary Response

A neutral stimulus that is consistently followed by an unconditioned stimulus for salivation will become a conditioned stimulus for salivation. But when this conditioned stimulus is then repeatedly presented without the unconditioned stimulus, the conditioned salivary response will weaken and eventually disappear; it has been extinguished.

extinction
The weakening and eventual disappearance of a learned response; in classical conditioning, it occurs when the conditioned stimulus is no longer paired with the unconditioned stimulus.

spontaneous recovery
The reappearance of a learned response after its apparent extinction.

higher-order conditioning
In classical conditioning, a procedure in which a neutral stimulus becomes a conditioned stimulus through association with an already established conditioned stimulus.

Extinction. Conditioned responses do not necessarily last forever. If, after conditioning, the conditioned stimulus is repeatedly presented without the unconditioned stimulus, the conditioned response eventually disappears, and **extinction** is said to have occurred (see Figure 8.2). Suppose that you train your dog Milo to salivate to the sound of a bell, but then you ring the bell every five minutes and do *not* follow it with food. Milo will salivate less and less to the bell and will soon stop salivating altogether; salivation will have been extinguished. However, if you come back the next day and ring the bell, Milo may salivate again for a few trials. The reappearance of the response, which is called **spontaneous recovery,** explains why completely eliminating a conditioned response usually requires more than one extinction session.

Higher-Order Conditioning. Sometimes a neutral stimulus can become a conditioned stimulus by being paired with an already established CS, a procedure known as **higher-order conditioning.** Say Milo has learned to salivate to the sight of a food dish. Now you flash a bright light before you present the dish. With repeated pairings of the light and the dish, Milo may learn to salivate to the light. The procedure for higher-order conditioning is illustrated in Figure 8.3.

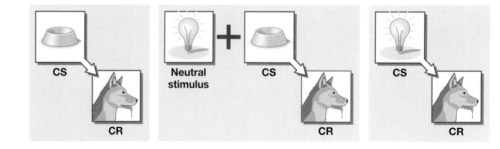

Figure 8.3
Higher-order Conditioning

In this illustration of higher-order conditioning, the food dish is a previously conditioned stimulus for salivation (left). When the light, a neutral stimulus, is paired with the dish (center), the light, too, becomes a conditioned stimulus for salivation (right).

GET INVOLVED

CONDITIONING AN EYE-BLINK RESPONSE

Try out your behavioral skills by conditioning an eye-blink response in a friend, using classical-conditioning procedures. You will need a drinking straw and something to make a ringing sound—a spoon tapped on a water glass works well. Tell your friend that you are going to blow in his or her eye through the straw, but don't say why. Immediately before each puff of air, make the ringing sound. Repeat this procedure ten times. Then make the ringing sound while holding the straw up to the person's eye, but *don't* puff. Your friend will probably blink anyway and may continue to do so for one or two more repetitions of the sound before the response extinguishes. Can you identify the US, the UR, the CS, and the CR in this exercise?

Higher-order conditioning may explain why some words trigger emotional responses in us—why they can inflame us to anger or evoke warm, sentimental feelings. When words are paired with objects or other words that already elicit some emotional response, they, too, may come to elicit that response (Chance, 1999; Staats & Staats, 1957). For example, a child may learn a positive response to the word *birthday* because of its association with gifts and attention. Conversely, the child may learn a negative response to ethnic or national labels, such as *Swede, Turk,* or *Jew,* if those words are paired with words that the child has already learned are disagreeable, such as *dumb* or *dirty.* Higher-order conditioning, in other words, may contribute to the formation of prejudices.

Stimulus Generalization and Discrimination.

After a stimulus becomes a conditioned stimulus for some response, other, similar stimuli may produce a similar reaction—a phenomenon known as **stimulus generalization.** For example, if you condition your patient pooch Milo to salivate to middle C on the piano, Milo may also salivate to D, which is one tone above C, even though you did not pair D with food. Stimulus generalization is described nicely by an old English proverb: "He who hath been bitten by a snake fears a rope."

The mirror image of stimulus generalization is **stimulus discrimination,** in which *different* responses are made to stimuli that resemble the conditioned stimulus in some way. Suppose that you have conditioned Milo to salivate to middle C on the piano by repeatedly pairing the sound with food. Now you play middle C on a guitar, *without* following it by food (but you continue to follow C on the piano by food). Eventually, Milo will learn to salivate to a C on the piano and not to salivate

to the same note on the guitar; that is, he will discriminate between the two sounds. If you keep at this long enough, you could train Milo to be a pretty discriminating drooler!

What Is Actually Learned in Classical Conditioning?

For classical conditioning to be most effective, the stimulus to be conditioned should *precede* the unconditioned stimulus rather than follow it or occur simultaneously with it. This makes sense, because in classical conditioning, the conditioned stimulus becomes a kind of signal for the unconditioned stimulus. It enables the organism to prepare for an event that is about to happen. In Pavlov's studies, for instance, a bell or buzzer was a signal that meat was coming, and the dog's salivation was preparation for digesting food.

Today, therefore, many psychologists contend that what an animal or person actually learns in classical conditioning is not merely an association between two paired stimuli that occur close together in time, but rather *information* conveyed by one stimulus about another: for example, "If a tone sounds, food is likely to follow" (Davey, 1992). This view is supported by the research of Robert Rescorla (1988), who showed, in a series of imaginative studies, that the mere pairing of an unconditioned stimulus and a neutral stimulus is not enough to produce learning. To become a conditioned stimulus, the neutral stimulus must reliably signal, or *predict*, the unconditioned stimulus. If food occurs just as often without a preceding tone as with it, the tone is unlikely to become a conditioned stimulus for salivation—because the tone does not

stimulus generalization
After conditioning, the tendency to respond to a stimulus that resembles one involved in the original conditioning; in classical conditioning, it occurs when a stimulus that resembles the CS elicits the CR.

stimulus discrimination
The tendency to respond differently to two or more similar stimuli; in classical conditioning, it occurs when a stimulus similar to the CS fails to evoke the CR.

provide any information about the likelihood of getting food.

In everyday life, too, a potential CS may sometimes predict an unconditioned stimulus and sometimes not, so conditioning is less certain than when the CS and US always occur together in the laboratory. A friend of ours, behaviorist Paul Chance, gave us this example: Suppose you work in an office where you are allowed to receive routine calls only from other employees; you may take outside calls only in emergencies. One day, your lover calls to jilt you, the police to report that your new car was stolen, and your landlord to tell you that a broken water pipe has flooded your apartment. If these were the only calls you got, the next time you heard the phone ring (the CS) you might freak out (the CR). But if they occurred randomly among 50 routine calls for supplies, the phone's ringing would probably not upset you (any more than you already are!) because it would not necessarily signal another disaster.

Rescorla (1988) concluded that "Pavlovian conditioning is not a stupid process by which the organism willy-nilly forms associations between any two stimuli that happen to co-occur. Rather, the organism is better seen as an information seeker using logical and perceptual relations among events, along with its own preconceptions, to form a sophisticated representation of its world." Not all learning theorists agree with this conclusion; an orthodox behaviorist would say that it is silly to talk about the preconceptions of a rat. The important point, however, is that concepts such as "information seeking," "preconceptions," and "representations of the world" open the door to a more cognitive view of classical conditioning.

QUICK QUIZ

Classical-conditioning terms can be hard to learn, so be sure to take this quiz before going on.

A. Name the unconditioned stimulus, unconditioned response, conditioned stimulus, and conditioned response in these two situations:

   1. Five-year-old Samantha is watching a storm from her window. A huge bolt of lightning is followed by a tremendous thunderclap, and Samantha jumps at the noise. This happens several more times. There is a brief lull and then another lightning bolt. Samantha jumps in response to the bolt.

   2. Gregory's mouth waters whenever he eats anything with lemon in it. One day, while reading an ad that shows a big glass of lemonade, Gregory notices his mouth watering.

B. In the view of many learning theorists, pairing a neutral and an unconditioned stimulus is not enough to produce learning; the neutral stimulus must _____ the unconditioned stimulus.

Answers:

A. 1. US = the thunderclap; UR = jumping elicited by the noise; CS = the sight of the lightning; CR = jumping elicited by the lightning. 2. US = the taste of lemon; UR = salivation elicited by the taste of lemon; CS = the picture of a glass of lemonade; CR = salivation elicited by the picture. B. signal or predict

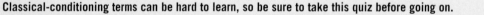

What's Ahead

- Why do advertisers often include pleasant music and gorgeous scenery in ads for their products?

- How would a classical-conditioning theorist explain your irrational fear of heights or mice?

- If you eat licorice and then happen to get the flu, how might your taste for licorice change?

- How can sitting in a doctor's office make you feel sick?

8.2 Classical Conditioning in Real Life

If a dog can learn to salivate to the ringing of a bell, so can you. In fact, you probably have learned to salivate to the sound of a lunch bell, not to mention the phrase *hot fudge sundae*, "mouth-watering" pictures of food in magazines, the sight of a waiter in a restaurant, and a voice calling out "Dinner's ready!" But the role of classical conditioning goes far beyond the learning of simple reflexive responses; conditioning affects us every day in many ways.

One of the first researchers to recognize the real-life implications of Pavlovian theory was John B. Watson, who founded American behaviorism and enthusiastically promoted Pavlov's ideas. Watson believed that the whole rich array of human emotion and behavior could be accounted for by conditioning principles. For example, he thought you learned to love another person when stroking and cuddling (unconditioned stimuli) were paired with the person doing the stroking and cuddling. (Watson, who was married five times, apparently tried many such pairings.) Watson turned out to be wrong about love, which is a lot more complicated than he thought (see Chapter 13). But he was right about the power of classical conditioning to affect our emotions, preferences, and tastes.

Learning to Like

Classical conditioning plays a big role in our emotional responses to objects, events, and places. It can explain why sentimental feelings sweep over us when we see a school mascot, a national flag, or the logo of the Olympic games: These objects have been associated in the past with positive feelings.

Many Madison Avenue techniques for getting us to like clients' products are also based on the principles first demonstrated by Pavlov, whether advertising executives realize it or not. In one study, college students looked at slides of either a beige pen or a blue pen. During the presentation, half the students heard a song from a recent musical film, and half heard a selection of traditional music from India. (The experimenter made the reasonable assumption that the show tune would be more appealing to the young Americans participating in the study.) Later the students were allowed to choose one of the pens. Almost three-fourths of those who heard the popular music chose a pen that was the same color as the one they had seen in the slides. An equal number of those who heard the Indian music chose a pen that *differed* in color from the one they had seen (Gorn, 1982).

In classical-conditioning terms, the music in this study was an unconditioned stimulus for internal responses associated with pleasure or displeasure, and the pens became conditioned stimuli for similar responses. You can see why television commercials often pair products with music, attractive people, or other appealing sounds and images.

Learning to Fear

Positive emotions are not the only ones that can be classically conditioned; so can dislikes and negative emotions such as fear. A person can learn to fear just about anything if it is paired with something that elicits pain, surprise, or embarrassment. But human beings are biologically primed to be especially susceptible to certain kinds of acquired fears: It is far easier to establish a conditioned fear of spiders, snakes, and heights than of butterflies, flowers, and toasters. The former can be dangerous to your health, and in the process of evolution, human beings therefore acquired a tendency to be wary of them.

When fear of an object or situation is irrational and interferes with normal activities, it qualifies as a *phobia*. To demonstrate how a phobia might be acquired, John Watson and Rosalie Rayner (1920) deliberately established a rat phobia in an 11-month-old boy named Albert. For ethical reasons, no psychologist today would do such a thing to a child. Nevertheless, the study remains a classic, and its main conclusion, that fears can be conditioned, is still well accepted.

"Little Albert" was a placid child who rarely cried. When Watson and Rayner gave him a furry white rat to play with (a live one, not a toy), Albert showed no fear; in fact, he was delighted. However, like most children, Albert was afraid of loud noises. When the researchers made a loud noise behind his head by striking a steel bar with a hammer, he would jump and fall sideways onto the mattress he was sitting on. The noise made by the hammer was an unconditioned stimulus for the unconditioned response of fear.

Having established that Albert liked rats, Watson and Rayner set about teaching him to fear them. Again they offered him a rat, but this time, as Albert reached for it, one of the researchers struck the steel bar. Startled, Albert fell onto the mattress. The researchers repeated this procedure several times. Albert began to whimper and tremble. Finally, the rat was offered alone, without the noise. Albert fell over, cried, and crawled away as fast as he could; the rat had become a conditioned stimulus for fear (see Figure 8.4). Tests done a few days later showed that Albert's fear had generalized to other hairy or furry objects, including white rabbits, cotton wool, a Santa Claus mask, and even John Watson's hair.

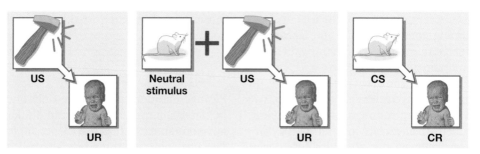

Figure 8.4

In the Little Albert study, noise from a hammer striking a steel bar was an unconditioned stimulus for fear (left). When a white rat, a neutral stimulus, was paired with the noise (center), the rat then became a conditioned stimulus for fear (right).

8.1

Unfortunately, Watson and Rayner lost access to Little Albert, so they were unable to reverse the conditioning. However, Watson and Mary Cover Jones did reverse another child's conditioned fear—one that was, as Watson put it, "home-grown" rather than psychologist-induced (Jones, 1924).

A 3-year-old named Peter was deathly afraid of rabbits. Watson and Jones eliminated this fear with a method called **counterconditioning,** in which a conditioned stimulus is paired with some other stimulus that elicits a response incompatible with the unwanted response. In this case, the rabbit (the CS) was paired with a snack of milk and crackers, and the snack produced pleasant feelings incompatible with the conditioned response of fear. At first, the researchers kept the rabbit some distance from Peter, so that his fear would remain at a low level. Otherwise, Peter might have learned to fear milk and crackers! But gradually, over several days, they brought the rabbit closer and closer. Eventually Peter was able to sit with the rabbit in his lap, playing with it with one hand while he ate with the other. A variation of this procedure, called *systematic desensitization,* was later devised for treating phobias in adults (see Chapter 11).

Accounting for Taste

Classical conditioning can also explain how we learn to like and dislike many foods and odors. In the laboratory, researchers have taught animals to dislike foods or odors by pairing them with drugs that cause nausea or other unpleasant symptoms. One researcher trained slugs to associate the smell of carrots, which slugs normally like, with a bitter-tasting chemical that they detest. Soon the slugs were avoiding the smell of carrots. The researcher then demonstrated higher-order conditioning by pairing the smell of carrots with

the smell of potato. Sure enough, the slugs began to avoid the smell of potato, as well (Sahley, Rudy, & Gelperin, 1981).

Many people have learned to dislike a food after eating it and then falling ill, even though the two events were unrelated. The food, previously a neutral stimulus, becomes a conditioned stimulus for nausea or for other symptoms produced by the illness. Psychologist Martin Seligman once told how he himself was conditioned to hate béarnaise sauce. One night, shortly after he and his wife ate a delicious filet mignon with béarnaise sauce, he came down with the flu. Naturally, he felt wretched. His misery had nothing to do with the béarnaise sauce, of course, yet the next time he tried it, he found he disliked the taste (Seligman & Hager, 1972).

Notice that unlike conditioning in the laboratory, Seligman's aversion to the sauce occurred after only one pairing of the sauce with illness and

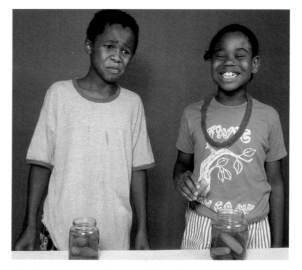

Whether we say "yum" or "yuck" to a food may depend on a past experience involving classical conditioning.

counterconditioning
In classical conditioning, the process of pairing a conditioned stimulus with a stimulus that elicits a response that is incompatible with an unwanted conditioned response.

with a considerable delay between the conditioned and unconditioned stimuli. Moreover, neither Seligman's wife nor his dinner plate became conditioned stimuli for nausea, even though they, too, had been paired with illness. Apparently, many animals (including psychologists) are biologically primed to associate sickness with taste more readily than with sights or sounds (Garcia & Koelling, 1966; Seligman & Hager, 1972). Like the tendency to acquire certain fears, this biological tendency enhances the species' survival: Eating bad food is more likely to be followed by illness than are particular sights or sounds.

Reacting to Medical Treatments

Because of classical conditioning, medical treatments can create unexpected misery or relief from symptoms, for reasons that are entirely unrelated to the treatment itself.

For example, unpleasant reactions to a treatment can generalize to a wide range of other stimuli. This is a particular problem for cancer patients. The nausea and vomiting resulting from chemotherapy often generalize to the place where the therapy takes place, the waiting room, the sound of a nurse's voice, or the smell of rubbing alcohol. The drug treatment is an unconditioned stimulus for nausea and vomiting, and through association, the other, previously neutral stimuli become conditioned stimuli for these responses. Even *mental*

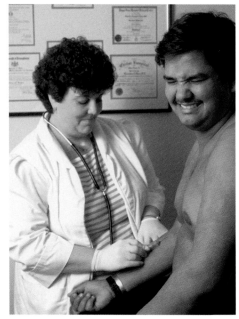

The anxiety of getting a shot can generalize to the nurse, the room, the sight of needles. . . .

images of the sights and smells of the clinic may become conditioned stimuli for nausea (Dadds et al., 1997; Redd et al., 1993).

Some cancer patients also acquire a classically conditioned anxiety response to anything associated with their chemotherapy. In one study, patients who drank lemon-lime Kool-Aid before their therapy sessions developed an anxiety response to the drink—an example of higher-order conditioning. They continued to feel anxious even when the drink was offered in their homes rather than at the clinic (Jacobsen et al., 1995).

On the other hand, patients may have *reduced* pain and anxiety when they take *placebos*—pills and injections with no active ingredients. Why do placebos work? The bottle containing the drug, the room in which the medication is given, the doctor's white coat, and the pill or injection itself may all become conditioned stimuli for relief from symptoms, because these stimuli have been associated in the past with *real* drugs (Ader, 1997). The real drugs are the unconditioned stimuli; the relief they bring is the unconditioned response; and the placebos acquire the ability to elicit similar reactions (conditioned responses).

 QUICK QUIZ

We hope you haven't acquired a classically conditioned fear of quizzes. See whether you can supply the correct term to describe the outcome in each of these situations.

1. After a child learns to fear spiders, he also responds with fear to ants, beetles, and other crawling bugs.

2. A toddler is afraid of the bath, so her father puts just a little water in the tub and gives the child a lollipop to suck on while she is being washed. Soon, the little girl loses her fear of the bath.

3. A factory worker's mouth waters whenever a noontime bell signals the beginning of his lunch break. One day, the bell goes haywire and rings every half hour. By the end of the day, the worker has stopped salivating to the bell.

Answers:
1. stimulus generalization   2. counterconditioning   3. extinction

What's Ahead

- What do praising a child and quitting your nagging have in common?
- How can operant principles account for superstitious rituals?
- What is the best way to discourage a friend from interrupting you while you're studying?
- How do trainers teach guide dogs to perform the amazing services they do for their owners?

8.3 Operant Conditioning

At the end of the nineteenth century, in the first known scientific study of anger, G. Stanley Hall (1899) asked people to describe angry episodes they had experienced or observed. One person told of a 3-year-old girl who broke out in furious, seemingly uncontrollable sobs when she was punished by being kept home from a ride. In the middle of her tantrum, the child suddenly stopped crying and asked in a perfectly calm voice if her father was in. Told no, she immediately resumed her sobbing.

Children, of course, cry for many valid reasons—pain, discomfort, fear, illness, fatigue—and these cries deserve an adult's sympathy and attention. The child in Hall's study, however, was crying for a different reason. She had learned from prior experience that an outburst of sobbing would bring her attention and possibly the ride she wanted. Her behavior, though some might call it "naughty," was perfectly understandable because it followed one of the most basic laws of learning: *Behavior becomes more likely or less likely, depending on its consequences.*

An emphasis on environmental consequences is at the heart of **operant conditioning** (also called *instrumental conditioning*), the second type of conditioning studied by behaviorists. In classical conditioning, it does not matter whether an animal's or person's behavior has consequences; in Pavlov's procedure, for example, the dog got food whether it salivated or not. But in operant conditioning, the organism's response (the little girl's sobbing, for example) *operates* or produces effects on the environment. These effects, in turn, influence whether the response will occur again.

Classical and operant conditioning also tend to differ in the types of responses they involve. In classical conditioning, the response is reflexive, an automatic reaction to something happening in the environment, such as the sight of food or the sound of a bell. Generally, responses in operant conditioning are complex and are not reflexive—for instance, riding a bicycle, writing a letter, climbing a mountain, . . . or throwing a tantrum.

The Birth of Radical Behaviorism

Operant conditioning has been studied since the start of the twentieth century, although it was not called that until later. Edward Thorndike (1898), then a young doctoral candidate, set the stage by observing cats as they tried to escape from a "puzzle box" to reach a scrap of fish that was just outside the box. At first, the cat would scratch, bite, or swat at parts of the cage in an unorganized way. Then, after a few minutes, it would chance on the successful response (loosening a bolt, pulling a string, or hitting a button) and rush out to get the reward. Placed in the box again, the cat now took a little less time to escape, and after several trials, the animal immediately made the correct response. According to Thorndike, the correct response had been "stamped in" by its satisfying effects (getting the food). In contrast, annoying or unsatisfying effects "stamped out" behavior. Behavior, said Thorndike, is controlled by its consequences.

This general principle was elaborated and extended to more complex forms of behavior by B. F. (Burrhus Frederic) Skinner, whose ideas we introduced in Chapter 2. Skinner called his approach "radical behaviorism" to distinguish it from the behaviorism of John Watson, who emphasized classical conditioning. Skinner argued

An instantaneous learning experience.

operant conditioning
The process by which a response becomes more likely to occur or less so, depending on its consequences.

that to understand behavior we should focus on the external causes of an action and the action's consequences. He avoided terms that Thorndike used, such as "satisfying" and "annoying," which reflect assumptions about what an organism feels and wants. To explain behavior, he said, we should look outside the individual, not inside.

The Consequences of Behavior

In Skinner's analysis, which has inspired an immense body of research, a response ("operant") can lead to one of three types of consequences.

1 A *neutral consequence does not alter the response.* That is, it neither increases nor decreases the probability that the behavior will recur. If a door handle squeaks each time you turn it, but you ignore the sound and it has no effect on your likelihood of opening the door in the future, the squeak is considered a neutral consequence. We will not be concerned further with neutral consequences.

2 **Reinforcement** *strengthens the response or makes it more likely to recur.* When your dog begs for food at the table, and you give her the lamb chop off your plate, her begging is likely to increase:

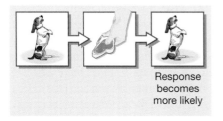

Response becomes more likely

Reinforcers are roughly equivalent to rewards, and many psychologists use *reward* and *reinforcer* as approximate synonyms. However, strict behaviorists avoid the word *reward* because it implies that something has been earned that results in happiness or satisfaction. To a behaviorist, a stimulus is a reinforcer if it strengthens the preceding behavior, whether or not the organism experiences pleasure or a positive emotion. Conversely, no matter how pleasurable a stimulus is, it is not a reinforcer if it does not increase the likelihood of a response. It's great to get a paycheck, but if you get paid regardless of the effort you put into your work, the money will not reinforce "hard-work behavior."

3 **Punishment** *weakens the response or makes it less likely to recur.* Any aversive (unpleasant) stimulus or event may be a *punisher.* If your dog begs for food from the table and you shout "No," her begging is likely to decrease—as long as you don't then feel guilty and give her the lamb chop anyway:

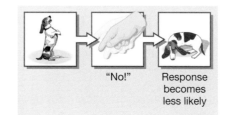

"No!" Response becomes less likely

Parents, employers, and governments resort to reinforcers and punishers all the time—to get kids to behave well, employees to work hard, and constituents to pay taxes—but they do not always use them effectively. In general, the sooner a reinforcer or punisher follows a response, the greater its effect; you are likely to respond more reliably when you do not have to wait too long for a paycheck, a smile, or a grade. When there is a delay, other responses occur in the interval, and the connection between the desired or undesired response and the consequence may not be made.

Primary and Secondary Reinforcers and Punishers.
Food, water, light stroking of the skin, and a comfortable air temperature are naturally reinforcing because they satisfy biological needs. They are therefore known as **primary reinforcers.** Similarly, pain and extreme heat or cold are inherently punishing and are therefore known as **primary punishers.** Primary reinforcers and punishers can be very powerful, but they also have some drawbacks, both in real life and in research. For one thing, a primary reinforcer may be ineffective if an animal or person is not in a deprived state; a glass of water is not much of a reward if you just drank three glasses. Also, for obvious ethical reasons, psychologists cannot go around using primary punishers (say, hitting their subjects) or taking away primary reinforcers (say, starving their subjects).

Fortunately, behavior can be controlled just as effectively by **secondary reinforcers** and **secondary punishers,** which are learned. Money, praise, applause, good grades, awards, and gold stars are common secondary reinforcers. Criticism, demerits, catcalls, scolding, fines, and bad grades are common secondary punishers. Most behaviorists believe that secondary reinforcers and punishers acquire their ability to influence behavior by being paired with primary

reinforcement
The process by which a stimulus or event strengthens or increases the probability of the response that it follows.

punishment
The process by which a stimulus or event weakens or reduces the probability of the response that it follows.

primary reinforcer
A stimulus that is inherently reinforcing, typically satisfying a physiological need; an example is food.

primary punisher
A stimulus that is inherently punishing; an example is electric shock.

secondary reinforcer
A stimulus that has acquired reinforcing properties through association with other reinforcers.

secondary punisher
A stimulus that has acquired punishing properties through association with other punishers.

reinforcers and punishers. (If that reminds you of classical conditioning, reinforce your excellent thinking with a pat on the head! Indeed, secondary reinforcers and punishers are often called *conditioned* reinforcers and punishers.) Money, a secondary reinforcer, has considerable power over most people's behavior because it can be exchanged for primary reinforcers such as food and shelter. It is also associated with other secondary reinforcers, such as praise and respect.

Positive and Negative Reinforcers and Punishers.

Reinforcement and punishment may seem pretty straightforward, but they are not always simple. Consider, first, reinforcement. In our example of the begging dog, something pleasant (getting the lamb chop) followed the dog's begging response, so the response increased. Similarly, if a good grade follows your studying, your efforts to study are likely to continue or increase. This kind of process, in which a pleasant consequence makes a response more likely, is known as **positive reinforcement.** But there is another type of reinforcement, **negative reinforcement,** which involves the *removal* of something *unpleasant.* For example, if someone nags you all the time to study, but stops nagging when you comply, your studying is likely to increase—because you will then avoid the nagging:

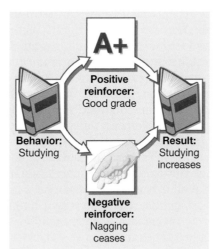

The positive–negative distinction can also be applied to punishment: Something unpleasant may occur following some behavior (positive punishment), or something *pleasant* may be removed (negative punishment). For example, if your friends tease you for being an egghead (positive punishment) or if studying makes you lose time with your friends (negative punishment), you may stop studying:

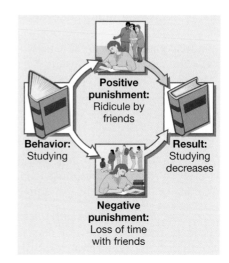

The distinction between positive and negative reinforcement has been a source of confusion and frustration for generations of students, turning strong people into quivering heaps. You will master these terms more quickly if you understand that "positive" and "negative" have nothing to do with "good" or "bad." They refer to *procedures*—giving something or taking something away.

In the case of reinforcement, think of a positive reinforcer as something that is added or obtained, and a negative reinforcer as avoidance of, or escape from, something unpleasant. *In either case, a response becomes more likely.* Do you recall what happened when Little Albert learned to fear rats through a process of classical conditioning? After he acquired this fear, crawling away was negatively reinforced by escape from the now-fearsome rodent. The negative reinforcement that results from escaping or avoiding something unpleasant explains why so many fears are long-lasting. When you avoid a feared object or situation, you also cut off all opportunities for extinguishing your fear.

Understandably, people often confuse negative reinforcement with positive punishment, because both involve an unpleasant stimulus. With punishment, though, you are subjected to the unpleasant stimulus, and with negative reinforcement, the unpleasant stimulus is taken away. To keep these terms straight, remember that punishment—whether positive or negative—*decreases* the likelihood of a response, whereas reinforcement—whether positive or negative—*increases* it.

positive reinforcement
A reinforcement procedure in which a response is followed by the presentation of, or increase in intensity of, a reinforcing stimulus; as a result, the response becomes stronger or more likely to occur.

negative reinforcement
A reinforcement procedure in which a response is followed by the removal, delay, or decrease in intensity of an unpleasant stimulus; as a result, the response becomes stronger or more likely to occur.

In real life, punishment and negative reinforcement often go hand in hand. If you use a choke collar on your dog to teach it to heel, a yank on the collar punishes the act of walking ahead of you, but release of the collar negatively reinforces the act of staying by your side.

You can positively reinforce your studying of this material by taking a refreshment break. As you master the material, a decrease in your anxiety will negatively reinforce studying. But we hope you won't punish your efforts by telling yourself "I'll never get it" or "It's too hard"!

QUICK QUIZ

What kind of consequence will follow if you can't answer these questions?

1. A child nags her father for a cookie; he keeps refusing, but finally, unable to stand the nagging any longer, he hands over the cookie. For him, the ending of the child's pleas is a _____. For the child, the cookie is a _____.

2. An able-bodied driver is careful not to park in a handicapped space anymore after paying a large fine for doing so. The loss of money is a _____.

3. Which of the following are secondary reinforcers: quarters spilling from a slot machine, a winner's blue ribbon, a piece of candy, an A on an exam, frequent-flyer miles.

4. During late-afternoon "happy hours," bars and restaurants sell drinks at reduced prices, and appetizers are often free. What undesirable behavior may be rewarded by this practice?

Answers:

1. negative reinforcer; positive reinforcer 2. punisher—or more precisely, a negative punisher (because something desirable, money, was taken away) 3. All but the candy are secondary reinforcers. 4. One possible answer: The reduced prices, free appetizers, and cheerful atmosphere all reinforce heavy alcohol consumption just before the commuter rush hour, thus possibly contributing to drunk driving.

Principles of Operant Conditioning

Thousands of operant-conditioning studies have been done, many using animals. A favorite experimental tool is the *Skinner box,* a cage equipped with a device that delivers food or water when an animal makes a desired response (see Figure 8.5 on the next page). In the original version, a machine connected to the cage recorded each response and produced a graph on a piece of paper, showing the cumulative number of responses across time; nowadays, computers are used.

Early in his career, Skinner (1938) used the Skinner box for a classic demonstration of operant conditioning. A rat that had previously learned to eat from the food-releasing device was placed in the box. Because no food was present, the animal proceeded to do typical ratlike things, scurrying about the box, sniffing here and there, and randomly touching parts of the floor and walls. Quite by accident, it happened to press a lever mounted on one wall, and immediately, a pellet of tasty rat food fell into the food dish. The rat continued its movements and again happened to press the bar, causing another pellet to fall into the dish. With additional repetitions of bar pressing followed by food, the animal began to behave less randomly and to press the bar more consistently. Eventually, Skinner had the rat pressing the bar as fast as it could.

A cartoon well known to behaviorists, originally published in a student newspaper, shows two rats in a Skinner box, with one saying to the other, "Boy, do we have this guy conditioned. Every time I press the bar down he drops a pellet in." But, in characteristic fashion, Skinner didn't think it was a joke. To Skinner, the environment was a place where organisms reinforced and punished each other, *reciprocally:* Yes, he conditioned the rat—but the rat also conditioned him (Bjork, 1993).

By using the Skinner box and similar devices, researchers have discovered many important techniques and applications of operant conditioning.

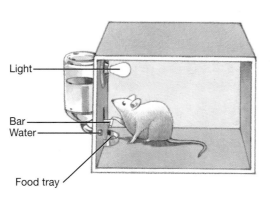

Figure 8.5
The Skinner Box

When a rat in a Skinner box presses a bar, a food pellet or drop of water is automatically released. The photo shows Skinner at work on one of the boxes.

Light

Bar
Water

Food tray

extinction
The weakening and eventual disappearance of a learned response; in operant conditioning, it occurs when a response is no longer followed by a reinforcer.

stimulus generalization
In operant conditioning, the tendency for a response that has been reinforced (or punished) in the presence of one stimulus to occur (or be suppressed) in the presence of other, similar stimuli.

stimulus discrimination
In operant conditioning, the tendency of a response to occur in the presence of one stimulus but not in the presence of other, similar stimuli that differ from it on some dimension.

discriminative stimulus
A stimulus that signals when a particular response is likely to be followed by a certain type of consequence.

continuous reinforcement
A reinforcement schedule in which a particular response is always reinforced.

intermittent (partial) schedule of reinforcement
A reinforcement schedule in which a particular response is sometimes but not always reinforced.

Extinction. In operant conditioning, as in classical, **extinction** is a procedure that causes a previously learned response to stop. In operant conditioning, extinction takes place when the reinforcer that maintained the response is removed or is no longer available. At first, there may be a spurt of responding, but then the responses gradually taper off and eventually cease. Suppose you put a coin in a vending machine and get nothing back. You may throw in another coin, or perhaps even two, but then you will probably stop trying. The next day, you may put in yet another coin, an example of *spontaneous recovery.* Eventually, however, you will give up on that machine. Your response will have been extinguished.

Stimulus Generalization and Discrimination. In operant conditioning, as in classical, **stimulus generalization** may occur. That is, responses may generalize to stimuli that were not present during the original learning situation but that resemble the original stimuli. For example, a pigeon that has been trained to peck at a picture of a circle may also peck at a slightly oval figure. But if you wanted to train the bird to discriminate between the two shapes, you would present both the circle and the oval, giving reinforcers whenever the bird pecked at the circle and withholding reinforcers when it pecked at the oval. Eventually, **stimulus discrimination** would occur.

Sometimes an animal or human being learns to respond to a stimulus only when some other stimulus, called a **discriminative stimulus,** is present. The discriminative stimulus signals whether a response, if made, will pay off. In a Skinner box containing a pigeon, a light may serve as a discriminative stimulus for pecking at a circle. When the light is on, pecking brings a reward; when it is off, pecking is futile.

Human behavior is controlled by many discriminative stimuli, both verbal ("Store hours are 9 to 5") and nonverbal (traffic lights, doorbells, the ring of a telephone). Learning to respond correctly when such stimuli are present is an essential part of a person's socialization. In a public place, if you have to go to the bathroom, the words *Women* and *Men* are discriminative stimuli for entering one door or the other. One word tells you the response will be rewarded by the opportunity to empty a full bladder, the other that it will be punished by the jeers or protests of other people.

Learning on Schedule. When a response is first acquired, learning is usually most rapid if the response is reinforced each time it occurs; this procedure is called **continuous reinforcement.** However, once a response has become reliable, it will be more resistant to extinction if it is rewarded on an **intermittent (partial) schedule of reinforcement,** which involves reinforcing only some responses, not all of them. Skinner (1956) learned this when he ran short of food pellets for his rats and was forced to deliver reinforcers less often. (Not all scientific discoveries are planned!)

Intermittent reinforcement helps explain why people often get attached to "lucky" hats, charms, and rituals. A batter pulls his earlobe, gets a home run, and from then on always pulls his earlobe before a pitch. A student takes an exam with a purple pen and gets an A, and from then on will not take an exam without a purple pen. Such rituals persist because *sometimes* they are followed, purely coincidentally, by a reinforcer—a hit, a good grade—and so they became resistant to extinction.

Skinner (1948) once demonstrated this phenomenon by creating eight "superstitious" pigeons in his laboratory. He rigged the pigeon's cages so that food was delivered every 15 seconds, even if the bird didn't lift a feather. Pigeons are often in motion, so when the food came, each animal was likely to be doing *something.* That something was then reinforced by delivery of the food. The behavior, of course, was reinforced entirely by chance, but it still became more likely to occur, and thus to be reinforced again. Within a short time, six of the pigeons were practicing some sort of consistent ritual—turning in counterclockwise circles, bobbing the head up and down, or swinging their heads to and fro. None of these activities had the least effect on the delivery of the reinforcer; the birds were behaving "superstitiously." It was as if they thought their movements were responsible for bringing the food.

The moral is, if you don't want to be a pigeon, you should examine how intermittent reinforcement might be perpetuating your own superstitious rituals or belief in good-luck charms.

Many kinds of intermittent schedules have been studied. Some deliver a reinforcer only after a certain number of responses has occurred; others do so only if a response is made after a certain amount of time has passed since the last reinforcer. The number of responses that must occur or the amount of time that must pass may be fixed (e.g., three responses or five seconds) or may vary around some average. These patterns of reinforcement affect the rate, form, and timing of behavior. The details are beyond the scope of this book, but here's an example. Suppose your sweetheart sends you ten e-mail messages each day, playfully spacing them at unpredictable intervals, although they come on average every hour or so. You will probably check your e-mail regularly, at a low but steady rate. But if your sweetheart sends you just one e-mail every day, at around dinnertime, you'll probably start checking around 5:00 P.M., keep doing so until the message arrives (your reward), and then stop looking at all until the next evening.

A basic principle of operant conditioning is that if you want a response to persist after it has been learned, you should reinforce it intermittently, not continuously. If you are continuously giving Harry, your hamster, a treat for pushing a ball with his nose, and then you suddenly stop the reinforcement, Harry will soon stop pushing that ball. Because the change in reinforcement is large, from continuous to none at all, Harry will easily discern the change. But if you have been reinforcing Harry's behavior only every so often, the change will not be so dramatic, and your hungry hamster will keep responding for quite a while. Pigeons, rats, and people on intermittent schedules of reinforcement have responded in the laboratory thousands of times without reinforcement before throwing in the towel, especially when the timing of the reinforcer varies. Animals will sometimes work so hard for an unpredictable, infrequent bit of food that the energy they expend is greater than that gained from the reward; theoretically, they could actually work themselves to death!

It follows that if you want to get rid of a response, you should be careful *not* to reinforce it intermittently. If you are going to extinguish undesirable behavior by ignoring it—a child's tantrums, a friend's midnight phone calls, a parent's unasked-for advice—you must be absolutely consistent in withholding reinforcement (your attention). Otherwise, the other person will learn that if he or she keeps up the screaming, calling, or advice-giving long enough, it will eventually be rewarded. One of the most common errors people make, from a behavioral point of view, is to reward intermittently the very responses that they would like to eliminate.

shaping
An operant-conditioning procedure in which successive approximations of a desired response are reinforced.

successive approximations
In the operant-conditioning procedure of shaping, behaviors that are ordered in terms of increasing similarity or closeness to the desired response.

Shaping. For a response to be reinforced, it must first occur. But suppose you want to train Harry the hamster to pick up a marble, a child to use a knife and fork properly, or a friend to play terrific tennis. Such behaviors, and most others in everyday life, have almost no probability of appearing spontaneously. You could grow old and gray waiting for them to occur so that you could reinforce them. The operant solution to this dilemma is a procedure called **shaping.**

In shaping, you start by reinforcing a tendency in the right direction, and then you gradually require responses that are more and more similar to the final, desired response. The responses that you reinforce on the way to the final one are called **successive approximations.** In the case of Harry and the marble, you might deliver a food pellet if the hamster merely turned toward the marble. Once this response was well established, you might then reward Harry for taking a step toward the marble. After that, you could reward him for approaching the marble, then for touching the marble, then for putting both paws on the marble, and finally for holding it. With the achievement of each approximation, the next one would become more likely, making it available for reinforcement.

Using shaping and other techniques, Skinner was able to train pigeons to play Ping-Pong with their beaks and to "bowl" in a miniature alley, complete with a wooden ball and tiny bowling pins. (Skinner had a great sense of humor.) Animal trainers routinely use shaping to teach dogs to act as the "eyes" of the blind and to act as the "limbs" of people with spinal-cord injuries by turning on light switches, opening refrigerator doors, and reaching for boxes on supermarket shelves.

Biological Limits on Learning. All principles of operant conditioning, like those of classical conditioning, are limited by an animal's genetic dispositions and physical characteristics; a fish cannot be trained to climb a ladder. That is why operant- and classical-conditioning procedures always work best when they capitalize on inborn tendencies.

Years ago, two psychologists who became animal trainers, Keller and Marian Breland (1961), learned what happens when you ignore biological constraints on learning. They found that their animals were having trouble learning tasks that should have been easy. For example, a pig was supposed to drop large wooden coins in a box. Instead, the pig would drop the coin, push at it

Behavioral techniques such as shaping have many useful applications. Monkeys like this one have been trained to assist their paralyzed owners by performing such everyday tasks as picking up objects, opening doors, helping with feeding, and turning the pages of books.

with its snout, throw it in the air, and push at it some more. This odd behavior actually delayed delivery of the reinforcer (food, which is *very* reinforcing to a pig), so it was hard to explain in terms of operant principles. The Brelands finally realized that the pig's rooting instinct—using its snout to uncover and dig up edible roots—was keeping it from learning the task. They called such a reversion to instinctive behavior *instinctive drift*.

In human beings, too, operant learning is affected by genetics, biology, and the evolutionary history of our species. As we saw in Chapter 3, human children are biologically disposed to learn language without much effort, and they may be disposed to learn some arithmetic operations, as well. Moreover, as we saw in Chapter 2, temperaments and other inborn dispositions may set limits on how a person responds to rewards and punishments. In Chapter 10, we will see that people with antisocial personality disorder (popularly called "sociopaths" or "psychopaths") often do not respond to punishment the way other people do.

Skinner: The Man and the Myth

Because of his groundbreaking work on operant conditioning, B. F. Skinner has often been called the greatest of American psychologists. Certainly he is one of the best known—and also one of the most misunderstood. For example, many people (even some psychologists) think that Skinner denied the existence of human consciousness and the value of studying it. In reality, Skinner (1972, 1990) maintained that we *can* study private, internal events—what we call perceptions, emotions, and thoughts—by observing our own sensory responses, the verbal reports of others, and the conditions under which such events occur. Internal events, he said, are as real as any others. But he insisted that thoughts and feelings cannot *explain* behavior; these components of "consciousness," he said, are themselves simply behaviors that occur because of reinforcement and punishment.

Because Skinner thought the environment should be manipulated to alter behavior, some critics have portrayed him as cold-blooded. One famous controversy regarding Skinner occurred when he invented an enclosed "living space," the Air-Crib, for his younger daughter Deborah when she was an infant. This "baby box," as it came to be known, had temperature and humidity con-

An animal's natural responses sometimes interfere with operant learning. For example, it is hard for pigs to learn to drop wooden coins into a "piggy bank" because the animal's rooting instinct causes them to lower their snouts and throw the coin in the air. Keller and Marian Breland were able to solve this problem by making the coins heavier so that the pigs could not easily toss them around.

trols to eliminate the usual discomforts suffered by babies: heat, cold, wetness, and confinement by blankets and clothing. Skinner believed that to reduce a baby's cries of distress and make infant care easier for the parents, you should fix the environment. But people imagined, incorrectly, that the Skinners were leaving their child in the baby box all the time without cuddling and holding her, and rumors later circulated that Deborah

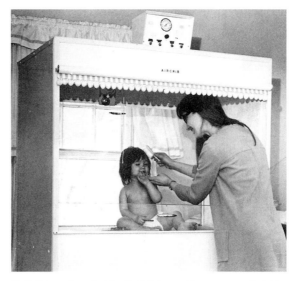

B. F. Skinner invented the Air-Crib to provide a more comfortable, less restrictive infant bed than the traditional crib with its bars and blankets. The baby in this Air-Crib is Skinner's granddaughter Lisa, with her mother, Julie.

had gone insane or killed herself. Actually, both of Skinner's daughters turned out to be perfectly normal and very successful.

Skinner aroused strong passions in both his supporters and his detractors. Perhaps the issue that most provoked and angered people was his insistence that free will is an illusion. Human beings, he said, just like any other animal, are shaped by their environments and their genetic heritage. Skinner therefore refused to credit personal traits (such as curiosity) or mental events (such as goals and motives) for anyone's accomplishments, including his own. Indeed, he regarded himself not as a "self" but as a "repertoire of behaviors"

resulting from an environment that encouraged looking, searching, and investigating (Bjork, 1993).

Skinner, who was a kind and mild-mannered man, felt that it would be unethical *not* to try to improve human behavior by applying behavioral principles. He practiced what he preached, proposing many ways to improve society and reduce human suffering. In old age, he wrote a book showing how behavioral principles can help the elderly cope with mental and physical losses. At the height of public criticism of Skinner, in 1972, the American Humanist Association recognized his efforts on behalf of humanity by honoring him with its Humanist of the Year Award.

QUICK QUIZ

Can you apply the principles of operant conditioning to your own quiz-taking behavior?

In each of the following situations, choose the best alternative, and give your reason for choosing it.

1. You want your 2-year-old to ask for water with a word instead of a grunt. Should you give him water when he says "wa-wa" or wait until his pronunciation improves?

2. Your roommate keeps interrupting your studying even though you have asked her to stop. Should you ignore her completely or occasionally respond for the sake of good manners?

3. Your father, who rarely writes to you, has finally sent a letter. Should you reply quickly or wait a while so he will know how it feels to be ignored?

Answers:

1. You should reinforce "wa-wa," an approximation of *water,* because complex behaviors need to be shaped.   2. From a behavioral view, you should ignore her completely because intermittent reinforcement (attention) could cause her interruptions to persist.   3. If you want to encourage letter writing, you should reply quickly because immediate reinforcement is more effective than delayed reinforcement.

What's Ahead

- Why do efforts to "crack down" on wrongdoers often go awry?
- What's the best way to discourage a child from throwing tantrums?
- Why does paying children for good grades sometimes backfire?

8.4 Operant Conditioning in Real Life

Operant principles can clear up many mysteries about why people behave as they do, and why, in spite of all the well-meaning motivational semi-

behavior modification
The application of conditioning techniques to teach new responses or to reduce or eliminate maladaptive or problematic behavior.

nars they attend or resolutions they make, they have trouble changing when they want to. If life at work and at home remains full of the same old reinforcers, punishers, and discriminative stimuli (a grumpy boss, an unresponsive spouse, a refrigerator stocked with high-fat goodies), any new responses that have been acquired may fail to generalize.

To help people change unwanted, dangerous, or self-defeating habits, behaviorists have carried operant principles out of the laboratory and into the wider world of the classroom, athletic field, prison, mental hospital, nursing home, rehabilitation ward, child-care center, factory, and office. The use of operant techniques (and classical ones) in such real-world settings is called **behavior modification.**

Behavior modification has had some enormous successes. Behaviorists have taught parents how to toilet-train their children in only a few sessions (Azrin & Foxx, 1974). They have taught autistic children who have never before spoken to use a vocabulary of several hundred words (Lovaas, 1977). They have trained disturbed and mentally retarded adults to communicate, mingle socially with others, and earn a living (Lent, 1968; McLeod, 1985). They have taught brain-damaged patients to control inappropriate behavior, focus their attention, and improve their language abilities (McGlynn, 1990). And they have helped ordinary folk eliminate unwanted habits, such as smoking and nail biting, or acquire wanted ones, such as practicing the piano or studying.

Yet when people try to apply the principles of conditioning to commonplace problems, their efforts sometimes miss the mark. Both punishment and reinforcement have their pitfalls, as we are about to see.

The Pros and Cons of Punishment

In his novel *Walden Two* (1948/1976), Skinner imagined a utopia in which reinforcers were used so wisely that undesirable behavior was rare. Unfortunately, we do not live in a utopia; bad habits and antisocial acts abound, and we are faced with how to get rid of them.

An obvious approach might seem to be punishment. Most Western countries have banned physical punishment of schoolchildren by principals and teachers, but in many parts of the United States, schools still permit it for disruptiveness, vandalism, and other kinds of misbehavior. The United States is also far more likely than any other developed country to jail its citizens for nonviolent crimes such as drug use and to enact the ultimate punishment—the death penalty—for violent crimes. And of course in daily life, people punish one another constantly, by yelling, scolding, fining, and sulking. Does all this punishment work?

When Punishment Works. Sometimes punishment is unquestionably effective. Some highly disturbed children have been known to chew their own fingers to the bone, stick objects in their eyes, or tear out their hair. You cannot ignore such behavior because the children will seriously injure themselves. You cannot respond with concern and affection because you may unwittingly reward the behavior. But immediately punishing the self-destructive behavior eliminates it (Lovaas,

Thinking Critically About Punishment

1977; Lovaas, Schreibman, & Koegel, 1974). Mild punishers, such as a spray of water in the face, or even a firm "No!" are often just as effective as strong ones, such as electric shock.

Punishment can also deter some young criminals from repeating their offenses. A study of the criminal records of all Danish men born between 1944 and 1947 (nearly 29,000 men), focused on repeat arrests (recidivism) through age 26 (Brennan & Sarnoff, 1994). After any given arrest, punishment reduced rates of subsequent arrests, for both minor and serious crimes (though recidivism still remained fairly high). Contrary to the researchers' expectations, however, the severity of punishment made no difference: Fines and probation were about as effective as jail time. What mattered most was the *consistency* of the punishment. This is understandable: When punishment is inconsistent—when lawbreakers sometimes get away with their crimes—their behavior is intermittently reinforced and therefore becomes resistant to extinction.

Unfortunately, that is exactly the situation in the United States. Young offenders are punished far less consistently than they are in Denmark, often because prosecutors, juries, and judges do not want to condemn them to mandatory prison terms. Because the courts have no other options for punishment, they may merely admonish the offenders and set them free (Brennan & Sarnoff, 1994). Ironically, then, policies that mandate severe punishment can actually lead to ineffective punishment—or to no punishment at all.

In sum, these results show that punishment can reduce recidivism, but they also show why harsh sentencing laws and simplistic efforts to "crack down" on wrongdoers often fail or even backfire. Indeed, despite its high incarceration rates, the United States has a far higher rate of violent crime than other developed countries do. Moreover, crime rates in the various states show no consistent correlation with rates of incarceration or the imposition of the death penalty (Currie, 1998).

When Punishment Fails. What about punishment that occurs every day, in families, schools, and workplaces? Laboratory and field studies find that it, too, often fails, for several reasons:

1 *People often administer punishment inappropriately or mindlessly.* They swing in a blind rage or shout things they don't mean, applying punishment so broadly that it covers all sorts of irrelevant behaviors. And even when people are not carried away by anger, they often misunderstand

Why do so many people ignore warnings and threats of punishment?

the proper application of punishment. One student told us his parents used to punish their children before leaving them alone for the evening because of all the naughty things they were *going* to do. Naturally, the children did not bother to behave like angels.

2 *The recipient of punishment often responds with anxiety, fear, or rage.* Through a process of classical conditioning, these emotional side effects may then generalize to the entire situation in which the punishment occurs—the place, the person delivering the punishment, and the circumstances. These negative emotional reactions can create more problems than the punishment solves. A teenager who has been severely punished may strike back or run away. A spouse who is constantly abused will feel bitter and resentful and is likely to retaliate with small acts of hostility. Being physically punished in childhood is a risk factor for depression, low self-esteem, violent behavior, and many other problems (Barrish, 1996; Straus & Kantor, 1994; Weiss et al., 1992).

3 *The effectiveness of punishment is often temporary, depending heavily on the presence of the punishing person or circumstances.* All of us can probably remember some transgressions of childhood that we never dared commit when our parents were around but that we promptly resumed as soon as they were gone. All we learned was not to get caught.

4 *Most misbehavior is hard to punish immediately.* Punishment, like reward, works best if it quickly follows a response. But outside the laboratory, rapid punishment is often hard to achieve,

and during the delay, the behavior may be reinforced many times. For example, if you punish your dog when you get home for getting into the doggie treats and eating them all up, the punishment will not do any good: Your pet's misbehavior has already been reinforced by all those delicious goodies.

5 *Punishment conveys little information.* If it immediately follows the misbehavior, punishment may tell the recipient what *not* to do. But it does not communicate what the person (or animal) *should* do. For example, spanking a toddler for messing in her pants will not teach her to use the potty chair, and scolding a student for learning slowly will not teach him to learn more quickly.

6 *An action intended to punish may instead be reinforcing because it brings attention.* Indeed, in some cases, angry attention may be just what the offender is after. If a mother yells at a child who is throwing a tantrum, the very act of yelling may give him what he wants—a reaction from her. In the schoolroom, teachers who scold children in front of other students, thus putting them in the limelight, often unwittingly reward the very misbehavior they are trying to eliminate.

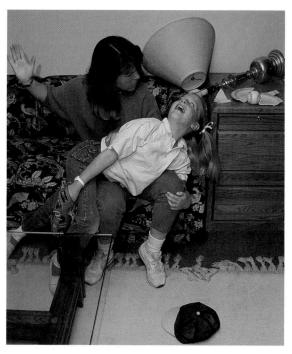

Many harried parents resort to physical punishment without being aware of its many negative consequences for themselves and their children. Based on your reading of this chapter, what alternatives does this mother have?

Because of these drawbacks, most psychologists believe that punishment, especially severe punishment, is a poor way to eliminate unwanted behavior in most situations. When punishment must be used, these guidelines should be kept in mind: (1) It should not involve physical abuse—for example, parents can use "time-outs" and loss of privileges instead of hitting; (2) it should be accompanied by information about what kind of behavior would be appropriate; and (3) it should be followed, whenever possible, by the reinforcement of desirable behavior.

Fortunately, a good alternative to punishment exists: extinction of the responses you want to discourage. Of course, the simplest form of extinction—ignoring the behavior—is often hard to carry out. It is not easy to ignore a child nagging for a cookie before dinner, a roommate interrupting your concentration, or a dog barking its lungs out. And ignoring the behavior is not always appropriate. A teacher cannot ignore a child who is hitting a playmate. The dog owner who ignores Fido's backyard barking may soon hear "barking" of another sort from the neighbors. A parent whose child is a video-game addict cannot ignore the behavior, because playing video games is rewarding to the child. One solution: Combine extinction of undesirable acts with reinforcement of alternative ones. For example, the parent of a video-game addict might ignore the child's pleas for "just one more game" and at the same time praise the child for doing something else that is incompatible with video-game playing, such as reading or playing basketball.

The Problems with Reward

So far, we have been praising the virtues of reinforcement. But like punishers, rewards do not always work as expected. Let's look at two complications that arise when people try to use them.

Thinking Critically About Rewards

Misuse of Rewards. Suppose you are a fourth-grade teacher, and a student has just turned in a paper full of grammatical and punctuation errors. This child has little self-confidence and is easily discouraged. What should you do?

Many people think you should give the paper a high mark anyway, in order to bolster the child's self-esteem. Teachers everywhere are handing out lavish praise and high grades in hopes that students' academic performance will improve as they

GABLE
THE GLOBE AND MAIL
Toronto
CANADA

learn to "feel good about themselves." One obvious result has been grade inflation at all levels of education. In many colleges and universities, C's, which once meant "average" or "satisfactory," are nearly extinct.

The problem, from a behavioral point of view, is that to be effective, rewards *must be tied to the behavior you are trying to increase.* When rewards are dispensed indiscriminately, they become meaningless because they no longer reinforce desired behavior. As behavioral principles would predict, when teachers or parents praise mediocre work, that is just what they get (Kohn, 1993). Lillian Katz (1993), a professor of early childhood education, once wrote that real self-esteem does not come from "cheap success in a succession of trivial tasks," or from phony flattery, gold stars, or happy faces drawn by the teacher. It emerges from effort, persistence, and the gradual acquisition of skills, and it is nurtured by a teacher's genuine appreciation of the *content* of the child's work (Damon, 1995). In the case of the child who turned in a poorly written paper, the teacher can praise its strengths but should also give feedback on the paper's weaknesses and show the child how to correct them.

Why Rewards Can Backfire. A little girl we know came home from school one day in a huff after her teacher announced that good work would be rewarded with play money that could later be exchanged for privileges. "Doesn't she think I can learn without being bribed?" the child asked her mother indignantly.

This child's reaction illustrates another problem in the use of reinforcers. Most of our examples

GET INVOLVED

WHAT'S REINFORCING YOUR BEHAVIOR?

For each activity that you do, indicate whether the reinforcers are extrinsic or intrinsic.

	Reinforcers mostly extrinsic	Reinforcers mostly intrinsic	Reinforcers about equally extrinsic and intrinsic
Studying	_____	_____	_____
Housework	_____	_____	_____
Worship	_____	_____	_____
Grooming	_____	_____	_____
Job	_____	_____	_____
Dating	_____	_____	_____
Attending class	_____	_____	_____
Reading unrelated to school	_____	_____	_____
Sports	_____	_____	_____
Cooking	_____	_____	_____

Is there an area of your life in which you'd like intrinsic reinforcement to play a larger role? What can you do to make that happen?

---

extrinsic reinforcers
Reinforcers that are not inherently related to the activity being reinforced, such as money, prizes, and praise.

intrinsic reinforcers
Reinforcers that are inherently related to the activity being reinforced, such as enjoyment of the task and the satisfaction of accomplishment.

of operant conditioning have involved **extrinsic reinforcers,** which come from an outside source and are not inherently related to the activity being reinforced. Money, praise, gold stars, applause, hugs, and thumbs-up signs are all extrinsic reinforcers. But people (and probably some other animals, too) also work for **intrinsic reinforcers,** such as enjoyment of the task and the satisfaction of accomplishment. As psychologists have applied operant conditioning in real-world settings, they have found that extrinsic reinforcement sometimes becomes too much of a good thing: If you focus on it exclusively, it can kill the pleasure of doing something for its own sake.

Consider what happened when psychologists gave nursery-school children the chance to draw with felt-tipped pens (Lepper, Greene, & Nisbett, 1973). The children already liked this activity and readily took it up during free play. First, the researchers recorded how long each child spontaneously played with the pens. Then they told some of the children that if they would draw with felt-tipped pens for a man who had

come "to see what kinds of pictures boys and girls like to draw with Magic Markers," they would get a prize, a "Good Player Award" complete with gold seal and red ribbon. After drawing for six minutes, each child got the award, as promised. Other children did not expect a reward and were not given one.

A week later, the researchers again observed the children's free play. Those children who had expected and received a reward were spending much less time with the pens than they had before the start of the experiment. In contrast, children who were not given an award continued to show as much interest in playing with the pens as they had initially, as you can see in Figure 8.6. Similar results occurred when older children were or were not rewarded for working on academic tasks.

Because promised rewards (otherwise known as bribes) can be effective in the short term and can sometimes increase test scores by boosting students' motivation, some educators advocate using more of them. But motivation to do well on a test is not the same thing as motivation to learn. In a study of 9-year-olds and their mothers, half of the mothers were told to encourage learning for the intrinsic pleasure of it, and half were told to reward high grades and punish low ones. A year later, the children in the first group had higher motivation and better school performance. For those in the second group, extrinsic rewards and punishments actually seemed to impede academic achievement (Gottfried, Fleming, & Gottfried, 1994).

Why should extrinsic rewards undermine the pleasure of doing something for its own sake? One possibility is that when we are paid for an activity, we interpret it as work. It is as if we say to ourselves, "I'm doing this because I'm being paid for it. Because I'm being paid, it must be something I wouldn't do if I didn't have to." When the reward is withdrawn, we refuse to "work" any longer. Or perhaps, because we regard extrinsic rewards as controlling, they reduce our sense of autonomy and choice ("I guess I should just do what I'm told to do—and *only* what I'm told to do") (Deci & Ryan, 1987). A third, more behavioral explanation is that extrinsic reinforcement sometimes raises the rate of responding above some optimal, enjoyable level. Then the activity really does become work.

However, extrinsic rewards do not always weaken the impact of intrinsic ones. If you get money, a high grade, or a trophy for doing a task *well,* rather than for just doing it, your intrinsic motivation is not likely to decline (Dickinson, 1989; Eisenberger & Cameron, 1996, 1998). If you have always been crazy about reading or playing the banjo, you will probably keep reading or playing even when you are not getting a grade or applause for doing so (Mawhinney, 1990).

So, what is the take-home message about extrinsic rewards? First, sometimes they are necessary: Few people would trudge off to work every morning if they never got paid; and in the classroom, teachers may need to offer incentives to unmotivated students. Second, extrinsic rewards should be used sparingly, so that intrinsic pleasure in an activity can blossom. As one mother wrote in *Newsweek,* children need to discover for themselves "the joy of music from songs, the power of mathematics from counting and all of human wisdom from reading" (Skreslet, 1987). And finally, educators and employers can avoid the trap of either–or thinking by recognizing that most people do their best

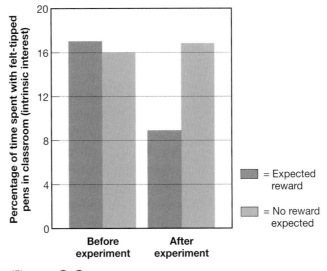

Figure 8.6
Turning Play into Work

Extrinsic rewards can sometimes reduce the intrinsic pleasure of an activity. When preschoolers were promised a prize for drawing with felt-tipped pens, the behavior temporarily increased. But after the children got their prizes, they spent less time with the pens than they had before the study began.

when they get tangible rewards *and* when they have interesting, challenging, and varied kinds of work to do.

Effective behavior modification, as you can see, is not only a science but an art. In "Taking Psychology with You," we offer additional guidelines for mastering that art.

"That is the correct answer, Billy, but I'm afraid you don't win anything for it."

QUICK QUIZ

We know that you are mastering the art of mastering quizzes.

A. According to behavioral principles, what is happening here?

   1. An adolescent whose parents have hit him for minor transgressions since he was small runs away from home.

   2. A young woman whose parents paid her to clean her room while she was growing up is a slob when she moves to her own apartment.

   3. Two parents scold their young daughter every time they catch her sucking her thumb. The thumb sucking continues anyway.

B. In a fee-for-service system of health care, doctors are paid for each visit by a patient or for each service performed; the longer the visit, the higher the fee. In contrast, some American health maintenance organizations (HMOs) pay their doctors a fixed amount per patient for the entire year. If the amount spent is less, the physician gets a bonus, and in some systems, if the amount spent is more, the physician must pay a penalty. Given what you know about operant conditioning, what are the potential advantages and disadvantages of each system?

Answers:

A. 1. The physical punishment was painful, and through a process of classical conditioning, the situation in which it occurred also became unpleasant. Because escape from an unpleasant stimulus is negatively reinforcing, the boy ran away. 2. Extrinsic reinforcers are no longer available, and room-cleaning behavior has been extinguished. Also, extrinsic rewards may have displaced the intrinsic satisfaction of having a tidy room. 3. Punishment has failed, possibly because it rewards thumb sucking with attention or because thumb sucking still brings the child pleasure whenever the parents are not around. B. In a fee-for-service system, the doctor is likely to provide the attention and tests that ill patients need. However, this system also rewards doctors for unnecessary tests and patient visits, contributing to the explosion in health-care costs. The policies of the HMOs help contain these costs, but because doctors are rewarded for reducing costs and in some cases penalized for running up charges, some patients may not get the attention or services they need.

What's Ahead

- How might watching violence on TV make (some) people more aggressive?

- Why do two people often learn different lessons from exactly the same experience?

8.5 Social–Cognitive Learning Theories

8.2

For half a century, most American learning theories held that learning could be explained by specifying the behavioral "ABCs"—*antecedents* (events preceding behavior), *behaviors,* and *consequences.* Yet even during the early glory years of behaviorism, a few behaviorists rebelled against explanations of behavior that relied solely on conditioning principles.

In the 1940s, two social scientists proposed a modification they called *social-learning theory* (Dollard & Miller, 1950). Most human learning, they argued, is acquired by observing other people in a social context, rather than through standard conditioning procedures. By the 1960s and 1970s, social-learning theory was in full bloom, and a new element had been added: the human capacity for higher-level cognitive processes. Its proponents agreed with behaviorists that human beings, along with the rat and the rabbit, are subject to the laws of operant and classical conditioning. But they added that human beings, unlike the rat and the rabbit, are full of attitudes, beliefs, and expectations that affect the way they acquire information, make decisions, reason, and solve problems. These mental processes affect what individuals will do at any given moment and also, more generally, the personality traits they develop (see Chapter 2).

Because of this emphasis on mental processes, one leading theorist, Walter Mischel, has called his approach *cognitive social-learning theory* (Mischel, 1973; Mischel & Shoda, 1995); and another, Albert Bandura, calls his *social–cognitive theory* (Bandura, 1986). We will use the general term **social–cognitive theories** to include all modern social-learning approaches (Barone, Maddux, & Snyder, 1997).

Learning by Observing

Late one night, a friend who lives in a rural area was awakened by a loud clattering and banging. Her whole family raced outside to find the source of the commotion. A raccoon had knocked over a "raccoon-proof" garbage can and seemed to be demonstrating to an assembly of other raccoons how to open it: If you jump up and down on the can's side, the lid will pop off.

According to our friend, the observing raccoons learned from this episode how to open stubborn garbage cans, and the observing humans learned how smart raccoons can be. In short, they all benefited from **observational learning:** learning by watching what others do and what happens to them for doing it.

Behaviorists have always acknowledged the importance of observational learning, which they call *vicarious conditioning,* and have tried to explain it in stimulus–response terms. But social–cognitive theorists believe that in human beings, observational learning cannot be fully understood without taking into account the thought processes of the learner (Meltzoff & Gopnik, 1993). They emphasize the knowledge that results when a person sees a model—another person—behaving in certain ways and experiencing the consequences (Bandura, 1977).

None of us would last long without observational learning. We would have to learn to avoid oncoming cars by walking into traffic and suffering the consequences or learn to swim by jumping into a deep pool and flailing around. Learning would be not only dangerous but also inefficient. Parents and teachers would be busy 24 hours a day shaping children's behavior. Bosses would have to stand over their employees' desks, rewarding every little link in the complex behavioral chains we call typing, report writing, and accounting.

Many years ago, Albert Bandura and his colleagues showed just how important observational learning is, especially for children who are learning the rules of social behavior (Bandura, Ross, & Ross, 1963). The researchers had nursery-school children watch a short film of two men, Rocky and Johnny, playing with toys. (Apparently the chil-

dren did not think this behavior was the least bit odd.) In the film, Johnny refuses to share his toys, and Rocky responds by clobbering him. Rocky's aggressive actions are rewarded because he winds up with all the toys. Poor Johnny sits dejectedly in the corner, while Rocky marches off in triumph with a sack full of his loot and a hobbyhorse under his arm.

After viewing the film, each child was left alone for 20 minutes in a playroom full of toys, including some of the items shown in the film. Watching through a one-way mirror, the researchers found that the children were much more aggressive in their play than a control group that had not seen the film. Some children imitated Rocky almost exactly. At the end of the session, one little girl even asked the experimenter for a sack!

Like father, like daughter. Parents can be powerful role models.

Of course, children imitate positive activities, too. Matt Groening, the creator of the cartoon *The Simpsons,* decided it would be funny if the Simpsons' 8-year-old daughter Lisa played the baritone sax. Sure enough, across the country, little girls began imitating her. Cynthia Sikes, a saxophone teacher in New York, told *The New York Times* (January 14, 1996) that "when the show started, I got an influx of girls coming up to me saying, 'I want to play the saxophone because Lisa Simpson plays the saxophone.'" And Groening says his mail regularly includes photos of girls holding up their saxophones.

Behavior and the Mind

Early behaviorists liked to compare the mind to an engineer's hypothetical "black box," a device whose workings must be inferred because they cannot be observed directly. To them, the box contained irrelevant wiring; it was enough to know that pushing a button on the box would produce a predictable response.

But even as early as the 1930s, a few behaviorists could not resist peeking into that black box. Edward Tolman (1938) committed virtual heresy at the time by noting that his rats, when pausing at turning points in a maze, seemed to be *deciding* which way to go. Moreover, the animals

social–cognitive theories
Theories that emphasize how behavior is learned and maintained through observation and imitation of others, positive consequences, and cognitive processes such as plans, expectations, and beliefs.

observational learning
A process in which an individual learns new responses by observing the behavior of another (a model) rather than through direct experience; sometimes called *vicarious conditioning.*

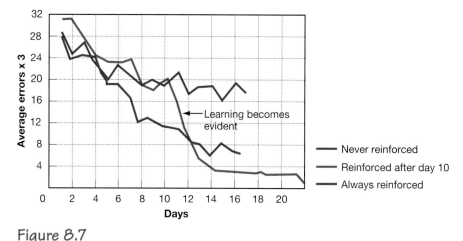

Figure 8.7

Latent Learning

In a classic experiment, rats that always found food in a maze made fewer and fewer errors in reaching the food (green curve). Rats that never found food showed little improvement (blue curve). Rats in a third group got no food for ten days, and then were given food on the eleventh (red curve). These animals showed rapid improvement from then on, quickly equaling the performance of the rats that had received food from the start. This result suggests that learning involves cognitive changes that can occur in the absence of reinforcement and that may not be acted on until a reinforcer becomes available (Tolman & Honzik, 1930).

sometimes seemed to be learning even without any reinforcement. What, he wondered, was going on in their little rat brains that might account for this puzzle?

In a classic experiment, Tolman and his colleague Chase Honzik (1930) placed three groups of rats in mazes and observed the rats' behavior each day for more than two weeks. The rats in Group 1 always found food at the end of the maze. Group 2 never found food. Group 3 found no food for ten days but then received food on the eleventh. The Group 1 rats, whose behavior had been reinforced with food, quickly learned to head straight for the end of the maze without going down blind alleys, whereas Group 2 rats did not learn to go to the end. But the Group 3 rats were different. For ten days they appeared to follow no particular route. Then, on the eleventh day, when food was introduced, they quickly learned to run to the end of the maze. By the next day, they were doing as well as the Group 1 rats, which had been rewarded from the beginning (see Figure 8.7).

Group 3 had demonstrated **latent learning,** learning that is not immediately expressed. A great deal of human learning also remains latent until circumstances allow or require it to be expressed. A driver finds her way to Fourth and Kumquat Streets using a new route she has never used before. A little boy observes a parent setting the

table or tightening a screw but does not act on this learning for years; then he finds he knows how to do these things, even though he has never done them before.

Latent learning not only occurs without any obvious reinforcer; it also raises questions about what, exactly, is learned during learning. In the Tolman and Honzik study, the rats that did not get any food until the eleventh day seemed to have acquired a mental representation of the maze. Similarly, the driver taking a new route can do so because she already knows how the city is laid out. More generally, according to social–cognitive theories, what we learn in both observational and latent learning is not a specific response, but *knowledge* about responses and their consequences. We learn how the world is organized, which paths lead to which places, and which actions can produce which payoffs. This knowledge permits us to be creative and flexible in reaching our goals.

Social–cognitive theories also emphasize the importance of people's *perceptions* in what they learn: perceptions of the models they observe and also perceptions of themselves (Bandura, 1994). Because people differ in their attitudes, expectations, and perceptions, they can live through the same event and come away with entirely different lessons from it. All siblings know this. One may

latent learning
A form of learning that is not immediately expressed in an overt response; it occurs without obvious reinforcement.

regard being grounded by their father as evidence of his all-around meanness, and another may see the same behavior as evidence of his care and concern for his children.

Individual differences in perceptions and interpretations help explain why violent television programs do not have the same impact on all children. As the Rocky and Johnny findings would predict, some children do imitate the incessant aggression they observe on television and in movies (APA Commission on Violence and Youth, 1993; Eron, 1995). But not all of them do; some just are not interested, and others find violence too scary or stupid to watch.

As we saw in Chapter 2, behaviorists would say that we acquire habitual ways of behaving because they have been rewarded over a lifetime. Social–cognitive theorists, however, maintain that our learned habits and beliefs eventually acquire a life of their own, coming to exert their own effects on behavior. In fact, internalized beliefs, perceptions, and goals may have a greater impact than external rewards and punishers, as when people sacrifice money and love for the sake of a great ambition or persist in the quest of a life's dream in spite of constant setbacks and losses.

Today, most psychologists accept the social–cognitive emphasis on mental processes, believing that people act as they do in part because of their beliefs, expectations, and perceptions. To the true behaviorist, however, cognitive explanations are misleading fictions, and nothing is to be gained by using them; people act as they do because of reinforcers and punishers in the environment. As behaviorist William Baum (1994) wrote, "I no more have a mind than I have a fairy godmother. I can talk to you about my mind or about my fairy godmother; that cannot make either of them less fictional. No one has ever seen either one . . . such talk is no help in a science."

The debates between behaviorists and cognitive psychologists over the nature of learning promise to continue. Yet in practice, behavioral and cognitive approaches are often combined. Many therapists, for example, use a combination of behavioral and cognitive strategies to treat people in psychotherapy (see Chapter 11).

The behavioral and social–cognitive approaches to learning share a fundamental optimism about the possibilities of change for individuals and societies. In Skinner's utopian novel *Walden Two,* the main character, Frazier, exclaims, "The one fact that I would cry from every housetop is this: The Good Life is waiting for us—here and now! We have the necessary techniques, both material and psychological, to create a full and satisfying life for everyone."

To modify self-defeating, inappropriate, or dangerous behavior, say learning theorists—to achieve that "good life"—we can do more than just sit around hoping that people will magically have a change of heart. Instead, we can focus on changing the reinforcers, role models, and media messages that affect people's attitudes and actions. In our homes and workplaces, have we arranged things so that reinforcers are given for creativity and active participation, or merely for mindless consumerism and passive entertainments? Do we find intrinsic satisfaction and pride in what we do, or do we settle for extrinsic rewards such as money or gold stars?

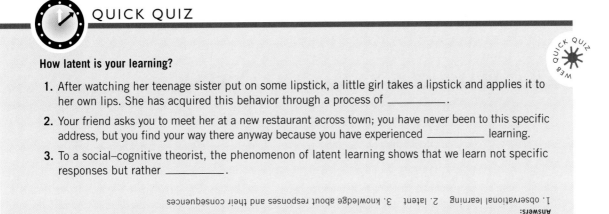

QUICK QUIZ

How latent is your learning?

1. After watching her teenage sister put on some lipstick, a little girl takes a lipstick and applies it to her own lips. She has acquired this behavior through a process of _____.

2. Your friend asks you to meet her at a new restaurant across town; you have never been to this specific address, but you find your way there anyway because you have experienced _____ learning.

3. To a social–cognitive theorist, the phenomenon of latent learning shows that we learn not specific responses but rather _____.

Answers:
1. observational learning   2. latent   3. knowledge about responses and their consequences

PSYCHOLOGY IN THE NEWS, REVISITED

How can the behavioral and social–cognitive learning principles covered in this chapter help us think about the zero-tolerance policies described in our opening story?

Findings on learning certainly do not rule out all use of punishment: Few people would want school authorities to ignore students who bring guns and knives to class. But severe punishment is not always the answer. In the study of the Danish criminals, you will recall, jail was no more effective than fines and probation; what mattered most was the consistency of punishment.

Moreover, as we have seen, punishment often brings its own set of problems. When children or adults have behaved badly, punishing them conveys little information about why their behavior was wrong or about how they might solve their problems constructively. And for students who are the recipients of punishment that is applied mindlessly and rigidly, as in the cases cited in our opening news story, punishment often backfires, creating a climate of fear, tension, and anger at authorities for going after trivial offenses with the same punitiveness as serious ones. Human beings, as we have seen, bring their *minds* to their experiences, and if they perceive that their punishment is unfair, inequitable, or overly harsh, their bad behavior is unlikely to change.

Crackdowns that lump together all kinds of wrongdoing, with one-size-fits-all penalties, also deflect attention from other ways of dealing with truly serious cases of antisocial behavior—such as treatment programs for troubled children and teenagers. (Such programs of course, are less con- venient and more costly than simplistic zero-tolerance rules.) Learning principles also direct us to identify the rewards and payoffs that promote disruptive or dangerous behavior, withdraw those rewards and payoffs, and train parents and teachers to reinforce civility, order, and friendly behavior instead. In addition, as social–cognitive theories remind us a society that truly wishes to reduce violence and crime will not glamorize bullies or vigilantes, glorify violence in sports, or look the other way when parents model violence by using it against their children or each other. For example, schools that want to eliminate student violence will not tolerate parents who verbally or physically assault umpires at a Little League game.

Three of the critical–thinking guidelines emphasized in this book—"examine the evidence," "avoid emotional reasoning," and "examine assumptions"—are especially important as we assess zero-tolerance policies. Although school violence and bullying are indeed pressing problems, overall rates of violent crime among young people have actually been falling for several years. It is easy, when you hear about a horrible but unusual incident of violence, to react by wanting to cast a wide punitive net, one that catches the minnows along with the piranhas. But the results may not be what you intended, for the reasons we have discussed.

The real world, alas, will never be as peaceful and law-abiding as Skinner's Walden Two. Violence, whether among children or adults, is a complex problem with many causes, not all of them easily controllable. Still, learning principles do give us cause for hope about our ability to change things for the better. By using learning techniques, we can fashion healthier environments for ourselves, our families, and our fellow human beings—so long as we exercise those techniques with patience, care, and good judgment.

TAKING PSYCHOLOGY WITH YOU

Shape Up!

Operant conditioning can seem deceptively simple—a few rewards here, a bit of shaping there, and you're done. In practice, though, behavior modification can be full of unwanted surprises, even in the hands of experts. Here are a few things to keep in mind if you want to modify someone's behavior:

• *Accentuate the positive.* Most people notice bad behavior more than good and therefore miss opportunities to use reinforcers. Parents, for example, often scold a child for bed-wetting but fail to give praise for dry sheets in the morning; or they punish a child for poor grades but fail to reward studying.

• *Reinforce small improvements.* A common error is to withhold reinforcement until behavior is perfect (which may be never). Has your child's grade in math improved from a D to a C? Has your favorite date, who is usually an awful cook, managed to serve up a half-decent omelet? Has your messy roommate left some dirty dishes in the sink but vacuumed the rug? It's probably time for a reinforcer. On the other hand, you don't want to overdo praise or give it insincerely. Gushing about every tiny step in the right direction will cause your praise to lose its value, and soon nothing less than a standing ovation will do.

• *Find the right reinforcers.* You may have to experiment a bit to find which reinforcers a person (or animal) actually wants. In general, it is good to use a variety of reinforcers because the same ones used again and again can get boring. Reinforcers, by the way, do not have to be *things.* You can also use valued activities, such as going out to dinner, to reinforce other behavior.

• *Always examine what you are reinforcing.* It is easy to reinforce undesirable behavior simply by responding to it. Suppose someone is always yelling at you at the slightest provocation, and you want the shouting to stop. If you respond to it at all, whether by crying, apologizing, or yelling back, you are likely to reinforce it. An alternative might be to explain in a calm voice that you will henceforth not respond to complaints unless they are communicated without yelling—and then, if the yelling continues, walk away. When the person does speak civilly, you can reward this behavior with your attention and goodwill.

• *Analyze the reasons for a person's undesirable behavior before responding to it.* A child screaming in a supermarket may be saying, "I'm going out of my head with boredom. Help!" A lover who sulks may be saying, "I'm not sure you really care about me; I'm frightened." Once you understand the purpose of someone's behavior, you may be more effective in dealing with it.

These guidelines apply to your own behavior, as well. Assume, for example, that you want to get yourself to study more. Here are some behavioral strategies for increasing the time you spend with your books:

• *Analyze the situation.* Are there circumstances that keep you from studying, such as a friend who is always pressuring you to go out or a rock band that practices next door? If so, you need to change the discriminative stimuli in your environment during study periods. Try to find a comfortable, cheerful, quiet, well-lit place. Not only will you concentrate better, but you may also have positive emotional responses to the environment, which may generalize to the activity of studying.

• *Set realistic goals.* Goals should be demanding but achievable. If a goal is too vague, as in "I'm going to work harder," you don't know what action to take to reach it or how to know when you have done so (what does "harder" mean?). If your goal is focused, as in "I am going to study two hours every evening instead of one," or "I will read 25 pages instead of 15," you have specified both a course of action and a goal you can achieve (and reward).

• *Keep records.* Chart your progress in some way, perhaps by making a graph. This will keep you honest, and the progress you see on the graph will serve as a secondary reinforcer.

• *Don't punish yourself.* If you did not study enough last week, don't brood about it or berate yourself with self-defeating thoughts, such as "I'll never be a good student" or "I'm a failure." Think about the coming week instead.

Above all, be patient. Shaping behavior is a creative skill that takes time to learn. Like Rome, new habits cannot be built in a day.

SUMMARY

• Research on *learning* has been heavily influenced by *behaviorism,* which accounts for behavior in terms of observable events without reference to mental entities such as "mind" or "will." Behaviorists have focused on two types of *conditioning:* classical conditioning and operant conditioning.

• *Classical conditioning* was first studied by Russian physiologist Ivan Pavlov. In this type of learning, when a neutral stimulus is paired with an *unconditioned stimulus (US)* that elicits some reflexive *unconditioned response (UR),* the neutral stimulus comes to elicit a similar or related response. The neutral stimulus is then called a *conditioned stimulus (CS),* and the response it elicits is a *conditioned response (CR).* Nearly any kind of involuntary response can become a CR.

• In *extinction,* the conditioned stimulus is repeatedly presented without the unconditioned stimulus, and the conditioned response eventually disappears—although later it may reappear (*spontaneous recovery*). In *higher-order conditioning,* a neutral stimulus becomes a conditioned stimulus by being paired with an already established conditioned stimulus.

In *stimulus generalization,* after a stimulus becomes a conditioned stimulus for some response, other, similar stimuli may produce the same reaction. In *stimulus discrimination,* different responses are made to stimuli that resemble the conditioned stimulus in some way.

• Many theorists believe that what an animal or person learns in classical conditioning is not just an association between the unconditioned and the conditioned stimulus, but information conveyed by one stimulus about another. They cite evidence that the neutral stimulus does not become a CS unless it reliably signals or predicts the US.

Classical Conditioning in Real Life

• Classical conditioning may account for positive emotional responses to particular objects and events, fears and phobias, the acquisition of likes and dislikes, and reactions to medical treatments and placebos. John Watson showed how fears may be learned and then may be unlearned through a process of *counterconditioning.*

Operant Conditioning

- In *operant conditioning*, behavior becomes more likely to occur or less so, depending on its consequences. Responses are generally not reflexive and are more complex than in classical conditioning. Research in this area is closely associated with B. F. Skinner, who called his approach "radical behaviorism."

- In the Skinnerian analysis, a response ("operant") can lead to neutral, reinforcing, or punishing consequences. *Reinforcement* strengthens or increases the probability of a response. *Punishment* weakens or decreases the probability of a response. Immediate consequences usually have a greater effect on a response than do delayed consequences.

- Reinforcers are called *primary* when they are naturally reinforcing (e.g., because they satisfy a biological need) and *secondary* when they have acquired their ability to strengthen a response through association with other reinforcers. A similar distinction is made for punishers.

- Reinforcement (and punishment) may be positive or negative, depending on whether the consequence involves a stimulus that is presented, or one that is removed or avoided. In *positive reinforcement,* something pleasant follows a response; in *negative reinforcement,* something unpleasant is removed following a response. In *positive punishment,* something unpleasant follows the response; in *negative punishment,* something pleasant is removed.

- Using the Skinner box and similar devices, behaviorists have shown that *extinction, stimulus generalization,* and *stimulus discrimination* occur in operant as well as in classical conditioning. A *discriminative stimulus* signals that a response is likely to be followed by a certain type of consequence.

- The pattern of responding in operant conditioning depends in part on the *schedule of reinforcement. Continuous reinforcement* leads to the most rapid learning. However, *intermittent (partial) reinforcement* makes a response more resistant to extinction (and therefore helps account for the persistence of superstitious rituals). One of the most common errors people make is to reward intermittently the responses they would like to eliminate.

- *Shaping* is used to train behaviors with a low probability of occurring spontaneously. Reinforcers are given for *successive approximations* to the desired response, until the desired response is achieved.

- Biology places limits on what an animal or person can learn through operant conditioning. For example, animals sometimes have trouble learning a task because of *instinctive drift.*

Operant Conditioning in Real Life

- *Behavior modification,* the application of conditioning principles, has been used successfully in many settings, but punishment and reinforcement both have their pitfalls.

- Punishment, when used properly, can be effective in discouraging undesirable behavior, including criminal behavior. But it is frequently misused and may have unintended consequences. It is often administered inappropriately because of the emotion of the moment; it may produce rage and fear; its effects are often only temporary; it is hard to administer immediately; it conveys little information about the kind of behavior that is desired; and it may provide attention that is rewarding. Extinction of undesirable behavior, combined with reinforcement of desired behavior, is generally preferable to the use of punishment.

- Reinforcers can also be misused. Rewards that are given out indiscriminately, as in efforts to raise children's self-esteem, do not reinforce desirable behavior. An exclusive reliance on *extrinsic reinforcement* can sometimes undermine the power of *intrinsic reinforcement.* But money and praise do not usually interfere with intrinsic pleasure when a person is rewarded for doing well rather than for merely participating in an activity, or when a person is already highly interested in the activity.

Social–Cognitive Learning Theories

- The 1960s and 1970s saw the increased influence of *social–cognitive theories* of learning, which focus on observational learning and the role played by beliefs, interpretations of events, and other cognitions. In *observational learning,* the learner imitates the behavior of a model. In *latent learning,* no obvious reinforcer may be present during learning, and a response is not expressed until later. Social–cognitive theorists argue that in these types of learning, knowledge, rather than a specific response, is acquired. Because people differ in their perceptions and beliefs, they may learn different lessons from the same event or situation.

- Behavioral and social–cognitive learning theories share a fundamental optimism about the prospects for changing individuals and societies. Learning techniques, however, must be used wisely and carefully, as we saw in our discussion of zero-tolerance policies.

KEY TERMS

LOOKING BACK

- Why would a dog salivate when it sees a lightbulb or hears a buzzer, even though it can't eat these things? (pp. 264–265)

- How can classical conditioning help explain prejudice? (p. 267)

- If you have learned to fear collies, why might you also be scared of sheepdogs? (p. 267)

- Why do advertisers often include pleasant music and gorgeous scenery in ads for their products? (p. 269)

- How would a classical-conditioning theorist explain your irrational fear of heights or mice? (p. 269)

- If you eat licorice and then happen to get the flu, how might your taste for licorice change? (pp. 270–271)

- How can sitting in a doctor's office make you feel sick? (p. 271)

- What do praising a child and quitting your nagging have in common? (p. 274)

- How can operant principles account for superstitious rituals? (pp. 276–277)

- What is the best way to discourage a friend from interrupting you while you're studying? (p. 277)

- How do trainers teach guide dogs to perform the amazing services they do for their owners? (p. 278)

- Why do efforts to "crack down" on wrongdoers often go awry? (pp. 281–282)

- What is the best way to discourage a child from throwing tantrums? (p. 283)

- Why does paying children for good grades sometimes backfire? (pp. 283–285)

- How might watching violence on TV make (some) people more aggressive? (p. 287)

- Why do two people often learn different lessons from exactly the same experience? (pp. 288–289)

Homeowner Fatally Shoots Exchange Student in Cultural Misunderstanding

BATON ROUGE, LA, NOVEMBER 1, 1992. A mistake over the address of a Halloween party yesterday had tragic consequences. Sixteen-year-old Japanese exchange student Yoshihiro Hattori and his friend Webb Haymaker stopped at a house that was covered in Halloween decorations while looking for the party they had been invited to attend. But they had the wrong house. When no one answered the doorbell, Hattori went to see if the party might be in the back yard. The homeowner, Bonnie Peairs, then opened the front door, saw Haymaker in his Halloween costume,

Slain exchange student Yoshihiro Hattori (right) posed with his new American friends after arriving in the United States.

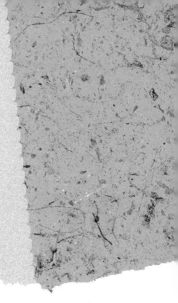

and spotted Hattori running back toward her waving an object (which turned out to be a camera). She panicked and called for her husband to get his gun; Rodney Peairs then grabbed a loaded .44 Magnum and shouted at Yoshihiro to "freeze." The young student, not understanding the command, kept running, and Peairs shot him in the heart, killing him instantly.

Little more than a minute passed between the time that Yoshihiro Hattori rang the doorbell and the time that Rodney Peairs shot him to death.

BEHAVIOR IN SOCIAL AND CULTURAL CONTEXT

How would you explain the actions taken by Bonnie and Rodney Peairs? A learning theorist might seek an explanation in their individual histories, in the examples of violence that all Americans see in the media, and in the ways that the availability of handguns might literally trigger violence. Similarly, researchers in the fields of *social psychology* and *cultural psychology* address the many puzzles of human behavior by emphasizing the external environment rather than internal personality dynamics or individual pathology. But social and cultural psychologists also broaden our vision by examining the entire sociocultural context in which an individual lives. Social psychologists study how social roles, attitudes, relationships, and groups influence people to do things they would not necessarily do on their own—act bravely, mindlessly, aggressively, or even cruelly. Cultural psychologists study the origins of roles, attitudes, and group norms in people's larger cultural worlds—their ethnic, regional, and national communities.

In this book, we have included discussions of social and cultural influences on child-rearing practices, moral development, scores on intelligence tests, love and attachment, the communication of emotion, and many other topics. In this chapter, however, we will focus on the basic social and cultural forces that affect behavior and make human beings less independent than they might think. As you read, ask yourself whether *you* would ever "shoot now and ask questions later," as Rodney

- **ROLES AND RULES**

- **SOCIAL INFLUENCES ON BELIEFS**

- **INDIVIDUALS IN GROUPS**

- **US VERSUS THEM: GROUP IDENTITY**

- **GROUP CONFLICT AND PREJUDICE**

- **PSYCHOLOGY IN THE NEWS, REVISITED**

- **TAKING PSYCHOLOGY WITH YOU TRAVELS ACROSS THE CULTURAL DIVIDE**

Peairs did. Could a social situation or cultural requirement ever induce you to behave in a way that violates your code of ethics? Would you vote to convict Rodney Peairs or acquit him, and how does your culture affect your answer?

When Bonnie Peairs took the witness stand, she wept. "There was no thinking involved," she said. "I wish I could have thought. If I could have just thought." An awareness of social and cultural influences might help us all to act more mindfully and think more critically.

them. Norms are the conventions of everyday life that make interactions with other people predictable and orderly; like a cobweb, they are often as invisible as they are strong. Every society has norms for just about everything in human experience: for conducting courtships, raising children, making decisions, behaving in public places. Some norms are enshrined in law, such as, "A person may not beat up another person, except in self-defense." Some are unspoken cultural understandings, such as, "A man may beat up another man who insults his masculinity." And some are tiny, unspoken regulations that people learn to follow unconsciously, such as, "You may not sing at the top of your lungs on a public bus."

In every society, people also fill a variety of social **roles,** positions that are regulated by norms about how people in those positions should behave. Gender roles define the proper behavior for a man and a woman. Occupational roles determine the correct behavior for a manager and an employee, a professor and a student. Family roles set tasks for parent and child, husband and wife. Certain aspects of every role must be carried out, or there will be penalties—emotional, financial, professional. As a student, for instance, you know just what you have to do to pass your psychology course (or you should by now!).

Most people follow the social roles required of them without being conscious that they are doing so. When they do violate a role requirement, intentionally or unintentionally, they are likely to feel uncomfortable—or other people will try to make them feel uncomfortable. For instance, in your family, whose job is it to buy gifts for parents, send greeting cards to friends, organize parties and prepare the food, remember

What's Ahead

- How do social rules regulate behavior—and what is likely to happen when you violate them?

- Do you have to be mean or disturbed to inflict pain on someone just because an authority tells you to?

- How can ordinary college students be transformed into sadistic prison guards?

- How can people be "entrapped" into violating their moral principles?

norms (social)
Rules that regulate human life, including social conventions, explicit laws, and implicit cultural standards.

role
A given social position that is governed by a set of norms for proper behavior.

9.1 Roles and Rules

"We are all fragile creatures entwined in a cobweb of social constraints," social psychologist Stanley Milgram once said. The constraints he referred to are social **norms,** rules about how we are supposed to act, enforced by threats of punishment if we violate them and promises of reward if we follow

---

GET INVOLVED

DARE TO BE DIFFERENT

Either alone or with a friend, try a mild form of "norm violation" (nothing alarming, obscene, dangerous, or offensive!). For example, stand backwards in line at the grocery store or cafeteria; sit right next to a stranger in the library or at a movie, even when other seats are available; sing or hum loudly for a couple of minutes in a public place; stand "too close" to a friend in conversation. Notice the reactions of onlookers, as well as your own feelings, while you violate this norm. If you do this exercise with someone else, one of you can be the "violator," and your friend can write down the responses of others; then switch places. Was it easy to do this exercise? Why or why not?

an aunt's birthday, and call friends to see how they're doing? Chances are you are thinking of a woman. These activities are considered part of the woman's role in most cultures, and women are usually blamed if they do not carry them out (di Leonardo, 1987; Lott & Maluso, 1993).

Likewise, in your culture what are the role requirements of a "real man"? According to studies conducted with a test called the Male Role Norms Scale, traditional male norms require a man to be strong (e.g., "A man should never back down in the face of trouble"), reject qualities associated with women (e.g., "It bothers me when a man does something that I consider 'feminine'"), keep his problems to himself (e.g., "Nobody respects a man very much who frequently talks about his worries, fears, and problems"), and behave aggressively if threatened (e.g., "Fists are sometimes the only way to get out of a bad situation") (Fischer et al., 1998). When men violate these norms—for example by revealing their fears and worries—they are frequently regarded by both sexes as being "too feminine" and poorly adjusted (Kimmel, 1995; Taffel, 1990).

However, the requirements of the male role, like those for women, are changing rapidly in Western cultures. Many men do not think it is such a great idea to use their fists to "get out

In most cultures, men are required to take on the dangerous, life-threatening roles . . . but it's not always easy to get all of them to do it.

of a bad situation." And many men think it is healthy and appropriate to express their feelings. Male politicians and athletes even cry in public—an act that not long ago would have cost them their careers.

Naturally, people bring their own personalities and interests to the roles they play. Just as two actors will play James Bond differently although they are reading from the same script, you will have your own "reading" of how to play the role of student, friend, parent, or employer. Nonetheless, the requirements of a social role are pretty strong, so strong that they may even cause you to behave in ways that shatter your fundamental sense of the kind of person you are. We turn now to two classic studies that illuminate the power of social roles in our lives.

Many roles in modern life require us to give up individuality, as conveyed by this dazzling image of white-suited referees at the Seoul Olympics. If each referee behaved out of role, the games could not continue. When is it appropriate to suppress your personal desires for the sake of the role, and when not?

The Obedience Study

In the early 1960s, Stanley Milgram (1963, 1974) designed a study that would become world famous. Milgram wanted to know how many people would obey an authority figure when directly ordered to violate their own ethical standards. Participants in the study, however, thought they were part of an experiment on the effects of punishment on learning. Each was assigned, apparently at random, to the role of "teacher." Another person, introduced as a fellow volunteer, was the "learner." Whenever the learner, seated in an adjoining room, made an error in reciting a list of word pairs he was supposed to have memorized, the teacher had to give him an electric shock by depressing a lever on a machine (see Figure 9.1). With each error, the voltage (marked from 0 to 450) was to be increased by another 15 volts. The shock levels on the machine were labeled from "SLIGHT SHOCK" to "DANGER—SEVERE SHOCK" and, finally, ominously, "XXX." In reality, the learners were confederates of Milgram and did not receive any shocks, but none of the teachers ever realized this during the study. The actor-victims played their parts convincingly: As the study continued, they shouted in pain and pleaded to be released, all according to a prearranged script.

Before doing this study, Milgram asked a number of psychiatrists, students, and middle-class adults how many people they thought would "go all the way" to "XXX" on orders from the researcher. The psychiatrists predicted that most people would refuse to go beyond 150 volts, when the learner first demanded to be freed, and that only one person in a thousand, someone who was disturbed and sadistic, would administer the highest voltage. The nonprofessionals agreed with

this prediction, and all of them said that they personally would disobey early in the procedure.

That is not, however, the way the results turned out. Every single person administered some shock to the learner, and about two-thirds of the participants, of all ages and from all walks of life, obeyed to the fullest extent. Many protested to the experimenter, but they backed down when he merely asserted, "The experiment requires that you continue." They obeyed no matter how much the victim shouted for them to stop and no matter how painful the shocks seemed to be. They obeyed even when they themselves were anguished about the pain they believed they were causing. As Milgram (1974) noted, participants would "sweat, tremble, stutter, bite their lips, groan, and dig their fingernails into their flesh"—but still they obeyed.

More than 1,000 people at several American universities eventually went through replications of the Milgram study. Most of them, men and women equally, inflicted what they thought were dangerous amounts of shock to another person. Researchers in other countries have also found high percentages of obedience, ranging to more than 90 percent in Spain and the Netherlands (Meeus & Raaijmakers, 1995; Smith & Bond, 1994).

Milgram and his team subsequently set up several variations of the study to determine the circumstances under which people might disobey the experimenter. They found that virtually nothing the victim did or said changed the likelihood of compliance—even when the victim said he had a heart condition, screamed in agony, or stopped responding entirely, as if he had collapsed. However, people *were* more likely to disobey under the following conditions:

 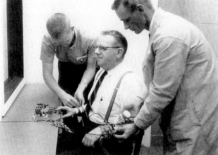

Figure 9.1
The Milgram Obedience Experiment

On the left is Milgram's original shock machine; in 1963, it looked pretty ominous. On the right, the "learner" is being strapped into his chair by the experimenter and the "teacher."

© 1965 By Stanly Milgram. From the filmObedience, distributed by Penn State Media Sales.

- *When the experimenter left the room.* Many people then subverted authority by giving low levels of shock but reporting that they had followed orders.

- *When the victim was right there in the room,* and the teacher had to administer the shock directly to the victim's body.

- *When two experimenters issued conflicting demands* to continue the experiment or to stop at once. In this case, no one kept inflicting shock.

- *When the person ordering them to continue was an ordinary man,* apparently another volunteer, instead of the authoritative experimenter.

- *When the subject worked with peers who refused to go further.* Seeing someone else rebel gave subjects the courage to disobey.

Obedience, Milgram concluded, was more a function of the situation than of the particular personalities of the participants. "The key to [their] behavior," Milgram (1974) summarized, "lies not in pent-up anger or aggression but in the nature of their relationship to authority. They have given themselves to the authority; they see themselves as instruments for the execution of his wishes; once so defined, they are unable to break free."

The Milgram study has had its critics. Some consider it unethical because people were kept in the dark about what was really happening until the session was over (of course, telling them in advance would have invalidated the study) and because many suffered emotional pain (Milgram countered that they would not have felt pain if they had simply disobeyed instructions). Others question the conclusion that personality traits always have less influence on behavior than the demands of the situation; certain traits, such as hostility and rigidity, do increase obedience to authority in real life (Blass, 1993, 2000).

Some psychologists also object to the parallel Milgram drew between the behavior of the study's participants and the brutality of the Nazis and others who have committed acts of barbarism in the name of duty (Berkowitz, 1999; Darley, 1995). The people in Milgram's study obeyed only when the experimenter was hovering right there, and many of them felt enormous discomfort and conflict. In contrast, the Nazis acted without direct supervision by authorities, without external pressure, and without feelings of anguish. There is a big difference, critics note, between people who initiate sadistic, barbarous policies and those who follow orders (Berkowitz, 1999).

Nevertheless, this famous and compelling study has had a tremendous influence on public awareness of the dangers of uncritical obedience (Blass, 2000). As John Darley (1995) observed, "Milgram shows us the beginning of a path by means of which ordinary people, in the grip of social forces, become the origins of atrocities in the real world."

The Prison Study

Imagine that one day, as you are walking home from school, a police car pulls up. Two uniformed officers get out, arrest you, and take you to a prison cell. There you are stripped of your clothes, sprayed with a delousing fluid, assigned a prison uniform, photographed with your prison number, and put behind bars. You feel a little queasy but you are not panicked. You have agreed to play the part of prisoner for a two-week study, and your arrest is merely part of the script. Your prison cell, while apparently authentic, is located in the basement of a university building.

So began an effort to discover what happens when ordinary college students take on the roles of prisoners and guards (Haney, Banks, & Zimbardo, 1973). The young men who volunteered for this experience were paid a nice daily fee. They were randomly assigned to be prisoners or guards, but other than that, they were given no instructions about how to behave. The results were dramatic. Within a short time, the prisoners became distressed, helpless, and panicky. They developed emotional symptoms and physical ailments. Some became apathetic; others became rebellious. After a few days, half of the prisoners begged to be let out. They were more than willing to forfeit their pay to gain an early release.

Within an equally short time, the guards adjusted to their new power. Some tried to be nice, helping the prisoners and doing little favors for them. Some were "tough but fair," holding strictly to "the rules." But about a third became tyrannical. Although they were free to use any method to maintain order, they almost always chose to be harsh and abusive, even when the prisoners were not resisting in any way. One guard, unaware that he was being observed by the researchers, paced the corridor while the prisoners were sleeping, pounding his nightstick into his hand. Another put a prisoner in solitary confinement (a small closet) and tried to keep him there all night. He concealed this information from the researchers, who, he thought, were "too soft" on the prisoners. Not one of the less actively cruel guards, by the way, ever

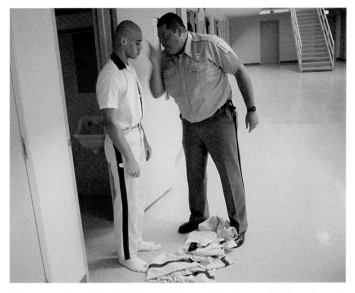

Prisoners and guards quickly learn their respective roles, as they have done at this correctional facility.

intervened or complained about the behavior of their more abusive peers.

The researchers, who had not expected such a speedy and terrifying transformation of healthy students, ended this study after only six days. The prisoners were relieved by this decision, but most of the guards were disappointed. They had enjoyed their short-lived authority.

Critics of this study maintain that you cannot learn much from such an artificial setup. They argue that the volunteers already knew, from movies, TV, and games, how they were supposed to behave. The guards acted their parts to the hilt in order to have fun and please the researchers. Their behavior was no more surprising than if they had been dressed in football gear and had then been found to be willing to bruise each other. The prison study made a great story, say some critics, but it wasn't *research*. That is, the researchers did not carefully investigate relationships among factors; for all the study's drama, it provided no new information (Festinger, 1980).

Craig Haney and Philip Zimbardo, who designed the prison study, responded that this dramatization illustrated the power of roles in a way that no ordinary lab experiment ever could. If the guards were just having fun, why did they lose sight of the "game" and behave as if it were a real job? Twenty-five years after the prison study was done, Haney and Zimbardo (1998) reflected on its contribution to understanding the behavior of real prisoners and guards in prisons, and also to increasing public awareness of how situations can outweigh personality and private values in influencing behavior.

The Power of Roles

The two imaginative studies we have described vividly demonstrate the power of social roles and obligations to influence the behavior of individuals. When people in the Milgram study believed they had to follow the orders of an authority, most of them put their private values and personality dispositions aside. Some prisoners were more rebellious than others, some guards were more abusive than others, but ultimately what the students did depended on the roles they were assigned.

Obedience, of course, is not always harmful or bad. A certain amount of routine compliance with rules is necessary in any group, and obedience to authority has many benefits for individuals and society. A nation could not operate if all its citizens ignored traffic signals, cheated on their taxes, dumped garbage wherever they chose, or assaulted each other. An organization could not function if its members came to work only when they felt like it. But obedience also has a darker aspect. Throughout history, the plea "I was only following orders" has been offered to excuse actions carried out on behalf of orders that were foolish, destructive, or illegal. The writer C. P. Snow once observed that "more hideous crimes have been committed in the name of obedience than in the name of rebellion."

Most people follow orders because of the obvious consequences of disobedience: They can be suspended from school, fired from their jobs, or arrested. They may also obey because of what they hope to gain: being liked, getting certain advantages or promotions from the authority, or learning from the authority's greater knowledge or experience. Primarily, though, people obey because they are deeply convinced of the authority's legitimacy. They obey not in hopes of gaining some tangible benefit, but because they like and respect the authority and value the relationship (Tyler, 1997).

But what about all those obedient people in Milgram's study who felt they were doing wrong and who wished they were free, yet could not untangle themselves from the cobweb of social constraints? Why do people obey when it is not in their interests, or when obedience requires them to ignore their own values or even commit a crime? How do they become morally disengaged from the consequences of their actions?

Researchers looking at the social context of behavior draw our attention to several factors that cause people to obey when they would rather not (Bandura, 1999; Gourevich, 1998; Kelman & Hamilton, 1989; Staub, 1999):

1 *Allocating responsibility to the authority.* In situations in which people have an exceptionally strong respect for authority, they hand over responsibility and thereby absolve themselves of accountability for their actions. In Milgram's study, many of those who administered the highest levels of shock adopted the attitude, "It's his problem; I'm just following orders." In contrast, individuals who refused to give high levels of shock took responsibility for their own actions and refused to grant the authority legitimacy. "One of the things I think is very cowardly," said a 32-year-old engineer, "is to try to shove the responsibility onto someone else. See, if I now turned around and said, 'It's your fault . . . it's not mine,' I would call that cowardly" (Milgram, 1974).

2 *Routinizing the task.* When people define their actions in terms of routine duties and roles, their behavior starts to feel normal, just a job to be done. Becoming absorbed in busywork distracts them from doubts or ethical questions, and it fosters an uncritical, mindless attention to details rather than the larger picture. In the Milgram study, some people became so fixated on the "learning task" that they shut out any moral concerns about the learner's demands to be let out. Routinization is typically the mechanism by which governments enlist citizens to aid and abet programs of genocide. Nazi bureaucrats kept meticulous records of every victim, and in Cambodia the Khmer Rouge recorded the names and histories of the millions of victims they tortured and killed. "I am not a violent man," said Sous Thy, one of the clerks who recorded these names, to a reporter from *The New York Times*. "I was just making lists."

3 *Wanting to be polite.* Good manners protect people's feelings and make relationships and civilization possible. But once people are caught in what they perceive to be legitimate roles and are obeying a legitimate authority, good manners ensnare them into further obedience. They do not want to rock the boat, appear to doubt the experts, or be rude, because they know they will be disliked for doing so (Collins & Brief, 1995).

Most people learn the language of manners ("please," "thank you," "I'm sorry for missing your birthday"), but they literally lack the words to justify disobedience and rudeness toward an authority they respect. In the Milgram study, many people could not find the words to justify

The routinization of horror enables people to commit or collaborate in atrocities. More than 16,000 political prisoners were tortured and killed at Tuol Sleng prison by members of Cambodia's Khmer Rouge, during the regime of Pol Pot. Prison authorities kept meticulous records and photos of each victim in order to make their barbarous activities seem mundane and normal. This man, Ing Pech, was one of only seven survivors, spared because he had skills useful to his captors. He now runs a memorial museum at the prison.

walking out, so they stayed. One woman kept apologizing to the experimenter, trying not to offend him with her worries for the victim: "Do I go right to the end, sir? I hope there's nothing wrong with him there." (She did go right to the end.) A man repeatedly protested and questioned the experimenter, but he too obeyed, even when the victim had apparently collapsed in pain. "He thinks he is killing someone," Milgram (1974) commented, "yet he uses the language of the tea table."

4 *Becoming entrapped.* **Entrapment** is a process in which individuals escalate their commitment to a course of action in order to justify their investment in it (Brockner & Rubin, 1985). The first steps of entrapment pose no difficult choices, but one step leads to another, and before you realize it, you have become committed to a course of action that poses problems. In Milgram's study, once subjects had given a 15-volt shock, they had committed themselves to the experiment. The next level was "only" 30 volts. Because each increment was small, before they knew it, most people were administering what they believed were dangerously strong shocks. At that point, it was difficult to explain a sudden decision to quit. Participants who resisted early in the study, questioning the procedure, were less likely to become entrapped and more likely to eventually disobey (Modigliani & Rochat, 1995).

Individuals and nations alike are vulnerable to the sneaky process of entrapment. You start dating someone you like moderately; before you know it,

entrapment
A gradual process in which individuals escalate their commitment to a course of action to justify their investment of time, money, or effort.

you have been together so long that you can't break up, although you don't want to become committed, either. Government leaders start a war they think will end quickly. Years later, the nation has lost so many soldiers and so much money that the leaders believe they cannot retreat without losing face.

A chilling study of entrapment was conducted with 25 men who had served in the Greek military police during the authoritarian regime that ended in 1974 (Haritos-Fatouros, 1988). A psychologist interviewed the men, identifying the steps used in training them to use torture in questioning prisoners. First the men were ordered to stand guard outside the interrogation and torture cells. Then they stood guard inside the detention rooms, where they observed the torture of prisoners. Then they "helped" beat up prisoners. Once they had obediently followed these orders and became actively involved, the torturers found their actions easier to carry out.

Many people expect solutions to moral problems to fall into two clear categories, with right on one side and wrong on the other. Yet in everyday life, as in the Milgram study, people often set out on a morally ambiguous path, only to find that they have traveled a long way toward violating their own principles. From Greece's torturers to the Khmer Rouge's dutiful clerks, from Milgram's well-meaning volunteers to all of us in our everyday lives, people face the difficult task of drawing a line beyond which they will not go. For many, the demands of the role defeat the inner voice of conscience.

 QUICK QUIZ

Step into your role of student to answer these questions.

1. About what percentage of the people in Milgram's obedience study administered the highest level of shock? (a) two-thirds, (b) one-half, (c) one-third, (d) one-tenth

2. Which of the following actions by the "learner" reduced the likelihood of being shocked by the "teacher" in Milgram's study? (a) protesting noisily, (b) screaming in pain, (c) complaining of having a heart ailment, (d) nothing he did made a difference

3. A friend of yours, who is moving, asks you to bring over a few boxes. Since you are there anyway, he asks you to fill them with books. Before you know it, you have packed up his entire kitchen, living room, and bedroom. What social-psychological process is at work here?

Answers:
1. a 2. d 3. entrapment

What's Ahead

- What is one of the most common mistakes people make when explaining the behavior of others?

- Why would a person blame victims of rape or torture for having brought their misfortunes on themselves?

- What is the "Big Lie," and why does it work so well?

- What is the difference between ordinary techniques of persuasion and the coercive techniques used by cults?

9.2 Social Influences on Beliefs

Social psychologists are interested not only in what people do in social situations, but also in what goes on in their heads while they're doing it. Researchers in the area of **social cognition** examine how the social environment and relationships influence thoughts, beliefs, and memories, and how people's perceptions of themselves and one another affect their relationships (A. Fiske & Haslam, 1996). We will consider two important topics in this area: explanations about behavior and the formation of attitudes.

Attributions

People read detective stories to find out *who* did the dirty deed, but in real life we also want to know *why* people do things—was it because of a terrible childhood, a mental illness, possession by a demon, or what? According to **attribution theory,** the explanations we make of our behavior and the behavior of others generally fall into two categories. When we make a *situational attribution,* we are identifying the cause of an action as something in the situation or environment: "Joe stole the money because his family is starving." When we make a *dispositional attribution,* we are identifying the cause of an action as something in the person, such as a trait or a motive: "Joe stole the money because he is a born thief."

When people are trying to find reasons for someone else's behavior, they reveal a common

bias: They tend to overestimate personality traits and underestimate the influence of the situation (Forgas, 1998; Nisbett & Ross, 1980). In terms of attribution theory, they tend to ignore situational attributions in favor of dispositional ones. This tendency has been called the **fundamental attribution error** (sometimes called the *correspondence bias,* because of the underlying assumption that people's dispositions correspond to their behavior) (Jones, 1990; Van Boven, Kamada, & Gilovich, 1999). Were the hundreds of people who obeyed Milgram's experimenters sadistic by nature? Were the student guards in the prison study sadistic and the prisoners cowardly? Those who think so are committing the fundamental attribution error.

People are especially likely to overlook situational attributions when they are in a good mood and not inclined to think about other people's motives critically, or when they are distracted and preoccupied and don't have time to stop and ask themselves, "Why, exactly, *is* Aurelia behaving like a dork today?" (Forgas, 1998). Instead, they leap to the easiest attribution, which is dispositional: Aurelia simply has a dorky personality.

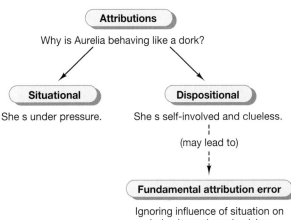

Attributions

Why is Aurelia behaving like a dork?

Situational

She s under pressure.

Dispositional

She s self-involved and clueless.

(may lead to)

Fundamental attribution error

Ignoring influence of situation on behavior and emphasizing personality traits alone

The fundamental attribution error is especially prevalent in Western nations, where middle-class people tend to believe that individuals are responsible for their own actions. In countries such as India, where everyone is embedded in caste and family networks, and in Japan, China, and Hong Kong, where people are more group oriented than in the West, people are more likely to be aware of situational constraints on behavior (Choi, Nisbett, & Norenzayan, 1999; Morris & Peng, 1994). Thus, if someone is behaving oddly,

social cognition
An area in social psychology concerned with social influences on thought, memory, perception, and other cognitive processes.

attribution theory
The theory that people are motivated to explain their own and other people's behavior by attributing causes of that behavior to a situation or a disposition.

fundamental attribution error
The tendency, in explaining other people's behavior, to overestimate personality factors and underestimate the influence of the situation.

9.1

Calvin and Hobbes

by Bill Watterson

Children learn the value of excuses at an early age.

makes a mistake, or plays badly in a soccer match, a person from India or China, unlike a Westerner, is more likely to make a situational attribution of the person's behavior ("He's under pressure") than a dispositional one ("He's incompetent") (Menon et al., 1999).

Westerners do not always prefer dispositional attributions, however. When it comes to explaining their *own* behavior, they often reveal a **self-serving bias:** They tend to choose attributions that are favorable to them, taking credit for their good actions (a dispositional attribution) but letting the situation account for their failures, embarrassing mistakes, or harmful actions (Campbell & Sedikides, 1999). For instance, most North Americans, when angry, will say, "I am furious for good reason; this situation is intolerable." They are less likely to say, "I am furious because I am an ill-tempered grinch." On the other hand, if they do something admirable, such as donating to charity, they are likely to attribute their motives to a personal disposition ("I'm so generous") instead of the situation ("That guy on the phone pressured me into it").

According to the **just-world hypothesis,** attributions are also affected by the need to believe that the world is fair and that justice prevails, and particularly that good people are rewarded and bad guys punished. This belief, which is especially prevalent in North America, helps people make sense out of senseless events and feel safe in the presence of threatening events (Lerner, 1980). Unfortunately, it also leads to a dispositional attribution called *blaming the victim*. If a friend is fired, a woman is raped, or an innocent bystander is shot

41 times by the police (as happened in a tragic case in New York), it is reassuring to think that they all must have done something to deserve what happened or to provoke it: The friend wasn't doing his work, the woman was dressed too "provocatively," the bystander shouldn't have been standing in a dark hallway. Blaming the victim is virtually universal when people are ordered to harm others or find themselves entrapped into harming others (Bandura, 1999). In the Milgram study, some "teachers" made comments such as, "[The learner] was so stupid and stubborn he deserved to get shocked" (Milgram, 1974).

Of course, sometimes dispositional attributions *do* explain a person's behavior. The point to remember is that attributions, whether they are accurate or not, have tremendously important consequences. Here's an example that will apply to your own relationships. Happy couples tend to attribute their partners' occasional lapses to something in the situation ("Poor Horace is under a lot of stress at work"), and the partners' positive actions to stable, internal dispositions ("Horace has the sweetest nature"). But unhappy couples do just the reverse, attributing lapses to their partners' personalities ("Henry is a hopeless mama's boy") and good behavior to the situation ("Yeah, he gave me a present, but only because his mother told him to."). These attributional habits, which can change over time, are strongly related to satisfaction with the partner (Karney & Bradbury, 2000). The attributions you make about your partner, your parents, and your friends will make a big difference in how you get along with them—and how long you will put up with their failings.

self-serving bias
The tendency, in explaining one's own behavior, to take credit for one's good actions and rationalize one's mistakes.

just-world hypothesis
The notion that many people need to believe that the world is fair and that justice is served, that bad people are punished and good people rewarded.

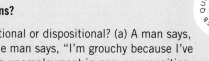

QUICK QUIZ

Attitudes

People hold attitudes about all sorts of things—politics, people, food, children, movies, sports heroes, you name it. An *attitude* is a relatively stable opinion containing beliefs about the topic and also emotional feelings about it. Most people think that their attitudes are based on thinking, a result of reasoned conclusions about how things work. Sometimes, of course, that's true! But some attitudes are a result of not thinking at all. They are a result of conformity, habit, rationalization, economic self-interest, and many subtle social and environmental influences.

For example, some attitudes arise because of the shared experiences of an age group or generation. Each generation has its own defining social and political events, economic interests, job and marital opportunities, and other shared concerns, and therefore its own characteristic attitudes. (That is why people speak of the Depression generation, the Baby Boomers, and Generation X.) The ages of 16 to 24 appear to be critical for the formation of a *generational identity* that lasts throughout adulthood. The experiences that occur during these years—wars, financial busts or booms, increases or drops in rates of violence, technological breakthroughs—make deeper impressions and exert more lasting influence than those that happen later in life (Inglehart, 1990; Schuman & Scott, 1989).

Two sociologists have proposed that the generation that entered college in 2000—whom they call the "Millennials"—is team-oriented, optimistic, and practical, unlike their passionate, rebellious Baby Boom parents and their cynical Generation X older siblings (Howe & Strauss, 2000). Millennials grew up in a time of falling rates of violent crime, teen pregnancy, and teen suicide; and, unlike the Baby Boomers, they are accustomed to following rules and accepting authority on matters from uniforms to metal detectors in school. If you are a "millennial" or know a few of them, does this description seem accurate?

Of course, attitudes change. People change their attitudes not only as a result of new information or experience, but also because of the need for consistency. In Chapter 6, we discussed *cognitive dissonance*, the uncomfortable feeling that occurs when two attitudes, or an attitude and behavior, are in conflict (are dissonant). To resolve this dissonance, something has to change. For example, if a politician or celebrity you admire does something stupid, immoral, or illegal, you can restore consistency by lowering your opinion of the person or by deciding the alleged act wasn't so stupid or immoral, or maybe not *very* illegal, after all.

Our attitudes are also influenced constantly by other people. Sometimes people persuade us to change our minds using reasoned argument; sometimes they use subtle manipulation; and sometimes they use outright coercion.

Friendly Persuasion. All around you, every day, advertisers, politicians, and friends are trying to influence your attitudes. One weapon they use is the drip, drip, drip of a repeated idea. Repeated exposure even to a nonsense syllable

The more familiar things are, the more we tend to like them. The Oreo name on these cereal boxes takes advantage of the fact that Oreo cookies have been advertised since 1912!

such as *zug* is enough to make a person feel more positive toward it (Zajonc, 1968). The effectiveness of familiarity has long been known to politicians and advertisers: Repeat something often enough, even the basest lie, and eventually the public will believe it—the reason that Hitler's propaganda minister, Joseph Goebbels, called this technique the "Big Lie." Its formal name is the **validity effect.**

In a series of experiments, Hal Arkes and his associates demonstrated how the validity effect operates (Arkes, 1993; Arkes, Boehm, & Xu, 1991). In a typical study, people read a list of statements, such as "Mercury has a higher boiling point than copper" or "Over 400 Hollywood films were produced in 1948." They had to rate each statement for its validity, on a scale of 1 (definitely false) to 7 (definitely true). A week or two later, they again rated the validity of some of these statements and also rated others that they had not seen previously. The result: Mere repetition increased the perception that the familiar statements were true. The same effect also occurred for other kinds of statements, including unverifiable opinions (e.g., "At least 75 percent of all politicians are basically dishonest"), opinions that subjects initially felt were true, and even opinions they initially felt were false. "Note that no attempt has been made to persuade," said Arkes (1993). "No supporting arguments are offered. We just have subjects rate the statements. Mere repetition seems to increase rated validity. This is scary."

Another effective influence technique is to have arguments presented by someone who is considered admirable, knowledgeable, or beautiful; this is why advertisements are full of sports heroes, experts, and models (Cialdini, 1993). Persuaders may also try to link their message with a nice, warm, fuzzy feeling. In one classic study, students who were given peanuts and Pepsi while listening to a speaker's point of view were more likely to be convinced by it than were students who listened to the same words without the pleasant munchies and soft drinks (Janis, Kaye, & Kirschner, 1965). This finding has been replicated many times (Pratkanis & Aronson, 1992), perhaps explaining why so much business is conducted over lunch, and so many courtships over dinner!

validity effect
The tendency of people to believe that a statement is true or valid simply because it has been repeated many times.

In sum, here are three good ways to influence attitudes:

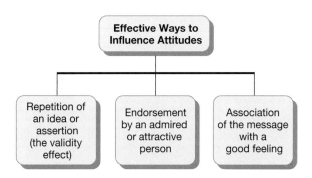

In contrast, the emotion of fear can cause people to resist arguments that are in their own best interest (Pratkanis & Aronson, 1992). Fear tactics are often used to try to persuade people to quit smoking or abusing other drugs, drive only when sober, use condoms, check for signs of cancer, and prepare for earthquakes. Fear tactics can be effective if the message also provides information about how to avoid the danger and if people feel competent to take advantage of this information (Aronson, 1999). But when messages about a future disaster are terrifying *and* people believe that they can do nothing to avoid it, they tend to deny the danger. How successful do you think this image, from an ad linking smoking to impotence in men, is likely to be?

Ad portrays smoking's effect on sexual potency.

Coercive Persuasion. Some manipulators use harsher tactics, not just hoping that people will change their minds but attempting to force them to. These tactics are sometimes referred to as *brainwashing,* a term first used during the Korean War to describe techniques used on American prisoners of war to get them to collaborate with their Chinese Communist captors and to endorse anti-American propaganda. Most psychologists, however, prefer the phrase *coercive persuasion.* "Brainwashing"

Thinking Critically About "Brainwashing"

implies that a person has a sudden change of mind and is unaware of what is happening; it sounds mysterious and strange. In fact, the methods involved are neither mysterious nor unusual. The difference between "persuasion" and "brainwashing" is often only a matter of degree and the observer's bias, just as a group that is a crazy cult to one person may be a group of devoutly religious people to another.

How, then, might we distinguish coercive persuasion from its more benign form? Persuasion techniques become coercive when they suppress an individual's ability to reason, think critically, and make choices in his or her own best interests. Studies of religious, political, and other cults have identified some of the key processes of coercive persuasion (Galanter, 1989; Mithers, 1994; Ofshe & Watters, 1994; Singer, Temerlin, & Langone, 1990; Zimbardo & Leippe, 1991):

1 *The person is put under physical or emotional distress.* The individual may not be allowed to eat, sleep, or exercise; may be isolated in a dark room with no stimulation; or may be induced into a trancelike state through repetitive chanting or fatigue.

2 *The person's problems are reduced to one simple explanation, which is repeatedly emphasized.* There are as many simplistic explanations as there are cults, but here are two real examples: Are you afraid or unhappy? It all stems from the pain of being born. Are you struggling financially? It's your fault for not fervently wanting to be rich. Members may also be taught to simplify their problems by blaming a particular enemy: Jews, blacks, whites, nonbelievers.

3 *The leader offers unconditional love, acceptance, and attention.* The new recruit may be given a "love bath" from the group—constant praise, support, and affection. Euphoria and well-being are intense because they typically follow exhaustion and fatigue. In exchange, the leader demands everyone's adoration and obedience.

4 *A new identity based on the group is created.* The recruit is told that he or she is part of the chosen, the elite, or the saved. To foster this new identity, many cults require their members to wear special clothes or eat special diets, and they assign each member a new name. All members of the Philadelphia group MOVE were given the last name "Africa"; all members of the Church of Armageddon took the last name "Israel."

5 *The person is subjected to entrapment.* At first, the new member agrees only to do small things,

These members of the Aum Shinrikyo ("Supreme Truth") sect in Japan, wearing masks of their leader's face, take the uniformity of cult identity to an extreme. The group's founder instructed his devotees to place a nerve gas in a Japanese subway, killing ten and sickening thousands of other passengers. One former member said of the sect, "Their strategy is to wear you down and take control of your mind. They promise you heaven, but they make you live in hell."

but gradually the demands increase: for example, to spend a weekend with the group, then another weekend, then take weekly seminars, then advanced courses. During the Korean War, the Chinese first got the American prisoners to agree with mild remarks, such as "The United States is not perfect." Then the prisoners had to add their own examples of American imperfections. At the end, they were signing their names to anti-American broadcasts (Schein, Schneier, & Barker, 1961).

6 *The person's access to information is severely controlled.* As soon as a person is a committed believer or follower, the group limits the person's choices, denigrates critical thinking, makes fun of doubts, and insists that any private distress is due to lack of belief in the group. Total conformity is demanded. The person may be physically isolated from the outside world and thus from antidotes to the leader's ideas. In many groups, members are encouraged or required to break all ties with their families, who are the most powerful link to the members' former world and thus the greatest threat to the leader's control.

Some people may be more vulnerable than others to coercive tactics, but these techniques are powerful enough to overwhelm even mentally healthy and well-educated individuals. The first step in increasing people's resistance to coercive persuasion, therefore, is to dispel their illusion of invulnerability to these tactics (Sagarin, Cialdini, & Rice, 1998).

QUICK QUIZ

Now, how can we persuade you to take this quiz without coercing you?

1. Candidate Carson spends $3 million to make sure his name is seen and heard frequently, and to repeat unverified charges that his opponent is a thief. What psychological process is he relying on to win?

2. A friend urges you to join a "life-renewal" group called "The Feeling Life." Your friend has been spending increasing amounts of time with her fellow Feelies, and you have some doubts about them. What questions would you want to have answered before joining up?

Answers:

1. the validity effect   2. A few things to consider: Is there an autocratic leader who tolerates no dissent or criticism, while rationalizing this practice as a benefit for members? ("Doubt and disbelief are signs that your feeling side is being repressed.") Have long-standing members given up their friends, families, interests, and ambitions for this group? Does the leader offer simple but unrealistic promises to repair your life and all that troubles you? Are members required to make extreme sacrifices by donating large amounts of time and money?

What's Ahead

- Why do people in groups often go along with the majority even when the majority is dead wrong?

- How can "groupthink" lead to bad, even catastrophic, decisions?

- Why is it common for a group of people to hear someone shout for help without one of them calling the police?

- What enables some people to dissent, take moral action, or blow the whistle on wrongdoers?

9.3 Individuals in Groups

Even when a group is not at all coercive, something happens to us when we join a bunch of other people. We act differently than we would on our own, regardless of whether the group has convened to solve problems and make decisions, has gathered to have fun, consists of anonymous bystanders, or is just a loose collection of individuals waiting around in a room. The decisions we make and the actions we take in groups may depend less on our personal desires than on the structure and dynamics of the group itself.

Conformity

One thing people in groups do is conform, taking action or adopting attitudes as a result of real or imagined group pressure.

Suppose that you are required to appear at a psychology laboratory for an experiment on perception. You join seven other students seated in a room. You are shown a 10-inch line and asked which of three other lines is identical to it:

Test line   A   B   C

The correct answer, line A, is obvious, so you are amused when the first person in the group chooses line B. "Bad eyesight," you say to yourself. "He's off by 2 whole inches!" The second person also chooses line B. "What a dope," you think. But by the time the fifth person has chosen line B, you are beginning to doubt yourself. The sixth and seventh students also choose line B, and now you are worried about *your* eyesight. The experimenter looks at you. "Your turn," he says. Do you follow the evidence of your own eyes or the collective judgment of the group?

This was the design for a series of famous studies of conformity conducted by Solomon Asch

Sometimes people like to conform in order to feel part of the group . . .

. . . and sometimes, like this playful bride, they like assert their individuality.

9.2

(1952, 1965). The seven "nearsighted" students were actually Asch's confederates. Asch wanted to know what people would do when a group unanimously contradicted an obvious fact. He found that when people made the line comparisons on their own, they were almost always accurate. But in the group, only 20 percent of the students remained completely independent on every trial, and often they apologized for not agreeing with the others. One-third conformed to the group's incorrect decision more than half the time, and the rest conformed at least some of the time. Whether they conformed or not, the students often felt uncertain of their decision. As one participant later said, "I felt disturbed, puzzled, separated, like an outcast from the rest."

Asch's experiment has been replicated many times over the years, in the United States and other countries. According to a meta-analysis of 133 studies in 17 countries, conformity depends on social and cultural norms, which can change over time. Americans are less likely to conform in the Asch paradigm today than they were in the 1950s, when the experiment was first done. People in individual-oriented cultures, such as the United States, are less conformist than are people in group-oriented cultures, where social harmony is considered more important than individual rights (see Chapter 2). But regardless of culture, we are all more likely to conform when the group consists of people like us—in age, sex, and ethnicity—and as the group's size increases (Bond & Smith, 1996).

People conform for all sorts of reasons. Some do so because they identify with group members and want to be like them. Some want to be liked and know that disagreeing with a group can make them unpopular. Some believe the group has knowledge that is superior to their own. And some conform out of pure self-interest, to keep their jobs, win promotions, or win votes. Also, being a nonconformist is not so easy! Group members are often uncomfortable with nonconformists and will try to persuade a deviant to conform. If pleasant persuasion fails, the group may punish, isolate, or reject the deviant (Moscovici, 1985).

Like obedience, conformity has both its positive and its negative sides. Society runs more smoothly when people know how to behave in a given situation and when they go along with cultural rules of dress and manners. But conformity can also suppress critical thinking and creativity. In a group, many people will suppress their private beliefs, agree with silly notions, and even repudiate their own values (Cialdini, 1993).

Groupthink

Close, friendly groups usually work well together. But they face the problem of getting the best ideas and efforts of their members while avoiding an extreme form of conformity called **groupthink,** the tendency to think alike and suppress dissent. According to Irving Janis (1982, 1989), groupthink occurs when a group's need for total agreement

groupthink
In close-knit groups, the tendency for all members to think alike and to suppress disagreement for the sake of harmony.

overwhelms its need to make the wisest decision. The symptoms of groupthink include the following:

- *An illusion of invulnerability.* The group believes it can do no wrong and is 100 percent correct in its decisions.

- *Self-censorship.* Dissenters decide to keep quiet rather than make trouble, offend their friends, or risk being ridiculed.

- *Pressure on dissenters to conform.* The leader teases or humiliates dissenters or otherwise pressures them to go along.

- *An illusion of unanimity.* By discouraging dissent, leaders and group members create an illusion of consensus; they may even explicitly deny suspected dissenters the chance to say what they think.

Janis (1982) examined the records of historical military decisions and identified typical features of groups that are vulnerable to groupthink: Their members feel that they are part of a tightly connected team; they are isolated from other viewpoints; they feel under pressure from outside forces; and they have a strong, directive leader. Do you notice the similarities between these features and those of coercive cults?

Throughout history, groupthink has led to disastrous decisions in military and civilian life. One example occurred in 1961, when President John F. Kennedy, after meeting with his advisers, approved a CIA plan to invade Cuba at the Bay of Pigs and overthrow the government of Fidel Castro; the invasion was a humiliating defeat. Another occurred in the mid-1960s, when President Lyndon Johnson and his cabinet escalated the war in Vietnam in spite of obvious signs that further bombing and increased troops were not

bringing the war to an end. A third example occurred in 1986, when NASA officials made the fatal decision to launch the space shuttle *Challenger,* which exploded shortly after takeoff. Apparently they insulated themselves from the objections of dissenting engineers who tried to warn them that the rocket was unsafe (Moorhead, Ference, & Neck, 1991).

Groupthink can be counteracted by creating conditions that explicitly encourage and reward the expression of doubt and dissent and by basing decisions on majority rule instead of unanimity (Kameda & Sugimori, 1993). President Kennedy apparently learned this lesson from the Bay of Pigs decision. In his next political crisis, provoked by missiles placed in Cuba by the then–Soviet Union in 1962, Kennedy brought in outside experts to advise his inner circle, often absented himself from the group so as not to influence its discussions, and encouraged free debate between the "hawks" and the "doves" (Aronson, Wilson, & Akert, 1999). The crisis, one of the most dangerous in post–World War II history, was resolved peacefully.

Of course, it is easy to see after the fact how conformity contributed to a bad decision or open debate to a good one, as Janis did. Predicting whether a group will make good or bad decisions in the *future* is far more complicated (Aldag & Fuller, 1993). Nevertheless, Janis put his finger on a phenomenon confirmed all too often by the historical record, as well as by research: individual members of a group suppressing their real opinions and doubts, so as to be good team players.

The Anonymous Crowd

Suppose you were in trouble on a city street or in another public place—say, being mugged or having a sudden appendicitis attack. Do you think you would be more likely to get help if (a) one other person was passing by, (b) several other people were in the area, or (c) dozens of people were in the area?

Most people would choose the third answer, but that is not how human beings operate. On the contrary, the more people there are around you, the *less* likely it is that one of them will come to your aid. The reason has to do with a group process called the **diffusion of responsibility,** in which responsibility for an outcome is diffused, or spread, among many people. In crowds, individuals often fail to take action because they believe that someone else will do so. The many

diffusion of responsibility

In organized or anonymous groups, the tendency of members to avoid taking responsibility for actions or decisions because they assume that others will do so.

news reports of *bystander apathy* reflect the diffusion of responsibility. When others are near, people fail to call for help as a woman is attacked on the street, as a man collapses, or as a child is neglected and beaten by a parent.

In work groups, the diffusion of responsibility sometimes takes the form of *social loafing:* Each member of a team slows down, letting others work harder (Karau & Williams, 1993; Latané, Williams, & Harkins, 1979). Social loafing occurs when individual group members are not accountable for the work they do; when people feel that working harder would only duplicate their colleagues' efforts; when workers feel that others are getting a "free ride"; or when the work itself is uninteresting (Shepperd, 1995). When the challenge of the job is increased or when each member of the group has a different, important job to do, the sense of individual responsibility rises and social loafing declines (Harkins & Szymanski, 1989; Williams & Karau, 1991).

The most extreme instances of the diffusion of responsibility occur in large, anonymous mobs or crowds—whether they are cheerful ones, such as sports spectators, or angry ones, such as rioters. In crowds like these, people often lose all awareness of their individuality and seem to "hand themselves over" to the mood and actions of the crowd, a state called **deindividuation** (Festinger, Pepitone, & Newcomb, 1952). You are more likely to feel deindividuated in a large city, where no one recognizes you, than a small town, where it is hard to hide. Sometimes organizations actively promote the deindividuation of their members in order to enhance conformity and allegiance to the group. This is an important function of uniforms or masks, which eliminate each member's distinctive identity.

Deindividuation has long been considered a primary reason for mob violence. According to this explanation, because deindividuated people in crowds "forget themselves" and do not feel accountable for their actions, they are more likely to violate social norms and laws than they would be on their own: breaking store windows, looting, getting into fights, or rioting at a sports event (Aronson, Wilson, & Akert, 1999). But deindividuation does not always make people more combative. Sometimes it makes them more friendly; think of all the chatty, anonymous people on buses and planes who reveal things to their seatmates they would never tell anyone they knew.

What really seems to be happening when people are in large crowds or anonymous situations is not that they become "mindless" or "uninhibited," but that they are simply more likely to conform to the norms of the *specific situation* (Postmes & Spears, 1998). College students who go on wild sprees during spring break may be violating the local laws and norms of Palm Springs or Key West, not because their "aggressiveness" has been released but because they are conforming to the "let's party!" norms of their fellow students.

Two classic experiments illustrate the power of the situation to influence what deindividuated people will do. In one, women who wore Ku Klux Klan–like disguises, which completely covered their faces and bodies, delivered twice as much apparent electric shock to another woman as did women who were not only undisguised but also wore large name tags (Zimbardo, 1970). In a second experiment, women who were wearing nurses' uniforms gave *less* shock than did women in regular dress (Johnson & Downing, 1979). Evidently, the KKK disguise was a signal to behave

deindividuation
In groups or crowds, the loss of awareness of one's own individuality.

Wearing a uniform or disguise can increase deindividuation and mindlessness, and provide a cue for how to behave. These women wearing Ku Klux Klan-like disguises behaved more aggressively than individuated women (Zimbardo, 1970).

aggressively; the nurses' uniforms were a signal to behave nurturantly.

In real life, too, members of crowds, conforming to the goals and norms of the situation, can be induced to take part in either collective violence or collective kindness. Peer pressure and conformity to an angry mob can induce people to commit hate crimes, such as violence against gay men or lesbians, attacks on black people or Jews, and the rape of women by gangs of civilians or soldiers (Franklin, 1998; Green, Glaser, & Rich, 1998). On the other hand, when collective norms are positive, anonymous members of a community will behave in constructive ways. When Swissair Flight 111 crashed over Halifax, Nova Scotia, in 1998, killing 229 people, the entire community—which holds a group norm about the importance of helping one another in that tough terrain—turned out to join in the rescue effort and comfort families in distress.

QUICK QUIZ

On your own, take responsibility for identifying which phenomenon discussed in the previous section is illustrated in the following situations.

1. The president's closest advisers are afraid to disagree with his views on arms negotiations.

2. You are at a costume party wearing a silly gorilla suit. When you see a chance to play a practical joke on the host, you do it.

3. Walking down a busy street, you see that fire has broken out in a store window. "Someone must have called the fire department," you say.

Answers: 1. groupthink 2. deindividuation 3. diffusion of responsibility

Courage and Nonconformity

We have seen how social roles, norms, and pressures to obey authority and conform to one's group can cause people to behave in ways they might not otherwise do. Yet, throughout history, men and women have disobeyed orders they believed to be wrong and have gone against prevailing cultural beliefs; their actions have changed the course of history.

Dissent and *altruism,* the willingness to take selfless or dangerous action on behalf of others, are in part a matter of personal convictions and conscience. In 1942, Wladyslaw Misiuna, a Polish

teenager, was ordered by the Germans to supervise inmates at a concentration camp. One day, an inmate named Devora Salzberg came to see him about an infection that had covered her arms with open lesions. Misiuna knew that he could never get a doctor to the camp to treat her. So he infected himself with her blood, contracted the lesions himself, and went to a doctor. Then he shared with Devora the medication he was given. Both were cured, and both survived the war (Fogelman, 1994).

Obviously, Misiuna was a young man of tremendous courage and conscience. However, just as there are situational reasons for obedience and conformity, so there are external influences

Many people retain their individuality and courage even at great risk. On the left, Terri Barnett and Gregory Alan Williams were honored at Los Angeles City Hall for rescuing white people during the violence that followed the 1992 acquittal of four white police officers who beat black motorist Rodney King. On the right are Ria Solomon, Sylvia Robins, and Al Bray, three whistle-blowers from Rockwell International who tried to inform NASA that the space shuttle Challenger was unsafe.

on a person's decision to state an unpopular opinion, choose conscience over conformity, or help a stranger in trouble. Here are some of the situational factors involved in deciding to "rock the boat" (Aronson, Wilson, & Akert, 1999):

1 *You perceive the need for intervention or help.* It may seem obvious, but before you can take independent action, you must realize that such action is necessary. Sometimes people willfully blind themselves to wrongdoing to justify their own inaction ("I'm just minding my business"; "I have no idea what they're doing over there at Dachau"). But blindness to the need for action also occurs when a situation imposes too many demands on people's attention. Workers who must juggle many pressures from work and family cannot stop to make a fuss about every problem or bureaucratic misdeed they notice. Likewise, residents of densely populated cities cannot stop to offer help to everyone who seems to need it; they would never do anything else (Levine et al., 1994).

2 *The situation makes it more likely that you will take responsibility.* When you are in a large crowd of observers or in a large organization, it is easy to avoid action because of the diffusion of responsibility. Even when you might like to help a stranger in trouble, in some places it is impossible to help everyone who needs it, as in cities where homeless persons number in the thousands. The decision to take responsibility also depends on the degree of risk involved. It is easier to be a whistle-blower or to protest a company policy when you know you can find another job, but what if jobs in your field are scarce and you have a family to sup-

port? People are less likely to take an independent position if situational risks are high.

3 *The cost-benefit ratio supports your decision to get involved.* The cost of helping or protesting might be embarrassment and wasted time or, more seriously, lost income, loss of friends, and even physical danger. The cost of not helping or remaining silent might be guilt, blame from others, loss of honor, or, in some tragic cases, the injury or death of others. Three employees of Rockwell International weighed these two sets of costs and ended up trying to convince NASA that the space shuttle *Challenger* was unsafe. The NASA authorities (perhaps influenced by groupthink, as we noted earlier) weighed the costs differently and refused to postpone the launch. The price of their decision was an explosion that caused the deaths of the entire crew.

4 *You have an ally.* In Asch's conformity experiment, the presence of one other person who gave the correct answer was enough to overcome agreement with the majority. In Milgram's experiment, the presence of a peer who disobeyed the experimenter's instruction to shock the learner sharply increased the number of people who also disobeyed. One dissenting member of a group may be viewed as a troublemaker and two dissenting members as a conspiracy, but several are a coalition. An ally reassures a person of the rightness of the protest, and their combined efforts may eventually persuade the majority (Wood et al., 1994).

5 *You become entrapped.* Once having taken the initial step of getting involved, most people will increase their commitment. In one study, nearly 9,000 federal employees were asked whether they had observed wrongdoing at work, whether they had told anyone about it, and what happened if they had told. Nearly half of the sample had observed some serious cases of wrongdoing, such as stealing federal funds, accepting bribes, or creating a situation that was dangerous to public safety. Of that half, 72 percent had done nothing at all, but the other 28 percent reported

the problem to their immediate supervisors. Once they had taken that step, a majority of the whistle-blowers eventually took the matter to higher authorities (Graham, 1986).

As you can see, certain social factors make altruism, disobedience, and dissent more likely to occur, just as other factors suppress them.

QUICK QUIZ

We hope you won't dissent from our suggestion to take this quiz.

Imagine that you are chief executive officer of a new electric-car company. You want your employees to feel free to offer their suggestions for improving productivity and satisfaction, and to inform managers if they find any evidence that your cars are unsafe, even if that means delaying production. What concepts from this chapter could you use in setting company policy?

Answers:
Some possibilities: You could encourage and acknowledge deviant ideas, and not require unanimity of group decisions (to avoid groupthink); reward individual innovation and suggestions by paying attention to them and implementing the best ones (to avoid social loafing and deindividuation); stimulate commitment to the task (building a car that will solve the world's pollution problem); and establish a written policy to protect whistle-blowers. What else can you think of?

What's Ahead

● **In what different ways do people balance their ethnic identity and their membership in the larger culture?**

● **What is an effective antidote to "us-them" thinking?**

● **How do stereotypes benefit us, and how do they distort reality?**

9.4 Us Versus Them: Group Identity

Each of us develops a personal identity that is based on our particular traits and unique life history. But we also develop **social identities** based on the groups we belong to, including our national, religious, political, and occupational groups (Brewer & Gardner, 1996; Tajfel & Turner, 1986). Social identities are important because they give us a sense of place and position in the world. Without them, most of us would feel like loose marbles

rolling around in an unconnected universe. In this section, we will consider the benefits and problems of social identities. It feels good to be part of an "us," but does that mean that we must automatically feel superior to "them"?

Ethnic Identity

In multicultural societies such as the United States, different social identities sometimes collide. In particular, people often face the dilemma of balancing an **ethnic identity,** a close identification with a religious or ethnic group, with **acculturation,** an identification with the dominant culture (Cross, 1971; Phinney, 1996; Spencer & Dornbusch, 1990).

As Table 9.1 shows, four outcomes are possible, depending on whether ethnic identity is strong or weak, and whether identification with the larger culture is strong or weak (Berry, 1994; Phinney, 1990). People who are *bicultural* have strong ties both to their ethnicity and to the larger culture: They say, "I am proud of my ethnic heritage, but I identify just as much with my new country." They can alternate easily between their culture of origin and the majority culture, slipping into the customs

---

social identity
The part of a person's self-concept that is based on identification with a nation, culture, or group or with gender or other roles in society.

ethnic identity
A person's identification with a racial, religious, or ethnic group.

acculturation
The process by which members of minority groups come to identify with and feel part of the mainstream culture.

These children are observing the December festival of Kwanzaa, an African-American holiday that celebrates traditional African spiritual values. In culturally diverse societies, many people maintain a strong attachment to their ethnic heritage.

ethnic identity but weak feelings of acculturation: They may say, "My ethnicity comes first; if I join the mainstream, I'm betraying my origins." And some people feel *marginal,* connected to neither their ethnicity nor the dominant culture: They may say, "I'm an individual and don't identify with any group" or "I don't belong anywhere."

The way a person balances ethnic identity and acculturation, however, may change in response to experiences and social and historical events (Berry, 1998). Thus, many immigrants arrive in North America with every intention of becoming "true" Canadians or Americans. If they encounter discrimination or setbacks, however, they may decide that acculturation is harder than they anticipated or that ethnic separatism offers greater solace. Moreover, acculturation is rarely a complete accommodation to mainstream culture. Most people pick and choose among customs of their own ethnicity and those of the dominant culture, or set limits on how far they want acculturation to go (Segall et al., 1999). You might become acculturated to another ethnic group's food and customs, but believe in the importance of marrying within your own group.

As groups develop a strong ethnic identity, they often reject the name that was imposed on them by the majority culture and choose their own. The Eskimos of Canada are now called the Inuit, their own name for themselves, and the Sioux are now the Lakota. A group's name reflects its history, status, and self-concept. The shift from Negro (a label based on racial categories) to black (based on skin color) to African-American (based on geographical origin) reflects the evolution of ethnic identity, self-concept, and political strength (Cross, 1971, 1991; Fairchild, 1985).

and language of each, as circumstances dictate (LaFromboise, Coleman, & Gerton, 1993). People who choose *assimilation* have weak feelings of ethnicity but a strong sense of acculturation: Their attitude, for example, might be "I'm an American, period." *Ethnic separatists* have a strong sense of

| Table 9.1 | Patterns of Ethnic Identity and Acculturation |

		Ethnic Identity Is	
		Strong	Weak
Acculturation Is	Strong	Bicultural	Assimilated
	Weak	Separatist	Marginal

The tension in America between ethnic identity and acculturation was apparent during the 1996 Hispanic March on Washington, when thousands of Hispanic Americans demanded rights for immigrants—while waving flags from their countries of origin. To the demonstrators, the flags symbolized pride in their heritage, but many other Americans regarded the flags as evidence of the demonstrators' lack of commitment to the United States. What would be your interpretation?

To add to the confusion, not all members of each ethnic group agree on a group label. Not all—blacks?—feel a kinship to Africa. The American Indian Movement and the National Congress of American Indians continue to use the term *American Indian* even though the "correct" term is supposed to be *Native American* (Trimble & Medicine, 1993). *Hispanic* is a label used by the U.S. government to include all Spanish-speaking groups; but many "Hispanics" dislike the term, pointing out that Spaniards, Mexican-Americans (Chicanos), Latin Americans (Latinos), Cubans, and Puerto Ricans differ in their cultures and histories, and therefore in their ethnic identity. And not all "white" Americans want to be called Anglos, which refers to a British heritage, or European-American, as if all European countries from Greece to Norway were the same. These tensions over group names are likely to continue, as ethnic groups struggle to define their place, raise their status, and secure their identity in a medley of cultures.

Thinking Critically About Ethnic Labels

Ethnocentrism

Having an ethnic or national identity is clearly important to many people, psychologically and socially. Unfortunately, it often leads to **ethno**-

centrism, the belief that your own culture or ethnic group is superior to all others. Ethnocentrism is universal, probably because it aids survival by increasing people's attachment to their own group and willingness to work on its behalf. It is even embedded in some languages: The Chinese word for China means "the center of the world" and the Navajo and the Inuit call themselves simply "The People."

Ethnocentrism rests on a fundamental social identity: us. As soon as people have created a category called "us," however, they invariably perceive everybody else as "not-us." It almost does not matter what the "us" category is, as Henri Tajfel and his colleagues (1971) demonstrated in a classic experiment with British schoolboys. Tajfel showed the boys slides with varying numbers of dots on them and asked the boys to guess how many dots there were. The boys were arbitrarily told that they were "overestimators" or "underestimators" and were then asked to work on another task. In this phase, they had a chance to give points to other boys identified as overestimators or underestimators. Although each boy worked alone in his cubicle, almost every single one assigned far more points to boys he thought were like him, an overestimator or an underestimator. As the boys emerged from their rooms, they were asked, "Which were you?"—and the answers received a mix of cheers and boos from the others.

Us-them social identities are strengthened when two groups compete with one another. Years ago, Muzafer Sherif and his colleagues used a natural setting, a Boy Scout camp called Robbers Cave, to demonstrate the effects of competition on hostility and conflict between groups (Sherif, 1958; Sherif et al., 1961). Sherif randomly assigned 11- and 12-year-old boys to two groups, the Eagles and the Rattlers. To build a sense of in-group identity and team spirit, he had each group work together on projects such as making a rope bridge and building a diving board. Sherif then put the Eagles and Rattlers in competition for prizes. During fierce games of football, baseball, and tug-of-war, the boys whipped up a competitive fever that soon spilled off of the playing fields. They began to raid each other's cabins, call each other names, and start fistfights. No one dared to have a friend from the rival group. Before long, the Rattlers and the Eagles were as hostile toward each other as any two gangs fighting for turf or any two nations fighting for dominance. Their hostility continued even when they were just sitting around together watching movies.

Then Sherif decided to try to undo the hostility he had created and make peace between the

ethnocentrism
The belief that one's own ethnic group, nation, or religion is superior to all others.

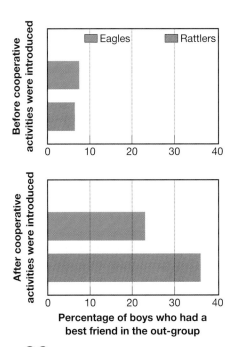

Figure 9.2

The Experiment at Robbers Cave

In this study, competitive games such as tug-of-war fostered hostility between the Rattlers and the Eagles. Very few boys had a best friend from the other group (top graph). But after the boys had to cooperate to solve various problems, such as repairing the camp's water-supply system, the percentage who made friends across "enemy lines" shot up (bottom graph) (Sherif et al., 1961).

Eagles and Rattlers. He and his associates set up a series of predicaments in which both groups needed to work together to reach a desired goal—pooling their resources to get a movie they all wanted to see, or pulling a staff truck up a hill on a camping trip. This policy of *interdependence in reaching mutual goals* was highly successful in reducing the boys' "ethnocentrism," competitiveness, and hostility; the boys eventually made friends with their former enemies (see Figure 9.2). Interdependence has a similar effect in adult groups. The reason, it seems, is that cooperation causes people to think of themselves as members of one big group—a new social identity—instead of two opposed groups, *us* and *them* (Gaertner et al., 1990).

Stereotypes

Most people know that "we"—the members of their own social and ethnic groups—have all sorts of personalities and quirks. But it is easy to assume that "they" are all alike. A **stereotype** is a summary impression of a group of people in which all members of the group are viewed as sharing a common trait or traits. Stereotypes may be negative or positive. There are stereotypes of people who drive Jeeps or BMWs, of men who wear earrings and of women who wear business suits, of engineering students and art students, of feminists and fraternity men.

Stereotypes play an important role in human thinking. They help us quickly process new information and retrieve memories. They allow us to organize experience, make sense of differences among individuals and groups, and predict how people will behave. They are, as some psychologists have called them, useful "tools in the mental toolbox"—energy-saving devices that allow us to make efficient decisions (Macrae, Milne, & Bodenhausen, 1994).

The problem is that stereotypes also distort reality in three ways (Judd et al., 1995). First, *they exaggerate differences between groups,* making the stereotyped group seem odd, unfamiliar, or dangerous, not like "us." Second, *they produce selective perception;* people tend to see only the evidence that fits the stereotype and reject any perceptions that do not fit. Third, *they underestimate differences within other groups.* Stereotypes create the impression that all members of other groups (say, all Texans or all teenagers) are the same.

Some stereotypes stem from a person's cultural values. For example, white Americans tend to have strongly negative stereotypes about fat people

Which woman is the chemical engineer and which is the assistant? The Western stereotype holds that (a) women are not engineers in the first place, but (b) if they are, they are Western. Actually, the engineer at this refinery is the Kuwaiti woman on the left.

stereotype
A cognitive schema or a summary impression of a group, in which a person believes that all members of the group share a common trait or traits (positive, negative, or neutral).

because of a cultural ideology that individuals are responsible for what happens to them and for how they look. In contrast, Mexicans (in Mexico and the United States) and African-Americans are significantly more accepting of heavy people (Crandall & Martinez, 1996; Hebl & Heatherton, 1998).

Cultural values also affect how people evaluate a particular action (Taylor & Porter, 1994). Chinese students in Hong Kong, where communalism and respect for elders are valued, think

that a student who comes late to class or argues with a parent about grades is being selfish and disrespectful of adults. But Australian students, who value individualism, think that the same behavior is perfectly appropriate (Forgas & Bond, 1985). You can see how the Chinese might form negative stereotypes of "disrespectful" Australians, and how the Australians might form negative stereotypes of the "spineless" Chinese. And it is a small step from negative stereotypes to prejudice.

QUICK QUIZ

Do you have a positive or a negative stereotype of quizzes?

1. Frank, an African-American college student, finds himself caught between two philosophies on his campus. One holds that blacks should move toward full integration into mainstream culture. The other holds that blacks should immerse themselves in the history, values, and contributions of African culture. The first group values _____, whereas the second emphasizes _____.

2. John knows and likes the Mexican-American minority in his town, but he privately believes that Anglo culture is superior to all others. His belief is evidence of his _____.

3. What strategy does the Robbers Cave study suggest for reducing "us-them" thinking and hostility between groups?

Answers:
1. acculturation, ethnic identity   2. ethnocentrism   3. interdependence in reaching mutual goals

---

What's Ahead

- Is prejudice more likely to be a *cause* of war or a *result* of it?

- What *is* prejudice exactly—discomfort with people of another group or active dislike?

- How can well-meaning members of different ethnic groups get caught in a "cycle of distrust"?

- Why isn't mere contact between cultural groups enough to resolve their conflicts? What does work?

9.5 Group Conflict and Prejudice

A *prejudice* consists of a negative stereotype and a strong, unreasonable dislike or hatred of a group—feelings that often remain immune to evidence or

even to experience with individual members of the group. In his classic book *The Nature of Prejudice,* Gordon Allport (1954/1979) described the responses characteristic of a prejudiced person when confronted with evidence contradicting his or her beliefs:

MR. X: The trouble with Jews is that they only take care of their own group.

MR. Y: But the record of the Community Chest campaign shows that they give more generously, in proportion to their numbers, to the general charities of the community, than do non-Jews.

MR. X: That shows they are always trying to buy favor and intrude into Christian affairs. They think of nothing but money; that is why there are so many Jewish bankers.

MR. Y: But a recent study shows that the percentage of Jews in the banking business is negligible, far smaller than the percentage of non-Jews.

MR. X: That's just it; they don't go in for respectable business; they are only in the movie business or run night clubs.

Notice that Mr. X doesn't even try to respond to Mr. Y's evidence; he just moves along to another reason for his dislike of Jews. That is the slippery nature of prejudice.

The Origins of Prejudice

Prejudice is a universal human experience because it has so many sources: psychological, social, economic, and cultural.

Psychologically, prejudice often serves to ward off feelings of doubt and fear. Prejudiced persons may transfer their worries onto the target group; thus, a person who has doubts or anxieties about his own sexuality may develop a hatred of gay people. Prejudice also allows people to use the target group as a scapegoat: "Those people are the source of all my troubles." And, as research from many nations has confirmed, prejudice is a tonic for low self-esteem: People puff up their own low self-worth by disliking or hating groups they see as inferior (Islam & Hewstone, 1993; Stephan et al., 1994; Tajfel & Turner, 1986).

However, not all prejudices have deep-seated psychological roots. Some are acquired through groupthink and other pressures to conform to the views of friends, relatives, or associates. Some prejudices are passed along mindlessly from one generation to another, as when parents communicate to their children that "We don't associate with people like that." And some are acquired uncritically from advertising, TV shows, and news reports that contain derogatory images and stereotypes of certain groups.

Prejudice also has important economic functions. It makes official forms of discrimination seem legitimate, by justifying the majority group's dominance, status, or greater wealth (Sidanius, Pratto, & Bobo, 1996). Historically, for example, white men in positions of power have justified their exclusion of women and minorities from the workplace and politics by claiming these individuals were inferior, irrational, and incompetent (Gould, 1996). But it's not only white men who do this. Any majority group—of any ethnicity, gender, or nationality—that discriminates against a minority will call upon prejudice to legitimize its actions (Islam & Hewstone, 1993).

Although it is widely believed that prejudice is the primary cause of conflict and war between groups, prejudice is actually more often a *result* of conflict and war; it *legitimizes* them. When any two groups are in direct competition for jobs, or when people are worried about their incomes and the stability of their communities, prejudice between them increases (Doty, Peterson, & Winter, 1991). Social psychologist Elliot Aronson (1999) traced the rise and fall of attitudes toward Chinese immigrants in the United States in the nineteenth century, as reported in newspapers of the time. When the Chinese were working in the gold mines and potentially taking jobs from white laborers, whites described them as depraved, vicious, and bloodthirsty. Just a decade later, when the Chinese began working on the transcontinental railroad—doing difficult and dangerous jobs that few white men wanted—prejudice against them declined. Whites described them as hardworking, industrious, and law-abiding. Then, after the railroad was finished and the Chinese had to compete with Civil War veterans for scarce jobs, white attitudes changed again. Whites now considered the Chinese to be "criminal," "crafty," "conniving," and "stupid". (The white newspapers did not report the attitudes of the Chinese.)

9.3

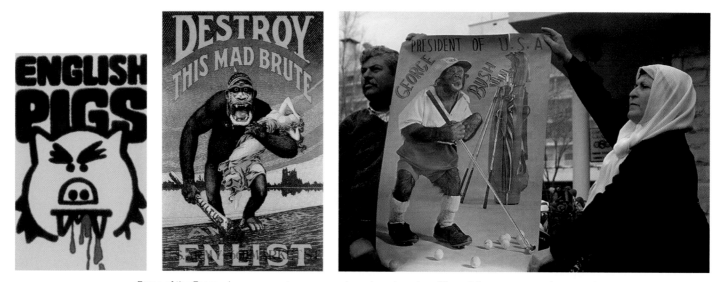

Faces of the Enemy: In every country, propaganda posters stereotype "them," the enemy, as ugly, aggressive, brutish, and greedy, and usually not quite human. These examples show an IRA poster of bloodthirsty "English pigs"; an American depiction of the German enemy in World War I as a "mad brute"; and a Jordanian caricature of former President George Bush as a golf-playing monkey.

The ultimate competition between groups, of course, is war. When two nations are at war, prejudice against the enemy allows each side to continue feeling righteous about its cause. As you can see in the propaganda posters on this page, each side portrays the other in stereotyped ways to demonize and dehumanize the enemy, making it seem that the enemy deserves to be killed. Fomenting prejudice against the perceived enemy—calling them traitors, heathens, vermin, subhuman, baby-killers, brutes, or monsters—legitimizes the attackers' motives for war.

Finally, prejudice against other groups also serves cultural purposes, bonding people to their own ethnic or national group and its ways; indeed, this may be a major evolutionary reason for the universal persistence of prejudice (Fishbein, 1996). In this respect, prejudice is the flip side of ethnocentrism; it is not only that *we* are good and kind, but also that *they* are bad and evil (Brewer, 1999).

The Varieties of Prejudice

One problem in studying prejudice is that not all prejudiced people are prejudiced in the same way or to the same extent. A person might wish to be unprejudiced, yet feel uncomfortable with members of certain groups. Should we put this person in the same category as one who is an outspoken bigot or who actively discriminates against others because of their membership in some category? Do good intentions count? What if a person knows nothing about another culture and mindlessly blurts out a dopy remark that reflects that ignorance? Does that count as prejudice or thoughtlessness? These questions complicate the measurement of prejudice.

If you ask people directly about their attitudes, you might conclude that prejudice in the United States and Canada is declining. White attitudes toward integration have become steadily more favorable, and the once-common beliefs that blacks are inferior to whites, and women inferior to men, have declined sharply (Plant & Devine, 1998; Tougas et al., 1995; Twenge, 1997)

But prejudice is a weasel—hard to grasp and hold on to. For example, male "sexism" is not only a matter of animosity toward women. In research with 15,000 men and women in 19 nations, psychologists have found that "hostile sexism," which reflects active dislike, is different from "benevolent sexism"—superficially positive attitudes toward women that put women on a pedestal but nonetheless reinforce their subordination. The latter type of sexism is affectionate but patronizing, conveying the attitude that women are so wonderful, good, kind, and moral

Thinking Critically About Defining and Measuring Prejudice

that they should stay at home and out of public life (Glick et al., 2000).

In addition, overt attitudes are often not an accurate measure of prejudice because people know they should not admit their prejudices. For example, when white students fill out a prejudice questionnaire in the presence of a black experimenter, they have lower prejudice scores than they do when the experimenter is white (Fazio et al., 1995). So researchers have turned to other ways of measuring prejudice. Some argue that prejudice against blacks lurks behind a mask of *symbolic racism,* in which whites focus not on dislike of black individuals but on issues such as "reverse discrimination" or "hard-core criminals." In this view, such issues have become code words for the continuing animosity that many whites feel toward blacks (Bell, 1992; Jones, 1997). Instead of asking respondents about blacks as individuals or about feelings of prejudice in general, therefore, researchers might probe for hostile feelings that lie beneath surface attitudes. The same whites who will not admit to disliking blacks, for example, might agree that "blacks are getting too demanding in their push for equal rights" (Brauer, Wasel, & Niedenthal, 2000).

Another method of measuring prejudice is to observe how people who say they are unprejudiced actually behave when they are angered or stressed (Jones, 1991; Sinclair & Kunda, 1999). In one experiment, students thought they were giving shock to other students in a study of biofeedback. White students initially showed *less* aggression toward blacks than toward whites. But as soon as the white students were angered by overhearing derogatory remarks about themselves, they showed *more* aggression toward blacks than toward whites (Rogers & Prentice-Dunn, 1981). The same pattern appears in studies of how English-speaking Canadians behave toward French-speaking Canadians (Meindl & Lerner, 1985), straights toward homosexuals, and non-Jewish students toward Jews (Fein & Spencer, 1997). These findings imply that people are willing to control negative feelings toward targets of prejudice under normal conditions. But as soon as they are angry or frustrated, or get a jolt to their self-esteem, their real prejudice reveals itself.

A third approach to measuring prejudice relies on unobtrusive, *implicit* measures rather than direct, *explicit* attitude questionnaires or behavioral indicators (Fazio et al., 1995; Guglielmi, 1999). Implicit processes are assumed to be nonconscious, auto-

matic, and unintentional, and hence a truer measure of a person's "real" feelings. One implicit measure taps people's unconscious associations between a stimulus and its degree of pleasantness or unpleasantness (Greenwald, McGhee, & Schwartz, 1998). Applying this approach, researchers have found that many people who describe themselves as being unprejudiced nonetheless have unconscious negative associations for certain groups.

For example, the Japanese and the Koreans have a long history of mutual antagonism. In one experiment, ethnically Korean students found it more difficult to process Japanese names associated with pleasant words than to process Korean names with pleasant associations, and the reverse was true for the Japanese students (Greenwald, McGhee, & Schwartz, 1998). This approach has also been used to identify allegedly unconscious prejudices against blacks, women, and the elderly. However, it is difficult to know what these implicit measures actually measure: true prejudice, unfamiliarity with the target stimulus, or activation of a stereotype. As we saw earlier, people find familiar names, products, and even nonsense syllables to be more pleasant than unfamiliar ones. So is this test measuring true prejudice toward a target or merely unfamiliarity with it?

As you can see, defining and measuring prejudice are not easy tasks. They involve distinguishing explicit attitudes from unconscious hostility, active dislike from simple discomfort, and what people say from how they actually behave (Brauer, Wasel, & Niedenthal, 2000).

Reducing Conflict and Prejudice

Given the many sources and varieties of prejudice, no one method of reducing it is likely to work in all situations. That is why social and cultural psychologists have designed different programs to try to reduce misunderstanding and prejudice, depending on the origins of a given conflict and the factors that are supporting it.

For example, according to Patricia Devine (1995), people who are actively trying to break their "prejudice habit" should not be lumped together with bigots. Their discomfort could reflect an honest effort to put old prejudices aside or simple unfamiliarity with another group's ways. When people are unfamiliar or uncomfortable with members of another group, a "cycle of distrust" and animosity can emerge even when individuals start off with the

9.2

best intentions to get along. Some majority-group members, although highly motivated to work well with minorities, may be self-conscious and anxious about doing the wrong thing. Their anxiety makes them behave awkwardly, for instance by blurting out dumb remarks and avoiding eye contact with minority-group members. The minority members, based on their own history of discrimination, may interpret the majority-group members' behavior as evidence of hostility and respond with withdrawal or anger. The majority members, not understanding that their own anxieties have been interpreted as evidence of prejudice, regard the minority members' behavior as unreasonable or mysterious, so they reciprocate the hostility or withdraw. This behavior confirms the minority members' suspicions about the majority's true feelings (Devine, Evett, & Vasquez-Suson, 1996). By understanding this cycle, Devine argues, people of good will can learn to break out of it.

What happens, however, when two groups really do bear enormous animosity toward each other, for historical, economic, or emotional reasons? How then might their conflicts be reduced?

Sociocultural research emphasizes the importance of changing people's circumstances, rather than waiting around for individuals to undergo a moral or psychological conversion. They have identified four conditions that must be met before conflict and prejudice between groups can be lessened (Allport, 1954/1979; Dovidio, Gaertner, & Validzic, 1998; Fisher, 1994; Pettigrew, 1998; Rubin, 1994; Slavin & Cooper, 1999; Staub, 1996; Stephan, 1999; Wittig & Grant-Thompson, 1998):

1 *Both sides must have equal legal status, economic opportunities, and power.* This requirement is the spur behind efforts to change laws that permit discrimination. Integration of public facilities in the American South would never have occurred if civil-rights advocates had waited for segregationists to have a change of heart. Women would never have gotten the right to vote, attend college, or do "men's work" without persistent challenges to the laws that permitted gender discrimination. Laws, however, do not necessarily change attitudes if all they do is produce unequal contact between groups or if competition for jobs continues.

THE MANY TARGETS OF PREJUDICE

Prejudice has a long history, everywhere in the world. Why do new prejudices keep emerging and some old ones persist? In the 1920s and during World War II, anti-Japanese feelings ran high, and returned during America's economic competition with Japan in the early 1990s. Prejudice toward gay men and lesbians has often erupted in virulent protest, anger, and violence. Antisemitism is one of the world's oldest prejudices, and still continues among those who make Jews the scapegoats for their problems.

2 *Authorities and community institutions must endorse egalitarian norms and provide moral support and legitimacy for both sides.* Society must establish norms of equality and support them in the actions of its officials—teachers, employers, the judicial system, government officials, and the police.

3 *Both sides must have opportunities to work and socialize together, formally and informally.* According to the *contact hypothesis*, prejudice declines when people have the chance to get used to one another's rules, food, music, customs, and attitudes. By making friends with one another, people of different groups and cultures can discover their shared interests and shared humanity, and stereotypes are shattered (Pettigrew, 1998). The contact hypothesis has been supported by many studies in the laboratory and in the "real world": studies of newly integrated housing projects in the American South during the 1950s and 1960s; relationships between German and immigrant Turkish children in German schools; young people's attitudes toward the elderly; healthy people's attitudes toward the mentally ill; nondisabled children's attitudes toward the disabled; and straight people's prejudices against gay men and lesbians (Fishbein, 1996; Herek, 1999; Herek & Capitanio, 1996; Pettigrew, 1997; Wilner, Walkley, & Cook, 1955). When people make friends with members of another group, they do tend to become less prejudiced against the group as a whole.

Nevertheless, contact and friendship alone are not enough to reduce prejudice and achieve harmony between groups. This is sadly apparent at multiethnic schools, where students often form ethnic cliques, fighting other groups and defending their own ways.

4 *Both sides must cooperate, working together for a common goal.* Cooperation often reduces us-them thinking and prejudice by creating an encompassing social identity ("We're all in this together"). Many successful cooperative situations have been established in schools, businesses, and communities, requiring formerly antagonistic groups to work together for a common goal—the Eagles and the Rattlers solution. For example, some elementary schools have experimented with having children from different ethnic groups work

Segregated facilities for blacks were legal in America until the 1950s, and today many neighborhoods and schools remain separate and unequal. During the economic recession of the early 1990s, Iranians and other immigrants became targets of American hostility. Native Americans have been objects of hatred since Europeans first arrived on the continent. And anti-female prejudice continues.

Tensions between groups often subside when people work together on a common goal. Here, volunteers from Habitat for Humanity, a group that constructs housing for low-income people, build a new home in the Watts area of Los Angeles.

together on a task that is broken up like a jigsaw puzzle; each child needs to cooperate with the others to put the assignment together. Children in such "jigsaw" classes tend to do better, like their classmates better, and become less stereotyped in their thinking than children in competitive classrooms (Aronson & Patnoe, 1997; Slavin & Cooper, 1999). However, cooperation does not work when members of a group have unequal status, blame one another for loafing or "dropping the ball," or believe that their teachers or employers are playing favorites.

Each of these four approaches to reducing prejudice is important, but none is sufficient on its own. Perhaps one reason that group conflicts and prejudice are so persistent is that all four conditions are rarely met at the same time.

QUICK QUIZ

Try to overcome your prejudice against quizzes by taking this one.

1. What are four important conditions required for reducing prejudice and conflict between groups?

2. Surveys find that large percentages of African-Americans, Asian-Americans, and Latinos hold negative stereotypes of one another and resent other minorities almost as much as they resent whites. What are some reasons that people who have themselves been victims of stereotyping and prejudice would hold the same attitudes toward others?

Answers:

1. Both sides must have equal status and power; have the moral, legal, and economic support of authorities; have opportunities to socialize formally and informally; and cooperate for a common goal.   2. low self-esteem, conformity with relatives and friends who share these prejudices, parental lessons and messages conveyed by the media, and economic competition for jobs and resources

PSYCHOLOGY IN THE NEWS, REVISITED

If ever an incident illustrated the power of social norms and cultural differences, the shooting of Yoshihiro Hattori is it. When Rodney Peairs's case came to trial, the jury acquitted him of manslaughter after only three hours of deliberation. The Japanese were appalled at this verdict. To them, it illustrated everything that is wrong with America. In their view, the United States is a nation rife with guns and violence—a "developing nation," as one news

commentator put it, that is still growing out of its Wild West past. The Japanese cannot imagine a nation in which private individuals are allowed to keep guns. The murder rate in Japan is a tiny percentage of what it is in America.

"I think for Japanese the most remarkable thing is that you could get a jury of Americans together, and they could conclude that shooting someone before you even talked to him was reasonable behavior," Masako Notoji, a professor of American cultural studies in Tokyo, told *The New York Times*. "We are more civilized. We rely on words." In contrast, the citizens of Baton Rouge were surprised that the case came to trial at all. What is more right and natural, they asked, than protecting yourself and your family from intruders? "A man's home is his castle," said one potential juror, expressing puzzlement that Peairs had even been arrested. A local man, joining the many sympathizers of Rodney Peairs, said, "It would be to me what a normal person would do under those circumstances."

But what is normal? As findings in cultural psychology have shown, what is normal in some cultures may be considered abnormal, immoral, or unnatural in other cultures. Within culturally diverse nations, the customs of one group often conflict sharply with those of another. In California, for example, an immigrant from Laos killed a puppy, a sacrifice he believed would help his wife recover from illness but one that enraged his neighbors and violated the animal-cruelty laws. The use of a gun to protect one's "home and castle" is more accepted in Southern and Western states in America, where a "culture of honor" flourishes, than in the North and East—where men who behave like Rodney Peairs usually go to jail (Nisbett, 1993).

Research from social and cultural psychology therefore knocks us off our ethnocentric pedestal. It is reassuring to divide the world into cultures and individuals who are good or bad, kind or cruel, moral or immoral. Most people want to believe that harm to others is done only by evil people who

Thinking Critically About "Evil" Cultures

are bad down to their bones, or that wars are started only by evil cultures that don't have a single good custom to recommend them. In fact, no culture can claim to be wholly virtuous, and no culture is entirely villainous, either.

The Nazis have come to symbolize the evil in human nature, because they systematically exterminated millions of Jews, Gypsies, homosexuals, disabled people, and anyone else not of the "pure" Aryan "race." But the Nazis were not a strange historical oddity; torture, genocide, and massacres are all too common in history. Americans and Canadians slaughtered native peoples in North America, Turks slaughtered Armenians, the Khmer Rouge slaughtered millions of fellow Cambodians, the Spanish conquistadors slaughtered native peoples in Mexico and South America, Idi Amin waged a reign of terror against his own people in Uganda, the Japanese slaughtered Koreans and Chinese, Iraqis slaughtered Kurds, despotic political regimes in Argentina and Chile killed thousands of dissidents and rebels. In Rwanda in the 1990s, hundreds of thousands of Tutsis were shot or hacked to death with machetes by members of the rival Hutu tribe;

and in the former Yugoslavia, Bosnian Serbs massacred thousands of Bosnian Muslims in the name of "ethnic cleansing."

Many people assume that these outbreaks of horrifying violence are a result of inner aggressive drives or, in the case of Rwanda and Yugoslavia, "age-old tribal hatreds." In fact, policies of genocide against a perceived outside enemy are almost always generated by governments that feel weakened and vulnerable (D. Smith, 1998; Staub, 1996). Governments then rely on the social-psychological processes discussed in this chapter—including obedience to authority, conformity, rationalization, groupthink, deindividuation, stereotyping, and prejudice—to carry out their policies.

That is why, from the standpoint of social and cultural psychology, all human beings, like all cultures, contain the potential for good *and* bad; how most of us actually behave in a given situation depends more on human social-organization than on human nature. The philosopher Hannah Arendt (1963) covered the trial of Adolf Eichmann, the Nazi officer who supervised the deportation and death of millions of Jews. Arendt used the phrase *the banality of evil* to describe how it was possible for Eichmann and other ordinary people in Nazi Germany to commit the monstrous acts they did. (*Banal* means "commonplace" or "unoriginal.")

Adolf Eichmann at his trial. Was he an "evil monster" or an example of the "banality of evil"?

The compelling evidence for the banality of evil is, perhaps, the hardest lesson in psychology. Of course, some people do stand out as being unusually sadistic—or unusually heroic. But everyone, from Rodney Peairs to Yoshihiro Hattori, is embedded in cultural norms and traditions. And within any culture, otherwise good people can do terribly disturbing things when the situation "takes over" and, like Bonnie Peairs, they do not stop to think critically. They may join self-destructive cults, inflict pain on others if ordered to, and go along with a violent crowd.

The research discussed in this chapter suggests that ethnocentrism and prejudice will always be with us, as long as differences exist among groups. But it can also help us formulate realistic yet nonviolent ways of living in a diverse world. By identifying the conditions that create the banality of evil, perhaps we can create others that foster the "banality of virtue"—everyday acts of kindness, selflessness, and generosity.

TAKING PSYCHOLOGY WITH YOU

Travels Across the Cultural Divide

A French salesman worked for a company that was bought by Americans. When the new American manager ordered him to step up his sales within the next three months, the employee quit in a huff, taking his customers with him. Why? In France, it takes years to develop customers; in family-owned businesses, relationships with customers may span generations. The American wanted instant results, as Americans often do, but the French salesman knew this was impossible and quit. The American view was, "He wasn't up to the job; he's lazy and disloyal, so he stole my customers." The French view was, "There is no point in explaining anything to a person who is so stupid as to think you can acquire loyal customers in three months" (Hall & Hall, 1987).

Both men were committing the fundamental attribution error: assuming that the other person's behavior was due to personality rather than the situation—in this case, a situation governed by cultural rules. Many corporations now realize that such rules are not trivial and that success in a global economy depends on understanding them. You, too, can benefit from the psychological research on culture, whether you plan to do business abroad, visit as a tourist, or just want to get along better in your own society.

● *Be sure you understand the other culture's rules, manners, and customs.* If you find yourself getting angry over something a person from another culture is doing, try to find out whether your expectations and perceptions of that person's behavior are appropriate. For example, Koreans typically do not shake hands when greeting strangers, whereas most North Americans and Europeans do. People who shake hands as a gesture of friendship and courtesy are likely to feel insulted if another person refuses to do the same unless they understand this cultural difference.

Or suppose that you are shopping in the Middle East or Latin America, where bargaining on a price is the usual practice. If you are not used to bargaining, the experience is likely to be exasperating—you will not know whether you got taken or got a great buy. On the other hand, if you are from a bargaining culture, you will feel just as exasperated if a seller offers you a flat price. "Where's the fun in this?" you'll say. "The whole human transaction of shopping is gone!" Whichever kind of culture you come from, you may need a "translator" to help you navigate the unfamiliar system. For example, in Los Angeles, a physician we know could not persuade his Iranian patients that office fees are fixed, not negotiable. They kept offering him half, then 60 percent . . . and each time he said "no" they thought he was just taking a hard negotiating position. It took a bicultural relative of the patients to explain the odd American custom of fixed prices for service.

● *When in Rome, do as the Romans do—as much as possible.* Most of the things you really need to know about a culture are not to be found in the guidebooks or travelogues. To learn the unspoken rules of a culture, look, listen, and observe. What is the pace of life like? Do people regard brash individuality as admirable or embarrassing? When customers enter a shop, do they greet and chat with the shopkeeper or ignore the person as they browse?

Remember, though, that even when you know the rules, you may find it difficult to carry them out. For example, cultures differ in their tolerance for prolonged gazes (Keating, 1994). In the Middle East, two men will look directly at one another as they talk, but such direct gazes would be deeply uncomfortable to most Japanese and a sign of insult or confrontation to some African-Americans. Knowing this fact about gaze rules can help people

accept the reality of different customs, but most of us will still feel uncomfortable trying to change our own ways.

● *Avoid stereotyping.* Try not to let your awareness of general cultural differences cause you to overlook individual variations within cultures. During a dreary Boston winter, social psychologist Roger Brown (1986) went to the Bahamas for a vacation. To his surprise, he found the people he met unfriendly, rude, and sullen. He decided that the reason was that Bahamians had to deal with spoiled, demanding foreigners, and he tried out this hypothesis on a cab driver. The cab driver looked at Brown in amazement, smiled cheerfully, and told him that Bahamians don't mind tourists; just *unsmiling* tourists.

And then Brown realized what had been going on. "Not tourists generally, but this tourist, myself, was the cause," he wrote. "Confronted with my unrelaxed wintry Boston face, they had assumed I had no interest in them and had responded non-committally, inexpressively. I had created the Bahamian national character. Everywhere I took my face it sprang into being. So I began smiling a lot, and the Bahamians changed their national character. In fact, they lost any national character and differentiated into individuals."

Wise travelers can use their knowledge of cultural differences to expand their understanding of human behavior, while avoiding the trap of stereotyping. Sociocultural research teaches us to appreciate the countless explicit and implicit cultural rules that govern our behavior, values, and attitudes, and those of others. Yet we should not forget Roger Brown's lesson that every human being is an individual: one who not only reflects his or her culture, but shares the common concerns of all humanity.

SUMMARY

● Like learning theorists, *social and cultural psychologists* emphasize environmental influences on behavior, but they broaden their attention to include the entire sociocultural context. Social psychologists study the influence of *norms, roles,* and groups on behavior and cognition; cultural psychologists study the cultural origins of and variations in norms and roles.

Roles and Rules

● Two classic studies illustrate the power of roles to affect individual actions. In Milgram's obedience study, most people in the role of "teacher" inflicted what they thought was extreme shock on another person because of the authority of the experimenter. Nothing the victim said or did affected the subjects' behavior, but people were less likely to inflict shock under certain conditions—for example, when the experimenter left the room, when the victim was right there in the room, and when the subject had an ally who refused to go further. In Zimbardo's prison study, college students quickly fell into the role of "prisoner" or "guard."

● Obedience to authority contributes to the smooth running of society, but obedience can also lead to actions that are deadly, foolish, or illegal. People obey orders because they can be punished if they d o not, because they are convinced of the authority's legitimacy, and because they hope to gain advantages. Even when they would rather not obey, they may do so because they allocate responsibility to the authority; because their role is *routinized* into duties that are performed mindlessly; because they are embarrassed to violate the rules of good manners and lack the words to protest; or because they have been *entrapped*.

Social Influences on Beliefs

● Researchers in the area of *social cognition* study how people's relationships and social environment affect their beliefs and perception. For example, according to *attribution theory*, people are motivated to search for causes to which they can attribute their own and other people's behavior. Their attributions may be *situational* or *dispositional*. The *fundamental attribution error* occurs when people overestimate personality traits as a cause of behavior and underestimate the influence of the situation. A *self-serving bias* allows people to excuse their mistakes by blaming the situation yet also take credit for their good deeds. According to the *just-world hypothesis*, most people need to believe that the world is fair and that people get what they deserve. To preserve this belief, they may *blame victims* of abuse or injustice for provoking or deserving it, instead of blaming the perpetrators.

● People hold many *attitudes*, which include cognitions and feelings about a subject. One important influence on attitudes is the shared experiences of a person's age group or generation, which form their *generational identity*. Attitudes may change as an effort to reduce *cognitive dissonance*. Another influence is the *validity effect:* Simply hearing a statement over and over again makes it seem more believable. Techniques of attitude change include associating a product or message with someone who is famous, attractive, or expert; and linking the product with good feelings. Fear tactics tend to backfire.

● Some methods of attitude change are intentionally manipulative. Tactics of *coercive persuasion* include putting a person under extreme distress, defining problems simplistically, offering the appearance of unconditional love and acceptance in exchange for unquestioning loyalty, creating a new identity for the person, using entrapment, and controlling access to outside information.

Individuals in Groups

● In groups, individuals often behave differently than they would on their own. They may *conform* to social pressure because they identify with a group, trust the group's judgment or knowledge, hope for personal gain, or wish to be liked. But they also may conform mindlessly and self-destructively, violating their own preferences and values because "everyone else is doing it."

● Groups that are strongly cohesive, are isolated from other views, are under outside pressure, and have strong leaders are vulnerable to *groupthink,* the tendency of group members to think alike, censor themselves, actively suppress disagreement, and feel that their decisions are invulnerable. Groupthink often produces faulty decisions because group members fail to seek disconfirming evidence for their ideas. However, groups can be structured to counteract groupthink.

● *Diffusion of responsibility* in a group can lead to inaction on the part of individuals, such as *bystander apathy* or, in work groups, *social loafing.* The diffusion of responsibility is likely to occur under conditions that promote *deindividuation,* the loss of awareness of one's individuality. Deindividuation increases when people feel anonymous, as in a large group or crowd, or when they are wearing masks or uniforms. In some situations, crowd norms lead deindividuated people to behave aggressively, but in others, crowd norms foster helpfulness.

- The willingness to speak up for an unpopular opinion, blow the whistle on illegal practices, or help a stranger in trouble and perform other acts of *altruism* is partly a matter of personal belief and conscience. But several situational factors are also important. These include being in a situation that fosters the perception that help and intervention are necessary, and that increases the likelihood that a person will take responsibility. Other factors include deciding that the costs of not doing anything are greater than the costs of getting involved, having an ally, and becoming entrapped in a commitment to help or dissent.

Us Versus Them: Group Identity

- In addition to having their own individual identities, people develop *social identities,* aspects of self-identity that are based on nationality, ethnicity, and social roles. Social identities provide a feeling of place and connection in the world.

- In culturally diverse societies, many people face the problem of balancing their *ethnic identity* with *acculturation* into the larger society. Depending on whether ethnic identity and acculturation are strong or weak, a person may become *bicultural,* choose *assimilation,* become an *ethnic separatist,* or feel *marginal.*

- *Ethnocentrism,* the belief that your own ethnic group or culture is superior to all others, promotes "us-them" thinking. One effective strategy for reducing us-them thinking and hostility between groups is cooperation, when both sides must work together to reach a common goal.

- *Stereotypes* help people rapidly process new information, retrieve memories, organize experience, and predict how others will behave. But they distort reality by exaggerating differences between groups, producing selective perception, and underestimating the differences within groups.

Group Conflict and Prejudice

- A *prejudice* is an unreasonable negative feeling toward a category of people. The sources of prejudice are partly psychological: Prejudice wards off feelings of anxiety and doubt, provides a scapegoat, and bolsters self-esteem when a person feels threatened. But other causes of prejudice are social (people acquire prejudices through conformity and groupthink, parental lessons, and media images); economic (prejudice justifies a majority group's economic interests and dominance, and, in extreme cases, it legitimizes war); and cultural (prejudice bonds people to their nation and social groups).

- People often disagree on whether racism and other prejudices are declining or have merely taken new forms. Because many people are unwilling to admit their prejudices openly, some researchers measure *symbolic racism* (prejudice disguised in opinions about race-related social issues); people's actual behavior toward a target group when they are stressed, provoked, or insulted; or nonconscious, *implicit* prejudice.

- Efforts to reduce prejudice and group conflict must take into account the origins of the conflict and the factors that support it. In groups where members of majority and minority groups are unfamiliar with one another's ways, it is important to break the "cycle of distrust," by not inferring prejudice or hostility when none is intended.

- Four conditions are required for reducing prejudice and conflict between groups: Both sides must have equal legal status, economic standing, and power; both sides must have the legal and moral support of authorities and the larger culture; both sides must have opportunities to work and socialize together (the *contact hypothesis*); and both sides must work together for a common goal.

- Although many people believe that only bad people do bad deeds, the principles of social and cultural psychology show that under certain conditions, good people are often induced to do bad things, too. All individuals are affected by the rules and norms of their cultures; and by the social processes of obedience and conformity, bystander apathy, groupthink, diffusion of responsibility, deindividuation, ethnocentrism, stereotyping, and prejudice.

KEY TERMS

LOOKING BACK ◄

- How do social rules regulate behavior—and what is likely to happen when you violate them? (p. 296)

- Do you have to be mean or disturbed to inflict pain on someone just because an authority tells you to? (p. 298)

- How can ordinary college students be transformed into sadistic prison guards? (p. 299)

- How can people be "entrapped" into violating their moral principles? (p. 302)

- What is one of the most common mistakes people make when explaining the behavior of others? (p. 303)

- Why would a person blame victims of rape or torture for having brought their misfortunes on themselves? (p. 304)

- What is the "Big Lie," and why does it work so well? (p. 306)

- What is the difference between ordinary techniques of persuasion and the coercive techniques used by cults? (p. 307)

- Why do people in groups often go along with the majority even when the majority is dead wrong? (pp. 308–309)

- How can "groupthink" lead to bad, even catastrophic, decisions? (p. 310)

- Why is it common for a group of people to hear someone shout for help without one of them calling the police? (pp. 310–311)

- What enables some people to dissent, take moral action, or blow the whistle on wrongdoers? (p. 313)

- In what different ways do people balance their ethnic identity and their membership in the larger culture? (pp. 314–315)

- What is an effective antidote to "us-them" thinking? (p. 317)

- How do stereotypes benefit us, and how do they distort reality? (p. 317)

- Is prejudice more likely to be a *cause* of war or a *result* of it? (p. 319)

- What *is* prejudice exactly—discomfort with people of another group or active dislike? (pp. 320–321)

- How can well-meaning members of different ethnic groups get caught in a "cycle of distrust"? (pp. 321–322)

- Why isn't mere contact between cultural groups enough to resolve their conflicts? What does work? (pp. 322–324)

Internet Addiction Growing

For Some "Internet Vampires," Lure of the Internet Is Stronger Than That of Sleep, Classes, or Meals

TROY, NY, JULY 11, 2000. A young man wandered into the counseling center at his college to seek help for his failing grades. For a year he had been a good student, but now he was depressed, skipping classes, and arguing with his parents. He had also spent 2,000 hours on the Internet that semester.

According to a survey of students at eight colleges and universities, "Internet dependence" and addiction are growing problems. "We had an honors student who was spending 12 to 15 hours a day on the Internet, and essentially flunked out of school," said one psychologist at the University of Maryland. Barbara McMullen, director of e-commerce initiatives at Marist College in Poughkeepsie, calls these students "Internet vampires," because

"Addiction" to the Internet is a growing problem, according to some psychologists.

they sleep all day and then stay up all night until dawn, chatting online, sending countless e-mails, or playing multiuser dimension games (MUDs).

So widespread is the problem that the Internet now has "Internet addiction" message boards and support groups. One student wrote to an Internet-addiction message board that his time online was "seriously hurting both my schoolwork and my social life, and therefore it must stop. But I'm not sure what to do to keep myself off the net. My self-discipline isn't what it should be."

PSYCHOLOGICAL DISORDERS

Do these students have a plain old problem—not being able to organize their time, wanting to procrastinate and have fun rather than study—or do they have an addiction, a disorder comparable to an addiction to drugs? Is their weakened "self-discipline" something they can control?

You don't have to be a psychologist to recognize the more extreme forms of abnormal behavior. When people think of "mental illness," they usually think of people with delusions, people who behave in bizarre ways, or people who, like the Unabomber Theodore Kaczynski, plant bombs or commit random murders. But most psychological problems, like those of students with "Internet dependence," are far less dramatic and far more common. Some people go through episodes of complete inability to function, yet get along fine between those episodes. Many people function adequately every day, yet suffer chronic feelings of melancholy—always feeling below par in happiness.

In this chapter, you will learn how psychologists and psychiatrists define disorder and how they diagnose a wide range of psychological problems. One of the most common worries that people have is "Am I normal?" It is normal to fear being abnormal—especially when you are reading about psychological problems! But it is also normal to have problems. All of us on occasion have difficulties that seem too much to handle. As you read, ask yourself how you would pinpoint precisely when "normal" problems shade into "abnormal" ones on the spectrum of human behavior.

What's Ahead

- Is insanity the same thing as having a mental disorder?

- What are three approaches to defining "mental disorder"?

- Why were slaves who dreamed of freedom once considered to be mentally ill?

- Why is the standard guide to the diagnosis of mental disorders so controversial?

- Can an "inkblot" test reveal your psychological problems?

10.1 Defining and Diagnosing Disorder

Many people confuse *abnormal behavior*—behavior that deviates from the norm—with *mental disorder*, but the two are not the same. A person may behave in ways that are statistically rare (collecting ceramic pigs, being a genius at math, committing murder)

without having a mental illness. Conversely, some mental disorders, such as depression and anxiety, are extremely common. If frequency of the problem is not a guide, how then should we define mental disorder?

In the law, the definition of mental disorder rests primarily on whether a person is aware of the consequences of his or her actions and can control his or her behavior. If not, the person may be declared insane and therefore incompetent to stand trial. But *insanity* is a legal term only; psychologists and psychiatrists do not use it in either research or diagnosis.

Dilemmas of Definition

One problem with trying to define "mental disorder" is that the definition depends on whether we are taking society's point of view, the view of people who are personally affected by the troubled individual, or the perspective of troubled individuals themselves:

1 *Mental disorder as a violation of cultural standards.* Every society sets up standards for its members to follow, and those who break the most important rules that define appropriate behavior are usually considered deviant or disturbed. However, many of these rules are specific to a particular time or group. For example, in most North American cultural groups, having visions of a deceased relative, though not uncommon, is considered abnormal; bereaved people tend to keep their hal-

People the world over paint their bodies, but what is normal in one culture may be considered abnormal or eccentric in another. What is your reaction to the "normal" facial painting of the Samburu tribesman of Kenya, on the left, and the tattoos of the American bikers, on the right? Do you think these body decorations are beautiful, amusing, disgusting, or creepy? Why?

lucinations secret, for fear of being labeled "crazy" (Bentall, 1990). But the Chinese, the Hopi, and members of many other cultures regard such visions as perfectly normal.

Sometimes a society's notions of mental disorder serve the interests of those in power. In the early years of the nineteenth century, for instance, a physician named Samuel Cartwright argued that many slaves were suffering from *drapetomania,* an urge to escape from slavery (the label was concocted from the Latin *drapetes,* "runaway slave," and *mania,* "mad" or "crazy") (Kutchins & Kirk, 1997; Landrine, 1988). Thus doctors could assure slave owners that a mental illness, not the intolerable condition of slavery, made slaves seek freedom. Today, of course, psychologists consider "drapetomania" foolish and cruel. But decisions about what should count as a mental disorder often still depend on the prevailing cultural climate, as we will see.

2 *Mental disorder as maladaptive or harmful behavior.* Another approach to defining mental disorder emphasizes the negative consequences of a person's behavior. Some behavior is harmful to the individual—for example, the behavior of a woman who is so afraid of crowds that she cannot leave her house, a man who drinks so much that he cannot keep a job, and a student who is so anxious that he cannot take exams. In other cases, the individual may report feeling fine and deny that anything is wrong, yet behave in ways that are disruptive or dangerous to the community, or out of touch with reality—as when a child sets fires, a compulsive gambler loses the family savings, or a woman hears voices telling her to stalk a celebrity.

3 *Mental disorder as emotional distress.* A third approach identifies mental disorder in terms of a person's suffering. By this criterion, according to nationwide surveys, about 28 percent of all Americans in any given year have one or more mental disorders, including depression, anxiety, incapacitating fears, and problems with alcohol or other drugs (Kessler et al., 1994; Regier et al., 1993). This definition recognizes that a behavior that is unendurable or upsetting for one person, such as lack of interest in sex, may be acceptable and normal for another. But it does not cover the behavior of people who are clearly disturbed and dangerous to others, yet are not troubled about their actions.

In this chapter, we define **mental disorder** broadly, as any behavior or emotional state that causes an individual great suffering or worry, is self-defeating or self-destructive, or is maladaptive and disrupts either the person's relationships or the larger community. By this definition, many people will have some mental-health problem in the course of their lives, or their loved ones will.

Diagnosis: Art or Science?

Even armed with a broad definition of mental disorder, psychologists have found that agreeing on specific diagnoses is easier said than done. As George Albee (1985), a past president of the American Psychological Association, put it, "Appendicitis, a brain tumor and chicken pox are the same everywhere, regardless of culture or class; mental conditions, it seems, are not." In this section we will examine why it is often difficult to get psychologists to agree on what those mental conditions are, and how you might classify and assess them.

The DSM. The standard reference manual used to diagnose all mental disorders is the *Diagnostic and Statistical Manual of Mental Disorders* (DSM), published by the American Psychiatric Association (1994, 2000). The first edition of the DSM, in 1952, was only 86 pages long and contained just nine basic categories, including brain disorders, "mental deficiency," and personality problems. The DSM-IV, published in 1994, and a "transition" volume published in 2000, are both 900 pages long and contain more than 300 mental disorders. The DSM's primary aim is *descriptive:* to provide clear diagnostic categories, so that clinicians and researchers can agree on which disorders they are talking about, and then can study and treat these disorders. (For a list of the DSM's major categories, see Table 10.1.)

The DSM lists the symptoms of each disorder, and, wherever possible, gives information about the typical age of onset, predisposing factors, course of the disorder, prevalence of the disorder, sex ratio of those affected, and cultural issues that might affect diagnosis. In addition, clinicians are encouraged to evaluate each client according to five *axes,* or dimensions:

1. The primary clinical problem, such as depression.
2. Ingrained aspects of the client's personality that are likely to affect the person's ability to be treated, such as self-involvement or dependency.

mental disorder
Any behavior or emotional state that causes an individual great suffering or worry, is self-defeating or self-destructive, or is maladaptive and disrupts the person's relationships or the larger community.

Table 10.1　Major Diagnostic Categories in the DSM-IV

Disorders usually first diagnosed in infancy, childhood, or adolescence include mental retardation, attention deficit disorders (such as hyperactivity or an inability to concentrate), and developmental problems.

Delirium, dementia, amnesia, and other cognitive disorders are those resulting from brain damage, degenerative diseases such as syphilis or Alzheimer's, toxic substances, or drugs.

Substance-related disorders are problems associated with excessive use of or withdrawal from alcohol, amphetamines, caffeine, cocaine, hallucinogens, nicotine, opiates, or other drugs.

Schizophrenia and other psychotic disorders are disorders characterized by delusions, hallucinations, and severe disturbances in thinking and emotion.

Mood disorders include major depression, bipolar disorder (manic depression), and dysthymia (chronic depressed mood).

Anxiety disorders include generalized anxiety disorder, phobias, panic attacks with or without agoraphobia, posttraumatic stress disorder, and obsessive thoughts or compulsive rituals.

Eating disorders include anorexia nervosa (self-starvation because of an irrational fear of being or becoming fat) and bulimia nervosa (episodes of binge eating and vomiting).

Somatoform disorders involve physical symptoms (e.g., paralysis, heart palpitations, fatigue) for which no organic cause can be found. This category includes hypochondria (an extreme preoccupation with health and the unfounded conviction that one is ill) and conversion disorder (in which a physical symptom, such as a paralyzed arm or blindness, serves a psychological function).

Dissociative disorders include dissociative amnesia (in which important events cannot be remembered after a traumatic event) and dissociative identity disorder (formerly "multiple personality disorder"), characterized by the presence of two or more distinct identities or personalities.

Sexual and gender identity disorders include problems of sexual (gender) identity, such as transsexualism (wanting to be the other gender), problems of sexual performance (such as premature ejaculation or lack of orgasm), and paraphilias (unusual or bizarre imagery or acts that are necessary for sexual arousal, as in sadomasochism or exhibitionism).

Impulse-control disorders involve an inability to resist an impulse to perform some act that is harmful to the individual or to others, such as pathological gambling, stealing (kleptomania), setting fires (pyromania), or having violent rages.

Personality disorders are inflexible and maladaptive patterns that cause distress to the individual or impair the ability to function; they include paranoid, narcissistic, and antisocial personality disorders.

Additional conditions that may be a focus of clinical attention include "problems in living" such as bereavement, academic difficulties, spiritual problems, and acculturation problems.

3. Medical conditions that are relevant to the disorder, such as respiratory or digestive problems.

4. Social and environmental problems that can make the disorder worse, such as job and housing troubles or having recently left a network of close friends.

5. A global assessment of the client's overall level of functioning in work, relationships, and leisure time, including whether the problem is of recent origin or of long duration, and how incapacitating it is.

The DSM has had an extraordinary impact worldwide. Virtually all textbooks in psychiatry and psychology base their discussions of mental disorders on the DSM. Insurance companies require clinicians to assign their clients an appropriate DSM code number for the diagnosed disorder, which puts pressure on compilers of the manual to add more diagnoses so that physicians and psychologists will be compensated. Attorneys and judges often refer to the manual's list of mental disorders, even though the DSM warns that its categories "may not be wholly relevant to legal judgments."

Because of the DSM's powerful influence, it is important to be aware of its limitations. Critics point to the following concerns about the very effort to classify and label mental disorders, and the DSM's efforts in particular:

> **Thinking Critically About Diagnosing Disorders**

1 *The danger of overdiagnosis.* "If you give a small boy a hammer," wrote Abraham Kaplan (1967), "it will turn out that everything he runs into needs pounding." Likewise, say critics, if you give mental-health professionals a diagnostic label, it will turn out that everyone they run into has the symptoms of it.

Consider "attention deficit/hyperactivity disorder" (ADHD), a diagnostic label given to children (and adults) who are impulsive, messy, restless, and easily frustrated, and who have trouble concentrating. Since ADHD was added to the DSM, it has become the fastest-growing disorder in America, where it is diagnosed at least ten times as often as it is in Europe. It may reflect a true disorder in a minority of cases, but critics fear that parents, teachers, and mental-health professionals are overusing this diagnosis, especially on boys, who make up 80 to 90 percent of all ADHD cases. The critics argue that normal boy behavior—being rambunctious, refusing to nap, being playful, not listening to teachers in school—is being pathologized (Panksepp, 1998).

2 *The power of diagnostic labels.* Being given a diagnosis reassures people who are seeking an explanation for their emotional symptoms or problems ("Whew! So *that's* what I've got!"). But it can also create a self-fulfilling prophecy: The client tries to conform to the assigned diagnosis, and the clinician interprets everything the client does as confirmation of the diagnosis (Maddux, 1996).

Moreover, once a person has been given a diagnosis, other people begin to see that person primarily in terms of the label; it sticks like lint. For example, when a rebellious, disobedient teenager is diagnosed as having "oppositional defiant disorder," people tend to see him as a person with a permanent, official problem (something is wrong with his personality) and often fail to consider other explanations of his actions: Maybe he is defiant because he has been mistreated or his parents never listen to him. And

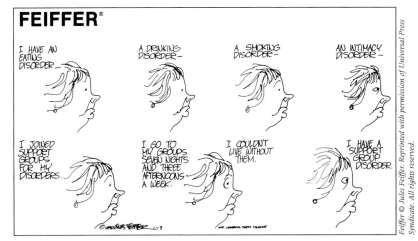

What's the difference between a common life problem and a mental disorder? And does it make a difference which one people think they have?

once he is labeled, observers tend to ignore changes in his behavior and the times when he is not being "defiant."

In a classic study, David Rosenhan (1973) demonstrated how rigid many people become when they are dealing with a person who has been given a psychiatric diagnosis. Eight healthy adults, including Rosenhan himself, got themselves admitted to psychiatric hospitals with diagnoses of schizophrenia or manic depression. Once inside, they stopped faking any symptoms and behaved normally. Nonetheless, the hospital staff regarded everything they did as odd behavior that further confirmed the diagnosis. For example, when the pseudopatients took notes on their experiences, several nurses recorded this act (one wrote "patient engages in writing behavior") as if writing were further evidence of illness!

3 *Confusion of serious mental disorders with normal problems.* The DSM is not called "The Diagnostic and Statistical Manual of Mental Disorders and a Whole Bunch of Everyday Problems." Yet the compilers of the DSM keep adding everyday problems. The latest version actually contains "disorder of written expression" (having trouble writing clearly), "mathematics disorder" (not doing well in math), and "caffeine-induced sleep disorder" (which at least is easy to cure; just switch to decaf). Some critics fear that by lumping together such normal difficulties with true mental illnesses, such as schizophrenia, the DSM implies that everyday problems are comparable to disorders—and equally likely to require treatment (Kutchins & Kirk, 1997; Maddux, 1993).

Harriet Tubman (on the left) poses with some of the people she helped to escape from slavery on her "underground railroad." Slaveholders welcomed the idea that Tubman and others who insisted on their freedom had a "mental disorder" called "drapetomania."

4 *The illusion of objectivity.* Finally, some psychologists argue that the whole enterprise of the DSM is a vain attempt to impose a veneer of science on an inherently subjective process (Kutchins & Kirk, 1997; Maddux, 1993; Tiefer, 1995). Many decisions about what to include as a diagnosis, say these critics, are based not on empirical evidence, but on group consensus. The problem is that group consensus often reflects prevailing attitudes and prejudices rather than objective evidence; physicians, in contrast, do not have to vote on whether diabetes is a disease.

Group consensus has sometimes led to self-correcting decisions. Over the years, psychiatrists have quite properly rejected many "disorders" that reflected cultural prejudices and lacked empirical validation, such as drapetomania, lack of vaginal orgasm, childhood masturbation disorder, and homosexuality. But they have also voted in new disorders that reflect today's prejudices and values. Nymphomania (wanting to have sex "too often") is no longer considered a disorder, but not wanting to have sex often "enough" is; it's called "hypoactive sexual desire disorder" (Groneman, 2000; Tiefer, 1995). The point to underscore is that as times change, so does the

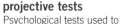

projective tests
Psychological tests used to infer a person's motives, conflicts, and unconscious dynamics on the basis of the person's interpretations of ambiguous stimuli.

cultural consensus about what is normal—and thus what constitutes a "mental disorder."

Psychological Tests. Clinical psychologists and psychiatrists usually base their diagnoses on interviews and observations of a person's behavior when he or she arrives at a hospital or clinic (Luhrmann, 2000). But many also use psychological tests to help them arrive at a diagnosis. Such tests are most commonly used in schools (e.g., to determine whether a child has a learning disorder or emotional problem) and in court settings (e.g., to try to determine which parent should have custody in a divorce case, or whether a defendant is legally insane or suffering from a mental disorder that might affect sentencing).

All of the problems regarding the DSM—the charges of subjectivity, clinicians' bias, overlabeling, and so on—are apparent in the difficulty of devising psychological tests to determine which "mental disorder" in the DSM a person might have. As you can imagine, if a diagnostic category itself is fuzzy, or if clinicians can't agree on its symptoms, you aren't going to be able to invent a reliable test to measure it!

Projective tests are based on psychodynamic assumptions (see Chapter 2); they are designed to reveal unconscious motives, feelings, and conflicts. These tests consist of ambiguous pictures, sentences, or stories that the test-taker interprets or completes. A child or adult may be asked to draw a person, a house, or some other object, or to finish a sentence (such as "My father . . ." or "Women are . . ."). The assumption behind all projective tests is that the person's unconscious thoughts and feelings will be "projected" onto the test and revealed in the person's responses.

Projective tests can help clinicians establish rapport with their clients and encourage clients to open up about anxieties and conflicts they might be ashamed to discuss. But the evidence is overwhelming that they are too unreliable to be used, as they often currently are, for assessing personality traits or diagnosing mental disorders (Dawes, 1994; Lilienfeld, 1999). Different clinicians often interpret the same person's scores differently; they may be "projecting" their own beliefs and assumptions when they decide what a specific response means. The tests also have low *validity,* failing to measure what they claim to measure. One reason is that responses to a projective test are significantly affected by sleepiness, hunger, drugs, worry, verbal ability, the clinician's instructions, the clinician's own personality (friendly and warm, or cool and remote), and other events occurring that day (Anastasi, 1988; Lilienfeld, Wood, & Garb, 2000).

One of the most popular projectives is the **Rorschach Inkblot Test,** which was devised by Swiss psychiatrist Hermann Rorschach in 1921. It consists of ten cards with symmetrical abstract patterns, originally formed by spilling ink on paper and folding the paper in half. The test-taker reports what he or she sees in the inkblots, and the clinician interprets the answers according to the symbolic meanings emphasized by psychodynamic theories. One kind of response, for example, might be interpreted as a sign of dependency, and another as a sign of self-involvement.

What do you see in this Rorschach inkblot?

Although the Rorschach is widely used among clinicians, efforts to confirm its reliability and validity have repeatedly failed (Garb, Florio, & Grove, 1998; Lilienfeld, Wood, & Garb, 2000). Clinicians often fail to agree with one another on what various answers mean, and test–retest reliability is also low. The Rorschach does not reliably diagnose depression, posttraumatic stress reactions, personality disorders, serious mental disorders, or evidence of sexual abuse (Garb, Wood, & Nezworski, 2000). In recent years, a scoring method called the Comprehensive System has become popular (Exner, 1993). But this method, too, has significant problems with reliability and validity. Claims of the system's success often come from Rorschach workshops where clinicians are taught how to use the test, which is hardly an impartial way of assessing it (Wood, Nezworski, & Stejskal, 1996). Positive claims for the Rorschach have rarely been independently replicated by investigators who have no vested interest in the use of the test. Because of the vast potential for error in interpreting Rorschach tests, some clinicians and researchers are calling for

a moratorium on its use in clinical and forensic settings, until impartial research settles the matter (Garb, 1999).

Many therapists also use *objective tests,* or **inventories.** These are standardized questionnaires that ask about the test-taker's behavior and feelings. Some inventories, such as the Beck Depression Inventory, the Spielberger State-Trait Anger Inventory, and the Taylor Manifest Anxiety Scale, reliably assess specific emotional problems. The most widely used objective test, the **Minnesota Multiphasic Personality Inventory (MMPI),** is organized into hundreds of clinical categories, or *scales,* covering such problems as depression, paranoia, schizophrenia, and introversion.

Inventories are more reliable and more valid than either projective methods or subjective clinical judgments based on observations and interviews (Anastasi & Urbina, 1997; Dawes, 1994). But inventories also have problems. For example, critics of the MMPI feel that in spite of recent revisions, the test's standards of normality do not sufficiently reflect differences among cultural, ethnic, and socioeconomic groups. Two psychologists who reviewed the history and validity of the MMPI concluded that correctly interpreting it requires "substantial experience and sophistication" (Helmes & Reddon, 1993), and, unfortunately, this condition is not always met.

What, then, should we conclude about the overall problem of subjectivity in diagnosis and testing? Defenders of the DSM point out that new studies are improving empirical support for many of the DSM's categories. They argue that when the manual is used carefully and correctly, along with empirically validated objective tests, it improves the accuracy of diagnosis and increases agreement among clinicians (Barlow, 1991; Spitzer & Williams, 1988; Wittchen et al., 1995). The DSM's labels, its supporters feel, help people identify the source of their unhappiness and help clinicians decide on appropriate treatment (Kessler et al., 1994).

Moreover, some clinicians point out, not all diagnoses reflect society's biases; as cross-cultural studies using objective psychological tests reveal, certain disorders are universal. All over the world, from the Inuit of Alaska to the Yorubas of Nigeria, some individuals do have delusions, are severely depressed, suffer panic attacks, or cannot control their behavior. In every culture, such individuals are considered to have mental illnesses (Butcher, Lim, & Nezami, 1998; Kleinman, 1988).

Rorschach Inkblot Test
A projective personality test that asks respondents to interpret abstract, symmetrical inkblots.

inventories
Standardized objective questionnaires requiring written responses; they typically include scales on which people are asked to rate themselves.

Minnesota Multiphasic Personality Inventory (MMPI)
A widely used objective personality test.

 QUICK QUIZ

Your mental health will be enhanced if you can answer these questions.

1. Ruthie is afraid to leave her apartment unless she is with a close friend or relative, yet she says she feels fine and she angrily resists her friends' advice that she get help. What criterion of mental disorder does Ruthie's behavior meet?

2. The primary purpose of the DSM is to (a) provide descriptive criteria for diagnosing mental disorders, (b) help psychologists assess normal as well as abnormal behavior, (c) describe the causes of common disorders, (d) keep the number of diagnostic categories of mental disorders to a minimum.

3. List four criticisms of the DSM.

4. What is the advantage of inventories, compared with clinical judgments and projective tests, in diagnosing mental disorders?

Answers:

1. maladaptive behavior   2. a   3. It can foster overdiagnosis; it fails to acknowledge the power of diagnostic labels on the perceptions of clinicians and the behavior of clients; it confuses normal problems in living with serious mental disorders; and it falsely implies that its diagnoses are always based on objective evidence.   4. They have better reliability and validity.

What's Ahead

- **What is the difference between ordinary anxiety and an anxiety disorder?**

- **Why is the most disabling of all phobias known as the "fear of fear"?**

- **When is checking the stove before leaving home a sign of caution, and when does it signal a disorder?**

10.2 Anxiety Disorders

Anyone who is waiting for important news, or living in a situation that is unpredictable and uncontrollable, quite sensibly feels *anxiety,* a general state of apprehension or psychological tension. And anyone who is in a dangerous and unfamiliar situation, such as making a first parachute jump or being accosted by a hungry hippopotamus on the attack, quite sensibly feels flat-out fear. In the short run, these emotions are adaptive because they energize us to cope with danger. They ensure that we don't make that first jump without knowing how to operate the parachute, and that we get away from that hippo as fast as we can.

But in some individuals, fear and anxiety become detached from any actual danger, or these feelings continue even when danger and uncer-

tainty are past. Such individuals may be suffering from *chronic anxiety,* marked by long-lasting feelings of apprehension and doom; *panic attacks,* short-lived but intense feelings of spontaneous anxiety; *phobias,* excessive fears of specific things or situations; or *obsessive-compulsive disorder,* in which repeated thoughts and rituals are used to ward off anxious feelings.

Anxiety and Panic

The chief characteristic of **generalized anxiety disorder** is continuous, uncontrollable anxiety or worry—a feeling of foreboding and dread—that occurs on a majority of days during a six-month period and that is not brought on by physical causes such as disease, drugs, or drinking too much coffee. Symptoms include restlessness or feeling keyed up, difficulty concentrating, irritability, muscle tension and jitteriness, sleep disturbance, and disturbing, unwanted, intrusive worries.

Some people suffer from generalized anxiety disorder without having lived through any specific anxiety-producing event. They may have a physiological tendency to experience anxiety symptoms—sweaty palms, a racing heart, shortness of breath—when they are in challenging or uncontrollable situations. Other chronically anxious people may have a history, starting in childhood,

generalized anxiety disorder
A continuous state of anxiety marked by feelings of worry and dread, apprehension, difficulties in concentration, and signs of motor tension.

of being unable to control or predict their environments (Chorpita & Barlow, 1998). Whatever the origins of their anxiety, chronically anxious people tend to have mental habits that foster their worries and keep their anxiety bubbling along; they perceive everything as an opportunity for disaster (McNally, 1996; Riskind et al., 2000).

Sometimes, however, chronic anxiety occurs in the aftermath of traumatic experiences. People who survive uncontrollable and unpredictable dangers—such as war, rape, torture, or natural disasters—may suffer from **posttraumatic stress disorder (PTSD).** Typical anxiety symptoms in PTSD include reliving the trauma in recurrent, intrusive thoughts or dreams; "psychic numbing," a sense of detachment from others and an inability to feel happy or loving; and increased physiological arousal, reflected in insomnia, irritability, and impaired concentration. These symptoms can occur either immediately after a trauma or after a delay of many weeks or months; episodes may recur for months, years, or even decades (Kessler et al., 1995).

Another kind of anxiety disorder is **panic disorder,** in which a person has recurring attacks of intense fear or panic, with feelings of impending doom or death (Clark & Ehlers, 1993; McNally, 1998). These panic attacks may last from a few minutes to (more rarely) several hours. Symptoms include trembling and shaking, dizziness, chest pain or discomfort, heart palpitations, feelings of unreality, hot and cold flashes, sweating, and, as a result of all these physical reactions, a fear of dying, going crazy, or losing control.

Although panic attacks seem to occur out of nowhere, they in fact usually occur in the aftermath of stress, prolonged emotion, exercise, specific worries, or frightening experiences (Beck, 1988; McNally, 1998). For example, a friend of ours was on a plane that was a target of a bomb threat while airborne at 33,000 feet. He coped beautifully at the time, but two weeks later, seemingly out of nowhere, he had a panic attack.

Such delayed attacks after life-threatening scares are common. The essential difference between people who develop panic disorder and those who do not lies in *how they interpret their bodily reactions* (Clark & Ehlers, 1993; McNally, 1998). Healthy people who have occasional panic attacks see them correctly as a result of a passing crisis or period of stress, comparable to another person's migraines. But people who develop panic disorder regard the attack as a sign of illness or impending death, and they begin to live their lives in restrictive ways, trying to avoid future attacks.

Fear is normal when you jump out of a plane for the first time. But people with anxiety disorders feel as if they are jumping out of planes all the time.

People who have panic disorder are found throughout the world, although culture influences the particular symptoms they experience (Barlow, Chorpita, & Turovsky, 1996). Feelings of choking or being smothered, numbness, and fear of dying are most common in Latin America and southern Europe; fear of public places is most common in northern Europe and America; and a fear of going crazy is more common in the Americas than in Europe. In Greenland, some fishermen suffer from "kayak-angst": a sudden attack of dizziness and fear that occurs while they are fishing in small, one-person kayaks (Amering & Katschnig, 1990).

Fears and Phobias

Are you afraid of bugs, snakes, or dogs? Are you so afraid that you can't stand to be around one, or are you just vaguely uncomfortable? A **phobia** is an exaggerated fear of a specific situation, activity, or thing. Some common phobias—such as fear of snakes and insects, heights (acrophobia), thunder (brontophobia), or enclosed spaces (claustrophobia)—may have evolved in human beings because these fears were adaptive for the species. Other, more idiosyncratic phobias, such as a fear of the color purple (porphyrophobia), may be acquired through classical conditioning, as we saw in Chapter 8. Still other phobias, such as fear of dirt and germs (mysophobia) or of the number 13

posttraumatic stress disorder (PTSD)
An anxiety disorder in which a person who has experienced a traumatic or life-threatening event has symptoms such as psychic numbing, reliving of the trauma, and increased physiological arousal.

panic disorder
An anxiety disorder in which a person experiences recurring panic attacks, feelings of impending doom or death, accompanied by physiological symptoms such as rapid breathing and dizziness.

phobia
An exaggerated, unrealistic fear of a specific situation, activity, or object.

agoraphobia
A set of phobias, often set off by a panic attack, involving the basic fear of being away from a safe place or person.

(triskaidekaphobia), reflect personality differences or cultural traditions. Whatever its source, a phobia is truly frightening and often incapacitating for its sufferer. It is not just a tendency to say "ugh" at tarantulas or skip the snake display at the zoo.

People who have a *social phobia* fear situations in which they will be observed by others. They worry that they will do or say something that will humiliate or embarrass them. Common social phobias are fears of speaking or performing in public, using public restrooms, eating in public, and writing in the presence of others. Again, these phobias are more severe forms of the occasional shyness and social anxiety that everyone experiences.

By far the most disabling fear disorder is **agoraphobia,** which accounts for more than half of the phobia cases for which people seek treatment. In ancient Greece, the *agora* was the social, political, business, and religious center of town, the public meeting place away from home. The fundamental fear in agoraphobia is of being alone in a public place, where escape might be difficult or where help might be unavailable. Individuals with agoraphobia report many specific fears—of public buses, driving in traffic or tunnels, eating in restaurants, or going to parties—but the underlying fear is of being away from a safe place, usually home, or a safe person, usually a parent or spouse.

Agoraphobia usually begins with a panic attack that seems to have no reason (McNally, 1998). The attack is so unexpected and scary that the agoraphobic-to-be begins to avoid situations that he or she thinks may provoke another one. For example, a woman we know had a panic attack while driving on a freeway. This was a perfectly normal posttraumatic response to the suicide of her husband a few weeks earlier. She pulled over and calmed down, but thereafter avoided freeways—as if the freeway, and not the suicide, had caused the attack. Because so many of the actions associated with agoraphobia arise as a mistaken effort to avoid a panic attack, psychologists regard agoraphobia as a "fear of fear" rather than a fear of places.

THE FAR SIDE   By GARY LARSON

Luposlipaphobia: The fear of being pursued by timber wolves around a kitchen table while wearing socks on a newly waxed floor.

Obsessions and Compulsions

Obsessive-compulsive disorder (OCD) is characterized by recurrent, persistent, unwished-for thoughts or images (*obsessions*) and by repetitive, ritualized, stereotyped behaviors that the person feels must be carried out to avoid disaster (*compulsions*). Of course, many people have trivial compulsions and practice superstitious rituals; baseball players are famous for them. Obsessions and compulsions become a disorder when they become uncontrollable and interfere with a person's life.

Obsessive thoughts are often experienced as frightening or repugnant. For example, the person may have repetitive thoughts of killing a child, of becoming contaminated by shaking hands, or of having unknowingly hurt someone in a traffic accident. Obsessive thoughts take many forms, but they are alike in reflecting maladaptive ways of reasoning and processing information.

People who suffer from compulsions likewise feel they have no control over them. The most common compulsions are hand washing, counting, touching, and checking. A woman *must* check the furnace, lights, locks, oven, and fireplace three times before she can sleep; or a man *must* wash his hands and face precisely eight times before he leaves the house. Most sufferers of OCD do not enjoy such rituals and realize that the behavior is senseless. But if they try to forgo the ritual, they feel mounting anxiety that is relieved only by giving in to it. For one young man with OCD, stairs became a treadmill he could not get off: "At first I'd walk up and down the stairs only three or four times," he recalled. "Later I had to run up and down 63 times in 45 minutes. If I failed, I had to start all over again from the beginning" (quoted in King, 1989).

Some cases of obsessive-compulsive disorder may involve a brain abnormality, because several parts of the brain are hyperactive in people with OCD (Schwartz et al., 1996). Normally, once danger is past or a person realizes that there is no cause for fear, the brain's alarm signal turns off. In people with OCD, however, false alarms keep clanging and the emotional networks keeping sending out mistaken "fear!" messages. The sufferer feels in a constant state of danger and tries repeatedly to reduce the resulting anxiety.

obsessive-compulsive disorder (OCD) An anxiety disorder in which a person feels trapped in repetitive, persistent thoughts (*obsessions*) and repetitive, ritualized behaviors (*compulsions*) designed to reduce anxiety.

QUICK QUIZ

We hope you don't feel anxious about matching each term on the left with its description on the right.

1. social phobia
2. generalized anxiety disorder
3. posttraumatic stress disorder
4. agoraphobia
5. compulsion
6. obsession

a. need to perform a ritual
b. fear of fear, of being trapped in public
c. continuing sense of doom and worry
d. repeated, unwanted thoughts
e. fear of meeting new people
f. anxiety following a severe shock

Answers:
1.e 2.c 3.f 4.b 5.a 6.d

What's Ahead
- How can you tell whether you have major depression or just the blues?
- What are the "poles" in bipolar disorder?
- How do some people think themselves into depression?

10.3 Mood Disorders

In the DSM, *mood disorders* include disturbances in mood ranging from extreme depression to extreme mania. Of course, most people feel sad from time to time, and also joyful. These feelings, however, are a far cry from the clinical disorders described by the DSM.

Depression and Bipolar Disorder

Some people go through life with constant but low-grade depression; they can do what they need to but nearly always report their mood as sad or "down in the dumps." Others, however, suffer from **major depression,** a serious mood disorder that is so widespread it has been called the common cold of psychiatric problems. Major depression involves emotional, behavioral, cognitive, and physical changes severe enough to disrupt a person's ordinary functioning for six months or longer. The writer William Styron, who fought and recovered from it, used the beginning of Dante's classic poem, *The Divine Comedy,* to convey his suffering:

> *In the middle of the journey of our life*
> *I found myself in a dark wood.*
> *For I had lost the right path.*

"For those who have dwelt in depression's dark wood," wrote Styron in *Darkness Visible,* "and known its inexplicable agony, the return from the abyss is not unlike the ascent of the poet, trudging upward and upward out of hell's black depths and at last emerging into what he saw as 'the shining world.'"

People with major depression, like Styron, feel despairing and hopeless. They may think often of death or suicide. They lose interest or pleasure in their usual activities. They feel unable to get up and do normal things; it takes an enormous effort just to get dressed. Their thinking patterns feed their bleak moods. They exaggerate minor failings, ignore or discount positive events ("She didn't mean that compliment; she was only being polite"), and interpret any little thing that goes wrong as evidence that nothing will ever go right. Emotionally healthy people who are sad or grieving do not see themselves as completely worthless and unlovable, and they know at some level that their sadness or grief will pass. But depressed people interpret losses as signs of personal failure and conclude that they will never be happy again.

Depression is accompanied by physical changes, as well. The depressed person may overeat or stop eating, have difficulty falling asleep or sleeping through the night, have trouble concentrating, and feel tired all the time. Some sufferers have other physical reactions for which no organic causes are apparent, such as inexplicable pain or headaches.

Even people who are rich, successful, and adored by millions can suffer from major depression. The suicide of Nirvana's lead singer, Kurt Cobain, shocked and saddened his many fans.

At the opposite pole from depression is *mania,* an abnormally high state of exhilaration. You might think it's impossible to feel too good, but mania is not the normal joy of being in love or winning the Pulitzer Prize. Someone in a manic state is expansive to an extent that is out of character. The symptoms are exactly the opposite of those in depression. Instead of feeling fatigued and listless, the person is full of energy. Instead of feeling hopeless and powerless, the person feels full of ambitions, plans, and power. The depressed person speaks slowly and monotonously. The manic person speaks rapidly, dramatically, often with many jokes and puns. The depressed person has low self-esteem. The manic person has inflated self-esteem.

When people alternate between episodes of depression and one or more episodes of mania, they are said to have **bipolar disorder** (formerly called *manic-depressive disorder*), a much rarer problem than depression. The great humorist Mark Twain had bipolar disorder, which he described as "periodical and sudden changes of mood . . . from

10.1

major depression
A mood disorder involving disturbances in emotion (excessive sadness), behavior (loss of interest in one's usual activities), cognition (thoughts of hopelessness), and body function (fatigue and loss of appetite).

bipolar disorder
A mood disorder in which episodes of both depression and mania (excessive euphoria) occur.

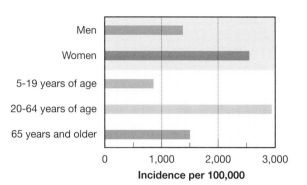

Figure 10.1

Gender, Age, and Depression

Almost everywhere in the world, women are more likely than men to be diagnosed with depression. Yet after age 65, rates of depression drop sharply in both sexes.

deep melancholy to half-insane tempests and cyclones." Other writers, artists, musicians, and scientists have suffered from this disorder, too, including Charles Dickens and Isaac Newton. During the "highs," many of these artists create their best work, but the price of the "lows" is disastrous relationships, bankruptcy, and sometimes suicide (Barondes, 1998).

Although bipolar disorder occurs equally in both sexes, major depression occurs two or three times as often among women as among men, all over the world (Culbertson, 1997; McGrath et al., 1990) (see Figure 10.1). Some psychologists think that women are truly more likely to become depressed than men are, but others think the difference is more apparent than real. Because women are more likely to talk about their feelings than men are and more likely to seek help, depression in males may be overlooked or misdiagnosed. Men who are depressed often try to mask the feeling by denying their unhappiness, abusing drugs, or committing acts of violence (Canetto, 1992; Kessler et al., 1994).

Theories of Depression

Explanations of depression generally emphasize five possible causes: biological predispositions, social conditions, problems with close attachments, cognitive habits, or a combination of individual vulnerability and external events.

1 *Biological explanations emphasize genetics and brain chemistry.* Studies of adopted children and twins support the notion that depression and bipolar

disorder have a genetic component, but the precise gene or genes have yet to be identified (DiLalla et al., 1996). Genes may exert their influence by creating biochemical imbalances in neurotransmitters, which permit messages to be transmitted from one neuron to another in the brain. Two neurotransmitters that may be implicated in depressive disorders are serotonin and norepinephrine. In the view of some researchers, depression is caused by a deficient production of one or both of these neurotransmitters, and manic moods are caused by an excessive production. Drugs that increase the levels of serotonin and norepinephrine sometimes alleviate symptoms of depression, and drugs that reduce norepinephrine sometimes alleviate those of mania. However, as we will see in the next chapter, these drugs do not help everyone.

Researchers are now using brain-scan technologies to identify changes that occur in the brain during depressive and manic episodes (see Figure 10.2). In general, the brains of depressed people seem less active, especially the left frontal lobes, which are involved in positive emotions. However, brain scans alone do not tell us whether low activation in the brain causes depression, or whether depression changes the brain. It may work both ways, of course.

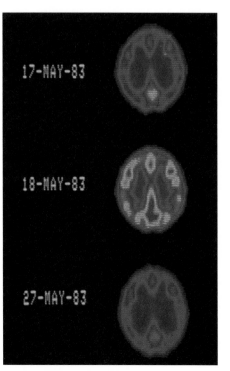

Figure 10.2

The Bipolar Brain

These PET scans show changes in the metabolism of glucose, the brain's energy supply, in a patient with bipolar disorder. On May 17 and 27, the patient was depressed, and glucose metabolism throughout the brain was lower than normal. On May 18, the patient became manic, and metabolic activity increased to near normal levels. Keep in mind that such changes do not show the direction of cause and effect: A drop in glucose might bring on depression, but depression might also cause a drop in glucose levels.

Any doubt what emotion this painting conveys? The artist Jacob Lawrence has captured the body language of depression in the posture, downcast eyes, somber mood, and drooping heads and shoulders of his figures.

Source: Jacob Lawrence (1917–2000), *Depression*, 1950. Tempera on paper, 22 × 30 1/2 in. (55.9 × 77.5 cm). Collection of Whitney Museum of American Art, New York. Gift of David M. Solinger. 66.98. Photo © 2000: Whitney Museum of American Art, New York. Photo by Geoffery Clements. Artwork © Gwendolyn Knight Lawrence. Courtesy of Jacob and Gwendolyn Lawrence Foundation.

2 *Social explanations emphasize the stressful circumstances of people's lives.* In the social view, women are more likely than men to suffer from depression because they have less satisfying work and family lives, lower status than men in work and society, and higher rates of poverty and sexual victimization. Mothers are especially vulnerable to depression: The more children a woman has, the more likely she is to become depressed, especially if she is unemployed (McGrath et al., 1990). In contrast, men are more likely than women to be both married and working full time, a combination of activities that is strongly associated with mental health and low rates of depression (G. Brown, 1993; Culbertson, 1997). Violence is also a risk factor for depression: Inner-city adolescents of both sexes who are exposed to high rates of violence report higher levels of depression and more attempts to commit suicide than those who are not subjected to constant violence in their lives or communities (Mazza & Reynolds, 1999).

Social analyses, however, fail to explain why *most* victims of violence, let alone most mothers and poor people, do not become clinically depressed. Nor do they explain why some people become depressed even though their lives are comfortable and secure.

3 *Attachment explanations emphasize problems with close relationships.* In this view, depression results from disturbed relationships; separations and losses, both past and present; and a history of insecure attachments (Klerman et al., 1984;

Roberts, Gotlib, & Kassel, 1996). This explanation is supported by the fact that depressive episodes are frequently set off by disruption of a primary relationship.

However, it is not always clear whether a broken relationship caused depression, or the relationship dissolved because one partner was chronically depressed. Depressed people often seem demanding and "depressing" to family and friends, who in turn feel angry or sad when they cannot help the sufferer cheer up. Eventually, the depressed person's partner and friends may leave (Alloy et al., 1998; Coyne, 1990). One longitudinal study found that the direction of cause and effect may be different for husbands and wives: In general, for wives, marital problems made them depressed; for husbands, being depressed caused the marital problems (Fincham et al., 1997).

4 *Cognitive explanations emphasize particular habits of thinking and ways of interpreting events.* Depression often involves three negative habits of thinking:

- *Internality.* Depressed people tend to believe that the reason for their misery is internal, an entrenched aspect of their personality. They will say, for example, "I'm unattractive and awkward; no wonder I'm not making friends." They rarely consider external explanations, such as "This school is so big and impersonal it's hard to meet new people" (Anderson et al., 1994).

■ *Stability.* Depressed people tend to believe that their situation is permanent ("Nothing good will ever happen to me"). Expecting nothing to get better, they do nothing to improve their lives, and therefore they remain unhappy.

■ *Lack of control.* Depressed people tend to believe that they have no control over their emotions or the situations that caused those emotions ("I'm depressed because I'm ugly and horrible and I can't do anything about it").

Where do these ways of thinking come from? In the 1970s, a leading theory held that people become depressed when their efforts to avoid pain or to control the environment consistently fail; their depression results from "learned helplessness" (Seligman, 1975). However, the fatal flaw with this theory was that not all depressed people have actually failed in their lives, and even living in painful or difficult situations does not make everyone depressed. The real problem for depressed people is not that they are helpless, but that they feel hopeless. They have a *pessimistic explanatory style* (see Chapter 12), believing that nothing good will ever happen to them and that they are powerless to change the future (Abramson, Metalsky, & Alloy, 1989; Seligman, 1991).

Another cognitive bad habit strongly associated with depression is brooding. People who ruminate endlessly about their negative feelings tend to have longer and more intense periods of depression than do those who are able to distract themselves, look outward, and seek solutions. Beginning in adolescence, women are more likely than men to develop a ruminating, introspective style, rehearsing the reasons for their unhappiness. This tendency may contribute both to longer-lasting depressions in women and to the sex difference in reported rates (Bromberger & Matthews, 1996; Nolen-Hoeksema & Girgus, 1994).

Of course, when you are already feeling sad, gloomy thoughts come more easily. But negative thinking is also an independent cause of depression. People with pessimistic, ruminating cognitive styles that foster hopelessness are at greater risk of developing full-blown, major depression than are people who think positively (Alloy & Abramson, 1998; Chorpita & Barlow, 1998).

5 *"Vulnerability-stress" explanations draw on all four explanations just discussed.* They hold that depression results from an *interaction* between individual vulnerabilities—in personality traits, habits of thinking, and genetic predispositions—and stress or sad events.

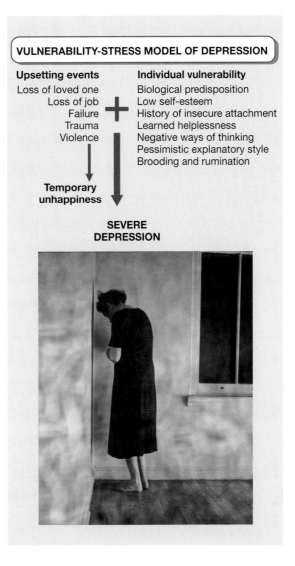

VULNERABILITY-STRESS MODEL OF DEPRESSION

Upsetting events	**Individual vulnerability**
Loss of loved one	Biological predisposition
Loss of job	Low self-esteem
Failure	History of insecure attachment
Trauma	Learned helplessness
Violence	Negative ways of thinking
	Pessimistic explanatory style
	Brooding and rumination

Temporary unhappiness

SEVERE DEPRESSION

Interaction models are an improvement over theories implying that everyone is equally vulnerable to depression, given a certain experience, gene, or biological disposition. These models try to specify which personality traits interact with which events to produce depression. For example, in one study, students who got worse grades than they expected reported feeling temporarily depressed (not a surprise). But depression persisted only in those who *also* had a pessimistic explanatory style ("I'm stupid and always will be") *and* low self-esteem, resulting in hopelessness (Metalsky et al., 1993).

By understanding the causes of depression as an interaction among an individual's biology, ways of thinking, and experiences, we can see why the same precipitating event, such as a minor setback or even the loss of a loved one, might produce normal sadness in one person and extreme depression in another.

QUICK QUIZ

Don't let another quiz make you vulnerable to depression.

1. In the view of some biological researchers, depression involves a deficit in the neurotransmitters _____ and/or _____.

2. Depressed people tend to believe that the reasons for their unhappiness are (a) controllable, (b) temporary, (c) internal, (d) caused by the situation.

3. Vulnerability-stress theories attribute depression to an interaction between _____ and _____.

4. A news headline announces that a single gene has been identified as the cause of depression, but the article itself notes that other studies have failed to replicate this research. What might explain these contradictory findings?

Answers:

1. serotonin, norepinephrine   2. c   3. individual vulnerabilities; stress or sad events   4. The conflicting evidence may mean that if a genetic predisposition for depression exists, it is not due to a single gene, but involves several genes working in the context of environmental events. It may mean that the right gene has not yet been identified. Or it may mean that genes are not a factor in any or all forms of depression.

What's Ahead

● **When does being self-centered become a disorder?**

● **What do a charming but heartless tycoon and a remorseless killer have in common?**

● **Why are some people seemingly incapable of feeling guilt and shame?**

10.4 Personality Disorders

Personality disorders involve rigid, maladaptive traits that cause great distress or an inability to get along with others. The DSM-IV describes such a disorder as "an enduring pattern of inner experience and behavior that deviates markedly from the expectations of the individual's culture [and] is pervasive and inflexible." That means it is not caused by depression, drugs, or a situation that temporarily induces a person to behave in ways that are out of character.

Problem Personalities

One personality disorder, **narcissistic personality disorder,** involves an exaggerated sense of self-importance and self-absorption. (Narcissism gets its name from the Greek myth of Narcissus, a beautiful young man who fell in love with his own image.) Individuals who are narcissistic are preoccupied with fantasies of unlimited success,

personality disorders
Rigid, maladaptive personality patterns that cause personal distress or an inability to get along with others.

narcissistic personality disorder
A disorder characterized by an exaggerated sense of self-importance and self-absorption.

Narcissus fell in love with his own image, and now he has a personality disorder named after him—just what a narcissist would want!

power, brilliance, or ideal love. They demand constant attention and admiration and feel entitled to special favors, without, however, being willing to reciprocate. They fall in love quickly and out of love just as fast, when the beloved proves to have some annoying human flaw.

Another personality disorder, **paranoid personality disorder,** involves pervasive, unfounded suspiciousness and mistrust of other people; irrational jealousy; secretiveness; and doubt about the loyalty of others. People with paranoid personalities have delusions of being persecuted by everyone from their closest relatives to government agencies, and their beliefs are immune to disconfirming evidence.

Notice that although these descriptions evoke flashes of recognition ("I know that type!"), it is hard to know where value judgments end and a clear disorder begins (Maddux & Mundell, 1997). Cultures draw the line differently. For example, American society often encourages people to pursue dreams of unlimited success and ideal love, but such dreams might be considered signs of serious disturbance in a more group-oriented society. How would you distinguish between having a "narcissistic personality disorder" and being a normal member of a group or culture that encourages putting your own needs ahead of those of your family and friends, and puts a premium on youth and beauty?

Antisocial Personality Disorder

Throughout history, societies have recognized and feared the few members in their midst who lack all human connection to anyone else—who can cheat, con, and kill without flinching. In the 1830s these individuals were said to be afflicted with "moral insanity," and in the twentieth century they came to be called "psychopaths" or "sociopaths." The DSM, trying to avoid such emotionally charged terms, refers to **antisocial personality disorder (APD).** By any name, this condition is fascinating and frightening because of the great harm these people inflict on their victims and on society.

According to the DSM, people diagnosed with APD must meet at least three of seven criteria: (1) They repeatedly break the law; (2) they are deceitful, using aliases and lies to con others; (3) they are impulsive and unable to plan ahead; (4) they repeatedly get into physical fights or assaults; (5) they show reckless disregard for their own safety or that of others; (6) they are constantly irresponsible, failing to meet obligations to others; and (7) they lack remorse for actions that harm others.

Lacking conscience and remorse, people with APD can lie, seduce, and manipulate others and then drop them without a qualm. They can steal your heart and your wallet in a minute. If caught in a lie

paranoid personality disorder
A disorder characterized by habitually unreasonable and excessive suspiciousness or jealousy.

antisocial personality disorder (APD)
A disorder characterized by antisocial behavior such as lying, stealing, manipulating others, and sometimes violence; and a lack of guilt, shame, and empathy. (Sometimes called *psychopathy* or *sociopathy.*)

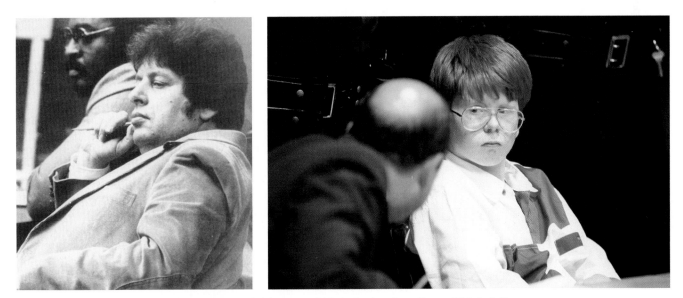

Some people with antisocial personalities use charm and elaborate con tricks to deceive others. Giovanni Vigliotto (left) married 105 women over 33 years, seized their assets, and then abandoned them. He was convicted of bigamy and fraud, and sentenced to 34 years in prison. But other people with APD are sadistic and violent, starting in childhood. At age 13, Eric Smith (right) bludgeoned and strangled a 4-year-old boy to death. He was tried as an adult and sentenced to a prison term of nine years to life.

or a crime, they may seem sincerely sorry and promise to make amends, but it is all an act. Some are sadistic, able to kill a pet, a child, or a random adult without a twinge of regret. Others direct their energies into con games or career advancement, abusing other people emotionally or economically rather than physically (Robins, Tipp, & Przybeck, 1991).

Antisocial personality disorder occurs in only about 3 percent of all males and less than 1 percent of all females. Yet people with APD may account for more than half of all serious crimes committed in the United States (Hare, 1993). Terrie Moffitt (1993), who observed the development of APD over time, reported that remorselessness and law-breaking start early and take different forms at different ages: "Biting and hitting at age 4, shoplifting and truancy at age 10, selling drugs and stealing cars at age 16, robbery and rape at age 22, and fraud and child abuse at age 30 . . . [people with APD] lie at home, steal from shops, cheat at school, fight in bars, and embezzle at work."

Researchers studying APD, like those studying other mental disorders, are investigating possible biological and social factors that contribute to antisocial personalities.

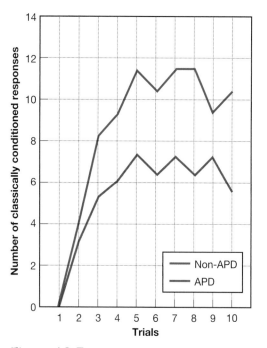

Figure 10.3

Emotions and Antisocial Personality Disorder

In several experiments, people with antisocial personality disorder (APD) were slow to develop classically conditioned responses to anticipated danger, pain, or shock—responses that indicate normal anxiety (Hare, 1965). This deficit may be related to the ability of people with APD to behave in destructive ways without remorse or regard for the consequences (Hare, 1993).

1 *Abnormalities in the central nervous system.* Antisocial individuals do not respond physiologically to punishments the way other people do; this may be why they can behave fearlessly in situations that would scare others to death. Normally, when a person is anticipating danger, pain, or punishment, the electrical conductance of the skin changes, a classically conditioned response that indicates anxiety or fear. But people with APD are slow to develop such responses, which suggests that they are unable to feel the anxiety necessary for learning that their actions will have unpleasant consequences (see Figure 10.3). Their inability to feel emotional arousal—empathy, guilt, fear of punishment, anxiety under stress—suggests some abnormality in the brain and central nervous system (Hare, 1965, 1993; Lykken, 1995; Raine, 1996).

Further evidence for the role of biology and temperament in APD comes from a team of psychologists and primatologists who observed the behavior of 34 chimpanzees and scored it according to their Chimpanzee Psychopathy Measure (Lilienfeld et al., 1999). Some chimps behave in ways that are comparable to the actions of human psychopaths: They use deception and manipulate others to get their way, they are unmoved by the suffering of others of their kind, they completely lack emotional ties to others, they are aggressive, and they are fearless. These findings are sure interesting!

2 *Problems with impulse control.* People who are antisocial, hyperactive, addicted, or impulsive may share a common inherited disorder involving an inability to control responses to frustration and provocation (Luengo et al., 1994; Raine, 1996). The biological children of parents with antisocial personality disorder, substance-abuse problems, or impulsivity disorders are at greater than normal risk of developing these disorders themselves, even when these children are reared by others (Nigg & Goldsmith, 1994).

3 *Brain abnormalities.* Psychopaths show abnormalities in left-hemisphere activation when they are processing information, a fact that appears to be related to their impaired ability to regulate their behavior (Bernstein et al., 2000). Damage to the prefrontal cortex may also be implicated in some cases of APD. One PET-scan study found that cold-blooded "predatory" murderers had less brain activity in this area than did men who murdered in the heat of passion or controls who hadn't murdered anybody (Raine et al., 1998). These brain abnormalities may result from genes, birth complications, or physical abuse and neglect. High percentages of violent teenagers—those who have

been arrested for vicious assault, rape, or murder, in contrast to those who just get into fistfights or normal teenage trouble—have a history of physical neglect, battering, and head injury (Lewis, 1981, 1992; Milner & McCanne, 1991; Moffitt, 1993).

4 *Vulnerability-stress explanations.* Brain damage or genetic predispositions alone are rarely enough to create a violent or antisocial individual. But according to the *vulnerability-stress model of APD,* when biological vulnerability is combined with physical abuse, parental neglect, lack of love and contact comfort, environmental stresses, and a larger culture that rewards ruthlessness and hard-heartedness, individuals are far more likely to develop the disorder.

For example, a study of more than 4,000 boys, followed from birth to age 18, found that many of those who became violent offenders had experi-

enced two risk factors: birth complications that caused damage to the prefrontal cortex, *and* early maternal rejection. Their mothers had not wanted the pregnancy, and the babies were put in institutional care for at least four months during their first year. Although only 4.4 percent of the boys had both risk factors, these boys accounted for 18 percent of all violent crimes committed by the sample as a whole (Raine, Brennan, & Mednick, 1994).

It seems, then, that several routes lead to the development of antisocial personality disorder: neurological abnormalities; a genetic disposition toward impulsivity, which leads to rule breaking and crime; brain damage; parental neglect or rejection; and a cultural environment that rewards and fosters antisocial traits. These multiple origins may explain why rates of antisocial personality disorder vary across societies and history.

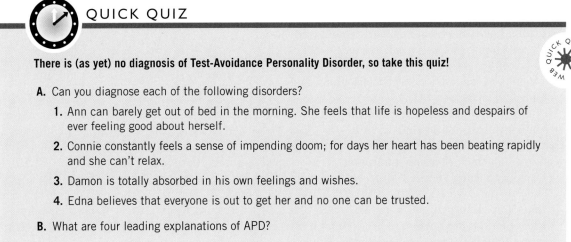

QUICK QUIZ

There is (as yet) no diagnosis of Test-Avoidance Personality Disorder, so take this quiz!

A. Can you diagnose each of the following disorders?

  1. Ann can barely get out of bed in the morning. She feels that life is hopeless and despairs of ever feeling good about herself.

  2. Connie constantly feels a sense of impending doom; for days her heart has been beating rapidly and she can't relax.

  3. Damon is totally absorbed in his own feelings and wishes.

  4. Edna believes that everyone is out to get her and no one can be trusted.

B. What are four leading explanations of APD?

Answers:
A. 1. major depression   2. generalized anxiety disorder   3. narcissistic personality disorder   4. paranoid personality disorder
B. Central nervous system abnormalities, problems with impulse control, brain damage, and an interaction among biological and environmental factors (the vulnerability-stress model).

What's Ahead

- Why are many clinicians and researchers skeptical about multiple personality disorder?

- Why did the number of "personalities" in "multiple personality" patients jump from two or three in early cases to thousands in recent ones?

10.5 Dissociative Identity Disorder ("Multiple Personality")

Have you ever been out driving on a highway and suddenly realized you have lost all track of time and distance? This is a small but common everyday example of *dissociation,* a split in awareness:

Part of you is driving the car and attending to other drivers, and part of you is daydreaming about a holiday in Paris. Dissociation also occurs when we must deal with stress or shock and we feel temporarily cut off from ourselves—strange, dazed, or "unreal."

In **dissociative disorders,** however, consciousness, behavior, and identity are more severely split or altered. The symptoms are intense, last a long time, and appear to be out of the individual's control. Like posttraumatic stress disorder, dissociative disorders often occur in response to shocking or harmful events. But whereas people with PTSD cannot get the trauma out of their minds and waking thoughts, people with dissociative disorders apparently escape the trauma by putting it out of their minds, erasing it from memory (Cardeña et al., 1994). Psychogenic amnesia, which we discussed in Chapter 7, is considered by many to be a dissociative disorder.

The DSM uses the term **dissociative identity disorder** to describe the appearance, within one person, of two or more distinct identities. In our discussion, however, we will retain the more commonly used term, *multiple personality disorder* (MPD). In this disorder, each identity appears to have its own memories, preferences, personality traits, and even medical problems.

Cases of multiple personality portrayed on TV, in popular books, and in films such as *The Three Faces of Eve* and *Sybil* have captivated the public for years. Among mental-health professionals, however, two competing views of MPD exist. On one side are those who think that MPD is common, but often unrecognized or misdiagnosed. On the other side are those who believe that most cases of MPD are generated by clinicians themselves, knowingly or unknowingly, during their interactions with vulnerable clients, and that if the condition exists at all, it is extremely rare.

Those in the MPD-is-real camp believe that it originates in childhood, as a means of coping with unspeakable, repeated traumas, such as torture (Gleaves, 1996; Kluft, 1993; Ross, 1995). In this view, the trauma produces a mental "splitting"; one personality emerges to handle everyday experiences and another emerges to cope with the bad ones. MPD patients are frequently described as having lived for years with several personalities of which they were unaware, until hypnosis revealed them.

Those who are skeptical about MPD point out that before 1980, only a handful of MPD cases

had ever been diagnosed anywhere in the world; yet since 1980, *tens of thousands* of cases have been reported, virtually all of them in North America (see Table 10.2). Critics of MPD think such numbers are suspicious, a sign that the disorder is being wildly overdiagnosed by its proponents. They have shown that the evidence used to support the diagnosis of MPD is highly questionable, for several reasons (Acocella, 1999; Ganaway, 1995; Merskey, 1995; Piper, 1997; Spanos, 1996):

Thinking Critically About "Multiple Personalities"

1 *Flaws in the research.* Claims have been made that MPD patients show different physiological responses (e.g., brain-wave patterns) for different personalities, but such claims rely mostly on anecdotes or on studies that lacked control groups (P. Brown, 1994). When researchers compare MPD patients with healthy people who are merely role-playing different personalities, they find differences in physiology between "personalities" in the *healthy* people, too (Miller & Triggiano, 1992; Spanos, 1996). People can alter physiological measures such as brain-wave activity by changing their moods, energy levels, and concentration, so these measures are not a valid way to verify MPD.

2 *Pressure and suggestion by clinicians.* Some clinicians may actually be creating the disorder in their clients through the power of suggestion, sometimes bordering on coercion (McHugh, 1993a; Merskey, 1992, 1995; Spanos, 1996). For example, one prominent believer in MPD, psychiatrist Richard Kluft (1987), wrote that efforts to determine the presence of MPD—that is, to get the person to reveal a dissociated personality—may require "between 2½ and 4 hours of continuous interviewing. Interviewees must be prevented from taking breaks to regain composure. . . . In one recent case of singular difficulty, the first sign of dissociation was noted in the 6th hour, and a definitive spontaneous switching of personalities occurred in the 8th hour." But think about it: After eight hours of "continuous interviewing" without a single break, how many of us wouldn't do what the interviewer wanted?

Clinicians who conduct such interrogations argue that they are merely *permitting* other personalities to reveal themselves. However, in numerous malpractice cases across the country, courts have ruled, on the basis of the testimony of scientific experts in psychiatry and psychology,

dissociative disorders
Conditions in which consciousness or identity is split or altered.

dissociative identity disorder
A controversial disorder marked by the appearance within one person of two or more distinct personalities, each with its own name and traits; commonly known as *multiple personality disorder (MPD).*

Table 10.2   The Rise of Multiple Personality Disorder

1789	An early case is reported of a young German woman with several "personalities" (including a French woman and a little boy).
1816	The first recorded case of "multiple personality" appears in America.
1875	The condition is officially named "multiple personality" in France.
1886	Robert Louis Stevenson's *Dr. Jekyll and Mr. Hyde* popularizes the notion of two personalities in one body.
1800s–1960	**A few cases are reported worldwide.**
1957	*The Three Faces of Eve* is published and the film is released.
1960–1970	**8 cases are reported.**
1976	The movie *Sybil* is released.
1980	**The DSM includes the MPD diagnosis for the first time.**
1980	The book *Michelle Remembers* claims that "Satanic ritual abuse" is a leading cause of MPD.
1980–1991	Media coverage escalates in popular books and on talk shows that feature MPD "victims."
1985	Psychiatrist Richard Kluft claims to have treated 250 MPD patients.
By 1986	**6,000 cases are reported in North America.**
1987	The first MPD inpatient treatment unit is established at Rush Presbyterian Hospital in Chicago; others follow across the country.
By 1995	**More than 40,000 cases are reported in North America.**
1995	Diane Humenansky becomes the first psychiatrist found guilty of malpractice for inducing multiple personalities in a vulnerable patient.
1996–present	Other successful lawsuits are won against major proponents of the MPD diagnosis and against treatment units in hospitals.

Sources: Acocella, 1999; Kenny, 1986; Loftus, 1996; Nathan, 1994; Pendergrast, 1995; Piper, 1997.

that it is more likely that these clinicians were actively *creating* personalities through suggestion and sometimes outright intimidation (Loftus, 1996; Spanos, 1996).

3 *The influence of the media.* Media coverage of sensational MPD cases has played a major role in fostering MPD diagnoses (Acocella, 1999). When Canadian psychiatrist Harold Merskey (1992) reviewed the published cases of MPD, including Sybil, he was unable to find a single one in which a patient developed MPD without being influenced by the therapist's sug-

gestions or reports about the disorder in books and the media. Even the authors of *The Three Faces of Eve* were alarmed by the media hype and the proliferation of questionable cases. Thirty years later, they reported that of the hundreds of alleged MPD patients that had been referred to them over the decades, they thought only one really had multiple personality disorder (Thigpen & Cleckley, 1984).

No one disputes that some troubled, highly imaginative individuals can produce many different "personalities" when asked. The question is

Popular books and films about multiple personality, such as The Three Faces of Eve *and* Sybil, *spawned countless imitators like* Lizzie—*and thousands of reported cases. According to critics, most of this increase was a result of unwitting therapist influence and sensational stories in the media (Acocella, 1999; Showalter, 1997).*

The *sociocognitive explanation* of multiple personality disorder holds that it is simply an extreme form of the ability we all have to present different aspects of our personalities to others (Piper, 1997; Spanos, 1996). In this view, the diagnosis of MPD provides a culturally acceptable way for some troubled people to make sense of their problems (Kenny, 1986; Showalter, 1997). It allows them to account, for example, for sexual or criminal behavior that they now regret or find intolerably embarrassing; they can claim their "other personality did it." Therapists who are looking for MPD reward such patients with attention and praise for revealing more and more personalities (Ofshe & Watters, 1994). These rewards would explain why the early cases of MPD involved only two or three personalities, whereas in recent years MPD patients have reported having hundreds and even thousands of them—including animals.

And of course, as the evidence of media involvement in the escalating numbers of MPD cases suggests, there can be big financial incentives for patients and therapists. The combination of a sensational, fascinating new disorder plus the allure of books, talk shows, and conferences can produce a "social contagion" in which the new disorder seems widespread—until the bubble pops and it disappears (Showalter, 1997).

The fact that MPD is controversial and has little empirical evidence to support it does not mean that no legitimate cases exist. Each case must be examined on its own merits. But the story of MPD teaches us to think critically about disorders that suddenly become trendy: to consider other explanations, to examine assumptions and biases, and to demand good evidence.

whether these people are suffering from an actual disorder over which they have no control—one in which different personalities just pop up—or whether they are going along with the clinician's diagnosis and expectations, in a process of reciprocal influence.

QUICK QUIZ

Any one of your personalities may answer this question.

Suppose you are on a jury in which the defendant, who killed six prostitutes, claims he suffers from multiple personality disorder. He has no memory of committing the murders, he says, and his psychiatrist testifies that the man has a true case of MPD. As a critical thinker, what questions would you want to ask about this defense? (By the way, this is a real case.)

Answers:
Some possible questions to ask: Was the diagnosis of MPD made *before* the man committed murder—that is, did he have a history of MPD or any other mental disorder—or did he conveniently "discover" his other personalities after being arrested? Is the psychiatrist a believer in MPD or a skeptic? Did any other psychiatrist or psychologist interview the defendant and agree on the diagnosis?

- In what ways might genes contribute to alcoholism?

- Why is alcoholism more common in Ireland than in Italy?

- Why don't policies of abstinence from alcohol reduce problem drinking?

- If you take morphine to control chronic pain, does that mean you will become addicted to it?

10.6 Drug Abuse and Addiction

In November, 2000, actor Robert Downey, Jr., was arrested for possession of cocaine and speed and for violating the terms of his parole (substance abuse had landed him in prison twice). Fans and the public were shocked, because Downey had finally seemed to be mending his ways and his career was soaring. With every reason in the world to stay off drugs, why did Downey succumb to their lure again, risking his family, his career, and his freedom? And what treatment program, if any, could help him?

Most people use drugs (legal, illegal, or prescription) in moderation and for short-lived effects, but some people depend too much on them, and others abuse drugs even at the cost of their own health. The DSM-IV defines *substance abuse* as "a maladaptive pattern of substance use leading to clinically significant impairment or distress." Symptoms of such impairment include the failure to hold a job, care for children, or complete schoolwork; use of the drug in hazardous situations (e.g., while driving a car or operating machinery); and frequent conflicts with others about use of the drug or as a result of using the drug.

In this section, focusing on the example of alcoholism, we will consider the two dominant approaches to understanding addiction and drug abuse—the biological model and the learning model—and conclude with an effort to integrate the contributions of both.

Biology and Addiction

In 1960, a book was published that profoundly changed the way most people thought about alcoholics. In *The Disease Concept of Alcoholism*, E. M.

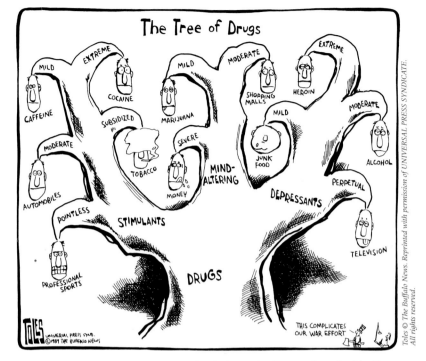

The Tree of Drugs

By poking fun at the things people do to make themselves feel better, this cartoon reminds us that many "addictions" are not biochemical.

Jellinek argued that alcoholism is a disease over which an individual has no control and from which he or she never recovers. Drunkenness is not an inevitable property of alcohol, he said, but a characteristic of some people who have an inborn vulnerability to liquor; for them, complete abstinence is the only solution. The disease theory of alcoholism transformed the moral condemnation of the addict as a bad and sinful person into concern for someone who is sick.

Today, many people continue to regard alcoholism as a disease, and the *biological model of addiction* is widely accepted by researchers and the public. The biological model holds that addiction, whether to alcohol or any other drug, is due primarily to a person's biochemistry, metabolism, and genetic predisposition. Twin and other family studies suggest that alcoholism may sometimes involve an inherited vulnerability (Cloninger, 1990; Goodwin et al., 1994; Schuckit & Smith, 1996). For alcoholics who begin heavy drinking in adulthood, genetic factors do not seem to be involved. But there may be a heritable component in the kind of alcoholism that begins in adolescence and is linked to impulsivity, antisocial behavior, and violent criminality (Bohman et al., 1987; McGue, Pickens, & Svikis, 1992).

Research Navigator.com
RESOURCES FOR COLLEGE RESEARCH ASSIGNMENTS
10.2

Live! psych
10.1

Genes could contribute to alcoholism by contributing to traits or temperaments that predispose a person to become alcoholic. Or they may affect biochemical processes in the brain that make some people more susceptible to alcohol or cause them to respond to it differently than others do (Reich et al., 1998; Schuckit & Smith, 1996). For example, genes may affect how much a person needs to drink before feeling high. In an ongoing longitudinal study of 450 young men (half of whom had alcoholic fathers and half of whom did not), the men who at age 20 had to drink more than others to feel any reaction were at increased risk of becoming alcoholic within the decade. This was true regardless of their current drinking habits or family history (Schuckit, 1998; Schuckit & Smith, 1996).

Virtually all geneticists agree that if genes are involved in alcoholism, there is more than one and that these genes interact in complex ways. As with so many other disorders, however, tracking down such genes has been difficult. When one research team finds a likely candidate (e.g., Noble, 1998; Noble et al., 1991), that work is promptly contradicted by others (e.g., Baron, 1993; Edenberg et al., 1998).

The usual way of looking at the relationship between biological factors and addiction is to assume that the former somehow cause the latter. However, there is growing evidence that the relationship also works the other way: that addictions

In cultures in which people drink moderately with meals and children learn the rules of social drinking from their families, as at this Jewish family's gathering for the traditional Passover seder, alcoholism rates are much lower than in cultures in which drinking occurs mainly in bars, in binges, or in privacy.

result from the abuse of drugs. For example, heavy drinking alters brain function, reduces the level of painkilling endorphins, produces nerve damage, shrinks the cerebral cortex, and damages the liver. These changes then create biological dependence, and inability to metabolize alcohol, and psychological problems. Further, in the view of some researchers, heavy use of alcohol, cocaine, amphetamines, or other drugs cause certain nerve cells in the brain to adapt to the rush of pleasure. When these cells are then deprived of the stimulation, the result is that addicts like Robert Downey, Jr., experience a physiological craving that feels almost irresistible, in spite of every realistic reason in the world to "just say no."

Learning, Culture, and Addiction

The biological model, popular though it is, has been challenged by another approach. According to the *learning model,* drug addiction is neither a sin nor a disease but "a central activity of the individual's way of life" that depends on learning and culture (Fingarette, 1988). Four arguments support this view:

1 *Addiction patterns vary according to cultural practices and the social environment.* Alcoholism is much more likely to occur in societies that forbid children to drink but condone drunkenness in adults (as in Ireland) than in societies that teach children how to drink responsibly and moderately but condemn adult drunkenness (as in Italy, Greece, and France). In cultures with low rates of alcoholism (except for those committed to a religious rule that forbids use of all psychoactive drugs), adults demonstrate correct drinking habits to their children, gradually introducing them to alcohol in safe family settings. Alcohol is not used as a rite of passage into adulthood, nor is it associated with masculinity and power (Peele & Brodsky, 1991; Vaillant, 1983). Abstainers are not sneered at and drunkenness is not considered charming, comical, or manly; it is considered stupid or obnoxious.

Within a particular country, addiction rates can rise or fall rapidly in response to cultural changes. In colonial America, the average person actually drank two to three times the amount of liquor consumed today, yet alcoholism was not the serious social problem it is now. Drinking was a universally accepted social activity; families drank and ate together. Alcohol was believed to produce pleasant feelings and relaxation. The Puritan minister Cotton Mather even called liquor "the good creature of God" (Critchlow, 1986). Then, between 1790 and 1830, when the American frontier was expanding, drinking came to symbolize masculine independence and toughness. The saloon became the place for drinking away from home, and, as the learning model would predict, alcoholism rates shot up.

Substance abuse and addiction problems increase not only when people fail to learn how to take drugs in moderation, but also when they move from their own culture of origin into another that has different drinking rules (Westermeyer, 1995). For example, in most Latino cultures, such as those of Mexico and Puerto Rico, drinking and drunkenness are considered male activities. Thus Latina women tend to drink little, if at all, and they have few drinking problems—until they move into an Anglo environment, where their rates of alcoholism rise (Canino, 1994).

2 *Policies of total abstinence tend to increase rates of addiction rather than reduce them.* In the United States, the temperance movement of the early twentieth century held that drinking inevitably leads to drunkenness, and drunkenness to crime. The solution it won for the Prohibition years (1920 to 1933) was national abstinence. But this victory backfired: Again in accordance with the learning model, Prohibition actually *increased* rates of alcoholism. Because people were denied the opportunity to learn to drink moderately, they drank excessively when given the chance (McCord, 1989). Something similar happened in Canada with the Inuit and other native groups, who were prohibited from drinking alcohol—and would therefore drink as much as they could when they could get hold of it. In 1951, they were permitted to drink only in licensed bars and would therefore drink as much as possible while in a bar. Both policies were guaranteed to create drunkenness. (The 1951 law was repealed in 1960.)

3 *Not all addicts have withdrawal symptoms when they stop taking a drug.* When heavy users of a drug stop taking it, they often suffer such unpleasant symptoms as nausea, abdominal cramps, muscle spasms, depression, and sleep problems, depending on the drug. But these symptoms are far from universal. During the Vietnam War, nearly 30 percent of American soldiers were taking heroin in doses far stronger than those available on the streets of U.S. cities.

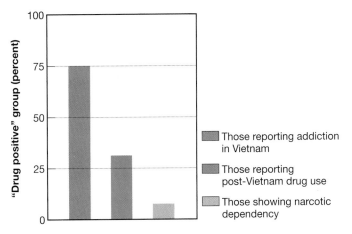

Figure 10.4

Drugs and Vietnam Veterans: Failure of the Addiction Prediction

U.S. soldiers who tested "drug positive" when they were in Vietnam showed a dramatic drop in drug use when they returned to civilian life—contrary to what the disease model of addiction would predict (Robins, Davis, & Goodwin, 1974).

These men believed themselves to be addicted, and experts predicted a drug-withdrawal disaster among the returning veterans. It never materialized; over 90 percent of the men simply gave up the drug, without significant withdrawal pain, when they came home to new circumstances (Robins, Davis, & Goodwin, 1974; see Figure 10.4). Similarly, most people who are addicted to cigarettes, tranquilizers, or painkillers are able to stop taking these drugs, without outside help and without severe withdrawal symptoms (Prochaska, Norcross, & DiClemente, 1994).

4 *Addiction does not depend on properties of the drug alone, but also on the reason for taking it.* Addicts use drugs to escape from the real world, but people living with chronic pain use some of the same drugs, including morphine and other opiates, in order to function in the real world—and they do not become addicted (Portenoy, 1994). In a study of 100 hospital patients who had been given strong doses of narcotics for postoperative pain, 99 had no withdrawal symptoms upon leaving the hospital (Zinberg, 1974). And of 10,000 burn patients who received narcotics as part of their hospital care, not one became an addict (Perry & Heidrich, 1982).

To understand why people abuse drugs, therefore, the learning model focuses on the reasons for taking them. In the case of alcohol, most people drink simply to be sociable, to conform to the group they are with, or to relax when they are stressed.

But those who drink in order to disguise or suppress anxiety, depression, or fear have significantly more drinking problems than sociable drinkers do (Cooper et al., 1995). College students who feel uninvolved with their studies or their school are more likely to drink in binges, with the intention of getting drunk (Flacks & Thomas, 1998). And although marijuana is relatively safe and not chemically addictive, adolescents who are *already* troubled and antisocial quickly become dependent on marijuana after starting to use it and do show withdrawal symptoms when they try to stop (Crowley et al., 1998). In all of these cases, the reason for abusing the drug lies in the individual's motives, not just in the chemical properties of the drug itself.

Debating the Causes of Addiction

The biological and learning models both contribute to our understanding of drug abuse and addiction. Yet among many researchers and public-health professionals, these views are quite polarized (see Table 10.3). What we have here is a case of either-or thinking on a national scale, with passions running high because of the implications for the treatment of alcoholics and other addicts.

The argument is most heated in the debate over whether former alcoholics can learn to drink moderately without becoming intoxicated and dependent again on alcohol. Those who advocate the disease model say there is no such thing as a "former" alcoholic; once an addict has even a single drink, he or she will not be able to stop. In this

The Rastafarian church regards marijuana as a "wisdom weed." Will these young Jamaican members react to the drug in the same way as someone who buys it illegally on a street and smokes it alone or at a party? Reactions to drugs are heavily influenced by a person's social and cultural environment, and reasons for taking the drug.

Table 10.3   Biological and Learning Models of Addiction Contrasted

The biological and learning models of addiction differ in how they explain drug abuse and the solutions they propose:

The Biological Model	The Learning Model
Addiction is genetic, biological.	Addiction is a way of coping.
Once an addict, always an addict.	A person can grow beyond the need for alcohol or other drugs.
An addict must abstain from the drug forever.	Most problem drinkers can learn to drink in moderation.
A person is either addicted or not.	The degree of addiction will vary, depending on the situation.
The solution is medical treatment and membership in groups that reinforce one's permanent identity as a recovering addict.	The solution involves learning new coping skills and changing one's environment.
An addict needs the same treatment and group support forever.	Treatment lasts only until the person no longer abuses the drug.

Source: Adapted from Peele & Brodsky, 1991.

view, problem drinkers who learn to cut back to social-drinking levels were never true alcoholics in the first place. Those who champion the learning model, on the other hand, argue that once a person no longer *needs* to become drunk, he or she can learn to drink socially and in moderation (Marlatt, 1996). Longitudinal studies find that many people do shift from problem drinking to moderate drinking—if they change from a hard-drinking environment to one that supports moderation; if they no longer have a psychological need to drink heavily; and if they learn better ways of coping with problems than by getting smashed (Marlatt et al., 1993; Vaillant, 1983).

Thinking Critically About "Either-Or" Views of Addiction

How can we assess these two positions critically? Can we locate a common ground between them? Because alcoholism and problem drinking occur for many reasons, neither model offers the only solution. Many alcoholics cannot learn to drink moderately, especially if they have had drinking problems for many years (Vaillant, 1995). On the other hand, although total-abstinence groups like Alcoholics Anonymous (AA) have saved lives, they do not work for everyone. According to its own surveys and those done independently, one-third to one-half of all people who join AA drop out. Many of these dropouts benefit from programs such as Rational Recovery, Moderation Management, and DrinkWise, which teach people how to drink moderately and keep their drinking under control (Marlatt, 1996; Peele & Brodsky, 1991; Rosenberg, 1993).

So instead of asking, "Can addicts and problem drinkers learn to drink moderately?" we should ask, "What are the factors that make it more likely that someone can learn to control problem drinking?" Alcoholics who are most likely to become controlled drinkers have a history of less severe dependence on the drug; they lead more stable lives, having jobs and families; and they believe that controlled drinking is possible (Rosenberg, 1993). Alcoholics who believe that one drink will set them off—those who accept the alcoholics' creed, "first drink, then drunk"—are in fact more likely to behave that way. Ironically, then, the course that alcoholism takes may reflect, in part, a person's belief in the disease model or the learning model.

As you can see, abuse and addiction reflect an interaction of physiology and psychology, person and culture. In sum, problems with drugs are most likely to occur under these conditions:

- When a person has a physiological vulnerability to a drug;

- When a person believes he or she has no control over the drug;

- When laws or customs encourage or teach people to take a drug in binges, and moderate use is neither encouraged nor taught;

- When a person comes to rely on a drug as a way of coping with problems, suppressing anger or fear, or relieving pain;

- When members of a person's peer group drink heavily or use other drugs excessively, forcing the person to choose between staying in the group and going along, or dropping out and losing friends.

QUICK QUIZ

If you are addicted to passing exams, answer these questions.

1. What is the most reasonable conclusion about the role of genes in alcoholism? (a) Without a key gene, a person cannot become alcoholic; (b) the presence of a key gene will almost always cause a person to become alcoholic; (c) genes may work in combination to increase a person's vulnerability to some kinds of alcoholism.

2. Which cultural practice is associated with *low* rates of alcoholism? (a) gradual introduction to drinking in family settings, (b) infrequent but binge drinking, (c) drinking as a rite of passage into adulthood, (d) policies of prohibition

3. In a national survey, 52 percent of American college students said they drink to get drunk and 42 percent said they usually binge when drinking. To reduce this problem, some schools and fraternities are instituting "zero tolerance" programs—permitting no alcohol at all. Others are basing solutions on "social norming"—trying to change the norms from binge drinking to moderate drinking. According to the research described in this section, which policies are more likely to work? Why or why not?

Answers:

1. c 2. a 3. Abstinence policies are likely to be much less effective than social-norming policies. "Zero tolerance" programs do not address the *reasons* that students binge, do not affect the student culture that fosters binge drinking, and do not teach students how to drink moderately.

What's Ahead

- What's the difference between schizophrenia and a "split personality"?

- Why do most researchers consider schizophrenia a brain disorder?

- Could schizophrenia begin in the womb?

schizophrenia
A psychotic disorder marked by positive symptoms (e.g., delusions, hallucinations, and incoherent speech) and negative symptoms (e.g., emotional flatness and loss of motivation).

psychosis
An extreme mental disturbance involving distorted perceptions and irrational behavior. (Plural: *psychoses*.)

10.7 Schizophrenia

To be schizophrenic is best summed up in a repeating dream that I have had since childhood. In this dream I am lying on a beautiful sunlit beach but my body is in pieces. . . . I realize that the tide is coming in and that I am unable to gather the parts of my dismembered body together to run away. . . . This to me is what schizophrenia feels like; being fragmented in one's personality and constantly afraid that the tide of illness will completely cover me. (Quoted in Rollin, 1980)

In 1911, Swiss psychiatrist Eugen Bleuler coined the term **schizophrenia** to describe cases in which the personality loses its unity. People with schizophrenia do *not* have a "split" or "multiple" personality. As this haunting quotation illustrates, schizophrenia is a fragmented condition in which words are split from meaning, actions from motives, perceptions from reality. It is an example of a **psychosis,** a mental condition that involves distorted perceptions of reality and an inability to function in most aspects of life.

Symptoms of Schizophrenia

If depression is the common cold of psychological disorder, said psychiatrist Donald Klein (1980), schizophrenia is its cancer: elusive, complicated, and varying in form. In general, schizophrenia produces two categories of symptoms. *Active* or *positive symptoms* involve an exaggeration or distortion of normal thinking processes and behavior. These symptoms are called "positive" because they are *additions* to normal behavior; healthy people do not have delusions that their brains are receiving Martian signals. In contrast, *negative symptoms* involve the *loss* or absence of normal traits and abilities, such as the ability to speak fluently and feel warm emotions.

The most common active symptoms include the following:

1 *Bizarre delusions,* such as the belief that dogs are extraterrestrials disguised as pets. Some people with schizophrenia have paranoid delusions, taking innocent events—a stranger's cough, a helicopter overhead—as evidence that the world is plotting against them. Some have delusions of identity, believing that they are Moses, Jesus, or some other famous person. A woman named Margaret Mary Ray suffered from the delusion that talk-show host David Letterman was in love with her; she

stalked him day and night for ten years before finally killing herself.

2 *Hallucinations and heightened sensory awareness,* which feel intensely real to the sufferer. Hallucinations usually take the form of voices speaking odd, garbled words; a running conversation in the head; or two or more voices conversing with each other. But some are visual (e.g., one patient thought she kept seeing Elizabeth Taylor in the mirror) or tactile (e.g., some patients feel insects crawling all over their bodies). People with schizophrenia also have difficulty in filtering out sensory stimulation and distracting sounds, making it difficult and sometimes impossible for them to concentrate.

3 *Disorganized, incoherent speech,* consisting of an illogical jumble of ideas and symbols, linked by meaningless rhyming words or by remote associations called *word salads.* Homeless people who are suffering from schizophrenia often seem strange or frightening to observers because of their incoherent associations and ideas. A patient of Bleuler's wrote, "Olive oil is an Arabian liquorsauce which the Afghans, Moors and Moslems use in ostrich farming. The Indian plantain tree is the whiskey of the Parsees and Arabs. Barley, rice and sugar cane called artichoke, grow remarkably

When people with schizophrenia are asked to draw pictures, their drawings are often distorted, lack color, include words, and reveal flat emotion. One patient was asked to copy a picture of flowers from a magazine (top right). The initial result is shown on the left. The drawing in the center shows improvement, and the drawing on the right shows how much the patient had progressed after several months of treatment.

well in India. The Brahmins live as castes in Baluchistan. The Circassians occupy Manchuria and China. China is the Eldorado of the Pawnees" (Bleuler, 1911/1950).

4 *Grossly disorganized and inappropriate behavior,* which may range from childlike silliness to unpredictable outbursts and violent agitation. The person may wear three overcoats and gloves on a hot day, start collecting garbage, or hoard scraps of food.

In contrast to these positive symptoms, negative symptoms include loss of motivation; poverty of speech (making only brief, empty replies in conversation, because of diminished thought rather than an unwillingness to speak); and, most notably, emotional flatness—unresponsive facial expressions, poor eye contact, and diminished emotionality. Some people with schizophrenia completely withdraw into a private world, sitting for hours without moving, a condition called *catatonic stupor.* These negative symptoms may appear months before active ones do, and they often persist even when the active symptoms are in remission.

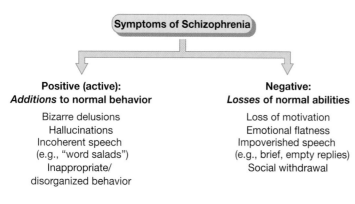

Symptoms of Schizophrenia

Positive (active):	Negative:
Additions to normal behavior	*Losses* of normal abilities
Bizarre delusions	Loss of motivation
Hallucinations	Emotional flatness
Incoherent speech	Impoverished speech
(e.g., "word salads")	(e.g., brief, empty replies)
Inappropriate/	Social withdrawal
disorganized behavior	

In some individuals, schizophrenic symptoms appear abruptly, often in response to a stressful situation; in such cases, the prognosis for recovery is relatively good. In other individuals, the onset is more gradual; negative symptoms slowly emerge, and friends and family report a slow change in personality. The person may stop working or bathing, become isolated and withdrawn, and start behaving in peculiar ways. In these cases, the outlook is less predictable. The more breakdowns and relapses the individual has had, the poorer the chances for complete recovery. Yet many people suffering from this illness learn to control the symptoms, while working and having good family relationships (Harding, Zubin, & Strauss, 1992).

The mystery of schizophrenia is that we could go on listing symptoms and variations all day and never finish. Some people with schizophrenia are almost completely impaired in all spheres; others do extremely well in certain areas. Still others have normal moments of lucidity in otherwise withdrawn lives. One adolescent crouched in a rigid catatonic posture in front of a television for the month of October; later, he was able to report on all the highlights of the World Series he had seen. A middle-aged man, hospitalized for 20 years, believing he was a prophet of God and that monsters were coming out of the walls, was able to interrupt his ranting to play a good game of chess (Wender & Klein, 1981).

Theories of Schizophrenia

Any disorder that has so many variations and symptoms will pose many problems for diagnosis and explanation. Early psychodynamic and learning theories—that schizophrenia results from being raised by an erratic, cold, rejecting mother or from living in an unpredictable environment—have not been supported. The leading theories today come primarily from the biological perspective, although biological explanations are, as usual, not the whole story.

Using brain-imaging techniques, longitudinal studies, and dissections of brains, many researchers are trying to pinpoint the biological factors that might be causes of schizophrenia. They are searching for genetic factors, abnormalities in the brain and neurotransmitters, and abnormalities in prenatal development. Here are some of their major findings:

1 *Genetic predispositions.* A person has a considerably greater risk of developing schizophrenia if an identical twin develops the disorder, and this is true even if the person is reared apart from the affected sibling (Gottesman, 1991, 1994). Moreover, children with one schizophrenic parent have a lifetime risk of 12 percent, and children with two schizophrenic parents have a lifetime risk of 35–46 percent, compared to a risk in the general population of only 1–2 percent (Goldstein, 1987). (See Figure 10.5.)

These and similar findings indicate the existence of a genetic contribution to the disorder, and researchers all over the world are trying to track down the genes that might be involved in specific symptoms, such as hallucinations and sensitivity to sounds (Blouin et al., 1998; Leonard et al., 1998). However, no single gene has been found—or is likely to be found, many researchers believe, given all the different forms that schizophrenia takes (Levinson et al., 1998). In addition, genes alone cannot predict who will develop the disorder. Even among identical twins, when one develops it, the chances that the other will do so are slightly less than half (Torrey et al., 1994). And remember that even if 12 percent of all children with one schizophrenic parent develop the disorder, that means that 88 percent of them do not.

2 *Structural brain abnormalities.* Some individuals with schizophrenia show signs of cerebral damage: decreased brain weight, a decrease in the volume of the temporal lobe or limbic regions, reduced numbers of neurons in the prefrontal cortex, or enlargement of the *ventricles,* the spaces in the brain filled with cerebrospinal fluid (see Figure 10.6) (Akbarian et al., 1996; Heinrichs, 1993; Zorrilla et al., 1997). Schizophrenics are also more likely than healthy individuals to have abnormalities in the thalamus, the traffic-control center that filters sensations and focuses attention (Andreasen et al., 1994; Gur et al., 1998).

A major problem in brain research, however, is that the antipsychotic medications that many schizophrenics take can affect the brain. Thus a brain difference that appears to be a cause of schizophrenia might instead be a result of medication. In one study, schizophrenic patients who had never taken medication did not differ from healthy control subjects except in the size of the thalamus (Gur et al., 1998).

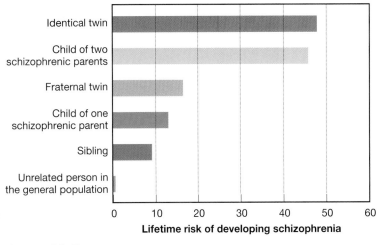

Figure 10.5
Genetic Vulnerability to Schizophrenia
This graph, based on combined data from 40 European twin and adoption studies conducted over seven decades, shows that the closer the genetic relationship to a person with schizophrenia, the higher the risk of developing the disorder (Gottesman, 1991).

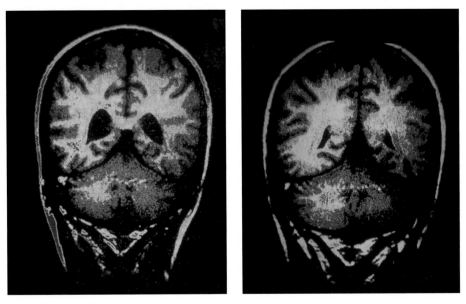

Figure 10.6
Schizophrenia and the Brain
MRI scans show that a person with schizophrenia (left) is more likely than a healthy person (right) to have enlarged ventricles, or spaces, in the brain (see arrows) (Andreasen et al., 1994).

3 *Neurotransmitter abnormalities.* Abnormalities in several neurotransmitters, including serotonin, glutamate, and most notably dopamine, have been associated with schizophrenia. For example, many schizophrenics have high levels of activity in brain areas served by dopamine, and a particular kind of dopamine receptor is more common in their brains than in those of healthy people (Seeman, Guan, & Van Tol, 1993). However, similar neurotransmitter abnormalities are also found in many other mental disorders, such as depression and alcoholism. This fact makes it difficult to know whether these abnormalities play a specific role in schizophrenia (Spoont, 1992).

4 *Prenatal abnormalities.* Damage to the fetal brain increases the likelihood of schizophrenia (and, again, of other mental disorders). In some cases, the damage may occur because of malnutrition: Babies conceived during times of famine have twice the schizophrenia rate as babies whose mothers ate normal diets during pregnancy (Susser et al., 1996). Another culprit, surprisingly enough, may be an infectious virus during prenatal development (Hooper, 1999; Torrey et al., 1994). There is a significant association between a mother's exposure to the influenza virus during the second trimester of pregnancy, when the fetal brain is forming crucial connections, and the onset of schizophrenia in the child 20 to 30 years later (Mednick, Huttunen, & Machón, 1994).

Although the evidence for brain abnormalities in schizophrenia is compelling, many researchers believe that the onset and course of this disorder— like those of depression, antisocial personality disorder, and addiction—are best explained by an interactive theory that combines biological and environmental factors (Gottesman, 1991). Proponents of the *vulnerability-stress model of schizophrenia* observe that genes or brain damage alone will not inevitably produce schizophrenia, and a vulnerable person who lives in a good environment may never show full-fledged signs of it.

For many years, the Copenhagen High-Risk Project has followed 207 children at risk for schizophrenia (because they had a schizophrenic parent) and a control group of 104 low-risk children. The project has identified several factors that, in combination, increase the likelihood of schizophrenia: the existence of schizophrenia in the family; physical trauma during childbirth that might damage the brain; exposure to the flu virus or other prenatal trauma during the second trimester of gestation; and unstable, stressful environments (Mednick, Parnas, & Schulsinger, 1987; Olin & Mednick, 1996).

The interaction of individual vulnerabilities and environmental stresses shows how several factors may combine to produce any given case of schizophrenia. To make matters even more complicated, different factors may predominate in different kinds of schizophrenia; this may explain why some schizophrenics recover and others do not. For example, the kind of schizophrenia caused primarily by prenatal exposure to the flu may be different from the kind caused primarily by genetic predispositions. The riddle of schizophrenia is likely to be several riddles, each remaining to be solved.

QUICK QUIZ

The following quiz is not a hallucination.

1. A patient with schizophrenia hears voices in her head when no one is around. Is this an example of a positive symptom or a negative one?

2. *True or false:* Most people with schizophrenia have a schizophrenic parent.

3. A research team compares the brains of schizophrenics and nonschizophrenics and finds an abnormality in the brains of the former group. What competing explanation should they rule out before concluding that they may have found a cause of schizophrenia?

Answers:

1. positive 2. false 3. They need to rule out the possibility that the brain difference was due to medication the schizophrenics were taking.

PSYCHOLOGY IN THE NEWS, REVISITED

We have come to the end of a long walk along the spectrum of psychological problems—from those that are normal conditions of life, such as occasional anxiety or "caffeine-induced sleep disorder," to mental disorders that can be severely disabling, such as schizophrenia. Where on this spectrum would you place "Internet dependence," the complaint of the students in our opening story?

Some psychologists think that Internet addiction is a true disorder, analogous to drug addiction or any other compulsive behavior. After all, it meets some of the criteria for a mental disorder: It can be maladaptive, disrupting the lives of those who spend thousands of hours in cyberspace instead of the real world; it often causes them emotional distress, and distresses their friends and families as well. Like addicts and people with obsessive-compulsive disorder, some people claim they have no control over the time they spend on the Internet, much as they might wish to change it.

Other psychologists think that students who spend too much time on the Internet are no different from previous generations who also sought ways of distracting themselves from the common problems students have—insecurity in a new environment, worry about grades, or a dull social life. This is not a "mental disorder," they say, it's a normal problem, called Learning to Pass Courses and Figure Out Life.

Thinking Critically About Mental Illness and Responsibility One of the great debates generated by all diagnoses of mental disorder concerns the question of personal responsibility. Growing numbers of students are claiming that they suffer from attention deficit/hyperactivity disorder so that they may be given more time for exams and papers (Ranseen, 1998). Before long, we will probably hear from some students claiming that Internet addiction disorder was the reason they flunked out.

Of course, many people *do* suffer from mental impairments that make it difficult or even impossible for them to focus their attention or control their behavior. How can we distinguish impairments that legitimately reduce a person's responsibility for his or her actions from unjustified excuses?

This issue of responsibility is not confined only to problems that affect students, like "Internet addiction." It becomes extremely urgent in civil and criminal cases when defendants use psychological diagnoses to try to exonerate themselves or rationalize their behavior. Romance writer Janet Dailey, accused of plagiarizing whole passages from another writer, said she was suffering from "a psychological problem that I never even suspected I had." Lyle and Erik Menendez, convicted of murdering their wealthy parents, claimed they suffered from a form of posttraumatic stress disorder resulting from years of abuse. (A jury rejected this claim and sentenced them to life in prison.)

In the United States and Canada, in order to prove that a defendant had diminished responsibility for a crime, the defense must show clear and convincing evidence that the defendant had a severe mental condition and not just a personality defect or a bad day at work. Few lawyers take advantage of the insanity defense; in fact, it is used in fewer than 1 percent of all U.S. felony cases, and it succeeds in only about a quarter of those cases (Silver, Cirincione, & Steadman, 1994). Nonetheless, some defense attorneys, aided by the testimony of psychiatrists and psychologists, keep trying to expand the legal grounds for diminished responsibility, searching for mental disorders that might lessen the severity of the sentence a guilty person receives.

When thinking about the relationship of mental disorder to personal responsibility, we face a dilemma. The law recognizes, rightly, that people who are mentally incompetent, delusional, or disturbed should not be judged by the same standards as mentally healthy individuals. At the same time, society has an obligation to protect its citizens from harm and to reject easy excuses for violations of the law. To balance these two positions, we need to find ways to ensure that people who commit crimes or behave reprehensibly face the consequences of their behavior. We also must ensure that people who are suffering from psychological problems have the compassionate support of society in their search for help. After all, psychological problems of one kind or another are problems that all of us will have at some time in our lives.

TAKING PSYCHOLOGY WITH YOU

When a Friend Is Suicidal

Suicide can be frightening to those who find themselves fantasizing about it, and it is devastating to the family and friends of those who go through with it. In North America, most people who commit suicide are over the age of 45, but suicide is a leading cause of death for teenagers and college students (Garland & Zigler, 1994; *The New York Times,* March 20, 1998).

Although many people believe that women are more likely than men to attempt suicide, whereas men are more likely to succeed, this gender difference is more apparent than real, and it depends on culture and circumstances. In Finland, for example, more males than females attempt suicide; and in Canada and the United States, men in prison have high rates of attempted suicide (Canetto & Sakinofsky, 1998). Moreover, men's efforts to commit suicide are not always as obvious as those of women: Some men provoke confrontations with the police, hoping to be shot and killed; others try to destroy themselves with drugs.

Suicidal people believe that life is unendurable. This belief may be rational in the case of people who are terminally ill and in pain, but more often it reflects the distorted thinking of someone suffering from depression. Friends and family members can help prevent a suicide by becoming informed and by recognizing the danger signs:

- *Take all suicide threats seriously.* Some people assume they can't do anything about it when a friend talks about committing suicide. "He'll just do it at another place, another time," they think. In fact, most suicides occur during an acute crisis. Once the person gets through the crisis, the desire to die fades. One researcher tracked down 515 people who had attempted suicide by jumping off the Golden Gate Bridge many years earlier. Less than 5 percent had actually committed suicide in the subsequent decades (Seiden, 1978).

Some people believe that if a friend is talking about suicide, he or she will not really do it. This belief is also false. Few people commit suicide without signaling their intentions. Most are ambivalent: "I want to kill myself, but I don't want to be dead—at least not forever." Most suicidal people want relief from the terrible pain of feeling that nobody cares, that life is not worth living (Baumeister, 1990). Getting these thoughts and fears out in the open is an important first step.

- *Know the danger signs.* A depressed person is at risk of trying to commit suicide if he or she has tried to do it before; has become withdrawn and listless; has a history of depression; reveals specific plans for carrying out the suicide or gives away cherished possessions; expresses no concern about religious prohibitions or the impact on family members; and has access to a lethal method, such as a gun (Garland & Zigler, 1994).

- *Take constructive action.* If you believe a friend is in danger of suicide, do not be afraid to ask, "Are you thinking of suicide?" This question does not "put the idea" in anyone's mind. If your friend is contemplating the action, he or she will probably be relieved to talk about it, and you will know that it is time to get help. Let your friend talk without argument or disapproval. Don't try to talk your friend out of it by debating whether suicide is right or wrong, and don't put on phony cheerfulness. If your friend's words or actions scare you, say so. By listening nonjudgmentally, you are showing that you care. By allowing your friend to unburden his or her grief, you help the person get through the immediate crisis.

Most of all, do not leave your friend alone. If necessary, get the person to a clinic or a hospital emergency room, or call a local suicide hot line. Don't worry about doing the wrong thing. In an emergency, the worst thing you can do is nothing at all.

SUMMARY

Defining and Diagnosing Disorder

- The prevalence of a behavior does not indicate whether it is a sign of "mental disorder." When defining *mental disorder,* mental-health professionals emphasize the violation of cultural standards, whether the behavior is maladaptive for the individual or society, and the emotional suffering caused by the behavior.

- *The Diagnostic and Statistical Manual of Mental Disorders* (DSM), which is used throughout the world, is designed to provide objective criteria and categories for diagnosing mental disorder. Critics argue that the diagnosis of mental disorders, unlike the diagnosis of medical diseases, is inherently a subjective process that can never be entirely objective. They believe the DSM fosters overdiagnosis, overlooks the influence of diagnostic labels on clients and therapists, confuses serious disorders with normal problems, and creates an illusion of objectivity.

- In diagnosing psychological disorders, clinicians often use *projective tests* such as the *Rorschach Inkblot Test,* which are based on psychodynamic assumptions. However, these tests have serious problems with reliability and validity, which cause further problems when they are used in the legal arena or in diagnosing disorders. In general, *objective tests* or *inventories,* such as the *MMPI,* are more reliable and valid than projective ones.

- Supporters of the DSM believe that when the DSM criteria are used correctly and when empirically validated objective tests are used, reliability in diagnosis improves. Athough some diagnoses are indeed subjective and culture specific, not all diagnoses reflect society's biases, and some disorders, including depression and schizophrenia, are found all over the world.

Anxiety Disorders

- *Generalized anxiety disorder* involves continuous, chronic anxiety, with signs of nervousness, worry, and irritability. When anxiety results from exposure to uncontrollable or unpredictable danger, it can lead to *posttraumatic stress disorder,* which involves mentally reliving the trauma, "psychic numbing," and increased physiological arousal. *Panic disorder* involves sudden, intense attacks of profound fear, with feelings of impending doom. Panic attacks are common in the aftermath of stress or frightening experiences; those who go on to develop a disorder tend to interpret the attacks as a sign of impending disaster rather than a normal response to great stress.

- *Phobias* are unrealistic fears of specific situations, activities, or things. Common *social phobias* include fears of speaking in public, using public restrooms, or being observed by others. *Agoraphobia,* the fear of being away from a safe place or person, is the most disabling phobia. It often begins with a panic attack, which the person tries to avoid in the future by staying close to "safe" places.

- *Obsessive-compulsive disorder* (OCD) involves recurrent, unwished-for thoughts or images (*obsessions*) and repetitive, ritualized behaviors (*compulsions*) that a person feels unable to control. Parts of the brain having to do with fear and response to threat are more active than normal in people with OCD.

Mood Disorders

- Symptoms of *major depression* include distorted thinking patterns, low self-esteem, physical ailments such as fatigue and loss of appetite, and prolonged grief and despair. In *bipolar disorder,* a person experiences episodes of both depression and *mania* (excessive euphoria). Women are more likely than men to be treated for major depression, but psychologists disagree on whether the difference is real or due to misdiagnosis of men's symptoms.

- *Biological* explanations of depression emphasize low levels of the neurotransmitters serotonin and norepinephrine, and the role of genetic predispositions. *Social* explanations emphasize the circumstances of people's lives, such as work and family life, motherhood, and experiences with violence. *Attachment* theories hold that depression results from broken or conflicted relationships or a history of insecure attachment. *Cognitive* explanations link depression to particular ways of thinking (believing that the origin of one's unhappiness is internal, stable, and uncontrollable), a *pessimistic explanatory style*, and habits of brooding or rumination. *Vulnerability-stress models* look at interactions between individual vulnerabilities (genetic dispositions, cognitive habits, and personality traits) and external stress.

Personality Disorders

- *Personality disorders* are characterized by rigid, self-destructive traits that cause distress or an inability to get along with others. They include *paranoid, narcissistic,* and *antisocial personality disorders.*

- A person with antisocial personality disorder lacks empathy and remorse, is unafraid of punishment, and is impulsive and lacks self-control. The disorder may stem from abnormalities in the central nervous system; problems with impulse control; brain abnormalities (especially in left-hemisphere activation and in damage to the prefrontal cortex) caused by genes, birth complications, or injury; or a combination of biological *vulnerability* and *stressful* or violent environments.

Dissociative Identity Disorder ("Multiple Personality")

- *Dissociative disorders* involve a split in consciousness or identity. In *dissociative identity disorder* (commonly called *multiple personality disorder,* or MPD), two or more distinct personalities and identities appear to exist within one person. Considerable controversy surrounds the validity and nature of MPD. Some clinicians think it is common, often goes undiagnosed, and originates in childhood trauma. Others have a *sociocognitive explanation.* They argue that most cases result from pressure and suggestion by clinicians who believe in the disorder, interacting with vulnerable patients who find MPD a plausible explanation for their problems. Media coverage of sensational alleged cases of

MPD has also contributed to the rise in the number of cases since 1980.

Drug Abuse and Addiction

• The effects of drugs depend on whether they are used moderately or are abused. Signs of *substance abuse* include impaired ability to work or get along with others, use of the drug in hazardous situations, recurrent arrests for drug use, and conflicts with others caused by drug use.

• According to the *biological* or *disease model of addiction*, some people have a biological vulnerability to alcoholism and other addictions, due to a genetic factor that affects their metabolism, biochemistry, or personality traits. Advocates of the *learning model of addiction* point out that addiction patterns vary according to culture, learning, and accepted practice; that many people can stop taking drugs without experiencing withdrawal symptoms; that drug abuse depends on the reasons for taking a drug; and that abuse increases when people are not taught moderate use.

• Although the biological and learning models are polarized on many issues, the evidence suggests that addiction and abuse result from an interaction between biological and psychological vulnerability and a person's culture, learning history, motives for taking a drug, and situation.

Schizophrenia

• *Schizophrenia* is a psychotic disorder involving *positive* or *active symptoms* (including delusions, hallucinations, disorganized speech called *word salads*, and inappropriate behavior) and *negative symptoms* (including loss of motivation, poverty of speech, emotional flatness, and *catatonic stupor*). Cases of schizophrenia vary in severity, duration, and prognosis.

• Causes of schizophrenia may involve genetic predispositions; structural brain abnormalities; neurotransmitter abnormalities; abnormalities of prenatal development resulting from maternal malnutrition, viral infection, or other trauma during the second trimester; and, according to the *vulnerability-stress model*, interactions between such factors and a person's environment during childhood or young adulthood.

Psychology in the News, Revisited

• The diagnosis of mental disorder raises important questions for issues of personal responsibility in the law and everyday life. Psychologists and others struggle to decide when a mental disorder is merely an excuse for bad or troubled behavior, and when it truly does reduce people's responsibility for actions they cannot control.

KEY TERMS

insanity   332
mental disorder   333
Diagnostic and Statistical Manual of Mental Disorders (DSM)   333
projective tests   336
Rorschach Inkblot Test   337
inventories (objective tests)   337
Minnesota Multiphasic Personality Inventory (MMPI)   337
generalized anxiety disorder   338
posttraumatic stress disorder (PTSD)   339
panic disorder (panic attack)   339
phobia   339
social phobia   340
agoraphobia   340
obsessive-compulsive disorder (OCD)   340

mood disorder   341
major depression   342
mania   342
bipolar disorder   342
pessimistic explanatory style   345
vulnerability-stress model of depression   345
personality disorders   346
narcissistic personality disorder   346
paranoid personality disorder   347
antisocial personality disorder (APD)   347
vulnerability-stress model of APD   349
dissociative disorders   350

dissociative identity disorder (multiple personality disorder, MPD)   350
sociocognitive explanation of MPD   352
substance abuse   353
biological or disease model of addiction   353
learning model of addiction   354
schizophrenia   358
psychosis   358
positive and negative symptoms of schizophrenia   359
word salads   359
catatonic stupor   360
vulnerability-stress model of schizophrenia   362

LOOKING BACK ◄

- Is insanity the same thing as having a mental disorder? (p. 332)

- What are three approaches to defining "mental disorder"? (pp. 332–333)

- Why were slaves who dreamed of freedom once considered to be mentally ill? (p. 333)

- Why is the standard guide to the diagnosis of mental disorders so controversial? (pp. 335–336)

- Can an "inkblot" test reveal your psychological problems? (p. 337)

- What is the difference between ordinary anxiety and an anxiety disorder? (p. 338)

- Why is the most disabling of all phobias known as the "fear of fear"? (p. 340)

- When is checking the stove before leaving home a sign of caution, and when does it signal a disorder? (p. 341)

- How can you tell whether you have major depression or just the blues? (p. 342)

- What are the "poles" in bipolar disorder? (p. 342)

- How do some people think themselves into depression? (pp. 344–345)

- When does being self-centered become a disorder? (pp. 346–347)

- What do a charming but heartless tycoon and a remorseless killer have in common? (p. 347)

- Why are some people seemingly incapable of feeling guilt and shame? (p. 348)

- Why did the number of "personalities" in "multiple personality" patients jump from two or three in early cases to thousands in recent ones? (p. 352)

- In what ways might genes contribute to alcoholism? (p. 354)

- Why is alcoholism more common in Ireland than in Italy? (p. 354)

- Why don't policies of abstinence from alcohol reduce problem drinking? (p. 355)

- If you take morphine to control chronic pain, does that mean you will become addicted to it? (p. 355)

- What's the difference between schizophrenia and a "split personality"? (p. 358)

- Why do most researchers consider schizophrenia a brain disorder? (p. 360)

- Could schizophrenia begin in the womb? (p. 362)

Colorado Girl Dies After Controversial Therapy

DENVER, CO, MAY 23, 2000. Police have charged four people with recklessly causing the death of 10-year-old Candace Newmaker during a session of "rebirthing" therapy. The procedure, aimed at helping adopted children form attachments to their adoptive parents by "reliving" birth, was captured on closed-circuit television as the girl's mother watched in a nearby room.

The child was completely wrapped in a blanket that supposedly simulated the womb, and was surrounded by large pillows. The therapists then pressed in on the pillows to simulate contractions and told the girl to push her way out of the blanket over her head. Candace repeatedly said that she could not breathe and felt she was

Connell Watkins arrives at the Jefferson County District court with her attorney (left), for a hearing on charges stemming from the death of a child during a "rebirthing" therapy session.

going to die. But instead of unwrapping her, the therapists said, "You've got to push hard if you want to be born—or do you want to stay in there and die?"

The girl, who was adopted four years ago and had been treated for attention deficit disorder and depression, lost consciousness and was rushed to a local hospital, where she died the next day. Connell Watkins, an unlicensed social worker who operated the counseling center, unregistered psychotherapist Julie Ponder, and two other employees were charged with reckless child abuse resulting in death. The child's mother, Jeane Newmaker, was also charged with child abuse.

APPROACHES TO TREATMENT AND THERAPY

Were the techniques used by these therapists standard practice in psychotherapy? How is a layperson like Jeane Newmaker, who wanted to help her troubled adopted child, supposed to tell the difference between good therapy and bad? When does psychotherapy help people with their problems and when does it do emotional damage—or cause even greater harm?

These questions are especially pressing today, when new kinds of therapies keep emerging, all claiming successful cures. Some are benign, but others are not, and malpractice claims are rising. In Pennsylvania, 13 former patients of Genesis Associates, a "therapeutic cult" in which patients were told they had to "detach" from their "toxic" families and make their primary allegiance to the therapists, filed lawsuits claiming that they had been victims of mind-control techniques. In California, a psychoanalyst was convicted of malpractice because he had treated a woman for 12 years for her alleged "repressed rage" at her mother, and never diagnosed her worsening muscle weakness as the disease it was, myasthenia gravis. And growing numbers of licensed psychotherapists and psychiatrists have been convicted of malpractice for using coercive or suggestive techniques to convince patients that they had multiple personality disorder and had participated in satanic cults. In Chicago, two well-known psychiatrists agreed to pay $10.6 million to one such patient and her family, although the psychiatrists did not admit any negligence or renounce the unorthodox techniques they had used.

Fortunately, these cases are not the norm. Many legitimate, well-tested therapies are available for treating psychological problems ranging from normal life difficulties (such as marital conflict or fear of public speaking) to the delusions of schizophrenia. In this chapter, we will evaluate two major approaches to treatment. *Biological* *treatments* include drugs or direct intervention in brain function; they are prescribed by psychiatrists or other physicians in a hospital or on an outpatient basis. *Psychotherapy* covers an array of psychological approaches, including psychodynamic therapies, cognitive and behavioral therapies, family therapy, and humanist therapies.

Each of these approaches can successfully handle some problems but not others. Each can help some individuals but not others. And in some cases, the misuse of medication or of therapeutic techniques can be terribly harmful. As you read what psychologists have learned about the effectiveness of drugs and psychotherapy, see whether you can come up with some things you would want to know when evaluating any form of therapy, including unorthodox ones such as "rebirthing therapy."

What's Ahead

- What kinds of drugs are used to treat psychological disorders?

- Are antidepressants always the best treatment for depression?

- Can mental disorders be cured by brain surgery?

- Why is "shock therapy" hailed by some clinicians but condemned by others?

11.1 Biological Treatments

For hundreds of years, people have tried to explain the origins of mental illness. Is it due to spirits, pressure in the skull, disease, or bad environments? Since the early 1900s, the mental-health world has alternated between viewing mental disorders as diseases that can be treated medically and as emotional problems that can be treated psychologically.

antipsychotic drugs
Drugs used primarily in the treatment of schizophrenia and other psychotic disorders.

antidepressant drugs
Drugs used primarily in the treatment of mood disorders, especially depression and anxiety.

Do we need to fix the person's brain or the person's mind? Today, biological explanations and treatments are in the ascendance. This is partly because of evidence that some disorders have a genetic component or involve a biochemical or neurological abnormality (see Chapter 10), and partly because economic and social forces are fostering biomedical solutions.

The Question of Drugs

The most widespread biological treatment is medication. Because drugs are so widely prescribed these days, both for severe disorders such as schizophrenia and for more common problems such as anxiety and depression, consumers need to understand what these drugs are, how they can best be used, and their limitations.

Drugs Commonly Prescribed for Mental Disorders. The main classes of drugs used in the treatment of mental and emotional disorders are these:

1 **Antipsychotic drugs,** also called *neuroleptics*—older ones such as chlorpromazine and haloperidol and newer, "second-generation" ones such as clozapine and risperidone—are used in the treatment of schizophrenia and other psychoses. Many antipsychotic drugs block or reduce the sensitivity of brain receptors that respond to dopamine. Some also increase levels of serotonin, a neurotransmitter that inhibits dopamine activity. Antipsychotic drugs can reduce a patient's agitation and delusions, and they can shorten schizophrenic episodes. However, they offer little relief from other symptoms of schizophrenia, such as jumbled thoughts, difficulty concentrating, or inability to interact with others. Although they allow many people to be released from hospitals, these individuals cannot always care for themselves, and they often fail to keep taking their medication because of its unpleasant side effects (Luhrmann, 2000; Masand, 2000). And in spite of the enthusiasm that welcomes each new generation of antipsychotic medication, for many people with schizophrenia these drugs are still not effective (Valenstein, 1998).

2 **Antidepressant drugs** are used primarily in the treatment of depression, anxiety, phobias, and obsessive–compulsive disorder. *Monoamine oxidase (MAO) inhibitors,* such as Nardil, elevate the level of norepinephrine and serotonin in the brain by blocking or inhibiting an enzyme that deacti-

These photos show the effects of antipsychotic drugs on the symptoms of a young man with schizophrenia. In the photo on the left, he was unmedicated; in the photo on the right, he had taken medication. However, these drugs do not help all people with psychotic disorders.

Live!
psych

11.1

vates these neurotransmitters. *Tricyclic antidepressants,* such as Elavil, boost norepinephrine and serotonin levels by preventing the normal reabsorption, or "reuptake," of these substances by the cells that have released them. *Selective serotonin reuptake inhibitors (SSRIs),* such as Prozac, work on the same principle as the tricyclics but specifically target serotonin. Antidepressants are nonaddictive, but they can produce some unpleasant physical reactions, including dry mouth, headaches, consti-

pation, nausea, gastrointestinal problems, weight gain, and, in as many as one-third of all patients, decreased sexual desire and blocked or delayed orgasm (Glenmullen, 2000).

3 **Tranquilizers,** such as Valium and Xanax, increase the activity of the neurotransmitter gamma-aminobutyric acid (GABA). They are the drugs most often prescribed by physicians in general practice for patients who complain of depressed mood, panic, or anxiety—but they are the wrong drugs for such problems. They are not effective for depression or panic disorder, and while they may help an anxious person temporarily feel calmer during an acute experience of anxiety, they are not considered the treatment of choice over a long period of time. One reason is that a significant percentage of people who take tranquilizers overuse the drugs and develop problems with withdrawal and tolerance (i.e., they need larger and larger doses). Xanax can also result in rebound panic attacks if it is not taken exactly on schedule.

4 A special category of drug, a salt called **lithium carbonate,** often helps people who suffer from bipolar disorder. It may produce its effects by moderating levels of norepinephrine or by protecting brain cells from being overstimulated by another neurotransmitter, glutamate (Nonaka, Hough, & Chuang, 1998). Lithium must be given in exactly the right dose, and levels of the drug in the blood must be carefully monitored, because too little will not help and too much is toxic.

"Before Prozac, she loathed company."

tranquilizers
Drugs commonly but often inappropriately prescribed for patients who complain of unhappiness, anxiety, or worry.

lithium carbonate
A drug frequently given to people suffering from bipolar disorder.

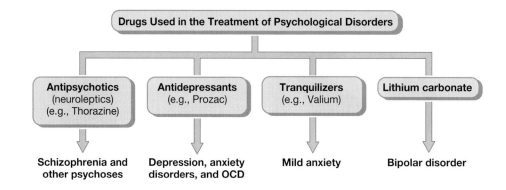

Antipsychotics (neuroleptics) (e.g., Thorazine)	**Antidepressants** (e.g., Prozac)	**Tranquilizers** (e.g., Valium)	**Lithium carbonate**
Schizophrenia and other psychoses	Depression, anxiety disorders, and OCD	Mild anxiety	Bipolar disorder

The increasing popularity of drugs as a method of treatment poses a problem for clinical psychologists, who, unlike psychiatrists, are not currently licensed to prescribe medication. Many psychologists are now lobbying for prescription rights, arguing that they should have access to the full range of treatment possibilities. But they have run into resistance from the medical profession, which argues that even with increased training, psychologists will not be qualified to prescribe medication. Many psychologists too are concerned about the medicalizing of their field and want psychology to remain a distinct alternative to psychiatry (DeNelsky, 1996).

Some Cautions About Drug Treatments.

Without question, drugs have rescued some people from emotional despair, suicide, or years in a mental hospital. They have enabled severely depressed or disturbed people to function and respond to psychotherapy. Although medication cannot magically eliminate people's problems, it can be a useful first step in treatment. Yet many psychiatrists and drug companies are trumpeting the benefits of medication without informing the public of its limitations, so a few words of caution are in order.

Thinking Critically About Drug Treatments

1 *The placebo effect.* New drugs, like new psychotherapies, often promise quick and effective cures. But the **placebo effect** (see Chapter 1) ensures that some people will respond positively to new drugs just because of the enthusiasm surrounding them and their own expectations that the drug will make them feel much better. After a while, when placebo effects decline, many drugs turn out to be neither as effective as promised nor as widely applicable. This has happened repeatedly with each new generation of tranquilizer and is happening again with antidepressants.

The belief that antidepressants are the treatment of choice for depression is widespread, so we were as surprised as anyone to discover the large amount of evidence questioning that belief (Antonuccio et al., 1999; Valenstein, 1998). One meta-analysis found that although clinicians considered antidepressants helpful, the patients' ratings showed no advantage for the drugs beyond the placebo effect (Greenberg et al., 1992). Another meta-analysis, of 19 double-blind studies involving more than 2,000 depressed patients, found that 75 percent of the drugs' effectiveness was due to the placebo effect or other nonchemical factors, and only 25 percent to the chemical properties of the drug (Kirsch & Sapirstein, 1998). Even Prozac, which arrived with much fanfare and enthusiasm, is generally no more effective than the older generation of antidepressants (Greenberg et al., 1994).

2 *High relapse and dropout rates.* A person may have short-term success with antipsychotic or antidepressant drugs. However, in part because of their unpleasant side effects, half to two-thirds of people stop taking them (Glenmullen, 2000; Torrey, 1988). Individuals who take antidepressants without also learning how to cope with their problems are also more likely to relapse in the future (Antonuccio et al., 1999).

3 *Dosage problems.* The challenge with drugs is to find the *therapeutic window,* the amount that is enough but not too much. This problem is compounded by the fact that the same dose of a drug may be metabolized differently in men and women, old people and young people, and different ethnic groups (Willie et al., 1995). When psychiatrist Keh-Ming Lin moved from Taiwan to the United States, he was amazed to learn that the dosage of antipsychotic drugs given to American patients with schizophrenia was often 10 times higher than the dose for Chinese patients. In subsequent studies,

placebo effect
The apparent success of a medication or treatment that is due to the patient's expectations or hopes, rather than to the drug or treatment itself.

Lin and his colleagues confirmed that Asian patients require significantly lower doses of the medication for optimal treatment (Lin, Poland, & Chien, 1990). Similarly, African- Americans suffering from depression or bipolar disorder seem to need lower dosages of tricyclic antidepressants and lithium than other ethnic groups do (Strickland et al., 1991, 1995). Groups may differ in the dosages they can tolerate because of variations in metabolic rates, amount of body fat, the number or type of neurotransmitter receptors in the brain, or cultural practices such as smoking and eating habits.

4 *Long-term risks.* Antipsychotic drugs can have dangerous, even fatal consequences if taken for many years. Antidepressants, in contrast, are assumed to be quite safe, but the effects of taking them for many years are still unknown. The general public and even many physicians do not realize that new drugs are often tested on only a few hundred people for only a few weeks or months, even when the drug is one that patients might take for many years. For example, clozapine was tested in controlled trials that lasted only six weeks (*FDA Drug Bulletin,* 1990). And none of the other second-generation antipsychotic drugs have been used long enough to determine their long-term risks (Gupta et al., 1999). Many physicians and the public, feeling reassured if a drug is effective in the short run, overlook the possibility of long-term dangers.

These cautions are the reason that it is important to think critically about the popularity of an exclusively biological approach to mental disorders. Many American doctors prescribe drugs routinely, often without accompanying psychotherapy for the person's problems. The overprescription of drugs in the United States is partly a result of pressure from managed-care organizations, which prefer to pay for one patient visit for a prescription rather than multiple visits for psychotherapy.

But it is also a result of advertising by drug companies, which are spending fortunes to study and market these highly profitable products. (In 1997 the Food and Drug Administration [FDA] permitted pharmaceutical companies to advertise directly to consumers, a practice still forbidden in Canada and Europe.) Most consumers do not realize that once a drug is approved by the FDA, doctors are then permitted to prescribe it for other conditions and to other populations than those on which it was originally tested. That is why antidepressants are now being marketed for "social

phobias"; Ritalin, widely used in the treatment of attention deficit disorder in school-aged children, is being prescribed for 2- and 3-year-olds; and antipsychotics are being used for nonpsychotic disorders such as bipolar disorder and impulsive aggression. Most worrisome for the future of impartial research, many if not most of the researchers who are studying the effectiveness of medication have strong financial ties to the pharmaceutical industry, in the form of lucrative consulting fees, funding for studies, stock investments, and patents (Angell, 2000; Bodenheimer, 2000; Critser, 1996).

The overprescription of drugs for mood disorders in North America also occurs because of a common but mistaken assumption: that if a disorder appears to have biological origins or involve biochemical abnormalities, then biological treatments must be most appropriate. But in fact, changing your behavior and thoughts, through psychotherapy or other new experiences, can also change the way your brain functions. This point was dramatically illustrated in two PET-scan studies of people with obsessive–compulsive disorder. Among those who were taking Prozac, the metabolism of glucose in the brain improved, suggesting that the drug was having a beneficial effect. But exactly the *same* brain changes occurred in patients who were getting cognitive–behavior therapy and no medication (see Figure 11.1) (Baxter et al., 1992; Schwartz et al., 1996). Cognitive–behavior therapy with depressed patients also restores their brain-wave sleep profiles to normal, unlike antidepressants (Thase et al., 1998).

In sum, consumers must think critically and carefully about the benefits and limitations of

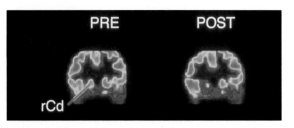

Figure 11.1

Psychotherapy and the Brain

These PET scans show the brain of a person with obsessive–compulsive disorder before and after behavior therapy. Before therapy, the glucose metabolic rates in the right caudate nucleus (rCd) were elevated. After therapy, this area "calmed down," becoming less active, just as it did with medication (Schwartz et al., 1996).

11.1

medication for psychological problems. These drugs are neither totally miraculous nor totally worthless. Their effectiveness depends on the individual, the problem, and whether medication is combined with psychotherapy.

Surgery and Electroshock

For centuries, physicians treated mental illness by trying to change brain function directly. In the seventeenth century, for example, physicians tried to release the "psychic pressures" they believed were causing a person's symptoms by drilling holes in the person's skull. (This method didn't work.) **Psychosurgery**—surgery designed to destroy selected areas of the brain thought to be responsible for emotional disorders or disturbed behavior—continued well into this century.

The most famous form of modern psychosurgery was invented in 1935, when a Portuguese neurologist, Egas Moniz, drilled two holes into the skull of a mental patient and used a specially designed instrument to cut or crush nerve fibers running from the prefrontal lobes to other areas. This operation, called a *prefrontal lobotomy,* was supposed to reduce the patient's emotional symptoms without impairing intellectual ability. The procedure—which, incredibly, was never assessed or validated scientifically—was performed on tens of thousands of people. In America, the lobotomy was popularized by Walter Freeman, who personally performed more than 3,500 operations. Tragically, lobotomies left many patients apathetic, withdrawn, and unable to care for themselves (Valenstein, 1986). Yet Moniz won a Nobel Prize for his work.

Today, psychosurgery is rare, but some neurosurgeons have not given up on the effort to cure mental illness by operating on the brains of severely depressed or anxious patients whose symptoms have not responded to other treatments (Marino & Cosgrove, 1997). Although the physicians usually claim success, these reports are anecdotal and, to date, the procedures have no greater scientific support than lobotomy did (Vertosick, 1997). Sometimes the criterion for success is only the psychiatrist's report, not even the patient's!

Another controversial procedure is **electroconvulsive therapy (ECT),** or "shock therapy," which is used for the treatment of severe depression. An electrode is placed on one or both sides of the head, and a current of between 70 and 130 volts is turned on. The current triggers a seizure that typically lasts one minute, causing the body to convulse. Unlike in the past, patients are given muscle relaxants and anesthesia, so they sleep through the procedure, and their convulsions are minimized. ECT is sometimes used effectively on people who are suicidal, when there is a life-threatening risk of waiting for drugs or psychotherapy to help, although no one knows how or why it

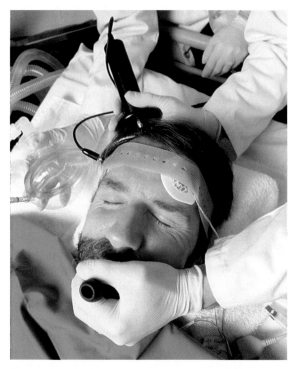

Electroconvulsive therapy has been used successfully to treat severe depression that has not responded to other treatments. But its supporters and critics continue to disagree vehemently about its use and potential for misuse.

psychosurgery
Any surgical procedure that destroys selected areas of the brain believed to be involved in emotional disorders or violent, impulsive behavior.

electroconvulsive therapy (ECT)
A procedure used in cases of prolonged and severe major depression, in which a brief brain seizure is induced.

works (Davison & Neale, 2001). However, ECT is *ineffective* with other disorders, such as schizophrenia or alcoholism, though it is occasionally misused for these conditions.

ECT's supporters argue that it is foolish to deny suffering, depressed patients a way out of their misery, especially if their misery is making them suicidal. They cite research showing that when ECT is used properly, it is safe and effective and causes no long-term cognitive impairment, memory loss, or detectable brain damage (Devanand et al., 1994; Fink, 1999). One psychologist, Norman Endler (1990), used ECT successfully to treat his own severe depression, later diagnosed as bipolar disorder. Critics counter that ECT is often used improperly, and that it can indeed damage the brain (Breggin, 1991); we know a woman whose brain function was severely impaired as a result of a series of inappropriate ECT treatments. The ECT controversy promises to continue.

 **QUICK QUIZ**

You won't be shocked by taking this quiz.

A. Match these treatments with the problems for which they are typically used.

1. antipsychotic drugs
2. antidepressant drugs
3. lithium carbonate
4. electroconvulsive therapy

a. suicidal depression
b. obsessive–compulsive disorder
c. bipolar disorder
d. schizophrenia
e. depression and anxiety

B. Give four reasons that the public should be cautious about concluding that particular drugs are miracle cures for emotional disorders.

C. Jezebel has had occasional episodes of depression. Her physician prescribes an antidepressant. Before taking it, what questions should Jezebel ask herself—and the doctor?

Answers:

A. 1.d 2.e 3.c 4.a B. Placebo effects are common; dropout and relapse rates are high; appropriate dosages can be difficult to determine and can vary by sex, age, and ethnicity; and some drugs have unknown or long-term risks. C. Jezebel might ask whether her physician has considered possible medical reasons for her depression. Has she been given a complete physical exam? Has the physician explored with her the possible emotional and psychological reasons for her depression or referred her to a mental-health professional who will do so? Would psychotherapy be appropriate, either with or without medication? Does the medication have any unpleasant physical effects or long-term risks? Will the doctor monitor her reactions to the drug on a regular basis?

What's Ahead

- Why are psychodynamic therapies called "depth" therapies?
- How can therapies based on learning principles help you change your bad habits?
- How do cognitive therapists help people get rid of self-defeating thoughts?
- Why do humanist therapists focus on the "here and now" instead of the "why and how"?
- Why do family therapists prefer to treat families rather than individuals?

11.2 Kinds of Psychotherapy

All good psychotherapists want to help clients think about their lives in new ways and find solutions to the problems that plague them. In this section we will consider the major schools of psychotherapy, and to illustrate the philosophy and methods of each one, we will focus on a fictional fellow named Murray. Murray is a smart guy whose problem is all too familiar to many students: He procrastinates. He just can't seem to settle down and write his term papers. He keeps getting incompletes, and before long the incompletes turn to F's. Why does Murray procrastinate, manufacturing his own misery? What kind of therapy might help him?

Psychodynamic Therapy

Sigmund Freud was the father of the "talking cure," as one of his patients called it. He believed that intensive analysis of a patient's past and unconscious motives would produce *insight*, the patient's awareness of the reason for his or her symptoms and unhappiness. With insight and emotional release, the symptoms would disappear. Freud's method of *psychoanalysis* has evolved into many different forms of *psychodynamic therapy*, which share the goal of exploring the unconscious dynamics of personality, such as defenses and conflicts (see Chapter 2). Their proponents also refer to them as "depth" therapies because the goal is to delve into unconscious processes rather than concentrate on "superficial" symptoms and conscious beliefs.

To bring unconscious conflicts into awareness, psychoanalytic and psychodynamic therapists often ask the client to talk about his or her dreams, fantasies, and memories. They encourage the person to **free associate,** saying whatever comes to mind. For example, by free associating to his dreams, his fantasies about work, and his early memories, our friend Murray might gain the insight that he pro-

crastinates as a way of expressing anger toward his parents. He might realize that he is angry because they insist that he study for a career he dislikes. Ideally, Murray will come to this insight by himself. If the analyst suggests it, Murray might feel too defensive to accept it.

A major element of psychodynamic therapy is **transference,** the client's transfer (displacement) of emotional elements of his or her inner life—usually feelings about the parents—outward onto the analyst. Have you ever found yourself responding to a new acquaintance with unusually quick affection or dislike, and later realized it was because the person reminded you of a relative that you loved or loathed? That experience is similar to transference. In therapy, a woman who failed to resolve her Oedipal love for her father might believe she has fallen in love with the analyst. A man who is unconsciously angry at his mother for rejecting him might become furious with his analyst for going on vacation. Through analysis of transference, psychodynamic therapists believe, clients can resolve their emotional conflicts.

In orthodox psychoanalysis, the client meets with the therapist as often as several times a week, for a period of years. The analyst listens to the client's free associations and dreams, but rarely comments. There is no rush to solve the problem that brought the client into therapy. In fact, a person may come in complaining of a symptom such as anxiety or headaches, and the therapist may not get around to that symptom for months or even years. The analyst views the symptom as only the tip of the mental iceberg. Some traditional analysts do not attempt cures at all. The goal, they say, is understanding, not change.

Today, however, most psychodynamic therapists reject the orthodox psychoanalytic approach, while retaining the key ideas of transference, free association, and probing for unconscious motives that stem from childhood experiences (Westen, 1998). They sit facing the client, they participate more actively, and they are more goal-directed. Many practice time-limited psychodynamic therapy, consisting of 15, 20, or 25 sessions. Without delving into the client's entire history, the therapist listens to the client's problems and formulates the main issue (Strupp & Binder, 1984). The rest of the therapy focuses on the person's self-defeating habits and recurring problems. The therapist looks for clues in the client's behavior in therapy to identify and change these patterns.

free association
In psychoanalysis, a method of uncovering unconscious conflicts by saying freely whatever comes to mind.

transference
In psychodynamic therapies, a critical step in which the client transfers unconscious emotions or reactions, such as conflicts about his or her parents, onto the therapist.

"Have a couple of dreams, and call me in the morning."

Behavior and Cognitive Therapy

Unlike psychodynamic therapists, psychologists who practice behavioral or cognitive therapy (or, more commonly, a mixture of the two) would focus on helping Murray change his current behavior and attitudes rather than on striving for insight. "Mur," they would say, "you have lousy study habits. And you have a set of beliefs about studying, writing papers, and success that are woefully unrealistic." Such therapists would not worry much about Murray's past, his parents, or his unconscious anxieties.

Behavioral Techniques. Behavior therapists draw on techniques derived from the behavioral principles of classical and operant conditioning discussed in Chapter 8. (You may want to review those principles before going on.)

1 *Systematic desensitization is a step-by-step process of desensitizing a client to a feared object or experience.* **Systematic desensitization** is based on the classical-conditioning procedure of *counterconditioning,* in which a stimulus for an unwanted response (such as fear) is paired with some other stimulus or situation that elicits a response incompatible with the undesirable one (see Chapter 8). In this case, the incompatible response is usually relaxation. The client learns to relax deeply while imagining or looking at a sequence of feared stimuli, arranged in a hierarchy ranging from the least frightening to the most frightening. The sequence for a person who is terrified of flying might be to read about airplane safety, look at pictures or models of airplanes, visit an airport and watch planes taking off, sit in a plane while it is on the ground, take a short flight, and then take a long flight. At each step the person must become relaxed and comfortable before going on. Eventually, the fear responses are extinguished.

2 *Aversive conditioning substitutes punishment for the reinforcement that has perpetuated a bad habit.* Suppose a woman who bites her nails is reinforced each time she does so by relief from her anxiety and a brief good feeling. A behavior therapist might have her wear a rubber band around her wrist and ask her to snap it (hard!) each time she bites her nails or feels the desire to do so. In **aversive conditioning,** the goal is to make sure that she receives no continuing rewards for the undesirable behavior.

3 *Exposure treatments, sometimes called "flooding," require clients who are suffering from specific anxieties to confront the feared situation or memory directly.* Normally, people who are afraid of some situation or traumatic memory do everything they can to *avoid* confronting or thinking of it. This only makes the fear worse. **Exposure treatments** therefore reverse this tendency. For example, a person who is trying to avoid thinking of a traumatic event might be asked to imagine the event over and over, until it no longer evokes the same degree of panic. Likewise, a person suffering from agoraphobia might be taken into the very situation that he or she fears most—a department store, say, or a subway—and would remain there, with the therapist, until the panic and anxiety declined. Notice

systematic desensitization
In behavior therapy, a step-by-step process of desensitizing a client to a feared object or experience; it is based on the classical-conditioning procedure of counterconditioning.

aversive conditioning
In behavior therapy, a method in which punishment is substituted for the reinforcement that is perpetuating a bad habit.

exposure treatment
In behavior therapy, a method in which a person suffering from an anxiety disorder, such as a phobia or panic attacks, is taken directly into the feared situation until the anxiety subsides.

GET INVOLVED

▶ CURE YOUR FEARS

In Chapter 10, a Get Involved exercise asked you to identify your greatest fear. Now see whether systematic desensitization procedures will help you conquer it. Write down a list of situations that evoke your fear, starting with one that produces little anxiety (e.g., seeing a photo of a tiny brown spider) and ending with the most frightening one possible (e.g., touching a live tarantula at the pet store). Then find a quiet room where you will have no distractions or interruptions, sit in a comfortable reclining chair, and relax all the muscles of your body. Breathe slowly and deeply. Imagine the first, easiest scene, remaining as relaxed as possible. Do this until you can confront the image without becoming the least bit anxious. When that happens, go on to the next scene in your hierarchy. Do not try this all at once; space out your sessions over time.

In this "virtual reality" version of systematic desensitization, people with spider phobias are gradually exposed to computerized but extremely lifelike images of spiders in a realistic, three-dimensional environment.

how different this approach is from a psychodynamic one, in which the goal is to uncover the presumably unconscious reason that the agoraphobic feels afraid of going out.

4 *Behavioral records and contracts help clients identify the reinforcers (rewarding consequences) that are keeping their unwanted habits going.* For example, a man who wants to curb his overeating may not be aware of how much he eats throughout the day to relieve tension; a behavioral record might show that he eats more junk food in the late afternoon than he realized. Once the unwanted behavior is identified, along with the reinforcers that have been maintaining it, a treatment program can be designed to change it. For instance, the man might find other ways to reduce stress and make sure that he is nowhere near junk food in the late afternoon.

The therapist also helps people set *behavioral goals,* small step by small step. A husband and wife who fight over housework, for instance, might be asked to draw up a contract indicating who will do what, with specified rewards for carrying out their duties. With such a contract, they can't fall back on accusations such as "You never do anything around here."

5 *Skills training provides practice in behaviors that are necessary for achieving the person's goals.* It is not enough to tell someone "Don't be shy" if the person does not know how to make small talk with others; skills training would teach the shy person how to converse in social settings (for example, by focusing on other people rather than on his or her own insecurity). Countless skills-training programs are available—for parents who don't know how to discipline children, for people who don't know how to manage anger, for children and adults who don't know how to express their wishes clearly, and so on.

A behaviorist would treat Murray's procrastination in several ways. Murray might not be aware of how he actually spends his time when he is avoiding his studies. Afraid that he hasn't time to do everything, he does nothing. Keeping a behavioral diary would let Murray know exactly how he spends his time, and how much time he should realistically allot to a project. Instead of having a vague, impossibly huge goal, such as "I'm going to reorganize my life," Murray would establish specific small goals, such as reading the two books necessary for an English paper and writing one page of an assignment. The therapist might also offer skills training to make sure Murray knows how to reach these goals.

Cognitive Techniques. Of course, people's thoughts, feelings, and motivations can influence their behavior. *Cognitive therapy* helps clients identify the beliefs and expectations that might be unnecessarily prolonging their unhappiness, conflicts, and other problems (Persons, Davidson, and Tompkins, 2001). For example, as we saw in Chapter 10, depression often arises from pessimistic, self-defeating thoughts, such as the belief that the sources of your misery are permanent, have do to with your failings rather than temporary circumstances, and will never change. So cognitive therapists require clients to examine the evidence for their beliefs—say, that everyone is mean and selfish, that ambition is hopeless, or that love is doomed. They would ask you to consider other explanations for the behavior of people who annoy you. By asking clients to identify their assumptions and biases, examine the evidence, and consider other interpretations, cognitive therapy, as you can see, teaches critical thinking!

One of the oldest and best-known schools of cognitive therapy is Albert Ellis's *rational emotive behavior therapy* (Ellis, 1993; Ellis & Blau, 1998). In this approach, the therapist uses rational arguments to directly challenge a client's unrealistic beliefs or expectations. For example, people who are emotionally upset often overgeneralize: They decide that one annoying act by someone means that person is totally bad in every way. Or they interpret their own normal failings and mistakes as evidence that they are totally incompetent and

---

GET INVOLVED

MIND OVER MOOD

See whether cognitive-therapy techniques can help you control your moods. Think of a time recently when you felt a particularly strong emotion, such as depression, anger, or anxiety. On a piece of paper, record (1) the situation—who was there, what happened, and when; (2) the intensity of your feeling at the time, from weak to strong; and (3) the thoughts that were going through your mind (e.g., "She never cares about what I want to do"; "This relationship is never going to make it"). Then examine your thoughts. What is the worst thing that could happen if those thoughts are true? *Are* your thoughts accurate, or are you "mind reading" another person's intentions and motives? Is there another way to think about this situation or the other person's behavior? If you practice this exercise repeatedly, you may learn how your thoughts affect your moods—and find out that you have more control over your feelings than you realized (from Greenberger & Padesky, 1995).

---

worthless individuals. The rational emotive behavior therapist directly challenges these thoughts and interpretations, showing the client why they are irrational and misguided.

Another popular cognitive approach, devised by Aaron Beck (1976, 1991), avoids direct challenges to the client's beliefs. Instead, the therapist encourages the person to test those beliefs against the evidence, to stop trying to read other people's minds ("I *know* he's out to get me"), and to avoid turning normal upsets and setbacks into catastrophes—a common mental habit that cognitive therapists call "catastrophizing."

A cognitive therapist might treat Murray's procrastination by having Murray write down his thoughts about work, read the thoughts as if someone else had said them, and then write a rational response to each one. This technique would encourage Murray to examine the validity of his beliefs. Many procrastinators are perfectionists; if they cannot do something perfectly, they will not do it at all. Unable to accept their limitations, they set impossible standards and catastrophize:

Negative thought	Rational response
This paper isn't good enough; I'd better rewrite it for the twentieth time.	Good enough for what? It won't win a Pulitzer Prize, but it is a pretty good paper.
If I don't get an A+ on this paper, my life will be ruined.	My life will be a lot worse if I keep getting incompletes. It's better to get a B or even a C than to do nothing at all.

Strict behaviorists consider thoughts to be "behaviors" that are modifiable by learning principles; they do not regard thoughts as causes of behavior. But most psychologists believe that thoughts and behavior influence each other, which is why cognitive-behavior therapy is more common than either form alone.

Humanist and Existential Therapy

Humanist therapies, like their parent philosophy humanism, start from the assumption that people seek self-actualization and self-fulfillment. The therapist generally does not dig into past conflicts but aims instead to help clients feel better about themselves and free themselves from self-imposed limits. (It was the humanists who changed the term for a person in therapy from "patient," which implies that the person is ill, to "client," which implies that the person simply has a problem.) Humanist therapists want to know how clients subjectively perceive their own situations, so they can help them develop the will and confidence to bring about change. That is why they explore what is going on "here and now," not the issues of "why and how."

In *client-centered* or *nondirective therapy,* developed by Carl Rogers, the therapist's role is to listen to the client's needs in an accepting, nonjudgmental way and offer what Rogers called *unconditional positive regard* (see Chapter 2). Whatever the client's specific complaint is, the goal is to build the client's self-esteem and help the person feel that he or she is accepted and respected. Thus a Rogerian might assume that Murray's procrastination masks his low self-regard, and that Murray is out of touch with his real feelings and

Humanist therapists focus on the inner, private self that exists beneath the external masks we present to the world.

our experiences may be, he believes, "they contain the seeds of wisdom and redemption." Perhaps the most remarkable example of a man able to find seeds of wisdom in a barren landscape was Victor Frankl (1905–1997), who developed a form of existential therapy after surviving a Nazi concentration camp. Even in that pit of horror, Frankl (1955) observed, some people maintained their sanity because they were able to find meaning in the experience, shattering though it was.

Some observers believe that, ultimately, all therapies are existential. In different ways, therapy helps people determine what is important to them, what values guide them, and what changes they will have the courage to make. An existential therapist might help Murray think about the significance of his procrastination, what his ultimate goals in life are, and how he might find the strength to carry out his ambitions.

Family Therapy

Murray's situation is getting worse. His father has begun to call him "Tomorrow Man," which upsets his mother, and his younger brother the math major has been calculating how much tuition money Murray's incompletes are costing. His older sister Isabel, the biochemist who never had an incomplete in her life, now proposes that all of them go to a *family therapist*. "Murray's not the only one in this family with complaints," she says.

Family therapists would maintain that Murray's problem developed in a social context, that it is sustained by a social context, and that any change he makes will affect that context. One leading family therapist, Salvador Minuchin (1984), compared the family to a kaleidoscope, a changing pattern of mosaics in which the pattern is larger than any one piece. In this view, efforts to isolate and treat one member of the family without the others are doomed. Only if all family members reveal their differing perceptions of each other can mistakes and misperceptions be identified. A teenager, for instance, may see his mother as crabby and nagging when actually she is tired and worried. A parent may see a child as rebellious when in fact the child is lonely and desperate for attention.

Family members are usually unaware of how they influence one another. By observing the entire family (or, in the case of couples, both partners), the family therapist hopes to discover tensions and imbalances in power and communication. For example, in some families a child may develop an

wishes. Perhaps he is not passing his courses because he is trying to please his parents by majoring in prelaw, when he would secretly rather become an artist.

Rogers (1951) believed that effective therapists must be warm, genuine, and honest in expressing their feelings, and must show accurate, empathic understanding of the client's problems. The therapist's support for the client, according to Rogers, will eventually be adopted by the client, who will become more self-accepting. Once that is accomplished, the person can accept the limitations of others, too.

Existential therapy helps clients explore the meaning of existence and face with courage the great issues of death, freedom, free will, alienation from oneself and others, loneliness, and meaninglessness. Existential therapists, like humanist therapists, believe that our lives are not inevitably determined by our pasts or our circumstances—that we have the power to choose our own destinies. As Irvin Yalom (1989) explained, "The crucial first step in therapy is the patient's assumption of responsibility for his or her life predicament. As long as one believes that one's problems are caused by some force or agency outside oneself, there is no leverage in therapy."

Yalom argues that the goal of therapy is to help clients cope with the inescapable realities of life and death and the struggle for meaning. However grim

GET INVOLVED

▶ CLIMB YOUR FAMILY TREE

Using the example of the genogram in Figure 11.2 on the next page, draw a diagram of a trait or behavior that has recurred in your family. It might be a problem, such as alcoholism, violence, or parental abandonment; an illness or disability that affected family dynamics, such as asthma or diabetes; or a positive quality, such as creativity or musical ability. What does this exercise show you about patterns across generations?

illness or a psychological problem that affects the workings of the whole family. One parent may become overinvolved with the sick child while the other parent retreats, and each may start blaming the other. The child, in turn, may cling to the illness as a way of expressing anger, keeping the parents together, getting the parents' attention, or asserting control (Luepnitz, 1988).

Some family therapists look for patterns of behavior across generations (Kerr & Bowen, 1988). The therapist and client may create a *genogram,* a family tree of psychologically significant events across as many generations as possible (Carter & McGoldrick, 1988; Coupland, Serovich, & Glenn,

1995). This method often reveals the origins of current problems, as you can see in Figure 11.2.

Even when it is not possible to treat the whole family, some therapists will treat individuals from a *family systems perspective,* which recognizes that people's behavior in a family is as interconnected as that of any two dancers (Bowen, 1978; Carter & McGoldrick, 1988). Clients learn that if they change in any way, even for the better, their families may protest noisily or may send subtle messages that read, "Change back!" Why? Because when one family member changes, each of the others must change too. As the saying goes, it takes two to tango, and if one dancer stops, so must

Family therapist Alan Entin uses photographs to help people identify themes and problems in their family histories. When one woman was asked to talk about a photo of her parents (left), she began to cry; she felt that it revealed her father's alienation from her and the rest of his family. Does the picture on the right convey a happy cohesive family to you, or a divided one? Shortly after it was taken, the couple divorced; the father took custody of the children . . . and the mother kept the dog (Entin, 1992).

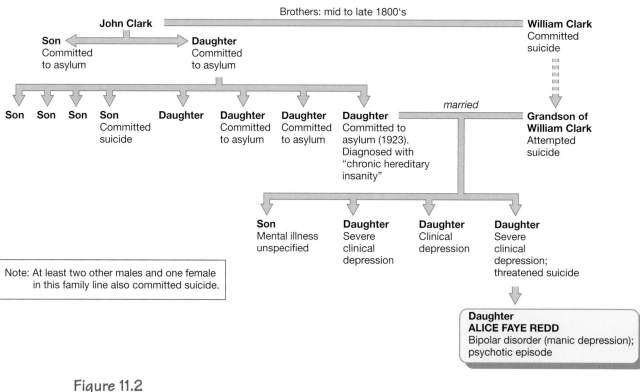

Brothers: mid to late 1800's

John Clark

Son
Committed
to asylum

Daughter
Committed
to asylum

William Clark
Committed
suicide

Son **Son** **Son** **Son**
Committed
suicide

Daughter

Daughter
Committed
to asylum

Daughter
Committed
to asylum

Daughter
Committed to
asylum (1923).
Diagnosed with
"chronic hereditary
insanity"

married

**Grandson of
William Clark**
Attempted
suicide

Son
Mental illness
unspecified

Daughter
Severe
clinical
depression

Daughter
Clinical
depression

Daughter
Severe
clinical
depression;
threatened suicide

Note: At least two other males and one female
in this family line also committed suicide.

**Daughter
ALICE FAYE REDD**
Bipolar disorder (manic depression);
psychotic episode

Figure 11.2

One Family's Genogram of Mental Illness

Genograms can reveal patterns of behavior and mental disorders across family generations (McGoldrick & Gerson, 1985). Alice Faye Redd was convicted of defrauding elderly investors of $10 million, money she then lost in lavish spending and extravagant investment schemes. Prosecution and defense psychiatrists agreed that she suffers from a form of manic depression (bipolar disorder). Alice Redd's daughter constructed this multigeneration family record of depression and suicide in an effort to have her mother committed for treatment, but the court sentenced Redd to 15 years in prison.

the other. But most people don't like change. They are comfortable with old patterns and habits, even those that cause them trouble. They want to keep tangoing, even if their feet hurt.

In general, family therapists would observe how Murray's procrastination fits his family dynamics. Perhaps it allows Murray to get his father's attention and his mother's sympathy. Perhaps it keeps Murray from facing his greatest fear: that if he does finish his work, it won't measure up to his father's high standards. The therapist will not only help Murray change his work habits, but also help his family deal with a changed Murray.

Psychotherapy in Practice

The four approaches to psychotherapy that we have discussed may seem quite different. In theory, they are, and so are the techniques resulting from them (see Table 11.1). Yet in practice, most psychotherapists draw on methods and ideas from various approaches, avoiding strong allegiances to any one theory or school of thought. This flexibility enables them to treat clients with whatever methods are most appropriate and effective.

Some therapists also take advantage of a lesson from social psychology—namely, that the influence of other people may accomplish what a single therapist cannot. In *group therapy*, people with the same or different problems are put together to find solutions. Members learn that their problems are not unique. They also learn that they cannot get away with their usual excuses because others in the group have tried them all (Yalom, 1995). Group therapies are commonly used in institutions, such as prisons and mental hospitals. They are also popular among people who have a range of social difficulties, such as shyness and anxiety, or who share a common traumatic experience, such as sexual assault. (Keep in mind that therapy groups are not

Table 11.1 The Major Schools of Therapy Compared

	Primary goal	Methods
Psychodynamic	Insight into unconscious motives and feelings	Probing the unconscious through dream analysis, free association, transference, other forms of "depth therapy"
Cognitive-behavioral	Modification of behavior and irrational beliefs	Behavioral techniques such as systematic desensitization, exposure, and flooding; cognitive exercises to identify and change faulty beliefs
Humanist	Insight; self-acceptance and self-fulfillment	Providing a safe, nonjudgmental setting in which to discuss life issues
Family	Modification of individual habits and family patterns	Working with couples, families, and sometimes individuals to identify and change patterns that perpetuate problems

the same as self-help groups, which we will discuss in "Taking Psychology with You," or motivational or spiritual programs designed for personal growth rather than psychotherapy.)

All successful therapies, regardless of approach, share a key element: They are able to replace a client's self-defeating, pessimistic, or unrealistic life story—the "story" each of us develops over time to explain our lives—with one that is more hopeful or attainable (Freedman & Combs, 1996; Howard, 1991). Some therapists explicitly focus on helping clients change their life stories and hence to change their own role in them. For example, therapist

David Epston worked with an immigrant woman named Marisa, who had been abused and rejected all her life. "To tell a story about your life turns it into a history," he told her, "one that can be left behind, and makes it easier for you to create a future of your own design" (quoted in O'Hanlon, 1994). Marisa came to see that she could tell a new story about her experiences. Instead of seeing the tragedies that had befallen her as evidence that she was a worthless victim, as she always had, she now saw the same events as evidence of her strength and endurance. "My life has a future now," she told him. "It will never be the same again."

QUICK QUIZ

Have you formed a good story about the benefits of taking quizzes? Match each method with the therapy most likely to use it.

1. free association
2. systematic desensitization
3. facing the fear of death
4. reappraisal of thoughts
5. unconditional positive regard
6. genogram
7. contract specifying duties

a. cognitive therapy
b. psychoanalysis
c. humanist therapy
d. behavior therapy
e. family therapy
f. existential therapy

Answers:
1.b 2.d 3.f 4.a 5.c 6.e 7.d

WEB READING

What's Ahead

- What is the "scientist–practitioner gap"— and why has it been widening?

- What sorts of people make the best therapists—and the best clients?

- What is the "therapeutic alliance" and why does it matter?

- Which form of psychotherapy is most likely to help if you are anxious or depressed?

- Under what conditions can psychotherapy be harmful?

11.3 Evaluating Psychotherapy

Poor Murray! He's getting a little baffled by all these therapies. He'd like to make a choice soon—no sense in procrastinating about that, too! Is there any scientific evidence, he wonders, that might help him decide which therapy to seek?

The Scientist–Practitioner Gap

Thinking Critically About Research and Psychotherapy

Many psychotherapists believe that trying to evaluate psychotherapy using the standard methods of empirical research is an exercise in futility. Psychotherapy is an art, they say, not a science; laboratory and survey studies capture only a small and shadowy image of the complex exchange that takes place between a therapist and a client (Edelson, 1994; Elliott & Morrow-Bradley, 1994). Clinical experience is therefore more valuable to therapists than research is.

Scientific psychologists agree that research has little to say about the existential aims of therapy, such as helping people come to terms with illness and death or helping them choose which values to live by (Cushman, 1995). But scientists are concerned that when therapists fail to keep up with empirical findings in the field—findings on the most beneficial methods for particular problems, on ineffective or potentially harmful techniques, and on topics relevant to their practice, such as memory, hypnosis, and child development—their clients may pay the price (Dawes, 1994).

Over the years, the breach between scientists and therapists has widened on this issue of the relevance and importance of research findings, leading to what some psychologists call the *scientist–practitioner gap*. This gap can have powerful individual and social consequences, as we saw in earlier chapters, when we discussed the controversy about repressed memories of sexual abuse (Chapter 7) and the popularity of unvalidated projective tests (Chapter 10).

Despite the skepticism about research on the part of many clinicians, economic pressures and health costs are requiring the empirical assessment of psychotherapy. For example, consider the traditional psychodynamic assumption that the longer therapy goes on, the more successful it will be. (Orthodox psychoanalysts often see clients for many years. Woody Allen was in analysis for at least 17 years, and for all we know still is.) Of course, people with severe mental disorders do often require and benefit from continued therapeutic care. But because of research, we now know that for the common emotional problems of life, short-term treatment is usually sufficient (see Figure 11.3). About half of all people in therapy improve within 8 to 11 sessions, according to self-reports and objective measures of improvement. And 76 percent improve within six months to a year; after that, further change is minimal (Howard et al., 1986; Kopta et al., 1994).

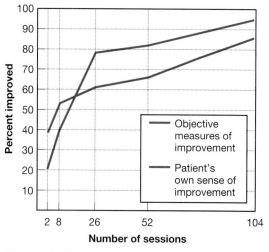

Figure 11.3
Is More Therapy Better?

In this study, about half of all patients improved in only 8 sessions and about three-fourths improved by the 26th session (Howard et al., 1986).

Psychotherapists are also being called on to produce clear, research-based guidelines for which therapies are most effective, which therapies are best for which disorders, and which therapies are ineffective or potentially harmful (Barlow, 1996; Chambless et al., 1998). To develop these guidelines, clinical researchers conduct *controlled clinical trials,* in which people with a given problem or disorder are randomly assigned to one or more treatment groups or to a control group. Hundreds of studies have been designed to test virtually every aspect of therapy.

Most of the research on psychotherapy today is directed toward three questions: What are the common ingredients in all successful therapies? Which kinds of therapy are best suited for which problems? And under what conditions can therapy be harmful?

When Therapy Helps

Overall, people who receive almost any professional kind of psychotherapy improve more than people who do not get help (Lambert & Bergin, 1994; Maling & Howard, 1994; Robinson, Berman, & Neimeyer, 1990; Weisz et al., 1995). But psychotherapy is a social exchange, and like all relationships, its success depends on the relationship between the client and therapist.

Qualities of the Participants.
Clients who are most likely to do well in therapy are, not surprisingly, motivated to improve and solve their problems (Orlinsky & Howard, 1994). They tend to have support from their families and a personal style of dealing actively with difficulties instead of avoiding them (Gaston et al., 1989). Basic personality traits also influence whether a person will be helped by therapy. As we saw in Chapter 2, some people are temperamentally negative and bitter; others are more agreeable and positive, even in the midst of emotional crises. Hostile, negative individuals are more resistant to treatment and are less likely to benefit from it. So are people with long-standing personality problems or psychotic disorders (Kopta et al., 1994).

The personality of the therapist affects the outcome of therapy, too, particularly the qualities that Carl Rogers praised: empathy, expressiveness, warmth, and genuineness. The most successful therapists make their clients feel respected, accepted, and understood. They are actively invested in the interaction with the client, instead

of detached in the manner of Freud (Orlinsky & Howard, 1994).

The Therapeutic Alliance.
Successful therapy also depends on the bond the therapist and client establish between them, called the **therapeutic alliance.** When both parties respect and understand one another and agree on the goals of treatment, the client is more likely to improve. For example, in one large-scale study of people being treated for alcohol abuse or dependence, those who had a strong therapeutic alliance with their therapists (as measured by a questionnaire filled out by both parties) were drinking much less alcohol a year after therapy ended. This was true regardless of which of three different treatment programs they had been in (Connors et al., 1997).

Many therapists and clients establish successful therapeutic alliances in spite of coming from different backgrounds. But sometimes cultural differences cause misunderstandings that result from ignorance or prejudice (Comas-Díaz & Greene, 1994; Cross & Fhagen-Smith, 1996; Franklin, 1993; Sue, 1998). For example, a lifetime of experience with racism may keep some African-American clients from revealing feelings that they believe a white therapist would not understand or accept. And black therapists frequently have to deal with clients and co-workers who are bigoted or uncomfortable with them, or who fail to understand or accept them (Boyd-Franklin, 1989; Markowitz, 1993). Misunderstandings and prejudice may be a major reason that Asian-, Mexican-, and African-American clients are more likely to stay in therapy, and thus benefit from it, when their therapists match their own ethnicity (Sue, 1998). If such

therapeutic alliance
The bond of confidence and mutual understanding established between therapist and client, which allows them to work together to solve the client's problems.

The therapist's warmth and empathy contribute to a successful therapeutic alliance with the client.

clients stay in therapy and do not drop out early, however, most do as well with an "unmatched" therapist as with a matched one.

Connection and Culture.

In establishing a bond with clients, therapists must distinguish normal cultural patterns from individual psychological problems (Pedersen et al., 1996). Two Irish-American clinicians, Monica McGoldrick and John Pearce (1996), described some problems that are typical of Irish-American families. These problems arise from Irish history and religious beliefs, and they are deeply ingrained. "In general, the therapist cannot expect the family to turn into a physically affectionate, emotionally intimate group, or to enjoy being in therapy very much," they observed. "The notion of Original Sin—that you are guilty before you are born—leaves them with a heavy sense of burden. Someone not sensitized to these issues may see this as pathological. It is not. But it is also not likely to change and the therapist should help the family tolerate this inner guilt rather than try to get rid of it."

More and more psychotherapists are becoming "sensitized to the issues" caused by cultural differences (Sue, 1998). For example, Latino and Asian clients are likely to react to a formal interview with a therapist with relative shyness and passivity, leading some therapists to diagnose a shyness problem that is only a cultural norm. Latinos may respond to

catastrophic stress with an *ataque nervioso,* a nervous attack of screaming, swooning, and agitation. The attack is a culturally determined response, but an uninformed clinician might label it as a sign of pathology (Malgady, Rogler, & Costantino, 1987). Similarly, *susto,* or "loss of the soul," is a syndrome common in Latin American cultures as a response to extreme grief over loss; the person believes his or her soul has departed along with that of the deceased relative. A psychiatrist unfamiliar with this culturally determined response might conclude that the sufferer was delusional or psychotic.

The American Psychiatric Association (1994) recommends that therapists consider a person's cultural background when making a diagnosis or suggesting treatment. For example, one New York psychiatrist, originally from Peru, treated a woman who was suffering from *susto* by prescribing a tradition important in her culture: a mourning ritual to help her accept the loss of her uncle. This ritual "was quite powerful for her," the psychiatrist told *The New York Times* (December 5, 1995). "She didn't need any antidepressants, and within a few meetings, including two with her family, her symptoms lifted and she was back participating fully in life once again."

Being aware of cultural differences, however, does not mean that the therapist should stereotype clients (Sue, 1998). Some Asians, after all, do have problems with excessive shyness, some Latinos do

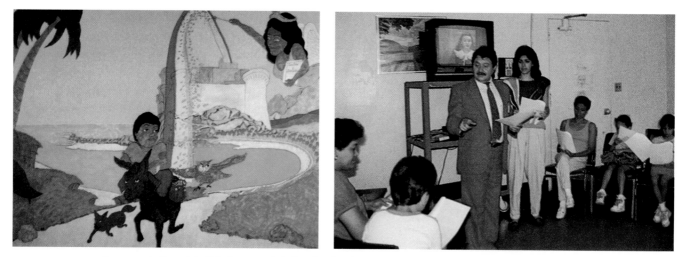

Some psychotherapists fit their approach to the client's cultural background. For example, most Puerto Rican children know the tales of Juan Bobo (left), a foolish child ("bobo") who is always getting into trouble. The therapists on the right have adapted these stories for Puerto Rican children who are coping with new problems and temptations in America. The children and their mothers watch a videotape of the folktale, discuss it together, and later role-play its major themes, such as controlling aggression and understanding right from wrong. This method has been more successful than traditional therapies in reducing the children's transitional anxieties and improving their attention spans and imaginations (Costantino, Malgady, & Rogler, 1986).

have emotional disorders, and some Irish do not carry burdens of guilt! It does mean that therapists must ensure that their clients find them to be trustworthy and effective; and it means that clients must be aware of their own prejudices, too.

Which Therapy for Which Problem?

By now, Murray is really motivated to change. He just read a study showing that procrastinators not only get worse grades than other students, but they also have more stress and illness during the semester (Tice & Baumeister, 1997). It is time to choose a therapeutic approach that would be best for him. But how?

Problems of Assessing Therapy. In studying the effectiveness of specific therapies, researchers must face a common problem: No matter what kind of therapy is involved, clients are motivated to tell you it worked—"Dr. Blitznik is a genius! I would *never* have taken that job (or moved to Cincinnati, or found my true love) if it hadn't been for Dr. Blitznik! I was cured in a week!" Every kind of therapy ever devised, including "rebirthing" therapy mentioned at the start of this chapter, produces enthusiastic testimonials from people who feel it saved their lives.

Thinking Critically About Evaluating Psychotherapy

The problem with testimonials is that none of us can be our own control group. How do people know they wouldn't have taken the job, moved to Cincinnati, or found true love anyway—maybe even sooner, if Dr. Blitznik had not kept them in treatment? Second, Dr. Blitznik's success could be due to the *placebo effect* (which we discussed earlier in this chapter in the context of new medications): The client's anticipation of success and the buzz about Dr. B.'s fabulous new method might be the active ingredients, rather than Dr. B.'s therapy itself. And third, notice that you never hear testimonials from the people who dropped out, who weren't helped, or who actually got worse.

So researchers cannot be satisfied with testimonials, no matter how glowing. They know that thanks to the *justification of effort* effect (see Chapter 6), people who have put time, money, and effort into something will tell you it was worth it. No one wants to say, "Yeah, I saw Dr. Blitznik for five years, and was it ever a waste of time."

It is important for consumers to be aware of the Dr. Blitznik problem because many new ther-apies are started by a charismatic leader solely on the basis of testimonials of happy clients. The method is then endorsed by enthusiastic practitioners who have been "certified" in the method, usually by attending a weekend workshop promoted by the therapy's founder. Some of these therapies are packaged and promoted with virtually no scientific support at all (Beyerstein, 1999). For example, Thought Field Therapy (TFT), originated by Roger Callahan, assumes that emotional problems are caused by "perturbations" (disturbances) in "a subtle energy field" rather than by cognitions, environmental events, or chemical imbalances. Callahan claims he can successfully cure people on the phone, using his special patented Voice Technology™ method to assess their perturbations (Gallo, 1998). There is no solid empirical research to support these assumptions and claims, or to show that TFT offers anything other than a temporary placebo effect (Gaudiano & Herbert, 2000; McNally, 2001).

What Works? To guard against these problems, the APA's Division of Clinical Psychology convened a task force to assess the research evaluating specific methods for specific problems. Before it could qualify as an *empirically validated treatment,* a method had to have been tested repeatedly against a placebo or another treatment, and it had to have its efficacy demonstrated by at least two different investigators (Chambless et al., 1996, 1998). Although the task force could not assess every therapy in existence, one key finding emerged clearly: For many problems and most emotional disorders, cognitive and behavior therapies are the method of choice. These therapies are particularly effective for the following problems:

- *Depression.* Cognitive therapy's greatest success has been in the treatment of mood disorders, especially depression. It is often more effective than antidepressant drugs alone, and people in cognitive therapy are also less likely than those on drugs to relapse when the treatment is over. The reason may be that the lessons learned in cognitive therapy last a long time, according to follow-ups done from 15 months to many years after treatment (Antonuccio et al., 1999; McNally, 1994; Seligman et al., 1998; Whisman, 1993).

- *Anxiety disorders.* Exposure techniques are more effective than any other treatment for posttraumatic stress disorder, simple phobias, and agoraphobia. Systematic desensitization

Research Navigator.com
RESOURCES FOR COLLEGE RESEARCH ASSIGNMENTS

11.2

IN THE BLEACHERS   By Steve Moore

THERE. SEE? IT'S JUST STITCHED ANIMAL HIDE... HERE. TOUCH IT. CARESS IT. CLUTCH IT TO YOUR BOSOM.

Batters overcoming bonkinogginophobia, a fear of the ball.

is usually all that is necessary in effectively treating phobias such as fear of dogs or of public speaking. And cognitive-behavior therapy is also more effective than medication for panic disorder, generalized anxiety disorder, and obsessive–compulsive disorder (Heisel, 1998; Kozak, Liebowitz, & Foa, 2000; Schwartz et al., 1996).

■ *Anger and impulsive violence.* Cognitive therapy is extremely successful, for males and females alike, in reducing hotheadedness, chronic anger, abusiveness, and hostility; it also teaches people how to express anger more calmly and constructively (Deffenbacher et al., 1998). It has been used to help young male athletes learn to control angry outbursts that lead to physical and verbal abuse (Abrams & Feindler, 1998).

■ *Health problems.* Cognitive and behavior therapies are highly successful in helping people cope with pain, chronic fatigue syndrome, headaches, and irritable bowel syndrome; quit smoking or overcome cocaine and alcohol dependence; recover from eating disorders such as bulimia and binge eating; and manage other health problems (Butler et al., 1991; J. Skinner et al., 1990; Wilson & Fairburn, 1993).

■ *Childhood and adolescent behavior problems.* Behavior therapy is the most effective treatment for behavior problems that range from bed-wetting to defiant rebelliousness, and even for problems that have biological origins, such as autism (Green, 1996). A meta-analysis of more than 100 studies of children and adolescents found that behavioral treatments worked better than others regardless of the child's age, the therapist's experience, or the specific problem (Weisz et al., 1995).

Cognitive therapy can even prevent mood disorders from developing in the first place. One such intervention program targeted 69 fifth- and sixth-grade children who were considered at risk of depression because they scored high on a children's depression inventory, came from homes with high levels of parental conflict, or both. The children were taught to identify pessimistic beliefs, examine the evidence for and against those beliefs, and generate positive ways of coping. A control group of children who were also at risk of depression did not get this training. As you can see in Figure 11.4, after the training, children in the prevention group had lower depression scores than did those in the control group at all four follow-up sessions. The differences still held two years later, when the children were entering adolescence and when depression rates in the control group shot up steeply (Gillham et al., 1995). A later study of more than 200 college students at risk of depression got similarly positive results (Seligman et al., 1998).

The APA task force also reported that young adults with schizophrenia are greatly helped by family intervention therapies that teach parents behavioral skills in dealing with their troubled children, and that educate the family in coping with the illness constructively (Chambless et al., 1998; Goldstein & Miklowitz, 1995). Nine studies found that in a two-year period, only 30 percent of the schizophrenic patients in such family intervention treatments relapsed, compared to 65 percent of those whose families were not involved.

Of course, as the APA task force acknowledged, these important findings have limitations. Cognitive-behavior therapies are designed for specific, identifiable problems, but sometimes people seek therapy for less clearly defined reasons. They may wish to introspect about their feelings and lives, find solace and courage, or explore moral issues. "Depth" approaches may be well suited for such individuals. Moreover, in

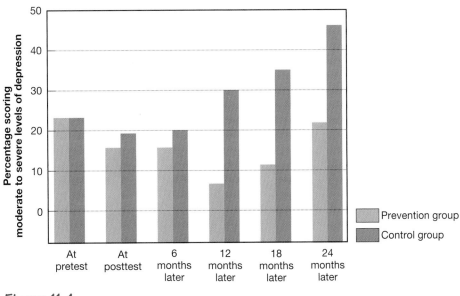

Figure 11.4

A Cognitive Inoculation Against Depression

This graph shows the percentage of children who were at moderate to high risk of depression (pretest), and their depression scores after a cognitive intervention (posttest) and during four follow-up assessments. Notice that the effects of the intervention were still strong two years later, as the children entered adolescence (Gillham et al., 1995).

spite of their many successes, behavior and cognitive therapies have had failures, especially with people unmotivated to carry out a behavioral or cognitive program or who have deeply ingrained personality disorders or psychoses (Brody, 1990; Foa & Emmelkamp, 1983).

Some problems, and some clients, are immune to any single kind of therapy but may respond to *combined* methods. For example, people who have severe and recurrent episodes of depression sometimes respond better to a combination of antide-pressants and psychotherapy than to either method alone (Keller et al., 2000; Thase et al., 1997). A promising treatment for sex offenders combines cognitive therapy, aversive conditioning, sex education, group therapy, reconditioning of sexual fantasies, and social-skills training (Abel et al., 1988; Kaplan, Morales, & Becker, 1993).

Figure 11.5 summarizes the factors contributing to successful therapy: qualities of the participants, the nature of the therapy, and the affinity between therapist and client.

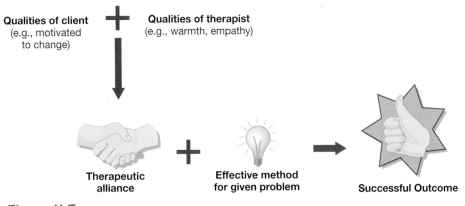

Figure 11.5

Factors in Successful Therapy

As this illustration summarizes, the outcome of psychotherapy depends not only on the methods used but also on the qualities of the therapist and the client, and on the "alliance" between them.

When Therapy Harms

Thinking Critically
About Harmful
Therapeutic
Practices

Every treatment and intervention carries risks, and so does psychotherapy. Some people are seriously harmed or unduly influenced by the treatment or by the therapist; their emotional state may deteriorate and their symptoms may worsen. Some clients become excessively dependent, relying on the therapist for all decisions; some therapists actively foster this dependency for financial or psychological motives (Johnson, 1988). Clients can also be harmed by the following:

1 *Animosity or biased treatment on the part of a therapist.* Some therapists may be prejudiced against their clients because of the client's gender, culture, religion, or sexual orientation. A therapist may try to induce the client to conform to the therapist's standards and values, even if they are not appropriate to the client or in the client's best interest (Brodsky, 1982; López, 1989). For example, for many years gay men and lesbians who entered therapy were told that homosexuality is a mental illness that could be "cured." Some of the so-called treatments were harsh and painful, such as shock applied to the genitals for "inappropriate" arousal. Although the American Psychological Association and the American Psychiatric Association have gone on record opposing therapies that claim to turn gays into heterosexuals, these therapies still surface from time to time, and were recently promoted in a campaign by Christian fundamentalists who believe homosexuality is a sin.

2 *Coercion to accept the therapist's advice, sexual intimacies, or other unethical behavior.* Some therapists abuse their clients' trust, pressuring them, in subtle or overt ways, to behave in ways the clients would otherwise find reprehensible (Peterson, 1992). Some therapy groups even acquire cultlike attributes, persuading their members that their mental health depends on staying in the group and severing their connections to their families (Mithers, 1994; Watters & Ofshe, 1999). Such "psychotherapy cults" are created by the therapist's use of techniques that foster the client's dependency and isolation, prevent the client from terminating therapy, and reduce the client's ability to think critically (Temerlin & Temerlin, 1986).

3 *Therapist-induced disorders resulting from inadvertent suggestions or influence.* In a good therapeutic alliance, therapists and clients come to agree on

Movies often portray therapists as silly, evil, or unethical. In *Prince of Tides*, Barbra Streisand plays a psychiatrist who becomes sexually involved with her client's brother, who then becomes her client too. Such films imply that having sex with a client is a common, accepted, harmless practice. But it can be harmful to clients and it is prohibited by the APA's ethical guidelines.

an explanation for the client's problems. Of course, the therapist will influence this explanation, according to his or her training and philosophy. This is why Freudian patients dream of erotic symbols, and patients in Jungian therapy dream of archetypes! However, some therapists so zealously believe in the prevalence of certain problems that they induce the client to produce the symptoms they are looking for (McHugh, 1993b; Merskey, 1995; Watters & Ofshe, 1999).

Therapist influence is a likely reason for the growing number of people diagnosed with multiple personality disorder in the 1980s and 1990s (see Chapter 10). It also helps account for *pseudomemories,* memories that clients construct about events that did not happen. For example, people in primal-scream therapy "remember" being born, people in fetal therapy "remember" their lives in the womb, and people in past-lives therapy "remember" being Julius Caesar (or whomever) (Spanos, 1996). The risk to clients increases when a therapist uses hypnosis, sodium amytal (a barbiturate misleadingly called "truth serum"), guided imagery, dream analysis, and other techniques that enhance the client's suggestibility (Mazzoni, Loftus, & Kirsch, 2001). When a therapist tells a client that his or her dreams are memories of something that really happened, suggestible clients will begin to confuse their dreams with reality (Mazzoni et al., 1999). As we noted in Chapter 7, a significant minority of therapists, between one-fourth and one-third, have used one or more of these techniques specifically to help clients "retrieve" memories of abuse (Poole et al., 1995), and many still are.

To avoid these risks and take advantage of what good therapy has to offer, it is important to become an educated consumer of psychotherapeutic services.

QUICK QUIZ

Have you formed a therapeutic alliance with quizzes?

1. The most important predictor of successful therapy is (a) how long it lasts, (b) the insight it provides the client, (c) the bond between therapist and client, (d) whether the therapist and client are matched according to gender, ethnicity, and culture.

2. In general, anxiety and depression are most effectively treated by which type of psychotherapy?

3. What are three possible sources of harm in psychotherapy?

4. Ferdie, who spends all his free time playing softball, joins a therapy group called "Sportaholics Anonymous" (SA). The therapist tells him he is suffering from sport addiction and that the only cure is SA. After a few months, Ferdie announces that the group doesn't seem to be helping him and he's going to quit. The other members reply with personal testimonials of how SA has helped them. They tell Ferdie that he is in denial, and that his doubts about the group are actually a sign that it's working. What are some problems with their argument?

Answers:

1. c 2. cognitive-behavior 3. coercion, bias, and therapist-induced disorders 4. The group members have violated the principle of falsifiability (see Chapter 1): That is, they will accept no evidence that contradicts their claims. If a person is helped by the group, they say it works; if a person is not helped by the group, they still say it works but the person doesn't know it yet or is "denying" its benefits. They are also arguing by anecdote: Ferdie is not hearing from people who have dropped out of the group and were not helped by it. Personal testimonials are not a scientific way to determine a therapy's effectiveness.

PSYCHOLOGY IN THE NEWS, REVISITED

Now that we have reviewed some of the benefits and hazards of psychotherapy, let's return to the issues raised by the charges against the "rebirthing" therapists in Colorado. How can you, as a potential consumer of psychological services, distinguish between techniques that are beneficial and techniques that can harm? As a critical thinker, what questions should you ask about the therapist and the therapist's approach?

The first step is to make sure you are dealing with a reputable individual with appropriate credentials and training. As we saw in Chapter 1, to become a licensed psychologist, a person must have an advanced degree and a period of supervised training. However, the word *psychotherapist* is unregulated; anyone can set up any kind of program and call it "therapy." Increasingly in the United States and Canada, people can get credentialed as "experts" in various techniques and therapies—doing hypnosis or "hypnotherapy," diagnosing child sexual abuse, becoming a devotee of Thought Field Therapy or its many relatives—simply by attending a weekend seminar or a training program lasting a week or two.

In Colorado, for example, it is legal to practice psychotherapy without a license, although therapists must register with the state. In our news story, the woman who ran the treatment center, Connell Watkins, a social worker, and her associate Julie Ponder were both unlicensed, and their registrations had lapsed. Watkins and Ponder had been trained in "rebirthing" by a California promoter of the method, Douglas Gosney, in a two-week training course. One of the members of the Colorado

Mental Health Grievance Board noted with dismay that her *hairdresser's* training took 1,500 hours, whereas anyone could take Gosney's course and become "certified" in a method that could take a child's life.

Second, it is important to ask whether a therapist practices one of the empirically validated methods described in this chapter, and also whether the basic *assumptions* of the therapist are likewise validated by empirical research. There is nothing especially new about "rebirthing" therapy, which has been around since the 1970s, when its founder claimed he had reexperienced his own birth while taking a bath. (Many psychological problems, he somehow decided, can be traced to a traumatic experience in the womb or during birth.) Many of rebirthing's practitioners even have advanced degrees and licenses. But the basic assumptions of this method—that people can recover from trauma, insecure attachment, or other psychological problems by "reliving their births"—are utterly unsupported by the vast research on infancy, attachment, memory, or posttraumatic stress disorder and its treatment. For that matter, why should the experience of being born be traumatic? Isn't it pretty nice to be let out of cramped quarters and see daylight and beaming parental faces?

Besides choosing a therapist carefully, consumers need to be realistic about what they expect of psychotherapy. In the hands of an empathic and knowledgeable practitioner, psychotherapy can help you make decisions and clarify your values and goals. It can teach you new skills and new ways of thinking. It can help you get along better with your family and break out of destructive family patterns. It can get you through bad times when no one seems to care or to understand what you are feeling. It can teach you how to manage depression, anxiety, and anger.

However, despite its many benefits, psychotherapy cannot transform you into someone you're not. It cannot turn an introvert into an extrovert. It cannot cure an emotional disorder overnight. It cannot provide a life without problems. And it is not intended to substitute for experience—for work that is satisfying, relationships that are sustaining, activities that are enjoyable. As Socrates knew, the unexamined life is not worth living. But as we would add, the unlived life is not worth examining.

TAKING PSYCHOLOGY WITH YOU

How to Evaluate Self-help Groups and Books

Not all psychological problems require the aid of a professional. Nowadays, thousands of programs and books are designed to help people help themselves. More than 2,000 self-help books are published every year, and an estimated 7 to 15 million adults belong to self-help groups (Christensen & Jacobson, 1994). Do these books and groups help?

Self-help groups are available for alcoholics, people who live with alcoholics, abusive parents, people suffering from depression or schizophrenia, gay fathers, divorced people, women who have had mastectomies, parents of murdered children, diabetics, rape victims, widows, widowers, stepparents, cancer patients, relatives of patients, and people with just about any other concern you can think of. Members say that the primary benefits are the awareness that they are not alone, encouragement when they are feeling down, and help in feeling better about themselves (Wuthnow, 1995).

Self-help groups offer understanding, empathy, and solutions to shared problems. Such groups can be reassuring and supportive in ways that family, friends, and psychotherapists sometimes may not be (Dunkel-Schetter, 1984). For example, people with disabilities face unique challenges that involve coping not only with physical problems but also with the condescension, hostility, and prejudice of many nondisabled people (Linton, 1998; Robertson, 1995). Other disabled people, who share these challenges, may be able to offer useful advice.

Self-help groups, however, do not provide psychotherapy for specific problems, and they are not designed to help people with serious psychological difficulties. Moreover, unlike group therapies, which are usually supervised by a licensed therapist, self-help groups are not regulated by law or by professional standards, and they vary widely in their philosophies and methods. Some are accepting and

tolerant, offering support, cohesiveness, and spiritual guidance. Others are confrontational and coercive, and members who disagree with the premises of the group may be made to feel deviant, crazy, or "in denial." If you choose to become part of a support group, you need to be sure it falls in the first category.

As for self-help books, there is one for every problem that ails you. These books will tell you how to make money, how to use your mind to cure your body, how to recover from heartbreak, and how to find happiness in seven easy steps. They will help you find a relationship, fix a relationship, or end a relationship. Which are helpful, which are harmful, and which are just innocuous?

Some self-help books, if they propose a specific program for the reader to follow, can actually be as effective as treatment administered by a therapist—*if* the reader follows through with the program (Christensen & Jacobson, 1994). After serving as chair of the APA's Task Force on Self-Help Therapies, which investigated the proliferation and promises of self-help books and tapes, Gerald Rosen (1981) concluded, "Unfortunately, the involvement of psychologists in the development, assessment, and marketing of do-it-yourself treatment programs has often been less than responsible. Psychologists have published untested materials, advanced exaggerated claims, and accepted the use of misleading titles that encourage unrealistic expectations regarding outcome." The situation remains the same today.

Rosen recognizes that self-help books and programs can be effective in helping people, however, and thus offered consumers some research-based criteria for evaluating a self-help book:

● *The authors should be qualified,* which means that they have conducted good research or are thoroughly versed in the field. Personal accounts by people who have survived difficulties can be helpful and inspirational, of course, but an author's own experience is not grounds for generalizing to everyone.

● *The book's advice should be based on sound scientific theory,* not on the author's hunches, pseudoscientific theories, or armchair observations. This criterion rules out, among other kinds of books, all the weight-loss manuals based on crash diets or goofy nutritional advice ("Eat popcorn and watermelon for a week").

● *The book should include evidence of the program's effectiveness* and not simply the author's claims that it works. Many self-help books offer programs that have not been tested for efficacy.

● *The book should not promise the impossible.* This lets out books that promise you perfect sex, total love, or high self-esteem in 30 days. It also lets out books, programs, or tapes that promote techniques whose effectiveness has been disconfirmed by psychological research, such as "subliminal" tapes, discussed in Chapter 5 (Moore, 1995).

● *The advice should be organized in a systematic program,* step by step, not as a vague pep talk to "take charge of your life" or "find love in your heart"; and the reader should be told how to evaluate his or her progress.

Some books do meet all these criteria. One is *Changing for Good* (Prochaska, Norcross, & DiClemente, 1994), which describes the common ingredients of effective change that apply to people in and out of therapy. But as long as people yearn for a magic bullet to cure their problems—a pill, a book, a subliminal tape—quick-fix solutions will find a ready audience.

SUMMARY

Biological Treatments

● Over the past century, people trying to understand and treat mental disorders have alternated between taking a biological approach or a psychological one. Today, biological approaches are in the ascendance because of research findings on the genetic and biological causes of some disorders, and because of economic and social factors.

● The medications most commonly prescribed for mental disorders include *antipsychotic drugs,* used in treating schizophrenia and other psychotic disorders; *antidepressants,* used in treating depression, anxiety disorders, and obsessive–compulsive disorder; *tranquilizers,* often prescribed for emotional problems; and *lithium carbonate,* a salt used to treat bipolar disorder. Antidepressants are generally more effective for mood disorders than are tranquilizers, which can become addictive.

● Drawbacks of drug treatment include the *placebo effect;* high dropout and relapse rates among people who take medications without also learning how to cope with their problems; the difficulty of finding the correct dose (the *therapeutic window*) for each individual, compounded by the fact that a person's ethnicity, sex, and age can influence a drug's effectiveness; and the long-term risks of medication, known and unknown. Medication can be helpful and can even save lives, but in an age when commercial interests are heavily invested in promoting drugs for psychological problems, the public is largely unaware of drugs' limitations. Medication should not be prescribed mindlessly and routinely, especially when nondrug therapies can work as well as drugs for many mood and behavioral problems.

● When drugs or psychotherapy have failed to help seriously disturbed people, some psychiatrists have intervened directly in the brain. *Psychosurgery,* which destroys selected areas of the brain thought to be responsible for a psychological problem, is rarely done today. *Electroconvulsive therapy (ECT),* in which a brief current is sent through the brain, has been used successfully to treat suicidal depression. However, controversy exists about its effects on the brain and the appropriateness of its use.

Kinds of Psychotherapy

● The hundreds of existing psychotherapies basically fall into four schools: (1) *Psychodynamic ("depth") therapies* include Freudian psychoanalysis and its modern variations, which explore unconscious dynamics by using *free association* and relying on the process of *transference. Brief psychodynamic therapy* is a time-limited version that focuses on one major dynamic issue. (2) *Behavior and cognitive therapies* draw on principles of learning and cognition. Behavior therapists use such methods as *systematic desensitization, aversive conditioning, flooding or exposure, behavioral contracts,* and *skills training.* Cognitive therapists aim to change the irrational thoughts involved in clients' negative emotions and self-defeating actions. (3) *Humanist and existential therapies* attempt to help people feel better about themselves by focusing on here-and-now issues and helping people cope with philosophical dilemmas, such as the meaning of life and the fear of death. Humanist Carl Rogers' *client-centered therapy* emphasized the importance of *unconditional positive regard.* (4) *Family therapies* share the view that individual problems develop in the context of the whole family network. Some *family-systems* therapists use *genograms* to identify patterns of behavior across generations.

● In practice, most therapists are flexible, drawing on many methods and ideas. Some therapists treat individuals in *group therapy,* hoping that the influence of other people with psychological problems will help the participants improve. Whatever their method, successful therapies share the goal of helping clients form more adaptive "life stories."

Evaluating Psychotherapy

● A *scientist–practitioner gap* has developed because of the different assumptions held by researchers and many clinicians regarding the value of empirical research for doing psychotherapy and for assessing its effectiveness. However, economic pressures and health costs are requiring the empirical assessment of psychotherapy using *controlled clinical trials.* Such research finds, for example, that for problems other than chronic mental disorders, short-term treatment is usually as effective as long-term therapy.

● The clients most likely to succeed in therapy are motivated to improve and solve their problems. Hostile, temperamentally negative individuals or those with personality disorders are less likely to benefit. For their part, good therapists are empathic, warm, and constructive. Successful therapy requires a *therapeutic alliance* between the therapist and the client, so that they understand each other and can work together. Therapists must also understand potential misunderstandings due to cultural differences. When the therapist and the client are of different ethnicities, both must try to avoid prejudice, misunderstanding, and stereotyping.

● Some therapies are demonstrably better than others for specific problems. Behavior therapy and cognitive-behavior therapies are the most effective for depression, anxiety disorders, anger, certain health problems and eating disorders, and childhood and adolescent behavior problems. Depth therapies may be most effective for people who want to introspect about their lives. And some individuals, such as sex offenders and chronic sufferers of schizophrenia, respond well to combined techniques.

● In some cases, therapy is harmful. The therapist may foster the client's dependency; be prejudiced against a client; be coercive, biased, or unethical; or inadvertently create disorders through undue influence or suggestion, as in the case of therapist-induced *pseudomemories.*

● Because of the growing number of unlicensed psychotherapists and the rise of new therapies whose methods and assumptions have little or no empirical validation, consumers need to choose a therapist carefully and be realistic about what they expect of psychotherapy.

KEY TERMS

antipsychotic drugs (neuroleptics) 370

antidepressant drugs 370
   monoamine oxidase (MAO) inhibitors 370
   tricyclic antidepressants 371
   selective serotonin reuptake inhibitors (SSRIs) 371

tranquilizers 371
lithium carbonate 371
placebo effect 372
therapeutic window 372
psychosurgery 374
prefrontal lobotomy 374
electroconvulsive therapy (ECT) 374

psychoanalysis 376
psychodynamic ("depth") therapies 376
free association 376
transference 376
behavior therapies 377
systematic desensitization 377
aversive conditioning 377

LOOKING BACK ◀

- What kinds of drugs are used to treat psychological disorders? (pp. 370–371)

- Are antidepressants always the best treatment for depression? (p. 372)

- Can mental disorders be cured by brain surgery? (p. 374)

- Why is "shock therapy" hailed by some clinicians but condemned by others? (p. 374)

- Why are psychodynamic therapies called "depth" therapies? (p. 376)

- How can therapies based on learning principles help you change your bad habits? (pp. 377–378)

- How do cognitive therapists help people get rid of self-defeating thoughts? (pp. 378–379)

- Why do humanist therapists focus on the "here and now" instead of the "why and how"? (p. 379)

- Why do family therapists prefer to treat families rather than individuals? (pp. 380–381)

- What is the "scientist–practitioner gap"— and why has it been widening? (p. 384)

- What sorts of people make the best therapists—and the best clients? (p. 385)

- What is the "therapeutic alliance" and why does it matter? (p. 385)

- Which form of psychotherapy is most likely to help if you are anxious or depressed? (p. 387)

- Under what conditions can psychotherapy be harmful? (p. 390)

PSYCHOLOGY IN THE NEWS

Ticket Agent and Passenger Injured During Altercation at Newark Airport

NEWARK, NJ, SEPTEMBER 5, 2000. A clash between an irate father and a Continental ticket agent yesterday at Newark International Airport resulted in a broken neck for the agent and aggravated assault charges against the father.

The confrontation took place at Gate 115 in Terminal C, when James C. Davis, Jr., 29, punched the agent,

Angelo Sottile, 50, and threw him to the ground. Davis said he was trying to protect his wife and his 23-month-old daughter, who had run off and was headed down the jetway. According to one witness, when the mother went after the child, the ticket agent

grabbed them both and shoved them up against the wall, which infuriated the father. Davis claimed that he acted in self-defense when Sottile then turned on him, shoved him, and put him in a choke hold. But other witnesses said that Davis attacked Sottile

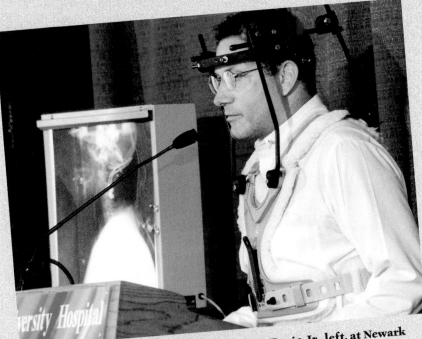

After an altercation with passenger James C. Davis, Jr., left, at Newark Airport, ticket agent Angelo Sottile, right, had two shattered vertebrae and a fractured skull. Some witnesses support Davis's claim that Sottile had grabbed him by the neck and dug in his fingers.

while the agent was trying to control a hostile and impatient crowd at the gate.

The incident is being viewed as an extreme example of "air rage." A spokesperson for the International Airline Passengers Association said that passengers' anger and frustration are on the rise as a result of airport crowding, delays, and increased air traffic. Agents are angrier, too. "The airplanes are completely full," he said. "People who are working for the airlines are completely stressed out."

EMOTION, STRESS, AND HEALTH

A ir rage, road rage, workplace rage—these are often in the news these days. Why do so many people "lose it" when they are traveling, whereas others are able to keep things in perspective and stay cool? More generally, why do some people respond to the inevitable stresses of life by losing control of their emotions, whereas others are able to keep unpleasant feelings from turning into abusive or self-destructive actions?

In this chapter we will examine two fundamental experiences in everyone's life—emotions and stress—and the links between them. Prolonged negative emotions such as anger can certainly be stressful, and, as stories of air rage tell us, stress can produce negative emotions. To understand emotion and stress, and how they interact, we will need to draw on all of the psychological perspectives described in this book: We will need to consider the biology of the brain and body, the mental processes of perception and belief, and the situational and cultural contexts that shape experience. As you read, see whether you can come up with some ideas for reducing unpleasant emotions and stressful experiences in your own life.

What's Ahead

● Which facial expressions of emotion do people recognize all over the world?

● Which side of your brain is most active when you're filled with joy—or despair?

● Which two hormones can make you "too excited to eat"?

● In a competition, who is likely to be happier, the third-place winner or the second-place winner?

● Why can't an infant feel shame or guilt?

12.1 The Nature of Emotion

People often curse their emotions, wishing to be freed from anger, jealousy, shame, guilt, and grief. Yet imagine a life without emotions. You would be unmoved by the magic of music. You would never care about losing someone you love, not only because you would not know sadness but also because you would not know love. You would never laugh because nothing would strike you as funny. And you would be a social klutz because you would not be able to identify other people's feelings.

Because emotions can get us into trouble, for centuries, emotion was regarded as the opposite of thinking, and an inferior opposite at that. The heart (emotion) was said to go its own way, in spite of what the head (reason) wanted. Today, psychologists avoid such either–or thinking. As

Thinking Critically About "Irrational" Emotions

we saw in Chapters 6 and 7, normal thought processes involve many "irrational" biases, such as the confirmation bias, the hindsight bias, and biases in the construction of memories. Conversely, emotions are not always irrational, even when they are uncomfortable. Emotions bind people together, motivate them to achieve their goals, and help them make decisions and plans (Damasio, 1994; Oatley, 1990). When you are faced with a decision between two appealing and justifiable career alternatives, for example, your sense of which one "feels right" emotionally may help you make the best choice. Emotions themselves, then, are not a problem. Too much uncontrolled emotionality, however, can lead to trouble and can even threaten your health.

emotion
A state of arousal involving facial and bodily changes, brain activation, cognitive appraisals, subjective feelings, and tendencies toward action.

The full experience of **emotion** is like a tree: The *biological* capacity for emotion is the trunk; *thoughts and explanations* create the many branches; and *culture* is the gardener that shapes the tree and prunes it, cutting off some limbs and cultivating others. Let's begin with the trunk.

Emotion and the Body

When you are feeling an emotion, where in your body are you feeling it? The answer may be just about everywhere—on the face, in the brain, and in the activity of the autonomic nervous system.

The Face of Emotion. The most obvious place to look for emotion is on the face, where emotions are often visibly expressed. In his classic book *The Expression of the Emotions in Man and Animals* (1872/1965), Charles Darwin argued that human facial expressions—the smile, the frown, the grimace, the glare—are as "wired in" as the wing flutter of a frightened bird, the purr of a contented cat, and the snarl of a threatened wolf. Such expressions evolved, he said, because they allowed our forebears to tell at a glance the difference between a friendly stranger and a hostile one.

Modern psychologists have supported Darwin's idea by showing that certain emotional displays are recognized the world over (see Figure 12.1). For example, Paul Ekman and his colleagues have gathered abundant evidence for the universality of seven basic facial expressions of emotion: anger, happiness, fear, surprise, disgust, sadness, and contempt (Ekman, 1994; Ekman & Heider, 1988; Ekman et al., 1987). In every culture they have studied—in Brazil, Chile, Estonia, Germany, Greece, Hong Kong, Italy, Japan, New Guinea, Scotland, Sumatra, Turkey, and the United States—a large majority of people recognize the emotional expressions portrayed by those in other cultures. Even most members of isolated tribes that have never watched a movie or read *People* magazine, such as the Foré of New Guinea or the Minangkabau of West Sumatra, can recognize the emotions expressed in pictures of people who are entirely foreign to them, and we can recognize theirs.

These findings do not mean that everybody in a society can recognize the same expressions in all situations. Ekman (1994) calls his theory *neurocultural* to emphasize that two factors are involved in facial expression: a universal neurophysiology in the facial muscles associated with certain emotions, and culture-specific variations in the expres-

Figure 12.1
Some Universal Expressions of Emotion
Can you tell what feelings are being conveyed here? Most people around the world can readily identify expressions of surprise, disgust, happiness, sadness, anger, fear, and contempt—no matter what the age, culture, or historical epoch of the person conveying the emotion.

12.1

sion and recognition of emotion. Thus, while most people in most cultures do recognize basic emotions as portrayed in photographs, sometimes a large minority does not. Across 20 studies of Western cultures, for example, fully 95 percent of the participants agreed in their judgments of happy faces, but only 78 percent agreed on expressions of sadness and anger. And across 11 non-Western societies, 88 percent recognized happiness, but only 74 percent agreed on sadness and 59 percent on anger (Ekman, 1994).

Of course, people do not always reveal their emotions on their faces. Most of us do not go around scowling and clenching our jaws whenever we are angry. We can grieve and feel enormously sad without weeping. We can feel worried and tense, yet try to look cheerful. We use facial expressions, in short, to lie about our feelings, as well as to reveal them. In Shakespeare's play *Henry VI*, the villain who will become the evil King Richard III says,

> *Why, I can smile, and murder while I smile;*
> *And cry content to that which grieves my heart;*
> *And wet my cheeks with artificial tears,*
> *And frame my face to all occasions.*

To get around the human ability to mask emotions, Ekman and his associates developed a way to peek under the mask. A special coding system allows researchers to analyze and identify each of the nearly 80 muscles of the face, as well as the combinations of muscles associated with various

Facial expressions do not always convey the emotion being felt. A posed, social smile like Gloria Vanderbilt's (left) may have nothing to do with true feelings of happiness. Conversely, you would never know from the apparently anguished face of Oksana Baiul (right) that she was actually feeling jubilant over winning an Olympic medal for figure skating.

emotions. When people try to hide their real emotions, they use different groups of muscles. For example, when people try to pretend that they feel grief, only 15 percent manage to get the eyebrows, eyelids, and forehead wrinkle exactly right, mimicking the way grief is expressed spontaneously. Authentic smiles last only two seconds; false smiles may last ten seconds or more (Ekman, 1994; Ekman, Friesen, & O'Sullivan, 1988).

Facial expressions not only reflect internal states, but also help us communicate our intentions to others. You can see this even in infants. A baby's expressions of misery, angry frustration, or happiness send a clear message to most parents, who respond by soothing an uncomfortable baby, feeding a grumpy, hungry one, and cuddling a happy one (Izard, 1994b; Stenberg & Campos, 1990). Babies, in turn, react to the facial expressions of their parents; American, German, Greek, Japanese, Trobriand Island, and Yanomamo mothers all "infect" their babies with happy moods by displaying happy expressions (Keating, 1994).

Starting at the end of their first year, babies begin to alter their own behavior after observing their parents' emotions and reactions, and this ability has survival value. Do you recall the visual-cliff studies described in Chapter 5 (p. 177)? These studies were originally designed to test for depth perception, which emerges early in infancy. But in one experiment, 1-year-old babies were put on a more ambiguous visual cliff that did not drop off sharply and thus did not automatically evoke fear, as the original one did. In this case, 74 percent of the babies crossed the cliff when their mothers showed a happy, reassuring expression, but not a single one crossed when their mothers showed an expression of fear (Sorce et al., 1985). If you have ever watched a toddler take a tumble and then look at his or her parent before deciding whether to cry or forget it, you will understand the influence of parental facial expressions.

Interestingly, facial expressions may help us communicate not only with others, but also with ourselves, so to speak, by helping us identify our own emotions. In the process of **facial feedback,** the facial muscles send messages to the brain

facial feedback
The process by which the facial muscles send messages to the brain about the basic emotion being expressed.

Great moms have always understood the importance of facial feedback.

about the basic emotion being expressed: A smile tells us that we're happy, a frown that we're angry or perplexed (Izard, 1990). When people are told to look pleased or happy, their positive feelings increase; when they are told to look angry, displeased, or disgusted, positive feelings decrease (Kleinke, Peterson, & Rutledge, 1998). And when they are asked to contort their facial muscles into patterns associated with happiness or anger, that is often the emotion they feel. As one young man put it, "When my jaw was clenched and my brows down, I tried not to be angry but it just fit the position" (Laird, 1974). The reason seems to be that facial expressions affect the sympathetic nervous system. If you put on an "angry" face, your heart rate will rise faster than if you put on a "happy" face (Levenson, Ekman, & Friesen, 1990). (The next time you are feeling sad or afraid, try purposely smiling, even if no one is around. Keep smiling. Does facial feedback work for you?)

Facial expressions are important clues to a person's emotions, but they are only part of the emotional picture. Even Ekman, who has been studying them for years, concludes, "There is obviously emotion without facial expression and facial expression without emotion." Later we will see that culture and circumstance play an important role in when and how people express their feelings.

Emotion and the Brain. Another line of research seeks to identify parts of the brain responsible for the components of emotional experience: recognizing another person's emotion, feeling an emotion, expressing an emotion, and acting on an emotion. Many of these components are quite specifically localized in the brain. For example, the right hemisphere is especially important for processing incoming emotional information and for expressing the emotions you feel. People with damage in a particular part of the right hemisphere have trouble understanding jokes or getting the emotions portrayed in films and stories. And if you ask them to express emotions, for instance by repeating sentences in happy, sad, or angry tones of voice, they cannot do it very well (Heller, Nitschke, & Miller, 1998).

The two cerebral hemispheres also play different roles in the experience of positive and negative emotions (Davidson, 1992). Regions of the left hemisphere appear to be specialized for positive emotions such as happiness, whereas regions of the right hemisphere are specialized for negative emotions such as fear and sadness. People with damage to the left hemisphere sometimes experience

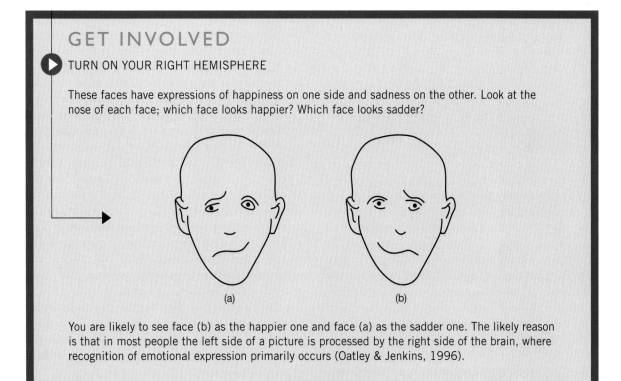

GET INVOLVED

TURN ON YOUR RIGHT HEMISPHERE

These faces have expressions of happiness on one side and sadness on the other. Look at the nose of each face; which face looks happier? Which face looks sadder?

(a)   (b)

You are likely to see face (b) as the happier one and face (a) as the sadder one. The likely reason is that in most people the left side of a picture is processed by the right side of the brain, where recognition of emotional expression primarily occurs (Oatley & Jenkins, 1996).

excessive anger or depression; people with damage to the right hemisphere may feel excessively manic and euphoric. Even in people without brain damage, those who are clinically depressed have less activation in the left frontal regions than non-depressed people do (Davidson, 1995).

The *amygdala,* a small structure in the brain's limbic system, plays a key role in emotion (see Chapter 4). The amygdala appears to be responsible for evaluating sensory information, determining its emotional importance, and making the initial decision to approach or withdraw from a person or situation (LeDoux, 1994, 1996). The amygdala quickly assesses danger or threat, which is a good thing, because otherwise you could be standing in the street asking, "Is it wise to cross now, while that very large truck is coming toward me?" The amygdala's initial response may then be overridden by a more accurate appraisal from the cerebral cortex (LeDoux, 1996). This is why you jump with fear when you suddenly feel a hand on your back in a dark alley, and why your fear evaporates when the cortex registers that the hand belongs to a friend whose lousy idea of humor is to scare you in a dark alley.

2. The cerebral cortex generates a more complete picture; it can override signals sent by the amygdala ("It's only Mike in a down coat").

1. The amygdala scrutinizes information for its emotional importance ("It's a bear! Be afraid! Run!").

If either the amygdala or critical areas of the cortex are damaged, emotional abnormalities result. A rat with a damaged amygdala "forgets" to be afraid when it should be. Likewise, people with damage to the amygdala often have difficulty recognizing fear in themselves or others (Damasio, 1994). But rats or people with damage to critical areas of the cortex often lose the capacity to put aside their fear when the emotion is no longer necessary. The result can be constant, irrational feelings of impending doom and anxiety, and obsessive thoughts of danger—as is the case in obsessive–compulsive disorder, discussed in Chapter 10.

The Energy of Emotion. A third line of physiological research focuses on hormones, which produce the energy of emotion. In particular, the inner part of the adrenal gland sends out two hormones, *epinephrine* and *norepinephrine* (see Chapter 4). These chemical messengers activate the sympathetic division of the autonomic nervous system and produce a state of arousal and alertness. The pupils dilate, widening to allow in more light; the heart beats faster; breathing speeds up; and blood sugar rises, providing the body with more energy. Digestion slows down, so that blood flow can be diverted from the stomach and intestines to the muscles and surface of the skin. (This is why, when you are excited, scared, furious, or wildly in love, you may not want to eat.) The ultimate purpose of all these physiological changes is to prepare the body to respond quickly when it needs to (Brehm, 1999; Frijda, 1988). When you feel an emotion, you generally feel motivated to do something specific: embrace the person who instills joy in you, yell at the person who is angering you, run from the situation that is frightening you, avoid a situation that makes you sad (Harmon-Jones & Allen, 1998).

The adrenal glands produce epinephrine and norepinephrine in response to many challenges in the environment. These hormones will surge if you are laughing at a comedian, playing a video game, worrying about an exam, cheering at a sports event, reacting to an insult, or driving on a hot day in terrible traffic. Epinephrine in particular provides the energy of an emotion—that familiar tingle, excitement, and sense of animation. At high levels, it can create the sensation of being "seized" or "flooded" by an emotion that is out of your control. In a sense, the release of epinephrine does cause us to lose control, because few people can consciously alter their heart rates, blood pressures, and digestive tracts. However, people *can* learn to control their actions when they are under the sway of an emotion. And no emotion, no matter how urgent or compelling, lasts forever. As arousal subsides, a "hot" emotion turns into its "cool" counterpart. Anger may pale into annoyance, ecstasy into contentment, fear into suspicion, past emotional whirlwinds into calm breezes.

Drivers all over the world often get impatient with other cars that get in their way or slow them down. But why don't passengers feel as irritated as drivers? One reason is that only the driver feels physiological arousal from the stress of driving. (You'll find another reason on page 417.)

Although epinephrine and norepinephrine are released during many emotions, emotions also differ from one another biochemically. The brain has a variety of chemical messengers at its disposal— neurotransmitters, hormones, and neuromodulators—and these play different roles in different emotions (Oatley & Jenkins, 1996). Fear, disgust, anger, sadness, surprise, and happiness are also associated with somewhat different patterns of autonomic nervous system activity, as measured by heart rate, electrical conductivity of the skin, and finger temperature (Levenson, 1992; Levenson, Ekman, & Friesen, 1990). These distinctive patterns may explain why people say they feel "hot and bothered" when they are angry, but "cold and clammy" when they are afraid. These metaphors capture what is going on in their bodies.

In sum, the physiology of emotion involves characteristic facial expressions; activity in specific parts of the brain, notably the amygdala and specialized parts of the two cerebral hemispheres; and hormones that stimulate sympathetic nervous system activity, which prepares the body for action. But the physical changes involved in emotion cannot explain why, of two students about to take an exam, one feels psyched up and the other feels overwhelmed by anxiety. Different patterns of hemispheric activation in cheerful and depressed people won't tell us why the former see the world through rose-tinted glasses and the latter through foggy gray ones. And hormones alone won't tell you whether you are thrilled or frightened, sick or just in love.

QUICK QUIZ

We hope that a little surge of hormonal energy will help you answer these questions.

1. A 3-year-old sees her dad dressed as a gorilla and runs away in fear. What brain structure is probably involved in her emotional reaction?

2. Casey is watching *Hatchet Murders in the Dorm: Sequel XVII*. What hormones cause his heart to pound and his palms to sweat when the murderer is stalking an unsuspecting victim?

3. Melissa is watching an old Laurel and Hardy film, which makes her chuckle and puts her in a good mood. Which hemisphere of her brain is likely to be most active?

Answers:

1. the amygdala   2. epinephrine and norepinephrine   3. the left

Emotion and the Mind

What gives you the feeling of a feeling? What would happen if you were injected with the hormones that create the physical arousal associated with emotion, but while you were sitting in a quiet, boring room with no *reason* to feel an emotion? In the 1960s, Stanley Schachter and Jerome Singer (1962) proposed a **two-factor theory of emotion** to answer this question. They argued that bodily changes are necessary to experience an emotion but are not enough. Emotion, they said, depends on two things: *physiological arousal* and a *cognitive interpretation* of that arousal. Your body may be churning away in high gear, but unless you can interpret, explain, and label those changes, you will not feel a true emotion.

Schachter and Singer's own studies investigating this theory were never successfully replicated, but their ideas had an electrifying effect on emotion research. The two-factor theory spurred other investigators to study how emotions are created or influenced by beliefs, perceptions of the situation, expectations, and *attributions*—the explanations that people make of their own and other people's behavior (see Chapter 9). Human beings, after all, are the only species that can say, "The more I thought about it, the madder I got." That remark shows that we can think ourselves into an emotional state—in this case, anger—and by implication, we can think ourselves out of it.

Psychologists have studied the role of cognitions in all kinds of emotions, from joy to sadness. For example, imagine that you get an A on your psychology midterm; how will you feel? Or perhaps you get a D on that midterm; how will you feel then? The answers are not so obvious. The emotions you will feel in response to your grade will depend more on how you *explain* your grade than on what you actually get—on whether you attribute your grade to your own efforts (or lack of effort), to the teacher, or to fate. In one series of experiments, students who believed they did well because of their own efforts tended to feel proud, competent, and satisfied. Those who believed they did well because of a lucky fluke or chance tended to feel gratitude, surprise, or guilt ("I don't deserve this"). Those who believed their failures were their own fault tended to feel regretful, guilty, or resigned. And those who blamed others tended to feel angry or hostile (Weiner, 1986).

Here is another interesting example of how thoughts affect emotions: Of two Olympic contenders, one who wins a second-place silver medal and one who wins a third-place bronze medal, which will feel happier? Won't it be the silver medalist? Nope. In a study of athletes' reactions to placing second and third in the 1992 Olympics and the 1994 Empire State games, the bronze medalists were happier than the silver medalists (Medvec, Madey, & Gilovich, 1995). Apparently, the athletes were comparing their performance to "what might have been." The second-place winners, comparing themselves to the gold medalists, were unhappy that they didn't get the gold. But the third-place winners, comparing themselves to those who did worse than they, were happy that they earned a medal at all!

Cognitive research on emotion helps explain a puzzle of emotional experience: why people sometimes feel an emotion that is inappropriate to the situation. The reason is that they mislabel their own physical state, making an incorrect attribution. For example, people sometimes decide that they are suffering from anxiety because they can't sleep and have a rapid, pounding heartbeat, when their symptoms are really due to too much coffee or to partying late. Or they may decide that they are feeling angry and all "riled up," when their physical arousal is actually

two-factor theory of emotion
The theory that emotions depend on both physiological arousal and a cognitive interpretation of that arousal.

due to exercise, heat, cold, crowds, stress, or traffic (Sinclair et al., 1994). Misattributions may also explain why the driver of a car feels angrier at other drivers than a passenger does ("That jerk tried to kill me!"). Presumably, the jerky other driver could have killed the passenger along with the driver, but only the driver is already tense and physically worked up from the stress of driving.

Cognitions play a greater role in some emotions than in others. A conditioned sentimental response to a patriotic symbol, an acquired disgust response to an ugly bug, or a warm fuzzy feeling toward a familiar object all involve simple, nonconscious reactions (Izard, 1994a; Murphy, Monahan, & Zajonc, 1995). But most of our emotions require complex cognitive capacities, such as the ability to decide that you have been humiliated, shamed, or betrayed. Infants cannot feel shame or guilt because these emotions require a sense of self and the ability to perceive that you have behaved badly or let down another person (Baumeister, Stillwell, & Heatherton, 1994; Tangney et al., 1996). With increasing mental maturity, the child becomes capable of complex cognitive evaluations of a situation, and emotions accordingly become more complex too (Malatesta, 1990; Oatley & Jenkins, 1996).

Today, almost all theories of emotion hold that attributions, beliefs, and the meanings people give to events are essential to the creation of most emotions. But where do these attributions, beliefs, and meanings come from? When people

Surprisingly, third place winners tend to be happier about their performance than those who come in second. Certainly Olympic fencing bronze medalist Jean-Michel Henry of France (left) is happier than silver medalist Pavel Kolobkov of the Unified Team (right). (Eric Srecki, center, won the gold for France.)

decide that it is shameful for a man to dance on a table with a lampshade on his head, or for a woman to walk down a street with her arms and legs uncovered, where do their ideas about shame originate? If you are a motorist who curses others for driving too slowly, where did you learn that cursing is acceptable on the highway? To answer these questions, we turn to the third major aspect of emotional experience: the role of culture.

QUICK QUIZ

How are your thoughts affecting your feelings about this quiz?

1. What are the two factors in Schachter and Singer's two-factor theory of emotion?

2. Dara and Dinah get B's on their psychology midterm, but Dara is ecstatic and proud, and Dinah is furious. What expectations and attributions are probably affecting their emotional reactions?

3. At a party, you see a stranger flirting with your date. You are flooded with jealousy. What cognitions might be causing this emotion? *Be specific.* What alternative thoughts might reduce your jealous feelings?

Answers:

1. physiological arousal and a cognitive interpretation of that arousal 2. Dara was probably expecting a lower grade and is attributing her B to her own efforts; Dinah was probably expecting a higher grade and is attributing her B to the instructor's unfairness, bad luck, or other external reasons. 3. Possible thoughts causing jealousy are "My date finds other people more attractive," "That person is trying to steal my date," or "My date's behavior is humiliating me." But you could be saying, "It's a compliment to me that other people find my date attractive," or "It pleases me that my date is getting such deserved attention."

What's Ahead

- Are the "basic" emotions basic everywhere?

- Do Germans, Japanese, and Americans always mean the same thing when they smile at others?

- Why do people feel obliged to show sadness at funerals even when they are not feeling sad?

- Are women really more emotional than men?

12.2 Emotion and Culture

A young wife leaves her house one morning to draw water from the local well as her husband watches from the porch. On her way back from the well, a male stranger stops her and asks for some water. She gives him a cupful and then invites him home to dinner. He accepts. The husband, wife, and guest have a pleasant meal together. The husband, in a gesture of hospitality, invites the guest to spend the night—with his wife. The guest accepts. In the morning, the husband leaves early to bring home breakfast. When he returns, he finds his wife again in bed with the visitor.

At what point in this story will the husband feel angry? The answer depends on his culture (Hupka, 1981, 1991). A North American husband would feel rather angry at a wife who had an extra-marital affair, and a wife would feel rather angry at being offered to a guest as if she were a lamb chop. But these reactions are not universal. A Pawnee husband of the nineteenth century would be enraged at any man who dared ask his wife for water. An Ammassalik Inuit husband finds it perfectly honorable to offer his wife to a stranger, but only once; he would be angry to find his wife and the guest having a second encounter. And a Toda husband at the turn of the century in India would not be angry at all because the Todas allowed both husband and wife to take lovers. Both spouses might feel angry, though, if one of them had a *sneaky* affair, without announcing it publicly.

As you can see, people in most cultures feel angry in response to insult and the violation of social rules, but they often disagree about what an insult is or what the correct rule should be. In this section, we will explore how culture influences the emotions we feel and the ways in which we express them.

primary emotions Emotions that are considered to be universal and biologically based; they generally include fear, anger, sadness, joy, surprise, disgust, and contempt.

secondary emotions Emotions that are specific to certain cultures.

The Varieties of Emotion

Earlier we saw that certain emotional expressions are recognizable throughout the world. Many psychologists believe that the emotions corresponding to these expressions—fear, anger, sadness, joy, surprise, disgust, and contempt—are universal and biologically based. These **primary emotions** are evoked by the same situations everywhere: Sadness follows perception of loss, fear follows perception of threat and bodily harm, anger follows perception of insult or injustice (Scherer, 1997). People in different cultures even give similar physical descriptions of these emotions, saying, for example, that they feel hot in response to anger and have a "lump in the throat" in response to sadness (Mesquita & Frijda, 1992; Oatley & Duncan, 1994).

In this view, **secondary emotions** are the cultural variations. Germans, for example, talk about *schadenfreude*, a feeling of joy at another's misfortune. The Japanese have *ijirashii*, a feeling associated with seeing an admirable person overcoming an obstacle, and *hagaii*, helpless anguish tinged with frustration. *Litost* is a Czech word that combines grief, sympathy, remorse, and longing; the Czech writer Milan Kundera used it to describe "a state of torment caused by a sudden insight into one's own miserable self."

Other psychologists, however, think that the effort to distinguish primary and secondary emo-

This father is clearly proud of his family, but pride is not on most lists of primary emotions—although it is probably a universal emotional feeling. Should it be considered a "primary" emotion or is it just a variation of happiness?

tions masks the profound influence of culture on every aspect of emotional experience, starting with which feelings a culture even considers "basic." For example, anger is a basic emotion in the United States, which emphasizes independence and personal rights, but it is caused and experienced quite differently in community-oriented cultures, where shame and loss of face are more central (Kitayama & Markus, 1994). On the tiny Micronesian atoll of Ifaluk, everyone would say that *fago* is the most fundamental emotion. *Fago*, translated as "compassion/love/sadness," reflects the sad feeling one has when a loved one is absent or in need, and the pleasurable sense of compassion in being able to care and help (Lutz, 1988). What, then, would theories of primary emotions look like from a non-Western perspective? They might start with shame or *fago*, which are far from central in Western emotion research.

Thinking Critically About "Basic" Emotions

Even if some basic emotions are hard-wired biologically, cultures clearly determine much of what people feel emotional *about*. Among the Bedouins and other "shame-oriented" cultures, shame is produced by violations of a complex code of honor; on Bali and Java, shame and embarrassment are generated by perceived challenges to one's status (Mesquita & Frijda, 1992). In Ifaluk, it is cause for anger if someone next to you is smoking without offering you the cigarette; it means the smoker is unwilling to share—a terrible offense (Lutz, 1988). Increasingly in the United States and Canada, it is cause for anger if someone is smoking at all! To nonsmokers, smoking means an infringement on their right to clean air.

Communicating Emotions

Suppose that someone who was dear to you died. Would you cry, and if so, would you do it alone or in public? Would you wail and tear your clothes, or try to keep your feelings to yourself? Your answer will depend in part on your culture's **display rules** for emotion (Ekman et al., 1987). In some cultures, grief is expressed by weeping; in others, by tearless resignation; and in still others by dance, drink, and song. The 1997 death of Diana, Princess of Wales, revealed a major shift in England's display rules for grief—from "keep a stiff upper lip" (don't express your grief publicly) to "let it all hang out."

Even the smile, which seems a straightforward signal of friendliness, has many meanings and uses that are not universal. Americans smile more frequently than Germans, not because

display rules
Social and cultural rules that regulate when, how, and where a person may express (or suppress) emotions.

Around the world, the cultural rules for expressing emotions (or suppressing them) differ. The display rule for a formal Japanese wedding portrait is "no expressions of emotion"—but not every member of this family has learned that rule yet.

Arms and hands communicate interest, emphasis, and feeling as much as words do. Some people are more fluent in "body language" than others.

Americans are friendlier but because they differ in their notions of when a smile is appropriate. After a German–American business session, Americans often complain that the Germans are cold and aloof. For their part, Germans often complain that Americans are excessively cheerful, hiding their real feelings under the mask of a smile (Hall & Hall, 1990). The Japanese smile even more than Americans, to disguise embarrassment, anger, or other negative emotions whose public display is considered rude and incorrect.

Display rules also govern emotional *body language,* the nonverbal signals of body movement, posture, gesture, and gaze that people constantly express (Birdwhistell, 1970). Some signals of body language, like some facial expressions, seem to be "spoken" universally; when people are depressed, for example, it shows in their walk, stance, and head position. However, most aspects of body language are specific to particular spoken languages and cultures, which makes even the simplest gesture subject to misunderstanding and offense. The sign of the University of Texas football team, the Longhorns, is to extend the index finger and the pinkie. In Italy and other parts of Europe, this gesture means a man's wife has been unfaithful to him—a serious insult!

Cultural misunderstandings of emotional display rules can lead to major misunderstandings, hostilities, and sometimes even tragedy (Triandis, 1994). On January 9, 1991, the Foreign Minister of Iraq, Tariq Aziz, met with the American Secretary of State, James Baker, to discuss Iraq's invasion of Kuwait. Seated next to Aziz was the half-brother of Iraq's president, Saddam Hussein. Baker said, "If you do not move out of Kuwait we will attack you." A clear statement, right? But his *nonverbal* language was that of an American diplomat, moderate and restrained. He did not shout, stamp his feet, or wave his hands. Saddam Hussein's brother, for his part, behaved like a normal Iraqi. He paid attention to Baker's nonverbal language, which he considered the important form of communication. He reported to Saddam Hussein that Baker was "not at all angry. The Americans are just talking, and they will not attack." Saddam therefore instructed Aziz to be inflexible and to yield nothing. This misunderstanding contributed to the outbreak of a bloody war in which thousands of people died.

Display rules tell us not only what to do when we *are* feeling an emotion, but also how and when to show an emotion we do *not* feel. Acting out an emotion we do not really feel, or trying to create the right emotion for the occasion, has been called **emotion work.** People are expected to demonstrate sadness at funerals, happiness at weddings, and affection toward relatives, whether they feel these emotions or not. Sometimes emotion work is a job requirement: Flight attendants, waiters, and customer-service representatives must "put on a happy face" to convey cheerfulness, even if they are angry about rude customers. And bill collectors must put on a stern face to convey threat, even if they feel sorry for the person they are collecting money from (Hochschild, 1983).

Smiling to convey friendliness is part of the job description for flight attendants, whether they are male or female—but not necessarily for the passengers they serve.

emotion work
Expression of an emotion, often because of a role requirement, that a person does not really feel.

Gender and Emotion

Thinking Critically
About Gender
Differences in
Emotionality

"Women are so emotional," men often complain. "Men are too uptight," women often reply. Are women really "more emotional" than men, as the stereotype suggests? We need to define our terms here.

To begin with, there is little evidence that one sex *feels* any of the everyday emotions more often than the other, including anger, worry, embarrassment, love, or grief (Fischer et al., 1993; Kring & Gordon, 1998; Oatley & Duncan, 1994; Shields, 1991). The major difference between the sexes has less to do with whether they *feel* emotions than with how those emotions are *expressed.*

Women in North America smile more than men do, gaze at their listeners more, have more emotionally expressive faces, use more expressive hand and body movements, and touch other people more (DePaulo, 1992; Kring & Gordon, 1998). Women also talk about their emotions more than men do. They are far more likely to cry, and to acknowledge emotions that reveal vulnerability and weakness, such as "hurt feelings," fear, sadness, loneliness, shame, and guilt (Grossman & Wood, 1993; L. Smith & Reise, 1998; Timmers, Fischer, & Manstead, 1998). In contrast, most North American men express only one emotion more freely than women: anger toward strangers, especially other men. Otherwise, men are expected to control and mask negative feelings. When they are worried or afraid, they are more likely than women to use vague terms, saying that they feel moody, frustrated, or "on edge" (Fehr et al., 1999; L. Smith & Reise, 1998).

Women in North America also smile more often than men as part of their role requirements and emotion work. They smile to pacify others, convey deference to someone of higher status, or smooth over conflicts (Hecht & LaFrance, 1998; Henley, 1995). In fact, women who don't smile when others expect them to do so are often disliked, even if they are actually smiling as often as men would. Men's emotion work tends to be the reverse: persuading others that they are strong, controlled, and unemotional, even if they are welling up with softer feelings inside.

These North American gender differences, however, are by no means universal. Italian,

Israeli parents (left) and a Palestinian father (right) react to the death of their children in the endless Middle Eastern conflict. Notice that the men are following different cultural display rules for the expression of grief, rules that govern whether they should try to suppress it or completely let go. Your own culture's rules may affect your reactions to these scenes: Is the Israeli father "cold and uptight" or "mature and manly"? Is the Palestinian father being "hysterical" or "humanly expressive"?

12.1

French, Spanish, and Middle Eastern men can have entire conversations using highly expressive hand gestures and facial expressions, and you won't find sex differences in nonverbal expressiveness in their cultures. In contrast, in Asian cultures, both sexes are taught to control emotional expression (Matsumoto, 1996; Mesquita & Frijda, 1992). Cultures also determine which emotions men and women express most freely. Israeli and Italian men are more likely than women to mask feelings of sadness, but British, Spanish, Swiss, and German men are more likely than their female counterparts to *express* this emotion (Wallbott, Ricci-Bitti, & Bänninger-Huber, 1986).

Even within a culture, the influence of a particular situation often overrides gender rules. An American man is as likely as an American woman to control his temper when the target of anger is someone with higher status or power; few people, no matter how angry, will readily sound off at a professor, police officer, or employer. And you won't find many gender differences in emotional expressiveness at a football game or the World Series!

The emotion "tree," as we have seen, can take many shapes, depending on physiology, cognitive processes, and cultural rules. Next we will see how these three factors can help us understand those difficult situations in which stress and negative emotions threaten to overwhelm us and even to make us ill.

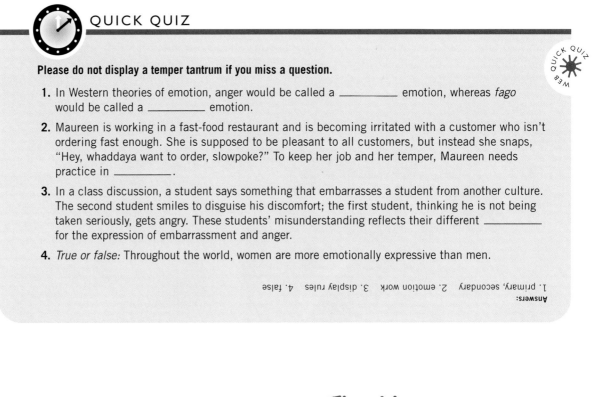

QUICK QUIZ

Please do not display a temper tantrum if you miss a question.

1. In Western theories of emotion, anger would be called a _____ emotion, whereas *fago* would be called a _____ emotion.

2. Maureen is working in a fast-food restaurant and is becoming irritated with a customer who isn't ordering fast enough. She is supposed to be pleasant to all customers, but instead she snaps, "Hey, whaddaya want to order, slowpoke?" To keep her job and her temper, Maureen needs practice in _____.

3. In a class discussion, a student says something that embarrasses a student from another culture. The second student smiles to disguise his discomfort; the first student, thinking he is not being taken seriously, gets angry. These students' misunderstanding reflects their different _____ for the expression of embarrassment and anger.

4. *True or false:* Throughout the world, women are more emotionally expressive than men.

Answers:

1. primary, secondary   2. emotion work   3. display rules   4. false

---

What's Ahead

- Why are you more likely to get a cold when you're "stressed out"?

- Which stressors pose the greatest hazard to your health?

- Why do optimists tend to live longer than pessimists?

- When is a sense of control good for you, and when is it not?

12.3 The Nature of Stress

No life is entirely free of stress. We are all vulnerable to *stressors*—conflicts that annoy us, pressures that fatigue us, and traumatic experiences that shatter our sense of safety. The question that most fascinates everyone is whether these events are linked to illness, and whether, by controlling our emotional reactions to events, we can improve our health and well-being.

Stress and the Body

The modern era of stress research began in 1956, when the Canadian physician Hans Selye (1907–1982) published *The Stress of Life*. Environmental stressors such as heat, cold, pain, toxins, and danger, Selye wrote, disrupt the body's equilibrium. The body then mobilizes its resources to fight off these stressors and restore normal functioning. Drawing on data from animal studies, Selye concluded that "stress" consists of a series of physiological reactions that occur in three phases:

1 *The alarm phase*, in which your body mobilizes to meet the immediate threat, whether the "threat" is an angry bear or a test you haven't studied for. As we saw earlier, these physiological responses occur with any intense emotion and include a boost in energy, tense muscles, reduced sensitivity to pain, the shutting down of digestion (so that blood flow will get more efficiently to the brain, muscles, and skin), a rise in blood pressure, and increased output of adrenal hormones.

2 *The resistance phase*, in which your body attempts to resist or cope with a stressor that cannot be avoided, but which persists over time. During this phase, the physiological responses of the alarm phase continue, but these very responses make the body more vulnerable to *other* stressors. For example, when your body has mobilized to fight off the flu, you may find you are more easily annoyed by minor frustrations. In most cases, the body will eventually adapt to the stressor and return to normal.

3 *The exhaustion phase*, in which persistent stress depletes the body of energy and therefore increases vulnerability to physical problems and eventually illness. The same reactions that allow the body to respond effectively in the alarm and resistance phases are unhealthy as long-range responses. Tense muscles can cause headache and neck pain. Increased blood pressure can become chronic hypertension. If normal digestive processes are interrupted or shut down for too long, digestive disorders may result.

A diagram of Selye's view would therefore look like this:

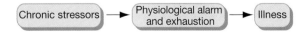

Selye did not believe that people should aim for a stress-free life. Some stress, he said, is posi-

tive and productive, even if it also requires the body to produce short-term energy: competing in an athletic event, falling in love, working hard on a project you enjoy. And some negative stress is simply unavoidable. The goal is to minimize its wear and tear on the system, not get rid of it entirely.

Of the many bodily systems affected by stress, one of the most intensively studied has been the immune system, which enables the body to fight disease and infection. The white blood cells of the immune system are designed to recognize foreign substances (*antigens*), such as flu viruses, bacteria, and tumor cells, and then destroy or deactivate them. When an antigen invades the body, the immune system deploys different kinds of white blood cells as weapons, depending on the nature of the enemy.

Prolonged stress can suppress some or many of these white blood cells. In one study of medical students who had the herpes virus, herpes outbreaks were more likely to occur when the students were feeling lonely or were under pressure from exams. Loneliness and tension apparently suppressed the immune system's capabilities, permitting the existing herpes virus to erupt (Kiecolt-Glaser et al., 1985a).

A phagocyte, magnified many millions of times, looks more fantastical than any alien creature Hollywood could design. This one is about to engulf and destroy a cigarette-shaped parasite that causes a tropical disease.

Live **psych**

12.2

Stressors Affecting the Body. Some kinds of stressors are especially likely to increase the risk of illness or poor health:

1 *Noise.* Loud noise becomes stressful (apart from what it does to your hearing) when it goes on day in and day out without relief. Children who live or go to school near noisy airports have higher blood pressure and higher levels of stress hormones, are more distractible, and have more learning and attention difficulties than do children in quieter environments (Cohen et al., 1980; Evans, Bullinger, & Hygge, 1998). In adults, constant loud noise contributes to cardiovascular problems, irritability, fatigue, and aggressiveness, probably because of overstimulation of the autonomic nervous system (Staples, 1996).

2 *Bereavement and loss.* One of life's most powerful stressors is the loss of a loved one or a close relationship, especially through divorce or death. In the two years following bereavement, widowed people are more susceptible to illness and physical ailments, and their mortality rate is higher than would otherwise be expected. Divorce can also take a long-term toll on health: Divorced adults have higher rates of heart disease, pneumonia, and other diseases than their counterparts who are not divorced (Laudenslager, 1988). Bereaved and divorced people may be vulnerable to illness in part because, feeling unhappy, they don't sleep well, they stop eating properly, and they consume more drugs and cigarettes. But broken attachments also seem to affect the body at a cellular level, producing cardiovascular changes, fewer white blood cells, and other abnormal responses of the immune system (Stroebe et al., 1996).

3 *Work-related problems.* Because work is central in most people's lives, the effects of unemployment or of a chronically stressful work environment can be more severe than other kinds of stressors. A Swedish study found that people who reported a history of severe workplace problems over a decade had 5.5 times the risk of developing colon or rectal cancers, even when diet and other factors linked to these malignancies were taken into account (Courtney et al., 1993).

Work-related stress can also increase a person's vulnerability to a more mundane illness—the common cold. Heroic volunteers in the war against winter colds were given either ordinary nose drops or nose drops containing a cold virus. Everyone was then quarantined for five days. The people most likely to get a cold's miserable symptoms were those who had been underemployed or unemployed for at least a month (see Figure 12.2). The longer the work problems had lasted, the greater the likelihood of illness (Cohen et al., 1998).

At work, the people who suffer most from job stress and who are at greatest risk of illness are not executives and managers, but those who have little opportunity to exercise initiative and who are trapped doing repetitive tasks (Karasek & Theorell, 1990). For example, the women who are most at risk of heart disease are clerical workers who feel

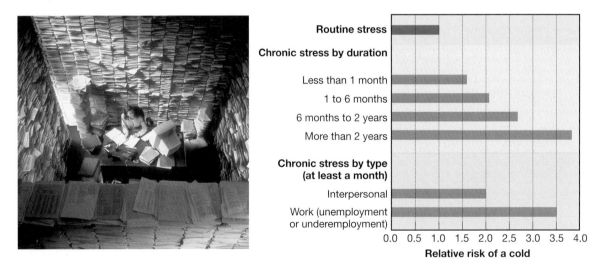

Figure 12.2
Stress and the Common Cold
Chronic stress lasting a month or more boosts the risk of catching a cold. The risk is increased among people who feel overwhelmed by work or who are undergoing problems with their friends or loved ones—but it is highest among people who are unemployed (Cohen et al., 1998).

they have no support from their bosses, who are stuck in low-paying jobs without hope of promotion, and who have financial problems at home (Haynes & Feinleib, 1980).

4 *Poverty, powerlessness, and racism.* People at the lower rungs of the socioeconomic ladder have worse health and higher mortality rates for almost every disease and medical condition than do those at the top (Adler et al., 1994). In America, one obvious reason is that poor people cannot afford medical care and preventive examinations, and they are more likely to eat high-fat, high-salt fast food. Another reason, however, has to do with the continuous environmental stressors that low-income people often endure: higher crime rates, discrimination, fewer community services, run-down housing, and greater exposure to hazards such as chemical contamination (Taylor, Repetti, & Seeman, 1997; Wandersman & Nation, 1998).

In North America, these conditions affect urban blacks disproportionately and may help account for their relatively high incidence of hypertension (high blood pressure), which can lead to kidney disease, strokes, and heart attacks. The anger and exhaustion that comes from dealing with persistent racial discrimination is another major stressor (Clark et al., 1999). In one study of 4,000 workers, the emotional stress brought on by racial discrimination was a stronger predictor of hypertension than were diet and smoking (Krieger & Sidney, 1996).

The Stress–Illness Mystery. Before you try to persuade your instructors that the stress of chronic studying is bad for your health, consider this mystery: None of the chronic stressors we just discussed leads in a direct, simple way to illness or affects everyone in the same way (Basic Behavioral Science Task Force, 1996). Some people exposed to a flu virus are sick all winter; others don't even get the sniffles. Some people in high-pressure careers wind up with heart disease; others work just as hard but remain healthy.

To understand the reasons that people differ so much in their susceptibility to stress and disease, researchers have considerably modified and expanded Selye's model of stress. They look not only at the external stressors in your life, but also at qualities in you (such as how you perceive the stressor, your emotional state, and your personality traits) and whether you feel able to control or cope with the stressor. Thus a modern view of *psychological stress*—the interaction between external stressors and illness—looks like this:

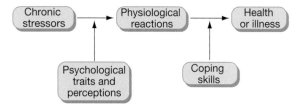

Earlier we saw that emotions involve not only the body but also the mind and a person's social and cultural context; the same is true for reactions to stress.

Stress and the Mind

Some people manufacture their own misery. Send them to a beach for a week to escape the pressures of civilization, and they bring along a suitcase full of worries and irritations. Others stay serene in the midst of chaos and conflict; they seem to carry along their own inner tranquilizer. These two kinds of people are distinguished by how they explain events and by the degree of control they think they exert over events.

Optimism and Pessimism. When something bad happens to you, what's your first reaction? Do you tell yourself that you will somehow come through it okay, or do you gloomily mutter, "More proof that if something can go wrong for me, it will"? These two responses reflect *pessimistic* and *optimistic explanatory styles,* and as far as health is concerned, optimism is a lot better for you (Carver & Scheier, 1999; Peterson, 2000). Pessimism is associated with depression (see Chapter 10), lower

12.2

self-esteem, reduced achievement, more illness, and slower recovery from setbacks.

If you are a pessimist, you will probably protest that optimism is just a *result*, not a cause, of good health or good fortune; it's easy to think positively when you feel good. But optimism actually seems to produce good health. In one imaginative study of baseball Hall-of-Famers who had played between 1900 and 1950, 30 players were rated according to their explanatory style. A pessimist would attribute a bad performance to a permanent failing in himself, as in: "We didn't win because my arm is shot, and it'll never get better." An optimist would attribute the same performance to external and changing conditions, as in: "We didn't win because we got a couple of lousy calls, just bad luck in this game, but we'll be great tomorrow." The optimists were significantly more likely to have lived well into old age than were the pessimists (Seligman, 1991).

Optimists may have better health than pessimists in part because they take better care of themselves when they get sick, whether their ailment is a simple cold or a life-threatening disease like AIDS. Pessimists, in contrast, often do self-destructive things: They drink too much, smoke, fail to wear seat belts, drive too fast, and refuse to take medication for illness. This may be why pessimists, especially males, are more likely than optimists to die untimely deaths as a result of accidents or violence (Peterson et al., 1998). But optimism is also directly associated with better immune function, such as a rise in the white blood cells that fight infection (Räikkönen et al., 1999; Segerstrom et al., 1998).

Pessimists, naturally, accuse optimists of being unrealistic. Yet health and well-being often depend on having some "positive illusions" about yourself and your circumstances (Taylor et al., 2000). Positive illusions, however, are not the same as denial. Optimists do not deny their problems or avoid facing bad news. On the contrary, they are more likely than pessimists to be active problem solvers and to seek information that can help them (Aspinwall & Taylor, 1997). They do not give up at the first sign of a setback or escape into wishful thinking. They keep their senses of humor, plan for the future, and reinterpret the situation in a positive light (Aspinwall & Brunhart, 1996; Chang, 1998).

Can pessimists be "cured" of their gloomy outlook? Optimists, naturally, think so! In Chapter 11, we discussed cognitive therapy, which teaches pessimists to test their dim predictions against the evidence. There we also described an effective

Explanatory style—pessimism or optimism—may affect health and longevity. Zack Wheat (left), an outfielder for the Brooklyn Dodgers, had an optimistic explanatory style: "I'm a better hitter than I used to be because my strength has improved and my experience has improved." Wheat lived to be 83. Walter Johnson (right), a star pitcher for the Washington Senators, had a pessimistic explanatory style: "I can't depend on myself to pitch well. I'm growing old. I've had my day." Johnson died at the age of 59.

intervention program that inoculates elementary-school children against pessimism and depression by teaching them optimistic explanatory styles (Gillham et al., 1995). Another method worked for psychologist Rachel Hare-Mustin, whose mother cured her budding childhood pessimism with humor. "Nobody likes me," Rachel lamented. "Don't say that," her mother said. "Everybody hasn't met you yet."

The Sense of Control. Optimism is related to another important cognitive ingredient in psychological and physical health: having an internal locus of control (Chang, 1998; Marshall et al., 1994). **Locus of control,** as we saw in Chapter 2, refers to your general expectation about whether you can control the things that happen to you. People who have an *internal locus of control* ("internals") tend to believe that they are responsible for what happens to them; those who have an *external locus of control* ("externals") tend to believe that they are the victims of circumstance (Rotter, 1990).

The Benefits of Control. People can tolerate all kinds of stressors if they feel able to predict or control them. The crowd you choose to join for a football game is not as stressful as the crowd you can't escape on a busy street; the music you choose to play at ear-splitting volume is not as stressful as the rotten music you are forced to listen to when you are put on hold on the phone! The greatest threat to health and well-being occurs when you feel caught in a situation you cannot escape. Conversely, feelings of control can reduce or even eliminate the relationship between stressors and illness described earlier. People who have an internal locus of control are better able than externals to resist exposure to cold viruses and even the health-impairing effects of poverty and discrimination (Cohen, Tyrrell, & Smith, 1993; Krieger & Sidney, 1996; Lachman & Weaver, 1998).

Feeling in control also helps to reduce pain, improve adjustment to surgery and illness, and speed up recovery from some diseases (Shapiro, Schwartz, & Astin, 1996; E. Skinner, 1996). As with optimism, feeling in control makes people more likely to take action to improve their health when necessary. In a group of patients recovering from heart attacks, for example, those who believed the heart attack occurred because they smoked, didn't exercise, or had a stressful job were more likely to change their bad habits and recover more quickly. In contrast, those who thought their illness was due to bad luck or fate—factors outside their control—

were less likely to generate plans for recovery and more likely to resume their old unhealthy habits (Affleck et al., 1987; Ewart, 1995).

A sense of control, like optimism, affects the immune system (Cohen & Herbert, 1996). This finding may explain why feeling in control is especially beneficial to old people, whose immune systems normally decline. When elderly residents of nursing homes are given more choices over their activities, environment, and day-to-day events—even small but engrossing activities such as tending plants—the results are dramatic. They become more alert, more active, and happier, and they live longer (Langer, 1983).

The Limits of Control. Overall, then, a sense of control is a good thing. But the question must always be asked: control over what? It is surely not beneficial for people to believe they can control absolutely every aspect of their lives; some things, such as death, taxes, or being a random victim of a crime, are out of anyone's control. Health and well-being are not enhanced by self-blame ("Whatever goes wrong with my health is my fault") or the belief that all disease can be prevented by doing the right thing ("If I just take vitamins and work out nine times a week, I'll never get sick").

Eastern and Western cultures tend to hold different attitudes toward the ability and desirability of controlling our own lives. In general, Western cultures celebrate **primary control,** in which people try to influence existing reality by trying to exert control over it: If you do not like a situation, you are supposed to change it, fix it, or fight it. The Eastern approach emphasizes **secondary control,** in which people try to accommodate to reality by changing their own aspirations or desires: If you have a problem, you are supposed to live with it or act in spite of it (Rothbaum, Weisz, & Snyder, 1982).

A Japanese psychologist once offered some examples of Japanese proverbs that teach the benefits of yielding to the inevitable (Azuma, 1984): "To lose is to win" (giving in, to protect the harmony of a relationship, demonstrates the superior trait of generosity); "Willow trees do not get broken by piled-up snow" (no matter how many problems pile up in your life, flexibility will help you survive them); and "The true tolerance is to tolerate the intolerable" (some "intolerable" situations are facts of life that no amount of protest will change). You can imagine how long "to lose is to win" would survive on an American

Thinking Critically About the Benefits of Control

locus of control
A general expectation about whether the results of your actions are under your own control (internal locus) or beyond your control (external locus).

primary control
An effort to modify reality by changing other people, the situation, or events; a "fighting back" philosophy.

secondary control
An effort to accept reality by changing your own attitudes, goals, or emotions; a "learn to live with it" philosophy.

Having a sense of control over your life is generally a good thing. But how much control does a factory worker, whose job is routine and closely supervised, actually have? What about a farm couple who are at the mercy of losing their lands and livelihoods when the economy changes? When is it realistic to believe we can control what happens to us, and when is such a belief counterproductive?

football field, or how long most Americans would be prepared to tolerate the intolerable!

People who are ill or under stress can reap the benefits of both Western and Eastern forms of control by taking responsibility for future actions, while not blaming themselves unduly for past ones (Thompson, Nanni, & Levine, 1994). Among women coping with cancer, for example, adjustment is related to a woman's belief that she is not to blame for getting sick but that she *is* in charge of taking care of herself from now on (Taylor, Lichtman, & Wood, 1984). "I felt that I had lost control of my body somehow," said one woman, "and the way for me to get back some control was to find out as much as I could." This way of thinking allows a person to avoid guilt and self-blame while retaining a sense of self-efficacy. Most problems require us to decide what we can change and to accept what we cannot; perhaps the secret of healthy control lies in knowing the difference.

QUICK QUIZ

We hope these questions are not sources of stress for you.

1. Steve is unexpectedly called on in class to discuss a question. He hasn't the faintest idea of the answer, and he feels his heart start to pound and his palms to sweat. According to Selye, Steve is in the _____ phase of his stress response.

2. Maria has worked as a file clerk for 17 years, in a job that is closely supervised, predictable, and boring. Her boss must make many rapid-fire decisions every day and always complains about the pressures of responsibility. Which of them probably has the more stressful job? (a) Maria, (b) the boss, (c) both equally, (d) neither job is stressful

3. "I'll never find anyone else to love because I'm not good-looking; that one romance was a fluke" illustrates a(n) _____ explanatory style.

4. On television, a self-described health expert explains that "no one gets sick if they don't want to be sick," because we can all control our bodies. As a critical thinker, how should you assess this claim?

Answers:
1. alarm   2. a   3. pessimistic   4. Skeptically. First, you would define your terms: What does "control" mean, and what kind of control is the supposed expert referring to? People can control some things, such as the decision to exercise and quit smoking, and they can control some aspects of treatment once they become ill; but they do not have control over everything that happens to them. Second, you would examine the assumption that control is always a good thing; the belief that we have total control over our lives could lead to depression and unwarranted self-blame when illness strikes.

What's Ahead

- Why are people who are chronically angry and mistrustful their own worst enemy?

- Which disease is depression most clearly linked to?

- How can revealing your unresolved feelings about a past trauma help your health?

12.4 Stress and Emotion

Perhaps you have heard people say things like "She was so depressed, it's no wonder she got cancer" or "He's always so angry he's going to give himself a heart attack one day." Are negative emotions—anger, anxiety, and depression—hazardous to your health?

There is good evidence that *once a person has a virus or medical condition,* negative emotions are indeed influential in affecting the course of the illness. Feeling anxious, helpless, and depressed, for example, can delay the healing of wounds after surgery and recovery from illness, whereas feeling optimistic and able to cope can speed healing and recovery significantly (Frasure-Smith et al., 1999; Kiecolt-Glaser et al., 1998).

However, evidence for the popular idea that negative emotions can *cause* illness all on their own is much murkier. Unfortunately, we will all have to live with some uncertainty on this matter. Let's see why.

Hostility and Depression

One of the first modern efforts to link emotions and illness was research in the 1970s on the *Type A personality,* a set of qualities thought to be associated with heart disease (Friedman & Rosenman, 1974).

Type A people are determined to achieve, have a sense of time urgency, are irritable, respond physiologically to threat and challenge very quickly, and are impatient with anyone who gets in their way. Type B people are calmer and less intense. It seemed logical that Type A's would be at greater risk of heart trouble than Type B's.

It turned out, however, that being highly reactive to stress and challenge is not in itself a risk factor in heart disease (Krantz & Manuck, 1984). The next round of research uncovered what it was about the behavior of some Type A's that *is* dangerous to health: hostility. By "hostility" we do not mean the irritability or anger that everyone feels on occasion. The toxic kind is *cynical* or *antagonistic hostility,* which characterizes people who are mistrustful of others and ready to provoke mean, furious arguments (Marshall et al., 1994; T. Miller et al., 1996). In a study of male physicians who had been interviewed as medical students 25 years earlier, those who were chronically angry and resentful were five times as likely as nonhostile men to get heart disease, even when other risk factors, such as smoking and a poor diet, were taken into account (Ewart & Kolodner, 1994; Williams, Barefoot, & Shekelle, 1985) (see Figure 12.3). These findings have been repeated in other large-scale studies, with blacks and whites, and with women as well as men. Proneness to anger is a significant risk factor, all on its own, for coronary heart disease (Williams et al., 2000).

Can depression also lead to illness? In two studies that each followed more than 1,000 people for many years, those who had been clinically depressed at the outset were two to four times more likely to have a heart attack than nondepressed people were. This finding, too, held up even after the researchers controlled for high blood pressure and smoking (Pratt et al., 1996), and even when they controlled for obesity, amount of exercise, and family history of heart disease (Ford et al., 1998). Yet other studies get different results; for example, a large study of elderly people found no link between depression and heart disease (Mendes de Leon et al., 1998). Maybe the connection depends on the age or generation of the people being studied.

A classic Type A personality in action.

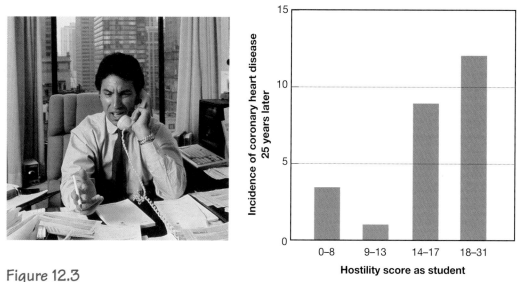

Figure 12.3
Hostility and Heart Disease

Anger is more hazardous to health than is a heavy work load. Men who had the highest hostility scores as young medical students were the most likely to have coronary heart disease 25 years later (Williams, Barefoot, & Shekelle, 1985).

Evidence that depression is involved in other diseases, such as cancer and AIDS, is also conflicting (Lyketsos et al., 1993; Penninx et al., 1998). All we can say at present, therefore, is that chronic depression *may* be a risk factor for heart disease and possibly other diseases as well.

Emotional Inhibition

Now pay attention: *Don't think of a white bear.* Are you not thinking of it?

You might assume by now that the safest thing to do when you feel angry, depressed, or worried is to try to suppress the feeling. But anyone who has tried to banish an unwelcome thought, bitter memory, or pangs of longing for an absent lover knows how hard it can be to do this. In an actual study, people who were told not to think of a white bear mentioned it nine times in a five-minute stream-of-consciousness session (Wegner et al., 1987). When you are trying to avoid a thought, you are in fact processing the thought more frequently—rehearsing it. That is why, when you are obsessed with someone you were once romantically involved with, trying not to think of the person actually prolongs your emotional responsiveness to him or her (Wegner & Gold, 1995).

Most people try to suppress their feelings some of the time, but some people, "suppressors," do so almost all of the time; they have a personality trait called *emotional inhibition* (Basic Behavioral Science Task Force, 1996). Suppressors tend to deny feelings of anxiety, anger, or fear and pretend that everything is fine. Yet, when they are in stressful or emotion-producing situations, their physiological responses, such as heart rate and blood pressure, rise sharply. Suppressors are at greater risk of becoming ill than people who can acknowledge their fears, and once they contract a serious disease, they may even die sooner (Cohen & Herbert, 1996).

Why should emotional inhibition increase the risk of health problems? One possibility is that the prolonged inhibition of thoughts and emotions requires physical effort that is stressful to the body (Pennebaker, 1995; Smyth & Pennebaker, 1999). The inability or unwillingness to confide important or traumatic events also seems to place continuing stress on the immune system. People who are able to express matters of great emotional importance to them show elevated levels of circulating white blood cells, whereas people who suppress such feelings tend to have decreased levels of these disease-fighting cells (Petrie, Booth, & Pennebaker, 1998).

Given these findings, it would seem that divulging private thoughts and feelings that make you ashamed or depressed would be helpful, both psychologically and physically. It certainly was for a class of students going through a normal but stressful transition: starting college. Freshmen who wrote about their feelings about leaving home and being in college reported greater homesickness and anxiety in the short run, compared to students who wrote about trivial topics. But by the end of the school year they had had fewer bouts of flu and visits to the infirmary than the control group (Pennebaker, Colder, & Sharp, 1990).

Confession is also beneficial for people who feel they are carrying the burden of painful secrets.

Everyone has secrets and private moments of sad reflection. But when you feel sad, anxious, or fearful for too long, keeping your feelings to yourself may increase your stress.

A group of college students was assigned to write about either a personal, traumatic experience or a neutral topic for 20 minutes a day for four days. Those who were asked to reveal their "deepest thoughts and feelings" about a traumatic event all had something to talk about. Many told stories of sexual coercion, physical beatings, humiliation, or parental abandonment. Yet most had never discussed these feelings with anyone. The researchers collected data on the students' physical symptoms, white-blood-cell counts, emotions, and visits to the health center. On every measure, the students who wrote about traumatic experiences were better off than those who did not (Pennebaker, Kiecolt-Glaser, & Glaser, 1988). Some of them showed short-term increases in anger and depression; writing about an unpleasant experience, after all, was disturbing. But over time, their health and well-being improved.

Confession works when it produces insight and understanding, thereby ending the stressful repetition of obsessive thoughts and unresolved feelings (Lepore, 1997). One young woman, who had been molested at age 9 by a boy a year older, at first wrote about her feelings of embarrassment and guilt. By the third day, she was writing about how angry she felt at the boy. By the last day, she had begun to see the whole event differently; he was a child too, after all. When the study was over, she said, "Before, when I thought about it, I'd lie to myself. . . . Now, I don't feel like I even have to think about it because I got it off my chest. I finally admitted that it happened."

How strong, overall, is the link between emotion and illness? Some researchers believe that the inhibition or expression of specific negative emotions can be tied to specific illnesses, such as cancer

Thinking Critically About Emotions and Health

or heart disease (Eysenck, 1993). Others caution against exaggerating the role of emotion in health, arguing that we must not overlook the stronger influences of chronic stressors in the environment, the biology of the disease, and the individual's health habits, such as smoking (Jorgensen et al., 1996).

Both sides, however, agree that the links between emotions and illness should not be oversimplified. Living with unresolved negative emotions can be stressful to the body, but a life of con-

stant stress also tends to foster negative emotions. Depression and anxiety may contribute to illness in some individuals, but illness also makes some people depressed or anxious. Emotional inhibition is hazardous to some people's health, but so is constant emotional ventilation, which violates social and cultural rules and can alienate others (Kelly & McKillop, 1996; Wellenkamp, 1995). Health psychology suggests a middle path: learning to identify, express, and deal with our negative emotions, without ruminating on them and letting them dominate our lives or erode our relationships.

QUICK QUIZ

You'll reduce stress and experience positive emotions if you can answer these questions.

1. Which aspect of Type A behavior seems most hazardous to men's health? (a) working hard, (b) being in a hurry, (c) cynical hostility, (d) high physical reactivity to work, (e) general grumpiness

2. Alexa has many worries about being in college, but she is afraid to tell anyone. What might be the healthiest solution for her? (a) exercise, (b) writing down her feelings in a diary, (c) talking frequently to strangers who won't judge her, (d) expressing her hostility whenever she feels it

Answers: 1.c 2.b

What's Ahead

- When you're feeling overwhelmed, what are some ways to calm yourself?
- Why is it important to move beyond the emotions caused by a problem and deal with the problem itself?
- How can you learn to rethink your problems?
- When do friends reduce your stress, and when do they just make matters worse?

12.5 Emotions, Stress, and Health: How to Cope

We have noted that most people who are under stress, even those living in continuing, difficult situations, do not become ill. In addition to feeling

optimistic and in control, and not wallowing around in negative emotions, how do they manage to cope?

Cooling Off

The most immediate way to cope with the physiological tension of stress and negative emotions is to calm down: to take time out and reduce the body's physical arousal.

One of the best ways to calm yourself is to meditate or use conscious relaxation techniques. *Relaxation training*—learning to alternately tense and relax the muscles, to lie or sit quietly, or to meditate by clearing your mind and banishing worries of the day—has beneficial effects on the body, by lowering stress hormones and enhancing immune function (Gruber et al., 1993; Kiecolt-Glaser et al., 1985b).

Another excellent buffer between stressors and physical symptoms is exercise. A low level of physical activity is associated with decreased life expectancy for both sexes and contributes independently to the development of many chronic diseases (Dubbert, 1992). As you can see in Figure 12.4, when people are experiencing the same objective pressures, those who are physically fit have fewer health problems than people who are less fit; they also show less physiological arousal to stressors and pay fewer visits to the doctor. The more that people exercise, the less anxious, depressed, and irritable they are, and the fewer physical symptoms and colds they have (Hendrix et al., 1991).

Perhaps you can think of other ways to cool off when you're hot and bothered. Many people respond beneficially to the soothing touch of massage (Field, 1998). Others listen to music, write in a journal, or bake bread. Such activities give the body a chance to recover from the "alarm phase" of its stress response and from the intensity of negative emotions. However, you can't always jog away from your problems. Relaxation is not going to change the fact that you may lose your job, your best friend has betrayed a confidence, or you need a serious operation. Sometimes other coping strategies are necessary.

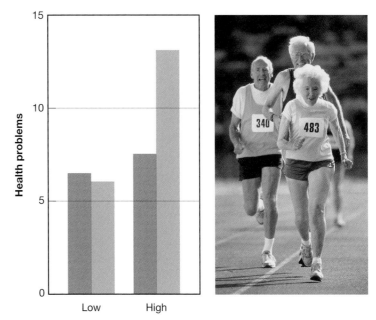

Figure 12.4
Fitness and Health
Among people under low stress, aerobically fit individuals had about the same number of health problems as those who were less fit. But among people under high stress, fit individuals had fewer health problems (Roth & Holmes, 1985).

Solving the Problem

A woman we know, whom we will call Nancy, was struck by tragedy when she was 22. She and her new husband were driving home one evening when a car went out of control and crashed into them. When Nancy awoke in a hospital room, she learned that her husband had been killed and that she herself had permanent spinal injury and would never walk again. For many months, Nancy reacted with understandable rage and despair. "Get it out of your system," her friends said. "You need to get in touch with your feelings." "But I know I'm miserable," Nancy lamented. "What do I *do?*"

Nancy's friends' advice and her reply illustrate the difference between *emotion-focused* and *problem-focused coping* (Lazarus & Folkman, 1984; Stanton & Franz, 1999). Emotion-focused coping concentrates on the emotions the problem has caused, whether anger, anxiety, or grief. For a period of time after any personal tragedy or traumatic natural disaster, it is normal to give in to these emotions and feel overwhelmed by them. In this stage, people often need to talk about the event in order to come to terms with it and make sense of it, before deciding

what to do about it (Lepore, Ragan, & Jones, 2000; Lepore et al., 1996).

Eventually, though, most people are ready to move beyond their emotional state and concentrate on solving the problem itself, whether it is preparing for an operation, learning how to adjust to a continuing situation, or recovering from a major setback. The coper can learn as much as possible about the problem from professionals, friends, books, and others in the same predicament (Clarke & Evans, 1998). Over time, problem-focused strategies are associated with better adjustment than are emotion-focused ones. Problem-focused coping tends to increase self-efficacy and reduce anger, anxiety, and physiological stress (Folkman & Moskowitz, 2000). By requiring you to think critically—that is, to consider alternatives and resist emotional reasoning—it often leads to constructive solutions.

In Nancy's case, she learned more about her medical condition and prognosis, how other accident victims had coped, and the occupations that were possible for her (which was most of them). Nancy stayed in school, remarried, got a Ph.D. in psychology, and now does research and counseling with disabled people.

Rethinking the Problem

Some problems cannot be "solved"; these are the tragedies that occur out of the blue and the unavoidable facts of life, such as getting older or becoming ill. Even when you cannot fix a problem, however, you can change the way you think about it. Here are four effective cognitive coping methods that help people not only *survive* a crisis, but *thrive* as a result of it—coming out stronger than they were before (Carver, 1998; Folkman & Moskowitz, 2000).

1 *Reappraising the situation.* Although you may not be able to get rid of a stressor (that nasty neighbor is unlikely to move; you cannot undo the fact that you lost your job), you can choose to think about it differently. Problems can be turned into challenges, and losses into unexpected gains. Maybe that job you lost was pretty dismal but you were too afraid to look for another; now you can. *Reappraisal* is also effective because it changes your emotional responses, turning anger into sympathy, worry into determination, or feelings of loss into feelings of opportunity.

2 *Learning from the experience.* Even when people suffer major losses, traumas, and serious illnesses, they can often find useful lessons in them. For example, a study of people with spinal-cord injuries found that two-thirds of them felt the disability had had positive side effects. They named such benefits as becoming a better person, seeing the value in other people, and gaining a

The ultimate example of rethinking your problems.

new appreciation of "brain, not brawn" (Schulz & Decker, 1985).

Some people emerge from adversity with newfound or newly acquired skills, having been forced to learn something they had not known before—how to cope with the medical system, say, or how to manage a deceased parent's estate. Others discover sources of courage and strength they did not know they had. People who are able to draw lessons from the inescapable tragedies of life, or find meaning in them, are far better off psychologically than are people who remain stuck in the past (Davis, Nolen-Hoeksema, & Larson, 1998; Taylor et al., 2000).

3 *Making social comparisons.* In a difficult situation, successful copers often compare themselves to others who are either doing better than they are or who are even less fortunate (Wood & VanderZee, 1997). In the former case, the coper says, in effect, "I'm devastated about this diagnosis of cancer, but look at how well those survivors are doing; I'd better learn how they did it." But sometimes the coper's most therapeutic comparison is to someone who is worse off (Taylor & Lobel, 1989). One AIDS sufferer said, "I made a list of all the other diseases I would rather not have than AIDS. Lou Gehrig's disease, being in a wheelchair; rheumatoid arthritis, when you are in knots and in terrible pain. So I said, 'You've got to get some perspective on this, and where you are on the Great Nasty Disease List'" (Reed, 1990).

4 *Cultivating a sense of humor.* "A merry heart doeth good like a medicine," says Proverbs in the Old Testament, and so it does. People who can see the absurd or whimsical aspects of a bad situation are less prone to depression, anger, and physical tension than are people who give in to gloom, moping, and tears (P. Fry, 1995; J. Solomon, 1996). In people with serious illnesses, humor reduces distress, improves immune functioning, and hastens recovery from surgery (Carver et al., 1993; Martin & Dobbin, 1988). It may also stimulate the flow of endorphins, the painkilling chemicals in the brain (W. Fry, 1994). Humor also has mental benefits. When you laugh at a problem, you are putting it in a new perspective—seeing its silly aspects—and gaining a sense of control over it.

Looking Outward

A final way to deal with negative emotions and stress is to reach out to others. Think of all the ways in which family members, friends, neighbors, and co-workers can help you. They can offer concern and affection. They can help you evaluate problems and plan a course of action. They can offer resources and services such as lending you money or a car, or taking notes in class for you when you are sick. Most of all, they are sources of attachment and connection, which everyone needs throughout life.

When Friends Help You Cope . . .

Friends are not just a nice part of life; they can improve your health and even save your life. Remember the study we described earlier, showing that stress increases your risk of getting a cold? Well, having a lot of friends and social contacts reduces that risk. In a group of nearly 300 volunteers exposed to a flu virus, those with the most friends were the least likely to get sick (Cohen et al., 1997). Social support is even more important for people who have extremely stressful jobs that require high cardiovascular responsiveness day after day, such as firefighters. Something about social support literally helps the heart rate return to normal more quickly after a stressful episode (Roy, Steptoe, & Kirschbaum, 1998).

People who live in a network of close connections even live longer than those who do not. In two major studies that followed thousands of adults for ten years, people who had many friends, social connections, or memberships in church and other groups were more likely to live longer than those who had few. The importance of having social networks was unrelated to physical health at the time the studies began, to socioeconomic status, and to risk factors like smoking (Berkman & Syme, 1979; House, Landis, & Umberson, 1988). In some cases, social-support groups can even extend the survival time of people with serious illnesses. In a group of older men and women who had had heart attacks, 58 percent of those who reported having no close contacts died within the year, compared with only 27 percent of those who said they had two or more people they could count on (Berkman, Leo-Summers, & Horwitz, 1992). Even when social support does not lengthen the lives of people with terminal illnesses, it often lessens their suffering and pain.

. . . And Coping with Friends.

Of course, sometimes other people *aren't* helpful. Sometimes they themselves are the source of unhappiness, stress, and anger.

In close relationships, the same person who is a source of support can also become a source of stress, especially if the two parties are arguing all the time. Constant fights can elevate both partners' blood pressures and suppress the immune system, too. Married couples who argue in a hostile fashion—criticizing, interrupting, or insulting the other person, and becoming angry and defensive—show significant elevations of stress hormones and impairments of immune

Friends can be our greatest source of warmth, support, and fun . . . .

. . . and also sources of exasperation, anger, and misery.

function afterward. Couples who argue in a positive fashion—trying to find common ground, compromising, listening to each other's concerns, and using humor to defuse tension—do not show these impairments (Kiecolt-Glaser et al., 1993; Malarkey et al., 1994). As one student of ours observed, "This study gives new meaning to the accusation 'You make me sick!'" It also suggests that learning to argue fairly and constructively may have physical as well as psychological benefits.

In addition to being sources of conflict, friends and relatives may be unsupportive in times of disaster or illness simply out of ignorance or awkwardness. They may abandon you or say something stupid and hurtful. Sometimes they actively block your efforts to change bad health habits—say, to cut down on binge drinking or smoking—by making fun of you or pressuring you to conform to what "everyone" does. And sometimes, because they have never been in the same situation and don't know what to do to help, they offer the wrong kind of support. For example, they may try to cheer you up, saying "Everything will be fine," rather than let you talk about your fears or find solutions (Bolger et al., 1996). That is why support groups of people experiencing the same illness (such as breast cancer or AIDS), problem (such as a parent's alcoholism), or tragedy (such as the death of a child) are often more helpful than friends who haven't "been there" (see Chapter 11).

When thinking about stress and social support, we should also not forget the benefits of *giving* support, rather than always being on the receiving end. Julius Segal (1986), a psychologist who worked with Holocaust survivors, hostages, refugees, and other survivors of catastrophe, wrote that a key element in their recovery was compassion for others, "healing through helping." Why? The ability to look outside yourself is related to all of the successful coping mechanisms we have discussed. It encourages you to solve problems instead of blaming others or just venting your emotions, helps you reappraise the situation by seeing it from another person's perspective, and allows you to gain perspective on your own problems. "Healing through helping" thus helps you live with situations that are facts of life.

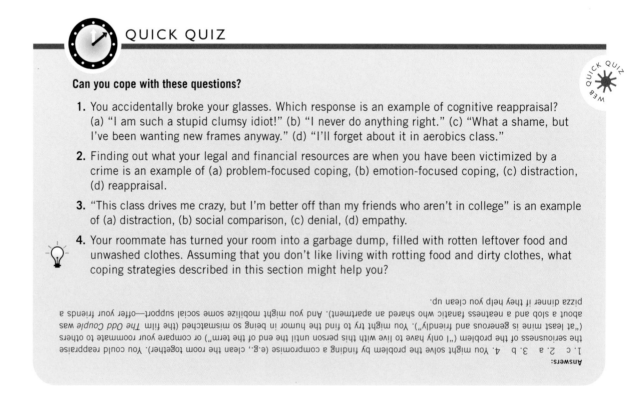

QUICK QUIZ

Can you cope with these questions?

1. You accidentally broke your glasses. Which response is an example of cognitive reappraisal? (a) "I am such a stupid clumsy idiot!" (b) "I never do anything right." (c) "What a shame, but I've been wanting new frames anyway." (d) "I'll forget about it in aerobics class."

2. Finding out what your legal and financial resources are when you have been victimized by a crime is an example of (a) problem-focused coping, (b) emotion-focused coping, (c) distraction, (d) reappraisal.

3. "This class drives me crazy, but I'm better off than my friends who aren't in college" is an example of (a) distraction, (b) social comparison, (c) denial, (d) empathy.

4. Your roommate has turned your room into a garbage dump, filled with rotten leftover food and unwashed clothes. Assuming that you don't like living with rotting food and dirty clothes, what coping strategies described in this section might help you?

Answers:

1. c   2. a   3. b   4. You might solve the problem by finding a compromise (e.g., clean the room together). You could reappraise the seriousness of the problem ("I only have to live with this person until the end of the term") or compare your roommate to others ("at least mine is generous and friendly"). You might try to find the humor in being so mismatched (the film *The Odd Couple* was about a slob and a neatness fanatic who shared an apartment). And you might mobilize some social support—offer your friends a pizza dinner if they help you clean up.

PSYCHOLOGY IN THE NEWS, REVISITED

Let us now consider how a better understanding of stress and emotion might help us understand the growing problem of "air rage" and what we can do about it. In a world that is getting noisier and more crowded, being stuck in a crowd at the airport or being caught in an endless traffic jam may feel like the last straw to some people, especially to those who are already anxious, hostile, or impatient. In 1991, there were only 99 reports of unruly behavior by airplane passengers, but in 1998 there were 283. The Air Transport Association told *The New York Times* that a big factor contributing to air rage is airport crowding and delays. Newark Airport, where the confrontation in our opening story occurred, was the eighth busiest American airport in 1999; departures and arrivals there had increased 55 percent since 1989. Newark was also ranked last among the nation's major airports for on-time arrivals.

However, as we have seen, your perceptions of a situation are as important as the situation itself in influencing your emotional response to it and the degree of stress you feel. When you are stuck in traffic or waiting for a delayed flight, if you tell yourself that being late to your destination is a horrible act of injustice and will be disastrous for your entire life, you are likely to feel extremely distressed. But if you decide that being late is trivial, as problems go, and that you can't do anything about it anyway, you may take the situation more calmly. If you interpret another person's poor driving habits as a personal insult or challenge, you are likely to be furious at that stupid driver who cut in front of you. But if you interpret the other driver's behavior more empathically—perhaps he or she is racing to a hospital, or just doesn't know any better, poor dolt—you are less likely to feel angry. A therapist we know has a wonderful reappraisal tactic: He helps motorists reduce their stress and rage on the highway by having them visualize other drivers as donkeys—certainly a better technique than *calling* another driver a donkey!

In "Taking Psychology with You," we offer further suggestions for handling anger in the sky, on the road, or anywhere else. Keep in mind, though, that successful coping does not mean eliminating all sources of stress or all difficult emotions. It does not mean constant happiness or a life without pain and frustration. The healthy person faces problems, deals with them, and gets beyond them, but the problems are necessary if the person is to acquire coping skills that endure. To wish for a life without stress, or a life without emotion, would be like wishing for a life without friends. The result might be calm, but it would be joyless and ultimately hazardous to your health. The stresses and passions of life—the daily hassles, the emotional ups and downs, and the occasional tragedies—force us to grow, and to grow up.

TAKING PSYCHOLOGY WITH YOU

The Dilemma of Anger—"Let It Out" or "Bottle It Up"?

What do you do when you feel angry? Do you tend to brood and sulk, collecting your righteous complaints like acorns for the winter, or do you erupt, hurling your wrath upon anyone or anything at hand? Do you discuss your feelings when you have calmed down? Does "letting anger out" get rid of it for you, or does it only make it more intense? The answer is crucial for how you get along with your family, neighbors, employers, and strangers.

Chronic feelings of anger and an inability to control anger can be as emotionally devastating and unhealthy as chronic problems

with depression or anxiety. In contrast to much pop-psych advice, research shows that expressing anger does not always get it "out of your system"; often people feel worse after an angry confrontation, both physically and mentally (Bushman, Baumeister, & Stack, 1999; Tavris, 1989). When people talk incessantly about their anger or act on that feeling, they tend to rehearse their grievances and pump up their blood pressure. Conversely, when people learn to control their tempers and express anger constructively, they usually feel better, not

worse; calmer, not angrier (Deffenbacher et al., 1998).

When people are feeling angry, they have a choice of doing any number of things. They can write letters, play the piano, jog, try to solve the problem that is causing their anger, abuse their friends or family, hit a punching bag, or yell. If a particular action soothes their feelings or gets the desired response from others, they are likely to acquire a habit. Soon that habit feels "natural," as if it could never be changed; indeed, many people justify their violent tempers by saying, "I just couldn't help myself." But they can. If you have learned an abusive or aggressive habit, the research in this chapter offers practical suggestions for relearning constructive ways of managing anger:

● *Don't sound off in the heat of anger; let bodily arousal cool down.* Whether your arousal comes from background stresses such as heat, crowds, or loud noise, or from conflict with another person, take time to relax. Time allows you to decide whether you are really angry or just tired and tense. This is the reason for that sage old advice to count to 10, count to 100, or sleep on it. Other cooling-off strategies include taking a time-out in the middle of an argument, meditating or relaxing, and calming yourself with a distracting activity.

● *If you feel that you have been insulted, check your perception for its accuracy.* Could there be another reason for the behavior you find offensive? People who are quick to feel anger tend to interpret other people's actions as intentional offenses. People who are slow to anger tend to give others the benefit of the doubt, and they are not as focused on their own injured pride. Empathy ("Poor guy, he's feeling rotten") is usually incompatible

with anger, so practice seeing the situation from the other person's perspective. And be sure you understand another person's nonverbal communication before you decide that you have been insulted! In Stockton, California, a driver used a hand signal to alert a car behind him at a stoplight that his headlights were off. The driver of the second car interpreted this gesture as a sign of disrespect, shot at the first car—and killed a passenger.

● *If you decide that expressing anger is appropriate, be sure you use the right verbal and nonverbal language to make yourself understood.* Because different cultures have different display rules, be sure the recipient of your anger understands what you are feeling and what complaint you are trying to convey. Some people come from cultures in which the direct expression of anger is considered rude, aggressive, and childish; others come from cultures in which the direct expression of anger is considered healthy, desirable, and mature. (If a person from the former culture marries someone from the latter, you can image the misunderstandings they might have!) Within cultures, too, people differ in the display roles they have learned from their families or through their own experiences. If your way of expressing

anger is to sulk, expecting everyone else to read your mind and apologize to you, you are probably not communicating clearly.

● *Think carefully about how to express anger so that you will get the results you want.* What do you want your anger to accomplish? Do you just want to make the other person feel bad, or do you want the other person to understand your concerns and make amends? Shouting "You turkey! How *could* you be so stupid!" might accomplish the former goal, but it's not likely to get the person to apologize, let alone to change his or her behavior.

If your goal in expressing anger is to restore your rights, persuade the other person to change in some way, improve a bad situation, or achieve justice, then learning how to express anger so the other person will listen is essential. People who have been the targets of injustice have learned that outbursts of anger may draw society's attention to a problem, but real change requires sustained political effort, challenges to unfair laws, and the use of tactics that persuade rather than alienate the opposition.

Of course, if you just want to blow off steam, go right ahead; but you risk becoming a hothead.

SUMMARY

The Nature of Emotion

● Thoughts and emotions are not "opposite"; each influences the other. Both processes can be rational or irrational, and both are necessary for making plans and wise decisions. The complex experience of *emotion* involves physiological changes in the face, brain, and autonomic nervous system; cognitive processes; and cultural norms and regulations.

● Some basic facial expressions—anger, fear, sadness, happiness, disgust, surprise, contempt—are widely recognized across cultures. But, as the *neurocultural theory* emphasizes, culture interacts with physiology to influence when and how emotions are displayed.

● Emotional expressions probably evolved to express internal states and communicate with others, functions that are apparent even in infancy. The *facial feedback* provided by emotional expressions also helps us to identify our own emotional states. However, because people can and do disguise their emotions, their expressions do not always communicate accurately.

● Many aspects of emotion are associated with specific parts of the brain. The right hemisphere is specialized for experiencing negative emotions (such as depression) and the left hemisphere for positive ones (such as happiness). The *amygdala* is responsible for initially evaluating the emotional importance of incoming sensory information. The *cerebral cortex* provides the cognitive ability to override this initial appraisal.

● During the experience of any emotion, *epinephrine* and *norepinephrine* produce a state of physiological arousal to prepare the body for an output of energy. But different emotions are also associated with different patterns of autonomic nervous system activity.

● The *two-factor theory of emotion* held that emotions result from physiological arousal and the labeling or interpretation of that arousal. Research spurred by this theory has investigated the cognitive processes involved in different emotions, such as the *attributions* people make about others' behavior and the way people interpret and evaluate events. When people mislabel their own physiological state, making an incorrect attribution, they may feel an emotion that is inappropriate to the situation.

● Some emotions involve simple, nonconscious reactions, such as a conditioned response to an emotional symbol. Others, such as shame and guilt, require complex cognitive capacities. As children mature, their cognitions and therefore their emotions become more complex.

Emotion and Culture

● Some researchers distinguish *primary emotions,* which are thought to be universal, from *secondary emotions,* which are specific to cultures. The list of primary emotions typically includes fear, anger, sadness, joy, surprise, disgust, and contempt. Other psychologists question the effort to find primary emotions. They argue that culture affects every aspect of emotional experience, including which emotions are considered basic and what people feel emotional about.

● Cultural *display rules* regulate how, when, and where a person may express or must suppress an emotion, and the *emotion work* a person is expected to do to convey an emotion that he or she does not feel. Cultural differences in the rules governing facial expressions and *body language* can lead to misunderstandings. Men and women experience the same emotions, but often differ in the display rules that govern how and when they express their feelings. The influence of a particular situation, however, can override gender rules. Cultures differ in the display rules that govern men's and women's emotional expressions.

The Nature of Stress

● Hans Selye argued that environmental *stressors* such as heat, pain, and toxins cause the body to respond in three stages: *alarm, resistance,* and *exhaustion.* If a stressor persists, it may overwhelm the body's ability to cope, and fatigue or illness may result. Studies of the immune system have confirmed that stress can suppress the activity of white blood cells and make illness more likely.

● Stressors especially likely to affect the body include uncontrollable, chronic noise; bereavement and loss; unemployment and work-related problems; and poverty, powerlessness, and racism. But even these stressors do not have the same effect on everyone. Therefore, modern views of the stress-illness link include psychological factors (such as the individual's perceptions of the stressor) and how the individual copes with the stressor.

● Two important cognitive factors that intervene between stress and illness are having an *optimistic explanatory style* (in contrast to a *pessimistic* one) and having an internal rather than external *locus of control.* Optimism and a sense of control improve immune function and also increase a person's ability to tolerate pain, live with ongoing problems, and recover more rapidly from illness. Optimists and people with an internal locus of control are more likely to actively solve their problems, and they may be more likely to take care of themselves. Optimists may rely on some "positive illusions" to keep themselves going, but they do not deny or avoid their problems.

● Health and well-being may depend on the right combination of *primary control* (trying to change the stressful situation) and *secondary control* (learning to accept and accommodate to a stressful situation). Cultures differ in the kind of control they emphasize and value.

Stress and Emotion

● Researchers have sought links between personality traits and illness. Having a competitive, impatient *Type A personality* is not itself related to heart disease, but *cynical or antagonistic hostility,* which is often part of the Type A pattern, is. Chronic depression also seems to be a risk factor in causing heart disease, but its link to other illnesses remains unclear.

• People who are emotionally inhibited are at greater risk of illness than people who acknowledge and cope with negative emotions. The effort to suppress worries, secrets, and memories of upsetting experiences can paradoxically lead to obsessively ruminating on these thoughts and become stressful to the body.

Emotions, Stress, and Health: How to Cope

• One way to cope with stress and negative emotions is to reduce their physical effects, for example, through relaxation and exercise. Another is to focus on solving the problem (*problem-focused coping*) rather than on ventilating the emotions caused by the problem (*emotion-focused coping*). A third is to rethink the problem by *reappraising* the situation, learning from the experience, comparing yourself with others who are less fortunate, or applying humor.

• Social support—the help, advice, and emotional connection provided by family and friends—is essential in maintaining physical health and emotional well-being; it even prolongs life and speeds recovery from illness. However, friends and family can also be sources of stress themselves. In close relationships, couples who fight in a hostile and negative way show impaired immune function. *Giving* social support to others—"healing by helping"—is also an important positive form of coping.

• Coping with stress does not mean trying to live without pain or problems. It means learning how to live with them.

KEY TERMS

emotion 398
neurocultural theory of emotional expressions 398
facial feedback 400
amygdala 402
epinephrine 402
norepinephrine 402
two-factor theory of emotion 404
attributions 404
primary emotions 406
secondary emotions 406

display rules 407
body language 408
emotion work 408
stressors 410
alarm, resistance, and exhaustion phases of stress 411
psychological stress 413
pessimistic and optimistic explanatory styles 413
internal versus external locus of control 415

primary control 415
secondary control 415
Type A personality 417
cynical/antagonistic hostility 417
emotional inhibition 418
relaxation training 420
emotion-focused coping 421
problem-focused coping 421
reappraisal 422
social comparison 422

LOOKING BACK

• Which facial expressions of emotion do people recognize all over the world? (p. 398)

• Which side of your brain is most active when you're filled with joy—or despair? (p. 401)

• Which two hormones can make you "too excited to eat"? (p. 402)

• In a competition, who is likely to be happier—the third-place winner or the second-place winner? (p. 404)

• Why can't an infant feel shame or guilt? (p. 405)

• Are the "basic" emotions basic everywhere? (pp. 406–407)

• Do Germans, Japanese, and Americans always mean the same thing when they smile at others? (pp. 407–408)

• Why do people feel obliged to show sadness at funerals even when they are not feeling sad? (p. 408)

- Are women really more emotional than men? (pp. 409–410)

- Why are you more likely to get a cold when you're "stressed out"? (p. 411)

- Which stressors pose the greatest hazard to your health? (pp. 412–413)

- Why do optimists tend to live longer than pessimists? (p. 414)

- When is a sense of control good for you, and when is it not? (pp. 415–416)

- Why are people who are chronically angry and mistrustful their own worst enemy? (p. 417)

- Which disease is depression most clearly linked to? (p. 417)

- How can revealing your unresolved feelings about a past trauma help your health? (p. 419)

- When you're feeling overwhelmed, what are some ways to calm yourself? (pp. 420–421)

- Why is it important to move beyond the emotions caused by a problem and deal with the problem itself? (p. 421)

- How can you learn to rethink your problems? (p. 422)

- When do friends reduce your stress, and when do they just make matters worse? (pp. 423–424)

PSYCHOLOGY IN THE NEWS

"Titanic" Refuses to Sink, Draws Huge Repeat Business

LOS ANGELES, CA, MARCH 11, 1998. *Titanic* has passed *Star Wars* as the top moneymaking film of all time, thanks to loyalists who have returned to view it two, three, or even more times. Software engineer Jim Sadur, 42, saw the movie twice and cried both times. "If you didn't," he said, "you may not have a pulse." A 23-year-old teacher, having seen the film a third time with her sister, said, "That's the kind of love I want for myself. Now that I know it exists, I'm going to wait for exactly the right man."

Naval Academy Football Stars Charged with Rape

WASHINGTON, DC, JULY 3, 2000. Three midshipmen at the Naval Academy in Annapolis have been charged with raping a female midshipman at an off-campus party. The woman, who apparently had passed out after drinking at the party, awoke to find the men assaulting her and tried to push them away. The three men, star football players at the Academy, face a maximum prison sentence of 20 years if convicted. The case has renewed debate over what some critics regard as the "climate of privilege and leniency" that many athletes are accorded across the country.

Lance Armstrong Defeats Cancer, Wins Tour de France for Second Time

PARIS, FRANCE, JULY 23, 2000. Amid throngs of jubilant fans lining the streets of Paris to greet his arrival, Lance Armstrong won the three-week Tour de France today. Victory in the grueling bicycle race, which covers 2,300 miles across the mountains of France, was particularly dramatic for Armstrong because of his recovery from testicular cancer that had spread to his abdomen, lungs, and brain. The cancer, diagnosed in 1996, was arrested by two operations and intensive chemotherapy. By 1998, Armstrong was ready to retire from the sport, but eventually he came back to win the Tour de France in both 1999 and again today.

▲ **Lance Armstrong arriving at the finish line of the Tour de France as thousands cheer him on.**

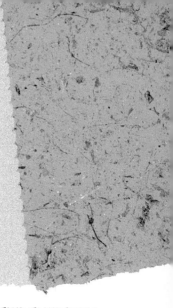

Dying to Be Thin

WASHINGTON, DC, NOVEM-BER 7, 2000. More bad news for dieters was revealed today. A new study reports that ephedra, a powerful herbal stimulant commonly used for weight loss, can cause strokes, permanent disability, and even death from heart attacks. The news follows on a recent federal decision upholding a multi-million-dollar settlement against the makers of fenfluramine, part of the diet drug "fen-phen," which was removed from the market after being linked to heart-valve damage in otherwise healthy users, and to numerous deaths.

THE MAJOR MOTIVES OF LIFE: LOVE, SEX, FOOD, AND WORK

What attracts so many women and men to the love story in *Titanic*? What are the reasons for sexual misunderstandings and aggression? Why do so many people struggle to lose weight, even subjecting themselves to the risks of drugs and surgery, and why do so many dieters fail? What motivates people like Lance Armstrong to pursue their dreams, in spite of setbacks that would cause so many others to give up?

The word *motivation,* like the word *emotion,* comes from the Latin root meaning "to move," and the psychology of motivation is indeed the study of what moves us, why we do what we do. To psychologists, **motivation** refers to an inferred process within a person or animal, which causes that organism to move *toward* a goal or *away from* an unpleasant situation. The goal may be to escape a scorpion or to satisfy a biological need, as in eating a sandwich to reduce hunger. The goal may be to fulfill an ambition, such as discovering a vaccine for AIDS or winning a Nobel Prize.

For many decades, the study of motivation was dominated by a focus on biological *drives,* states of tension resulting from the deprivation of physical needs, such as those for food or water. An organism in such a deprived state is motivated to satisfy the need—for example, by eating or drinking. Human beings, however, have only a few primary, unlearned drives, including the need to reduce hunger and thirst and avoid cold and pain. Most human motivations are psychological or social rather than biological: the determination to be famous, to study butterflies, or to be the first person to row across the Atlantic in a dinghy.

Today, therefore, motivation researchers emphasize the fact that people are conscious creatures who think and plan ahead, set goals for themselves, and plot strategies to reach those goals. In this chapter, we have chosen four examples to illustrate the cognitive, cultural, and biological components of human motivation: love, sex, eating, and achievement in work and other domains of life. As you read, see whether this information helps you understand the appeal of *Titanic,* the rape charges against the Navy athletes, the desperate risks some people take to lose weight, and the determination of Lance Armstrong to conquer both his illness and the mountains of France.

The gaze of love is unmistakable, even after years together.

did. Let's begin our examination of love by defining our terms.

The Varieties of Love

Do you have a favorite love story? Is it one where the couple falls madly in love at first sight, and, after a couple of silly misunderstandings, lives happily ever after, without a single quarrel or miserable moment? Or is your ideal love story captured by Rhett Butler's famous concluding remark to Scarlett in *Gone with the Wind:* "Frankly, my dear, I don't give a damn"?

What *is* love, exactly? Perhaps the oldest distinction is that between *passionate (romantic) love,* characterized by a turmoil of intense emotions and sexual passion, and *companionate love,* characterized by affection and trust (Hatfield & Rapson, 1996). Passionate love is the stuff of crushes, infatuations, "love at first sight," and the early stage of love affairs. It may burn out completely or subside into companionate love. But psychologists who study love (it's a tough job, but someone's got to do it) think that love comes in more varieties than two. Here are three leading theories about what they are.

1 *The six styles of love.* After surveying hundreds of people, John Alan Lee (1973, 1988) proposed that there are six distinct kinds of love, which he labeled with Greek names. Psychologists have empirically validated Lee's work by administering a Love Attitudes Scale to thousands of adults in such ethnically diverse cities as Miami (Hendrick & Hendrick, 1992, 1997) and Toronto (Dion & Dion, 1993). The six "styles" of love that Lee described are:

What's Ahead

- What kind of lover defines love as jealousy and possessiveness, and what kind defines it as just the opposite—calm compatibility?

- Do men and women differ in the ability to love?

- How are your beliefs about love affected by your income?

13.1 The Social Animal: Motives for Love

Everybody needs somebody; even Batman has Robin. One of the deepest and most universal of human motives is the **need for affiliation,** the need to be with others, make friends, cooperate, love. Human survival depends on the child's ability to form attachments and learn from others, and on the adult's ability to form relationships with intimate partners, family, friends, and colleagues.

While the need for attachment and companionship is universal, however, the meanings and experiences of love—that most intense of attachments—are more diverse. "How do I love thee? Let me count the ways," wrote Elizabeth Barrett Browning in a love sonnet to Robert Browning. Social scientists have also counted the ways of loving, although not as poetically as Browning

motivation
An inferred process within a person or animal that causes movement either toward a goal or away from an unpleasant situation.

need for affiliation
The motive to associate with other people, as by seeking friends, companionship, or love.

> ## GET INVOLVED
> ▶ WHAT IS THIS THING CALLED LOVE?
>
> What qualities do you look for in a partner in a close relationship? Write down five qualities that matter most to you: intelligence, looks, sexiness, abilities, background, values, income, whatever. Now examine your list. What does it tell you about your own style of love, according to the theories discussed in the text? If you have a current partner—and have the nerve—ask the person which five qualities he or she regards as most important. Do your lists match?

■ *Eros* (romantic, passionate love). People who score high on eros believe in love at first sight and instant chemistry. They would agree, for example, that "My lover and I were attracted to each other immediately after we first met."

■ *Ludus* (game-playing love). Those who score high on ludic love like to play the game of love with several partners at once. They enjoy the chase more than the catch, agreeing that "I try to keep my lover a little uncertain about my commitment."

■ *Storge* [STOR-gay] (affectionate, friendly love). Those who score high on storge believe that true love grows out of friendship. They value companionship and trust, and they agree that "It is hard for me to say exactly when our friendship turned into love."

■ *Pragma* (logical, pragmatic love). Pragmatic lovers choose partners on the basis of a list of compatible traits. For example, they agree that "I considered what my lover was going to become in life before I committed myself to him or her."

■ *Mania* (possessive, dependent, "crazy" love). People who score high on mania yearn desperately for love but suffer from jealousy and worry when they find it. "When things aren't right with my lover and me," they would agree, "my stomach gets upset."

■ *Agape* [ah-GAH-pay] (unselfish love). Those who score high on agape think of love as a selfless, almost spiritual form of giving to the partner. They will say, "I always try to help my lover through difficult times."

2 *The triangle theory of love.* Robert Sternberg (1997) argues that the three ingredients of love are *passion* (euphoria and sexual excitement), *intimacy* (feeling free to talk about anything, feeling close to and understood by the loved one), and *commitment* (needing to be with the other person, being loyal). In this view, varieties of love occur because of the ways people combine the three elements. *Liking* is intimacy alone; *companionate love* is intimacy plus commitment, without passion; *romantic love* is intimacy plus passion, without commitment; *infatuation* is passion alone; *fatuous* (illusory or shallow) *love* is

passion plus commitment, without intimacy—like the whirlwind celebrity courtships that end in marriage but generally don't last; and *empty love* is commitment alone, without passion or intimacy. In Sternberg's view, the ideal or *consummate* form of love combines all three elements: passion, closeness, and the secure attachment that comes from commitment.

When people are asked to define the key ingredients of love, most do agree that love is a mix of passion, intimacy, and commitment (Aron & Westbay, 1996). However, in most relationships, over the years, romantic passion subsides and intimacy increases. Intimacy is based on deep knowledge of the other person, which accumulates gradually and thus needs time to reach a maximum degree of closeness; but passion is based on emotion, which is generated by novelty and change. That is why passion is usually highest at the beginning of a relationship, when two people begin to disclose things about themselves to each other, and lowest when knowledge of the other person's beliefs and habits is at its maximum—when it seems that there is nothing left to learn about the beloved. The negative correlation between passion and intimacy explains why passion is often reawakened when a couple is separated or unexpected crises occur, or when the couple takes up a new shared activity that brings them closer (Baumeister & Bratslavsky, 1999).

3 *The attachment theory of love.* The theory that has generated the most research and interest, by far, relates adult styles of love to types of infant attachment. According to Phillip Shaver and Cindy Hazan (1993), adults, just like babies, can be secure, avoidant, or anxious-ambivalent in their attachments (see Chapter 3). Securely attached lovers are, well, secure: They are rarely jealous or worried about being abandoned. Anxious or ambivalent lovers are always fretting about their relationships; they want to be close but worry that their partners will leave them. Other people often describe them as "clingy," which may be why they are more likely than secure lovers to suffer from unrequited love (Aron, Aron, & Allen, 1998). Avoidant people distrust and avoid intimate attachments.

In this view, people acquire their attachment styles in large part from how their parents cared for them. Surveys find that the distribution of the three basic styles of attachment among adults is very similar to that found for infants: about 59 percent secure, 25 percent avoidant, and 11 percent anxious. Further, the kind of relationships that people have as adults is strongly related to their reports of how their parents treated them (Mickelson, Kessler, & Shaver, 1997). Securely attached adults report having had warm, close relationships with their parents. Although they recognize their parents' flaws, they describe their parents as having been more benevolent and kind than insecurely attached people do. Anxious-ambivalent people report feeling more ambivalence toward their parents, especially their mothers, and also describe their parents ambivalently—as having been both punitive and kind. And people with an avoidant attachment style describe their parents in almost entirely negative terms, as having been cold, punishing, and rejecting (Levy, Blatt, & Shaver, 1998).

Keep in mind, however, that people's self-reports about their parents or childhoods may be influenced more by their *current* perceptions of their parents, and by their own positive or negative temperaments, than by how the parents actually treated them.

These three theories differ in key ways, but the general overlap among them suggests that they are describing many of the same things. However, a person's style of love is not necessarily permanent. Many people change their styles of love over time and with new partners. People

"My preference is for someone who's afraid of closeness, like me."

An avoidant lover in action.

who are in love for the first time are apt to be especially romantic and idealistic, but by their third love relationship they tend to be more realistic and even a touch cynical (Carducci & McGuire, 1990). The most pragmatic person can have an "erotic" interlude. The most game-playing ludic lover may become committed to an affectionate relationship. Older couples are far less likely to show signs of mania than younger couples are, suggesting that the desperation and insecurity of mania subside with time and experience (Waller & Shaver, 1994).

Many people believe that critical thinking and love are mutually exclusive: If you are thinking critically about love, you kill the emotion; and if you are in love, you stop thinking altogether! Yet psychologists have found repeatedly that the way we define love, and the love stories we choose to guide our lives, deeply affect our satisfaction with relationships—and even whether relationships last. If you believe that love "just happens," that you have no control over it, that love is defined by sexual passion and hot emotion, then you may decide you are "out of love" when the initial phase of attraction fades, as it eventually must—and you will be repeatedly disappointed. Robert Solomon (1994) argued that "We conceive of [love] falsely—as a feeling, as novelty, as bound up with youth and beauty. . . . We expect an explosion at the beginning powerful enough to fuel love through all of its ups and downs instead of viewing love as a process over which we have control, a process that tends to increase with time rather than wane." Perhaps, then, a little critical thinking about love, far from killing it, can make it a truer and richer experience.

Thinking Critically About Love

Gender, Culture, and Love

Gender stereotypes tell us that men are more ludic and avoidant than women, and that women are more romantic and anxious than men, but like all stereotypes, these oversimplify. Neither sex loves more than the other in terms of "love at first sight," manic (possessive) love, erotic (passionate) love, selfless love, or companionate love over the long haul (Dion & Dion, 1993; Fehr, 1993; Hatfield & Rapson, 1996). Both sexes suffer when a love relationship ends, if they did not want it to.

However, women and men do differ, on average, in how they *express* love. As we saw in Chapter 12, males in many cultures learn early that revelations of emotion can be construed as evidence of vulnerability and weakness, which are considered unmasculine. Thus, men in such cultures often develop ways of expressing love that differ from women's. In contemporary Western society, many women express feelings of love in words, whereas many men express these feelings in actions—doing things for the partner, supporting the family financially, or just sharing the same activity, such as watching TV or a football game together (Baumeister & Bratslavsky, 1999; Cancian, 1987; Swain, 1989). Similarly, many women tend to define "intimacy" as shared revelations of feelings, but many men define intimacy as just hanging out together comfortably.

These gender differences in ways of expressing the universal motives of love and intimacy do not just pop up from nowhere; they reflect social, economic, and cultural forces. For example, for many years, Western men were more romantic than women in their choice of partner, and women in turn were far more pragmatic than men. One reason was that a woman did not just marry a man; she married a standard of living. Therefore she could not afford to marry someone "unsuitable" or waste her time in a relationship that was "not going anywhere," even if she loved him. In contrast, a man could afford to be sentimental in his choice of partner. In the 1960s, two-thirds of a sample of college men said they would not marry someone they did not love, but only one-fourth of the women ruled out the possibility (Kephart, 1967).

As women entered the workforce and as two incomes became necessary in most families, however, the gender difference in romantic love waned, and so did pragmatic reasons for marriage—all over the world. Nowadays, in every developed and developing nation, only tiny numbers of women and men would consider marrying someone who had all the "right" qualities if they weren't in love with the person. Pragmatic reasons for marriage, with romantic love being a remote luxury, persist only in economically underdeveloped countries, such as India and Pakistan, where the extended family still controls the rules of marriage (Hatfield & Rapson, 1996).

As you can see, our beliefs about love, and the kind of love we feel, are influenced by the culture we live in, the historical era that shapes us, and something as unromantic as economic self-sufficiency. How do these influences affect your own style of love?

QUICK QUIZ

Are you passionately committed to quizzes yet?

A. Of Lee's six styles of loving, which kind does each of the following examples illustrate?

1. The nineteenth-century historian Thomas Carlyle and his friend Jane Welsh enjoy exchanging ideas and confidences for years before realizing they love each other.

2. In choosing his last four wives, Henry VIII makes sure they are likely to bear children and are of suitably high status for his court.

3. Romeo and Juliet think only of each other and hate to be separated for even an hour.

4. Casanova tries to seduce every woman he meets for the thrill of the conquest.

B. Tiffany is wildly in love with Timothy, and he with her, but she can't stop worrying about him and doubting his love. She wants to be with him constantly, but when she feels jealous she pushes him away. According to the attachment theory of love, which style of attachment does Tiffany have? In terms of the six styles of love, which style does she have?

Answers:
A. 1. friendship (storge) 2. pragmatic love (pragma) 3. romantic, passionate love (eros) 4. game-playing love (ludus)
B. anxious-ambivalent; mania

What's Ahead

- What part of the anatomy do psychologists think is the "sexiest sex organ"?

- How do the sexual rules for heterosexual couples foster misunderstandings?

- Can psychological theories about "smothering mothering" or absent fathers explain why some men are gay?

13.2 The Erotic Animal: Motives for Sex

Most people believe that sex is a biological drive like hunger, just a matter of doing what comes naturally. This is certainly true among lower species, where sexual behavior is genetically programmed. Without instruction, a male stickleback fish knows exactly what to do with a female stickleback, and a whooping crane knows when to whoop. But as sex researcher Leonore Tiefer (1995) has observed, for human beings "sex is not a natural act." For one thing, the activities that one culture considers "natural" are often considered "unnatural" in another culture or his-torical time. For another, people have to learn from experience and culture what they are supposed to do with their sexual desires and how they are expected to behave sexually. Human sexuality is a blend of biological, psychological, and cultural factors.

The Biology of Desire

Biological researchers have contributed to our understanding of sexual motivation by sweeping away the cobwebs of superstition and ignorance about how the body works. They have disproved the idea that the sexes are physically opposite and have documented the capacity for sexual arousal, orgasm, and pleasure in both sexes.

Hormones and Sexual Response. One biological factor that seems to promote sexual desire, in both sexes, is the hormone testosterone. Its role has been documented in studies of men who have been given synthetic hormones that suppress the production of testosterone; of men and women who have abnormally low testosterone levels; of women who have taken androgens after having had their ovaries removed; and of women who kept diaries of their sexual activity while also having their hormone levels periodically measured (Bradford & Pawlak, 1993; Carani et al., 1992; Sherwin, 1998b).

However, hormones do not *cause* sexual behavior, or any other behavior, in a simple, direct way, even though some pop-psych books and media personalities claim that they do. Hormones and behavior travel a two-way street: Testosterone contributes to sexual arousal, but sexual activity also produces higher levels of testosterone (Sapolsky, 1997). More important, testosterone is almost always trumped by psychological factors. Thus, raising testosterone levels may increase sexual desire in some women who have unusually low amounts, as might occur if their ovaries were removed; but for most women the qualities of their relationship affect sexual desire far more than hormone levels do (Bancroft et al., 1991). Conversely, *lowering* testosterone levels, as has been done by giving some sex offenders a medication that suppresses production of the hormone, does not always produce a loss of sexual desire.

Arousal and Orgasm.

Physiological research has dispelled a lot of nonsense written about female sexuality. Freud, for example, claimed that when women reach puberty, their locus of sexual sensation shifts from the "childish" clitoris to the "mature" vagina, and women can then have healthy "vaginal" orgasms instead of immature "clitoral" orgasms. (Freud's theory was at least an improvement on the Victorian notion, still held in some cultures, that normal or "good" women don't have orgasms at all.) Freudian ideas caused countless women to worry that they were mentally disturbed or sexually repressed if they were not having the correct kind of orgasm (Ehrenreich, 1978).

The first modern attack on these beliefs came from Alfred Kinsey and his associates (1948, 1953), in their pioneering books on male and female sexuality. In *Sexual Behavior in the Human Female,* they observed that "males would be better prepared to understand females, and females to understand males, if they realized that they are alike in their basic anatomy and physiology." For example, the penis and the clitoris develop from the same embryonic tissues; they differ in size, of course, but not in sensitivity.

Kinsey's survey findings were expanded in the 1960s in the laboratory research of physician William Masters and his associate Virginia Johnson (1966). In studies of physiological changes during sexual arousal and orgasm, they confirmed that male and female arousal and orgasms are indeed

Desire and sensuality are lifelong pleasures.

remarkably similar and that all orgasms are physiologically the same, regardless of the source of stimulation. Masters and Johnson even argued, in contrast to the popular wisdom of the times, that women's capacity for sexual response "infinitely surpasses that of men" because women, unlike most men, are physiologically able to have repeated orgasms until exhaustion or a persistent telephone make them stop.

Masters and Johnson's work, like Kinsey's, had limitations. Perhaps the most serious one was that Masters and Johnson did not do research to learn how people's sexual response might vary according to their age, experience, and culture. They accepted as research subjects only those volunteers who met their predetermined notions of normalcy—for instance, who were readily orgasmic. (Leonore Tiefer [1995] observed that this was like studying the range of human singing abilities by selecting only international recording stars.) But not all women, or even all men, are easily orgasmic, let alone multiply orgasmic.

In addition, Masters and Johnson assumed that people's *physiological* responses would be indications of their *subjective* experience of desire and arousal, but this is not always the case (Irvine, 1990). For example, vaginal lubrication is not always a sign of arousal; it is sometimes a response to nervousness, excitement, disgust, or fear. Similarly, a man's erection is not always due to sexual stimulation; a man can also have an erection as a response to fear, anger, or other emotions.

The question of whether men and women are alike or different in sexual drive and responsiveness continues to provoke lively debate. Some researchers argue that we cannot answer this question until economic and cultural conditions are the same for both sexes. As long as large numbers of women are taught to fear, dislike, or avoid sex, they say, it is impossible to know what women's "sexual drive" would be like. Others argue that certain behaviors, such as frequency of masturbation, sexual fantasies, and orgasm, are universally higher among men than women, even when men are forbidden by social or religious rules to engage in sex of any kind (Baumeister, Catanese, & Vohs, 2001; Oliver & Hyde, 1993). One possibility is that men's sex drive is more biologically influenced than is women's, whereas women's sexual desires and responsiveness are more affected by circumstances, the relationship, and culture (Baumeister, 2000; Peplau et al., 2000).

The Evolutionary View. Biological approaches to sexuality have had a boost in recent years from *evolutionary psychologists,* who believe that sex differences in courtship and mating practices evolve in response to a species' survival needs (Buss, 1994). In this view, it is evolutionarily adaptive for males to compete with other males for access to young and fertile females, and to try to win and then inseminate as many females as possible. The more females a male mates with, the more genes he can pass along. (The human record in this regard was achieved by a man who fathered 899 children [Daly & Wilson, 1983]. What else he did with his time is not known.) But according to evolutionary psychologists, females need to shop for the best genetic deal, as it were, because they can conceive and bear only a limited number of offspring. Having such a large biological investment in each pregnancy, they can't afford to make mistakes. Besides, mating with a lot of different males would produce no more offspring than staying with just one. So, in the evolutionary view, females try to attach themselves to dominant males, who have resources and status and are likely to have "superior" genes.

The result of these two opposite sexual strategies, in this view, is that males generally want sex more often than females do; males are often fickle and promiscuous, whereas females are usually devoted and faithful; males are drawn to sexual novelty, whereas females want stability and security; males will sometimes resort to sexual coercion and rape; males are relatively undiscriminating in their choice of partners, whereas females are cautious and choosy; and males are competitive and concerned about dominance, whereas females are less so (Buss, 1994, 1996).

This Kenyan man has 40 wives and 349 children (all of whom, apparently, come to visit). Although he is unusual, around the world it is more common for men to have many wives than for women to have many husbands. Evolutionary psychologists think the reason is that men have evolved to sow as many wild oats as they can, whereas women have evolved to be happy with just a few grains.

Some sex differences do appear to be universal, or at least very common. In one massive project, 50 scientists studied 10,000 people in 37 cultures located on six continents and five islands (Buss, 1994). Around the world, they found, men are more violent than women and more socially dominant. They are more interested in the youth and beauty of their sexual partners, presumably because youth is associated with fertility. They are more sexually jealous and possessive, presumably because males can never be 100 percent sure that their children are really theirs genetically. They are quicker to have sex with partners they don't know well, and more inclined toward promiscuity, presumably so that their sperm will be distributed as widely as possible. Women, in contrast, tend to emphasize the financial resources or prospects of a potential mate, his status, and his willingness to commit to a relationship (Bailey et al., 1994; Buss, 1996; Buunk et al., 1996; Daly & Wilson, 1983; Sprecher, Sullivan, & Hatfield, 1994).

Critics maintain that the evolutionary view is an after-the-fact explanation of a *stereotype,* and that the actual behavior of human beings and other animals often contradicts the image of the sexually promiscuous male and the coy and choosy female (Fausto-Sterling, 1997; Hrdy, 1988, 1999; Hubbard, 1990). In many species—birds, fish, mammals, and primates, including humans—females are sexually ardent and often have many male partners. The female's sexual behavior does not seem to depend only on the goal of being fertilized by the male: Females have sex when they are not ovulating and even when they are already pregnant. And in many species, from penguins to primates, males do not just mate and run. They stick around, feeding the infants, carrying them, and protecting them against predators (Hrdy, 1988; Snowdon, 1997; Taub, 1984).

These findings have sent evolutionary theorists scurrying to figure out the evolutionary benefits of female promiscuity and male nurturance. Perhaps, in some species, females need sperm from several males in order to ensure conception by the healthiest sperm (Baker, 1996). Or perhaps females have multiple partners in order to increase the number of males who will support the female's offspring. This motive is quite explicit among the Barí people of Venezuela. A man who impregnates a woman is considered the child's primary father. But if she takes a lover during her pregnancy (an approved practice), he is considered a secondary father, and he is expected to supply mother and baby with extra food (Beckerman et al., 1998).

A basic assumption of evolutionary approaches to sexuality is that females across species have greater involvement in child rearing than males do. But there are many exceptions. Female emperor penguins, for example, take off every winter, leaving behind males like this doting dad to care for the kids.

Critics, however, argue that all evolutionary explanations, whether of female fidelity or "promiscuity," are inadequate when applied to human beings (Fausto-Sterling, 1997). Human sexual behavior is extremely varied and changeable. Cultures range from those in which women have many children to those in which they have very few; from those in which men are intimately involved in child rearing to those in which they do nothing at all; from those in which women may have many lovers to those in which women may be killed if they have sex outside of marriage (Hatfield & Rapson, 1996). In some places, the chastity of a potential mate is much more important to men than to women, but in other places, it is important to both sexes—or to neither one (see Figure 13.1).

Even within a culture, sexual attitudes and practices vary tremendously and can change dramatically in one person's lifetime (Laumann et al.,

Thinking Critically
About Evolutionary
Theories of Sex

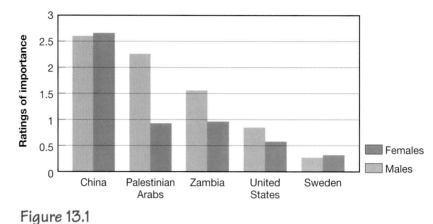

Figure 13.1
Attitudes Toward Chastity

In many places, men care more about a partner's chastity than women do, as evolutionary psychologists would predict. But culture has a powerful effect on attitudes. This graph shows the importance that men and women in five countries place on their partner's chastity. In China, both partners prefer a partner who has not yet had intercourse, whereas in Sweden, chastity is a nonissue (Buss, 1995).

1994). Plenty of women are not attracted to rich men, nor men to stereotypically beautiful women, happily finding partners who are physical shlubs, financially challenged, or merely average Joes and Janes. Such variations, say the critics, argue against a universal, genetically determined sexual strategy. We will discuss social and cultural explanations of gender differences in sexuality shortly.

The Psychology of Desire

Psychologists are fond of observing that the sexiest sex organ is the brain, where perceptions begin. People's values, fantasies, and beliefs profoundly affect their sexual desire and behavior. That is why a touch on the knee by an exciting new date feels terrifically sexy, but the same touch by a creepy stranger on a bus feels disgusting. It is why a distracting thought can kill sexual arousal in a second, and why a fantasy can be more erotic than reality.

The Many Motives for Sex. To most people, the primary motives for sex are pretty obvious: to enjoy the pleasure of it, to express love and intimacy, or to make babies. But there are other motives, too, not all of them so positive. Studies of several hundred college students and more than 1,500 older adults identified six factors underlying the many reasons that people give for having sex (Cooper, Shapiro, & Powers, 1998):

- *Enhancement*—having sex for the emotional satisfaction or physical pleasure of it.

- *Intimacy*—having sex to feel emotionally close to the partner.

- *Coping*—having sex to cope with negative emotions and disappointments.

- *Self-affirmation*—having sex to be reassured of one's attractiveness or desirability.

- *Partner approval*—having sex to please or appease one's partner (e.g., to avoid the partner's anger or rejection).

- *Peer approval*—having sex to impress one's friends, be part of the group, and conform to what "everyone else" seems to be doing.

In this research, men and women did not differ in their motives for intimacy, but men more strongly endorsed all the other motives, especially peer approval. The older that people were, the more likely they were to have sex for intimacy and for self-enhancement (pleasure), and the less likely they were to have sex for peer or partner approval. White adolescents more strongly endorsed intimacy motives than black adolescents did, and black teenagers more strongly endorsed coping and peer-pressure motives.

People's motives for having sex affect many aspects of their sexual behavior, including whether they engage in sex in the first place, whether

There are many motivations for sex, including physical lust and financial gain, intimacy and love, and joyful playfulness.

they enjoy it, whether they have unprotected or otherwise risky sex, and whether they have few or many partners. Coping and approval motives are most strongly associated with risky sexual behavior, including having many partners and not using effective birth control, and also with having more unplanned pregnancies (Cooper, Shapiro, & Powers, 1998).

Many studies of college students find that women and men often have sex not for pleasure or intimacy, but because of feelings of inadequacy or peer pressure. In one survey of nearly a thousand college students, fully two-thirds of the men reported having had unwanted intercourse (Muehlenhard & Cook, 1988). The main reasons for doing so, the men said, were peer pressure, inexperience, a desire for popularity, and a fear of seeming homosexual or "unmasculine." Women too said they "gave in," but for different reasons: because it was easier than having an argument; because they did not want to lose the relationship; because they felt obligated, once the partner had spent time and money on them; or because the partner made them feel guilty.

Sexual Coercion and Rape. One of the most persistent differences in the sexual experiences of women and men has to do with their perceptions of, and experiences with, sexual coercion. In a nationally representative survey of more than 3,000 Americans ages 18 to 59, nearly one-fourth of the women said that a man—usually a husband or boyfriend—had forced them to do something sexually that they did not want to do (Laumann et al., 1994). But only about 3 percent of the men said they had ever forced a woman into a sexual act. Obviously, what many women regard as coercion is not always seen as coercive by men.

The most extreme form of sexual coercion, of course, is rape. Although the public image of the rapist tends to be one of a menacing stranger, in most cases the rapist is known to the victim. They may have dated once or a few times; they may have been friends for years; they may even be married (Koss, 1993; Russell, 1990). According to a representative survey of more than 4,000 women in the United States, 14 percent of all American women have been the victims of forcible rape at least once in their lives, most by men they knew; only 22 percent of rape victims were assaulted by strangers (National Victim Center, 1992). The survey did not include men; children and teenagers under age 18; women in college residences, prisons, or the military; and homeless women. So the percentage of people who have been raped is undoubtedly even higher (Koss, 1993; Merrill et al., 1998).

What motivates some men to rape? For many, the answer is peer approval. College men who have physically coerced their dates into having sex have often been pressured by male friends, since early adolescence, to prove their masculinity by "scoring" (Kanin, 1985). For other men who rape, the motive is anger, revenge, or a desire to dominate; by its very nature, rape is an act of hostility that reflects a devaluing and dehumanizing of the victim. Sexually aggressive males are characterized by a cluster of traits: insecurity, defensiveness, hostility toward women and a wish to control them, and a preference for promiscuous, impersonal sex. They misperceive women's behavior in social situations, equate feelings of power with sexuality, regard women as being entirely responsible for whatever happens to them, and tend to have coercive sexual fantasies (Drieschner & Lange, 1999; Malamuth et al., 1995). Convicted rapists have a mixture of even more disturbed motives: anger at women or the world, a need for power, contempt for women, a desire to act out a sexual fantasy, and sometimes sexual sadism (Knight, Prentky, & Cerce, 1994).

The argument that rape is primarily an act of dominance and aggression, rather than a sexual act for the evolutionary purpose of disseminating a man's sperm, is also supported by the fact that during war, many soldiers rape captive women and then often kill them (Olujic, 1998). Aggressive motives also occur in the rape of men by other men (King & Woollett, 1997). Male–male rape, which usually involves anal penetration, typically occurs in youth gangs, where the intention is to humiliate rival gang members, and in prison, where again the motive is to conquer and degrade the victim.

As you can see, the answer to the question "Why do people have sex?" is not obvious after all, and by no means a simple matter of biology. In addition to intimacy, pleasure, procreation, and love, psychological motives include intimidation and dominance, insecurity, a wish to appease the partner, the need for reassurance, the need for approval from peers, and the wish to prove oneself a real man or a desirable woman.

The Culture of Desire

Think about kissing. Westerners like to think about kissing, and to do it, too. But if you think kissing is "natural," try to remember your first serious kiss—and all you had to learn about noses, breathing, and the position of teeth and tongue. The sexual kiss is so complicated that some cultures have never even gotten around to it. They think that kissing another

Kissing is a learned skill—one that some people start practicing earlier than others.

person's mouth—the very place that food enters!—is disgusting (Tiefer, 1995). Others have elevated the sexual kiss to high art; why do you suppose one version is called "French" kissing?

As the kiss illustrates, having the physical equipment to perform a sexual act is not all there is to sexual motivation. People acquire their notions of proper sexual behavior from cultural norms and parental lessons (Lottes & Kuriloff, 1994). They learn what is supposed to "turn them on" (and off), what parts of the body and what activities are erotic (or repulsive), and even how to have sexual relations. To men of the Victorian era, the sight of a woman's ankle was highly arousing; to men of the modern era, an ankle doesn't do it. In some cultures, oral sex is regarded as a bizarre sexual deviation and may even be against the law; in others, oral sex is considered not only normal but also supremely desirable.

Cultures also differ in their attitudes toward sex itself: whether sex is seen as something joyful and beautiful, an art to cultivate as one might cultivate the art of cooking or dancing, or as something ugly and dirty, something to "get through" as quickly as possible.

How do cultures transmit their rules and requirements about sex to their members? During childhood and adolescence, people learn their culture's *gender roles*—collections of rules that determine the proper attitudes and behavior for men and women, sexual and otherwise (see Chapter 9). Just as an actor in the role of Hamlet needs a script to learn his part, a person following a gender role needs a **sexual script** that teaches men and women how to behave in sexual matters (Gagnon

sexual scripts
Sets of implicit rules that specify proper sexual behavior for a person in a given situation, varying with the person's age, culture, and gender.

& Simon, 1973; Laumann & Gagnon, 1995). Sexual scripts differ from culture to culture, as members act in accordance with the scripts for their gender, sexual orientation, and age.

In many parts of the world, boys acquire their attitudes about sex in a competitive atmosphere where the goal is to impress other males, and they talk and joke about masturbation and other sexual experiences with their friends. While boys are learning to value physical sex, however, girls are learning to value relationships and to make themselves attractive. They learn that their role is to be sexually desirable (which is good), but not to indulge in their own sexual pleasures (which would be bad). One psychologist summarized the different sexual scripts that many North American boys and girls learn as, "'Nice women' don't say yes and 'real men' don't say no" (Muehlenhard, 1988). You can see how the different sexual scripts for heterosexual couples are almost guaranteed to create conflicting motives for sexuality and misreadings of one another's behavior. Is she dressing that way to look sexy or to tell me she wants sex? Is he really interested in me or just in hooking up for tonight? (How would you describe the sexual script that your own culture has written for you and for the other sex? Are the rules the same or different for women and men?)

Gay men and lesbians follow sexual scripts, too. In number of sexual partners, sexual practices, and acceptance of casual sex, gay men are generally similar to heterosexual men, and lesbians are similar to heterosexual women. But lesbians and gay men tend to be more innovative and flexible than heterosexuals in establishing rules for their relationships; often, neither partner is clearly the pursuer or the pursued or the one who makes the sexual decisions (Peplau & Spalding, 2000; Rose, Zand, & Cini, 1993).

Where do sexual scripts and gender differences in sexuality come from? We described the evolutionary answer earlier, and certainly one key biological difference does affect men's and women's attitudes and behavior: Only one sex gets pregnant. But for social and cultural psychologists, the primary answer has to do with a culture's economic and social arrangements.

Historically, for example, when women have needed to find and keep a relationship in order to have financial security, they have tended to regard sex as a bargaining chip—an asset to be rationed, rather than an activity to be enjoyed for its own sake (Hatfield & Rapson, 1996). A woman cannot afford to seek and enjoy sex if that means risking an unwanted pregnancy, the security of marriage,

Is she dressing provocatively or comfortably? Boys and girls often disagree on the answer.

her reputation, or her physical safety. When women become self-supporting and able to control their own fertility, however, they are more likely to want sex for pleasure rather than as a means to another goal.

All over the world, as industrialization and modernization are transforming gender roles, the sexual behavior of women and men is indeed becoming more alike (Laumann et al., 1994). Although this transformation is slow and uneven, and although change always brings protest and confusion in its wake, social scientists have documented a growing endorsement, worldwide, of birth control, premarital sex, sexual freedom in general, and the entitlement of both sexes to love and sexual pleasure (Ellison, 2000; Hatfield & Rapson, 1996).

The Riddle of Sexual Orientation

Why do some people become heterosexual, others homosexual, and still others bisexual? Although same-sex sexual behavior has existed throughout history, the words *homosexual* and *heterosexual* were not even invented until the late nineteenth century (Katz, 1995). Only then did homosexuality become a "problem" to be studied, an entity distinct from heterosexuality.

Psychological Versus Biological Explanations. Exclusively psychological theories of homosexuality (or heterosexuality), although taken for granted by many lay people, have never been supported. Homosexuality is not a result of having a "smothering mother," an absent father, or emotional problems, as was once thought. It is not caused by same-sex sexual play in childhood or adolescence, which is actually quite common. It is not caused by "seduction" by an older adult (Rind, Tromovich, & Bauserman, 1998). It is not caused by parental practices or role models. Most gay men recall that they rejected the typical "boy" role and boys' toys and games from a very early age, in spite of enormous pressures from their parents and peers to conform to the traditional male role (Bailey & Zucker, 1995). Conversely, the overwhelming majority of children of gay parents do not become gay, as a learning model would predict (Bailey et al., 1995; C. Patterson, 1992).

Many researchers, therefore, have been turning to biological explanations of sexual orientation. One candidate is prenatal exposure to androgens, which affect certain neural structures in the brain (Bailey & Pillard, 1995; Gladue, 1994). A few stud-

In most relationships, whether gay or straight, people seek the pleasures of love, family, and companionship.

ies of gay men have reported associations between sexual orientation and very specific areas of the brain (Allen & Gorski, 1992; LeVay, 1991). These studies have gotten lots of press, but they have not been replicated (Byne, 1995). Other studies have suggested that female babies accidentally exposed in the womb to masculinizing hormones—androgens or other chemicals—are more likely than other girls to become bisexual or lesbian (Collaer & Hines, 1995; Meyer-Bahlburg et al., 1995). However, most of these "androgenized" women do not become lesbians, and most lesbians were not exposed to atypical prenatal hormones (Peplau et al., 2000).

There is some evidence that sexual orientation is moderately heritable, particularly in men (Bailey & Pillard, 1995; Whitam, Diamond, & Martin, 1993). One research team made headlines when they reported finding a genetic marker on the X chromosome in pairs of gay brothers (Hamer et al., 1993; Hu et al., 1995). However, a later study of 52 pairs of gay brothers did not replicate this finding (Rice et al., 1999). Moreover, the vast majority of gay men and lesbians do *not* have a close gay relative, and their siblings, including twins, are overwhelmingly likely to be heterosexual (Peplau et al., 2000). So we are left with a real puzzle.

One problem with trying to find "the" origin of sexual orientation is that sexual identity and behavior take different forms. Many people are neither exclusively homosexual nor exclusively heterosexual; others are heterosexual in behavior but have homosexual fantasies (Baumrind, 1995; Byne, 1995). In some cultures, boys go through a homosexual phase that they do not define as homosexual and that does not affect their future relations with women. In the Sambian society of Papua New Guinea, for example, adolescent males are required to engage in oral sex with older men as part of their initiation into manhood; it is believed that a boy cannot mature unless he ingests another man's semen for several years. But all Sambian boys eventually marry women (Herdt, 1984). In Lesotho, in South Africa, women have intimate relations with other women, including passionate kissing and oral sex, but the women do not define these acts as sexual, as they do when a man is the partner (Kendall, 1999).

Genetics cannot account for such customs, nor can genetics explain the flexible sexual histories of most lesbians across cultures. Some lesbians do have an exclusively same-sex orientation their whole lives, but many others have sex with the person they fall in love with, regardless of his or her gender, rather than loving someone only of one sex (Kitzinger & Wilkinson, 1995; Peplau et al., 2000).

At present, therefore, the most reasonable conclusions may be that sexual identity and behavior involve an interaction of biology, cultural norms, and experiences; that the routes to homosexual orientation may differ for males and females; and that the origins of sexual orientation may differ among individuals (Gladue, 1994; Patterson, 1995).

Homosexuality and Politics. How are you reacting to these findings? Your responses are probably affected by your feelings about homosexuality. Many gay men and lesbians welcome biological research on the grounds that it supports what they have been saying all along: Sexual orientation is not a matter of choice, but a fact of nature. Others fear that people who are prejudiced against homosexuals will use this research to argue that gay people have a biological "defect" that should be eradicated or "corrected" (as the talk-show host Laura Schlessinger has advocated). But people who are hostile to homosexuals will use any theory—biological or psychological—to justify their wish to eliminate homosexuality. For example, they have used learning theories to argue, mistakenly, that "if it's learned, it can be unlearned," and to justify subjecting gay men, and even "unboyish" boys as young as 3 years old, to harsh forms of behavior modification (Burke, 1996).

> Thinking Critically
> About Findings on
> Homosexuality

In any case, the *scientific* question of the origins of sexual orientation is logically unrelated to *political and moral* questions of the rights of gay men and lesbians (Strickland, 1995). In a democracy, civil rights do not depend on whether one's beliefs or practices are a matter of choice, nor do they depend on how popular those beliefs are. A person's religion is not biologically inherited, yet America and Canada guarantee freedom of religion to everyone—whether your religion is shared by 75 percent of the population or 2 percent.

Research on sexuality can be used for many contradictory purposes and political goals, depending on the values and attitudes of the popular culture in which such findings emerge. As long as a society is uncomfortable about homosexuality, preconceptions and prejudice are likely to cloud its reactions to anything that psychologists learn about it.

QUICK QUIZ

Were you motivated to learn about sexual motivation?

1. Which of the following behaviors would an evolutionary psychologist expect to be more typical of males than of females? (a) promiscuity, (b) choosiness about sexual partners, (c) concern with dominance, (d) interest in young partners, (e) emphasis on physical attractiveness of partners

2. Biological research finds that (a) male and female sexual responses are physiologically very different, (b) vaginal orgasms are healthier than clitoral ones, (c) testosterone promotes sexual desire in both sexes, (d) all women have multiple orgasms.

3. Research on the motives of rapists finds that rape is usually (a) a result of thwarted sexual desire, (b) the result of hostility or a need for power, (c) a matter of crossed signals, (d) an unconscious wish to disseminate their sperm.

4. *True or false:* Exclusively psychological theories of the origins of homosexuality have never been supported.

Answers:

1. all but b   2. c   3. b   4. true

What's Ahead

- Is overweight usually a result of psychological problems?

- What genetic theory explains why it's so hard for heavy people to lose weight—and just as hard for thin people to gain it?

- Why are people all over the world getting fatter?

- Why are bright, academically motivated college women the most vulnerable to eating disorders?

13.3 The Hungry Animal: Motives to Eat

Some people are skinny; others are plump. Some are shaped like string beans; others look more like pears. Some can eat anything they want without gaining an ounce; others struggle unsuccessfully their whole lives to shed pounds. Some people eat when they aren't hungry—say, to be sociable—and others refuse to eat even when they *are* hungry—say, to lose weight, even when they are already thin. How much do genes and environment contribute to these differences in the motivation to eat—or not eat?

The Genetics of Weight

At one time, most psychologists thought that being overweight was a sign of emotional disturbance. If you were fat, it was because you hated your mother, feared intimacy, or were trying to fill an emotional hole in your psyche by loading up on rich desserts. The evidence for psychological theories of overweight, however, came mainly from self-reports and from studies that were seriously flawed: For example, many studies lacked control groups and objective measures of how much people were actually eating (Allison & Heshka, 1993). When researchers did controlled experiments, they learned that fat people, on average, are no more and no less emotionally disturbed than average-weight people (Stunkard, 1980).

Even more surprising, studies showed that *heaviness is not always caused by overeating.* Many heavy people do eat large quantities of food, but so do some thin people. Many thin people eat very little, but so do some obese people. In one study that carefully monitored everything that subjects were eating, two 260-pound women maintained their weights while consuming only 1,000 calories a day (Wooley, Wooley, & Dyrenforth, 1979). In another study, which had volunteers gorge themselves for months, it was as hard for slender people to gain weight as it is for most heavy people to lose weight. The minute the study was over, the slender people lost weight as fast as dieters gain it back (Sims, 1974).

The leading explanation for such findings is that a biological mechanism keeps your body weight at a genetically influenced **set point**—the weight you stay at when you are not consciously trying to gain or lose (Lissner et al., 1991). The set point can vary about 10 percent in either direction. For example, a woman with a set point of 150 pounds might weigh anywhere from 135 to 165. But if her weight dips below 135 or goes above 165, her body will produce either an insatiable urge to eat or a feeling of disgust at the sight of food, to bring its fat levels back into line.

Set-point theory helps explain why most people who diet eventually gain their weight back: They are returning to their set-point weight (Leibel, Rosenbaum, & Hirsch, 1995; Levitan & Ronan, 1988). Everyone has a genetically programmed *basal metabolism rate,* the rate at which the body burns calories for energy, and a fixed number of *fat cells,* which store fat for energy and can change in size. A complex interaction of metabolism, fat cells, and hormones keeps people at the weight their bodies are designed to be, much in the way that a thermostat keeps a house at a preset temperature. When a heavy person diets, the body's metabolism slows down to conserve energy and fat reserves. When a thin person overeats, metabolism speeds up, burning energy.

Set-point theory predicts that the heritability of weight and body fat should be high, and indeed it is: In twin and adoption studies, heritability estimates fall between .40 and .70 (Comuzzie & Allison, 1998). It seems clear, therefore, that genes contribute to size and weight differences among people. Consider some further evidence for the role of genes:

■ In a study of 171 Pima Indians in Arizona, two-thirds of the women and half of the men became obese over time, and the slower their metabolisms, the greater the weight gain. After adding anywhere from 20 to 45 pounds, however, the Pimas stopped gaining weight. Their metabolism rates rose, and their weights

set point
The genetically influenced weight range for an individual, maintained by biological mechanisms that regulate food intake, fat reserves, and metabolism.

Body weight and shape are strongly affected by genetic factors. Set-point theory helps explain why the Pimas of the American Southwest gain weight easily but lose it slowly, whereas the Bororo nomads of Nigeria can eat a lot of food yet remain slender.

Both of these mice have a mutation in the ob gene, which usually makes mice chubby, like the one on the left. But when leptin is injected daily, the mice remain almost normal in weight, like the one on the right, because they eat less and burn more calories.

stabilized at the new, higher level (Ravussin et al., 1988). Many Pimas apparently have a set point for plumpness.

■ Infants born to overweight mothers generate less energy than the babies of normal-weight mothers, even when the infants are eating the same amount. By the age of 1 year, these lower-metabolism babies are more likely to be overweight (Roberts et al., 1988).

■ Pairs of adult identical twins who grow up in different families are just as similar in body weight and shape as twins raised together. The early family environment has almost *no effect at all* on body shape, weight gain, or percentage of fat in the body (Stunkard et al., 1990). When identical twins gain weight, they gain it in the same place: Some pairs store extra pounds around their waists, others on their hips and thighs (C. Bouchard et al., 1990).

Enormous progress has been made in identifying the genes involved in some types of obesity. One team of researchers isolated a genetic variation that causes mice to become obese (Zhang et al., 1994). The usual form of the gene, called "obese," or *ob* for short, causes fat cells to secrete a protein, which the researchers named *leptin* (from the Greek *leptos,* "slender"). Leptin travels through the blood to the brain's *hypothalamus,* which is involved in the regulation of appetite. Rising and falling levels of leptin signal how large or small the body's fat cells are, so that the brain can maintain the animal's or person's set point by adjusting appetite and metabolism. Injecting leptin into mice reduces the animals' appetites, speeds up their metabolisms, and makes them more active; as a result, the animals shed weight, even if they are not overweight to begin with (Halaas et al., 1995).

Alas, the role of leptin in human obesity is more complicated than it is in mice. (We are tempted to say "rats!" to this news.) Some obese people may gain weight rapidly because their secretion of leptin is impaired (Ravussin et al., 1997). Other obese people may produce plenty of leptin but be insensitive to it, perhaps because of a gene that prevents brain cells from responding normally to leptin's signals (Chua et al., 1996; Considine et al., 1996). But for most obese people, leptin does not play a major role (Comuzzie & Allison, 1998).

Dozens of other genes and many body chemicals besides leptin are thought to be involved in appetite, metabolism rates, and weight regulation. Yet despite the obvious involvement of genes in weight and body shape, set-point theory cannot explain the dramatic worldwide increase in rates of overweight and extreme obesity (Pinel, Assanand, & Lehman, 2000). If most people have normal set points, why are so many people everywhere getting fatter? Half of all American adults are overweight, and rates of obesity jumped from 12.8 percent of the population in the early 1960s to 22.5 percent by the mid-1990s. Increases have occurred in both sexes, all social classes, and all age groups, including children, and in many other countries around the world (Taubes, 1998). And these increases continue in spite of large percentages of people who say they are dieting. Why?

Culture, Psychology, and Weight

The answer has to do with the interaction between genes and the environment. Genes have not changed in the last decades, but the environment has. The leading environmental culprits in the causes of the worldwide weight-gain epidemic are the increased abundance of low-cost, high-fat foods; the habit of eating high-calorie food on the run rather than leisurely meals; the rise in energy-saving (fat-conserving) devices; the popularity of driving over walking or biking; the preference for watching television rather than exercising; and "couch-potato" lifestyles (Brownell & Rodin, 1994; Hill & Peters, 1998).

Diet and Exercise. Most human beings are predisposed to gain weight when rich food is abundant because, in the past, starvation was all too often a real possibility. Therefore, a tendency to store calories in the form of fat provided a definite survival advantage. Unfortunately, evolution did not design a mechanism to prevent us from gaining weight when food is easily available, tasty, and cheap—precisely the situation today in many countries (Pinel, Assanand, & Lehman, 2000). If you consume the high-fat food that so many North Americans love—all those cheap and tasty burgers, fries, cokes, chips, tacos, candy bars, and pizzas—and if you eat such food in the large quantities that most Europeans and Asians find excessive and alarming, you are likely to be heavier than if you eat a low-fat diet in moderate portions.

Many people, however, are unaware of the fats and hidden calories in the foods they eat. For example, many Mexican-Americans born in the United States are fatter than those who were born in Mexico. Why? In Mexico, poor people eat corn tortillas, which are cheapest; and their diet overall is lower in fat and higher in fiber than that of their relatives in the north. But Mexican-Americans born in the United States tend to eat flour tortillas, which are made with lard and are thus much higher in calories, and they eat other high-fat foods that result from acculturation to American ways. As a result, they have higher obesity rates than their kin in Mexico

(Dixon, Sundquist, & Winkleby, 2000; Sundquist & Winkleby, 2000).

Another nongenetic influence on weight is exercise, which boosts the body's metabolic rate and may lower its set point. When obese women are put on severely restricted diets, their metabolic rates drop sharply, as set-point theory would predict. But when they combine the diet with moderate physical activity—daily walking—they lose weight and their metabolic rates rise almost to previous levels (Wadden et al., 1990). This evidence suggests why changes in weight often accompany changes in habits and activity levels. People take a job that is near where they live, so they start walking or biking to work and lose weight. Or they move to a climate that is boiling hot, so they stop walking as much as they did and gain weight. A study that compared Pima Indians living in Arizona and Mexico found that although both groups are genetically susceptible to obesity (as we saw), the physical activity of the Pimas in Mexico is higher—and their weight therefore significantly lower—than that of American Pimas (Esparza et al., 2000).

Cultural Attitudes. Eating habits and activity levels, in turn, are shaped by a culture's customs and standards of what the ideal body should look like: fat, thin, muscular, soft. In many places around the world, especially in places like Africa, where famine and crop failures are common, fat is taken as a sign of health, affluence in men, and sexual desirability in women (Stearns, 1997). Among the Calabari of Nigeria, for example, brides are put in special "fattening huts" where they do nothing but eat, so as to become obese enough to please their husbands. And at the Hangandi festival in Niger, the fattest woman wins the beauty contest. In the United States, many African-Americans and Mexican-Americans are more accepting of fat people and less concerned about being "overweight" than are white Americans (Crandall & Martinez, 1996; Hebl & Heatherton, 1998).

While people of all ethnicities and social classes have been getting fatter, the cultural ideal for white women in the United States, Canada, and Europe has been getting thinner and thinner. The ideal of the voluptuously curvy woman, big-breasted and big-hipped, was popular before World War I and after World War II. But in the flapper era of the 1920s and again starting in the 1960s, big breasts and hips became unfashionable. Today the female ideal is an odd combination:

big breasts but no hips. The cultural ideal for American men has changed, too. Until relatively recently, most of the men who were heavily muscled were laborers and farmers, so being physically strong and muscular was a sign of being working class. In the past decade, pressures have increased for middle-class men to be "fit," highly toned, and strong (Bordo, 2000).

Why did these changes occur? One explanation is that white men and women associate overweight, in either sex, with softness, laziness, and weakness (Crandall & Martinez, 1996). In particular, the curvy, big-breasted female body is associated in people's minds with femininity, nurturance, and motherhood. Hence big breasts are fashionable in eras that celebrate women's role as mothers—such as after World War II, when women were encouraged to give up their wartime jobs and have many children (Bennett & Gurin, 1982; Stearns, 1997). However, people also associate femininity with incompetence. Thus, whenever women have entered traditionally male spheres of education and work, as they did in the 1920s and between the 1970s and the present, bright, ambitious women have tried to look boyishly thin and muscular in order to avoid appearing "soft," feminine, and dumb (Silverstein & Perlick, 1995; Silverstein, Peterson, & Perdue,

Should a woman be voluptuous and curvy or slim as a reed? Should a man be thin and unmuscled or strong and buff? Genes and evolution cannot explain cultural changes in attitudes toward the ideal body. During the 1950s, actresses like Diana Dors embodied the post-war ideal: curvy, buxom, and "womanly." Today, many women struggle to look like Calista Flockhart: skinny, angular, and boyish. Men, too, have been caught up in body-image mania. The hippie ideal of the 1960s is a far cry from the muscular, macho standards of the ideal man in the 2000's.

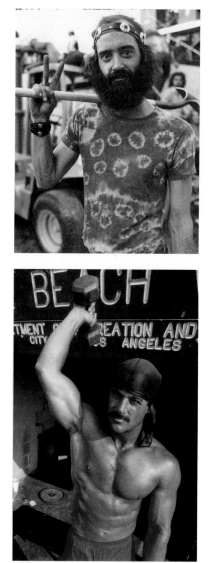

1986). Today's big-breasted but otherwise skinny female ideal may reflect cultural ambivalence about whether women's proper role is domestic or professional. And in men, having a strong, muscular body is now a sign of affluence rather than poverty—it means a man has the money and the time to join a gym and work out.

Weight and Health: Biology Versus Culture

What happens when your set point clashes with your culture's notions of the ideal body? The battle between biology and culture can cause health problems and emotional problems, because being extremely overweight *or* starving to be underweight can both be harmful.

Cultures that regard overweight as a sign of health and sexiness—the "more to love" school of thought—are obviously more accepting of people who are naturally heavy. But obesity is now a serious health problem of epidemic proportions; it is a leading risk factor in diabetes, high blood pressure, heart disease, stroke, cancer, infertility, and many other disorders. Otelio Randall and his colleagues at Howard University have established a program to teach African-Americans about the risks of obesity, which are especially high among this population. About two-thirds of all black women are overweight, compared to 47 percent of white women, and one in ten middle-aged black women is more than 100 pounds overweight—explaining in part why black women are four times as likely as white women to die young of heart disease (Angier, 2000).

Other researchers are trying to combat similar cultural pressures to be overweight among white farm and rural families, who often associate eating large amounts of food with sociability and family togetherness. In the Farm Belt states of the American Midwest, for example, people are expected to eat huge, hearty meals and plenty of sweets and cakes. If you don't join in, an anthropologist from Iowa told *The New York Times*, you are being antisocial—insulting your hosts and rejecting your kin (Angier, 2000).

On the other hand, efforts to match a cultural standard of excessive thinness can also pose serious risks to health. Evolution has programmed women for a reserve of fat necessary for the onset of menstruation, healthy childbearing, nursing, and, after menopause, the production and storage of the

The sad revelation that the late Princess Diana suffered from bulimia showed that even women of great beauty, wealth, and power are vulnerable to the insecurities that can lead to an eating disorder. Wealthy, upper-class women who seem to "have it all" are actually under the greatest cultural pressure to be extremely thin.

hormone estrogen (Bennett & Gurin, 1982). In cultures that think women should look like the TV character Ally McBeal, therefore, many women become obsessed with weight and are continually dieting, forever fighting their bodies' need for a minimum of fat.

In such a climate, a significant minority of women develop serious eating disorders that reflect an irrational terror of being "too fat" (Walsh & Devlin, 1998). In **bulimia,** the person binges (eats vast quantities of rich food) and then purges by inducing vomiting or using laxatives. In **anorexia nervosa,** the person eats hardly anything and therefore becomes dangerously thin; anorexics have severely distorted body images, thinking they are "fat" even when they are emaciated and near death. Bulimia and anorexia are at least ten times more common in women than in men (Davison & Neale, 2001). Although many people

bulimia
An eating disorder characterized by episodes of excessive eating (bingeing) followed by forced vomiting or use of laxatives (purging).

anorexia nervosa
An eating disorder characterized by fear of being fat, a distorted body image, radically reduced consumption of food, and emaciation.

13.2

with these disorders recover, others damage their health permanently, or, in the case of anorexia, eventually die of self-starvation. The estimated mortality rate from anorexia—from 10 to 20 percent of its victims—is the highest of any emotional disorder.

Eating disorders and body-image distortions among boys and men are increasing too, though they take different forms (Bordo, 2000). Just as anorexic women see their gaunt bodies as being too fat, men with the comparable delusion, which one group of researchers calls an "Adonis complex," see their muscular bodies as being too puny. So they abuse steroids and exercise or pump iron compulsively (Pope, Phillips, & Olivardia, 2000).

Genetic vulnerabilities may play a role in the development of eating disorders (Allison & Faith, 1997). However, genetic dispositions clearly interact with cultural pressures—as we saw in the case of professionally ambitious women who feel the need to look thin, "masculine," and competent—and with a person's psychological conflicts. For example, college women who develop eating disorders are often caught between their desires to achieve and their parents' messages about "women's place"; the body becomes a battleground to resolve this conflict. They are more likely than other women to say that their parents believe a woman's place is in the home,

that their mothers are unhappy with their lives, that their fathers think their mothers are unintelligent, and that their fathers think their sons are more intelligent than their daughters (Silverstein & Perlick, 1995). Perhaps this is why women who have eating disorders tend to be depressed, perfectionistic, and more self-critical than healthy eaters (Lehman & Rodin, 1989; Walsh & Devlin, 1998).

But why are many men becoming as vulnerable as women to media images of nearly impossible body shapes, devouring magazines that promise "Perfect Abs in 10 Days!" and "Fat to Flat: Drop 20 Pounds the Easy Way!" and spending billions on cosmetic surgery and gym equipment? One explanation is that, in an era of growing equality and challenges to their masculinity, men want to look strong and "manly" to distinguish themselves from women (Pope, Phillips, & Olivardia, 2000). Another is that commercial interests just know a vulnerable audience when they see one—and they also know how to create one.

These findings on the forces that influence eating habits, weight, and eating disorders contain a lesson that applies to many other areas of behavior: Within a given environment, genes interact with cultural rules, psychological needs, and individual habits to shape—sometimes quite literally—who we are.

QUICK QUIZ

Is all this information about eating making you hungry for knowledge?

1. *True or false:* Emotional problems explain why fat people are heavy.

2. Falling and rising levels of leptin help the brain regulate appetite and _____ in order to maintain a person's genetically influenced _____.

3. Rising rates of obesity can best be explained by (a) genetic changes over the past few decades, (b) a lack of willpower, (c) an abundance of high-fat food and sedentary lifestyles, (d) the increase in eating disorders.

4. Bill, who is thin, reads in the newspaper that genes set the range of body weight and shape. "Oh, good," he exclaims, "now I can eat all the junk food I want; I was born to be skinny." What's wrong with Bill's conclusion?

Answers:

1. false 2. metabolism, set point 3. c 4. Bill is right to recognize that there may be limits to how heavy he can become. But he may also be oversimplifying and jumping to conclusions. Even people who have a set point for leanness will gain considerable weight on fatty foods and excess calories, especially if they don't exercise; also, rich junk food is unhealthy for reasons that have nothing to do with becoming overweight.

What's Ahead

- Why is "doing your best" an ineffective goal to set for yourself?

- When you are learning a new skill, should you concentrate on mastering it or on performing it well in front of others?

- Which aspects of a job are more important than money in increasing your work satisfaction and involvement?

- How is the *desire* to achieve affected by the *opportunity* to achieve?

13.4 The Competent Animal: Motives to Achieve

Almost every adult works. But "work" does not only mean paid employment. Students work at studying. Homemakers work, often more hours than salaried employees, at running a household. Artists, poets, and actors work, even if they are paid erratically (or not at all). And some people work to make a living, but they put their passion for achievement into other activities—learning to become an accomplished trail rider or adding an Australian crimson rosella to their list of birds sighted. What keeps everybody doing what they do?

Psychologists, particularly those in the field of *industrial/organizational psychology,* have studied work motivation in the laboratory, where they have measured internal motives such as the desire for achievement, and in organizations, where they study the conditions that influence productivity and satisfaction. Their findings apply not only to understanding why people thrive or wilt in the work environment, but also to understanding people's aspirations and achievements in general.

Goals and Aspirations

One of the strongest findings about the motivation to achieve, in any sphere of life, is the importance of having goals—but not just any old goals. Goals are most likely to improve motivation and performance when three conditions are met (Cooper, Shapiro, & Powers, 1998; Higgins, 1998; Locke & Latham, 1990; Smither, 1998):

- *The goal must be specific.* Defining a goal as "doing your best" is as ineffective as having no goals at all. You need to be specific about what you are going to do and when you are going to do it: "I will write four pages of this paper today."

- *The goal must be challenging but achievable.* You are apt to work harder for tough but realistic goals that make you feel gratified when you reach them, than for either easy goals that pose no challenge or impossible goals that can never be attained.

- *The goal should be framed in terms of getting what you want rather than avoiding what you do not want.* Approach goals are positive experiences that you seek directly, such as "trying to be smarter" or "learning to scuba dive." *Avoidance goals* involve escaping from unpleasant experiences, such as "trying not to make a fool of myself" or "trying to avoid being dependent."

People who frame their goals in specific, achievable approach terms (e.g., "I'm going to lose weight by jogging three times a week") feel better about themselves, feel more competent, are more optimistic and less depressed, and even have fewer colds and other physical symptoms than people who frame the same goals in avoidance terms (e.g., "I'm going to lose weight by staying away from rich foods"). Can you guess why? Approach goals allow you to focus on what you can actively do to accomplish them, whereas avoidance goals make you focus on what you have to give up (Coats, Janoff-Bulman, & Alpert, 1996; Elliot & Sheldon, 1998).

Defining your goals is only the first step on the road to success; next you need to know what to do when you hit a pothole. Some people give up when a goal becomes difficult or they are faced with a setback, whereas others become even more determined to succeed. Talent or ambition alone does not predict who will push on and who will give up. The crucial factor is whether their main motivation is to perform well in front of others or to learn the task for the satisfaction of it (Utman, 1997).

People who are motivated by **performance goals** are concerned with doing well, being judged favorably, and avoiding criticism (Dweck, 1992; Dweck & Sorich, 1999). When such people are focused on how well they are performing and then do poorly, they often decide the fault is theirs, and they stop trying to improve. Because their goal is to demonstrate their abilities, they set themselves

performance goals
Goals framed in terms of performing well in front of others, being judged favorably, and avoiding criticism.

up for grief when they temporarily fail—as all of us must if we are to learn anything new.

In contrast, those who are motivated by **mastery (learning) goals** are concerned with increasing their competence and skills. Therefore, they regard failure as a source of useful information that will help them improve. Failure and criticism do not discourage them because they know that learning takes time. In addition, people who focus on mastery rather than performance usually feel greater intrinsic pleasure in the task they are doing or the goal they are pursuing. (However, there is an exception to this rule for highly ambitious, performance-driven people, such as great athletes and musicians. For them, focusing on specific ways of improving their performance raises intrinsic motivation and satisfaction [Elliot & Harackiewicz, 1994].)

Children acquire performance or mastery goals early, from the actions adults praise them for and from what they observe in their environments. For example, many parents believe in the importance of praising their child's intelligence and ability when the child does well ("Wow, Katie, are you smart!").

mastery (learning) goals
Goals framed in terms of increasing one's competence and skills.

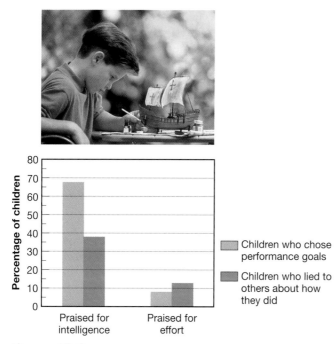

Figure 13.2

Mastery and Motivation

Children praised for being smart rather than for working hard tend to lose the pleasure of learning and focus on how well they are doing. Nearly 70 percent of fifth graders who were praised for intelligence later chose performance goals (doing "problems that aren't too hard, so I don't get many wrong") rather than learning goals (doing "problems that I'll learn a lot from, even if I won't look so smart")—compared to fewer than 10 percent of children who were praised for their efforts (Mueller & Dweck, 1998).

Yet, surprisingly, such praise can backfire (see Chapter 8). In several studies, children who were praised for their intelligence and ability later cared more about performance goals and less about learning goals than did children praised for their *efforts* (see Figure 13.2). And after the "smart" children failed a problem-solving game, they tended to give up on subsequent ones, enjoyed them less, lied to other kids about how well they had done, and actually performed less well than children who had been praised for their efforts (Mueller & Dweck, 1998). The reason seems to be that most American children regard intelligence and ability as fixed traits that you can't do anything about. Therefore, if you fail, you might as well give up. But effort is subject to improvement; you can always try again, and that is the key to mastery. As one learning-oriented child said, "Mistakes are our friends" (Dweck & Sorich, 1999).

The Effects of Motivation on Work

Most people are motivated to work in order to meet the basic needs for food and shelter. Yet survival does not explain why some people want to do their work well and others want just to get it done. It doesn't explain the difference between Aristotle's view ("All paid employments absorb and degrade the mind") and Noël Coward's ("Work is more fun than fun"). What psychological factors might account for these variations in the motivation to work?

Expectations and Values. How hard you work for something depends, first, on what you expect to accomplish. If you are fairly certain of success, you will work much harder to reach your goal than if you are fairly certain of failure.

A classic experiment showed how quickly experience affects these expectations. Young women were asked to solve 15 anagram puzzles. Before working on each one, they had to estimate their chances of solving it. Half of the women started off with very easy anagrams, but half began with insoluble ones. Sure enough, those who started with the easy ones increased their estimates of success on later ones. Those who began with the impossible ones decided they would all be impossible. These expectations, in turn, affected the young women's ability to actually solve the last 10 anagrams, which were the same for everyone. The higher the expectation of success, the more anagrams the women solved

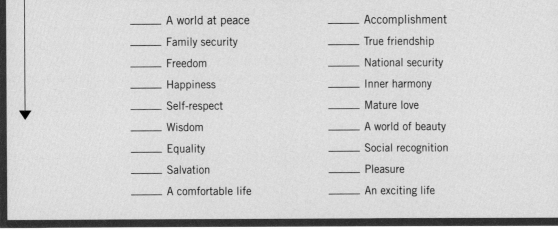

GET INVOLVED

▶ WHAT DO YOU VALUE MOST IN LIFE?

Rank the following values in terms of their importance to you, with 1 the most important and 18 the least. Then ask some friends and relatives to do the same. How does your ranking differ from theirs? Do your values affect your goals, relationships, level of community activism, or decisions? Do any of your key values conflict with your daily actions—and if so, does that conflict motivate you to change in any way? (From Rokeach and Ball-Rokeach, 1989.)

_____ A world at peace	_____ Accomplishment
_____ Family security	_____ True friendship
_____ Freedom	_____ National security
_____ Happiness	_____ Inner harmony
_____ Self-respect	_____ Mature love
_____ Wisdom	_____ A world of beauty
_____ Equality	_____ Social recognition
_____ Salvation	_____ Pleasure
_____ A comfortable life	_____ An exciting life

(Feather, 1966). Once acquired, therefore, expectations can create a *self-fulfilling prophecy,* in which a person predicts how he or she will do and then behaves in such a way as to make the prediction come true (see Chapter 2).

How hard you work for something, of course, also depends on how much you want it, which in turn depends on your general value system (Feather, 1982). A *value* is a central motivating belief, reflecting a person's fundamental goals and ideals: freedom, beauty, equality, friendship, fame, wisdom, and so on (Rokeach & Ball-Rokeach, 1989). The values that motivate people can themselves have psychological consequences. For example, American culture puts a high value on wealth and financial success. But the pursuit of material wealth for its own sake has a dark side. Young adults whose central value is the acquisition of wealth have poorer overall emotional adjustment and lower well-being than do people whose primary values are self-acceptance, affiliation with others, or wanting to make the world a better place (Kasser & Ryan, 1996; Ryan et al., 1999).

Competence and Self-efficacy. A feeling of competence is another spur to continued motivation. Albert Bandura (1994) calls it **self-efficacy,** the conviction that you can accomplish what you set out to do. You aren't born with

Talk about self-efficacy! Aimee Mullins was born without the bones that connect the knee to the ankle, and her legs were amputated below the knee on her first birthday. Mullins learned to ski, and set records in running and jumping at the 1996 Paralympics. In 1998 she became a professional model. "[People] relate to what I'm doing, which is challenging the norm," says Mullins.

self-efficacy
A person's belief that he or she is capable of producing desired results, such as mastering new skills and reaching goals.

self-efficacy; you acquire it, through experience in mastering new skills, overcoming obstacles, and learning from occasional failures. Self-efficacy also comes from having successful role models who teach you that your ambitions are possible, and from having people around to give you constructive feedback and encouragement.

People who have a strong sense of self-efficacy are quick to cope with problems that befall them, and they keep striving for their goals even in the face of setbacks and failures. Research in North America, Europe, and Russia has found that self-efficacy has a positive effect on just about every aspect of people's lives: how well they do on a task, how persistently they pursue their goals, the kind of career choices they make, their ability to solve complex problems, their motivation to work for political and social goals, their health habits, and even their chances of recovery from heart attack (Bandura, 1994; Ewart, 1995; Maddux, 1995; Stajkovic & Luthans, 1998).

The Need for Achievement. In the early 1950s, David McClelland and his associates (1953) speculated that some people have a **need for achievement** that motivates them as much as hunger motivates people to eat. To measure the strength of this motive, McClelland used the **Thematic Apperception Test (TAT),** which requires the test taker to make up a story about a set of ambiguous pictures. A standardized scoring system permits the test to be scored for different motives, including the needs for achievement, power, and affiliation. The strength of these internal motives, said McClelland (1961), is captured in the fantasies the test-taker reveals. "In fantasy anything is at least symbolically possible," he explained. "A person may rise to great heights, sink to great depths, kill his grandmother, or take off for the South Sea Islands on a pogo stick."

Needless to say, people with high achievement motivation do not fantasize about taking off for the South Seas or sinking to great depths. They tell stories about working hard, becoming rich and famous, and clobbering the opposition with their wit and brilliance; or of feeling miserable and depressed if they do not succeed. For example, here is what two people wrote in response to a

need for achievement
A learned motive to meet personal standards of success and excellence in a chosen area.

Thematic Apperception Test (TAT)
A personality test that asks respondents to interpret a series of drawings showing ambiguous scenes of people; usually scored for motives such as the needs for achievement, power, and affiliation.

THE MANY MOTIVES OF ACCOMPLISHMENT

IMMORTALITY
WILLIAM FAULKNER
(1897–1962)
Novelist

"Really the writer doesn't want success . . . He wants to leave a scratch on that wall [of oblivion]—Kilroy was here—that somebody a hundred or a thousand years later will see."

KNOWLEDGE
HELEN KELLER
(1880–1968)
Blind/deaf author and lecturer

"Knowledge is happiness, because to have knowledge—broad, deep knowledge—is to know true ends from false, and lofty things from low."

JUSTICE
MARTIN LUTHER KING, JR.
(1929–1968)
Civil rights activist

"I have a dream . . . that my four little children will one day live in a nation where they will not be judged by the color of their skin but by the content of their character."

AUTONOMY
GEORGIA O'KEEFFE
(1887–1986)
Artist

"[I] found myself saying to myself—I can't live where I want to, go where I want to, do what I want to . . . I decided I was a very stupid fool not to at least paint as I wanted to."

neutral illustration of a man named George, sitting at his desk (McClelland, 1985):

High need for achievement: George is an engineer who wants to win a competition in which the man with the most practicable drawing will be awarded the contract to build a bridge. He is taking a moment to think how happy he will be if he wins. He has been baffled by how to make such a long span strong, but remembers to specify a new steel alloy of great strength, submits his entry, but does not win and is very unhappy.

High need for affiliation: George is an engineer who is working late. He is worried that his wife will be annoyed with him for neglecting her. She has been objecting that he cares more about his work than his wife and family. He seems unable to satisfy both his boss and his wife, but he loves her very much, and will do his best to finish up fast and get home to her.

When high achievers are in situations that arouse their competitiveness and desire to succeed—when, for example, they believe that the TAT is measuring their intelligence and leadership ability—their achievement-related themes increase (Atkinson, 1958). In the laboratory and real life, people who score high on the need for achievement consistently differ from those who score low. High scorers are more likely, for example, to start their own businesses. They set high personal standards and prefer to work with capable colleagues who can help them succeed rather than with co-workers who are merely friendly (McClelland, 1987).

The Effects of Work on Motivation

Psychologists who study achievement motivation ask, "How does having an internal motive to achieve affect a person's chances of success?" But others reverse the question, asking, "How does a person's chances of success affect the motive to achieve?" Achievement, they find, does not depend solely on internal expectations, values, and motives—that is, on enduring, unchanging

POWER

HENRY KISSINGER
(b. 1923)
Former Secretary of State

"Power is the ultimate aphrodisiac."

DUTY

ELEANOR ROOSEVELT
(1884–1962)
Humanitarian, lecturer, stateswoman

"As for accomplishments, I just did what I had to do as things came along."

EXCELLENCE

FLORENCE GRIFFITH JOYNER
(1959–1998)
Olympic gold medalist

"When you've been second best for so long, you can either accept it, or try to become the best. I made the decision to try and be the best."

GREED

IVAN BOESKY
(b. 1937)
Financier, convicted of insider trading violations

"Greed is all right . . . I think greed is healthy. You can be greedy and still feel good about yourself."

qualities of the individual. It also depends on conditions of the work you do.

Working Conditions.

Several specific aspects of the work environment are known to increase job involvement, work motivation, and job satisfaction (S. Brown, 1996; Kohn & Schooler, 1983):

- The work provides a sense of meaningfulness.

- Employees have control over many aspects of their work—for example, they can set their own hours and make decisions.

- Tasks are varied rather than repetitive.

- The company maintains clear and consistent rules for its workers.

- Employees have supportive relationships with their superiors and co-workers.

- Employees receive useful feedback about their work, so they know what they have accomplished and what they need to do to improve.

- The company offers opportunities for its employees' growth and development.

Companies that foster these conditions tend to have more productive and satisfied employees, and this is true in countries as diverse as the Netherlands, Hungary, and Bulgaria (Roe et al., 1998). Workers tend to become more creative in

their thinking and feel better about themselves and their work than they do if they feel stuck in routine, boring jobs that give them no control or flexibility over their daily tasks (Karasek & Theorell, 1990; Locke & Latham, 1990). Conversely, when people with high power or achievement motivation are put in situations that frustrate their desire and ability to express these motives, they become dissatisfied and stressed, and their power and achievement motives decline (Jenkins, 1994).

Did you notice anything missing from that list of beneficial working conditions? Where is money, supposedly the great motivator? Actually, work motivation is related not to the amount of money you get, but to how and when you get it. The strongest motivator is *incentive pay*, bonuses that are given upon completion of a goal rather than as an automatic raise (Locke et al., 1981). Incentive pay increases people's feelings of competence and accomplishment ("I got this raise because I deserved it"). This doesn't mean that people should accept low pay so they will like their jobs better, or that they should never demand cost-of-living raises!

Opportunities to Achieve.

Another important working condition that affects achievement is having the *opportunity* to achieve. When someone does not do well at work, others are apt to say it is the individual's own fault because he or she lacks the internal drive to "make it." But what the person may really lack is a fair chance to make it, and this is especially true for those who have been subjected to systematic discrimination, such as women and ethnic

> Thinking Critically About Why People Achieve—or Don't

minorities. At one time, for example, women were said to be less successful than men in the workplace because women had an internalized "fear of success." Yet as opportunities for women improved and sex discrimination was made illegal, this apparent "motive" vanished.

Similarly, when the proportion of men and women in an occupation changes, so do people's motivations to work in that field (Kanter, 1977/1993). Many occupations are still highly segregated by gender; there are few male secretaries or female auto mechanics. As a result, many people form gender stereotypes of the requirements of such careers: "Female" jobs require kindness and nurturance, "male" jobs require strength and smarts. These stereotypes, in turn, stifle many people's aspirations to enter a nontraditional career

Like employees, students can have poor working conditions that affect their motivation. They may have to study in crowded quarters or may have small siblings who interrupt and distract them.

(Cejka & Eagly, 1999). As job segregation breaks down, however, people's motivations change. When law and bartending were almost entirely male professions, few women aspired to become lawyers or bartenders. Now that women make up a large percentage of both occupations, their motivation to become lawyers or bartenders has changed rapidly.

Once in a career, people may become more motivated to advance up the ladder or less so, depending on how many rungs they are permitted to climb. Men *and* women who work in jobs with no prospect of promotion tend to play down the importance of achievement, fantasize about quitting, and emphasize the social benefits of their jobs instead of the intellectual or financial benefits (Kanter, 1977/1993). Consider the comments of a man who realized in his mid-30s that he was never going to be promoted to top management and who scaled down his ambitions accordingly (Scofield, 1993). As organizational psychologists would predict, he began to emphasize the benefits of not achieving: "I'm freer to speak my mind," "I can choose not to play office politics." He had time, he learned, for coaching Little League and could stay home when the kids were sick. "Of course," he wrote, "if I ever had any chance for upward corporate mobility it's gone now. I couldn't take the grind. Whether real or imagined, that glass ceiling has become an invisible shield."

Women and members of minority groups are especially likely to encounter a real "glass ceiling" in management—a barrier to promotion that is so subtle as to be transparent, yet strong enough to prevent advancement. Researchers can determine that a company has a glass ceiling when a woman or minority person's educational level, work experience, and professional accomplishments do not predict advancement as they do for white men (Graham, 1994; Valian, 1998).

As you can see, work motivation and satisfaction depend on the right fit between qualities of the individual and conditions of the work. Increasingly, in a global economy dependent on an ethnically diverse workforce, companies face the challenge of how best to structure the work environment so that employees will be productive and satisfied, striving to do their best rather than feeling apathetic, resentful, or burned out.

QUICK QUIZ

Work on your understanding of work motivation.

1. Ramón and Ramona are learning to ski. Every time she falls, Ramona says, "This is the most humiliating experience I've ever had! Everyone is watching me behave like a clumsy dolt!" When Ramón falls, he says, "&*!!@$@! I'll show these dratted skis who's boss!" Why is Ramona more likely than Ramón to give up? (a) She *is* a clumsy dolt; (b) she is less competent at skiing; (c) she is focused on performance; (d) she is focused on learning.

2. Which of these factors significantly increase work motivation? (a) specific goals, (b) regular pay, (c) feedback, (d) general goals, (e) being told what to do, (f) being able to make decisions, (g) the chance of promotion, (h) having routine, predictable work

3. Phyllis works at an umbrella company. Her work is competent, but she rarely arrives on time, doesn't seem as motivated as others to do well, and has begun to take an unusual number of sick days. This behavior is annoying her boss, who is thinking of firing her. What guidelines of critical thinking is the boss overlooking, and what research should the boss consider before taking this step?

Answers:

1. c 2. a, c, f, g 3. The boss is jumping to the conclusion that Phyllis has low achievement motivation. This may be true, but because her work is competent, the boss should consider other explanations and examine the evidence. Perhaps the work conditions are unsatisfactory: There may be few opportunities for promotion; she may get no feedback; perhaps the company does not provide child care, so Phyllis arrives late because she has child-care obligations. What other possible explanations come to mind?

What's Ahead

- What kind of conflict do you have when you want to study for a big exam but you also want to go out partying?

- Do you have to satisfy basic needs for security and belonging before you can become "self-actualized"?

13.5 When Motives Conflict

Throughout this chapter we have been looking at the specific motives involved in love, sex, eating, and work. But the many motives of human life rarely coexist in perfect harmony. Two motives are in conflict when the satisfaction of one leads to the inability to act on the other—when, that is, you want to eat your cake and have it, too. Researchers have identified four kinds of motivational conflicts (Lewin, 1948):

1 *Approach–approach conflicts* occur when you are equally attracted to two or more possible activities or goals. For example, you would like to go out with Tom, Dick, *and* Harry, all at the same time; you would like to be a veterinarian *and* a rock singer; you would like to go out with friends (an affiliation motive) *and* study like mad for an exam (an achievement motive).

2 *Avoidance–avoidance conflicts* require you to choose between "the lesser of two evils" because you dislike both alternatives. Novice parachute jumpers, for example, must choose between the fear of jumping and the fear of losing face if they don't jump.

3 *Approach–avoidance conflicts* occur when one activity or goal has both a positive and a negative aspect. For example, you want to be a powerful executive but you worry about losing your friends if you succeed. You want power and yet you fear it at the same time. In culturally diverse nations, differing cultural values produce many approach–avoidance conflicts. Our students have offered many examples. A Chicano student said he wants to succeed in the mainstream culture, but his parents, valuing the family's closeness, worry that if he goes to college and graduate school, he will become too independent and eventually leave them behind. An African-American student from a poor neighborhood, in college on a prestigious scholarship, is torn between wanting to leave his background behind him and returning to help his home community. And a white student wants to be a marine biologist, but her friends tell her that only nerdy guys and dweebs go into science.

4 *Multiple approach–avoidance conflicts* occur in situations that offer several possible choices, each containing advantages and disadvantages. For example, you want to marry while you are still in school, and you think you have found the right person. On the other hand, you also want to establish a career and have some money in the bank, and lately you and the right person have been quarreling a lot.

Conflicts like these are inevitable, part of the price and pleasure of living. But if they remain unresolved, they can take an emotional toll. In students, high levels of conflict and ambivalence are associated with anxiety, depression, headaches and other symptoms, and more visits to the health center (Emmons & King, 1988). In contrast, students who are "true to themselves," who strive for goals that are consistent with the qualities they value most, have greater self-integrity and a greater sense of meaning and purpose in life than do those who are pursuing goals discrepant with their core values (McGregor & Little, 1998).

Another way of thinking about the competing motives in our lives comes from a theory proposed by humanist psychologist Abraham Maslow (1970). Maslow envisioned people's motives as forming a pyramid, a *hierarchy of needs* ranked by their importance for survival. At the bottom level of the pyramid were basic *survival needs,* for food, sleep, and water; at the next level were *security needs,* for shelter and safety; at the third level were *social needs,* for belonging and affection; at the fourth level were *esteem needs,* for self-respect and the respect of others; and at the top were *needs for self-actualization* and "self-transcendence." Maslow argued that your needs must be met at each level before you can even think of the matters posed by the level above it. You can't worry about achievement if you are hungry, cold, and poor. You can't

THE FAR SIDE By GARY LARSON

"C'mon, c'mon—it's either one or the other."

A classic avoidance–avoidance conflict.

become self-actualized if you haven't satisfied your needs for self-esteem and love. Human beings behave badly, he argued, only when their lower needs are frustrated.

This theory, which was intuitively logical and optimistic about human progress, became immensely popular, and "motivational experts" still often refer to it, but it has not been well supported by research (Smither, 1998). People have *simultaneous* needs for comfort and safety and for attachments, self-esteem, and competence. Individuals who have met their "lower" needs do not inevitably seek "higher" ones, nor is it the case that people behave badly only when their lower needs are frustrated. Higher needs may even take precedence over lower ones. History is full of examples of people who would rather starve than be humiliated; who would rather die of torture than sacrifice their convictions; who would rather explore, risk, or create new art than be safe and secure at home.

PSYCHOLOGY IN THE NEWS, REVISITED

Understanding the biological, psychological, and cultural influences on motivation can help us understand the stories that opened this chapter and the many other stories that make the news every day.

The love story in *Titanic* appeals most to those whose ideal is romantic or passionate love—the kind that involves emotional turmoil, sexual longing, and idealization of the loved one. As pragmatic reasons for marriage have faded, this ideal has become increasingly popular throughout the world. But as we saw, "eros" is only one kind of love, and it is not the most long-lasting type. It characterizes the early stage of love affairs, when the lovers still don't know much about each other, and it often creates unrealistic expectations that can lead to disappointment. If a relationship is to last, the lovers must also pass the tests of intimacy and commitment. What would have happened to the young couple in *Titanic* if the ship had not gone down? Would they have been as happy clearing the table together and diapering the kids as they were in the swanky salons of a luxury liner? Would the original flame of passion have left a satisfying afterglow? If so, their relationship would probably

have endured, but it would no longer be the type that makes grown men cry.

Our second news item, about the rape charges against the three star football players at the Naval Academy, illustrates the tragedy and conflict that can occur when women and men have different sexual motives and learn different sexual scripts. As we saw, the motives for sex among sexually aggressive men have less to do with physical pleasure than with hostility toward women, peer pressure to prove their masculinity, and a cultural script that endorses promiscuous, impersonal sex for men. In addition, the sexual scripts for star athletes in American culture may foster a sense of dominance over women and a sense of "entitlement" to sex.

The news item about the risks of diet drugs reveals the problems that arise when people seek miracle cures for their weight problems. As each quick-fix solution fails, others arise to tempt a gullible and desperate public: earplugs that curb the appetite; "Slimming Insoles" for your shoes that help you lose weight by pressing on nerves in the foot; tablets that "block the absorption of fat" in the body; and even a shiny "Fat-Be-Gone" ring, said to produce the same effect as jogging six miles.

Save your money. As research in this chapter suggests, the first question dieters should ask is why they want to lose weight: to conform to a cultural ideal, or to be healthier? As we saw, some people have a genetic tendency to be plump. Understanding this fact may help people accept the normal diversity of body shapes and sizes, lose their prejudices against fat people, and set realistic goals for themselves. Instead of trying to conform to a pencil-thin or hypermuscular cultural ideal that is impossible for all but a minority of women and men, for example, people can find the best weight within their own set-point range.

On the other hand, obesity is associated with many severe health risks, including heart disease, high blood pressure, and diabetes, so it is important for people to realize what they *can* control. As we saw, major reasons for weight gain are lack of exercise; the availability of inexpensive, high-fat, high-calorie food; the rapid pace of life, which encourages people to eat fattening "convenience" meals and snacks on the run; and social and cultural pressures to overeat.

Finally, the story of Lance Armstrong shows the importance of having self-efficacy, setting challenging but achievable goals, and persisting in the pursuit of one's dreams despite inevitable failures. After winning his war with cancer, Armstrong was ready to give up racing, but his coaches wouldn't let him. They took him on a weeklong training retreat in the mountains, where they rode hard for hours a day, just for the pleasure of riding. "I tried to remind Lance how gifted he is as a bike racer," said Bob Roll, one of the coaches, "how important it was for his peace of mind that he try his hardest and take whatever comes. . . . If you turn away from the sport without having made your best effort, it would always bug you." "That week was the turning point, absolutely," Armstrong told *The New York Times*. "I learned there that I still loved racing and training. I learned I really loved it."

At the end of the first chapter of this book, we discussed not only what psychology can do for you but also what it cannot. As we hope this final chapter has shown, psychology can teach us a great deal about the many motives of human life: the mean-ings of love, the mysteries of sex, the dilemmas we create for ourselves about eating and weight, and the conditions that enhance or suppress the pursuit of achievement.

What psychology cannot tell us is which motives, goals, and values to choose in the first place: love, wealth, security, passion, freedom, fame, the desire to improve the world, or anything else. In a commencement address some years ago, Mario Cuomo, the former governor of New York, had these words of wisdom for the graduating stu-dents: "When you've parked the second car in the garage, and installed the hot tub, and skied in Colorado, and wind-surfed in the Caribbean, when you've had your first love affair and your second and your third, the question will remain: Where does the dream end for me?"

TAKING PSYCHOLOGY WITH YOU

Improving Your Motivation

Why are you in school? What do you hope to accomplish in your life? Are you motivated primarily by the intrinsic goals of a job well done and the satisfaction of the work itself or by extrinsic goals such as getting a job and a big salary? Do you have a burning ambition, or are you burned out? If you are feeling unmoti-vated these days, research on work motivation suggests some steps you might take:

● *Seek activities that are intrinsically pleasur-able, even if they don't "pay off."* If you really, really want to study Swahili or Swedish even though these languages are not in your prelaw requirements, try to find a way to do it. If you are not enjoying your major or your job, con-sider finding a career that would be more intrinsically pleasurable; or at least make sure you have other projects and activities that you do enjoy for their own sake.

● *Set specific goals that have a target date.* Remember to be as specific as you can in what you hope to achieve; "do my best" is too vague. If you know you have to meet a goal by a specific date, you are more likely to succeed than if you give yourself an indef-inite amount of time ("by next year").

● *Focus on learning goals rather than on performance goals.* In general, you will be better able to cope with setbacks if your goal is to learn rather than to show off how good you are. Regard failure as a chance to learn rather than as a sign of incompetence. The more you are able to focus on improvement, the better your performance will be.

● *Get accurate feedback on your perform-ance.* Once you have specified a goal, continued motivation depends in part on getting feedback about your performance. Edward Koch, the former mayor of New York, used to go around asking people, "How'm I doing?" We all need to know how we are doing and what steps we can take to do better. If you are not getting enough feedback, ask for it—and then remember that criticism is useful.

● *Assess your working conditions.* Are you getting support from co-workers, employers, or instructors? Do you have opportunities to develop ideas and vary your routine, or are you expected to toe the line and do the same thing day after day? Do you perceive a glass ceiling that might limit your advancement in your chosen field, and are your perceptions accurate? If you have entered school or a job with enthusiasm, optimism, and expecta-tions of success, only to have these feelings slowly dwindle and dissipate, you might con-sider whether your working conditions are causing your burnout. And then you might see whether changing some of those condi-tions could recharge your batteries.

● *Take steps to resolve motivational con-flicts.* Many students in an approach–avoidance conflict tend to think a great deal about their conflicts but not do any-thing to resolve them. A student in one study, for instance, remained unhappily stuck between his goal of achieving inde-pendence and his desire to be cared for by his parents (Emmons & King, 1988). The reconciliation of conflicts like these is important for your well-being.

Abraham Maslow may have been wrong about a universal hierarchy of motives, but perhaps each of us develops our own hier-archy as we grow from childhood to old age. For some people, needs for love, secu-rity, and safety will dominate. For others, the need for achievement or power will rule. Some of us will wrestle with conflict-ing motives; for others, one consuming ambition will hold sway over all others. The motives and goals that inspire us, and the choices we make in their pursuit, are what give our lives passion, color, and meaning. Choose wisely.

SUMMARY

- *Motivation* refers to an inferred process within a person or animal that causes that organism to move toward a goal—satisfy a biological need or achieve a psychological ambition—or away from an unpleasant situation. A few primary motivating *drives* are based on physiological needs, but most human motives are psychological or social in nature.

The Social Animal: Motives for Love

- All human beings have a *need for affiliation*—for connection, attachment, and love. But love takes many forms. Traditionally, *passionate ("romantic") love* has been distinguished from *companionate love*. But psychologists have analyzed other kinds as well. One theory describes *six styles of love* (romantic, game-playing, affectionate, pragmatic, possessive, and selfless). In the *triangle theory of love*, love consists of different combinations of passion, intimacy, and commitment. And the *attachment theory of love* views adult love relationships, like those of infants, as being secure, avoidant, or anxious-ambivalent. Adults' attachment styles tend to be stable from childhood throughout adulthood and affect their own close relationships. A person's style of love can change over time and in different relationships. The love "stories" that guide our lives affect our satisfaction in relationships; for example, people who expect to feel highly passionate forever are likely to experience disappointment.

- Men and women are equally likely to feel love and need attachment, but gender roles affect how they express feelings of love and how they define "intimacy." In Western societies, women often express love in words, whereas men express it in actions. But as women have entered the workforce in large numbers and pragmatic reasons for marriage have faded, the two sexes have become more alike in endorsing romantic love as a requirement for marriage.

The Erotic Animal: Motives for Sex

- Biological research finds that testosterone influences sexual desire in both sexes, that there is no "right" kind of orgasm for women to have, and that both sexes are capable of sexual arousal and response. Kinsey and, later, Masters and Johnson were the first modern investigators to show that physiologically, male and female sexuality are more similar than different, although some researchers believe that the sexes differ in whether their sexual motivation is governed primarily by physiology or by culture and circumstance.

- *Evolutionary psychologists* argue that men and women have evolved different sexual strategies and behavior in response to survival problems faced in the distant past. In this view, it has been more adaptive for males to be promiscuous, be attracted to young partners, and want sexual novelty, and for females to be monogamous, be choosy about partners, and prefer security to novelty. Critics argue that research on many species, including primates, does not support these allegedly universal sex differences and that human sexual behavior is too varied and changeable to fit a single evolutionary explanation.

- Psychological, social, and cultural approaches to sexual motivation emphasize the ways that values, beliefs, and fantasies affect sexual desire and response. Men and women have sex to satisfy many different psychological motives, including pleasure, intimacy, coping, self-affirmation, the partner's approval, or peer approval. Both sexes may agree to intercourse for nonsexual motives: Men sometimes feel obligated to "make a move" to prove their masculinity, and women sometimes feel obliged to "give in" to preserve the relationship.

- A major gender difference in sexual experience has to do with rape and perceptions of sexual coercion: What many women regard as coercion is not always seen as such by men. Men who rape do so for diverse reasons, including peer pressure, insecurity, hostility toward women, a wish to dominate or humiliate the victim, and sometimes sadism.

- Cultures differ widely in determining what parts of the body people learn are erotic, which sexual acts are erotic or repulsive, and whether sex itself is good or bad. Cultures transmit these ideas through *gender roles* and *sexual scripts*, which specify appropriate behavior during courtship and sex, depending on a person's gender, age, and sexual orientation. Scripts for heterosexual women and men often lead to different sexual goals and misunderstandings. As in the case of love, gender differences (and growing similarities) in sexuality are affected by cultural and economic factors.

- The origins of sexual orientation are still unknown. Traditional psychological explanations do not account for why some people become homosexual despite strong social pressures for heterosexuality. Genetic and hormonal factors may be involved, although the evidence is stronger for gay men than for lesbians, whose sexuality is more varied and flexible. Biology, culture, learning, and circumstance interact in complex ways to produce a given person's orientation. Research on this issue is sensitive because people often confuse scientific questions about the origins of homosexuality with political and moral questions about the rights of gays and lesbians.

The Hungry Animal: Motives to Eat

- Overweight and obesity are not simply a result of failed willpower, emotional disturbance, or overeating. Hunger, weight, and eating are regulated by a set of bodily mechanisms that keep people within a genetically influenced *set point*. Genes influence body shape, distribution of fat, and whether the body will convert excess calories into fat. Genes may also account for certain types of obesity. Some obese people have low levels of, or are insensitive to, *leptin*, which enables the *hypothalamus* to regulate appetite and metabolism. But for most obese people, leptin does not play a major role.

- However, set-point theory alone cannot explain why rates of overweight and obesity are rising all over the world, among all social classes, ethnicities, and ages. The reasons reflect the interaction of a genetic disposition to gain weight when rich food is plentiful, and an environment that provides cheap, high-fat food and rewards sedentary lifestyles. Eating habits and activity levels are, in turn, affected by cultural standards of what the ideal body should look like—heavy or thin, soft or muscular.

- When genetic predispositions clash with culture, physical problems and mental disorders can result. In cultures that foster overeating and regard overweight as a sign of attractiveness and health, obesity is acceptable, but obesity is associated with a greatly elevated risk of many diseases and disabilities. In cultures that idealize unrealistically thin bodies, eating disorders increase, especially *bulimia* and *anorexia*. These disorders, which are far more common in women than in men, are associated with a desire for a boyish body and a conflict between the desire to achieve and parental messages about "women's place."

The Competent Animal: Motives to Achieve

- The motivation to achieve depends not only on ability, but also on whether people set *mastery (learning) goals*, in which the focus is on learning the task well, or *performance goals*, in which the focus is on performing well for others. Mastery goals lead to persistence in the face of failures and setbacks; performance goals often lead to giving up.

- Work motivation also depends on people's expectations of success, which can create *self-fulfilling prophecies* of success or failure; the *value* they place on the goal; and *self-efficacy*, the conviction that they have the ability to accomplish their goals. Self-efficacy comes from experience in mastering new skills and learning from failure, having successful role models, and getting feedback and encouragement from others. People who are motivated by a high *need for achievement*, as measured by the *Thematic Apperception Test (TAT)*, set high but realistic standards for success and excellence.

- Work motivation also depends on circumstances of the job itself. Key working conditions that promote motivation and satisfaction are those that provide workers with a sense of meaningfulness, control, variation in tasks, clear rules, supportive relationships, feedback, and opportunities for advancement and learning. *Incentive pay* is more effective than predictable raises in elevating work motivation. For women, one factor in the motivation to enter a career is its gender ratio. The motivation to achieve also depends on having the opportunity to be promoted, in contrast to hitting a glass ceiling.

When Motives Conflict

- Human motives often conflict. In an *approach–approach conflict*, a person is equally attracted to two goals. In an *avoidance–avoidance conflict*, a person is equally repelled by two goals. An *approach–avoidance conflict* is the most difficult to resolve, because the person is both attracted to and repelled by the same goal. Prolonged conflict can lead to physical symptoms and reduced well-being.

- Abraham Maslow believed that human motives could be ranked along a *hierarchy of needs*, from basic biological needs for survival to higher psychological needs for self-actualization. This popular theory has not been supported. People can have simultaneous motives; "higher" motives can outweigh "lower" ones; and people do not always become kinder or more self-actualized when their "lower" needs are met.

KEY TERMS

motivation 431

drives 431

need for affiliation 432

passionate and companionate love 432

six styles of love 432

triangle theory of love 433

attachment theory of love 434

evolutionary psychology 438

gender roles 442

sexual scripts 442

set point 447

leptin 448

hypothalamus 448

bulimia 451

anorexia 451

industrial/organizational psychology 453

approach goals versus avoidance goals 453

performance goals 453

mastery (learning) goals 454

self-fulfilling prophecy 455

values 455

self-efficacy 455

need for achievement 456

Thematic Apperception Test (TAT) 456

incentive pay 458

approach and avoidance conflicts 460

Maslow's hierarchy of needs 460

LOOKING BACK ◄

- What kind of lover defines love as jealousy and possessiveness, and what kind defines it as just the opposite—calm compatibility? (p. 433)

- Do men and women differ in the ability to love? (p. 435)

- How are your beliefs about love affected by your income? (p. 435)

- What part of the anatomy do psychologists think is the "sexiest sex organ"? (p. 440)

- How do the sexual rules for heterosexual couples foster misunderstandings? (p. 443)

- Can psychological theories about "smothering mothering" or absent fathers explain why some men are gay? (p. 444)

- Is overweight usually a result of psychological problems? (p. 446)

- What genetic theory explains why it's so hard for heavy people to lose weight—and just as hard for thin people to gain it? (p. 447)

- Why are people all over the world getting fatter? (pp. 448–449)

- Why are bright, academically motivated college women the most vulnerable to eating disorders? (p. 452)

- Why is "doing your best" an ineffective goal to set for yourself? (p. 453)

- When you are learning a new skill, should you concentrate on mastering it or on performing it well in front of others? (p. 454)

- Which aspects of a job are more important than money in increasing your work satisfaction and involvement? (p. 458)

- How is the *desire* to achieve affected by the *opportunity* to achieve? (pp. 458–459)

- What kind of conflict do you have when you want to study for a big exam but you also want to go out partying? (p. 460)

- Do you have to satisfy basic needs for security and belonging before you can become "self-actualized"? (p. 461)

APPENDIX: STATISTICAL METHODS

Nineteenth-century English statesman Benjamin Disraeli reportedly once named three forms of dishonesty: "lies, damned lies, and statistics." It is certainly true that people can lie with the help of statistics. It happens all the time: Advertisers, politicians, and others with some claim to make either use numbers inappropriately or ignore certain critical ones. (When hearing that "four out of five doctors surveyed" recommended some product, have you ever wondered just how many doctors were surveyed and whether they were representative of all doctors?) People also use numbers to convey a false impression of certainty and objectivity when the true state of affairs is uncertainty or ignorance. But it is people, not statistics, that lie. When statistics are used correctly, they neither confuse nor mislead. On the contrary, they expose unwarranted conclusions, promote clarity and precision, and protect us from our own biases and blind spots.

If statistics are useful anywhere, it is in the study of human behavior. If human beings were all alike, and psychologists could specify all the influences on behavior, there would be no need for statistics. But any time we measure human behavior, we are going to wind up with different observations or scores for different individuals. Statistics can help us spot trends amid the diversity.

This appendix will introduce you to some basic statistical calculations used in psychology. Reading the appendix will not make you into a statistician, but it will acquaint you with some ways of organizing and assessing research data. If you suffer from a "math phobia," relax: You do not need to know much math to understand this material. However, you should have read Chapter 1, which discussed the rationale for using statistics and described various research methods. You may want to review the basic terms and concepts covered in that chapter. Be sure that you can define *hypothesis, sample, correlation, independent variable, dependent variable, random assignment, experimental group, control group, descriptive statistics, inferential statistics* and *test of statistical significance.* (Correlation coefficients, which are described in some detail in Chapter 1, will not be covered here.)

To read the tables in this appendix, you will also need to know the following symbols:

N = the total number of observations or scores in a set

X = an observation or score

Σ = the Greek capital letter sigma, read as "the sum of"

$\sqrt{}$ = the square root of

(*Note:* Boldfaced terms in this appendix are defined in the glossary at the end of the book.)

Organizing Data

Before we can discuss statistics, we need some numbers. Imagine that you are a psychologist and that you are interested in that most pleasing of human qualities, a sense of humor. You suspect that a well-developed funny bone can protect people from the negative emotional effects of stress. You already know that in the months following a stressful event, people who score high on sense-of-humor tests tend to feel less tense and moody than more sobersided individuals do. You realize, though, that this correlational evidence does not prove cause and effect. Perhaps people with a healthy sense of humor have other traits, such as flexibility or creativity, that act as the true stress buffers. To find out whether humor itself really softens the impact of stress, you do an experiment.

First, you randomly assign subjects to two groups, an experimental group and a control group. To keep our calculations simple, let's assume there are only 15 people per group. Each person individually views a silent film that most North Americans find fairly stressful, one showing Australian aboriginal boys undergoing a puberty rite involving genital mutilation. Subjects in the experimental group are instructed to make up a humorous monologue while watching the film. Those in the control group are told to make up a straightforward narrative. After the film, each person answers a mood questionnaire that measures current feelings of tension, depression, aggressiveness, and anxiety. A person's overall score on the questionnaire can range from 1 (no mood disturbance) to 7 (strong mood disturbance). This procedure provides you with 15 "mood disturbance" scores for each group. Have people who tried to be humorous reported less disturbance than those who did not?

Constructing a Frequency Distribution

Your first step might be to organize and condense the "raw data" (the obtained scores) by constructing a **frequency distribution** for each group. A frequency distribution shows how often each possible score actually occurred. To construct one, you first order all the possible scores from highest to lowest. (Our mood disturbance scores will be ordered from 7 to 1.) Then you tally how often each score was actually obtained. Table A.1 gives some hypothetical raw data for the two groups, and Table A.2 shows

Table A.1
Some Hypothetical Raw Data

These scores are for the hypothetical humor-and-stress study described in the text.

Experimental group
4,5,4,4,3,6,5,2,4,3,5,4,4,3,4

Control group
6,4,7,6,6,4,6,7,7,5,5,5,7,6,6

Table A.2 Two Frequency Distributions

The scores are from Table A.1.

Experimental Group			Control Group		
Mood Disturbance Score	Tally	Frequency	Mood Disturbance Score	Tally	Frequency
7		0	7	////	4
6	/	1	6	ЖН /	6
5	///	3	5	///	3
4	ЖН //	7	4	//	2
3	///	3	3		0
2	/	1	2		0
1		0	1		0
	N = 15			*N* = 15	

the two frequency distributions based on these data. From these distributions you can see that the two groups differed. In the experimental group, the extreme scores of 7 and 1 did not occur at all, and the most common score was the middle one, 4. In the control group, a score of 7 occurred four times, the most common score was 6, and no one obtained a score lower than 4.

Because our mood scores have only seven possible values, our frequency distributions are quite manageable. Suppose, though, that your questionnaire had yielded scores that could range from 1 to 50. A frequency distribution with 50 entries would be cumbersome and might not reveal trends in the data clearly. A solution would be to construct a *grouped frequency distribution* by grouping adjacent scores into equal-sized *classes* or *intervals*. Each interval could cover, say, five scores (1–5, 6–10, 11–15, and so forth). Then you could tally the frequencies within each *interval*. This procedure would reduce the number of entries in each distribution from 50 to only 10, making the overall results much easier to grasp. However, information would be lost. For example, there would be no way of knowing how many people had a score of 43 versus 44.

Graphing the Data

As everyone knows, a picture is worth a thousand words. The most common statistical picture is a **graph,** a drawing that depicts numerical relationships. Graphs appear at several points in this book, and are routinely used by psychologists to convey their findings to others. From graphs, we can get a general impression of what the data are like, note the relative frequencies of different scores, and see which score was most frequent.

In a graph constructed from a frequency distribution, the possible score values are shown along a horizontal line (the *x-axis* of the graph) and frequencies along a vertical line (the *y-axis*), or vice versa. To construct a **histogram,** or **bar graph,** from our mood scores, we draw rectangles (bars) above each score, indicating the number of times it occurred by the rectangle's height (see Figure A.1).

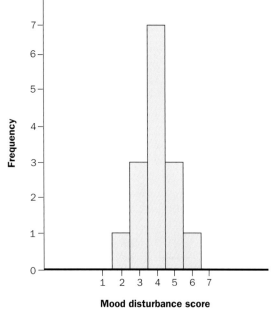

Figure A.1
A Histogram

This graph depicts the distribution of mood disturbance scores shown on the left side of Table A.2.

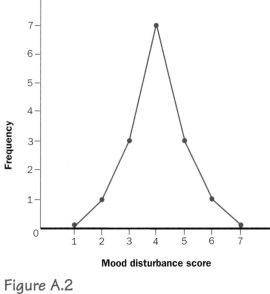

Figure A.2

A Frequency Polygon

This graph depicts the same data as Figure A.1.

A slightly different kind of "picture" is provided by a **frequency polygon,** or **line graph.** In a frequency polygon, the frequency of each score is indicated by a dot placed directly over the score on the horizontal axis, at the appropriate height on the vertical axis. The dots for the various scores are then joined together by straight lines, as in Figure A.2. When necessary an "extra" score, with

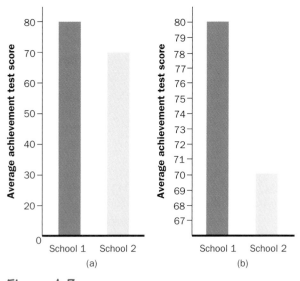

Figure A.3

Same Data, Different Impressions

These two graphs depict the same data, but have different units on the vertical axis.

a frequency of zero, can be added at each end of the horizontal axis, so that the polygon will rest on this axis instead of floating above it.

A word of caution about graphs: They may either exaggerate or mask differences in the data, depending on which units are used on the vertical axis. The two graphs in Figure A.3, although they look quite different, actually depict the same data. Always read the units on the axes of a graph; otherwise, the shape of a histogram or frequency polygon may be misleading.

Describing Data

Having organized your data, you are now ready to summarize and describe them. As you will recall from Chapter 1, procedures for doing so are known as **descriptive statistics.** In the following discussion, the word *score* will stand for any numerical observation.

Measuring Central Tendency

Your first step in describing your data might be to compute a **measure of central tendency** for each group. Measures of central tendency characterize an entire set of data in terms of a single representative number.

The Mean. The most popular measure of central tendency is the arithmetic mean, usually called simply the **mean.** It is often expressed by the symbol *M*. Most people are thinking of the mean when they say "average." We run across means all the time: in grade point averages, temperature averages, and batting averages. The mean is valuable to the psychologist because it takes all the data into account and it can be used in further statistical analyses. To compute the mean, you simply add up a set of scores and divide the total by the number of scores in the set. Recall that in mathematical notation, Σ means "the sum of," X stands for the individual scores, and N represents the total number of scores in a set. Thus the formula for calculating the mean is:

$$M = \frac{\Sigma X}{N}$$

Table A.3 shows how to compute the mean for our experimental group. Test your ability to perform this calculation by computing the mean for the control group yourself. (You can find the answer, along with other control group statistics, on page 473.) Later, we will describe how a psychologist would compare the two means statistically to see if there is a significant difference between them.

The Median. Despite its usefulness, sometimes the mean can be misleading, as we noted in Chapter 1. Suppose you piled some children on a seesaw in such a way that it was perfectly balanced, and then a 200-pound adult came and sat on one end. The center of gravity would quickly shift toward the adult. In the same way, one extremely high score can dramatically raise the mean (and one extremely low score can dramatically lower it). In real life, this can be a serious problem. For example, in the calculation of a town's mean income, one millionaire would offset hundreds of poor people. The mean income would be a misleading indication of the town's actual wealth.

When extreme scores occur, a more representative measure of central tendency is the **median,** or midpoint in a set of scores or observations ordered from highest to lowest. In any set of scores, the same *number* of scores falls above the median as below it. The median is not affected by extreme scores. If you were calculating the *median* income of that same town, the one millionaire would offset only one poor person.

When the number of scores in the set is odd, calculating the median is a simple matter of counting in from the ends to the middle. However, if the number of scores is even, there will be two middle scores. The simplest solution is to find the mean of those two scores and use that number as the median. (When the data are from a grouped frequency distribution, a more complicated procedure is required, one beyond the scope of this appendix.) In our experimental group, the median score is 4 (see Table A.3). What is it for the control group?

The Mode. A third measure of central tendency is the **mode,** the score that occurs most often. In our experimental group, the modal score is 4. In our control group, it is 6. In some distributions, all scores occur with equal frequency, and there is no mode. In others, two or more scores "tie" for the distinction of being most frequent. Modes are used less often than other measures of central tendency. They do not tell us anything about the other scores in the distribution; they often are not very "central"; and they tend to fluctuate from one random sample of a population to another more than either the median or the mean.

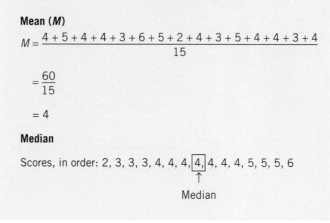

Table A.3   Calculating a Mean and a Median

The scores are from the left side of Table A.1.

Mean (*M*)

$$M = \frac{4 + 5 + 4 + 4 + 3 + 6 + 5 + 2 + 4 + 3 + 5 + 4 + 4 + 3 + 4}{15}$$

$$= \frac{60}{15}$$

$$= 4$$

Median

Scores, in order: 2, 3, 3, 3, 4, 4, 4, 4, 4, 4, 4, 5, 5, 5, 6
↑
Median

Measuring Variability

A measure of central tendency may or may not be highly representative of other scores in a distribution. To understand our results, we also need a **measure of variability** that will tell us whether our scores are clustered closely around the mean or widely scattered.

The Range. The simplest measure of variability is the **range,** which is found by subtracting the lowest score from the highest one. For our hypothetical set of mood disturbance scores, the range in the experimental group is 4 and in the control group it is 3. Unfortunately, though, simplicity is not always a virtue. The range gives us some information about variability but ignores all scores other than the highest and lowest ones.

The Standard Deviation. A more sophisticated measure of variability is the **standard deviation (SD).** This statistic takes every score in the distribution into account. Loosely speaking, it gives us an idea of how much, on the average, scores in a distribution differ from the mean. If the scores were all the same, the standard deviation would be zero. The higher the standard deviation, the more variability there is among scores.

To compute the standard deviation, we must find out how much each individual score deviates from the mean. To do so we simply subtract the mean from each score. This gives us a set of *deviation scores.* Deviation scores for numbers above the mean will be positive, those for numbers below the mean will be negative, and the positive scores will exactly balance the negative ones. In other words, the sum of the deviation scores will be zero. That is a problem, since the next step in our calculation is to add. The solution is to *square* all the deviation scores (that is, to multiply each score by itself). This step gets rid of negative values. Then we can compute the average of the *squared* deviation scores by adding them up and dividing the sum by the number of scores (N). Finally, we take the square root of the result, which takes us from squared units of measurement back to the same units that were used originally (in this case, mood disturbance levels).

The calculations just described are expressed by the following formula:

$$SD = \sqrt{\frac{\Sigma(X - M)^2}{N}}$$

Table A.4 shows the calculations for computing the standard deviation for our experimental group. Try your hand at computing the standard deviation for the control group.

Remember, a large standard deviation signifies that scores are widely scattered, and that therefore the mean is not terribly typical of the entire population. A small standard deviation tells us that most scores are clustered near the mean, and that therefore the mean is representative. Suppose two classes took a psychology exam, and both classes had the same mean score, 75 out of a possible 100. From the means alone, you might conclude that the classes were similar in performance. But if Class A had a standard deviation of 3 and Class B had a standard deviation of 9, you would know that there was much more variability in performance in Class B. This information could be useful to an instructor in planning lectures and making assignments.

Transforming Scores

Sometimes researchers do not wish to work directly with raw scores. They may prefer numbers that are more manageable, such as when the raw scores are tiny fractions. Or they may want to work with scores that reveal where a person stands relative to others. In such cases, raw scores can be transformed to other kinds of scores.

Percentile Scores. One common transformation converts each raw score to a **percentile score** (also called a *centile rank*). A percentile score gives

Table A.4
Calculating a Standard Deviation

Scores (X)	Deviation scores (X − M)	Squared deviation scores (X − M)²
6	2	4
5	1	1
5	1	1
5	1	1
4	0	0
4	0	0
4	0	0
4	0	0
4	0	0
4	0	0
4	0	0
3	−1	1
3	−1	1
3	−1	1
2	−2	4
	0	14

$$SD = \sqrt{\frac{\Sigma(X - M)^2}{N}} = \sqrt{\frac{14}{15}} = \sqrt{.93} = .97$$

Note: When data from a sample are used to estimate the standard deviation of the population from which the sample was drawn, division is by $N - 1$ instead of N, for reasons that will not concern us here.

the percentage of people who scored at or below a given raw score. Suppose you learn that you have scored 37 on a psychology exam. In the absence of any other information, you may not know whether to celebrate or cry. But if you are told that 37 is equivalent to a percentile score of 90, you know that you can be pretty proud of yourself; you have scored as well as, or higher than, 90 percent of those who have taken the test. On the other hand, if you are told that 37 is equivalent to a percentile score of 50, you have scored only at the median— only as well as, or higher than, half of the other students. The highest possible percentile rank is 99, or more precisely, 99.99, because you can never do better than 100 percent of a group when you are a member of the group. (Can you say what the lowest possible percentile score is? The answer is on page 473.) Standardized tests such as those described in previous chapters often come with tables that allow for the easy conversion of any raw score to the appropriate percentile score, based on data from a larger number of people who have already taken the test.

Percentile scores are easy to understand and easy to calculate. However, they also have a drawback: They merely rank people and do *not* tell us how far apart people are in terms of raw scores. Suppose you scored in the 50th percentile on an exam, June scored in the 45th, Tricia scored in the 20th, and Sean scored in the 15th. The difference between you and June may seem identical to that between Tricia and Sean (five percentiles). But in terms of *raw* scores you and June are probably more alike than Tricia and Sean, because exam scores usually cluster closely together around the midpoint of the distribution and are farther apart at the extremes. Because percentile scores do not preserve the spatial relationships in the original distribution of scores, they are inappropriate for computing many kinds of statistics. For example, they cannot be used to calculate means.

Z-scores. Another common transformation of raw scores is to **z-scores,** or **standard scores.** A z-score tells you how far a given raw score is above or below the mean, using the standard deviation as the unit of measurement. To compute a z-score, you subtract the mean of the distribution from the raw score and divide by the standard deviation:

$$z = \frac{X - M}{SD}$$

Unlike percentile scores, z-scores preserve the relative spacing of the original raw scores. The mean itself always corresponds to a z-score of zero, since it cannot deviate from itself. All scores above the mean have positive z-scores and all scores below the mean have negative ones. When the raw scores form a certain pattern called a *normal distribution* (to be described shortly), a z-score tells you how high or low the corresponding raw score was, relative to the other scores. If your exam score of 37 is equivalent to a z-score of +1.0, you have scored 1 standard deviation above the mean. Assuming a roughly normal distribution, that's pretty good, because in a normal distribution only about 16 percent of all scores fall at or above 1 standard deviation above the mean. But if your 37 is equivalent to a z-score of −1.0, you have scored 1 standard deviation below the mean—a poor score.

Z-scores are sometimes used to compare people's performance on different tests or measures. Say that Elsa earns a score of 64 on her first psy-

chology test and Manuel, who is taking psychology from a different instructor, earns a 62 on his first test. In Elsa's class, the mean score is 50 and the standard deviation is 7, so Elsa's z-score is $(64 - 50)/7 = 2.0$. In Manuel's class, the mean is also 50, but the standard deviation is 6. Therefore, his z-score is also 2.0 [$(62 - 50)/6$]. Compared to their respective classmates, Elsa and Manuel did equally well. *But be careful:* This does *not* imply that they are equally able students. Perhaps Elsa's instructor has a reputation for giving easy tests and Manuel's for giving hard ones, so Manuel's instructor has attracted a more industrious group of students. In that case, Manuel faces stiffer competition than Elsa does, and even though he and Elsa have the same z-score, Manuel's performance may be more impressive.

You can see that comparing z-scores from different people or different tests must be done with caution. Standardized tests, such as IQ tests and various personality tests, use z-scores derived from a large sample of people assumed to be representative of the general population taking the tests. When two tests are standardized for similar populations, it is safe to compare z-scores on them. But z-scores derived from special samples, such as students in different psychology classes, may not be comparable.

Curves

In addition to knowing how spread out our scores are, we need to know the *pattern* of their distribution. At this point we come to a rather curious phenomenon. When researchers make a very large number of observations, many of the physical and psychological variables they study have a distribution that approximates a pattern called a **normal distribution.** (We say "approximates" because a *perfect* normal distribution is a theoretical construct and is not actually found in nature.) Plotted in a frequency polygon, a normal distribution has a symmetrical, bell-shaped form known as a **normal curve** (see Figure A.4 on the next page).

A normal curve has several interesting and convenient properties. The right side is the exact mirror image of the left. The mean, median, and mode all have the same value and are at the exact center of the curve, at the top of the "bell." Most observations or scores cluster around the center of the curve, with far fewer out at the ends, or "tails," of the curve. Most important, as Figure A.4 shows, when standard deviations (or z-scores) are used on the horizontal axis of the curve, the percentage of scores falling between the mean and

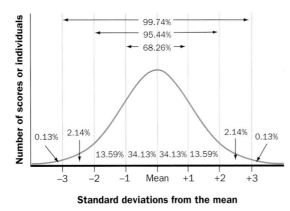

Figure A.4

A Normal Curve

When standard deviations (or z-scores) are used along the horizontal axis of a normal curve, certain fixed percentages of scores fall between the mean and any given point. As you can see, most scores fall in the middle range (between +1 and −1 standard deviations from the mean).

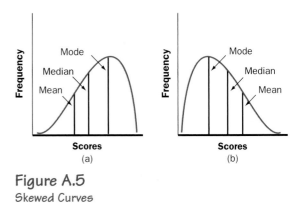

Figure A.5

Skewed Curves

Curve (a) is skewed negatively, to the left. Curve (b) is skewed positively, to the right. The direction of a curve's skewness is determined by the position of the long tail, not by the position of the bulge. In a skewed curve, the mean, median, and mode fall at different points.

any given point on the horizontal axis is always the same. For example, 68.26 percent of the scores will fall between plus and minus 1 standard deviation from the mean; 95.44 percent of the scores will fall between plus and minus 2 standard deviations from the mean; and 99.74 percent of the scores will fall between plus and minus 3 standard deviations from the mean. These percentages hold for any normal curve, no matter what the size of the standard deviation. Tables are available showing the percentages of scores in a normal distribution that lie between the mean and various points (as expressed by z-scores).

The normal curve makes life easier for psychologists when they want to compare individuals on some trait or performance. For example, since IQ scores from a population form a roughly normal curve, the mean and standard deviation of a test are all the information you need in order to know how many people score above or below a particular score. On a test with a mean of 100 and a standard deviation of 15, about 68.26 percent of the population scores between 85 and 115— 1 standard deviation below and 1 standard deviation above the mean (see Chapter 6).

Not all types of observations, however, are distributed normally. Some curves are lopsided, or *skewed,* with scores clustering at one end or the other of the horizontal axis (see Figure A.5). When the "tail" of the curve is longer on the right than on the left, the curve is said to be positively, or right, skewed. When the opposite is true, the curve is said to be negatively, or left, skewed. In experiments, reaction times typically form a right-

skewed distribution. For example, if people must press a button whenever they hear some signal, most will react quite quickly; but a few will take an unusually long time, causing the right "tail" of the curve to be stretched out.

Knowing the shape of a distribution can be extremely valuable. Paleontologist Stephen Jay Gould (1985) has told how such information helped him cope with the news that he had a rare and serious form of cancer. Being a researcher, he immediately headed for the library to learn all he could about his disease. The first thing he found was that it was incurable, with a median mortality of only eight months after discovery. Most people might have assumed that a "median mortality of eight months" means "I will probably be dead in eight months." But Gould realized that although half of all patients died within eight months, the other half survived longer than that. Since his disease had been diagnosed in its early stages, he was getting top-notch medical treatment, and he had a strong will to live, Gould figured he could reasonably expect to be in the half of the distribution that survived beyond eight months. Even more cheering, the distribution of deaths from the disease was right-skewed: The cases to the left of the median of eight months could only extend to zero months, but those to the right could stretch out for years. Gould saw no reason why he should not expect to be in the tip of that right-hand tail.

For Stephen Jay Gould, statistics, properly interpreted, were "profoundly nurturant and lifegiving." They offered him hope and inspired him to fight his disease. Today, Gould is as active professionally as he ever was. The initial diagnosis was made in July of 1982.

ANSWERS:

Control group statistics:

Mean $= \dfrac{\Sigma X}{N} = \dfrac{87}{15} = 5.8$

Median = 6

Standard Deviation $= \sqrt{\dfrac{\Sigma(X - M)^2}{N}} = \sqrt{\dfrac{14.4}{15}}$

$$= \sqrt{.96} = .98$$

Lowest possible percentile score: 1
(or, more precisely, .01)

Drawing Inferences

Once data are organized and summarized, the next step is to ask whether they differ from what might have been expected purely by chance (see Chapter 1). A researcher needs to know whether it is safe to infer that the results from a particular sample of people are valid for the entire population from which the sample was drawn. **Inferential statistics** provide this information. They are used in both experimental and correlational studies.

The Null Versus the Alternative Hypothesis

In an experiment, the scientist must assess the possibility that his or her experimental manipulations will have no effect on the subjects' behavior. The statement expressing this possibility is called the **null hypothesis.** In our stress-and-humor study, the null hypothesis states that making up a funny commentary will not relieve stress any more than making up a straightforward narrative will. In other words, it predicts that the difference between the means of the two groups will not deviate significantly from zero. Any obtained difference will be due solely to chance fluctuations. In contrast, the **alternative hypothesis** (also called the experimental or research hypothesis) states that on the average the experimental group will have lower mood disturbance scores than the control group.

The null hypothesis and the alternative hypothesis cannot both be true. Our goal is to reject the null hypothesis. If our results turn out to be consistent with the null hypothesis, we

will not be able to do so. If the data are inconsistent with the null hypothesis, we will be able to reject it with some degree of confidence. Unless we study the entire population, though, we will never be able to say that the alternative hypothesis has been proven. No matter how impressive our results are, there will always be some degree of uncertainty about the inferences we draw from them. Since we cannot prove the alternative hypothesis, we must be satisfied with showing that the null hypothesis is unreasonable.

Students are often surprised to learn that in traditional hypothesis testing it is the null hypothesis, not the alternative hypothesis, that is tested. After all, it is the alternative hypothesis that is actually of interest. But this procedure does make sense. The null hypothesis can be stated precisely and tested directly. In the case of our fictitious study, the null hypothesis predicts that the difference between the two means will be zero. The alternative hypothesis does not permit a precise prediction because we don't know how much the two means might differ (if, in fact, they do differ). Therefore, it cannot be tested directly.

Testing Hypotheses

Many computations are available for testing the null hypothesis. The choice depends on the design of the study, the size of the sample, and other factors. We will not cover any specific tests here. Our purpose is simply to introduce you to the kind of *reasoning* that underlies hypothesis testing. With that in mind, let us return once again to our data. For each of our two groups we have calculated a mean and a standard deviation. Now we want to compare the two sets of data to see if they differ enough for us to reject the null hypothesis. We wish to be reasonably certain that our observed differences did not occur entirely by chance.

What does it mean to be "reasonably certain"? How different from zero must our result be to be taken seriously? Imagine, for a moment, that we had infinite resources and could somehow repeat our experiment, each time using a new pair of groups, until we had "run" the entire population through the study. It can be shown mathematically that if only chance were operating, our various experimental results would form a normal distribution. This theoretical distribution is called "the sampling distribution of the difference between means," but since that is quite a mouthful, we will simply call it the *sampling distribution* for short. If the null hypothesis were true, the mean of the sampling distribution would be zero. That is, on the average, we would find no difference between the two groups. Often, though, because of chance influences or *random error*, we would get a result that deviated to one degree or another from zero. On rare occasions, the result would deviate a great deal from zero.

We cannot test the entire population, though. All we have are data from a single sample. We would like to know whether the difference between means that we actually obtained would be close to the mean of the theoretical sampling distribution (if we *could* test the entire population) or far away from it, out in one of the "tails" of the curve. Was our result highly likely to occur on the basis of chance alone or highly unlikely?

Before we can answer that question, we must have some precise way to measure distance from the mean of the sampling distribution. We must know exactly how far from the mean our obtained result must be to be considered "far away." If only we knew the standard deviation of the sampling distribution, we could use it as our unit of measurement. We don't know it, but fortunately, we can use the standard deviation of our *sample* to estimate it. (We will not go into the reasons that this is so.)

Now we are in business. We can look at the mean difference between our two groups and figure out how far it is (in terms of standard deviations) from the mean of the sampling distribution. As mentioned earlier, one of the convenient things about a normal distribution is that a certain fixed percentage of all observations falls between the mean of the distribution and any given point above or below the mean. These percentages are available from tables. Therefore, if we know the "distance" of our obtained result from the mean of the theoretical sampling distribution, we automatically know how likely our result is to have occurred strictly by chance.

To give a specific example, if it turns out that our obtained result is 2 standard deviations above the mean of the theoretical sampling distribution, we know that the probability of its having occurred by chance is less than 2.3 percent. If our result is 3 standard deviations above the mean of the sampling distribution, the probability of its having occurred by chance is less than .13 percent—less than 1 in 800. In either case, we might well suspect that our result did not occur entirely by chance after all. We would call the result **statistically significant.** (Psychologists usually consider any highly unlikely result to be of interest, no matter which direction it takes. In other words, the result may be in either "tail" of the sampling distribution.)

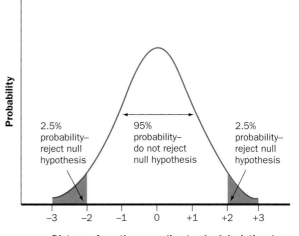

Distance from the mean (in standard deviations)

Figure A.6
Statistical Significance
This curve represents the theoretical sampling distribution discussed in the text. The curve is what we would expect by chance if we did our hypothetical stress-and-humor study many times, testing the entire population. If we used the conventional significance level of .05, we would regard our obtained result as significant only if the probability of getting a result that far from zero by chance (in either direction) totaled 5 percent or less. As shown, the result must fall far out in one of the tails of the sampling distribution. Otherwise, we cannot reject the null hypothesis.

To summarize: Statistical significance means that if only chance were operating, our result would be highly improbable, so we are fairly safe in concluding that more than chance was operating—namely, the influence of our independent variable. We can reject the null hypothesis, and open the champagne. As we noted in Chapter 1, psychologists usually accept a finding as statistically significant if the likelihood of its occurring by chance is 5 percent or less (see Figure A.6). This cutoff point gives the researcher a reasonable chance of confirming reliable results as well as reasonable protection against accepting unreliable ones.

Some cautions are in order, though. As noted in Chapter 1, conventional tests of statistical significance have drawn serious criticisms in recent years. Statistically significant results are not always psychologically interesting or important. Further, statistical significance is related to the size of the sample. A large sample increases the likelihood of reliable results. But there is a trade-off: The larger the sample, the more probable it is that a small result having no practical importance will reach statistical significance. On the other hand, with the sample sizes typically used in psychological research, there is a good chance of falsely concluding that an experimental effect has *not* occurred when one actually has (Hunter, 1997). For these reasons, it is always useful to know how much of the total variability in scores was accounted for by the independent variable (the **effect size**). (The computations are not discussed here.) If only 3 percent of the variance was accounted for, then 97 percent was due either to chance factors or to systematic influences of which the researcher was unaware. Because human behavior is affected by so many factors, the amount of variability accounted for by a single psychological variable is often modest. But sometimes the effect size is considerable even when the results don't quite reach significance.

Oh, yes, about those humor findings: Our fictitious study is similar to two more-complicated ones done by Herbert M. Lefcourt and Rod A. Martin (1986). Women who tried to be funny reported less mood disturbance than women who merely produced a straightforward narrative. They also grimaced and fidgeted less during the film, suggesting that they really did feel less stress. The results were not statistically significant for men, for reasons that were not clear. Other findings, however, suggest that humor can shield both sexes from stress (see Chapter 12). *The moral:* When gravity gets you down, try a little levity.

SUMMARY

● When used correctly, statistics expose unwarranted conclusions, promote precision, and help researchers spot trends amid diversity.

● Often, the first step in data analysis is to organize and condense data in a *frequency distribution*, a tally showing how often each possible score (or interval of scores) occurred. Such information can also be depicted in a *histogram* (bar graph) or a *frequency polygon* (line graph).

● Descriptive statistics summarize and describe the data. *Central tendency* is measured by the *mean, median,* or, less frequently, the *mode.* Since a measure of central tendency may or may not be highly representative of other scores in a distribution, it is also important to analyze variability. A large *standard deviation* means that scores are widely scattered about the mean; a small one means that most scores are clustered near the mean.

● Raw scores can be transformed into other kinds of scores. *Percentile scores* indicate the percentage of people who scored at or below a given raw score. *Z-scores* (*standard scores*) indicate how far a given raw score is above or below the mean of the distribution.

● Many variables have a distribution approximating a *normal distribution*, depicted as a *normal curve.* The normal curve has a convenient property: When standard deviations are used as the units on the horizontal axis, the percentage of scores falling between any two points on the horizontal axis is always the same. Not all types of observations are distributed normally, however. Some distributions are *skewed* to the left or right.

● Inferential statistics can be used to test the *null hypothesis* and to tell a researcher whether a result differed significantly from what might have been expected purely by chance. Basically, hypothesis testing involves estimating where the obtained result would have fallen in a theoretical *sampling distribution* based on studies of the entire population in question. If the result would have been far out in one of the "tails" of the distribution, it is considered statistically significant. A statistically significant result may or may not be psychologically interesting, important, or informative so many researchers also compute the *effect size.*

KEY TERMS

frequency distribution   466
graph   467
histogram/bar graph   467
frequency polygon/line
    graph   468
descriptive statistics   468
measure of central tendency   468
mean   468
median   469

mode   469
measure of variability   469
range   469
standard deviation   469
deviation score   469
percentile score   470
z-score (standard score)   471
normal distribution   471
normal curve   471

right- and left-skewed
    distributions   472
inferential statistics   473
null hypothesis   473
alternative hypothesis   473
sampling distribution   473
statistically significant   474
effect size   475

absolute threshold   The smallest quantity of physical energy that can be reliably detected by an observer.

accommodation   In Piaget's theory, the process of modifying existing cognitive structures in response to experience and new information.

acculturation   The process by which members of minority groups come to identify with and feel part of the mainstream culture.

activation-synthesis theory   The theory that dreaming results from the cortical synthesis and interpretation of neural signals triggered by activity in the lower part of the brain.

adrenal hormones   Hormones that are produced by the adrenal glands and that are involved in emotion and stress.

agoraphobia   A set of phobias, often set off by a panic attack, involving the basic fear of being away from a safe place or person.

algorithm   A problem-solving strategy guaranteed to produce a solution even if the user does not know how it works.

alternative hypothesis   An assertion that the independent variable in a study will have a certain predictable effect on the dependent variable; also called an experimental or research hypothesis.

amygdala   A brain structure involved in the arousal and regulation of emotion and the initial emotional response to sensory information.

anorexia nervosa   An eating disorder characterized by fear of being fat, a distorted body image, radically reduced consumption of food, and emaciation.

antidepressant drugs   Drugs used primarily in the treatment of mood disorders, especially depression and anxiety.

antipsychotic drugs   Drugs used primarily in the treatment of schizophrenia and other psychotic disorders.

antisocial personality disorder (APD)   A disorder characterized by antisocial behavior such as lying, stealing, manipulating others, and sometimes violence; and a lack of guilt, shame, and empathy. (Sometimes called *psychopathy* or *sociopathy*.)

applied psychology   The study of psychological issues that have direct practical significance; also, the application of psychological findings.

archetypes (AR-ki-tipes)   Universal, symbolic images that appear in myths, art, stories, and dreams; to Jungians, they reflect the collective unconscious.

arithmetic mean   An average that is calculated by adding up a set of quantities and dividing the sum by the total number of quantities in the set.

assimilation   In Piaget's theory, the process of absorbing new information into existing cognitive structures.

attribution theory   The theory that people are motivated to explain their own and other people's' behavior by attributing causes of that behavior to a situation or a disposition.

autonomic nervous system   The subdivision of the peripheral nervous system that regulates the internal organs and glands.

availability heuristic   The tendency to judge the probability of a type of event by how easy it is to think of examples or instances.

aversive conditioning   In behavior therapy, a method in which punishment is substituted for the reinforcement that is perpetuating a bad habit.

axon   A neuron's extending fiber, which conducts impulses away from the cell body and transmits them to other neurons or to muscle or gland cells.

basic psychology   The study of psychological issues in order to seek knowledge for its own sake rather than for its practical application.

behavior modification   The application of conditioning techniques to teach new responses or to reduce or eliminate maladaptive or problematic behavior.

behavioral genetics   An interdisciplinary field of study concerned with the genetic bases of behavior and personality.

behaviorism   An approach to psychology that emphasizes the study of observable behavior and the role of the environment as a determinant of behavior.

binocular cues   Visual cues to depth or distance requiring two eyes.

biological perspective   A psychological approach that emphasizes bodily events and changes associated with actions, feelings, and thoughts.

bipolar disorder   A mood disorder in which episodes of both depression and mania (excessive euphoria) occur.

brain stem   The part of the brain at the top of the spinal cord, consisting of the medulla and the pons.

brightness   Lightness or luminance; the dimension of visual experience related to the amount of light emitted from or reflected by an object.

bulimia   An eating disorder characterized by episodes of excessive eating (bingeing) followed by forced vomiting or use of laxatives (purging).

case study   A detailed description of a particular individual being studied or treated.

cell body   The part of the neuron that keeps it alive and determines whether it will fire.

central nervous system (CNS)   The portion of the nervous system consisting of the brain and spinal cord.

cerebellum   A brain structure that regulates movement and balance, and that is involved in the learning of certain kinds of simple responses.

cerebral cortex   A collection of several thin layers of cells covering the cerebrum; it is largely responsible for higher mental functions; cortex is Latin for "bark" or "rind."

cerebral hemispheres   The two halves of the cerebrum.

cerebrum (suh-REE-brum)   The largest brain structure, consisting of the upper part of the brain; it is in charge of most sensory, motor, and cognitive processes. (From the Latin for "brain.")

childhood (infantile) amnesia   The inability to remember events and experiences that occurred during the first two or three years of life.

chunk   A meaningful unit of information; it may be composed of smaller units.

classical conditioning   The process by which a previously neutral stimulus acquires the capacity to elicit a response through association with a stimulus that already elicits a similar or related response.

cochlea (KOCK-lee-uh)   A snail-shaped, fluid-filled organ in the inner ear, containing the receptors for hearing.

coefficient of correlation   A measure of correlation that ranges in value from −1.00 to +1.00.

cognitive dissonance   A state of tension that occurs when a person simultaneously holds two cognitions that are psychologically inconsistent, or when a person's belief is incongruent with his or her behavior.

cognitive ethology   The study of cognitive processes in nonhuman animals.

cognitive perspective   A psychological approach that emphasizes mental processes in perception, memory, language, problem solving, and other areas of behavior.

cognitive schema   An integrated mental network of knowledge, beliefs, and expectations concerning a particular topic or aspect of the world.

collective unconscious   In Jungian theory, the universal memories and experiences of humankind, represented in the symbols, stories, and images (archtypes) that occur across all cultures.

collectivist cultures   Cultures in which the self is regarded as embedded in relationships, and harmony with one's group is prized above individual goals and wishes.

concept   A mental category that groups objects, relations, activities, abstractions, or qualities having common properties.

conditioned response (CR)   The classical-conditioning term for a response that is elicited by a conditioned stimulus; it occurs after the conditioned stimulus is associated with an unconditioned stimulus.

conditioned stimulus (CS)   The classical-conditioning term for an initially neutral stimulus that comes to elicit a conditioned response after being associated with an unconditioned stimulus.

conditioning   A basic kind of learning that involves associations between environmental stimuli and the organism's responses.

cones   Visual receptors involved in color vision.

confabulation   Confusion of an event that happened to someone else with one that happened to you, or a belief that you remember something when it never actually happened.

confirmation bias   The tendency to look for or pay attention only to information that confirms one's own belief.

conservation   The understanding that the physical properties of objects—such as the number of items in a cluster or the amount of liquid in a glass—can remain the same even when their form or appearance changes.

contact comfort   In primates, the innate pleasure derived from close physical contact; it is the basis of an infant's first attachment.

continuous reinforcement   A reinforcement schedule in which a particular response is always reinforced.

control condition   In an experiment, a comparison condition in which subjects are not exposed to the same treatment as in the experimental condition.

convergence   The turning inward of the eyes, which occurs when they focus on a nearby object.

corpus callosum   The bundle of nerve fibers connecting the two cerebral hemispheres.

correlation   A measure of how strongly two variables are related to one another.

correlational study   A descriptive study that looks for a consistent relationship between two phenomena.

counterconditioning   In classical conditioning, the process of pairing a conditioned stimulus with a stimulus that elicits a response that is incompatible with an unwanted conditioned response.

critical thinking   The ability and willingness to assess claims and make objective judgments on the basis of well-supported reasons and evidence, rather than emotion or anecdote.

cross-sectional study   A study in which subjects of different ages are compared at a given time.

crystallized intelligence   Cognitive skills and specific knowledge of information acquired over a lifetime; it depends heavily on education and tends to remain stable over the lifetime.

cue-dependent forgetting   The inability to retrieve information stored in memory because of insufficient cues for recall.

culture   A program of shared rules that govern the behavior of members of a community or society, and a set of values, beliefs, and attitudes shared by most members of that community.

dark adaptation A process by which visual receptors become maximally sensitive to dim light.

decay theory The theory that information in memory eventually disappears if it is not accessed; it applies more to short-term than to long-term memory.

declarative memories Memories of facts, rules, concepts, and events ("knowing that"); they include semantic and episodic memories.

deep processing In the encoding of information, the processing of meaning rather than simply the physical or sensory features of a stimulus.

defense mechanisms Methods used by the ego to prevent unconscious anxiety or threatening thoughts from entering consciousness.

deindividuation In groups or crowds, the loss of awareness of one's own individuality.

dendrites The branches of a neuron that receive information from other neurons and transmit it toward the cell body.

dependent variable A variable that an experimenter predicts will be affected by manipulations of the independent variable.

descriptive methods Methods that yield descriptions of behavior but not necessarily causal explanations.

descriptive statistics Statistics that organize and summarize research data.

dialectical reasoning A process in which opposing facts or ideas are weighed and compared, with a view to determining the best solution or to resolving differences.

difference threshold The smallest difference in stimulation that can be reliably detected by an observer when two stimuli are compared; also called *just noticeable difference (jnd)*.

diffusion of responsibility In organized or anonymous groups, the tendency of members to avoid taking responsibility for actions or decisions because they assume that others will do so.

discriminative stimulus A stimulus that signals when a particular response is likely to be followed by a certain type of consequence.

display rules Social and cultural rules that regulate when, how, and where a person may express (or suppress) emotions.

dissociative disorders Conditions in which consciousness or identity is split or altered.

dissociative identity disorder A controversial disorder marked by the appearance within one person of two or more distinct personalities, each with its own name and traits; commonly known as *multiple personality disorder (MPD)*.

dizygotic twins *See* fraternal twins.

doctrine of specific nerve energies The doctrine that different sensory modalities, such as vision and hearing, exist because signals received by the sense organs stimulate different nerve pathways leading to different areas of the brain.

double-blind study An experiment in which neither the subjects nor the individuals running the study know which subjects are in the control group and which are in the experimental group until after the results are tallied.

effect size In an experiment, the amount of variance in the data accounted for by the independent variable.

ego In psychoanalysis, the part of personality that represents reason, good sense, and rational self-control.

egocentric thinking Seeing the world from only your own point of view; the inability to take another person's perspective.

elaborative rehearsal Association of new information with already stored knowledge and analysis of the new information to make it memorable.

electroconvulsive therapy (ECT) A procedure used in cases of prolonged and severe major depression, in which a brief brain seizure is induced.

electroencephalogram (EEG) A recording of neural activity detected by electrodes.

emotion A state of arousal involving facial and bodily changes, brain activation, cognitive appraisals, subjective feelings, and tendencies toward action.

emotion work Expression of an emotion, often because of a role requirement, that a person does not really feel.

emotional intelligence The ability to identify your own and other people's emotions accurately, express your emotions clearly, and regulate emotions in yourself and others.

empirical Relying on or derived from observation, experimentation, or measurement.

endocrine glands Internal organs that produce hormones and release them into the bloodstream.

endorphins (en-DOR-fins) Chemical substances in the nervous system that are similar in structure and action to opiates; they are involved in pain reduction, pleasure, and memory, and are known technically as *endogenous opioid peptides*.

entrapment A gradual process in which individuals escalate their commitment to a course of action to justify their investment of time, money, or effort.

episodic memories Memories of personally experienced events and the contexts in which they occurred.

equilibrium The sense of balance.

ethnic identity A person's identification with a racial, religious, or ethnic group.

ethnocentrism The belief that one's own ethnic group, nation, or religion is superior to all others.

experiment A controlled test of a hypothesis in which the researcher manipulates one variable to discover its effect on another.

experimenter effects Unintended changes in subjects' behavior due to cues inadvertently given by the experimenter.

explicit memory Conscious, intentional recollection of an event or of an item of information.

exposure treatment In behavior therapy, a method in which a person suffering from an anxiety disorder, such as a phobia or panic attacks, is taken directly into the feared situation until the anxiety subsides.

extinction The weakening and eventual disappearance of a learned response. In classical conditioning, it occurs when the conditioned stimulus is no longer paired with the unconditioned stimulus; in operant conditioning, it occurs when a response is no longer followed by a reinforcer.

extrinsic reinforcers Reinforcers that are not inherently related to the activity being reinforced, such as money, prizes, and praise.

facial feedback The process by which the facial muscles send messages to the brain about the basic emotion being expressed.

factor analysis A statistical method for analyzing the intercorrelations among different measures or test scores; clusters of measures or scores that are highly correlated are assumed to measure the same underlying trait or ability (factor).

feature detectors Cells in the visual cortex that are sensitive to specific features of the environment.

field research conducted in a natural setting outside the laboratory.

fluid intelligence The capacity for deductive reasoning and the ability to use new information to solve problems; it is relatively independent of education and tends to decline in old age.

fraternal (dizygotic) twins Twins that develop from two separate eggs fertilized by different sperm; they are no more alike genetically than any other pair of siblings.

free association In psychoanalysis, a method of uncovering unconscious conflicts by saying freely whatever comes to mind.

frequency distribution A summary of how frequently each score in a set occurred.

frequency polygon (line graph) A graph showing a set of points obtained by plotting score values against score frequencies; adjacent points are joined by straight lines.

frontal lobes Lobes at the front of the brain's cerebral cortex; they contain areas involved in short-term memory, higher-order thinking, initiative, social judgment, and (in the left lobe, typically) speech production.

functionalism An early psychological approach that emphasized the function or purpose of behavior and consciousness.

fundamental attribution error The tendency, in explaining other people's behavior, to overestimate personality factors and underestimate the influence of the situation.

g factor A general intellectual ability assumed by many theorists to underlie specific mental abilities and talents.

ganglion cells Neurons in the retina of the eye, which gather information from receptor cells (by way of intermediate bipolar cells); their axons make up the optic nerve.

gate-control theory The theory that the experience of pain depends in part on whether pain impulses get past a neurological "gate" in the spinal cord and thus reach the brain.

gender identity The fundamental sense of being male or female; it is independent of whether the person conforms to the social and cultural rules of gender.

gender schema A cognitive schema (mental network) of knowledge, beliefs, metaphors, and expectations about what it means to be male or female.

gender typing The process by which children learn the abilities, interests, personality traits, and behaviors associated with being masculine or feminine in their culture.

generalized anxiety disorder A continuous state of anxiety marked by feelings of worry and dread, apprehension, difficulties in concentration, and signs of motor tension.

genes The functional units of heredity; they are composed of DNA and specify the structure of proteins.

Gestalt principles Principles that describe the brain's organization of sensory building blocks into meaningful units and patterns.

glial cells Nervous-system cells that aid the neurons by providing them with nutrients, insulating them, and removing cellular debris when they die.

graph A drawing that depicts numerical relationships.

groupthink In close-knit groups, the tendency for all members to think alike and to suppress disagreement for the sake of harmony.

heritability A statistical estimate of the proportion of the total variance in some trait that is attributable to genetic differences among individuals within a group.

heuristic A rule of thumb that suggests a course of action or guides problem solving but does not guarantee an optimal solution.

higher-order conditioning In classical conditioning, a procedure in which a neutral stimulus becomes a conditioned stimulus through association with an already established conditioned stimulus.

hindsight bias The tendency to overestimate one's ability to have predicted an event once the outcome is known; the "I knew it all along" phenomenon.

hippocampus A brain structure involved in the storage of new information in memory.

histogram (bar graph) A graph in which the heights (or lengths) of bars are proportional to the frequencies of individual scores or classes of scores in a distribution.

hormones Chemical substances, secreted by organs called glands, that affect the functioning of other organs.

hue The dimension of visual experience specified by color names and related to the wavelength of light.

humanist psychology A psychological approach that emphasizes personal growth and the achievement of human potential rather than the scientific understanding and assessment of behavior.

hypnosis A procedure in which the practitioner suggests changes in the sensations, perceptions, thoughts, feelings, or behavior of the subject, who cooperates by altering his or her normal cognitive functioning accordingly.

hypothalamus A brain structure involved in emotions and drives vital to survival, such as fear, hunger, thirst, and reproduction; it regulates the autonomic nervous system.

hypothesis A statement that attempts to predict or to account for a set of phenomena; scientific hypotheses specify relationships among events or variables and are empirically tested.

id In psychoanalysis, the part of personality containing inherited psychological energy, particularly sexual and aggressive instincts.

identical (monozygotic) twins Twins that develop when a fertilized egg divides into two parts that develop into separate embryos.

implicit memory Unconscious retention in memory, as evidenced by the effect of a previous experience or previously encountered information on current thoughts or actions.

independent variable A variable that an experimenter manipulates.

individualist cultures Cultures in which the self is regarded as autonomous, and individual goals and wishes are prized above duty and relations with others.

induction A method of child rearing in which the parent appeals to the child's own resources, abilities, sense of responsibility, and feelings for others in correcting the child's misbehavior.

infantile amnesia *See* childhood amnesia.

inferential statistics Statistical procedures that allow researchers to draw inferences about how statistically meaningful a study's results are.

intelligence An inferred characteristic of an individual, usually defined as the ability to profit from experience, acquire knowledge, think abstractly, act purposefully, or adapt to changes in the environment.

intelligence quotient (IQ) A measure of intelligence originally computed by dividing a person's mental age by his or her chronological age and multiplying the result by 100; now derived from norms provided for standardized intelligence tests.

intermittent (partial) schedule of reinforcement A reinforcement schedule in which a particular response is sometimes but not always reinforced.

intrapsychic Within the mind (psyche) or self.

intrinsic reinforcers Reinforcers that are inherently related to the activity being reinforced, such as enjoyment of the task and the satisfaction of accomplishment.

inventories Standardized objective questionnaires requiring written responses; they typically include scales on which people are asked to rate themselves.

just-world hypothesis The notion that many people need to believe that the world is fair and that justice is served, that bad people are punished and good people rewarded.

justification of effort The tendency of individuals to increase their liking for something that they have worked hard or suffered to attain; a common form of dissonance reduction.

kinesthesis (KIN-es-THEE-sis) The sense of body position and movement of body parts; also called *kinesthesia.*

language acquisition device According to many psycholinguists, an innate mental module that allows young children to develop language if they are exposed to an adequate sampling of conversation.

latent learning A form of learning that is not immediately expressed in an overt response; it occurs without obvious reinforcement.

lateralization Specialization of the two cerebral hemispheres for particular operations.

learning perspective A psychological approach that emphasizes how the environment and experience affect a person's or animal's actions; it includes behaviorism and social-cognitive learning theories.

learning A relatively permanent change in behavior (or behavioral potential) due to experience.

libido [li-BEE-dough] In psychoanalysis, the psychic energy that fuels the sexual or life instincts of the id.

limbic system A group of brain areas involved in emotional reactions and motivated behavior.

lithium carbonate A drug frequently given to people suffering from bipolar disorder.

localization of function Specialization of particular brain areas for particular functions.

locus of control A general expectation about whether the results of your actions are under your own control (internal locus) or beyond your control (external locus).

long-term memory (LTM) In the three-box model of memory, the memory system involved in the long-term storage of information.

longitudinal study A study in which subjects are followed and periodically reassessed over a period of time.

loudness The dimension of auditory experience related to the intensity of a pressure wave.

magnetic resonance imaging *See* MRI.

maintenance rehearsal Rote repetition of material in order to maintain its availability in memory.

major depression A mood disorder involving disturbances in emotion (excessive sadness), behavior (loss of interest in one's usual activities), cognition (thoughts of hopelessness), and body function (fatigue and loss of appetite).

mastery (learning) goals Goals framed in terms of increasing one's competence and skills.

mean *See* arithmetic mean.

measure of central tendency A number intended to characterize an entire set of data.

measure of variability A number that indicates how dispersed scores are around the mean of the distribution.

median A measure of central tendency; the value at the midpoint of a distribution of scores when the scores are ordered from highest to lowest.

medulla A structure in the brain stem responsible for certain automatic functions, such as breathing and heart rate.

melatonin A hormone, secreted by the pineal gland, that is involved in the regulation of daily biological rhythms.

menarche (men-ARR-kee) The onset of menstruation.

menopause The cessation of menstruation and of the production of ova; it is usually a gradual process lasting up to several years.

mental age (MA) A measure of mental development expressed in terms of the average mental ability at a given age.

mental disorder Any behavior or emotional state that causes an individual great suffering or worry, is self-defeating or self-destructive, or is maladaptive and disrupts the person's relationships or the larger community.

mental image A mental representation that mirrors or resembles the thing it represents; it can occur in many and perhaps all sensory modalities.

mental set A tendency to solve problems using procedures that worked before on similar problems.

meta-analysis A procedure for combining and analyzing data from many studies; it determines how much of the variance in scores across all studies can be explained by a particular variable.

metacognition The knowledge or awareness of one's own cognitive processes.

Minnesota Multiphasic Personality Inventory (MMPI) A widely used objective personality test.

mnemonics (neh-MON-iks) Strategies and tricks for improving memory, such as the use of a verse or a formula.

mode A measure of central tendency; the most frequently occurring score in a distribution.

monochronic cultures Cultures in which time is organized sequentially; schedules and deadlines are valued over people.

monocular cues Visual cues to depth or distance that can be used by one eye alone.

monozygotic twins *See* identical twins.

motivation An inferred process within a person or animal that causes movement either toward a goal or away from an unpleasant situation.

MRI (magnetic resonance imaging) A method for studying body and brain tissue, using magnetic fields and special radio receivers.

multiple personality disorder *See* dissociative identity disorder.

myelin sheath A fatty insulation that may surround the axon of a neuron.

narcissistic personality disorder A disorder characterized by an exaggerated sense of self-importance and self-absorption.

need for achievement A learned motive to meet personal standards of success and excellence in a chosen area.

need for affiliation The motive to associate with other people, as by seeking friends, companionship, or love.

negative correlation An association between increases in one variable and decreases in another.

negative reinforcement A reinforcement procedure in which a response is followed by the removal, delay, or decrease in intensity of an unpleasant stimulus; as a result, the response becomes stronger or more likely to occur.

nerve A bundle of nerve fibers (axons and sometimes dendrites) in the peripheral nervous system.

neuromatrix theory The theory that a matrix of neurons in the brain is capable of generating pain (and other sensations) in the absence of signals from sensory nerves.

neuron A cell that conducts electrochemical signals; the basic unit of the nervous system; also called a *nerve cell.*

neurotransmitter A chemical substance that is released by a transmitting neuron at the synapse and that alters the activity of a receiving neuron.

nonconscious processes Mental processes occurring outside of and not available to conscious awareness.

normal curve A symmetrical, bell-shaped frequency polygon representing a normal distribution.

normal distribution A theoretical frequency distribution having certain special characteristics. For example, the distribution is symmetrical; the mean, mode, and median all have the same value; and the farther a score is from the mean, the less the likelihood of obtaining it.

norms In test construction, established standards of performance.

norms (social) Rules that regulate human life, including social conventions, explicit laws, and implicit cultural standards.

null hypothesis An assertion that the independent variable in a study will have no effect on the dependent variable.

object permanence The understanding, which develops late in the first year, that an object continues to exist even when you cannot see it or touch it.

object-relations school A psychodynamic approach that emphasizes the importance of the infant's first two years of life and the baby's formative relationships, especially with the mother.

observational learning A process in which an individual learns new responses by observing the behavior of another (a model) rather than through direct experience; sometimes called *vicarious conditioning.*

observational study A study in which the researcher carefully and systematically observes and records behavior without interfering with the behavior; it may involve either naturalistic or laboratory observation.

obsessive-compulsive disorder (OCD) An anxiety disorder in which a person feels trapped in repetitive, persistent thoughts (obsessions) and repetitive, ritualized behaviors (compulsions) designed to reduce anxiety.

occipital [ahk-SIP-uh-tuhl] lobes Lobes at the lower back part of the brain's cerebral cortex; they contain areas that receive visual information.

Oedipus complex In psychoanalysis, a conflict in which a child desires the parent of the other sex and views the same-sex parent as a rival; this is the key issue in the phallic stage of development.

operant conditioning The process by which a response becomes more likely to occur or less so, depending on its consequences.

operational definition A precise definition of a term in a hypothesis, which specifies the operations for observing and measuring the process or phenomenon being defined.

operations In Piaget's theory, mental actions that are cognitively reversible.

opponent-process theory A theory of color perception, which assumes that the visual system treats pairs of colors as opposing or antagonistic.

panic disorder An anxiety disorder in which a person experiences recurring panic attacks, feelings of impending doom or death, accompanied by physiological symptoms such as rapid breathing and dizziness.

papillae (pa-PILL-ee) Knoblike elevations on the tongue, containing the taste buds. (Singular: papilla.)

parallel distributed processing (PDP) A model of memory in which knowledge is represented as connections among thousands of interacting processing units, distributed in a vast network and all operating in parallel.

paranoid personality disorder A disorder characterized by habitually unreasonable and excessive suspiciousness or jealousy.

parapsychology The study of purported psychic phenomena such as ESP and mental telepathy.

parasympathetic nervous system The subdivision of the autonomic nervous system that operates during relaxed states and that conserves energy.

parietal [puh-RYE-uh-tuhl] lobes Lobes at the top of the brain's cerebral cortex; they contain areas that receive information on pressure, pain, touch, and temperature.

pattern recognition The identification of a stimulus on the basis of information already contained in long-term memory.

percentile score A score that indicates the percentage of people who scored at or below a given raw score; also called *centile rank.*

perception The process by which the brain organizes and interprets sensory information.

perceptual constancy The accurate perception of objects as stable or unchanged despite changes in the sensory patterns they produce.

perceptual illusion An erroneous or misleading perception of reality.

perceptual set A habitual way of perceiving, based on expectations.

performance goals Goals framed in terms of performing well in front of others, being judged favorably, and avoiding criticism.

peripheral nervous system (PNS) All portions of the nervous system outside the brain and spinal cord; it includes sensory and motor nerves.

personality A distinctive and relatively stable pattern of behavior, thoughts, motives, and emotions that characterizes an individual.

personality disorders Rigid, maladaptive personality patterns that cause personal distress or an inability to get along with others.

PET scan (positron-emission tomography) A method for analyzing biochemical activity in the brain, using injections of a glucoselike substance containing a radioactive element.

phobia An exaggerated, unrealistic fear of a specific situation, activity, or object.

pitch The height or depth of a tone; the dimension of auditory experience related to the frequency of a pressure wave.

pituitary gland A small endocrine gland at the base of the brain, which releases many hormones and regulates other endocrine glands.

placebo An inactive substance or fake treatment used as a control in an experiment or given by a medical practitioner to a patient.

placebo effect The apparent success of a medication or treatment that is due to the patient's expectations or hopes, rather than to the drug or treatment itself.

polychronic cultures Cultures in which time is organized horizontally; people tend to do several things at once and value relationships over schedules.

pons A structure in the brain stem involved in, among other things, sleeping, waking, and dreaming.

positive correlation An association between increases in one variable and increases in another—or between decreases in one and in the other.

positive reinforcement A reinforcement procedure in which a response is followed by the presentation of, or increase in intensity of, a reinforcing stimulus; as a result, the response becomes stronger or more likely to occur.

positron-emmission tomography *See* PET scan.

posttraumatic stress disorder (PTSD) An anxiety disorder in which a person who has experienced a traumatic or life-threatening event has symptoms such as psychic numbing, reliving of the trauma, and increased physiological arousal.

power assertion A method of child rearing in which the parent uses punishment and authority to correct the child's misbehavior.

primary control An effort to modify reality by changing other people, the situation, or events; a "fighting back" philosophy.

primary emotions Emotions that are considered to be universal and biologically based; they generally include fear, anger, sadness, joy, surprise, disgust, and contempt.

primary punisher A stimulus that is inherently punishing; an example is electric shock.

primary reinforcer A stimulus that is inherently reinforcing, typically satisfying a physiological need; an example is food.

priming A method for measuring implicit memory in which a person reads or listens to information and is later tested to see whether the information affects performance on another type of task.

principle of falsifiability The principle that a scientific theory must make predictions that are specific enough to expose the theory to the possibility of disconfirmation; that is, the theory must predict not only what will happen, but also what will not happen.

proactive interference Forgetting that occurs when previously stored material interferes with the ability to remember similar, more recently learned material.

procedural memories Memories for the performance of actions or skills ("knowing how").

projective tests Psychological tests used to infer a person's motives, conflicts, and unconscious dynamics on the basis of the person's interpretations of ambiguous stimuli.

proposition A unit of meaning that is made up of concepts and expresses a single idea.

prototype An especially representative example of a concept.

psychoanalysis A theory of personality and a method of psychotherapy originally developed by Sigmund Freud; it emphasizes unconscious motives and conflicts.

psychodynamic perspective A psychological approach that emphasizes unconscious dynamics within the individual, such as inner forces, conflicts, or the movement of instinctual energy.

psychodynamic theories Theories that explain behavior and personality in terms of unconscious energy dynamics within the individual.

psychogenic amnesia The partial or complete loss of memory (due to nonorganic causes) for threatening information or traumatic experiences.

psychological tests Procedures used to measure and evaluate personality traits, emotional states, aptitudes, interests, abilities, and values.

psychology The discipline concerned with behavior and mental processes and how they are affected by an organism's physical state, mental state, and external environment; often represented by Ψ, the Greek letter psi (usually pronounced "sy").

psychometrics The measurement of mental abilities, traits, and processes.

psychosis An extreme mental disturbance involving distorted perceptions and irrational behavior. (Plural: psychoses.)

psychosurgery Any surgical procedure that destroys selected areas of the brain believed to be involved in emotional disorders or violent, impulsive behavior.

puberty The age at which a person becomes capable of sexual reproduction.

punishment The process by which a stimulus or event weakens or reduces the probability of the response that it follows.

random assignment A procedure for assigning people to experimental and control groups in which each individual has the same probability as any other of being assigned to a given group.

range A measure of the spread of scores, calculated by subtracting the lowest score from the highest score.

rapid eye movement (REM) sleep Sleep periods characterized by fast eye movement, loss of muscle tone, and dreaming.

reasoning The drawing of conclusions or inferences from observations, facts, or assumptions.

recall The ability to retrieve and reproduce from memory previously encountered material.

recognition The ability to identify previously encountered material.

reinforcement The process by which a stimulus or event strengthens or increases the probability of the response that it follows.

reinforcer A stimulus or event that strengthens or increases the probability of the response it follows.

relearning method A method for measuring retention that compares the time required to relearn material with the time used in the initial learning of the material.

reliability In test construction, the consistency of scores derived from a test, from one time and place to another.

REM sleep *See* rapid eye movement sleep.

representative sample A group of subjects, selected from a population for study, which matches the population on important characteristics such as age and sex.

reticular activating system (RAS) A dense network of neurons found in the core of the brain stem; it arouses the cortex and screens incoming information.

retina Neural tissue lining the back of the eyeball's interior, which contains the receptors for vision.

retinal disparity The slight difference in lateral separation between two objects as seen by the left eye and the right eye.

retroactive interference Forgetting that occurs when recently learned material interferes with the ability to remember similar material stored previously.

rods Visual receptors that respond to dim light.

role A given social position that is governed by a set of norms for proper behavior.

Rorschach Inkblot Test A projective personality test that asks respondents to interpret abstract, symmetrical inkblots.

saturation Vividness or purity of color; the dimension of visual experience related to the complexity of light waves.

schizophrenia A psychotic disorder marked by positive symptoms (e.g., delusions, hallucinations, and incoherent speech) and negative symptoms (e.g., emotional flatness and loss of motivation).

secondary control An effort to accept reality by changing your own attitudes, goals, or emotions; a "learn to live with it" philosophy.

secondary emotions Emotions that are specific to certain cultures.

secondary punisher A stimulus that has acquired punishing properties through association with other punishers.

secondary reinforcer A stimulus that has acquired reinforcing properties through association with other reinforcers.

selective attention The focusing of attention on selected aspects of the environment and the blocking out of others.

self-efficacy A person's belief that he or she is capable of producing desired results, such as mastering new skills and reaching goals.

self-serving bias The tendency, in explaining one's own behavior, to take credit for one's good actions and rationalize one's mistakes.

semantic memories Memories of general knowledge, including facts, rules, concepts, and propositions.

semicircular canals Sense organs in the inner ear, which contribute to equilibrium by responding to rotation of the head.

sensation The detection of physical energy emitted or reflected by physical objects; it occurs when energy in the external environment or the body stimulates receptors in the sense organs.

sense receptors Specialized cells that convert physical energy in the environment or the body to electrical energy that can be transmitted as nerve impulses to the brain.

sensory adaptation The reduction or disappearance of sensory responsiveness that occurs when stimulation is unchanging or repetitious.

sensory deprivation The absence of normal levels of sensory stimulation.

sensory memory A memory system that momentarily preserves extremely accurate images of sensory information.

separation anxiety The distress that most children develop, at about 7 to 9 months of age, when their primary caregivers temporarily leave them with strangers or in a new situation; it varies according to cultural practices.

serial-position effect The tendency for recall of the first and last items on a list to surpass recall of items in the middle of the list.

set point The genetically influenced weight range for an individual, maintained by biological mechanisms that regulate food intake, fat reserves, and metabolism.

sex hormones Hormones that regulate the development and functioning of reproductive organs and that stimulate the development of male and female sexual characteristics; they include androgens, estrogens, and progesterone.

sex-typing   *See* gender typing.

sexual scripts   Sets of implicit rules that specify proper sexual behavior for a person in a given situation, varying with the person's age, culture, and gender.

shaping   An operant-conditioning procedure in which successive approximations of a desired response are reinforced.

short-term memory (STM)   In the three-box model of memory, a limited-capacity memory system involved in the retention of information for brief periods; it is also used to hold information retrieved from long-term memory for temporary use.

signal-detection theory   A psychophysical theory that divides the detection of a sensory signal into a sensory process and a decision process.

significance tests   Statistical tests that assess how likely it is that a study's results occurred merely by chance.

single-blind study   An experiment in which subjects do not know whether they are in an experimental or a control group.

social cognition   An area in social psychology concerned with social influences on thought, memory, perception, and other cognitive processes.

social identity   The part of a person's self-concept that is based on identification with a nation, culture, or group or with gender or other roles in society.

socialization   The processes by which children learn the behaviors, attitudes, and expectations required of them by their society or culture.

social–cognitive learning theory   A theory that emphasizes how behavior is learned and maintained through the interaction between individuals and their environments, an interaction strongly influenced by such cognitive processes as observations, expectations, perceptions, and motivating beliefs.

social–cognitive theories   Theories that emphasize how behavior is learned and maintained through observation and imitation of others, positive consequences, and cognitive processes such as plans, expectations, and beliefs.

sociocultural perspective   A psychological approach that emphasizes social and cultural influences on behavior.

somatic nervous system   The subdivision of the peripheral nervous system that connects to sensory receptors and to skeletal muscles; sometimes called the *skeletal nervous system*.

source amnesia   The inability to distinguish what you originally experienced from what you heard or were told about an event later.

spinal cord   A collection of neurons and supportive tissue running from the base of the brain down the center of the back, protected by a column of bones (the spinal column).

spontaneous recovery   The reappearance of a learned response after its apparent extinction.

standard deviation   A commonly used measure of variability that indicates the average difference between scores in a distribution and their mean.

standardize   In test construction, to develop uniform procedures for giving and scoring a test.

state-dependent memory   The tendency to remember something when the rememberer is in the same physical or mental state as during the original learning or experience.

statistically significant   A term used to refer to a result that is extremely unlikely to have occurred by chance.

stereotype   A cognitive schema or a summary impression of a group, in which a person believes that all members of the group share a common trait or traits (positive, negative, or neutral).

stereotype threat   A burden of doubt a person feels about his or her performance, due to negative stereotypes about his or her group's abilities.

stimulus discrimination   The tendency to respond differently to two or more similar stimuli. In classical conditioning, it occurs when a stimulus similar to the conditioned stimulus fails to evoke the conditioned response; in operant conditioning, it occurs when an organism learns to make a response in the presence of other, similar stimuli that differ from it on some dimension.

stimulus generalization   After conditioning, the tendency to respond to a stimulus that resembles one involved in the original conditioning. In classical conditioning, it occurs when a stimulus that resembles the conditioned stimulus elicits the conditioned response; in operant conditioning, it occurs when a response that has been reinforced (or punished) in the presence of one stimulus occurs (or is suppressed) in the presence of other, similar stimuli.

subconscious processes   Mental processes occurring outside of conscious awareness but accessible to consciousness when necessary.

successive approximations   In the operant-conditioning procedure of shaping, behaviors that are ordered in terms of increasing similarity or closeness to the desired response.

superego   In psychoanalysis, the part of personality that represents conscience, morality, and social standards.

surveys   Questionnaires and interviews that ask people directly about their experiences, attitudes, or opinions.

sympathetic nervous system   The subdivision of the autonomic nervous system that mobilizes bodily resources and increases the output of energy during emotion and stress.

synapse   The site where a nerve impulse is transmitted from one nerve cell to another; it includes the axon terminal, the synaptic cleft, and receptor sites in the membrane of the receiving cell.

systematic desensitization   In behavior therapy, a step-by-step process of desensitizing a client to a feared object or experience; it is based on the classical-conditioning procedure of counterconditioning.

tacit knowledge   Strategies for success that are not explicitly taught but that instead must be inferred.

taste buds   Nests of taste-receptor cells.

telegraphic speech   A child's first word combinations, which omit (as a telegram did) unnecessary words.

temperaments   Physiological dispositions to respond to the environment in certain ways; they are present in infancy and are assumed to be innate.

temporal lobes   Lobes at the sides of the brain's cerebral cortex; they contain areas involved in hearing, memory, perception, emotion, and (in the left lobe, typically) language comprehension.

thalamus   A brain structure that relays sensory messages to the cerebral cortex.

Thematic Apperception Test (TAT)   A personality test that asks respondents to interpret a series of drawings showing ambiguous scenes of people; usually scored for motives such as the needs for achievement, power, and affiliation.

theory   An organized system of assumptions and principles that purports to explain a specified set of phenomena and their interrelationships.

therapeutic alliance   The bond of confidence and mutual understanding established between therapist and client, which allows them to work together to solve the client's problems.

timbre   The distinguishing quality of a sound; the dimension of auditory experience related to the complexity of the pressure wave.

trait   A characteristic of an individual, describing a habitual way of behaving, thinking, and feeling.

tranquilizers   Drugs commonly but often inappropriately prescribed for patients who complain of unhappiness, anxiety, or worry.

transference   In psychodynamic therapies, a critical step in which the client transfers unconscious emotions or reactions, such as conflicts about his or her parents, onto the therapist.

triarchic theory of intelligence   A cognitive theory of intelligence that emphasizes information-processing strategies, the ability to transfer skills to new situations, and the practical application of intelligence.

trichromatic theory   A theory of color perception, which proposes three mechanisms in the visual system, each sensitive to a certain range of wavelengths; their interaction is assumed to produce all the different experiences of hue.

two-factor theory of emotion   The theory that emotions depend on both physiological arousal and a cognitive interpretation of that arousal.

unconditional positive regard   To Carl Rogers, love or support given to another person, with no conditions attached.

unconditioned response (UR)   The classical-conditioning term for a reflexive response elicited by a stimulus in the absence of learning.

unconditioned stimulus (US)   The classical-conditioning term for a stimulus that elicits a reflexive response in the absence of learning.

validity   The ability of a test to measure what it was designed to measure.

validity effect   The tendency of people to believe that a statement is true or valid simply because it has been repeated many times.

variables   Characteristics of behavior or experience that can be measured or described by a numeric scale; variables are manipulated and assessed in scientific studies.

volunteer bias   A shortcoming of findings derived from a sample of volunteers instead of a representative sample, the volunteers may differ from those who did not volunteer.

z-score (standard score)   A number that indicates how far a given raw score is above or below the mean, using the standard deviation of the distribution as the unit of measurement.

Abel, Gene G.; Mittelman, Mary; Becker, Judith V.; et al. (1988). Predicting child molesters' response to treatment. *Annals of the New York Academy of Sciences, 528,* 223–234.

Abrams, Mitchell, & Feindler, Eva (1998). Violence reduction via anger management for male athletes. Paper presented at the annual meeting of the American Psychological Association, San Francisco.

Abramson, Lyn Y.; Metalsky, Gerald I.; & Alloy, Lauren B. (1989). Hopelessness depression: A theory-based subtype of depression. *Psychological Review, 96,* 358–372.

Acocella, Joan (1999). *Creating hysteria: Women and multiple personality disorder.* San Francisco: Jossey-Bass.

Adams, James L. (1986). *Conceptual blockbusting: A guide to better ideas* (3rd ed.). Boston: Addison-Wesley.

Ader, Robert (1997). The role of conditioning. In A. Harrington (ed.), *The placebo effect: An interdisciplinary exploration.* Cambridge, MA: Harvard University Press.

Adler, Nancy E.; Boyce, Thomas; Chesney, Margaret A.; et al. (1994). Socioeconomic status and health: The challenge of the gradient. *American Psychologist, 49,* 15–24.

Affleck, Glenn; Tennen, Howard; Croog, Sydney; & Levine, Sol (1987). Causal attribution, perceived control, and recovery from a heart attack. *Journal of Social and Clinical Psychology, 5,* 339–355.

Ainsworth, Mary D. S. (1973). The development of infant-mother attachment. In B. M. Caldwell & H. N. Ricciuti (eds.), *Review of child development research* (Vol. 3). Chicago: University of Chicago Press.

Ainsworth, Mary D. S. (1979). Infant-mother attachment. *American Psychologist, 34,* 932–937.

Akbarian, Schahram; Kim, J. J.; Potkin, Steven G.; et al. (1996). Maldistribution of interstitial neurons in prefrontal white matter of the brains of schizophrenic patients. *Archives of General Psychiatry, 53,* 425–436.

Albee, George W. (1985, February). The answer is prevention. *Psychology Today,* 60–64.

Aldag, Ramon J., & Fuller, Sally R. (1993). Beyond fiasco: A reappraisal of the group think phenomenon and a new model of group decision processes. *Psychological Bulletin, 113,* 533–552.

Allen, Laura S., & Gorski, Robert A. (1992). Sexual orientation and the size of the anterior commissure in the human brain. *Proceedings of the National Academy of Sciences, 89,* 7199–7202.

Allison, David B.; & Faith, Myles S. (1997). Issues in mapping genes for eating disorders. *Psychopharmacology Bulletin, 33,* 359–368.

Allison, David B., & Heshka, Stanley (1993). Emotion and eating in obesity? A critical analysis. *International Journal of Eating Disorders, 13,* 289–295.

Alloy, Lauren B., & Abramson, Lyn Y. (1998). The Temple-Wisconsin cognitive vulnerability to depression (CVD) project. Paper presented at the annual meeting of the American Psychological Association, San Francisco.

Alloy, Lauren B.; Fedderly, Sharon S.; Kennedy-Moore, Eileen; & Cohan, Catherine L. (1998). Dysphoria and social interaction: An integration of behavioral confirmation and interpersonal perspectives. *Journal of Personality and Social Psychology, 74,* 1566–1579.

Allport, Gordon W. (1937). *Personality: A psychological interpretation.* New York: Holt, Rinehart and Winston.

Allport, Gordon W. (1954/1979). *The nature of prejudice.* Reading, MA: Addison-Wesley.

Allport, Gordon W. (1961). *Pattern and growth in personality.* New York: Holt, Rinehart and Winston.

Amabile, Teresa M. (1983). *The social psychology of creativity.* New York: Springer-Verlag.

Amabile, Teresa M.; Phillips, Elise D.; & Collins, Mary Ann (1993). Creativity by contract: Social influences on the creativity of professional artists. Paper presented at the annual meeting of the American Psychological Association, Toronto, Canada.

Amato, Paul R. (1994). Life-span adjustment of children to their parents' divorce. *Social Forces, 73,* 895–915.

Amato, Paul R.; & Keith, Bruce (1991). Parental divorce and the well-being of children: A meta-analysis. *Psychological Bulletin, 110,* 26–46.

Ambert, Anne-Marie (1997). *Parents, children, and adolescents: Interactive relationships and development in context.* New York: Haworth Press.

American Psychiatric Association (1994). *The diagnostic and statistical manual of mental disorders* (4th ed.). Washington, DC: American Psychiatric Association.

American Psychiatric Association (2000). *The diagnostic and statistical manual of mental disorders, IV-TR.* Washington, DC: American Psychiatric Association.

Amering, Michaela, & Katschnig, Heinz (1990). Panic attacks and panic disorder in cross-cultural perspective. *Psychiatric Annals, 20,* 511–516.

Anastasi, Anne (1988). *Psychological testing* (6th ed.). New York: Macmillan.

Anastasi, Anne, & Urbina, Susan (1997). *Psychological testing* (7th ed.). Upper Saddle River, NJ: Prentice-Hall.

Andersen, Susan M., & Berk, Michele S. (1998). The social-cognitive model of transference: Experiencing past relationships in the present. *Current Directions in Psychological Science, 7,* 109–115.

Anderson, Craig A.; Miller, Rowland S.; Riger, Alice L.; et al. (1994). Behavioral and characterological attributional styles as predictors of depression and loneliness: Review, refinement, and test. *Journal of Personality and Social Psychology, 66,* 549–558.

Anderson, John R. (1990). *The adaptive nature of thought.* Hillsdale, NJ: Erlbaum.

Andreasen, Nancy C.; Arndt, Stephan; Swayze, Victor, II; et al. (1994). Thalamic abnormalities in schizophrenia visualized through magnetic resonance image averaging. *Science, 266,* 294–298.

Angell, Marcia (2000, May 18). Is academic medicine for sale? [Editorial]. *New England Journal of Medicine, 342,* 1516–1518.

Angell, Marcia, & Kassirer, Jermone P. (1998, September 17). Alternative medicine: The risks of untested and unregulated remedies. *New England Journal of Medicine, 339,* 839–841.

Angier, Natalie (2000, November 7). Who is fat? It depends on culture. *New York Times,* Science Times, D1–2.

Antonuccio, David O.; Danton, William G.; & DeNelsky, Garland Y.; et al. (1999). Raising questions about antidepressants. *Psychotherapy and Psychosomatics, 68,* 3–14.

APA Commission on Violence and Youth (1993). *Violence and youth: Psychology's response.* Washington, DC: American Psychological Association.

APA Research Office (1998). *APA doctorate employment survey, 1996.* Washington, DC: American Psychological Association.

Arendt, Hannah (1963). *Eichmann in Jerusalem: A report on the banality of evil.* New York: Viking.

Arkes, Hal R. (1993). Some practical judgment and decision-making research. In N. J. Castellan, Jr., et al. (eds.), *Individual and group decision making: Current issues.* Hillsdale, NJ: Erlbaum.

Arkes, Hal R.; Boehm, Lawrence E.; & Xu, Gang (1991). The determinants of judged validity. *Journal of Experimental Social Psychology, 27,* 576–605.

Arkes, Hal R.; Faust, David; Guilmette, Thomas J.; & Hart, Kathleen (1988). Eliminating the hindsight bias. *Journal of Applied Psychology, 73,* 305–307.

Arnett, Jeffrey J. (1999). Adolescent storm and stress, reconsidered. *American Psychologist, 54,* 317–326.

Aron, Arthur; Aron, Elaine N.; & Allen, Joselyn (1998). Motivations for unreciprocated love. *Personality and Social Psychology Bulletin, 24,* 787–796.

Aron, Arthur, & Westbay, Lori (1996). Dimensions of the prototype of love. *Journal of Personality and Social Psychology, 70,* 535–551.

Aronson, Elliot (1999). *The social animal* (8th ed.). New York: W. H. Freeman.

Aronson, Elliot, & Mills, Judson (1959). The effect of severity of initiation on liking for a group. *Journal of Abnormal and Social Psychology, 59,* 177–181.

Aronson, Elliot, & Patnoe, Shelley (1997). *Cooperation in the classroom: The jigsaw method.* New York: Longman.

Aronson, Elliot; Wilson, Timothy D.; & Akert, Robin A. (1999). *Social psychology: The heart and the mind* (3rd ed.). New York: Longman.

Arroyo, Carmen G., & Zigler, Edward (1995). Racial identity, academic achievement, and the psychological well-being of economically disadvantaged adolescents. *Journal of Personality and Social Psychology, 69,* 903–914.

Asch, Solomon E. (1952). *Social psychology.* Englewood Cliffs, NJ: Prentice-Hall.

Asch, Solomon E. (1965). Effects of group pressure upon the modification and distortion of judgments. In H. Proshansky & B. Seidenberg (eds.), *Basic studies in social psychology.* New York: Holt, Rinehart and Winston.

Aserinsky, Eugene, & Kleitman, Nathaniel (1955). Two types of ocular motility occurring in sleep. *Journal of Applied Physiology, 8,* 1–10.

Aspinwall, Lisa G., & Brunhart, Susanne M. (1996). Distinguishing optimism from denial: Optimistic beliefs predict attention to health threats. *Personality and Social Psychology Bulletin, 22,* 993–1003.

Aspinwall, Lisa G., & Taylor, Shelley E. (1997). A stitch in time: Self-regulation and proactive coping. *Psychological Bulletin, 121,* 417–436.

Atkinson, John W. (ed.) (1958). *Motives in fantasy, action, and society.* Princeton, NJ: Van Nostrand.

Atkinson, Richard C., & Shiffrin, Richard M. (1968). Human memory: A proposed system and its control processes. In K. W. Spence & J. T. Spence (eds.), *The psychology of learning and motivation: Vol. 2. Advances in research and theory.* New York: Academic Press.

Atkinson, Richard C., & Shiffrin, Richard M. (1971, August). The control of short-term memory. *Scientific American, 225*(2), 82–90.

Axel, Richard (1995, October). The molecular logic of smell. *Scientific American,* 154–159.

Azrin, Nathan H., & Foxx, Richard M. (1974). *Toilet training in less than a day.* New York: Simon & Schuster.

Azuma, Hiroshi (1984). Secondary control as a heterogeneous category. *American Psychologist, 39,* 970–971.

Bahill, A. Terry, & Karnavas, William J. (1993). The perceptual illusion of baseball's rising fastball and breaking curveball. *Journal of Experimental Psychology: Human Perception & Performance, 19,* 3–14.

Bahrick, Harry P. (1984). Semantic memory content in permastore: Fifty years of memory for Spanish learned in school. *Journal of Experimental Psychology: General, 113,* 1–29.

Bahrick, Harry P.; Bahrick, Phyllis O.; & Wittlinger, Roy P. (1975). Fifty years of memory for names and faces: A cross-sectional approach. *Journal of Experimental Psychology: General, 104,* 54–75.

Bailey, J. Michael; Bobrow, David; Wolfe, Marilyn; & Mikach, Sarah (1995). Sexual orientation of adult sons of gay fathers. *Developmental Psychology, 31,* 124–129.

Bailey, J. Michael; Gaulin, Steven; Agyei, Yvonne; & Gladue, Brian A. (1994). Effects of gender and sexual orientation on evolutionarily relevant aspects of human mating psychology. *Journal of Personality and Social Psychology, 66,* 1081–1093.

Bailey, J. Michael, & Pillard, Richard C. (1995). Genetics of human sexual orientation. *Annual Review of Sex Research, 6,* 126–150.

Bailey, J. Michael, & Zucker, Kenneth J. (1995). Childhood sex-typed behavior and sexual orientation: A conceptual analysis and quantitative review. *Developmental Psychology, 31,* 43–55.

Baillargeon, Renée (1994). How do infants learn about the physical world? *Current Directions in Psychological Science, 5,* 133–140.

Baker, Mark C. (1999). Innateness and the universality of universal grammar: Evidence from Mohawk. Paper presented at the annual meeting of the American Association for the Advancement of Science, Anaheim, CA.

Baker, Robin (1996). *The sperm wars: The science of sex.* New York: Basic Books.

Baltes, Paul B. (1983). Life-span developmental psychology: Observations on history and theory revisited. In R. M. Lerner (ed.), *Developmental psychology: Historical and philosophical perspectives.* Hillsdale, NJ: Erlbaum.

Baltes, Paul B., & Graf, Peter (1996). Psychological aspects of aging: Facts and frontiers. In D. Magnusson (ed.), *The lifespan development of individuals.* Cambridge, England: Cambridge University Press.

Baltes, Paul B.; Sowarka, Doris; & Kliegl, Reinhold (1989). Cognitive training research on fluid intelligence in old age: What can older adults achieve by themselves? *Psychology and Aging, 4,* 217–221.

Bancroft, John; Sherwin, Barbara B.; Alexander, G. M.; et al. (1991). Oral contraceptives, androgens, and the sexuality of young women: II. The role of androgens. *Archives of Sexual Behavior, 20,* 121–135.

Bandura, Albert (1977). *Social learning theory.* Englewood Cliffs, NJ: Prentice-Hall.

Bandura, Albert (1986). *Social foundations of thought and action: A social cognitive theory.* Englewood Cliffs, NJ: Prentice-Hall.

Bandura, Albert (1994). Self-efficacy. In *Encyclopedia of human behavior* (Vol. 4). Orlando, FL: Academic Press.

Bandura, Albert (1999). Moral disengagement in the perpetration of inhumanities. *Personality and Social Psychology Review, 3,* 193–209.

Bandura, Albert; Ross, Dorothea; & Ross, Sheila A. (1963). Vicarious reinforcement and imitative learning. *Journal of Abnormal and Social Psychology, 67,* 601–607.

Banks, Martin S., with Philip Salapatek (1984). Infant visual perception. In P. Mussen (series ed.) & M. M. Haith & J. J. Campos (vol. eds.), *Handbook of child psychology: Vol. 2. Infancy and developmental psychobiology* (4th ed.). New York: Wiley.

Bargh, John A. (1999, January 29). The most powerful manipulative messages are hiding in plain sight. *Chronicle of Higher Education,* B6.

Barinaga, Marcia (1992). Challenging the "no new neurons" dogma. *Science, 255,* 1646.

Barlow, David H. (1996). Health care policy, psychotherapy research, and the future of psychotherapy. *American Psychologist, 51,* 1050–1058.

Barlow, David H. (ed.) (1991). Special issue on diagnoses, dimensions, and DSM-IV: The science of classification. *Journal of Abnormal Psychology, 100,* 243–412.

Barlow, David H.; Chorpita, Bruce F.; & Turovsky, Julia (1996). Fear, panic, anxiety, and disorders of emotion. In D. A. Hope et al. (eds.), *Nebraska Symposium on Motivation, 1995: Perspectives on anxiety, panic, and fear.* Lincoln, NE: University of Nebraska Press.

Baron, Miron (1993). The D2 dopamine receptor gene and alcoholism: A tempest in a wine cup? *Biological Psychiatry, 34,* 821–823.

Barondes, Samuel H. (1998). *Mood genes: Hunting for origins of mania and depression.* New York: W. H. Freeman.

Barone, David F.; Maddux, James E.; & Snyder, C. R. (1997). *Social cognitive psychology: History and current domains.* New York: Plenum Press.

Barrish, Barbara M. (1996). The relationship of remembered parental physical punishment to adolescent self-concept. *Dissertation Abstracts International, Section B, 57,* 2171.

Bartlett, Frederic C. (1932). *Remembering.* Cambridge, England: Cambridge University Press.

Bartoshuk, Linda M. (1993). Genetic and pathological taste variation: What can we learn from animal models and human disease? In D. J. Chadwick, J. Marsh, & J. Goode (eds.), *The molecular basis of smell and taste transduction* (CIBA Foundation Symposia Series, No. 179). New York: Wiley.

Bartoshuk, Linda M. (1998). Born to burn: Genetic variation in taste. Paper presented at the annual meeting of the American Psychological Association, San Francisco.

Bartoshuk, Linda M., & Beauchamp, Gary K. (1994). Chemical senses. *Annual Review of Psychology, 45,* 419–449.

Bartoshuk, Linda M.; Duffy, V. B.; Lucchina, L. A.; Prutkin, J.; & Fast, K. (1998). PROP (6-n-propylthiouracil) supertasters and the saltiness of NaCl. *Annals of the New York Academy of Sciences, 855,* 793–796.

Bashore, Theodore R.; Ridderinkhof, K. Richard; & van der Molen, Maurits W. (1997). The decline of cognitive processing speed in old age. *Current Directions in Psychological Science, 6,* 163–169.

Basic Behavioral Science Task Force of the National Advisory Mental Health Council (1996). Basic behavioral science research for mental health: Vulnerability and resilience. *American Psychologist, 51,* 22–28.

Bauer, Patricia J., & Dow, Gina A. (1994). Episodic memory in 16- and 20-month-old children: Specifics are generalized but not forgotten. *Developmental Psychology, 30,* 403–417.

Baum, William M. (1994). *Understanding behaviorism: Science, behavior, and culture.* New York: Addison Wesley Education.

Baumeister, Roy F. (1990). Suicide as escape from self. *Psychological Review, 97,* 90–113.

Baumeister, Roy F. (2000). Gender differences in erotic plasticity: The female sex drive as socially flexible and responsive. *Psychological Bulletin, 126,* 347–374.

Baumeister, Roy F., & Bratslavsky, Ellen (1999). Passion, intimacy, and time: Passionate love as a function of change in intimacy. *Personality and Social Psychology Review, 3,* 49–67.

Baumeister, Roy F.; Catanese, Kathleen R.; & Vohs, Kathleen D. (2001). Is there a gender difference in strength of sex drive? Theoretical views, conceptual distinctions, and a review of relevant evidence. *Personality and Social Psychology Review,* in press.

Baumeister, Roy F.; Stillwell, Arlene M.; & Heatherton, Todd F. (1994). Guilt: An interpersonal approach. *Psychological Bulletin, 115,* 243–267.

Baumrind, Diana (1989). Rearing competent children. In W. Damon (ed.), *Child development today and tomorrow.* San Francisco: Jossey-Bass.

Baumrind, Diana (1991). Parenting styles and adolescent development. In R. Lerner, A. C. Petersen, & J. Brooks-Gunn (eds.), *The encyclopedia of adolescence.* New York: Garland.

Baumrind, Diana (1995). Commentary on sexual orientation: Research and social policy implications. *Developmental Psychology, 31,* 130–136.

Baxter, Lewis R.; Schwartz, Jeffrey M.; Bergman, Kenneth S.; et al. (1992). Caudate glucose metabolic rate changes with both drug and behavior therapy for obsessive-compulsive disorder. *Archives of General Psychiatry, 49,* 681–689.

Bechara, Antoine; Dermas, Hanna; Tranel, Daniel; & Damasio, Antonio R. (1997). Deciding advantageously before knowing the advantageous strategy. *Science, 275,* 1293–1294.

Beck, Aaron T. (1976). *Cognitive therapy and the emotional disorders.* New York: International Universities Press.

Beck, Aaron T. (1988). Cognitive approaches to panic disorder: Theory and therapy. In S. Rachman & J. D. Maser (eds.), *Panic: Psychological perspectives.* Hillsdale, NJ: Erlbaum.

Beck, Aaron T. (1991). Cognitive therapy: A 30-year retrospective. *American Psychologist, 46,* 368–375.

Beckerman, Stephen; Lizarralde, Roberto; Ballew, Carol; et al. (1998). The Bari partible paternity project: Preliminary results. *Current Anthropology, 39,* 164–167.

Bee, Helen (1997). *The developing child* (8th ed.). New York: Longman.

Beer, Jeremy M.; Arnold, Richard D.; & Loehlin, John C. (1998). Genetic and environmental influences on MMPI factor scales: Joint model fitting to twin and adoption data. *Journal of Personality and Social Psychology, 74,* 818–827.

Bekenstein, Jonathan W., & Lothman, Eric W. (1993). Dormancy of inhibitory interneurons in a model of temporal lobe epilepsy. *Science, 259,* 97–100.

Bell, Derrick (1992). *Faces at the bottom of the well: The permanence of racism.* New York: Basic Books.

Belmont, Lillian, & Marolla, Francis A. (1973). Birth order, family size, and intelligence. *Science, 182,* 1096–1101.

Belsky, Jay; Campbell, Susan B.; Cohn, Jeffrey F.; & Moore, Ginger (1996). Instability of infant parent attachment security. *Developmental Psychology, 32,* 921–924.

Belsky, Jay; Hsieh, Kuang-Hua; & Crnic, Keith (1996). Infant positive and negative emotionality: One dimension or two? *Developmental Psychology, 32,* 289–298.

Bem, Daryl J., & Honorton, Charles (1994). Does psi exist? Replicable evidence for an anomalous process of information transfer. *Psychological Bulletin, 115,* 4–18.

Bem, Sandra L. (1993). *The lenses of gender.* New Haven, CT: Yale University Press.

Benet-Martinez, Verónica, & John, Oliver P. (1998). *Los Cinco Grandes* across cultures and ethnic groups: Multitrait multimethod analyses of the Big Five in Spanish and English. *Journal of Personality and Social Psychology, 75,* 729–750.

Benjamin, Ludy T., Jr. (1999). Why Gorgeous George, and not Wilhelm Wundt, was the founder of psychology: A history of popular psychology in America. Invited address presented at the National Institute on the Teaching of Psychology, St. Petersburg Beach, FL.

Bennett, William, & Gurin, Joel (1982). *The dieter's dilemma: Eating less and weighing more.* New York: Basic Books.

Bentall, R. P. (1990). The illusion of reality: A review and integration of psychological research on hallucinations. *Psychological Bulletin, 107,* 82–95.

Bereiter, Carl, & Bird, Marlene (1985). Use of thinking aloud in identification and teaching of reading comprehension strategies. *Cognition and Instruction, 2,* 131–156.

Berenbaum, Sheri A., & Snyder, Elizabeth (1995). Early hormonal influences on childhood sex-typed activity and playmate preferences: Implications for the development of sexual orientation. *Developmental Psychology, 31,* 31–42.

Berger, F.; Gage, F. H.; & Vijayaraghavan, S. (1998). Nicotinic receptor-induced apoptotic cell death of hippocampal progenitor cells. *Journal of Neuroscience, 18,* 6871–6881.

Berkman, Lisa F.; Leo-Summers, L.; & Horwitz, R. I. (1992). Emotional support and survival after myocardial infarction: A prospective, population-based study of the elderly. *Annals of Internal Medicine, 117,* 1003–1009.

Berkman, Lisa, & Syme, S. Leonard (1979). Social networks, host resistance, and mortality: A nine-year follow-up study of Alameda County residents. *American Journal of Epidemiology, 109,* 186–204.

Berkowitz, Leonard (1999). Evil is more than banal: Situationism and the concept of evil. *Personality and Social Psychology Review, 3,* 246–253.

Bernstein, Amit; Newman, Joseph P.; Wallace, John F.; & Luh, Karen E. (2000). Left-hemisphere activation and deficient response modulation in psychopaths. *Psychological Science, 11,* 414–418.

Berry, John W. (1994). Acculturative stress. In W. J. Lonner & R. S. Malpass (eds.), *Psychology and culture.* Needham Heights, MA: Allyn & Bacon.

Berry, John W. (1998). Acculturation strategies: Theory, measurement and application. Paper presented at the annual meeting of the International Association for Cross-Cultural Psychology, Bellingham, WA.

Beutler, Larry F. (2000). David and Goliath: When empirical and clinical standards of practice meet. *American Psychologist, 55,* 997–1007.

Beyerstein, Barry L. (1996). Graphology. In G. Stein (ed.), *The encyclopedia of the paranormal.* Amherst, NY: Prometheus Books.

Beyerstein, Barry L. (1999). Fringe psychotherapies: The public at risk. In W. Sampson (ed.), *A guide to alternative medicine.* London: Gordon and Breech.

Birdwhistell, Ray L. (1970). *Kinesics and context: Essays on body motion communication.* Philadelphia: University of Pennsylvania Press.

Bishop, Katherine M., & Wahlsten, Douglas (1997). Sex differences in the human corpus callosum: Myth or reality? *Neuroscience and Biobehavioral Reviews, 21,* 581–601.

Bjork, Daniel W. (1993). *B. F. Skinner: A life.* New York: Basic Books.

Blakemore, Colin, & Cooper, Grahame F. (1970). Development of the brain depends on the visual environment. *Nature, 228,* 477–478.

Blass, Thomas (1993). What we know about obedience: Distillations from 30 years of research on the Milgram paradigm. Paper presented at the annual meeting of the American Psychological Association, Toronto.

Blass, Thomas (ed.) (2000). *Obedience to authority: Current perspectives on the Milgram paradigm.* Mahwah, NJ: Erlbaum.

Bleuler, Eugen (1911/1950). *Dementia praecox or the group of schizophrenias.* New York: International Universities Press.

Blouin, J. L.; Dombroski, B. A.; Nath, S. K.; et al. (1998). Schizophrenia susceptibility loci on chromosomes 13q32 and 8p21. *Nature Genetics, 20,* 70–73.

Blum, Deborah (1997). *Sex on the brain: The biological differences between men and women.* New York: Viking.

Bodenheimer, Thomas (2000, May 18). Uneasy alliance—clinical investigators and the pharmaceutical industry [Health policy report]. *New England Journal of Medicine, 342,* 1539–1544.

Boesch, Cristophe (1991). Teaching among wild chimpanzees. *Animal Behavior, 41,* 530–532.

Bohannon, John N., & Stanowicz, Laura (1988). The issue of negative evidence: Adult responses to children's language errors. *Developmental Psychology, 24,* 684–689.

Bohman, Michael; Cloninger, R.; Sigvardsson, S.; & von Knorring, Anne-Liis (1987). The genetics of alcoholisms and related disorders. *Journal of Psychiatric Research, 21,* 447–452.

Bolger, Niall; Foster, Mark; Vinokur, Amiram D.; & Ng, Rosanna (1996). Close relationships and adjustment to a life crisis: The case of breast cancer. *Journal of Personality and Social Psychology, 70,* 283–294.

Bond, Rod, & Smith, Peter B. (1996). Culture and conformity: A meta-analysis of studies using Asch's (1952b, 1956) line judgment task. *Psychological Bulletin, 119,* 111–137.

Bordo, Susan (2000). *The male body.* New York: Farrar, Straus and Giroux.

Bornstein, Robert F.; Leone, Dean R.; & Galley, Donna J. (1987). The generalizability of subliminal mere exposure effects: Influence of stimuli perceived without awareness on social behavior. *Journal of Personality and Social Psychology, 53,* 1070–1079.

Bosworth, H. B., & Schaie, K. Warner (1999). Survival effects in cognitive function, cognitive style, and sociodemographic variables in the Seattle Longitudinal Study. *Experimental Aging Research, 25,* 121–139.

Bothwell, R. K., Deffenbacher, K. A., & Brigham, J. C. (1987). Correlation of eyewitness accuracy and confidence: Optimality hypothesis revised. *Journal of Applied Psychology, 72,* 691–698.

Bouchard, Claude; Tremblay, A.; Despres, J. P.; et al. (1990, May 24). The response to long-term overfeeding in identical twins. *New England Journal of Medicine, 322,* 1477–1482.

Bouchard, Thomas J., Jr. (1995). Nature's twice-told tale: Identical twins reared apart—what they tell us about human individuality. Paper presented at the annual meeting of the Western Psychological Association, Los Angeles.

Bouchard, Thomas J., Jr. (1997a). The genetics of personality. In K. Blum & E. P. Noble (eds.), *Handbook of psychiatric genetics.* Boca Raton, FL: CRC Press.

Bouchard, Thomas J., Jr. (1997b). IQ similarity in twins reared apart: Findings and responses to critics. In R. J. Sternberg & E. Grigorenko (eds.), *Intelligence: Heredity and environment.* New York: Cambridge University Press.

Bouchard, Thomas J., Jr., & McGue, Matthew (1981). Familial studies of intelligence: A review. *Science, 212,* 1055–1058.

Bousfield, W. A. (1953). The occurrence of clustering in the recall of randomly arranged associates. *Journal of General Psychology, 49,* 229–240.

Bowen, Murray (1978). *Family therapy in clinical practice.* New York: Jason Aronson.

Bower, Bruce (1998, February 21). All fired up: Perception may dance to the beat of collective neuronal rhythms. *Science News, 153,* 120–121.

Bower, Gordon H., & Clark, M. C. (1969). Narrative stories as mediators of serial learning. *Psychonomic Science, 14,* 181–182.

Bowers, Kenneth S.; Regehr, Glenn; Balthazard, Claude; & Parker, Kevin (1990). Intuition in the context of discovery. *Cognitive Psychology, 22,* 72–110.

Bowlby, John (1958). The nature of the child's tie to his mother. *International Journal of Psycho-Analysis, 39,* 350–373.

Bowlby, John (1969). *Attachment and loss: Vol. 1. Attachment.* New York: Basic Books.

Bowlby, John (1973). *Attachment and loss: Vol. 2. Separation.* New York: Basic Books.

Boyd-Franklin, Nancy (1989). *Black families in therapy: A multisystems approach.* New York: Guilford Press.

Boysen, Sarah T., & Berntson, Gary G. (1989). Numerical competence in a chimpanzee (*Pan troglodytes*). *Journal of Comparative Psychology, 103*, 23–31.

Bradford, John M., & Pawlak, Anne (1993). Effects of cyproterone acetate on sexual arousal patterns of pedophiles. *Archives of Sexual Behavior, 22*, 629–641.

Brainerd, C. J.; Reyna, V. F.; & Brandse, E. (1995). Are children's false memories more persistent than their true memories? *Psychological Science, 6*, 359–364.

Brannon, Elizabeth M., & Terrace, Herbert S. (1998). Ordering of the numerosities 1 to 9 by monkeys. *Science, 282*, 746–749.

Brauer, Markus; Wasel, Wolfgang; & Niedenthal, Paula (2000). Implicit and explicit components of prejudice. *Review of General Psychology, 4*, 79–101.

Breggin, Peter R. (1991). *Toxic psychiatry*. New York: St. Martin's Press.

Brehm, Jack W. (1999). The intensity of emotion. *Personality and Social Psychology Review, 3*, 2–22.

Breland, Keller, & Breland, Marian (1961). The misbehavior of organisms. *American Psychologist, 16*, 681–684.

Brennan, Patricia A., & Mednick, Sarnoff A. (1994). Learning theory approach to the deterrence of criminal recidivism. *Journal of Abnormal Psychology, 103*, 430–440.

Brewer, Marilynn B. (1999). The psychology of prejudice: Ingroup love or outgroup hate? *Journal of Social Issues, 55*, 429–444.

Brewer, Marilynn B., & Gardner, Wendi (1996). Who is this "we"? Levels of collective identity and self representations. *Journal of Personality and Social Psychology, 71*, 83–93.

Briggs, John (1984, December). The genius mind. *Science Digest, 92*(12), 74–77, 102–103.

Brigham, John C., & Malpass, Roy S. (1985, Fall). The role of experience and contact in the recognition of faces of own- and other-race persons. *Journal of Social Issues, 41*, 139–155.

Brockner, Joel, & Rubin, Jeffrey Z. (1985). *Entrapment in escalating conflicts: A social psychological analysis*. New York: Springer-Verlag.

Brodsky, Annette M. (1982). Sex, race, and class issues in psychotherapy research. In J. H. Harvey & M. M. Parks (eds.), *Psychotherapy research and behavior change: Vol. 1. The APA Master Lecture Series*. Washington, DC: American Psychological Association.

Brody, D. J.; Pirkle, J. L.; Kramer, R. A.; et al. (1994). Blood lead levels in the US population: Phase 1 of the Third National Health and Nutrition Examination Survey (NHANES III, 1988 to 1991). *Journal of the American Medical Association, 272*, 277–283.

Brody, Nathan (1990). Behavior therapy versus placebo: Comment on Bowers and Clum's meta-analysis. *Psychological Bulletin, 107*, 106–109.

Bromberger, Joyce T., & Matthews, Karen A. (1996). A "feminine" model of vulnerability to depressive symptoms: A longitudinal investigation of middle-aged women. *Journal of Personality and Social Psychology, 70*, 591–598.

Brown, George W. (1993). Life events and affective disorder: Replications and limitations. *Psychosomatic Medicine, 55*, 248–259.

Brown, Paul (1994). Toward a psychobiological study of dissociation. In S. J. Lynn & J. Rhue (eds.), *Dissociation: Clinical, theoretical and research perspectives*. New York: Guilford Press.

Brown, Roger (1986). *Social psychology* (2nd ed.). New York: Free Press.

Brown, Roger; Cazden, Courtney; & Bellugi, Ursula (1969). The child's grammar from I to III. In J. P. Hill (ed.), *Minnesota Symposium on Child Psychology* (Vol. 2). Minneapolis: University of Minnesota Press.

Brown, Roger, & Kulik, James (1977). Flashbulb memories. *Cognition, 5*, 73–99.

Brown, Roger, & McNeill, David (1966). The "tip of the tongue" phenomenon. *Journal of Verbal Learning and Verbal Behavior, 5*, 325–337.

Brown, Ryan P., & Josephs, Robert A. (1999). A burden of proof: Stereotype relevance and gender differences in math performance. *Journal of Personality and Social Psychology, 76*, 246–257.

Brown, Steven P. (1996). A meta-analysis and review of organizational research on job involvement. *Psychological Bulletin, 120*, 235–255.

Brownell, Kelly D., & Rodin, Judith (1994). The dieting maelstrom: Is it possible and advisable to lose weight? *American Psychologist, 49*, 781–791.

Buck, Linda, & Axel, Richard (1991). A novel multigene family may encode odorant receptors: A molecular basis for odor recognition. *Cell, 65*, 175–187.

Budiansky, Stephen (1998). *If a lion could talk: Animal intelligence and the evolution of consciousness*. New York: Free Press.

Burgess, Cheryl A.; Kirsch, Irving; Shane, Howard; et al. (1998). Facilitated communication as an ideomotor response. *Psychological Science, 9*, 71–74.

Burke, Deborah M.; MacKay, Donald G.; Worthley, Joanna S.; & Wade, Elizabeth (1991). On the tip of the tongue: What causes word finding failures in young and older adults? *Journal of Memory and Language, 30*, 237–246.

Burke, Phyllis (1996). *Gender shock*. New York: Basic Books.

Bushman, Brad J.; Baumeister, Roy; & Stack, Angela D. (1999). Catharsis, aggression, and persuasive influence: Self-fulfilling or self-defeating prophecies? *Journal of Personality and Social Psychology, 76*, 367–376.

Buss, David M. (1994). *The evolution of desire: Strategies of human mating*. New York: Basic Books.

Buss, David M. (1996). Sexual conflict: Can evolutionary and feminist perspectives converge? In D. M. Buss & N. Malamuth (eds.), *Sex, power, conflict: Evolutionary and feminist perspectives*. New York: Oxford University Press.

Bussey, Kay, & Bandura, Albert (1992). Self-regulatory mechanisms governing gender development. *Child Development, 63*, 1236–1250.

Butcher, James N.; Lim, Jeeyoung; & Nezami, Elahe (1998). Objective study of abnormal personality in cross-cultural settings: The MMPI-2. *Journal of Cross-Cultural Psychology, 29*, 189–211.

Butler, S.; Chalder, T.; Ron, M.; et al. (1991). Cognitive behaviour therapy in chronic fatigue syndrome. *Journal of Neurology, Neurosurgery & Psychiatry, 54*, 153–158.

Buunk, Bram; Angleitner, Alois; Oubaid, Viktor; & Buss, David M. (1996). Sex differences in jealousy in evolutionary and cultural perspective: Tests from the Netherlands, Germany, and the United States. *Psychological Science, 7*, 359–363.

Byne, William (1993). Sexual orientation and brain structure: Adding up the evidence. Paper presented at the annual meeting of the International Academy of Sex Research, Pacific Grove, CA.

Byne, William (1995). Science and belief: Psychobiological research on sexual orientation. *Journal of Homosexuality, 28*, 303–344.

Cahill, Larry; Prins, Bruce; Weber, Michael; & McGaugh, James L. (1994). ß-Adrenergic activation and memory for emotional events. *Nature, 371*, 702–704.

Campbell, Frances A., & Ramey, Craig T. (1995). Cognitive and school outcomes for high risk students at middle adolescence: Positive effects of early intervention. *American Educational Research Journal, 32*, 743–772.

Campbell, Jennifer; Trapnell, Paul D.; Heine, Steven J.; et al. (1996). Self-concept clarity: Measurement, personality correlates, and cultural boundaries. *Journal of Personality and Social Psychology, 70*, 141–156.

Campbell, Joseph (1949/1968). *The hero with 1,000 faces* (2nd ed.). Princeton, NJ: Princeton University Press.

Campbell, W. Keith, & Sedikides, Constantine (1999). Self-threat magnifies the self-serving bias: A meta-analytic integration. *Review of General Psychology, 3,* 23–43.

Cancian, Francesca M. (1987). *Love in America: Gender and self-development.* Cambridge, England: Cambridge University Press.

Canetto, Silvia S. (1992). Suicide attempts and substance abuse: Similarities and differences. *Journal of Psychology, 125,* 605–620.

Canetto, Silvia S., & Sakinofsky, Isaac (1998). The gender paradox in suicide. *Suicide and Life-Threatening Behavior, 28,* 1–23.

Canino, Glorisa (1994). Alcohol use and misuse among Hispanic women: Selected factors, processes, and studies. *International Journal of the Addictions, 29,* 1083–1100.

Carani, C.; Bancroft, J.; Granata, A.; et al. (1992). Testosterone and erectile function, nocturnal penile tumescence and rigidity, and erectile response to visual erotic stimuli in hypogonadal and eugonadal men. *Psychoneuroendocrinology, 17,* 647–654.

Cardeña, Etzel; Lewis-Fernández, Roberto; Bear, David; et al. (1994). Dissociative disorders. In *DSM-IV Sourcebook.* Washington, DC: American Psychiatric Press.

Carducci, Bernardo J., & McGuire, Jay C. (1990). Behavior and beliefs characteristic of first-, second-, and third-time lovers. Paper presented at the annual meeting of the American Psychological Association, Boston.

Carstensen, Laura L., & Charles, Susan T. (1998). Emotion in the second half of life. *Current Directions in Psychological Science, 7,* 144–149.

Carter, Betty, & McGoldrick, Monica (eds.) (1988). *The changing family life cycle: A framework for family therapy* (2nd ed.). New York: Gardner Press.

Carver, Charles S. (1998). Resilience and thriving: Issues, models, and linkages. *Journal of Social Issues, 54,* 245–266.

Carver, Charles S.; Pozo, Christina; Harris, Suzanne D.; et al. (1993). How coping mediates the effect of optimism on distress: A study of women with early stage breast cancer. *Journal of Personality and Social Psychology, 65,* 375–390.

Carver, Charles S., & Scheier, Michael F. (1999). Optimism. In C. R. Snyder (ed.), *Coping: The psychology of what works.* New York: Oxford University Press.

Caspi, Avshalom, & Moffitt, Terrie E. (1991). Individual differences are accentuated during periods of social change: The sample case of girls at puberty. *Journal of Personality and Social Psychology, 61,* 157–168.

Cattell, Raymond B. (1965). *The scientific analysis of personality.* Baltimore, MD: Penguin.

Cattell, Raymond B. (1973). *Personality and mood by questionnaire.* San Francisco: Jossey-Bass.

Ceci, Stephen J. (1996). *On intelligence: A bioecological treatise on intellectual development.* Cambridge, MA: Harvard University Press.

Ceci, Stephen J., & Bruck, Maggie (1995). *Jeopardy in the courtroom: A scientific analysis of children's testimony.* Washington, DC: American Psychological Association.

Cejka, Mary Ann, & Eagly, Alice H. (1999). Gender-stereotypic images of occupations correspond to the sex segregation of employment. *Personality and Social Psychology Bulletin, 25,* 413–423.

Cermak, Laird S., & Craik, Fergus I. M. (eds.) (1979). *Levels of processing in human memory.* Hillsdale, NJ: Erlbaum.

Chambless, Dianne L., and members of the Division 12 Task Force (1996). An update on empirically validated therapies. *Clinical Psychologist, 49,* 5–18.

Chambless, Dianne L.; and the Task Force on Psychological Interventions (1998). Update on empirically validated therapies: II. *Clinical Psychologist, 51,* 3–16.

Chance, June E., & Goldstein, Alvin G. (1995). The other-race effect in eyewitness identification. In S. L. Sporer, G. Koehnken, & R. S. Malpass (eds.), *Psychological issues in eyewitness identification.* Hillsdale, NJ: Erlbaum.

Chance, Paul (1999). *Learning and behavior* (4th ed.). Pacific Grove, CA: Brooks/Cole.

Chang, Edward C. (1998). Dispositional optimism and primary and secondary appraisal of a stressor. *Journal of Personality and Social Psychology, 74,* 1109–1120.

Chang, Kenneth (2000, September 12). Can robots rule the world? Not yet. *New York Times,* Science section, B1.

Chehab, Farid F.; Mounzih, K.; Lu, R.; & Lim, M. E. (1997, January 3). Early onset of reproductive function in normal female mice treated with leptin. *Science, 275,* 88–90.

Chipuer, Heather M.; Rovine, Michael J.; & Plomin, Robert (1990). LISREL modeling: Genetic and environmental influences on IQ revisited. *Intelligence, 14,* 11–29.

Chodorow, Nancy (1978). *The reproduction of mothering.* Berkeley: University of California Press.

Chodorow, Nancy (1992). *Feminism and psychoanalytic theory.* New Haven, CT: Yale University Press.

Choi, Incheol; Nisbett, Richard E.; & Norenzayan, Ara (1999). Causal attribution across cultures: Variation and universality. *Psychological Bulletin, 125,* 47–63.

Chomsky, Noam (1957). *Syntactic structures.* The Hague, Netherlands: Mouton.

Chomsky, Noam (1980). Initial states and steady states. In M. Piatelli-Palmerini (ed.), *Language and learning: The debate between Jean Piaget and Noam Chomsky.* Cambridge, MA: Harvard University Press.

Chorney, M. J.; Chorney, K.; Seese, N.; et al. (1998). A quantitative trait locus associated with cognitive ability in children. *Psychological Science, 9,* 159–166.

Chorpita, Bruce F., & Barlow, David H. (1998). The development of anxiety: The role of control in the early environment. *Psychological Bulletin, 124,* 3–21.

Christensen, Andrew, & Jacobson, Neil S. (1994). Who (or what) can do psychotherapy: The status and challenge of non-professional therapies. *Psychological Science, 5,* 8–14.

Christensen, Larry, & Burrows, Ross (1990). Dietary treatment of depression. *Behavior Therapy, 21,* 183–194.

Chua, Streamson C., Jr.; Chung, Wendy K.; Wu-Peng, S. Sharon; et al. (1996). Phenotypes of mouse *diabetes* and rat *fatty* due to mutations in the OB (leptin) receptor. *Science, 271,* 994–996.

Chudacoff, Howard P. (1990). *How old are you? Age consciousness in American culture.* Princeton, NJ: Princeton University Press.

Church, A. Timothy, & Lonner, Walter J. (1998). The cross-cultural perspective in the study of personality: Rationale and current research. *Journal of Cross-Cultural Psychology, 29,* 32–62.

Cialdini, Robert B. (1993). *Influence: The psychology of persuasion.* New York: Quill/Morrow.

Cialdini, Robert B.; Trost, Melanie R.; & Newsom, Jason T. (1995). Preference for consistency: The development of a valid measure and the discovery of surprising behavioral implications. *Journal of Personality and Social Psychology, 69,* 318–328.

Cinque, Guglielmo (1999). *Adverbs and functional heads: A cross-linguistic approach.* New York: Oxford University Press.

Cioffi, Delia, & Holloway, James (1993). Delayed costs of suppressed pain. *Journal of Personality and Social Psychology, 64,* 274–282.

Cioffi, Frank (1998). *Freud and the question of pseudoscience.* Chicago, IL: Open Court.

Clark, David M., & Ehlers, A. (1993). An overview of the cognitive theory and treatment of panic disorder. *Applied and Preventive Psychology, 2,* 131–139.

Clark, Margaret S.; Milberg, Sandra; & Erber, Ralph (1991). Arousal cues state dependent memory: Evidence and some implications for understanding social judgments and social behavior. In K. Fiedler & J. P. Forgas (eds.), *Affect, cognition and social behavior*. Toronto, Canada: Hogrefe and Huber.

Clark, Rodney; Anderson, Norman B.; Clark, Vernessa R.; & Williams, David R. (1999). Racism as a stressor for African Americans: A biopsychosocial model. *American Psychologist, 54*, 805–816.

Clarke, Peter, & Evans, Susan H. (1998). *Surviving modern medicine*. New Brunswick, NJ: Rutgers University Press.

Cloninger, C. Robert (1990). *The genetics and biology of alcoholism*. Cold Springs Harbor, ME: Cold Springs Harbor Press.

Clopton, Nancy A., & Sorell, Gwendolyn T. (1993). Gender differences in moral reasoning: Stable or situational? *Psychology of Women Quarterly, 17*, 85–101.

Coats, Erik J.; Janoff-Bulman, Ronnie; & Alpert, Nancy (1996). Approach versus avoidance goals: Differences in self-evaluation and well-being. *Personality and Social Psychology Bulletin, 22*, 1057–1067.

Cohen, David B. (1999). *Stranger in the nest: Do parents really shape their child's personality, intelligence, or character?* New York: Wiley.

Cohen, Sheldon; Doyle, W. J.; Skoner, D. P.; et al. (1997). Social ties and susceptibility to the common cold. *Journal of the American Medical Association, 277*, 1940–1944.

Cohen, Sheldon; Evans, Gary W.; Krantz, David S.; & Stokols, Daniel (1980). Physiological, motivational, and cognitive effects of aircraft noise on children. *American Psychologist, 35*, 231–243.

Cohen, Sheldon; Frank, Ellen; Doyle, William J.; et al. (1998). Types of stressors that increase susceptibility to the common cold in healthy adults. *Health Psychology, 17*, 214–223.

Cohen, Sheldon, & Herbert, Tracy B. (1996). Health psychology: Psychological factors and physical disease from the perspective of human psychoneuroimmunology. *Annual Review of Psychology, 47*, 113–142.

Cohen, Sheldon; Tyrrell, David A.; & Smith, Andrew P. (1993). Negative life events, perceived stress, negative affect, and susceptibility to the common cold. *Journal of Personality and Social Psychology, 64*, 131–140.

Cohn, Lawrence D. (1991). Sex differences in the course of personality development: A meta-analysis. *Psychological Bulletin, 109*, 252–266.

Cole, Michael, & Cole, Sheila R. (1993). *The development of children* (2nd ed.). New York: W. H. Freeman.

Collaer, Marcia L., & Hines, Melissa (1995). Human behavioral sex differences: A role for gonadal hormones during early development? *Psychological Bulletin, 118*, 55–107.

Collins, Allan M., & Loftus, Elizabeth F. (1975). A spreading-activation theory of semantic processing. *Psychological Review, 82*, 407–428.

Collins, Barry E., & Brief, Diana E. (1995). Using person-perception vignette methodologies to uncover the symbolic meanings of teacher behaviors in the Milgram paradigm. *Journal of Social Issues, 51*, 89–106.

Comas-Díaz, Lillian, & Greene, Beverly (1994). *Women of color: Integrating ethnic and gender identities in psychotherapy*. New York: Guilford Press.

Comuzzie, Anthony G., & Allison, David B. (1998). The search for human obesity genes. *Science, 280*, 1374–1377.

Connors, Gerard J.; Carroll, Kathleen M.; DiClemente, Carlo C.; et al. (1997). The therapeutic alliance and its relationship to alcoholism treatment participation and outcome. *Journal of Consulting and Clinical Psychology, 65*, 588–598.

Considine, R. V.; Sinha, M. K.; Heiman, M. L.; et al. (1996). Serum immunoreactive-leptin concentrations in normal-weight and obese humans. *New England Journal of Medicine, 334*, 292–295.

Cooper, M. Lynne; Frone, Michael R.; Russell, Marcia; & Mudar, Pamela (1995). Drinking to regulate positive and negative emotions: A motivational model of alcohol use. *Journal of Personality and Social Psychology, 69*, 990–1005.

Cooper, M. Lynne; Shapiro, Cheryl M.; & Powers, Anne M. (1998). Motivations for sex and risky sexual behavior among adolescents and young adults: A functional perspective. *Journal of Personality and Social Psychology, 75*, 1528–1558.

Coren, Stanley (1996). Daylight saving time and traffic accidents. *New England Journal of Medicine, 334*, 924.

Corkin, Suzanne (1984). Lasting consequences of bilateral medial temporal lobectomy: Clinical course and experimental findings in H. M. *Seminars in Neurology, 4*, 249–259.

Corkin, Suzanne; Amaral, David G.; Gonzalez, R. Gilberto; et al. (1997). H. M.'s medial temporal lobe lesion: Findings from magnetic resonance imaging. Journal of *Neuroscience, 17*, 3964–3979.

Cose, Ellis (1994). *The rage of a privileged class*. New York: Harper-Collins.

Costa, Paul T., Jr.; McCrae, Robert R.; Martin, Thomas A.; et al. (1999). Personality development from adolescence through adulthood: Further cross-cultural comparisons of age differences. In V. J. Molfese & D. Molfese (eds.), *Temperament and personality development across the life span*. Hillsdale, NJ: Erlbaum.

Coupland, Scott K.; Serovich, Julianne; & Glenn, J. Edgar (1995). Reliability in constructing genograms: A study among marriage and family therapy doctoral students. *Journal of Marital and Family Therapy, 21*, 251–263.

Courtney, J. G.; Longnecker, M. P.; Theorell, T.; & Gerhardsson de Verdier, M. (1993). Stressful life events and the risk of colorectal cancer. *Epidemiology, 4*, 407–414.

Cowen, Emory L.; Wyman, Peter A.; Work, William C.; & Parker, Gayle R. (1990). The Rochester Child Resilience Project (RCRP): Overview and summary of first year findings. *Development and Psychopathology, 2*, 193–212.

Coyne, J. C. (1990). Interpersonal processes in depression. In G. I. Keitner (ed.), *Depression and families: Impact and treatment*. Washington, DC: American Psychiatric Press.

Craik, Fergus I. M., & Tulving, Endel (1975). Depth of processing and the retention of words in episodic memory. *Journal of Experimental Psychology: General, 104*, 268–294.

Crain, Stephen (1991). Language acquisition in the absence of experience. *Behavioral & Brain Sciences, 14*, 597–650.

Crair, Michael C.; Gillespie, Deda C.; & Stryker, Michael P. (1998). The role of visual experience in the development of columns in cat visual cortex. *Science, 279*, 566–570.

Cramer, Phebe (2000). Defense mechanisms in psychology today. *American Psychologist, 55*, 637–646.

Crandall, Christian S., & Martinez, Rebecca (1996). Culture, ideology, and antifat attitudes. *Personality and Social Psychology Bulletin, 22*, 1165–1176.

Crews, Frederick (ed.) (1998). *Unauthorized Freud: Doubters confront a legend*. New York: Viking.

Crick, Francis, & Mitchison, Graeme (1995). REM sleep and neural nets. *Behavioural Brain Research, 69*, 147–155.

Critchlow, Barbara (1986). The powers of John Barleycorn: Beliefs about the effects of alcohol on social behavior. *American Psychologist, 41*, 751–764.

Critser, Greg (1996, June). Oh, how happy we will be: Pills, paradise, and the profits of the drug companies. *Harper's*, 39–48.

Croizen, Jean-Claude, & Claire, Theresa (1998). Extending the concept of stereotype threat to social class: The intellectual underperformance of students from low socioeconomic backgrounds. *Personality and Social Psychology Bulletin, 24*, 588–594.

Cronbach, Lee J. (1990). *Essentials of psychological testing* (5th ed.). New York: Harper & Row.

Cross, William E. (1971). The Negro-to-Black conversion experience: Toward a psychology of Black liberation. *Black World, 20,* 13–27.

Cross, William E. (1991). *Shades of Black: Diversity in African-American identity.* Philadelphia, PA: Temple University Press.

Cross, William E., Jr., & Fhagen-Smith, Peony (1996). Nigrescence and ego identity development: Accounting for differential black identity patterns. In P. B. Pedersen, J. G. Draguns, W. J. Lonner, & J. E. Trimble (eds.), *Counseling across cultures* (4th ed.). Thousand Oaks, CA: Sage.

Crowley, Thomas J.; MacDonald, Marilyn J.; Whitmore, Elizabeth A.; & Mikulich, Susan K. (1998). Cannabis dependence, withdrawal and reinforcing effects among adolescents with conduct symptoms and substance use disorders. *Drug and Alcohol Dependence, 50,* 27–37.

Csikszentmihalyi, Mihaly, & Larson, Reed (1984). *Being adolescent: Conflict and growth in the teenage years.* New York: Basic Books.

Culbertson, Frances M. (1997). Depression and gender: An international review. *American Psychologist, 52,* 25–31.

Currie, Elliot (1998). *Crime and punishment in America.* New York: Henry Holt.

Curtiss, Susan (1977). *Genie: A psycholinguistic study of a modern-day "wild child."* New York: Academic Press.

Curtiss, Susan (1982). Developmental dissociations of language and cognition. In L. Obler & D. Fein (eds.), *Exceptional language and linguistics.* New York: Academic Press.

Cushman, Philip (1995). *Constructing the self, constructing America: A cultural history of psychotherapy.* New York: Addison-Wesley.

Cvetkovich, George T., & Earle, Timothy C. (1994). Risk and culture. In W. J. Lonner & R. Malpass (eds.), *Psychology and culture.* Boston: Allyn & Bacon.

Dadds, Mark R.; Bovbjerg, Dana H.; Redd, William H.; & Cutmore, Tim R. H. (1997). Imagery in human classical conditioning. *Psychological Bulletin, 122,* 89–103.

Daly, Martin, & Wilson, Margo (1983). *Sex, evolution, and behavior* (2nd ed.). Belmont, CA: Wadsworth.

Damasio, Antonio R. (1994). *Descartes' error: Emotion, reason, and the human brain.* New York: Grosset/Putnam.

Damasio, Hanna; Grabowski, Thomas J.; Frank, Randall; Galaburda, Albert M.; & Damasio, Antonio R. (1994). The return of Phineas Gage: Clues about the brain from the skull of a famous patient. *Science, 264,* 1102–1105.

Damasio, Hanna; Grabowski, Thomas J.; Tranel, Daniel; Hichwa, R. D.; & Damasio, Antonio R. (1996). A neural basis for lexical retrieval. *Nature, 380,* 499–505.

Damon, William (1995). *Greater expectations.* New York: Free Press.

Darley, John M. (1995). Constructive and destructive obedience: A taxonomy of principal agent relationships. *Journal of Social Issues, 51*(3), 125–154.

Darwin, Charles (1872/1965). *The expression of the emotions in man and animals.* Chicago: University of Chicago Press.

Dasen, Pierre R. (1994). Culture and cognitive development from a Piagetian perspective. In W. J. Lonner & R. S. Malpass (eds.), *Psychology and culture.* Needham Heights, MA: Allyn & Bacon.

Daum, Irene, & Schugens, Markus M. (1996). On the cerebellum and classical conditioning. *Psychological Science, 5,* 58–61.

Davey, Graham C. (1992). Classical conditioning and the acquisition of human fears and phobias: A review and synthesis of the literature. *Advances in Behaviour Research and Therapy, 14,* 29–66.

Davidson, Richard J. (1992). Anterior cerebral asymmetry and the nature of emotion. *Brain and Cognition, 20,* 125–151.

Davidson, Richard J. (1995). Cerebral asymmetry, emotion, and affective style. In R. J. Davidson & K. Hugdahl (eds.), *Brain asymmetry.* Cambridge, MA: Massachusetts Institute of Technology.

Davies, Michaela; Stankov, Lazar; & Roberts, Richard D. (1998). Emotional intelligence: In search of an elusive construct. *Journal of Personality and Social Psychology, 75,* 989–1015.

Davis, Christopher G.; Nolen-Hoeksema, Susan; & Larson, Judith (1998). Making sense of loss and benefiting from the experience: Two construals of meaning. *Journal of Personality and Social Psychology, 75,* 561–574.

Davis, Karen D.; Kiss, Z. H.; Luo, L.; et al. (1998). Phantom sensations generated by thalamic microstimulation. *Nature, 391,* 385–387.

Davison, Gerald C., & Neale, John M. (2001). *Abnormal psychology* (8th ed.). New York: Wiley.

Dawes, Robyn M. (1994). *House of cards: Psychology and psychotherapy built on myth.* New York: Free Press.

Dawson, Neal V.; Arkes, Hal R.; Siciliano, C.; et al. (1988). Hindsight bias: An impediment to accurate probability estimation in clinicopathologic conferences. *Medical Decision Making, 8*(4), 259–264.

de Lacoste-Utamsing, Christine, & Holloway, Ralph L. (1982). Sexual dimorphism in the human corpus callosum. *Science, 216,* 1431–1432.

de Rivera, Joseph (1989). Comparing experiences across cultures: Shame and guilt in America and Japan. *Hiroshima Forum for Psychology, 14,* 13–20.

de Waal, Frans (1997, July). Are we in anthropodenial? *Discover,* 50–53.

De Wolff, Marianne, & van IJzendoorn, Marinus H. (1997). Sensitivity and attachment: A meta-analysis on parental antecedents of infant attachment. *Child Development, 68,* 571–591.

Dean, Geoffrey (1987, Spring). Does astrology need to be true? II. The answer is no. *Skeptical Inquirer, 11,* 257–273.

Deaux, Kay (1985). Sex and gender. *Annual Review of Psychology, 36,* 49–81.

Deci, Edward L., & Ryan, Richard M. (1987). The support of autonomy and the control of behavior. *Journal of Personality and Social Psychology, 53,* 1024–1037.

Deffenbacher, Jerry L.; Dahlen, Eric R.; Lynch, Rebekah S.; et al. (1998). Application of Beck's cognitive therapy to general anger reduction. Paper presented at the annual meeting of the American Psychological Association, San Francisco.

DeLoache, Judy S. (1995). Early understanding and use of symbols: The model model. *Current Directions in Psychological Science, 4,* 109–113.

Dement, William (1978). *Some must watch while some must sleep.* New York: Norton.

Dement, William (1992). *The sleepwatchers.* Stanford, CA: Stanford Alumni Association.

DeNelsky, Garland Y. (1996). The case against prescription privileges for psychologists. *American Psychologist, 51,* 207–212.

DePaulo, Bella M. (1992). Nonverbal behavior and self-presentation. *Psychological Bulletin, 111,* 203–243.

DeValois, Russell L., & DeValois, Karen K. (1975). Neural coding of color. In E. C. Carterette & M. P. Friedman (eds.), *Handbook of perception* (Vol. 5). New York: Academic Press.

Devanand, Devangere P.; Dwork, Andrew J.; Hutchinson, Edward R.; et al. (1994). Does ECT alter brain structure? *American Journal of Psychiatry, 151,* 957–970.

Devine, Patricia G. (1995). Breaking the prejudice habit: Progress and prospects. Award address presented at the annual meeting of the American Psychological Association, New York.

Devine, Patricia G.; Evett, Sophia R.; & Vasquez-Suson, Kristin A. (1996). Exploring the interpersonal dynamics of inter-group contact. In R. M. Sorrentino & E. T. Higgins (eds.), *Handbook of motivation and cognition: Vol. 3. The interpersonal context.* New York: Guilford Press.

Devlin, B.; Daniels, Michael; & Roeder, Kathryn (1997). The heritability of IQ. *Nature, 388,* 468–471.

di Leonardo, Micaela (1987). The female world of cards and holidays: Women, families, and the work of kinship. *Signs, 12,* 1–20.

Diamond, Marian C. (1993, Winter-Spring). An optimistic view of the aging brain. *Generations, 17,* 31–33.

Dickinson, Alyce M. (1989). The detrimental effects of extrinsic reinforcement on "intrinsic motivation." *Behavior Analyst, 12,* 1–15.

Dien, D. S. (1982). A Chinese perspective on Kohlberg's theory of moral development. *Developmental Review, 2,* 331–341.

Dien, Dora S. (1999). Chinese authority-directed orientation and Japanese peer-group orientation: Questioning the notion of collectivism. *Review of General Psychology, 3,* 372–385.

Digman, John M. (1996). The curious history of the five-factor model. In J. S. Wiggins (ed.), *The five-factor model of personality: Theoretical perspectives.* New York: Guilford Press.

Digman, John M., & Shmelyov, Alexander G. (1996). The structure of temperament and personality in Russian children. *Journal of Personality and Social Psychology, 71,* 341–351.

DiLalla, David; Carey, Gregory; Gottesman, Irving I.; & Bouchard, Thomas J., Jr. (1996). Heritability of MMPI personality indicators of psychopathology in twins reared apart. *Journal of Abnormal Psychology, 105,* 491–499.

Dinges, David F.; Whitehouse, Wayne G.; Orne, Emily C.; et al. (1992). Evaluating hypnotic memory enhancement (hypermnesia and reminiscence) using multitrial forced recall. *Journal of Experimental Psychology: Learning, Memory, and Cognition, 18,* 1139–1147.

Dion, Kenneth L., & Dion, Karen K. (1993). Gender and ethnocultural comparisons in styles of love. *Psychology of Women Quarterly, 17,* 463–474.

Dixon, L. B.; Sundquist, J.; Winkleby, M. (2000, September 15). Differences in energy, nutrient, and food intakes in a US sample of Mexican-American women and men: Findings from the Third National Health and Nutrition Examination Survey, 1988–1994. *American Journal of Epidemiology, 152,* 548–557.

Dollard, John, & Miller, Neal E. (1950). *Personality and psychotherapy: An analysis in terms of learning, thinking, and culture.* New York: McGraw-Hill.

Domhoff, G. William (1996). *Finding meaning in dreams: A quantitative approach.* New York: Plenum.

Doty, Richard M.; Peterson, Bill E.; & Winter, David G. (1991). Threat and authoritarianism in the United States, 1978–1987. *Journal of Personality and Social Psychology, 61,* 629–640.

Dovidio, John F.; Gaertner, Samuel L.; & Validzic, Ana (1998). Intergroup bias: Status, differentiation, and a common in-group identity. *Journal of Personality and Social Psychology, 75,* 109–120.

Downey, Geraldine; Freitas, Antonio L.; Michaelis, Benjamin; & Khouri, Hala (1998). The self-fulfilling prophecy in close relationships: Rejection sensitivity and rejection by romantic partners. *Journal of Personality and Social Psychology, 75,* 545–560.

Drieschner, K., & Lange, A. (1999). A review of cognitive factors in the etiology of rape: Theories, empirical studies, and implications. *Clinical Psychology Review, 19,* 57–77.

Druckman, Daniel, & Swets, John A. (eds.) (1988). *Enhancing human performance: Issues, theories, and techniques.* Washington, DC: National Academy Press.

Dubbert, Patricia M. (1992). Exercise in behavioral medicine. *Journal of Consulting and Clinical Psychology, 60,* 613–618.

Duncan, Paula D.; Ritter, Philip L.; Dornbusch, Sanford M.; et al. (1985). The effects of pubertal timing on body image, school behavior, and deviance. *Journal of Youth and Adolescence, 14,* 227–235.

Dunkel-Schetter, Christine (1984). Social support and cancer: Findings based on patient interviews and their implications. *Journal of Social Issues, 40*(4), 77–98.

Dweck, Carol S. (1992). The study of goals in psychology. *Psychological Science, 3,* 165–167.

Dweck, Carol S., & Sorich, Lisa A. (1999). Mastery-oriented thinking. In C. R. Snyder (ed.), *Coping: The psychology of what works.* New York: Oxford University Press.

Ebbinghaus, Hermann M. (1885/1913). *Memory: A contribution to experimental psychology* (H. A. Ruger & C. E. Bussenius, trans.). New York: Teachers College Press, Columbia University.

Eccles, Jacquelynne S. (1993). Parents and gender-role socialization during the middle childhood and adolescent years. In S. Oskamp & M. Costanzo (eds.), *The Claremont Symposium on Applied Social Psychology: Gender issues in contemporary society.* Newbury Park, CA: Sage.

Eccles, Jacquelynne S.; Midgley, Carol; Wigfield, Allan; et al. (1993). Development during adolescence: The impact of stage-environment fit on young adolescents' experiences in schools and in families. *American Psychologist, 48,* 90–101.

Eckensberger, Lutz H. (1994). Moral development and its measurement across cultures. In W. J. Lonner & R. Malpass (eds.), *Psychology and culture.* Needham Heights, MA: Allyn & Bacon.

Edelson, Marshall (1994). Can psychotherapy research answer this psychotherapist's questions? In P. F. Talley, H. H. Strupp, & S. F. Butler (eds.), *Psychotherapy research and practice: Bridging the gap.* New York: Basic Books.

Edenberg, Howard J.; Foroud, Tatiana; Koller, D. L.; et al. (1998). A family-based analysis of the association of the dopamine D2 receptor (DRD2) with alcoholism. *Alcohol Clinical and Experimental Research, 22,* 505–512.

Edwards, Kari, & Smith, Edward E. (1996). A disconfirmation bias in the evaluation of arguments. *Journal of Personality and Social Psychology, 71,* 5–24.

Ehrenreich, Barbara (1978). *For her own good: 150 years of the experts' advice to women.* New York: Doubleday.

Eich, E., & Hyman, R. (1992). Subliminal self-help. In D. Druckman & R. A. Bjork (eds.), *In the mind's eye: Enhancing human performance.* Washington, DC: National Academy Press.

Eisenberg, Nancy (1995). Prosocial development: A multifaceted model. In W. M. Kurtines & J. L. Gewirtz (eds.), *Moral development: An introduction.* Boston: Allyn & Bacon.

Eisenberg, Nancy; Fabes, Richard A.; Murphy, Bridget; et al. (1996). The relations of children's dispositional empathy-related responding to their emotionality, regulation, and social functioning. *Developmental Psychology, 32,* 195–209.

Eisenberger, Robert; Armeli, Stephen; & Pretz, Jean (1998). Can the promise of reward increase creativity? *Journal of Personality and Social Psychology, 74,* 704–714.

Eisenberger, Robert, & Cameron, Judy (1996). Detrimental effects of reward: Reality or myth? *American Psychologist, 51,* 1153–1166.

Eisenberger, Robert, & Cameron, Judy (1998). Reward, intrinsic interest, and creativity: New findings [Comment]. *American Psychologist, 53,* 676–679.

Ekman, Paul (1994). Strong evidence for universals in facial expressions: A reply to Russell's mistaken critique. *Psychological Bulletin, 115,* 268–287.

Ekman, Paul; Friesen, Wallace V.; & O'Sullivan, Maureen (1988). Smiles when lying. *Journal of Personality and Social Psychology, 54,* 414–420.

Ekman, Paul; Friesen, Wallace V.; O'Sullivan, Maureen; et al. (1987). Universals and cultural differences in the judgments of facial expression of emotion. *Journal of Personality and Social Psychology, 53,* 712–717.

Ekman, Paul, & Heider, Karl G. (1988). The universality of a contempt expression: A replication. *Motivation and Emotion, 12,* 303–308.

Elliot, Andrew J., & Harackiewicz, Judith M. (1994). Goal setting, achievement orientation, and intrinsic motivation: A mediational analysis. *Journal of Personality and Social Psychology, 66,* 968–980.

Elliot, Andrew J., & Sheldon, Kennon M. (1998). Avoidance personal goals and the personality-illness relationship. *Journal of Personality and Social Psychology, 75,* 1282–1299.

Elliott, Robert, & Morrow-Bradley, Cheryl (1994). Developing a working marriage between psychotherapists and psychotherapy researchers: Identifying shared purposes. In P. F. Talley, H. H. Strupp, & S. F. Butler (eds.), *Psychotherapy research and practice: Bridging the gap.* New York: Basic Books.

Ellis, Albert (1993). Changing rational-emotive therapy (RET) to rational emotive behavior therapy (REBT). *Behavior Therapist, 16,* 257–258.

Ellis, Albert, & Blau, Shawn (1998). Rational emotive behavior therapy. *Directions in Clinical and Counseling Psychology, 8,* 41–56.

Ellison, Carol R. (2000). *Women's sexualities.* Oakland, CA: New Harbinger.

Emmons, Robert A., & King, Laura A. (1988). Conflict among personal strivings: Immediate and long-term implications for psychological and physical well-being. *Journal of Personality and Social Psychology, 54,* 1040–1048.

Endler, Norman S. (1990). *Holiday of darkness.* New York: Wiley-Interscience.

Epstein, Seymour (1994). Integration of the cognitive and the psychodynamic unconscious. *American Psychologist, 49,* 709–724.

Erikson, Erik H. (1950/1963). *Childhood and society* (2nd ed.). New York: Norton.

Erikson, Erik H. (1982). *The life cycle completed.* New York: Norton.

Eriksson, P. S.; Perfilieva, E.; Bjork-Eriksson, T.; et al. (1998). Neurogenesis in the adult human hippocampus. *Nature Medicine, 4,* 1313–1317.

Eron, Leonard D. (1995). Media violence: How it affects kids and what can be done about it. Invited address presented at the annual meeting of the American Psychological Association, New York.

Ervin-Tripp, Susan (1964). Imitation and structural change in children's language. In E. H. Lenneberg (ed.), *New directions in the study of language.* Cambridge, MA: MIT Press.

Esparza, J.; Fox, C.; Harper, I. T.; et al. (2000, January 24). Daily energy expenditure in Mexican and USA Pima Indians: Low physical activity as a possible cause of obesity. *International Journal of Obesity and Related Metabolic Disorders, 1,* 55–59.

Evans, Gary W.; Bullinger, Monika; & Hygge, Staffan (1998). Chronic noise exposure and physiological response: A prospective study of children living under environmental stress. *Psychological Science, 9,* 75–77.

Ewart, Craig K. (1995). Self-efficacy and recovery from heart attack. In J. E. Maddux (ed.), *Self-efficacy, adaptation, and adjustment: Theory, research, and application.* New York: Plenum.

Ewart, Craig K., & Kolodner, Kenneth B. (1994). Negative affect, gender, and expressive style predict elevated ambulatory blood pressure in adolescents. *Journal of Personality and Social Psychology, 66,* 596–605.

Exner, John E. (1993). *The Rorschach: A comprehensive system: Vol. 1. Basic foundations* (3rd ed.). New York: Wiley.

Eyferth, Klaus (1961). [The performance of different groups of the children of occupation forces on the Hamburg-Wechsler Intelligence Test for Children.] *Archiv für die Gesamte Psychologie, 113,* 222–241.

Eysenck, Hans J. (1993). Prediction of cancer and coronary heart disease mortality by means of a personality inventory: Results of a 15-year follow-up study. *Psychological Reports, 72,* 499–516.

Fagan, Joseph F., III (1992). Intelligence: A theoretical viewpoint. *Current Directions in Psychological Science, 1,* 82–86.

Fagot, Beverly I. (1985). Beyond the reinforcement principle: Another step toward understanding sex role development. *Developmental Psychology, 2,* 1097–1104.

Fagot, Beverly I. (1993, June). Gender role development in early childhood: Environmental input, internal construction. Invited address presented at the annual meeting of the International Academy of Sex Research, Monterey, CA.

Fagot, Beverly I.; Hagan, R.; Leinbach, Mary D.; & Kronsberg, S. (1985). Differential reactions to assertive and communicative acts of toddler boys and girls. *Child Development, 56,* 1499–1505.

Fagot, Beverly I., & Leinbach, Mary D. (1993). Gender-role development in young children: From discrimination to labeling. *Developmental Review, 13,* 205–224.

Fairchild, Halford H. (1985). Black, Negro, or Afro-American? The differences are crucial! *Journal of Black Studies, 16,* 47–55.

Falk, Ruma, & Greenbaum, Charles W. (1995). Significance tests die hard: The amazing persistence of a probabilistic misconception. *Theory & Psychology, 5*(1), 75–98.

Fausto-Sterling, Anne (1997). Beyond difference: A biologist's perspective. *Journal of Social Issues, 53,* 233–258.

Fazio, Russell H.; Jackson, Joni R.; Dunton, Bridget C.; & Williams, Carol J. (1995). Variability in automatic activation as an unobtrusive measure of racial attitudes: A bona fide pipeline? *Journal of Personality and Social Psychology, 69,* 1013–1027.

FDA Drug Bulletin (1990, April). Two new psychiatric drugs. *20*(1), 9.

Feather, N. T. (1966). Effects of prior success and failure on expectations of success and subsequent performance. *Journal of Personality and Social Psychology, 3,* 287–298.

Feather, N. T. (ed.) (1982). *Expectations and actions: Expectancy value models in psychology.* Hillsdale, NJ: Erlbaum.

Fehr, Beverley (1993). How do I love thee . . . ? Let me consult my prototype. In S. Duck (ed.), *Individuals in relationships* (Vol. 1). Newbury Park, CA: Sage.

Fehr, Beverley; Baldwin, Mark; Collins, Lois; et al. (1999). Anger in close relationships: An interpersonal script analysis. *Personality and Social Psychology Bulletin, 25,* 299–312.

Fein, Steven, & Spencer, Steven J. (1997). Prejudice as self-image maintenance: Affirming the self through derogating others. *Journal of Personality and Social Psychology, 73,* 31–44.

Feingold, Alan (1988). Cognitive gender differences are disappearing. *American Psychologist, 43,* 95–103.

Feldman, Robert S. (1997). *Development across the life span.* Upper Saddle River, NJ: Prentice Hall.

Fernald, Anne (1990). Emotion in the voice: Meaningful melodies in mother's speech to infants. Paper presented at the annual meeting of the American Psychological Association, Boston.

Fernald, Anne, & Mazzie, Claudia (1991). Prosody and focus in speech to infants and adults. *Developmental Psychology, 27,* 209–221.

Fernandez, Ephrem, & Turk, Dennis C. (1992). Sensory and affective components of pain: Separation and synthesis. *Psychological Bulletin, 112,* 205–217.

Fernea, Elizabeth, & Fernea, Robert (1994). Cleanliness and culture. In W. J. Lonner & Malpass (eds.), *Psychology and culture.* Boston: Allyn & Bacon.

Festinger, Leon (1957). *A theory of cognitive dissonance.* Evanston, IL: Row, Peterson.

Festinger, Leon (1980). Looking backward. In L. Festinger (ed.), *Retrospections on social psychology.* New York: Oxford University Press.

Festinger, Leon, & Carlsmith, J. Merrill (1959). Cognitive consequences of forced compliance. *Journal of Abnormal and Social Psychology, 58,* 203–210.

Festinger, Leon; Pepitone, Albert; & Newcomb, Theodore (1952). Some consequences of deindividuation in a group. *Journal of Abnormal and Social Psychology, 47,* 382–389.

Festinger, Leon; Riecken, Henry W.; & Schachter, Stanley (1956). *When prophecy fails.* Minneapolis: University of Minnesota Press.

Field, Tiffany M. (1998). Massage therapy effects. *American Psychologist, 53,* 1270–1281.

Fields, Howard (1991). Depression and pain: A neurobiological model. *Neuropsychiatry, Neuropsychology, and Behavioral Neurology, 4,* 83–92.

Fiez, J. A. (1996). Cerebellar contributions to cognition. *Neuron, 16,* 13–15.

Fincham, Frank D.; Beach, Steven R. H.; Harold, Gordon T.; & Osborne, Lori N. (1997). Marital satisfaction and depression: Different causal relationships for men and women? *Psychological Science, 8,* 351–357.

Fingarette, Herbert (1988). *Heavy drinking: The myth of alcoholism as a disease.* Berkeley: University of California Press.

Fink, Max (1999). *Electroshock: Restoring the mind.* New York: Oxford University Press.

Fischer, Ann R.; Tokar, David M.; Good, Glenn E.; & Snell, Andrea F. (1998). More on the structure of male role norms. *Psychology of Women Quarterly, 22,* 135–155.

Fischer, Pamela C.; Smith, Randy J.; Leonard, Elizabeth; et al. (1993). Sex differences on affective dimensions: Continuing examination. *Journal of Counseling and Development, 71,* 440–443.

Fischhoff, Baruch (1975). Hindsight is not equal to foresight: The effect of outcome knowledge on judgment under uncertainty. *Journal of Experimental Psychology: Human Perception and Performance, 1,* 288–299.

Fishbein, Harold D. (1996). *Peer prejudice and discrimination.* Boulder, CO: Westview Press.

Fisher, Ronald J. (1994). Generic principles for resolving intergroup conflict. *Journal of Social Issues, 50,* 47–66.

Fiske, Alan P., & Haslam, Nick (1996). Social cognition is thinking about relationships. *Current Directions in Psychological Science, 5,* 143–148.

Fivush, Robyn, & Hamond, Nina R. (1991). Autobiographical memory across the school years: Toward reconceptualizing childhood amnesia. In R. Fivush & J. A. Hudson (eds.), *Knowing and remembering in young children.* New York: Cambridge University Press.

Flacks, Richard, & Thomas, Scott L. (1998, November 27). Among affluent students, a culture of disengagement. *Chronicle of Higher Education,* A48.

Flavell, John H. (1996). Piaget's legacy. *Psychological Science, 7,* 200–203.

Flor, Herta; Kerns, Robert D.; & Turk, Dennis C. (1987). The role of spouse reinforcement, perceived pain, and activity levels of chronic pain patients. *Journal of Psychosomatic Research, 31,* 251–259.

Flynn, James R. (1987). Massive IQ gains in 14 nations: What IQ tests really measure. *Psychological Bulletin, 95,* 29–51.

Flynn, James R. (1999). Searching for justice: The discovery of IQ gains over time. *American Psychologist, 54,* 5–20.

Foa, Edna, & Emmelkamp, Paul (eds.) (1983). *Failures in behavior therapy.* New York: Wiley.

Fogelman, Eva (1994). *Conscience and courage: Rescuers of Jews during the Holocaust.* New York: Anchor Books.

Folkman, Susan, & Moskowitz, Judith T. (2000). Stress, positive emotion, and coping. *Current Directions in Psychological Science, 9,* 115–118.

Ford, D. E.; Mead, L. A.; Chang, P. P.; et al. (1998). Depression is a risk factor for coronary artery disease in men: The precursors study. *Archives of Internal Medicine, 158,* 1422–1426.

Forgas, Joseph P. (1998). On being happy and mistaken: Mood effects on the fundamental attribution error. *Journal of Personality and Social Psychology, 75,* 318–331.

Forgas, Joseph P., & Bond, Michael H. (1985). Cultural influences on the perception of interaction episodes. *Personality and Social Psychology Bulletin, 11,* 75–88.

Forrest, F.; Florey, C. du V.; Taylor, D.; et al. (1991, July 6). Reported social alcohol consumption during pregnancy and infants' development at 18 months. *British Medical Journal, 303,* 22–26.

Foulkes, D. (1962). Dream reports from different states of sleep. *Journal of Abnormal and Social Psychology, 65,* 14–25.

Fouts, Roger, with Stephen T. Mills (1997). *Next of kin: What chimpanzees have taught me about who we are.* New York: William Morrow.

Fouts, Roger S., & Rigby, Randall L. (1977). Man-chimpanzee communication. In T. A. Seboek (ed.), *How animals communicate.* Bloomington: University of Indiana Press.

Frankl, Victor E. (1955). *The doctor and the soul: An introduction to logotherapy.* New York: Knopf.

Franklin, Anderson J. (1993, July/August). The invisibility syndrome. *Family Therapy Networker,* 33–39.

Franklin, Karen (1998). Psychosocial motivations of hate crimes perpetrators: Implications for educational interventions. Paper presented at the annual meeting of the American Psychological Association, San Francisco.

Franz, Carol E. (1997). Stability and change in the transition to midlife: A longitudinal study of midlife adults. In M. E. Lachman & J. B. James (eds.), *Multiple paths of midlife development.* Chicago: University of Chicago Press.

Frasure-Smith, Nancy; Lesperance, F.; Juneau, M.; Talajic, M.; & Bourassa, M. G. (1999). Gender, depression, and one-year prognosis after myocardial infarction. *Psychosomatic Medicine, 61,* 26–37.

Freed, C. R.; Breeze, R. E.; Rosenberg, N. L.; & Schneck, S. A. (1993). Embryonic dopamine cell implants as a treatment for the second phase of Parkinson's disease: Replacing failed nerve terminals. *Advances in Neurology, 60,* 721–728.

Freedman, Hill, & Combs, Gene (1996). *Narrative therapy.* New York: Norton.

Freud, Anna (1967). *Ego and the mechanisms of defense (The writings of Anna Freud,* Vol. 2) (rev. ed.). New York: International Universities Press.

Freud, Sigmund (1900/1953). The interpretation of dreams. In J. Strachey (ed.), *Standard edition of the complete psychological works of Sigmund Freud* (Vols. 4 and 5). London: Hogarth Press.

Freud, Sigmund (1905a). Fragment of an analysis of a case of hysteria. In J. Strachey (ed.), *Standard edition of the complete psychological works of Sigmund Freud* (Vol. 7).

Freud, Sigmund (1905b). Three essays on the theory of sexuality. In J. Strachey (ed.), *Standard edition* (Vol. 7).

Freud, Sigmund (1920/1960). *A general introduction to psychoanalysis* (Joan Riviere, trans.). New York: Washington Square Press.

Freud, Sigmund (1923/1962). *The ego and the id* (Joan Riviere, trans.). New York: Norton.

Freud, Sigmund (1924a). The dissolution of the Oedipus complex. In J. Strachey (ed.), *Standard edition* (Vol. 19).

Freud, Sigmund (1924b). Some psychical consequences of the anatomical distinction between the sexes. In J. Strachey (ed.), *Standard edition* (Vol. 19).

Freud, Sigmund (1961). *Letters of Sigmund Freud, 1873–1939* (Ernst L. Freud, ed.). London: Hogarth Press.

Freyd, Jennifer J. (1996). *Betrayal trauma: The logic of forgetting childhood abuse.* Cambridge, MA: Harvard University Press.

Friedman, Meyer, & Rosenman, Ray (1974). *Type A behavior and your heart.* New York: Knopf.

Friedman, William; Robinson, Amy; & Friedman, Britt (1987). Sex differences in moral judgments? A test of Gilligan's theory. *Psychology of Women Quarterly, 11,* 37–46.

Friedrich, W. (1998). Normative sexual behavior in children: A contemporary sample. *Pediatrics, 101,* 4.

Frijda, Nico H. (1988). The laws of emotion. *American Psychologist, 43,* 349–358.

Frome, Pamela M., & Eccles, Jacquelynne S. (1998). Parents' influence on children's achievement-related perceptions. *Journal of Personality and Social Psychology, 74,* 435–452.

Fry, P. S. (1995). Perfectionism, humor, and optimism as moderators of health outcomes and determinants of coping styles of women executives. *Genetic, Social, and General Psychology Monographs, 121,* 211–245.

Fry, William F. (1994). The biology of humor. *Humor: International Journal of Humor Research, 7,* 111–126.

Frye, Richard E.; Schwartz, B. S.; & Doty, Richard L. (1990). Dose-related effects of cigarette smoking on olfactory function. *Journal of the American Medical Association, 263,* 1233–1236.

Gaertner, Samuel L.; Mann, Jeffrey A.; Dovidio, John F.; et al. (1990). How does cooperation reduce intergroup bias? *Journal of Personality and Social Psychology, 59,* 692–704.

Gage, Fred H.; Kempermann, G.; Palmer, T. D.; et al. (1998). Multipotent progenitor cells in the adult dentate gyrus. *Journal of Neurobiology, 36,* 249–266.

Gagnon, John, & Simon, William (1973). *Sexual conduct: The social sources of human sexuality.* Chicago: Aldine.

Galanter, Eugene (1962). Contemporary psychophysics. In R. Brown, E. Galanter, H. Hess, & G. Mandler (eds.), *New directions in psychology.* New York: Holt, Rinehart and Winston.

Galanter, Marc (1989). *Cults: Faith, healing, and coercion.* New York: Oxford University Press.

Gallant, Jack L.; Braun, Jochen; & Van Essen, David C. (1993). Selectivity for polar, hyperbolic, and Cartesian gratings in macaque visual cortex. *Science, 259,* 100–103.

Gallo, Fred (1998). *Energy therapies.* Washington, DC: American Psychological Association.

Galotti, Kathleen (1989). Approaches to studying formal and everyday reasoning. *Psychological Bulletin, 105,* 331–351.

Ganaway, George (1995). Hypnosis, childhood trauma, and dissociative identity disorder: Toward an integrative theory. *International Journal of Clinical and Experimental Hypnosis, 33,* 127–144.

Gao, Jia-Hong; Parsons, Lawrence M.; Bower, James M.; et al. (1996). Cerebellum implicated in sensory acquisition and discrimination rather than motor control. *Science, 272,* 545–547.

Garb, Howard N. (1999). Call for a moratorium on the use of the Rorschach Inkblot Test in clinical and forensic settings. *Assessment, 6,* 313–315.

Garb, Howard N.; Florio, Colleen M.; & Grove, William M. (1998). The validity of the Rorschach and the Minnesota Multiphasic Personality Inventory: Results from meta-analyses. *Psychological Science, 9,* 402–404.

Garb, Howard N.; Wood, James M.; & Nezworski, M. Teresa (2000). Projective techniques and the detection of child sexual abuse. *Child Maltreatment, 5,* 161–168.

Garcia, John, & Koelling, Robert A. (1966). Relation of cue to consequence in avoidance learning. *Psychonomic Science, 4,* 23–124.

Gardner, Howard (1983). *Frames of mind: The theory of multiple intelligences.* New York: Basic Books.

Gardner, Howard (1993). *Creating minds.* New York: Basic Books.

Gardner, Howard (1995). Perennial antinomies and perpetual redrawings: Is there progress in the study of mind? In R. L. Solso & D. W. Massar (eds.), *The science of the mind: 2001 and beyond.* New York: Oxford University Press.

Gardner, R. Allen, & Gardner, Beatrice T. (1969). Teaching sign language to a chimpanzee. *Science, 165,* 664–672.

Garland, Ann F., & Zigler, Edward (1994). Adolescent suicide prevention: Current research and social policy implications. *American Psychologist, 48,* 169–182.

Garmezy, Norman (1991). Resilience and vulnerability to adverse developmental outcomes associated with poverty. *American Behavioral Scientist, 34,* 416–430.

Garry, Maryanne; Manning, Charles G.; & Loftus, Elizabeth F. (1996). Imagination inflation: Imagining a childhood event inflates confidence that it occurred. *Psychonomic Bulletin & Review, 3,* 208–214.

Garven, Sena; Wood, James M.; Malpass, Roy S.; & Shaw, John S., III (1998). More than suggestion: The effect of interviewing techniques from the McMartin Preschool case. *Journal of Applied Psychology, 83,* 347–359.

Gaston, Louise; Marmar, Charles R.; Gallagher, Dolores; & Thompson, Larry W. (1989). Impact of confirming patient expectations of change processes in behavioral, cognitive, and brief dynamic psychotherapy. *Psychotherapy, 26,* 296–302.

Gaudiano, Brandon A., & Herbert, James D. (2000, July/August). Can we really tap our problems away? A critical analysis of Thought Field Therapy. *Skeptical Inquirer,* 29–33, 36.

Gawande, Atul (1998, September 21). The pain perplex. *New Yorker,* 86, 88, 90, 92–94.

Gay, Peter (1988). *Freud: A life for our time.* New York: Norton.

Gazzaniga, Michael S. (1967). The split brain in man. *Scientific American, 217*(2), 24–29.

Gazzaniga, Michael S. (1983). Right hemisphere language following brain bisection: A 20-year perspective. *American Psychologist, 38,* 525–537.

Gazzaniga, Michael S. (1988). *Mind matters.* Boston: Houghton Mifflin.

Geary, David C. (1995). Reflections of evolution and culture in children's cognition: Implications for mathematical development and instruction. *American Psychologist, 50,* 24–37.

Gelernter, David (1997, May 19). How hard is chess? *Time,* 72–73.

Gibson, Eleanor, & Walk, Richard (1960). The "visual cliff." *Scientific American, 202,* 80–92.

Gillham, Jane E.; Reivich, Karen J.; Jaycox, Lisa H.; & Seligman, Martin E. P. (1995). Prevention of depressive symptoms in schoolchildren: A two-year follow-up. *Psychological Science, 6,* 343–351.

Gilligan, Carol (1982). *In a different voice.* Cambridge, MA: Harvard University Press.

Gladue, Brian A. (1994). The biopsychology of sexual orientation. *Current Directions in Psychological Science, 3,* 150–154.

Glanzer, Murray, & Cunitz, Anita R. (1966). Two storage mechanisms in free recall. *Journal of Verbal Learning and Verbal Behavior, 5,* 351–360.

Gleaves, David H. (1996). The sociocognitive model of dissociative identity disorder: A reexamination of the evidence. *Psychological Bulletin, 120,* 42–59.

Glenmullen, Joseph (2000). *Prozac backlash: Overcoming the dangers of Prozac, Zoloft, Paxil, and other antidepressants with safe, effective alternatives.* New York: Simon & Schuster.

Glick, Peter; Fiske, Susan T.; Mladinic, Antonio; et al. (2000). Beyond prejudice as simple antipathy: Hostile and benevolent sexism across cultures. *Journal of Personality and Social Psychology, 79,* 763–775.

Goldman-Rakic, Patricia S. (1996). Opening the mind through neurobiology. Invited address at the annual meeting of the American Psychological Association, Toronto, Canada.

Goldstein, Michael J. (1987). Psychosocial issues. *Schizophrenia Bulletin, 13*(1), 157–171.

Goldstein, Michael, & Miklowitz, David (1995). The effectiveness of psychoeducational family therapy in the treatment of schizophrenic disorders. *Journal of Marital and Family Therapy, 21,* 361–376.

Goleman, Daniel (1995). *Emotional intelligence.* New York: Bantam.

Goodman, Gail S.; Qin, Jianjian; Bottoms, Bette L.; & Shaver, Phillip R. (1995). Characteristics and sources of allegations of ritualistic child abuse. Final report to the National Center on Child Abuse and Neglect [NCCAN], Washington, DC. (Executive summary and complete report available from NCCAN, 1-800-394-3366.)

Goodwin, Donald W.; Knop, Joachim; Jensen, Per; et al. (1994). Thirty-year follow-up of men at high risk for alcoholism. In T. F. Babor & V. M. Hesselbrock (eds.), *Types of alcoholics: Evidence from clinical, experimental, and genetic research.* New York: New York Academy of Sciences.

Goodwyn, Susan, & Acredolo, Linda (1998). Encouraging symbolic gestures: A new perspective on the relationship between gesture and speech. In J. Iverson & S. Goldin-Meadow (eds.), *The nature and functions of gesture in children's communication.* San Francisco: Jossey-Bass.

Gore, P. M., & Rotter, Julian B. (1963). A personality correlate of social action. *Journal of Personality, 31,* 58–64.

Goren, C. C.; Sarty, J.; & Wu, P. Y. (1975). Visual following and pattern discrimination of face-like stimuli by newborn infants. *Pediatrics, 56,* 544–549.

Gorn, Gerald J. (1982). The effects of music in advertising on choice behavior: A classical conditioning approach. *Journal of Marketing, 46,* 94–101.

Gottesman, Irving I. (1991). *Schizophrenia genesis: The origins of madness.* New York: W. H. Freeman.

Gottesman, Irving I. (1994). Perils and pleasures of genetic psychopathology. Distinguished Scientist Award address presented at the annual meeting of the American Psychological Association, Los Angeles.

Gottfried, Adele Eskeles; Fleming, James S.; & Gottfried, Allen W. (1994). Role of parental motivational practices in children's academic intrinsic motivation and achievement. *Journal of Educational Psychology, 86,* 104–113.

Gould, Elizabeth; Beylin, A.; Tanapat, Patima; et al. (1999). Learning enhances adult neurogenesis in the hippocampal formation. *Nature Neuroscience, 2,* 260–265.

Gould, Elizabeth; Tanapat, Patima; McEwen, Bruce S.; et al. (1998). Proliferation of granule cell precursors in the dentate gyrus of adult monkeys is diminished by stress. *Proceedings of the National Academy of Science, 95,* 3168–3171.

Gould, Stephen Jay (1994, November 28). Curveball [Review of *The bell curve,* by Richard J. Herrnstein and Charles Murray]. *New Yorker,* 139–149.

Gould, Stephen Jay (1996). *The mismeasure of man* (rev. ed.). New York: Norton.

Gourevich, Philip (1998). *We wish to inform you that tomorrow we will be killed with our families: Stories from Rwanda.* New York: Farrar, Straus and Giroux.

Graf, Peter, & Schacter, Daniel A. (1985). Implicit and explicit memory for new associations in normal and amnesic subjects. *Journal of Experimental Psychology: Learning, Memory, and Cognition, 11,* 501–518.

Graham, Jill W. (1986). Principled organizational dissent: A theoretical essay. *Research in Organizational Behavior, 8,* 1–52.

Graham, Sandra (1994). Motivation in African Americans. *Review of Educational Research, 64,* 55–117.

Green, Donald P.; Glaser, Jack; & Rich, Andrew (1998). From lynching to gay bashing: The elusive connection between economic conditions and hate crime. *Journal of Personality and Social Psychology, 75,* 82–92.

Green, Gina (1996). Behavioral treatment of autistic persons: A review of research from 1980 to the present. *Research in Developmental Disabilities, 17,* 433–465.

Greenberg, Roger P.; Bornstein, Robert F.; Greenberg, Michael D.; & Fisher, Seymour (1992). A meta-analysis of antidepressant outcome under "blinder" conditions. *Journal of Consulting and Clinical Psychology, 60,* 664–669.

Greenberg, Roger P.; Bornstein, Robert F.; Zborowski, Michael J.; et al. (1994). A meta-analysis of fluoxetine outcome in the treatment of depression. *Journal of Nervous and Mental Disease, 182,* 547–551.

Greenberger, Dennis, & Padesky, Christine A. (1995). *Mind over mood: A cognitive therapy treatment manual for clients.* New York: Guilford Press.

Greene, Robert L. (1986). Sources of recency effects in free recall. *Psychological Bulletin, 99,* 221–228.

Greenfield, Patricia (1976). Cross-cultural research and Piagetian theory: Paradox and progress. In K. F. Riegel & J. A. Meacham (eds.), *The developing individual in a changing world: Vol. 1. Historical and cultural issues.* The Hague, Netherlands: Mouton.

Greenough, William T., & Anderson, Brenda J. (1991). Cerebellar synaptic plasticity: Relation to learning vs. neural activity. *Annals of the New York Academy of Sciences, 627,* 231–247.

Greenough, William T., & Black, James E. (1992). Induction of brain structure by experience: Substrates for cognitive development. In M. Gunnar & C. A. Nelson (eds.), *Behavioral developmental neuroscience: Vol. 24. Minnesota Symposium on Child Psychology.* Hillsdale, NJ: Erlbaum.

Greenwald, Anthony G.; Draine, Sean C.; & Abrams, Richard L. (1996). Three cognitive markers of unconscious semantic activation. *Science, 273,* 1699–1702.

Greenwald, Anthony G.; McGhee, Debbie E.; & Schwartz, Jordan L. K. (1998). Measuring individual differences in implicit cognition: The Implicit Association Test. *Journal of Personality and Social Psychology, 74,* 1464–1480.

Greenwald, Anthony G.; Spangenberg, Eric R.; Pratkanis, Anthony R.; & Eskenazi, Jay (1991). Double-blind tests of subliminal self-help audiotapes. *Psychological Science, 2,* 119–122.

Gregory, Richard L. (1963). Distortion of visual space as inappropriate constancy scaling. *Nature, 199,* 678–679.

Griffin, Donald R. (1992). *Animal minds.* Chicago: University of Chicago Press.

Grigorenko, Elena L., & Sternberg, Robert J. (1998). Dynamic testing. *Psychological Bulletin, 124,* 75–111.

Groneman, Carol (2000). *Nymphomania: A history.* New York: Norton.

Grossman, Michele, & Wood, Wendy (1993). Sex differences in intensity of emotional experience: A social role interpretation. *Journal of Personality and Social Psychology, 65,* 1010–1022.

Gruber, Barry L.; Hersh, Stephen P.; Hall, Nicholas R.; et al. (1993). Immunological responses of breast cancer patients to behavioral interventions. *Biofeedback and Self-Regulation, 18,* 1–22.

Guglielmi, R. Sergio (1999). Psychophysiological assessment of prejudice: Past research, current status, and future directions. *Personality and Social Psychology Review, 3,* 123–157.

Guilford, J. P. (1988). Some changes in the structure-of-intellect model. *Educational and Psychological Measurement, 48,* 1–4.

Gupta, S.; Mosnik, D.; Black, D. W.; et al. (1999). Tardive dyskinesia: Review of treatments past, present, and future. *Annals of Clinical Psychiatry, 11,* 257–266.

Gur, R. E.; Maany, V.; Mozley, P. D.; et al. (1998). Subcortical MRI volumes in neuroleptic-naive and treated patients with schizophrenia. *American Journal of Psychiatry, 155,* 1711–1717.

Guralnick, M. J. (ed.) (1997). *The effectiveness of early intervention.* Baltimore: Brookes.

Haber, Ralph N. (1970, May). How we remember what we see. *Scientific American, 222,* 104–112.

Haimov, I., & Lavie, P. (1996). Melatonin—a soporific hormone. *Current Directions in Psychological Science, 5,* 106–111.

Halaas, Jeffrey L.; Gajiwala, Ketan S.; Maffei, Margherita; et al. (1995). Weight-reducing effects of the plasma protein encoded by the *obese* gene. *Science, 269,* 543–546.

Hall, Edward T. (1959). *The silent language.* Garden City, NY: Doubleday.

Hall, Edward T. (1976). *Beyond culture.* New York: Anchor.

Hall, Edward T. (1983). *The dance of life: The other dimension of time.* Garden City, NY: Anchor Press/Doubleday.

Hall, Edward T., & Hall, Mildred R. (1987). *Hidden differences: Doing business with the Japanese.* Garden City, NY: Anchor Press/Doubleday.

Hall, Edward T., & Hall, Mildred R. (1990). *Understanding cultural differences.* Yarmouth, ME: Intercultural Press.

Hall, G. Stanley (1899). A study of anger. *American Journal of Psychology, 10,* 516–591.

Halliday, G. (1993). Examination dreams. *Perceptual and Motor Skills, 77,* 489–490.

Halpern, Diane (1995). *Thought and knowledge: An introduction to critical thinking* (3rd ed.). Hillsdale, NJ: Erlbaum.

Hamer, Dean H.; Hu, Stella; Magnuson, Victoria L.; et al. (1993). A linkage between DNA markers on the X chromosome and male sexual orientation. *Science, 261,* 321–327.

Haney, Craig; Banks, Curtis; & Zimbardo, Philip (1973). Interpersonal dynamics in a simulated prison. *International Journal of Criminology and Penology, 1,* 69–97.

Haney, Craig, & Zimbardo, Philip (1998). The past and future of U.S. prison policy: Twenty-five years after the Stanford Prison Experiment. *American Psychologist, 53,* 709–727.

Harding, Courtenay M.; Zubin, Joseph; & Strauss, John S. (1992). Chronicity in schizophrenia: Revisited. *British Journal of Psychiatry, 161*(Suppl. 18), 27–37.

Hare, Robert D. (1965). Temporal gradient of fear arousal in psychopaths. *Journal of Abnormal Psychology, 70,* 442–445.

Hare, Robert D. (1993). *Without conscience: The disturbing world of the psychopaths among us.* New York: Pocket Books.

Haritos-Fatouros, Mika (1988). The official torturer: A learning model for obedience to the authority of violence. *Journal of Applied Social Psychology, 18,* 1107–1120.

Harkins, Stephen G., & Szymanski, Kate (1989). Social loafing and group evaluation. *Journal of Personality and Social Psychology, 56,* 934–941.

Harlow, Harry F. (1958). The nature of love. *American Psychologist, 13,* 673–685.

Harlow, Harry F., & Harlow, Margaret K. (1966). Learning to love. *American Scientist, 54,* 244–272.

Harmon-Jones, Eddie, & Allen, John J. B. (1998). Anger and frontal brain activity: EEG asymmetry consistent with approach motivation despite negative affective valence. *Journal of Personality and Social Psychology, 74,* 1310–1316.

Harmon-Jones, Eddie; Brehm, Jack W.; Greenberg, Jeff; et al. (1996). Evidence that the production of aversive consequences is not necessary to create cognitive dissonance. *Journal of Personality and Social Psychology, 70,* 5–16.

Harris, Judith R. (1998). *The nurture assumption.* New York: Free Press.

Hart, John, Jr.; Berndt, Rita S.; & Caramazza, Alfonso (1985, August 1). Category-specific naming deficit following cerebral infarction. *Nature, 316,* 339–340.

Hasher, Lynn, & Zacks, Rose T. (1984). Automatic processing of fundamental information: The case of frequency of occurrence. *American Psychologist, 39,* 1372–1388.

Hatfield, Elaine, & Rapson, Richard L. (1996). *Love and sex: Cross-cultural perspectives.* Boston: Allyn & Bacon.

Hauser, Marc (2000). *Wild minds: What animals really think.* New York: Holt.

Hawkins, Scott A., & Hastie, Reid (1990). Hindsight: Biased judgments of past events after the outcomes are known. *Psychological Bulletin, 107,* 311–327.

Haynes, Suzanne, & Feinleib, Manning (1980). Women, work, and coronary heart disease: Prospective findings from the Framingham heart study. *American Journal of Public Health, 70,* 133–141.

Hebl, Michelle R., & Heatherton, Todd F. (1998). The stigma of obesity in women: The difference in black and white. *Personality and Social Psychology Bulletin, 24,* 417–426.

Hecht, Marvin A., & LaFrance, Marianne (1998). License or obligation to smile: The effect of power and sex on amount and type of smiling. *Personality and Social Psychology Bulletin, 24,* 1332–1342.

Heinrichs, R. Walter (1993). Schizophrenia and the brain: Conditions for a neuropsychology of madness. *American Psychologist, 48,* 221–233.

Heisel, Marnin J. (1998). A meta-analysis of psychotherapy and pharmacotherapy for panic disorder. Paper presented at the annual meeting of the American Psychological Association, San Francisco.

Heller, Wendy; Nitschke, Jack B.; & Miller, Gregory A. (1998). Lateralization in emotion and emotional disorders. *Current Directions in Psychological Science, 7,* 26–32.

Helmes, Edward, & Reddon, John R. (1993). A perspective on developments in assessing psychopathology: A critical review of the MMPI and MMPI-2. *Psychological Bulletin, 113,* 453–471.

Helson, Ravenna, & McCabe, Laurel (1993). The social clock project in middle age. In B. F. Turner & L. E. Troll (eds.), *Women growing older.* Newbury Park, CA: Sage.

Helson, Ravenna; Roberts, Brent; & Agronick, Gail (1995). Enduringness and change in creative personality and the prediction of occupational creativity. *Journal of Personality and Social Psychology, 6,* 1173–1183.

Hendrick, Susan S., & Hendrick, Clyde (1992). *Romantic love.* Newbury Park, CA: Sage.

Hendrick, Susan S., & Hendrick, Clyde (1997). Love and satisfaction. In R. J. Sternberg & M. Hojjat (eds.), *Satisfaction in close relationships.* New York: Guilford Press.

Hendrix, William H.; Steel, Robert P.; Leap, Terry L.; & Summers, Timothy P. (1991). Development of a stress-related health promotion model: Antecedents and organizational effectiveness outcomes. *Journal of Social Behavior and Personality, 6,* 141–162.

Henley, Nancy (1995). Body politics revisited: What do we know today? In P. J. Kalbfleisch & M. J. Cody (eds.), *Gender, power, and communication in human relationships.* Hillsdale, NJ: Erlbaum.

Henry, Bill; Caspi, Avshalom; Moffitt, Terrie E.; & Silva, Phil A. (1996). Temperamental and familial predictors of violent and nonviolent criminal convictions: Age 3 to age 18. *Developmental Psychology, 32,* 614–623.

Herdt, Gilbert (1984). *Ritualized homosexuality in Melanesia.* Berkeley: University of California Press.

Herek, Gregory M. (1999). Interpersonal contact and sexual prejudice. Paper presented at the annual meeting of the American Psychological Society, Denver.

Herek, Gregory M., & Capitanio, J. P. (1996). "Some of my best friends": Intergroup contact, concealable stigma, and heterosexuals' attitudes toward gay men and lesbians. *Personality and Social Psychology Bulletin, 22,* 412–424.

Herman, Louis M.; Kuczaj, Stan A.; & Holder, Mark D. (1993). Responses to anomalous gestural sequences by a language-trained dolphin: Evidence for processing of semantic relations and syntactic information. *Journal of Experimental Psychology: General, 122,* 184–194.

Herman, Louis M., & Morrel-Samuels, Palmer (1996). Knowledge acquisition and asymmetry between language comprehension and production: Dolphins and apes as general models for animals. In M. Bekoff, D. Jamieson, et al. (eds.), *Readings in animal cognition.* Cambridge, MA: MIT Press.

Herman-Giddens, Marcia E.; Slora, E. J.; Wasserman, R. C.; et al. (1997). Secondary sexual characteristics and menses in young girls seen in office practice: A study from the Pediatric Research in Office Settings network. *Pediatrics, 99,* 505–512.

Heron, Woodburn (1957). The pathology of boredom. *Scientific American, 196*(1), 52–56.

Herrnstein, Richard J., & Murray, Charles (1994). *The bell curve: Intelligence and class structure in American life.* New York: Free Press.

Higgins, E. Tory (1998). Promotion and prevention: Regulatory focus as a motivational principle. *Advances in Experimental Social Psychology, 30,* 1–46.

Higley, J. D.; Hasert, M. L.; Suomi, S. J.; & Linnoila, M. (1991). A nonhuman primate model of alcohol abuse: Effects of early experience, personality, and stress on alcohol consumption. *Proceedings of the National Academy of Science, 88,* 7261–7265.

Hill, Harlan F.; Chapman, C. Richard; Kornell, Judy A.; et al. (1990). Self-administration of morphine in bone marrow transplant patients reduces drug requirement. *Pain, 40,* 121–129.

Hill, James O., & Peters, John C. (1998). Environmental contributions to the obesity epidemic. *Science, 280,* 1371–1374.

Hilts, Philip J. (1995). *Memory's ghost: The strange tale of Mr. M. and the nature of memory.* New York: Simon & Schuster.

Hirsch, Helmut V. B., & Spinelli, D. N. (1970). Visual experience modifies distribution of horizontally and vertically oriented receptive fields in cats. *Science, 168,* 869–871.

Hirst, William; Neisser, Ulric; & Spelke, Elizabeth (1978, January). Divided attention. *Human Nature, 1,* 54–61.

Hobson, J. Allan (1988). *The dreaming brain.* New York: Basic Books.

Hobson, J. Allan (1990). Activation, input source, and modulation: A neurocognitive model of the state of the brain mind. In R. R. Bootzin, J. F. Kihlstrom, & D. L. Schacter (eds.), *Sleep and cognition.* Washington, DC: American Psychological Association.

Hochschild, Arlie (1983). *The managed heart.* Berkeley: University of California Press.

Hodges, Ernest V. E., & Perry, David G. (1999). Personal and interpersonal antecedents and consequences of victimization by peers. *Journal of Personality and Social Psychology, 76,* 677–685.

Hoffman, Martin L. (1990). Empathy and justice motivation. *Motivation and Emotion, 14,* 151–172.

Hoffman, Martin L. (1994). Discipline and internalization. *Developmental Psychology, 30,* 26–28.

Hofstede, Geert, & Bond, Michael H. (1988). The Confucius connection: From cultural roots to economic growth. *Organizational Dynamics, 18,* 5–21.

Holden, Constance (1997). Thumbs up for acupuncture [News report]. *Science, 278,* 1231.

Holden, George W., & Miller, Pamela C. (1999). Enduring and different: A meta-analysis of the similarity in parents' child rearing. *Psychological Bulletin, 125,* 223–254.

Holmes, David S. (1990). The evidence for repression: An examination of sixty years of research. In J. L. Singer (ed.), *Repression and dissociation.* Chicago: University of Chicago Press.

Hooker, Evelyn (1957). The adjustment of the male overt homosexual. *Journal of Projective Techniques, 21,* 18–31.

Hoon, M. A.; Adler, E.; Lindemeier, J.; et al. (1999). Putative mammalian taste receptors: A class of taste-specific GPCRs with distinct topographic selectivity. *Cell, 96,* 541–551.

Hooper, Judith (1999, February). A new germ theory. *Atlantic,* 41–53.

Hoptman, Matthew J., & Davidson, Richard J. (1994). How and why do the two cerebral hemispheres interact? *Psychological Bulletin, 116,* 195–219.

Horgan, John (1995, November). Get smart, take a test: A long-term rise in IQ scores baffles intelligence experts. *Scientific American, 273,* 12, 14.

Horner, Althea J. (1991). *Psychoanalytic object relations therapy.* New York: Jason Aronson.

Hornstein, Gail (1992). The return of the repressed: Psychology's problematic relations with psychoanalysis, 1909–1960. *American Psychologist, 47,* 254–263.

House, James S.; Landis, Karl R.; & Umberson, Debra (1988, July 19). Social relationships and health. *Science, 241,* 540–545.

Howard, George S. (1991). Culture tales: A narrative approach to thinking, cross-cultural psychology, and psychotherapy. *American Psychologist, 46,* 187–197.

Howard, Kenneth; Kopta, S. Mark; Krause, Merton S.; & Orlinsky, David (1986). The dose-effect relationship in psychotherapy. *American Psychologist, 41,* 159–164.

Howe, Mark L., & Courage, Mary L. (1993). On resolving the enigma of infantile amnesia. *Psychological Bulletin, 113,* 305–326.

Howe, Mark L.; Courage, Mary L.; & Peterson, Carole (1994). How can I remember when "I" wasn't there? Long-term retention of traumatic experiences and emergence of the cognitive self. *Consciousness and Cognition, 3,* 327–355.

Howe, Neil, & Strauss, William (2000). *Millennials rising: The next great generation.* New York: Vintage.

Hrdy, Sarah B. (1988). Empathy, polyandry, and the myth of the coy female. In R. Bleier (ed.), *Feminist approaches to science.* New York: Pergamon.

Hrdy, Sarah B. (1999). *Mother nature: A history of mothers, infants, and natural selection.* New York: Pantheon.

Hu, S.; Pattatucci, A. M.; Patterson C.; et al. (1995). Linkage between sexual orientation and chromosome Xq28 in males but not in females. *Nature Genetics, 11,* 248–256.

Hubbard, Ruth (1990). *The politics of women's biology.* New Brunswick, NJ: Rutgers University Press.

Hubel, David H., & Wiesel, Torsten N. (1962). Receptive fields, binocular interaction and functional architecture in the cat's visual cortex. *Journal of Physiology* (London), *160,* 106–154.

Hubel, David H., & Wiesel, Torsten N. (1968). Receptive fields and functional architecture of monkey striate cortex. *Journal of Physiology* (London), *195,* 215–243.

Hughes, Judith M. (1989). *Reshaping the psychoanalytic domain: The work of Melanie Klein, W. R. D. Fairbairn, & D. W. Winnicott.* Berkeley, CA: University of California Press.

Hultsch, David F.; Hertzog, Christopher; Small, Brent J.; & Dixon, Roger A. (1999). Use it or lose it: Engaged lifestyle as a buffer of cognitive decline in aging? *Psychology and Aging, 14,* 245–263.

Hunt, Earl; Streissguth, Ann P.; Kerr, Beth; & Olson, Heather C. (1995). Mothers' alcohol consumption during pregnancy: Effects on spatial-visual reasoning in 14-year-old children. *Psychological Science, 6,* 339–342.

Hunt, Morton M. (1993). *The story of psychology.* New York: Doubleday.

Hunter, John E. (1997). Needed: A ban on the significance test. *Psychological Science, 8,* 3–7.

Hupka, Ralph B. (1981). Cultural determinants of jealousy. *Alternative Lifestyles, 4,* 310–356.

Hupka, Ralph B. (1991). The motive for the arousal of romantic jealousy. In P. Salovey (ed.), *The psychology of jealousy and envy.* New York: Guilford Press.

Hur, Yoon-Mi; McGue, Matt; & Iacono, William G. (1998). The structure of self-concept in female preadolescent twins: A behavioral genetic approach. *Journal of Personality and Social Psychology, 74,* 1069–1077.

Hyde, Janet S. (2000). A gendered brain? [Review of *Sex and cognition,* by Doreen Kimura]. *Journal of Sex Research, 37,* 191.

Hyde, Janet S.; Fennema, Elizabeth; & Lamon, Susan J. (1990). Gender differences in mathematics performance: A meta-analysis. *Psychological Bulletin, 107,* 139–155.

Hyde, Janet S., & Linn, Marcia C. (1988). Gender differences in verbal ability: A meta-analysis. *Psychological Bulletin, 104,* 53–69.

Hyman, Ira E., Jr., & Pentland, Joel (1996). The role of mental imagery in the creation of false childhood memories. *Journal of Memory and Language, 35,* 101–117.

Hyman, Ray (1994). Anomaly or artifact? Comments on Bem and Honorton. *Psychological Bulletin, 115,* 25–27.

Inglehart, Ronald (1990). *Culture shift in advanced industrial society.* Princeton, NJ: Princeton University Press.

Inglis, James, & Lawson, J. S. (1981). Sex differences in the effects of unilateral brain damage on intelligence. *Science, 212,* 693–695.

Irvine, Janice M. (1990). *Disorders of desire: Sex and gender in modern American sexology.* Philadelphia: Temple University Press.

Islam, Mir Rabiul, & Hewstone, Miles (1993). Intergroup attributions and affective consequences in majority and minority groups. *Journal of Personality and Social Psychology, 64,* 936–950.

Izard, Carroll E. (1990). Facial expressions and the regulation of emotions. *Journal of Personality and Social Psychology, 58,* 487–498.

Izard, Carroll E. (1994a). Four systems for emotion activation: Cognitive and noncognitive processes. *Psychological Review, 100,* 68–90.

Izard, Carroll E. (1994b). Innate and universal facial expressions: Evidence from developmental and cross-cultural research. *Psychological Bulletin, 115,* 288–299.

Jacobsen, Paul B.; Bovbjerg, Dana H.; Schwartz, Marc D.; et al. (1995). Conditioned emotional distress in women receiving chemotherapy for breast cancer. *Journal of Consulting & Clinical Psychology, 63,* 108–114.

Jaffee, Sara, & Hyde, Janet S. (2000). Gender differences in moral orientation: A meta-analysis. *Psychological Bulletin, 126,* 703–726.

James, Jacquelyn B., & Lewkowicz, Corinne J. (1997). Themes of power and affiliation across time. In M. E. Lachman & J. B. James (eds.), *Multiple paths of midlife development.* Chicago: University of Chicago Press.

James, William (1890/1950). *Principles of psychology* (Vol. 1). New York: Dover.

Jancke, Lutz; Schlaug, Gottfried; & Steinmetz, Helmuth (1997). Hand skill asymmetry in professional musicians. *Brain and Cognition, 34,* 424–432.

Jang, Kerry L.; McCrae, Robert R.; Angleitner, Alois; et al. (1998). Heritability of facet-level traits in a cross-cultural twin sample: Support for a hierarchical model of personality. *Journal of Personality and Social Psychology, 74,* 1556–1565.

Janis, Irving L. (1982). *Groupthink: Psychological studies of policy decisions and fiascoes* (2nd ed.). Boston: Houghton Mifflin.

Janis, Irving L. (1989). *Crucial decisions: Leadership in policymaking and crisis management.* New York: Free Press.

Janis, Irving L.; Kaye, Donald; & Kirschner, Paul (1965). Facilitating effects of "eating-while-reading" on responsiveness to persuasive communications. *Journal of Personality and Social Psychology, 1,* 181–186.

Jellinek, E. M. (1960). *The disease concept of alcoholism.* New Haven, CT: Hillhouse Press.

Jenkins, John G., & Dallenbach, Karl M. (1924). Obliviscence during sleep and waking. *American Journal of Psychology, 35,* 605–612.

Jenkins, Sharon Rae (1994). Need for power and women's careers over 14 years: Structural power, job satisfaction, and motive change. *Journal of Personality and Social Psychology, 66,* 155–165.

Jensen, Arthur R. (1969). How much can we boost IQ and scholastic achievement? *Harvard Educational Review, 39,* 1–123.

Jensen, Arthur R. (1981). *Straight talk about mental tests.* New York: Free Press.

Johnson, Catherine (1988). *When to say goodbye to your therapist.* New York: Simon & Schuster.

Johnson, Marcia K. (1995). The relation between memory and reality. Paper presented at the annual meeting of the American Psychological Association, New York.

Johnson, Mark H.; Dziurawiec, Suzanne; Ellis, Hadyn; & Morton, John (1991). Newborns' preferential tracking of face-like stimuli and its subsequent decline. *Cognition, 40,* 1–19.

Johnson, Robert, & Downing, Leslie (1979). Deindividuation and valence of cues: Effects of prosocial and antisocial behavior. *Journal of Personality and Social Psychology, 37,* 1532–1538.

Jones, Edward E. (1990). *Interpersonal perception.* New York: Macmillan.

Jones, James M. (1991). Psychological models of race: What have they been and what should they be? In J. D. Goodchilds (ed.), *Psychological perspectives on human diversity in America.* Washington, DC: American Psychological Association.

Jones, James M. (1997). *Prejudice and racism* (2nd ed.). New York: McGraw-Hill.

Jones, Mary Cover (1924). A laboratory study of fear: The case of Peter. *Pedagogical Seminary, 31,* 308–315.

Jones, Russell A. (1977). *Self-fulfilling prophecies.* Hillsdale, NJ: Erlbaum.

Jorgensen, Randall S.; Johnson, Blair T.; Kolodziej, Monika E.; & Schreer, George E. (1996). Elevated blood pressure and personality: A meta-analytic review. *Psychological Bulletin, 120,* 293–320.

Judd, Charles M.; Park, Bernadette; Ryan, Carey S.; et al. (1995). Stereotypes and ethnocentrism: Diverging interethnic perceptions of African American and white American youth. *Journal of Personality and Social Psychology, 69,* 460–481.

Jung, Carl (1967). *Collected works.* Princeton, NJ: Princeton University Press.

Jusczyk, Peter W. (1997). Finding and remembering words: Some beginnings by English-learning infants. *Current Directions in Psychological Science, 6,* 170–174.

Kagan, Jerome (1984). *The nature of the child.* New York: Basic Books.

Kagan, Jerome (1989). *Unstable ideas: Temperament, cognition, and self.* Cambridge, MA: Harvard University Press.

Kagan, Jerome (1993). The meanings of morality. *Psychological Science, 4,* 353, 357–360.

Kagan, Jerome (1994). *Galen's prophecy: Temperament in human nature.* New York: Basic Books.

Kagan, Jerome (1998a). How we become what we are. Paper presented at the annual meeting of the Family Therapy Network Symposium, Washington, DC.

Kagan, Jerome (1998b). *Three seductive ideas.* Cambridge, MA: Harvard University Press.

Kagan, Jerome; Kearsley, Richard B.; & Zelazo, Philip R. (1978). *Infancy: Its place in human development.* Cambridge, MA: Harvard University Press.

Kahneman, Daniel, & Treisman, Anne (1984). Changing views of attention and automaticity. In R. Parasuraman, D. R. Davies, & J. Beatty (eds.), *Varieties of attention.* New York: Academic Press.

Kameda, Tatsuya, & Sugimori, Shinkichi (1993). Psychological entrapment in group decision making: An assigned decision rule and a groupthink phenomenon. *Journal of Personality and Social Psychology, 65,* 282–292.

Kanin, Eugene J. (1985). Date rapists: Differential sexual socialization and relative deprivation. *Archives of Sexual Behavior, 14,* 219–231.

Kanter, Rosabeth Moss (1977/1993). *Men and women of the corporation.* New York: Basic Books.

Kaplan, Abraham (1967). A philosophical discussion of normality. *Archives of General Psychiatry, 17,* 325–330.

Kaplan, Meg S.; Morales, Miguel; & Becker, Judith V. (1993). The impact of verbal satiation of adolescent sex offenders: A preliminary report. *Journal of Child Sexual Abuse, 2,* 81–88.

Karasek, Robert, & Theorell, Tores (1990). *Healthy work: Stress, productivity, and the reconstruction of working life.* New York: Basic Books.

Karau, Steven J., & Williams, Kipling D. (1993). Social loafing: A meta-analytic review and theoretical integration. *Journal of Personality and Social Psychology, 65,* 681–706.

Karney, Benjamin, & Bradbury, Thomas N. (2000). Attributions in marriage: State or trait? A growth curve analysis. *Journal of Personality and Social Psychology, 78,* 295–309.

Karni, Avi; Tanne, David; Rubenstein, Barton S.; et al. (1994). Dependence on REM sleep of overnight improvement of a perceptual skill. *Science, 265,* 679–682.

Kashima, Yoshihisa; Yamaguchi, Susumu; Kim, Uichol; et al. (1995). Culture, gender, and self: A perspective from individualism-collectivism research. *Journal of Personality and Social Psychology, 69,* 925–937.

Kasser, Tim, & Ryan, Richard M. (1996). Further examining the American dream: Correlates of financial success as a central life aspiration. *Personality and Social Psychology Bulletin, 22,* 280–287.

Katigbak, Marcia S.; Church, A. Timothy; & Akamine, Toshio X. (1996). Cross-cultural generalizability of personality dimensions: Relating indigenous and imported dimensions in two cultures. *Journal of Personality and Social Psychology, 70,* 99–114.

Katz, Jonathan Ned (1995). *The invention of heterosexuality.* New York: Dutton.

Katz, Lilian G. (1993, Summer). All about me. *American Educator, 17*(2), 18–23.

Katz, Phyllis A., & Ksansnak, Keith R. (1994). Developmental aspects of gender role flexibility and traditionality in middle childhood and adolescence. *Developmental Psychology, 30,* 272–282.

Kaufman, Joan, & Zigler, Edward (1987). Do abused children become abusive parents? *American Journal of Orthopsychiatry, 57,* 186–192.

Keating, Caroline F. (1994). World without words: Messages from face and body. In W. J. Lonner & R. Malpass (eds.), *Psychology and culture.* Needham Heights, MA: Allyn & Bacon.

Keller, Martin B.; McCullough, James P.; Klein, Daniel N.; et al. (2000, May 18). A comparison of nefazodone, the cognitive behavioral-analysis system of psychotherapy, and their combination for the treatment of chronic depression. *New England Journal of Medicine, 342,* 1462–1470.

Kelly, Anita E., & McKillop, Kevin J. (1996). Consequences of revealing personal secrets. *Psychological Bulletin, 120,* 450–465.

Kelman, Herbert C., & Hamilton, V. Lee (1989). *Crimes of obedience: Toward a social psychology of authority and responsibility.* New Haven, CT: Yale University Press.

Kempermann, G.; Brandon, E. P.; & Gage, F. H. (1998). Environmental stimulation of 120/SvJ mice causes increased cell proliferation and neurogenesis in the adult dentate gyrus. *Current Biology, 8,* 939–942.

Kendall [no first name] (1999). Women in Lesotho and the (Western) construction of homophobia. In E. Blackwood & S. E. Wieringa (eds.), *Female desires: Same-sex relations and transgender practices across cultures.* New York: Columbia University Press.

Kenny, Michael G. (1986). *The passion of Ansel Bourne: Multiple personality in American culture.* Washington, DC: Smithsonian Press.

Kephart, William M. (1967). Some correlates of romantic love. *Journal of Marriage and the Family, 29,* 470–474.

Kerr, Michael E., & Bowen, Murray (1988). *Family evaluation: An approach based on Bowen theory.* New York: Norton.

Kessler, Ronald C.; McGonagle, Katherine A.; Zhao, Shanyang; et al. (1994). Lifetime and 12-month prevalence of DSM-III-R psychiatric disorders in the United States: Results from the National Comorbidity Survey. *Archives of General Psychiatry, 51,* 8–19.

Kessler, Ronald C.; Sonnega, A.; Bromet, E.; et al. (1995). Posttraumatic stress disorder in the National Comorbidity Survey. *Archives of General Psychiatry, 52,* 1048–1060.

Kiecolt-Glaser, Janice; Garner, Warren; Speicher, Carl; et al. (1985a). Psychosocial modifiers of immunocompetence in medical students. *Psychosomatic Medicine, 46,* 7–14.

Kiecolt-Glaser, Janice; Glaser, Ronald; Williger, D.; et al. (1985b). Psychosocial enhancement of immunocompetence in a geriatric population. *Health Psychology, 4,* 25–41.

Kiecolt-Glaser, Janice; Malarkey, William B.; Chee, MaryAnn; et al. (1993). Negative behavior during marital conflict is associated with immunological down-regulation. *Psychosomatic Medicine, 55,* 395–409.

Kiecolt-Glaser, Janice; Page, Gayle G.; Marucha, Phillip T.; et al. (1998). Psychological influences on surgical recovery: Perspectives from psychoneuroimmunology. *American Psychologist, 53,* 1209–1218.

Kihlstrom, John F. (1994). Hypnosis, delayed recall, and the principles of memory. *International Journal of Clinical and Experimental Hypnosis, 40,* 337–345.

Kihlstrom, John F. (1995). From a subject's point of view: The experiment as conversation and collaboration between investigator and subject. Invited address presented at the annual meeting of the American Psychological Society, New York.

Kihlstrom, John F.; Barnhardt, Terrence M.; & Tataryn, Douglas J. (1992). The psychological unconscious: Found, lost, and regained. *American Psychologist, 47,* 788–791.

Kihlstrom, John F., & Harackiewicz, Judith M. (1982). The earliest recollection: A new survey. *Journal of Personality, 50,* 134–148.

Kim, Karl H. S.; Relkin, Norman R.; Lee, Kyoung-Min; & Hirsch, Joy (1997). Distinct cortical areas associated with native and second languages. *Nature, 388,* 171–174.

Kimmel, Michael (1995). *Manhood in America: A cultural history.* New York: Free Press.

King, M., & Woollett, E. (1997). Sexually assaulted males: 115 men consulting a counseling service. *Archives of Sexual Behavior, 26,* 579–588.

King, Pamela (1989, October). The chemistry of doubt. *Psychology Today*, 58, 60.

King, Patricia M., & Kitchener, Karen S. (1994). *Developing reflective judgment: Understanding and promoting intellectual growth and critical thinking in adolescents and adults.* San Francisco: Jossey-Bass.

Kinsey, Alfred C.; Pomeroy, Wardell B.; & Martin, Clyde E. (1948). *Sexual behavior in the human male.* Philadelphia: Saunders.

Kinsey, Alfred C.; Pomeroy, Wardell B.; Martin, Clyde E.; & Gebhard, Paul H. (1953). *Sexual behavior in the human female.* Philadelphia: Saunders.

Kirsch, Irving, & Lynn, Steven Jay (1995). The altered state of hypnosis: Changes in the theoretical landscape. *American Psychologist, 50,* 846–858.

Kirsch, Irving; Montgomery, G.; & Sapirstein, Guy (1995). Hypnosis as an adjunct to cognitive behavioral psychotherapy: A meta-analysis. *Journal of Consulting and Clinical Psychology, 63,* 214–220.

Kirsch, Irving, & Sapirstein, Guy (1998). Listening to Prozac but hearing placebo: A meta-analysis of antidepressant medication. *Prevention & Treatment, 1, Article 0002a*, posted electronically June 26, 1998, on the website of the American Psychological Association.

Kirschenbaum, B.; Nedergaard, M.; Preuss, A.; et al. (1994). In vitro neuronal production and differentiation by precursor cells derived from the adult human forebrain. *Cerebral Cortex, 4,* 576–589.

Kitayama, Shinobu, & Markus, Hazel R. (1994). Introduction to cultural psychology and emotion research. In S. Kitayama & H. R. Markus (eds.), *Emotion and culture: Empirical studies of mutual influence.* Washington, DC: American Psychological Association.

Kitchener, Karen S., & King, Patricia M. (1990). The Reflective Judgment Model: Ten years of research. In M. L. Commons (ed.), *Models and methods in the study of adolescent and adult thought: Vol. 2. Adult development.* Westport, CT: Greenwood Press.

Kitchener, Karen S.; Lynch, Cindy L.; Fischer, Kurt W.; & Wood, Phillip K. (1993). Developmental range of reflective judgment: The effect of contextual support and practice on developmental stage. *Developmental Psychology, 29,* 893–906.

Kitzinger, Celia, & Wilkinson, Sue (1995). Transitions from heterosexuality to lesbianism: The discursive production of lesbian identities. *Developmental Psychology, 31,* 95–104.

Kleim, J. A.; Swain, R. A.; Armstrong, K. A.; et al. (1998). Selective synaptic plasticity within the cerebellar cortex following complex motor skill learning. *Neurobiology of Learning and Memory, 69,* 274–289.

Klein, Donald F. (1980). Psychosocial treatment of schizophrenia, or psychosocial help for people with schizophrenia? *Schizophrenia Bulletin, 6,* 122–130.

Klein, Stanley B., & Kihlstrom, John F. (1998). On bridging the gap between social-personality psychology and neuropsychology. *Personality and Social Psychology Review, 2,* 228–242.

Kleinke, Chris L.; Peterson, Thomas R.; & Rutledge, Thomas R. (1998). Effects of self-generated facial expressions on mood. *Journal of Personality and Social Psychology, 74,* 272–279.

Kleinman, Arthur (1988). *Rethinking psychiatry: From cultural category to personal experience.* New York: Free Press.

Klerman, Gerald L.; Weissman, Myrna M.; Rounsaville, Bruce J.; & Chevron, Eve S. (1984). *Interpersonal psychotherapy of depression.* New York: Basic Books.

Klima, Edward S., & Bellugi, Ursula (1966). Syntactic regularities in the speech of children. In J. Lyons & R. J. Wales (eds.), *Psycholinguistics papers.* Edinburgh, Scotland: Edinburgh University Press.

Klimoski, R. (1992). Graphology and personnel selection. In B. Beyerstein & D. Beyerstein (eds.), *The write stuff: Evaluations of graphology—the study of handwriting analysis.* Buffalo, NY: Prometheus Books.

Klopfenstein, Glenn D. (1997, May 30). Cheating at chess, 200 million times a second. *Chronicle of Higher Education*, B8.

Kluft, Richard P. (1987). The simulation and dissimulation of multiple personality disorder. *American Journal of Clinical Hypnosis, 30,* 104–118.

Kluft, Richard P. (1993). Multiple personality disorders. In D. Spiegel (ed.), *Dissociative disorders: A clinical review.* Lutherville, MD: Sidran.

Kluger, Richard (1996). *Ashes to ashes: America's hundred-year cigarette war, the public health, and the unabashed triumph of Philip Morris.* New York: Knopf.

Knight, Raymond A.; Prentky, Robert A.; & Cerce, David D. (1994). The development, reliability, and validity of an inventory for the multidimensional assessment of sex and aggression. *Criminal Justice and Behavior, 21,* 72–94.

Kohlberg, Lawrence (1964). Development of moral character and moral ideology. In M. Hoffman & L. W. Hoffman (eds.), *Review of child development research.* New York: Russell Sage Foundation.

Kohlberg, Lawrence (1976). Moral stages and moralization: The cognitive-developmental approach. In T. Lickona (ed.), *Moral development and behavior.* New York: Holt, Rinehart and Winston.

Kohlberg, Lawrence (1984). *Essays on moral development: Vol. 2. The psychology of moral development: The nature and validity of moral stages.* San Francisco: Harper & Row.

Köhler, Wolfgang (1925). *The mentality of apes.* New York: Harcourt, Brace.

Kohn, Alfie (1993). *Punished by rewards.* Boston: Houghton Mifflin.

Kohn, Melvin, & Schooler, Carmi (1983). *Work and personality: An inquiry into the impact of social stratification.* Norwood, NJ: Ablex.

Kolata, Gina (2001, March 8). Parkinson's research is set back by failure of fetal cell implants. *New York Times,* A1, A12.

Kolb, B., & Whishaw, I. Q. (1998). Brain plasticity and behavior. *Annual Review of Psychology, 49,* 43–64.

Kolbert, Elizabeth (1995, June 5). Public opinion polls swerve with the turns of a phrase. *New York Times, 144,* A1.

Koocher, Gerald P.; Goodman, Gail S.; White, C. Sue; et al. (1995). Psychological science and the use of anatomically detailed dolls in child sexual-abuse assessments. *Psychological Bulletin, 118,* 199–222.

Kopta, Stephen M.; Howard, Kenneth I.; Lowry, Jenny L.; & Beutler, Larry E. (1994). Patterns of symptomatic recovery in psychotherapy. *Journal of Consulting and Clinical Psychology, 62,* 1009–1016.

Koss, Mary P. (1993). Rape: Scope, impact, interventions, and public policy responses. *American Psychologist, 48,* 1062–1069.

Kosslyn, Stephen M. (1980). *Image and mind.* Cambridge, MA: Harvard University Press.

Kozak, Michael J.; Liebowitz, Michael R.; & Foa, Edna B. (2000). Cognitive-behavior therapy and pharmacotherapy for OCD: The NIMH-sponsored collaborative study. In W. K. Goodman, M. Rudorfer, & J. Maser (eds.), *Treatment challenges in obsessive compulsive disorder.* Mahwah, NJ: Erlbaum.

Krantz, David S., & Manuck, Stephen B. (1984). Acute psychophysiologic reactivity and risk of cardiovascular disease: A review and methodological critique. *Psychological Bulletin, 96,* 435–464.

Krieger, Nancy, & Sidney, S. (1996). Racial discrimination and blood pressure: The CARDIA study of young black and white adults. *American Journal of Public Health, 86,* 1370–1378.

Kring, Ann M., & Gordon, Albert H. (1998). Sex differences in emotion: Expression, experience, and physiology. *Journal of Personality and Social Psychology, 74,* 686–703.

Kroll, Barry M. (1992). *Teaching hearts and minds: College students reflect on the Vietnam War in literature.* Carbondale: Southern Illinois University Press.

Krupa, David J.; Thompson, Judith K.; & Thompson, Richard F. (1993). Localization of a memory trace in the mammalian brain. *Science, 260,* 989–991.

Kuhl, Patricia K.; Andruski, Jean E.; Chistovich, Inna A.; et al. (1997, August 1). Cross-language analysis of phonetic units in language addressed to infants. *Science, 277,* 684–686.

Kuhl, Patricia K.; Williams, Karen A.; Lacerda, Francisco; et al. (1992, January 31). Linguistic experience alters phonetic perception in infants by 6 months of age. *Science, 255,* 606–608.

Kuhn, Deanna; Weinstock, Michael; & Flaton, Robin (1994). How well do jurors reason? Competence dimensions of individual variation in a juror reasoning task. *Psychological Science, 5,* 289–296.

Kunda, Ziva (1990). The case for motivated reasoning. *Psychological Bulletin, 108,* 480–498.

Kutchins, Herb, & Kirk, Stuart A. (1997). *Making us crazy: DSM. The psychiatric bible and the creation of mental disorders.* New York: Free Press.

Lachman, Margie E., & Weaver, Suzanne L. (1998). The sense of control as a moderator of social class differences in health and well-being. *Journal of Personality and Social Psychology, 74,* 763–773.

Lachman, Sheldon J. (1996). Processes in perception: Psychological transformations of highly structured stimulus material. *Perceptual and Motor Skills, 83,* 411–418.

LaFromboise, Teresa; Coleman, Hardin L. K.; & Gerton, Jennifer (1993). Psychological impact of biculturalism: Evidence and theory. *Psychological Bulletin, 114,* 395–412.

Laird, James D. (1974). Self-attribution of emotion: The effects of expressive behavior on the quality of emotional experience. *Journal of Personality and Social Psychology, 29,* 475–486.

Lakoff, Robin T., & Coyne, James C. (1993). *Father knows best: The use and abuse of power in Freud's case of "Dora."* New York: Teachers College Press.

Lambert, Michael J., & Bergin, Allen E. (1994). The effectiveness of psychotherapy. In A. E. Bergin & S. L. Garfield (eds.), *Handbook of psychotherapy and behavior change* (4th ed.). New York: Wiley.

Land, Edwin H. (1959). Experiments in color vision. *Scientific American, 200*(5), 84–94, 96, 99.

Landine, Jeffrey, & Stewart, John (1998). Relationship between metacognition, motivation, locus of control, self-efficacy, and academic achievement. *Canadian Journal of Counseling, 32,* 200–212.

Landrine, Hope (1988). Revising the framework of abnormal psychology. In P. Bronstein & K. Quina (eds.), *Teaching a psychology of people.* Washington, DC: American Psychological Association.

Langer, Ellen J. (1983). *The psychology of control.* Beverly Hills, CA: Sage.

Langer, Ellen J. (1989). *Mindfulness.* Reading, MA: Addison-Wesley.

Langer, Ellen J.; Blank, Arthur; & Chanowitz, Benzion (1978). The mindlessness of ostensibly thoughtful action: The role of placebic information in interpersonal interaction. *Journal of Personality and Social Psychology, 36,* 635–642.

Latané, Bibb; Williams, Kipling; & Harkins, Stephen (1979). Many hands make light the work: The causes and consequences of social loafing. *Journal of Personality and Social Psychology, 37,* 822–832.

Laudenslager, Mark L. (1988). The psychology of loss: Lessons from humans and nonhuman primates. *Journal of Social Issues, 44,* 19–36.

Laumann, Edward O., & Gagnon John H. (1995). A sociological perspective on sexual action. In R. G. Parker & J. H. Gagnon (eds.), *Conceiving sexuality: Approaches to sex research in a postmodern world.* New York: Routledge.

Laumann, Edward O.; Gagnon, John H.; Michael, Robert T.; & Michaels, Stuart (1994). *The social organization of sexuality.* Chicago: University of Chicago Press.

Laursen, Brett, & Collins, W. Andrew (1994). Interpersonal conflict during adolescence. *Psychological Bulletin, 115,* 197–209.

Lazarus, Richard S., & Folkman, Susan (1984). *Stress, appraisal, and coping.* New York: Springer.

LeDoux, Joseph E. (1994, June). Emotion, memory, and the brain. *Scientific American, 220,* 50–57.

LeDoux, Joseph E. (1996). *The emotional brain.* New York: Simon & Schuster.

Lee, John Alan (1973). *The colours of love.* Ontario, Canada: New Press.

Lee, John Alan (1988). Love-styles. In R. J. Sternberg & M. L. Barnes (eds.), *The psychology of love.* New Haven, CT: Yale University Press.

Lehman, Adam K., & Rodin, Judith (1989). Styles of self-nurturance and disordered eating. *Journal of Consulting and Clinical Psychology, 57,* 117–122.

Leibel, Rudolph L.; Rosenbaum, Michael; & Hirsch, Jules (1995). Changes in energy expenditure resulting from altered body weight. *New England Journal of Medicine, 332,* 621–628.

Lenneberg, Eric H. (1967). *Biological foundations of language.* New York: Wiley.

Lent, James R. (1968, June). Mimosa cottage: Experiment in hope. *Psychology Today,* 51–58.

Leonard, S.; Gault, J.; Moore, T.; et al. (1998, July 10). Further investigation of a chromosome 15 locus in schizophrenia: Analysis of affected sibpairs from the NIMH Genetics Initiative. *American Journal of Medical Genetics, 81,* 308–312.

Lepore, Stephen J. (1997). Expressive writing moderates the relation between intrusive thoughts and depressive symptoms. *Journal of Personality and Social Psychology, 73,* 1030–1037.

Lepore, Stephen J.; Ragan, Jennifer D.; & Jones, Scott (2000). Talking facilitates cognitive-emotional processes of adaptation to an acute stressor. *Journal of Personality and Social Psychology, 78,* 499–508.

Lepore, Stephen J.; Silver, Roxanne C.; Wortman, Camille B.; & Wayment, Heidi A. (1996). Social constraints, intrusive thoughts, and depressive symptoms among bereaved mothers. *Journal of Personality and Social Psychology, 70,* 271–282.

Lepper, Mark R.; Greene, David; & Nisbett, Richard E. (1973). Undermining children's intrinsic interest with extrinsic rewards. *Journal of Personality and Social Psychology, 28,* 129–137.

Leproult, Rachel; Van Reeth, Olivier; Byrne, Maria M.; et al. (1997). Sleepiness, performance, and neuroendocrine function during sleep deprivation: Effects of exposure to bright light or exercise. *Journal of Biological Rhythms, 12,* 245–258.

Lerner, Melvin J. (1980). *The belief in a just world: A fundamental delusion.* New York: Plenum.

Lester, Barry M.; LaGasse, Linda L.; & Seifer, Ronald (1998, October 23). Cocaine exposure and children: The meaning of subtle effects. *Science, 282,* 633–634.

LeVay, Simon (1991). A difference in hypothalamic structure between heterosexual and homosexual men. *Science, 253,* 1034–1037.

Levenson, Robert W. (1992). Autonomic nervous system differences among emotions. *Psychological Science, 3,* 23–27.

Levenson, Robert W.; Ekman, Paul; & Friesen, Wallace V. (1990). Voluntary facial action generates emotion-specific autonomic nervous system activity. *Psychophysiology, 27,* 363–384.

Levine, Robert V.; Martinez, Todd S.; Brase, Gary; & Sorenson, Kerry (1994). Helping in 36 U.S. cities. *Journal of Personality and Social Psychology, 67,* 69–82.

Levinson, D. F.; Mahtani, M. M.; Nancarrow, D. J.; et al. (1998). Genome scan of schizophrenia. *American Journal of Psychiatry, 155,* 741–750.

Levitan, Alexander A., & Ronan, William J. (1988). Problems in the treatment of obesity and eating disorders. *Medical Hypnoanalysis Journal, 3,* 131–136.

Levy, Becca (1996). Improving memory in old age through implicit self-stereotyping. *Journal of Personality and Social Psychology, 71,* 1092–1107.

Levy, David A. (1997). *Tools of critical thinking: Metathoughts for psychology.* Boston: Allyn & Bacon.

Levy, Jerre; Trevarthen, Colwyn; & Sperry, Roger W. (1972). Perception of bilateral chimeric figures following hemispheric deconnection. *Brain, 95,* 61–78.

Levy, Kenneth N.; Blatt, Sidney J.; & Shaver, Phillip R. (1998). Attachment styles are parental representations. *Journal of Personality and Social Psychology, 74,* 407–419.

Lewin, Kurt (1948). *Resolving social conflicts.* New York: Harper.

Lewis, Dorothy O. (ed.) (1981). *Vulnerabilities to delinquency.* New York: Spectrum Medical and Scientific Books.

Lewis, Dorothy O. (1992). From abuse to violence: Psychophysiological consequences of maltreatment. *Journal of the American Academy of Child and Adolescent Psychiatry, 31,* 383–391.

Lewis, Michael (1997). *Altering fate: Why the past does not predict the future.* New York: Guilford Press.

Lewontin, Richard C. (1970). Race and intelligence. *Bulletin of the Atomic Scientists, 26*(3), 2–8.

Lichtenstein, Sarah; Slovic, Paul; Fischhoff, Baruch; et al. (1978). Judged frequency of lethal events. *Journal of Experimental Psychology: Human Learning and Memory, 4,* 551–578.

Lickona, Thomas (1983). *Raising good children.* New York: Bantam.

Liepert, J.; Bauder, H.; Miltner, W. H.; et al. (2000). Treatment-induced cortical reorganization after stroke in humans. *Stroke, 31,* 1210–1216.

Lilienfeld, Scott O. (1999, September/October). Projective measures of personality and psychopathology: How well do they work? *Skeptical Inquirer,* 32–39.

Lilienfeld, Scott O.; Gershon, Jonathan; Duke, Marshall; Marino, Lori; & De Waal, Frans B. M. (1999). A preliminary investigation of the construct of psychopathic personality (psychopathy) in chimpanzees (*Pan troglodytes*). *Journal of Comparative Psychology, 113,* 365–375.

Lilienfeld, Scott O.; Wood, James M.; & Garb, Howard N. (2000). The scientific status of projective techniques. *Psychological Science in the Public Interest, 1,* 27–66.

Lin, Keh-Ming; Poland, Russell E.; & Chien, C. P. (1990). Ethnicity and psychopharmacology: Recent findings and future research directions. In E. Sorel (ed.), *Family, culture, and psychobiology.* New York: Legas.

Linday, Linda A. (1994). Maternal reports of pregnancy, genital, and related fantasies in preschool and kindergarten children. *Journal of the American Academy of Child and Adolescent Psychiatry, 33,* 416–423.

Lindsay, D. Stephen, & Read, J. Don (1994). Psychotherapy and memories of childhood sexual abuse: A cognitive perspective. *Applied Cognitive Psychology, 8,* 281–338.

Lindvall, O.; Sawle, G.; Widner, H.; et al. (1994). Evidence for long-term survival and function of dopaminergic grafts in progressive Parkinson's disease. *Annals of Neurology, 35,* 172–180.

Linton, Marigold (1978). Real-world memory after six years: An in vivo study of very long-term memory. In M. M. Gruneberg, P. E. Morris, & R. N. Sykes (eds.), *Practical aspects of memory.* London: Academic Press.

Linton, Simi (1998). *Claiming disability: Knowledge and identity.* New York: New York University Press.

Linville, P. W.; Fischer, G. W.; & Fischhoff, B. (1992). AIDS risk perceptions and decision biases. In J. B. Pryor & G. D. Reeder (eds.), *The social psychology of HIV infection.* Hillsdale, NJ: Erlbaum.

Lissner, L.; Odell, P. M.; D'Agostino, R. B.; et al. (1991, June 27). Variability of body weight and health outcomes in the Framingham population. *New England Journal of Medicine, 324*(26), 1839–1844.

Locke, Edwin A., & Latham, Gary P. (1990). Work motivation and satisfaction: Light at the end of the tunnel. *Psychological Science, 1,* 240–246.

Locke, Edwin A.; Shaw, Karyll; Saari, Lise; & Latham, Gary (1981). Goal-setting and task performance: 1969–1980. *Psychological Bulletin, 90,* 125–152.

Loehlin, John C. (1992). *Genes and environment in personality development.* Newbury Park, CA: Sage.

Loehlin, John C.; Horn, J. M.; & Willerman, L. (1996). Heredity, environment, and IQ in the Texas adoption study. In R. J. Sternberg & E. Grigorenko (eds.), *Intelligence: Heredity and environment.* New York: Cambridge University Press.

Loewen, E. Ruth; Shaw, Raymond J.; & Craik, Fergus I. (1990). Age differences in components of metamemory. *Experimental Aging Research, 16*(1–2), 43–48.

Loftus, Elizabeth F. (1980). *Memory.* Reading, MA: Addison-Wesley.

Loftus, Elizabeth F. (1996). Memory distortion and false memory creation. *Bulletin of the American Academy of Psychiatry and the Law, 24*(3), 281–295.

Loftus, Elizabeth F., & Greene, Edith (1980). Warning: Even memory for faces may be contagious. *Law and Human Behavior, 4,* 323–334.

Loftus, Elizabeth F., & Ketcham, Katherine (1994). *The myth of repressed memory.* New York: St. Martin's Press.

Loftus, Elizabeth F.; Miller, David G.; & Burns, Helen J. (1978). Semantic integration of verbal information into a visual memory. *Journal of Experimental Psychology: Human Learning and Memory, 4,* 19–31.

Loftus, Elizabeth F., & Palmer, John C. (1974). Reconstruction of automobile destruction: An example of the interaction between language and memory. *Journal of Verbal Learning and Verbal Behavior, 13,* 585–589.

Loftus, Elizabeth F., & Pickrell, Jacqueline E. (1995). The formation of false memories. *Psychiatric Annals, 25,* 720–725.

Loftus, Elizabeth F., & Zanni, Guido (1975). Eyewitness testimony: The influence of the wording of a question. *Bulletin of the Psychonomic Society, 5,* 86–88.

Lonner, Walter J. (1995). Culture and human diversity. In E. Trickett, R. Watts, & D. Birman (eds.), *Human diversity: Perspectives on people in context.* San Francisco: Jossey-Bass.

López, Steven R. (1989). Patient variable biases in clinical judgment: Conceptual overview and methodological considerations. *Psychological Bulletin, 106,* 184–203.

López, Steven R. (1995). Testing ethnic minority children. In B. B. Wolman (ed.), *The encyclopedia of psychology, psychiatry, and psychoanalysis.* New York: Henry Holt.

Lott, Bernice (1997). The personal and social consequences of a gender difference ideology. *Journal of Social Issues, 53,* 279–298.

Lott, Bernice, & Maluso, Diane (1993). The social learning of gender. In A. E. Beall & R. J. Sternberg (eds.), *The psychology of gender.* New York: Guilford Press.

Lottes, Ilsa L., & Kuriloff, Peter J. (1994). Sexual socialization differences by gender, Greek membership, and religious background. *Psychology of Women Quarterly, 18,* 203–219.

Louie, Therese A. (1999). Decision makers' hindsight bias after making favorable and unfavorable feedback. *Journal of Applied Psychology, 84,* 29–41.

Lovaas, O. Ivar (1977). *The autistic child: Language development through behavior modification.* New York: Halsted Press.

Lovaas, O. Ivar; Schreibman, Laura; & Koegel, Robert L. (1974). A behavior modification approach to the treatment of autistic children. *Journal of Autism and Childhood Schizophrenia, 4,* 111–129.

Lucchina, L. A.; Curtis, O. F.; Putnam, P.; et al. (1998). Psychophysical measurement of 6-n-propylthiouracil (PROP) taste perception. *Annals of the New York Academy of Sciences, 855,* 816–819.

Luengo, M. A.; Carrillo-de-la-Peña, M. T.; Otero, J. M.; & Romero, E. (1994). A short-term longitudinal study of impulsivity and antisocial behavior. *Journal of Personality and Social Psychology, 66,* 542–548.

Luepnitz, Deborah A. (1988). *The family interpreted: Feminist theory in clinical practice.* New York: Basic Books.

Luhrmann, T. M. (2000). *Of two minds: The growing disorder in American psychiatry.* New York: Knopf.

Luria, Alexander (1968). *The mind of a mnemonist* (L. Soltaroff, trans.). New York: Basic Books.

Luria, Alexander R. (1980). *Higher cortical functions in man* (2nd rev. ed.). New York: Basic Books.

Lutz, Catherine (1988). *Unnatural emotions.* Chicago: University of Chicago Press.

Lyketsos, C. G.; Hoover, D. R.; Guccione, M.; et al. (1993). Depressive symptoms as predictors of medical outcomes in HIV infection: Multicenter AIDS Cohort Study. *Journal of the American Medical Association, 270,* 2563–2567.

Lykken, David T. (1995). *The antisocial personalities.* Hillsdale, NJ: Erlbaum.

Lykken, David T., & Tellegen, Auke (1996). Happiness is a stochastic phenomenon. *Psychological Science, 7,* 186–189.

Lytton, Hugh, & Romney, David M. (1991). Parents' differential socialization of boys and girls: A meta-analysis. *Psychological Bulletin, 109,* 267–296.

Lyubomirsky, Sonja; Caldwell, Nicole D.; & Nolen-Hoeksema, Susan (1998). Effects of ruminative and distracting responses to depressed mood on retrieval of autobiographical memories. *Journal of Personality and Social Psychology, 75,* 166–177.

Maas, James B. (1998). *Power sleep.* New York: Villard.

MacArthur Foundation Research Network on Successful Midlife Development (1999). Report of latest findings (Orville G. Brim, director; 2145 14th Avenue, Vero Beach, FL 32960. Also reported 2/16/99 in *The New York Times,* "New study finds middle age is prime of life," by Erica Goode, Health & Fitness section.)

Maccoby, Eleanor E. (1998). *The two sexes: Growing up apart, coming together.* Cambridge, MA: Belknap Press/Harvard University Press.

MacKavey, William R.; Malley, Janet E.; & Stewart, Abigail J. (1991). Remembering autobiographically consequential experiences: Content analysis of psychologists' accounts of their lives. *Psychology and Aging, 6,* 50–59.

MacKinnon, Donald W. (1968). Selecting students with creative potential. In P. Heist (ed.), *The creative college student: An unmet challenge.* San Francisco: Jossey-Bass.

MacLean, Paul (1993). Cerebral evolution of emotion. In M. Lewis & J. M. Haviland (eds.), *Handbook of emotions.* New York: Guilford Press.

Macrae, C. Neil; Milne, Alan B.; & Bodenhausen, Galen V. (1994). Stereotypes as energy-saving devices: A peek inside the cognitive toolbox. *Journal of Personality and Social Psychology, 66,* 37–47.

Maddux, James E. (1993, Summer). The mythology of psychopathology: A social cognitive view of deviance, difference, and disorder. *General Psychologist, 29,* 34–45.

Maddux, James E. (ed.) (1995). *Self-efficacy, adaptation, and adjustment: Theory, research, and application.* New York: Plenum.

Maddux, James E. (1996). The social-cognitive construction of difference and disorder. In D. F. Barone, J. E. Maddux, & C. R. Snyder (eds.), *Social cognitive psychology: History and current domains.* New York: Plenum.

Maddux, James E., & Mundell, Clare E. (1997). Disorders of personality. In V. Derlega, B. Winstead, & W. Jones (eds.), *Personality: Contemporary theory and research* (2nd ed.). Chicago: Nelson-Hall.

Maguire, Eleanor A.; Gadian, David G.; Johnsrude, Ingrid S.; et al. (2000). Navigation-related structural change in the hippocampi of taxi drivers. *Proceedings of the National Academy of Sciences, 97,* 4398–4403.

Major, Brenda; Spencer, Steven; Schmader, Toni; et al. (1998). Coping with negative stereotypes about intellectual performance: The role of psychological disengagement. *Personality and Social Psychology Bulletin, 24,* 34–50.

Malamuth, Neil, & Dean, Karol (1990). Attraction to sexual aggression. In A. Parrot & L. Bechhofer (eds.), *Acquaintance rape: The hidden crime.* Newark, NJ: Wiley.

Malamuth, Neil M.; Linz, Daniel; Heavey, Christopher L.; et al. (1995). Using the confluence model of sexual aggression to predict men's conflict with women: A 10-year follow-up study. *Journal of Personality and Social Psychology, 69,* 353–369.

Malarkey, William B.; Kiecolt-Glaser, Janice K.; Pearl, Dennis; & Glaser, Ronald (1994). Hostile behavior during marital conflict alters pituitary and adrenal hormones. *Psychosomatic Medicine, 56,* 41–51.

Malatesta, Carol Z. (1990). The role of emotions in the development and organization of personality. In R. A. Thompson et al. (eds.), *Nebraska Symposium on Motivation, 1988: Socioemotional development.* Lincoln, NE: University of Nebraska Press.

Malgady, Robert G.; Rogler, Lloyd; & Costantino, Giuseppe (1987). Ethnocultural and linguistic bias in mental health evaluation of Hispanics. *American Psychologist, 42,* 228–234.

Maling, Michael S., & Howard, Kenneth I. (1994). From research to practice to research to. . . . In P. F. Talley, H. H. Strupp, & S. F. Butler (eds.), *Psychotherapy research and practice: Bridging the gap.* New York: Basic Books.

Malinosky-Rummell, Robin, & Hansen, David J. (1993). Long-term consequences of childhood physical abuse. *Psychological Bulletin, 114,* 68–79.

Malnic, B.; Hirono, J.; Sato, T.; & Buck, L. B. (1999). Combinatorial receptor codes for odors. *Cell, 96,* 713–723.

Mansfield, Elizabeth D., & McAdams, Dan P. (1996). Generativity and themes of agency and community in adult autobiography. *Personality and Social Psychology Bulletin, 22,* 721–731.

Marcus, Gary F.; Pinker, Steven; Ullman, Michael; et al. (1992). Overregularization in language acquisition. *Monographs of the Society for Research in Child Development, 57* (Serial No. 228), 1–182.

Marcus, G. F.; Vijayan, S.; Rao, S. Bandi; & Vishton, P. M. (1999, January 1). Rule learning by seven-month-old infants. *Science, 283,* 77–79.

Marcus-Newhall, Amy; Pedersen, William C.; Carlson, Mike; & Miller, Norman (2000). Displaced aggression is alive and well: A meta-analytic review. *Journal of Personality and Social Psychology, 78,* 670–689.

Marino, Raul, Jr., & Cosgrove, G. Rees (1997). Neurosurgical treatment of neuropsychiatric illness. *Psychiatric Clinics of North America, 20,* 933–943.

Markowitz, Laura M. (1993, July/August). Walking the walk. *Family Therapy Networker,* 19–31.

Markus, Hazel R., & Kitayama, Shinobu (1991). Culture and the self: Implications for cognition, emotion, and motivation. *Psychological Review, 98,* 224–253.

Marlatt, G. Alan (1996). Models of relapse and relapse prevention: A commentary. *Experimental and Clinical Psychopharmacology, 4,* 55–60.

Marlatt, G. Alan; Larimer, Mary E.; Baer, John S.; & Quigley, Lori A. (1993). Harm reduction for alcohol problems: Moving beyond the controlled drinking controversy. *Behavior Therapy, 24,* 461–503.

Marriott, Bernadette M. (ed.) (1994). *Food components to enhance performance.* Washington, DC: National Academy Press.

Marshall, Grant N.; Wortman, Camille B.; Vickers, Ross R., Jr.; et al. (1994). The five-factor model of personality as a framework for personality health research. *Journal of Personality and Social Psychology, 67,* 278–286.

Martin, Rod A., & Dobbin, James P. (1988). Sense of humor, hassles, and immunoglobulin A: Evidence for a stress-moderating effect of humor. *International Journal of Psychiatry in Medicine, 18,* 93–105.

Masand, P. S. (2000). Side effects of antipsychotics in the elderly. *Journal of Clinical Psychiatry, 61*(Suppl. 8), 43–49.

Maslow, Abraham H. (1970). *Motivation and personality* (2nd ed.). New York: Harper & Row.

Maslow, Abraham H. (1971). *The farther reaches of human nature.* New York: Viking.

Masten, Ann S., & Coatsworth, J. Douglas (1998). The development of competence in favorable and unfavorable environments. *American Psychologist, 53,* 205–220.

Masters, William H., & Johnson, Virginia E. (1966). *Human sexual response.* Boston: Little, Brown.

Mather, Mara; Shafir, Eldar; & Johnson, Marcia K. (2000). Misremembrance of options past: Source monitoring and choice. *Psychological Science, 11,* 132–138.

Matsumoto, David (1996). *Culture and psychology.* Pacific Grove, CA: Brooks-Cole.

Matthews, Karen A.; Wing, Rena R.; Kuller, Lewis H.; et al. (1990). Influences of natural menopause on psychological characteristics and symptoms of middle-aged healthy women. *Journal of Consulting and Clinical Psychology, 58,* 345–351.

Mawhinney, T. C. (1990). Decreasing intrinsic "motivation" with extrinsic rewards: Easier said than done. *Journal of Organizational Behavior Management, 11,* 175–191.

Maxfield, Michael, & Widom, Cathy S. (1996). The cycle of violence. Revisited 6 years later. *Archives of Pediatric and Adolescent Medicine, 150,* 390–395.

May, Rollo (1994). *The discovery of being: Writings in existential psychology.* New York: Norton.

Mayer, John D.; McCormick, Laura J.; & Strong, Sara E. (1995). Mood-congruent memory and natural mood: New evidence. *Personality and Social Psychology Bulletin, 21,* 736–746.

Mayer, John D., & Salovey, Peter (1997). What is emotional intelligence? In P. Salovey & D. Sluyter (eds.), *Emotional development and emotional intelligence: Implications for educators.* New York: Basic Books.

Mazza, James J., & Reynolds, William M. (1999). Exposure to violence in young inner-city adolescents: Relationships with suicidal ideation, depression, and PTSD symptomatology. *Journal of Abnormal Child Psychology, 27,* 203–213.

Mazzoni, Giuliana A.; Loftus, Elizabeth F.; & Kirsch, Irving (2001). Changing beliefs about implausible autobiographical events: A little plausibility goes a long way. *Journal of Experimental Psychology: Applied,* in press.

Mazzoni, Guiliana A. L.; Loftus, Elizabeth F.; Seitz, Aaron; & Lynn, Steven J. (1999). Changing beliefs and memories through dream interpretation. *Applied Cognitive Psychology, 13,* 125–144.

Mazzoni, Giuliana A.; Lombardo, Pasquale; Malvagia, Stefano; & Loftus, Elizabeth F. (1999). Dream interpretation and false beliefs. *Professional Psychology: Research and Practice, 30,* 45–50.

McAdams, Dan P. (1988). *Power, intimacy, and the life story: Personological inquiries into identity.* New York: Guilford Press.

McCarthy, John (1997). AI as sport [Review of *Kasparov versus Deep Blue: Computer chess comes of age,* by Monty Newborn]. *Science, 276,* 1518–1519.

McClearn, Gerald E.; Johanson, Boo; Berg, Stig; et al. (1997). Substantial genetic influence on cognitive abilities in twins 80 or more years old. *Science, 176,* 1560–1563.

McClelland, David C. (1961). *The achieving society.* New York: Free Press.

McClelland, David C. (1985). *Human motivation.* Glenview, IL: Scott, Foresman.

McClelland, David C. (1987). Characteristics of successful entrepreneurs. *Journal of Creative Behavior, 3,* 219–233.

McClelland, David C.; Atkinson, John W.; Clark, Russell A.; & Lowell, Edgar L. (1953). *The achievement motive.* New York: Appleton-Century-Crofts.

McClelland, James L. (1994). The organization of memory: A parallel distributed processing perspective. *Revue Neurologique, 150,* 570–579.

McCord, Joan (1989). Another time, another drug. Paper presented at the conference Vulnerability to the Transition from Drug Use to Abuse and Dependence, Rockville, MD.

McCord, Joan (1992). The Cambridge-Somerville study: A pioneering longitudinal-experimental study of delinquency prevention. In J. McCord & R. E. Tremblay (eds.), *Preventing antisocial behavior: Interventions from birth through adolescence.* New York: Guilford Press.

McCrae, Robert R. (1987). Creativity, divergent thinking, and openness to experience. *Journal of Personality and Social Psychology, 52,* 1258–1265.

McCrae, Robert R., & Costa, Paul T., Jr. (1988). Do parental influences matter? A reply to Halverson. *Journal of Personality, 56,* 445–449.

McCrae, Robert R., & Costa, Paul T., Jr. (1996). Toward a new generation of personality theories: Theoretical contexts for the five-factor model. In J. S. Wiggins (ed.), *The five-factor model of personality: Theoretical perspectives.* New York: Guilford Press.

McCrae, Robert R., & Costa, Paul T., Jr. (1997). Personality trait structure as a human universal. *American Psychologist, 52,* 509–516.

McDonough, Laraine, & Mandler, Jean M. (1994). Very long-term recall in infancy. *Memory, 2,* 339–352.

McEwen, Bruce S. (1983). Gonadal steroid influences on brain development and sexual differentiation. *Reproductive Physiology IV (International Review of Physiology), 27,* 99–145.

McGaugh, James L. (1990). Significance and remembrance: The role of neuromodulatory systems. *Psychological Science, 1,* 15–25.

McGaugh, James L. (1999). Making memories that linger: Emotional arousal, stress hormones and brain systems. Invited address at the annual meeting of the Western Psychological Association, Irvine, CA.

McGlone, Jeannette (1978). Sex differences in functional brain asymmetry. *Cortex, 14,* 122–128.

McGlynn, Susan M. (1990). Behavioral approaches to neuropsychological rehabilitation. *Psychological Bulletin, 108,* 420–441.

McGoldrick, Monica, & Gerson, Randy (1985). *Genograms in family assessment.* New York: Norton.

McGoldrick, Monica, & Pearce, John K. (1996). Family therapy with Irish Americans. In M. McGoldrick, J. Giordano, & J. K. Pearce (eds.), *Ethnicity and family therapy* (2nd ed.). New York: Guilford Press.

McGrath, Ellen; Keita, Gwendolyn P.; Strickland, Bonnie; & Russo, Nancy F. (eds.) (1990). *Women and depression: Risk fac-*

tors and treatment issues. Washington, DC: American Psychological Association.

McGregor, Ian, & Holmes, John G. (1999). How storytelling shapes memory and impressions of relationship events over time. *Journal of Personality and Social Psychology, 76,* 403–419.

McGregor, Ian, & Little, Brian R. (1998). Personal projects, happiness, and meaning: On doing well and being yourself. *Journal of Personality and Social Psychology, 74,* 494–512.

McGue, Matt; Bouchard, Thomas J., Jr.; Iacono, William G.; & Lykken, David T. (1993). Behavioral genetics of cognitive ability: A life-span perspective. In R. Plomin & G. E. McClearn (eds.), *Nature, nurture, and psychology.* Washington, DC: American Psychological Association.

McGue, Matt, & Lykken, David T. (1992). Genetic influence on risk of divorce. *Psychological Science, 3,* 368–373.

McGue, Matt; Pickens, Roy W.; & Svikis, Dace S. (1992). Sex and age effects on the inheritance of alcohol problems: A twin study. *Journal of Abnormal Psychology, 101,* 3–17.

McHugh, Paul R. (1993a). History and the pitfalls of practice. Unpublished paper, Johns Hopkins University.

McHugh, Paul R. (1993b, December). Psychotherapy awry. *American Scholar,* 17–30.

McKee, Richard D., & Squire, Larry R. (1992). Equivalent forgetting rates in long-term memory for diencephalic and medial temporal lobe amnesia. *Journal of Neuroscience, 12,* 3765–3772.

McKee, Richard D., & Squire, Larry R. (1993). On the development of declarative memory. *Journal of Experimental Psychology: Learning, Memory, and Cognition, 19,* 397–404.

McKim, Margaret K.; Cramer, Kenneth M.; Stuart, Barbara; & O'Connor, Deborah L. (1999). Infant care decisions and attachment security: The Canadian Transition to Child Care Study. *Canadian Journal of Behavioural Science, 31,* 92–106.

McKinlay, John B.; McKinlay, Sonja M.; & Brambilla, Donald (1987). The relative contributions of endocrine changes and social circumstances to depression in mid-aged women. *Journal of Health and Social Behavior, 28,* 345–363.

McLeod, Beverly (1985, March). Real work for real pay. *Psychology Today,* 42–44, 46, 48–50.

McNally, Richard J. (1994). *Panic disorder: A critical analysis.* New York: Guilford Press.

McNally, Richard J. (1996). Cognitive bias in the anxiety disorders. In D. A. Hope et al. (eds.), *Nebraska Symposium on Motivation, 1995: Perspectives on anxiety, panic, and fear.* Lincoln, NE: University of Nebraska Press.

McNally, Richard J. (1998). Panic attacks. In *Encyclopedia of mental health* (Vol. 3). New York: Academic Press.

McNally, Richard J. (2001). Tertullian's motto and Callahan's method [Invited commentary]. *Journal of Clinical Psychology,* in press.

McNaughton, B. L., & Morris, R. G. M. (1987). Hippocampal synaptic enhancement and information storage within a distributed memory system. *Trends in Neuroscience, 10,* 408–415.

McNeill, David (1966). Developmental psycholinguistics. In F. L. Smith & G. A. Miller (eds.), *The genesis of language: A psycholinguistic approach.* Cambridge, MA: MIT Press.

Medawar, Peter B. (1979). *Advice to a young scientist.* New York: Harper & Row.

Mednick, Sarnoff A. (1962). The associative basis of the creative process. *Psychological Review, 69,* 220–232.

Mednick, Sarnoff A.; Huttunen, Matti O.; & Machón, Ricardo (1994). Prenatal influenza infections and adult schizophrenia. *Schizophrenia Bulletin, 20,* 263–267.

Mednick, Sarnoff A.; Parnas, Josef; & Schulsinger, Fini (1987). The Copenhagen High-Risk Project, 1962–86. *Schizophrenia Bulletin, 13,* 485–495.

Medvec, Victoria H.; Madey, Scott F.; & Gilovich, Thomas (1995). When less is more: Counterfactual thinking and satisfaction among Olympic medalists. *Journal of Personality and Social Psychology, 69,* 603–610.

Meeus, Wim H. J., & Raaijmakers, Quinten A. W. (1995). Obedience in modern society: The Utrecht studies. *Journal of Social Issues, 51,* 155–175.

Meindl, J. R., & Lerner, M. J. (1985). Exacerbation of extreme responses to an out-group. *Journal of Personality and Social Psychology, 47,* 71–84.

Meltzoff, Andrew N., & Gopnik, Alison (1993). The role of imitation in understanding persons and developing a theory of mind. In S. Baron-Cohen, H. Tager-Flusberg, & D. Cohen (eds.), *Understanding other minds.* New York: Oxford University Press.

Melzack, Ronald (1992, April). Phantom limbs. *Scientific American, 266,* 120–126. [Reprinted in a special issue, "Mysteries of the Mind," 1997.]

Melzack, Ronald (1993). Pain: Past, present, and future. *Canadian Journal of Experimental Psychology, 47,* 615–629.

Melzack, Ronald, & Wall, Patrick D. (1965). Pain mechanisms: A new theory. *Science, 13,* 971–979.

Mendes de Leon, C. F.; Krumholz, H. M.; Seeman, T. S.; et al. (1998). Depression and risk of coronary heart disease in elderly men and women: New Haven EPESE, 1982–1991; Established Populations for the Epidemiologic Studies of the Elderly. *Archives of Internal Medicine, 158,* 2341–2348.

Menon, Tanya; Morris, Michael W.; Chiu, Chi-yue; & Hone, Ying-yi (1999). Culture and the construal of agency: Attribution to individual versus group dispositions. *Journal of Personality and Social Psychology, 76,* 701–717.

Merikle, Philip M., & Skanes, Heather E. (1992). Subliminal self-help audiotapes: A search for placebo effects. *Journal of Applied Psychology, 77,* 772–776.

Merrill, L. L.; Newell, C. E.; Milner, J. S.; Koss, M. P.; et al. (1998). Prevalence of premilitary adult sexual victimization and aggression in a Navy recruit sample. *Military Medicine, 163,* 209–212.

Merskey, Harold (1992). The manufacture of personalities: The production of MPD. *British Journal of Psychiatry, 160,* 327–340.

Merskey, Harold (1995). The manufacture of personalities: The production of multiple personality disorder. In L. M. Cohen, J. N. Berzoff, & M. R. Elin (eds.), *Dissociative identity disorder: Theoretical and treatment controversies.* Northvale, NJ: Jason Aronson.

Mesquita, Batja, & Frijda, Nico H. (1992). Cultural variations in emotions: A review. *Psychological Bulletin, 112,* 179–204.

Metalsky, Gerald I.; Joiner, Thomas E., Jr.; Hardin, Tammy S.; & Abramson, Lyn Y. (1993). Depressive reactions to failure in a naturalistic setting: A test of the hopelessness and self-esteem theories of depression. *Journal of Abnormal Psychology, 102,* 101–109.

Meyer-Bahlburg, Heino F. L.; Ehrhardt, Anke A.; Rosen, Laura R.; et al. (1995). Prenatal estrogens and the development of homosexual orientation. *Developmental Psychology, 31,* 12–21.

Mickelson, Kristin D.; Kessler, Ronald C.; & Shaver, Phillip R. (1997). Adult attachment in a nationally representative sample. *Journal of Personality and Social Psychology, 73,* 1092–1106.

Milgram, Stanley (1963). Behavioral study of obedience. *Journal of Abnormal and Social Psychology, 67,* 371–378.

Milgram, Stanley (1974). *Obedience to authority: An experimental view.* New York: Harper & Row.

Miller, George A. (1956). The magical number seven, plus or minus two: Some limits on our capacity for processing information. *Psychological Review, 63,* 81–97.

Miller, Inglis J., & Reedy, Frank E. (1990). Variations in human taste bud density and taste intensity perception. *Physiology and Behavior, 47,* 1213–1219.

Miller, Neal E. (1978). Biofeedback and visceral learning. *Annual Review of Psychology, 29,* 421–452.

Miller, Scott D., & Triggiano, Patrick J. (1992). The psychophysiological investigation of multiple personality disorder: Review and update. *American Journal of Clinical Hypnosis, 35,* 47–61.

Miller, Todd Q.; Smith, Timothy W.; Turner, Charles W.; et al. (1996). A meta-analytic review of research on hostility and physical health. *Psychological Bulletin, 119,* 322–348.

Miller-Jones, Dalton (1989). Culture and testing. *American Psychologist, 44,* 360–366.

Milner, Brenda (1970). Memory and the temporal regions of the brain. In K. H. Pribram & D. E. Broadbent (eds.), *Biology of memory.* New York: Academic Press.

Milner, J. S., & McCanne, T. R. (1991). Neuropsychological correlates of physical child abuse. In J. S. Milner (ed.), *Neuropsychology of aggression.* Norwell, MA: Kluwer Academic.

Milton, Julie, & Wiseman, Richard (1999). Does Psi exist? Lack of replication of an anomalous process of information transfer. *Psychological Bulletin, 125,* 387–391.

Minuchin, Salvador (1984). *Family kaleidoscope.* Cambridge, MA: Harvard University Press.

Mischel, Walter (1973). Toward a cognitive social learning reconceptualization of personality. *Psychological Review, 80,* 252–253.

Mischel, Walter, & Shoda, Yuichi (1995). A cognitive affective system theory of personality: Reconceptualizing situations, dispositions, dynamics, and invariance in personality structures. *Psychological Review, 102,* 246–268.

Mishkin, M.; Suzuki, W. A.; Gadian, D. G.; & Vargha-Khadem, F. (1997). Hierarchical organization of cognitive memory. *Philosophical Transactions of the Royal Society of London, B: Biological Science, 352,* 1461–1467.

Mistry, Jayanthi, & Rogoff, Barbara (1994). Remembering in cultural context. In W. J. Lonner & R. Malpass (eds.), *Psychology and culture.* Needham Heights, MA: Allyn & Bacon.

Mitchell, Valory, & Helson, Ravenna (1990). Women's prime of life: Is it the 50s? *Psychology of Women Quarterly, 14,* 451–470.

Mithers, Carol L. (1994). *Reasonable insanity: A true story of the seventies.* Reading, MA: Addison-Wesley.

Modigliani, Andre, & Rochat, François (1995). The role of interaction sequences and the timing of resistance in shaping obedience and defiance to authority. *Journal of Social Issues, 51,* 107–125.

Moffitt, Terrie E. (1993). Adolescence-limited and life-course-persistent antisocial behavior: A developmental taxonomy. *Psychological Review, 100,* 674–701.

Moore, Timothy E. (1992, Spring). Subliminal perception: Facts and fallacies. *Skeptical Inquirer, 16,* 273–281.

Moore, Timothy E. (1995). Subliminal self-help auditory tapes: An empirical test of perceptual consequences. *Canadian Journal of Behavioural Science, 27,* 9–20.

Moore, Timothy E., & Pepler, Debra J. (1998). Correlates of adjustment in children at risk. In G. W. Holden, R. Geffner, et al. (eds.), *Children exposed to marital violence: Theory, research, and applied issues.* Washington, DC: American Psychological Association.

Moorhead, Gregory; Ference, Richard; & Neck, Chris P. (1991). Group decision fiascoes continue: Space shuttle *Challenger* and a revised groupthink framework. *Human Relations, 44,* 539–550.

Morris, Michael W., & Peng, Kaiping (1994). Culture and cause: American and Chinese attributions for social and physical events. *Journal of Personality and Social Psychology, 67,* 949–971.

Moscovici, Serge (1985). Social influence and conformity. In G. Lindzey & E. Aronson (eds.), *Handbook of social psychology* (Vol. 2, 3rd ed.). New York: Random House.

Moscovitch, Morris; Winocur, Gordon; & Behrmann, Marlene (1997). What is special about face recognition? Nineteen experiments on a person with visual object agnosia and dyslexia but normal face recognition. *Journal of Cognitive Neuroscience, 9,* 555–604.

Mozell, Maxwell M.; Smith, Bruce P.; Smith, Paul E.; et al. (1969). Nasal chemoreception in flavor identification. *Archives of Otolaryngology, 90,* 367–373.

Mroczek, Daniel K., & Kolarz, Christian M. (1998). The effect of age on positive and negative affect: A developmental perspective on happiness. *Journal of Personality and Social Psychology, 75,* 1333–1349.

Muehlenhard, Charlene L. (1988). "Nice women" don't say yes and "real men" don't say no: How miscommunication and the double standard can cause sexual problems. *Women & Therapy, 7,* 95–108.

Muehlenhard, Charlene L., & Cook, Stephen (1988). Men's self-reports of unwanted sexual activity. *Journal of Sex Research, 24,* 58–72.

Mueller, Claudia M., & Dweck, Carol S. (1998). Praise for intelligence can undermine children's motivation and performance. *Journal of Personality and Social Psychology, 75,* 33–52.

Müller, Ralph-Axel; Courchesne, Eric; & Allen, Greg (1998). The cerebellum: So much more [Letter]. *Science, 282,* 879–880.

Murphy, Sheila T.; Monahan, Jennifer L.; & Zajonc, R. B. (1995). Additivity of nonconscious affect: Combined effects of priming and exposure. *Journal of Personality and Social Psychology, 69,* 589–602.

Nash, Michael R. (1987). What, if anything, is regressed about hypnotic age regression? A review of the empirical literature. *Psychological Bulletin, 102,* 42–52.

Nash, Michael R. (1994). Memory distortion and sexual trauma: The problem of false negatives and false positives. *International Journal of Clinical and Experimental Hypnosis, 42,* 346–362.

Nash, Michael R., & Nadon, Robert (1997). Hypnosis. In D. L. Faigman, D. Kaye, M. J. Saks, & J. Sanders (eds.), *Modern scientific evidence: The law and science of expert testimony.* St. Paul, MN: West.

Nathan, Debbie (1994, Fall). Dividing to conquer? Women, men, and the making of multiple personality disorder. *Social Text, 40,* 77–114.

Nathan, Debbie, & Snedeker, Michael (1995). *Satan's silence: Ritual abuse and the making of a modern American witch hunt.* New York: Basic Books.

National Victim Center & Crime Victims Research and Treatment Center (1992). *Rape in America: A report to the nation.* Fort Worth, TX: National Victim Center.

Needleman, Herbert L.; Riess, Julie A.; Tobin, Michael J.; et al. (1996). Bone lead levels and delinquent behavior. *Journal of the American Medical Association, 275,* 363–369.

Neher, Andrew (1996). Jung's theory of archetypes: A critique. *Journal of Humanistic Psychology, 36,* 61–91.

Neisser, Ulric (ed.) (1998). *The rising curve: Long-term gains in IQ and related measures.* Washington, DC: American Psychological Association.

Neisser, Ulric, & Harsch, Nicole (1992). Phantom flashbulbs: False recollections of hearing the news about *Challenger.* In E. Winograd & U. Neisser (eds.), *Affect and accuracy in recall: Studies of "flashbulb memories."* New York: Cambridge University Press.

Neitz, Maureen, & Neitz, Jay (1995). Numbers and ratios of visual pigment genes for normal red-green color vision. *Science, 267,* 1013–1016.

Nelson, Thomas O., & Dunlosky, John (1991). When people's judgments of learning (JOLs) are extremely accurate at predicting subsequent recall: The "delayed JOL effect." *Psychological Science, 2,* 267–270.

Nelson, Thomas O., & Leonesio, R. Jacob (1988). Allocation of self-paced study time and the "labor in vain effect." *Journal* *of Experimental Psychology: Learning, Memory, and Cognition, 14,* 676–686.

Neugarten, Bernice (1979). Time, age, and the life cycle. *American Journal of Psychiatry, 136,* 887–894.

Newcombe, Nora S.; Drummey, Anna Bullock; Fox, Nathan A.; et al. (2000). Remembering early childhood: How much, how, and why (or why not). *Current Directions in Psychological Science, 9,* 55–58.

Newman, Lucille F., & Buka, Stephen (1991, Spring). Clipped wings. *American Educator,* 27–33, 42.

NICHD Early Child Care Research Network (1997). The effects of infant-child care on infant-mother attachment security (Results of the NICHD study of early child care). *Child Development, 68,* 860–879.

Nickerson, Raymond S. (1998). Confirmation bias: A ubiquitous phenomenon in many guises. *Review of General Psychology, 2,* 175–220.

Nickerson, Raymond S., & Adams, Marilyn Jager (1979). Long-term memory for a common object. *Cognitive Psychology, 11,* 287–307.

Nigg, Joel T., & Goldsmith, H. Hill (1994). Genetics of personality disorders: Perspectives from personality and psychopathology research. *Psychological Bulletin, 115,* 346–380.

NIH Technology Assessment Panel on Integration of Behavioral and Relaxation Approaches into the Treatment of Chronic Pain and Insomnia (1996). *Journal of the American Medical Association, 276,* 313–318.

Nisbett, Richard E. (1993). Violence and U.S. regional culture. *American Psychologist, 48,* 441–449.

Nisbett, Richard E., & Ross, Lee (1980). *Human inference: Strategies and shortcomings of social judgment.* Englewood Cliffs, NJ: Prentice-Hall.

Noble, Ernest P. (1998, August 28). DRD2 gene and alcoholism. *Science, 281,* 1287–1288.

Noble, Ernest P.; Blum, Kenneth; Ritchie, T.; Montgomery, A.; & Sheridan, P. J. (1991). Allelic association of the D2 dopamine receptor gene with receptor-binding characteristics in alcoholism. *Archives of General Psychiatry, 48,* 648–654.

Nolen-Hoeksema, Susan, & Girgus, Joan S. (1994). The emergence of gender differences in depression during adolescence. *Psychological Bulletin, 115,* 424–443.

Nonaka, S.; Hough, C. J.; & Chuang, De-Maw (1998, March 3). Chronic lithium treatment robustly protects neurons in the central nervous system against excitotoxity by inhibiting N-methyl-D-aspartate receptor-mediated calcium influx. *Proceedings of the National Academy of Sciences, 95,* 2642–2647.

Norman, Donald A. (1988). *The psychology of everyday things.* New York: Basic Books.

Nowicki, Stephen, & Strickland, Bonnie R. (1973). A locus of control scale for children. *Journal of Consulting Psychology, 40,* 148–154.

Ó Scalaidhe, Séamas P.; Wilson, Fraser A. W.; & Goldman-Rakic, Patricia S. (1997). Areal segregation of face-processing neurons in prefrontal cortex. *Science, 278,* 1135–1138.

O'Hanlon, Bill (1994, November/December). The third wave. *Family Therapy Networker,* 18–29.

Oatley, Keith (1990). Do emotional states produce irrational thinking? In K. J. Gilhooly, M. T. G. Keane, R. H. Logie, & G. Erdos (eds.), *Lines of thinking* (Vol. 2). New York: Wiley.

Oatley, Keith, & Duncan, Elaine (1994). The experience of emotions in everyday life. *Cognition and Emotion, 8,* 369–381.

Oatley, Keith, & Jenkins, Jennifer M. (1996). *Understanding emotions.* Cambridge, MA: Blackwell.

Ofshe, Richard J., & Watters, Ethan (1994). *Making monsters: False memory, psychotherapy, and sexual hysteria.* New York: Scribners.

Ogden, Jenni A., & Corkin, Suzanne (1991). Memories of H. M. In W. C. Abraham, M. C. Corballis, & K. G. White (eds.), *Memory mechanisms: A tribute to G. V. Goddard.* Hillsdale, NJ: Erlbaum.

Olds, James (1975). Mapping the mind onto the brain. In F. G. Worden, J. P. Swazy, & G. Adelman (eds.), *The neurosciences: Paths of discovery.* Cambridge, MA: Colonial Press.

Olds, James, & Milner, Peter (1954). Positive reinforcement produced by electrical stimulation of septal area and other regions of the rat brain. *Journal of Comparative and Physiological Psychology, 47,* 419–429.

Olin, Su-Chin S., & Mednick, Sarnoff A. (1996). Risk factors of psychosis: Identifying vulnerable populations premorbidly. *Schizophrenia Bulletin, 22,* 223–240.

Oliver, Mary Beth, & Hyde, Janet S. (1993). Gender differences in sexuality: A meta-analysis. *Psychological Bulletin, 114,* 29–51.

Olujic, M. B. (1998). Embodiment of terror: Gendered violence in peacetime and wartime in Croatia and Bosnia-Herzegovina. *Medical Anthropology Quarterly, 12,* 31–50.

Orlinsky, David E., & Howard, Kenneth I. (1994). Unity and diversity among psychotherapies: A comparative perspective. In B. Bongar & L. E. Beutler (eds.), *Foundations of psychotherapy: Theory, research, and practice.* New York: Oxford University Press.

Page, Gayle G.; Ben-Eliyahu, Shamgar; Yirmiya, Raz; & Liebeskind, John C. (1993). Morphine attenuates surgery-induced enhancement of metastatic colonization in rats. *Pain, 54,* 21–28.

Panksepp, Jaak (1998). Attention deficit hyperactivity disorders, psychostimulants, and intolerance of childhood playfulness: A tragedy in the making? *Current Directions in Psychological Science, 7,* 91–98.

Panksepp, Jaak; Herman, B. H.; Vilberg, T.; et al. (1980). Endogenous opioids and social behavior. *Neuroscience and Biobehavioral Reviews, 4,* 473–487.

Park, Denise (2000). The basic mechanisms accounting for age-related decline in cognitive function. In D. C. Park, N. Schwarz, et al. (eds.), *Cognitive aging: A primer.* Philadelphia, PA: Psychology Press/Taylor & Francis.

Parker, Gwendolyn M. (1997). *Trespassing: My sojourn in the halls of privilege.* Boston: Houghton Mifflin.

Patterson, Charlotte J. (1992). Children of lesbian and gay parents. *Child Development, 63,* 1025–1042.

Patterson, Charlotte J. (1995). Sexual orientation and human development: An overview. *Developmental Psychology, 31,* 3–11.

Patterson, Francine, & Linden, Eugene (1981). *The education of Koko.* New York: Holt, Rinehart and Winston.

Patterson, Gerald R.; Forgatch, Marion S.; Yoerger, Karen L.; & Stoolmiller, Mike (1998). Variables that initiate and maintain an early-onset trajectory for juvenile offending. *Development and Psychopathology, 10,* 531–547.

Patterson, Gerald R.; Reid, John; & Dishion, Thomas (1992). *Antisocial boys.* Eugene, OR: Castalia.

Paul, Richard W. (1984, September). Critical thinking: Fundamental to education for a free society. *Educational Leadership,* 4–14.

Pearlin, Leonard (1982). Discontinuities in the study of aging. In T. K. Hareven & K. J. Adams (eds.), *Aging and life course transitions: An interdisciplinary perspective.* New York: Guilford Press.

Pedersen, Paul B.; Draguns, Juris G.; Lonner, Walter J.; & Trimble, Joseph E. (eds.) (1996). *Counseling across cultures* (4th ed.). Thousand Oaks, CA: Sage.

Peele, Stanton, & Brodsky, Archie, with Mary Arnold (1991). *The truth about addiction and recovery.* New York: Simon & Schuster.

Pendergrast, Mark (1995). *Victims of memory* (2nd ed.). Hinesburg, VT: Upper Access Press.

Pennebaker, James W. (1995). Emotion, disclosure, and health: An overview. In J. W. Pennebaker (ed.), *Emotion, disclosure, and health.* Washington, DC: American Psychological Association.

Pennebaker, James W.; Colder, Michelle; & Sharp, Lisa K. (1990). Accelerating the coping process. *Journal of Personality and Social Psychology, 58,* 528–527.

Pennebaker, James W.; Kiecolt-Glaser, Janice; & Glaser, Ronald (1988). Disclosure of traumas and immune function: Health implications for psychotherapy. *Journal of Consulting and Clinical Psychology, 56,* 239–245.

Penninx, B. W.; Guralnik, J. M.; Pahor, M.; et al. (1998). Chronically depressed mood and cancer risk in older persons. *Journal of the National Cancer Institute, 90,* 1888–1893.

Peplau, Letitia A., & Spalding, Leah R. (2000). The close relationships of lesbians, gay men and bisexuals. In C. Hendrick & S. Hendrick (eds.), *Close relationships: A sourcebook.* Thousand Oaks, CA: Sage.

Peplau, Letitia A.; Spalding, Leah R.; Conley, Terri D.; & Veniegas, Rosemary C. (2000). The development of sexual orientation in women. *Annual Review of Sex Research, 10,* 70–99.

Pepperberg, Irene (2000). *The Alex papers: The cognitive and communicative abilities of grey parrots.* Cambridge, MA: Harvard University Press.

Perry, Patrick (2000, September/October). Michael J. Fox's challenging new role. *Saturday Evening Post, 272,* 38ff.

Perry, Samuel W., & Heidrich, George (1982). Management of pain during debridement: A survey of U.S. burn units. *Pain, 13,* 267–280.

Persons, Jacqueline; Davidson, Joan; & Tompkins, Michael A. (2001). *Essential components of cognitive-behavior therapy for depression.* Washington, DC: American Psychological Association.

Pert, Candace B., & Snyder, Solomon H. (1973). Opiate receptor: Demonstration in nervous tissue. *Science, 179,* 1011–1014.

Pesetsky, David (1999). Introduction to symposium: "Grammar: What's Innate?" Paper presented at the annual meeting of the American Association for the Advancement of Science, Anaheim, CA.

Peterson, Christopher (2000). The future of optimism. *American Psychologist, 55,* 44–55.

Peterson, Christopher; Seligman, Martin E. P.; Yurko, Karen H.; et al. (1998). Catastrophizing and untimely death. *Psychological Science, 9,* 127–130.

Peterson, Lloyd R., & Peterson, Margaret J. (1959). Short-term retention of individual verbal items. *Journal of Experimental Psychology, 58,* 193–198.

Peterson, Marilyn R. (1992). *At personal risk: Boundary violations in professional-client relationships.* New York: Norton.

Petrie, Keith J.; Booth, Roger J.; & Pennebaker, James W. (1998). The immunological effects of thought suppression. *Journal of Personality and Social Psychology, 75,* 1264–1272.

Pettigrew, Thomas F. (1997). Generalized intergroup contact effects on prejudice. *Personality and Social Psychology Bulletin, 23,* 173–185.

Pettigrew, Thomas F. (1998). Intergroup contact theory. *Annual Review of Psychology* (Vol. 49, pp. 65–85). Palo Alto, CA: Annual Reviews.

Pfungst, Oskar (1911/1965). *Clever Hans (The horse of Mr. von Osten): A contribution to experimental animal and human psychology.* New York: Holt, Rinehart and Winston.

Phinney, Jean S. (1990). Ethnic identity in adolescents and adults: Review of research. *Psychological Bulletin, 108,* 499–514.

Phinney, Jean S. (1996). When we talk about American ethnic groups, what do we mean? *American Psychologist, 51,* 918–927.

Piaget, Jean (1929/1960). *The child's conception of the world.* Paterson, NJ: Littlefield, Adams.

Piaget, Jean (1932). *The moral judgment of the child.* New York: Macmillan.

Piaget, Jean (1952a). *The origins of intelligence in children.* New York: International Universities Press.

Piaget, Jean (1952b). *Play, dreams, and imitation in childhood.* New York: Norton.

Piaget, Jean (1984). Piaget's theory. In P. Mussen (series ed.) & W. Kessen (vol. ed.), *Handbook of child psychology: Vol. 1. History, theory, and methods* (4th ed.). New York: Wiley.

Pinel, John P. J.; Assanand, Sunaina; & Lehman, Darrin R. (2000). Hunger, eating, and ill health. *American Psychologist, 55,* 1105–1116.

Pinker, Steven (1994). *The language instinct: How the mind creates language.* New York: Morrow.

Piper, August, Jr. (1997). *Hoax and reality: The bizarre world of multiple personality disorder.* Northvale, NJ: Jason Aronson.

Plant, E. Ashby, & Devine, Patricia G. (1998). Internal and external motivation to respond without prejudice. *Journal of Personality and Social Psychology, 75,* 811–832.

Plomin, Robert (1989). Environment and genes: Determinants of behavior. *American Psychologist, 44,* 105–111.

Plomin, Robert; Corley, Robin; Caspi, Avshalom; et al. (1998). Adoption results for self-reported personality: Evidence for nonadditive genetic effects? *Journal of Personality and Social Psychology, 75,* 211–218.

Plomin, Robert; Corley, Robin; DeFries, J. C.; & Fulker, D. W. (1990). Individual differences in television viewing in early childhood: Nature as well as nurture. *Psychological Science, 1,* 371–377.

Plomin, Robert, & DeFries, John C. (1985). *Origins of individual differences in infancy: The Colorado Adoption Project.* New York: Academic Press.

Plutchik, Robert; Conte, Hope R.; Karasu, Toksoz; & Buckley, Peter (1988, Fall/Winter). The measurement of psychodynamic variables. *Hillside Journal of Clinical Psychology, 10,* 132–147.

Pollak, Richard (1997). *The creation of Dr. B: A biography of Bruno Bettelheim.* New York: Simon & Schuster.

Poole, Debra A. (1995). Strolling fuzzy-trace theory through eyewitness testimony (or vice versa). *Learning and Individual Differences, 7,* 87–93.

Poole, Debra A., & Lamb, Michael E. (1998). *Investigative interviews of children.* Washington, DC: American Psychological Association.

Poole, Debra A.; Lindsay, D. Stephen; Memon, Amina; & Bull, Ray (1995). Psychotherapy and the recovery of memories of childhood sexual abuse: U.S. and British practitioners' opinions, practices, and experiences. *Journal of Consulting and Clinical Psychology, 63,* 426–437.

Pope, Harrison G., Jr.; Phillips, Katharine A.; & Olivardia, Roberto (2000). *The Adonis complex: The secret crisis of male body obsession.* New York: Free Press.

Pope, Kenneth S. (1996). Memory, abuse, and science: Questioning claims about the false memory syndrome epidemic. *American Psychologist, 51,* 957–974.

Portenoy, Russell K. (1994). Opioid therapy for chronic non-malignant pain: Current status. In H. L. Fields & J. C. Liebeskind (eds.), *Progress in pain research and management: Vol. 1. Pharmacological approaches to the treatment of chronic pain.* Seattle: International Association for the Study of Pain.

Postmes, Tom, & Spears, Russell (1998). Deindividuation and antinormative behavior: A meta-analysis. *Psychological Bulletin, 123,* 238–259.

Potter, W. James (1987). Does television viewing hinder academic achievement among adolescents? *Human Communication Research, 14*, 27–46.

Poulin-Dubois, Diane; Serbin, Lisa A.; Kenyon, Brenda; & Derbyshire, Alison (1994). Infants' intermodal knowledge about gender. *Developmental Psychology, 30*, 436–442.

Powell, Russell A., & Boer, Douglas P. (1995). Did Freud misinterpret reported memories of sexual abuse as fantasies? *Psychological Reports, 77*, 563–570.

Pratkanis, Anthony, & Aronson, Elliot (1992). *Age of propaganda: The everyday use and abuse of persuasion.* New York: W. H. Freeman.

Pratt, L. A.; Ford, D. E.; Crum, R. M.; et al. (1996, December 15). Depression, psychotropic medication, and risk of myocardial infarction: Prospective data from the Baltimore ECA follow-up. *Circulation, 94*, 3123–3129.

Premack, David, & Premack, Ann James (1983). *The mind of an ape.* New York: Norton.

Prochaska, James O.; Norcross, John C.; & DiClemente, Carlo C. (1994). *Changing for good.* New York: Morrow.

Punamaeki, Raija-Leena, & Joustie, Marja (1998). The role of culture, violence, and personal factors affecting dream content. *Journal of Cross-Cultural Psychology, 29*, 320–342.

Pynoos, R. S., & Nader, K. (1989). Children's memory and proximity to violence. *Journal of the American Academy of Child and Adolescent Psychiatry, 28*, 236–241.

Radetsky, Peter (1991, April). The brainiest cells alive. *Discover, 12*, 82–85, 88, 90.

Radke-Yarrow, Marian; Zahn-Waxler, Carolyn; & Chapman, M. (1983). Prosocial dispositions and behavior. In P. Mussen (ed.), *Handbook of child psychology: Vol. 4. Socialization, personality, and social development.* New York: Wiley.

Räikkönen, Katri; Matthews, Karen A.; Flory, Janine D.; et al. (1999). Effects of optimism, pessimism, and trait anxiety on ambulatory blood pressure and mood during everyday life. *Journal of Personality and Social Psychology, 76*, 104–113.

Raine, Adrian (1996). Autonomic nervous system factors underlying disinhibited, antisocial, and violent behavior. Biosocial perspectives and treatment implications. *Annals of the New York Academy of Sciences, 794*, 46–59.

Raine, Adrian; Brennan, Patricia; & Mednick, Sarnoff A. (1994). Birth complications combined with early maternal rejection at age one year predispose to violent crime at age 18 years. *Archives of General Psychiatry, 51*, 984–988.

Raine, Adrian; Meloy, J. R.; Bihrle, S.; et al. (1998). Reduced prefrontal and increased subcortical brain functioning assessed using positron emission tomography in predatory and affective murderers. *Behavioral Science and Law, 16*, 319–332.

Ramey, Craig T., & Ramey, Sharon L. (1998). Early intervention and early experience. *American Psychologist, 53*, 109–120.

Ranseen, John D. (1998). Lawyers with ADHD: The special test accommodation controversy. *Professional Psychology: Research and Practice, 29*, 450–459.

Ratcliffe, Heather (2000, January 28). Midwest UFO sightings get once-over from scientists. *Detroit News*, Religion Section [online version].

Rathbun, Constance; DiVirgilio, Letitia; & Waldfogel, Samuel (1958). A restitutive process in children following radical separation from family and culture. *American Journal of Orthopsychiatry, 28*, 408–415.

Ravussin, Eric; Lillioja, Stephen; Knowler, William; et al. (1988). Reduced rate of energy expenditure as a risk factor for body-weight gain. *New England Journal of Medicine, 318*, 467–472.

Ravussin, Eric; Pratley, R. E.; Maffei, M.; et al. (1997). Relatively low plasma leptin concentrations precede weight gain in Pima Indians. *Nature Medicine, 3*, 238–240.

Redd, W. H.; Dadds, M. R.; Futterman, A. D.; et al. (1993). Nausea induced by mental images of chemotherapy. *Cancer, 72*, 629–636.

Redelmeier, Donald A., & Tversky, Amos (1996). On the belief that arthritis pain is related to the weather. *Proceedings of the National Academy of Sciences, 93*, 2895–2896.

Reed, Geoffrey M. (1990). Stress, coping, and psychological adaptation in a sample of gay and bisexual men with AIDS. Unpublished doctoral dissertation, University of California, Los Angeles.

Reedy, F. E.; Bartoshuk, L. M.; Miller, I. J.; et al. (1993). Relationships among papillae, taste pores, and 6-n-propylthiouracil (PROP) suprathreshold taste sensitivity. *Chemical Senses, 18*, 618–619.

Regier, Darrel A.; Narrow, William E.; Rae, Donald S.; et al. (1993). The de facto US mental and addictive disorders service system: Epidemiologic Catchment Area prospective 1-year prevalence rates of disorders and services. *Archives of General Psychiatry, 50*, 85–94.

Reich, Theodore; Edenberg, Howard J.; Goate, Alison; et al. (1998, May 8). Genome-wide search for genes affecting the risk for alcohol dependence. *American Journal of Medical Genetics, 81*, 207–215.

Rescorla, Robert A. (1988). Pavlovian conditioning: It's not what you think it is. *American Psychologist, 43*, 151–160.

Reuter-Lorenz, Patricia A.; Jonides, John; Smith, Edward E.; et al. (2000). Age differences in the frontal lateralization of verbal and spatial working memory revealed by PET. *Journal of Cognitive Neuroscience, 12*, 174–187.

Reuter-Lorenz, Patricia A.; Stanczak, Louise; & Miller, Andrea C. (1999). Neural recruitment and cognitive aging: Two hemispheres are better than one, especially as you age. *Psychological Science, 10*, 494–500.

Reynolds, Brent A., & Weiss, Samuel (1992). Generation of neurons and astrocytes from isolated cells of the adult mammalian central nervous system. *Science, 255*, 1707–1710.

Reynolds, Meredith A. (1998). Childhood sexual play games. Paper presented at the annual meeting of the American Psychological Association, San Francisco.

Rice, George; Anderson, Carol; Risch, Neil; & Ebers, George (1999, April 23). Male homosexuality: Absence of linkage to microsatellite markers at Xq28. *Science, 284*, 665–667.

Richards, Ruth L. (1991). Everyday creativity and the arts. Paper presented at the annual meeting of the American Psychological Association, San Francisco.

Richardson-Klavehn, Alan, & Bjork, Robert A. (1988). Measures of memory. *Annual Review of Psychology, 39*, 475–543.

Ridley-Johnson, Robyn; Cooper, Harris; & Chance, June (1983). The relation of children's television viewing to school achievement and I.Q. *Journal of Educational Research, 76*, 294–297.

Rind, Bruce, & Tromovitch, Philip (1997). A meta-analytic review of findings from national samples on psychological correlates of child sexual abuse. *Journal of Sex Research, 34*, 237–255.

Rind, Bruce; Tromovitch, Philip; & Bauserman, Robert (1998). A meta-analytic examination of assumed properties of child sexual abuse using college samples. *Psychological Bulletin, 124*, 22–53.

Riskind, John H.; Williams, Nathan L.; Gessner, Theodore L.; et al. (2000). The looming maladaptive style: Anxiety, danger, and schematic processing. *Journal of Personality and Social Psychology, 79*, 837–852.

Roberts, John E.; Gotlib, Ian H.; & Kassel, Jon D. (1996). Adult attachment security and symptoms of depression: The mediating roles of dysfunctional attitudes and low self-esteem. *Journal of Personality and Social Psychology, 70*, 310–320.

Roberts, Susan B.; Savage, J.; Coward, W. A.; et al. (1988). Energy expenditure and intake in infants born to lean and overweight mothers. *New England Journal of Medicine, 318*, 461–466.

Robertson, Barbara A. (1995). Creating a disability community. Paper presented at the annual meeting of the American Psychological Association, New York.

Robins, Lee N.; Davis, Darlene H.; & Goodwin, Donald W. (1974). Drug use by U.S. Army enlisted men in Vietnam: A follow-up on their return home. *American Journal of Epidemiology, 99,* 235–249.

Robins, Lee N.; Tipp, Jayson; & Przybeck, Thomas R. (1991). Antisocial personality. In L. N. Robins & D. A. Regier (eds.), *Psychiatric disorders in America.* New York: Free Press.

Robinson, Leslie A.; Berman, Jeffrey S.; & Neimeyer, Robert A. (1990). Psychotherapy for the treatment of depression: A comprehensive review of controlled outcome research. *Psychological Bulletin, 108,* 30–49.

Roe, R. A.; Zinovieva, I. L.; Dienes, E.; & Ten Horn, L. A. (1998). Test of a model of work motivation in the Netherlands, Hungary and Bulgaria. Paper presented at the annual meeting of the International Association for Cross-Cultural Psychology, Bellingham, WA.

Roediger, Henry L. (1990). Implicit memory: Retention without remembering. *American Psychologist, 45,* 1043–1056.

Roediger, Henry L., & McDermott, Kathleen B. (1995). Creating false memories: Remembering words not presented in lists. *Journal of Experimental Psychology; Learning, Memory, & Cognition, 21,* 803–814.

Rogers, Carl (1951). *Client-centered therapy: Its current practice, implications, and theory.* Boston: Houghton Mifflin.

Rogers, Carl (1961). *On becoming a person.* Boston: Houghton Mifflin.

Rogers, Ronald W., & Prentice-Dunn, Steven (1981). Deindividuation and anger-mediated interracial aggression: Unmasking regressive racism. *Journal of Personality and Social Psychology, 41,* 63–73.

Rokeach, Milton, & Ball-Rokeach, Sandra (1989). Stability and change in American value priorities, 1968–1981. *American Psychologist, 44,* 775–784.

Rollin, Henry (ed.) (1980). *Coping with schizophrenia.* London: Burnett.

Rosch, Eleanor H. (1973). Natural categories. *Cognitive Psychology, 4,* 328–350.

Rose, Suzanna; Zand, Debra; & Cini, Marie A. (1993). Lesbian courtship scripts. In E. D. Rothblum & K. A. Brehony (eds.), *Boston marriages.* Amherst: University of Massachusetts Press.

Rosen, Gerald M. (1981). Guidelines for the review of do-it-yourself treatment books. *Contemporary Psychology, 26,* 189–191.

Rosen, R. D. (1977). *Psychobabble.* New York: Atheneum.

Rosenberg, Harold (1993). Prediction of controlled drinking by alcoholics and problem drinkers. *Psychological Bulletin, 113,* 129–139.

Rosenhan, David L. (1973). On being sane in insane places. *Science, 179,* 250–258.

Rosenthal, Robert (1966). *Experimenter effects in behavioral research.* New York: Appleton-Century-Crofts.

Rosenthal, Robert (1994). Interpersonal expectancy effects: A 30-year perspective. *Current Directions in Psychological Science, 3,* 176–179.

Rosenzweig, Mark R. (1984). Experience, memory, and the brain. *American Psychologist, 39,* 365–376.

Ross, Colin (1995). The validity and reliability of dissociative identity disorder. In L. M. Cohen, J. N. Berzoff, & M. R. Elin (eds.), *Dissociative identity disorder: Theoretical and treatment controversies.* Northvale, NJ: Jason Aronson.

Ross, Michael (1989). Relation of implicit theories to the construction of personal histories. *Psychological Review, 96,* 341–357.

Roth, David L., & Holmes, David S. (1985). Influence of physical fitness in determining the impact of stressful life events on physical and psychologic health. *Psychosomatic Medicine, 47,* 164–173.

Rothbaum, Fred; Weisz, John; Pott, Martha; Miyake, Kazuo; & Morelli, Gilda (2000). Attachment and culture: Security in the United States and Japan. *American Psychologist, 55,* 1093–1104.

Rothbaum, Fred M.; Weisz, John R.; & Snyder, Samuel S. (1982). Changing the world and changing the self: A two-process model of perceived control. *Journal of Personality and Social Psychology, 42,* 5–37.

Rotter, Julian B. (1966). Generalized expectancies for internal versus external control of reinforcement. *Psychological Monographs, 80*(Whole No. 609), 1–28.

Rotter, Julian B. (1982). *The development and applications of social learning theory: Selected papers.* New York: Praeger.

Rotter, Julian B. (1990). Internal versus external control of reinforcement: A case history of a variable. *American Psychologist, 45,* 489–493.

Rowe, John W., & Kahn, Robert L. (1998). *Successful aging.* New York: Pantheon.

Rowe, Walter F. (1993, Winter). Psychic detectives: A critical examination. *Skeptical Inquirer, 17,* 159–165.

Roy, Mark P.; Steptoe, Andrew; & Kirschbaum, Clemens (1998). Life events and social support as moderators of individual differences in cardiovascular and cortisol reactivity. *Journal of Personality and Social Psychology, 75,* 1273–1281.

Rubin, Jeffrey Z. (1994). Models of conflict management. *Journal of Social Issues, 50,* 33–45.

Ruggiero, Vincent R. (1988). *Teaching thinking across the curriculum.* New York: Harper & Row.

Ruggiero, Vincent R. (1997). *The art of thinking: A guide to critical and creative thought* (5th ed.). New York: HarperCollins.

Rumbaugh, Duane M. (1977). *Language learning by a chimpanzee: The Lana project.* New York: Academic Press.

Rumbaugh, Duane M.; Savage-Rumbaugh, E. Sue; & Pate, James L. (1988). Addendum to "Summation in the chimpanzee (Pan troglodytes)." *Journal of Experimental Psychology: Animal Behavior Processes, 14,* 118–120.

Rumelhart, David E.; McClelland, James L.; & the PDP Research Group (1986). *Parallel distributed processing: Explorations in the microstructure of cognition* (Vols. 1 and 2). Cambridge, MA: MIT Press.

Rushton, J. Philippe (1988). Race differences in behavior: A review and evolutionary analysis. *Personality and Individual Differences, 9,* 1009–1024.

Russell, Diana E. H. (1990). *Rape in marriage* (rev. ed.). Bloomington: Indiana University Press.

Ryan, Richard M.; Chirkov, Valery I.; Little, Todd D.; et al. (1999). The American dream in Russia: Extrinsic aspirations and well-being in two cultures. *Personality and Social Psychology Bulletin, 25,* 1509–1524.

Ryff, Carol D., & Keyes, Corey L. M. (1995). The structure of psychological well-being revisited. *Journal of Personality and Social Psychology, 69,* 719–727.

Rymer, Russ (1993). *Genie: An abused child's flight from silence.* New York: HarperCollins.

Sack, Robert L., & Lewy, Alfred J. (1997). Melatonin as a chronobiotic: Treatment of circadian desynchrony in night workers and the blind. *Journal of Biological Rhythms, 12,* 595–603.

Sacks, Oliver (1985). *The man who mistook his wife for a hat and other clinical tales.* New York: Simon & Schuster.

Sagan, Eli (1988). *Freud, women, and morality: The psychology of good and evil.* New York: Basic Books.

Sagarin, Brad; Cialdini, Robert B.; & Rice, William E. (1998). Creating critical consumers: Instilling resistance to unethical persuasion. Paper presented at the annual meeting of the American Psychological Association, San Francisco.

Sahley, Christie L.; Rudy, Jerry W.; & Gelperin, Alan (1981). An analysis of associative learning in a terrestrial mollusk: I. Higher-order conditioning, blocking, and a transient US preexposure effect. *Journal of Comparative Physiology, 144,* 1–8.

Salthouse, Timothy A. (1998). The what and where of cognitive aging. Address presented at the annual meeting of the American Psychological Association, San Francisco.

Samelson, Franz (1979). Putting psychology on the map: Ideology and intelligence testing. In A. R. Buss (ed.), *Psychology in social context.* New York: Irvington.

Sameroff, Arnold J.; Seifer, Ronald; Barocas, Ralph; et al. (1987). Intelligence quotient scores of 4-year-old children: Social-environmental risk factors. *Pediatrics, 79,* 343–350.

Sapolsky, Robert M. (1997). *The trouble with testosterone: And other essays on the biology of the human predicament.* New York: Touchstone.

Sapolsky, Robert M. (1998, March/April). Is biology destiny? *Family Therapy Networker, 22,* 33–35.

Savage-Rumbaugh, Sue, & Lewin, Roger (1994). *Kanzi: The ape at the brink of the human mind.* New York: Wiley.

Savage-Rumbaugh, Sue; Shanker, Stuart; & Taylor, Talbot (1998). *Apes, language and the human mind.* New York: Oxford University Press.

Scarr, Sandra (1993). Biological and cultural diversity: The legacy of Darwin for development. *Child Development, 64,* 1333–1353.

Scarr, Sandra; Pakstis, Andrew J.; Katz, Soloman H.; & Barker, William B. (1977). Absence of a relationship between degree of white ancestry and intellectual skill in a black population. *Human Genetics, 39,* 69–86.

Scarr, Sandra, & Weinberg, Robert A. (1994). Educational and occupational achievement of brothers and sisters in adoptive and biologically related families. *Behavioral Genetics, 24,* 301–325.

Schachter, Stanley (1959). *The psychology of affiliation.* Stanford, CA: Stanford University Press.

Schachter, Stanley, & Singer, Jerome E. (1962). Cognitive, social, and physiological determinants of emotional state. *Psychological Review, 69,* 379–399.

Schacter, Daniel L. (1996). *Searching for memory: The brain, the mind, and the past.* New York: Basic Books.

Schacter, Daniel L.; Chiu, C.-Y. Peter; & Ochsner, Kevin N. (1993). Implicit memory: A selective review. *Annual Review of Neuroscience, 16,* 159–182.

Schaie, K. Warner (1993). The Seattle longitudinal studies of adult intelligence. *Current Directions in Psychological Science, 2,* 171–175.

Schaie, K. Warner (1994). The course of adult intellectual development. *American Psychologist, 49,* 304–313.

Schank, Roger C., with Peter Childers (1988). *The creative attitude.* New York: Macmillan.

Schein, Edgar; Schneier, Inge; & Barker, Curtis H. (1961). *Coercive persuasion.* New York: Norton.

Scherer, Klaus R. (1997). The role of culture in emotion-antecedent appraisal. *Journal of Personality and Social Psychology, 73,* 902–922.

Schlossberg, Nancy K. (1984). Exploring the adult years. In A. M. Rogers & C. J. Scheirer (eds.), *The G. Stanley Hall Lecture Series* (Vol. 4). Washington, DC: American Psychological Association.

Schlossberg, Nancy K., & Robinson, Susan P. (1996). *Going to plan B.* New York: Simon & Schuster/Fireside.

Schmelz, M.; Schmidt, R.; Bickel, A.; et al. (1997). Specific C-receptors for itch in human skin. *Journal of Neuroscience, 17,* 8003–8008.

Schmolck, H.; Buffalo, E. A.; & Squire, L. R. (2000). Memory distortions develop over time: Recollections of the O. J. Simpson trial verdict after 15 and 32 months. *Psychological Science, 11,* 39–45.

Schneider, Allen M., & Tarshis, Barry (1986). *An introduction to physiological psychology* (3rd ed.). New York: Random House.

Schneider, Edward L. (1999, February 5). Aging in the third millennium. *Science, 283,* 796–797.

Schnell, Lisa, & Schwab, Martin E. (1990, January 18). Axonal regeneration in the rat spinal cord produced by an antibody against myelin-associated neurite growth inhibitors. *Nature, 343,* 269–272.

Schuckit, Marc A. (1998). Relationship among genetic, environmental, and psychological variables in predicting alcoholism. Invited address presented at the annual meeting of the American Psychological Association, San Francisco.

Schuckit, Marc A., & Smith, T. L. (1996). An 8-year follow-up of 450 sons of alcoholic and control subjects. *Archives of General Psychiatry, 53,* 202–210.

Schulkin, Jay (1994). Melancholic depression and the hormones of adversity: A role for the amygdala. *Current Directions in Psychological Science, 3,* 41–44.

Schulman, Michael, & Mekler, Eva (1994). *Bringing up a caring child* (rev. ed.). New York: Doubleday.

Schulz, Richard, & Decker, Susan (1985). Long-term adjustment to physical disability: The role of social support, perceived control, and self-blame. *Journal of Personality and Social Psychology, 48,* 1162–1172.

Schuman, Howard, & Scott, Jacqueline (1989). Generations and collective memories. *American Journal of Sociology, 54,* 359–381.

Schwartz, Jeffrey; Stoessel, Paula W.; Baxter, Lewis R.; et al. (1996). Systematic changes in cerebral glucose metabolic rate after successful behavior modification treatment of obsessive-compulsive disorder. *Archives of General Psychiatry, 53,* 109–113.

Scofield, Michael (1993, June 6). About men: Off the ladder. *New York Times Magazine,* 22.

Sears, Pauline, & Barbee, Ann H. (1977). Career and life satisfactions among Terman's gifted women. In J. C. Stanley, W. C. George, & C. H. Solano (eds.), *The gifted and the creative: A fifty-year perspective.* Baltimore, MD: Johns Hopkins University Press.

Seeman, Philip; Guan, Hong-chang; & Van Tol, Hubert H. (1993). Dopamine D4 receptors elevated in schizophrenia. *Nature, 365,* 441–445.

Segal, Julius (1986). *Winning life's toughest battles.* New York: McGraw-Hill.

Segall, Marshall H. (1994). A cross-cultural research contribution to unraveling the nativist/empiricist controversy. In W. J. Lonner & R. Malpass (eds.), *Psychology and culture.* Needham Heights, MA: Allyn & Bacon.

Segall, Marshall H.; Campbell, Donald T.; & Herskovits, Melville J. (1966). *The influence of culture on visual perception.* Indianapolis: Bobbs-Merrill.

Segall, Marshall H.; Dasen, Pierre R.; Berry, John W.; & Poortinga, Ype H. (1999). *Human behavior in global perspective: An introduction to cross-cultural psychology* (2nd ed.). Boston, MA: Allyn & Bacon.

Segerstrom, Suzanne C.; Taylor, Shelley E.; Kemeny, Margaret E.; & Fahey, John L. (1998). Optimism is associated with mood, coping, and immune change in response to stress. *Journal of Personality and Social Psychology, 74,* 1646–1655.

Seiden, Richard (1978). Where are they now? A follow-up study of suicide attempters from the Golden Gate Bridge. *Suicide and Life-Threatening Behavior, 8,* 203–216.

Seidenberg, Mark S., & Petitto, Laura A. (1979). Signing behavior in apes: A critical review. *Cognition, 7,* 177–215.

Sekuler, Robert, & Blake, Randolph (1994). *Perception* (3rd ed.). New York: Knopf.

Seligman, Martin E. P. (1975). *Helplessness: On depression, development, and death.* San Francisco: W. H. Freeman.

Seligman, Martin E. P. (1991). *Learned optimism.* New York: Knopf.

Seligman, Martin E. P., & Hager, Joanne L. (1972, August). Biological boundaries of learning: The sauce-béarnaise syndrome. *Psychology Today,* 59–61, 84–87.

Seligman, Martin E. P.; Schulman, Peter; DeRubeis, Robert J.; & Hollon, Steven D. (1998). The prevention of depression and anxiety. Paper presented at the annual meeting of the American Psychological Association, San Francisco.

Selye, Hans (1956). *The stress of life.* New York: McGraw-Hill.

Serbin, Lisa A.; Powlishta, Kimberly K.; & Gulko, Judith (1993). The development of sex typing in middle childhood. *Monographs of the Society for Research in Child Development, 58*(2, Serial No. 232), v–74.

Serpell, Robert (1994). The cultural construction of intelligence. In W. J. Lonner & R. S. Malpass (eds.), *Psychology and culture.* Needham Heights, MA: Allyn & Bacon.

Shapiro, Deane H.; Schwartz, Carolyn E.; & Astin, John A. (1996). Controlling ourselves, controlling our world. *American Psychologist, 51,* 1213–1230.

Shatz, Marilyn, & Gelman, Rochel (1973). The development of communication skills: Modifications in the speech of young children as a function of the listener. *Monographs of the Society for Research in Child Development, 38.*

Shaver, Phillip R., & Hazan, Cindy (1993). Adult romantic attachment: Theory and evidence. In D. Perlman & W. H. Jones (eds.), *Advances in personal relationships* (Vol. 4). London: Kingsley.

Shaw, Daniel S.; Keenan, Kate; & Vondra, Joan I. (1994). Developmental precursors of externalizing behavior: Ages 1 to 3. *Developmental Psychology, 30,* 355–364.

Shaywitz, Bennett A.; Shaywitz, Sally E.; Pugh, Kenneth R.; et al. (1995). Sex differences in the functional organization of the brain for language. *Nature, 373,* 607–609.

Shepard, Roger N., & Metzler, Jacqueline (1971). Mental rotation of three-dimensional objects. *Science, 171,* 701–703.

Shepperd, James A. (1995). Remedying motivation and productivity loss in collective settings. *Current Directions in Psychological Science, 4,* 131–140.

Sherif, Muzafer (1958). Superordinate goals in the reduction of intergroup conflicts. *American Journal of Sociology, 63,* 349–356.

Sherif, Muzafer; Harvey, O. J.; White, B. J.; Hood, William; & Sherif, Carolyn (1961). *Intergroup conflict and cooperation: The Robbers Cave experiment.* Norman, OK: University of Oklahoma Institute of Intergroup Relations.

Sherman, Bonnie R., & Kunda, Ziva (1989). Motivated evaluation of scientific evidence. Paper presented at the annual meeting of the American Psychological Society, Arlington, VA.

Sherman, Jeffrey W., & Bessenoff, Gayle R. (1999). Stereotypes as source-monitoring cues: On the interaction between episodic and semantic memory. *Psychological Science, 10,* 106–110.

Shermer, Michael (1997). *Why people believe weird things: Pseudoscience, superstition, and other confusions of our time.* New York: W. H. Freeman.

Sherwin, Barbara B. (1998a). Estrogen and cognitive functioning in women. *Proceedings of the Society for Experimental Biological Medicine, 217,* 17–22.

Sherwin, Barbara B. (1998b). Use of combined estrogen-androgen preparations in the postmenopause: Evidence from clinical studies. *International Journal of Fertility & Women's Medicine, 43,* 98–103.

Shields, Stephanie A. (1975). Functionalism, Darwinism, and the psychology of women: A study in social myth. *American Psychologist, 30,* 739–754.

Shields, Stephanie A. (1991). Gender in the psychology of emotion: A selective research review. In K. T. Strongman (ed.), *International review of studies on emotion* (Vol. 1). New York: Wiley.

Showalter, Elaine (1997). *Hystories: Hysterical epidemics and modern culture.* New York: Columbia University Press.

Shweder, Richard A.; Mahapatra, Manamohan; & Miller, Joan G. (1990). Culture and moral development. In J. W. Stigler, R. A. Shweder, & G. Herdt (eds.), *Cultural psychology: Essays on comparative human development.* Cambridge, England: Cambridge University Press.

Sidanius, Jim; Pratto, Felicia; & Bobo, Lawrence (1996). Racism, conservatism, affirmative action, and intellectual sophistication: A matter of principled conservatism or group dominance? *Journal of Personality and Social Psychology, 70,* 476–490.

Siegler, Robert (1996). *Emerging minds: The process of change in children's thinking.* New York: Oxford University Press.

Silver, Eric; Cirincione, Carmen; & Steadman, Henry J. (1994). Demythologizing inaccurate perceptions of the insanity defense. *Law and Human Behavior, 18,* 63–70.

Silverstein, Brett, & Perlick, Deborah (1995). *The cost of competence: Why inequality causes depression, eating disorders, and illness in women.* New York: Oxford University Press.

Silverstein, Brett; Peterson, Barbara; & Perdue, Lauren (1986). Some correlates of the thin standard of bodily attractiveness in women. *International Journal of Eating Disorders, 5,* 145–155.

Sims, Ethan A. (1974). Studies in human hyperphagia. In G. Bray & J. Bethune (eds.), *Treatment and management of obesity.* New York: Harper & Row.

Sinclair, Lisa, & Kunda, Ziva (1999). Reactions to a Black professional: Motivated inhibition and activation of conflicting stereotypes. *Journal of Personality and Social Psychology, 77,* 885–904.

Sinclair, Robert C.; Hoffman, Curt; Mark, Melvin M.; et al. (1994). Construct accessibility and the misattribution of arousal: Schachter and Singer revisited. *Psychological Science, 5,* 15–19.

Singer, Jerome L. (1984). The private personality. *Personality and Social Psychology Bulletin, 10,* 7–30.

Singer, Margaret T.; Temerlin, Maurice K.; & Langone, Michael D. (1990). Psychotherapy cults. *Cultic Studies Journal, 7,* 101–125.

Skinner, B. F. (1938). *The behavior of organisms: An experimental analysis.* New York: Appleton-Century-Crofts.

Skinner, B. F. (1948). Superstition in the pigeon. *Journal of Experimental Psychology, 38,* 168–172.

Skinner, B. F. (1948/1976). *Walden two.* New York: Macmillan.

Skinner, B. F. (1956). A case history in the scientific method. *American Psychologist, 11,* 221–233.

Skinner, B. F. (1972). The operational analysis of psychological terms. In B. F. Skinner, *Cumulative record* (3rd ed.). New York: Appleton-Century-Crofts.

Skinner, B. F. (1990). Can psychology be a science of mind? *American Psychologist, 45,* 1206–1210.

Skinner, Ellen A. (1996). A guide to constructs of control. *Journal of Personality and Social Psychology, 71,* 549–570.

Skinner, J. B.; Erskine, A.; Pearce, S. A.; et al. (1990). The evaluation of a cognitive behavioural treatment programme in outpatients with chronic pain. *Journal of Psychosomatic Research, 34,* 13–19.

Skreslet, Paula (1987, November 30). The prizes of first grade. *Newsweek,* 8.

Slavin, Robert E., & Cooper, Robert (1999). Improving intergroup relations: Lessons learned from cooperative learning programs. *Journal of Social Issues, 55,* 647–663.

Slotkin, Theodore A. (1998). Fetal nicotine or cocaine exposure: Which one is worse? *Journal of Pharmacology and Experimental Therapeutics, 285,* 931–945.

Smith, Carolyn A.; Lizotte, Alan J.; Thornberry, Terence P.; et al. (1997). Resilient youth: Identifying factors that prevent high-risk youth from engaging in delinquency and drug use. In J. Hagan (ed.), *Delinquency and disrepute in the life course.* Greenwich, CT: JAI Press.

Smith, David N. (1998). The psychocultural roots of genocide: Legitimacy and crisis in Rwanda. *American Psychologist, 53,* 743–753.

Smith, James F., & Kida, Thomas (1991). Heuristics and biases: Expertise and task realism in auditing. *Psychological Bulletin, 109,* 472–489.

Smith, Larissa L., & Reise, Steven P. (1998). Gender differences on negative affectivity: An IRT study of differential item functioning on the Multidimensional Personality Questionnaire Stress Reaction Scale. *Journal of Personality and Social Psychology, 75,* 1350–1362.

Smith, Peter B., & Bond, Michael H. (1994). *Social psychology across cultures: Analysis and perspectives.* Boston: Allyn & Bacon.

Smither, Robert D. (1998). *The psychology of work and human performance* (3rd ed.). New York: Longman.

Smyth, Joshua M., & Pennebaker, James W. (1999). Sharing one's story: Translating emotional experiences into words as a coping tool. In C. R. Snyder (ed.), *Coping: The psychology of what works.* New York: Oxford University Press.

Snow, Barry R.; Pinter, Isaac; Gusmorino, Paul; et al. (1986). Sex differences in chronic pain: Incidence and causal mechanisms. Paper presented at the annual meeting of the American Psychological Association, Washington, DC.

Snowdon, Charles T. (1997). The "nature" of sex differences: Myths of male and female. In P. A. Gowaty (ed.), *Feminism and evolutionary biology.* New York: Chapman and Hall.

Snyder, C. R., & Shenkel, Randee J. (1975, March). The P. T. Barnum effect. *Psychology Today,* 52–54.

Snyder, James J., & Patterson, Gerald R. (1995). Individual differences in social aggression: A test of a reinforcer model of socialization in the natural environment. *Behavior Therapy, 26,* 371–391.

Solomon, Jennifer C. (1996). Humor and aging well: A laughing matter or a matter of laughing? *American Behavioral Scientist, 39,* 249–271.

Solomon, Paul R. (1979). Science and television commercials: Adding relevance to the research methodology course. *Teaching of Psychology, 6,* 26–30.

Solomon, Robert C. (1994). *About love.* Lanham, MD: Littlefield Adams.

Sommer, Robert (1969). *Personal space: The behavioral basis of design.* Englewood Cliffs, NJ: Prentice-Hall.

Sorce, James F.; Emde, Robert N.; Campos, Joseph; & Klinnert, Mary D. (1985). Maternal emotional signaling: Its effect on the visual cliff behavior of 1-year-olds. *Developmental Psychology, 21,* 195–200.

Spanos, Nicholas P. (1996). *Multiple identities and false memories: A sociocognitive perspective.* Washington, DC: American Psychological Association.

Spanos, Nicholas P.; Menary, Evelyn; Gabora, Natalie J.; et al. (1991). Secondary identity enactments during hypnotic past-life regression: A sociocognitive perspective. *Journal of Personality and Social Psychology, 61,* 308–320.

Spearman, Charles (1927). *The abilities of man.* London: Macmillan.

Spence, Janet T. (1985). Gender identity and its implications for concepts of masculinity and femininity. In T. Sonderegger (ed.), *Nebraska Symposium on Motivation, 1984.* Lincoln, NE: University of Nebraska Press.

Spencer, M. B., & Dornbusch, Sanford M. (1990). Ethnicity. In S. S. Feldman & G. R. Elliott (eds.), *At the threshold: The developing adolescent.* Cambridge, MA: Harvard University Press.

Sperling, George (1960). The information available in brief visual presentations. *Psychological Monographs, 74*(Whole No. 498).

Sperry, Roger W. (1964). The great cerebral commissure. *Scientific American, 210*(1), 42–52.

Sperry, Roger W. (1982). Some effects of disconnecting the cerebral hemispheres. *Science, 217,* 1223–1226.

Spilich, George J.; June, Lorraine; & Renner, Judith (1992). Cigarette smoking and cognitive performance. *British Journal of Addiction, 87,* 113–126.

Spitz, Herman H. (1997). *Nonconscious movements: From mystical messages to facilitated communication.* Mahwah, NJ: Erlbaum.

Spitzer, Robert L., & Williams, Janet B. (1988). Having a dream: A research strategy for DSM-IV. *Archives of General Psychiatry, 45,* 871–874.

Spoont, Michele R. (1992). Modulatory role of serotonin in neural information processing: Implications for human psychopathology. *Psychological Bulletin, 112,* 330–350.

Sporer, Siegfried L.; Penrod, Steven; Read, Don; & Cutler, Brian (1995). Choosing, confidence, and accuracy: A meta-analysis of the confidence-accuracy relation in eyewitness identification studies. *Psychological Bulletin, 118,* 315–327.

Sprecher, Susan; Sullivan, Quintin; & Hatfield, Elaine (1994). Mate selection preferences: Gender differences examined in a national sample. *Journal of Personality and Social Psychology, 66,* 1074–1080.

Spring, Bonnie; Chiodo, June; & Bowen, Deborah J. (1987). Carbohydrates, tryptophan, and behavior: A methodological review. *Psychological Bulletin, 102,* 234–256.

Springer, S. P., & Deutsch, G. (1998). *Left brain, right brain: Perspective from cognitive neuroscience.* New York: W. H. Freeman.

Squier, Leslie H., & Domhoff, G. William (1998). The presentation of dreaming and dreams in introductory psychology textbooks: A critical examination with suggestions for textbook authors and course instructors. *Dreaming, 8,* 149–168.

Squire, Larry R. (1987). *Memory and the brain.* New York: Oxford University Press.

Squire, Larry R., & Zola-Morgan, Stuart (1991). The medial temporal lobe memory system. *Science, 253,* 1380–1386.

Staats, Carolyn K., & Staats, Arthur W. (1957). Meaning established by classical conditioning. *Journal of Experimental Psychology, 54,* 74–80.

Stajkovic, Alexander D., & Luthans, Fred (1998). Self-efficacy and work-related performance: A meta-analysis. *Psychological Bulletin, 124,* 240–261.

Stanovich, Keith (1996). *How to think straight about psychology* (4th ed.). New York: HarperCollins.

Stanton, Annette L., & Franz, Robert (1999). Focusing on emotion: An adaptive coping strategy? In C. R. Snyder (ed.), *Coping: The psychology of what works.* New York: Oxford University Press.

Staples, Brent (1994). *Parallel time.* New York: Pantheon.

Staples, Susan L. (1996). Human response to environmental noise: Psychological research and public policy. *American Psychologist, 51,* 143–150.

Stattin, Haken, & Magnusson, David (1990). *Pubertal maturation in female development.* Hillsdale, NJ: Erlbaum.

Staub, Ervin (1996). Cultural-social roots of violence. *American Psychologist, 51,* 117–132.

Staub, Ervin (1999). The roots of evil: Social conditions, culture, personality, and basic human needs. *Personality and Social Psychology Review, 3,* 179–192.

Stearns, Peter N. (1997). *Fat history: Bodies and beauty in the modern West.* New York: New York University Press.

Steele, Claude M. (1992, April). Race and the schooling of Black Americans. *Atlantic Monthly,* 68–78.

Steele, Claude M. (1997). A threat in the air: How stereotypes shape intellectual identity and performance. *American Psychologist, 52,* 613–629.

Steele, Claude M., & Aronson, Joshua (1995). Stereotype threat and the intellectual test performance of African-Americans. *Journal of Personality and Social Psychology, 69,* 797–811.

Steinberg, Laurence D. (1990). Interdependence in the family: Autonomy, conflict and harmony in the parent-adolescent relationship. In S. S. Feldman & G. R. Elliott (eds.), *At the threshold: The developing adolescent.* Cambridge, MA: Harvard University Press.

Steinberg, Laurence D.; Dornbusch, Sanford M.; & Brown, B. Bradford (1992). Ethnic differences in adolescent achievement: An ecological perspective. *American Psychologist, 47,* 723–729.

Stenberg, Craig R., & Campos, Joseph (1990). The development of anger expressions in infancy. In N. Stein, B. Leventhal, & T. Trabasso (eds.), *Psychological and biological approaches to emotion.* Hillsdale, NJ: Erlbaum.

Stephan, K. M.; Fink, G. R.; Passingham, R. E.; et al. (1995). Functional anatomy of the mental representation of upper movements in healthy subjects. *Journal of Neurophysiology, 73,* 373–386.

Stephan, Walter G. (1999). *Reducing prejudice and stereotyping in schools.* New York: Teachers College Press.

Stephan, Walter G.; Ageyev, Vladimir; Coates-Shrider, Lisa; et al. (1994). On the relationship between stereotypes and prejudice: An international study. *Personality and Social Psychology Bulletin, 20,* 277–284.

Stephens, Mitchell (1991, September 20). The death of reading. *Los Angeles Times Magazine,* 10, 12, 16, 42, 44.

Stern, Marilyn, & Karraker, Katherine H. (1989). Sex stereotyping of infants: A review of gender labeling studies. *Sex Roles, 20,* 501–522.

Sternberg, Robert J. (1988). *The triarchic mind: A new theory of human intelligence.* New York: Viking.

Sternberg, Robert J. (1995). *In search of the human mind.* Orlando, FL: Harcourt Brace.

Sternberg, Robert J. (1997). Construct validation of a triangular love scale. *European Journal of Social Psychology, 27,* 313–335.

Sternberg, Robert J., & Wagner, Richard K. (1989). Individual differences in practical knowledge and its acquisition. In P. Ackerman, R. J. Sternberg, & R. Glaser (eds.), *Individual differences.* New York: W. H. Freeman.

Sternberg, Robert J.; Wagner, Richard K.; & Okagaki, Lynn (1993). Practical intelligence: The nature and role of tacit knowledge in work and at school. In H. Reese & J. Puckett (eds.), *Advances in lifespan development.* Hillsdale, NJ: Erlbaum.

Sternberg, Robert J.; Wagner, Richard K.; Williams, Wendy M.; & Horvath, Joseph A. (1995). Testing common sense. *American Psychologist, 50,* 912–927.

Sternberg, Robert J., & Williams, Wendy M. (1997). Does the GRE predict meaningful success in the graduate training of psychologists? A case study. *American Psychologist, 52,* 630–641.

Stevenson, Harold W.; Chen, Chuansheng; & Lee, Shin-ying (1993, January 1). Mathematics achievement of Chinese, Japanese, and American children: Ten years later. *Science, 259,* 53–58.

Stevenson, Harold W., & Stigler, James W. (1992). *The learning gap.* New York: Summit.

Stewart, Abigail J., & Ostrove, Joan M. (1998). Women's personality in middle age: Gender, history, and midcourse corrections. *American Psychologist, 53,* 1185–1194.

Stewart, Abigail J., & Vandewater, Elizabeth A. (1999). "If I had it to do over again . . . ": Midlife review, midcourse corrections, and women's well-being in midlife. *Journal of Personality and Social Psychology, 76,* 270–283.

Stoch, M. B., & Smythe, P. M. (1963). Does undernutrition during infancy inhibit brain growth and subsequent intellectual development? *Archives of Diseases in Childhood, 38,* 546–552.

Straus, Murray A., & Kantor, Glenda Kaufman (1994). Corporal punishment of adolescents by parents: A risk factor in the epidemiology of depression, suicide, alcohol abuse, child abuse, and wife beating. *Adolescence, 29,* 543–561.

Streissguth, Ann P.; Barr, Helen M.; Bookstein, Fred L.; et al. (1999). The long-term neurocognitive consequences of prenatal alcohol exposure: A 14-year study. *Psychological Science, 10,* 186–190.

Strickland, Bonnie R. (1989). Internal-external control expectancies: From contingency to creativity. *American Psychologist, 44,* 1–12.

Strickland, Bonnie R. (1995). Research on sexual orientation and human development: A commentary. *Developmental Psychology, 31,* 137–140.

Strickland, Tony L.; Lin, Keh-Ming; Fu, Paul; et al. (1995). Comparison of lithium ratio between African-American and Caucasian bipolar patients. *Biological Psychiatry, 37,* 325–330.

Strickland, Tony L.; Ranganath, Vijay; Lin, Keh-Ming; et al. (1991). Psychopharmacological considerations in the treatment of black American populations. *Psychopharmacology Bulletin, 27,* 441–448.

Stroebe, Wolfgang; Stroebe, Margaret; Abakoumkin, Georgios; & Schut, Henk (1996). The role of loneliness and social support in adjustment to loss: A test of attachment versus stress theory. *Journal of Personality and Social Psychology, 70,* 1241–1249.

Strupp, Hans H., & Binder, Jeffrey (1984). *Psychotherapy in a new key.* New York: Basic Books.

Stunkard, Albert J. (ed.) (1980). *Obesity.* Philadelphia: Saunders.

Stunkard, Albert J.; Harris, J. R.; Pedersen, N. L.; & McClearn, G. E. (1990, May 24). The body-mass index of twins who have been reared apart. *New England Journal of Medicine, 322,* 1483–1487.

Sue, Stanley (1998). In search of cultural competence in psychotherapy and counseling. *American Psychologist, 53,* 440–448.

Suedfeld, Peter (1975). The benefits of boredom: Sensory deprivation reconsidered. *American Scientist, 63*(1), 60–69.

Sullivan, Michael J. L.; Tripp, Dean A.; & Santor, Darcy (1998). Gender differences in pain and pain behaviour: The role of catastrophizing. Paper presented at the annual meeting of the American Psychological Association, San Francisco.

Sulloway, Frank J. (1992). *Freud, biologist of the mind: Beyond the psychoanalytic legend* (rev. ed.). Cambridge, MA: Harvard University Press.

Sundquist, J., & Winkleby, M. (2000, June). Country of birth, acculturation status and abdominal obesity in a national sample of Mexican-American women and men. *International Journal of Epidemiology, 29,* 470–477.

Suomi, Stephen J. (1987). Genetic and maternal contributions to individual differences in rhesus monkey biobehavioral development. In N. Krasnegor, E. Blass, M. Hofer, & W. Smotherman (eds.), *Perinatal development: A psychobiological perspective.* New York: Academic Press.

Suomi, Stephen J. (1991). Uptight and laid-back monkeys: Individual differences in the response to social challenges. In S. Branch, W. Hall, & J. E. Dooling (eds.), *Plasticity of development.* Cambridge, MA: MIT Press.

Super, Charles A., & Harkness, Sara (1994). The developmental niche. In W. J. Lonner & R. Malpass (eds.), *Psychology and culture.* Needham Heights, MA: Allyn & Bacon.

Susser, Ezra; Neugebauer, Richard; Hoek, Hans W.; et al. (1996). Schizophrenia after prenatal famine: Further evidence. *Archives of General Psychiatry, 53,* 25–31.

Swain, Scott (1989). Covert intimacy: Closeness in men's friendships. In B. J. Risman & P. Schwartz (eds.), *Gender in intimate relationships.* Belmont, CA: Wadsworth.

Taffel, Ronald (1990, September/October). The politics of mood. *Family Therapy Networker,* 49–53, 72.

Tajfel, Henri; Billig, M. G.; Bundy, R. P.; & Flament, C. (1971). Social categorization and intergroup behavior. *European Journal of Social Psychology, 1,* 149–178.

Tajfel, Henri, & Turner, John C. (1986). The social identity theory of intergroup behavior. In S. Worchel & W. G. Austin (eds.), *Psychology of intergroup relations.* Chicago: Nelson-Hall.

Tangney, June P.; Wagner, Patricia E.; Hill-Barlow, Deborah; et al. (1996). Relation of shame and guilt to constructive versus destructive responses to anger across the lifespan. *Journal of Personality and Social Psychology, 70,* 797–809.

Taub, David M. (1984). *Primate paternalism.* New York: Van Nostrand Reinhold.

Taubes, Gary (1998). As obesity rates rise, experts struggle to explain why. *Science, 280,* 1367–1368.

Tavris, Carol (1989). *Anger: The misunderstood emotion* (rev. ed.). New York: Simon & Schuster/Touchstone.

Taylor, Donald M., & Porter, Lana E. (1994). A multicultural view of stereotyping. In W. J. Lonner & R. Malpass (eds.), *Psychology and culture.* Needham Heights, MA: Allyn & Bacon.

Taylor, Shelley E.; Kemeny, Margaret E.; Reed, Geoffrey; et al. (2000). Psychological resources, positive illusions, and health. *American Psychologist, 55,* 99–109.

Taylor, Shelley E.; Lichtman, Rosemary R.; & Wood, Joanne V. (1984). Attributions, beliefs about control, and adjustment to breast cancer. *Journal of Personality and Social Psychology, 46,* 489–502.

Taylor, Shelley E., & Lobel, Marci (1989). Social comparison activity under threat: Downward evaluation and upward contacts. *Psychological Review, 96,* 569–575.

Taylor, Shelley E.; Repetti, Rena; & Seeman, Teresa (1997). Health psychology: What is an unhealthy environment and how does it get under the skin? *Annual Review of Psychology* (Vol. 48). Palo Alto, CA: Annual Reviews.

Temerlin, Jane W., & Temerlin, Maurice K. (1986). Some hazards of the therapeutic relationship. *Cultic Studies Journal, 3,* 234–242.

Terman, Lewis M., & Oden, Melita H. (1959). *Genetic studies of genius: Vol. 5. The gifted group at mid-life.* Stanford, CA: Stanford University Press.

Terrace, H. S. (1985). In the beginning was the "name." *American Psychologist, 40,* 1011–1028.

Thase, Michael E.; Fasiczka, A. L.; Berman, S. R.; et al. (1998). Electroencephalographic sleep profiles before and after cognitive behavior therapy of depression. *Archives of General Psychiatry, 55,* 138–144.

Thase, Michael E.; Greenhouse, J. B.; Frank, E.; et al. (1997). Treatment of major depression with psychotherapy or psychotherapy-pharmacotherapy combinations. *Archives of General Psychiatry, 54,* 1009–1015.

Thigpen, Corbett H., & Cleckley, Hervey M. (1984). On the incidence of multiple personality disorder: A brief communication. *International Journal of Clinical and Experimental Hypnosis, 32,* 63–66.

Thoma, Stephen J. (1986). Estimating gender differences in the comprehension and preference of moral issues. *Developmental Review, 6,* 165–180.

Thomassen, R.; van Schaick, H. W.; & Blansjaar, B. A. (1998). Prevalence of dementia over age 100. *Neurology, 50,* 283–286.

Thompson, Suzanne C.; Nanni, Christopher; & Levine, Alexandra (1994). Primary versus secondary and central versus consequence-related control in HIV-positive men. *Journal of Personality and Social Psychology, 67,* 540–547.

Thorndike, Edward L. (1898). Animal intelligence: An experimental study of the associative processes in animals. *Psychological Review Monograph Supplement, 2*(Whole No. 8).

Tice, Dianne M., & Baumeister, Roy F. (1997). Longitudinal study of procrastination, performance, stress, and health: The costs and benefits of dawdling. *Psychological Science, 8,* 454–458.

Tiefer, Leonore (1995). *Sex is not a natural act and other essays.* Boulder, CO: Westview Press.

Timmers, Monique; Fischer, Agneta H.; & Manstead, Antony S. R. (1998). Gender differences in motives for regulating emotions. *Personality and Social Psychology Bulletin, 24,* 974–985.

Todes, Daniel P. (1997). From the machine to the ghost within: Pavlov's transition from digestive physiology to conditional reflexes. *American Psychologist, 52,* 947–955.

Tolman, Edward C. (1938). The determiners of behavior at a choice point. *Psychological Review, 45,* 1–35.

Tolman, Edward C., & Honzik, Chase H. (1930). Introduction and removal of reward and maze performance in rats. *University of California Publications in Psychology, 4,* 257–275.

Torrey, E. Fuller (1988). *Surviving schizophrenia* (rev. ed.). New York: Harper & Row.

Torrey, E. Fuller; Bowler, Ann E.; Taylor, Edward H.; & Gottesman, Irving I. (1994). *Schizophrenia and manic-depressive disorder.* New York: Basic Books.

Tougas, Francine; Brown, Rupert; Beaton, Ann M.; & Joly, Stéphane (1995). Neosexism: Plus ça change, plus c'est pareil. *Personality and Social Psychology Bulletin, 21,* 842–849.

Triandis, Harry C. (1994). *Culture and social behavior.* New York: McGraw-Hill.

Triandis, Harry C. (1996). The psychological measurement of cultural syndromes. *American Psychologist, 51,* 407–415.

Trimble, Joseph E., & Medicine, Beatrice (1993). Diversification of American Indians: Forming an indigenous perspective. In U. Kim & J. W. Berry (eds.), *Indigenous psychologies: Research and experience in cultural context.* Newbury Park, CA: Sage.

Tronick, Edward Z.; Morelli, Gilda A.; & Ivey, Paula K. (1992). The Efe forager infant and toddler's pattern of social relationships: Multiple and simultaneous. *Developmental Psychology, 28,* 568–577.

Tulving, Endel (1985). How many memory systems are there? *American Psychologist, 40,* 385–398.

Tversky, Amos, & Kahneman, Daniel (1973). Availability: A heuristic for judging frequency and probability. *Cognitive Psychology, 5,* 207–232.

Tversky, Amos, & Kahneman, Daniel (1981). The framing of decisions and the psychology of choice. *Science, 211,* 453–458.

Twenge, Jean M. (1997). Attitudes toward women, 1970–1995: A meta-analysis. *Psychology of Women Quarterly, 21,* 35–51.

Tyler, Tom R. (1997). The psychology of legitimacy: A relational perspective on voluntary deference to authorities. *Personality and Social Psychology Review, 1,* 323–345.

Uchida, K., & Toya, S. (1996). Grafting of genetically manipulated cells into adult brain: Toward graft-gene therapy. *Keio Journal of Medicine* (Japan), *45,* 81–89.

Usher, JoNell A., & Neisser, Ulric (1993). Childhood amnesia and the beginnings of memory for four early life events. *Journal of Experimental Psychology: General, 122,* 155–165.

Utman, Christopher H. (1997). Performance effects of motivational state: A meta-analysis. *Personality and Social Psychology Review, 1,* 170–182.

Vaillant, George E. (1983). *The natural history of alcoholism: Causes, patterns, and paths to recovery.* Cambridge, MA: Harvard University Press.

Vaillant, George E. (ed.) (1992). *Ego mechanisms of defense.* Washington, DC: American Psychiatric Press.

Vaillant, George E. (1995). *The natural history of alcoholism revisited.* Cambridge, MA: Harvard University Press.

Valenstein, Elliot (1986). *Great and desperate cures: The rise and decline of psychosurgery and other radical treatments for mental illness.* New York: Basic Books.

Valenstein, Elliot (1998). *Blaming the brain: The truth about drugs and mental health.* New York: Free Press.

Valian, Virginia (1998). *Why so slow? The advancement of women.* Cambridge, MA: MIT Press.

Van Boven, Leaf; Kamada, Akiko; & Gilovich, Thomas (1999). The perceiver as perceived: Everyday intuitions about the correspondence bias. *Journal of Personality and Social Psychology, 77,* 1188–1199.

Van Cantfort, Thomas E., & Rimpau, James B. (1982). Sign language studies with children and chimpanzees. *Sign Language Studies, 34,* 15–72.

Van de Castle, R. (1994). *Our dreaming mind.* New York: Ballantine Books.

van Praag, H.; Kempermann, G.; & Gage, F. H. (1999). Running increases cell proliferation and neurogenesis in the adult mouse dentate gyrus. *Nature Neuroscience, 2,* 266–270.

Vandello, Joseph A., & Cohen, Dov (1999). Patterns of individualism and collectivism across the United States. *Journal of Personality and Social Psychology, 77,* 279–292.

Verhaeghen, Paul, & Salthouse, Timothy A. (1997). Meta-analyses of age-cognition relations in adulthood: Estimates of linear and nonlinear age effects and structural models. *Psychological Bulletin, 122,* 231–249.

Vertosick, Frank T. (1997, October). Lobotomy's back. *Discover,* 66–72.

Voyer, Daniel; Voyer, Susan; & Bryden, M. P. (1995). Magnitude of sex differences in spatial abilities: A meta-analysis and consideration of critical variables. *Psychological Bulletin, 117,* 250–270.

Wadden, Thomas A.; Foster, G. D.; Letizia, K. A.; & Mullen, J. L. (1990, August 8). Long-term effects of dieting on resting metabolic rate in obese outpatients. *Journal of the American Medical Association, 264,* 707–711.

Wagenaar, Willem A. (1986). My memory: A study of autobiographical memory over six years. *Cognitive Psychology, 18,* 225–252.

Walker, Lawrence J. (1995). Sexism in Kohlberg's moral psychology? In W. M. Kurtines & J. L. Gurwitz (eds.), *Moral development: An introduction.* Boston: Allyn & Bacon.

Walker, Lawrence J.; de Vries, Brian; & Trevethan, Shelley D. (1987). Moral stages and moral orientations in real-life and hypothetical dilemmas. *Child Development, 58,* 842–858.

Wallbott, Harald G.; Ricci-Bitti, Pio; & Bänninger-Huber, Eva (1986). Non-verbal reactions to emotional experiences. In K. R. Scherer, H. G. Wallbott, & A. B. Summerfield (eds.), *Experiencing emotion: A cross-cultural study.* Cambridge, England: Cambridge University Press.

Waller, Niels G.; Kojetin, Brian A.; Bouchard, Thomas J., Jr.; et al. (1990). Genetic and environmental influences on religious interests, attitudes, and values: A study of twins reared apart and together. *Psychological Science, 1,* 138–142.

Waller, Niels G., & Shaver, Phillip (1994). The importance of nongenetic influences on romantic love styles: A twin-family study. *Psychological Science, 5,* 268–274.

Wallerstein, Judith; Lewis, Julia; & Blakeslee, Sandra (2000). *The unexpected legacy of divorce: A 25-year landmark study.* New York: Hyperion.

Walsh, B. Timothy, & Devlin, Michael J. (1998). Eating disorders: Progress and problems. *Science, 280,* 1387–1390.

Wandersman, Abraham, & Nation, Maury (1998). Urban neighborhoods and mental health: Psychological contributions to understanding toxicity, resilience, and interventions. *American Psychologist, 53,* 647–656.

Wang, Alvin Y.; Thomas, Margaret H.; & Ouellette, Judith A. (1992). The keyword mnemonic and retention of second-language vocabulary words. *Journal of Educational Psychology, 84,* 520–528.

Wark, Gillian R., & Krebs, Dennis (1996). Gender and dilemma differences in real-life moral judgment. *Developmental Psychology, 32,* 220–230.

Washburn, David A., & Rumbaugh, Duane M. (1991). Ordinal judgments of numerical symbols by macaques (*Macaca mulatta*). *Psychological Science, 2,* 190–193.

Watson, John B. (1913). Psychology as the behaviorist views it. *Psychological Review, 20,* 158–177.

Watson, John B., & Rayner, Rosalie (1920). Conditioned emotional reactions. *Journal of Experimental Psychology, 3,* 1–14.

Watters, Ethan, & Ofshe, Richard (1999). *Therapy's delusions.* New York: Scribner.

Webb, Wilse B., & Cartwright, Rosalind D. (1978). Sleep and dreams. In M. Rosenzweig & L. Porter (eds.), *Annual Review of Psychology, 29,* 223–252.

Webster, Richard (1995). *Why Freud was wrong.* New York: Basic Books.

Wechsler, David (1955). *Manual for the Wechsler Adult Intelligence Scale.* New York: Psychological Corporation.

Wegner, Daniel M., & Gold, Daniel B. (1995). Fanning old flames: Emotional and cognitive effects of suppressing thoughts of a past relationship. *Journal of Personality and Social Psychology, 68,* 782–792.

Wegner, Daniel M.; Schneider, David J.; Carter, Samuel R., III; & White, Teri L. (1987). Paradoxical effects of thought suppression. *Journal of Personality and Social Psychology, 53,* 5–13.

Weil, Andrew T. (1974a, June). Parapsychology: Andrew Weil's search for the true Geller. *Psychology Today,* 45–50.

Weil, Andrew T. (1974b, July). Parapsychology: Andrew Weil's search for the true Geller—II. The letdown. *Psychology Today,* 74–78, 82.

Weiner, Bernard (1986). *An attributional theory of motivation and emotion.* New York: Springer-Verlag.

Weiss, Bahr; Dodge, Kenneth A.; Bates, John E.; & Petitt, Gregory S. (1992). Some consequences of early harsh discipline: Child aggression and a maladaptive social information processing style. *Child Development, 63,* 1321–1335.

Weisz, John R.; Weiss, Bahr; Han, Susan S.; et al. (1995). Effects of psychotherapy with children and adolescents revisited: A meta-analysis of treatment outcome studies. *Psychological Bulletin, 117,* 450–468.

Weiten, Wayne, & Wight, Randall D. (1992). Portraits of a discipline: An examination of introductory psychology textbooks in America. In A. E. Puente, J. R. Matthews, & C. L. Brewer (eds.), *Teaching psychology in America: A history.* Washington, DC: American Psychological Association.

Wellenkamp, Jane (1995). Cultural similarities and differences regarding emotional disclosure: Some examples from Indonesia and the Pacific. In J. W. Pennebaker (ed.), *Emotion, disclosure, and health.* Washington, DC: American Psychological Association.

Wells, Gary L.; Small, Mark; Penrod, Steven; et al. (1998). Eyewitness identification procedures: Recommendations for lineups and photospreads. *Law and Human Behavior, 22,* 602–647.

Wender, Paul H., & Klein, Donald F. (1981). *Mind, mood, and medicine: A guide to the new biopsychiatry.* New York: Farrar, Straus and Giroux.

Werner, Emmy E. (1989). High-risk children in young adulthood: A longitudinal study from birth to 32 years. *American Journal of Orthopsychiatry, 59,* 72–81.

West, Melissa O., & Prinz, Ronald J. (1987). Parental alcoholism and childhood psychopathology. *Psychological Bulletin, 102,* 204–218.

Westen, Drew (1998). The scientific legacy of Sigmund Freud: Toward a psychodynamically informed psychological science. *Psychological Bulletin, 124,* 333–371.

Westermeyer, Joseph (1995). Cultural aspects of substance abuse and alcoholism: Assessment and management. *Psychiatric Clinics of North America, 18,* 589–605.

Wheeler, David L. (1998, September 11). Neuroscientists take stock of brain-imaging studies. *Chronicle of Higher Education,* A20–A21.

Whisman, Mark A. (1993). Mediators and moderators of change in cognitive therapy of depression. *Psychological Bulletin, 114,* 248–265.

Whitam, Frederick L.; Diamond, Milton; & Martin, James (1993). Homosexual orientation in twins: A report on 61 pairs and 3 triplet sets. *Archives of Sexual Behavior, 22,* 187–206.

Wickelgren, Ingrid (1997). Estrogen stakes claim to cognition [Research news]. *Science, 276,* 675–678.

Widner, H.; Tetrud, J.; Rehncrona, S.; et al. (1993). Fifteen months' follow-up on bilateral embryonic mesencephalic grafts in two cases of severe MPTP-induced Parkinsonism. *Advances in Neurology, 60,* 729–733.

Wiggins, Jerry S. (ed.) (1996). *The five-factor model of personality: Theoretical perspectives.* New York: Guilford Press.

Williams, Janice E.; Paton, Catherine C.; Siegler, Ilene C.; et al. (2000). Anger proneness predicts coronary heart disease risk. *Circulation, 101,* 2034–2039.

Williams, Kipling D., & Karau, Steven J. (1991). Social loafing and social compensation: The effects of expectations of co-worker performance. *Journal of Personality and Social Psychology, 61,* 570–581.

Williams, Redford B., Jr.; Barefoot, John C.; & Shekelle, Richard B. (1985). The health consequences of hostility. In M. A. Chesney & R. H. Rosenman (eds.), *Anger and hostility in cardiovascular and behavioral disorders.* New York: Hemisphere.

Willie, Charles V.; Rieker, Patricia P.; Kramer, Bernard M.; & Brown, Bertram S. (eds.) (1995). *Mental health, racism, and sexism* (rev. ed.). Pittsburgh: University of Pittsburgh Press.

Willis, Sherry L. (1987). Cognitive training and everyday competence. In K. W. Schaie (ed.), *Annual review of gerontology and geriatrics* (Vol. 7). New York: Springer.

Wilner, Daniel; Walkley, Rosabelle; & Cook, Stuart (1955). *Human relations in interracial housing.* Minneapolis: University of Minnesota Press.

Wilson, G. Terence, & Fairburn, Christopher G. (1993). Cognitive treatments for eating disorders. *Journal of Consulting and Clinical Psychology, 61,* 261–269.

Winick, Myron; Meyer, Knarig Katchadurian; & Harris, Ruth C. (1975). Malnutrition and environmental enrichment by early adoption. *Science, 190,* 1173–1175.

Winnicott, D. W. (1957/1990). *Home is where we start from.* New York: Norton.

Wispé, Lauren G., & Drambarean, Nicholas C. (1953). Physiological need, word frequency, and visual duration thresholds. *Journal of Experimental Psychology, 46,* 25–31.

Witelson, Sandra F.; Glazer, I. I.; & Kigar, D. L. (1994). Sex differences in numerical density of neurons in human auditory association cortex. *Society for Neuroscience Abstracts, 30*(Abstr. No. 582.12).

Wittchen, Hans-Ulrich; Kessler, Ronald C.; Zhao, Shanyang; & Abelson, Jamie (1995). Reliability and clinical validity of UM-CIDI DSM-III-R generalized anxiety disorder. *Journal of Psychiatric Research, 29,* 95–110.

Wittig, Michele A., & Grant-Thompson, Sheila (1998). The utility of Allport's conditions of intergroup contact for predicting perceptions of improved racial attitudes and beliefs. *Journal of Social Issues, 54,* 795–812.

Wood, James M.; Nezworski, Teresa; & Stejskal, William J. (1996). The comprehensive system for the Rorschach: A critical examination. *Psychological Science, 7,* 3–10.

Wood, Joanne V., & VanderZee, K. (1997). Social comparisons among cancer patients: Under what conditions are comparisons upward and downward? In B. P. Buunk & F. X. Gibbons (eds.), *Health and coping: Perspectives from social comparison theory.* Hillsdale, NJ: Erlbaum.

Wood, Wendy; Lundgren, Sharon; Ouellette, Judith A.; et al. (1994). Minority influence: A meta-analytic review of social influence processes. *Psychological Bulletin, 115,* 323–345.

Wooley, Susan; Wooley, O. Wayne; & Dyrenforth, Susan (1979). Theoretical, practical, and social issues in behavioral treatments of obesity. *Journal of Applied Behavior Analysis, 12,* 3–25.

Wright, Daniel B. (1993). Recall of the Hillsborough disaster over time: Systematic biases of "flashbulb" memories. *Applied Cognitive Psychology, 7,* 129–138.

Wright, R. L. D. (1976). *Understanding statistics: An informal introduction for the behavioral sciences.* New York: Harcourt Brace Jovanovich.

Wurtman, Richard J. (1982). Nutrients that modify brain function. *Scientific American, 264*(4), 50–59.

Wurtman, Richard J., & Lieberman, Harris R. (eds.) (1982–1983). Research strategies for assessing the behavioral effects of foods and nutrients [Whole issue]. *Journal of Psychiatric Research, 17*(2).

Wuthnow, Robert (1995). *Sharing the journey: Support groups and America's new quest for community.* New York: Free Press.

Wygant, Steven A. (1997). Moral reasoning about real-life dilemmas: Paradox in research using the Defining Issues Test. *Personality and Social Psychology Bulletin, 23,* 1022–1033.

Yalom, Irvin D. (1989). *Love's executioner and other tales of psychotherapy.* New York: Basic Books.

Yalom, Irvin D. (1995). *The theory and practice of group psychotherapy* (4th ed.). New York: Basic Books.

Yang, Kuo-shu, & Bond, Michael H. (1990). Exploring implicit personality theories with indigenous or imported constructs: The Chinese case. *Journal of Personality and Social Psychology, 58,* 1087–1095.

Yapko, Michael (1994). *Suggestions of abuse: True and false memories of childhood sexual trauma.* New York: Simon & Schuster.

Yazigi, R. A.; Odem, R. R.; & Polakoski, K. L. (1991, October 9). Demonstration of specific binding of cocaine to human spermatozoa. *Journal of the American Medical Association, 266*(14), 1956–1959.

Yoder, Janice D. (1999). *Women and gender: Transforming psychology.* Upper Saddle River, NJ: Prentice Hall.

Young, Malcolm P., & Yamane, Shigeru (1992). Sparse population coding of faces in the inferotemporal cortex. *Science, 256,* 1327–1331.

Young-Eisendrath, Polly (1993). *You're not what I expected: Learning to love the opposite sex.* New York: Morrow.

Zahn-Waxler, Carolyn (1996). Environment, biology, and culture: Implications for adolescent development. *Developmental Psychology, 32,* 571–573.

Zajonc, Robert B. (1968). Attitudinal effects of mere exposure. *Journal of Personality and Social Psychology, 9*(Monograph Suppl. 2), 1–27.

Zhang, Yiying; Proenca, Ricardo; Maffei, Margherita; et al. (1994). Positional cloning of the mouse obese gene and its human homologue. *Nature, 372*(6505), 425–432.

Zimbardo, Philip G. (1970). The human choice: Individuation, reason, and order versus deindividuation, impulse, and chaos. In W. J. Arnold & D. Levine (eds.), *Nebraska Symposium on Motivation, 1969.* Lincoln, NE: University of Nebraska Press.

Zimbardo, Philip G., & Leippe, Michael R. (1991). *The psychology of attitude change and social influence.* New York: McGraw-Hill.

Zinberg, Norman (1974). The search for rational approaches to heroin use. In P. G. Bourne (ed.), *Addiction.* New York: Academic Press.

Zorrilla, L. T.; Cannon, T. D.; Kronenberg, S.; Mednick, S. A.; et al. (1997, December 15). Structural brain abnormalities in schizophrenia: A family study. *Biological Psychiatry, 42,* 1080–1086.

CREDITS

Text, Table, and Figure Credits

CHAPTER 1 *Page 23:* Figure 1.2, adapted from *Understanding Statistics: An Informal Introduction for the Behavioral Sciences* by R. L. Wright, copyright © 1976 by Harcourt Brace & Company. Reprinted by permission of the publisher.

CHAPTER 2 *Page 54:* Table 2.1, from Harry C. Triandis, "The Psychological measurement of cultural syndrome," *American Psychologist, 51,* 407–415, 1996. Copyright © 1996 by the American Psychological Association. Adapted with permission; pp. 68-69, from "The P. T. Barnum Effect" by C. R. Snyder, *Psychology Today,* March 1975. Reprinted with permission from Psychology Today Magazine. Copyright © 1975 Sussex Publishers, Inc.

CHAPTER 3 *Page 76:* Table 3.1, from Helen Bee, *The Developing Child.* Copyright © 1989 by Harper & Row, Publishers, Inc. Reprinted by permission of Allyn & Bacon; *p. 86:* Figure 3.3, from Rene Baillargeon, "How do infants learn about the physical world" *Current Directions in Psychological Science,* Vol. 5 (1994). Reprinted by permission of Blackwell Publishers.

CHAPTER 4 *Page 121:* Figure 4.6, Orietta Agostoni from ABC's of the Human Mind, *Reader's Digest,* 1990, p. 64; *p. 127:* Figure 4.8a (L) Hank Morgan/Science Source/Photo Researchers, Inc., (R) Dr. Michal E. Phelps/Mazziotta UCLA School of Medicine.

CHAPTER 5 *Page 158:* Table 5.1, Reprinted with permission from the American Academy of Otolaryngology–Head and Neck Surgery, Washington, DC.; *p. 161:* Figure 5.5, copyright © Josef Albers Foundation/Yale University Press. Reprinted by permission of Yale University Press.

CHAPTER 6 *Page 194:* from Kathleen Galotti, "Two kinds of reasoning." *Psychological Bulletin, 105,* 331–351, Table 1, p. 335, 1989. Copyright © 1989 by the American Psychological Association. Adapted with permission; *pp. 195–197,* from Patricia King and Karen Kitchener, *Developing Reflexive Judgment: Understanding and Promoting Intellectual Growth and Critical Thinking in Adolescents and Adults.* Copyright © 1994 by Jossey-Bass, Inc., Publishers. Reprinted by permission of John Wiley & Sons, Inc.; *p. 201:* from CONCEPTUAL BLOCKBUSTING by James L. Adams. Copyright © 1986 by James L. Adams. Reprinted by permission of Perseus Books Publishers, a member of Perseus Books, L.L.C.; *p. 206:* Table 6.2, copyright © 1972 by The Riverside Publishing Company. Reproduced from *Stanford Binet Intelligence Scale, Form L-M, Manual for 3rd Revision, Part 2,* pages 68–111 by Lewis M. Terman and Maude A. Merrill, with permission of the publisher. All rights reserved; *p. 207:* Figure 6.3, from "Performance Tasks on the Weschler Tests" by Lee. J. Cronbach from *Essentials of Psychological Testing,* 5th edition, p. 247. Copyright © 1990 by Harper-Collins Publishers. Reprinted by permission of Allyn & Bacon; *p. 221:* from Mednick, Sarnoff. A. (1962). The associative basis of the creative process. *Psychological Review, 69,* 220–232; *p. 214:* Figure 6.6, from J. Horgan, "Get smart, take a test: A long term rise in IQ scores baffles intelligence experts" from *Scientific American* November 1995, p. 14 Reprinted by permission of Demitry Schildlovsky.

CHAPTER 7 *Page 234:* Figure 7.2, from Gaven, Sena, Wood, James, M., Malpass, Roy S., & Shaw, John S., II (1998). More than suggestion: The effect of interviewing techniques from the McMartin Preschool Case. *Journal of Applied Psychology, 83,* 347–359. Figure 1, p. 353. Copyright © 1998 by the American Psychological Association. Adapted with permission; *p. 245:* Figure 7.6, from "Serial Position Effect" in *Memory* by Elizabeth Loftus, 1980, p. 25. Copyright © 1980 by Addison Wesley Publishing Co. Reprinted by permission of the author; *p. 250:* Figure 7.8, from "I Remember It Well" by Marigold Linton in *Psychology Today,* Vol. 13-2, July 1979. Reprinted with permission from psychology Today Magazine. Copyright © 1979 (Sussex Publishers, Inc.).

CHAPTER 8 *Page 226:* Figure 8.2, from "Acquisition and Extinction of a Salivary Response," Conditioned Reflexes, copyright © 1927. Reprinted by permission of Oxford University Press; *p. 285:* Figure 8.6, from "Turning Play into Work" by David Greene and Mark R. Lepper, *Psychology Today,* September 1974. Reprinted with permission from Psychology Today Magazine. Copyright © 1974 Sussex Publishers, Inc.; *p. 288:* Figure 8.7, from "Introduction and removal of reward and maze performance in rats" by E. C. Tolman and C. H. Honzik from *Psychology, 4* (1930). University of California Publications.

CHAPTER 9 *Pages 318–319:* from The Nature of Prejudice by Gordon Allport. Copyright © 1979, 1958, 1954. Reprinted by permission of Perseus Books Publishers, a member of Perseus Book, L.L.C.

CHAPTER 10 *Page 343:* Figure 10.1, from "Depression's double standard," by Kristin Leutwyler in "Mysteries of the Mind," special issue published by *Scientific American,* June 1995, p. 54. Figure reprinted by permission of Bran Christie; *p. 348:* Figure 10.3, from Robert Hare, "Antisocial personality disorder" in *Journal of Psychology,* F, 1A, 1985. Reprinted with permission of the Helen Dwight Reid Educational Foundation. Published by Heldref Publications, 1319 18th St. N. W., Washington, DC 20036-1802. Copyright © 1985; *p. 355:* Figure 10.4, from "Drug Use by U.S. Army Enlisted Men in Vietnam: A Follow Up on the Return Home" by Robins, Davis & Goodwin in American *Journal of Epidemiology,* Vol. 99, pp. 239–249, 1974. Reprinted by permission of Oxford University Press.

CHAPTER 11 *Page 384:* Figure 11.3, from "The close-effect relationship in psychotherapy" by Kenneth l. Howard from *American Psychologist, 41,* February 1986, pp. 159–164, Figure 1, p. 160. Copyright © 1986 by the American Psychological Association. Reprinted with permission.

CHAPTER 12 *Page 401:* from Chimeric faces, Figure 5.5, p. 146 in Keith Oatley and Jennifer J. Jenkins, *Understanding Emotions,* 1996. Reproduced by permission of Blackwell Publishers; *p. 412:* Figure 12.2, from "Stress and the Cold," *The New York Times Health,* May 12, 1998. Adapted with permission; *p. 421:* Figure 12.4, from Roth, David L. and Holmes, Davis S. (1985). Influence of physical fitness in determining the impact of stressful life events on physical and psychological health. *Psychosomatic Medicine, 47,* 164–173. Reprinted by permission of Lippincott, Williams, & Wilkins.

CHAPTER 13 *Page 440:* Adapated from Evolutionary Psychology: a new paradigm for psychological

Photographs and Cartoons

SUBJECT INDEX